personally, critically, actively

An Emphasis on Critical Thinking

Challenge Your Thinking features involve you in debates over findings from psychological research. Thought-provoking questions encourage you to examine the evidence on both sides. See, for example, pg. 254.

It's time to become a memory detective and explore the accuracy of your own memory for major events. Think about an event for which you might have a flashbulb memory. You might choose from a major event in recent history, such as the 9/11 attacks, Hurricane Katrina, or the Indian Ocean tsunami. Then ask yourself some easily verifiable questions about it, such as what day of the week did it happen? What time of day? What were the date and year? How many people were involved? When you have done your best to answer these questions, go to the library or go online and check out the facts. Were your memories accurate?

challenge your thinking

Does Gender Influence Language?

Common stereotypes suggest that women are the talkative sex. The best-seller *The Female Brain* by Louann Brizendine (2006) claims that women talk three times as much as men. Brizendine suggests that women's brains are wired from birth to be extraordinarily sensitive to social information. Women, she says, have an "eight-lane superhighway" for processing emotion, whereas men have only "a single country road."

The notion that men are somehow missing out on an emotional expressway is also reflected in the *extreme male brain theory* of autism. Recall from Chapter 4 that autism is a disorder in which individuals have particular difficulty processing social information. Simon Baron-Cohen (2002, 2003, 2008; Baron-Cohen, Knickmeyer, & Belmonte, 2006) has suggested that characteristics associated with autism might be considered simply extreme forms of the "male brain" (that is, one that is well suited to math and spatial reasoning but less well geared to verbal and social skills). This controversial notion certainly shows that people seem to be prone to extreme positions and stereotypes when discussing gender differences.

Recent research challenges the idea that women are the talkers of the world. Matthias Mehl and his colleagues (Mehl & others, 2007) examined this notion in an innovative way. Nearly 400 male and female college students wore a device that recorded them for a few minutes every 12½ minutes as they went about their daily routines. The device allowed the researchers to count how much each participant spoke in the course of the day. The results of the study showed that women

uttered slightly more than 16,000 words a day. And men? They spoke slightly less than 16,000 words a day. No significant difference emerged. Interestingly, the biggest talkers in the study (averaging 47,000 words per day) were all men. So was the quietest person in the study, speaking just 700 words per day.

The sheer number of best-selling books about gender differences highlights our fascination with male–female contrasts. Boys, men, girls, and women live in a social world that poses different expectations and different challenges. It is easy to think of male–female differences as rooted exclusively in the biological differences of sex. A more realistic and balanced viewpoint might acknowledge that men and women are, after all, human beings and that working out our conflicts with the other sex is about negotiating common human needs rather than simply living with biologically programmed characteristics.

What Do You Think?

- Is research on gender differences in language ability potentially damaging to men or women? Why or why not?

- Why are gender differences so fascinating to people in general?

- Who are the biggest talkers you know? Do they have any characteristics (aside from gender) in common?

An Emphasis on Active Engagement

Do It! is a brief, reoccurring activity that gives you an opportunity to test your assumptions and learn through hands-on exploration and discovery. Such exercises provide you with a more active experience of psychology. See, for example, pg. 212.

experience psychology

Laura A. King

University of Missouri, Columbia

Connect
Learn
Succeed™

Published by McGraw-Hill, an imprint of The McGraw-Hill Companies, Inc., 1221 Avenue of the Americas, New York, NY 10020. Copyright © 2010. All rights reserved. No part of this publication may be reproduced or distributed in any form or by any means, or stored in a database or retrieval system, without the prior written consent of The McGraw-Hill Companies, Inc., including, but not limited to, in any network or other electronic storage or transmission, or broadcast for distance learning.

This book is printed on acid-free paper.

3 4 5 6 7 8 9 0 DOW/DOW 0

ISBN: 978-0-07-340547-6
MHID: 0-07-340547-7

Editor in Chief: *Michael Ryan*
Editorial Director: *Beth Mejia*
Publisher: *Mike Sugarman*
Executive Marketing Manager: *James Headley*
Marketing Manager: *Yasuko Okada*
Executive Market Development Manager: *Sheryl Adams*
Director of Development: *Dawn Groundwater*
Developmental Editor: *Sylvia Mallory*
Supplements Development Editor: *Sarah Colwell*
Editorial Coordinator: *AJ Laferrera*
Market Development Coordinator: *Emory Davis*
Senior Production Editor: *Catherine Morris*
Manuscript Editor: *Jennifer Gordon*
Art Manager: *Robin Mouat*
Design Manager: *Cassandra Chu*
Text and Cover Designer: *Linda Beaupré*
Illustrators: *John and Judy Waller*
Lead Photo Editor: *Alexandra Ambrose*
Photo Researcher: *David Tietz*
Senior Production Supervisor: *Tandra Jorgensen*
Permissions Editor: *Marty Moga*
Media Project Manager: *Thomas Brierly*
Composition: *10/12 Times Roman by Aptara®, Inc.*
Printing: *45# Publisher's Matte, R. R. Donnelley & Sons*

Cover: © Foodcollection/Getty Images

Credits: The credits section for this book begins on page C1 and is considered an extension of the copyright page.

Library of Congress Cataloging-in-Publication Data

King, Laura.
    Experience psychology / Laura King.—1st ed.
      p. cm.
    Includes bibliographical references and index.
    ISBN-13: 978-0-07-340547-6 (alk. paper)
    ISBN-10: 0-07-340547-7 (alk. paper)
    1. Psychology.   I. Title.
    BF121.K536 2010
    150–dc22

2009034029

The Internet addresses listed in the text were accurate at the time of publication. The inclusion of a Web site does not indicate an endorsement by the authors or McGraw-Hill, and McGraw-Hill does not guarantee the accuracy of the information presented at these sites.

www.mhhe.com

For Sam

Laura A. King

Laura King did her undergraduate work at Kenyon College, where, an English major, she declared a second major, in psychology, during the second semester of her junior year. She completed her A.B. in English with high honors and distinction and in psychology with distinction in 1986. Laura then did graduate work at Michigan State University and the University of California, Davis, receiving her Ph.D. in personality psychology in 1991.

Laura began her career at Southern Methodist University in Dallas, moving to the University of Missouri in 2001, where she now holds the Frederick A. Middlebush chair in psychology. In addition to seminars in the development of character, social psychology, and personality psychology, she has taught undergraduate lecture courses in introductory psychology, introduction to personality psychology, and social psychology. At SMU, she received six different teaching awards, including the "M" award for "sustained excellence" in 1999. At the University of Missouri, she received the Chancellor's Award for Outstanding Research and Creative Activity in 2004.

Her research, which has been funded by the National Institutes for Mental Health, has focused on a variety of topics relevant to the question of what it is that makes for a good life. She has studied goals, life stories, happiness, well-being, and meaning in life. In general, her work reflects an enduring interest in studying what is good and healthy in people. In 2001, her research accomplishments were recognized by a Templeton Prize in positive psychology. Laura's research (often in collaboration with undergraduate and graduate students) has been published in *American Psychologist,* the *Journal of Personality and Social Psychology, Personality and Social Psychology Bulletin, Cognition and Emotion,* the *Journal of Personality,* and other publications.

Currently the editor of the *Journal of Personality and Social Psychology: Personality and Individual Differences,* Laura has also served as editor of *The Journal of Research in Personality;* as associate editor of *Personality and Social Psychology Bulletin,* the *Journal of Personality and Social Psychology,* and *Social and Personality Psychology Compass;* and on numerous grant panels. She has edited or co-edited special sections of the *Journal of Personality and the American Psychologist.* In "real life," Laura is an accomplished cook and enjoys listening to music (mostly jazz vocalists and singer-songwriters), gardening, and chasing Sam, her five-year-old son.

brief contents

contents

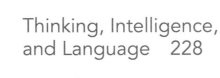

12 Psychological Disorders 411

13 Therapies 449

14 Health Psychology 480

preface
to the student

Experience Psychology is about, well, experience—our own behaviors; our relationships at home and in our communities, in school and at work. Some of the content will be familiar to you, though much of it, especially the underlying science, may not be so familiar and may even come as a surprise. In keeping with the experiential theme, *Experience Psychology* is also a complete learning system designed to provide you with a personally meaningful, hands-on path to success in this course. An online diagnostic tool automatically adapts to your level of understanding—what you know and what you may not know—guiding you to specific activities, exercises, or readings that will improve understanding and likely your grade in the course. The book you hold in your hands (or are viewing on-screen), *Experience Psychology,* is designed to immerse you in a fascinating area of study and to guide you in connecting the science of psychology with your life.

Building on a strong research foundation, I emphasize function before dysfunction—what works more so than what does not—in keeping with how most of us, our families, our friends, and our colleagues experience our world. The text provides recurring opportunities for you, the student of psychology, to make connections between your coursework and your life. Drawn from our everyday world, *Experience Psychology*'s contemporary examples and applied exercises speak directly to you. They invite you to engage with psychology and to learn verbally, visually, and experientially—that is, by reading, seeing, and doing. I firmly believe that to get the most out of this course, you must not just "take" psychology but actively *experience* it.

Some people take introductory psychology; others experience it.

Experience Psychology Personally, Actively, Critically

My goal is to involve you in experiencing the science of psychology by helping you understand and appreciate, really *appreciate,* the research basis of the field. This means learning not just what psychologists know but also how they know it. I find in my experience as an author and a teacher that the best way to develop the analytical thinking required for successful learning is to model it. As a result, I have devoted attention throughout *Experience Psychology* to stimulating critical thinking—to asking you thought-provoking questions as you read or make your way through an on-line simulation, guiding you, with concrete examples relevant to you and your world, toward an understanding of the principles and processes of psychological science.

In support of this dynamic, personalized approach, *Experience Psychology* includes innovative pedagogical elements in all of its components:

- *Experience Psychology* **Online:** *Experience Psychology* includes a digital element to help you make the most of your introductory psychology experience. Whether explicitly assigned by your instructor or not, I encourage you to use Connect Psychology to help you master the concepts of introductory psychology in the most efficient and effective way for *you*. I emphasize "you" because one of the most exciting pieces of Connect psychology is an adaptive diagnostic tool that will help you to quickly and consistently identify your areas of strength as well as areas and concepts where you may need some additional practice. As you answer the questions in this diagnostic, the program is constantly adjusting to provide you with a personalized study plan tailored to your needs.

- *Margin Notes:* **Margin notes** are personal asides from me—Laura King—to you. The main purpose of these notes, like the one on the right, is to highlight facts and concepts in your study that are especially important, counterintuitive, or particularly complex. Some of the notes remind you that, yes, you really must grasp the technicalities of what you are reading at a given moment—for instance, what independent and dependent variables are—if you are genuinely to understand later concepts. Other notes encourage you to apply what you have learned to new situations; for example, after you have finished reading about research methods, you need to consider whether a given study is correlational or experimental. Still other margin notes speak to complexities such as the difference between random assignment and random selection.

Note that the operational definition of the dependent variable here was any brain differences at all. The researchers looked at more and less activation of a variety of brain areas—and still, no dice. As the researchers noted, "We found nothing. But we found nothing in an interesting way!"

    In addition, many margin notes bring a particular topic or issue to life by presenting real-world associations to it. After the text describes a classic study mapping areas of the brain, for example, a margin note describes brain surgery patients, such as the late Senator Ted Kennedy, who are routinely awake during their procedures and why this is so.

    The margin notes have a broader purpose that goes beyond *Experience Psychology*: to foster critical thinking and engagement with respect to processing *any* information, whether communicated in your classes, around the dinner table, in a newspaper or periodical, or in a media broadcast. Through my "mini-conversations" with you in these margin notes, I aim to help you develop the kinds of analytical skills that will make you a thoughtful and informed citizen throughout your life.

- *Do It!* **Do It!** activities give you an opportunity to experience psychology actively by testing your assumptions and learning through hands-on exploration and discovery. Do It! selections include going online to research topics such as a "happiness gene" and intelligence tests, pulling out one's old diaries for critical analysis, and conducting an informal study in which you observe and classify behaviors in a public setting. The Do It! activities provide a holistic experience of psychology by getting you away from the assigned reading and out into the world.

- *Psychology in Our World:* **Psychology in Our World** sections demonstrate the relevance of psychology for a variety of real-world contexts, including the workplace, the media, and current events. The selection in Chapter 2 (The Brain and Behavior), for example, looks at traumatic brain injury, the signature wound of the Iraq War. The example in Chapter 8 (Human Development) probes the role of infant and child perception research on toy design. Psychology in Our World seeks to open your eyes to the presence of the psychological science all around you.

Experience Contemporary Scientific Research and Debate

Experience Psychology connects you intimately to the methods and discoveries of the science of psychology. Built on the foundations of John Santrock's work, each chapter's main text interweaves discussion and analysis of the most current research with examination of classic studies. Such integration provides well-balanced coverage of how psychologists "do" psychology and what each study has contributed to advancing knowledge about ourselves, others, and our interactions in the world. Current scholarship gives you and your instructor the very latest that psychology has to offer on each topic and shows the ever-changing nature of this dynamic field.

In addition, each chapter presents a special **Intersection** feature that showcases research at the crossroads of two subfields or that shows the influence of one field of psychology on another. Students have often told me that they have difficulty seeing the relationships among these various areas. Through the Intersections, you can develop an understanding of how psychology is interconnected and how research in one area can build on a discovery in a quite different subfield. For example, in the neuroscience section of Chapter 2 (The Brain and Behavior), I discuss links between happiness and the brain; in Chapter 6 (Memory), I discuss the connections between sensation and memory by looking at studies of the influence of smell on remembering.

A contemporary perspective also means providing you with opportunities to experience current controversies in the field. To this end, the **Challenge Your Thinking** feature in each chapter involves you in debates over findings from psychological research. Through accompanying critical thinking questions, you examine the evidence on both sides. For example, Chapter 7's selection asks you to reflect on the debate over whether gender influences language, and Chapter 11's "Challenge" directs you to consider whether violent video games lead to violence.

Experience the Breadth of Psychology

Many students show up on the first day of class thinking that psychology is all about the study of psychological disorders. I have aimed to break this mindset by highlighting examples and research topics that "bring psychology home" to the lives of people of all backgrounds and ages. My goal is to demonstrate that studying psychology as a field of human behavior and functioning is just as interesting, as a whole, as focusing on the segment of the field that is occupied with psychological problems and mental illness. Even when things are going right, the science of psychology has important knowledge to share. After all, what is *not* interesting about happiness, love, gratitude, altruism, and the experience of meaning in life? The science of psychology offers important clues about these positive aspects of human existence, as I emphasize throughout the narrative.

Experience Psychology Visually

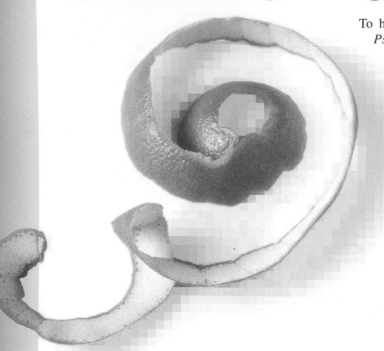

To help you master challenging concepts, *Experience Psychology* includes a special insert, "Touring the Brain and Nervous System," featuring detailed full-color transparency overlays of important figures. Conceived and developed with the input of an expert in this area, the overlays offer you hands-on practice in grasping key biological structures and processes that are essential to your success in the course. (In addition, Connect Psychology, described above, also offers a wealth of multimedia resources to assist your mastery in this area.) In keeping with the book's central theme of experiencing psychology, a feature called **Apply It to Our World** links the subject matter of the transparency overlays to common real-life situations such as fear of spiders. On-page assessment questions and answers, as well as critical thinking questions, accompany each figure.

Experience Mastery: Study Aids

In addition to the dynamic resources that I have already discussed, the fourteen chapters offer several tools to guide your learning, review, and test preparation:

- *Key Terms:* **Key terms** appear in bold type in the narrative and are formally defined both there and in adjacent margin definitions. A handy list of the chapter's key terms can also be found at the end of each chapter, including the relevant page number for ease of study and review.

- *Self-Quiz:* Each major section of reading concludes with a **Self-Quiz** consisting of multiple-choice and Apply It! questions. The multiple-choice quiz items help you assess your grasp of the section's main facts and concepts. The Apply It! question prompts you to apply what you have learned to a concrete situation. Inability to answer these questions accurately is a signal that you should reread the material until you master it. Answers appear at the end of the book. Using these Self-Quizzes along with the Connect Psychology diagnostic is a sure-fire way to improving your performance in the course.

- *Summary:* Each chapter ends with a **Summary** organized by the main chapter headings. The summary recaps the key take-away points section by section and is a valuable aid to organizing your reading, review, and test preparation.

- *Self-Test:* The **Self-Test** at the end of each chapter comprises multiple-choice questions and a short-essay Apply It! question. The Self-Test serves as a realistic practice test, simulating what a real chapter test might look like. The Test Bank uses some of the self-test questions in modified form. Answers appear at the end of the book.

resources for instructors and students

All the resources of Experience Psychology help students perform to their maximum potential in and out of the classroom.

Experience Psychology Online

What if . . .

■ You could re-create the one-on-one experience of working through difficult concepts in office hours with every one of your students without having to invest any office-hour time to do so?

■ You could see at a glance how well each of your students (and sections) was performing in each segment of your course?

■ You had all of the assignments and resources for your course pre-organized by learning objective and with point-and-click flexibility?

Over the course of developing *Experience Psychology,* we have been asking a lot of these questions and many more for some time now. We did not stop at simply asking questions either. We visited with faculty across the country and also observed you doing what you do to prepare and deliver your courses. We observed students as they worked through assignments and studied for exams. The result of these thousands of hours of research and development is *Experience Psychology,* a state of the art learning environment tool that bolsters student performance at the same time as it makes instructors' lives easier and more efficient. To experience this environment for yourself, please visit **www.mcgraw-hillconnect.com.**

Adaptive Questioning Diagnostic This diagnostic tool is at the heart of *Experience Psychology.* It is an unparalleled, intelligent learning system based on cognitive mapping that *diagnoses* your students' knowledge of a particular subject and then creates an individualized learning path geared toward student success in your course. It offers individualized assessment by delivering appropriate learning material in the form of questions at the right time, helping students attain mastery of the content. Whether the system is assigned by you or used independently by students as a study tool, the results can be recorded in an easy-to-use grade report that allows you to measure student progress at all times and coach your students to success.

As an added benefit, all content covered in this adaptive diagnostic is tied to learning objectives for your course and competencies set forth by accrediting bodies so that you can use the results as evidence of subject mastery. This tool also provides a personal study plan that allows the student to estimate the time it will take and number of questions required to learn the subject matter. You will find your students will learn faster, study more efficiently, and retain more knowledge when using *Experience Psychology*.

Instructor Resources

All of the instructor resources described below can be found on the password-protected instructor's side of *Experience Psychology's* Online Learning Center. Contact your local McGraw-Hill publishing representative for log-in information: **www.mhhe.com/kingep.**

Testing Program by Brandy Young, Cypress College By increasing the rigor of the **Test Bank** development process, Laura King has raised the bar for student assessment. Over 100 test items for each chapter of King's *Experience Psychology* were prepared by a coordinated team of subject-matter experts. Each question and set of possible answers were methodically vetted by the team for accuracy, clarity, effectiveness, and accessibility, and each is annotated for level of difficulty, Bloom's Taxonomy, and corresponding coverage in the text. The Test Bank is compatible with McGraw-Hill's computerized testing program EZ Test and most course management systems.

We are grateful to the following people for reviewing the items in the *Experience Psychology* Testing Program:

Sonya Lott Harrison, *Community College of Philadelphia*
Kelly Henry, *Missouri Western State University*
Tanya Renner, *Kapi'olani Community College*
Nick Salter, *Ramapo College*
David Schneider, *Rice University*

Instructor's Manual by Ruth Wallace, Butler Community College The **Instructor's Manual** provides a wide variety of tools and resources for enhancing your course instruction, including learning objectives, ideas for lectures and discussions, and handouts. The Connections section serves as a roadmap outlining all the other ancillaries for that chapter and points out all the unique and interesting resources available.

PowerPoint Presentations by Eva Szeli, Arizona State University The **PowerPoint Presentations** cover the key points of each chapter and include charts and graphs from the text. The presentations serve as an organizational and a navigational tool integrated with examples and activities from an expert teacher. The slides can be used as is or modified to meet the needs of the individual instructor.

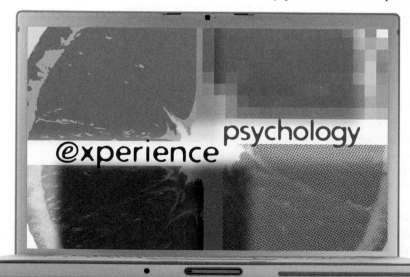

Classroom Performance System (CPS) by Alisha Janowsky, University of Central Florida The mix of factual and opinion questions in the **Classroom Performance System** allows instructors to know what concepts their students are variously mastering and those with which students are having difficulty. CPS, a "clicker" system, is a great way to give interactive quizzes, maximize student participation in class discussions, and take attendance.

Image Gallery The **Image Gallery** features the complete set of figures and tables from the text. These images are available for download and can be easily embedded into instructors' PowerPoint slides.

Student Resources

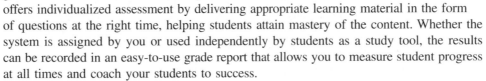

Adaptive Questioning Diagnostic This diagnostic tool is at the heart of *Experience Psychology*. It is an unparalleled, intelligent learning system based on cognitive mapping that *diagnoses* your students' knowledge of a particular subject and then creates an individualized learning path geared toward student success in your course. It offers individualized assessment by delivering appropriate learning material in the form of questions at the right time, helping students attain mastery of the content. Whether the system is assigned by you or used independently by students as a study tool, the results can be recorded in an easy-to-use grade report that allows you to measure student progress at all times and coach your students to success.

As an added benefit, all content covered in this adaptive diagnostic is tied to learning objectives for your course and competencies set forth by accrediting bodies so that you can use the results as evidence of subject mastery. This tool also provides a personal study plan that allows the student to estimate the time it will take and number of questions required to learn the subject matter. You will find your students will learn faster, study more efficiently, and retain more knowledge when using *Experience Psychology*.

Student Online Learning Center by Rachelle Tannenbaum, Anne Arundel Community College The **Student Online Learning Center** contains chapter-by-chapter quizzes, outlines, learning objectives, and key terms in English and Spanish. The multiple-choice, fill-in-the-blank, and true/false quizzes ask questions that build on conscientious use of the Student Study Guide. To access the Online Learning Center, go to **www.mhhe.com/kingep**.

Psych 2.0 An innovative blend of print and online components, **Psych 2.0** combines the best of a study guide with the best of online interactivity. The Psych 2.0 Online Experience Guide, written by Tammy Rahhal of the University of Massachusetts-Amherst and Matthew Schulkind of Amherst College, provides a synopsis, pre-activity tips, and post-activity questions for each online activity. The activities themselves offer experiential, observational, and visual learning opportunities for more than 90 key concepts in introductory psychology. Accessible as a stand-alone site or enhanced course cartridge, Psych 2.0 can be easily added to any syllabus or online course. To view a demonstration of Psych 2.0, please visit **http://www.mhhe.com/psych2demo**.

CourseSmart **CourseSmart** is a new way find and buy eTextbooks. At CourseSmart you can save up to 50% off the cost of a print textbook, reduce your impact on the environment, and gain access to powerful web tools for learning. CourseSmart has the largest selection of eTextbooks available anywhere, offering thousands of the most commonly adopted textbooks from a wide variety of higher education publishers. CourseSmart eTextbooks are available in one standard online reader with full text search, notes and highlighting, and e-mail tools for sharing notes between classmates. For further details contact your sales representative or go to **www. coursesmart.com**.

acknowledgments

The quality of Experience Psychology is a testament to the suggestions and insights of instructors and students alike. I am tremendously grateful to the following individuals whose contributions during the project's development and production have improved it immeasurably.

Manuscript Reviewers

David W. Alfano, *Community College of Rhode Island–Warwick*

Carol Anderson, *Bellevue Community College*

Marina Baratian, *Brevard Community College–Melbourne*

Marlena Barber, *Lee University*

David Baskin, *Delta College*

Paul George Billmeyer, *Chippewa Valley Technical College*

Ken Callis, *Southeast Missouri State University*

Carrie Canales, *West Los Angeles College*

Jack Chuang, *San Jacinto College–Central*

Mark Cloud, *Lock Haven University*

Mary Coplen, *Hutchinson Community College*

Pamela Costa, *Tacoma Community College*

Christopher Cronin, *Saint Leo University*

Patricia Crow, *Hawkeye Community College*

Christopher L. Curtis, *Delta College*

Katherine Demitrakis, *Central New Mexico Community College*

Nancy-Lee Devane, *Community College of Rhode Island–Warwick*

Christina Downey, *Indiana University–Kokomo*

Jenna P. Duke, *Lehigh Carbon Community College*

Curt Dunkel, *Western Illinois University*

Darlene Earley-Hereford, *Southern Union State Community College*

Penny S. Edwards, *Tri-County Technical College*

Carla Fanning, *Grayson County College*

Meredyth G. Fellows, *West Chester University of Pennsylvania*

Michael Flohr, *Brown Mackie College*

Tony Foster, *Lone Star College–Kingwood*

Judy Gentry, *Columbus State Community College*

Tracy Grandy, *Hawkeye Community College*

Robert Guttentag, *University of North Carolina–Greensboro*

Ericka Hamilton, *Moraine Valley Community College*

Christine Harrington, *Middlesex County College*

Kelly Bouas Henry, *Missouri Western State University*

Raquel Henry, *Lone Star College–Kingwood*

Julie L. Hernandez, *Rock Valley College*

Suzanne Hester, *Oakton Community College*

Michael Hillard, *Central New Mexico Community College*

Theresa T. Holt, *Middlesex County College*

David P. Hurford, *Pittsburg State University*

Steven Isonio, *Golden West College*

Nita Jackson, *Butler Community College*

Cameron R. John, *Utah Valley University*

Susan T. Johnson, *Cypress College*

Pete Johnson, *North Platte Community College*

Carolyn Kaufman, *Columbus State Community College*

Barbara Kennedy, *Brevard Community College–Palm Bay*

Rosalyn M. King, *Northern Virginia Community College–Loudoun*

Burton F. Krain, *College of Lake County*

Juliana K. Leding, *University of North Florida*

Jeffrey Lee, *West Los Angeles College*

James Leppien–Christiansen, *Saddleback College*

Cynthia Lofaso, *Central Virginia Community College*

Karsten Look, *Columbus State Community College*

Wade Lueck, *Mesa Community College*

Mike Majors, *Delgado Community College*

Amy J. Marin, *Phoenix College*

Karen Marsh, *University of Minnesota–Duluth*

Randy Martinez, *Cypress College*

Donna Marie McElroy, *Atlantic Cape Community College*

Lee Merchant, *Modesto Junior College*

J. Trevor Milliron, *Lee University*

Dan Muhwezi, *Butler Community College*

Robin Musselman, *Lehigh Carbon Community College*

Elizabeth Nelson, *American River College*

David Neufeldt, *Hutchinson Community College*

Allison D. O'Neal, *Chandler–Gilbert Community College*

Keith Pannell, *El Paso Community College*

Jeffrey J. Pedroza, *Santa Ana College*

Russell Phillips, *Missouri Western State University*

Andrea Phronebarger, *York Technical College*

Rebecca Rahschulte, *Ivy Tech Community College*

Belinda Ramos, *Chandler–Gilbert Community College*

Evette F. Reagan, *Orange Coast College*

Shannon Rich, *Texas Woman's University*

Linda Robertson-Schule, *San Antonio College*

James Rodgers, *Hawkeye Community College*

Susan Rogers, *Columbus State Community College*

Lilian M. Romero, *San Jacinto College–Central*

Traci Sachteleben, *Southwestern Illinois College*

Nancy A. Schaab, *Delta College*

David Shepard, *South Texas College*

Susan A. Shodahl, *San Bernardino Valley College*

Donald R. Shull, *Ivy Tech Community College*

Barry Silber, *Hillsboro Community College*

Christopher L. Smith, *Tyler Junior College*

Brian D. Smith, *Seattle Central Community College*

Wayne S. Stein, *Brevard Community College–Melbourne*

Pamela E. Stewart, *Northern Virginia College*

David Stout, *Brookdale Community College*

Maurianna Swanson, *Miami-Dade College–Kendall*

Eva Szeli, *Arizona State University–Tempe*

Helen Taylor, *Bellevue Community College*

Lynne Ticke, *Bronx Community College*

Joe M. Tinnin, *Richland College*

David Tom, *Columbus State Community College*

Isabel A. Trombetti, *Community College of Rhode Island–Warwick*

Karl J. Ullrich, *Ivy Tech Community College*

Victoria Van Wie, *Lone Star College–CyFair*
Ruth A. Wallace, *Butler Community College*
Robert W. Wildblood, *Indiana University–Kokomo*
David K. Williams, *Spartanburg Community College*
John W. Wright, *Washington State University*
Jennifer Yanowitz, *Utica College*
Stefani Yorges, *West Chester University of Pennsylvania*
Brandy Young, *Cypress College*
Adena Young, *Missouri State University*
R. Lee Zasloff, *American River College*

Introductory Psychology Symposia

Every year McGraw-Hill conducts several Introductory Psychology Symposia that are attended by instructors from across the country. These events are an opportunity for editors from McGraw-Hill to gather information about the needs and challenges of instructors teaching the introductory psychology course. They also offer a forum for the attendees to exchange ideas and experiences with colleagues whom they might not otherwise have met. The feedback we have received has been invaluable and has contributed—directly or indirectly—to the development of *Experience Psychology* and its supplements.

Terry Scott Adcock, *Parkland College*
Mark Alicke, *Ohio University*
Cheryl Almeida, *Johnson & Wales University*
Susan A. Anderson, *University of South Alabama*
Diane Davis Ashe, *Valencia Community College*
Thomas C. Bailey, *University of Maryland*
David E. Baskind, *Delta College*
Scott C. Bates, *Utah State*

James L. Becker, *Pulaski Technical College*
Aileen M. Behan–Collins, *Chemeketa Community College*
Dan Bellack, *Trident Technical College*
Andrew Berns, *Milwaukee Area Tech*
Joy L. Berrenberg, *University of Colorado–Denver*
Jennifer Bizon, *Texas A & M University*
Ginette Blackhart, *East Tennessee State*
Stephen Blessing, *University of Tampa*
Jeffrey Blum, *Los Angeles City College*
Susan Boatright, *University of Rhode Island*
Deb Briihl, *Valdosta State University*
Tamara Brown, *University of Kentucky*
Brad Brubaker, *Indiana State University*
Lorelei A. Carvajal, *Triton Community College*
Karen Christoff, *University of Mississippi*
Jack Chuang, *San Jacinto College*
Douglas L. Chute, *Drexel University*
Diana Ciesko, *Valencia Community College*
Marsha G. Clarkson, *Georgia State University*
Alexis Collier, *Ohio State University*
Doreen Collins-McHugh, *Seminole Community College*
Laurie L. Couch, *Morehead State University*
Layton Curl, *Metro State College–Denver*
Chris Curtis, *Delta College*
Michaela DeCataldo, *Johnson & Wales University*
Barbara De Filippo, *Lane Community College*
Suzanne Delaney, *University of Arizona*
Bonnie Dennis, *Virginia Western Community College*
Peggy Dombrowski, *Central Pennsylvania Community College*
Carol Donnelly, *Northwestern University/Purdue University*
Dale Doty, *Monroe Community College*
Katherine Dowdell, *Des Moines Area Community College*
Shari Dunlavy, *Ivy Tech–Ft. Wayne*
Laura Duvall, *Heartland Community College*
Jay Brophy Ellison, *University of Central Florida*
Michael Erickson, *University of California–Riverside*

Dan Fawaz, *Georgia Perimeter College*
Greg J. Feist, *San Jose State University*
Dave Filak, *Joliet Junior College*
Tom Fischer, *Wayne State University*
Raymond Fleming, *University of Wisconsin–Madison*
Dan Forsyth, *Virginia Commonwealth*
Eric Fox, *Western Michigan University*
Paula A. Fox, *Appalachian State University*
Debra L. Frame, *University of Cincinnati*
Paula Frioli, *Truckee Meadows Community College*
Dale Fryxell, *Chaminade University*
John Gambon, *Ozarks Technical College*
Travis Gibbs, *Riverside Community College*
Charles W. Ginn, *University of Cincinnati*
Robert L. Gordon, *Wright State University*
Jerry Green, *Tarrant County College*
Daine Grey, *Middlesex Community College*
Sara Grison, *University of Illinois–Urbana-Champaign*
Regan Gurung, *University of Wisconsin–Green Bay*
David T. Hall, *Baton Rouge Community College*
Laura Harpster, *Salt Lake Community College*
Gregory Eugene Harris, *Polk Community College*
Leslie Hathorn, *Metropolitan State College of Denver*
Jeffrey Henriques, *University of Wisconsin–Madison*
Carmon Weaver Hicks, *Ivy Tech Community College*
Debra Hollister, *Valencia Community College*
Theresa Holt, *Middlesex County College*
Natalie W. Hopson, *Salisbury University*
Vahan Hovsepian, *Butte College*
Mark Hoyert, *Indiana University–Northwest*
John Huber, *Texas State University*
Charlie Huffman, *James Madison University*
Rachel Hull, *Texas A & M University*
Nita Jackson, *Butler Community College*
Sean P. Jennings, *Valencia Community College*

Linda Jones, *Blinn College*
Barbara Kennedy, *Brevard Community College*
Sheila Kennison, *Oklahoma State University*
Shirin Khosropour, *Austin Community College*
Christina Knox, *College of the Sequoias*
Dana Kuehn, *Florida Community College*
Mark Laumakis, *San Diego State University*
Natalie Kerr Lawrence, *James Madison University*
Tera Letzring, *Idaho State University*
Dawn Lewis, *Prince Georges Community College*
Deborah Licht, *Pikes Peak Community College*
Mark Licht, *Florida State University*
Mario Lopez, *Mt. San Jacinto College*
Sonya L. Lott-Harrison, *Community College of Philadelphia*
Jeff Love, *Penn State University*
Lea Ann Lucas, *Sinclair Community College*
Linda Mae, *Arizona State University*
Clem Magner, *Milwaukee Area Tech West*
Mike Majors, *Delgado Community College*
Brian Malley, *University of Michigan–Ann Arbor*
Karen Marsh, *University of Minnesota–Duluth*
Randall Martinez, *Cypress College*
Wanda C. McCarthy, *University of Cincinnati*
Jason McCoy, *Cape Fear Community College–Downtown*
Sean Meegan, *University of Utah*
Charlene Melrose, *Orange Coast College*
Kathleen Mentink, *Chippewa Valley Technical College*
Steven P. Mewaldt, *Marshall University*
Sean Mikulay, *Elgin Community College*
Michelle D. Miller, *Northern Arizona University*
Joel Morgovsky, *Brookdale Community College*
Glenn Musgrove, *Broward Community College*
Bethany Neal-Beliveau, *Indiana University/Perdue University–Indianapolis*
Jeff Neubauer, *Pima Community College West*
Jonathan Nezlek, *College of William & Mary*
Glenda Nichols, *Tarrant County College–South*
Jane Noll, *University of Southern Florida*
Brian Oppy, *Chico State*
Donald Orso, *Anne Arundel Community College*
Randall Osborne, *Texas State University–San Marcos*
Jack A. Palmer, *University of Louisiana–Monroe*
Debra Parish, *Tomball College*
Jennifer Peluso, *Florida Atlantic University*
Julie A. Penley, *El Paso Community College*
David Perkins, *University of Louisiana*
Deb Podwika, *Kankakee Community College*

Bryan Porter, *Old Dominion University*
Alida Quick, *Wayne County Community College*
Reginald Rackley, *Southern University*
Chris Randall, *Kennesaw State University*
Diane Reddy, *University of Wisconsin–Milwaukee*
Laura Reichel, *Front Range Community College*
Tanya Renner, *Kapi'olani Community College*
Tonja Ringgold, *Baltimore City Community College*
Vicki Ritts, *Saint Louis Community College*
Alan Roberts, *Indiana University*
Caton F. Roberts, *University of Wisconsin*
Edna Ross, *University of Louisville–Louisville*
Debra Rowe, *Oakland Community College*
Larry Rudiger, *University of Vermont*
Phyllis Rundhaug, *San Jacinto College*
Sharleen Sakai, *Michigan State University*
Dave Schroeder, *University of Arkansas*
Donna Love Seagle, *Chattanooga State Technical*
James Shannon, *Citrus College*
Wayne Shebilske, *Wright State University*
Elisabeth Sherwin, *University of Arkansas–Little Rock*
Maria Shpurik, *Florida International University*
Harvey Shulman, *Ohio State University*
Jennifer Siciliani, *University of Missouri–St. Louis*
Barry Silber, *Hillsborough Community College*
Nancy Simpson, *Trident Technical College*
Peggy Skinner, *South Plains College*
Chris Smith, *Tyler Community College*
Jamie Smith, *Ohio State University*
Lilliette Johnson Smith, *Southwest Tennessee*
Vivian Smith, *Lakeland Community College*
Genevieve Stevens, *Houston Community College*
Mark Stewart, *American River College–Los Rios*

Pam Stewart, *Northern Virginia Community College*
Claire St. Peter Pipkin, *West Virginia University*
Eva Szeli, *Arizona State University*
Nina Tarner, *Sacred Heart University*
Rachelle Tannenbaum, *Anne Arundel Community College–Arnold*
Helen Taylor, *Bellevue Community College*
Felicia Friendly Thomas, *California State Polytechnic*
Lisa Thomassen, *Indiana University*
Stephen Tracy, *Community College of Southern Nevada*
Margot Underwood, *Joliet Junior College*
Lisa Valentino, *Seminole Community College*
Barbara Van Horn, *Indian River Community College*
Ruth Wallace, *Butler Community College*
Martin Wolfger, *Ivy Tech Bloomington*
John W. Wright, *Washington State University*
Mona Yektaparast, *Central Piedmont Community College*

Student Focus Groups

Judy Bowker, *Pace University*
Sam Fryer, *Baruch College*
Richard Herrera, *Bronx Community College*
Mahir Hossein, *Baruch College*
Jasmine Rivera, *Bronx Community College*
Bhabana Shakya, *Baruch College*

Board of Advisors

I would like to give special thanks to the members of *Experience Psychology* Board of Advisors, who read every chapter from start to finish—not just once but twice. Their suggestions, criticisms, references, and edits have helped to shape *Experience Psychology*. I am very grateful to them for all their hard work under demanding deadlines.

Carol Anderson, *Bellevue Community College*
Marlena Barber, *Lee University*
Kendra Gilds, *Lane Community College*
David Stout, *Brookdale Community College*
Eva Szeli, *Arizona State University–Tempe*
Ruth Wallace, *Butler Community College*
Brandy Young, *Cypress College*

Top, L-R: Carol Anderson, Marlena Barber, David Stout, Eva Szeli.
Bottom, L-R: Ruth Wallace, Brandy Young.

Teleconference Participants

Gary Bothe, *Pensacola Junior College*
David T. Hall, *Baton Rouge Community College*
Gregory E. Harris, *Polk Community College*
Carmon Weaver Hicks, *Ivy Tech Community College*
Kathleen Mentink, *Chippewa Valley Technical College*
MaryEllen Vandenberg, *Potomac State College*
Ruth A. Wallace, *Butler Community College*

Supplement Reviewers

David W. Alfano, *Community College of Rhode Island–Warwick*
Patricia Crowe, *Hawkeye Community College*
Kathy Demitrakis, *Central New Mexico Community College*
Penny S. Edwards, *Tri-County Technical College*
Tracy Grandy, *Hawkeye Community College*
Ericka Hamilton, *Moraine Valley Community College*
Raquel Henry, *Missouri Western State University*
Sachi Horback, *Bucks County Community College*
Carolyn Kaufman, *Columbus State Community College*

Barbara Kennedy, *Brevard Community College (Palm Bay)*
Wade Lueck, *Mesa Community College*
Dan Muhwezi, *Butler Community College*
Robin Musselman, *Lehigh Carbon Community College*
Elizabeth Nelson, *American River College*
Andrea Phronebarger, *York Technical College*
Wendy Quinton, *SUNY Buffalo*
Shannon Rich, *Texas Woman's University*
James Rodgers, *Hawkeye Community College*
Brian Smith, *Seattle Central Community College*

Survey Participants

Laura Billings, *Southwestern Illinois College*
Elliott Bonem, *Eastern Michigan University*
Ann Ewing, *Mesa Community College*
Carla Fanning, *Grayson County College*
Paula Frioli, *Truckee Meadows Community College*
Kevin B. Handley, *Germanna Community College*
Sachi Horback, *Bucks County Community College*
David Leung, *Lane Community College*
Andrew Peck, *Penn State University*
Eric Reittinger, *South Texas College*
Vivian Smith, *Lakeland Community College*
Mary West, *Tri-County Technical College*

Cover and Design Reviewers

Carol Anderson, *Bellevue Community College*
Marlena Barber, *Lee University*
Kendra Gilds, *Lane Community College*
David Stout, *Brookdale Community College*
Eva Szeli, *Arizona State University–Tempe*
Brandy Young, *Cypress College*
Ruth Wallace, *Butler Community College*

Personal Acknowledgments

To close, I want to express my deepest appreciation to the many people at McGraw-Hill who have contributed so substantially to making *Experience Psychology* the best it could be. Foremost, I owe a very large debt of gratitude to Sylvia Mallory, my best reader, editor, and (sometimes) partner in crime as we saw this volume to completion. Thanks as well to Mike Sugarman, Dawn Groundwater, Sheryl Adams, Beth Mejia, and James Headley, who supported and contributed to the innovative features of *Experience Psychology*. Every hesitant suggestion from me ("Could we, maybe, do . . .?") was met by them with a resounding "Yes!" making this volume a true adventure. In addition, I am in awe of the amazing contributions made to this book by those in production (especially Catherine Morris, Cassandra Chu, Robin Mouat, Alexandra Ambrose, and Linda Beaupré). *Experience Psychology* is beautiful because of their creativity and resourcefulness. A big shout-out as well to Jennifer Gordon, whose copyediting was painstaking and enormously helpful.

Thanks to my colleagues and students at the University of Missouri, for their enthusiasm, advice, patience, and support. I must acknowledge the artists whose music kept me sane and engaged throughout this process, including Regina Spektor, Rufus Wainwright, Polyphonic Spree, Sufjan Stevens, Citizen Cope, and Radiohead. And a heartfelt thank-you goes to my family and friends who have supported and inspired me, especially Lisa and Sam.

L.A.K.

experience psychology

1 The Science of Psychology

The Mystery That Is You

Do you have a hero? When you think about someone you admire, a politician, film star, or high-achieving athlete might come to mind. In a December 2008 Gallup poll, the most admired American man was Barack Obama (Saad, 2008). The most admired woman was Hillary Rodham Clinton. Both are famous people who have made significant contributions in public life.

At the right moment, an ordinary person can become a hero. On January 15, 2009, US Airways Captain Chesley "Sully" Sullenberger was piloting a routine flight out of New York City. Shortly after takeoff, the plane hit a flock of birds, rendering the engines useless. With 155 people on board, Sullenberger faced a potential catastrophe. Realizing that the available runways were unreachable, he made a split-second decision to land the plane in the Hudson River. Just six minutes after takeoff, all 155 on board began deplaning from the floating plane into rescue boats. Sullenberger had calmly saved everyone on board, becoming a hero to the world (CBS News, 2009).

Even in ordinary circumstances, people make choices that we might call heroic. They are generous when they might be selfish. They work hard when they could slack off. Thinking about the admirable people we encounter every day, we can see how ordinary human behavior can be extraordinary if we view it in the right light and with a close lens.

Scientists, including psychologists, bring such powerful observations to their work. As scientists, moreover, psychologists are passionate about what they study—and what they study is you. As you read this book, thousands of dedicated scientists are studying things about you that you might have never considered, such as how your brain responds to a picture flashed on a screen and how your eyes adjust to a sunny day. There is not a single thing about you that is not fascinating to some psychologist somewhere. ■

- **What is the most admirable thing you saw someone do today? Was the act heroic?**

- **What is the most admirable thing *you* did in the last week?**

- **What could you do in your life to become someone's hero?**

This chapter begins by defining psychology and reviewing the history of the field. Next we survey seven broad approaches that characterize psychological science today. Then, in sequence, we examine the elements of the scientific method, review the different kinds of research psychologists do, and consider the importance of conducting psychological research according to ethical guidelines. We conclude with a look at the many applications of psychology to daily life—a central theme of this book.

1 Defining Psychology and Exploring Its Roots

Formally defined, **psychology** is the scientific study of behavior and mental processes. Let's consider the three key terms in this definition: *science, behavior,* and *mental processes.*

As a **science,** psychology uses systematic methods to observe human behavior and draw conclusions. The goals of psychological science are to describe, predict, and explain behavior. In addition, psychologists are often interested in controlling or changing behavior and use scientific methods to examine interventions that might help, for example, reduce violence or promote happiness.

Researchers might be interested in knowing whether individuals will help a stranger who has fallen down. The researchers could devise a study in which they observe people walking past a person who needs help. Through many observations, the researchers could come to *describe* helping behavior by counting how many times it occurs in particular circumstances. The researchers may also try to *predict* who will help, and when, by examining characteristics of the individuals studied. Are happy people more likely to help? Are women or men more likely to help? After psychologists have analyzed their data, they also will want to *explain* why helping behavior occurred when it did. Finally, these researchers might be interested in changing helping behavior, by devising strategies to increase helping.

Behavior is everything we do that can be directly observed—two people kissing, a baby crying, a college student riding a motorcycle to campus. **Mental processes** are the thoughts, feelings, and motives that each of us experiences privately but that cannot be observed directly. Although we cannot directly see thoughts and feelings, they are

What is your definition of psychology? When you think of the word psychology, what first comes to mind?

behavior
Everything we do that can be directly observed.

Behavior includes the observable act of two people kissing; mental processes include their unobservable thoughts about kissing.

psychology
The scientific study of behavior and mental processes.

science
The use of systematic methods to observe the natural world, including human behavior, and to draw conclusions.

mental processes
The thoughts, feelings, and motives that each of us experiences privately but that cannot be observed directly.

nonetheless real. They include *thinking* about kissing someone, a baby's *feelings* when its mother leaves the room, and a student's *memory* of a motorcycle trip.

The Psychological Frame of Mind

What makes for a good job, a good marriage, or a good life? Although there are a variety of ways to come to answer the big questions of life, psychologists approach these questions as scientists. Psychology is a rigorous discipline that tests assumptions, bringing scientific data to bear on the questions of central interest to human beings (Neuman, 2009; Salkind, 2009). Psychologists conduct research and rely on that research to provide evidence for their conclusions. They examine the available evidence about some aspect of mind and behavior, evaluate how strongly the data (information) support their hunches, analyze disconfirming evidence, and carefully consider whether they have explored all of the possible factors and explanations (Sternberg, Roediger, & Halpern, 2007). At the core of this scientific approach are four attitudes: critical thinking, curiosity, skepticism, and objectivity.

Like all scientists, psychologists are critical thinkers. **Critical thinking** is the process of thinking deeply and actively, asking questions, and evaluating the evidence. Thinking critically means asking ourselves *how* we know something. Critical thinkers question and test what some people say are facts. They examine research to see how soundly it supports an idea (McMillan, 2008). Critical thinking reduces the likelihood that conclusions will be based on unreliable personal beliefs, opinions, and emotions. *Critical thinking is very important as you are reading this book.* Some of the things you read might fit with what you already believe, and some might challenge you to reconsider your assumptions about the world. Actively engaging in critical thinking is vital to making the most of psychology. As you read about and study the field, think about how what you are learning relates to your life experiences and the assumptions you might have about people.

Scientists are also curious. The scientist notices things in the world (a star in the sky, an insect, a happy person) and wants to know what it is and why it is that way. Science involves asking questions, even very big questions such as where did the earth come from, and how does love between two people endure for 50 years? Thinking like a psychologist means opening your mind and imagination to wondering why things are the way they are.

In addition, scientists are skeptical (Stanovich, 2007). Skeptical people challenge whether a supposed fact is really true. Being skeptical can mean questioning what "everybody knows." There was a time when "everybody knew" that women were morally inferior to men, that race could influence a person's IQ, and that the earth was flat. Psychologists, like all scientists, look at assumptions in new and questioning ways. Psychology is different from common sense because psychologists are skeptical of commonsensical answers. Psychology researchers often turn up the unexpected in human behavior. For example, it might seem obvious that couples who live together before marriage have a better chance of making the marriage last. After all, practice makes perfect, right? Yet researchers have found a higher rate of marital success for couples who marry *before* living together (Liefbroer & Dourleijn, 2006; Popenoe, 2007; Wilson & Smallwood, 2008). You might use scientific skepticism the next time you encounter an infomercial about the latest diet craze that promises to help people lose weight "without diet or exercise." A skeptic knows that if something sounds too good to be true, it probably is.

Last, practicing science also means being objective. Scientists believe that one of the best ways to be objective is to use empirical methods to learn about the world (Beins, 2009; Martin, 2008). Using the *empirical method* means gaining knowledge through observation of events and logical reasoning. Being objective involves trying to see things as they really are, not just as we would like them to be. Objectivity means waiting to see what the evidence tells us rather than going with our hunches. Does the latest herbal

critical thinking
The process of thinking deeply and actively, asking questions, and evaluating the evidence.

dietary supplement really help relieve depression? An objective thinker knows that we have to have sound evidence before answering that question.

Once you start to think like a psychologist, you might notice that the world starts to look like a different place. Easy answers and simple assumptions will not do. As you can probably imagine, psychologists, as a group, are people with many different opinions about many different things. If a number of these critical thinkers were to gather around a table, it is a safe bet that they would have a lively conversation.

Indeed, as you will see throughout this book, there are many things about which psychologists disagree, and psychology (like any science) is filled with debate and controversy. For example, a recent controversy in psychology concerns the emergence of so-called Generation Me (Twenge, 2006). Jean Twenge and her colleagues (Twenge, 2006; Twenge & Foster, 2008) argue that Americans born since the 1980s are different from previous generations in that they are unusually self-confident, self-assertive, and self-centered. Based on her research examining scores on questionnaires concerning *narcissism* (a condition of intense, unhealthy self-love) over many years, Twenge (2006) refers to these individuals as Generation Me. She suggests that we are in the midst of an epidemic of narcissism. Other psychologists, however, sharply challenge this claim. In doing so, they present data showing no changes in narcissism over the last three decades (Donnellan, Trzesniewski, & Robins, 2009).

Debate and controversy are a natural part of thinking like a psychologist. Psychology has advanced as a field *because* psychologists do not always agree with one another about why mind and behavior work the way they do. Psychologists have reached a more accurate understanding of human behavior *because* psychology fosters controversies and *because* psychologists think deeply and reflectively and examine the evidence on all sides. A good place to try out your critical thinking skills is by revisiting the definition of psychology.

Psychology as the Science of All Human Behavior

As you consider the general definition of psychology as the science of human behavior, you might be thinking, okay, where's the couch? Where's the mental illness? Psychology certainly includes the study of therapy and psychological disorders. *Clinical psychologists* in particular are psychologists who specialize in studying and treating psychological disorders. By definition, though, psychology is a much more general science (Ash & Sturm, 2007), practiced in several other environments in addition to clinical settings (Figure 1.1). How did we end up with the idea that psychology is only about mental illness? Surely, psychological disorders are very interesting, and the media often portray psychologists as therapists. Yet the view of psychology as the science of what is wrong with people started long before TV was even invented.

When they think of psychology, many people think of Sigmund Freud (1856–1939). Freud believed that most of human behavior is caused by dark, unpleasant, unconscious impulses pressing for expression. For Freud, even the average person on the street is a mysterious well of unconscious desires. Certainly, Freud has had a lasting impact on psychology and on society; as recently as March 2006, on the occasion of his 150th birthday, Freud was featured on the cover of *Newsweek*. Consider, though, that Freud based his ideas about human nature on the patients that he saw

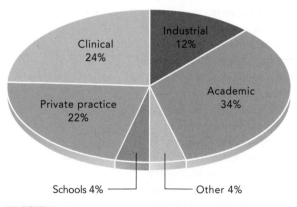

FIGURE 1.1

Settings in Which Psychologists Work More psychologists work in academic settings (34 percent), such as colleges and universities, than any other setting. However, clinical (24 percent) and private practice (22 percent) settings—both contexts in which many psychologists in the mental health professions work—together make up almost half of the total settings.

in his clinical practice—individuals who were struggling with psychological problems. His experiences with these individuals, as well as his analysis of himself, colored his outlook on all of humanity. Freud (1918/1996) once wrote, "I have found little that is 'good' about human beings on the whole. In my experience most of them are trash."

Freud's view of human nature has crept into general perceptions of what psychology is all about. Imagine, for example, that you are seated on a plane, having a pleasant conversation with the woman (a stranger) sitting next to you. At some point you ask your seatmate what she does for a living, and she informs you she is a psychologist. You might think to yourself, "Uh oh. What have I already told this person? What secrets does she know about me that I don't know about myself? Has she been analyzing me this whole time?" Would you be surprised to discover that this psychologist studies happiness? Or intelligence? Or the processes related to the experience of vision? The study of psychological disorders is a very important aspect of psychology, but represents only one part of the science of psychology.

The murder in 2006 of five Amish schoolgirls evoked feelings in the community not of hatred and revenge but of forgiveness.

Psychology seeks to understand the truths of human life in *all* its dimensions, including people's best and worst experiences. Psychologists acknowledge that as in the heroism of Sully Sullenberger, sometimes an individual's best moments emerge amid the most difficult circumstances. Research on the human capacity for forgiveness demonstrates this point (Bono, McCullough, & Root, 2008; Lawler-Row & others, 2008; Legaree, Turner, & Lollis, 2007). Forgiveness is the act of letting go of our anger and resentment toward someone who has done something harmful to us. Through forgiveness we cease seeking revenge or avoiding the person who did us harm, and we might even wish that person well.

In October 2006, after Charles Carl Roberts IV took 10 young Amish girls hostage in a one-room schoolhouse in Pennsylvania, eventually killing 5 of them and wounding 5 others before killing himself, the grief-stricken Amish community focused not on hatred and revenge but on forgiveness. As funds were being set up for the victims' families, the Amish insisted that one be established for the murderer's family. As they prepared simple funerals for the dead girls, the community invited the wife of the killer to attend. The science of psychology has much to offer to our understanding not only of the violent acts of the perpetrator but also of the forgiveness of the victims.

The willingness of these Amish people to forgive this horrible crime is both remarkable and puzzling. Can we scientifically understand the human ability to forgive even what might seem to be unforgivable? A number of psychologists have taken up the topic of forgiveness in research and clinical practice (Bono & McCullough, 2006; Cohen & others, 2006). Michael McCullough and his colleagues (2007) have shown that the capacity to forgive is an unfolding process that often takes time. For the Amish, their deep religious faith led them to embrace forgiveness, where many people might have been motivated to seek revenge and retribution. Researchers also have explored the relation between religious commitment and forgiveness (McCullough, Bono, & Root, 2007).

Some psychologists argue that the field has focused too much on the negative aspects of humanity and neglected topics that reflect the best of human life (Seligman & Csikszentmihalyi, 2000). Others insist that human weaknesses are the most important aspects of life to study (Lazarus, 2003). The fact is that in order to be a truly general science of human behavior, psychology must address *all* sides of human experience. Surely, controversy is a part of any science. Healthy debate characterizes the field of psychology, and a new psychological perspective sometimes arises when one scientist questions the views of another. Such ongoing debate is a sign of a lively discipline. Indeed, the very birth of the field was marked by debate. Great minds do not always think alike, especially when they are thinking about psychology.

Psychology in Historical Perspective

Psychology seeks to answer questions that people have been asking for thousands of years—for example:

- How do we learn?
- What is memory?
- Why does one person grow and flourish while another struggles?

The notion that such questions might be answered through scientific inquiry is a relatively new idea. From the time human language included the word *why* and became rich enough to let people talk about the past, we have been creating myths to explain why things are the way they are. Ancient myths attributed most important events to the pleasure or displeasure of the gods: When a volcano erupted, the gods were angry; if two people fell in love, they had been struck by Cupid's arrows. Gradually, myths gave way to *philosophy*—the rational investigation of the underlying principles of being and knowledge. People attempted to explain events in terms of natural rather than supernatural causes (Viney & King, 2003).

Western philosophy came of age in ancient Greece in the fourth and fifth centuries B.C.E. Socrates, Plato, Aristotle, and others debated the nature of thought and behavior, including the possible link between the mind and the body. Later philosophers, especially René Descartes, argued that the mind and body were completely separate, and they focused their attention on the mind. Psychology grew out of this tradition of thinking about the mind and body. The influence of philosophy on contemporary psychology persists today, as researchers who study emotion still talk about Descartes, and scientists who study happiness often refer to Aristotle (Kashdan, Biswas-Diener, & King, 2008).

In addition to philosophy, psychology also has roots in the natural sciences of biology and physiology (Johnson, 2008; Pinel, 2009). Indeed, it was Wilhelm Wundt (1832–1920), a German philosopher-physician, who put the pieces of the philosophy–natural science puzzle together to create the academic discipline of psychology. Some historians like to say that modern psychology was born in December 1879 at the University of Leipzig, when Wundt and his students (most notably E. B. Titchener) performed an experiment to measure the time lag between the instant a person heard a sound and when that person pressed a telegraph key to signal that he had heard it.

What was so special about this experiment? Wundt's study was about the workings of the brain: He was trying to measure the time it took the human brain and nervous system to translate information into action. At the heart of this experiment was the idea that mental processes could be measured. This focus ushered in the new science of psychology.

Wundt and his collaborators concentrated on discovering the basic elements, or "structures," of mental processes. Their approach was called **structuralism** because of its focus on identifying the structures of the human mind. The method they used in the study of mental structures was *introspection* (literally, "looking inside"). For this type of research, a person was placed in a laboratory setting and was asked to think (introspect) about what was going on mentally as various events took place. For example, the individual might be subjected to a sharp, repetitive clicking sound and then might be asked to report whatever conscious feelings the clicking produced. What made this method scientific was the systematic, detailed self-reports required of the person in the controlled laboratory setting.

Although Wundt is most often regarded as the founding father of modern psychology, it was psychologist and philosopher William James (1842–1910), perhaps more than anyone else, who gave the field an American stamp. From

Wilhelm Wundt (1832–1920)
Wundt founded the first psychology laboratory (with his two co-workers) in 1879 at the University of Leipzig in Germany.

William James (1842–1910)
James's approach became known as functionalism.

structuralism
Wundt's approach to discovering the basic elements, or structures, of mental processes.

James's perspective, the key question for psychology is not so much what the mind *is* (that is, its structures) as what it *is for* (its purpose or function). James's view was eventually named *functionalism*.

What mental processes have become so automatic for you that you no longer think about them?

In contrast to structuralism, which emphasized the components of the mind, **functionalism** probed the functions and purposes of the mind and behavior in the individual's adaptation to the environment. Whereas structuralists were looking inside the mind and searching for its structures, functionalists focused on what was going on in human interactions with the outside world and trying to understand the purpose of thoughts. If structuralism is about the "what" of the mind, functionalism is about the "why."

functionalism
James's approach to mental processes, emphasizing the functions and purposes of the mind and behavior in the individual's adaptation to the environment.

A central question in functionalism is, why is human thought *adaptive*—that is, why are people better off because they can think than they would be otherwise? When we talk about whether a characteristic is adaptive, we are talking about how it makes an organism better able to survive. Unlike Wundt, James did not believe in the existence of rigid structures of the mind. Instead, James saw the mind as flexible and fluid, characterized by constant change in response to a continuous flow of information from the world. Not surprisingly, James called the natural flow of thought a "stream of consciousness."

Why are you better off because you can think than you would be if you could not? How have you used your ability to think today?

Functionalism fit well with the theory of evolution through natural selection proposed by British naturalist Charles Darwin (1809–1882). In 1859, Darwin published his ideas in *On the Origin of Species.* He proposed the principle of **natural selection,** an evolutionary process in which organisms that are best adapted to their environment will survive and, importantly, produce offspring. Darwin noted that members of any species are often locked in competition for scarce resources such as food and shelter. Natural selection is the process by which the environment determines who wins that competition. Darwin asserted that organisms with biological features that led to survival and reproduction would be better represented in subsequent generations. Over many generations, organisms with these characteristics would constitute a larger percentage of the population. Eventually this process could change an entire species. If environmental conditions changed, however, other characteristics might become favored by natural selection, moving the process in a different direction.

natural selection
Darwin's principle of an evolutionary process in which organisms that are best adapted to their environment will survive and produce offspring.

If you are unfamiliar with Darwin's theory of evolution, it might be helpful to consider the simple question, why do giraffes have long necks? An early explanation might have been that giraffes live in places where the trees are very high, and so the creatures must stretch their necks to get to their favorite food—leaves. Lots of stretching might lead to adult giraffes that have longer necks. This explanation does not tell us, though, why giraffes are *born* with long necks. A characteristic cannot be passed from one generation to the next unless it is recorded in the *genes,* those collections of molecules that are responsible for heredity.

According to evolutionary theory, species change through random genetic mutation. That means that essentially by accident, some members of a species are born with genetic characteristics that make them different from other members (for instance, some lucky giraffes being born with unusually long necks). If these changes are adaptive (for example, if they help those giraffes compete for food, survive, and reproduce), they become more common in members of the species. So, presumably long, long ago, some giraffes were genetically predisposed to have longer necks, and some giraffes were genetically predisposed to have shorter necks. Only those with the long necks survived to reproduce, giving us the giraffes we see today. The survival of the giraffes with long necks is a product of natural selection. Evolutionary theory implies that the way we are, at least partially, is the way that is best suited to survival in our environment (Kardong, 2008; Mader, 2009).

The survival of giraffes with long necks (and not giraffes with short necks) vividly illustrates natural selection at work.

Darwin's theory continues to influence psychologists today because it is strongly supported by observation. We can make such observations every day. Right now, for example, in your kitchen sink, various bacteria are locked in competition for scarce resources in the form of those tempting food particles from your last meal. When you use an antibacterial cleaner, you are playing a role in natural selection, because you are effectively killing off the bacteria that cannot survive the cleaning agents. However, you are also letting the bacteria that are genetically adapted to survive that cleaner to take over the sink. The same principle applies to taking an antibiotic medication at the first sign of a sore throat or an earache. By killing off the bacteria that may be causing the illness, you are creating an environment where their competitors (so-called antibiotic-resistant bacteria) may flourish. These observations powerfully demonstrate Darwinian selection in action.

If structuralism won the battle to be the birthplace of psychology, functionalism won the war. To this day, psychologists continue to talk about the adaptive nature of human characteristics. Indeed, from these beginnings, psychologists have branched out to study more aspects of human behavior than Wundt or James might have imagined. We now examine various contemporary approaches to the science of psychology.

self-quiz

1. The one *correct* statement among the following is
   A. there are many controversies in the field of psychology.
   B. psychologists on the whole agree among themselves on most aspects of the field.
   C. psychologists do not engage in critical thinking.
   D. there are few controversies in the field of psychology.

2. Of the following, the characteristic that is *not* at the heart of the scientific approach is
   A. skepticism.
   B. critical thinking.

C. prejudging.
D. curiosity.

3. Charles Darwin's work is relevant to psychology because
   A. Darwin's research demonstrated that there are few differences between humans and animals.
   B. Darwin's principle of natural selection suggests that human behavior is partially a result of efforts to survive.
   C. Darwin stated that humans descended from apes, a principle that allows psychologists to understand human behavior.
   D. Darwin created functionalism.

Apply It! 4. Two psychologists, Clayton and Sam, are interested in studying emotional expressions. Clayton wants to determine whether emotional expression is healthy and if it has an influence on well-being. Sam is interested in describing the types of emotions people express and building a catalog of all of the emotions and emotional expressions that exist. In this example. Clayton is most like _____ and Sam is most like _____.
   A. Wilhelm Wundt; William James
   B. William James; Wilhelm Wundt
   C. Wilhelm Wundt; Sigmund Freud
   D. Sigmund Freud; Wilhelm Wundt

2 Contemporary Approaches to Psychology

In this section we briefly survey seven different approaches that represent the intellectual backdrop of psychological science: biological, behavioral, psychodynamic, humanistic, cognitive, evolutionary, and sociocultural.

The Biological Approach

neuroscience
The scientific study of the structure, function, development, genetics, and biochemistry of the nervous system, emphasizing that the brain and nervous system are central to understanding behavior, thought, and emotion.

Some psychologists examine behavior and mental processes through the **biological approach,** which is a focus on the body, especially the brain and nervous system. For example, researchers might investigate the way your heart races when you are afraid or how your hands sweat when you tell a lie. Although a number of physiological systems may be involved in thoughts and feelings, perhaps the largest contribution to physiological psychology has come through the emergence of neuroscience (Nelson, 2009).

Neuroscience is the scientific study of the structure, function, development, genetics, and biochemistry of the nervous system. Neuroscience emphasizes that the brain and nervous system are central to understanding behavior, thought, and emotion. Neuroscientists believe that thoughts and emotions have a physical basis in the brain. Electrical impulses zoom

biological approach
An approach to psychology focusing on the body, especially the brain and nervous system.

throughout the brain's cells, releasing chemical substances that enable us to think, feel, and behave. Our remarkable human capabilities would not be possible without the brain and nervous system, which constitute the most complex, intricate, and elegant system imaginable. Although biological approaches might sometimes seem to reduce complex human experience into simple physical structures, developments in neuroscience have allowed psychologists to understand the brain as an amazingly complex organ, perhaps just as complex as the psychological processes linked to its functioning.

The Behavioral Approach

behavioral approach
An approach to psychology emphasizing the scientific study of observable behavioral responses and their environmental determinants.

The **behavioral approach** emphasizes the scientific study of observable behavioral responses and their environmental determinants. It focuses on an organism's visible interactions with the environment—that

Richard J. Davidson of the University of Wisconsin, Madison, shown with the Dalai Lama, is a leading researcher in behavioral neuroscience.

is, behaviors, not thoughts or feelings. The principles of the behavioral approach have been widely applied to help people change their behavior for the better (Miltenberger, 2008). The psychologists who adopt this approach are called *behaviorists.* Under the intellectual leadership of John B. Watson (1878–1958) and B. F. Skinner (1904–1990), behaviorism dominated psychological research during the first half of the twentieth century.

Skinner (1938) emphasized that psychology should be about what people do—their actions and behaviors—and should not concern itself with things that cannot be seen, such as thoughts, feelings, and goals. He believed that rewards and punishments determine our behavior. For example, a child might behave in a well-mannered fashion because her parents have rewarded this behavior. We do the things we do, say behaviorists, because of the environmental conditions we have experienced and continue to experience.

Contemporary behaviorists still emphasize the importance of observing behavior to understand an individual, and they use rigorous methods advocated by Watson and Skinner (Cooper, Heron, & Heward, 2007). They also continue to stress the importance of environmental determinants of behavior (DeSantis-Moniaci & Altshuler, 2007). However, not every behaviorist today accepts the earlier behaviorists' rejection of thought processes, which are often called *cognition* (M. G. Kushner, 2007).

The Psychodynamic Approach

psychodynamic approach
An approach to psychology emphasizing unconscious thought, the conflict between biological drives (such as the drive for sex) and society's demands, and early childhood family experiences.

The **psychodynamic approach** emphasizes unconscious thought, the conflict between biological drives (such as the drive for sex) and society's demands, and early childhood family experiences. Practitioners of this approach believe that sexual and aggressive impulses buried deep within the unconscious mind influence the way people think, feel, and behave.

Sigmund Freud, the founding father of the psychodynamic approach, theorized that early relationships with parents shape an individual's personality. Freud's (1917) theory was the basis for the therapeutic technique that he called *psychoanalysis,* which involves an analyst's unlocking a person's unconscious conflicts by talking with the individual about his or her childhood memories, dreams, thoughts, and feelings. Certainly, Freud's views have been controversial, but they remain a part of contemporary psychology. Today's psychodynamic theories tend to place less emphasis on sexual drives and more on cultural or social experiences as determinants of behavior.

Sigmund Freud (1856–1939)
Freud was the founding father of the psychodynamic approach.

The Humanistic Approach

The **humanistic approach** emphasizes a person's positive qualities, the capacity for positive growth, and the freedom to choose one's destiny. Humanistic psychologists stress that people have the ability to control their lives and are not simply controlled by the environment (Maslow, 1971; Rogers, 1961). They theorize that rather than being driven by unconscious impulses (as the psychodynamic approach dictates) or by external rewards (as the behavioral approach emphasizes), people can choose to live by higher human values such as *altruism*—unselfish concern for other people's well-being—and free will. Many aspects of this optimistic approach appear in research on motivation, emotion, and personality psychology (Diaz-Laplante, 2007; Patterson & Joseph, 2007).

humanistic approach
An approach to psychology emphasizing a person's positive qualities, the capacity for positive growth, and the freedom to choose any destiny.

According to humanistic psychologists, warm, supportive behavior toward others helps us to realize our tremendous capacity for self-understanding.

The Cognitive Approach

According to cognitive psychologists, your brain houses a "mind" whose mental processes allow you to remember, make decisions, plan, set goals, and be creative (Grigorenko & others, 2009; Sternberg, 2009). The **cognitive approach,** then, emphasizes the mental processes involved in knowing: how we direct our attention, perceive, remember, think, and solve problems. For example, cognitive psychologists want to know how we solve math problems, why we remember some things for only a short time but others for a lifetime, and how we can use our imaginations to plan for the future.

Cognitive psychologists view the mind as an active and aware problem-solving system (Robinson-Riegler & Robinson-Riegler, 2008). This view contrasts with the behavioral view, which portrays behavior as controlled by external environmental forces. In the cognitive view, an individual's mental processes are in control of behavior through memories, perceptions, images, and thinking.

cognitive approach
An approach to psychology emphasizing the mental processes involved in knowing: how we direct our attention, perceive, remember, think, and solve problems.

The Evolutionary Approach

evolutionary approach
An approach to psychology centered on evolutionary ideas such as adaptation, reproduction, and natural selection as the basis for explaining specific human behaviors.

Although arguably all of psychology emerges out of evolutionary theory, some psychologists emphasize an **evolutionary approach** that uses evolutionary ideas such as adaptation, reproduction, and natural selection as the basis for explaining specific human behaviors. David Buss (2008) argues that just as evolution molds our physical features, such as body shape, it also influences our decision making, level of aggressiveness, fears, and mating patterns. Thus, evolutionary psychologists argue, the way we adapt is traceable to problems early humans faced in adapting to their environments (Dunbar & Barrett, 2007).

Evolutionary psychologists believe that their approach provides an umbrella that unifies the diverse fields of psychology (Bjorklund, 2007). Not all psychologists agree with this

F-Minus: © United Feature Syndicate. Inc.

conclusion, however. For example, some critics stress that the evolutionary approach provides an inaccurate explanation of why men and women have different social roles and does not adequately account for cultural diversity and experiences (Wood & Eagly, 2007). Yet keep in mind that even psychologists who disagree with the application of the evolutionary approach to psychological characteristics still agree with the general principles of evolutionary theory.

The Sociocultural Approach

The **sociocultural approach** examines the ways in which social and cultural environments influence behavior. Socioculturalists argue that understanding a person's behavior requires knowing about the cultural context in which the behavior occurs (Brettell & Sargent, 2009; Matsumoto & Juang, 2008).

We find an example of the sociocultural approach in recent research examining responses to failure in Western versus Eastern cultures. Imagine that you are in a psychological study in which you are asked to solve a number of puzzles. Some of the puzzles are quite easy, and you complete them with no problem. The other puzzles are more difficult; try as you might, you cannot figure them out. After the study you are left alone with the puzzles, and the researcher informs you that if you like, you can keep playing with the puzzles while he or she prepares the rest of the study materials. Which puzzles will you be likely to work on?

If you are like most U.S. college students, you will gravitate toward the easy puzzles, choosing to work on what you know you are already good at. However, if you are like most Asian students, you will pick up the difficult puzzles and keep working on those that you have not yet solved (Heine, 2005; Norenzayan & Heine, 2005). These cultural differences are thought to emerge out of differing views of the self, goals, and learning. Compared to U.S. students, Asian students may be more likely to view failure as an opportunity to learn.

The sociocultural approach focuses not only on comparisons of behavior across countries but also on the behavior of individuals from different ethnic and cultural groups within a country (Gollnick & Chinn, 2009; Taylor & Whittaker, 2009). Thus, there is increasing interest in the behavior of African Americans, Latinos, and Asian Americans, especially in terms of the factors that have restricted or enhanced their ability to adapt and cope with living in a predominantly White society (Banks, 2008).

Summing up the Seven Contemporary Approaches

These seven approaches to understanding psychology provide different views of the same behavior, and all of them may provide valuable insights that the other perspectives miss. Think about the simple experience of seeing a cute puppy. Looking at that puppy involves physical processes in the eyes, nervous system, and brain—the focus of the biological approach to psychology. The moment you spot that puppy, though, you might smile without thinking and reach down to pet the little guy. That reaction might be a learned response based on your past learning with your own dog (behavioral perspective), or unconscious memories of a childhood dog (psychodynamic perspective), or conscious memories that you especially like this breed of dogs (cognitive perspective), or even evolutionary processes that promoted cuteness to help offspring survive (evolutionary approach). You might find yourself striking up a conversation with the puppy's owner, based on your shared love of dogs (humanistic perspective). Further, sociocultural factors might play a role in your decision about whether to ask the owner if holding the puppy would be okay, whether to share those warm feelings about the puppy with others, and even whether (as in some cultures) to view that puppy as food.

These broad approaches to psychology are reflected in the variety of specialties within which psychologists work (Figure 1.2). Many of these specialties are represented by chapters in this book. As you read the text, keep in mind that psychology is a collaborative

Human beings originally evolved long ago in a very different environment than we occupy today. The survivors were those who were most able to endure extremely difficult circumstances, struggling to find food, avoid predators, and create social groups. What do you think were the most adaptive traits for these early folk? To what specific environments are humans adapting even now?

Specialization and Relevant Chapters in This Book	Focus of Specialists
Behavioral Neuroscience (Chapter 2)	Behavioral neuroscience focuses on biological processes, especially the brain's role in behavior.
Sensation and Perception (Chapter 3)	Sensation and perception researchers focus on the physical systems and psychological processes of vision, hearing, touch, and smell that allow us to experience the world.
Learning (Chapter 5)	Learning specialists study the complex process by which behavior changes to adapt to shifting circumstances.
Cognitive (Chapters 4, 6, & 7)	Cognitive psychology examines attention, consciousness, information processing, and memory. Cognitive psychologists are also interested in cognitive skills and abilities such as problem solving, decision making, expertise, and intelligence.
Developmental (Chapter 8)	Developmental psychology examines how people become who they are, from conception to death, concentrating on biological and environmental factors.
Motivation and Emotion (Chapter 9)	Researchers from a variety of specializations are interested in these two aspects of experience. Motivation researchers examine questions such as how individuals attain difficult goals. Emotion researchers study the physiological and brain processes that underlie emotional experience, the role of emotional expression in health, and the possibility that emotions are universal.
Personality (Chapter 10)	Personality psychology focuses on the relatively enduring characteristics of individuals, including traits, goals, motives, genetics, and personality development.
Social (Chapter 11)	Social psychology studies how social contexts influence perceptions, social cognition, and attitudes. Social psychologists study how groups influence attitudes and behavior.
Clinical and Counseling (Chapters 12 & 13)	Clinical and counseling psychology, the most widely practiced specialization, involves diagnosing and treating people with psychological problems.
Health (Chapter 14)	Health psychology emphasizes psychological factors, lifestyle, and behavior that influence physical health.
Industrial and Organizational (I/O)	I/O psychology applies findings in all areas of psychology to the workplace.
Community	Community psychology is concerned with providing accessible care for people with psychological problems. Community-based mental health centers are one means of delivering such services as outreach programs.
School and Educational	School and educational psychology centrally concerns children's learning and adjustment in school. School psychologists in elementary and secondary school systems test children and make recommendations about educational placement, and work on educational planning teams.
Environmental	Environmental psychologists explore the effects of physical settings in most major areas of psychology, including perception, cognition, learning, and others. An environmental psychologist might study how different room arrangements influence behavior or what strategies might be used to reduce human behavior that harms the environment.
Psychology of Women	Psychology of women stresses the importance of integrating information about women with current psychological knowledge and applying that information to society and its institutions.
Forensic	Forensic psychology applies psychology to the legal system. Forensic psychologists might help with jury selection or provide expert testimony in trials.
Sport	Sport psychology applies psychology to improving sport performance and enjoyment of sport participation.
Cross-Cultural	Cross-cultural psychology studies culture's role in understanding behavior, thought, and emotion, with a special interest in whether psychological phenomena are universal or culture-specific.

FIGURE 1.2

Areas of Specialization in Psychology Psychology has many subfields that overlap.

science in which psychologists work together to examine a wide range of research questions. Indeed, many times scholars from different specialties within psychology join forces to understand some aspect of human behavior. It is the purpose of this book's Intersection feature (see an example on page 24) to review research that represents collaboration among scientists from different specialties to answer the same question.

(see an example on page 24)

1. The approach to psychology that is most interested in early childhood relationships is
   A. evolutionary psychology.
   B. cognitive psychology.
   C. psychodynamic psychology.
   D. behavioral psychology.

2. The approach to psychology that views psychological distress as a result of persistent negative thoughts is
   A. the humanistic approach.
   B. the behavioral approach.
   C. the sociocultural approach.
   D. the cognitive approach.

3. The approach to psychology that focuses on self-fulfillment, altruism, and personal growth is
   A. the cognitive approach.
   B. the behavioral approach.
   C. the psychodynamic approach.
   D. the humanistic approach.

Apply It! 4. A video clip called "The Evolution of Dance" was posted to YouTube by comedian Judson Laipply and quickly went viral, receiving more than 116 *million* views. In the clip, Laipply dances to music by artists as varied as the Brady Bunch, Vanilla Ice, and New Kids on the Block. Why would a video of a guy dancing to a variety of pop songs, be so popular? All of the contemporary approaches we reviewed might offer an explanation. Which of the following is most like what a *psychodynamic* thinker might say?
   A. Human beings have been *rewarded* for watching people dance in funny ways.
   B. Watching a young male dance is a *socially* and *culturally* defined pastime, and it is likely most of the "hits" came from Western web surfers.
   C. Human beings have an *unconscious* desire to see someone looking foolish.
   D. This is clearly evidence of serious worldwide brain damage.

3 Psychology's Scientific Method

Science is not defined by *what* it investigates but by *how* it investigates. Whether you study photosynthesis, butterflies, Saturn's moons, or happiness, the *way* you study your question of interest determines whether your approach is scientific. The scientific method is how psychologists gain knowledge about mind and behavior.

It is the use of the scientific method that makes psychology a science (Rosnow & Rosenthal, 2008). Indeed, most of the studies psychologists publish in research journals follow the scientific method, which may be summarized in these five steps (Figure 1.3):

1. Observing some phenomenon
2. Formulating hypotheses and predictions
3. Testing through empirical research
4. Drawing conclusions
5. Evaluating conclusions

1. Observing Some Phenomenon The first step in conducting a scientific inquiry involves observing some phenomenon in the world. The critical-thinking, curious psychologist sees something in the world and wants to know why or how it is the way it is. The phenomena that scientists study are called variables, a word related to the verb *to vary*. A **variable** is anything that can change. For example, one variable that interests psychologists is happiness. Some people seem to be generally happier than others. What might account for these differences? As they consider answers to these questions, scientists often develop theories. A **theory** is a broad idea or set of closely related ideas that attempts to explain observations. Theories seek to explain why certain things have happened, and they can be used to make predictions about future observations. For instance, some psychologists believe that the most important human need is the need to belong to a social group (Baumeister & Leary, 2000).

variable
Anything that can change.

theory
A broad idea or set of closely related ideas that attempts to explain observations and to make predictions about future observations.

Science is defined not by what it studies but by how it investigates. Photosynthesis, butterflies, and relationships among people all can be studied in a scientific manner.

1

Observing Some Phenomenon

We feel good when we give someone a gift. However, do we genuinely feel better giving something away than we might feel if we could keep it? Elizabeth Dunn, Lara Aknin, and Michael Norton (2008) decided to test this question.

2

Formulating Hypotheses and Predictions

These researchers hypothesized that spending money on other people would lead to greater happiness than spending money on oneself.

3

Testing Through Empirical Research

In an experiment designed to examine this prediction, the researchers randomly assigned undergraduate participants to receive money ($5 or $20) that they had to spend either on themselves or on someone else by 5 P.M. that day. Those who spent the money on *someone else* reported greater happiness that night.

4

Drawing Conclusions

The experiment supported the hypothesis that spending money on others can be a strong predictor of happiness. Money might not buy happiness, the researchers concluded, but spending money in a particular way, that is, on other people, may enhance happiness.

5

Evaluating Conclusions

The experimental results were published in the prestigious journal *Science*. Now that the findings are public, other researchers might investigate related topics and questions inspired by this work, and their experiments might shed further light on the original conclusions.

FIGURE 1.3

Steps in the Scientific Method: Is It Better to Give Than to Receive? This figure shows how the steps in the scientific method were applied in a research experiment examining how spending money on ourselves or others can influence happiness (Dunn, Aknin, & Norton, 2008).

hypothesis
An educated guess that derives logically from a theory; a prediction that can be tested.

2. Formulating Hypotheses and Predictions The second step in the scientific method is stating a hypothesis. A **hypothesis** is an educated guess that derives logically from a theory. It is a prediction that can be tested. A theory can generate many hypotheses. If more and more hypotheses related to a theory turn out to be true, the theory gains in credibility. So, a researcher who believes that social belonging is the most important aspect of human functioning might predict that people who belong to social groups will be happier than others.

3. Testing Through Empirical Research The next step in the scientific method is to test the hypotheses by conducting *empirical research,* that is, by collecting and analyzing data. At this point, it is time to design a study that will test our predictions. To do so, we first need a concrete way to measure the variables of interest.

operational definition
A definition that provides an objective description of how a variable is going to be measured and observed in a particular study.

An **operational definition** provides an objective description of how a variable is going to be measured and observed in a particular study. Operational definitions eliminate the fuzziness that might creep into thinking about a problem. Imagine that everyone in your psychology class is asked to observe a group of children and keep track of kind behaviors. Do you think that everyone will define "kind behaviors" in the same way? An operational definition allows us to be sure that everyone agrees on what a variable means. To measure personal happiness, for example, prominent psychologist Ed Diener and his students (Diener & others, 1985) devised a self-report questionnaire that measures how satisfied a person is with his or her life, called the Satisfaction with Life Scale. (You will get a chance to complete the questionnaire later in this chapter.) Scores on this questionnaire are then used as measures of happiness. Research using this scale and others like it has shown that certain specific factors are strongly related to being happy: marriage, religious faith, purpose in life, and good health (Diener, 1999; Pavot & Diener, 2008).

Importantly, there is not just one operational definition for any variable. For example, in a study that examined happiness as a predictor of important life outcomes, Lee Anne Harker and Dacher Keltner (2001) looked at the yearbook pictures of college women who had graduated three decades earlier and coded the pictures for the appearance of *Duchenne smiling.* This type of smiling refers to genuine smiling—the kind that creates little wrinkles around the outer corner of the eyes. Duchenne smiling has been shown to be a sign of genuine happiness. (If you want to see whether someone in a photograph is smiling genuinely, cover the bottom of the person's face. Can you still tell that he or she is smiling? A genuine smile can be seen in the eyes, not just the mouth.) So, while Diener and colleagues operationally defined happiness as a score on a questionnaire, Harker and Keltner operationally defined happiness as Duchenne smiling. Harker and Keltner found that happiness, as displayed in these yearbook pictures, predicted positive life outcomes, such as successful marriages and satisfying lives, some 30 years later.

Coming up with operational definitions for the variables in a study is a crucial step in designing psychological research. To study anything, we have to have a way to see it or measure it. Clearly, in order to devise an operational definition for any variable, we first must agree on what it is that we are trying to measure. If we think of happiness as something that people know about themselves, then a questionnaire score might be a good operational definition of the variable. If we think that people

Researchers have identified Duchenne smiling (notice the wrinkles) as a sign of genuine happiness.

might not be aware of how happy they are (or are not), then facial expression might be a better operational definition. In other words, our definition of a variable must be set out clearly before we operationally define it.

Because operational definitions allow researchers to measure variables, they have a lot of numbers to deal with once they have conducted a study. A key aspect of the process of testing hypotheses is *data analysis. Data* refers to all the information (all those numbers) researchers collect in a study—say, the questionnaire scores or the behaviors observed. Data analysis means "crunching" those numbers mathematically to see if they support predictions. In other words, data analysis involves applying mathematical procedures to understand what the data mean (Agresti & Finlay, 2009; Jackson, 2009). Many students of psychology are surprised to learn that much of the work in the psychological sciences relies heavily on sophisticated *statistics,* or numbers that help us describe what the data have to tell us.

The following example demonstrates the first three steps in the scientific method. One theory of well-being is *self-determination theory* (Deci & Ryan, 2000; Ryan, Huta, & Deci, 2008). According to this theory, people are likely to feel fulfilled when their lives meet three important needs: relatedness (warm relations with others), autonomy (independence), and competence (mastering new skills). One hypothesis that follows logically from this theory is that people who value money, material possessions, prestige, and physical appearance (that is, *extrinsic rewards*) over the needs of relatedness, autonomy, and competence should be less fulfilled, less happy, and less well adjusted. In a series of studies entitled "The Dark Side of the American Dream," researchers Timothy Kasser and Richard Ryan asked participants to complete self-report measures of values and of psychological and physical functioning (Kasser & Ryan, 1993, 1996; Kasser & others, 2004). Thus, the operational definitions of values and psychological functioning were questionnaire scores. The researchers found that individuals who value material rewards over more intrinsic rewards do indeed tend to suffer as predicted.

Try operationally defining the following variables: generosity, love, maturity, liberal, conservative, exhaustion, stress, attractiveness. What are some things that you find interesting that you think a psychologist should study? How might you operationally define them?

4. Drawing Conclusions

Based on the results of the data analyses, scientists then draw conclusions from their research. It is important to keep in mind that usually a theory is revised only after a number of studies produce similar results. Before we change a theory, we want to be sure that the research can be replicated, or repeated, by other scientists using different methods. If a research finding is shown again and again across different researchers and different specific methods, it is considered reliable—in other words, it is a result we can depend on.

5. Evaluating Conclusions

The final step in the scientific method is one that never really ends. Researchers submit their work for publication, and it undergoes rigorous review. Afterward, the published studies are there for all to see, read, and evaluate continually.

The research community maintains an active conversation about what scientists know, and it constantly questions conclusions. From published studies, a scholar may come up with a new idea that will eventually change the thinking on some topic. Steps 3, 4, and 5 in the scientific method are part of an ongoing process. That is, researchers go back and do more research, revise their theories, hone their methods, and draw and evaluate their new conclusions.

1. Any changeable phenomenon that a scientist studies is called a
   A. differential.
   B. predictor.
   C. variation.
   D. variable.

2. The statement "I believe this research will demonstrate that students who study in groups will get better grades than those who study alone" is an example of
   A. a theory.
   B. an observation.
   C. a conclusion.
   D. a hypothesis.

3. The last step in the scientific method, and one that never ends, is
   A. drawing conclusions.
   B. evaluating conclusions.
   C. testing through empirical research.
   D. running a statistical analysis.

Apply It! 4. Paul believes that physically attractive people are selfish. He decides to conduct a study to see if he is right. He goes up to five people he thinks are good-looking and asks them for spare change. They all turn him down. Paul concludes, "Aha! I knew it all along." The operational definition of "selfish" in Paul's study is
   A. physical attractiveness.
   B. whether people gave Paul spare change.
   C. whether Paul thought the person was attractive.
   D. asking for spare change.

Bonus: As you practice thinking like a scientist and learn about research design, give some thought to Paul's study. Can you spot at least four big problems with it?

4 Types of Psychological Research

The five steps of the scientific method are reflected differently in three types of research commonly used in psychology. *Descriptive research* involves finding out about the basic dimensions of some variable (for example, what is the average level of happiness of men in the United States?). *Correlational research* is interested in discovering relationships between variables (for instance, are married men happier than single men?). *Experimental research* concerns establishing causal relationships between variables (if we make men smile, do women perceive them as more attractive?). Let's examine each of these types of research.

Descriptive Research

Just as its name suggests, descriptive research is about describing some phenomenon—determining its basic dimensions and defining what this thing is, how often it occurs, and so on. By itself, descriptive research cannot prove what causes some phenomenon, but it can reveal important information about people's behaviors and attitudes (Given, 2008). Descriptive research methods include observation, surveys and interviews, and case studies.

Observation   Imagine that you are going to conduct a study on how children who are playing a game resolve conflicts that arise during the game. The data that are of interest to you concern conflict resolution. As a first step, you might go to a playground and simply observe what the children do—how often you see conflict resolution occur and how it unfolds. You would likely keep careful notes of what you observe.

This type of scientific observation requires an important set of skills. Unless you are a trained observer and practice your skills regularly, you might not know what to look for, you might not remember what you saw, you might not realize that what you are looking for is changing from one moment to the next, and you might not communicate your observations effectively. Furthermore, it might be important to have one or more others do the observations as well, to develop a sense of how accurate your observations are. For observations to be effective, they must be systematic. You must know whom you are observing, when and where you will observe, and how you will make the observations. Also, you need to know in advance in what form you will document them: in writing, by sound recording, or by video.

Surveys and Interviews   Sometimes the best and quickest way to get information about people is to ask them for it. One technique is to interview them directly. A related method that is especially useful when information from many people is needed is the *survey,* or questionnaire. A survey presents a standard set of questions, or *items,* to obtain people's self-reported attitudes or beliefs about a particular topic.

Although surveys can be a straightforward way to measure psychological variables, constructing them requires care. For example, surveys can measure only what people think about themselves. Thus, if we are interested in studying a variable that we think is unconscious, like a psychodynamic drive, we cannot use a survey. Furthermore, people do not always know the truth about themselves. If you were answering a survey that asked, "Are you a generous person?" how might your answer compare to that of a friend who is asked to make that same rating about you? One particular problem with surveys and interviews is the tendency of participants to answer questions in a way that will make them look good rather than in a way that communicates what they truly think or feel (Nardi, 2006). Another challenge in survey construction is that when questionnaires are used to operationally define variables, it is crucial that the items clearly probe the specific topic of interest and not some other characteristic. The language used in surveys therefore must be clear and understandable for responses to reflect the participants' actual feelings.

Surveys and interviews can probe a wide range of topics, from religious beliefs to sexual habits to attitudes about gun control (Rosnow & Rosenthal, 2008). Some survey and interview questions are unstructured and open-ended, such as "How fulfilling would you say your marriage is?" Such questions allow for unique responses from each person surveyed. Other survey and interview questions are more structured and ask about quite specific things. For example, a structured question might ask, "How many times have you talked with your partner about a personal problem in the past month: 0, 1–2, 3–5, 6–10, 11–30, every day?"

case study
Also called a case history, an in-depth look at a single individual.

Case Studies   A **case study,** or *case history,* is an in-depth look at a single individual. Case studies are performed mainly by clinical psychologists when, for either practical or ethical reasons, the unique aspects of an individual's life cannot be duplicated and tested in other individuals. A case study provides information about one person's goals, hopes, fantasies, fears, traumatic experiences, family relationships, health, or anything else that helps the psychologist understand the person's mind and behavior. Case studies can also involve in-depth explorations of particular families or social groups.

An example of a case study is the analysis of India's spiritual leader Mahatma Gandhi (1869–1948) by psychodynamic theorist Erik Erikson (1969). Erikson studied

Mahatma Gandhi was the spiritual leader of India in the middle of the twentieth century. Erik Erikson conducted an extensive case study of his life to determine what contributed to his identity development.

Gandhi's life in great depth to discover insights into how his positive spiritual identity developed, especially during his youth. In piecing together Gandhi's identity development, Erikson described the contributions of culture, history, family, and various other factors that might affect the way other people form an identity.

Case histories provide dramatic, detailed portrayals of people's lives, but we must be cautious about applying what we learn from one person's life to other people. The subject of a case study is unique, with a genetic makeup and personal history that no one else shares. Case studies can be very valuable at the first step of the scientific method, in that they often provide vivid observations that can then be tested in a variety of ways in psychological research.

The Value of Descriptive Research

Descriptive research allows researchers to get a sense of something but cannot answer questions about how and why things are the way they are. Such research can nonetheless be intriguing, such as descriptive research on the experience of happiness in different cultures. Before reading about that research, complete the measure below. Using the 7-point scale below, indicate your agreement with each item that follows.

7	6	5	4	3	2	1
Strongly Agree	Agree	Slightly Agree	Neither Agree Nor Disagree	Slightly Disagree	Disagree	Strongly Disagree

1. In most ways my life is close to my ideal.
2. The conditions of my life are excellent.
3. I am satisfied with my life.
4. So far I have gotten the important things I want in life.
5. If I could live my life over, I would change almost nothing.

You have just completed the Satisfaction with Life Scale (or SWLS; Diener & others, 1985), one operational definition of happiness. To find out your score, add up your ratings and divide by 5. This average rating could be considered your level of general happiness. A broad range of studies in many different countries have used this scale and others like it to measure happiness levels. Based on such research, Ed and Carol Diener (1996) concluded that most people are quite happy because they score above the midpoint, 3.5, on the scale you just completed. However, research on happiness in various cultures has generally centered on relatively industrialized countries. What about non-industrialized cultures?

One study examined levels of happiness in groups of people who have not generally been included in psychological studies (Biswas-Diener, Vitterso, & Diener, 2005). The research included three groups: the Inuits of Greenland, the Masai of southern Kenya, and American Old Order Amish. All three groups completed measures essentially the same as the one you just did.

The Inuit tribe studied (the Inughuit) live at 79 degrees latitude (very far north), in the harshest climate inhabited by a traditional human society. The landscape consists of rocks, glaciers, and the sea. Farming is impossible. The Inughuits have some modern conveniences, but they generally adhere to a traditional hunting culture. It is not uncommon to find an Inughuit hunter carving a seal or caribou on the kitchen floor while children in the next room watch TV. Most of us might feel a little blue in the winter months when gloomy weather seems to stretch on, day after day. For the Inughuits, however, the sun never rises at all throughout the winter months, and in the summer, it never sets. How happy could an individual be in such a difficult setting? Pretty happy, it turns out, as the Inughuits averaged a 5.0 on the Satisfaction with Life Scale.

The Masai are an indigenous (native) African nomadic group who live in villages of about 20 people, with little exposure to the West. The Masai are fierce warriors, and their culture has many traditional ceremonies built around a boy's passage from childhood to manhood. Boys are circumcised between the ages of 15 and 22, and they are forbidden from moving or making a sound during the procedure. Girls also experience circumcision as they enter puberty, a controversial rite that involves the removal of the clitoris and that makes childbirth extremely difficult. The Masai practice child marriage and polygamy. Masai women have very little power and are generally expected to do most of the work. How happy could an individual be in this context? Masai men and women who completed the measure orally in their native tongue, Maa, averaged a 5.4 on the life satisfaction scale (Biswas-Diener, Vitterso, & Diener, 2005).

Finally, the Old Order Amish of the midwestern and northeastern United States belong to a strict religious sect that explicitly rejects modern aspects of life. The Amish separate themselves from mainstream society and travel by horse and buggy. The women wear bonnets, and the men sport beards, dark clothes, and dark brimmed hats. The Amish farm without modern machinery and dedicate their lives to simplicity—without radios, TVs, CDs, DVDs, iPods, cell phones, washing machines, and cars. Still, the Amish are relatively happy, averaging 4.4 on the 7-point happiness scale (Biswas-Diener, Vitterso, & Diener, 2005).

Like a host of other studies in industrialized nations, these results indicate that most individuals are pretty happy. Such descriptive findings provide researchers on well-being a foundation for further examining the processes that lead to feelings of happiness in different cultural settings. If a researcher wanted to extend these findings to examine predictors of happiness in different cultures, he or she would use a correlational design.

How does your score compare to the score of the Inughuits, the Masai, or the Old Order Amish? Do you think the Satisfaction with Life Scale is a good measure of happiness? Why or why not?

Correlational Research

We have seen that descriptive research tells us about the basic dimensions of a variable. In contrast, **correlational research** tells us about the relationships between variables, and its purpose is to examine whether and how two variables *change together*. That is, correlational research looks at a co-relationship. For instance, if one of the variables increases, what happens to the other one? When two variables change together, we can predict one from the other, and we say that the variables are correlated.

Correlational research is so named because of the statistical technique, *correlation*, that is typically used to analyze these type of data. The key feature of a correlational study is that the variables of interest are measured or observed to see how they relate. If we wanted to know whether shy people are happy, we might give the same people two questionnaires, one that measures shyness and another that measures happiness. For each person we would have two scores, and we would then see whether shyness and happiness relate to each other in a systematic way.

The degree of relationship between two variables is expressed as a numerical value called a *correlational coefficient,* which is most commonly represented by the letter *r.* The correlation coefficient is a statistic that tells us two things about the relationship between two variables—its strength and its direction. The value of a correlation always falls between -1.00 and $+1.00$. The number or magnitude of the correlation tells us about the *strength* of the relationship. The closer the number is to ± 1.00, the stronger the relationship. The sign ($+$ or $-$) tells us about the *direction* of the relationship between the variables. A positive sign means that as one variable increases, the other also increases. A negative sign means that as one variable increases, the other decreases. A zero correlation means that there is no systematic relationship between the variables. Examples of scatter plots (a type of graph that plots scores on the two variables) showing positive and negative correlations appear in Figure 1.4. Note that every dot in this figure represents both scores for one person.

correlational research
Research that examines the relationships between variables, whose purpose is to examine whether and how two variables change together.

FIGURE 1.4

Scatter Plots Showing Positive and Negative Correlations A positive correlation is a relationship in which two factors vary in the same direction, as shown in the two scatter plots on the left. A negative correlation is a relationship in which two factors vary in opposite directions, as shown in the two scatter plots on the right.

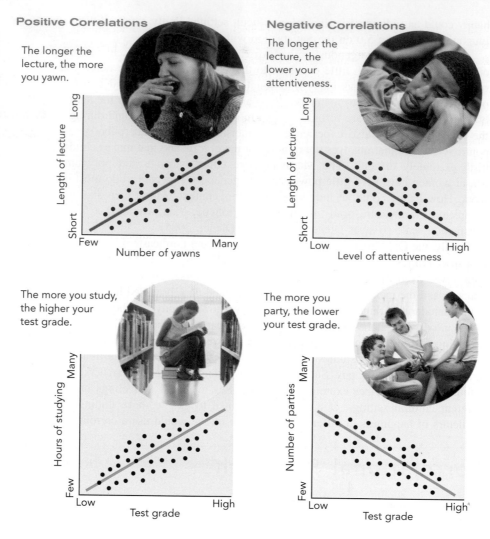

Positive Correlations

The longer the lecture, the more you yawn.

Length of lecture (Short → Long) vs. *Number of yawns* (Few → Many)

The more you study, the higher your test grade.

Hours of studying (Few → Many) vs. *Test grade* (Low → High)

Negative Correlations

The longer the lecture, the lower your attentiveness.

Length of lecture (Short → Long) vs. *Level of attentiveness* (Low → High)

The more you party, the lower your test grade.

Number of parties (Few → Many) vs. *Test grade* (Low → High)

Correlation Is Not Causation

Look at the terms in bold type in the following newspaper headlines:

Researchers **Link** Coffee Consumption to Cancer of Pancreas

Scientists Find **Connection** Between Ear Hair and Heart Attacks

Psychologists Discover **Relationship** Between Marital Status and Health

Reading these headlines, one might conclude that coffee causes pancreatic cancer, ear hair causes heart attacks, and so on. The words in bold type are synonymous only with correlation, however, not with causality. *Correlation does not equal causation.* Remember, correlation means only that two variables change together. Being able to predict one event based on the occurrence of another event does not necessarily tell us anything about the cause of either event (Howell, 2008). Sometimes some other variable that has not been measured accounts for the relationship between two others. Researchers refer to this circumstance as the **third variable problem.**

To understand the third variable problem, consider the following example. A researcher measures two variables: the number of ice cream cones sold in a town and the number of violent crimes that occur in that town throughout the year. The researcher finds that ice cream cone sales and violent crimes are positively correlated, to the magnitude of +.50. This high positive correlation would indicate that as ice cream sales increase, so does violent crime. Would it be reasonable for the local paper to run the headline "Ice Cream Consumption Leads to Violence"? Should concerned citizens gather outside the local Frosty Freeze to stop the madness? Probably not. Perhaps you have already thought of the third

third variable problem
The circumstance where a variable that has not been measured accounts for the relationship between two other variables.

variable that might explain this correlation—heat. Indeed, when it is hot outside, people are more likely both to purchase ice cream and to act aggressively (Anderson & Bushman, 2002). These "third variables" are also called *confounds*.

Given the potential problems with third variables, why do researchers bother to conduct correlational studies? There are several very good reasons. One reason is that some important questions can be investigated only by using correlational designs. Such questions may involve variables that can only be measured or observed, such as biological sex, personality traits, genetic factors, and ethnic background. Another reason why researchers conduct correlational studies is that sometimes the variables of interest are real-world events that influence people's lives, such as the effects of a natural disaster such as Hurricane Katrina. Correlational research is also valuable in cases where it would not be ethical to do research in any other way. For example, it would be unethical for an experimenter to direct expectant mothers to smoke varying numbers of cigarettes in order to see how cigarette smoke affects birth weight and fetal activity.

Although we have focused on relationships between just two variables, researchers often measure many variables in their studies. This way, they can examine whether a relationship between two variables is explained by a third variable (or a fourth or fifth variable). An interesting research question that has been addressed in this fashion is, do happy people live longer? In one study, 2000 Mexican Americans aged 65 and older were interviewed twice over the course of two years (Ostir & others, 2000). In the first assessment, participants completed measures of happiness but also reported about potential third variables such as diet, physical health, smoking, marital status, and distress. Two years later, the researchers contacted the participants again to see who was still alive. Even with these many potential third variables taken into account, happiness predicted who was still living two years later.

Correlational studies are useful, too, when researchers are interested in everyday experience. For example, correlational researchers have begun to use daily diary methodologies, known as the *experience sampling method (ESM)*, to study people in their natural settings. These studies involve having people report on their daily experiences in a diary a few times a day or complete measures of their mood and behavior whenever they are beeped by an electronic organizer.

Longitudinal Designs One way that correlational researchers can deal with the issue of causation is to employ a special kind of systematic observation called a **longitudinal design.** Longitudinal research involves obtaining measures of the variables of interest in multiple waves over time. Longitudinal research can suggest potential causal relationships because if one variable is thought to cause changes in another, it should at least come before that variable in time.

One intriguing longitudinal study is the Nun Study, conducted by David Snowdon and his colleagues (Grossi & others, 2007; Snowdon, 2003; Tyas & others, 2007). The study began in 1986 and has followed a sample of 678 School Sisters of Notre Dame ever since. The nuns ranged in age from 75 to 103 when the study began. These women complete a variety of psychological and physical measures annually. This sample is unique in many respects. However, some characteristics render the participants an excellent group for correlational research. For one thing, many potential extraneous third variables are relatively identical for all the women in the group. Their gender, living conditions, diet, activity levels, marital status, and religious participation are essentially held constant, providing little chance that differences in these variables can explain results.

Researchers recently examined the relationship between happiness and longevity using this rich dataset. All of the nuns had been asked to write a spiritual autobiography when they entered the convent (for some, as many as 80 years before). Deborah Danner and her colleagues (2001) were given access to these documents and used them as indicators of happiness earlier in life by counting the number of positive emotions expressed in the autobiographies (note that here we have yet another operational definition

longitudinal design
A special kind of systematic observation, used by correlational researchers, that involves obtaining measures of the variables of interest in multiple waves over time.

of happiness). Higher levels of positive emotion expressed in autobiographies written at an average age of 22 were associated with a 2.5-fold difference in risk of mortality when the nuns were in their 80s and 90s. That is, women who included positive emotion in their autobiographies when they were in their early 20s were two-and-a-half times more likely to survive some 60 years later.

Longitudinal designs provide ways by which correlational researchers may attempt to demonstrate causal relations among variables. Still, it is important to be aware that even in longitudinal studies, causal relationships are not completely clear. For example, the nuns who wrote happier autobiographies may have had happier childhood experiences that might be influencing their longevity, or a particular genetic factor might explain both their happiness and their survival. As you read about numerous correlational research studies throughout this book, do so critically, and with some skepticism, and consider that even the brightest scientist may not have thought of all of the potential third variables that might have explained his or her results. Keep in mind how easy it is to assume causality when two events or characteristics are merely correlated. Think about those innocent ice cream cones and critically evaluate conclusions that may be drawn from simple observation.

Experimental Research

experiment
A carefully regulated procedure in which the researcher manipulates one or more variables that are believed to influence some other variable.

To determine whether a causal relationship exists between variables, researchers must use experimental methods (Gravetter, 2009). An **experiment** is a carefully regulated procedure in which the researcher manipulates one or more variables that are believed to influence some other variable. Imagine that a researcher notices that people who listen to classical music seem to be of above average intelligence. A correlational study on this question would not tell us if listening to classical music *causes* increases in intelligence. In order to demonstrate causation, the researcher would manipulate whether or not people listen to classical music. He or she might create two groups: one that listens to classical music and one that listens to pop music. To test for differences in intelligence, the researcher would then measure intelligence.

If that manipulation led to differences between the two groups on intelligence, we could say that the manipulated variable *caused* those differences In other words, the experiment has demonstrated cause and effect. This notion that experiments can demonstrate causation is based on the idea that if participants are *randomly assigned* to groups, the only systematic difference between them must be the manipulated variable. **Random assignment** means that researchers assign participants to groups by chance. This technique reduces the likelihood that the experiment's results will be due to any preexisting differences between groups (Kantowitz, Roediger, & Elmes, 2009).

random assignment
Researchers' assignment of participants to groups by chance, to reduce the likelihood that an experiment's results will be due to preexisting differences between groups.

To get a sense of what experimental studies, as compared to correlational studies, can tell us, consider the following example. Psychologists have long assumed that experiencing one's life as meaningful is an important aspect of psychological well-being (Frankl, 1963/1984; Steger & Frazier, 2005). Because surveys that measure meaning in life and well-being correlate positively (that is, the more meaningful your life, the happier you are), the assumption has been that experiencing meaning in life causes greater happiness. Because the studies involved in exploring this relationship have been correlational, however, the causal pathway is unknown. Meaning

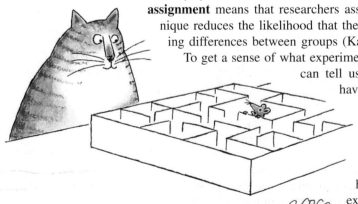

"Well, you don't look like an experimental psychologist to me."

in life may lead people to be happier, but the reverse might also be true: Happiness might make people feel that their lives are more meaningful.

To address this issue, Laura King and colleagues (2006; Hicks & King, 2008) conducted a series of laboratory experiments. The researchers had some people listen to happy music and other participants listen to neutral music. Participants who listened to happy music rated their lives as more meaningful than did individuals who listened to neutral music. Note that participants were randomly assigned to one of two conditions, happy music or neutral music, and then rated their meaning in life using a questionnaire. In this case happiness was operationally defined by the type of music participants listened to, and meaning in life was operationally defined by ratings on a questionnaire. Because participants were randomly assigned to conditions, we can assume that the only systematic difference between the two groups was the type of music they heard. As a result, we can say that the happy music caused people to rate their lives as more meaningful.

Independent and Dependent Variables

Experiments have two types of variables: independent and dependent. An **independent variable** is a manipulated experimental factor. The independent variable is the variable that the experimenter changes to see what its effects are; it is a potential cause. Any experiment may include several independent variables or factors that are manipulated to determine their effect on some outcome. In the study of positive mood and meaning in life, the independent variable is mood (positive versus neutral), operationally defined by the type of music participants listened to.

Sometimes the independent variable is the social context in which a person finds him- or herself. Social psychologists often manipulate the social context with the help of a confederate. A **confederate** is a person who is given a role to play in a study so that the social context can be manipulated. For example, if a researcher is interested in reactions to being treated rudely, he or she might have a confederate treat participants rudely (or not).

A **dependent variable** is the outcome—the factor that can change in an experiment in response to changes in the independent variable. As researchers manipulate the independent variable, they measure the dependent variable for any resulting effect. In the study of mood and meaning in life, meaning in life was the dependent variable.

Experimental and Control Groups

Experiments can involve one or more experimental groups and one or more control groups. In an experiment, the researcher manipulates the independent variable to create these groups. An **experimental group** consists of the participants in an experiment who receive the drug or other treatment under study—that is, those who are exposed to the change that the independent variable represents. A **control group** in an experiment is as much like the experimental group as possible and is treated in every way like the experimental group except for that change. The control group provides a comparison against which the researcher can test the effects of the independent variable. In the study of meaning in life above, participants who listened to happy music were the experimental group, and those who heard neutral music were the control group. To see how experimental and correlational research can be applied to the same research question, check out the Intersection.

Some Cautions About Experimental Research

Validity refers to the soundness of the conclusions that a researcher draws from an experiment. Two broad types of validity matter to experimental designs. The first is **external validity,** which refers to the degree to which an experimental design really reflects the real-world issues it is supposed to address. That is, external validity is concerned with the question, do the experimental methods and the results *generalize*—do they apply—to the real world?

confederate
A person who is given a role to play in a study so that the social context can be manipulated.

dependent variable
The outcome—the factor that can change in an experiment in response to changes in the independent variable.

control group
The participants in an experiment who are as much like the experimental group as possible and who are treated in every way like the experimental group except for a manipulated factor, the independent variable.

validity
The soundness of the conclusions that a researcher draws from an experiment.

external validity
The degree to which an experimental design actually reflects the real-world issues it is supposed to address.

independent variable
A manipulated experimental factor, the variable that the experimenter changes to see what its effects are.

Independent variable and dependent variable are two of the most important concepts in psychological research. Remember that the independent variable is the cause, and the dependent variable is the effect.

experimental group
The participants in an experiment who receive the drug or other treatment under study—that is, those who are exposed to the change that the independent variable represents.

Coming up with a good control group can be a challenge. Let's say you want to do a study on the influence of smiling on social behaviors. Your experimental group will interact with a confederate who smiles a lot during the interaction. What would you have happen in your control group? Would the confederate keep a blank expression? A frown? Smile just a little?

intersection

Low self-esteem is frequently implicated in society's ills, from juvenile delinquency to violent acts of aggression. It often seems as if we could make the world a better place if we could just help everyone achieve higher self-esteem. Yet in the late 1990s, psychologist Roy Baumeister presented a provocative idea: He suggested that *high* self-esteem, not low self-esteem, is associated with aggressive acts (Baumeister, 1999; Baumeister, Bushman, & Campbell, 2000; Baumeister & Butz, 2005;

Social Psychology and Developmental Psychology: Is High Self-Esteem Such a Good Thing?

Baumeister & others, 2007; Bushman & Baumeister, 2002). In a variety of experimental studies, he showed that individuals who scored very high on a measure of self-esteem were more likely than their low self-esteem counterparts to aggress against others when their self-esteem was threatened. These findings conflicted with a long-held belief in psychology that self-esteem was a central component of psychological health.

Following the publication of Baumeister's work, research conducted by developmental psychologists (who study the ways human beings mature

from earliest childhood to old age) challenged the notion that high self-esteem was bad. These researchers used longitudinal data collected from a large sample of individuals in Dunedin, New Zealand, to show that contrary to Baumeister's conclusions, low (not high) self-esteem was associated with a variety of negative outcomes, including aggression, delinquency, poor health, and limited economic prospects through the middle adulthood years (Donnellan & others, 2005; Trzesniewski & others, 2006).

How can we resolve this apparent conflict between experimental evidence and longitudinal evidence? One possibility is that Baumeister was talking about a particular kind of high self-esteem: inflated and unstable high self-esteem (Campbell & others, 2004; Konrath, Bushman, & Campbell, 2006). Individuals with unrealistically high self-esteem appear to be prone to respond with aggression in response to a threat. For most people, though, it is more likely that low self-esteem rather than high self-esteem is linked to higher levels of aggression.

Which is more likely to lead to aggression—high or low self-esteem?

How would you show that in research?

Imagine, for example, that a researcher is interested in the influence of stress (the independent variable) on creative problem solving (the dependent variable). He or she randomly assigns individuals to be blasted with loud noises at random times during the session (the high-stress or experimental group) or to complete the task in relative quiet (the control group). As the task, the researcher gives all participants a chance to be creative by asking them to list all of the uses they can think of for a cardboard box. Counting up the number of uses that people list, the researcher discovers that those in the high-stress group generated fewer uses of the box. This finding might indicate that stress reduces creativity. In considering the external validity of this study, however, we might ask some questions: How similar are the blasts of loud, random noises to the stresses we experience every day? Is listing uses for a cardboard box really an indicator of creativity? We are asking, in other words, if these operational definitions do a good job of reflecting the real-world processes they are supposed to represent.

The second type of validity is **internal validity,** which refers to the degree to which changes in the dependent variable are due to the manipulation of the independent variable. In the case of internal validity, we want to know whether the experimental methods are free from biases and logical errors that may render the results suspect. Although experimental research is a powerful tool, it requires safeguards (Leary, 2008). Expectations and biases can, and sometimes do, tarnish results (Ray, 2009; Rosnow & Rosenthal, 2008), as we next consider.

internal validity
The degree to which changes in the dependent variable are due to the manipulation of the independent variable.

Experimenter Bias   Experimenters may subtly (and often unknowingly) influence their research participants. **Experimenter bias** occurs when the experimenter's expectations influence the outcome of the research. No one designs an experiment without wanting meaningful results. Consequently, experimenters can sometimes subtly communicate to participants what they want the participants to do. **Demand characteristics** are any aspects of a study that communicate to the participants how the experimenter wants them to behave. The influence of experimenter expectations can be very difficult to avoid.

In a classic study, Robert Rosenthal (1966) turned college students into experimenters. He randomly assigned the participants rats from the same litter. Half of the students were told that their rats were "maze bright," whereas the other half were told that their rats were "maze dull." The students then conducted experiments to test their rats' ability to navigate mazes. The results were stunning. The so-called maze-bright rats were more successful than the maze-dull rats at running the mazes. The only explanation for the results is that the college students' expectations affected the rats' performance.

Often the participants in psychological studies are not rats but people. Imagine that you are an experimenter and you know that a participant is going to be exposed to disgusting pictures in a study. Is it possible that you might treat the person differently than you would if you were about to show him photos of cute kittens? The reason experimenter bias is important is that it introduces systematic differences between the experimental and control groups, so that we cannot know if those who looked at disgusting pictures were more, say, upset because of the pictures or because of different treatment by the experimenter. Like third variables in correlational research, these systematic biases are called *confounds*. In experimental research, confounds are factors that "ride along" with the experimental manipulation, systematically and undesirably influencing the dependent variable. Experimenter bias, demand characteristics, and confounds may all lead to differences between groups on the dependent variable that bias results.

Research Participant Bias and the Placebo Effect   Like the experimenters, research participants may have expectations about what they are supposed to do and how they should behave, and these expectations may affect the results of experiments (L. B. Christensen, 2007). **Research participant bias** occurs when the behavior of research participants during the experiment is influenced by how they think they are supposed to behave or their expectations about what is happening to them.

One example of the power of participant expectations is the placebo effect. The **placebo effect** occurs when participants' expectations, rather than the experimental treatment, produce an outcome. Participants in a drug study might be assigned to an experimental group that receives a pill containing an actual painkiller or a control group that receives a placebo pill. A **placebo** is a harmless substance that has no physiological effect. This placebo is given to participants in a control group so that they are treated identically to the experimental group except for the active agent—in this case, the painkiller. Giving individuals in the control group a placebo pill allows researchers to determine whether changes in the experimental group are due to the active drug agent and not simply to participants' expectations.

Experimenters often use placebos to ensure that the effects of a medication are not simply due to expectations. Placebo effects can be surprisingly strong. Research has shown that a substantial part of the treatment effects for antidepressants, for example, may come out of the beliefs of the doctors and patients who use them (Kirsch & Sapirstein, 1999). Sometimes just taking a pill can make people feel better. A recent survey of 231 doctors in the Chicago area showed that nearly half of the doctors surveyed reported prescribing placebos for their patients (Sherman & Hickner, 2008).

Another way to ensure that neither the experimenter's nor the participants' expectations affect the outcome is to design a **double-blind experiment.** In this design, neither the experimenter administering the treatment nor the participants

Volunteering for a double-blind drug study might seem risky. Would you do it? How might differences in willingness to volunteer to participate in this research influence its external validity?

Observation
Psychologists are using observational methods to examine President Obama's inaugural address, focusing on the words he used and the themes he stressed to make predictions about his presidency. Other observational data might include facial expressions of the crowd during the inaugural ceremony and the content of various post-election blogs.

Survey and Interview
Researchers can use surveys and telephone interviews to track popular approval of the president and to gauge public support for his various initiatives and programs. Survey research can also probe how different demographic groups (for example, African Americans and Euro-Americans) might differ in their expectations about the president.

Case Study
President Obama has published two autobiographical books, *The Audacity of Hope* and *Dreams from My Father*. These works provide valuable data for psychologists who are interested in using case studies to understand his life story and his path to presidential office.

Correlational Research
Correlational research can track the ways that attitudes toward African Americans may have changed with Obama's candidacy and election. In addition, examining the aspirations of children of various ethnicities before and after the election allows psychologists to study the influence of this new role model on American children.

Experimental Research
Psychologists interested in attitudes and behaviors toward different ethnic groups can use images of President Obama in experimental research to examine how visual reminders of the president influence such attitudes and behaviors.

FIGURE 1.5
Psychology's Research Methods Applied to Studying President Barack Obama
Psychologists can apply very different methods to study the same phenomenon. The historic election of Barack Obama, the first African American president, opened up a host of new research questions for psychologists.

are aware of which participants are in the experimental group and which are in the control group until the results are calculated. This setup ensures that the experimenter cannot, for example, make subtle gestures signaling who is receiving a drug and who is not. A double-blind study allows researchers to identify the specific effects of the independent variable from the possible effects of the experimenter's and the participants' expectations about it.

Applications of the Three Types of Research

All three types of research that we have considered—descriptive, correlational, and experimental—can be used to address the same research topic (Figure 1.5). For instance, researchers have been interested in examining the role of intensely positive experiences in human functioning. Abraham Maslow believed that the healthiest, happiest people in the world were capable of having intense moments of awe, and he used the descriptive case study approach (1971) to examine the role of such "peak experiences" in the lives of individuals who seemed to exemplify the best in human life. Through correlational research, Dan McAdams (2001) probed individuals' descriptions of the most intensely positive experiences of their lives. He found that individuals who were motivated toward warm interpersonal experiences tended to mention such experiences as the best memories of their lives. Experimental researchers have also investigated this question. In their work, people who were randomly assigned to write about their most intensely positive experience for a few minutes each day for two or three days experienced enhanced positive mood as well as fewer physical illnesses two months later, compared to individuals in control groups who wrote about unemotional topics (Burton & King, 2004, 2008).

1. A correlation of −.67 indicates
   A. a strong positive relationship.
   B. a strong negative relationship.
   C. a weak positive relationship.
   D. a weak negative relationship.

2. A study on obesity had four groups, each with a different assignment. One group of participants read a brochure about diet and nutrition; another group had a 30-minute nutrition counseling session; a third group read the newspaper; a fourth group watched a video about exercise and fitness. The control group is
   A. the group that had a counseling session.
   B. the group that read the newspaper.
   C. the group that read the brochure.
   D. the group that watched the video.

3. Which of the following statements is *correct?*
   A. Only correlational research allows researchers to determine causality.
   B. Only experimental research allows researchers to determine causality.
   C. Both correlational and experimental research allow researchers to determine causality.
   D. Neither correlational nor experimental research allows researchers to determine causality.

Apply It! 4. Jacob wants to study the relationship between falling in love and a person's academic performance. He asks students to fill out a questionnaire in which they answer "true" or "false" to the question, "Did you fall in love this semester?" Then he asks them for their GPA for the semester. Jacob's study is _____ study.
A. a correlational
B. an experimental
C. a sociological
D. a longitudinal

5 Research Samples and Settings

Among the important decisions to be made about collecting data are whom to choose as the participants and where to the conduct the research. Will the participants be people or animals? Will they be children, adults, or both? Where will the research take place—in a lab or in a natural setting?

The Research Sample

When psychologists conduct a study, they usually want to be able to draw conclusions that will apply to a larger group of people than the participants they actually study. The entire group about which the investigator wants to draw conclusions is the **population.** The subset of the population chosen by the investigator for study is a **sample.** The researcher might be interested only in a particular group, such as all children who are gifted and talented, all young women who embark on science and math careers, or all gay men. The key is that the sample studied must be representative of the population to which the investigator wants to generalize his or her results. That is, the researcher might only study 100 gifted adolescents, but he or she wants to apply these results to all gifted and talented adolescents.

To mirror the population as closely as possible, the researcher uses a **random sample,** a sample that gives every member of the population an equal chance of being selected. A representative sample would reflect the U.S. population's age, socioeconomic status,

sample
The subset of the population chosen by the investigator for study.

population
The entire group about which the investigator wants to draw conclusions.

random sample
A sample that gives every member of the population an equal chance of being selected.

The research sample might include a particular group, such as all gay men or all women runners.

Data Detectives

Being an expert in sampling and research design is useful in a broad range of careers. During the 2008 presidential election campaigns, Americans were bombarded with daily polls tracking Barack Obama and John McCain. Every time you read about a poll, someone has used such expertise to recruit and collect data from the sample. In industry, research design is used in consumer testing and evaluation. Market research analysts translate a business's questions into testable hypotheses and design studies to analyze the results. Have you tried a new product lately? Chances are, that product was thoroughly tested using market research.

Whoa. A random sample is not the same thing as random assignment. Further, even though both of these terms include the word random, they are not at all haphazard. Random assignment is about making sure experimental and control groups are equivalent, and a random sample is about selecting participants from a population so that the sample is representative of that population.

ethnic origins, marital status, geographic location, religion, and so forth. A random sample provides much better grounds for generalizing the results to a population than a nonrandom sample, because random selection improves the chances that the sample is representative of the population.

In selecting a sample, researchers must strive to minimize bias, including gender bias. Because psychology is the scientific study of human behavior, it should pertain to *all* humans, and so the participants in psychological studies ought to be representative of humanity as a whole. Early research in the field often included just the male experience—not only because the researchers themselves were often male, but also because the participants too were typically male (Matlin, 2008). For a long time, the human experience studied by psychologists was primarily the male experience.

There is also a growing realization that psychological research needs to include more people from diverse ethnic groups (Robinson-Wood, 2008). Because a great deal of psychological research involves college student participants, individuals from groups that have not had as many educational opportunities have not been strongly represented in that research. Given the fact that individuals from diverse ethnic groups have been excluded from psychological research for so long, we might reasonably conclude that people's real lives are more varied than past research data have indicated.

These issues are important because scientists want to be able to predict *human* behavior, not just White, male college student behavior. Imagine if policymakers planned their initiatives for a broad range of Americans based on research derived from only a small group of individuals from a particular background. What might the results be?

The Research Setting

All three types of research we examined in the preceding section can take place in different settings. The setting of the research does not determine the type of research it is. Common settings include the research laboratory and natural settings.

Because psychological researchers often want to control as many aspects of the situation as possible, they conduct much of their research in a laboratory, a controlled setting with many of the complex factors of the real world, including potential confounds, removed (Kantowitz, Roediger, & Elmes, 2009). Although laboratory research provides a great deal of control, doing research in the laboratory has drawbacks. First, it is almost impossible to conduct research in the lab without the participants knowing they are being

Natural settings and laboratories are common locales for psychological studies. (Left) Jane Goodall, who specializes in animal behavior, has carried out extensive research on chimpanzees in natural settings. Her work has contributed a great deal to our understanding of these intelligent primates. (Right) Barbara L. Fredrickson, a psychologist at the University of North Carolina, Chapel Hill, whose work investigates topics such as positive emotions and human flourishing, conducts a laboratory study.

studied. Second, the laboratory setting is not the real world and therefore can cause the participants to behave unnaturally. A third drawback of laboratory research is that people who are willing to go to a university laboratory may not be representative of groups from diverse cultural backgrounds. Those who are unfamiliar with university settings and with the idea of "helping science" may be intimidated by the setting. Fourth, some aspects of the mind and behavior are difficult if not impossible to examine in the laboratory.

Research can also take place in a natural setting. **Naturalistic observation** is observing behavior in a real-world setting (McMillan, 2008). Psychologists conduct naturalistic observations at sporting events, child care centers, work settings, shopping malls, and other places that people frequent. If you wanted to study the level of civility on your campus for a research project, most likely you would include naturalistic observation of how people treat one another in such gathering places as the cafeteria and the library reading room. In another example of a natural setting, researchers who use survey methods are increasingly relying on web-based assessments that allow participants to complete the measures using the Internet.

The type of research a psychologist conducts, the operational definitions of the variables of interest, and the choice of sample and setting are decisions that ideally are guided by the research question itself. However, sometimes these decisions represent a compromise between the psychologist's key objective (for example, to study a representative sample of Americans) and the available resources (for instance, a sample of 100 college students).

naturalistic observation
The observation of behavior in a real-world setting.

self-quiz

1. The *entire group* of people about whom a researcher wants to draw conclusions is the
   A. sample.
   B. random sample.
   C. population.
   D. field.

2. When a researcher decides to study a particular group, such as Latino factory workers, the researcher is specifically determining the study's
   A. population.
   B. sample.
   C. research setting.
   D. scope.

3. A drawback of laboratory research is that
   A. it is hard to conduct without the participants' knowledge that they are being studied.
   B. people unfamiliar with the university environment and culture may be intimidated and thus underrepresented.
   C. the lab setting is unnatural and may thus cause participants to behave unnaturally.
   D. all of the above

Apply It! 4. Emily, a committed environmentalist, reads a report that among a nationally representative sample, 60 percent of people polled support drilling for oil off the shores of California. The poll includes 1,000 people. Emily scoffs at the results, noting that all of the people she knows do not support offshore drilling. The poll must be flawed, she insists. How do you evaluate Emily's statement?
A. Emily is likely to be wrong. A representative sample is more likely to reflect the general population than the small sample of Emily's friends.
B. Emily is likely to be wrong because 1,000 people is a high number.
C. Emily is probably right because, as an environmentalist, she is probably more in tune with these issues than any polling organization.
D. Emily is probably right because even representative polls are usually biased.

Conducting Ethical Research

Ethics is an important consideration for all science. This fact came to the fore in the aftermath of World War II, for example, when it became apparent that Nazi doctors had used concentration camp prisoners as unwilling participants in experiments. These atrocities spurred scientists to develop a code of appropriate behavior—a set of principles about the treatment that participants in research have a right to expect. In general, ethical principles of research focus on balancing the rights of the participants with the rights of scientists to ask important research questions (Leary, 2008).

The issue of ethics in psychological research may affect you personally if at some point you serve as a participant in a study. In that event, you need to know your rights as a participant and the researchers' responsibilities in ensuring that these rights are safeguarded. Experiences in research can have unforeseen effects on people's lives.

One investigation of young dating couples asked them to complete a questionnaire that coincidentally stimulated some of the participants to think about potentially troublesome issues in the relationship (Rubin & Mitchell, 1976). One year later, when the researchers followed up with the original sample, 9 of 10 participants said they had discussed their answers with their dating partners. In most instances, the discussions helped to strengthen the relationships. In some cases, however, the participants used the questionnaire as a springboard to discuss problems or concerns previously hidden. One participant said, "The study definitely played a role in ending my relationship with Larry." In this case, the couple had different views about how long they expected to be together. She was thinking of a short-term dating relationship, whereas he was thinking in terms of a lifetime. Their answers to the questions brought the disparity in their views to the surface and led to the end of their relationship. Researchers have a responsibility to anticipate the personal problems their study might cause and, at least, to inform the participants of the possible fallout.

Ethics comes into play in every psychological study. Even smart, conscientious students sometimes think that members of their church, athletes in the Special Olympics, or residents of the local nursing home where they volunteer present great samples for psychological research. Without proper permission, though, the most well-meaning, kind, and considerate researchers still violate the rights of the participants.

Ethics Guidelines

A number of guidelines have been developed to ensure that research is conducted ethically. At the base of all of these guidelines is the notion that a person participating in psychological research should be no worse off coming out of the study than he or she was on the way in.

Today colleges and universities have a review board (typically called the *institutional review board,* or *IRB*) that evaluates the ethical nature of research conducted at their institutions. Proposed research plans must pass the scrutiny of a research ethics committee before the research can be initiated. In addition, the American Psychological Association (APA) has developed ethics guidelines for its members. The code of ethics instructs psychologists to protect their participants from mental and physical harm. The participants' best interests need to be kept foremost in the researcher's mind (Gravetter, 2009; Ray, 2009). APA's guidelines address four important issues:

- *Informed consent:* All participants must know what their participation will involve and what risks might develop. For example, participants in a study on dating should be told beforehand that a questionnaire might stimulate thoughts about issues in their relationships that they have not considered. Participants also should be informed that in some instances a discussion of the issues might improve their relationships but that in others it might worsen the relationships and even end them. Even after informed consent is given, participants must retain the right to withdraw from the study at any time and for any reason.

- *Confidentiality:* Researchers are responsible for keeping all of the data they gather on individuals completely confidential and, when possible, completely anonymous. Confidential data are not the same as anonymous. When data are confidential, it is possible to link a participant's identity to his or her data.

- *Debriefing:* After the study has been completed, the researchers should inform the participants of its purpose and the methods they used. In most cases, the experimenters also can inform participants in a general manner beforehand about the purpose of the research without leading the participants to behave in a way that they think that the experimenters are expecting. When preliminary information about the study is likely to affect the results, participants can at least be debriefed after the study's completion.

- *Deception:* This is an ethical issue that psychologists debate extensively. In some circumstances, telling the participants beforehand what the research study is about substantially alters the participants' behavior and invalidates the researcher's data. For example, suppose a psychologist wants to know whether bystanders will report a theft. A mock theft is staged, and the psychologist observes which bystanders report it. Had the psychologist informed the participants beforehand that the study intended to discover the percentage of bystanders who will report a theft, the whole study would have been ruined. Thus, the researcher deceives participants about the purpose of the study, perhaps leading them to believe that it has some other purpose. In all cases of deception, however, the psychologist must ensure that the deception will not harm the participants and that the participants will be told the true nature of the study (will be debriefed) as soon as possible after the study is completed.

The federal government also takes a role in ensuring that research involving human participants is conducted ethically. The Federal Office for Protection from Research Risks is devoted to ensuring the well-being of participants in research studies. Over the years, the office has dealt with many challenging and controversial issues—among them, informed consent rules for research on mental disorders, regulations governing research on pregnant women and fetuses, and ethical issues regarding AIDS vaccine research.

The Ethics of Research with Animals

For generations, psychologists have used animals in some research. Animal studies have provided a better understanding of and solutions for many human problems (Pinel, 2009). Neal Miller (1985), who has made important discoveries about the effects of biofeedback on health, listed the following areas in which animal research has benefited humans:

- Psychotherapy techniques and behavioral medicine
- Rehabilitation of neuromuscular disorders
- Alleviation of the effects of stress and pain
- Drugs to treat anxiety and severe mental illness
- Methods for avoiding drug addiction and relapse
- Treatments to help premature infants gain weight so they can leave the hospital sooner
- Methods used to alleviate memory deficits in old age

challenge your thinking

Would Reality TV Pass the Institutional Review Board?

Survivor, American Idol, The Bachelor, Big Brother—these are just a few of many popular reality TV shows. While critics debate the quality of these shows, reality TV watchers may think that they are learning a lot about human nature by tuning in to see who will willingly eat ground-up rats or who will be ridiculed by Simon Cowell.

For you as a psychology student, an appropriate question might be, would these shows ever gain the approval of the IRB of an institution of higher learning? This issue was of interest to psychologist Barbara Spellman, who examined reality TV programming with an eye toward the ethical issues these shows present. If we were to consider reality TV from the perspective of the APA ethical guidelines, at least five issues that Spellman (2005) identified would come to the fore.

First, how do reality shows achieve informed consent? Informed consent means that all participants must know what their participation will involve and what risks might develop. Yet the very thing that makes reality shows exciting is the element of the unknown. Clearly the producers of *Survivor* are not going to inform contestants upfront that for their particular episode they will be asked to eat live bugs, because the element of shock and the dramatic moment of the decision would diminish greatly if it occurred off camera while the person read the consent form. On the other hand, it is unlikely that anyone who participates on such a show has not watched a few episodes, and therefore most participants will have a pretty good idea that they must expect the unexpected.

A second, related problem with at least some reality shows is the use of deception. Fooling a group of women into believing that

Reality TV shows would face high hurdles in trying to win over members of an institutional review board.

the individual to act in ways he or she might later regret or be judged for?

Ethical considerations involve balancing the rights of participants with the scientist's right to know. Thus, a fifth question pertinent to a study of reality TV is, what is the value of what we can learn from these "experiments"? This brings up the issue of how "natural" reality shows are. Are people truly themselves when the cameras are rolling?

a semi-employed construction worker is actually a millionaire is probably not likely to satisfy APA ethical considerations.

A third issue that might arise is that of risk. Many reality shows pose psychological and/or physical risk. Some reality shows include children (for example, *Trading Spouses*), and it is very unlikely that an IRB would consider posing any kind of risk to children justified.

A fourth major stumbling block for reality TV is the potential for huge cash awards to compel people to behave in ways they would not otherwise do. Is it "really" lying if you are doing it in order to win a million dollars? If a person does something to "play the game" that he or she would never do outside of the game, haven't we shown that money has compelled

What Do You Think?

- Do reality TV shows represent natural human behavior? Explain.

- What kind of reality show would you design if you were interested in exploring important psychological processes? What ethical safeguards would you use to protect participants?

Only about 5 percent of APA members use animals in their research. Rats and mice account for 90 percent of all psychological research with animals. It is true that researchers sometimes use procedures with animals that would be unethical with humans, but they are guided by a set of standards for housing, feeding, and maintaining the psychological and physical well-being of their animal subjects. Researchers are required to weigh potential benefits of the research against possible harm to the animal and to avoid inflicting unnecessary pain. Animal abuse is not as common as animal activist groups charge. In short, researchers must follow stringent ethical guidelines, whether animals or humans are the subjects in their studies.

The Place of Values in Psychological Research

Questions are asked not only about the ethics of psychology but also about its values and its standards for judging what is worthwhile and desirable. Some psychologists argue that psychology should be value-free and morally neutral. From their perspective, the psychologist's role as a scientist is to present facts as objectively as possible. Others believe that because psychologists are human, they cannot possibly be value-free. Indeed, some people go so far as to argue that psychologists should take stands on certain issues. For example, psychological research shows that children reared by gay male and lesbian parents are no more likely to be gay than other children and tend to show levels of psychological health that are equal to or higher than those of children reared by heterosexual parents (Patterson & Hastings, 2007). To the extent that some have argued against the rights of gay individuals to adopt children or to retain custody of their biological children, psychologists may have a role to play in the debate about these issues.

To further explore questions about the ethics of research, read the Challenge Your Thinking feature about reality TV.

self-quiz

1. Providing research participants with information about the purpose of a study at the study's conclusion is called
   A. informed consent.
   B. deception.
   C. debriefing.
   D. confidentiality.

2. The organization that provides ethical guidelines for psychologists is the
   A. American Psychiatric Association.
   B. Institutional Review Board.
   C. American Medical Association.
   D. American Psychological Association.

3. A study could possibly put participants at risk of harm, but the participants are not told about that risk. The ethical standard that has been violated is
   A. debriefing.
   B. informed consent.
   C. deception.
   D. confidentiality.

Apply It! 4. Amanda is participating in a psychological study as part of her Intro Psychology course. While filling out items on a questionnaire, Amanda finds that some of them embarrass her, and she decides to skip them. As she leaves the study, the experimenter notices these blank questions and asks Amanda to complete them because the research will be ruined without complete data from all participants. Which of the following accurately assesses the ethics of this situation?
   A. Amanda should really complete those questions. What's the big deal?
   B. Amanda is within her rights to leave any question blank if she chooses, and the experimenter has definitely "crossed a line."
   C. Amanda is ethically wrong because she agreed to be in the study, and so she must see it through.
   D. If Amanda read and signed the consent form, she is obligated to do as the experimenter says.

7 Learning About Psychology Means Learning About You

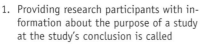

Throughout your life you have been exposed to a good deal of information about psychological research. In this book and your introductory psychology class, you will also learn about a multitude of research findings. In this last section, we consider the ways that learning about psychological studies can help you learn about yourself. We start by looking at some guidelines for evaluating psychological research findings that you might encounter in your everyday life.

Encountering Psychology in Everyday Life

Not all psychological information that is presented for public consumption comes from professionals with excellent credentials and reputations at colleges or universities or in applied mental health settings (Stanovich, 2007). Because journalists, television reporters, and other media personnel are not usually trained in psychological research, they often have trouble sorting through the widely varying material they find and making sound decisions about the best information to present to the public. In addition, the media often focus on sensationalistic and dramatic psychological findings to capture public attention. They tend to go beyond what actual research articles and clinical findings really say.

Even when the media present the results of excellent research, they have trouble accurately informing people about the findings and their implications for people's lives. This entire book is dedicated to carefully introducing, defining, and elaborating on key concepts and issues, research, and clinical findings. The media, however, do not have the luxury of so much time and space to detail and specify the limitations and qualifications of research. In the end, *you* have to take responsibility for evaluating media reports on psychological research. To put it another way, you have to consume psychological information critically and wisely. Five guidelines follow.

Avoid Overgeneralizing Based on Little Information
Media reports of psychological information often leave out details about the nature of the sample used in a given study. Without information about sample characteristics, such as the number of participants, their gender, or their ethnic representation, it is wise to take research results with a grain of salt.

Distinguish Between Group Results and Individual Needs
Just as we cannot generalize from a small group to all people, we also cannot apply conclusions from a group to an individual. When you learn about psychological research through the media, you might be disposed to apply the results to your life. It is important to keep in mind that statistics about a group do not necessarily represent each individual in the group equally well. Imagine, for example, taking a test in a class and being told that the class average was 75 percent, but you got 98 percent. It is unlikely that you would want the instructor to apply the group average to your score.

Sometimes consumers of psychological research can get the wrong idea about whether their experience is "normal" if it does not match group statistics. New parents face this issue all the time. They read about developmental milestones that supposedly characterize an entire age group of children; one such milestone might be that most 2-year-olds are conversing with their parents. However, this group information does not necessarily characterize *all* children who are developing normally. Albert Einstein did not start talking until he was the ripe old age of 3.

Look for Answers Beyond a Single Study
The media might identify an interesting piece of research and claim that it is something phenomenal with far-reaching implications. Although such pivotal studies do occur, they are rare. It is safer to assume that no single study will provide conclusive answers to an important question, especially answers that apply to all people. In fact, in most psychological domains that prompt many investigations, conflicting results are common. Answers to

Snapshots

"This just in from the AMA: New studies reveal that life is bad for you."

www.CartoonStock.com

questions in research usually emerge after many scientists have conducted similar investigations that yield similar conclusions. Remember that you should not take one research study as the absolute, final answer to a problem, no matter how compelling the findings.

Avoid Attributing Causes Where None Have Been Found

Drawing causal conclusions from correlational studies is one of the most common mistakes the media make. When a true experiment has not been conducted—that is, when participants have not been randomly assigned to treatments or experiences—two variables might have only a noncausal relationship to each other. Remember from the discussion of correlation earlier in the chapter that causal interpretations cannot be made when two or more factors are simply correlated. We cannot say that one causes the other. When you hear about correlational studies, be skeptical of words indicating causation until you know more about the particular research.

Consider the Source of Psychological Information

Studies conducted by psychologists are not automatically accepted by the rest of the research community. The researchers usually must submit their findings to a journal for review by their colleagues, who make a decision about whether to publish the paper, depending on its scientific merit. Although the quality of research and findings is not uniform among all psychology journals, in most cases journals submit the findings to far greater scrutiny than the popular media do (Stanovich, 2007).

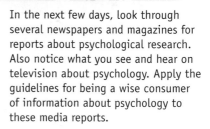

Within the media, though, you can usually draw a distinction. The reports of psychological research in respected newspapers such as the *New York Times* and the *Washington Post,* as well as in credible magazines such as *Time* and *Newsweek,* are far more trustworthy than reports in tabloids such as the *National Enquirer* and *Star.* Yet whatever the source—serious publication, tabloid, or even academic journal—you are responsible for reading the details behind the reported findings and for analyzing the study's credibility.

In the next few days, look through several newspapers and magazines for reports about psychological research. Also notice what you see and hear on television about psychology. Apply the guidelines for being a wise consumer of information about psychology to these media reports.

Appreciating Psychology as the Science of You

In taking introductory psychology, you have an amazing opportunity. You will learn a great deal about human beings, especially one particular human being: you. Whether the psychological research presented is about emotions and motivation or the structures of the nervous system, it is still essentially about you.

When you think of psychology, you might think first and foremost about the mind and its complex mental processes such as those involved in love, gratitude, hate, and anger. However, psychology has come to recognize more and more that the mind and its operations are intricately connected to the body. As you will see when we examine neuroscience in Chapter 2, observations of the brain at work reveal that when mental processes change, so do physical processes. This mind–body link has fascinated philosophers for centuries. Psychology occupies the very spot where the mind and the body meet.

It might be helpful to think concretely about the ways the mind and body can relate to each other even as they are united in the physical reality of a person. Let's say you experience a mental event such as seeing a "Buns of Steel" infomercial on TV. You decide to embark on a quest for these legendary buns. Dedication, goal setting, and self-discipline will be the kinds of mental processes necessary to transform your body. The mind can work on the body, prompting changes to its shape and size.

Similarly, the body can dramatically influence the mind. Consider how fuzzy your thinking is after you stay out too late and how much easier it is to solve life's problems after a good night's sleep. Also think about your outlook on the first day of true recovery from a nagging cold: Everything seems better. Your mood and your work improve. Clearly, physical states such as illness and health influence how we think.

The relationship between the body and mind is illustrated in a major dilemma that countless psychologists have faced: the impact of nature versus nurture. Essentially, psychologists have wondered and debated which of the two is more important to a person—nature (that is, genetic heritage) or nurture (social experiences). The influence of genetics on a variety of psychological characteristics, and the ways that genetic influence can itself be altered by experience, will be addressed in many of the main topics in this book, from development (Chapter 8) to personality traits (Chapter 10) to psychological disorders (Chapter 12). You will see that at every turn, your physical and mental self are intertwined in ways you may have never considered.

Throughout this book, we investigate the ways that all of the various approaches to psychology matter to your life. Psychology is crucially about you, essential to your understanding of your life, your goals, and the ways that you can use the insights of thousands of scientists to make your life healthier and happier.

summary

① Defining Psychology and Exploring Its Roots

Psychology is the scientific study of human behavior and mental processes. Psychologists approach human behavior as scientists who think critically, are curious, skeptical, and objective. Psychology emerged as a science from philosophy and physiology. Two founders of the science of psychology are Wilhelm Wundt and William James.

② Contemporary Approaches to Psychology

Seven different approaches to psychology include biological, behavioral, psychodynamic, humanistic, cognitive, evolutionary, and sociocultural. All of these approaches consider important questions about human behavior from different but complementary perspectives.

③ Psychology's Scientific Method

Psychologists use the scientific method to address research questions. This method involves starting with a theory and then making observations, formulating hypotheses, testing these through empirical research, drawing conclusions, and evaluating these conclusions. The science of psychology is an ongoing conversation among scholars.

④ Types of Psychological Research

Three types of research commonly used in psychology are descriptive research (finding out about the basic dimensions of some variable), correlational research (finding out if and how two variables change together), and experimental research (determining the causal relationship between variables). In an experiment, the independent variable is manipulated to see if it produces changes in the dependent variable. Experiments involve comparing two groups: the experimental group (the one that receives the treatment or manipulation of the independent variable) and the control group (the comparison group or baseline that is equal to the experimental group in every way except for the independent variable). Experimental research relies on random assignment to ensure that the groups are roughly equivalent before the manipulation of the independent variable.

⑤ Research Samples and Settings

Two important decisions that must be made for psychological research are whom to study and where to study them. A sample is the group that participates in a study; the population is the group to which the researcher wishes to generalize the results. A random sample is the best way of ensuring that the sample reflects the population. Research settings include the laboratory but also real-world, naturalistic contexts. The laboratory allows a great deal of control, but naturalistic settings may give a truer sense of natural behavior.

⑥ Conducting Ethical Research

For all kinds of research, ethical treatment of participants is very important. Participants should leave a psychological study no worse off than they were when they entered. Some guiding principles for ethical research in psychology include informed consent, confidentiality, debriefing (participants should be fully informed about the purpose of a study once it is over), and explaining fully the use of deception in a study.

⑦ Learning About Psychology Means Learning About You

In your everyday life and in introductory psychology, you will be exposed to psychological research findings. In approaching psychological research in the media, you should adopt the attitude of a scientist and critically evaluate the research presented. In introductory psychology, you should make the most of the experience by applying it to your life. Psychology is, after all, the scientific study of you—your behavior, thoughts, goals, and well-being.

key terms

self-test

Multiple Choice

1. The beginning of psychology as a science began in the discipline of
   A. philosophy.   C. sociology.
   B. physics.   D. biology.

2. Of the following experimental situations that a structuralist might conduct, the one that reflects the method of introspection is
   A. documenting subjects' descriptions of an experience.
   B. asking subjects to remember a list of words.
   C. testing rats in a maze to see how fast they learn.
   D. rewarding subjects for solving problems.

3. Structuralism focuses on _____, and functionalism focuses on _____.
   A. thoughts; behaviors
   B. the components of the mind; the purposes of the mind
   C. pragmatism; idealism
   D. natural selection; environment

4. The individual most closely associated with behaviorism is
   A. B. F. Skinner.
   B. Charles Darwin.
   C. Wilhelm Wundt.
   D. William James.

5. Of the following, the topic that would be of most interest to a psychodynamic psychologist is
   A. altruism.
   B. unconscious drives.

C. the adaptiveness of behaviors.
D. people's thought processes.

6. The type of research design that allows a researcher to test for causation is
   A. correlational design.
   B. longitudinal design.
   C. case study design.
   D. experimental design.

7. A researcher finds that as scores on optimism go up, scores on depression go down. Moreover, she finds a strong relationship between optimism and depression. Which of the following correlation coefficients would be most consistent with her findings?
   A. .38   C. −.11
   B. .79   D. −.68

8. An experimenter told a research participant that the purpose of the study was to examine people's reaction to media violence. In reality, the purpose was to examine group dynamics. A potential ethical problem for this study would be
   A. debriefing.
   B. confidentiality.
   C. informed consent.
   D. deception.

9. Alfonso is in a study testing the effectiveness of a new type of medication. He is given a pill that contains no actual medicine (a sugar pill). After taking the pill, he reports significantly fewer symptoms. Which of the following is at play?
   A. experimenter bias
   B. placebo effect

C. external validity
D. internal validity

10. An example of selecting a random sample is
    A. randomly choosing a group of 50 students from a roster of all students in a school.
    B. randomly choosing a classroom from all classrooms in a school.
    C. randomly choosing students who attended a soccer game.
    D. choosing each 50th student who enters the building's front entrance.

Apply It!

11. Georgia believes that people are more likely to behave kindly toward others if they are in a good mood. She randomly assigns participants (who are psychology students participating for research credits) to one of two groups. In one group, participants are told to write for 10 minutes about the happiest moment of their life. In the other group, participants write for 10 minutes about a typical day in their life.
    A. Why did Georgia assign participants to groups *randomly?*
    B. In Georgia's study, what are the *independent variable* and the *dependent variable,* and how are each of these operationally defined?
    C. Identify the *experimental group* and the *control group* in Georgia's study.

2 The Brain and Behavior

Tommy McHugh: From Violent Heroin Addict to Accomplished Artist

Tommy McHugh, a builder in Liverpool, England, was a gruff, sometimes violent heroin addict. At age 51, he suffered a stroke that caused permanent changes to his brain (Lythgoe & others, 2005). During his recovery, Tommy found himself talking and writing in rhymes. Soon he was writing poetry, and drawing and sculpting too. This man who had previously shown no interest in such pursuits emerged as an accomplished artist. Tommy was happier as well, calling the changes in his life "fantastic" (BBC News, 2004).

Tommy's experience is rare, but it offers a fascinating glimpse of the brain's ability to change itself. It points to untapped hidden potential in the brain. Further, it suggests that changes to the brain can alter what we do, how we think, and even who we are.

The brain is extraordinarily complex, containing about 100 billion nerve cells (Nolte, 2009). Imagine: The intricate organ you are reading about is the engine that is doing the work of learning this material. The brain is also responsible for the research presented here. In other words, the brain is at once an object of study and *the studier*.

You might think of the mind that is reading this book as separate from the small organ housed inside your skull. Perhaps you consider thinking a mental process, not a physical one. Yet thinking *is* a physical event. Every thought you have is reflected in physical activity in the brain. In fact, the brain can be changed by experience. London cab drivers who have developed a familiarity with the city show increases in the size of the area of the brain thought to be responsible for reading maps (Maguire & others, 2000). Think about that: When you change the way you think, you are *literally* changing the brain's physical processes and even its shape. ■

- **If a person's brain is changed, is he or she the *same person*?**

- **What goals do you have that might involve changing the way you think?**

- **What special activities do you do that may have already modified the working of your brain?**

In this chapter, our focus is the nervous system and its command center—the brain. We review the essentials of what the brain has come to know about itself, including the biological foundations of human behavior and the brain's extraordinary capacity for adaptation and repair. We end with a look at how genetic processes influence who we are as individuals and how we behave.

1 The Nervous System

nervous system
The body's electrochemical communication circuitry.

The **nervous system** is the body's electrochemical communication circuitry. The field that studies the nervous system is called *neuroscience,* and the people who study it are *neuroscientists.*

The human nervous system is made up of billions of communicating cells, and it is likely the most intricately organized aggregate of matter on the planet. A single cubic centimeter of the human brain consists of well over 50 million nerve cells, each of which communicates with many other nerve cells in information-processing networks that make the most elaborate computer seem primitive.

One cubic centimeter of brain = 50 million nerve cells. Think about it—that's about the size of a snack cube of cheese.

Characteristics of the Nervous System

The brain and nervous system guide our interaction with the world around us, move the body through the world, and direct our *adaptation* to our environment. Several extraordinary characteristics allow the nervous system to direct our behavior: complexity, integration, adaptability, and electrochemical transmission.

Adaptation, adaptability, adapt: Psychologists use these words a lot in referring to your ability to function in your environment. When you adapt to something, you adjust your behavior to promote your own survival.

Complexity The human brain and nervous system are enormously complex. The orchestration of all of the billions of nerve cells in the brain—to allow you to sing, dance, write, talk, and think—is an awe-inspiring task. As you are reading, your brain is carrying out a multitude of tasks, including seeing, reading, learning, and (we hope) breathing. Extensive assemblies of nerve cells participate in each of these activities, all at once.

Integration Neuroscientist Steven Hyman (2001) calls the brain the "great integrator," meaning that the brain does a wonderful job of pulling information together. Sounds, sights, touch, taste, smells, hearing—the brain integrates all of these as we function in our world.

The brain and the nervous system have different levels and many different parts. Brain activity is integrated across these levels through countless interconnections of brain cells and extensive pathways that link different parts of the brain. Each nerve cell communicates, on average, with 10,000 others, making an astronomical number of connections (Bloom, Nelson, & Lazerson, 2001). The evidence for these connections is observable, for example, when a loved one takes your hand. How does your brain know, and tell you, what has happened? Bundles of interconnected nerve cells relay information about the sensation in your hand through the nervous system in very orderly fashion, all the way to the areas of the brain involved in recognizing that someone you love is holding your hand. Then the brain might send a reply back and prompt your hand to give him or her a little squeeze.

Adaptability The world around us is constantly changing. To survive, we must adapt to new conditions. Our brain and nervous system together serve as our agent in adapting to the world. Although nerve cells reside in certain brain regions, they are not

fixed, unchanging structures. They have a hereditary, biological foundation, but they are constantly adapting to changes in the body and the environment (Coch, Fischer, & Dawson, 2007).

The term **plasticity** denotes the brain's special capacity for change. Tommy McHugh's amazing experience is an example of extreme plasticity. Less dramatic examples of plasticity occur in all of us. The experiences that we have contribute to the wiring or rewiring of the brain (Nelson, 2009), just like those London cab drivers.

Electrochemical Transmission

The brain and the nervous system function essentially as an information-processing system, powered by electrical impulses and chemical messengers (Chichilnisky, 2007). When an impulse travels down a nerve cell or *neuron,* it does so electrically. When that impulse gets to the end of the line, it communicates with the next neuron using chemicals, as we will describe in some detail later in this chapter.

When we touch or gaze at an object, electrical charges and chemical messages pulse through our brain, knitting the cells together into pathways and networks for processing the information.

Pathways in the Nervous System

As we interact with and adapt to the world, the brain and the nervous system receive and transmit sensory input (like sounds, smells, and flavors), integrate the information received from the environment, and direct the body's motor activities. Information flows into the brain through input from our senses, and the brain makes sense of that information, pulling it together and giving it meaning. In turn, information moves out of the brain to the rest of the body, directing all of the physical things we do (Fox, 2008).

The nervous system possesses specialized pathways that are adapted for different functions. These pathways are made up of afferent nerves, efferent nerves, and neural networks. **Afferent nerves,** or sensory nerves, carry information *to* the brain and spinal cord. These sensory pathways communicate information about the external environment (for example, seeing a sunrise) and things that are going on in our bodies (for example, feeling tired or hungry) from sensory receptors to the brain and spinal cord. **Efferent nerves,** or motor nerves, carry information *out of* the brain and spinal cord— that is, they carry the nervous system's output. These motor pathways communicate information from the brain and spinal cord to other areas of the body, including muscles and glands, telling them to get busy.

If you are sitting in a chair in the same position for too long, your bottom might start to feel uncomfortable. Those sensations are sent by afferent nerves to the brain and spinal cord. Efferent nerves in turn send the response to your muscles, "Shift a little, please!" and then afferent nerves might send the message, "Ah! Much better."

Most information processing occurs when information moves through **neural networks.** These networks of nerve cells integrate sensory input and motor output. For example, as you read your class notes, the input from your eyes is transmitted to your brain and then passed through many neural networks, which translate the characters on the page into neural codes for letters, words, associations, and meanings. Some of the information is stored in the neural networks, and, if you read aloud, some is passed on as messages to your lips and tongue. Neural networks make up most of the brain. Working in networks amplifies the brain's computing power.

Divisions of the Nervous System

This truly elegant system is highly ordered and organized for effective function. Figure 2.1 shows the two primary divisions of the human nervous system: the central nervous system and the peripheral nervous system.

The **central nervous system (CNS)** is made up of the brain and spinal cord. More than 99 percent of all nerve cells in our body are located in the CNS. The **peripheral nervous system (PNS)** is the network of nerves that connects the brain and spinal cord

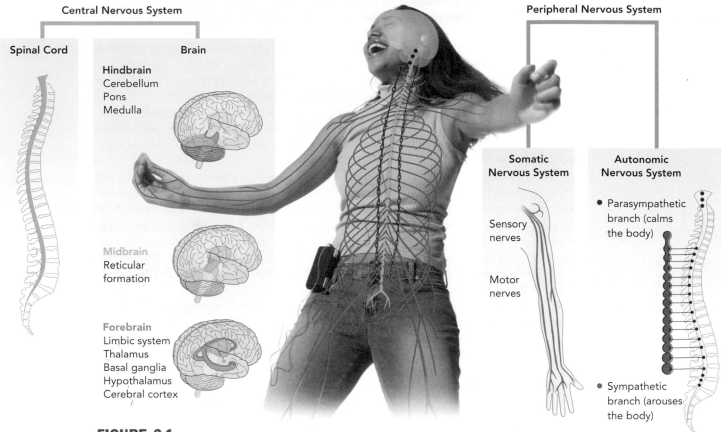

Human Nervous System

Central Nervous System

Spinal Cord

Brain

Hindbrain
Cerebellum
Pons
Medulla

Midbrain
Reticular
formation

Forebrain
Limbic system
Thalamus
Basal ganglia
Hypothalamus
Cerebral cortex

Peripheral Nervous System

Somatic Nervous System

Sensory nerves

Motor nerves

Autonomic Nervous System

• Parasympathetic branch (calms the body)

• Sympathetic branch (arouses the body)

FIGURE 2.1

Major Divisions of the Human Nervous System The nervous system has two main divisions. One is the *central nervous system* (*left*), which comprises the brain and the spinal cord. The nervous system's other main division is the *peripheral nervous system* (*right*), which itself has two parts—the *somatic nervous system*, which controls sensory and motor neurons, and the *autonomic nervous system*, which monitors processes such as breathing, heart rate, and digestion. These complex systems work together to help us successfully navigate the world.

autonomic nervous system
The body system that takes messages to and from the body's internal organs, monitoring such processes as breathing, heart rate, and digestion.

stressors
Circumstances and events that threaten individuals and tax their coping abilities and that cause physiological changes to ready the body to handle the assault of stress.

somatic nervous system
The body system consisting of the sensory nerves, whose function is to convey information from the skin and muscles to the CNS about conditions such as pain and temperature, and the motor nerves, whose function is to tell muscles what to do.

sympathetic nervous system
The part of the autonomic nervous system that arouses the body.

parasympathetic nervous system
The part of the autonomic nervous system that calms the body.

stress
The response of individuals to environmental stressors.

to other parts of the body. The functions of the peripheral nervous system are to bring information to and from the brain and spinal cord and to carry out the commands of the CNS to execute various muscular and glandular activities.

The peripheral nervous system has two major divisions: the somatic nervous system and the autonomic nervous system. The **somatic nervous system** consists of sensory nerves, whose function is to convey information from the skin and muscles to the CNS about conditions such as pain and temperature, and motor nerves, whose function is to tell muscles what to do. The function of the **autonomic nervous system** is to take messages to and from the body's internal organs, monitoring such processes as breathing, heart rate, and digestion. The autonomic nervous system also is divided into two parts: The first part, the **sympathetic nervous system,** arouses the body to mobilize it for action, while the second, the **parasympathetic nervous system,** calms the body. The sympathetic nervous system is involved in the experience of stress.

Stress is the response of individuals to **stressors,** which are the circumstances and events that threaten them and tax their coping abilities. When we experience stress, our body readies itself to handle the assault of stress; a number of physiological changes take place. You certainly know what stress feels like. Imagine, for example, that you show up for class one morning, and it looks as if everyone else knows that there is a test that day. You hear others talking about how much they have studied, and you nervously ask yourself: "Test? What test?" You might start to sweat, and your heart might thump fast and hard in your chest. Sure enough, the instructor shows up with a stack of exams. You are about to be tested on material you have not even thought about, much less studied.

The stress response begins with a "fight or flight" reaction, one of the functions of the sympathetic nervous system. This reaction quickly mobilizes the body's physiological resources to prepare the organism to deal with threats to survival. Clearly, an unexpected exam is not literally a threat to your survival, but the human stress response is such that it can occur in reaction to any threat to personally important motives (Sapolsky, 2004).

When you feel your heart pounding and your hands sweating under stress, those experiences reveal the sympathetic nervous system in action. If you need to run away from a stressor, the sympathetic nervous system sends blood out to your extremities to get you ready to take off.

When we undergo stress, we also experience the release of *corticosteroids,* which are powerful stress hormones (Maggio & Segal, 2009). Corticosteroids in the brain allow us to focus our attention on what needs to be done *now.* For example, in an emergency, people sometimes report feeling strangely calm and doing just what has to be done, whether it is calling 911 or applying pressure to a serious cut. Such experiences reveal the benefits of corticosteroids for humans in times of extreme acute stress (Holsboer & Ising, 2010). *Acute stress* is the momentary stress that occurs in response to life experiences. When the stressful situation ends, so does acute stress.

However, we are not in a live-or-die situation most of the time when we experience stress. Indeed, we can even "stress ourselves out" just by thinking. *Chronic stress*—that is, stress that goes on continuously—may lead to persistent autonomic nervous system arousal (Leonard & Myint, 2009). While the sympathetic nervous system is working to meet the demands of whatever is stressing us out, the parasympathetic nervous system is not getting a chance to do its job of maintenance and repair, of digesting food, or keeping our organs in good working order. Thus, over time, chronic autonomic nervous system activity can break down the immune system (Miller, Chen, & Cole, 2009). Chronic stress is clearly best avoided, although this objective is easier said than done.

Yet the brain, an organ that is itself powerfully affected by chronic stress, can be our ally in helping us avoid such continuous stress. Consider that when we face a challenging situation, we can exploit the brain's abilities and interpret the experience in a way that is not so stressful. For example, maybe we can approach an upcoming audition for a play not so much as a stressor but as an opportunity to shine. Many cognitive therapists believe that changing the way people think about their life opportunities and experiences can help them live less stressfully (Rachman, 2009; Watson, 2009).

At the beginning of this chapter, we considered how changing the way we think leads to physical changes in the brain and its processes. In light of this remarkable capacity, it is reasonable to conclude that we can use our brain's powers to change how we look at life experiences—and maybe even deploy the brain as a defense against stress.

self-quiz

1. The characteristics that allow the nervous system to direct our behavior are its complexity, integration, electrochemical transmission, and
   A. constancy.
   B. adaptability.
   C. sensitivity.
   D. "fight or flight" response.

2. Neural networks are networks of nerve cells that integrate sensory input and
   A. the "fight or flight" response.
   B. electrochemical transmission.
   C. bodily processes such as heart rate and digestion.
   D. motor output.

3. When you are in danger, the part of the nervous system that is responsible for an increase in your heart rate is the
   A. central nervous system.
   B. peripheral nervous system.
   C. sympathetic nervous system.
   D. parasympathetic nervous system.

Apply It! 4. Shannon and Terrell are two college students. Shannon is in a constant state of low-level stress. She spends a lot of time worrying about what might happen, and she gets herself worked up about imagined catastrophes. Terrell is generally more easygoing, but on his way to class one day he is in a near-miss traffic accident—at the moment he sees the truck coming at him, his body tenses up, his heart races, and he experiences extreme panic. Which answer most accurately identifies the individual who is most likely to catch the cold that is going around their dorm this semester?
A. Shannon, who is experiencing chronic stress
B. Terrell, who is experiencing acute stress
C. Shannon, who is experiencing acute stress
D. Terrell, who is experiencing chronic stress

2 Neurons

Within each division of the nervous system, much is happening at the cellular level. Nerve cells, chemicals, and electrical impulses work together to transmit information at speeds of up to 330 miles per hour. As a result, information can travel from your brain to your hands (or vice versa) in a matter of milliseconds (Shier, Butler, & Lewis, 2007).

There are two types of cells in the nervous system: neurons and glial cells. **Neurons** are the nerve cells that handle the information-processing function. The human brain contains about 100 billion neurons. The average neuron is a complex structure with as many as 10,000 physical connections with other cells. Recently, researchers have been particularly interested in a special type of neuron called *mirror neurons*. Mirror neurons seem to play a role in imitation and are activated (in primates and humans) when we perform an action but also when we watch someone else perform that same task (Rizzolatti & Craighero, 2004). In addition to imitation, these neurons are thought to play a role in empathy and in our understanding of others.

Glial cells provide support, nutritional benefits, and other functions in the nervous system (Kriegstein & Alvarez-Buylla, 2009). Glial cells keep neurons running smoothly. These cells are not specialized to process information in the way that neurons are, and there are many more of them in the nervous system than there are neurons. In fact, for every neuron there are about 10 glial cells.

neurons
One of two types of cells in the nervous system; neurons are the nerve cells that handle the information-processing function.

330 miles per hour? Most of us will never experience driving that fast. The supersonic rocket car, developed in Britain by the team that set the previous land record of over 700 miles per hour, is shooting for 1,000 miles per hour. Now, the wisdom of driving cars that go faster than we can think is another story...

glial cells
Cells in the nervous system that provide support, nutritional benefits, and other functions and keep neurons running smoothly.

Specialized Cell Structure

Not all neurons are alike, as they are specialized to handle different information-processing functions. However, all neurons do have some common characteristics. Most neurons are created very early in life, but their shape, size, and connections can change throughout the life span. The way neurons function reflects the major characteristic of the nervous system described at the beginning of the chapter: plasticity. Neurons can and do change.

Every neuron has a cell body, dendrites, and an axon (Figure 2.2). The **cell body** contains the nucleus, which directs the manufacture of substances that the neuron needs

cell body
The part of the neuron that contains the nucleus, which directs the manufacture of substances that the neuron needs for growth and maintenance.

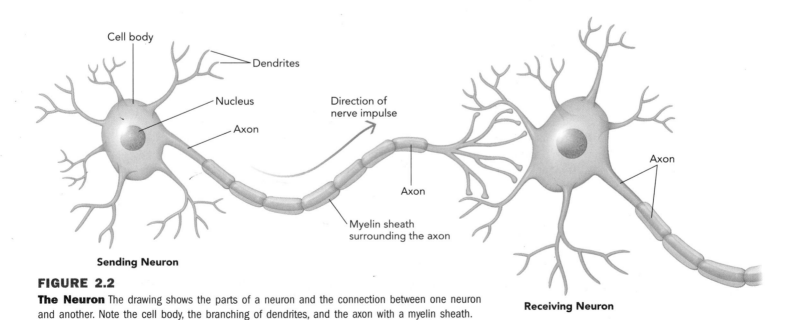

Cell body
Dendrites
Nucleus
Direction of nerve impulse
Axon
Axon
Myelin sheath surrounding the axon
Axon

Sending Neuron

Receiving Neuron

FIGURE 2.2

The Neuron The drawing shows the parts of a neuron and the connection between one neuron and another. Note the cell body, the branching of dendrites, and the axon with a myelin sheath.

for growth and maintenance. **Dendrites,** treelike fibers projecting from a neuron, receive information and orient it toward the neuron's cell body. Most nerve cells have numerous dendrites, which increase their surface area, allowing each neuron to receive input from many other neurons. The **axon** is the part of the neuron that carries information away from the cell body toward other cells. Although extremely thin (1/10,000th of an inch—a human hair by comparison is 1/1,000 of an inch), axons can be very long, with many branches. In fact, some extend more than 3 feet—all the way from the top of the brain to the base of the spinal cord.

Covering all surfaces of neurons, including the dendrites and axons, are very thin cellular membranes that are much like the surface of a balloon. The neuronal membranes are semipermeable, meaning that they contain tiny holes, or channels, that allow only certain substances to pass into and out of the neurons.

A **myelin sheath,** consisting of a layer of cells containing fat, encases and insulates most axons. By insulating axons, myelin sheaths speed up transmission of nerve impulses (Diamond, 2009). Multiple sclerosis (MS), a degenerative disease of the nervous system in which a hardening of myelin tissue occurs, disrupts neuronal communication. *Sclerosis* means, literally, "scars," and indeed, in such disorders as MS, myelin is replaced by scar tissue. There are numerous disorders that involve problems in either the creation or maintenance of myelin. For instance, adrenoleukodystrophy (ALD) is a genetic disorder that generally affects boys. If you have seen the film *Lorenzo's Oil,* you are familiar with the story of Lorenzo Odone, a boy with ALD whose parents became experts on the biochemistry of myelinization so that they could search for a cure for their son. Although ALD remains incurable, some boys are spared its worst effects by the early introduction of Lorenzo's oil (actually, a mixture of oils) to their diets, along with an extremely low-fat diet that prevents the buildup of long-chain fatty acids that results in demyelinization.

The myelin sheath developed as the nervous system evolved (Hartline & Colman, 2007). As brain size increased, it became necessary for information to travel over longer distances in the nervous system. Axons without myelin sheaths are not very good conductors of electricity. With the insulation of myelin sheaths, axons transmit electrical impulses and convey information much more rapidly (Diamond, 2009). We can compare the myelin sheath's development to the evolution of freeways as cities grew. A freeway is a shielded road. It keeps fast-moving, long-distance traffic from getting snarled by slow local traffic.

The Neural Impulse

To transmit information to other neurons, a neuron sends brief electrical impulses (let's call them "blips") through its axon to the next neuron. As you reach to turn this page, hundreds of such impulses will stream down the axons in your arm to tell your muscles when to flex and how quickly. By changing the rate of the signals, or blips, the neuron can vary its message.

The rate of the blips determines the intensity. So, if you are dying of suspense, the blips might happen faster as you rush to learn more about neurons on the next page.

Those impulses traveling down the axon are electrical. How does a neuron— a living cell—generate electricity? To answer this question, we need to take a moment to examine the axon. The axon is a tube encased in a membrane. The membrane has hundreds and thousands of tiny gates in it. These gates are generally closed, but they can open. We call the membrane *semipermeable* because fluids can sometimes flow in and out of these gates. Indeed, there are

dendrites
Treelike fibers projecting from a neuron, which receive information and orient it toward the neuron's cell body.

axon
The part of the neuron that carries information away from the cell body toward other cells.

myelin sheath
A layer of fat cells that encases and insulates most axons.

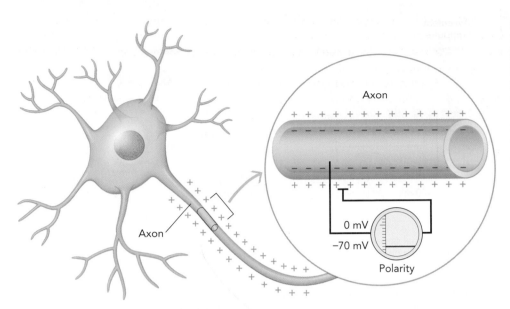

fluids both inside the axon and outside it as well. Floating in those fluids are electrically
charged particles called *ions*.

Some of these ions, notably sodium and potassium, carry positive charges. Negatively
charged ions of chlorine and other elements also are present. The membrane surrounding
the axon prevents negative and positive ions from randomly flowing into or out of the
cell. The neuron creates electrical signals by moving positive and negative ions back
and forth through its outer membrane. How does the movement of ions across
the membrane occur? Those tiny gates mentioned above, called *ion channels*,
open and close to let the ions pass into and out of the cell. Normally when
the neuron is resting, not transmitting information, the ion channels are
closed, and a slight negative charge is present along the inside of the cell
membrane. On the outside of the cell membrane, the charge is positive. Because
of the difference in charge, the membrane of the resting neuron is said to be *polarized*, with most negatively charged ions on the inside of the cell and most positively
charged ions on the outside. **Resting potential** is the stable, negative charge of an inactive neuron (Figure 2.3). That potential is between −60 and −75 millivolts, meaning each
tiny cell maintains the potential for about 0.075 volts of electricity.

For ions, it is true that opposites attract. The negatively charged ions inside the membrane and the positively charged ions outside the membrane will rush to each other if
given the chance. Impulses that travel down the neuron do so by opening and closing
ion channels, allowing the ions to flow in and out.

A neuron becomes activated when an incoming impulse—a reaction to, say, a pin-
prick or the sight of someone's face—raises the neuron's voltage, and the sodium gates
at the base of the axon open briefly. This action allows positively charged sodium ions
to flow into the neuron, creating a more positively charged neuron and *depolarizing* the
membrane by decreasing the charge difference between the fluids inside and outside of
the neuron. Then potassium channels open, and positively charged potassium ions move
out through the neuron's semipermeable membrane. This outflow returns the neuron to
a negative charge. Then the same process occurs as the next group of channels flips
open briefly.

So it goes all the way down the axon, like a long row of cabinet doors opening and
closing in sequence. It is hard to imagine, but this simple system of opening and closing
tiny doors is responsible for the fluid movements of a ballet dancer and the flying fingers
of a pianist playing a concerto.

resting potential
The stable, nega-
tive charge of an
inactive neuron.

*So, human neural
transmission uses relatively little
electricity. Not thinking is not a
good way to "go green."*

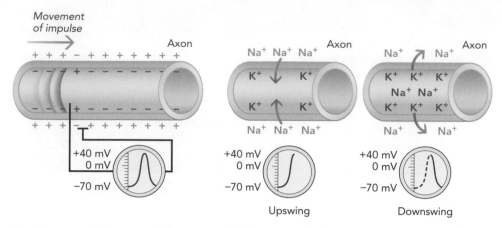

FIGURE 2.4

The Action Potential An action potential is a brief wave of positive electrical charge that sweeps down the axon as the sodium channels in the axon membrane open and close. (*a*) The action potential causes a change in electrical potential as it moves along the axon. (*b*) The movements of sodium ions (Na⁺) and potassium ions (K⁺) into and out of the axon cause the electrical changes.

(a) Action potential generated by an impulse within a neuron

(b) Movement of sodium (Na⁺) and potassium (K⁺) ions responsible for the action potential

action potential
The brief wave of positive electrical charge that sweeps down the axon.

The term **action potential** describes the brief wave of positive electrical charge that sweeps down the axon (Figure 2.4). An action potential lasts only about 1/1,000th of a second, because the sodium channels can stay open for only a very brief time. They quickly close again and become reset for the next action potential. When a neuron sends an action potential, it is commonly said to be "firing." The action potential abides by the **all-or-nothing principle:** Once the electrical impulse reaches a certain level of intensity, called its *threshold,* it fires and moves all the way down the axon without losing any of its intensity. The impulse traveling down an axon can be compared to the burning fuse of a firecracker. Whether you use a match or blowtorch to light the fuse, once the fuse has been lit, the spark travels quickly and with the same intensity down the fuse.

all-or-nothing principle
The principle that once the electrical impulse reaches a certain level of intensity (its threshold), it fires and moves all the way down the axon without losing any intensity.

Synapses and Neurotransmitters

The movement of an impulse down an axon may be compared to a crowd's "wave" motion in a stadium. With the wave, there is a problem, however—the aisles. How does the wave get across the aisle? Similarly, neurons do not touch each other directly, and electricity cannot travel over the space between them. Yet somehow neurons manage to communicate. This is where the chemical part of electrochemical transmission comes in. Neurons communicate with each other through chemicals that carry messages across the space. This connection between one neuron and another is one of the most intriguing and highly researched areas of contemporary neuroscience (McAllister, 2007). Figure 2.5 gives an overview of how this connection between neurons takes place.

neurotransmitters
Chemical substances that are stored in very tiny sacs within the terminal buttons and involved in transmitting information across a synaptic gap to the next neuron.

Synaptic Transmission **Synapses** are tiny spaces between neurons; the gap between neurons is referred to as a *synaptic gap.* Most synapses lie between the axon of one neuron and the dendrites or cell body of another neuron. Before an impulse can cross the synaptic gap, it must be converted into a chemical signal.

Each axon branches out into numerous fibers that end in structures called *terminal buttons.* Stored in very tiny synaptic vesicles (*sacs*) within the terminal buttons are chemical substances called **neurotransmitters.** As their name suggests, neurotransmitters transmit, or carry, information across the synaptic gap to the next neuron. When a nerve impulse reaches the terminal button, it triggers the release of neurotransmitter molecules from the synaptic vesicles (Brooks, 2006; Zhao & others, 2006). The neurotransmitter molecules flood the synaptic gap. Their movements are random, but some of them bump into receptor sites in the next neuron.

The neurotransmitters are like pieces of a puzzle, and the receptor sites on the next neuron are differently shaped spaces. If the shape of the receptor site corresponds to the shape of the neurotransmitter molecule, the neurotransmitter acts like a key to open the

synapses
Tiny spaces between neurons; the gaps between neurons are referred to as synaptic gaps.

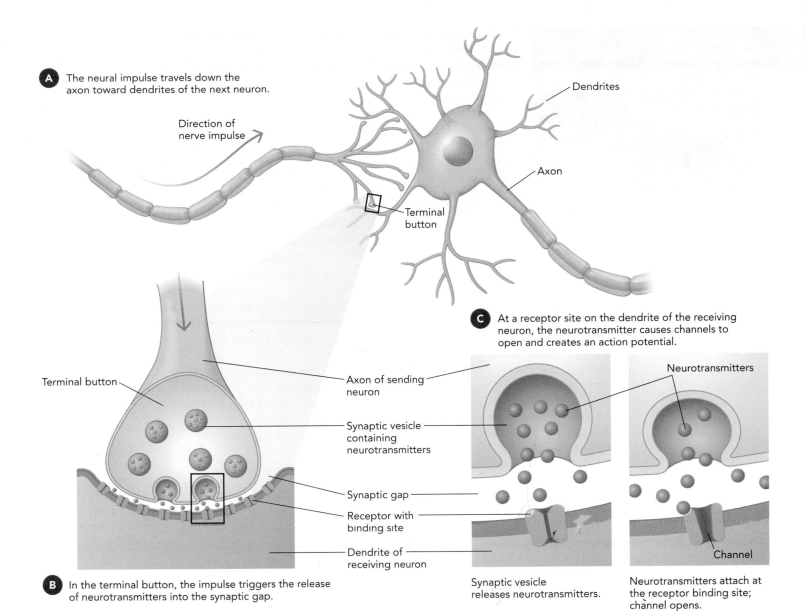

A The neural impulse travels down the axon toward dendrites of the next neuron.

Direction of nerve impulse

Dendrites

Axon

Terminal button

C At a receptor site on the dendrite of the receiving neuron, the neurotransmitter causes channels to open and creates an action potential.

Neurotransmitters

Terminal button

Axon of sending neuron

Synaptic vesicle containing neurotransmitters

Synaptic gap

Receptor with binding site

Dendrite of receiving neuron

B In the terminal button, the impulse triggers the release of neurotransmitters into the synaptic gap.

Synaptic vesicle releases neurotransmitters.

Channel

Neurotransmitters attach at the receptor binding site; channel opens.

FIGURE 2.5

How Synapses and Neurotransmitters Work (A) The axon of the *presynaptic* (sending) neuron meets dendrites of the *postsynaptic* (receiving) neuron. (B) This is an enlargement of one synapse, showing the synaptic gap between the two neurons, the terminal button, and the synaptic vesicles containing a neurotransmitter. (C) This is an enlargement of the receptor site. Note how the neurotransmitter opens the channel on the receptor site, triggering the neuron to fire.

receptor site, so that the neuron can receive the signals coming from the previous neuron. After delivering its message, some of the neurotransmitter is used up in the production of energy, and some of it is reabsorbed by the axon that released it to await the next neural impulse. This reabsorption is termed *reuptake*. Essentially, a message in the brain is delivered across the synapse by a neurotransmitter, which pours out of the terminal button just as the message approaches the synapse.

Neurochemical Messengers   There are many different neurotransmitters. Each plays a specific role and functions in a specific pathway. Whereas some neurotransmitters stimulate or excite neurons to fire, others can inhibit neurons from firing (Feldman, 2009). Some neurotransmitters are both excitatory *and* inhibitory.

The neurotransmitter-like venom of the black widow spider does its harm by disturbing neurotransmission.

As the neurotransmitter moves across the synaptic gap to the receiving neuron, its molecules might spread out, or they might be confined to a small space. The molecules might come in rapid sequence or might be spaced out. The receiving neuron integrates this information before reacting to it.

Neurotransmitters fit into the receptor sites like keys in keyholes. Other substances, such as drugs, can sometimes fit into those receptor sites as well, producing a variety of effects. Similarly, many animal venoms, such as that of the black widow spider, are neurotransmitter-like substances that act by disturbing neurotransmission.

Most neurons secrete only one type of neurotransmitter, but often many different neurons are simultaneously secreting different neurotransmitters into the synaptic gaps of a single neuron. At any given time, a neuron is receiving a mixture of messages from the neurotransmitters. At its receptor sites, the chemical molecules bind to the membrane and either excite the neuron, bringing it closer to the threshold at which it will fire, or inhibit the neuron from firing. Usually the binding of an excitatory neurotransmitter from one neuron will not be enough to trigger an action potential in the receiving neuron. Triggering an action potential often takes a number of neurons sending excitatory messages simultaneously or fewer neurons sending rapid-fire excitatory messages.

So far, researchers have identified more than 50 neurotransmitters, each with a unique chemical makeup. The rapidly growing list likely will grow to more than 100 (G. B. Johnson, 2008). In organisms ranging from snails to whales, neuroscientists have found the same neurotransmitter molecules that our own brains use. To get a better sense of what neurotransmitters do, let's consider seven that have major effects on behavior.

Acetylcholine

Acetylcholine (ACh) usually stimulates the firing of neurons and is involved in the action of muscles, learning, and memory (Brooks, 2006). ACh is found throughout the central and peripheral nervous systems. The venom of the black widow spider causes ACh to gush out of the synapses between the spinal cord and skeletal muscles, producing violent spasms.

Got wrinkles? Injections of Botox—a brand-name product made from botulin, a poison—act by destroying ACh, so that the recipient's facial muscles (which are activated by ACh) do not move. Wrinkles, as well as many genuine facial expressions, are prevented.

Individuals with Alzheimer disease, a degenerative brain disorder that involves a decline in memory, have an acetylcholine deficiency (Orhan & others, 2009). Some of the drugs that alleviate the symptoms of Alzheimer disease do so by compensating for the loss of the brain's supply of acetylcholine.

GABA

GABA (gamma aminobutyric acid) is found throughout the central nervous system. It is believed to be the neurotransmitter in as many as one-third of the brain's synapses. GABA is important in the brain because it keeps many neurons from firing (Burkhalter, 2008). In this way, it helps to control the precision of the signal being carried from one neuron to the next. Low levels of GABA are linked with anxiety. Antianxiety drugs increase the inhibiting effects of GABA.

Norepinephrine

Norepinephrine inhibits the firing of neurons in the central nervous system, but it excites the heart muscle, intestines, and urogenital tract. Stress stimulates the release of norepinephrine (Katzman, 2009). This neurotransmitter also helps to control alertness. Too little norepinephrine is associated with depression, and too much triggers agitated, manic states. For example, amphetamines and cocaine cause hyperactive, manic states of behavior by rapidly increasing brain levels of norepinephrine (Nelson & Gehlert, 2006).

Recall from the beginning of the chapter that one of the most important characteristics of the brain and nervous system is integration. In the case of neurotransmitters, they may work in teams of two or more. For example, norepinephrine works with acetylcholine to regulate states of sleep and wakefulness.

Dopamine   *Dopamine* helps to control voluntary movement and affects sleep, mood, attention, learning, and the ability to recognize rewards in the environment (Martin-Soelch, 2009). Stimulant drugs such as cocaine and amphetamines produce excitement, alertness, elevated mood, decreased fatigue, and sometimes increased motor activity mainly by activating dopamine receptors (Cox & others, 2009).

Low levels of dopamine are associated with Parkinson disease, in which physical movements deteriorate (Dagher & Robbins, 2009). High levels of dopamine are associated with schizophrenia, a severe psychological disorder that we will examine in Chapter 12.

Serotonin   *Serotonin* is involved in the regulation of sleep, mood, attention, and learning. In regulating states of sleep and wakefulness, it teams with acetylcholine and norepinephrine. Lowered levels of serotonin are associated with depression (Serrano-Blanco & others, 2009). The antidepressant drug Prozac works by slowing down the reuptake of serotonin into terminal buttons, thereby increasing brain levels of serotonin (Little, Zhang, & Cook, 2006). Figure 2.6 shows the brain pathways for serotonin. There are 15 known types of serotonin receptors in the brain (Hoyer, Hannon, & Martin, 2002), and each type of antidepressant drug has its effects on different receptors.

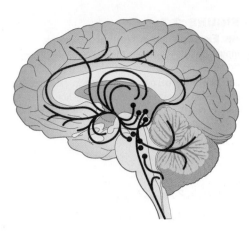

FIGURE 2.6
Serotonin Pathways Each of the neurotransmitters in the brain has specific pathways in which it functions. Shown here are the pathways for serotonin.

Endorphins   *Endorphins* are natural opiates that mainly stimulate the firing of neurons. Endorphins shield the body from pain and elevate feelings of pleasure. A long-distance runner, a woman giving birth, and a person in shock after a car wreck all have elevated levels of endorphins (Mahler & others, 2009).

As early as the fourth century B.C.E., the Greeks used wild poppies to induce euphoria. More than 2,000 years later, the magical formula behind opium's addictive action was finally discovered. In the early 1970s, scientists found that opium plugs into a sophisticated system of natural opiates that lie deep within the brain's pathways (Pert, 1999; Pert & Snyder, 1973). Morphine (the most important narcotic of opium) mimics the action of endorphins by stimulating receptors in the brain involved with pleasure and pain (Vetter & others, 2006).

Oxytocin   *Oxytocin* is a hormone and neurotransmitter that plays an important role in the experience of love and social bonding. A powerful surge of oxytocin is released in mothers who have just given birth, and oxytocin is related to the onset of lactation and breast feeding (P. D. Hill & others, 2009). Oxytocin, however, is not only involved in a mother's ability to provide nourishment for her baby (Carter & others, 2007). It is also a factor in the experience of parents who find themselves "in love at first sight" with their newborn (Young, 2009).

Oxytocin is released as part of the sexual orgasm and is thought to play a role in the human tendency to feel pleasure during orgasm and to form emotional bonds with romantic partners (Neumann, 2007). Provocative research has related oxytocin to the way that women respond to stress. According to Shelley Taylor (2001, 2007), women under stress do not experience the classic "fight or flight" response—rather, the influx of oxytocin suggests that women may seek bonds with others when under stress. Taylor refers to this response as "tend and befriend."

Drugs and Neurotransmitters   Most drugs that influence behavior do so mainly by interfering with the work of neurotransmitters (Wecker & others, 2010). Drugs can mimic or increase the effects of a neurotransmitter, or they can block those effects. An **agonist** is a drug that mimics or increases a neurotransmitter's effects. For example, the drug morphine mimics the actions of endorphins by stimulating receptors in the brain and spinal cord associated with pleasure and pain. An **antagonist** is a drug that blocks a neurotransmitter's effects. For example, drugs used to treat schizophrenia interfere with the activity of dopamine.

agonist
A drug that mimics or increases a neurotransmitter's effects.

antagonist
A drug that blocks a neurotransmitter's effects.

FIGURE 2.7

An Example of a Neural Network
Inputs (information from the environment and from sensory receptors, such as the details of a person's face) become embedded in extensive connections between neurons in the brain. This embedding process leads to outputs such as remembering the person's face.

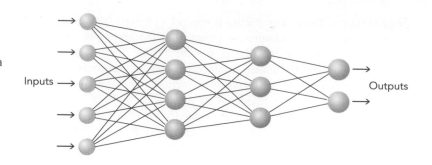

Inputs → Outputs

Neural Networks

Hello? There's a big hint here about how to study successfully. When your goal is to remember something, the best way is to build a neural network. That means creating connections between the material and other things—your experiences, your family, your everyday habits. As you read, try to create networks of associations around the course material. Neural networks: They work hard so you don't have to.

So far, we have focused mainly on how a single neuron functions and on how a nerve impulse travels from one neuron to another. Now let's look at how large numbers of neurons work together to integrate incoming information and coordinate outgoing information. Figure 2.7 shows a simplified drawing of a neural network, or pathway. This diagram gives you an idea of how the activity of one neuron is linked with that of many others.

Some neurons have short axons and communicate with other, nearby neurons. Other neurons have long axons and communicate with circuits of neurons some distance away. These neural networks are not static (Tang, Fang, & Miao, 2009). They can be altered through changes in the strength of synaptic connections. Any piece of information, such as a name, might be embedded in hundreds or even thousands of connections between neurons (Larson-Prior & others, 2009). In this way, human activities such as being attentive, memorizing, and thinking are distributed over a wide range of connected neurons. The strength of these connected neurons determines how well you remember the information (Goldman, 2009).

self-quiz

1. The part of the neuron that carries information away from the cell body toward other cells is the
   A. dendrite.
   B. synapse.
   C. nucleus.
   D. axon.

2. The law stating that once the electrical impulse reaches its threshold, it fires and moves down the axon without losing intensity is called
   A. neurotransmission.
   B. the action potential.

C. the neural impulse.
D. the all-or-nothing principle.

3. The chemical substances that carry information across the synaptic gap to the next neuron are called
   A. neurotransmitters.
   B. synapses.
   C. endorphins.
   D. hormones.

Apply It! 4. Many years ago some researchers found that when people were experiencing stressful, threatening

circumstances—in this case, getting a painful electrical shock—they did not "fight" and they did not "flee." Instead, they asked for a friend to sit by them during the shocks. Which of the following helps to explain this "misery loves company" effect?
A. The participants were all men.
B. The participants were all women.
C. The participants had faulty autonomic nervous systems.
D. The participants had serious psychological disorders.

3 Structures of the Brain and Their Functions

The extensive and intricate networks of neurons that we have just studied are not visible to the naked eye. Fortunately technology is available to help neuroscientists form pictures of the structure and organization of neurons and the larger structures they make up without harming the organism being studied. This section explores techniques that scientists use in brain research and discusses what these tools reveal about the brain's structures and functions. We pay special attention to the cerebral cortex, the region of the brain that is most relevant to the topics in this book.

How Researchers Study the Brain and Nervous System

Early knowledge of the human brain came mostly from studies of individuals who had suffered brain damage from injury or disease or who had brain surgery to relieve another condition. Modern discoveries have relied largely on technology that enables researchers to "look inside" the brain while it is at work. Let's examine some of these innovative techniques.

Brain Lesioning   *Brain lesioning* is an abnormal disruption in the tissue of the brain resulting from injury or disease. In a lab setting, neuroscientists produce lesions in laboratory animals to determine the effects on the animal's behavior (Pierucci & others, 2009). They create the lesions by surgically removing brain tissue, destroying tissue with a laser, or eliminating tissue by injecting it with a drug (Martin & Clark, 2007). Examining the person or animal that has the lesion gives the researchers a sense of the function of the part of the brain that has been damaged.

Do you know anyone who has experienced a stroke or brain-damaging head injury? These experiences create lesioned areas in the brain.

Electrical Recording   The electroencephalograph (EEG) records the brain's electrical activity. Electrodes placed on the scalp detect brain-wave activity, which is recorded on a chart known as an electroencephalogram (Figure 2.8). This device can assess brain damage, epilepsy, and other problems (Erdem & others, 2009). Researchers have also used the electroencephalograph in studying the neuroscience of happiness, as we see in the Intersection later in this chapter.

Not every recording of brain activity is made with surface electrodes that are attached to the scalp. In *single-unit recording,* which provides information about a single neuron's electrical activity, a thin probe is inserted in or near an individual neuron. The probe transmits the neuron's electrical activity to an amplifier so that researchers can "see" the activity.

Brain Imaging   For years, medical practitioners have used X rays to reveal damage inside or outside our bodies, both in the brain and in other locations. A single X ray of the brain is hard to interpret, however, because it shows a two-dimensional image of the three-dimensional interior of the brain. An improved technique called *computerized axial tomography* (CAT scan or CT scan) produces a three-dimensional image obtained from X rays of the head that are assembled into a composite image by a computer. The CT scan provides valuable information about the location and extent of damage involving stroke, language disorder, or loss of memory (Patel & others, 2009).

Positron-emission tomography (PET scan) is based on metabolic changes in the brain related to activity. PET measures the amount of glucose in various areas of the brain and then sends this information to a computer for analysis. Neurons use glucose for energy, so glucose levels vary with the levels of activity throughout the brain. Tracing the amounts of glucose generates a picture of activity levels throughout the brain.

An interesting application of the PET technique is the work of Stephen Kosslyn and colleagues (1996) on mental imagery, the brain's ability to create perceptual states in the absence of external stimuli. For instance, if you were to think of your favorite song right now, you could "hear" it in your mind's ear; or if you reflected on your mother's face, you could probably "see" it in your mind's eye. Research using PET scans has shown that often the same area of the brain—a location called Area 17—is activated when we think of seeing something as

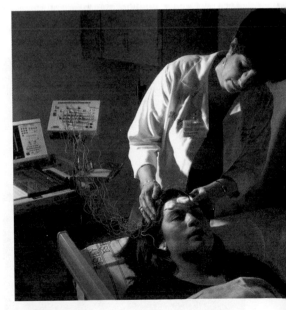

FIGURE 2.8

An EEG Recording The electroencephalograph (EEG) is widely used in sleep research. It has led to some major breakthroughs in understanding sleep by showing how the brain's electrical activity changes during sleep.

when we are actually seeing it. However, Area 17 is not always activated for all of us when we imagine a visual image. Kosslyn and his colleagues asked their participants to visualize a letter in the alphabet and then asked those individuals to answer some yes or no questions about the letter. For instance, a person might be thinking of the letter *C* and have to answer the question "Does it have curvy lines?" The answer would be yes. If the person was thinking of *F*, the answer would be no. The fascinating result of this work was that individuals who showed brain activation on the PET scan in Area 17 while engaged in the visualization task answered the questions faster than those who were not using Area 17.

Another technique, *magnetic resonance imaging (MRI)*, involves creating a magnetic field around a person's body and using radio waves to construct images of the person's tissues and biochemical activities. The magnetic field of the magnet used to create an MRI image is over 50,000 times more powerful than the earth's magnetic field (Parry & Matthews, 2002). MRI takes advantage of the fact that our brains contain a great deal of water (like the rest of the body, the brain is 70 percent water). Within each water molecule there are hydrogen atoms (remember, water is H_2O). These hydrogen atoms can be thought of as tiny magnets. When these magnetlike hydrogen atoms encounter a very strong magnetic field, they align themselves with it. Neurons have more water in them than do other brain tissues, and that contrast is what provides the nuanced brain images that MRI is able to produce (Parry & Matthews, 2002).

MRI generates very clear pictures of the brain's interior, does not require injecting the brain with a substance, and (unlike X rays) does not pose a problem of radiation overexposure (Nyberg, 2004). Getting an MRI scan involves lying still in a large metal barrellike tunnel. MRI scans provide an excellent picture of the architecture of the brain and allow us to see if and how experience affects brain structure. In one MRI study, Katrin Amunts and colleagues (1997) documented a link between the number of years a person has practiced musical skills (playing the piano, for example) and the size of the brain region that is responsible for controlling hand movements. Clearly, our behavior can influence the structure of our brains.

Although MRI scans can reveal considerable information about brain *structure*, they cannot portray brain *function*. Other techniques, however, can serve as a window on the brain in action (Schnitzer, 2009). The newest such method, *functional magnetic resonance imaging*, or *fMRI*, allows scientists literally to see what is happening in the brain while it is working (Figure 2.9). Like the PET scan, fMRI rests on the idea that mental activity is associated with changes in the brain. While PET is about the use of glucose as fuel for thinking, fMRI exploits changes in blood oxygen that occur in association with brain activity. When part of the brain is working, oxygenated blood rushes into the area. This oxygen, however, is more than is needed. In a sense, fMRI is based on the fact that thinking is like running sprints. When you run the 100-yard dash, blood rushes to the muscles in your legs, carrying oxygen. Right after you stop, you might feel a tightness in your leg, because the oxygen has not all been used. Similarly, if an area of the brain is hard at work—for example, solving a math problem—the increased activity leads to a surplus of oxygenated blood. This "extra" oxygen allows the brain activity to be imaged.

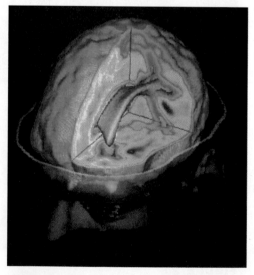

FIGURE 2.9
Functional Magnetic Resonance Imaging (fMRI) Through fMRI, scientists can literally see what areas of the brain are active during a task by monitoring oxygenated blood levels.

Getting an fMRI involves reclining in the same large metal barrel as does an MRI, but in the case of fMRI, the person is active—listening to audio signals sent by the researcher through headphones or watching visual images that are presented on a screen mounted overhead. Pictures of the brain are taken, both while the brain is at rest and while it is engaging in an activity such as listening to music, looking at a picture, or making a decision. By comparing the at-rest picture to the active picture, fMRI tells us what specific brain activity is associated with the mental experience being studied. fMRI technology is one of the most exciting methodological advances to hit psychology in a long time.

How the Brain Is Organized

As a human embryo develops inside its mother's womb, the nervous system begins forming as a long, hollow tube on the embryo's back (Nelson, 2009). At 3 weeks or so after conception, cells making up the tube differentiate into a mass of neurons, most of which then develop into three major regions of the brain: the hindbrain, which is adjacent to the top part of the spinal cord; the midbrain, which rises above the hindbrain; and the forebrain, which is the uppermost region of the brain (Figure 2.10).

hindbrain
Located at the skull's rear, the lowest portion of the brain, consisting of the medulla, cerebellum, and pons.

Hindbrain The **hindbrain,** located at the skull's rear, is the lowest portion of the brain. The three main parts of the hindbrain are the medulla, cerebellum, and pons. Figure 2.11 locates these brain structures.

The *medulla* begins where the spinal cord enters the skull. This structure controls many vital functions, such as breathing and heart rate. It also regulates our reflexes.

The *cerebellum* extends from the rear of the hindbrain, just above the medulla. It consists of two rounded structures thought to play important roles in motor coordination (Glickstein, Strata, & Voogd, 2009; I. S. Park & others, 2009). Leg and arm movements are coordinated by the cerebellum, for example. When we play golf, practice the piano, or learn a new dance, the cerebellum is hard at work. If another portion of the brain commands us to write the number 7, it is the cerebellum that integrates the muscular activities required to do so. Damage to the cerebellum impairs the performance of coordinated movements. When this damage occurs, people's movements become awkward and jerky. Extensive damage to the cerebellum even makes it impossible to stand up.

The *pons* is a bridge in the hindbrain that connects the cerebellum and the brain stem. It contains several clusters of fibers involved in sleep and arousal (Thankachan, Kaur, & Shiromani, 2009).

A region called the **brain stem** includes much of the hindbrain (it does not include the cerebellum) and the midbrain (which we discuss below) and gets its name because it looks like a stem. Embedded deep within the brain, the brain stem connects with the spinal cord at its lower end and then extends upward to encase the reticular formation in the midbrain. The most ancient part of the brain, the brain stem evolved more than 500 million

brain stem
The stemlike brain area that includes much of the hindbrain (excluding the cerebellum) and the midbrain; connects with the spinal cord at its lower end and then extends upward to encase the reticular formation in the midbrain.

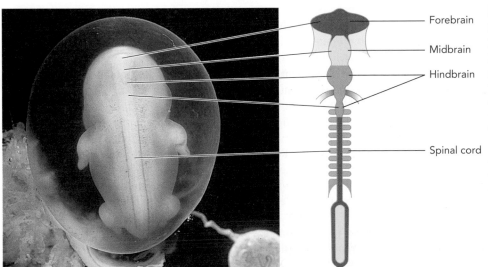

Forebrain

Midbrain

Hindbrain

Spinal cord

FIGURE 2.10
Embryological Development of the Nervous System The photograph shows the primitive tubular appearance of the nervous system at 6 weeks in the human embryo. The drawing shows the major brain regions and spinal cord as they appear early in the development of a human embryo.

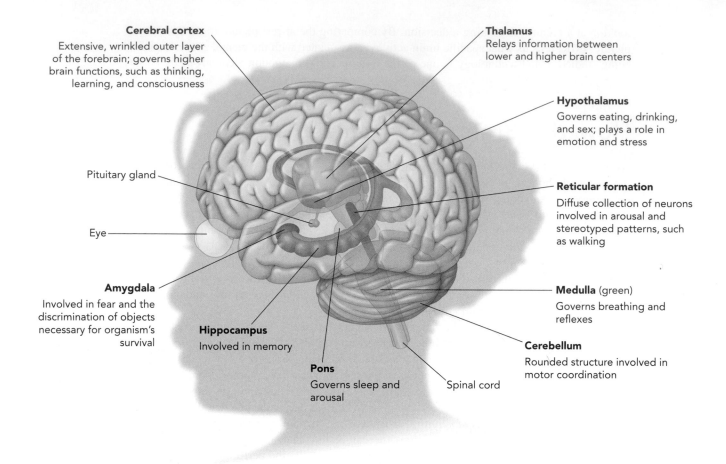

Cerebral cortex
Extensive, wrinkled outer layer of the forebrain; governs higher brain functions, such as thinking, learning, and consciousness

Pituitary gland

Eye

Amygdala
Involved in fear and the discrimination of objects necessary for organism's survival

Hippocampus
Involved in memory

Pons
Governs sleep and arousal

Spinal cord

Thalamus
Relays information between lower and higher brain centers

Hypothalamus
Governs eating, drinking, and sex; plays a role in emotion and stress

Reticular formation
Diffuse collection of neurons involved in arousal and stereotyped patterns, such as walking

Medulla (green)
Governs breathing and reflexes

Cerebellum
Rounded structure involved in motor coordination

FIGURE 2.11

Structure and Regions in the Human Brain To get a feel for where these structures are in your own brain, use the eye (pictured on the left of the figure) as a landmark. Note that structures such as the thalamus, hypothalamus, amygdala, pituitary gland, pons, and reticular formation reside deep within the brain.

years ago (Carter, 1998). Clumps of cells in the brain stem determine alertness and regulate basic survival functions such as breathing, heartbeat, and blood pressure.

Midbrain The **midbrain,** located between the hindbrain and forebrain, is an area in which many nerve-fiber systems ascend and descend to connect the higher and lower portions of the brain (Prescott & Humphries, 2007). In particular, the midbrain relays information between the brain and the eyes and ears. The ability to attend to an object visually, for example, is linked to one bundle of neurons in the midbrain. Parkinson disease, a deterioration of movement that produces rigidity and tremors, damages a section near the bottom of the midbrain.

Two systems in the midbrain are of special interest. One is the **reticular formation** (see Figure 2.11), a diffuse collection of neurons involved in stereotyped patterns of behavior such as walking, sleeping, and turning to attend to a sudden noise. The other system consists of small groups of neurons that use the neurotransmitters serotonin, dopamine, and norepinephrine. Although these groups contain relatively few cells, they send their axons to a remarkable variety of brain regions, an operation that perhaps explains their involvement in complex, integrative functions.

Forebrain You try to understand what all of these terms and parts of the brain mean. You talk with friends and plan a party for this weekend. You remember that it has been 6 months since you went to the dentist. You are confident you will do

midbrain
Located between the hindbrain and forebrain, an area in which many nerve-fiber systems ascend and descend to connect the higher and lower portions of the brain; in particular, the midbrain relays information between the brain and the eyes and ears.

reticular formation
A system in the midbrain comprising a diffuse collection of neurons involved in stereotyped patterns of behavior such as walking, sleeping, and turning to attend to a sudden noise.

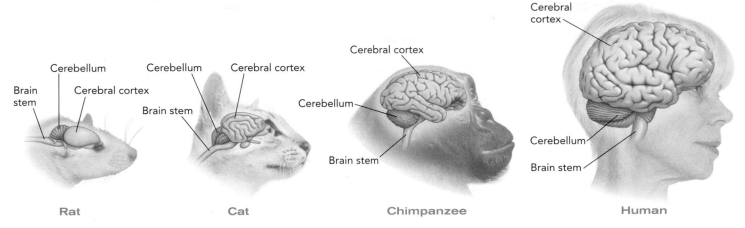

Rat Cat Chimpanzee Human

FIGURE 2.12

The Brain in Different Species Note how much larger the cerebral cortex becomes as we go from the brain of a rat to the brain of a human.

well on the next exam in this course. All of these experiences and millions more would not be possible without the **forebrain,** the brain's largest division and its most forward part.

Before we explore the structures and function of the forebrain, though, let's stop for a moment and examine how the brain evolved. The brains of the earliest vertebrates were smaller and simpler than those of later animals. Genetic changes during the evolutionary process were responsible for the development of more complex brains with more parts and more interconnections (Johnson & Losos, 2008). Figure 2.12 compares the brains of a rat, cat, chimpanzee, and human. In both the chimpanzee's brain and (especially) the human's brain, the hindbrain and midbrain structures are covered by a forebrain structure called the *cerebral cortex.* The human hindbrain and midbrain are similar to those of other animals, so it is the relative size of the forebrain that mainly differentiates the human brain from the brains of animals such as rats, cats, and chimps. The human forebrain's most important structures are the limbic system, thalamus, basal ganglia, hypothalamus, and cerebral cortex.

Limbic System   The **limbic system,** a loosely connected network of structures under the cerebral cortex, is important in both memory and emotion. Its two principal structures are the amygdala and the hippocampus (see Figure 2.11).

The **amygdala** is an almond-shaped structure located inside the brain toward the base. In fact there is an amygdala on each side of the brain. The amygdala is involved in the discrimination of objects that are necessary for the organism's survival, such as appropriate food, mates, and social rivals. Neurons in the amygdala often fire selectively at the sight of such stimuli, and lesions in the amygdala can cause animals to engage in inappropriate behavior such as attempting to eat, fight, or even mate with an object like a chair. Throughout this book you will encounter the amygdala whenever we turn to discussions of intense emotions such as fear and rage. The amygdala also is involved in emotional awareness and expression through its many connections with a variety of brain areas (Roy & others, 2009; van de Riet, Grezes, & de Gelder, 2009).

The **hippocampus** has a special role in the storage of memories (Reitz & others, 2009). Individuals who suffer extensive hippocampal damage cannot retain any new conscious memories after the damage. It is fairly certain, though, that memories are not stored "in" the limbic system. Instead, the limbic system seems to determine what parts of the information passing through the cortex should be "printed" into durable, lasting neural traces in the cortex.

forebrain
The brain's largest division and its most forward part.

limbic system
A loosely connected network of structures under the cerebral cortex, important in both memory and emotion. Its two principal structures are the amygdala and the hippocampus.

amygdala
An almond-shaped structure within the base of the temporal lobe that is involved in the discrimination of objects that are necessary for the organism's survival, such as appropriate food, mates, and social rivals.

hippocampus
The structure in the limbic system that has a special role in the storage of memories.

Thalamus

The **thalamus** is a forebrain structure that sits at the top of the brain stem in the central core of the brain (see Figure 2.11). It serves as a very important relay station, functioning much like a server in a computer network. That is, an important function of the thalamus is to sort information and send it to the appropriate places in the forebrain for further integration and interpretation (Jia, Goldstein, & Harrison, 2009). For example, one area of the thalamus receives information from the cerebellum and projects it to the motor area of the cerebral cortex. Indeed, most neural input to the cerebral cortex goes through the thalamus. Whereas one area of the thalamus works to orient information from the sense receptors (hearing, seeing, and so on), another region seems to be involved in sleep and wakefulness, having ties with the reticular formation.

Basal Ganglia

Above the thalamus and under the cerebral cortex lie large clusters, or *ganglia,* of neurons called basal ganglia. The **basal ganglia** work with the cerebellum and the cerebral cortex to control and coordinate voluntary movements. Basal ganglia enable people to engage in habitual behaviors such as riding a bicycle. Individuals with damage to basal ganglia suffer from either unwanted movement, such as constant writhing or jerking of limbs, or too little movement, as in the slow and deliberate movements of people with Parkinson disease (Beste & others, 2009).

Hypothalamus

The **hypothalamus,** a small forebrain structure just below the thalamus, monitors three pleasurable activities—eating, drinking, and sex—as well as emotion, stress, and reward (see Figure 2.11 for the location of the hypothalamus). As we will see later, the hypothalamus also helps direct the endocrine system. Perhaps the best way to describe the function of the hypothalamus is as a regulator of the body's internal state. It is sensitive to changes in the blood and neural input, and it responds by influencing the secretion of hormones and neural outputs. For example, if the temperature of circulating blood near the hypothalamus is increased by just 1 or 2 degrees, certain cells in the hypothalamus start increasing their rate of firing. As a result, a chain of events is set in motion. Increased circulation through the skin and sweat glands occurs immediately to release this heat from the body. The cooled blood circulating to the hypothalamus slows down the activity of some of the neurons there, stopping the process when the temperature is just right—37.1 degrees Celsius (98.6 degrees Fahrenheit). These temperature-sensitive neurons function like a finely tuned thermostat in maintaining the body in a balanced state.

The hypothalamus also is involved in emotional states, playing an important role as an integrative location for handling stress. Much of this integration is accomplished through the hypothalamus's action on the pituitary gland, an important endocrine gland located just below it (Susman & Dorn, 2009).

If certain areas of the hypothalamus are electrically stimulated, a feeling of pleasure results. In a classic experiment, James Olds and Peter Milner (1954) implanted an electrode in the hypothalamus of a rat's brain. When the rat ran to a corner of an enclosed area, a mild electric current was delivered to its hypothalamus. The researchers thought the electric current would cause the rat to avoid the corner. Much to their surprise, the rat kept returning to the corner. Olds and Milner believed they had discovered a pleasure center in the hypothalamus. Olds (1958) conducted further experiments and found that rats would press bars until they dropped over from exhaustion just to continue to receive a mild electric shock to their hypothalamus. One rat pressed a bar more than 2,000 times an hour for a period of 24 hours to receive the stimulation to its hypothalamus (Figure 2.13). Today researchers agree that the hypothalamus is involved in pleasurable feelings but that other areas of the brain, such as the limbic system and a bundle of fibers in the forebrain, are also important in the link between the brain and pleasure.

The Olds studies have implications for drug addiction. In these studies, the rat pressed the bar mainly because it produced a positive, rewarding effect (pleasure), not

Pleasure center receptors can become inactive after use of drugs such as Ecstasy and methamphetamine. The damaging effects of these drugs on the brain's reward system are what lead individuals into a hopeless pursuit of the same feelings they had during their "first high"—they will never feel that high again.

because it wanted to avoid or escape a negative effect (pain). Cocaine users talk about the drug's ability to heighten pleasure in food, in sex, and in a variety of activities, highlighting the reward aspects of the drug (Kalivas, 2007). We will discuss the effects of drugs on the reward centers of the brain in Chapter 5.

The Cerebral Cortex

cerebral cortex
Part of the forebrain, the outer layer of the brain, responsible for the most complex mental functions, such as thinking and planning.

neocortex
The outermost part of the cerebral cortex, making up 80 percent of the human brain's cortex.

The **cerebral cortex** is part of the forebrain and is the most recently developed part of the brain in the evolutionary scheme. The word *cortex* means "bark" (as in the bark of a tree) in Latin, and the cerebral cortex is, in fact the outer layer of the brain. It is in the cerebral cortex that the most complex mental functions, such as thinking and planning, take place.

The **neocortex** (or "new bark") is the outermost part of the cerebral cortex. In humans, this area makes up 80 percent of the cortex (compared with just 30 to 40 percent in most other mammals). The size of the neocortex in mammals is strongly related to the size of the social group in which the organisms live. Some scientists theorize that this part of the human brain, which is responsible for high-level thinking, evolved so that we could figure each other out (Dunbar & Schultz, 2007).

The neural tissue that makes up the cerebral cortex covers the lower portions of the brain like a sheet that is laid over the brain's surface. In humans the cerebral cortex is greatly convoluted with lots of grooves and bulges, and these considerably enlarge its surface area (compared with a brain with a smooth surface). The cerebral cortex is highly connected with other parts of the brain. Millions of axons connect the neurons of the cerebral cortex with those located elsewhere in the brain.

Lobes The wrinkled surface of the cerebral cortex is divided into two halves called *hemispheres* (Figure 2.14). Each hemisphere is subdivided into four regions or *lobes*—occipital, temporal, frontal, and parietal (Figure 2.15).

occipital lobes
Structures located at the back of the head that respond to visual stimuli.

The **occipital lobes,** located at the back of the head, respond to visual stimuli. Connections among various areas of the occipital lobes allow for the processing of information about such aspects of visual stimuli as their color, shape, and motion. A person can have perfectly functioning eyes, but the eyes only detect and transport information. That information must be interpreted in the occipital lobes for the viewer to "see it." A stroke or a wound in an occipital lobe can cause blindness or, at a minimum, can wipe out a portion of the person's visual field.

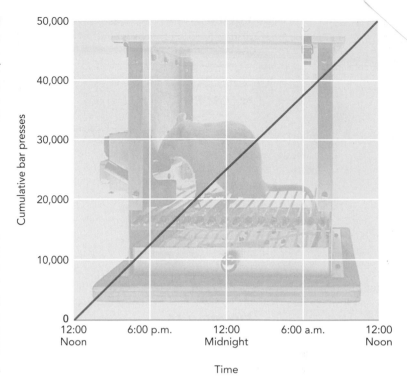

FIGURE 2.13
Results of the Experiment on the Role of the Hypothalamus in Pleasure The graphed results for one rat show that it pressed the bar more than 2,000 times an hour for a period of 24 hours to receive stimulation to its hypothalamus. One of the rats in Olds and Milner's experiments is shown pressing the bar.

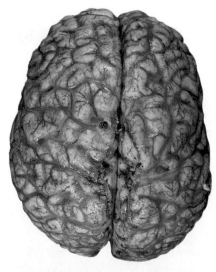

FIGURE 2.14
The Human Brain's Hemispheres
The two halves (hemispheres) of the human brain can be seen clearly in this photograph.

Lobes of the Brain

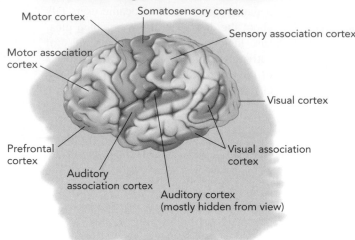

Functional Regions within the Lobes

FIGURE 2.15

The Cerebral Cortex's Lobes and Association Areas The cerebral cortex (*left*) is roughly divided into four lobes: occipital, temporal, frontal, and parietal. The cerebral cortex (*right*) also consists of the motor cortex and somatosensory cortex. Further, the cerebral cortex includes association areas, such as the visual association cortex, auditory association cortex, and sensory association cortex.

temporal lobes
Structures in the cerebral cortex that are located just above the ears and are involved in hearing, language processing, and memory.

The **temporal lobes,** the part of the cerebral cortex just above the ears, are involved in hearing, language processing, and memory. The temporal lobes have a number of connections to the limbic system. For this reason, people with damage to the temporal lobes cannot file experiences into long-term memory. Some researchers argue that the temporal lobes are the location of humans' ability to process information about faces. To read further about this topic, see Challenge Your Thinking.

The **frontal lobes,** the portion of the cerebral cortex behind the forehead, are involved in personality, intelligence, and the control of voluntary muscles. A fascinating case study illustrates how damage to the frontal lobes can significantly alter personality. Phineas T. Gage, a 25-year-old foreman who worked for the Rutland and Burlington Railroad, was the victim of a terrible accident in 1848. Phineas and several co-workers were using blasting powder to construct a roadbed. The crew drilled holes in the rock and gravel, poured in the blasting powder, and then tamped down the powder with an iron rod. While Phineas was still tamping it down, the powder exploded, driving the iron rod up through the left side of his face and out through the top of his head. Although the wound in his skull healed in a matter of weeks, Phineas had become a different person. Previously he had been a mild-mannered, hardworking, emotionally calm individual, well liked by all who knew him. Afterward he was obstinate, moody, irresponsible, selfish, and incapable of participating in any planned activities. Damage to the frontal lobe area of his brain had dramatically altered Phineas's personality.

frontal lobes
The portion of the cerebral cortex behind the forehead, involved in personality, intelligence, and the control of voluntary muscles.

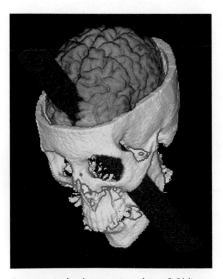

A computerized reconstruction of Phineas T. Gage's accident, based on measurements taken of his skull.

Without intact frontal lobes, humans are emotionally shallow, distractible, listless, and so insensitive to social contexts that they may belch with abandon at dinner parties. Individuals with frontal lobe damage become so distracted by irrelevant stimuli that they often cannot carry out some basic directions. In one such case, an individual, when asked to light a candle, struck a match correctly, but instead of lighting the candle, he put it in his mouth and acted as if he were smoking it (Luria, 1973).

The frontal lobes of humans are especially large when compared with those of other animals. For example, the frontal cortex of rats barely exists;

challenge your thinking

Are Human Brains Uniquely Wired to Recognize Faces?

It seems hard to argue with the idea that faces have a unique importance to humans and a special capacity to attract our attention. Even infants are drawn to human faces when given a choice of things to look at. Moreover, there is a disorder (*prosopagnosia*) that involves the inability to recognize faces but not other objects, and this condition would seem to suggest a specific region of brain damage. If faces are so special, might there be a particular place in the brain for processing faces?

Research by Nancy Kanwisher and colleagues has provided evidence of just such a specialized area (Kanwisher, Livingstone, & Tsao, 2007; Kanwisher & Yovel, 2009; Yovel & Kanwisher, 2008). Situated in the fusiform gyrus in the right temporal lobe, this location is called the *fusiform face area* (FFA). The FFA is a dime-size spot behind your right ear. Using fMRI, researchers have shown that the FFA is especially active when a person is viewing a face—a human face, a cat's face, or a cartoon face—but not cars, butterflies, or other objects (Tong & others, 2000).

The theory that humans have a brain area specialized to process the most important visual information of life—other people's faces—is appealing. It makes sense that organisms like us who live in groups and need others to survive would be especially tuned to social stimuli. However, other researchers have challenged this idea. They argue that, as human beings, we are all experts in perceiving humans. So, what if the FFA is in fact more involved with processing any expert knowledge, not just faces?

To explore this alternative theory, Isabel Gauthier and her colleagues have conducted a number of studies (Bukach & others, 2006; Gauthier, Behrmann, & Tarr, 2004; Gauthier & Bukach, 2007; Wong, Palmeri, & Gauthier, 2009; Wong & others, 2009).

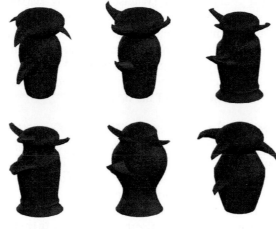

FIGURE 2.16

Some Greebles Used in Gauthier's Study
In individuals who had reached a level of expertise in recognizing greebles, the fusiform face area became active during greeble identification.

In one investigation, Gauthier and her colleagues (2000) examined individuals who were experts on cars or birds. The FFAs of these experts "lit up" when the individuals were presented with the objects about which they had expertise. In a provocative study, participants were trained to recognize imaginary, faceless creatures called *greebles,* small plantlike objects made of pink clay (Tarr & Gauthier, 2000) (see Figure 2.16). Participants quickly learned to classify the greebles according to sex and family. During fMRI, the FFA was active during these judgments, suggesting that the FFA is concerned with recognition more generally rather than just with facial recognition. These results have been countered, however, by studies showing that at the very least, the FFA is far more activated during facial recognition than during recognition of other objects (Tong & others, 2000).

The status of the FFA as a specific brain area for face recognition is at the center of a lively debate in neuroscience (Dricot & others, 2008; Large & others, 2008; McKone, Kanwisher, & Duchaine, 2007). This area of research demonstrates that as scientists' experimental tools develop, so does their understanding of the brain. Moreover, the new questions they are asking can profoundly impact the advancement of scientific knowledge.

What Do You Think?

- What other aspects of our social worlds might the brain to be specially designed to perceive?

- How does the debate over the FFA illustrate the role of controversy in science more generally?

in cats, it occupies a paltry 3.5 percent of the cerebral cortex; in chimpanzees, 17 percent; and in humans, approximately 30 percent.

An important part of the frontal lobes is the *prefrontal cortex,* which is at the front of the motor cortex (see Figure 2.15). The prefrontal cortex is involved in higher cognitive functions such as planning, reasoning, and self-control (Sternberg, 2009). Some neuroscientists refer to the prefrontal cortex as an executive control system

DOG TRAINING (ADVANCED)

BOWL   HUMAN BRAIN

"The prefrontal cortex is involved in higher mental functioning, like using a can opener and remembering to feed you."

www.CartoonStock.com

because of its role in monitoring and organizing thinking (Kuhn, 2009).

The **parietal lobes,** located at the top and toward the rear of the head, are involved in registering spatial location, attention, and motor control (Jax & Coslett, 2009; Stanley & Miall, 2009). Thus, the parietal lobes are at work when you are judging how far you have to throw a ball to get it to someone else, when you shift your attention from one activity to another (turn your attention away from the TV to a noise outside), and when you turn the pages of this book. The brilliant physicist Albert Einstein said that his reasoning often was best when he imagined objects in space. It turns out that his parietal lobes were 15 percent larger than average (Witelson, Kigar, & Harvey, 1999).

A word of caution is in order about going too far in localizing function within a particular lobe. Although this discussion has attributed specific functions to a particular lobe (such as vision in the occipital lobe), there are considerable integration and connection between any two or more lobes and between lobes and other parts of the brain.

Somatosensory Cortex and Motor Cortex

Two other important regions of the cerebral cortex are the somatosensory cortex and the motor cortex (see Figure 2.15). The **somatosensory cortex** processes information about body sensations. It is located at the front of the parietal lobes. The **motor cortex,** just behind the frontal lobes, processes information about voluntary movement.

The map in Figure 2.17 shows which parts of the somatosensory and motor cortexes are associated with different parts of the body. It is based on research done by Wilder Penfield (1947), a neurosurgeon at the Montreal Neurological Institute. He worked with patients who had severe epilepsy, and he often performed surgery to remove portions of the epileptic patients' brains. However, he was concerned that removing a portion of the brain might impair some of the individuals' functions. Penfield's solution was to map the cortex during surgery by stimulating different cortical areas and observing the responses of the patients, who were given a local anesthetic so they would remain awake during the operation. He found that when he stimulated certain somatosensory and motor areas of the brain, patients reported feeling different sensations, or different parts of a patient's body moved. For both somatosensory and motor areas, there is a point-to-point relation between a part of the body and a location on the cerebral cortex.

In Figure 2.17, the face and hands are given proportionately more space than other body parts because the face and hands are capable of finer perceptions and movements than are other body areas and therefore need more cerebral cortex representation.

The point-to-point mapping of somatosensory fields onto the cortex's surface is the basis of our orderly and accurate perception of the world (Beauchamp, Laconte, & Yasar, 2009). When something touches your lip, for example, your brain knows what body part has been touched because the nerve pathways from your lip are the only pathways that project to the lip region of the somatosensory cortex.

The Association Cortex

Embedded in the brain's lobes, the association cortex makes up 75 percent of the cerebral cortex (see Figure 2.15). Processing information about sensory input and motor output is not all that is taking place in the cerebral cortex. The **association cortex** (sometimes called *association areas*) is the region of the cerebral cortex that integrates this information. The highest intellectual functions, such as thinking and problem solving, occur in the association cortex.

Interestingly, damage to a specific part of the association cortex often does not result in a specific loss of function. With the exception of language areas (which are localized),

parietal lobes
Structures at the top and toward the rear of the head that are involved in registering spatial location, attention, and motor control.

somatosensory cortex
A region in the cerebral cortex that processes information about body sensations, located at the front of the parietal lobes.

motor cortex
A region in the cerebral cortex that processes information about voluntary movement, located just behind the frontal lobes.

association cortex
Sometimes called association areas, the region of the cerebral cortex that is the site of the highest intellectual functions, such as thinking and problem solving.

In 2008 Senator Edward ("Ted") Kennedy had a malignant brain tumor removed. Like other brain surgery patients, he was wide awake during the procedure. The brain doesn't feel pain, so this surgery can be done with just a local anesthetic. Keeping the patient awake allows the neurosurgeon to ask questions about what the patient is seeing, hearing, and feeling and to be sure that the parts of the brain that are being affected are not essential for consciousness, speech, and other important functions.

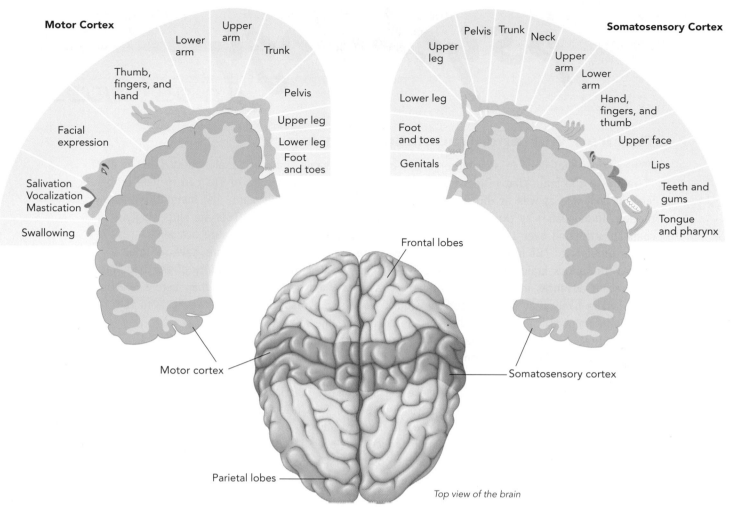

Motor Cortex

Upper arm

Lower arm

Trunk

Thumb, fingers, and hand

Pelvis

Facial expression

Upper leg

Lower leg

Foot and toes

Salivation Vocalization Mastication

Swallowing

Somatosensory Cortex

Pelvis Trunk Neck

Upper leg

Upper arm

Lower leg

Lower arm

Foot and toes

Hand, fingers, and thumb

Genitals

Upper face

Lips

Teeth and gums

Tongue and pharynx

Frontal lobes

Motor cortex

Somatosensory cortex

Parietal lobes

Top view of the brain

FIGURE 2.17

Disproportionate Representation of Body Parts in the Motor and Somatosensory Areas of the Cortex The amount of cortex allotted to a body part is not proportionate to the body part's size. Instead, the brain has more space for body parts that require precision and control. Thus, the thumb, fingers, and hand require more brain tissue than does the arm.

loss of function seems to depend more on the extent of damage to the association cortex than on the specific location of the damage. By observing brain-damaged individuals and using a mapping technique, scientists have found that the association cortex is involved in linguistic and perceptual functioning.

The largest portion of the association cortex is located in the frontal lobes, directly under the forehead. Damage to this area does not lead to somatosensory or motor loss but rather to problems in planning and problem solving. Personality also may be linked to the frontal lobes. Recall the misfortune of Phineas Gage, whose personality radically changed after he experienced frontal lobe damage.

The Cerebral Hemispheres and Split-Brain Research

Recall that the cerebral cortex is divided into two halves—left and right (see Figure 2.14). Do these hemispheres have different functions? In 1861, French surgeon Paul Broca saw a patient who had received an injury to the left side of his brain about

psychology in our world

The Iraq War and Traumatic Brain Injury

The brain is not only an amazing organ, it is also vulnerable. Traumatic brain injury (TBI) is an injury to the brain that results from an abrupt trauma. The symptoms of TBI can include problems in language as well as difficulty in controlling emotions, making plans, and maintaining attention. Individuals may experience headaches, fatigue, and memory loss. TBIs are surprisingly common, affecting over 1 million people as a result of experiences such as auto accidents.

The problem of TBI has become increasingly acute as many Iraq War veterans have returned home with serious brain injuries. In fact, TBI has been called the signature injury of the Iraq War. With recent advances in body armor, soldiers' vital organs are better protected than before, and it is now more likely that they will survive a blast from, say, a roadside bomb. However, even the best body armor still leaves a soldier's head and brain vulnerable.

Rehabilitation psychologists help to diagnose and treat brain injuries. These specialists work with Veterans Administration personnel to test returning vets for brain injury and to treat them to prevent further damage to the brain. Rehabilitation therapists help injured vets to regain lost functioning and to make the best of the functions they still possess. These services are vital for aiding troops to resume their lives after combat. The Defense and Veterans Brain Injury Center was set up in 1992 to address brain injuries in combat veterans. However, funding for rehabilitation services has been scarce, and improving the lives of men and women who have sacrificed for the country and suffered combat-related head injuries in the process remains a challenge for U.S. society and policymakers.

30 years earlier. The patient became known as Tan because *tan* was the only word he could speak. Tan suffered from *aphasia,* a language disorder associated with brain damage. Tan died several days after Broca evaluated him, and an autopsy revealed that the injury was to a precise area of the left hemisphere. Today we refer to this area of the brain as *Broca's area,* and we know that it plays an important role in the production of speech. Another area of the brain's left hemisphere that has an important role in language is *Wernicke's area,* which, if damaged, causes problems in comprehending language. Figure 2.18 shows the locations of Broca's area and Wernicke's area.

Today there continues to be considerable interest in the degree to which the brain's left hemisphere or right hemisphere is involved in various aspects of thinking, feeling, and behavior. For many years, scientists speculated that the **corpus callosum,** the large bundle of axons that connects the brain's two hemispheres, has something to do with relaying information between the two sides

corpus callosum
The large bundle of axons that connects the brain's two hemispheres, responsible for relaying information between the two sides.

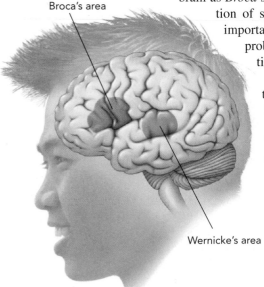
Broca's area

Wernicke's area

FIGURE 2.18
Broca's Area and Wernicke's Area Broca's area is located in the brain's left hemisphere, and it is involved in the control of speech. Individuals with damage to Broca's area have problems saying words correctly. Also shown is Wernicke's area, the portion of the left hemisphere that is involved in understanding language. Individuals with damage to this area cannot comprehend words; they hear the words but do not know what they mean.

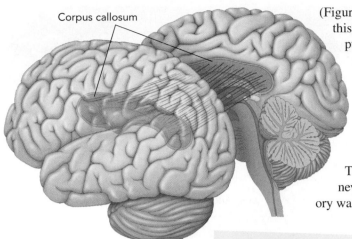

Corpus callosum

FIGURE 2.19

The Corpus Callosum The corpus callosum is a thick band of about 80 million axons that connects the brain cells in one hemisphere to those in the other. In healthy brains, the two sides engage in a continuous flow of information via this neural bridge.

Plane of cut

(Figure 2.19). Roger Sperry (1974) confirmed this in an experiment in which he cut the corpus callosum in cats. He also severed certain nerves leading from the eyes to the brain. After the operation, Sperry trained the cats to solve a series of visual problems with one eye blindfolded. After a cat learned the task—say, with only its left eye uncovered—its other eye was blindfolded, and the animal was tested again. The "split-brain" cat behaved as if it had never learned the task. It seems that the memory was stored only in the left hemisphere, which could no longer directly communicate with the right hemisphere.

Further evidence of the corpus callosum's function has come from studies of patients with severe, even life-threatening, forms of epilepsy. Epilepsy is caused by electrical "brainstorms" that flash uncontrollably across the corpus callosum. In one famous case, neurosurgeons severed the corpus callosum of an epileptic patient now known as W. J. in a final attempt to reduce his unbearable seizures. Sperry (1968) examined W. J. and found that the corpus callosum functions the same in humans as in animals—cutting the corpus callosum seemed to leave the patient with "two separate minds" that learned and operated independently.

As it turns out, the right hemisphere receives information only from the left side of the body, and the left hemisphere receives information only from the right side of the body. When you hold an object in your left hand, for example, only the right hemisphere of your brain detects the object. When you hold an object in your right hand, only the left hemisphere of the brain detects it (Figure 2.20). In individuals with a normally functioning corpus callosum, both hemispheres receive this information eventually, as it travels between the hemispheres through the corpus callosum. In fact, although we might have two minds, we usually use them in tandem.

You can appreciate how well the corpus callosum rapidly integrates our experience by considering how hard it is to do two things at once (Stirling, 2002). Recall, for example, when you were a kid and you tried to tap your head and rub your stomach at the same time. Even with two separate hands controlled by two separate hemispheres, such dual activity is hard.

In people with intact brains, specialization of function occurs in some areas. Researchers have uncovered evidence for hemispheric differences in function by sending different information to each ear. Remember, the left hemisphere gets its information (first) from the right ear, and the right hemisphere hears what is going on (first) in the left ear. Such research has shown that the brain tends to divide its functioning into one hemisphere or the other as follows:

■ *Left hemisphere:* The most extensive research on the brain's two hemispheres has focused on language. Speech and grammar are localized to the left hemisphere (Hornickel, Skoe, & Kraus, 2009). Although it is a common misconception that *all* language processing occurs in the brain's left hemisphere, much language processing and production does come from this hemisphere (Harpaz, Levkovitz, & Lavidor, 2009). For example, in reading, the left hemisphere comprehends syntax and grammar, but the right hemisphere does not. The left hemisphere

The right side of the brain is really good at recognizing faces. Researchers have asked people to watch images on a computer screen and to press a button with either their right or left hand if they recognize a face. Even right-handed people are faster to recognize faces with their left hand, because the information goes directly from the part of the brain that recognizes faces (the right hemisphere) to the left hand. In contrast, to press the button with the right hand, the information has to travel from the right hemisphere, across the corpus callosum, to the left hemisphere, and then to the right hand.

FIGURE 2.20

Information Pathways from the Eyes to the Brain Each of our eyes receives sensory input from both our left and our right field of vision. Information from the left half of our visual field goes to the brain's right hemisphere (which is responsible for simple comprehension), and information from the right half of our visual field goes to the brain's left hemisphere (the brain's main language center, which controls speech and writing). The input received in either hemisphere passes quickly to the other hemisphere across the corpus callosum. When the corpus callosum is severed, however, this transmission of information cannot occur.

Fixation point

Left visual field

Right visual field

Optic nerve

Speech

R

L

Writing

Main language center

Simple comprehension

Visual half field R

Visual half field L

Corpus callosum severed

is also keenly involved in singing the words of a song.

- *Right hemisphere:* The right hemisphere dominates in processing nonverbal information such as spatial perception, visual recognition, and emotion (Kensinger & Choi, 2009). For example, as we saw in Challenge Your Thinking, the right hemisphere is mainly at work when we process information about people's faces (Kanwisher, 2006).

- The right hemisphere also may be more involved than the left hemisphere in processing information about emotions, both when we express emotions ourselves and when we recognize others' emotions (Carmona, Holland, & Harrison, 2009). People are more likely to remember emotion words if they hear them in the left ear. Much of our sense of humor resides in the right hemisphere (Bartolo & others, 2006; Coulson & Wu, 2005). In fact, if you want to be sure that someone laughs at your joke, tell it to the person's left ear.

One way to think about the right hemisphere is to consider what people do with their left hand. One study showed that girls and women (but not boys or men) automatically cradle a baby (or baby doll) in their left arm, regardless of whether they are right-handed or left-handed (Bourne and Todd, 2004). The researchers suggested that this tendency has something to do with the right hemisphere and emotional intimacy. Why would it make sense for women to cradle babies on the left, and why don't men show the effect?

- The right hemisphere is also good at picking up the meaning of a story or the intonation of a voice. Further, the right hemisphere excels at picking up the melody of a song. It is important to keep in mind that it is more difficult to learn what the right hemisphere can do because it cannot just tell us. We have to come up with a way for the right hemisphere to communicate what it knows. The right hemisphere certainly has some verbal abilities, for instance, because people with split brains can draw (with their left hand) pictures of words that have been spoken to them (in the left ear).

Because differences in the functioning of the brain's two hemispheres are known to exist, people commonly use the phrases *left-brained* (meaning logical and rational) and *right-brained* (meaning creative or artistic) as a way of categorizing themselves and others. Such generalizations

THIS IS THE RIGHT SIDE OF THE BRAIN CALLING THE LEFT SIDE OF THE BRAIN. COME IN, LEFT SIDE...

Yo!

www.CartoonStock.com

Are some brains happier than others? Put your hand on your forehead. The answer to the happy brain question may be lying in the palm of your hand. Indeed, research using a variety of techniques to study the neuroscience of emotion suggests that there might be a pattern of brain activity associated with feeling good, and that this activity takes place in the front of your brain, in the prefrontal lobes (van Reekum & others, 2007).

Emotion and Neuroscience: Is Your Brain Happy?

Paul Ekman, Richard Davidson, and Wallace Friesen (1990) measured EEG activity during emotional experiences provoked by film clips. Individuals in this study watched amusing film clips (such as a puppy playing with flowers and monkeys taking a bath) as well as clips likely to provoke fear or disgust (a leg amputation and a third-degree burn victim). How does the brain respond to such stimuli? The researchers found that while watching the amusing clips, people tended to exhibit more left than right prefrontal activity, as shown in EEGs. In contrast, when the participants viewed the fear-provoking films, the right prefrontal area was generally more active than the left.

Do these differences generalize to overall differences in feelings of happiness? They just might. Heather Urry and her colleagues (2004) found that individuals who have relatively more left than right prefrontal activity (what is called *prefrontal asymmetry*) tend to rate themselves higher on a number of measures of well-being, including self-acceptance, positive relations with others, purpose in life, and life satisfaction. The fact that certain neurons are active during an activity, however, does not prove that these brain processes cause the experience under study. Can experimental evidence clarify the picture?

John Allen and his colleagues (Allen, Harmon-Jones, & Cavender, 2001) have provided some experimental support for the role of prefrontal asymmetry in emotional responses. The researchers used biofeedback to train college women to increase right or left frontal activation, and they measured the participants' activation patterns using EEG. Through this training, the participants were generally able to accomplish the goal of changing either their right hemisphere or their left hemisphere activation, without any mention of emotional processes. After the training, researchers found that women who were trained to activate the left more than the right side of the prefrontal brain area were less likely to frown while watching a negative clip, whereas those who were trained to activate the right side more than the left responded with less smiling to the happy clips.

Research on the effects of mindfulness meditation on frontal activation also shows that changing the way we think can influence brain processes. *Mindfulness meditation* involves maintaining a floating state of consciousness and focusing on whatever comes to mind—a sensation, a thought, an image—at a particular moment. Richard Davidson and colleagues (2003; Davidson & Lutz, 2008; Lutz & others, 2008) have shown that mindfulness meditation training can enhance left frontal activation.

Bear in mind that brain structure and function depend on experience. Thus, savoring the enjoyable moments of life—looking at the flowers in your garden, getting a phone call from a friend, hearing your favorite song—may be an opportunity to train your brain to be happy.

You can train your brain to experience happiness by habitually taking a moment to appreciate life.

have little scientific basis, and that is a good thing. We have both hemispheres because we use them both.

Sperry did discover that the left hemisphere is superior in the kind of logic used to prove geometric theorems. In everyday life, however, our logic problems involve integrating information and drawing conclusions. In these instances, the right hemisphere is crucial. In most complex activities in which people engage, interplay occurs between the brain's two hemispheres (Ibrahim & Eviatar, 2009; Pinel & Dehaene, 2009). To grasp how the hemispheres might be involved in your happiness, see the Intersection.

Integration of Function in the Brain

How do all of the regions of the brain cooperate to produce the wondrous complexity of thought and behavior that characterizes humans? Neuroscience still does not have answers to questions such as how the brain solves a murder mystery or composes a poem or an essay. Even so, we can get a sense of integrative brain function by using a real-world scenario, such as the act of escaping from a burning building.

Imagine that you are sitting at your computer, writing an e-mail, when a fire breaks out behind you. The sound of crackling flames is relayed from your ear through the thalamus, to the auditory cortex, and on to the auditory association cortex. At each stage, the stimulus is processed to extract information, and at some stage, probably at the association cortex level, the sounds are finally matched with something like a neural memory representing sounds of fires you have heard previously. The association "fire" sets new machinery in motion. Your attention (guided in part by the reticular formation) shifts to the auditory signal being held in your association cortex and on to your auditory association cortex, and simultaneously (again guided by reticular systems) your head turns toward the noise. Now your visual association cortex reports in: "Objects matching flames are present." In other regions of the association cortex, the visual and auditory reports are synthesized ("We have things that look and sound like fire"), and neural associations representing potential actions ("flee") are activated. However, firing the neurons that code the plan to flee will not get you out of the chair. The basal ganglia must become engaged, and from there the commands will arise to set the brain stem, motor cortex, and cerebellum to the task of transporting you out of the room. All of this happens in mere seconds.

Which part of your brain did you use to escape? Virtually all systems had a role. By the way, you would probably remember this event because your limbic circuitry would likely have started memory formation when the association "fire" was triggered. The next time the sounds of crackling flames reach your auditory association cortex, the associations triggered would include this most recent escape. In sum, considerable integration of function takes place in the brain (Hamlin & others, 2009; Kwon & others, 2009). All of the parts of the nervous system work together as a team to keep you safe and sound.

self-quiz

1. Four ways that researchers study the brain and the nervous system are electrical recording, imaging, staining, and
   A. biopsy.
   B. lesioning.
   C. lobotomy.
   D. neurosurgery.

2. The brain's three major regions are the hindbrain, the midbrain, and the
   A. brain stem.
   B. reticular formation.

   C. forebrain.
   D. temporal lobes.

3. The most recently developed level of the human brain is the
   A. midbrain.
   B. forebrain.
   C. reticular formation.
   D. brain stem.

Apply It! 4. Because Miles suffers from extreme seizures, a surgeon severs his

corpus callosum. Using a special technique, researchers present a picture of a flower to Miles's right brain and a picture of a bumblebee to Miles's left brain. When Miles is asked to say out loud what he sees, he is likely to answer
   A. "A flower."
   B. "I don't know."
   C. "A bee."
   D. There is no way to know.

4 The Endocrine System

endocrine system
The body system consisting of a set of glands that regulate the activities of certain organs by releasing their chemical products into the bloodstream.

The nervous system works closely with another bodily system, the endocrine system. The **endocrine system** consists of a set of glands that regulate the activities of certain organs by releasing their chemical products into the bloodstream. **Glands** are organs or tissues in the body that create chemicals that control many of our bodily functions. Neuroscientists have discovered that the nervous system and endocrine system are intricately interconnected. They know that the brain's hypothalamus connects the nervous system and the endocrine system and that the two systems work together to control the body's activities. Yet the endocrine system differs significantly from the nervous system in a variety of ways. For one thing, the parts of the endocrine system are not all connected in the way that the parts of the nervous system are. For another thing, the endocrine system works more slowly than the nervous system, because the chemicals released by the endocrine glands are transported

glands
Organs or tissues in the body that create chemicals that control many of our bodily functions.

through the circulatory system, in the blood. Our hearts do a mind-boggling job of pumping blood throughout the body, but blood moves far more slowly than the neural impulses do.

The chemical messengers produced by the endocrine glands are called **hormones.** The bloodstream carries hormones to all parts of the body, and the membrane of every cell has receptors for one or more hormones.

The endocrine glands consist of the pituitary gland, the thyroid and parathyroid glands, the adrenal glands, the pancreas, the ovaries in women, and the testes in men (Figure 2.21). In much the same way that the brain's control of muscular activity is constantly monitored and altered to suit the information received by the nervous system, the action of the endocrine glands is continuously monitored and changed by nervous, hormonal, and chemical signals (Shier, Butler, & Lewis, 2010). Recall from earlier in the chapter that the autonomic nervous system regulates processes such as respiration, heart rate, and digestion. The autonomic nervous system acts on the endocrine glands to produce a number of important physiological reactions to strong emotions, such as rage and fear.

The **pituitary gland,** a pea-sized gland just beneath the hypothalamus, controls growth and regulates other glands (Figure 2.22). The anterior (front) part of the pituitary is known as the master gland, because almost all of its hormones direct the activity of target glands elsewhere in the body. In turn, the anterior pituitary gland is controlled by the hypothalamus.

The **adrenal glands,** located at the top of each kidney, regulate moods, energy level, and the ability to cope with stress (Wirtz & others, 2009). Each adrenal gland secretes epinephrine (also called *adrenaline*) and norepinephrine (also called *noradrenaline*). Unlike most hormones, epinephrine and norepinephrine act quickly. Epinephrine helps a person get ready for an emergency by acting on smooth muscles, the heart, stomach, intestines, and sweat glands. In addition, epinephrine stimulates the reticular formation, which in turn arouses the sympathetic nervous system, and this system subsequently excites the adrenal glands to produce more epinephrine. Norepinephrine also alerts the individual to emergency situations by interacting with the pituitary and the liver. You may remember that norepinephrine functions as a neurotransmitter when it is released by neurons. In the adrenal glands, norepinephrine is released as a hormone. In both instances, norepinephrine conveys information—in the first case, to neurons; in the second case, to glands (Mader, 2008).

The **pancreas,** located under the stomach, is a dual-purpose gland that performs both digestive and endocrine functions. The part of the pancreas that serves endocrine functions produces a number of hormones, including insulin. This part of the pancreas, the Islets of Langerhans, turns out hormones like a little factory. Insulin is an essential hormone that controls glucose (blood sugar) levels in the body and is related to metabolism, body weight, and obesity.

The **ovaries,** located in the pelvis on either sides of the uterus in women, and **testes,** located in the scrotum in men, are the sex-related endocrine glands

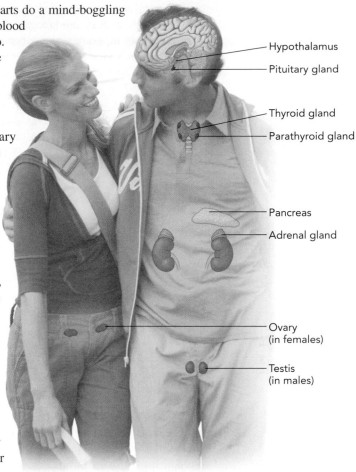

Hypothalamus
Pituitary gland
Thyroid gland
Parathyroid gland
Pancreas
Adrenal gland
Ovary (in females)
Testis (in males)

FIGURE 2.21

The Major Endocrine Glands The pituitary gland releases hormones that regulate the hormone secretions of the other glands. The pituitary gland is regulated by the hypothalamus.

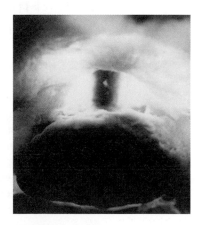

FIGURE 2.22

The Pituitary Gland The pituitary gland, which hangs by a short stalk from the hypothalamus, regulates the hormone production of many of the body's endocrine glands. Here it is enlarged 30 times.

that produce hormones related to sexual development and reproduction. These glands and the hormones they produce play important roles in developing sexual characteristics such as breasts in women and a beard in men. They are also involved in other characteristics and behaviors, as we will see throughout this book.

1. The endocrine glands produce chemicals called
   A. hormones.
   B. neurotransmitters.
   C. endocrine secretions.
   D. bile.

2. The endocrine glands include all of the following *except* the
   A. pituitary.
   B. pancreas.
   C. liver.
   D. thyroid.

3. The adrenal glands regulate energy level, the ability to deal with stress, and
   A. appetite.
   B. digestion.
   C. motor coordination.
   D. moods.

Apply It! 4. Diabetes is an increasingly common disorder worldwide. Diabetes involves problems in the body's regulation of glucose, or blood sugar. This disorder is often treated by diet, but sometimes individuals with diabetes must inject themselves with insulin. The endocrine system gland that is involved in diabetes is the
   A. pituitary.
   B. ovaries.
   C. pancreas.
   D. adrenal.

5 Brain Damage, Plasticity, and Repair

Recall from the discussion of the brain's important characteristics earlier in the chapter that plasticity is an example of the brain's remarkable adaptability. Neuroscientists have studied plasticity, especially following brain damage, and have charted the brain's ability to repair itself (Fisher & others, 2009; Ratan & Noble, 2009). Brain damage can produce horrific effects, including paralysis, sensory loss, memory loss, and personality deterioration. When such damage occurs, can the brain recover some or all of its functions? Recovery from brain damage varies considerably, depending on the age of the individual and the extent of the damage (Nelson, 2009).

The Brain's Plasticity and Capacity for Repair

The human brain shows the most plasticity in young children before the functions of the cortical regions become entirely fixed (Nelson, 2009). For example, if the speech areas in an infant's left hemisphere are damaged, the right hemisphere assumes much of this language function. However, after age 5, damage to the left hemisphere can permanently disrupt language ability. We examine the brain's plasticity further in Chapter 3 on sensation and perception and Chapter 8 on human development.

A key factor in recovery is whether some or all of the neurons in an affected area are just damaged or are completely destroyed (Huang & Chang, 2009). If the neurons have not been destroyed, brain function often becomes restored over time.

There are three ways in which repair of the damaged brain might take place:

■ *Collateral sprouting,* in which the axons of some healthy neurons adjacent to damaged cells grow new branches (Watt & others, 2009).

■ *Substitution of function,* in which the damaged region's function is taken over by another area or areas of the brain.

■ *Neurogenesis,* the process by which new neurons are generated. Researchers have found that neurogenesis does occur in mammals such as mice. Recent research

Touring the Nervous System and the Brain

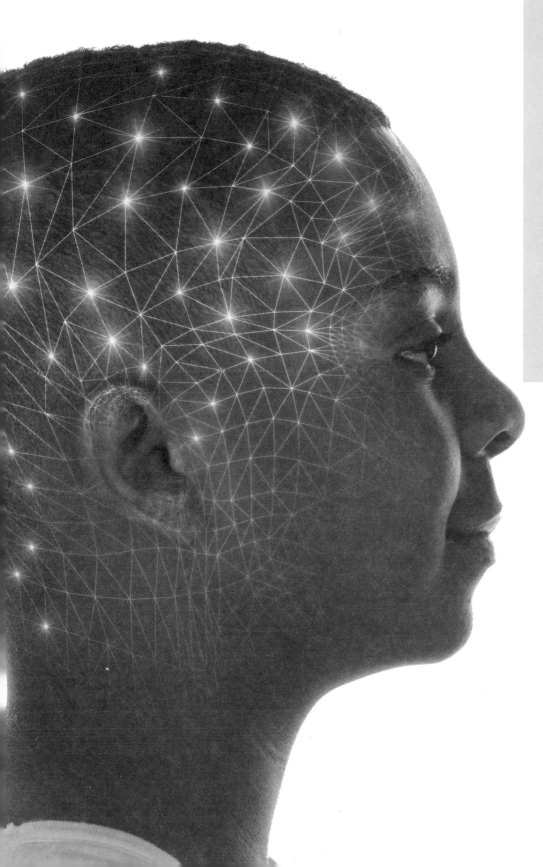

The Neuron and the Synapse

Identify parts of the neuron and synapse and describe how they communicate information.

The **neuron** consists of a **cell body, dendrites,** and an **axon.** Dendrites are branches of the neuron that receive information from other neurons. The axon sends information to other cells. Some axons are surrounded by a **myelin sheath** (fatty layer) that speeds up the transmission of the neural impulse down the axon. When a neuron "fires" it sends an electrical impulse down the axon, called an **action potential.** The arrival of the impulse at the axon terminal buttons causes the release of **neurotransmitter** molecules into the **synapse** (the gap junction between two neurons). Neurons communicate with each other by means of chemical signals provided by neurotransmitters. A neurotransmitter can cause a change in the membrane properties of the receiving neuron, allowing certain electrically charged particles (ions) to enter or leave the neuron. The entry of a positively charged ion, like sodium (Na+), will cause a change in the electrical charge (potential) of the receiving neuron making it more likely to fire (generate its own action potential).

Sending Neuron

1a **Neuron**
Stimulus to a neuron causes a neural impulse to travel down the axon toward dendrites of the next neuron.

Receiving Neuron

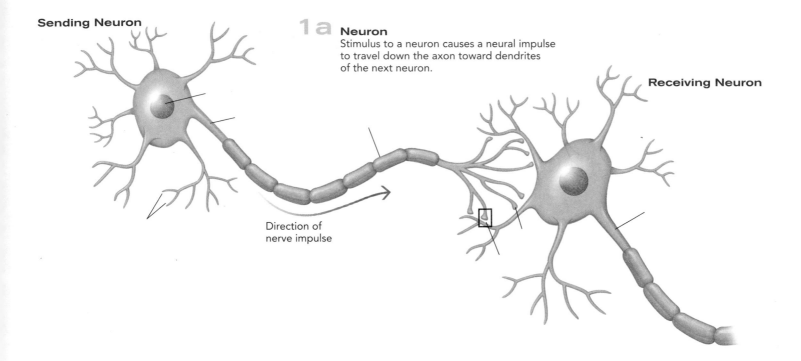

Direction of
nerve impulse

Structures and Functions of the Human Brain

2. Identify the brain's key structures and functions.

Brainstem structures are within the core of the brain and provide a number of vital functions for survival. *Medulla:* life-sustaining reflexes including breathing, coughing, vomiting, and heart rate. *Pons:* sleep and arousal. *Cerebellum:* motor coordination and balance; attention to visual and auditory stimuli. *Reticular formation:* arousal, attention, and sleep patterns; also involved in stereotyped patterns such as posture and locomotion. *Thalamus:* relays auditory, visual, and somatosensory (bodily senses) information to the cerebral cortex.

Limbic system comprises a number of structures involved in motivation, emotion, and memory. *Hypothalamus:* controls the autonomic nervous system and endocrine system; involved in eating, drinking, sexual behavior, and the expression of emotions. *Hippocampus:* special role in learning and memory. *Amygdala:* fear and anxiety; involved in discrimination of objects necessary for survival.

Cerebral cortex is the outer layer of the brain; it is involved in higher-order brain functions including thinking, consciousness, learning, memory, perception, and language.

2a Brain Stem Structures

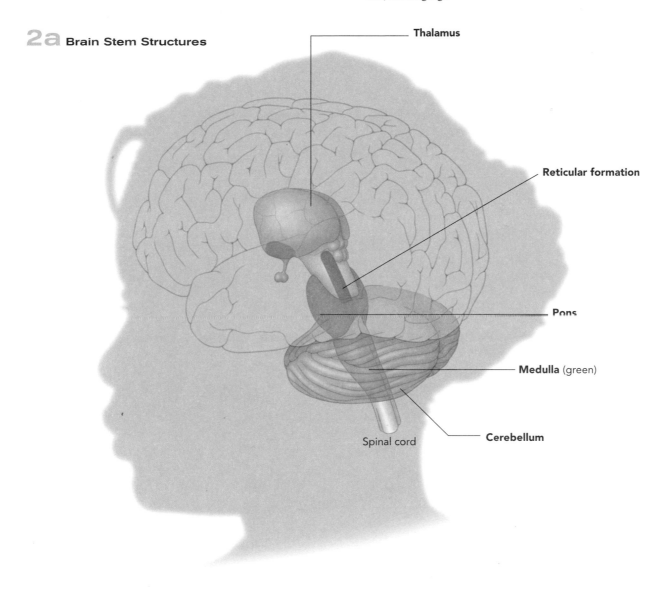

Thalamus

Reticular formation

Pons

Medulla (green)

Cerebellum

Spinal cord

Identify the location of the four cerebral cortex lobes and describe their primary functions.

The **cerebral cortex** is divided into four lobes. The *occipital lobe* is located in the back region of the cortex and is involved in *vision*. The *parietal lobe* is involved in *bodily senses* and lies between the occipital lobe and the *central sulcus.* The area just behind the central sulcus is called the *somatosensory cortex* because it is the primary target for the *touch senses* of the body. The *temporal lobe* is involved in *hearing* and lies behind the frontal lobe and below the lateral fissure. The *frontal lobe* extends forward from the central

sulcus. The region of the frontal lobe immediately adjacent to the central sulcus is called the *motor cortex* because it controls *voluntary movements*. The *prefrontal cortex* (forehead region) is involved in higher functions including *cognition, memory,* the *planning of movement,* and aspects of *emotion.*

Association areas are not primarily sensory or motor; rather, they associate various sensory and motor inputs that give rise to higher mental functions, such as perception, learning, remembering, thinking, and speaking.

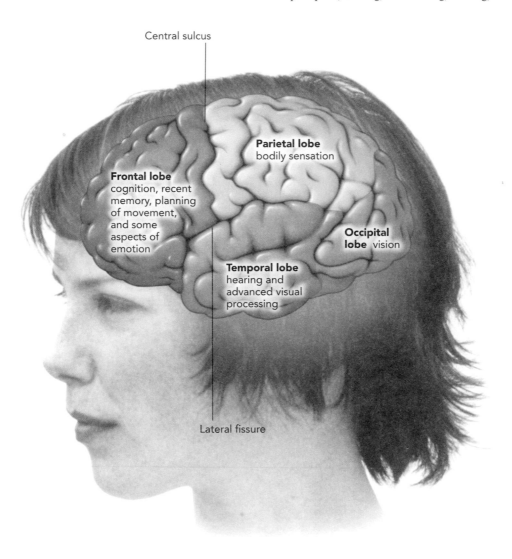

Central sulcus

Parietal lobe
bodily sensation

Frontal lobe
cognition, recent
memory, planning
of movement,
and some
aspects of
emotion

**Occipital
lobe** vision

Temporal lobe
hearing and
advanced visual
processing

Lateral fissure

Central and Peripheral Nervous Systems

Identify the bodily changes that occur when the sympathetic branch or the parasympathetic branch of the autonomic nervous system is activated.

The **central nervous system** is comprised of the brain and the spinal cord. The **peripheral nervous system** consists of all nerves outside the brain and spinal cord. The peripheral nervous system is made up of two major divisions: the *somatic division* and the *autonomic division.* The somatic division consists of nerve fibers that convey information from the brain and spinal cord to skeletal muscles to control movement and send information back to the brain via the spinal cord from sensory receptors. The autonomic division controls the glands and muscles of the internal organs such as the heart, digestive system, lungs, salivary glands, and so on. The autonomic division consists of two branches: the *sympathetic branch* and the *parasympathetic branch.* The sympathetic branch is involved in arousing the body and mobilizing its energy during physical exercise and in stressful situations. It also activates the adrenal glands to release epinephrine into the bloodstream. The parasympathetic branch calms the body and is involved in the conservation and replenishment of energy.

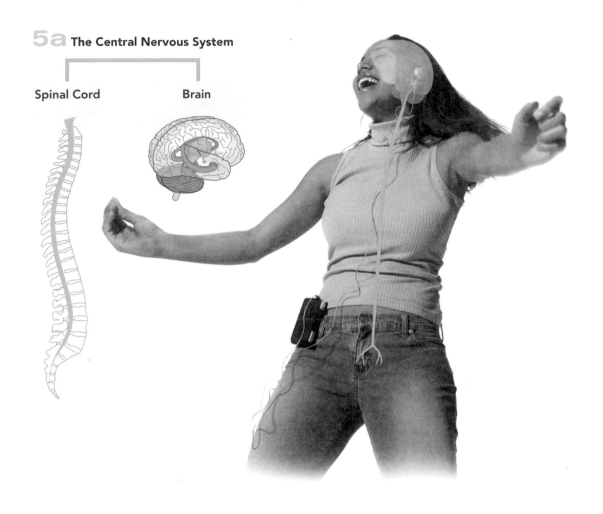

5a **The Central Nervous System**

Spinal Cord   **Brain**

5 Sympathetic and Parasympathetic Nervous System

Identify the parts of the sympathetic and parasympathetic nervous systems and describe their role in arousing and calming the body.

Sympathetic branch: general increase in arousal and excitation accompanied by an increase in heart rate, breathing rate, dilation of the pupils, release of epinephrine from the adrenal glands, and a halt in digestion.

Parasympathetic branch: relaxation and energy conservation accompanied by a reduction in heart rate, breathing rate, constriction of the pupils, and stimulation of digestion.

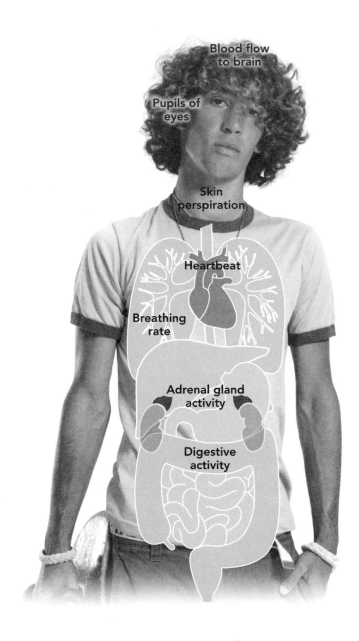

Blood flow
to brain

Pupils of
eyes

Skin
perspiration

Heartbeat

Breathing
rate

Adrenal gland
activity

Digestive
activity

revealed that exercise increased neurogenesis while social isolation decreased neurogenesis (Leasure & Decker, 2009; Van der Borght & others, 2009). It is now accepted that neurogenesis can occur in humans, but to date the presence of new neurons has only been documented in the hippocampus, which is involved in memory, and the olfactory bulb, which is involved in the sense of smell (Aimone, Wiles, & Gage, 2009; Hagg, 2009). If researchers can discover how new neurons are generated, possibly the information can be used to fight degenerative diseases of the brain such as Alzheimer disease and Parkinson disease (Mirochnic & others, 2009).

Brain Tissue Implants

The brain naturally recovers some functions that are lost following damage, but not all. Recent research has generated excitement about brain grafts—implants of healthy tissue into damaged brains (Capetian & others, 2009). The potential success of brain grafts is much better when brain tissue from the fetal stage (an early stage in prenatal development) is used (Thomas & others, 2009). The neurons of the fetus are still growing and have a much higher probability of making connections with other neurons than do the neurons of adults. In a number of studies, researchers have damaged part of an adult rat's brain, waited until the animal recovered as much as possible by itself, and assessed its behavioral deficits. Then they took the corresponding area of a fetal rat's brain and transplanted it into the damaged brain of the adult rat. In these studies, the rats that received the brain transplants demonstrated considerable behavioral recovery (Shetty, Rao, & Hattiangady, 2008).

Might such brain grafts be successful with humans suffering from brain damage? Research suggests that they might, but finding donors is a problem (Glaw & others, 2009). Aborted fetuses are a possibility, but using them as a source of graft tissue raises ethical issues. Another type of treatment has been attempted with individuals who have Parkinson disease, a neurological disorder that affects about a million people in the United States (D. H. Park & others, 2009). Parkinson disease impairs coordinated movement to the point that just walking across a room can be a major ordeal.

Perhaps one of the most heated debates in recent years has concerned the use of human embryonic stem cells in research and treatment (Capetian & others, 2009; Chae & others, 2009). The human body contains more than 220 different types of cells, but **stem cells** are unique because they are primitive cells that have the capacity to develop into most types of human cells. Stem cells were first harvested from embryos by researchers at the University of Wisconsin, Madison, and Johns Hopkins University, in 1998. Because of their amazing plasticity, stem cells might potentially replace damaged cells in the human body, including cells involved in spinal cord injury and brain damage.

Typically, researchers have harvested the stem cells from frozen embryos left over from in vitro fertilization procedures. In these procedures, a number of eggs, or *ova*, are collected from a woman's ovaries in order to be fertilized in a lab (rather than in the woman's body). In successful in vitro fertilization, the ova are brought together with sperm, producing human embryos. Because the procedure is difficult and delicate, doctors typically fertilize a large number of eggs with the hope that some will survive when implanted in the woman's uterus. In the typical procedure, there are leftover embryos. These embryos are in the *blastocyst* stage, which occurs five days after conception. At this stage the embryo has not yet attached to the uterus. The blastocyst has no brain, no central nervous system, and no mouth—it is an undifferentiated ball of cells.

Some supporters of stem cell technology (among them the late actor Christopher Reeve, 2000) emphasize that using these cells for research and treatment might relieve a great deal of human suffering. Opponents of abortion disapprove of the use of stem cells in research or treatment on the grounds that the embryos die when the stem cells are removed. (In fact, leftover embryos are likely to be destroyed in any case.) In 2009, President Barack Obama removed restrictions on stem cell research.

stem cells
Unique primitive cells that have the capacity to develop into most types of human cells.

Do you favor or oppose the use of stem cells in research? Why?

1. Repair of the damaged brain might take place by all of the following *except*
   A. substitution of function.
   B. psychotherapy.
   C. collateral sprouting.
   D. neurogenesis.

2. The process by which the axons of healthy neurons adjacent to damaged cells grow new branches is called
   A. substitution of function.
   B. neurogenesis.
   C. collateral sprouting.
   D. dendritic branching.

3. The primitive cells that have the capacity to develop into most types of human cells are called
   A. stem cells.
   B. blastocysts.
   C. collateral cells.
   D. neurogenetic cells.

Apply It! 4. Taylor is injured in a serious car accident, suffering head injuries. After the accident, Taylor, who used to be very talkative, seems to be unable to speak. Which of the following would best predict that Taylor is likely to regain the ability to talk?
   A. Taylor is male.
   B. Taylor is under 5 years old.
   C. Taylor is over the age of 21.
   D. Taylor is female.

6 Genetics and Behavior

In addition to the brain and nervous system, other aspects of our physiology also have consequences for psychological processes. Genes are one important contributor to these processes. As noted in Chapter 1, the influence of nature (genetic endowment) and nurture (experience) on psychological characteristics has fascinated psychologists. Here we begin by examining the central agent of nature: our genetic heritage.

Chromosomes, Genes, and DNA

chromosomes
In the human cell, threadlike structures that come in 23 pairs, one member of each pair originating from each parent, and that contain DNA.

Within the human body are literally trillions of cells. The nucleus of each human cell contains 46 **chromosomes,** threadlike structures that come in 23 pairs, one member of each pair originating from each parent. Chromosomes contain the remarkable substance **deoxyribonucleic acid,** or **DNA,** a complex molecule that carries genetic information. **Genes,** the units of hereditary information, are short segments of chromosomes composed of DNA. Genes enable cells to reproduce and manufacture the proteins that are necessary for maintaining life. The relation among cells, chromosomes, genes, and DNA is illustrated in Figure 2.23.

An international research program called the Human Genome Project (*genome* refers to an organism's complete genetic material, as discussed below) is dedicated to documenting the human genome. Human beings have approximately 20,500 genes (Ensembl Human, 2008). When these 20,500 genes from one parent combine at conception with the same number of genes from the other parent, the number of possibilities is staggering. Although scientists are still a long way from unraveling all the mysteries about the way genes work, some aspects of this process are well understood, starting with the fact that multiple genes interact to give rise to observable characteristics.

deoxyribonucleic acid (DNA)
A complex molecule in the cell's chromosomes that carries genetic information.

genes
The units of hereditary information, consisting of short segments of chromosomes composed of DNA.

A positive result from the Human Genome Project: Shortly after Andrew Gobea was born, his cells were genetically altered to prevent his immune system from failing.

The Study of Genetics

Historically speaking, genetics is a relatively young science. Its origins go back to the mid-nineteenth century, when an Austrian monk named Gregor Mendel studied heredity in generations of pea plants. By cross-breeding plants with different characteristics and noting the characteristics of the offspring, Mendel discovered predictable patterns of heredity and laid the foundation for modern genetics.

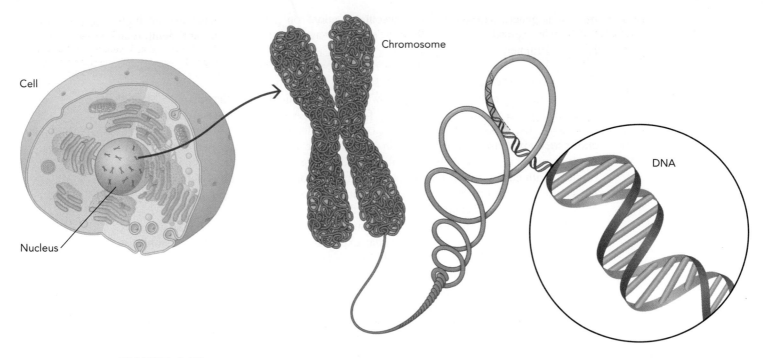

FIGURE 2.23

Cells, Chromosomes, Genes, and DNA (*Left*) The body contains trillions of cells, which are the basic structural units of life. Each cell contains a central structure, the nucleus. (*Middle*) Chromosomes and genes are located in the nucleus of the cell. Chromosomes are made up of threadlike structures composed mainly of DNA molecules. (*Right*) A gene is a segment of DNA that contains the hereditary code. The structure of DNA resembles a spiral ladder.

Mendel noticed that some genes seem to be more likely than others to show up in the physical characteristics of an organism. In some gene pairs, one gene is dominant over the other. If one gene of a pair is dominant and one is recessive, according to the **dominant-recessive genes principle,** the dominant gene overrides the recessive gene. A recessive gene exerts its influence only if both genes of a pair are recessive. If you inherit a recessive gene from only one parent, you may never know you carry the gene. In the world of dominant-recessive genes, brown eyes, farsightedness, and dimples rule over blue eyes, nearsightedness, and freckles. If you inherit a recessive gene for a trait from both of your parents, you will show the trait. That is why two brown-eyed parents can have a blue-eyed child: Each parent would have a dominant gene for brown eyes and a recessive gene for blue eyes. Because dominant genes override recessive genes, the parents have brown eyes. However, the child can inherit a recessive gene for blue eyes from each parent. With no dominant gene to override them, the recessive genes make the child's eyes blue.

Unlike eye color, complex human characteristics such as personality and intelligence are likely influenced by many different genes. Scientists use the term *polygenic inheritance* to describe the influences of multiple genes on behavior.

Today researchers continue to apply Mendel's methods, as well as modern technology, in their quest to expand our knowledge of genetics. This section discusses three ways to study genetics: molecular genetics, selective breeding, and behavior genetics.

Molecular Genetics
The field of *molecular genetics* involves the manipulation of genes using technology to determine their effect on behavior. There is currently a great deal of enthusiasm about the use of

dominant-recessive genes principle
The principle that if one gene of a pair is dominant and one is recessive, the dominant gene overrides the recessive gene. A recessive gene exerts its influence only if both genes of a pair are recessive.

Do It!

Search the web for information about a happiness gene. How would you evaluate research on such a gene given what you have read so far in this book? What (if anything) would the existence of such a gene mean for your ability to find happiness in your life?

molecular genetics to discover the specific locations on genes that determine an individual's susceptibility to many diseases and other aspects of health and well-being (van Driel & Brunner, 2006).

Selective Breeding

Selective breeding is a genetic method in which organisms are chosen for reproduction based on how much of a particular trait they display. Mendel developed this technique in his studies of pea plants. A more recent example involving behavior is the classic selective breeding study conducted by Robert Tryon (1940). He chose to study maze-running ability in rats. After he trained a large number of rats to run a complex maze, he then mated the rats that were the best at maze running ("maze bright") with each other and the ones that were the worst ("maze dull") with each other. He continued this process with 21 generations of rats. After several generations, the maze-bright rats significantly outperformed the maze-dull rats.

Selective breeding studies have demonstrated that genes are an important influence on behavior, but that does not mean that experience is unimportant. For example, in another study, maze-bright and maze-dull rats were reared in one of two environments: (1) an impoverished environment that consisted of a barren wire-mesh group cage or (2) an enriched environment that contained tunnels, ramps, visual displays, and other stimulating objects (Cooper & Zubeck, 1958). When they reached maturity, only the maze-dull rats that had been reared in an impoverished environment made more maze-learning errors than the maze-bright rats.

Behavior Genetics

Behavior genetics is the study of the degree and nature of heredity's influence on behavior. Behavior genetics is less invasive than molecular genetics and selective breeding. Using methods such as the *twin study,* behavior geneticists examine the extent to which individuals are shaped by their heredity and their environmental experiences (Plomin & others, 2009).

In the most common type of twin study, researchers compare the behavioral similarity of identical twins with the behavioral similarity of fraternal twins (Sartor & others, 2009). *Identical twins* develop from a single fertilized egg that splits into two genetically identical embryos, each of which becomes a person. *Fraternal twins* develop from separate eggs and separate sperm, and so they are genetically no more similar than non-twin siblings. They may even be of different sexes.

By comparing groups of identical and fraternal twins, behavior geneticists capitalize on the fact that identical twins are more similar genetically than are fraternal twins. In one twin study, researchers compared 7,000 pairs of Finnish identical and fraternal twins with respect to the personality traits of extraversion (being outgoing) and neuroticism (being psychologically unstable) (Rose & others, 1988). The identical twins were much more alike than the fraternal twins on both of these personality traits, suggesting that genes influence both traits.

One problem with twin studies is that adults might stress the similarities of identical twin children more than those of fraternal twins, and identical twins might perceive themselves as a "set" and play together more than fraternal twins do. If so, observed similarities in identical twins might be more strongly influenced by environmental factors than usually thought.

In another type of twin study, researchers evaluate identical twins who have been reared in separate environments. If their behavior is similar, the assumption is that heredity has played an important role in shaping their behavior. This strategy is the basis for the Minnesota Study of Twins Reared Apart, directed by Thomas Bouchard and his colleagues (1996). They bring identical twins who have been reared apart to Minneapolis from all over the world to study their behavior. They ask thousands of questions about their family, childhood, interests, and values. Detailed medical histories are obtained, including information about diet, smoking, and exercise habits.

The Jim twins: Springer (right) and Lewis were unaware of each other for 39 years.

One pair of twins in the Minnesota study, Jim Springer and Jim Lewis, were separated at 4 weeks of age and did not see each other again until they were 39 years old. They had an uncanny number of similarities, even though they had lived apart. For example, they both worked as part-time deputy sheriffs, had vacationed in Florida, had owned Chevrolets, had dogs named Toy, and had married and divorced women named Betty. Both liked math but not spelling. Both were good at mechanical drawing. Both put on 10 pounds at about the same time in their lives, and both started suffering headaches at 18 years of age. They did have a few differences. For example, one expressed himself better orally, and the other was more proficient at writing. One parted his hair over his forehead; the other wore his hair slicked back with sideburns.

How similar would Jim Springer be to any man who is also the same age and has the same name? Is it possible that some of his similarities to Jim Lewis were not so surprising after all?

Critics argue that some of the separated twins in the Minnesota study had been together several months prior to their adoption, that some had been reunited prior to testing (in certain cases, for a number of years), that adoption agencies often put identical twins in similar homes, and that even strangers are likely to have some coincidental similarities (Joseph, 2006).

Genes and the Environment

So far, we have talked a lot about genes, and you are probably getting the picture that genes are a powerful force in an organism. The role of genetics in some characteristics may seem obvious; for instance, how tall you are depends to a large degree on how tall your parents are. However, imagine a person growing up in a severely impoverished environment—with poor nutrition, inadequate shelter, little or no medical care, and a mother who had received no prenatal care. This individual may have genes that call for the height of an NBA or a WNBA center, but without environmental support for this genetic capacity, he or she may never reach that genetically programmed height. Thus, the relationship between an individual's genes and the actual person we see before us is not a perfect one-to-one correspondence. Even for a characteristic such as height, genes do not fully determine where a person will stand on this variable. We need to account for the role of nurture, or environmental factors, in the actual characteristics we see in the fully grown person.

If the environment matters for an apparently simple characteristic such as height, imagine the role it might play in complex characteristics such as being outgoing or intelligent. For these psychological characteristics, genes are, again, not directly reflected in the characteristics of the person. Indeed, genes cannot tell us exactly what a person will be like. Genes are simply related to some of the characteristics we see in a person.

To account for this gap between genes and actual observable characteristics, scientists distinguish between a genotype and a phenotype. A **genotype** is a person's genetic heritage, his or her actual genetic material. A **phenotype** is the individual's observable characteristics. The relationship between a genotype and phenotype is not always obvious. Recall that some genetic characteristics are dominant and others are recessive. Seeing that a person has brown eyes (his or her phenotype) tells us nothing about whether the person might also have a gene for

genotype
A person's genetic heritage; his or her actual genetic material.

phenotype
An individual's observable characteristics.

Our height depends significantly on the genes we inherit. However, even if we have genes that call for the stature of a basketball center, we many not reach that genetically programmed height if we lack good nutrition, adequate shelter, and medical care.

blue eyes (his or her genotype) hiding out as well. The phenotype is influenced by the genotype but also by environmental factors.

The term *phenotype* applies to both physical *and* psychological characteristics. Consider a trait such as extraversion, the tendency to be outgoing and sociable. Even if we knew the exact genetic recipe for extraversion, we still could not perfectly predict a person's level of (phenotypic) extraversion from his or her genes, because at least some of this trait comes from the person's experience. We will revisit the concepts of genotype and phenotype throughout this book, including in Chapter 7 when we look at intelligence, Chapter 8 when we explore development, and Chapter 10 when we examine personality.

One of the big surprises of the Human Genome Project was a report indicating that humans have about 20,500 genes ("Human gene count tumbles again," 2008). Scientists had thought that humans had as many as 100,000 or more genes and that each gene programmed just one protein. In fact, humans have far more proteins than they have genes, so there cannot be a one-to-one correspondence between genes and proteins (Commoner, 2002). Each gene is not translated into one and only one protein. A gene does not act independently (Diamond, 2009). Indeed, rather than being a group of independent genes, the human genome consists of many genes that collaborate both with each other and with nongenetic factors inside and outside the body. The collaboration operates at many points. For example, the cellular machinery mixes, matches, and links small pieces of DNA to reproduce the genes, and that machinery is influenced by what is going on around it.

Whether a gene is turned "on"—working to assemble proteins—is also a matter of collaboration. The activity of genes (*genetic expression*) is affected by their environment (Gottlieb, 2007). For example, hormones that circulate in the blood make their way into the cell where they can turn genes on and off. The flow of hormones, too, can be affected by environmental conditions, such as light, day length, nutrition, and behavior. Numerous studies have shown that external events outside of the original cell and the person, as well as events inside the cell, can excite or inhibit gene expression (Gottlieb, 2007). For example, one study revealed that an increase in the concentration of stress hormones such as cortisol produced a 5-fold increase in DNA damage (Flint & others, 2007).

The biological foundations of psychology are in evidence across the entire nervous system, including the brain, the intricately working neurotransmitters, the endocrine system, and our genes. These physical realities of our bodies work in amazing concert to produce our behaviors, thoughts, and feelings. The activities you do in the course of your daily life, from large to small, are all signs of the spectacular success of this physical system. Your mastery of the material in this chapter is but one reflection of the extraordinary capabilities of this biological miracle.

self-quiz

1. The threadlike structures that are present in the cell nucleus and contain genes and DNA are called
   A. genomes.
   B. polygenic markers.
   C. chromosomes.
   D. stem cells.

2. Researchers study genetics through all of the following methods *except*
   A. twin studies.
   B. selective breeding.
   C. environmental impact studies.
   D. molecular genetics.

3. The individual's *observable* characteristics, influenced by both genetic and environmental factors, are called the
   A. genome.
   B. genotype.
   C. phenotype.
   D. prototype.

Apply It! 4. Sarah and Jack both have brown hair. When their son Trent is born, he has bright red hair. Family and friends start making jokes about any male friends of Sarah's who have red hair. Should Jack be worried that he is not Trent's father?

A. Jack should not be worried because brown hair color is part of the phenotype, not necessarily Sarah's and Jack's genotypes.

B. Jack should not be worried because Trent's hair color is part of his genotype, not necessarily his phenotype.

C. Jack should be worried because there is no way for two brunettes to have a baby with red hair. Sarah's been up to no good.

D. Jack should be worried because Trent's phenotype should match his parents' exactly.

summary

① The Nervous System

The nervous system is the body's electrochemical communication circuitry. Four important characteristics of the brain and nervous system are complexity, integration, adaptability, and electrochemical transmission. The brain's special ability to adapt and change is called plasticity.

Decision making in the nervous system occurs in specialized pathways of nerve cells. Three of these pathways involve sensory input, motor output, and neural networks.

The nervous system is divided into two main parts: central (CNS) and peripheral (PNS). The CNS consists of the brain and spinal cord. The PNS has two major divisions: somatic and autonomic. The autonomic nervous system consists of two main divisions: sympathetic and parasympathetic. In particular, the sympathetic nervous system is involved in the experience of stress.

② Neurons

Neurons are cells that specialize in processing information. They make up the communication network of the nervous system. The three main parts of the neuron are the cell body, dendrite (receiving part), and axon (sending part). A myelin sheath encases and insulates most axons and speeds up transmission of neural impulses.

A neuron sends information along its axon in the form of brief electric impulses. Resting potential is the stable, slightly negative charge of an inactive neuron. The brief wave of electrical charge that sweeps down the axon, called the action potential, is an all-or-nothing response. The synapse is the space between neurons. At the synapse, neurotransmitters are released from the sending neuron, and some of these attach to receptor sites on the receiving neuron, where they stimulate another electrical impulse. Neurotransmitters include acetylcholine, GABA, norepinephrine, dopamine, serotonin, and endorphins. Neural networks are clusters of neurons that are interconnected to process information.

③ Structures of the Brain and Their Functions

Techniques used to study the brain include brain lesioning, electrical recording, and brain imaging. These methods have revealed much about the brain's major divisions—hindbrain, midbrain, and forebrain.

The cerebral cortex makes up most of the outer layer of the brain, and it is here that higher mental functions such as thinking and planning take place. The wrinkled surface of the cerebral cortex is divided into hemispheres, each with four lobes: occipital, temporal, frontal, and parietal. There is considerable integration and connection among the brain's lobes.

The brain has two hemispheres. Two areas in the left hemisphere that involve specific language functions are Broca's area (speech) and Wernicke's area (comprehending language). The corpus callosum is a large bundle of fibers that connects the two hemispheres. Research suggests that the left brain is more dominant in processing verbal information (such as language) and the right brain in processing nonverbal information (such as spatial perception, visual recognition, faces, and emotion). Nonetheless, in a person whose corpus callosum is intact, both hemispheres of the cerebral cortex are involved in most complex human functioning.

④ The Endocrine System

The endocrine glands release hormones directly into the bloodstream for distribution throughout the body. The pituitary gland is the master endocrine gland. The adrenal glands play important roles in moods, energy level, and ability to cope with stress. Other parts of the endocrine system include the pancreas, which produces insulin, and the ovaries and testes, which produce sex hormones.

⑤ Brain Damage, Plasticity, and Repair

The human brain has considerable plasticity, although this plasticity is greater in young children than later in development. Three ways in which a damaged brain might repair itself are collateral sprouting, substitution of function, and neurogenesis. Brain grafts are implants of healthy tissue into damaged brains. Brain grafts are more successful when fetal tissue is used. Stem cell research may allow for new treatments for damaged nervous systems.

⑥ Genetics and Behavior

Chromosomes are threadlike structures that occur in 23 pairs, with one member of each pair coming from each parent. Chromosomes contain the genetic substance deoxyribonucleic acid (DNA). Genes, the units of hereditary information, are short segments of chromosomes composed of DNA. According to the dominant-recessive genes principle, if one gene of a pair is dominant and one is recessive, the dominant gene overrides the recessive gene.

Two important concepts in the study of genetics are the genotype and phenotype. The genotype is an individual's actual genetic material. The phenotype is the observable characteristics of the person.

Three methods of studying heredity's influence are molecular genetics, selective breeding, and behavior genetics. Two methods used by behavior geneticists are twin studies and adoption studies. Both genes and environment play a role in determining the phenotype of an individual. Even for characteristics in which genes play a large role (such as height and eye color), the environment also is a factor.

key terms

nervous system, p. 39
plasticity, p. 40
afferent nerves, p. 40
efferent nerves, p. 40
neural networks, p. 40
central nervous system
  (CNS), p. 40
peripheral nervous system
  (PNS), p. 40
somatic nervous system, p. 41
autonomic nervous system, p. 41
sympathetic nervous system, p. 41
parasympathetic nervous
  system, p. 41
stress, p. 41
stressors, p. 41
neurons, p. 43

glial cells, p. 43
cell body, p. 43
dendrites, p. 44
axon, p. 44
myelin sheath, p. 44
resting potential, p. 45
action potential, p. 46
all-or-nothing principle, p. 46
synapses, p. 46
neurotransmitters, p. 46
agonist, p. 49
antagonist, p. 49
hindbrain, p. 53
brain stem, p. 53
midbrain, p. 54
reticular formation, p. 54
forebrain, p. 55

limbic system, p. 55
amygdala, p. 55
hippocampus, p. 55
thalamus, p. 56
basal ganglia, p. 56
hypothalamus, p. 56
cerebral cortex, p. 57
neocortex, p. 57
occipital lobes, p. 57
temporal lobes, p. 58
frontal lobes, p. 58
parietal lobes, p. 60
somatosensory cortex, p. 60
motor cortex, p. 60
association cortex, p. 60
corpus callosum, p. 62
endocrine system, p. 66

glands, p. 66
hormones, p. 67
pituitary gland, p. 67
adrenal glands, p. 67
pancreas, p. 67
ovaries, p. 67
testes, p. 67
stem cells, p. 69
chromosomes, p. 70
deoxyribonucleic acid
  (DNA), p. 70
genes, p. 70
dominant-recessive genes
  principle, p. 71
genotype, p. 73
phenotype, p. 73

self-test

Multiple Choice

1. Nerves that carry information from other parts of the body to the brain are called
   A. neural networks.
   B. afferent nerves.
   C. efferent nerves.
   D. neurotransmitters.

2. The purpose of myelin is to
   A. promote the release of presynaptic neurotransmitters.
   B. insulate axons to increase the speed of electrical impulses.
   C. open and close channels.
   D. create GABA.

3. When a neuron is resting, the inside of the cell membrane is _____, and the outside of the cell membrane is _____.
   A. positive; negative
   B. negative; positive
   C. negative; negative
   D. positive; positive

4. The structures at the end of the axon are called
   A. dendrites.
   B. terminal buttons.
   C. cell bodies.
   D. synaptic gaps.

5. The neurotransmitter most associated with love and bonding is
   A. serotonin.
   B. oxytocin.
   C. endorphins.
   D. norepinephrine.

6. The lobe of the cerebral cortex that responds to visual stimuli is the
   A. occipital lobe.
   B. parietal lobe.
   C. temporal lobe.
   D. frontal lobe.

7. The lobe of the cerebral cortex associated with personality is the
   A. occipital lobe.
   B. parietal lobe.
   C. temporal lobe.
   D. frontal lobe.

8. The part of the brain that acts as central relay station is the
   A. reticular formation.
   B. limbic system.
   C. hippocampus.
   D. thalamus.

9. Broca's area plays an important role in _____, while Wernicke's area plays an important role in _____.
   A. motor function; sensation
   B. sensation; motor function
   C. speech production; speech comprehension
   D. speech comprehension; speech production

10. The corpus callosum is responsible for
   A. verbal processing.
   B. relaying information between the right and left hemispheres.
   C. speech production.
   D. sleep.

Apply It!

11. After reading about the right brain and the left brain, Carl announces that it makes no sense to wear a helmet while skateboarding, because we all have an extra brain to spare anyway. He announces, "I am cool as long as I have my left brain, since that's the one that does the talking!" Explain to Carl what life might be like with no right hemisphere.

3 Sensation and Perception

Destiny Diaz, Seeing the World for the First Time

"I can see Mariah Carey. She's American and she has the same skin as me. Her pants are red," exclaimed 11-year-old Destiny Diaz, who had been legally blind since birth, after receiving an artificial cornea. Just 24 hours after her transplant—an artificial cornea was used because her immune system had rejected human transplants—Destiny's doctor asked her to tell him how many fingers he was holding up and then to touch his nose. As she reached out and touched it, her aunts, watching from a corner of the room, wept with joy. This formerly blind little girl could see.

The first organ transplant was a double cornea transplant performed about a century ago by a Czech doctor, Eduard Zirm, on a 43-year-old man named Alois Gloger. After the surgery, Gloger's eyes were sewn shut for 10 miserable days, but when the stitches were removed, he could see. Today, 40,000 cornea transplants are performed each year. These transplants generally depend on eye banks, to which individuals can promise to donate their organs after death. The operation is complex but not nearly as difficult as that first one. Imagine 40,000 people a year undergoing this procedure—in some cases seeing for the first time. For these individuals, sight is truly a gift bestowed not by nature but by science, technology, and the generosity of others.

Vision and all of our other senses connect us to the world. We see a beloved friend's face, feel a comforting hand on our shoulder, or hear our name called from across a room. Our ability to perceive the world is what allows us to reach out into that world in the many ways we do every day. ■

- ■ **What is your favorite song or food?**
- ■ **What role do your senses play in determining these favorite things?**
- ■ **How do these favorites relate to your self-identity?**

In this chapter we explore sensation and perception, the processes by which we connect with the world. We first examine vision, the sense about which scientists know the most. We then probe the nature of hearing, the skin senses, taste, smell, and the kinesthetic and vestibular senses.

1 How We Sense and Perceive the World

Sensation and perception researchers represent a broad range of specialties, including *ophthalmology,* the study of the eye's structure, function, and diseases; *audiology,* the science concerned with hearing; *neurology,* the scientific study of the nervous system; and many others. Understanding sensation and perception requires comprehending the physical properties of the objects of our perception—light, sound, the texture of material things, and so on. The psychological approach to these processes involves understanding the physical structures and functions of the sense organs, as well as the brain's conversion of the information from these organs into experience.

The Processes and Purposes of Sensation and Perception

Our world is alive with stimuli—all the objects and events that surround us. Sensation and perception are the processes that allow us to detect and understand these various stimuli. It may seem strange to think about it this way, but we do not actually experience these stimuli directly; rather, our senses allow us to get information about aspects of our environment, and we then take that information and form a perception of the world. **Sensation** is the process of receiving stimulus energies from the external environment and transforming those energies into neural energy. Physical energy such as light, sound, and heat is detected by specialized receptor cells in the sense organs—eyes, ears, skin, nose, and tongue. When the receptor cells register a stimulus, the energy is converted to an electrochemical impulse or action potential that relays information about the stimulus through the nervous system to the brain (Sani & others, 2009; Wang & Hatton, 2009). Recall from Chapter 2 that an action potential is the brief wave of electrical charge that sweeps down the axon of a neuron for possible transmission to another neuron. When it reaches the brain, the information travels to the appropriate area of the cerebral cortex (Gruber & O'Donnell, 2009).

The brain gives meaning to sensation through perception. **Perception** is the process of organizing and interpreting sensory information so that it makes

sensation
The process of receiving stimulus energies from the external environment and transforming those energies into neural energy.

perception
The process of organizing and interpreting sensory information so that it makes sense.

Through sensation we take in information from the world; through perception we identify meaningful patterns in that information. Thus sensation and perception work hand in hand when we enjoy a hug and the sweet fragrance of a flower.

sense. Receptor cells in our eyes record—that is, sense—a sleek silver object in the sky, but they do not "see" a jet plane. Recognizing that silver object as a plane is perception. Sensing and perceiving give us views of the setting sun, the sounds of a rock concert, the touch of soft caresses, the taste of sweets, and the fragrance of flowers. Of all the various stimuli that are present in your environment right now, you are able to sense and perceive only some of them. Every species is adapted to sense and perceives stimuli that matter to that species' ability to survive in its environment.

Humans cannot smell as well as dogs. Your dog might pick up the scent of another dog yards away, while you might never smell that other canine—because, unlike your dog, you don't need to.

Bottom-Up and Top-Down Processing

bottom-up processing
The operation in sensation and perception in which sensory receptors register information about the external environment and send it up to the brain for interpretation.

top-down processing
The operation in sensation and perception, launched by cognitive processing at the brain's higher levels, that allows the organism to sense what is happening and to apply that framework to information from the world.

Psychologists distinguish between bottom-up and top-down processing in sensation and perception. In **bottom-up processing,** sensory receptors register information about the external environment and send it up to the brain for interpretation. Bottom-up processing means taking in information and trying to make sense of it (Weidner & others, 2009). An example of bottom-up processing might be the way you experience a song the first time you hear it: You listen carefully to get a "feel" for it. In contrast, **top-down processing** starts with cognitive processing at the higher levels of the brain; in top-down processing we begin with some sense of what is happening and apply that framework to information from the world (Balaguer-Ballester & others, 2009; Johnson & Johnson, 2009). You can experience top-down processing by "listening" to your favorite song in your head right now. As you "hear" the song in your mind's ear, you are engaged in perceptual experience.

Both bottom-up and top-down processing take place in sensing and perceiving the world (Liu & others, 2009), and these processes work together to allow us to function accurately and efficiently. By themselves our ears provide only incoming information about sound in the environment. Only when we consider both what the ears hear (bottom-up processing) and what the brain interprets (top-down processing) can we fully understand how we perceive sounds in our world. In everyday life, the two processes of sensation and perception are essentially inseparable. For this reason, most psychologists refer to sensation and perception as a unified information-processing system (Goldstein, 2010).

Have you ever begged a friend to taste your favorite food or listen to your favorite song, only to be disappointed when your pal reacted to trying it out with a shrug and "Eh"? In this scenario, both tongues and all four ears register the same information, but perception is a very subjective interpretation of that information.

The Purposes of Sensation and Perception

Why do we perceive the world? From an evolutionary perspective, the purpose of sensation and perception is adaptation that improves a species' chances for survival (Hartman & Smith, 2009; Mader, 2010). An organism must be able to sense and respond quickly and accurately to events

Most predatory animals have eyes at the front of their faces; most animals that are prey have eyes on the side of their heads. Through these adaptations, predators perceive their prey accurately, and prey gain a measure of safety from their panoramic view of their environment.

in the immediate environment, such as the approach of a predator, the presence of prey, or the appearance of a potential mate. Not surprisingly, therefore, most animals—from goldfish to gorillas to humans—have eyes and ears, as well as sensitivities to touch and chemicals (smell and taste). Furthermore, a close comparison of sensory systems in animals reveals that each species is exquisitely adapted to the habitat in which it evolved (Molles, 2010). Animals that are primarily predators generally have their eyes at the front of their faces so that they can perceive their prey accurately. In contrast, animals that are more likely to be someone else's lunch have their eyes on either side of their heads, giving them a wide view of their surroundings at all times.

A marvelous example of evolutionary accomplishment appears in a fish called *Anableps microlepis,* which has four eyes. This remarkable adaptation allows the *Anableps microlepis* to swim just at the surface of the water, with two aerial eyes monitoring the dangerous world above the water and two aquatic eyes looking for food in the world below.

Sensory Receptors and the Brain

All sensation begins with sensory receptors. **Sensory receptors** are specialized cells that detect stimulus information and transmit it to sensory (*afferent*) nerves and the brain (Kaltenbach, Yu, & Holland, 2009). Sensory receptors are the openings through which the brain and nervous system experience the world. Figure 3.1 shows the human sensory receptors for vision, hearing, touch, smell, and taste.

The sensory receptors of all animal species have evolved so that animals are adapted to their environments. For example, the sensory receptors that a bat uses to find food are very different from—but no more specialized than—those that an eagle uses. Bats use sound to locate prey at night, whereas eagles hunt with their eyes from great heights to avoid detection from potential prey.

Figure 3.2 depicts the flow of information from the environment to the brain. Sensory receptors take in information from the environment, creating local electrical currents. These currents are *graded;* that means they are sensitive to the intensity of stimulation, such as the difference between a dim and a bright light. These receptors trigger action potentials in sensory neurons, which carry that information to the central

Yes, there it is again: afferent nerves. Remember that afferent nerves bring information to the brain, and efferent nerves send messages away from the brain to the body.

sensory receptors Specialized cells that detect stimulus information and transmit it to sensory (afferent) nerves and the brain.

FIGURE 3.1

Human Senses: Organs, Energy Stimuli, and Sensory Receptors The receptor cells for each sense are specialized to receive particular types of energy stimuli.

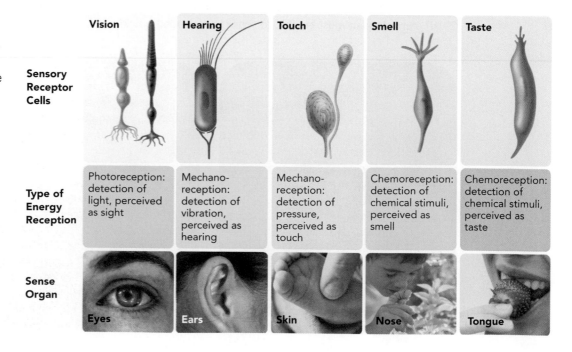

nervous system. Because sensory neurons (like all neurons) follow the all-or-nothing principle, described in Chapter 2, the intensity of the stimulus cannot be communicated to the brain by changing the strength of the action potential. Instead, the receptor varies the *frequency* of action potentials sent to the brain. So, if a stimulus is very intense, like the bright sun on a hot day, the neuron will fire more frequently (but with the same strength) to let the brain know that the light is, indeed, very, very bright.

Other than frequency, the action potentials of all sensory nerves are alike. This sameness raises an intriguing question: How can an animal distinguish among sight, sound, odor, taste, and touch? The answer is that sensory receptors are selective and have different neural pathways. They are specialized to absorb a particular type of energy—light energy, sound vibrations, or chemical energy, for example—and convert it into an action potential.

Sensation involves detecting and transmitting information about different kinds of energy. The sense organs and sensory receptors fall into several main classes based on the type of energy that is transmitted. The functions of these classes include

- *Photoreception:* detection of light, perceived as sight
- *Mechanoreception:* detection of pressure, vibration, and movement, perceived as touch, hearing, and equilibrium
- *Chemoreception:* detection of chemical stimuli, perceived as smell and taste

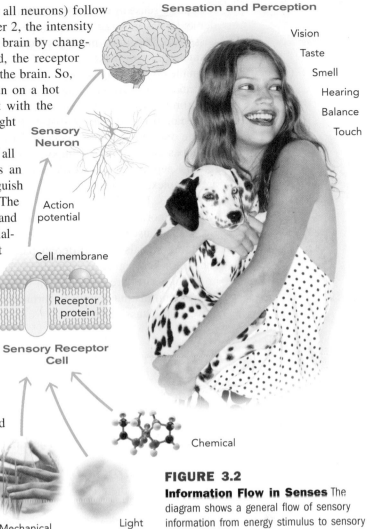

FIGURE 3.2
Information Flow in Senses The diagram shows a general flow of sensory information from energy stimulus to sensory receptor cell to sensory neuron to sensation and perception.

Each of these processes belongs to a particular class of receptors and brain processes. There are rare cases, however, in which the senses can become confused. The term *synaesthesia* describes an experience in which one sense (say, sight) induces an experience in another sense (say, hearing). Some individuals "see" music or "taste" a color, for example. One woman was able to taste sounds, so that a piece of music might taste like tuna fish (Beeli, Esslen, & Jancke, 2005). Neuroscientists are exploring the neurological bases of synaesthesia, especially in the connections between the various sensory regions of the cerebral cortex (Cohen & Henik, 2007). One proposal is that the posterior parietal cortex, which is linked to normal sensory integration, is a key brain region involved in synaesthesia (Muggleton & others, 2007; Mulvenna & Walsh, 2006).

Phantom limb pain might be another example of confused senses. As many as 95 percent of individuals who have lost an arm or a leg report alarming and puzzling pain in the amputated arm or leg. Although the limb that contains the sensory receptors is gone, the areas of the brain and nervous system that received information from those receptors are still there, causing confusion (Casale & others, 2009; Kollewe & others, 2009). Amputee veterans of combat in Iraq and Afghanistan have found some relief in an unexpected place: looking in a mirror. In this treatment, individuals place a mirror in front of their existing limb and move the limb around while watching the mirror. So, if a person's left leg has been amputated, the mirror is placed so that the right leg is seen moving in the mirror where the left leg would be if it had not been amputated. This procedure seems to trick the brain into perceiving the missing limb as still there, allowing it to make sense of incoming sensation (Young, 2008). The success of this mirror therapy demonstrates how our senses cooperate to produce experience—how the bottom-up processes (the incoming messages from the missing limb) and the top-down processes (the brain's efforts to make sense of these) work together.

In the brain, nearly all sensory signals go through the thalamus, the brain's relay station, described in Chapter 2. From the thalamus, the signals go to the sensory areas of the cerebral cortex, where they are modified and spread throughout a vast network of neurons.

Recall from Chapter 2 that certain areas of the cerebral cortex are specialized to handle different sensory functions. Visual information is processed mainly in the occipital lobes; hearing in the temporal lobes; and pain, touch, and temperature in the parietal lobes. Keep in mind, however, that the interactions and pathways of sensory information are complex, and the brain often must coordinate extensive information and interpret it (Dawson & List, 2009).

An important part of perception is interpreting the sensory messages (Schultz-Bosbach, Tausche, & Weiss, 2009). Many top-down factors determine this meaning, including signals from different parts of the brain, prior learning, the person's goals, and his or her degree of arousal (Hackley, 2009; Villemure & Bushnell, 2009). Moving in the opposite direction, bottom-up signals from a sensory area may help other parts of the brain maintain arousal, form an image of where the body is in space, or regulate movement (Stuss, 2006).

Thresholds

Any sensory system must be able to detect varying degrees of energy. This energy can take the form of light, sound, chemical, or mechanical stimulation. How much of a stimulus is necessary for you to see, hear, taste, smell, or feel something? What is the lowest possible amount of stimulation that will still be detected?

Absolute Threshold   One way to think about the lowest limits of perception is to assume that there is an **absolute threshold,** or minimum amount of stimulus energy that a person can detect. When the energy of a stimulus falls below this absolute threshold, we cannot detect its presence; when the energy of the stimulus rises above the absolute threshold, we can detect the stimulus (Markessis & others, 2009). As an example, find a clock that ticks; put it on a table and walk far enough away that you no longer hear it. Then gradually move toward the clock. At some point, you will begin to hear it ticking. Hold your position and notice that occasionally the ticking fades, and you may have to move forward to reach the threshold; at other times, it may become loud, and you can move backward.

In this experiment, if you measure your absolute threshold several times, you likely will record several different distances for detecting the stimulus. For example, the first time you try it, you might hear the ticking at 25 feet from the clock. However, you probably will not hear it every time at 25 feet. Maybe you hear it only 38 percent of the time at this distance, but you hear it 50 percent of the time at 20 feet away and 65 percent of the time at 15 feet. People have different thresholds. Some have better hearing than others, and some have better vision. Figure 3.3 shows one person's measured absolute threshold for detecting a clock's ticking sound. Psychologists have

absolute threshold The minimum amount of stimulus energy that a person can detect.

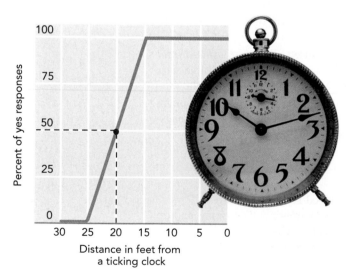

FIGURE 3.3

Measuring Absolute Threshold Absolute threshold is the minimum amount of energy we can detect. To measure absolute threshold, psychologists have arbitrarily decided to use the criterion of detecting the stimulus 50 percent of the time. In this graph, the person's absolute threshold for detecting the ticking clock is at a distance of 20 feet.

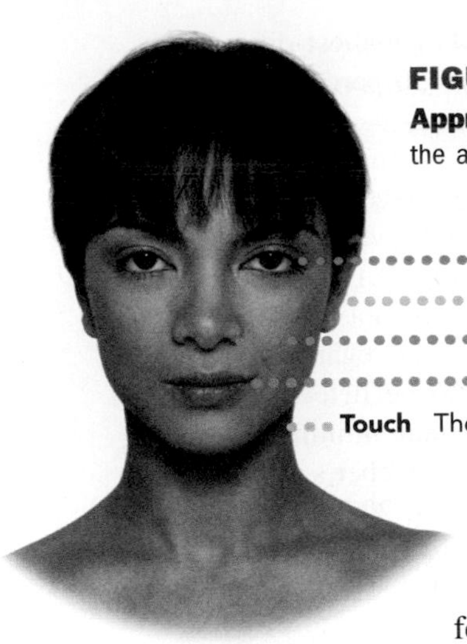

FIGURE 3.4

Approximate Absolute Thresholds for Five Senses These thresholds show the amazing power of our senses to detect even very slight variations in the environment.

Vision A candle flame at 30 miles on a dark, clear night

Hearing A ticking clock at 20 feet under quiet conditions

Smell One drop of perfume diffused throughout three rooms

Taste A teaspoon of sugar in 2 gallons of water

Touch The wing of a fly falling on your neck from a distance of 1 centimeter

arbitrarily decided that absolute threshold is the point at which the individual detects the stimulus 50 percent of the time—in this case, 20 feet away. Using the same clock, another person might have a measured absolute threshold of 26 feet, and yet another, 18 feet. Figure 3.4 lists the approximate absolute thresholds of five senses.

Under ideal circumstances, our senses have very low absolute thresholds, so we can be remarkably good at detecting small amounts of stimulus energy. You might be surprised to learn that the human eye can see a candle flame at 30 miles on a dark, clear night. However, our environment seldom gives us ideal conditions with which to detect stimuli. If the night were cloudy or the air smoky, for example, you would have to be much closer to see the candle flame. In addition, other lights on the horizon—car or house lights—would hinder your ability to detect the candle's flicker. **Noise** is the term given to irrelevant and competing stimuli—not just sounds but any distracting stimuli for our senses (Brown & van Kamp, 2009; van Kempen & others, 2009).

noise
Irrelevant and competing stimuli—not only sounds but also any distracting stimuli for our senses.

Subliminal Perception

Can sensations that occur below our absolute threshold affect us without our being aware of them? **Subliminal perception** refers to the detection of information below the level of conscious awareness. In 1957, James Vicary, an advertising executive, announced that he was able to increase popcorn and soft drink sales by secretly flashing the words "EAT POPCORN" and "DRINK COKE" on a movie screen in a local theater (Weir, 1984). Vicary's claims were a hoax, but people have continued to wonder whether behavior can be influenced by stimuli that are presented so quickly that we cannot perceive them.

subliminal perception
The detection of information below the level of conscious awareness.

Studies have shown that the brain responds to information that is presented below the conscious threshold, and such information can also influence behavior (Dupoux, de Gardelle, & Kouider, 2008; Tsushima, Sasaki, & Watanabe, 2006). In one study (Strahan, Spencer, & Zanna, 2002), researchers randomly assigned participants to observe either words related to being thirsty or control words of the same length being flashed on a computer screen for 16 milliseconds while they performed an unrelated task. All of the participants thought they were participating in a taste test study, and all were thirsty. None of the participants reported seeing the flashed words, but when given a chance to drink a beverage afterward, those who had seen thirst-related words drank more. Research has also supported the notion that people's performance on learning tasks is affected by stimuli that are too faint to be recognized at a conscious level (Cleeremans & Sarrazin, 2007). We examine these effects further in Chapter 6's discussion of priming.

Notice that this is an experiment. Those who saw the "thirsty words" were the experimental group, and those who saw the control words were the control group. Now, why were they randomly assigned to conditions?

Difference Threshold

In addition to studying how much energy is required for a stimulus to be detected, psychologists investigate the degree of *difference* that must exist between two stimuli before the difference is detected. This is the **difference threshold,** or *just noticeable difference.* An artist might detect the difference between two similar shades of color. A fashion designer might notice a difference in the texture of two fabrics. How different must the colors and textures be for someone to say, "These

difference threshold
The degree of difference that must exist between two stimuli before the difference is detected.

are different"? Like the absolute threshold, the difference threshold is the smallest difference in stimulation required to discriminate one stimulus from another 50 percent of the time.

Difference thresholds increase as a stimulus becomes stronger. That means that at very low levels of stimulation, small changes can be detected, but at very high levels, small changes are less noticeable. When music is playing softly, you may notice when your roommate increases the volume by even a small amount. If, however, he or she turns the volume up an equal amount when the music is playing very loudly, you may not notice. More than 150 years ago, E. H. Weber, a German physiologist, noticed that regardless of their magnitude, two stimuli must differ by a constant proportion to be detected. **Weber's law** is the principle that two stimuli must differ by a constant minimum percentage (rather than a constant amount) to be perceived as different. Weber's law generally holds true (Gao & Vasconcelos, 2009; Jimenez-Sanchez & others, 2009). For example, we add 1 candle to 20 candles and notice a difference in the brightness of the candles; we add 1 candle to 120 candles and do not notice a difference, but we would notice the difference if we added 6 candles to 120 candles.

Weber's law
The principle that two stimuli must differ by a constant minimum percentage (rather than a constant amount) to be perceived as different.

Perceiving Sensory Stimuli

As we just saw, the perception of stimuli is influenced by more than the characteristics of the environmental stimuli themselves. Two important factors in perceiving sensory stimuli are attention and perceptual set.

Attention   The world holds a lot of information to perceive. At this moment you are perceiving the letters and words that make up this sentence. Now gaze around you and fix your eyes on something other than this book. Afterward, curl up the toes on your right foot. In each of these circumstances, you engaged in **selective attention,** which involves focusing on a specific aspect of experience while ignoring others (Klumpp & Amir, 2009). A familiar example of selective attention is the ability to focus on one voice among many in a crowded airline terminal or noisy restaurant. Psychologists call this common occurrence the *cocktail party effect* (Kuyper, 1972).

selective attention
The act of focusing on a specific aspect of experience while ignoring others.

Not only is attention selective, but it also is *shiftable*. For example, you might be paying close attention to your instructor's lecture, but if the person next to you starts texting a friend, you might look to see what is going on over there. The fact that we can attend selectively to one stimulus and shift readily to another indicates that we must be monitoring many things at once.

Certain features of stimuli cause people to attend to them. Novel stimuli (those that are new, different, or unusual) often attract our attention. If a Ferrari convertible whizzes by, you are more likely to notice it than you would a Ford. Size, color, and movement also influence our attention. Objects that are large, vividly colored, or moving are more likely to grab our attention than objects that are small, dull-colored, or stationary.

Sometimes even very interesting stimuli can be missed, if our attention is otherwise occupied. *Inattentional blindness* (Mack & Rock, 1998) refers to the failure to detect unexpected events when attention is engaged by a task. When we are working intently on something, such as finding a seat in a packed movie theater, we might not even see an unusual stimulus, such as a friend waving to us in the crowd. Research conducted by Daniel Simons and Christopher Chabris (1999) provides a remarkable example of inattentional blindness. In that study, participants were asked to watch a video of two teams playing basketball. The participants were instructed to closely count the number of passes thrown by each team. During the video, a small woman dressed in a gorilla suit walked through the action, clearly visible for 5 seconds. Surprisingly, over half of the participants (who were apparently deeply engaged in the counting task) never noticed the gorilla. Inattentional blindness is more likely to occur when a task is difficult (Macdonald & Lavie, 2008) and when the distracting stimulus is very different from stimuli that are relevant to the task at hand (White & Aimola Davies, 2008).

When they later saw the video (without having to count passes), many of the participants were shocked and couldn't believe they missed a gorilla in their midst.

Perceptual Set Place your hand over the playing cards on the right in the illustration and look at the playing cards on the left. As quickly as you can, count how many aces of spades you see. Then place your hand over the cards on the left and count the number of aces of spades among the cards on the right.

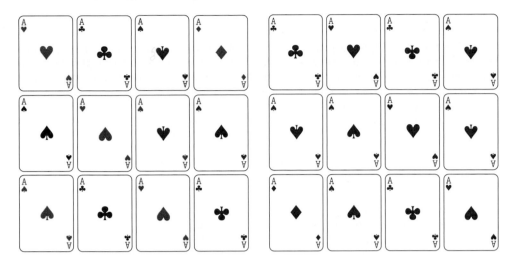

Most people report that they see two or three aces of spades in the set of cards on the left. However, if you look closely, you will see that there are five. Two of the aces of spades are black and three are red. When people look at the set of cards on the right, they are more likely to count five aces of spades. Why do we perceive the two sets of cards differently? We expect the ace of spades to be black because it is always black in a regular deck of cards. We do not expect red spades, so we skip right over the red ones: Expectations influence perceptions.

Psychologists refer to a predisposition or readiness to perceive something in a particular way as a **perceptual set.** Perceptual sets act as "psychological" filters in processing information about the environment (Fei-Fei & others, 2007). Perceptual sets reflect top-down influences on perception. Interestingly, young children are more accurate at the task involving the ace of spades than adults are. Why? Because they have not built up the perceptual set that the ace of spades is black. To read further about how perceptual sets can influence perceptions and subsequent actions, see the Intersection.

perceptual set
A predisposition or readiness to perceive something in a particular way.

Eating strawberries, cherries, and red popsicles— children sometimes get the idea that red things taste sweet. Then they get a taste of red beets. It's always a fun moment when top-down processing meets bottom-up sensation.

Sensory Adaptation

Turning out the lights in your bedroom at night, you stumble across the room to your bed, blind to the objects around you. Gradually the objects reappear and become clearer. The ability of the visual system to adjust to a darkened room is an example of **sensory adaptation**—a change in the responsiveness of the sensory system based on the average level of surrounding stimulation (Elliott & others, 2009; Preston, Kourtzi, & Welchman, 2009). You have experienced sensory adaptation countless times in your life—adapting to the temperature of a shower, to the water in an initially "freezing" swimming pool, and to the smell of the Thanksgiving dinner that is wonderful to you as an arriving guest but almost undetectable to the cook who spent all day laboring over it. When you first enter a room, you might be bothered by the hum of the air conditioner or the buzz of the fluorescent lights, but after a while you get used to these mild irritations. That is adaptation.

In the example of adapting to the dark, when you turn out the lights, everything is black. Conversely, when you step out into the bright sunshine after spending time in a dark basement, light floods your eyes and everything appears light. These momentary blips in sensation arise because adaptation takes time. Even though the pupil of the eye opens and closes rather rapidly when light levels change, the sensory receptors in your visual system adjust their response rates on the basis of the average light level of the surrounding room. This

sensory adaptation
A change in the responsiveness of the sensory system based on the average level of surrounding stimulation.

intersection

At midnight on February 4, 1999, in New York City, a 22-year-old Black man named Amadou Diallo was returning home. He was approached by four White plainclothes police officers, who told him to stop. As Diallo reached into his pocket, one of the officers

Perception and Social Psychology: Was That a Gun or a Cell Phone?

shouted "Gun!" setting off a flurry of 41 gunshots. Nineteen bullets hit Diallo, killing him. The object in his hand was in fact not a gun but his wallet. In Shreveport, Louisiana, in March 2003, Marquise Hudspeth, a 25-year-old African American, was shot and killed by three White police officers who mistook his cell phone for a gun.

In both cases, the police officers were cleared of wrongdoing. Juries and judges concluded that they had made terrible but honest mistakes. Could it be a coincidence, though, that the unarmed dead men were all African Americans? What role did ethnicity play in these "honest" perceptual mistakes?

Social psychologist Keith Payne (2001, 2008) has examined how ethnicity might influence the tendency to misperceive harmless objects such as wallets and cell phones as handguns. Participants were told that they would see two pictures on a computer screen. Their job was to decide, as quickly and accurately as possible, whether the second picture was a gun or a tool. The first picture—always an image of an African American man or a White man—cued the participants that the judgment was coming. After seeing an African American man's face, participants were quicker to recognize guns accurately in the second picture. In a second study using the same sequence of images, participants were required to respond very quickly. Here, participants were more likely to misperceive tools as guns when the tools were shown after a picture of an African American man.

Similar research has employed video games in which participants must decide whether to shoot or not shoot a potential suspect who is holding either a gun or a harmless object. Both African American and White participants have been found to shoot more quickly at an armed African American man and to decide more quickly not to shoot at an unarmed White man (Correll & others, 2002). Because African Americans and Whites were equally disposed to react in these ways, the researchers suggested that the automatic use of knowledge of stereotypes—or generalizations—about different ethnicities explains the tendency to let ethnicity guide the decision to shoot or not shoot (Payne, 2008).

In another study, 48 police officers, Whites and African Americans, played a video game in which they had to decide whether to shoot or not shoot the suspects (Plant & Peruche, 2005). The suspects were African American or White and were holding guns or other objects. The researchers were interested in whether *practice* with the game—in which African American and White suspects were randomly determined to be holding a gun or another object—would help the officers become less biased in their perceptions. In the early trials the officers were more likely to mistakenly shoot an unarmed suspect when he was African American. By the experiment's end, the officers treated African American and White suspects with equal restraint.

Amadou Diallo's life was cut short because someone "saw" a gun where there was only a wallet. Although the mistake police made may have been honest, it was not inevitable. Cases such as Diallo's highlight the crucial role of cultural beliefs and the social world in the process of perception. A society that does not view ethnic minority individuals as dangerous, aggressive, or likely to be criminals might be less inclined to misperceive a wallet or cell phone as a weapon—and might avoid tragedies such as the Diallo killing.

What do tragedies like the Diallo case tell you about the influence of ethnicity in U.S. society?

Why do you think that even African American police officers were more likely to shoot an unarmed African American?

---

adaptation takes longer than it does for the pupil to adjust. While these mechanisms allow the visual system to preserve the high level of contrast in our vision over an extremely large range of background illumination conditions, the price we pay for our ability to adapt to the average light level is *time*. Driving out of a dark tunnel under a mountain into the glistening and blinding reflection of the sun off the snow reminds us of this trade-off.

Extrasensory Perception

Our examination of the relationship between sensation and perception may leave you wondering, is there such a thing as ESP? ESP—*extrasensory perception*—means that a person can read another person's mind or perceive future events in the absence of concrete sensory input. More than half of adults in the United States believe in ESP (Moore, 2005), and many researchers have studied it. As an example of ESP, you might recall stories about someone's "just knowing" that a friend was in trouble and later finding out that at the moment of "knowing," the friend was in a car accident. Such an experience can be fascinating, spooky, and even thrilling, but does it reflect ESP—or simply coincidence?

There are many reasons to question the existence of ESP. Think about ESP in the ways we have considered sensation and perception so far. What sort of energy transmits psychic messages? Where do those messages register? Remember that scientists evaluate evidence critically, rely on research to draw conclusions, and expect that if a conclusion is valid, it will be reproducible. From a scientific perspective, despite some 75 years of research, no evidence supports the existence of ESP (French & others, 2008; Wiseman & Watt, 2006).

Recently, Samuel Moulton and Stephen Kosslyn (2008) conducted a fascinating study to test for the existence of ESP. The researchers went directly to the source: the brain. Using fMRI, they scanned the brains of individuals when they were shown (1) pictures that had been previously "sent" to them, mentally, by a partner, and (2) pictures that had not been thus sent. Did the brains respond differently to images that had been sent via ESP compared to images that had not been sent?

Moulton and Kosslyn (2008) designed the study to enhance the chances that if ESP exists, they would find it. They selected participant pairs who were related to each other biologically or emotionally (twins, sisters, mothers and sons, close friends, and romantic couples). The stimuli were emotionally evocative pictures (for example, a picture of eye surgery or a couple kissing). One member of each pair was given the role of "sender," and the other got the role of "receiver." The sender sat in a room alone, and the receiver was placed in the brain scanner. At the beginning of the study, senders were told to try their best to "send" the images they saw, mentally, to their partner in the next room. Then the receivers' brains were scanned as they were shown two images (the one that had been sent via ESP and a control image). The receivers also tried to guess which of the two images was the one that the partner had "sent" to them. To enhance motivation, receivers received a dollar for every correct response. The results? First, receivers were no more likely than chance to guess correctly which images had been sent. Second, their brains did not differ when they were exposed to ESP stimuli versus other stimuli, and this result suggested no special effects of ESP.

In the absence of empirical data for the existence of ESP, why does it remain so fascinating? One possibility is that human beings are not very good at dealing with random experiences. We find ourselves making up interesting stories to account for these unusual events. However, even really fun stories do not necessarily reflect reality. Sometimes believing that we can foretell the future brings a sense of comfort and predictability to the world.

www.CartoonStock.com

Note that the operational definition of the dependent variable here was any brain differences at all. The researchers looked at more and less activation of a variety of brain areas—and still, no dice. As the researchers noted, "We found nothing. But we found nothing in an interesting way!"

Maybe you've had an experience that seems to demonstrate ESP, such as thinking about a friend and then having her phone at that moment. You might ask yourself, how many times have I had similar thoughts without my friend's calling me? You probably would not recall those other occasions for the very reason that a phone call didn't follow them.

1. Every day, you see, hear, smell, taste, and feel stimuli from the outside world. Collecting data about that world is the function of _____, and interpreting the data collected is the function of _____.
   A. the brain; the spinal cord
   B. the spinal cord; the brain
   C. sensation; perception
   D. perception; sensation

2. The main classes into which the sense organs and sensory receptors fall include all of the following *except*
   A. chemoreception.
   B. electroreception.
   C. photoreception.
   D. mechanoreception.

3. An architect is designing apartments and wants them to be soundproof. She asks a psychologist what the smallest amount of sound is that can be heard. Her question is most related to
   A. the absolute threshold.
   B. the difference threshold.
   C. Weber's law.
   D. the sensory receptors.

Apply It! 4. Trina, a first-year college student, goes home at Thanksgiving break after being away from home (for the first time) for three months. She feels as if she has changed a lot, but her parents still treat her like a high school girl. At Thanksgiving dinner she confronts them, bursting out, "Stop top-down processing me!" Her parents think Trina has lost her mind. Which of the following explains her eruption?
   A. Trina feels that her parents are judging her sophisticated college ways too harshly.
   B. Trina probably ate too much turkey.
   C. Trina feels that her parents have spent too much time analyzing her behavior.
   D. Trina believes that her parents are letting their preconceived ideas of who she is prevent them from seeing her as the person she has become.

2 The Visual System

When Michael May of Davis, California, was 3 years old, an accident left him visually impaired, with only the ability to perceive the difference between night and day. He lived a rich, full life, marrying and having children, founding a successful company, and becoming an expert skier. Twenty-five years passed before doctors transplanted stem cells into May's right eye, a new procedure that gave him partial sight (Kurson, 2007). May can now see; his right eye is functional and allows him to detect color and negotiate the world without the use of a cane or reliance on his seeing-eye dog. His visual experience remains unusual, however: He sees the world as if it is an abstract painting. He can catch a ball thrown to him by his sons, but he cannot recognize his wife's face. His brain has to work at interpreting the new information that his right eye is providing. May's experience highlights the intimate connection between the brain and the sense organs in producing perception. Vision is a remarkable process that involves the brain's interpretation of the visual information sent from the eyes. We now explore the physical foundations of the visual system.

The Visual Stimulus and the Eye

Our ability to detect visual stimuli depends on the sensitivity of our eyes to differences in light.

Light   *Light* is a form of electromagnetic energy that can be described in terms of wavelengths. Light travels through space in waves. The *wavelength* of light is the distance from the peak of one wave to the peak of the next. Wavelengths of visible light range from about 400 to 700 nanometers (a nanometer is 1 billionth of a meter and is abbreviated nm). The wavelength of light that is reflected from a stimulus determines its *hue* or color.

Outside the range of visible light are longer radio and infrared radiation waves and shorter ultraviolet and X rays (Figure 3.5). These other forms of electromagnetic energy continually bombard us, but we do not see them.

We can also describe waves of light in terms of their height, or *amplitude,* which determines the brightness of the stimulus. Finally, the *purity* of the wavelengths—whether they are all the same or a mix of waves—determines the perceived *saturation,* or richness, of a visual stimulus (Figure 3.6). The color tree shown in Figure 3.7 can help you to understand saturation. Colors that are very pure have no white light in them. They are located on the outside of the color tree. Notice how the closer we get to the center of

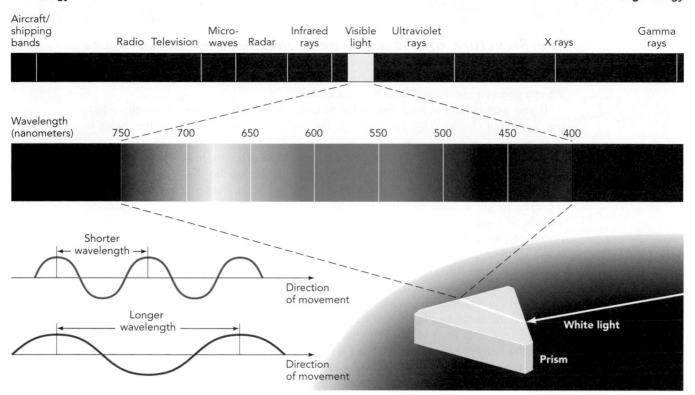

Longer Wavelengths
Low energy

Shorter Wavelengths
High energy

Aircraft/ shipping bands — Radio — Television — Micro-waves — Radar — Infrared rays — Visible light — Ultraviolet rays — X rays — Gamma rays

Wavelength (nanometers)   750   700   650   600   550   500   450   400

Shorter wavelength

Direction of movement

Longer wavelength

Direction of movement

White light

Prism

FIGURE 3.5

The Electromagnetic Spectrum and Visible Light (*Top*) Visible light is only a narrow band in the electromagnetic spectrum. Visible light wavelengths range from about 400 to 700 nanometers. X rays are much shorter, radio waves much longer. (*Bottom*) The two graphs show how waves vary in length between successive peaks. Shorter wavelengths are higher in frequency, as reflected in blue colors; longer wavelengths are lower in frequency, as reflected in red colors.

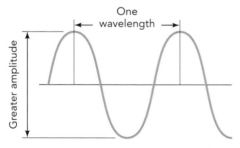

Light waves of greater amplitude make up brighter light.

One wavelength

Greater amplitude

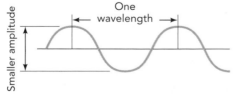

Light waves of smaller amplitude make up dimmer light.

One wavelength

Smaller amplitude

FIGURE 3.6
Light Waves of Varying Amplitude The top graph might suggest a spotlight on a concert stage; the bottom, a candlelit dinner.

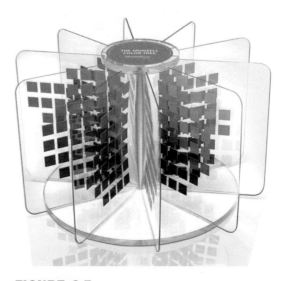

FIGURE 3.7
A Color Tree Showing Color's Three Dimensions: Hue, Saturation, and Brightness Hue is represented around the color tree, saturation horizontally, and brightness vertically.

the color tree, the more white light has been added to the single wavelength of a particular color. In other words, the deep colors at the edge fade into pastel colors toward the center.

The Structure of the Eye

The eye, like a camera, is constructed to get the best possible picture of the world. An accurate picture is in focus, is not too dark or too light, and has good contrast between the dark and light parts. Each of several structures in the eye plays an important role in this process.

If you look closely at your eyes in the mirror, you will notice three parts—the sclera, iris, and pupil (Figure 3.8). The *sclera* is the white, outer part of the eye that helps to maintain the shape of the eye and to protect it from injury. The *iris* is the colored part of the eye, which might be light blue in one individual and dark brown in another. The *pupil,* which appears black, is the opening in the center of the iris. The iris contains muscles that control the size of the pupil and, hence, the amount of light that gets into the eye. To get a good picture of the world, the eye needs to be able to adjust the amount of light that enters. In this sense, the pupil acts like the aperture of a camera, opening to let in more light when it is needed and closing to let in less light when there is too much.

Two structures bring the image into focus: the *cornea,* a clear membrane just in front of the eye, and the *lens,* a transparent and somewhat flexible, disklike structure filled with a gelatin-like material. The function of both of these structures is to bend the light falling on the surface of the eye just enough to focus it at the back. The curved surface of the cornea does most of this bending, while the lens fine-tunes things. When you are looking at faraway objects, the lens has a relatively flat shape because the light reaching the eye from faraway objects is parallel and the bending power of the cornea is sufficient to keep things in focus. However, the light reaching the eye from objects that are close is more scattered, so more bending of the light is required to achieve focus.

Without this ability of the lens to change its curvature, the eye would have a tough time focusing on close objects such as reading material. As we get older, the lens loses its flexibility and hence its ability to change from its normal flattened shape to the rounder shape needed to bring close objects into focus. That is why many people with normal vision throughout their young adult lives require reading glasses as they age.

retina
The multilayered light-sensitive surface in the eye that records electromagnetic energy and converts it to neural impulses for processing in the brain.

The parts of the eye we have considered so far work together to give us the sharpest picture of the world. This effort would be useless, however, without a vehicle for recording the images the eyes take of the world—in essence, the film of the camera. Photographic film is made of a material that responds to light. At the back of the eye is the eye's "film," the multilayered **retina,** which is the light-sensitive surface that records

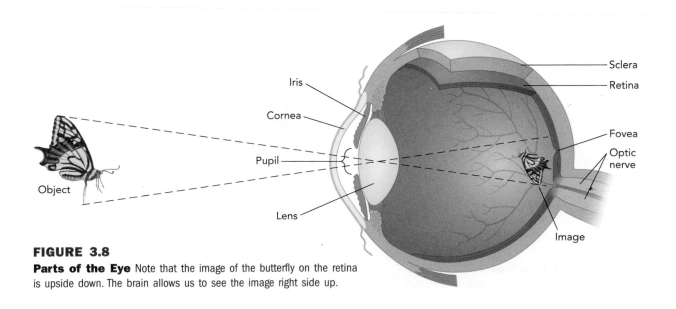

FIGURE 3.8
Parts of the Eye Note that the image of the butterfly on the retina is upside down. The brain allows us to see the image right side up.

electromagnetic energy and converts it to neural impulses for processing in the brain. The analogy between the retina and film only goes so far, however. The retina is amazingly complex and elegantly designed. It is, in fact, the primary mechanism of sight. Even after decades of intense study, the full marvel of this structure is far from understood (Field & Chichilnisky, 2007; van Hateren, 2007).

The human retina has approximately 126 million receptor cells. They turn the electromagnetic energy of light into a form of energy that the nervous system can process. There are two kinds of visual receptor cells: rods and cones. Rods and cones differ both in how they respond to light and in their patterns of distribution on the surface of the retina (Ramon, Mao, & Ridge, 2009; Warrant, 2009). **Rods** are the receptors in the retina that are sensitive to light, but they are not very useful for color vision. Rods function well under low illumination; they are hard at work at night. Humans have about 120 million rods. **Cones** are the receptors that we use for color perception. Like rods, cones are light-sensitive. However, they require a larger amount of light to respond than the rods do, so they operate best in daylight or under high illumination. There are about 6 million cone cells in human eyes. Figure 3.9 shows what rods and cones look like.

The most important part of the retina is the *fovea*, a tiny area in the center of the retina at which vision is at its best (see Figure 3.8). The fovea contains only cones and is vital to many visual tasks. Rods are found almost everywhere on the retina except in the fovea. Rods give us the ability to detect fainter spots of light on the peripheral retina than at the fovea. Thus, if you want to see a very faint star, you should gaze slightly away from it, to allow your rods to do their work.

Figure 3.10 shows how the rods and cones at the back of the retina convert light into electrochemical impulses. The signal is transmitted to the *bipolar cells* and then moves on to another layer of specialized cells called *ganglion cells* (tom Dieck & Brandstatter, 2006). The axons of the ganglion cells make up the **optic nerve,** which carries the visual information to the brain for further processing.

One place on the retina contains neither rods nor cones. This area, the *blind spot,* is the place on the retina where the optic nerve leaves the eye on its way to the brain

rods
The receptor cells in the retina that are sensitive to light but not very useful for color vision.

cones
The receptor cells in the retina that allow for color perception.

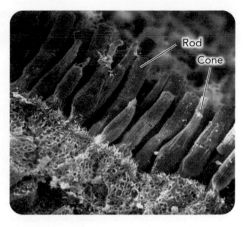

FIGURE 3.9
Rods and Cones In real life, rods and cones look somewhat like stumps and corncobs.

To get a sense of how well the cones in the fovea work, try reading out of the corner of your eye. It is difficult because the fovea doesn't get to do the reading for you.

optic nerve
The structure at the back of the eye, made up of axons of the ganglion cells, that carries visual information to the brain for further processing.

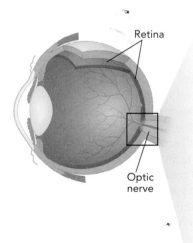

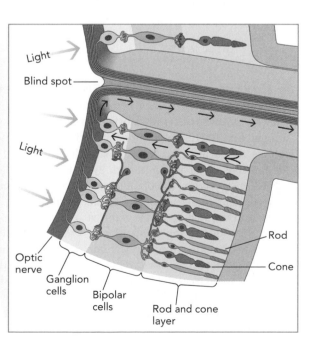

FIGURE 3.10
Direction of Light in the Retina After light passes through the cornea, pupil, and lens, it falls on the retina. Three layers of specialized cells in the retina convert the image into a neural signal that can be transmitted to the brain. First, light triggers a reaction in the rods and cones at the back of the retina, transducing light energy into electrochemical neural impulses. The neural impulses activate the bipolar cells, which in turn activate the ganglion cells. Then light information is transmitted to the optic nerve, which conveys it to the brain. The arrows indicate the sequence in which light information moves in the retina.

FIGURE 3.11
The Eye's Blind Spot There is a normal blind spot in your eye, a small area where the optic nerve leads to the brain. To find your blind spot, hold this book at arm's length, cover your left eye, and stare at the red pepper on the left with your right eye. Move the book slowly toward you until the yellow pepper disappears. To find the blind spot in your left eye, cover your right eye, stare at the yellow pepper, and adjust the book until the red pepper disappears.

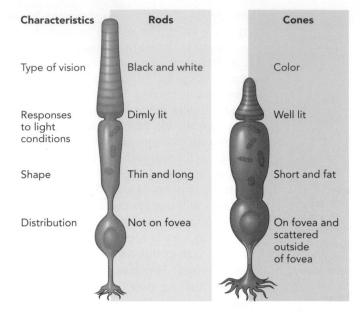

FIGURE 3.12
Characteristics of Rods and Cones Rods and cones differ in shape, location, and function.

Characteristics	Rods	Cones
Type of vision	Black and white	Color
Responses to light conditions	Dimly lit	Well lit
Shape	Thin and long	Short and fat
Distribution	Not on fovea	On fovea and scattered outside of fovea

Keep in mind that the visual information in the retina that is closest to the nose crosses over, and the visual information on the outer side of the retina stays on that side of the brain.

(see Figure 3.10). We cannot see anything that reaches only this part of the retina. To prove to yourself that you have a blind spot, look at Figure 3.11. Once you have seen the yellow pepper disappear, you have probably noticed it took a while to succeed at this task. Now shut one eye and look around. You see a perfectly continuous picture of the world around you; there is no blind spot. This is a great example of top-down processing and a demonstration of the constructive aspect of perception. Your brain fills in the gap for you (the one that ought to be left by your blind spot) with some pretty good guesses about what must be in that spot, like a creative artist painting in the blind spot. Figure 3.12 summarizes the characteristics of rods and cones.

Visual Processing in the Brain

The eyes are just the beginning of visual perception. The next step occurs when neural impulses generated in the retina are dispatched to the brain for analysis and integration.

The optic nerve leaves the eye, carrying information about light toward the brain. Light travels in a straight line; therefore, stimuli in the left visual field are registered in the right half of the retina in both eyes, and stimuli in the right visual field are registered in the left half of the retina in both eyes (Figure 3.13). In the brain, at a point called the *optic chiasm,* the optic nerve fibers divide, and approximately half of the nerve fibers cross over the midline of the brain. As a result, the visual information originating in the right halves of the two retinas is transmitted to the right side of the occipital lobe in the cerebral cortex, and the visual information coming from the left halves of the retinas is transmitted to the left side of the occipital lobe. These crossings mean that what we see in the left side of our visual field is registered in the right side of the brain, and what we see in the right visual field is registered in the left side of the brain (see Figure 3.13). Then this information is processed and combined into a recognizable object or scene in the visual cortex.

Stop and look closely at Figure 3.13. This is one place where things can get confusing. Notice that the blonde runner on the right side of the figure is detected on the left sides of the retinas and that the information then goes to the occipital lobe in the left hemisphere.

The Visual Cortex

The *visual cortex,* located in the occipital lobe at the back of the brain, is the part of the cerebral cortex involved in vision. Most visual information travels to the primary visual cortex, where it is processed, before moving to other visual areas for further analysis (Downing, 2009; Jermakowicz & others, 2009).

An important aspect of visual information processing is the specialization of neurons. Like the cells in the retina, many cells in the primary visual cortex are highly specialized (Lee & Maunsell, 2009). **Feature detectors** are neurons in the brain's visual system that respond to particular features of a stimulus. David Hubel and Torsten Wiesel (1963) won a Nobel Prize for their research on feature detectors. By recording the activity of a *single* neuron in a cat while it looked at patterns that varied in size, shape, color, and movement, the researchers found that the visual cortex has neurons that are individually sensitive to different types of lines and angles. One neuron might show a sudden burst of activity when stimulated by lines of a particular angle; another neuron might fire only when moving stimuli appear; yet another neuron might be stimulated when the object in the visual field has a combination of certain angles, sizes, and shapes.

Hubel and Wiesel also noted that when deprived of certain types of visual stimulation early on, kittens lost the ability to perceive these patterns. This finding suggested that there might be a critical period in visual development and that the brain requires stimulation in its efforts to delegate its resources to different perceptual tasks. The brain "learns" to perceive through experience. This explains Michael May's unusual experience, described at the beginning of our examination of the visual system. Once deprived of stimulation, the brain will redistribute its resources to other tasks.

feature detectors Neurons in the brain's visual system that respond to particular features of a stimulus.

Parallel Processing

Sensory information travels quickly through the brain because of **parallel processing,** the simultaneous distribution of information across different neural pathways (Joubert & others, 2008). A sensory system designed to process information about sensory qualities serially or consecutively (such as processing first the shapes of images, then their colors, then their movements, and finally their locations) would be too slow to keep us current with a rapidly changing world. To function in the world, we need to "see" all of these characteristics at once, which is parallel processing. There is some evidence suggesting that parallel processing also occurs for sensations of touch and hearing (Recanzone & Sutter, 2008).

parallel processing The simultaneous distribution of information across different neural pathways.

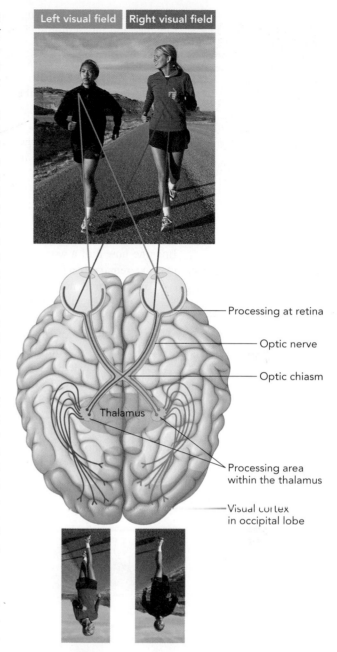

FIGURE 3.13

Visual Pathways to and Through the Brain Light from each side of the visual field falls on the opposite side of each eye's retina. Visual information then travels along the optic nerve to the optic chasm, where most of the visual information crosses over to the other side of the brain. From there visual information goes to the occipital lobe at the rear of the brain. All these crossings mean that what we see in the left side of our visual field (here, the shorter, dark-haired woman) is registered in the right side of our brain, and what we see in the right visual field (the taller, blonde woman) is registered in the left side of our brain.

Binding

Connections between neural pathways provide us with a unified sense of what we are seeing. For example, looking at a child's face, you see the pieces but also the whole. Even your perception of the child's nose or eyes is embedded in your perception of the overall face.

One of the most exciting topics in visual perception today is **binding,** the bringing together and integration of what is processed by different pathways or cells (Seymour & others, 2009; Shipp & others, 2009). Binding involves the coupling of the activity of various cells and pathways. Through binding, you can integrate information about the shape of the child's mouth, eyes, and nose; her skin color; and whether she is smiling into a complete image in the cerebral cortex. Exactly how binding occurs is a mystery that fascinates neuroscientists to this day (McMahon & Olson, 2009).

Researchers have found that all the neurons throughout pathways that are activated by a visual object pulse together at the same frequency (Engel & Singer, 2001). Within the vast network of cells in the cerebral cortex, this set of neurons appears to *bind* together all the features of the objects into a unified perception.

Color Vision

If you've seen The Wizard of Oz, you might remember that goose-bumps moment when Dorothy steps out of her house and the black-and-white of Kansas gives way to the Technicolor glory of Oz.

Imagine how dull a world without color would be. Art museums are filled with paintings that are remarkable for their use of color, and flowers would lose much of their beauty if we could not see their rich hues. The ability to see color evolved because it provides many advantages to animals, including the ability to detect and discriminate among various objects (Blake & Sekuler, 2006). For example, the edibility of foods depends on ripeness, which is reflected in color.

Interestingly enough, perceiving color involves the brain's interpretation of the sensory neurons' responses to a stimulus, not the wavelengths of light themselves (Solomon & Lennie, 2007). When we see that grass is green, that is not because the grass emits a green light but because of the way the sensory receptors in the retina respond to the grass. The study of human color vision using psychological methods has a long and distinguished history. A full century before the methods existed to study the anatomical and neurophysiological bases of color perception, psychological studies had discovered many of the basic principles of our color vision system. These studies produced two main theories: trichromatic theory and opponent-process theory. Both turned out to be correct.

The **trichromatic theory** states that color perception is produced by three types of cone receptors in the retina that are particularly sensitive to different, but overlapping, ranges of wavelengths. The trichromatic theory of color vision was proposed by Thomas Young in 1802 and extended by Hermann von Helmholtz in 1852. The theory is based on the results of experiments on human color-matching abilities, which show that a person with normal vision can match any color in the spectrum by combining three other wavelengths. In this type of experiment, individuals are given a light of a single wavelength and are asked to combine three other single-wavelength lights to match the first light. They can do this by changing the relative intensities of the three lights until the color of the combination light is indistinguishable from the color of the first light. Young and Helmholtz reasoned that, if the combination of any three wavelengths of different intensities is indistinguishable from any single pure wavelength, the visual system must base its perception of color on the relative responses of three receptor systems.

The study of defective color vision, or *color blindness* (Figure 3.14), provides further support for the trichromatic theory. Complete color blindness is rare; most color-blind people, the vast majority of whom are men,

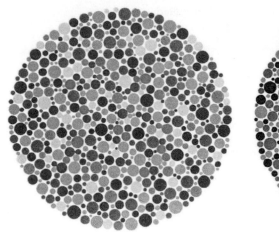
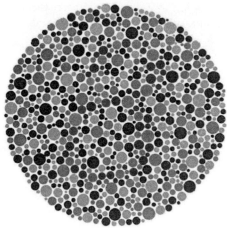

FIGURE 3.14
Examples of Stimuli Used to Test for Color Blindness People with normal vision see the number 16 in the left circle and the number 8 in the right circle. People with red-green color blindness may see just the 16, just the 8, or neither. A complete color-blindness assessment involves the use of 15 stimuli.

can see some colors but not others. The nature of color blindness depends on which of the three kinds of cones is inoperative (Deeb, 2006). The three cone systems are green, red, and blue. In the most common form of color blindness, the green cone system malfunctions in some way, rendering green indistinguishable from certain combinations of blue and red.

In 1878, the German physiologist Ewald Hering observed that some colors cannot exist together, whereas others can. For example, it is easy to imagine a greenish blue or a reddish yellow but nearly impossible to imagine a reddish green or a bluish yellow. Hering also noticed that trichromatic theory could not adequately explain *afterimages*, sensations that remain after a stimulus is removed (Figure 3.15 gives you a chance to experience an afterimage). Color afterimages are common and involve particular pairs of colors. If you look at red long enough, eventually a green afterimage will appear. If you look at yellow long enough, eventually a blue afterimage will appear.

Hering's observations led him to propose that there were not three types of color receptor cones (as proposed by trichromatic theory) but four, organized into complementary pairs: red-green and blue-yellow. Hering's view, **opponent-process theory,** states that cells in the visual system respond to red-green and blue-yellow colors; a given cell might be excited by red and inhibited by green, whereas another cell might be excited by yellow and inhibited by blue. Researchers have found that opponent-process theory does, indeed, explain afterimages (Hurvich & Jameson, 1969; Jameson & Hurvich, 1989). If you stare at red, for instance, your red-green system seems to "tire," and when you look away, it rebounds and gives you a green afterimage.

If the trichromatic theory of color perception is valid and we do, in fact, have three kinds of cone receptors like those predicted by Young and Helmholtz, then how can the

opponent-process theory
Theory stating that cells in the visual system respond to complementary pairs of red-green and blue-yellow colors; a given cell might be excited by red and inhibited by green, whereas another cell might be excited by yellow and inhibited by blue.

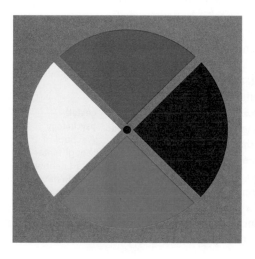

FIGURE 3.15
Negative Afterimage—Complementary Colors If you gaze steadily at the dot in the colored panel on the left for a few moments, then shift your gaze to the gray box on the right, you will see the original hues' complementary colors. The blue appears as yellow, the red as green, the green as red, and the yellow as blue. This pairing of colors has to do with the fact that color receptors in the eye are apparently sensitive as pairs: When one color is turned off (when you stop staring at the panel), the other color in the receptor is briefly turned on. The afterimage effect is especially noticeable with bright colors.

FIGURE 3.16
Trichromatic and Opponent-Process Theories: Transmission of Color Information in the Retina Cones responsive to green, blue, or red light form a trichromatic receptor system in the retina. As information is transmitted to the retina's ganglion cells, opponent-process cells are activated. As shown here, a retinal ganglion cell is inhibited by a green cone (−) and excited by a red cone (+), producing red-green color information.

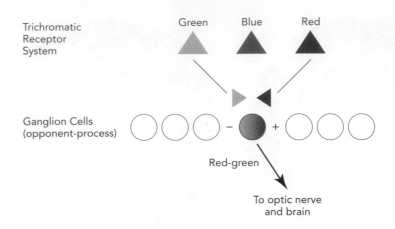

Trichromatic Receptor System

Green Blue Red

Ganglion Cells (opponent-process)

Red-green

To optic nerve and brain

In many instances, as with color vision, seemingly clashing theories or systems may work—and even work best together.

opponent-process theory also be accurate? The answer is that the red, blue, and green cones in the retina are connected to retinal ganglion cells in such a way that the three-color code is immediately translated into the opponent-process code (Figure 3.16). For example, a green cone might inhibit and a red cone might excite a particular ganglion cell. Thus, *both* the trichromatic and opponent-process theories are correct—the eye and the brain use both methods to code colors.

Perceiving Shape, Depth, Motion, and Constancy

Perceiving visual stimuli means organizing and interpreting the fragments of information that the eye sends to the visual cortex. Information about the dimensions of what we are seeing is critical to this process. Among these dimensions are shape, depth, motion, and constancy.

Shape Think about the visible world and its shapes—buildings against the sky, boats on the horizon, the letters on this page. We see these shapes because they are marked off from the rest of what we see by *contour,* a location at which a sudden change of brightness occurs (Norman & others, 2009). Now think about the letters on this page. As you look at the page, you see letters, which are shapes or figures, in a field or background—the white page. The **figure-ground relationship** is the principle by which we organize the perceptual field into stimuli that stand out (*figure*) and those that are left over (*background,* or *ground*). Generally this principle works well for us, but some figure-ground relationships are highly ambiguous, and it may be difficult to tell what is figure and what is ground. Figure 3.17 shows a well-known ambiguous figure-ground relationship. As you look at the figure, your perception is likely to shift from seeing two faces to seeing a single goblet.

The figure-ground relationship is a gestalt principle (Figure 3.18 shows others). *Gestalt* is German for "configuration" or "form," and **gestalt psychology** is a school of thought interested in how people naturally organize their perceptions according to certain patterns. One of gestalt psychology's main principles is that the whole is different from the sum of its parts. For example, when you watch a movie, the motion you see in the film cannot be found in the film itself; if you examine the film, you see only separate frames. When you watch the film, the frames move past a light source at a rate of many per second, and you perceive a whole that is very different from the separate frames that are the film's parts. Similarly, thousands of tiny pixels make up an image (whole) on a computer screen.

figure-ground relationship
The principle by which we organize the perceptual field into stimuli that stand out (figure) and those that are left over (ground).

gestalt psychology
A school of thought interested in how people naturally organize their perceptions according to certain patterns.

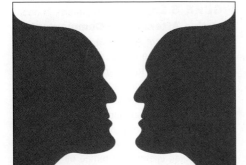

FIGURE 3.17
Reversible Figure-Ground Pattern Do you see the silhouette of a goblet or a pair of faces in profile?

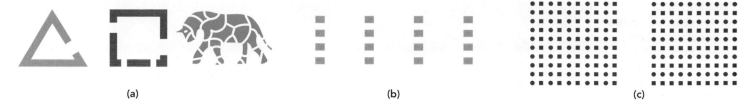

(a)   (b)   (c)

FIGURE 3.18

Gestalt Principles of Closure, Proximity, and Similarity (*a*) *Closure:* When we see disconnected or incomplete figures, we fill in the spaces and see them as complete figures. (*b*) *Proximity:* When we see objects that are near each other, they tend to be seen as a unit. You are likely to perceive the grouping as four columns of four squares, not one set of 16 squares. (*c*) *Similarity:* When we see objects that are similar to each other, they tend to be seen as a unit. Here, you are likely to see vertical columns of circles and squares in the left box but horizontal rows of circles and squares in the right box.

Depth Perception

Images appear on our retinas in two-dimensional form, yet remarkably we see a three-dimensional world. **Depth perception** is the ability to perceive objects three-dimensionally. Look around you. You do not see your surroundings as flat. You see some objects farther away, some closer. Some objects overlap each other. The scene and objects that you are looking at have depth. How do you see depth? To perceive a world of depth, we use two kinds of information, or cues—binocular and monocular.

depth perception
The ability to perceive objects three-dimensionally.

Because we have two eyes, we get two views of the world, one from each eye. **Binocular cues** are depth cues that depend on the combination of the images in the left and right eyes and on the way the two eyes work together. The pictures are slightly different because the eyes are in slightly different positions. Try holding your hand about 10 inches from your face. Alternately close and open your left and right eyes so that only one eye is open at a time. The image of your hand will appear to jump back and forth, because the image is in a slightly different place on the left and right retinas. The *disparity,* or difference, between the images in the two eyes is the binocular cue the brain uses to determine the depth, or distance, of an object. The combination of the two images in the brain, and the disparity between them in the eyes, give us information about the three-dimensionality of the world (Preston, Kourtzi, & Welchman, 2009).

binocular cues
Depth cues that depend on the combination of the images in the left and right eyes and on the way the two eyes work together.

Those 3-D glasses (with one green lens and one red one) that are used for some movies are also an example of depth from disparity. They work because your eyes are competing with each other and your brain makes sense of the conflict by creating the perception of three dimensions.

Convergence is another binocular cue to depth and distance. When we use our two eyes to look at something, they are focused on the same object. If the object is near us, our eyes converge, or move together, almost crossing. If the object is farther away, we can focus on it without pulling our eyes together. The muscle movements involved in convergence provide information about how far away or how deep something is.

convergence
A binocular cue to depth and distance in which the muscle movements in our two eyes provide information about how deep and/or far away something is.

In addition to using binocular cues to get an idea of objects' depth, we rely on a number of **monocular cues,** or depth cues, available from the image in one eye, either right or left. Monocular cues are powerful, and under normal circumstances they can provide a compelling impression of depth. Try closing one eye—your perception of the world still retains many of its three-dimensional qualities. Examples of monocular cues are:

monocular cues
Powerful depth cues available from the image in one eye, either the right or the left.

1. *Familiar size:* This cue to the depth and distance of objects is based on what we have learned from experience about the standard sizes of objects. We know how large oranges tend to be, so we can tell something about how far away an orange is likely to be by the size of its image on the retina.

2. *Height in the field of view:* All other things being equal, objects positioned higher in a picture are seen as farther away.

3. *Linear perspective and relative size:* Objects that are farther away take up less space on the retina. So, things that appear smaller are perceived to be farther away. As Figure 3.19 shows, as an object recedes into the distance, parallel lines in the scene appear to converge.

4. *Overlap:* We perceive an object that partially conceals or overlaps another object as closer.

FIGURE 3.19
An Artist's Use of the Monocular Cue of Linear Perspective
Famous landscape artist J. M. W. Turner used linear perspective to give the perception of depth in *Rain, Steam, and Speed* (1844).

5. *Shading:* This cue involves changes in perception due to the position of the light and the position of the viewer. Consider an egg under a desk lamp. If you walk around the desk, you will see different shading patterns on the egg.

6. *Texture gradient:* Texture becomes denser and finer the farther away it is from the viewer (Figure 3.20).

Depth perception is a remarkably complex adaptation. Individuals with only one functioning eye cannot see depth in the way that those with two eyes can. Other disorders of the eye can also lead to a lack of depth perception. Oliver Sacks (2006) described the case of Susan Barry, who had been born with crossed eyes. The operation to correct her eyes left her cosmetically normal, but she was unable to perceive depth throughout her life. As an adult, she became determined to see depth. With a doctor's aid, she found special glasses and undertook a process of eye muscle exercises to improve her chances of perceiving in three dimensions. It was a difficult and long process, but one day she noticed things starting to "stick out" at her—as you might when watching a film in 3-D. Although Barry had successfully adapted to life in a flat visual world, she had come to realize that relying on monocular cues was not the same as experiencing the rich visual world of binocular vision. She described flowers as suddenly appearing "inflated." She noted how "ordinary things looked extraordinary" as she saw the leaves of a tree, an empty chair, and her office door projecting out from the background. For the first time, she had a sense of being inside the world she was viewing.

FIGURE 3.20
Texture Gradient The gradients of texture create an impression of depth on a flat surface.

Motion Perception Motion perception plays an important role in the lives of many species (Takeuchi & De Valois, 2009). Indeed, for some animals, motion perception is critical for survival. Both predators and their prey depend on being able to detect motion quickly. Frogs and some other simple vertebrates may not even see an object unless it is moving. For example, if a dead fly is dangled motionlessly in front of a frog, the frog cannot sense its winged meal. The bug-detecting cells in the frog's retinas are wired only to sense movement.

Whereas the retinas of frogs can detect movement, the retinas of humans and other primates cannot. According to one neuroscientist, "The dumber the animal, the 'smarter' the retina" (Baylor, 2001). In humans the brain takes over the job of analyzing motion through highly specialized pathways (Fernandez & Farell, 2008). Recall from our discussion of the brain pathways in vision that the "where" pathway is involved in motion detection.

How do humans perceive motion? First, we have neurons that are specialized to detect motion. Second, feedback from our body tells us whether we are moving or whether someone or some object is moving; for example, you move your eye muscles as you watch a ball coming toward you. Third, the environment we see is rich in cues that give us information about movement (Badler & Heinen, 2006). For example, when we run, our surroundings appear to be moving.

apparent movement
The perception that a stationary object is moving.

Psychologists are interested in both real movement and **apparent movement,** which occurs when we perceive a stationary object as moving. You can experience apparent movement at IMAX movie theaters. In watching a film of a climb of Mount Everest, you may find yourself feeling breathless as your visual field floods with startling images. In theaters without seats, viewers of these films are often warned to hold the handrail because perceived movement is so realistic that they might fall.

FIGURE 3.21
Size Constancy Even though our retinal images of the hot air balloons vary, we still realize the balloons are approximately the same size. This illustrates the principle of size constancy.

Perceptual Constancy   Retinal images change constantly. Yet even though the stimuli that fall on our retinas change as we move closer to or farther away from objects, or as we look at objects from different orientations and in light or dark settings, our perception of them remains stable. **Perceptual constancy** is the recognition that objects are constant and unchanging even though sensory input about them is changing.

perceptual constancy
The recognition that objects are constant and unchanging even though sensory input about them is changing.

We experience three types of perceptual constancy—size constancy, shape constancy, and color constancy—as follows:

- *Size constancy* is the recognition that an object remains the same size even though the retinal image of the object changes (Figure 3.21). Experience is important to size perception: No matter how far away you are from your car, you know how large it is.

- *Shape constancy* is the recognition that an object retains the same shape even though its orientation to you changes. Look around. You probably see objects of various shapes—chairs and tables, for example. If you walk around the room, you will see these objects from different sides and angles. Even though the retinal image of the object changes as you walk, you still perceive the objects as having the same shape (Figure 3.22).

- *Color constancy* is the recognition that an object retains the same color even though different amounts of light fall on it. For example, if you are reaching for a green Granny Smith apple, it looks green to you whether you are having it for lunch, in the bright noon sun, or as an evening snack in the pale pink of sunset.

Note that perceptual constancy tells us about the crucial role of interpretation in perception: We *interpret* sensation. That is, we perceive objects as having particular characteristics regardless of the retinal image detected by our

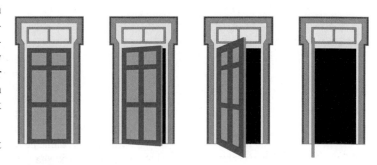

FIGURE 3.22
Shape Constancy The various projected images from an opening door are quite different, yet you perceive a rectangular door.

Rotational Illusion
The two rings appear to rotate in different directions when we approach or move away from this figure while fixing our eyes on the center.

Ponzo Illusion
The top line looks much longer than the bottom, but they are the same length.

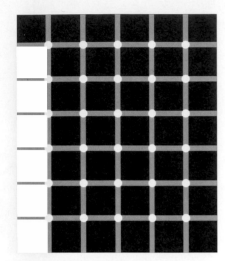

Blinking Effect Illusion
Stare at the white circles and notice the intermittent blinking effect. Your eyes make the static figure seem dynamic, attempting to fill in the white circle intersections with the black of the background.

FIGURE 3.23

Perceptual Illusions These illusions show how adaptive perceptual cues can lead to errors when taken out of context. They are definitely fun, but keep in mind that these illusions are based on processes that are quite adaptive in real life.

Pattern Recognition
Although the diagram contains no actual triangles, your brain "sees" two overlapping triangles. The explanation is that the notched circles and angled lines merely suggest gaps in which complete objects should be. The brain fills in the missing information.

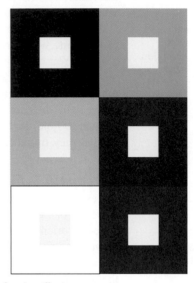

Induction Illusion
The yellow patches are identical, but they look different and seem to take on the characteristics of their surroundings when they appear against different-color backgrounds.

eyes. Images may flow across the retina, but experiences are made sensible through perception. The many cues we use to visually perceive the real world can lead to optical illusions when they are taken out of that real-world context, as you can experience for yourself in Figure 3.23.

1. When we refer to the hue of a light wave, we are referring to what we perceive as
   A. intensity.
   B. radiation.
   C. brightness.
   D. color.

2. To read this question, you are looking at it. After the light passes into your eyes, the incoming light waves are recorded by receptor cells located in the
   A. retina.
   B. cornea.
   C. blind spot.
   D. optic chiasm.

3. If you are in a well-lighted room, your rods are being used _____ and cones are being used _____.
   A. infrequently; frequently
   B. infrequently; infrequently
   C. frequently; infrequently
   D. frequently; frequently

Apply It! 4. Sondra was driving in the country one afternoon. There was not much traffic on the long, straight road, though Sondra noticed a man walking along the roadside some distance away. Suddenly, as she approached the person, he drifted toward the middle of the road, and Sondra, with screeching brakes, was shocked to realize she had nearly hit a child. Fortunately, the child was not harmed. It had become clear to Sondra that what had seemed like a man some distance away was actually a child who was much closer than she realized. What explains this situation?
   A. Sondra's occipital lobe must be damaged.
   B. Because objects that are smaller on the retina are typically further away, Sondra was fooled by relative size.
   C. Because objects in the mirror are closer than they appear, Sondra was not able to detect the just-noticeable difference.
   D. Because objects that are smaller on the retina are typically closer than they appear, Sondra was fooled by shape constancy.

3 The Auditory System

Just as light provides us with information about the environment, so does sound. Sounds tell us about the presence of a person behind us, the approach of an oncoming car, the force of the wind, and the mischief of a 2-year-old. Perhaps most important, sounds allow us to communicate through language and song.

The Nature of Sound and How We Experience It

At a fireworks display, you may feel the loud boom of the explosion in your chest. At a concert, you might have sensed that the air around you was vibrating. Bass instruments are especially effective at creating mechanical pulsations, even causing the floor to vibrate. When the bass is played loudly, we can sense air molecules being pushed forward in waves from the speaker. How does sound generate these sensations?

Sound waves are vibrations in the air that are processed by the *auditory* (hearing) system. Remember that light waves are much like the waves in the ocean moving toward the beach. Sound waves are similar. Sound waves also vary in length. Wavelength determines the sound wave's *frequency,* that is, the number of cycles (full wavelengths) that pass through a point in a given time interval. *Pitch* is the perceptual interpretation of the frequency of a sound. We perceive high-frequency sounds as having a high pitch, and low-frequency sounds as having a low pitch. A soprano voice sounds high-pitched. A bass voice has a low pitch. As with the wavelengths of light, human sensitivity is limited to a range of sound frequencies. It is common knowledge that dogs, for example, can hear higher frequencies than humans can.

Sound waves vary not only in frequency but also, like light waves, in amplitude (see Figure 3.6). A sound wave's *amplitude,* measured in decibels (dB), is the amount of pressure the sound wave produces relative to a standard. The typical standard —0 decibels—is

Practice "Safe Sound"

Many of us enjoy listening to our favorite tunes on a portable media player. We use these devices whenever we desire and wherever we are. These players use earbuds that transmit sound directly into the ear canal. How might this technology affect our hearing?

A study examined the safety of iPods for the hearing of listeners. Cory Portnuff and Brian Fligor (2006) found that a typical person could safely listen to an iPod for nearly 5 hours at 70 percent volume. The researchers concluded that those who like their tunes louder should not listen as long; if you listen at 90 percent volume, for example, keep yourself plugged in for no more than 90 minutes. One important issue is the environment in which the person is listening. Participants in the study were more likely to pump up the volume if they were listening to their iPods in already noisy environments. Effects on hearing did not depend on the participants' choice of music. So, whether it is Ne-Yo, Barry Manilow, or Mozart, sensible listening is wise.

FIGURE 3.24
Physical Difference in Sound Waves and the Qualities of Sound They Produce Here we can see how the input of sound stimuli requires our ears and brain to attend to varying characteristics of the rich sensory information that is sound.

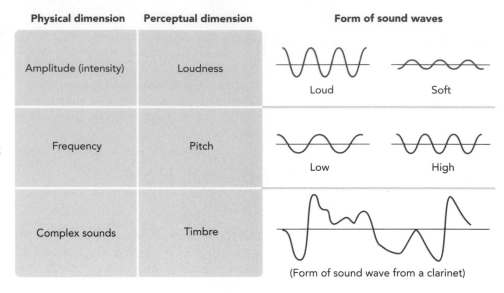

the weakest sound the human ear can detect. *Loudness* is the perception of the sound wave's amplitude. In general, the higher the amplitude of the sound wave, or the higher the decibel level, the louder we perceive the sound to be. Thus, in terms of amplitude, the air is pressing more forcibly against you and your ears during loud sounds and more gently during quiet sounds.

So far we have been describing a single sound wave with just one frequency. A single sound wave is similar to the single wavelength of pure colored light, discussed in the context of color matching. Most sounds, including those of speech and music, are *complex sounds,* those in which numerous frequencies of sound blend together. *Timbre* is the tone saturation, or the perceptual quality, of a sound. Timbre is responsible for the perceptual difference between a trumpet and a trombone playing the same note and for the quality differences we hear in human voices. Figure 3.24 illustrates the physical differences in sound waves that produce the different qualities of sounds.

Structures and Functions of the Ear

What happens to sound waves once they reach your ear? How do various structures of the ear transform sound waves into signals that the brain will recognize as sound? Functionally the ear is analogous to the eye. The ear serves the purpose of transmitting a high-fidelity version of sounds in the world to the brain for analysis and interpretation. Just as an image needs to be in focus and sufficiently bright for the brain to interpret it, a sound needs to be transmitted in a way that preserves information about its location, its frequency (which helps us distinguish the voice of a child from that of an adult), and its timbre (which allows us to identify the voice of a friend on the telephone). The ear is divided into three parts: *outer ear, middle ear,* and *inner ear* (Figure 3.25).

outer ear
The outermost part of the ear, consisting of the pinna and the external auditory canal.

Outer Ear The **outer ear** consists of the pinna and the external auditory canal. The funnel-shaped *pinna* (plural, *pinnae*) is the outer, visible part of the ear. (Elephants have very large pinnae.) The pinna collects sounds and channels them into the interior of the ear. The pinnae of many animals, such as cats, are movable and serve a more important role in sound localization than do the pinnae of humans. Cats turn their ears in the direction of a faint and interesting sound.

middle ear
The part of the ear that channels sound through the eardrum, hammer, anvil, and stirrup to the inner ear.

Middle Ear After passing the pinna, sound waves move through the auditory canal to the middle ear. The **middle ear** channels the sound through the eardrum, hammer, anvil, and stirrup to the inner ear. The *eardrum* or tympanic membrane separates the

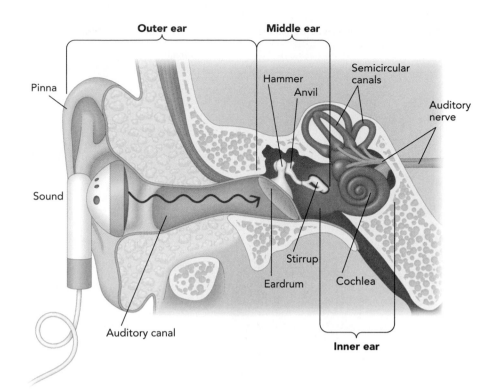

Outer ear   Middle ear

Pinna

Hammer
Anvil

Semicircular
canals

Auditory
nerve

Sound

Stirrup

Eardrum   Cochlea

Auditory canal

Inner ear

FIGURE 3.25

The Outer, Middle, and Inner Ear On entering the outer ear, sound waves travel through the auditory canal, where they generate vibrations in the eardrum. These vibrations are transferred via the hammer, anvil, and stirrup to the fluid-filled cochlea in the inner ear. There the mechanical vibrations are converted to an electrochemical signal that the brain will recognize as sound.

outer ear from the middle ear and vibrates in response to sound. It is the first structure that sound touches in the middle ear. The *hammer, anvil,* and *stirrup* are an intricately connected chain of the three smallest bones in the human body. When they vibrate, they transmit sound waves to the fluid-filled inner ear (Stenfelt, 2006). The muscles that operate these tiny bones take the vibration of the eardrum and transmit it to the oval window, the opening of the inner ear.

If you are a swimmer, you know that sound travels far more easily in air than in water. Sound waves entering the ear travel in air until they reach the inner ear. At this border between air and fluid, sound meets the same kind of resistance encountered by shouts directed at an underwater swimmer when they hit the surface of the water. To compensate, the muscles of the middle ear can maneuver the hammer, anvil, and stirrup to amplify the sound waves. Importantly, these muscles can also work to decrease the intensity of sound waves, to protect the inner ear if necessary.

Inner Ear   The function of the **inner ear,** which includes the oval window, cochlea, and basilar membrane, is to convert sound waves into neural impulses and send them on to the brain (Zou & others, 2006). The stirrup is connected to the membranous *oval window,* which transmits sound waves to the cochlea. The *cochlea* is a tubular, fluid-filled structure that is coiled up like a snail (Figure 3.26). The *basilar membrane* lines the inner wall of the cochlea and runs its entire length. It is narrow and rigid at the base of the cochlea but widens and becomes more flexible at the top. The variation in width and flexibility allows different areas of the basilar membrane to vibrate more intensely when exposed to different sound frequencies (Wojtczak & Oxenham, 2009). For example, the high-pitched tinkle of a little bell stimulates the narrow region of the basilar membrane at the base of the cochlea, whereas the low-pitched tones of a tugboat whistle stimulate the wide end.

In humans and other mammals, hair cells line the basilar membrane (see Figure 3.26). These *hair cells* are the sensory receptors of the ear. They are called hair cells because of the tufts of fine bristles, or *cilia,* which sprout from the top of them. The movement of the hair cells against the *tectorial membrane,* a jellylike flap above them, generates resulting impulses that are interpreted as sound by the brain (Gueta & others, 2006). Hair cells are so delicate that exposure to loud noise can destroy them, leading to deafness

inner ear

The part of the ear that includes the oval window, cochlea, and basilar membrane and whose function is to convert sound waves into neural impulses and send them to the brain.

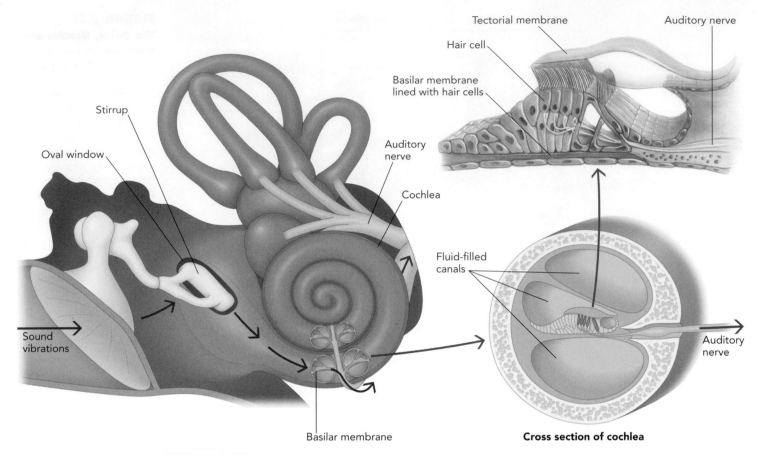

Tectorial membrane

Auditory nerve

Hair cell

Basilar membrane lined with hair cells

Auditory nerve

Cochlea

Stirrup

Oval window

Fluid-filled canals

Auditory nerve

Sound vibrations

Basilar membrane

Cross section of cochlea

FIGURE 3.26

The Cochlea The cochlea is a spiral structure consisting of fluid-filled canals. When the stirrup vibrates against the oval window, the fluid in the canals vibrates. Vibrations along portions of the basilar membrane correspond to different sound frequencies. The vibrations exert pressure on the hair cells (between the basilar and tectorial membranes); the hair cells in turn push against the tectorial membrane, and this pressure bends the hairs. This triggers an action potential in the auditory nerve.

or difficulties in hearing. Once lost, hair cells cannot regenerate. Cochlear implants are devices that were specifically developed to replace damaged hair cells. To read more about these implants, see Challenge Your Thinking.

Theories of Hearing

One of the auditory system's mysteries is how the inner ear registers the frequency of sound. Two theories aim to explain this mystery: place theory and frequency theory.

place theory
Theory on how the inner ear registers the frequency of sound, stating that each frequency produces vibrations at a particular spot on the basilar membrane.

Place theory states that each frequency produces vibrations at a particular spot on the basilar membrane. Georg von Békésy (1960) studied the effects of vibration applied at the oval window on the basilar membrane of human cadavers. Through a microscope, he saw that this stimulation produced a traveling wave on the basilar membrane. A traveling wave is like the ripples that appear in a pond when you throw in a stone. However, because the cochlea is a long tube, the ripples can travel in only one direction, from the oval window at one end of the cochlea to the far tip of the cochlea. High-frequency vibrations create traveling waves that maximally displace, or move, the area of the basilar membrane next to the oval window; low-frequency vibrations maximally displace areas of the membrane closer to the tip of the cochlea. Békésy won a Nobel Prize in 1961 for his research on the basilar membrane.

challenge your thinking

Are Cochlear Implants a "Cure" for Deafness?

Advances in science and technology have provided an option for people who cannot hear. A *cochlear implant*—a small electronic device that is surgically implanted in the ear and head—allows deaf or profoundly hard-of-hearing individuals to detect sound. Unlike a hearing aid, an implant does not amplify sound. It works by directly stimulating whatever working auditory nerves the recipient has in his or her cochlea with electronic impulses. In the United States, 22,000 adults and nearly 15,000 children have had cochlear implants (FDA, 2005).

Adults with hearing loss and parents of deaf children are often very interested in cochlear implants (Fitzpatrick & others, 2009; Hayes & others, 2009). For deaf adults who previously were able to hear and speak, implants work best if they are inserted shortly after the hearing loss. The reason? If a person is deaf for a long time, the brain adapts to this change and uses the auditory cortex for other tasks. Indeed, for older adults who receive a cochlear implant, the length of time spent profoundly deaf and the percentage of one's life lived as deaf are much stronger predictors of hearing success than age at implantation (Leung & others, 2005). Similarly, for children, time is of the essence. The brain is quite sensitive and responsive to sensory processes, and a young child's brain remains somewhat "up for grabs." It can be used to process sound or other stimuli, but once it dedicates itself, change is difficult. The language abilities of children implanted at the age of 2 tend to be superior to those who wait until the age of 4 (Niparko, 2004). Many parents are thus motivated to have their child receive the implant as early as possible. These parental motivations are where the controversy comes in.

Through the 1990s a debate raged over implants, especially with respect to children. On the pro-implant side were parents of deaf children, late-deafened adults, and medical professionals who emphasized the individual's right to hearing, as well as the benefits of hearing. On the other side were members of the deaf community. Spokespersons for the deaf stressed that life as a deaf person can be rich, rewarding, and successful. Deaf culture

Some critics say that parents who opt for a cochlear implant for their deaf daughter or son deprive the child of participation in the unique language and culture that is the child's right.

has its own language (*sign language*), opportunities, and valuable perspectives. Perhaps, some argued, hearing parents simply do not want to take on the daunting tasks of learning a new language and navigating this new world. Moreover, the use of cochlear implants in children implies that deafness is a problem that needs fixing, and in this way the procedure further undermines the many positive aspects of deaf culture.

In 2001 the National Association of the Deaf (NAD), an advocacy organization for deaf and hard-of-hearing individuals, issued a statement about the debate. The group emphasized that regardless of whether a deaf child receives an implant, he or she will live simultaneously in two worlds the deaf world and the hearing world. The NAD also stressed the importance of realistic perceptions of the promises and limitations of cochlear implants. A cochlear implant does not provide "normal" hearing. The implant substitutes just 22 electrodes wound around the cochlea for the 16,000 delicate hairs in an intact cochlea. Hence the auditory experience of a person who has a cochlear implant is limited compared with that of a hearing person. Nonetheless, cochlear implants can allow a person to comprehend spoken language, to communicate by phone, and to hear his or her own voice, in this way facilitating speech and conversation

Conflict is likely to continue over cochlear implants. The NAD has recognized that the deaf community itself is diverse—and emphasizes that all individuals are unique. So there is no one right answer to these dilemmas. As the motto of Hands and Voices, another deaf and hard-of-hearing advocacy group, stresses, "What works for your child is what makes the choice right."

What Do You Think?

- If you were the parent of a deaf child, would you opt for the cochlear implant? Why or why not?

- What values of deaf culture might be lost if deafness were "cured"?

Place theory adequately explains high-frequency sounds but not low-frequency sounds. The reason is that a high-frequency sound stimulates a precise area on the basilar membrane so displacement of the basilar membrane provides a good explanation for this kind of sound. In contrast, a low-frequency sound causes a large part of the basilar membrane to be displaced, making it hard to identify an exact location that is associated with hearing this kind of sound. Looking only at the movement of the basilar membrane, you would get the impression that humans are probably not very good at hearing low-frequency sounds, and yet we are quite good at hearing them. Therefore, some other factors must be at play in low-frequency hearing. **Frequency theory** gets at these other influences by stating that the perception of a sound's frequency depends on how often the auditory nerve fires. Higher-frequency sounds cause the auditory nerve to fire more often than do lower-frequency sounds. One limitation of frequency theory, however, is that a single neuron has a maximum firing rate of about 1,000 times per second. Therefore, frequency theory does not apply to tones with frequencies that would require a neuron to fire more rapidly.

To deal with this limitation of frequency theory, researchers developed the **volley principle,** which states that a cluster of nerve cells can fire neural impulses in rapid succession, producing a volley of impulses. Individual neurons cannot fire faster than 1,000 times per second, but if the neurons team up and alternate their neural firing, they can attain a combined frequency above that rate. To get a sense for how the volley principle works, imagine a troop of soldiers who are all armed with guns that can only fire one round at a time and that take time to reload. If all the soldiers fire at the same time, the frequency of firing is limited and cannot go any faster than it takes to reload those guns. If, however, the soldiers are coordinated as a group and fire at different times, some of them can fire while others are reloading, leading to a greater frequency of firing. Frequency theory better explains the perception of sounds below 1,000 times per second, whereas a combination of frequency and place theory is needed for sounds above 1,000 times per second.

frequency theory
Theory on how the inner ear registers the frequency of sound, stating that the perception of a sound's frequency depends on how often the auditory nerve fires.

volley principle
Modification of frequency theory stating that a cluster of nerve cells can fire neural impulses in rapid succession, producing a volley of impulses.

Auditory Processing in the Brain

As we considered in the discussion of the visual system, once our receptors pick up energy from the environment, that energy must be transmitted to the brain for processing and interpretation. We saw that in the retina, the responses of the rod and cone receptors feed into ganglion cells and leave the eye via the optic nerve. In the auditory system, information about sound moves from the hair cells of the inner ear to the **auditory nerve,** which carries neural impulses to the brain's auditory areas. Remember that it is the movement of the hair cells that transforms the physical stimulation of sound waves into the action potential of neural impulses.

Auditory information moves up the auditory pathway via electrochemical transmission in a more complex manner than does visual information in the visual pathway. Many synapses occur in the ascending auditory pathway, with most fibers crossing over the midline between the hemispheres of the cerebral cortex, although some proceed directly to the hemisphere on the same side as the ear of reception (Landau & Barner, 2009). This means that most of the auditory information from the left ear goes to the right side of the brain, but some also goes to the left side of the brain. The auditory nerve extends from the cochlea to the brain stem, with some fibers crossing over the midline. The cortical destination of most of these fibers is the temporal lobes of the brain (beneath the temples of the head). As in the case of visual information, researchers have found that features are extracted from auditory information and transmitted along parallel pathways in the brain (Recanzone & Sutter, 2008).

auditory nerve
The nerve structure that receives information about sound from the hair cells of the inner ear and carries these neural impulses to the brain's auditory areas.

Localizing Sound

When we hear the siren of a fire engine or the bark of a dog, how do we know where the sound is coming from? The basilar membrane gives us information about the frequency, pitch, and complexity of a sound, but it does not tell us where a sound is located.

Earlier in the chapter we saw that because our two eyes see slightly different images, we can determine how near or far away an object is. Similarly, having two ears helps us to localize a sound because each receives somewhat different stimuli from the sound source. A sound coming from the left has to travel different distances to the two ears, so if a barking dog is to your left, your left ear receives the sound sooner than your right ear. Also, your left ear will receive a slightly more intense sound than your right ear in this case. The sound reaching one ear is more intense than the sound reaching the other ear for two reasons: (1) It has traveled less distance and (2) the other ear is in what is called the *sound shadow* of the listener's head, which provides a barrier that reduces the sound's intensity (Figure 3.27). Blind individuals use the sound shadow to orient themselves.

Thus, differences in both the *timing* of the sound and the *intensity* of the sound help us to localize a sound (Van Deun & others, 2009). Humans often have difficulty localizing a sound that is coming from a source that is directly in front of them because it reaches both ears simultaneously. The same is true for sounds directly above your head or directly behind you.

FIGURE 3.27
The Sound Shadow The sound shadow is caused by the listener's head, which forms a barrier that reduces the sound's intensity. Here the sound is to the person's left, so the sound shadow will reduce the intensity of the sound that reaches the right ear.

The amazing echolocation ability of bats allows them to navigate through their environment with speed and precision and makes them very successful hunters.

Compared with some animals, humans are not very accurate at locating sounds (Benoit-Bird & Au, 2009). For example, bats are able to hunt insects at night because of their exquisitely developed sensitivity to their own echoes. They emit sounds that echo back to them, allowing them to detect objects in the darkness. Using this system—called *echolocation*—bats can fly through their environment at high speeds, avoid predators, and find prey (McDonald & others, 2009; Skowronski & Fenton, 2009). Why has evolution provided bats with such superb hearing? The answer is simple. Vision requires light, and bats are nocturnal animals. Any method of building internal representations of the environment that requires light would not be an effective perceptual system for the bat. Humans do not need echolocation ability because we do not hunt bugs at night. Rather, we use our eyes to pursue food by day.

1. Your mother's and sister's voices have the same pitch and loudness, but you can tell them apart on the telephone. This is due to the perceptual quality, or _____, of their voices.
   A. timbre
   B. wavelength
   C. frequency
   D. amplitude

2. The major function of the hammer, anvil, and stirrup of the middle ear is
   A. to soften the tone of incoming stimuli for appropriate processing.
   B. to stir cochlear fluid so that bone conduction hearing can occur.
   C. to amplify vibrations and pass them on to the inner ear.
   D. to clean the external auditory canal of any potential wax buildup.

3. The bones of the middle ear are set into motion by vibrations of the
   A. cochlea.
   B. eardrum.
   C. saccule.
   D. basilar membrane.

Apply It! 4. Conservative radio personality Rush Limbaugh experienced sudden hearing loss in 2001, after which he received a cochlear implant. He has described his ability to listen to music as dependent on what he heard before becoming deaf. If he had heard a song prior to becoming deaf, he could hear it, but if it was a new song, he could not make sense of it. Which of the following explains Limbaugh's experience?
   A. He is no longer able to listen to music from a top-down perspective.
   B. He is able to engage in top-down listening, but not bottom-up listening.
   C. He is likely to have experienced damage to the temporal lobes.
   D. He is not able to experience any auditory sensation.

4 Other Senses

We turn now to the body's other sensory systems. These include the skin senses and the chemical senses (smell and taste), as well as the kinesthetic and vestibular senses (systems that allow us to stay upright and to coordinate our movements).

The Skin Senses

You know when a friend has a fever by putting your hand to her head; you know how to find your way to the light switch in a darkened room by groping along the wall; and you know whether a pair of shoes is too tight by the way the shoes touch different parts of your feet when you walk. Many of us think of our skin as a canvas rather than a sense. We color it with cosmetics, dyes, and tattoos. In fact, the skin is our largest sensory system, draped over the body with receptors for touch, temperature, and pain. These three kinds of receptors form the *cutaneous senses*.

Standing in front of a vending machine, you find you need another nickel. Without looking, you are able to pull out the right coin. That is something that not even the most sophisticated robot can do. Engineers who design robots for use in surgical and other procedures have been unable to match the human hand's amazing sensitivity.

Touch   Touch is one of the senses that we most often take for granted, yet our ability to respond to touch is astounding. What do we detect when we feel "touch"? What kind of energy does our sense of touch pick up from our external environment? In vision we detect light energy. In hearing we detect the vibrations of air or sound waves pressing against our eardrums. In touch we detect mechanical energy, or pressure against the skin. The lifting of a single hair causes pressure on the skin around the shaft of hair. This tiny bit of mechanical pressure at the base of the hair is sufficient for us to feel the touch of a pencil point. More commonly we detect the mechanical energy of the pressure of a car seat against our buttocks or of a pencil in our hand. Is this energy so different from the kind of energy we detect in vision or hearing? Sometimes the only difference is one of intensity—the sound of a rock band playing softly is an auditory stimulus, but at the high volumes that make a concert hall reverberate, this auditory stimulus is also *felt* as mechanical energy pressing against our skin.

How does information about touch travel from the skin through the nervous system? Sensory fibers arising from receptors in the skin enter the spinal cord. From there the information travels to the brain stem, where most fibers from each side of the body cross over to the opposite side of the brain. Next the information about touch moves on to the thalamus, which serves as a relay station. The thalamus then projects the map of the body's surface onto the somatosensory areas of the parietal lobes in the cerebral cortex (Chen & others, 2009).

Just as the visual system is more sensitive to images on the fovea than to images in the peripheral retina, our sensitivity to touch is not equally good across all areas of the skin. Human toolmakers need excellent touch discrimination in their hands, but they require much less touch discrimination in other parts of the body, such as the torso and legs. The brain devotes more space to analyzing touch signals coming from the hands than from the legs.

Newborns can feel touch better than they can see, hear, or even taste (Eliot, 2001). The sense of touch is crucial to infants, as it helps them detect and explore the physical world and is important for health and emotional well-being (Diego, Field, & Hernandez-Reif, 2008). As we will see in Chapter 8, close, warm contact—touch—is a key aspect of attachment.

thermoreceptors
Sensory nerve endings under the skin that respond to changes in temperature at or near the skin and provide input to keep the body's temperature at 98.6 degrees Fahrenheit.

Temperature   We not only can feel the warmth of a comforting hand on our hand, we also can feel the warmth or coolness of a room. In order to maintain our body temperature, we have to be able to detect temperature. **Thermoreceptors,** sensory nerve endings under the skin, respond to changes in temperature at or near the skin and provide input to keep the body's temperature at 98.6 degrees Fahrenheit. There are two types of thermoreceptors: warm and cold. Warm thermoreceptors respond to the warming of the skin, and cold thermoreceptors respond to the cooling of the skin. When warm and cold receptors that are close to each other in the skin are stimulated simultaneously, we experience the sensation of hotness. Figure 3.28 illustrates this "hot" experience.

pain
The sensation that warns us of damage to our bodies.

Pain   **Pain** is the sensation that warns us of damage to our bodies. When contact with the skin takes the form of a sharp pinch, our sensation of mechanical pressure changes from touch to pain. When a pot handle is so hot that it burns our hand, our sensation of temperature becomes one of pain. Intense stimulation of any one of the senses can produce pain—too much light, very loud sounds, or too many habanero peppers, for example. Our ability to sense pain is vital for our survival as a species. It functions as a quick-acting messenger that tells the brain's motor systems that they must act fast to minimize or eliminate damage. We must immediately pull that hand away from the hot pan handle.

Pain receptors are dispersed widely throughout the body—in the skin, in the sheath tissue surrounding muscles, in internal organs, and in the membranes around bone. Although all pain receptors are anatomically similar, they differ in the type of physical stimuli to which they most readily respond. Mechanical pain receptors respond mainly to pressure, such as when we encounter a sharp object. Heat pain receptors respond primarily to strong heat that is capable of burning the tissue in which the receptors are embedded. Other pain receptors have a mixed function, responding to both types of painful stimuli. Many pain receptors are chemically sensitive and respond to a range of pain-producing substances.

Pain receptors have a much higher threshold for firing than receptors for temperature and touch (Bloom, Nelson, & Lazerson, 2001). Pain receptors react mainly to physical stimuli that distort them or to chemical stimuli that irritate them into action. Inflamed joints or sore, torn muscles produce *prostaglandins,* which stimulate the receptors and cause the experience of pain. Drugs such as aspirin likely reduce the feeling of pain by reducing prostaglandin production.

Two different neural pathways transmit pain messages to the brain: a fast pathway and a slow pathway (Bloom, Nelson, & Lazerson, 2001). In the *fast pathway,* fibers connect directly with the thalamus and then to the motor and sensory areas of the cerebral cortex. This pathway transmits information about sharp, localized pain, as when you cut your skin. The fast pathway may serve as a warning system, providing immediate information about an injury—it takes less than a second for the information in this pathway to reach the cerebral cortex. In the *slow pathway,* pain information travels through the limbic system, a detour that delays the arrival of information at the cerebral cortex by seconds. The unpleasant, nagging pain that characterizes the slow pathway may function to remind the brain that an injury has occurred and that we need to restrict normal activity and monitor the pain.

Many neuroscientists believe that the brain actually generates the experience of pain. There is evidence that turning pain signals on and off is a chemical process that probably involves *endorphins*. Recall from Chapter 2 that endorphins are neurotransmitters that function as natural opiates in producing pleasure and pain (Vetter & others, 2006). Endorphins are believed to be released mainly in the synapses of the slow pathway.

Perception of pain is complex and often varies from one person to the next (Finley, Kristjansdottir, & Forgeron, 2009). Some people rarely feel pain; others seem to be in great pain if they experience a minor bump or bruise. To some degree, these individual variations may be physiological. A person who experiences considerable pain even with a minor injury may have a neurotransmitter system that is deficient in endorphin production. However, perception of pain goes beyond physiology. Although it is true that all sensations are affected by factors such as motivation, expectation, and other related decision factors, the perception of pain is especially susceptible to these factors (Watson & others, 2006). A substantial research literature indicates that women experience more clinical pain, suffer more pain-related distress, and are more sensitive to experimentally induced pain than men are (Paller & others, 2009). Cultural and ethnic contexts also can greatly determine the

Warm water   Cold water

FIGURE 3.28
A "Hot" Experience
When two pipes, one containing cold water and the other warm water, are braided together, a person touching the pipes feels a sensation of "hot." The perceived heat coming from the pipes is so intense that the individual cannot touch them for longer than a couple of seconds.

The ability to perceive pain is adaptive. Individuals who cannot perceive pain often have serious difficulty navigating the world. They might not notice that they need to move away from a hot fire or that they have seriously injured themselves.

degree to which an individual experiences pain (Dawson & List, 2009). For example, one pain researcher described a ritual performed in India in which a chosen person travels from town to town delivering blessings to the children and the crops while suspended from metal hooks embedded in his back (Melzack, 1973). The individual apparently reports no sensation of pain and appears to be in ecstasy.

Most acute pain decreases over time with avoidance of activity or with pain-reducing medication. Treatment of chronic pain is often more complex. Often the most successful treatment of pain involves a combination of physical and psychological techniques (Watkins & Maier, 2000). A pain clinic may select from the following techniques to treat an individual's pain: surgery, drugs, acupuncture (the insertion of thin needles at specific points in the body to produce certain effects), electrical stimulation, massage, exercise, hypnosis, and relaxation (Hahn, Payne, & Lucas, 2007; Insel & Roth, 2008). Other strategies to reduce pain that people can do on their own include

- *Distraction:* When you are about to get a shot, do you focus on the needle as it is about to plunge into your flesh, or do you turn away and concentrate on something else? Distraction is usually the best way to reduce pain, because attention to the sensation can magnify it.

- *Focused breathing:* The next time you stub your toe, try panting—using short, fast breaths (similar to the breathing practiced in Lamaze childbirth). Focused breathing may diminish your agony.

- *Counterstimulation:* If you pinch your cheek after getting a bad cut, it likely will mute your pain, as will applying ice to a sprained or swollen area.

The Chemical Senses

The information processed through our senses comes in many diverse forms: electromagnetic energy in vision, sound waves in hearing, and mechanical pressure and temperature in the skin senses. The two senses we now consider, smell and taste, are responsible for processing chemicals in our environment. Through smell, we detect airborne chemicals, and through taste we detect chemicals that have been dissolved in saliva. Smell and taste are frequently stimulated simultaneously. We notice the strong links between the two senses when a nasty cold with lots of nasal congestion takes the pleasure out of eating. Our favorite foods become "tasteless" without their characteristic smells. Despite this link, taste and smell are two distinct systems.

Taste   Think of your favorite food. Why do you like it? Imagine that food without its flavor. The thought of giving up a favorite taste, such as chocolate, can be depressing. Indeed, eating food we love is a major source of pleasure.

How does taste happen? To get at this question, try this. Take a drink of milk and allow it to coat your tongue. Then go to a mirror, stick out your tongue, and look carefully at its surface. You should be able to see rounded bumps above the surface. Those bumps, called **papillae,** contain taste buds, the receptors for taste. Your tongue houses about 10,000 taste buds, and those taste buds are replaced about every two weeks. As we age, however, this replacement process is not quite as efficient, and an older individual may have just 5,000 working taste buds at any given moment. As with all of the other sensory systems we have studied, the information picked up by these taste receptors is transmitted to the brain for analysis and, when necessary, for a response (spitting something out, for example).

Researchers have traditionally categorized the taste qualities to which humans respond as sweet, sour, bitter, and salty (Scott, 2000). Though all areas of the tongue can detect each of these four tastes, different parts are more sensitive to some tastes than others. The tip of the tongue is the most sensitive to sweet and salty substances, the sides to sour, and the rear to bitter (Figure 3.29) (Bloom, Nelson, & Lazerson, 2001). However, today, many neuroscientists believe that the breakdown of taste into four independent, elementary

Smoking cigarettes can reduce the number of taste buds a person has.

papillae
Rounded bumps above the tongue's surface that contain the taste buds, the receptors for taste.

categories underestimates the complexity of taste (Cauller, 2001). The taste fibers leading from a taste bud to the brain often respond strongly to a range of chemicals spanning *multiple* taste elements, such as salty and sour. The brain processes these somewhat ambiguous incoming signals and integrates them into a perception of taste (Bartoshuk, 2008). So although people often categorize taste sensations along the four dimensions of sweet, bitter, salty, and sour, our tasting ability goes far beyond these.

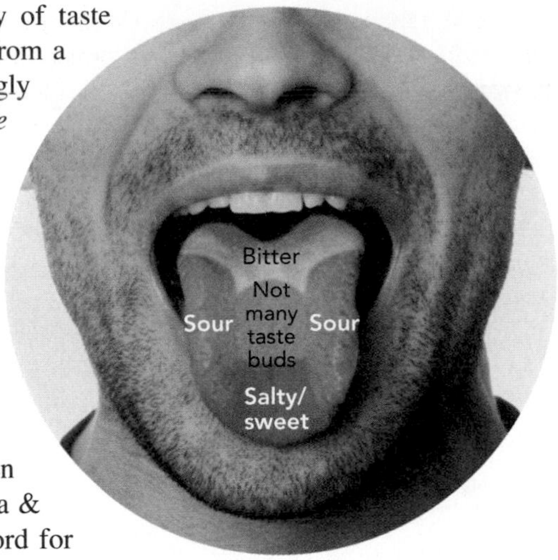

Recently, researchers and chefs have been exploring a taste called *umami* (Maruyama & others, 2006). *Umami* is the Japanese word for "delicious" or "yummy." The taste of umami, one that Asian cooks have long recognized, is the flavor of L-glutamate. What is that taste? Umami is a savory flavor that is present in many seafoods as well as soy sauce, parmesan and mozzarella cheese, anchovies, mushrooms, and hearty meat broths.

Culture certainly influences the experience of taste. Any American who has watched the Japanese version of the TV series *Iron Chef* quickly notices that some people enjoy the flavor of sea urchin, while others just do not get the appeal. In some cultures, food that is so spicy as to be practically inedible for the outsider may be viewed as quite delicious or umami. The culture in which we live can influence the foods we are exposed to as well as our sense of what tastes good. In some cultures, very spicy food is introduced slowly into children's diets so they can learn what is delicious at an early age.

FIGURE 3.29
Historical Description of the Location of Taste Sensitivity on the Tongue You might be familiar with this map of the tongue. We now know that taste is much more complex than this figure suggests.

Umami is also why you can't eat just one potato chip. When potato chips are fried, glutamate is concentrated.

Smell Why do we have a sense of smell? One way to appreciate the importance of smell is to think about animals with a more sophisticated sense of smell than our own. A dog, for example, can use smell to find its way back from a long stroll, to distinguish friend from foe, and even (with practice) to detect illegal drugs concealed in a suitcase. In fact, dogs can detect odors in concentrations 100 times lower than those detectable by humans. Given the nasal feats of the average dog, we might be tempted to believe that the sense of smell has outlived its usefulness in humans.

What do humans use smell for? For one thing, humans need the sense of smell to decide what to eat. We can distinguish rotten food from fresh food and remember (all too well) which foods have made us ill in the past. The smell of a food that has previously made us sick is often by itself enough to make us feel nauseated. Second, although tracking is a function of smell that we often associate only with animals, humans are competent odor trackers. We can follow the odor of gas to a leak, the smell of smoke to a fire, and the aroma of a hot apple pie to a windowsill.

What physical equipment do we use to process odor information? Just as the eyes scan the visual field for objects of interest, the nose is an active instrument. We actively sniff when we are trying to track down the source of a fire or an unfamiliar chemical odor. The **olfactory epithelium** lining the

olfactory epithelium
The lining the roof of the nasal cavity, containing a sheet of receptor cells for smell.

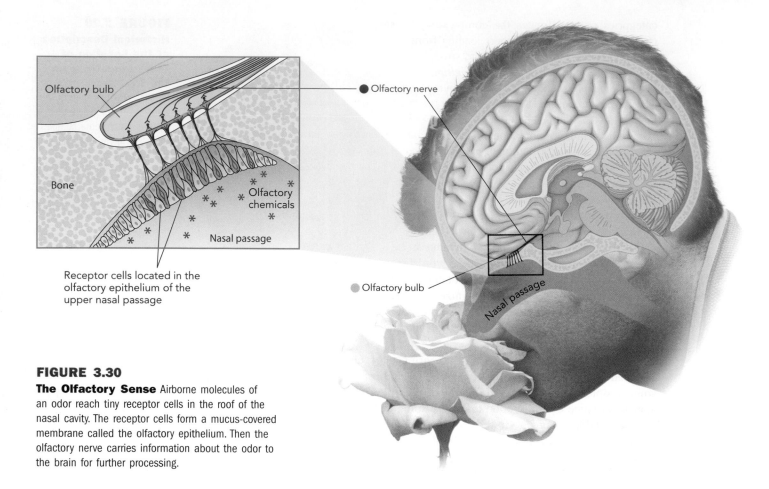

FIGURE 3.30

The Olfactory Sense Airborne molecules of an odor reach tiny receptor cells in the roof of the nasal cavity. The receptor cells form a mucus-covered membrane called the olfactory epithelium. Then the olfactory nerve carries information about the odor to the brain for further processing.

roof of the nasal cavity contains a sheet of receptor cells for smell (Figure 3.30), so sniffing maximizes the chances of detecting an odor. The receptor cells are covered with millions of minute, hairlike antennae that project through the mucus in the top of the nasal cavity and make contact with air on its way to the throat and lungs (Bartoshuk, 2008; Rawson & Yee, 2006). Interestingly, unlike the neurons of most sensory systems, the neurons in the olfactory epithelium tend to replace themselves after injury (Doty, 2001).

What is the neural pathway for information about smell? Although all other sensory pathways pass through the thalamus, the pathway for smell does not. In smell, the neural pathway first goes to the olfactory areas in the temporal lobes and then projects to various brain regions, especially the limbic system, which is involved in emotion and memory (Breer, Fleischer, & Strotmann, 2006). Unlike the other senses, smells take a superhighway to emotion and memory, a phenomenon we will consider in more detail in Chapter 6.

Smell might have a role to play in the chemistry of interpersonal attraction. From an evolutionary perspective, the goal of human mating is to find someone with whom to produce the healthiest offspring. Mates with differing sets of genes (known as the *major histocompatibility complex,* or *MHC*) produce healthier offspring with the broadest immune systems. How do we find these people, short of taking a blood test? Martie Haselton (2006) has conducted studies on interpersonal attraction using the "smelly T-shirt" paradigm. In this research, men are asked to wear a T-shirt to bed every day for a week without washing it. After they have been thoroughly imbued with a male's personal scent, the T-shirts are presented to women to smell and rate for attractiveness. Women reliably rate men whose MHCs are different from their own as more attractive, on the basis of the aroma of the T-shirts. Thus, although the eyes may be the window to the soul, the nose might be the gateway to love. Interestingly, researchers have not found these effects for women who are taking contraceptives that alter their hormonal cycles.

Why might women who are on contraceptives that affect hormonal cycles, such as the pill, not be influenced by these smelly T-shirts in the same way?

The Kinesthetic and Vestibular Senses

kinesthetic senses
Senses that provide information about movement, posture, and orientation.

vestibular sense
Sense that provides information about balance and movement.

You know the difference between walking and running and between lying down and sitting up. To perform even the simplest act of motor coordination, such as reaching out to take a book off a shelf or getting up out of a chair, the brain must constantly receive and coordinate information from every part of the body. Your body has two kinds of senses that give you information about your movement and orientation in space, as well as help you to maintain balance. The **kinesthetic senses** provide information about movement, posture, and orientation. The **vestibular sense** provides information about balance and movement.

No specific organ contains the kinesthetic senses. Instead, they are embedded in muscle fibers and joints. As we stretch and move, these receptors signal the state of the muscle. Kinesthesia is a sense that you often do not even notice until it is gone. Try walking when your leg is "asleep" or smiling (never mind talking) when you have just come from a dentist's office and are still under the effects of Novocain.

We can appreciate the sophistication of kinesthesis when we think about it in terms of memory. Even a mediocre typist can bang out 20 words per minute—but how many of us could write down the order of the letters on a keyboard without looking? Typing is a skill that relies on very coordinated sensitivity to the orientation, position, and movements of our fingers. We say that our fingers "remember" the positions of the keys. Likewise, the complicated movements a pitcher uses to throw a baseball cannot be written down or communicated easily using language. They involve nearly every muscle and joint in the body. Most information about the kinesthetic senses is transmitted from the joints and muscles along the same pathways to the brain as information about touch.

The vestibular sense tells us whether our head (and hence usually our body) is tilted, moving, slowing down, or speeding up. It works in concert with the kinesthetic senses to coordinate our *proprioceptive feedback,* which is information about the position of our limbs and body parts in relation to other body parts. Consider the combination of sensory abilities involved in the motion of an ice hockey player skating down the ice, cradling the puck, and pushing it forward with the hockey stick. The hockey player is responding simultaneously to a multitude of sensations, including those produced by the slickness of the ice, the position of the puck, the speed and momentum of the forward progression, and the requirements of the play to turn and to track the other players on the ice.

semicircular canals
Three fluid-filled circular tubes in the inner ear containing the sensory receptors that detect head motion caused when we tilt or move our heads and/or bodies.

The **semicircular canals** of the inner ear contain the sensory receptors that detect head motion caused when we tilt or move our heads and/or bodies (Figure 3.31). These canals consist of three fluid-filled, circular tubes that lie in the three planes of the body—right-left, front-back, and up-down. We can picture these as three intersecting hula hoops. As you move your head, the fluid of the semicircular canals flows in different directions and at different speeds (depending on the force of the head movement). Our perception of head movement and position is determined by the movements of these receptor cells (Tribukait, 2006). This ingenious system of using the motion of fluid in tubes to sense head position is similar to the auditory system of the inner ear. However,

The kinesthetic and vestibular senses play an essential role in a baseball pitcher's wind-up and delivery.

FIGURE 3.31

The Semicircular Canals and Vestibular Sense
The semicircular canals provide feedback to the gymnast's brain as her head and body tilt in different directions. Any angle of head rotation is registered by hair cells in one or more semicircular canals in both ears. (*Inset*) The semicircular canals.

the fluid movement in the cochlea results from the pressure sound exerts on the oval window, whereas the movements in the semicircular canals reflect physical movements of the head and body. Vestibular sacs in the semicircular canals contain hair cells embedded in a gelatin-like mass. Just as the hair cells in the cochlea trigger hearing impulses in the brain, the hair cells in the semicircular canals transmit information about balance and movement.

The brain pathways for the vestibular sense begin in the auditory nerve, which contains both the cochlear nerve (with information about sound) and the vestibular nerve (which has information about balance and movement). Most of the axons of the vestibular nerve connect with the medulla, although some go directly to the cerebellum. There also appear to be vestibular projections to the temporal cortex, but research has not fully charted their specific pathways.

Information from the sense of vision supplements the combination of kinesthetic and vestibular senses. This simple principle has made IMAX theaters profitable. When we watch films on screens that are large enough to fill our visual field, such as those found in many theme parks, the motion we perceive on the screen can make us feel as if *we* are moving. This same principle causes a motorist to slam on the brakes in his tiny sports car when the big truck next to him starts to move forward. When everything in our visual field appears to be moving, it is generally because *we are* moving.

Throughout this chapter we have viewed sensation and perception as our connections to the world. Our senses build a bridge between the objects in our environment and the creative interpreter that is our brain. Through perception our sensations become meaningful and our mental life engages with the environment. Sensation and perception allow us to survive in that environment, but also to experience the world in all its vibrancy. Sue Berry, a woman who achieved the ability to perceive depth only after a long, arduous effort, described her encounter with nature on a snowy day. "I felt myself within the snow fall, among the snowflakes. . . . I was overcome with a sense of joy. A snow fall can be quite beautiful—especially when you see it for the first time" (quoted in Sacks, 2006, p. 73). Also, recall Michael May, who was able to see after 25 years of blindness. One night, with his seeing-eye dog Josh at his side, he decided to go look at the sky. Lying on the grass in a field, he opened his eyes. He thought he was "seeing stars"—in the metaphorical sense. He thought that the thousands of white lights in the sky could not really be real, but they were. As he remarked in his vision diary: "How sweet it is" (May, 2003; Stein, 2003).

Do It!

If you have a few minutes and a strong stomach, give your vestibular system a workout. Spin around quickly and repeatedly for a minute. You can do it in a swivel chair or standing in the center of a room (be careful of sharp edges). When you stop, you will feel dizzy. Here's what's happening. The fluid in the semicircular canals moves rather slowly and changes direction very slowly. When we spin for a while, the fluid eventually catches up with our rate of motion and starts moving in the same direction. When we stop moving, however, the slow-moving fluid keeps on moving. It tells the hair cells in the vestibular canals (which in turn tell the brain) "We are still spinning"—and we feel as if we are.

self-quiz

1. Taste buds are bunched together in
   A. taste cells.
   B. the papillae.
   C. salivary glands.
   D. the olfactory epithelium.

2. _____ is/are involved in the sense of smell.
   A. The papillae
   B. The olfactory epithelium
   C. The thalamus
   D. The pinnae

3. The inner-ear structures that contain the sensory receptors that detect head motion as when we move our heads and/or bodies are the
   A. stirrups.
   B. semicircular canals.
   C. hammer.
   D. cochlea.

Apply It! 4. Sean loves anchovy, mushroom, and double-cheese pizza on a whole wheat crust from his hometown pizzeria. He brings a pie back from home to give his roommate Danny a chance to taste it. Sean is stunned by Danny's reaction to the pizza: "Dude! Epic Fail" (meaning he hates it). What does this example demonstrate?
   A. Danny may not have the taste receptors for umami.
   B. Although Sean and Danny have similar tongue anatomy, perception is still a subjective process. Sean is apparently a big umami fan, but Danny is not.
   C. Danny may have a disorder of the olfactory epithelium.
   D. Danny is engaged in top-down processing.

summary

① How We Sense and Perceive the World

Sensation is the process of receiving stimulus energies from the environment. Perception is the process of organizing and interpreting sensory information to give it meaning. Perceiving the world involves both bottom-up and top-down processing. All sensation begins with sensory receptors, specialized cells that detect and transmit information about a stimulus to sensory neurons and the brain. Sensory receptors are selective and have different neural pathways.

Psychologists have explored the limits of our abilities to detect stimuli. Absolute threshold refers to the minimum amount of energy that people can detect. The difference threshold, or just noticeable difference, is the smallest difference in stimulation required to discriminate one stimulus from another 50 percent of the time.

Perception is influenced by attention, beliefs, and expectations. Sensory adaptation is a change in the responsiveness of the sensory system based on the average level of surrounding stimulation, essentially the ways that our senses start to ignore a particular stimulus once it is around long enough.

② The Visual System

Light is the stimulus that is sensed by the visual system. Light can be described in terms of wavelengths. Three characteristics of light waves determine our experience: wavelength (hue), amplitude (brightness), and purity (saturation).

In sensation, light passes through the cornea and lens to the retina, the light-sensitive surface in the back of the eye that houses light receptors called rods (which function in low illumination) and cones (which react to color). The fovea of the retina contains only cones and sharpens detail in an image. The optic nerve transmits neural impulses to the brain. There it diverges at the optic chiasm, so that what we see in the left visual field is registered in the right side of the brain and vice versa. In the occipital lobes of the cerebral cortex, the information is integrated.

The trichromatic theory of color perception holds that three types of color receptors in the retina allow us to perceive three colors (green, red, and blue). The opponent-process theory states that cells in the visual system respond to red-green and blue-yellow colors. Both theories are probably correct—the eye and the brain use both methods to code colors.

Shape perception is the ability to distinguish objects from their background. Depth perception is the ability to perceive objects three-dimensionally and depends on binocular (two-eyes) cues and monocular (one-eye) cues. Motion perception by humans depends on specialized neurons, feedback from the body, and environmental cues. Perceptual constancy is the recognition that objects are stable despite changes in the way we see them.

③ The Auditory System

Sounds, or sound waves, are vibrations in the air that are processed by the auditory system. These waves vary in important ways that influence what we hear. Pitch (how high or low in tone a sound is) is the perceptual interpretation of wavelength frequency. Amplitude of wavelengths, measured in decibels, is perceived as loudness. Complex sounds involve a blending of frequencies. Timbre is the tone saturation, or perceptual quality, of a sound.

The outer ear consists of the pinna and external auditory canal and acts to funnel sound to the middle ear. In the middle ear, the eardrum, hammer, anvil, and stirrup vibrate in response to sound and transfer the vibrations to the inner ear. Important parts of the fluid-filled inner ear are the oval window, cochlea, and basilar membrane. The movement of hair cells between the basilar membrane and the tectorial membrane generates nerve impulses.

Place theory states that each frequency produces vibrations at a particular spot on the basilar membrane. Place theory adequately explains high-frequency sounds but not low-frequency sounds. Frequency theory holds that the perception of a sound's frequency depends on how often the auditory nerve fires. The volley principle states that a cluster of neurons can fire impulses in rapid succession, producing a volley of impulses.

Information about sound moves from the hair cells to the auditory nerve, which carries information to the brain's auditory areas. The cortical destination of most fibers is the temporal lobes of the cerebral cortex. Localizing sound involves both the timing of the sound and the intensity of the sound arriving at each ear.

④ Other Senses

The skin senses include touch, temperature, and pain. Touch is the detection of mechanical energy, or pressure, against the skin. Touch information travels through the spinal cord, brain stem, and thalamus and on to the somatosensory areas of the parietal lobes. Thermoreceptors under the skin respond to increases and decreases in temperature. Pain is the sensation that warns us about damage to our bodies.

The chemical senses of taste and smell enable us to detect and process chemicals in the environment. Papillae are bumps on the tongue that contain taste buds, the receptors for taste. The olfactory epithelium contains a sheet of receptor cells for smell in the roof of the nose.

The kinesthetic senses provide information about movement, posture, and orientation. The vestibular sense gives us information about balance and movement. Receptors for the kinesthetic senses are embedded in muscle fibers and joints. The semicircular canals in the inner ear contain the sensory receptors that detect head motion.

key terms

sensation, p. 78
perception, p. 78
bottom-up processing, p. 79
top-down processing, p. 79
sensory receptors, p. 80
absolute threshold, p. 82
noise, p. 83
subliminal perception, p. 83
difference threshold, p. 83
Weber's law, p. 84
selective attention, p. 84

perceptual set, p. 85
sensory adaptation, p. 85
retina, p. 90
rods, p. 91
cones, p. 91
optic nerve, p. 91
feature detectors, p. 93
parallel processing, p. 93
binding, p. 94
trichromatic theory, p. 94
opponent-process theory, p. 95

figure-ground relationship, p. 96
gestalt psychology, p. 96
depth perception, p. 97
binocular cues, p. 97
convergence, p. 97
monocular cues, p. 97
apparent movement, p. 99
perceptual constancy, p. 99
outer ear, p. 102
middle ear, p. 102
inner ear, p. 103

place theory, p. 104
frequency theory, p. 106
volley principle, p. 106
auditory nerve, p. 106
thermoreceptors, p. 108
pain, p. 109
papillae, p. 110
olfactory epithelium, p. 111
kinesthetic senses, p. 113
vestibular sense, p. 113
semicircular canals, p. 113

self-test

Multiple Choice

1. Bottom-up processing involves analysis that begins with the
   A. absolute threshold.
   B. sensory receptors.
   C. cerebral cortex.
   D. spinal cord.

2. When you first arrive at a party, the music is so loud that it almost hurts your ears. After a couple of hours, even though the music is still at the same volume, it does not bother you any more. This change over time describes the process of
   A. light adaptation.
   B. transduction.
   C. sensory adaptation.
   D. sensory deprivation.

3. You are outside enjoying a beautiful day. The sky is bright blue. When the sun sets, the sky turns a gorgeous salmon pink. After the sun has set, the sky turns to lavender; as it gets dark, it becomes a deeper purple, then midnight blue, and finally black. The color changes you perceive in the sky are due to the _____ of light that it reflects.
   A. amplitude
   B. purity
   C. wavelength
   D. saturation

4. The crossover point where the right visual field information goes to the left hemisphere is called the
   A. fovea.
   B. optic nerve.
   C. retina.
   D. optic chiasm.

5. Near the center of the retina there is a spot where there are no rods and no cones; this is because of the
   A. clouding of the lens.
   B. retinal degeneration.
   C. optic nerve.
   D. ciliary muscle.

6. The pinna is the _____, which is quite useful for collecting sounds from the environment.
   A. external part of the ear
   B. inner eardrum
   C. curled structure of the inner ear
   D. organ of Corti

7. The basilar membrane gives us information about all of the following aspects of sound *except*
   A. frequency.
   B. location.
   C. pitch.
   D. complexity.

8. The _____, which lines the roof of our nasal cavity, maximizes the chances of our detecting an odor such as smoke.
   A. nasoreceptive sheath
   B. olfactory epithelium
   C. semicircular canal
   D. cochlea

9. Our largest sensory system is
   A. the visual system.
   B. the auditory system.
   C. the skin.
   D. the chemical senses.

10. A skier is able to slide down a snowy slope, maneuver her poles and skis, and come to a stop at the bottom of the hill through
    A. biofeedback.
    B. proprioceptive feedback.
    C. multitasking.
    D. fast pathway activation.

Apply It!

11. Casey loves to go hiking and rock climbing with her friends. On one excursion, she notices that though she can tell when someone is calling to her from the right or left, she is not always sure if a friend is calling from just above. Should Casey be worried? Why or why not?

4 States of Consciousness

Terry Wallis—Awakened After Almost 20 Years

Imagine falling asleep at the age of 19 and waking up nearly 20 years later. You open your eyes to a drastically changed world. Major events have transpired, technology has advanced, and people you love have aged quite suddenly.

This is Terry Wallis's story. In 1984, Terry was 19 years old when the truck he was driving dove off a 25-foot bluff. Found paralyzed and in a coma, he persisted in a state of minimal consciousness for the next 19 years. His parents visited him frequently in the nursing home where he lived and continued to talk to him, never knowing whether he had any awareness of them. Then, one day in 2003, Terry shocked everyone by answering "Mom" when asked who his visitor was that day.

Recent years have seen improvements in Terry's functioning. He has in some ways become himself again, making jokes and expressing joy at being alive. Terry has taken a while to accommodate to his new world. Until recently he could not imagine that he is in his 40s, not his 20s.

Recoveries of Terry's type are extremely rare. Scientists have recently discovered how he recovered. Neuroscientists Henning Voss and his colleagues (2006) published the first evidence that Terry's brain had *rewired* itself, allowing him to regain consciousness. Using a new technology called diffusion tensor imaging, the researchers showed that during those 20 years, Terry's brain had undergone a complex process of healing. His neurons slowly formed new connections, finally making enough to create a network.

The sense that Terry is himself again is based on the recovery of conscious awareness. Such is the enormous importance of consciousness in human life, the focus of this chapter. ■

- Which do you think is more a reflection of who you are—your thoughts and feelings or your behaviors?

- How important are your private thoughts to your sense of yourself?

- How do you get inside the head of a person who is "hard to read"?

In this chapter, we review various states of consciousness, explore the world of sleep and dreams, and consider three topics related to altered states of consciousness—psychoactive drugs, hypnosis, and meditation.

1 The Nature of Consciousness

If we didn't have those private thoughts and feelings that occur in our conscious minds, we couldn't tell a lie—and others wouldn't be able to lie to us. Think about how boring soap operas would be if the characters could not hold back the truth in their private world.

In the 1989 *Dictionary of Psychology,* British psychologist Stuart Sutherland described consciousness as a "fascinating but elusive phenomenon" and said that "it is impossible to specify what it is, what it does, or why it evolved." Although Sutherland dismissed the potential for scientific research on consciousness, this "fascinating but elusive" aspect of life has interested psychologists for centuries, and for good reason: Consciousness is a crucial part of many human experiences (Owen & others, 2006; Pinker, 2007).

In the late nineteenth and early twentieth centuries, psychology pioneer, William James (1890/1950) described the mind as a **stream of consciousness,** a continuous flow of changing sensations, images, thoughts, and feelings. The content of our awareness changes from moment to moment. Information moves rapidly in and out of consciousness. Our minds can race from one topic to the next—from thinking about the person approaching us to our physical state today to our strategy for the test tomorrow to the café where we are going to have lunch. During much of the twentieth century, psychologists focused less on the study of mental processes and more on the study of observable behavior. More recently, the study of consciousness has regained widespread respectability in psychology (Hansimayr & others, 2009; Reder, Park, & Kieffaber, 2009). Scientists from many different fields are interested in consciousness (Cabanac, Cabanac, & Parent, 2009; McKenny-Fick & others, 2009; Yeates & others, 2009).

We can define consciousness in terms of its two parts: awareness and arousal. **Consciousness** is an individual's awareness of external events and internal sensations under a condition of arousal. *Awareness* includes awareness of the self and one's thoughts about one's experiences. Consider that on an autumn afternoon, when you see a beautiful tree, vibrant with color, you are not simply perceiving the colors; you are also *aware* that you are seeing them. The term *metacognition* refers to thinking about thinking (Efklides, 2009; Exner & others, 2009). When you think about your thoughts—for example, when you reflect on why you are so nervous before an exam—you are using your conscious awareness to examine your own thought processes. The second part of consciousness is *arousal,* the physiological state of being engaged with the environment. Thus, a sleeping person is not conscious in the same way that he or she would be while awake.

stream of consciousness Term used by William James to describe the mind as a continuous flow of changing sensations, images, thoughts, and feelings.

consciousness An individual's awareness of external events and internal sensations under a condition of arousal, including awareness of the self and thoughts about one's experiences.

Take 15 minutes and document your stream of consciousness. Just sit and write or type whatever comes into your head. Don't censor yourself or worry about spelling and grammar. When you've finished, take a look at your work. Does your stream of consciousness reveal particular things about you?

Consciousness and the Brain

The two aspects of consciousness, awareness and arousal, are associated with different parts of the brain. Awareness, the subjective state of being conscious of what is going on, typically involves the cerebral cortex, especially its association areas and frontal lobes (Bekinschtein & others, 2009). It may be that the integration of input from the senses, along with information about emotions and memories in the association areas, creates consciousness (Bloom, Nelson, & Lazerson, 2001). Depending on what a person is aware of—for example, music playing or a photograph of a friend—at a given moment, different areas of the brain are activated (Janata, 2009). Arousal is a physiological state determined by the reticular activating system, a network of structures including the brain stem, medulla, and thalamus. Damage to either the cerebral cortex or the reticular activating system may cause a coma.

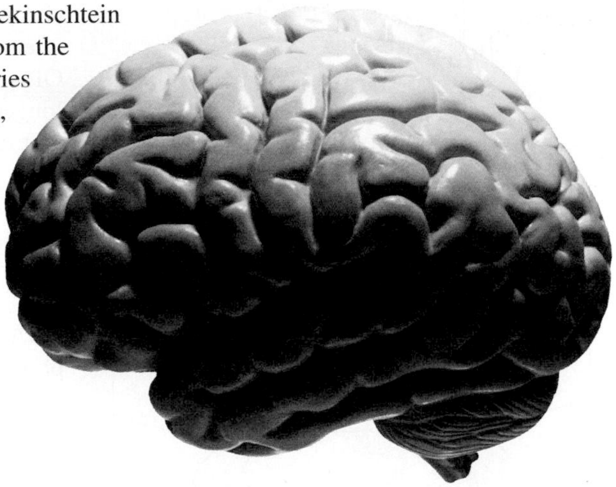

Levels of Awareness

The flow of sensations, images, thoughts, and feelings that William James spoke of can occur at different levels of awareness. Although we might think of consciousness as either present or not, there are in fact shades of awareness, observed in comatose patients as well as in everyday life. Here we consider five levels of awareness: higher-level consciousness, lower-level consciousness, altered states of consciousness, subconscious awareness, and no awareness (Figure 4.1).

Higher-Level Consciousness

In **controlled processes,** the most alert states of human consciousness, individuals actively focus their efforts toward a goal (Sibbald & others, 2009). For example, observe a classmate as he struggles to master the unfamiliar buttons on his new 10-function cell phone. He does not hear you humming or notice the intriguing shadow on the wall. His state of focused awareness illustrates the idea of controlled processes. Controlled processes require selective attention (see Chapter 3), the ability to concentrate on a specific aspect of experience while ignoring others

controlled processes
The most alert states of human consciousness; individuals actively focus their efforts toward a goal.

Level of Awareness	Description	Examples
Higher-Level Consciousness	Involves controlled processing, in which individuals actively focus their efforts on attaining a goal; the most alert state of consciousness	Doing a math or science problem; preparing for a debate; taking an at-bat in a baseball game
Lower-Level Consciousness	Includes automatic processing that requires little attention, as well as daydreaming	Punching in a number on a cell phone; typing on a keyboard when one is an expert; gazing at a sunset
Altered States of Consciousness	Can be produced by drugs, trauma, fatigue, possibly hypnosis, and sensory deprivation	Feeling the effects of having taken alcohol or psychedelic drugs; undergoing hypnosis to quit smoking or lose weight
Subconscious Awareness	Can occur when people are awake, as well as when they are sleeping and dreaming	Sleeping and dreaming
No Awareness	Freud's belief that some unconscious thoughts are too laden with anxiety and other negative emotions for consciousness to admit them	Having unconscious thoughts; being knocked out by a blow or anesthetized

FIGURE 4.1
Levels of Awareness
Each level of awareness has its time and place in human life.

"I'm sorry, dear. I must have lost consciousness.
What were you saying?"

(Klumpp & Amir, 2009). Because controlled processes require attention and effort, they are slower than automatic processes. Often, after we have practiced an activity a great deal, we no longer have to think about it while doing it. It becomes automatic and faster.

Lower-Level Awareness
Beneath the level of controlled processes are other levels of conscious awareness. Lower levels of awareness include automatic processes and daydreaming.

Automatic Processes
A few weeks after acquiring his cell phone, your classmate flips it open and sends a text message in the middle of a conversation with you. He does not have to concentrate on the keys and hardly seems aware of the gadget in his hand as he continues to talk to you while finishing his lunch. Using his cell phone has reached the point of automatic processing. **Automatic processes** are states of consciousness that require little attention and do not interfere with other ongoing activities. Automatic processes require less conscious effort than controlled processes (Gillard & others, 2009). When we are awake, our automatic behaviors occur at a lower level of awareness than controlled processes, but they are still conscious behaviors. Your classmate pushed the right buttons, so at some level he apparently was aware of what he was doing.

automatic processes
States of consciousness that require little attention and do not interfere with other ongoing activities. Automatic processes require less conscious effort than controlled processes.

Daydreaming
Another state of consciousness that involves a low level of conscious effort is *daydreaming,* which lies between active consciousness and dreaming while asleep. It is a little like dreaming while we are awake. Daydreams usually begin spontaneously when we are doing something that requires less than our full attention.

Mind wandering is probably the most obvious type of daydreaming. We regularly take brief side trips into our own private kingdoms of imagery and memory while reading, listening, or working. When we daydream, we drift into a world of fantasy. We perhaps imagine ourselves on a date, at a party, on television, in a faraway place, or at another time in our lives. Sometimes our daydreams are about everyday events such as paying the rent, going to the dentist, and meeting with somebody at school or work.

The semiautomatic flow of daydreaming can be useful. As you daydream while ironing a shirt or walking to the store, you may make plans, solve a problem, or come up with a creative idea. Daydreams can remind us of important things ahead. Daydreaming keeps our minds active while helping us to cope, create, and fantasize (Schupak & Rosenthal, 2009).

Altered States of Consciousness
Altered states of consciousness or awareness are mental states that are noticeably different from normal awareness. Altered states of consciousness can range from losing one's sense of self-consciousness to hallucinating. Such states can be produced by drugs, trauma, fever, fatigue, sensory deprivation, meditation, and possibly hypnosis (Avner, 2006). Drug use can also induce altered states of consciousness (Fields, 2010), as we will consider later.

Subconscious Awareness
In Chapter 3, we saw that a great deal of brain activity occurs beneath the level of conscious awareness. Psychologists are increasingly interested in the subconscious processing of information, which can take place while we are awake or asleep (Voss & Paller, 2009; Yamada & Decety, 2009).

Waking Subconscious Awareness

When we are awake, processes are going on just below the surface of awareness. For example, while you are grappling with a problem, the solution may just pop into your head. Such insights can occur when a subconscious connection between ideas is so strong that it rises into awareness, somewhat the way a cork held underwater bobs to the surface as soon as it is released (Csikszentmihalyi, 1996).

Evidence that we are not always aware of our brain's processing of information comes from studies of individuals with certain neurological disorders. In one case, a woman who suffered neurological damage was unable to describe or report the shape or size of objects in her visual field, although she was capable of describing other physical perceptions that she had (Milner & Goodale, 1995). Nonetheless, when she reached for an object, she could accurately adjust the size of her grip to allow her to grasp the object. Thus, she did possess some subconscious knowledge of the size and shape of objects, even though she had no awareness of this knowledge.

Subconscious information processing can occur simultaneously in a distributed manner along many parallel tracks. (Recall the discussion of parallel processing of visual information in Chapter 3.) For example, when you look at a dog running down the street, you are consciously aware of the event but not of the subconscious processing of the object's identity (a dog), its color (black), and its movement (fast). In contrast, conscious processing occurs in sequence and is slower than much subconscious processing. Note that the various levels of awareness often work together. You might rely on controlled processing when memorizing material for class, but later, the answers on a test just pop into your head as a result of automatic or subconscious processing.

Recall that in Chapter 1, we noted the limits of introspection. Now you can see that introspection relies on conscious awareness.

Subconscious Awareness During Sleep and Dreams

When we sleep and dream, our level of awareness is lower than when we daydream, but sleep and dreams are not best regarded as the absence of consciousness (Issa & Wang, 2008). Rather, they are low levels of consciousness.

Researchers have found that when people are asleep, they remain aware of external stimuli to some degree. In sleep laboratories, when people are clearly asleep (as determined by physiological monitoring devices), they are able to respond to faint tones by pressing a handheld button (Ogilvie & Wilkinson, 1988). In one study, the presentation of pure auditory tones to sleeping individuals activated auditory processing regions of the brain, whereas participants' names activated language areas, the amygdala, and the prefrontal cortex (Stickgold, 2001). We return to the topics of sleep and dreams in the next section.

No Awareness

The term *unconscious* generally applies to someone who has been knocked out by a blow or anesthetized, or who has fallen into a deep, prolonged unconscious state (Matis & Birbilis, 2009). However, Sigmund Freud (1917) used the term *unconscious* in a very different way: **Unconscious thought,** said Freud, is a reservoir of unacceptable wishes, feelings, and thoughts that are beyond conscious awareness. In other words, Freud's interpretation viewed the unconscious as a storehouse for vile thoughts. He believed that some aspects of our experience remain unconscious for good reason, as if we are better off not knowing about them. For example, from Freud's perspective, the human mind is full of disturbing impulses such as a desire to have sex with our parents.

unconscious thought According to Freud, a reservoir of unacceptable wishes, feelings, and thoughts that are beyond conscious awareness.

Although Freud's interpretation remains controversial, psychologists now widely accept the notion that unconscious processes do exist (Sampaio & Brewer, 2009; Voss & Paller, 2009). Recently, researchers have found that many mental processes (thoughts, emotions, and perceptions) can occur outside of awareness. Some psychologists term these processes *nonconscious* rather than *unconscious* to avoid the Freudian connotation (Finkbeiner & Palermo, 2009; Weyers & others, 2009).

For further insights on consciousness, see the Intersection, which explores children's beliefs and understanding of how the mind works and the implications of these beliefs and understanding for their social functioning.

Imagine yourself in a conversation with a friend, describing a complex issue. You search your friend's face for signs of understanding. Does she nod? Does her brow furrow? Consider that, in a sense, your observations reveal your belief in your friend's consciousness. When you pause and ask, "Do you see what I mean?" you are checking in on your conversation partner's mind.

Consciousness and Developmental Psychology: How Do We Develop a Sense for the Minds of Others?

Examining interactions like this provides clues about how we think others think. It might seem obvious that other people have minds of their own, but the human ability to recognize the subjective experience of another is a true developmental accomplishment. Developmental psychologists who study children's ideas about mental states use the phrase *theory of mind* to refer to individuals' understanding that they and others think, feel, perceive, and have private experiences (Gelman, 2009).

In subtle ways, children reveal early in life their sense that other people think. For example, if a 6-month-old sees a person talking to someone hidden behind a curtain, the child will be surprised if the curtain is opened to reveal an

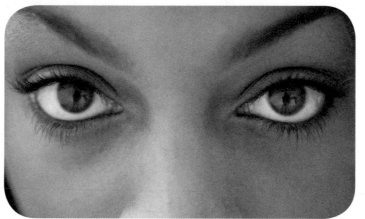

object rather than another person. This outcome suggests that even an infant knows that people talk to people (Legerstee, Barna, & DiAdamo, 2000). When a 9-month-old points to a wanted item, these actions imply that the infant recognizes that another person can understand that he or she wants something (Tomasello, 2008).

Developmental psychologists have used a procedure called the *false belief task* to examine children's theory of mind (Doherty, 2008). In one version of the false belief task, the child is asked to consider the following situation (Wellman & Woolley, 1990). Anna is a little girl who has some chocolate that she decides to save for later. She puts it in a blue cupboard and goes outside to play. While Anna is gone, her mother moves the chocolate to the red cupboard. When Anna comes back in, where will she look for her chocolate? Three-year-olds give the wrong answer—they assume that Anna will look in the red cupboard because they know (even though Anna does not) that Anna's mom moved the chocolate to the red one. Four-year-olds answer correctly—they recognize that Anna does not know everything they do and that she will believe the chocolate is where she left it (Wellman & Woolley, 1990). Success at the false belief task is associated with social competence, and children who perform well at it are better liked by their peers (Leslie, German, & Polizzi, 2005).

Theory of mind is essential to many valuable social capacities, such as empathy and sympathy (Boyd, 2008; Peterson & others, 2009). We know we have found a true kindred spirit when someone "gets" us—when a friend can say, "I know exactly what you mean."

Simon Baron-Cohen (1995, 2006, 2008) is an expert on *autism,* a disorder that affects communication and social interaction. He has proposed that the emergence of theory of mind is so central to human functioning that evolution would not leave it up to chance. Baron-Cohen suggests that we are born with a brain mechanism that is ready to develop a theory of mind. This theory of mind mechanism (or TOMM) accounts for the fact that nearly all children over the age of 4 pass the false belief task. Baron-Cohen has proposed that autistic individuals lack the TOMM, a condition that would explain their unique social deficits.

Even with our TOMM in full working order, however, our intuitions about others are sometimes inaccurate. We might love someone who does not return our feelings, or we might trust a person who does not have our best interest at heart. There is perhaps no greater mystery than what is going on behind another person's eyes. What another person knows, thinks, believes, and wants—these questions have fascinated human beings since the beginning of our species.

If you could, would you want to be able to read someone's mind? Why or why not?

2 Sleep and Dreams

Sleep takes up about one-third of the time in our lives, more than anything else we do. What is sleep? Why is it important? Before tackling these questions, let's first see how sleep is linked to our internal biological rhythms.

Biological Rhythms and Sleep

biological rhythms
Periodic physiological fluctuations in the body, such as the rise and fall of hormones and accelerated/decelerated cycles of brain activity, that can influence behavior.

Biological rhythms are periodic physiological fluctuations in the body. We are unaware of most biological rhythms, such as the rise and fall of hormones and accelerated and decelerated cycles of brain activity, but they can influence our behavior. These rhythms are controlled by biological clocks, which include annual or seasonal cycles such as the migration of birds and the hibernation of bears, and 24-hour cycles such as the sleep/wake cycle and temperature changes in the human body. Let's further explore the body's 24-hour cycles.

Circadian Rhythms **Circadian rhythms** are daily behavioral or physiological cycles. Daily circadian rhythms involve the sleep/wake cycle, body temperature, blood pressure, and blood sugar level (Habbal & Al-Jabri, 2009; Scheer & others, 2009). For example, body temperature fluctuates about 3 degrees Fahrenheit in a 24-hour day, peaking in the afternoon and reaching its lowest point between 2 A.M. and 5 A.M.

circadian rhythms
Daily behavioral or physiological cycles that involve the sleep/wake cycle, body temperature, blood pressure, and blood sugar level.

suprachiasmatic nucleus (SCN)
A small brain structure that uses input from the retina to synchronize its own rhythm with the daily cycle of light and dark; the body's way of monitoring the change from day to night.

Researchers have discovered that the body monitors the change from day to night by means of the **suprachiasmatic nucleus (SCN),** a small brain structure that uses input from the retina to synchronize its own rhythm with the daily cycle of light and dark (Borgs & others, 2009). Output from the SCN allows the hypothalamus to regulate daily rhythms such as temperature and hunger and the reticular formation to regulate daily rhythms of sleep and wakefulness (Figure 4.2). Although a number of biological clocks seem to be involved in regulating circadian rhythms, researchers have found that the SCN is the most important (Vimal & others, 2009).

Many individuals who are totally blind experience lifelong sleeping problems because their retinas cannot detect light. These people have a kind of permanent jet lag and periodic insomnia because their circadian rhythms often do not follow a 24-hour cycle (Waller, Bendel, & Kaplan, 2008).

 How, where, and with whom we sleep are all issues that are influenced by culture. In Western societies infants are trained to sleep alone. In many other cultures infants "co-sleep" with their parents, and some cultures encourage a family bed, in which everyone sleeps together.

Desynchronizing the Biological Clock Biological clocks can become *desynchronized,* or thrown off their regular schedules. Among the circumstances of life that can introduce irregularities into our sleep are jet travel, changing work shifts, and

FIGURE 4.2
Suprachiasmatic Nucleus

The suprachiasmatic nucleus (SCN) plays an important role in keeping our biological clock running on time. The SCN is located in the hypothalamus. It receives information from the retina about light, which is the external stimulus that synchronizes the SCN. Output from the SCN is distributed to the rest of the hypothalamus and to the reticular formation.

Cerebral cortex

Hypothalamus

Suprachiasmatic nucleus (SCN)

Reticular formation

Why would melatonin be particularly helpful for eastward but not westward travel?

insomnia. What effects might such irregularities have on circadian rhythms?

If you fly from Los Angeles to New York and then go to bed at 11 P.M. eastern time, you may have trouble falling asleep because your body is still on west coast time. Even if you sleep for 8 hours that night, you may have a hard time waking up at 7 A.M. eastern time, because your body thinks it is 4 A.M. If you stay in New York for several days, your body will adjust to this new schedule.

The jet lag you experience when you fly from Los Angeles to New York occurs because your body time is out of phase, or synchronization, with clock time (Sack, 2009). Jet lag is the result of two or more body rhythms being out of sync. You usually go to bed when your body temperature begins to drop, but in your new location, you might be trying to go to sleep when it is rising. In the morning, your adrenal glands release large doses of the hormone cortisol to help you wake up. In your new geographic time zone, the glands may be releasing this chemical just as you are getting ready for bed at night.

Circadian rhythms may also become desynchronized when shift workers change their work hours (Mitchell, Gallagher, & Thomas, 2008). A number of near accidents in air travel have been associated with pilots who have not yet become synchronized to their new shifts and are not working as efficiently as usual (Kim & Lee, 2007). Shift-work problems most often affect night-shift workers who never fully adjust to sleeping in the daytime after their work shifts. Such workers may fall asleep at work and are at increased risk for heart disease and gastrointestinal disorders (Sadeghniiat-Haghighi & others, 2008).

Resetting the Biological Clock

If your biological clock for sleeping and waking becomes desynchronized, how can you reset it? With regard to jet lag, if you take a transoceanic flight and arrive at your destination during the day, it is a good idea to spend as much time outside in the daylight as possible. Bright light during the day, especially in the morning, increases wakefulness, whereas bright light at night delays sleep (Goel & others, 2009).

Researchers are studying melatonin, a hormone that increases at night in humans, for its possible effects in reducing jet lag (G. M. Brown & others, 2009). Recent studies have shown that a small dosage of melatonin can reduce jet lag by advancing the circadian clock—an effect that makes it useful for eastward but not westward jet lag (Arendt, 2009).

Changing to a night-shift job can desynchronize our biological clocks and affect our circadian rhythms and performance.

Why Do We Need Sleep?

When we do not get enough sleep, we often do not function well, physically and mentally. The important benefits of sleep include restoration, adaptation, growth, and memory.

Because all animals require sleep, it seems that sleep is fundamental for survival. Examining the evolutionary basis for sleep, scientists have proposed that sleep restores, replenishes, and rebuilds the brain and body, which the day's waking activities can wear out. This idea fits with the feeling of being tired before we go to sleep and restored when we wake up.

In support of the restorative function of sleep, many of the body's cells show increased production and reduced breakdown of proteins during deep sleep (Aton & others, 2009; Vazquez & others, 2008). Protein molecules are the building blocks needed for cell growth and for repair of damages from factors such as stress. Also, neuroscientists recently have argued that sleep enhances synaptic connections between neurons (Aton & others, 2009).

From an evolutionary perspective, sleep may have developed because animals needed to protect themselves at night. For some animals the search for food and water is easier and safer when the sun is up. When it is dark, it is adaptive for these animals to save energy, prevent themselves from getting eaten, and avoid falling off a cliff that they cannot see. In general, animals that serve as food for other animals sleep the least. Figure 4.3 illustrates the average amount of sleep per day of various animals.

Sleep also may benefit physical growth and brain development in infants and children. For example, deep sleep coincides with the release of growth hormone in children. The lack of sleep is stressful, and stress hormones may interfere with the creation of neurons in the hippocampus, the part of the brain most associated with memory (Wierzynski & others, 2009). A recent research review concluded that sleep is vital to the consolidation of memory, whether memory is about specific information, memory for skills, or memory for emotional experiences (Diekelmann, Wilhelm, & Born, 2009). One possible explanation is that during sleep the cerebral cortex is free to conduct activities that strengthen memory associations, so that memories formed during recent waking hours can be integrated into long-term memory storage. Lost sleep often results in lost memories. This connection can be especially important if you have a test coming up.

Indeed, if you are thinking about studying all night for your next test, you might want to think again. In one study, a good night's sleep helped the brain to store the memory of what had been learned during the day (Stickgold & Hobson, 2000). The researchers found that the memory of individuals who stayed up all night for one of the nights during the study was inferior to the memory of individuals who got a good night's sleep every night during the study.

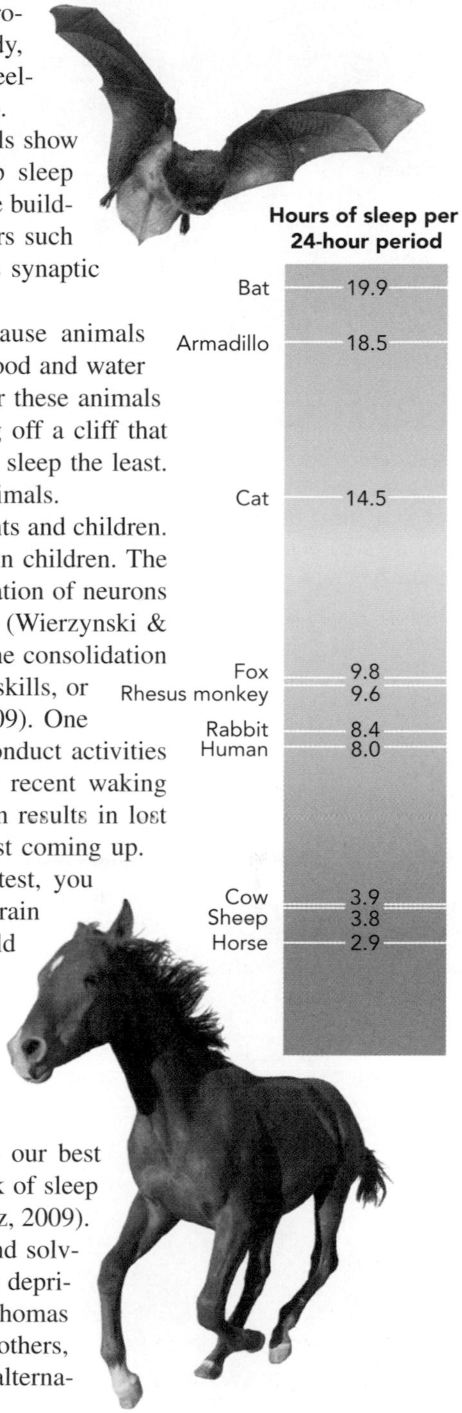

The Effects of Chronic Sleep Deprivation
We do our best when we sleep more than 8 hours a night (Habeck & others, 2004). Lack of sleep is stressful and has an impact on the body and the brain (Azboy & Kaygisiz, 2009). When deprived of sleep, people have trouble paying attention to tasks and solving problems (Mullington & others, 2009). Studies have shown that sleep deprivation decreased brain activity in the thalamus and the prefrontal cortex (Thomas & others, 2001) and reduced the complexity of brain activity (Jeong & others, 2001). The tired brain must compensate by using different pathways or alternative neural networks when thinking (Mander & others, 2008). Sleep deprivation can even influence moral judgment. Following 53 hours of wakefulness, participants in a recent study had more difficulty making moral decisions and were more likely to agree with decisions that violated their personal standards (Killgore & others, 2007).

Although sleep is unquestionably key to optimal physical and mental performance, many of us do not get sufficient sleep. In a national

Hours of sleep per 24-hour period

Animal	Hours
Bat	19.9
Armadillo	18.5
Cat	14.5
Fox	9.8
Rhesus monkey	9.6
Rabbit	8.4
Human	8.0
Cow	3.9
Sheep	3.8
Horse	2.9

FIGURE 4.3

From Bats to Horses: The Wide Range of Sleep in Animals We might feel envious of bats, which sleep nearly 20 hours a day, and more than a little in awe of horses, still running on just under 3 hours of rest.

Sleep researchers record Randy Gardner's behavior (he's the person doing push-ups) during his 264-hour period of sleep deprivation. Most people who try to stay up even one night have difficulty remaining awake from 3 A.M. to 6 A.M.

Developmental changes in sleep patterns during adolescence can influence alertness at school.

survey of more than 1,000 American adults conducted by the National Sleep Foundation (2001), 63 percent said that they get less than 8 hours of sleep a night, and 31 percent said that they get less than 7 hours of sleep a night. An estimated 50 to 70 million Americans chronically suffer from lack of sleep or a sleep disorder (Institute of Medicine, 2006). The Institute of Medicine declared that sleep deprivation is an unmet health problem in the United States (2006).

Why do Americans get too little sleep? Pressures at work and school, family responsibilities, and social obligations often lead to long hours of wakefulness and irregular sleep/wake schedules (Artazcoz & others, 2009). Not having enough hours to do all that we want or need to do in a day, we cheat on our sleep. As a result we may suffer from a "sleep debt," an accumulated level of exhaustion.

Sleep Deprivation from Adolescence to Old Age

Recently there has been a surge of interest in adolescent sleep patterns (Eaton & others, 2008; Rao, Hammen, & Poland, 2009; Vallido, Jackson, & O'Brien, 2009). During adolescence, the brain, especially the cerebral cortex, is continuing to develop, and the adolescent's need for sleep may be linked to this important work (Dahl & Spear, 2004).

The National Sleep Foundation (2006) conducted a U.S. survey of 1,602 caregivers and their 11- to 17-year-olds. Nearly half of the adolescents got inadequate sleep on school nights (less than 8 hours). Adolescents who logged less than 8 hours of sleep on school nights were more likely to feel tired, sleepy, cranky, and irritable. They were also more likely to fall asleep in school and to drink caffeinated beverages than their counterparts who got optimal sleep (9 or more hours).

Many adolescents stay up later at night and sleep longer in the morning than they did when they were children, and these changing sleep patterns may influence their academic work. Mary Carskadon and her colleagues have conducted a number of studies on adolescent sleep patterns (Carskadon, 2006; Carskadon, Mindell, & Drake, 2006; Tarokh & Caskadon, 2008). They found that when given the opportunity, adolescents will sleep an average of 9 hours and 25 minutes a night. Most get considerably less than 9 hours of sleep, especially during the week. This shortfall creates a sleep debt that adolescents often attempt to make up on the weekend. The researchers also found that older adolescents tend to be sleepier during the day than younger adolescents. They theorized that this sleepiness was not due to academic work or social pressures. Rather, their research suggests that adolescents' biological clocks undergo a shift as they get older, delaying their period of wakefulness by about an hour. A delay in the nightly release of the sleep-inducing hormone melatonin seems to underlie this shift. Melatonin is secreted at about 9:30 P.M. in younger adolescents and approximately an hour later in older adolescents.

Carskadon has suggested that early school starting times may cause grogginess, inattention in class, and poor performance on tests. Based on her research, school officials in Edina, Minnesota, decided to start classes at 8:30 A.M. rather than the usual 7:25 A.M. Since then there have been fewer referrals for discipline problems, and the number of students who report being ill or depressed has decreased. The school system reports that test scores have improved for high school students, but not for middle school students. This finding supports Carskadon's suspicion that early start times are likely to be more stressful for older than for younger adolescents.

Sleep patterns also change as people age through the middle-adult (40s and 50s) and late-adult (60s and older) years (Goldman & others, 2008). Many such adults go to bed earlier at night and wake up earlier in the morning. Beginning in the 40s, individuals report that they are less likely to sleep through the entire night than when they were younger. Middle-aged adults also spend less time in deep sleep than when they were younger. More than 50 percent of individuals in late adulthood report that they experience some problems falling asleep and staying asleep (Kamel & Gammack, 2006; Wolkove & others, 2007).

Stages of Wakefulness and Sleep

Have you ever been awakened from your sleep and been totally disoriented? Have you ever awakened in the middle of a dream and suddenly gone right back into the dream as if it were a movie running just under the surface of your consciousness? These two circumstances reflect two distinct stages in the sleep cycle.

Stages of sleep correspond to massive electrophysiological changes that occur throughout the brain as the fast, irregular, and low-amplitude electrical activity of wakefulness is replaced by the slow, regular, high-amplitude waves of deep sleep. Using the electroencephalograph (EEG) to monitor the brain's electrical activity, scientists have identified two stages of wakefulness and five stages of sleep.

Wakefulness Stages When people are awake, their EEG patterns exhibit two types of waves: beta and alpha. *Beta waves* reflect concentration and alertness. These waves are the highest in frequency and lowest in amplitude. This means that the waves go up and down a great deal, but they do not have very high peaks or very low ebbs. They also are more *desynchronous* than other waves, meaning they do not form a very consistent pattern. Inconsistent patterning makes sense given the extensive variation in sensory input and activities we experience when we are awake.

When we are relaxed but still awake, our brain waves slow down, increase in amplitude, and become more *synchronous,* or regular. These waves, associated with relaxation or drowsiness, are called *alpha waves.*

The five stages of sleep also are differentiated by the types of wave patterns detected with an EEG, and the depth of sleep varies from one stage to another, as we now consider.

Sleep Stages 1–4 *Stage 1 sleep* is characterized by drowsy sleep. In this stage, the person may experience sudden muscle movements called *myoclonic jerks.*

EEGs of individuals in this stage are characterized by *theta waves,* which are even slower in frequency and greater in amplitude than alpha waves. The difference between just being relaxed and stage 1 sleep is gradual. Figure 4.4 shows the EEG pattern of stage 1 sleep, along with the EEG patterns for the other four sleep stages and beta and alpha waves.

In *stage 2 sleep,* muscle activity decreases, and the person is no longer consciously aware of the environment. Theta waves continue but are interspersed with a defining characteristic of stage 2 sleep: *sleep spindles.* These involve a sudden increase in wave frequency (Bastien & others, 2009). Stages 1 and 2 are both relatively light stages of sleep, and if people awaken during one of these stages, they often report not having been asleep at all.

Stage 3 and *stage 4 sleep* are characterized by *delta waves,* the slowest and highest-amplitude brain waves during sleep. These two stages are often referred to as *delta sleep.*

Watch people in your classes fight to stay awake— you'll see their heads jerk up. This first stage of sleep often involves the feeling of falling.

FIGURE 4.4

Characteristics and Formats of EEG Recordings During Stages of Sleep Even while you are sleeping, your brain is busy. No wonder you sometimes wake up feeling tired.

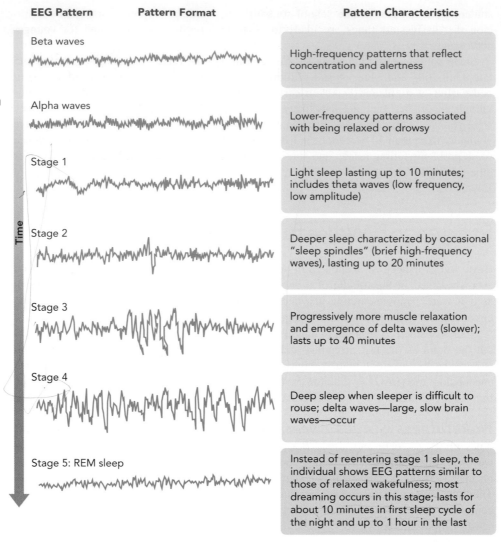

EEG Pattern	Pattern Format	Pattern Characteristics
Beta waves		High-frequency patterns that reflect concentration and alertness
Alpha waves		Lower-frequency patterns associated with being relaxed or drowsy
Stage 1		Light sleep lasting up to 10 minutes; includes theta waves (low frequency, low amplitude)
Stage 2		Deeper sleep characterized by occasional "sleep spindles" (brief high-frequency waves), lasting up to 20 minutes
Stage 3		Progressively more muscle relaxation and emergence of delta waves (slower); lasts up to 40 minutes
Stage 4		Deep sleep when sleeper is difficult to rouse; delta waves—large, slow brain waves—occur
Stage 5: REM sleep		Instead of reentering stage 1 sleep, the individual shows EEG patterns similar to those of relaxed wakefulness; most dreaming occurs in this stage; lasts for about 10 minutes in first sleep cycle of the night and up to 1 hour in the last

Distinguishing between stage 3 and stage 4 is difficult, although typically stage 3 is characterized by delta waves occurring less than 50 percent of the time and stage 4 by delta waves occurring more than 50 percent of the time. Delta sleep is our deepest sleep, the time when our brain waves are least like waking brain waves. It is during delta sleep that it is the most difficult to wake sleepers. This is also the stage when bed wetting (in children), sleep walking, and sleep talking occur. When awakened during this stage, people usually are confused and disoriented.

REM Sleep

After going through stages 1–4, sleepers drift up through the sleep stages toward wakefulness. Instead of reentering stage 1, however, they enter stage 5, a different form of sleep called *REM (rapid eye movement)* sleep (Ravassard & others, 2009). **REM sleep** is an active stage of sleep during which dreaming occurs. The EEG pattern for REM sleep shows fast waves similar to those of relaxed wakefulness, and the sleeper's eyeballs move up and down and from left to right (Figure 4.5).

Specialists refer to stages 1–4 as *non-REM sleep*. Non-REM sleep is characterized by a lack of rapid eye movement and little dreaming. A person who is awakened during REM sleep is more likely to report having dreamed than when awakened at any other stage (Schredl, 2009). Even people who claim they rarely dream frequently report dreaming

REM sleep
An active stage of sleep during which dreaming occurs.

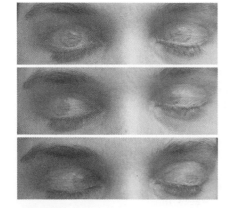

FIGURE 4.5
REM Sleep During REM sleep, your eyes move rapidly, as if following the images moving in your dreams.

when they are awakened during REM sleep. The longer the period of REM sleep, the more likely the person will report dreaming. Dreams also occur during slow-wave or non-REM sleep, but the frequency of dreams in these stages is relatively low (McNamara, McLaren, & Durso, 2007), and we are less likely to remember these dreams. Reports of dreaming by individuals awakened from REM sleep are typically longer, more vivid, more physically active, more emotionally charged, and less related to waking life than reports by those awakened from non-REM sleep (Hobson, 2004).

REM sleep also likely plays a role in memory (Diekelmann, Wilhelm, & Born, 2009). Researchers have presented individuals with unique phrases before they go to bed. When they are awakened just before they begin REM sleep, they remember less the next morning than when they are awakened during the other sleep stages (Stickgold & Walker, 2005).

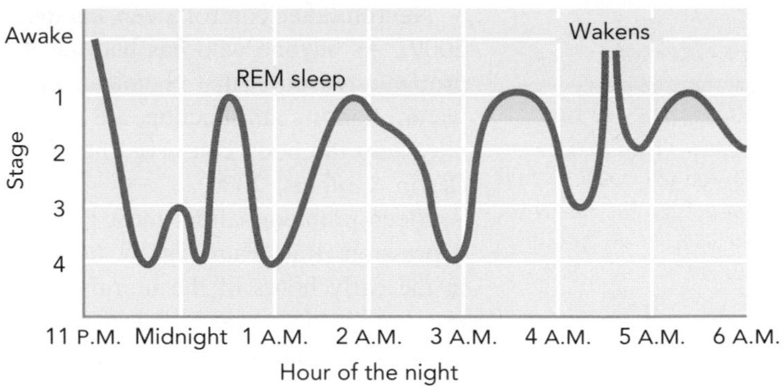

FIGURE 4.6

Cycling Through a Night's Sleep During a night's sleep, we go through several cycles. Depth of sleep decreases, and REM sleep (shown in light blue) increases as the night progresses. In this graph, the person is depicted as awakening at about 5 A.M. and then going back to sleep for another hour.

Sleep Cycling Through the Night   The five stages of sleep we have considered make up a normal cycle of sleep. As shown in Figure 4.6, one of these cycles lasts about 90 to 100 minutes and recurs several times during the night. The amount of deep sleep (stages 3 and 4) is much greater in the first half of a night's sleep than in the second half. Most REM sleep takes place toward the end of a night's sleep, when the REM stage becomes progressively longer. The night's first REM stage might last for only 10 minutes, but the final REM stage might continue for as long as an hour. During a normal night of sleep, individuals will spend about 60 percent of sleep in light sleep (stages 1 and 2), 20 percent in delta or deep sleep, and 20 percent in REM sleep (Webb, 2000).

Sleep and the Brain   The five sleep stages are associated with distinct patterns of neurotransmitter activity initiated in the reticular formation, the core of the brain stem. In all vertebrates, the reticular formation plays a crucial role in sleep and arousal (see Figure 4.2). As previously noted, damage to the reticular formation can result in coma and death.

Three important neurotransmitters involved in sleep are serotonin, epinephrine, and acetylcholine (Jellinger, 2009; Kalonia, Bishnoi, & Kumar, 2008). As sleep begins, the levels of neurotransmitters sent to the forebrain from the reticular formation start dropping, and they continue to fall until they reach their lowest levels during the deepest sleep stage—stage 4. REM sleep (stage 5) is initiated by a rise in acetylcholine, which activates the cerebral cortex while the rest of the brain remains relatively inactive. REM sleep ends when there is a rise in serotonin and norepinephrine, which increase the level of forebrain activity nearly to the awakened state (Miller & O'Callaghan, 2006). You are most likely to wake up just after a REM period. If you do not wake up then, the level of the neurotransmitters falls again, and you enter another sleep cycle.

Sleep and Disease

Sleep plays a role in a large number of diseases and disorders (Friese, Bruns, & Sinton, 2009; van Leeuwen & others, 2009). For example, stroke and asthma attacks are more common during the night and in the early morning, probably because of changes in hormones, heart rate, and other characteristics associated with sleep (Teodorescu & others, 2006). Sleeplessness is also associated with obesity and heart disease (Plante, 2006).

Neurons that control sleep interact closely with the immune system (Imeri & Opp, 2009). As anyone who has had the flu knows, infectious diseases make us sleepy. The probable reason is that chemicals called cytokines, produced by the body's cells while we are fighting an infection, are powerfully sleep-inducing (Patel & others, 2009). Sleep may help the body conserve energy and other resources it needs to overcome infection (Irwin & others, 2006).

Sleep problems afflict most people who have mental disorders, including those with depression (Rao, Hammen, & Poland, 2009). Individuals with depression often awaken in the early hours of the morning and cannot get back to sleep, and they often spend less time in delta wave or deep sleep than do non-depressed individuals.

Sleep problems are common in many other disorders as well, including Alzheimer disease, stroke, and cancer (Deschenes & McCurry, 2009; Parish, 2009). In some cases, however, these problems may be due not to the disease itself but to the drugs used to treat the disease.

Sleep Disorders

Many individuals suffer from undiagnosed and untreated sleep disorders that leave them struggling through the day, feeling unmotivated and exhausted (Ohayon, 2009). Some of the major sleep problems are insomnia, sleepwalking and sleep talking, nightmares and night terrors, narcolepsy, and sleep apnea.

Insomnia   A common sleep problem is *insomnia,* the inability to sleep. Insomnia can involve a problem in falling asleep, waking up during the night, or waking up too early. In the United States, as many as one in five adults have insomnia (Pearson, Johnson, & Nahin, 2006). Insomnia is more common among women and older adults, as well as individuals who are thin, stressed, or depressed (National Sleep Foundation, 2007).

For short-term insomnia, most physicians prescribe sleeping pills. However, most sleeping pills stop working after several weeks of nightly use, and their long-term use can interfere with good sleep. Mild insomnia often can be reduced by simply practicing good sleep habits, such as always going to bed at the same time, even on weekends, and sleeping in a dark, quiet place. In more serious cases, researchers are experimenting with light therapy, melatonin supplements, and other ways to alter circadian cycles (Garzon & others, 2009; Miyamoto, 2009). Behavioral changes (such as avoiding naps and setting an alarm in the morning) can help insomniacs increase their sleep time and to awaken less frequently in the night (Edinger & others, 2001).

"I probably shouldn't wake him. He needs the exercise."

Sleepwalking and Sleep Talking   *Somnambulism* is the formal term for sleepwalking, which occurs during the deepest stages of sleep (Harris & Grunstein, 2009). For many years, experts believed that somnambulists were acting out their dreams. However, somnambulism takes place during stages 3 and 4, usually early in the night, when a person is unlikely to be dreaming.

The specific causes of sleepwalking have not been identified, but it is more likely to occur when individuals are sleep deprived or when they have been drinking alcohol. There is nothing abnormal about sleepwalking, and despite superstition, it is safe to awaken sleepwalkers. In fact, they probably should be awakened, as they may harm themselves wandering around in the dark (Swanson, 1999).

Another quirky night behavior is sleep talking. If you interrogate sleep talkers, can you find out what they did, for instance, last Thursday night? Probably not. Although sleep talkers will converse with you and make fairly coherent statements, they are soundly asleep. Thus, even if a sleep talker mumbles a response to your question, do not count on its accuracy.

Recently, a few cases of an even rarer sleep behavior have come to light—sleep eating. Ambien is a widely prescribed sleep medication for insomnia. Some Ambien users began to notice odd things upon waking up from a much-needed good night's sleep, such as candy wrappers strewn around the room, crumbs in the bed, and food missing from the refrigerator. One woman gained 100 pounds without changing her waking, eating, or exercise habits. How could this be? Dr. Mark Mahowald, the medical director of the Minnesota Regional Sleep Disorders Center in Minneapolis, has confirmed that sleep eating may be a side effect of using Ambien (CBS News, 2006).

The phenomenon of sleep eating illustrates that even when we feel fast asleep, we may be "half-awake"—and capable of putting together some unusual late-night snacks, including buttered cigarettes, salt sandwiches, and raw bacon. The maker of Ambien has noted this unusual side effect on the label of the drug. Even more alarming than sleep eating may be recent reports of sleep driving under the influence of Ambien (Saul, 2006). Sleep experts agree that reports of sleep driving while taking Ambien are rare and extreme but plausible.

No one should abruptly stop taking any medication without talking to his or her doctor. For individuals who are battling persistent insomnia, a drug that provides a good night's rest may be worth the risk of these unusual side effects.

Nightmares and Night Terrors A *nightmare* is a frightening dream that awakens a dreamer from REM sleep (Zadra, Pilon, & Donderi, 2006). The nightmare's content invariably involves danger—the dreamer is chased, robbed, or thrown off a cliff. Nightmares are common. Most of us have had them, especially as young children. Nightmares peak at 3 to 6 years of age and then decline, although the average college student experiences four to eight nightmares a year (Hartmann, 1993). Reported increases in nightmares or worsening nightmares are often associated with an increase in life stressors such as the loss of a relative or a job and conflicts with others.

A *night terror* features sudden arousal from sleep and intense fear. Night terrors are accompanied by a number of physiological reactions, such as rapid heart rate and breathing, loud screams, heavy perspiration, and movement (Mason & Pack, 2005). Night terrors, which peak at 5 to 7 years of age, are less common than nightmares, and unlike nightmares, they occur during slow-wave, non-REM sleep.

Narcolepsy A disorder called *narcolepsy* involves the sudden, overpowering urge to sleep. The urge is so uncontrollable that the person may fall asleep while talking or standing up. Narcoleptics immediately enter REM sleep rather than progressing through the first four sleep stages (Stores, Montgomery, & Wiggs, 2006). Individuals with narcolepsy are often extremely tired during the day. Narcolepsy can be triggered by extreme emotional reactions, such as surprise, laughter, excitement, or anger. Researchers suspect that narcolepsy is inherited. Treatment usually involves prescribing stimulants as well as providing counseling to discover potential causes of the excessive sleepiness (Morrish & others, 2004).

Sleep Apnea *Sleep apnea* is a sleep disorder in which individuals stop breathing because the windpipe fails to open or because brain processes involved in respiration fail to work properly. People with sleep apnea experience numerous brief awakenings during the night so that they can breathe better, although they usually are not aware of their awakened state. During the day, these people may feel sleepy because they were deprived of sleep at night. A common sign of sleep apnea is loud snoring, punctuated by silence (the apnea).

According to the American Sleep Apnea Association (ASAA), sleep apnea affects approximately 12 million Americans (ASAA, 2006). The disorder is most common among infants and adults over the age of 65. Sleep apnea also occurs more frequently among obese individuals, men, and individuals with large necks and recessed chins (ASAA, 2006; Scott & others, 2006).

Untreated sleep apnea can cause high blood pressure, stroke, and sexual dysfunction. In addition, the daytime sleepiness caused by sleep apnea can result in accidents, lost productivity, and relationship problems (Hartenbaum & others, 2006). Sleep apnea is commonly treated by weight loss programs, side sleeping, propping the head on a pillow, or wearing a device (called a CPAP for continuous positive airway pressure) that sends pressurized air through a mask that prevents the airway from collapsing.

Keep a sleep journal for several nights. Compare your sleep patterns with those described in the text. Do you have a sleep debt? If so, which stages of sleep are you most likely missing? Does a good night's sleep affect your behavior? Keep a record of your mood and energy levels after a short night's sleep and then after you have had at least 8 hours sleep in one night. What changes do you notice, and how do they compare with the changes predicted by research on sleep deprivation described in the chapter?

Dreams

Have you ever dreamed that you left your long-term romantic partner for a former lover? If so, did you tell your partner about that dream? Probably not. However, you would have likely wondered about the dream's meaning, and if so you would not be alone. Since the dawn of language, human beings have attributed great meaning to dreams. As early as 5000 B.C.E., Babylonians recorded and interpreted their dreams on clay tablets. Egyptians built temples in honor of Serapis, the god of dreams. Dreams are described at length in more than 70 passages in the Bible. Psychologists have also examined this fascinating topic.

Sigmund Freud put great stock in dreams as a key to our unconscious minds. He believed that dreams (even nightmares) symbolize unconscious wishes and that analysis of dream symbols could uncover our hidden desires. Freud distinguished between a dream's manifest content and its latent content. **Manifest content** is the dream's surface content, which contains dream symbols that disguise the dream's true meaning; **latent content** is the dream's hidden content, its unconscious—and true—meaning. For example, if a person had a dream about riding on a train and talking with a friend, the train ride would be the dream's manifest content. Freud thought that this manifest content expresses a wish in disguised form. To get to the latent or true meaning of the dream, the person would have to analyze the dream images. In our example, the dreamer would be asked to think of all the things that come to mind when the person thinks of a train, the friend, and so forth. By following these associations to the objects in the manifest content, the latent content of the dream could be brought to light. Artists have sometimes incorporated the symbolic world of dreaming in their work (Figure 4.7).

More recently, psychologists have approached dreams not as expressions of unconscious wishes but as mental events that come from various sources. Research has revealed a great deal about the nature of dreams. A common misconception is that dreams are typically bizarre or strange, but many studies of thousands of dreams, collected from individuals in sleep labs and sleeping at home, have shown that dreams generally are not very strange. Instead, research shows that dreams are often very similar to waking life (Domhoff, 2007; Schredl, 2009).

Although some aspects of dreams *are* unusual, dreams often are no more bizarre than a typical fairy tale, TV show

FIGURE 4.7
Artists' Portrayals of Dreams Through the centuries, artists have captured the enchanting or nightmarish characteristics of our dreams. Marc Chagall (1887–1985) painted a world of dreams in *I and the Village* (1911).

manifest content
According to Freud, the surface content of a dream, containing dream symbols that disguise the dream's true meaning.

latent content
According to Freud, a dream's hidden content; its unconscious and true meaning.

episode, or movie plot. Dreams do generally contain more negative emotion than everyday life; and certainly some unlikely characters, including dead people, sometimes show up in dreams.

There is also no evidence that dreams provide opportunities for problem solving or advice about how to handle life's difficulties. We may dream about a problem we are dealing with, but we typically find the solution while we are awake and thinking about the dream, not during the dream itself (Domhoff, 2007). There is also no evidence that people who remember their dreams are better off than those who do not (Blagrove & Akehurst, 2000).

So, if the typical dream involves doing ordinary things, what are dreams? The most prominent theories that attempt to explain dreams are cognitive theory and activation-synthesis theory.

Many of us seem to believe that our dreams typically are very strange. Think critically about it. Why might this be so? The reason is that we are probably most likely to remember our more vividly bizarre dreams. Boring dreams end up being forgotten, and so we never realize how common they really are.

cognitive theory of dreaming
Theory proposing that we can understand dreaming by applying the same cognitive concepts we use in studying the waking mind.

Cognitive Theory   The **cognitive theory of dreaming** proposes that we can understand dreaming by applying the same cognitive concepts we use in studying the waking mind. The theory rests on the idea that dreams are essentially subconscious cognitive processing. Dreaming involves information processing and memory. Indeed, thinking during dreams appears to be very similar to thinking in waking life (Schredl & Erlacher, 2008).

In the cognitive theory of dreaming, there is little or no search for the hidden, symbolic content of dreams that Freud sought (Foulkes, 1993, 1999). Instead, dreams are viewed as dramatizations of general life concerns that are similar to relaxed daydreams. Even very unusual aspects of dreams, such as odd activities, strange images, or sudden scene shifts, can be understood as metaphorically related to a person's preoccupations while awake (Domhoff, 2007).

Critics of the cognitive theory of dreaming fault the theory's lack of attention to the roles of brain structures and brain activity in dreaming. These perceived shortcomings are the main emphasis of the activation-synthesis theory of dreams.

activation-synthesis theory
Theory that dreaming occurs when the cerebral cortex synthesizes neural signals generated from activity in the lower brain and that dreams result from the brain's attempts to find logic in random brain activity that occurs during sleep.

Activation-Synthesis Theory   According to **activation-synthesis theory,** dreaming occurs when the cerebral cortex synthesizes neural signals generated from activity in the lower part of the brain. Dreams result from the brain's attempts to find logic in random brain activity that occurs during sleep (Hobson, 1999).

When we are awake and alert, our conscious experience tends to be driven by *external stimuli,* all those things we see, hear, and respond to. During sleep, according to activation-synthesis theory, conscious experience is driven by *internally generated stimuli* that have no apparent behavioral consequence. A key source of such internal stimulation is spontaneous neural activity in the brain stem (Hobson, 2000). Some of the neural activity that produces dreams comes from external sensory experiences. If a fire truck with sirens blaring drives past your house, you might find yourself dreaming about an emergency. Many of us have had the experience of incorporating our alarm clock going off in an early morning dream.

You may have noticed how internal states influence your dreams if you have ever been very thirsty while sleeping and dream that you get a glass of water.

Supporters of activation-synthesis theory have suggested that neural networks in other areas of the forebrain play a significant role in dreaming (Hobson, Pace-Schott, & Stickgold, 2000). Specifically, they believe that the same regions of the forebrain that are involved in certain waking behaviors also function in particular aspects of dreaming (Lu & others, 2006). As levels of neurotransmitters rise and fall during the stages of sleep, some neural networks are activated and others shut down. Random neural firing in various areas of the brain lead to dreams that are the brain's attempts to makes sense of the activity. So, firing in the primary motor and sensory areas of the forebrain might be reflected in a dream of running and feeling wind on your face. From the activation-synthesis perspective, our nervous system is cycling through various activities, and our consciousness is simply along for the ride (Hobson, 2000, 2004). Dreams are merely a flashy sideshow, not the main event (Hooper & Teresi, 1993). Indeed, one activation-synthesis theorist has referred to dreams as so much "cognitive trash" (Hobson, 2002, p. 23).

Like all dream theories, activation-synthesis theory has its critics. A key criticism is that damage to the brain stem does not necessarily reduce dreaming, suggesting that this area of the brain is not the only starting point for dreaming. Furthermore, life experiences stimulate and shape dreaming more than activation-synthesis theory acknowledges (Domhoff, 2007; Malcolm-Smith & others, 2008).

3 Psychoactive Drugs

One way that people seek to alter their own consciousness is through the use of psychoactive drugs. Illicit drug use is a global problem. According to the United Nations Office on Drugs and Crime (UNODC), more than 200 million people worldwide use drugs each year (UNODC, 2008). Among those, 25 million individuals (2.7 percent of the world population) are characterized as problem drug users—individuals whose drug habit interferes with their ability to engage in work and social relationships (UNODC, 2008).

Drug use among youth is a special concern because of its relation to problems such as unsafe sex, sexually transmitted infections, unplanned pregnancy, depression, and school-related difficulties (Eaton & others, 2008; UNODC, 2008). The consumption of drugs among U.S. secondary school students declined in the 1980s but began to increase in the early 1990s (Johnston & others, 2009). Then in the late 1990s and early 2000s, the proportion of secondary school students reporting the use of any illicit drug again declined (Johnston & others, 2009).

Figure 4.8 shows the trends in drug use by U.S. high school seniors since 1975 and by U.S. eighth- and tenth-graders since 1991 (Johnston & others, 2009). The most notable declines in adolescent drug use in the twenty-first century have occurred for marijuana, LSD, Ecstasy, steroids, and cigarettes. Nonetheless, the United States still has the highest rate of adolescent drug use of any industrialized nation (Johnston & others, 2009).

Drug use increases further in emerging adulthood. In one national survey, approximately 20 percent of 18- to 25-year-old Americans reported recent illicit drug use compared with 11 percent of adolescents (Substance Abuse and Mental Health Services Administration, 2006).

Uses of Psychoactive Drugs

Psychoactive drugs act on the nervous system to alter consciousness, modify perceptions, and change moods. Some people use psychoactive drugs as a way to deal with life's difficulties. Drinking, smoking, and taking drugs reduce tension, relieve boredom and fatigue, and help people to escape from the harsh realities of life. Some people use drugs because they are curious about their effects.

The use of psychoactive drugs, whether it is to cope with problems or just for fun, can carry a high price tag. These include losing track of one's responsibilities, problems in the workplace and in relationships, drug dependence, and increased risk for serious, sometimes fatal diseases (Donatelle, 2009; Fields, 2010). For example, drinking alcohol may initially help people relax and forget about their worries. If, however, they turn more and more to alcohol to escape reality, they may develop a dependence that can destroy relationships, careers, and their bodies.

Continued use of psychoactive drugs leads to **tolerance,** the need to take increasing amounts of a drug to get the same effect (Ksir, Hart, & Ray, 2008). For example, the first time someone takes 5 milligrams of the tranquilizer Valium, the person feels very relaxed. However, after taking the pill every day for six months, the individual may need to consume twice as much to achieve the same calming effect.

Continuing drug use can also result in **physical dependence,** the physiological need for a drug that causes unpleasant *withdrawal* symptoms such as physical pain and a craving for the drug when it is discontinued. **Psychological dependence** is the strong desire to repeat the use of a drug for emotional reasons, such as a feeling of well-being and reduction of stress. Experts on drug abuse use the term **addiction** to describe either a physical or psychological dependence, or both, on the drug (Hales, 2008).

How does the brain become addicted? Psychoactive drugs increase dopamine levels in the brain's reward pathways (Wise, 2008). This reward pathway is located in the *ventral tegmental area* (VTA) and *nucleus accumbens* (NAc) (Figure 4.9). Only the limbic and prefrontal areas of the brain are directly activated

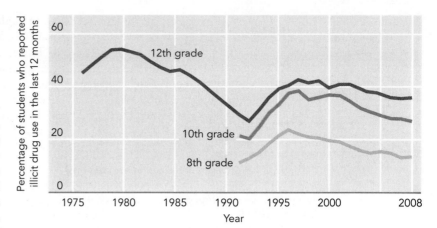

FIGURE 4.8

Trends in Drug Use by U.S. Eighth-, Tenth-, and Twelfth-Grade Students This graph shows the percentage of U.S. eighth-, tenth-, and twelfth-grade students who reported having taken an illicit drug in the last 12 months from 1991 to 2008 (for eighth- and tenth-graders) and from 1975 to 2009 (for twelfth-graders) (Johnston & others, 2009).

Ventral tegmental area and nucleus accumbens are mouthfuls, but these areas of the brain are vital to experiencing pleasure. Remember these structures—they will come up again and again.

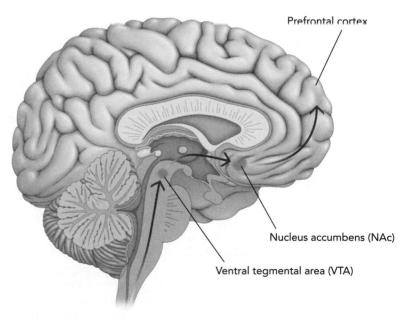

FIGURE 4.9

The Brain's Reward Pathway for Psychoactive Drugs The ventral tegmental area (VTA) and nucleus accumbens (NAc) are important locations in the reward pathway for psychoactive drugs. Information travels from the VTA to the NAc and then up to the prefrontal cortex. The VTA is located in the midbrain just above the pons, and the NAc is located in the forebrain, just beneath the prefrontal cortex.

Yes	No
☐	☐ I have gotten into problems because of using drugs.
☐	☐ Using alcohol or other drugs has made my college life unhappy at times.
☐	☐ Drinking alcohol or taking other drugs has been a factor in my losing a job.
☐	☐ Drinking alcohol or taking other drugs has interfered with my studying for exams.
☐	☐ Drinking alcohol or taking drugs has jeopardized my academic performance.
☐	☐ My ambition is not as strong since I've been drinking a lot or taking drugs.
☐	☐ Drinking or taking drugs has caused me to have difficulty sleeping.
☐	☐ I have felt remorse after drinking or taking drugs.
☐	☐ I crave a drink or other drugs at a definite time of the day.
☐	☐ I want a drink or other drug in the morning.
☐	☐ I have had a complete or partial loss of memory as a result of drinking or using other drugs.
☐	☐ Drinking or using other drugs is affecting my reputation.
☐	☐ I have been in the hospital or another institution because of my drinking or taking drugs.

College students who responded yes to items similar to these on the Rutgers Collegiate Abuse Screening Test were more likely to be substance abusers than those who answered no. If you responded yes to just 1 of the 13 items on this screening test, consider going to your college health or counseling center for further screening.

FIGURE 4.10

Do You Abuse Drugs? Take this short quiz to see if your use of drugs and alcohol might be a cause for concern.

Sometimes friends think someone who is dangerously drunk can simply be put to bed to "sleep it off." Drinking to the point of passing out is a symptom of alcohol poisoning. Call 911.

by dopamine, which comes from the VTA (Koob, 2006). Although different drugs have different mechanisms of action, each drug increases the activity of the reward pathway by increasing dopamine transmission. As we will see throughout this book, the neurotransmitter dopamine plays a vital role in the experience of rewards.

Types of Psychoactive Drugs

Three main categories of psychoactive drugs are depressants, stimulants, and hallucinogens. All have the potential to cause health or behavior problems or both. To evaluate whether you abuse drugs, see Figure 4.10.

Depressants **Depressants** are psychoactive drugs that slow down mental and physical activity. Among the most widely used depressants are alcohol, barbiturates, tranquilizers, and opiates.

depressants
Psychoactive drugs that slow down mental and physical activity.

Alcohol Alcohol is a powerful drug. It acts on the body primarily as a depressant and slows down the brain's activities. This effect might seem surprising, as people who tend to be inhibited may begin to talk, dance, and socialize after a few drinks. However, people "loosen up" after a few drinks because the brain areas involved in inhibition and judgment slow down. As people drink more, their inhibitions decrease even further, and their judgment becomes increasingly impaired. Activities that require intellectual functioning and motor skills, such as driving, become harder to perform. Eventually the drinker falls asleep. With extreme intoxication, the person may lapse into a coma and die. Figure 4.11 illustrates alcohol's main effects on the body.

The effects of alcohol vary from person to person. Factors in this variation are body weight, the amount of alcohol consumed, individual differences in the way body metabolizes alcohol, and the presence or absence of tolerance (Fields, 2010). Men and women differ in terms of the intoxicating effects of alcohol. Because of differences in body fat as well as stomach enzymes, women are likely to be more strongly affected by alcohol than men.

How does alcohol affect the brain? Like other psychoactive drugs, alcohol goes to the VTA and the NAc (Meyer, Meshul, & Phillips, 2009; Wanat & others, 2009). Alcohol also increases the concentration of the neurotransmitter gamma aminobutyric acid (GABA),

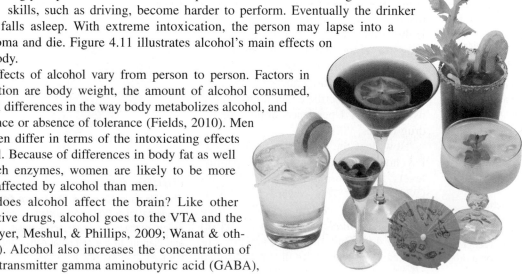

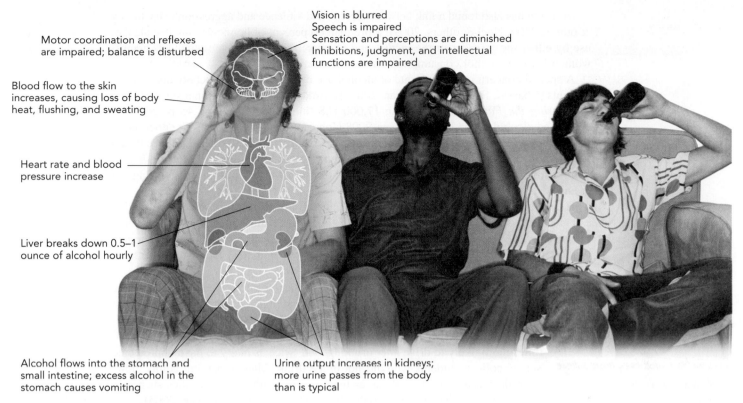

Motor coordination and reflexes are impaired; balance is disturbed

Vision is blurred
Speech is impaired
Sensation and perceptions are diminished
Inhibitions, judgment, and intellectual functions are impaired

Blood flow to the skin increases, causing loss of body heat, flushing, and sweating

Heart rate and blood pressure increase

Liver breaks down 0.5–1 ounce of alcohol hourly

Alcohol flows into the stomach and small intestine; excess alcohol in the stomach causes vomiting

Urine output increases in kidneys; more urine passes from the body than is typical

FIGURE 4.11

The Physiological and Behavioral Effects of Alcohol Alcohol has a powerful impact throughout the body. Its effects touch everything from the operation of the nervous, circulatory, and digestive systems to sensation, perception, motor coordination, and intellectual functioning.

which is widely distributed in many brain areas, including the cerebral cortex, cerebellum, hippocampus, amygdala, and nucleus accumbens (Guerrini, Thomson, & Gurling, 2009). Recall from Chapter 2 that GABA plays a role in inhibiting neurons from firing. Alcohol, then, increases this neurotransmitter that puts the brakes on other neurons.

Researchers believe that the frontal cortex holds a memory of the pleasure involved in prior alcohol use and contributes to continued drinking. Alcohol consumption also may affect the areas of the frontal cortex involved in judgment and impulse control (Mantere & others, 2002). It is further believed that the basal ganglia, which are involved in compulsive behaviors, may lead to a greater demand for alcohol, regardless of reason and consequences (Brink, 2001).

This explains how getting the next drink can become more important than anything else in a person's life.

After caffeine, alcohol is the most widely used drug in the United States. As many as two-thirds of U.S. adults drink beer, wine, or liquor at least occasionally, and in one recent survey approximately 30 percent reported drinking more than five drinks at one sitting at least once in the last year (National Center for Health Statistics, 2005). Approximately 18 million people in the United States are alcoholics (Grant & others, 2004).

Alcoholism is the third leading killer in the United States. Approximately 20,000 people are killed and 1.5 million injured each year by drivers who have been drinking. Approximately 32 percent of all fatal crashes and 40 percent of those during holidays involve alcohol (National Highway Traffic Safety Administration, 2007). The vast majority of offenses for driving under the influence are committed by social drinkers (Caetano & McGrath, 2005), and an estimated 3 in 10 Americans will be involved in an alcohol-related crash (National Highway Traffic Safety Administration, 2005).

Research has also found a link between alcohol and violence and aggression (McCloskey & others, 2009; Noel & others, 2009). More than 60 percent of homicides involve alcohol use by either the offender or the victim, and 65 percent of aggressive sexual acts against women involve alcohol consumption by the offender.

A special concern is the high rate of alcohol use by U.S. secondary school and college students (Chassin, Hussong, & Beltran, 2009; Hoffman, 2009). In a national survey (titled *Monitoring the Future*) of more than 17,000 U.S. high school seniors, 43 percent had consumed alcohol in the last 30 days in 2008 (Johnston & others, 2009). The good news is that 43 percent represents a decline from 54 percent in 1991. In the most recent survey, 28 percent of the high school seniors had engaged in binge drinking (having five or more drinks in a row at least once in the previous two weeks) at least once during the previous month, down from 34 percent in 1997.

Heavy binge drinking often increases during the first two years of college, and it can take its toll on students (C. L. Park, 2004). In the most recent *Monitoring the Future* survey, 41 percent of college students reported engaging in binge drinking in the last two weeks (49 percent of males, 33 percent of females) (Johnston & others, 2008).

In a national survey of drinking patterns on college campuses, almost half of the binge drinkers reported problems that included missed classes, injuries, trouble with police, and unprotected sex (Wechsler & others, 2000, 2002) (Figure 4.12). Binge-drinking college students were 11 times more likely to fall behind in school, 10 times more likely to drive after drinking, and twice as likely to have unprotected sex as college students who did not binge drink. Many emerging adults, however, decrease their alcohol use as they assume adult responsibilities such as a permanent job, marriage or cohabitation, and parenthood (Slutske, 2005).

Alcoholism is a disorder that involves long-term, repeated, uncontrolled, compulsive, and excessive use of alcoholic beverages and that impairs the drinker's health and social relationships. A recent longitudinal study linked early onset of

It's good news that most people seem to settle down and reduce their alcohol consumption once they leave college life. Think about it, though: They first have to survive their college years, and binge drinking can be deadly.

alcoholism
Disorder that involves long-term, repeated, uncontrolled, compulsive, and excessive use of alcoholic beverages and that impairs the drinker's health and social relationships.

FIGURE 4.12

Consequences of Binge Drinking Binge drinking has wide-ranging negative consequences.

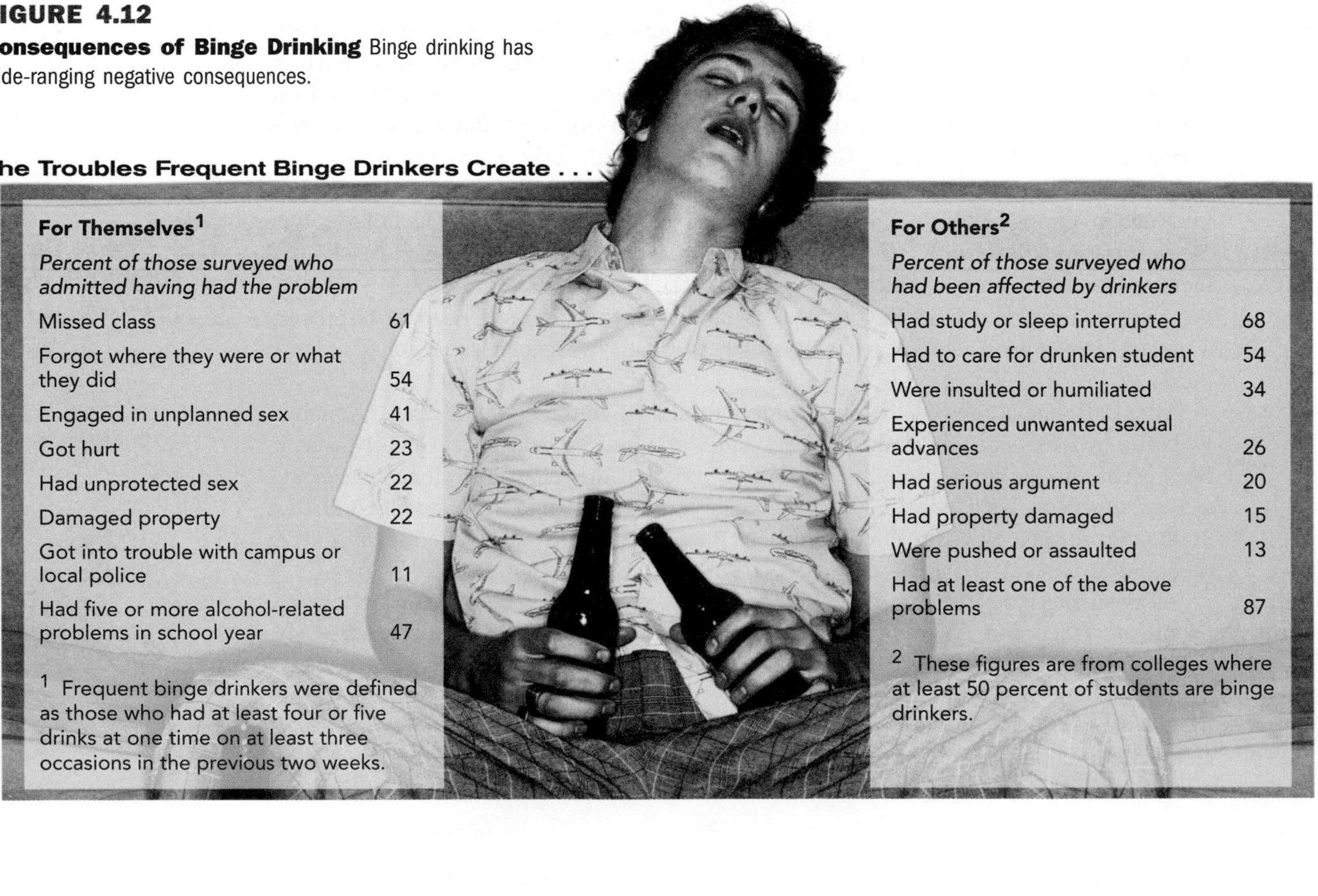

The Troubles Frequent Binge Drinkers Create . . .

For Themselves[1]		For Others[2]	
Percent of those surveyed who admitted having had the problem		*Percent of those surveyed who had been affected by drinkers*	
Missed class	61	Had study or sleep interrupted	68
Forgot where they were or what they did	54	Had to care for drunken student	54
Engaged in unplanned sex	41	Were insulted or humiliated	34
Got hurt	23	Experienced unwanted sexual advances	26
Had unprotected sex	22	Had serious argument	20
Damaged property	22	Had property damaged	15
Got into trouble with campus or local police	11	Were pushed or assaulted	13
Had five or more alcohol-related problems in school year	47	Had at least one of the above problems	87

[1] Frequent binge drinkers were defined as those who had at least four or five drinks at one time on at least three occasions in the previous two weeks.

[2] These figures are from colleges where at least 50 percent of students are binge drinkers.

drinking to later alcohol problems. Individuals who began drinking alcohol before 14 years of age were more likely to become alcohol dependent than their counterparts who began drinking alcohol at 21 years of age or older (Hingson, Heeren, & Winter, 2006). One in nine individuals who drink continues down the path to alcoholism. Those who do are disproportionately related to alcoholics; family studies consistently find a high frequency of alcoholism in the close biological relatives of alcoholics (Edenberg & Foroud, 2006). A possible explanation is that the brains of people genetically predisposed to alcoholism may be unable to produce adequate dopamine, that neurotransmitter that can make us feel pleasure (Tsuchihashi-Makay & others, 2009). For these individuals, alcohol may increase dopamine concentration and resulting pleasure to the point where it leads to addiction (Meyer, Meshul, & Phillips, 2009).

Like other psychological characteristics, though, alcoholism is not all nature: Nurture matters too. Indeed, research shows that experience also plays a role in alcoholism (Schuckit, 2009). Many alcoholics do not have close relatives who are alcoholics (Duncan & others, 2006), a finding that points to environmental influences.

What does it take to stop alcoholism? About one-third of alcoholics recover whether they are in a treatment program or not. This finding came from a long-term study of 700 individuals over 50 years (Vaillant, 1983, 1992) and has consistently been confirmed by other researchers. George Vaillant formulated the so-called one-third rule for alcoholism: By age 65, one-third are dead or in terrible shape; one-third are still trying to beat their addiction; and one-third are abstinent or drinking only socially. In his extensive research, Vaillant found that recovery from alcoholism was predicted by (1) having a strong negative experience with drinking, such as a serious medical emergency; (2) finding a substitute dependency, such as meditation, exercise, or overeating (which has its own adverse health effects); (3) developing new, positive relationships; and (4) joining a support group such as Alcoholics Anonymous.

Barbiturates

barbiturates
Depressant drugs, such as Nembutal and Seconal, that decrease central nervous system activity.

Barbiturates, such as Nembutal and Seconal, are depressant drugs that decrease central nervous system activity. Physicians once widely prescribed barbiturates as sleep aids. In heavy dosages, they can lead to impaired memory and decision making. When combined with alcohol (for example, sleeping pills taken after a night of binge drinking), barbiturates can be lethal. Heavy doses of barbiturates by themselves can cause death. For this reason, barbiturates are the drug most often used in suicide attempts. Abrupt withdrawal can produce seizures. Because of the addictive potential and relative ease of toxic overdose, barbiturates have largely been replaced by tranquilizers in the treatment of insomnia.

Handy survival tips: Never share prescription drugs. Never take someone else's prescription drugs. Never mix prescribed drugs with alcohol.

Tranquilizers

Tranquilizers, such as Valium and Xanax, are depressant drugs that reduce anxiety and induce relaxation. In small doses tranquilizers can induce a feeling of calm; higher doses can lead to drowsiness and confusion. Tolerance for tranquilizers can develop within a few weeks of usage, and these drugs are addictive. Widely prescribed in the United States to calm anxious individuals, tranquilizers can produce withdrawal symptoms when use is stopped (Voshaar & others, 2006). Prescription tranquilizers were part of the lethal cocktail of drugs that ended the life of actor Heath Ledger in 2008.

tranquilizers
Depressant drugs that reduce anxiety and induce relaxation.

Opiates

Narcotics, or **opiates,** consist of opium and its derivatives and depress the central nervous system's activity. These drugs are used as powerful painkillers. The most common opiate drugs—morphine and heroin—affect synapses in the brain that use endorphins as their neurotransmitter. When these drugs leave the brain, the affected synapses become understimulated. For several hours after taking an opiate, the person feels euphoric and pain-free and has an increased appetite for food and sex. Opiates are highly addictive, and users experience craving and painful withdrawal when the drug becomes unavailable.

opiates
Opium and its derivatives; narcotic drugs that depress the central nervous system's activity and eliminate pain.

Opiate addiction can also raise the risk of exposure to HIV, the virus that causes AIDS. Most heroin addicts inject the drug intravenously. When they share needles without sterilizing them, one infected addict can transmit the virus to others.

Stimulants

Stimulants are psychoactive drugs that increase the central nervous system's activity. The most widely used stimulants are caffeine, nicotine, amphetamines, and cocaine.

Caffeine   Often overlooked as a drug, caffeine is the world's most widely used psychoactive drug. Caffeine is a stimulant and a natural component of the plants that are the sources of coffee, tea, and cola drinks. Caffeine also is present in chocolate, in many nonprescription medications, and in energy drinks such as Red Bull. People often perceive the stimulating effects of caffeine as beneficial for boosting energy and alertness, but some experience unpleasant side effects.

Caffeinism refers to an overindulgence in caffeine. It is characterized by mood changes, anxiety, and sleep disruption. Caffeinism often develops in people who drink five or more cups of coffee (at least 500 milligrams) each day. Common symptoms are insomnia, irritability, headaches, ringing ears, dry mouth, increased blood pressure, and digestive problems (Hogan, Hornick, & Bouchoux, 2002).

off the mark.com   by Mark Parisi

ATLANTIC FEATURE © 1998 MARK PARISI   offthemark.com

ANSWERING THE QUESTION OF HOW THEY FLY AROUND THE WORLD IN ONE NIGHT

© Mark Parisi. Atlantic Feature Syndicate.

Caffeine affects the brain's pleasure centers, so it is not surprising that it is difficult to kick the caffeine habit. When individuals who regularly consume caffeinated beverages remove caffeine from their diet, they typically experience headaches, lethargy, apathy, and concentration difficulties. These symptoms of withdrawal are usually mild and subside after several days.

Nicotine   Nicotine is the main psychoactive ingredient in all forms of smoking and smokeless tobacco. Even with all the publicity given to the enormous health risks posed by tobacco, we sometimes overlook the highly addictive nature of nicotine. Nicotine stimulates the brain's reward centers by raising dopamine levels. Behavioral effects of nicotine include improved attention and alertness, reduced anger and anxiety, and pain relief (Knott & others, 2006). Figure 4.13 shows the main effects of nicotine on the body.

Tolerance develops for nicotine both in the long run and on a daily basis, so that cigarettes smoked later in the day have less effect than those

stimulants
Psychoactive drugs, including caffeine, nicotine, amphetamines, and cocaine, that increase the central nervous system's activity.

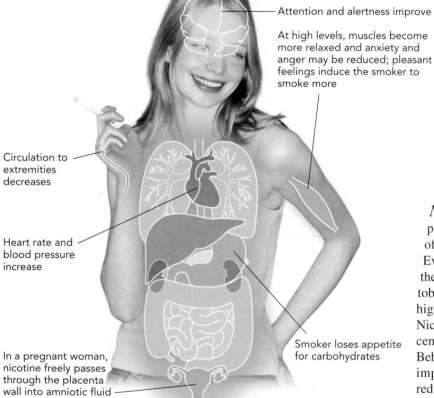

Attention and alertness improve

At high levels, muscles become more relaxed and anxiety and anger may be reduced; pleasant feelings induce the smoker to smoke more

Circulation to extremities decreases

Heart rate and blood pressure increase

In a pregnant woman, nicotine freely passes through the placenta wall into amniotic fluid

Smoker loses appetite for carbohydrates

FIGURE 4.13

The Physiological and Behavioral Effects of Nicotine Smoking has many physiological and behavioral effects. Highly addictive, nicotine delivers pleasant feelings that make the smoker smoke more, but tobacco consumption poses very serious health risks to the individual.

smoked earlier. Withdrawal from nicotine often quickly produces strong, unpleasant symptoms such as irritability, craving, inability to focus, sleep disturbance, and increased appetite. Withdrawal symptoms can persist for months or longer.

Tobacco poses a much larger threat to public health than illegal drugs. According to the Centers for Disease Control and Prevention (CDC), tobacco use kills more than 400,000 people each year in the United States (CDC, 2005). That is more than the total number killed by AIDS, alcohol, motor vehicles, homicide, illegal drugs, and suicide combined. Today there are approximately 1 billion smokers globally, and estimates are that by 2030, another 1 billion youth will have started to smoke (United Nations World Youth Report, 2005). In 2005, about 21 percent of U.S. adults smoked—a decline from 1996, when nearly a quarter of surveyed Americans smoked (CDC, 2006).

Cigarette smoking is decreasing among both adolescents and college students. In the national *Monitoring the Future* survey by the Institute of Social Research, the percentage of U.S. adolescents who are current cigarette smokers continued to decline in 2007 (Johnston & others, 2009). Cigarette smoking peaked in 1996 and 1997 and then decreased 13 to 16 percent, depending on grade level, from 1998 to 2008 (Figure 4.14).

The drop in cigarette use by U.S. youth may have several sources, including higher cigarette prices, less tobacco advertising reaching adolescents, more antismoking advertisements, and more negative publicity about the tobacco industry than before. Increasingly, adolescents report perceiving cigarette smoking as dangerous, disapprove of it, are less accepting of being around smokers, and prefer to date nonsmokers (Johnston & others, 2009). With respect to college students and young adults, smoking has shown a smaller decline than adolescent and adult smoking (Johnston & others, 2009).

Cigarette advertisements have long linked cigarette smoking with healthy, attractive people and the good life.

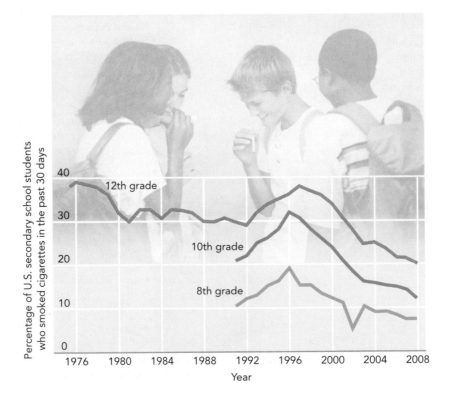

FIGURE 4.14

Trends in Cigarette Smoking by U.S. Secondary School Students Fortunately, cigarette smoking by American high school students is on the decline.

In sum, cigarette smoking appears to be generally on the decline. Most smokers recognize the serious health risks of smoking and wish they could quit. Chapter 14 explores the difficulty of giving up smoking and strategies for quitting.

Amphetamines Amphetamines, or uppers, are stimulant drugs that people use to boost energy, stay awake, or lose weight. Often prescribed in the form of diet pills, these drugs increase the release of dopamine, which enhances the user's activity level and pleasurable feelings.

Perhaps the most insidious illicit drug for contemporary society is crystal methamphetamine, or crystal meth. Smoked, injected, or swallowed, crystal meth (also called "crank" or "tina") is a synthetic stimulant that causes a powerful feeling of euphoria, particularly the first time it is ingested. Meth is made using household products such as battery acid, cold medicine, drain cleaner, and kitty litter, and its effects have been devastating, notably in rural areas of the United States.

Crystal meth releases enormous amounts of dopamine in the brain, producing intense feelings of pleasure. The drug is highly addictive. The extreme high of crystal meth leads to a severe "come down" experience that is associated with strong cravings. Because the person's very first experience with crystal meth can lead to ruinous consequences, the Drug Enforcement Agency has started a website, designed by and targeted at teenagers, http://www.justthinktwice.com, to share the hard facts of the horrific effects of this and other illicit substances.

Crystal meth also damages dopamine receptors. Essentially, the crystal meth addict is chasing a high that his or her brain can no longer produce.

Seriously, don't try it—not even once.

Cocaine Cocaine is an illegal drug that comes from the coca plant, native to Bolivia and Peru. Cocaine is either snorted or injected in the form of crystals or powder. Used this way, cocaine floods the bloodstream rapidly, producing a rush of euphoric feelings that lasts for about 15 to 30 minutes. Because the rush depletes the brain's supply of the neurotransmitters dopamine, serotonin, and norepinephrine, an agitated, depressed mood usually follows as the drug's effects decline. Figure 4.15 shows how cocaine affects dopamine levels in the brain.

Crack is a potent form of cocaine, consisting of chips of pure cocaine that are usually smoked. Scientists believe that crack is one of the most addictive substances known.

FIGURE 4.15

Cocaine and Neurotransmitters Cocaine concentrates in areas of the brain that are rich in dopamine synapses such as the ventral tegmental area (VTA) and the nucleus accumbens (NAc). (*Top*) What happens in normal reuptake. The transmitting neuron releases dopamine, which stimulates the receiving neuron by binding to its receptor sites. After binding occurs, dopamine is carried back into the transmitting neuron for later release. (*Bottom*) What happens when cocaine is present in the synapse. Cocaine binds to the uptake pumps and prevents them from removing dopamine from the synapse. The result is that more dopamine collects in the synapse, and more dopamine receptors are activated.

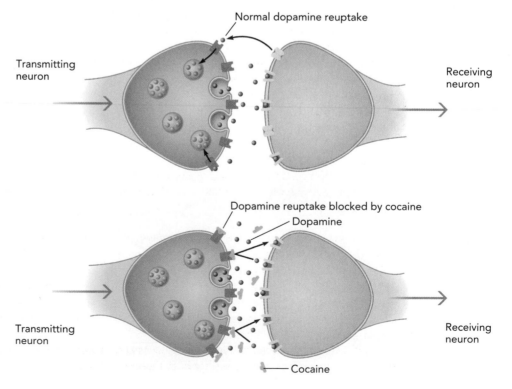

Normal dopamine reuptake

Transmitting neuron

Receiving neuron

Dopamine reuptake blocked by cocaine

Dopamine

Transmitting neuron

Receiving neuron

Cocaine

Treatment of cocaine addiction is difficult (Ahmadi & others, 2009). Cocaine's addictive properties are so strong that, six months after treatment, more than 50 percent of abusers return to the drug, a statistic that highlights the importance of prevention.

MDMA (Ecstasy)   MDMA—called Ecstasy, X, or XTC—is an illegal synthetic drug with both stimulant and hallucinogenic properties. People have called Ecstasy an "empathogen" because under its influence, users tend to feel warm bonds with others. MDMA produces its effects by releasing serotonin, dopamine, and norepinephrine. The effects of the drug on serotonin are particularly problematic. MDMA depletes the brain of this important neurotransmitter, producing lingering feelings of listlessness that often continue for days after use (NIDA, 2009).

MDMA impairs memory and cognitive processing. Heavy users of Ecstasy show cognitive deficits (Dafters, 2006) that persist even two years after they begin to abstain (Rogers & others, 2009; Ward, Hall, & Haslam, 2006). Because MDMA destroys axons that release serotonin, repeated use might lead to susceptibility to depression (Cowan, Roberts, & Joers, 2008).

Hallucinogens
Hallucinogens are psychoactive drugs that modify a person's perceptual experiences and produce visual images that are not real. Hallucinogens are also called *psychedelic* (from the Greek meaning "mind-revealing") drugs. Marijuana has a mild hallucinogenic effect; LSD, a stronger one.

hallucinogens
Psychoactive drugs that modify a person's perceptual experiences and produce visual images that are not real.

Marijuana   Marijuana is the dried leaves and flowers of the hemp plant *Cannabis sativa,* which originated in Central Asia but is now grown in most parts of the world. The plant's dried resin is known as hashish. The active ingredient in marijuana is THC (delta-9-tetrahydrocannabinol). Unlike other psychoactive drugs, THC does not affect a specific neurotransmitter. Rather, marijuana disrupts the membranes of neurons and affects the functioning of a variety of neurotransmitters and hormones.

The physical effects of marijuana include increased pulse rate and blood pressure, reddening of the eyes, coughing, and dry mouth. Psychological effects include a mixture of excitatory, depressive, and mildly hallucinatory characteristics that make it difficult to classify the drug. Marijuana can trigger spontaneous unrelated ideas; distorted perceptions of time and place; increased sensitivity to sounds, tastes, smells, and colors; and erratic verbal behavior. The drug can also impair attention and memory. Further, when used daily in large amounts, marijuana can alter sperm count and change hormonal cycles (Close, Roberts, & Berger, 1990). A review of research concluded that marijuana use by pregnant women is related to negative outcomes in memory and information processing in their offspring (Kalant, 2004).

Marijuana is the illegal drug most widely used by high school students. In the *Monitoring the Future* survey, 42 percent of U.S. high school seniors said they had tried marijuana in their lifetime, and 19 percent reported that they had used marijuana in the last 30 days (Johnston & others, 2009). One concern about adolescents' use of marijuana is that the drug might be a gateway to the use of other more serious illicit substances. Although there is a correlational relationship between using marijuana and using other illicit drugs, evidence for the notion that marijuana use leads to the use of other drugs is mixed (Tarter & others, 2006).

LSD   LSD (lysergic acid diethylamide) is a hallucinogen that even in low doses produces striking perceptual changes. Objects change their shapes and glow. Colors become kaleidoscopic and astonishing images unfold. LSD-induced images are sometimes pleasurable and sometimes grotesque. LSD can also influence a user's sense of time so that brief glances at objects are experienced as deep, penetrating, and lengthy examinations, and minutes turn into hours or even days. A bad LSD trip can trigger extreme anxiety, paranoia, and suicidal or homicidal impulses.

LSD's effects on the body can include dizziness, nausea, and tremors. LSD acts primarily on the neurotransmitter serotonin in the brain, though it also can affect dopamine

Drug Classification	Medical Uses	Short-Term Effects	Overdose Effects	Health Risks	Risk of Physical/ Psychological Dependence
Depressants					
Alcohol	Pain relief	Relaxation, depressed brain activity, slowed behavior, reduced inhibitions	Disorientation, loss of consciousness, even death at high blood-alcohol levels	Accidents, brain damage, liver disease, heart disease, ulcers, birth defects	Physical: moderate Psychological: moderate
Barbiturates	Sleeping pill	Relaxation, sleep	Breathing difficulty, coma, possible death	Accidents, coma, possible death	Physical and psychological: moderate to high
Tranquilizers	Anxiety reduction	Relaxation, slowed behavior	Breathing difficulty, coma, possible death	Accidents, coma, possible death	Physical: low to moderate Psychological: moderate to high
Opiates (narcotics)	Pain relief	Euphoric feelings, drowsiness, nausea	Convulsions, coma, possible death	Accidents, infectious diseases such as AIDS	Physical: high Psychological: moderate to high
Stimulants					
Amphetamines	Weight control	Increased alertness, excitability; decreased fatigue, irritability	Extreme irritability, feelings of persecution, convulsions	Insomnia, hypertension, malnutrition, possible death	Physical: possible Psychological: moderate to high
Cocaine	Local anesthetic	Increased alertness, excitability, euphoric feelings; decreased fatigue, irritability	Extreme irritability, feelings of persecution, convulsions, cardiac arrest, possible death	Insomnia, hypertension, malnutrition, possible death	Physical: possible Psychological: moderate (oral) to very high (injected or smoked)
MDMA (Ecstasy)	None	Mild amphetamine and hallucinogenic effects; high body temperature and dehydration; sense of well-being and social connectedness	Brain damage, especially memory and thinking	Cardiovascular problems; death	Physical: possible Psychological: moderate
Caffeine	None	Alertness and sense of well-being followed by fatigue	Nervousness, anxiety, disturbed sleep	Possible cardiovascular problems	Physical: moderate Psychological: moderate
Nicotine	None	Stimulation, stress reduction, followed by fatigue, anger	Nervousness, disturbed sleep	Cancer and cardio-vascular disease	Physical: high Psychological: high
Hallucinogens					
LSD	None	Strong hallucinations, distorted time perception	Severe mental disturbance, loss of contact with reality	Accidents	Physical: none Psychological: low
Marijuana	Treatment of the eye disorder glaucoma	Euphoric feelings, relaxation, mild hallucinations, time distortion, attention and memory impairment	Fatigue, disoriented behavior	Accidents, respiratory disease	Physical: very low Psychological: moderate

FIGURE 4.16

Categories of Psychoactive Drugs: Depressants, Stimulants, and Hallucinogens
Note that these various drugs have different effects and negative consequences.

(Gonzalez-Maeso & Sealfon, 2009). Emotional and cognitive effects may include rapid mood swings and impaired attention and memory. The use of LSD peaked in the 1960s and 1970s, and its consumption has been decreasing in the twenty-first century (Johnston & others, 2009). Figure 4.16 summarizes the effects of LSD and a variety of other psychoactive drugs.

There is ongoing public controversy over the question, should hallucinogenic drugs such as LSD and marijuana be used for medical purposes? To read about the issue, see Challenge Your Thinking.

challenge your thinking

Should Psychedelic Drugs Be Legalized for Medical Uses?

Psychedelic drugs such as LSD (acid), MDMA (Ecstasy), psilocybin (magic mushrooms), mescaline (peyote buttons), and cannabis (marijuana, or pot) have mind-altering effects. Could these effects be harnessed to promote healthier functioning in the mentally ill or to aid well-being more generally? John Halpern, an associate director of addiction research at Harvard University's McLean Hospital, and his colleagues think so (Halpern, 2003; Halpern & Sewell, 2005; Halpern & others, 2005; Passie & others, 2008; Sewell, Halpern, & Pope, 2006). They have been advocates for research using psychedelic drugs to treat a number of disorders.

The effects of LSD were discovered by a Swiss chemist. While working in a pharmaceutical lab, he accidentally ingested the substance and experienced a "trip" he described as terrifying yet thrilling. His experience led others to consider whether LSD might play a role in psychological treatment. During the 1960s, more than 100 scientific articles examined the effects and potential benefits of psychedelic drugs, and over 40,000 patients were given LSD for problems such as schizophrenia, alcoholism, and depression. The benefits of LSD were very publicly championed by Harvard psychologist Timothy Leary, who in the 1960s embarked on research dedicated to unlocking the secrets of consciousness through the use of the drug. Leary fell out of favor and lost his job over his tendency to sample the research stimuli (Greenfield, 2006).

Leary's behavior had a chilling effect on research into applications of psychedelic drugs (Horgan, 2005; Sessa, 2007). By the late 1960s, LSD and other psychedelic drugs were outlawed in the United States, Canada, and Europe. Slowly, however, researchers have again begun to consider the potential benefits of these now illegal substances for various disorders, although government restrictions make the research difficult (Halpern, 1996; Horgan, 2005). Promising initial results are leading some to consider whether these drugs should be legalized for medical use.

The controversy over medical marijuana illustrates the conflicts that can erupt over the possibility of an illicit drug's legalization. In the late 1970s, it became apparent that marijuana could be used as treatment for glaucoma because cannabis reduces pressure in the eye (American Academy of Ophthalmology, 2003). More recently, researchers have recognized marijuana as a potential treatment for diseases such as AIDS and cancer, as well as for the unpleasant side effects of treating these illnesses. For individuals dealing with such issues, "medical marijuana" may promote appetite, calm anxiety, and stimulate well-being (Joy, Watson, & Benson, 1999).

If marijuana were legalized for medical purposes, however, would drug use rise more generally, as many believe (Schwartz & others, 2003)? Researchers examined attitudes and marijuana use before and after the passage of Proposition 215 in California. "Prop 215" legalized the noncommercial possession, cultivation, and distribution of marijuana for medical purposes. The research

Medical marijuana is now legal in 13 states, and in 2009, Attorney General Eric Holder announced an end to federal raids on medical marijuana facilities unless these facilities violated both state and federal law.

results showed that while attitudes about marijuana were more lenient after Prop 215's passage, *usage* did not change (Khatapoush & Hallfors, 2004). Medical marijuana is now legal in 13 states. Although users of medical marijuana were previously subject to prosecution under U.S. federal laws, more recently Attorney General Eric Holder announced that the federal government would no longer raid medical marijuana facilities in states where they are legal.

In a related controversy, some people argue that psychedelic drugs should be legalized because they enhance everyday life and are an avenue for gaining creative insight. Whether hallucinogenic drugs provide insight into the mysteries of life is debatable. One of Timothy Leary's early participants noted that he had solved all the world's problems during an acid trip, yet the next day he could not remember how (Greenfield, 2006). The use of these drugs to help individuals struggling with serious life difficulties is certain to remain a subject of debate for years to come.

What Do You Think?

- Would the legalization of psychedelic drugs for medical purposes "send the wrong message" about drug use? Why or why not?

- Would you support the legalization of drugs for medical purposes? Explain.

1. The most widely consumed drug in the world as a whole is
   A. nicotine.
   B. marijuana.
   C. cocaine.
   D. caffeine.

2. Roger used to feel the effect of one or two alcoholic drinks; he now needs four or five to feel the same effect. Roger is experiencing
   A. physical dependence.
   B. psychological dependence.
   C. withdrawal symptoms.
   D. tolerance.

3. Of the following drugs, the one that is *not* a depressant is
   A. nicotine.
   B. alcohol.
   C. barbiturates.
   D. opiates.

Apply It! 4. In high school Kareem was a star student, and drinking alcohol did not fit with his academic ambitions. In college, he started drinking and eventually drank heavily every weekend. He has a lot of trouble making it to his Monday classes, and his grades have dropped from mostly *A*s to mainly *C*s, but otherwise he feels he is doing pretty well. A friend asks him about his drinking, and Kareem declares, "I will definitely stop drinking once I am out of college. Besides, no one in my family has ever been an alcoholic, so I am not at risk." Which of the statements below is an accurate assessment of Kareem's belief?

A. Kareem is probably not at risk for alcoholism, but he might be putting himself at risk for alcohol-related problems, such as drunk driving.
B. Kareem is at risk for alcohol-related problems only if he also drives while drinking.
C. Kareem is clearly already suffering from alcohol-related problems. Despite his lack of family history, his alcohol use could put him at risk for dependence. Furthermore, if Kareem is binge drinking, he is risking death by alcohol poisoning.
D. Kareem appears to have his alcohol use under control and accurately states his lack of risk—he has no family history of alcoholism, and he did not start drinking until he was college-age.

4 Hypnosis

Fifty-three-year-old Shelley Thomas entered a London Hospital for a 30-minute pelvic surgery. Before the operation, with her hypnotherapist guiding her, Shelley counted backward from 100 and entered a hypnotic trance. Her surgery was performed with no anesthesia (Song, 2006); rather, Shelley relied on hypnosis to harness her mind's powers to overcome pain.

You may have seen a hypnotist on TV or in a nightclub, putting a person into a trance and then perhaps making him or her act like a chicken or pretend to be a contestant on *American Idol* or enact some similarly strange behavior. When we observe someone in such a trance, we might be convinced that hypnosis involves a powerful manipulation of another person's consciousness. What is hypnosis, really? The answer to this question is itself the source of some debate.

Some psychologists think of hypnosis as an altered state of consciousness, while others believe that it is simply a product of more mundane processes such as focused attention and expectation (Lynne, Boycheva, & Barnes, 2008; Rossi, 2009). In fact, both views are reasonable, and we may define **hypnosis** as an altered state of consciousness or as a psychological state of altered attention and expectation in which the individual is unusually receptive to suggestions. People have used basic hypnotic techniques since the beginning of recorded history, in association with religious ceremonies, magic, and the supernatural.

hypnosis
An altered state of consciousness or a psychological state of altered attention and expectation in which the individual is unusually receptive to suggestions.

Today, psychology and medicine recognize hypnosis as a legitimate process, although researchers still have much to learn about how it works. In addition, there is continuing debate about whether hypnosis truly is an altered state of consciousness (Lynn, Boycheva, & Barnes, 2008; Poon, 2009).

The Nature of Hypnosis

When Shelley Thomas was in a hypnotic trance, what exactly was happening in her brain and mind? Patterns of brain activity during the hypnotic state suggest that hypnosis produces a state of consciousness similar to other states of consciousness. For example, individuals in a hypnotic state display a predominance of alpha and beta waves, characteristic of persons in a relaxed waking state, when monitored by an EEG (Graffin, Ray, & Lundy, 1995; Williams & Gruzelier, 2001). In a recent brain-imaging study, widespread areas of the cerebral cortex—including the occipital lobes, parietal lobes, sensorimotor cortex, and prefrontal cortex—were activated when individuals were in a hypnotic state (Faymonville, Boly, & Laureys, 2006). A similar activation pattern is found in individuals in a non-hypnotic waking state who are engaging in mental imagery. How does the hypnotist lead people into this state of relaxation and imagery?

www.CartoonStock.com

The Four Steps in Hypnosis
Hypnosis involves four steps. The hypnotist

1. Minimizes distractions and makes the person to be hypnotized comfortable.

2. Tells the person to concentrate on something specific, such as an imagined scene or the ticking of a watch.

3. Informs the person what to expect in the hypnotic state, such as relaxation or a pleasant floating sensation.

4. Suggests certain events or feelings he or she knows will occur or observes occurring, such as "Your eyes are getting tired." When the suggested effects occur, the person interprets them as being caused by the hypnotist's suggestions and accepts them as an indication that something is happening. This increase in the person's expectations that the hypnotist will make things happen in the future makes the person even more suggestible.

Individual Variations in Hypnosis
Some people are more easily hypnotized than others. About 65 percent of individuals are moderately hypnotizable, with an additional 15 percent being highly susceptible to hypnosis (Song, 2006). Ten percent or fewer cannot be hypnotized at all, and the remainder falls in between (Hilgard, 1965).

There is no simple way to tell beforehand who can be hypnotized. However, if you have the capacity to immerse yourself deeply in imaginative activities—listening to a favorite piece of music or reading a novel, for example—you are a likely candidate. People susceptible to hypnosis become completely absorbed in what they are doing, removing the boundaries between themselves and their experiences in their environment. Nonetheless, such absorption is at best a weak rather than a strong predictor of a person's likelihood of being hypnotized (Nash, 2001).

Explaining Hypnosis

How does hypnosis have its effects? Contemporary theorists disagree as to whether hypnosis is a divided state of consciousness or simply a learned social behavior.

divided consciousness view of hypnosis Hilgard's view that hypnosis involves a splitting of consciousness into two separate components, one of which follows the hypnotist's commands and the other of which acts as a "hidden observer."

A Divided State of Consciousness
Ernest Hilgard (1977, 1992), in his **divided consciousness view of hypnosis,** proposed that hypnosis involves a special divided state of consciousness, a splitting of consciousness into separate components. One component follows the hypnotist's commands, while another component acts as a "hidden observer."

Hilgard placed one hand of hypnotized individuals in a bucket of ice-cold water and told them that they would not feel pain but that a part of their mind—a hidden part that would be aware of what was going on—could signal any true pain by pressing a key with the hand that was not submerged (Figure 4.17). The individuals under hypnosis reported afterward that they had not experienced any pain; yet while

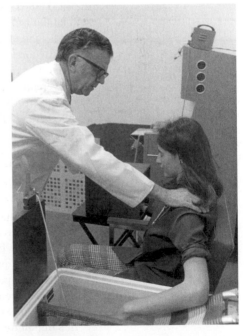

FIGURE 4.17
Hilgard's Divided Consciousness Experiment Ernest Hilgard tests a participant in the study in which he had individuals place one arm in ice-cold water.

their hand had been submerged in the ice-cold water, they had pressed the key with their non-submerged hand, and they had pressed it more frequently the longer their hand was in the cold water. Thus, in Hilgard's view, in hypnosis, consciousness has a hidden part that stays in contact with reality and feels pain while another part of consciousness feels no pain.

Critics of Hilgard's view suggest that the hidden observer simply demonstrates that the hypnotized person is not in an altered state of consciousness at all. From this perspective, the hidden observer is simply the person him- or herself, having been given permission to admit to the pain that he or she was always feeling (Green & others, 2005). This argument is part of the social cognitive behavior view of hypnosis.

Social Cognitive Behavior   Some experts are skeptical that hypnosis is an altered state of consciousness (Chaves, 2000; Green & others, 2005; Lynn, Boycheva, & Barnes, 2008). In the **social cognitive behavior view of hypnosis,** hypnosis is a normal state in which the hypnotized person behaves the way he or she believes that a hypnotized person should behave. The social cognitive perspective frames the important questions about hypnosis around cognitive factors—the attitudes, expectations, and beliefs of good hypnotic participants—and around the powerful social context in which hypnosis occurs (Lynn, 2007; Spanos & Chaves, 1989). Individuals being hypnotized surrender their responsibility to the hypnotist and follow the hypnotist's suggestions; and they have expectations about what hypnosis is supposed to be like.

Experts have continued to debate whether hypnosis is indeed an altered state of consciousness (Kihlstrom, 2005) or simply a reaction to a special social situation (Green & others, 2005). Although there may be no consensus about what hypnosis is, health professionals have begun to apply this powerful technique to a number of problems.

Applications of Hypnosis

In the United States, practitioners of hypnosis use the technique to treat alcoholism, somnambulism, suicidal tendencies, post-traumatic stress disorder, migraines, overeating, diabetes, and smoking (Carmody & others, 2008; Hammond, 2007; Holt & others, 2006; Lynn & Cardena, 2007; Sandor & Afra, 2005; Xu & Cardena, 2008). Among the least effective but most common applications of hypnosis are sessions aimed to help people stop overeating or quit smoking. Here individuals rarely achieve dramatic results unless they are already motivated to change. Hypnosis is most effective when combined with psychotherapy (Rossi, 2009).

A long history of research and practice has clearly demonstrated that hypnosis can reduce the experience of pain (Jensen, 2009). A fascinating study examined the pain perceptions of hypnotized individuals, with the goal of changing their pain threshold. In that study, the brains of participants were monitored while they received painful electrical shocks (rated 8 or higher on a 1 to 10 pain scale) (Schulz-Stubner & others, 2004). Those who were hypnotized to find the shocks less painful did rate them as lower in pain (giving them a 3 or less). The brain-scanning results were most interesting: The subcortical brain areas (the brain stem and midbrain) of the hypnotized patients responded the same as those of the patients who were not hypnotized, suggesting that these brain structures recognized the painful stimulation. However, the sensory cortex was not activated in the hypnotized patients, suggesting that although they sensed pain on some level, they were never conscious of it. In essence, the "ouch" signal never made it to awareness.

In sum, although the nature of hypnosis remains a bit of a mystery, there is increasing evidence that hypnosis can play a role in a variety of health contexts and that this procedure influences the brain in fascinating ways. Part of the uncertainty about the definition of hypnosis comes from the fact that it involves a very special social context. It is also possible to experience altered states of consciousness without a hypnotist guiding us along, as we next consider.

social cognitive behavior view of hypnosis
The perspective that hypnosis is a normal state in which the hypnotized person behaves the way he or she believes that a hypnotized person should behave.

1. The type of brain waves that hypnotized persons display include
   A. alpha waves.
   B. delta waves.
   C. gamma waves.
   D. theta waves.

2. The divided consciousness theory of hypnosis receives support from evidence that
   A. hypnosis can block sensory input.
   B. hypnosis can affect voluntary, but not involuntary, behaviors.
   C. hypnotized people often seem to play the role of "good hypnotic subjects."
   D. hypnotized people can be aware of pain sensation without experiencing emotional distress.

3. Hypnosis treatments tend to work best when they are accompanied by
   A. daily meditation.
   B. physical exercise.
   C. yoga.
   D. psychotherapy.

Apply It! 4. Ryan and his friends attend a show by the Great Chorizo, a hypnotist. Chorizo asks for volunteers to be hypnotized, and he picks the first five people who raise their hands. He puts the five people into a trance, and within minutes he has them lying on stage sizzling like slices of bacon in a frying pan. When it is all over, one of Ryan's friends remarks that Chorizo must have amazing powers: "That guy could make a person do anything!" Ryan, who has been working on his critical thinking and the psychology of hypnosis, wisely notes which of the following about Chorizo's act?

A. As long as Chorizo followed the steps of hypnosis described in this text, he probably does have amazing powers of suggestion.
B. Ryan would need to see Chorizo's training and qualifications prior to rendering judgment.
C. Chorizo selected the first five volunteers, and these individuals may have been especially motivated, suggestible, and likely to believe in the effects of hypnosis. There is no way to gauge whether Chorizo could have influence over anyone else.
D. Hypnotizability is similar for all people, so if Chorizo was able to get five people to act like frying bacon, he could probably do just about anything.

5 Meditation

Hypnosis involves a powerful social context, but harnessing the power of consciousness is also possible without the aid of a hypnotist—through meditation. Meditation involves attaining a peaceful state of mind in which thoughts are not occupied by worry. The meditator is mindfully present to his or her thoughts and feelings but is not consumed by them. Let's look at how meditation can enhance well-being and examine more closely what it is.

psychology in our world

Meditation at Work

More and more companies are discovering the benefits of giving their staff a chance to learn about meditation. Apple, Yahoo, and Google, along with more traditional organizations such as Deutsche Bank and McKinsey, have pioneered in making meditation a staple of their wellness programs. Trainers work with employees to reduce stress, sharpen mental focus, clarify thinking, boost productivity, improve communication, and help them balance work responsibilities with family life and outside interests.

Health and well-being can improve significantly for employees who take part in such programs. The corporation benefits, too. Andy Puddicombe, a former Buddhist monk with over 20 years of practical meditation experience, writes "These benefits make for a handsome return on investment, with a sharp decline in absenteeism and health costs accompanied by a significant increase in productivity and staff retention. The bottom line—it pays to meditate" (Puddicombe, 2008).

Mindfulness Meditation

Melissa Munroe, a Canadian woman diagnosed with Hodgkin lymphoma (a cancer of the immune system), was tormented by excruciating pain. Seeking ways to cope with the agony, Munroe enrolled in a meditation program. She was skeptical at first. "What I didn't realize," she said, "is that if people have ever found themselves taking a walk in the countryside or in the forest or on a nice pleasant autumn day . . . and find themselves in a contemplative state, that's a form of meditation." Munroe worked hard to use meditation to control her pain. Interestingly, the way she harnessed the power of her mind to overcome pain was by concentrating her thoughts on the pain—not trying to avoid it.

Using *mindfulness meditation,* a technique practiced by yoga enthusiasts and Buddhist monks, Munroe focused on her pain. By doing so, she was able to isolate the pain from her emotional response to it and to her cancer diagnosis. She grew to see her physical discomfort as bearable. Munroe's success shows that contrary to what a non-meditator might think, meditation is not about avoiding one's thoughts. Indeed, the effort involved in avoidance steers the person away from the contemplative state. Munroe described her thoughts as like people striding by her on the street, walking in the other direction; she explained, "They come closer and closer, then they pass you by."

Jon Kabat-Zinn (2006, 2009) has pioneered the use of meditation techniques in medical settings. Research by Kabat-Zinn and colleagues has demonstrated the beneficial effects of mindfulness meditation for a variety of conditions, including depression, panic attacks, and anxiety (Miller, Fletcher, & Kabat-Zinn, 1995), chronic pain (Kabat-Zinn, Lipworth, & Burney, 1985), and stress and the skin condition psoriasis (Kabat-Zinn & others, 1998). Many of these effects have also been shown to be long-lasting.

As noted in Chapter 2, Richard Davidson and colleagues (including Jon Kabat-Zinn) studied the brain and immune system changes that might underlie the health and wellness effects of meditation (Davidson & others, 2003). They performed MRIs on the brains of individuals who were in a standard eight-week meditation training program. After the training program and as compared to a control group, those in the meditation program reported reduced anxiety and fewer negative emotions. Furthermore, brain scans revealed that these individuals showed increased activation in the left hemisphere—the "happy brain" described in Chapter 2. In addition, the meditators showed better immune system response to a flu vaccine (Davidson & others, 2003). These results suggest that our conscious minds may have a role to play in enhancing our psychological and physical health (Arias & others, 2006; Ekman & others, 2005).

The Meditative State of Mind

What actually is the meditative state of mind? As a physiological state, meditation shows qualities of sleep and wakefulness, yet it is distinct from both. You may have experienced a state called *hypnagogic reverie*—an overwhelming feeling of wellness right before you fall asleep, the sense that everything is going to work out. Meditation has been compared to this relaxed sense that all is well (Friedman, Myers, & Benson, 1998).

In a study of Zen meditators, researchers examined what happens when people switch from their normal waking state to a meditative state (Ritskes & others, 2003). Using

Among those practicing altered states of consciousness are Zen monks who explore the Buddha-nature at the center of their being.

fMRI, the experimenters got images of the brain before and after the participants entered the meditative state. They found that the switch to meditation involved initial increases in activation in the basal ganglia and prefrontal cortex (the now familiar area that is often activated during consciousness). However, and interestingly, they also found that these initial activations led to decreases in the *anterior cingulate,* a brain area that is thought to be associated with acts of will. These results provide a picture of the physical events of the brain that are connected with the somewhat paradoxical state of meditation—controlling one's thoughts in order to let go of the need to control.

Getting Started with Meditation

Would you like to experience the meditative state? If so, you can probably reach that state by following some simple instructions:

- Find a quiet place and a comfortable chair.
- Sit upright in the chair, rest your chin comfortably on your chest, and place your arms in your lap. Close your eyes.
- Now focus on your breathing. Every time you inhale and every time you exhale, pay attention to the sensations of air flowing through your body, the feeling of your lungs filling and emptying.
- After you have focused on several breaths, begin to repeat silently to yourself a single word every time you breathe out. You can make a word up, use the word *one,* or try a word associated with an emotion you want to produce, such as *trust, love, patience,* or *happy.* Experiment with several different words to see which one works for you.
- If you find that thoughts are intruding and you are no longer attending to your breathing, refocus on your breathing and say your chosen word each time you exhale.

After you have practiced this exercise for 10 to 15 minutes, twice a day, every day for two weeks, you will be ready for a shortened version. If you notice that you are experiencing stressful thoughts or circumstances, simply meditate, on the spot, for several minutes. If you are in public, you do not have to close your eyes; just fix your gaze on a nearby object, attend to your breathing, and say your word silently every time you exhale.

Meditation is an age-old practice. Without explicitly mentioning meditation, some religions advocate related practices such as daily prayer and peaceful introspection. Whether the practice involves praying over rosary beads, chanting before a Buddhist shrine, or taking a moment to commune with nature, a contemplative state clearly has broad appeal and conveys many benefits (Kabat-Zinn, 2009; Sharma, Gupta, & Bijiani, 2008). Current research on the contemplative state suggests that there are good reasons why human beings have been harnessing its beneficial powers for centuries.

self-quiz

1. A pre-sleep state of calmness and wellness, with an accompanying feeling of optimism, is called
   A. a trance.
   B. a hypnagogic reverie.
   C. meditation.
   D. mindfulness.

2. Which of the following is *true* about mindfulness meditation?
   A. It involves clearing the mind of all thoughts.
   B. It has not been demonstrated to be effective in pain management.
   C. It increases activation of the right hemisphere of the brain.
   D. It focuses thoughts on specific bodily sensations.

3. In terms of physiology, meditation shows characteristics of
   A. sleep and wakefulness.
   B. sleep and hypnosis.
   C. sleep and hallucinations.
   D. sleep and daydreaming.

Apply It! 4. Prudence enjoys walking by a river next to her apartment building nearly every day. As she walks, she loses track of time and just thinks quietly about her life and experiences, letting her thoughts come and go without concern. Sometimes she stops to gaze at the river and enjoys its quiet glistening. After her walks, she always feels refreshed and ready for life's next challenges. One day a friend sees her while walking and says, "Oops, I didn't mean to interrupt your meditation." Prudence says, "Oh I'm not meditating, I'm just taking a walk." Is Prudence right?
   A. Prudence is right. If she does not think she is meditating, then she cannot be meditating.
   B. Prudence is right because she is not sitting down, and she is not repeating a word over and over.
   C. Prudence is not correct. She may not know it, but she is engaged in a contemplative state.
   D. Prudence is not correct. She is meditating because she is in a hypnotic state.

summary

① The Nature of Consciousness

Consciousness is the awareness of external events and internal sensations, including awareness of the self and thoughts about experiences. Most experts agree that consciousness is likely distributed across the brain. The association areas and prefrontal lobes are believed to play important roles in consciousness.

William James described the mind as a stream of consciousness. Consciousness occurs at different levels of awareness that include higher-level awareness (controlled processes and selective attention), lower-level awareness (automatic processes and daydreaming), altered states of consciousness (produced by drugs, trauma, fatigue, and other factors), subconscious awareness (waking subconscious awareness, sleep, and dreams), and no awareness (unconscious thought).

② Sleep and Dreams

The biological rhythm that regulates the daily sleep/wake cycle is the circadian rhythm. The part of the brain that keeps our biological clocks synchronized is the suprachiasmatic nucleus, a small structure in the hypothalamus that registers light. Biological clocks can become desynchronized by such things as jet travel and work shifts. Some strategies are available for resetting the biological clock.

We need sleep for physical restoration, adaptation, growth, and memory. Research studies increasingly reveal that people do not function optimally when they are sleep-deprived.

Stages of sleep correspond to massive electrophysiological changes that occur in the brain and that can be assessed by an EEG. Humans go through four stages of non-REM sleep and one stage of REM sleep, or rapid eye movement sleep. Most dreaming occurs during REM sleep. A sleep cycle of five stages lasts about 90 to 100 minutes and recurs several times during the night. The REM stage lasts longer toward the end of a night's sleep.

The sleep stages are associated with distinct patterns of neurotransmitter activity. Levels of the neurotransmitters serotonin, norepinephrine, and acetylcholine decrease as the sleep cycle progresses from stage 1 through stage 4. Stage 5, REM sleep, begins when the reticular formation raises the level of acetylcholine.

Sleep plays a role in a large number of diseases and disorders. Neurons that control sleep interact closely with the immune system, and when our bodies are fighting infection our cells produce a substance that makes us sleepy. Individuals with depression often have sleep problems.

Many Americans suffer from chronic, long-term sleep disorders that can impair normal daily functioning. These include insomnia, sleepwalking and sleep talking, nightmares and night terrors, narcolepsy, and sleep apnea.

Contrary to popular belief, most dreams are not bizarre or strange. Freud thought that dreams express unconscious wishes in disguise. The cognitive theory of dreaming attempts to explain dreaming in terms of the same cognitive concepts that are used in studying the waking mind. According to activation-synthesis theory, dreaming occurs when the cerebral cortex synthesizes neural signals emanating from activity in the lower part of the brain. In this view, the rising level of acetylcholine during REM sleep plays a role in neural activity in the brain stem that the cerebral cortex tries to make sense of.

③ Psychoactive Drugs

Psychoactive drugs act on the nervous system to alter states of consciousness, modify perceptions, and change moods. Humans are attracted to these types of drugs because they ease adaptation to change.

Addictive drugs activate the brain's reward system by increasing dopamine concentration. The reward pathway involves the ventral tegmental area (VTA) and nucleus accumbens (NAc). The abuse of psychoactive drugs can lead to tolerance, psychological and physical dependence, and addiction—a pattern of behavior characterized by a preoccupation with using a drug and securing its supply.

Depressants slow down mental and physical activity. Among the most widely used depressants are alcohol, barbiturates, tranquilizers, and opiates.

After caffeine, alcohol is the most widely used drug in America. The high rate of alcohol abuse by high school and college students is especially alarming. Alcoholism is a disorder that involves long-term, repeated, uncontrolled, compulsive, and excessive use of alcoholic beverages that impairs the drinker's health and work and social relationships.

Stimulants increase the central nervous system's activity and include caffeine, nicotine, amphetamines, cocaine, and MDMA (Ecstasy). Hallucinogens modify a person's perceptual experiences and produce visual images that are not real. Marijuana has a mild hallucinogenic effect; LSD has a strong one.

④ Hypnosis

Hypnosis is a psychological state or possibly altered attention and awareness in which the individual is unusually receptive to suggestions. The hypnotic state is different from a sleep state, as confirmed by EEG recordings. Inducing hypnosis involves four basic steps, beginning with minimizing distractions and making the person feel comfortable and ending with the hypnotist's suggesting certain events or feelings that he or she knows will occur or observes occurring.

There are substantial individual variations in people's susceptibility to hypnosis. People in a hypnotic state are unlikely to do anything that violates their morals or that involves a real danger.

Two theories have been proposed to explain hypnosis. In Hilgard's divided consciousness view, hypnosis involves a divided state of consciousness, a splitting of consciousness into separate components. One component follows the hypnotist's commands; the other acts as a hidden observer. In the social cognitive behavior view, hypnotized individuals behave the way they believe hypnotized individuals are expected to behave.

⑤ Meditation

Meditation refers to a state of quiet reflection. Meditation has benefits for a wide range of psychological and physical illnesses. Meditation can also benefit the body's immune system. Research using fMRI suggests that meditation allows an individual to control his or her thoughts in order to "let go" of the need to control.

Mindfulness meditation is a powerful tool for managing life's problems. How we think about our lives and experiences plays a role in determining whether we feel stressed and worried or challenged and excited about life. Seeking times of quiet contemplation can have a positive impact on our abilities to cope with life's ups and downs.

key terms

stream of consciousness, p. 118
consciousness, p. 118
controlled processes, p. 119
automatic processes, p. 120
unconscious thought, p. 121
biological rhythms, p. 123
circadian rhythms, p. 123
suprachiasmatic nucleus
  (SCN), p. 123

REM sleep, p. 128
manifest content, p. 132
latent content, p. 132
cognitive theory of
  dreaming, p. 133
activation-synthesis theory, p. 133
psychoactive drugs, p. 135
tolerance, p. 135

physical dependence, p. 135
psychological dependence, p. 135
addiction, p. 135
depressants, p. 136
alcoholism, p. 138
barbiturates, p. 139
tranquilizers, p. 139
opiates, p. 139

stimulants, p. 140
hallucinogens, p. 143
hypnosis, p. 146
divided consciousness view
  of hypnosis, p. 147
social cognitive behavior view
  of hypnosis, p. 148

self-test

Multiple Choice

1. You are aware of the thoughts running through your mind and the emotions triggered by those thoughts. You are also aware of sounds, things you see outside the window, and the smell of coffee. You are in a state of
   A. consciousness.
   B. transcendence.
   C. divided perception.
   D. heightened sensation.

2. Jordan has decided to go to sleep early. Although her eyes are closed and she is very relaxed, she has not yet fallen asleep. An EEG is most likely to indicate the presence of
   A. delta waves.
   B. alpha waves.
   C. sleep spindles.
   D. rapid eye movements.

3. Which of the following best characterizes a night's sleep?
   A. We begin the night in light sleep and end in deep sleep.
   B. We pass from light sleep to dream sleep to deep sleep.
   C. Our depth of sleep alternates up and down many times.
   D. We alternate from the waking state to dream sleep about six times.

4. Dreams occurring during _____ sleep are briefer, less fragmented, and less likely to involve visual images compared to _____ sleep.
   A. REM; non-REM
   B. non-REM; REM
   C. stage 2; REM
   D. stage 2; non-REM

5. The hormone _____ is a key factor in regulating a person's level of sleepiness.
   A. testosterone
   B. melatonin
   C. estrogen
   D. glutamate

6. Jane says she smokes marijuana because it makes her feel indescribably happy. This effect is indicative of
   A. transcendent experiences.
   B. psychological withdrawal.
   C. physical dependence.
   D. an altered state of consciousness.

7. Your friend reported feeling greater energy and a sense of well-being after taking a drug. Medical tests reveal increased activity of her central nervous system. The drug she took is most likely some type of
   A. depressant.
   B. tranquilizer.
   C. hallucinogen.
   D. stimulant.

8. Amphetamines are classified as a _____ and _____ in the same class as nicotine and caffeine.
   A. depressant; are not
   B. stimulant; are not
   C. depressant; are
   D. stimulant; are

9. In terms of states of consciousness, hypnosis involves a
   A. high degree of controlled processing.
   B. strong defense against suggestibility.
   C. sense of deep relaxation and altered body awareness.
   D. dependence on a belief in supernatural powers.

10. Meditation results in an altered state of consciousness by
    A. reducing the activity level.
    B. lowering the heart rate.
    C. decreasing the use of oxygen.
    D. refocusing attention.

Apply It!

11. Review the steps in hypnosis on page 147. Apply the social cognitive behavior view to each step. When and how, specifically, do social and cognitive factors play a role in hypnosis?

5 Learning

A Boy and His Dog

Like many other 6-year-olds, Xavier Ivy-Parris received a puppy for Christmas in 2003. Xavier's gift was no ordinary puppy, however. Xavier had suffered a traumatic brain injury that left him prone to blackouts and made it difficult for him to concentrate. As a result, he could not walk to school like his first-grade classmates. Xavier's puppy changed that and many other aspects of his life because it was a service dog, trained to help Xavier get to school and to alert others if he blacked out.

We have all seen such service dogs faithfully walking next to their human partners. The idea of guide dogs began in 1929 when Dorothy Eustis observed the German military using German shepherds as guides for war-blinded veterans of World War I. Today, there are approximately 15,000 service dogs in the United States (Partners for Life, 2007), trained to aid people with various disabilities. The dogs provide sound discrimination for the hearing impaired, assist with mobility, and retrieve items. They locate people, bathrooms, elevators, and lost cell phones. They open and close doors, help people dress and undress, flush toilets, and even put clothes in a washer and dryer.

Truly, service dogs are highly skilled professionals. They are trained to perform these complex acts using the principles that psychologists have uncovered in studying the processes that underlie learning, the focus of this chapter. ∎

- **How would you define learning?**

- **Does your definition apply both to animals and to humans?**

- **What is one thing you have learned in the past week, and how does it fit your definition?**

We begin by defining learning and sketching out its main types—associative learning and observational learning. We then turn our attention to two types of associative learning—classical conditioning and operant conditioning—followed by a close look at observational learning. We next probe into the role of cognitive processes in learning, before finally considering biological, cultural, and psychological constraints on learning. As you read, regularly ask yourself about your own beliefs concerning learning. If a dog can learn to do the laundry, surely the human potential for learning has barely been tapped.

1 Types of Learning

Learning anything new involves change. Once you learned the alphabet, it did not leave you; it became part of a "new you" who had been changed through the process of learning. Similarly, once you learn how to drive a car, you do not have to go through the process again at a later time. If you ever try out for the X-Games, you may break a few bones along the way, but at some point you probably will learn a trick or two through the experience, changing from a novice to an enthusiast who can at least stay on top of a skateboard.

By way of experience, too, you may have learned that you have to study to do well on a test, that there usually is an opening act at a rock concert, and that a field goal in U.S. football adds 3 points to the score. Putting these pieces together, we arrive at a definition of **learning**: a systematic, relatively permanent change in behavior that occurs through experience.

If someone were to ask you what you learned in class today, you might mention new ideas you heard about, lists you memorized, or concepts you mastered. However, how would you define learning if you could not refer to unobservable mental processes? You might follow the lead of behavioral psychologists. **Behaviorism** is a theory of learning that focuses solely on observable behaviors, discounting the importance of such mental activity as thinking, wishing, and hoping. Psychologists who examine learning from a behavioral perspective define learning as relatively stable, observable changes in behavior. The behavioral approach has emphasized general laws that guide behavior change and make sense of some of the puzzling aspects of human life (Olson & Hergenhahn, 2009).

Behaviorism maintains that the principles of learning are the same whether we are talking about animals or humans. Because of the influence of behaviorism, psychologists' understanding of learning started with studies of rats, cats, pigeons, and even raccoons. A century of research on learning in animals and in humans suggests that many of the principles generated initially in research on such animals also apply to humans (Domjan, 2006).

Notice that learning is relatively permanent, which means that we can sometimes forget things we've learned. Also, learning involves experience—so, changes in behavior that occur because of physical maturation are typically not considered learning.

learning
A systematic, relatively permanent change in behavior that occurs through experience.

behaviorism
A theory of learning that focuses solely on observable behaviors, discounting the importance of such mental activity as thinking, wishing, and hoping.

In this chapter we look at two types of learning: *associative learning* and *observational learning*. **Associative learning** occurs when we make a connection, or an association, between two events. *Conditioning* is the process of learning these associations (Chance, 2009; Klein, 2009). There are two types of conditioning: classical and operant, both of which have been studied by behaviorists.

In *classical conditioning,* organisms learn the association between two stimuli. As a result of this association, organisms learn to anticipate events. For example, lightning is associated with thunder and regularly precedes it. Thus, when we see lightning, we anticipate that we will hear thunder soon afterward. Fans of horror films know the power of classical conditioning. Watching one of the *Friday the 13th* movies, we find the tension building whenever we hear that familiar "Ch-ch-ch—ch-ha-ha-ha-ha" that signals Jason's arrival.

In *operant conditioning,* organisms learn the association between a behavior and a consequence, such as a reward. As a result of this association, organisms learn to increase behaviors that are followed by rewards and to decrease behaviors that are followed by punishment. For example, children are likely to repeat their good manners if their parents reward them with candy after they have shown good manners. Also, if children's bad manners are followed by scolding words and harsh glances by parents, the children are less likely to repeat the bad manners. Figure 5.1 compares classical and operant conditioning.

Much of what we learn, however, is not a result of direct consequences but rather of exposure to models performing a behavior or skill. For instance, as you watch someone shoot baskets, you get a sense of how it is done. The learning that takes place when a person observes and imitates another's behavior is called **observational learning.** Observational learning is a common way that people learn in educational and other settings. Observational learning is different from the associative learning described by behaviorism because it relies on mental processes: The learner has to pay attention, remember, and reproduce what the model did. Observational learning is especially important to human beings. In fact, watching other people is another way in which human infants acquire skills.

Human infants differ from baby monkeys in their strong reliance on imitation (MacLeod, 2006). After watching an adult model perform a task, a baby monkey will figure out its own way to do it, but a human infant will do exactly what the model did. Imitation may be the human baby's way to solve the huge problem it faces: to learn the

associative learning
Learning that occurs when we make a connection, or an association, between two events.

observational learning
Learning that takes place when a person observes and imitates another's behavior.

Classical Conditioning

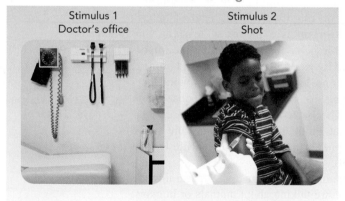

Stimulus 1
Doctor's office

Stimulus 2
Shot

Operant Conditioning

Behavior

Consequences

FIGURE 5.1

Associative Learning: Comparing Classical and Operant Conditioning (*Left*) In this example of classical conditioning, a child associates a doctor's office (stimulus 1) with getting a painful injection (stimulus 2). (*Right*) In this example of operant conditioning, performing well in a swimming competition (behavior) becomes associated with getting awards (consequences).

vast amount of cultural knowledge that is part of human life. Many of our behaviors are rather arbitrary. Why do we clap to show approval or wave "hello" or "bye-bye"? The human infant has a lot to learn and may be well served to follow the old adage, "When in Rome, do as the Romans do."

Learning applies to many areas of acquiring new behaviors, skills, and knowledge. Our focus in this chapter is on the two types of associative learning—classical conditioning and operant conditioning—and on observational learning.

Did you ever notice that human eyes are different from animals' eyes because you can see the "whites" of our eyes? It might be that this characteristic allows humans to model each other closely—because we can see what a model is looking at.

self-quiz

1. Any situation that involves learning
   A. requires some relatively permanent change to occur.
   B. requires a great deal of effort.
   C. involves conscious determination.
   D. is relatively automatic.

2. A cat that associates the sound of a can opener with being fed has learned through
   A. behaviorism.
   B. operant conditioning.
   C. classical conditioning.
   D. observational learning.

3. Which one of the following statements is *true* about learning?

   A. Learning can only be accomplished by higher-level species, such as mammals.
   B. Learning is not permanent.
   C. Learning occurs through experience.
   D. Learning processes in humans are distinct from learning processes in animals.

   Apply It! 4. After seeing dogs catching Frisbees in the park, Lionel decides that he wants to teach his dog Ivan to do it too. He takes Ivan to the park and sits with him, making sure that he watches the other dogs successfully catching Frisbees. What technique is Lionel using on Ivan, and what are the chances for success?

   A. He is using associative learning, and his chances for success are very good, because dogs and humans both learn this way.
   B. He is using operant conditioning, and his chances for success are very good, because dogs and humans both learn this way.
   C. He is using observational learning, and his chances for success are pretty bad, because dogs are not as likely as people to learn in this way.
   D. He is using classical conditioning, and his chances for success are pretty bad, because dogs are much less likely than people to learn in this way.

2 Classical Conditioning

It is a nice spring day. A father takes his baby out for a walk. The baby reaches over to touch a pink flower and is stung by a bumblebee sitting on the petals. The next day, the baby's mother brings home some pink flowers. She removes a flower from the arrangement and takes it over for her baby to smell. The baby cries loudly as soon as she sees it. The baby's panic at the sight of the pink flower illustrates the learning process of **classical conditioning,** in which a neutral stimulus (the flower) becomes associated with a meaningful stimulus (the pain of a bee sting) and acquires the capacity to elicit a similar response (fear).

classical conditioning
Learning process in which a neutral stimulus becomes associated with a meaningful stimulus and acquires the capacity to elicit a similar response.

Pavlov's Studies

Even before beginning this course, you might have heard about "Pavlov's dogs." The Russian physiologist Ivan Pavlov's work is very well known. Still, it is easy to take its true significance for granted. Importantly, Pavlov demonstrated that neutral aspects of the environment can attain the capacity to evoke responses through pairing with other stimuli and that bodily processes can be influenced by environmental cues.

In the early 1900s, Pavlov was interested in the way the body digests food. In his experiments, he routinely placed meat powder in a dog's mouth, causing the dog to salivate. By accident, Pavlov noticed that the meat powder was not the only stimulus that caused the dog to salivate. The dog salivated in response to a number of stimuli associated with the food, such as the sight of the food dish, the sight of the individual who

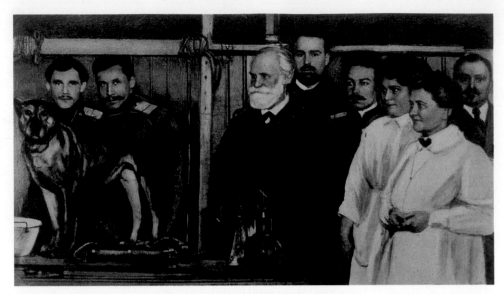

Pavlov (the white-bearded gentleman in the center) is shown demonstrating the nature of classical conditioning to students at the Military Medical Academy in Russia.

brought the food into the room, and the sound of the door closing when the food arrived. Pavlov recognized that the dog's association of these sights and sounds with the food was an important type of learning, which came to be called *classical conditioning*.

Pavlov wanted to know *why* the dog salivated in reaction to various sights and sounds before eating the meat powder. He observed that the dog's behavior included both unlearned and learned components. The unlearned part of classical conditioning is based on the fact that some stimuli automatically produce certain responses apart from any prior learning; in other words, they are inborn (innate). *Reflexes* are such automatic stimulus–response connections. They include salivation in response to food, nausea in response to spoiled food, shivering in response to low temperature, coughing in response to throat congestion, pupil constriction in response to light, and withdrawal in response to pain. An **unconditioned stimulus (UCS)** is a stimulus that produces a response without prior learning; food was the UCS in Pavlov's experiments. An **unconditioned response (UCR)** is an unlearned reaction that is automatically elicited by the UCS. Unconditioned responses are involuntary; they happen in response to a stimulus without conscious effort. In Pavlov's experiment, salivating in response to food was the UCR. In the case of the baby and the flower, the baby's learning and experience did not cause her to cry when the bee stung her. Her crying was unlearned and occurred automatically. The bee's sting was the UCS, and the crying was the UCR.

In classical conditioning, a **conditioned stimulus (CS)** is a previously neutral stimulus that eventually elicits a conditioned response after being paired with the unconditioned stimulus. The **conditioned response (CR)** is the learned response to the conditioned stimulus that occurs after CS–UCS pairing (Pavlov, 1927). Sometimes conditioned responses are quite similar to unconditioned responses, but typically they are not as strong.

In studying a dog's response to various stimuli associated with meat powder, Pavlov rang a bell before giving meat powder to the dog. Until then, ringing the bell did not have a particular effect on the dog, except perhaps to wake the dog from a nap. The bell was a neutral stimulus. However, the dog began to associate the sound of the bell with the food and salivated when it heard the bell. The bell had become a conditioned (learned) stimulus (CS), and salivation was now a conditioned response (CR). In the case of the unhappy baby, the flower was the CS, and crying was the CR after the sting (UCS) and the flower (CS) were paired. Figure 5.2 summarizes how classical conditioning works.

unconditioned stimulus (UCS)
A stimulus that produces a response without prior learning.

conditioned stimulus (CS)
A previously neutral stimulus that eventually elicits a conditioned response after being paired with the unconditioned stimulus.

Note that the association between food and salivating is natural (unlearned), while the link between a bell and salivating indicates a learned association.

unconditioned response (UCR)
An unlearned reaction that is automatically elicited by the unconditioned stimulus.

conditioned response (CR)
The learned response to the conditioned stimulus that occurs after conditioned stimulus–unconditioned stimulus pairing.

Before Conditioning

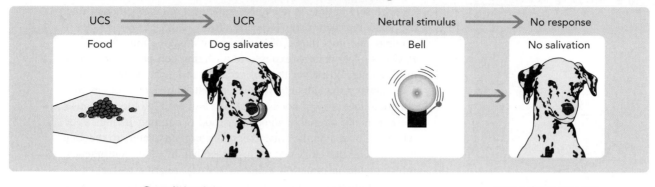

UCS ⟶ UCR		Neutral stimulus ⟶ No response	
Food	Dog salivates	Bell	No salivation

Conditioning

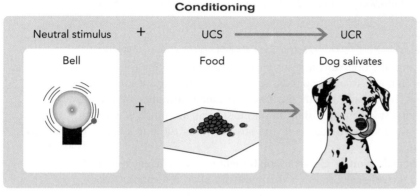

Neutral stimulus +	UCS ⟶ UCR	
Bell +	Food ⟶	Dog salivates

After Conditioning

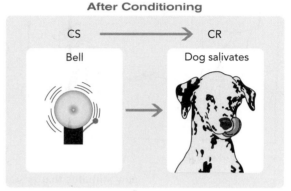

CS ⟶ CR	
Bell	Dog salivates

FIGURE 5.2

Pavlov's Classical Conditioning In one experiment, Pavlov presented a neutral stimulus (bell) just before an unconditioned stimulus (food). The neutral stimulus became a conditioned stimulus by being paired with the unconditioned stimulus. Subsequently, the conditioned stimulus (bell) by itself was able to elicit the dog's salivation.

Researchers have shown that salivation can be used as a conditioned response not only in dogs and humans but also in, of all things, cockroaches (Watanabe & Mizunami, 2007). These researchers paired the smell of peppermint (the CS, which was applied to the cockroaches' antennae) with sugary water (the UCS). Cockroaches naturally salivate (the UCR) in response to sugary foods, and after repeated pairings between peppermint smell and sugary water, the cockroaches salivated in response to the smell of peppermint (the CR). When they collected and measured the cockroach saliva, the researchers found that the cockroaches had slobbered over that smell for two minutes.

Wouldn't you love to be the research assistant who got to measure the cockroach saliva? What a great addition to any resume: "Cockroach saliva technician."

Acquisition Whether it is human beings, dogs, or cockroaches, the first part of classical conditioning is called acquisition. **Acquisition** is the initial learning of the connection between the UCS and CS when these two stimuli are paired (as with the smell of peppermint and the sugary water). During acquisition, the CS is repeatedly presented followed by the UCS. Eventually, the CS will produce a response. Note that classical conditioning is a type of learning that occurs without awareness or effort, based on the presentation of two stimuli together. For this pairing to work, however, two important factors must be present: contiguity and contingency.

Contiguity simply means that the CS and UCS are presented very close together in time—even a mere fraction of a second (Wheeler & Miller, 2008). In Pavlov's work, if the bell had rung 20 minutes before the presentation of the food, the dog probably would not have associated the bell with the food. However, pairing the CS and UCS close together in time is not all that is needed for conditioning to occur.

acquisition
The initial learning of the connection between the unconditioned stimulus and the conditioned stimulus when these two stimuli are paired.

www.CartoonStock.com

Contingency means that the CS must not only precede the UCS closely in time, it must also serve as a reliable indicator that the UCS is on its way (Rescorla, 1966, 1988, 2009). To get a sense of the importance of contingency, imagine that the dog in Pavlov's experiment is exposed to a ringing bell at random times all day long. Whenever the dog receives food, the delivery of the food always immediately follows a bell ring. However, in this situation, the dog will not associate the bell with the food, because the bell is not a reliable signal that food is coming: It rings a lot when no food is on the way. Whereas contiguity refers to the fact that the CS and UCS occur close together in time, contingency refers to the information value of the CS relative to the UCS. When contingency is present, the CS provides a systematic signal that the UCS is on its way.

Generalization and Discrimination

Pavlov found that the dog salivated in response not only to the tone of the bell but also to other sounds, such as a whistle. These sounds had not been paired with the unconditioned stimulus of the food. Pavlov discovered that the more similar the noise was to the original sound of the bell, the stronger was the dog's salivary flow.

Generalization in classical conditioning is the tendency of a new stimulus that is similar to the original conditioned stimulus to elicit a response that is similar to the conditioned response (Pearce & Hall, 2009). Generalization has value in preventing learning from being tied to specific stimuli. Once we learn the association between a given CS (say, flashing police lights behind our car) and a particular UCS (the dread associated with being pulled over), we do not have to learn it all over again when a similar stimulus presents itself (a police car with its siren moaning as it cruises directly behind our car).

Stimulus generalization is not always beneficial. For example, the cat that generalizes from a harmless minnow to a dangerous piranha has a major problem; therefore, it is important to also discriminate among stimuli. **Discrimination** in classical conditioning is the process of learning to respond to certain stimuli and not others. To produce discrimination, Pavlov gave food to the dog only after ringing the bell and not after any other sounds. In this way, the dog learned to distinguish between the bell and other sounds.

Extinction and Spontaneous Recovery

After conditioning the dog to salivate at the sound of a bell, Pavlov rang the bell repeatedly in a single session and did not give the dog any food. Eventually the dog stopped salivating. This result is **extinction,** which in classical conditioning is the weakening of the conditioned response when the unconditioned stimulus is absent (Joscelyne & Kehoe, 2007). Without continued association with the unconditioned stimulus (UCS), the conditioned stimulus (CS) loses its power to produce the conditioned response (CR).

Extinction is not always the end of a conditioned response (Urcelay, Wheeler, & Miller, 2009). The day after Pavlov extinguished the conditioned salivation to the sound of a bell, he took the dog to the laboratory and rang the bell but still did not give the dog any meat powder. The dog salivated, indicating that an extinguished response can spontaneously recur. **Spontaneous recovery** is the process in classical conditioning by which a conditioned response can recur after a time

Do It!

Demonstrate Pavlov's work among yourself and your friends. First buy some lemons and slice them. Then gather a group of friends to watch something on TV together, maybe the Academy Awards or the Super Bowl. Pick a CS that you know will come up a lot on the show—for example, someone saying "Thank you" during the Oscars or a soft drink or beer ad during the Super Bowl. For the first half hour, everyone has to suck on a lemon slice (the UCS) when the CS is presented. After the first half hour, take the lemons away. Have everyone report on their salivation levels (the CR) whenever the CS is presented later in the show. What happens?

generalization (classical conditioning) The tendency of a new stimulus that is similar to the original conditioned stimulus to elicit a response that is similar to the conditioned response.

discrimination (classical conditioning) The process of learning to respond to certain stimuli and not others.

extinction (classical conditioning) The weakening of the conditioned response when the unconditioned stimulus is absent.

spontaneous recovery The process in classical conditioning by which a conditioned response can recur after a time delay, without further conditioning.

delay, without further conditioning (Rescorla, 2005). Consider an example of spontaneous recovery you may have experienced: You thought that you had forgotten about (extinguished) an ex-girlfriend or boyfriend, but then you found yourself in a particular context (perhaps the restaurant where you always dined together), and you suddenly got a mental image of your ex, accompanied by an emotional reaction to him or her from the past (spontaneous recovery).

Figure 5.3 shows the sequence of acquisition, extinction, and spontaneous recovery. Spontaneous recovery can occur several times, but as long as the conditioned stimulus is presented alone (that is, without the unconditioned stimulus), spontaneous recovery becomes weaker and eventually ceases.

Extinction is not always the end of a conditioned response. **Renewal** refers to the recovery of the conditioned response when the organism is placed in a novel context. Renewal can be a powerful problem to overcome—as when a drug-addicted individual who spends time in a rehab facility leaves that setting (Stasiewicz, Brandon, & Bardizza, 2007). Indeed, drug addiction is one of the many areas in which classical conditioning has been applied to human beings.

renewal
The recovery of the conditioned response when the organism is placed in a novel context.

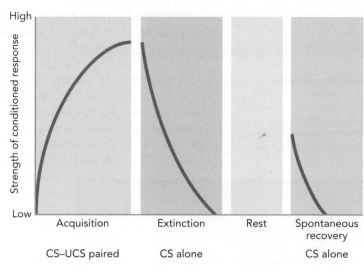

FIGURE 5.3

The Strength of a Classically Conditioned Response During Acquisition, Extinction, and Spontaneous Recovery During acquisition, the conditioned stimulus and unconditioned stimulus are associated. As the graph shows, when this association occurs, the strength of the conditioned response increases. During extinction, the conditioned stimulus is presented alone, and, as can be seen, the result is a decrease in the conditioned response. After a rest period, spontaneous recovery appears, although the strength of the conditioned response is not nearly as great at this point as it was after a number of CS–UCS pairings. When the CS is presented alone again, after spontaneous recovery, the response is extinguished rapidly.

Classical Conditioning in Humans

Since Pavlov conducted his experiments, researchers have conditioned individuals to respond to the sound of a buzzer, a glimpse of light, a puff of air, and the touch of a hand (J. A. Harris, 2006). Classical conditioning has a great deal of survival value for human beings (Powell, Symbaluk, & Honey, 2009). Here we review examples of classical conditioning at work in human life.

Explaining and Eliminating Fears Classical conditioning provides an explanation of fears (Wood & others, 2007). John B. Watson (who coined the term *behaviorism*) and Rosalie Rayner (1920) demonstrated classical conditioning's role in the development of fears with an infant named Albert. They showed Albert a white laboratory rat to see whether he was afraid of it. He was not (so the rat is a neutral stimulus or CS). As Albert played with the rat, the researchers sounded a loud noise behind his head (the bell is then the UCS). The noise caused little Albert to cry (the UCR). After only seven pairings of the loud noise with the white rat, Albert began to fear the rat even when the noise was not sounded (the CR). Albert's fear was generalized to a rabbit, a dog, and a sealskin coat.

Today, Watson and Rayner's (1920) study would violate the ethical guidelines of the American Psychological Association (see Chapter 1). Especially problematic is that the researchers did not reverse Albert's fear of furry objects, so presumably this phobia remained with him into old age. In any case, Watson correctly concluded that we learn many of our fears

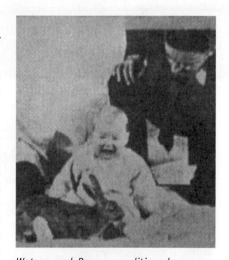

Watson and Rayner conditioned 11-month-old Albert to fear a white rat by pairing the rat with a loud noise. When little Albert was later presented with other stimuli similar to the rat, such as the rabbit shown here with Albert, he was afraid of them too. This study illustrates stimulus generalization in classical conditioning.

through classical conditioning. We might develop a fear of the dentist because of a painful experience, fear of driving after having been in a car crash, and fear of dogs after having been bitten by one.

If we can learn fears, we can possibly unlearn them too (Maier & Seligman, 2009; Powell, Symbaluk, & Honey, 2009). **Counterconditioning** is a classical conditioning procedure for changing the relationship between a conditioned stimulus and its conditioned response. One type of counterconditioning is systematic desensitization.

counterconditioning
A classical conditioning procedure for changing the relationship between a conditioned stimulus and its conditioned response.

Systematic desensitization is a method of therapy that treats anxiety by teaching the client to associate deep relaxation with increasingly intense anxiety-producing situations (Wolpe, 1963). A therapist might first ask the client which aspects of the feared situation are the most and least frightening. The therapist then arranges these circumstances in order from most to least frightening. The next step is to teach the individual to relax. The client learns to recognize the presence of muscular contractions or tensions in various parts of the body and then to contract and relax different muscles. Once the individual is relaxed, the therapist asks him or her to imagine the least feared stimulus in the hierarchy. Subsequently, the therapist moves up the list of items, from least to most feared, while the client remains relaxed. Eventually, the client can imagine the most fearsome circumstance without fear.

systematic desensitization
A method of therapy that treats anxiety by teaching the client to associate deep relaxation with increasingly intense anxiety-producing situations.

Therapists often use systematic desensitization successfully to treat phobias, irrational fears that interfere with a person's life, such as fear of heights, dogs, flying, and public speaking (we will discuss phobias more specifically in Chapter 12). If you are afraid of spiders, the therapist might initially have you watch someone handle a spider and then ask you to engage in increasingly more feared behaviors. You might first go into the same room with a spider, next approach the spider, then touch the spider; eventually, you might play with the spider.

Notice how systematic desensitization makes use of classical conditioning. It involves pairing a stimulus with a state of relaxation, extinguishing the person's fear association and linking the stimulus instead with a state of calm.

Explaining Pleasant Emotions
Classical conditioning is not restricted to unpleasant emotions such as fear. Things in our lives that might produce pleasure because they have become conditioned include Saturdays, a rainbow, and a favorite song. If you have a positive romantic experience, the location in which that experience took place can become a conditioned stimulus. This is the result of the pairing of a place (CS) with the event (UCS). Stimuli that are often associated with sex—such as mood music, seductive clothing, and a romantic restaurant—likely become conditioned stimuli that produce sexual arousal.

Sometimes, though, classical conditioning involves an experience that is both pleasant and deviant from the norm. Consider the fetishist who becomes sexually aroused by the sight and touch of certain clothing, such as undergarments or shoes. The fetish may have developed when the fetish object (undergarment, shoe) was associated with sexual arousal, especially when the individual was young. The

A breathtaking rainbow or some other beautiful natural event that you observed can serve as a conditioned stimulus. So can a restaurant where you enjoyed a positive romantic experience.

fetish object becomes a conditioned stimulus that can produce sexual arousal by itself (Chance, 2009).

Therapists have used counterconditioning to break apart the association between certain stimuli and positive feelings. **Aversive conditioning** is a form of treatment that consists of repeated pairings of a stimulus with a very unpleasant stimulus. Electric shocks and nausea-inducing substances are examples of noxious stimuli that are used in aversive conditioning (Sommer & others, 2006).

To reduce drinking, for example, every time a person drank an alcoholic beverage, he or she also would consume a mixture that induced nausea. In classical conditioning terminology, the alcoholic beverage is the conditioned stimulus and the nausea-inducing agent is the unconditioned stimulus. Through a repeated pairing of alcohol with the nausea-inducing agent, alcohol becomes the conditioned stimulus that elicits nausea, the conditioned response. As a consequence, alcohol no longer is associated with something pleasant but rather something highly unpleasant. Antabuse, a drug treatment for alcoholism since the late 1940s, is based on this association. When someone takes this drug, ingesting even the smallest amount of alcohol will make him or her quite ill, even if the exposure to the alcohol is through mouthwash or cologne.

Examples of aversive conditioning are evident in the classic film A Clockwork Orange (in which Malcolm McDowell's character is conditioned using nausea) and in the not-so-classic film Rollercoaster (presented in "Sensurround" in 1977 and featuring George Segal's character trying to quit smoking). These films do not present aversive conditioning as it is used these days!

Classical Conditioning and the Placebo Effect

Chapter 1 defined the placebo effect as the effect of a substance or procedure (such as taking a pill) that is used as a control to identify the actual effects of a treatment. Placebo effects are observable changes (such as a drop in pain) that cannot be explained by the effects of an actual treatment. The principles of classical conditioning can help to explain some of these effects (Price, Finniss, & Benedetti, 2008). In this case, the pill or syringe serves as a CS and the actual drug is the UCS. After the experience of pain relief following the consumption of a drug, for instance, the pill or syringe might lead to a CR of lowered pain even in the absence of actual painkiller. The strongest evidence for the role of classical conditioning on placebo effects comes from research on the immune system and the endocrine system.

Classical Conditioning and the Immune and Endocrine Systems

The immune system is the body's natural defense against disease. Robert Ader and Nicholas Cohen have conducted a number of studies that reveal that classical conditioning can produce *immunosuppression,* a decrease in the production of antibodies, which can lower a person's ability to fight disease (Ader, 2000; Ader & Cohen, 1975, 2000).

The initial discovery of this link between classical conditioning and immunosuppression came as a surprise. In studying classical conditioning, Ader (1974) was examining how long a conditioned response would last in some laboratory rats. He paired a conditioned stimulus (saccharin solution) with an unconditioned stimulus, a drug called Cytoxan, which induces nausea. Afterward, while giving the rats saccharin-laced water without the accompanying Cytoxan, Ader watched to see how long it would take the rats to forget the association between the two.

Unexpectedly, in the second month of the study, the rats developed a disease and began to die off. In analyzing this unforeseen result, Ader looked into the properties of the nausea-inducing drug he had used. He discovered that one of its side effects was immunosuppression. It turned out that the rats had been classically conditioned to associate sweet water not only with nausea but also with the shutdown of the immune system. The sweet water apparently had become a conditioned stimulus for immunosuppression. Researchers have found that conditioned immune responses also occur in humans (Ader, 2000; Goebel & others, 2002; Olness & Ader, 1992). For example, in one study, patients with multiple sclerosis were given a flavored drink prior to receiving a drug that suppressed the immune system. After this pairing, the flavored drink by itself lowered immune functioning, similarly to the drug (Giang & others, 1996).

Similar results have been found for the endocrine system. Recall from Chapter 2 that the endocrine system is a loosely organized set of glands that produce and circulate hormones. Research has shown that placebo pills can influence the secretion of hormones if patients had previous experiences with pills containing actual drugs that affected hormone secretion (Benedetti & others, 2003). Studies have revealed that the sympathetic nervous system (the part of the autonomic nervous systems that responds to stress) plays an important role in the learned associations between conditioned stimuli and immune and endocrine functioning (Saurer & others, 2008).

Through classical conditioning your body is learning things without your awareness.

Taste Aversion Learning

Consider this scenario: Mike goes out for sushi with some friends and eats tekka maki (tuna roll), his favorite dish. He then proceeds to a jazz concert. Several hours later, he becomes very ill with stomach pains and nausea. A few weeks later, he tries to eat tekka maki again but cannot stand it. Importantly, Mike does not experience an aversion to jazz music, even though he attended the jazz concert that night before getting sick. Mike's experience involves *taste aversion*: a special kind of classical conditioning involving the learned association between a particular taste and nausea (Bernstein & Koh, 2007; Ferreira & others, 2006; Garcia & Koelling, 1966; Masaki & Nakajima, 2006).

Taste aversion is special because it typically requires only one pairing of a neutral stimulus (a taste) with the unconditioned response of nausea to seal that connection, often for a very long time. As we consider later, it is highly adaptive to learn taste aversion in only one trial. An animal that required multiple pairings of taste with poison would likely not survive the acquisition phase. It is notable, though, that taste aversion can occur even if the "taste" had nothing to do with getting sick—perhaps, in Mike's case, he was simply coming down with a stomach bug. Taste aversion can even occur when a person has been sickened by a completely separate event, such as being spun around in a chair (Klosterhallfen & others, 2000).

Taste aversion learning is particularly important in the context of the traditional treatment of some cancers. Radiation and the chemical treatment of cancer often produce nausea in patients, with the result that cancer patients sometimes develop strong aversions to many foods that they ingest prior to treatment (Holmes, 1993; Jacobsen & others, 1993). Consequently, they may experience a general tendency to be turned off by food, a situation that can lead to nutritional deficits (Hutton, Baracos, & Wismer, 2007).

*These results show **discrimination** in classical conditioning—the kids developed aversions only to the specific scapegoat flavors.*

Researchers have used classical conditioning principles to combat these taste aversions, especially in children, for whom antinausea medication is often ineffective (Skolin & others, 2006) and for whom aversions to protein-rich food is particularly problematic (Ikeda & others, 2006). Early studies demonstrated that giving children a "scapegoat" conditioned stimulus prior to chemotherapy would help contain the taste aversion to only one flavor (Broberg & Bernstein, 1987). For example, children might be given a particular flavor of Lifesaver candy or ice cream before receiving treatment. For these children, the nausea would be more strongly associated with the Lifesaver or ice cream flavor than with the foods they needed to eat for good nutrition.

Drug Habituation

Chapter 4 described drug habituation and noted how, over time, a person might need a higher and higher dose of a drug to get the same effect. Classical conditioning helps to explain drug habituation. A mind-altering drug is an unconditioned stimulus: It naturally produces a response in the person's body. This unconditioned stimulus is often paired systematically with a previously neutral stimulus (CS). For instance, the physical appearance of the drug in a pill or syringe, and the room where the person takes the drugs, are conditioned stimuli that are paired with the UCS

psychology
in our world

Marketing Between the Lines

Classical conditioning provides the foundation of many of the commercials that the media bombard us with daily. (Appropriately, when John Watson left the field of psychology, he went on to advertising.) Think about it: Advertising involves creating an association between a product and pleasant feelings (buy that Caffe Misto grande and be happy). Watching TV, you can see how advertisers cunningly apply classical conditioning principles to consumers by showing ads that pair something pleasant (a UCS) with a product (a CS) in hopes that you, the viewer, will experience those positive feelings toward the product (CR). You might have seen the Hardee's ad showing Padma Lakshmi in a low-cut dress (the UCS) eating a giant messy hamburger (the CS). Of course, these days, hardly anyone seems to watch commercials anymore. Nonetheless, advertisers continue to exploit classical conditioning principles—for instance, through the technique of product placement, or what is known as *embedded marketing*.

This is how embedded marketing works. Viewing a TV show or movie, you might notice that a character is drinking a particular brand of soft drink or eating a particular type of cereal. By placing their products in the context of a show or movie you like, advertisers are hoping that your positive feelings about the show, movie plot, or a character (the UCR) rub off on their product (the CS). Sure, it may seem like a long shot—but all they need to do is enhance the chances that, navigating through, say, a car dealership or a grocery store, you will feel attracted to their product. If you saw *The Matrix Reloaded,* did you notice that all of the cars in the film were General Motors vehicles? Fans of the sitcom *The Office* might recognize that Jim classically conditioned Dwight Schrute with breath mints, modeling Pavlov's work, as you can check out on YouTube. Note that this pop culture moment explicitly demonstrated classical conditioning while also using classical conditioning in product placement for those curiously strong mints, Altoids.

of the drug. These repeated pairings should produce a conditioned response, and they do—but it is different from those we have considered so far. The conditioned response to a drug can be the body's way of *preparing* for the effects of a drug (Rachlin & Green, 2009). In this case, the body braces itself for the effects of the drug with a CR that is the opposite of the UCR. For instance, if the drug (the UCS) leads to an increase in heart rate (the UCR), the CR might be a drop in heart rate. The CS serves as a warning that the drug is coming, and the conditioned response in this case is the body's compensation for the drug's effects (Figure 5.4). In this situation the conditioned response works to decrease the effects of the UCS, making the drug experience less intense. Some drug users try to prevent habituation by varying the location where they take a drug.

This aspect of drug use can play a role in deaths caused by drug overdoses. How might classical conditioning be involved? A user typically takes a drug in a particular setting, such as a bathroom, and acquires a conditioned response to this location (Siegel, 1988). Because of classical conditioning, as soon as the drug user walks into the bathroom, his or her body begins to prepare for and anticipate the drug dose in order to lessen the effect of the drug. However, if the user takes the drug in a location other than the usual one, such as at a rock concert, the drug's effect is greater because no conditioned responses have built up in the new setting, and therefore the body is not prepared for the drug. In cases in which heroin causes death, researchers often have found that the individuals took the drug under unusual circumstances, at a different time, or in a

FIGURE 5.4

Drug Habituation
Classical conditioning is involved in drug habituation. As a result of conditioning, the drug user needs to take more of the drug to get the same effect as before the conditioning. Moreover, if the user takes the drug without the usual conditioned stimulus or stimuli—represented in the middle panel by the bathroom and the drug tablets—overdosing is likely.

UCS

The psychoactive drug is an unconditioned stimulus (UCS) because it naturally produces a response in a person's body.

CS

Appearance of the drug tablets and the room where the person takes the drug are conditioned stimuli (CS) that are paired with the drug (UCS).

CR

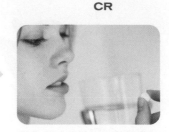

The body prepares to receive the drug in the room. Repeated pairings of the UCS and CS have produced a conditioned response (CR).

different place relative to the context in which they usually took the drug (Marlow, 1999). In these cases, with no CS signal, the body is unprepared for (and tragically overwhelmed by) the drug's effects.

self-quiz

1. Pavlov's dog salivates each time it hears a bell. Now, after several trials of salivating to the bell and *not* receiving any food, the dog stops salivating. The explanation is that
   A. the dog realizes that the bell is not food.
   B. extinction has occurred.
   C. the contingency loop has been disrupted.
   D. spontaneous recovery was not triggered.

2. A young boy goes to the zoo for the first time with his father and sister. While he is looking at a bird display, his sister sneaks up on him and startles him. He becomes very frightened, and now when he sees birds outside or on TV, he cries. The unconditioned response is
   A. fear.
   B. birds.

   C. being startled by his sister.
   D. going to the zoo.

3. A dog has learned to associate a small blue light coming on with being fed. Now, however, when a small light of any color comes on, the dog salivates. The reason is
   A. extinction.
   B. discrimination.
   C. counterconditioning.
   D. generalization.

Apply it! 4. Jake, a college student, goes out to eat with friends at a local Mexican restaurant and orders his favorite food, bean and cheese tamales. Jake and his friends are all dressed in fraternity T-shirts, and they spend the night talking about an upcoming charity event. When he gets home, Jake feels horribly ill and vomits through the night. Later he finds out that a

lot of people in his dorm also were sick and that apparently everyone had picked up a stomach bug.

Consider this as an example of classical conditioning. Based on the description of Jake's experience and your knowledge of classical conditioning, which of the following would you predict to happen in the future?
A. Jake will probably feel pretty sick the next time he puts on his fraternity T-shirt.
B. Jake will probably feel pretty sick the next time someone offers him tamales.
C. Jake will probably feel pretty sick at the charity event.
D. Jake should have no trouble eating tamales in the future, because he found that a stomach bug, not the tamales, made him sick.

3 Operant Conditioning

Recall from early in the chapter that classical conditioning and operant conditioning are forms of associative learning, which involves learning that two events are connected. In classical conditioning, organisms learn the association between two stimuli (UCS and CS). Classical conditioning is a form of *respondent behavior,* behavior that occurs in automatic response to a stimulus such as a nausea-producing drug, and later to a conditioned stimulus such as sweet water that was paired with the drug.

Classical conditioning explains how neutral stimuli become associated with unlearned, *involuntary responses.* Classical conditioning is not as effective, however, in explaining *voluntary behaviors* such as a student's studying hard for a test, a gambler's playing slot machines in Las Vegas, or a dog's searching for and finding his owner's lost cell phone. Operant conditioning is usually much better than classical conditioning at explaining such voluntary behaviors.

Defining Operant Conditioning

operant conditioning (instrumental conditioning)
A form of associative learning in which the consequences of a behavior change the probability of the behavior's occurrence.

The American psychologist B. F. Skinner (1938) developed the concept of operant conditioning. **Operant conditioning** (or *instrumental conditioning*) is a form of associative learning in which the consequences of a behavior change the probability of the behavior's occurrence. Skinner chose the term *operant* to describe the behavior of the organism. An operant behavior occurs spontaneously. According to Skinner, the consequences that follow such spontaneous behaviors determine whether the behavior will be repeated.

Imagine, for example, that you spontaneously decide to take a different route while driving to campus one day. You are more likely to repeat that route on another day if you have a pleasant experience, for instance, arriving at school faster or finding a new coffee place to try, than if you have a lousy experience such as getting stuck in traffic. In either case, the consequences of your spontaneous act influence whether that behavior happens again.

Recall that *contingency* is an important aspect of classical conditioning in which the occurrence of one stimulus can be predicted from the presence of another one. Contingency also plays a key role in operant conditioning. For example, when a rat pushes a lever (behavior) that delivers food, the delivery of food (consequence) is *contingent* on that behavior. This principle of contingency helps explain why passersby should never praise, pet, or feed a service dog while he is working (at least without asking first). Providing rewards during such times might interfere with the dog's training.

Thorndike's Law of Effect

Although Skinner emerged as the primary figure in operant conditioning, the experiments of E. L. Thorndike (1898) established the power of consequences in determining voluntary behavior. At about the same time that Pavlov was conducting classical conditioning experiments with salivating dogs, Thorndike, another American psychologist, was studying cats in puzzle boxes. Thorndike put a hungry cat inside a box and placed a piece of fish outside. To escape from the box and obtain the food, the cat had to learn to open the latch inside the box. At first the cat made a number of ineffective responses. It clawed or bit at the bars and thrust its paw through the openings. Eventually the cat accidentally stepped on the lever that released the door bolt. When the cat returned to the box, it went through the same random activity until it stepped on the lever once more. On subsequent trials, the cat made fewer and fewer random movements until finally it immediately stepped on the lever to open the door (Figure 5.5). Thorndike's resulting **law of effect** states that behaviors followed by positive outcomes are strengthened and that behaviors followed by negative outcomes are weakened (Brown & Jenkins, 2009).

law of effect
Thorndike's law stating that behaviors followed by positive outcomes are strengthened and that behaviors followed by negative outcomes are weakened.

The law of effect is important because it presents the basic idea that the consequences of a behavior influence the likelihood of that behavior's recurrence. Quite simply, a behavior can be followed by something good or something bad, and the

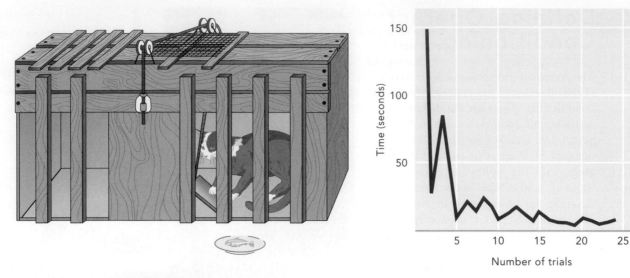

FIGURE 5.5

Thorndike's Puzzle Box and the Law of Effect (*Left*) A box typical of the puzzle boxes Thorndike used in his experiments with cats to study the law of effect. Stepping on the treadle released the door bolt; a weight attached to the door then pulled the door open and allowed the cat to escape. After accidentally pressing the treadle as it tried to get to the food, the cat learned to press the treadle when it wanted to escape the box. (*Right*) One cat's learning curve over 24 separate trials. Notice that the cat escaped much more quickly after about five trials. It had learned the consequences of its behavior.

probability of a behavior's being repeated depends on these outcomes. As we now explore, Skinner's operant conditioning model expands on this basic idea.

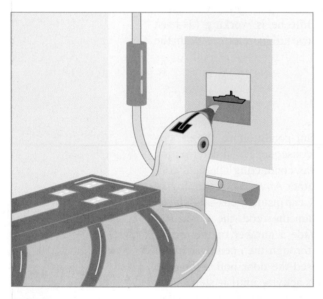

FIGURE 5.6

Skinner's Pigeon-Guided Missile Skinner wanted to help the military during World War II by using pigeons' tracking behavior. A gold electrode covered the tip of the pigeons' beaks. Contact with the screen on which the image of the target was projected sent a signal informing the missile's control mechanism of the target's location. A few grains of food occasionally given to the pigeons maintained their tracking behavior.

Skinner's Approach to Operant Conditioning

Skinner believed that the mechanisms of learning are the same for all species. This conviction led him to study animals in the hope that he could discover the components of learning with organisms simpler than humans, including pigeons. During World War II, Skinner trained pigeons to pilot missiles. Top navy officials just could not accept pigeons piloting their missiles in a war, but Skinner congratulated himself on the degree of control he was able to exercise over the pigeons (Figure 5.6).

Skinner and other behaviorists made every effort to study organisms under precisely controlled conditions so that they could examine the connection between the operant behavior and the specific consequences in minute detail (Hernstein, 2009). One of Skinner's creations in the 1930s to control experimental conditions was the Skinner box (Figure 5.7). A device in the box delivered food pellets into a tray at random. After a rat became accustomed to the box, Skinner installed a lever and observed the rat's behavior. As the hungry rat explored the box, it occasionally pressed the lever, and a food pellet was dispensed. Soon the rat learned that the consequences of pressing the lever were

FIGURE 5.7

The Skinner Box B. F. Skinner conducting an operant conditioning study in his behavioral laboratory. The rat being studied is in a Skinner box.

positive: It would be fed. Skinner achieved further control by soundproofing the box to ensure that the experimenter was the only influence on the organism. In many of the experiments, the responses were mechanically recorded, and the food (the consequence) was dispensed automatically. These precautions aimed to prevent human error.

These human errors might include cheering the rat on or rewarding it with food just because you feel bad for the hungry little guy.

Shaping

Imagine trying to teach even a really smart dog how to do the laundry. The challenge might seem insurmountable, as it is quite unlikely that a dog will spontaneously start putting the clothes in the washing machine. You could wait a very long time for such a feat to happen. It *is* possible, however, to train a dog or another animal to perform highly complex tasks through the process of shaping.

Shaping refers to rewarding approximations of a desired behavior (Krueger & Dayan, 2009). For example, shaping can be used to train a rat to press a bar to obtain food. When a rat is first placed in a Skinner box, it rarely presses the bar. Thus, the experimenter may start off by giving the rat a food pellet if it is in the same half of the cage as the bar. Then the experimenter might reward the rat's behavior only when it is within 2 inches of the bar, then only when it touches the bar, and finally only when it presses the bar.

shaping
Rewarding approximations of a desired behavior.

Returning to the service dog, rather than waiting for the dog spontaneously to put the clothes in the washing machine, we might reward the dog for carrying the clothes to the laundry room and for bringing them closer and closer to the washing machine. Finally, we might reward the dog only when it gets the clothes inside the washer. Indeed, trainers use this type of shaping technique extensively in teaching animals to perform tricks. A dolphin that jumps through a hoop held high above the water has been trained to perform this behavior through shaping.

Operant conditioning relies on the notion that a behavior is likely to be repeated if it is followed by a reward. A reasonable question is, what makes a reinforcer rewarding? Recent research reveals considerable interest in discovering the links between brain activity and operant conditioning (Chester & others, 2006; Fontanini & others, 2009). To explore this topic, see the Intersection.

Principles of Reinforcement

reinforcement
The process by which a rewarding stimulus or event (a reinforcer) following a particular behavior increases the probability that the behavior will happen again.

We noted earlier that a behavior can be followed by something pleasant or something unpleasant. *Reinforcement* refers to those nice things that follow a behavior. **Reinforcement** is the process by which a rewarding stimulus or event (a *reinforcer*) following a particular behavior increases the probability that the behavior will

Through operant conditioning, animal trainers can coax some amazing behaviors from their star performers.

intersection

When behaviorists talk about behaviors, they rarely focus on what is going on inside the head of the organism they are studying. With remarkable innovations in brain imaging, however, researchers—even those interested in associative learning—can examine the neural underpinnings of the relationships that underlie behavior (Koob, 2006). In effect, researchers can look inside the "black box" of the human brain and observe how learning takes place.

A key idea behind operant conditioning is that an organism is likely to repeat a behavior when that behavior is followed by a reward. However, what is rewarding about a reward? Food is an obvious reward. Hungry rats will work hard for food. Neuroscientists have identified a midbrain area called the nucleus accumbens (NAc), an extension of the amygdala that plays a vital role in our learning to repeat a rewarded behavior (Schultz, 2006). In essence, a special input into the NAc tells the organism to "do it again." The brain's response literally reinforces the synapses in the brain that connect the stimulus and response.

Behaviorism and Neuroscience: If It Feels Good, Is It Rewarding?

Researchers have found that the neurotransmitter dopamine plays a crucial role in the reinforcement of behaviors (Schlosser & others, 2009; Thomsen & others, 2009). An electrode that records dopamine cells in the brain of a monkey, for example, shows that dopamine is released not only when the monkey tastes food, but also when it sees signals in the environment suggesting that food is available (Schultz, Dayan, & Montague, 1997). By comparison, imagine that you are walking through a shopping mall and you see a "50 percent off" sign outside the shoe store. That sign might just start a dopamine explosion in your brain.

Dopamine's role in the activation of reinforcement is also demonstrated in animals that lack dopamine. Animals that have been given a drug that blocks dopamine find rewards less rewarding. They treat sugar as less sweet and fail to react to potential rewards in the environment (Smith, 1995). As researchers bring questions of basic learning principles into the neuroscience laboratory, they get ever-closer to understanding what "rewarding" really means.

Some people enjoy shopping, and others like playing competitive sports or video games. What are some rewarding experiences in your life that other people just don't understand? Why do you find them rewarding?

---

happen again. Pleasant or rewarding consequences of a behavior fall into two types, called *positive reinforcement* and *negative reinforcement*. Both of these types of consequences are experienced as pleasant, and both increase the frequency of a behavior.

positive reinforcement
The presentation of a rewarding stimulus following a given behavior in order to increase the frequency of that behavior.

negative reinforcement
The removal of an unpleasant stimulus following a given behavior in order to increase the frequency of that behavior.

Positive and Negative Reinforcement
In **positive reinforcement,** the frequency of a behavior increases because it is followed by the presentation of something that is good. For example, if someone you meet smiles at you after you say, "Hello, how are you?" and you keep talking, the smile has reinforced your talking. The same principle of positive reinforcement is at work when you teach a dog to "shake hands" by giving it a piece of food when it lifts its paw.

In contrast, in **negative reinforcement,** the frequency of a behavior increases because it is followed by the removal of something unpleasant. For example, if your father nagged you to clean out the garage and kept nagging until you cleaned out the garage, your response (cleaning out the garage) removed the unpleasant stimulus (your dad's nagging). Taking an aspirin when you have a headache works the same way: A reduction of pain reinforces the act of taking an aspirin. Similarly, if your TV is making an irritating buzzing sound, you might give it a good smack on the side, and if the buzzing stops, you are more likely to smack the set again if the buzzing resumes. Ending the buzzing sound rewards the TV-smacking.

Positive Reinforcement

Behavior	Rewarding Stimulus Provided	Future Behavior
You turn in homework on time.	Teacher praises your performance.	You increasingly turn in homework on time.
You wax your skis.	The skis go faster.	You wax your skis the next time you go skiing.
You randomly press a button on the dashboard of a friend's car.	Great music begins to play.	You deliberately press the button again the next time you get into the car.

Negative Reinforcement

Behavior	Unpleasant Stimulus Removed	Future Behavior
You turn in homework on time.	Teacher stops criticizing late homework.	You increasingly turn in homework on time.
You wax your skis.	People stop zooming by you on the slope.	You wax your skis the next time you go skiing.
You randomly press a button on the dashboard of a friend's car.	An annoying song shuts off.	You deliberately press the button again the next time the annoying song is on.

FIGURE 5.8

Positive and Negative Reinforcement Negative reinforcers involve taking something aversive away. Positive reinforcers mean adding something pleasant.

Notice that both positive and negative reinforcement involve rewarding behavior—but they do so in different ways. Positive reinforcement means following a behavior with something pleasant, and negative reinforcement means following a behavior with the removal of something unpleasant. Remember that in this case, "positive" and "negative" have nothing to do with "good" and "bad." Rather, they refer to processes in which something is given (positive reinforcement) or something is removed (negative reinforcement). Whether it is positive or negative, reinforcement is about increasing a behavior. Figure 5.8 provides further examples to help you understand the distinction between positive and negative reinforcement.

Positive reinforcement and negative reinforcement can be difficult concepts to grasp. The real-world examples and accompanying practice exercises on the following website should help to clarify the distinction for you: http://psych.athabascau.ca/html/prtut/reinpair.htm

Parents who are potty-training toddlers often rely on token economies.

primary reinforcer
A reinforcer that is innately satisfying; one that does not take any learning on the organism's part to make it pleasurable.

secondary reinforcer
A reinforcer that acquires its positive value through an organism's experience; a secondary reinforcer is a learned or conditioned reinforcer.

Types of reinforcers   Psychologists classify positive reinforcers as primary or secondary based on whether the rewarding quality of the consequence is innate or learned. A **primary reinforcer** is innately satisfying; that is, a primary reinforcer does not take any learning on the organism's part to make it pleasurable. Food, water, and sexual satisfaction are primary reinforcers. A **secondary reinforcer** acquires its positive value through an organism's experience; a secondary reinforcer is a learned or conditioned reinforcer. We encounter hundreds of secondary reinforcers in our lives, such as getting an *A* on a test and a paycheck for a job. Although we might think of these as quite positive outcomes, they are not innately positive. We learn through experience that *A*s and paychecks are good. Secondary reinforcers can be used in a system called a *token economy*. In a token economy behaviors are rewarded with tokens (such as poker chips or stars on a chart) that can be exchanged later for desired rewards (such as candy or money).

Generalization, Discrimination, and Extinction   Not only are generalization, discrimination, and extinction important in classical conditioning, they also are key principles in operant conditioning.

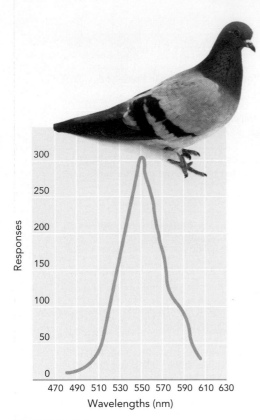

Responses — (y-axis: 0, 50, 100, 150, 200, 250, 300)

Wavelengths (nm) — (x-axis: 470 490 510 530 550 570 590 610 630)

FIGURE 5.9

Stimulus Generalization In the experiment by Norman Guttman and Harry Kalish (1956), pigeons initially pecked a disk of a particular color (in this graph, a color with a wavelength of 550 nm) after they had been reinforced for this wavelength. Subsequently, when the pigeons were presented disks of colors with varying wavelengths, they were likelier to peck those that were similar to the original disk.

Generalization In operant conditioning, **generalization** means performing a reinforced behavior in a different situation. For example, in one study pigeons were reinforced for pecking at a disk of a particular color (Guttman & Kalish, 1956). To assess stimulus generalization, researchers presented the pigeons with disks of varying colors. As Figure 5.9 shows, the pigeons were most likely to peck at disks closest in color to the original. When a student who gets excellent grades in a calculus class by studying the course material every night starts to study psychology and history every night as well, generalization is at work.

Discrimination In operant conditioning, **discrimination** means responding appropriately to stimuli that signal that a behavior will or will not be reinforced (de Wit & others, 2007). For example, you go to a restaurant that has a "University Student Discount" sign in the front window, and you enthusiastically flash your student ID with the expectation of getting the reward of a reduced-price meal. Without the sign, showing your ID might get you only a puzzled look, not cheap food.

The principle of discrimination helps to explain how a service dog "knows" when he is working. Typically, the dog wears a training harness while on duty but not at other times. Thus, when a service dog is wearing its harness, it is important to treat him like the professional that he is. Similarly, an important aspect of the training of service dogs is the need for selective disobedience. Selective disobedience means that in addition to obeying commands from its human partner, the service dog must at times override such commands if the context provides cues that obedience is not the appropriate response. So, if a guide dog is standing at the corner with his visually impaired human, and the human commands him to move forward, the dog might refuse if he sees the "Don't Walk" sign flashing. Stimuli in the environment serve as cues, informing the organism if a particular reinforcement contingency is in effect.

Extinction In operant conditioning, **extinction** occurs when a behavior is no longer reinforced and decreases in frequency (Leslie & others, 2006). If, for example, a soda machine that you frequently use starts "eating" your coins without dispensing soda, you quickly stop inserting more coins. Several weeks later, you might try to use the machine again, hoping that it has been fixed. Such behavior illustrates spontaneous recovery in operant conditioning.

Continuous Reinforcement, Partial Reinforcement, and Schedules of Reinforcement

Most of the examples of reinforcement we have considered so far involve *continuous reinforcement,* in which a behavior is reinforced every time it occurs. When continuous reinforcement takes place, organisms learn rapidly. However, when reinforcement stops, extinction takes place quickly. A variety of conditioning procedures have been developed that are particularly resistant to extinction. These involve *partial reinforcement,* in which a reinforcer follows a behavior only a portion of the time (Shull & Grimes, 2006). Partial reinforcement characterizes most life experiences. For instance, a golfer does not win every tournament she enters; a chess whiz does not win every match he plays; a student does not get a pat on the back each time she solves a problem.

Schedules of reinforcement are specific patterns that determine when a behavior will be reinforced (Killeen & others, 2009; Soreth & Hineline, 2009). There are four main schedules of partial reinforcement: fixed ratio, variable ratio, fixed interval, and variable

generalization (operant conditioning) Performing a reinforced behavior in a different situation.

discrimination (operant conditioning) Responding appropriately to stimuli that signal that a behavior will or will not be reinforced.

extinction (operant conditioning) Decreases in the frequency of a behavior when the behavior is no longer reinforced.

schedules of reinforcement Specific patterns that determine when a behavior will be reinforced.

interval. With respect to these, *ratio schedules* involve the number of behaviors that must be performed prior to reward, and *interval schedules* refer to the amount of time that must pass before a behavior is rewarded. In a fixed schedule, the number of behaviors or the amount of time is always the same. In a variable schedule, the required number of behaviors or the amount of time that must pass changes and is unpredictable from the perspective of the learner. Let's look concretely at how each of these schedules of reinforcement influences behavior.

A *fixed-ratio schedule* reinforces a behavior after a set number of behaviors. For example, if you are playing the slot machines in Atlantic City and if the machines are on a fixed-ratio schedule, you might get $5 back every 20th time you put money in the machine. It would not take long to figure out that if you watched someone else play the machine 18 or 19 times, not get any money back, and then walk away, you should step up, insert your coin, and get back $5. The business world often uses fixed-ratio schedules to increase production. For instance, a factory might require a line worker to produce a certain number of items in order to get paid a particular amount.

Of course, if the reward schedule for a slot machine were that easy to figure out, casinos would not be so successful. What makes gambling so tantalizing is the unpredictability of wins (and losses). Slot machines are on a *variable-ratio schedule,* a timetable in which behaviors are rewarded an average number of times but on an unpredictable basis. For example, a slot machine might pay off at an average of every 20th time, but the gambler does not know when this payoff will be. The

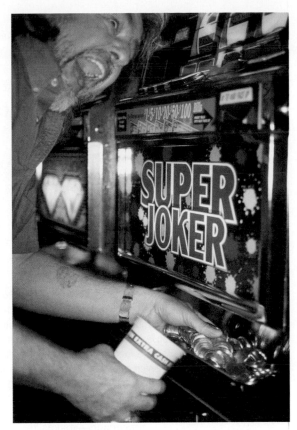

Slot machines are on a variable-ratio schedule of reinforcement.

slot machine might pay off twice in a row and then not again until after 58 coins have been inserted. This averages out to a reward for every 20 behavioral acts, but *when* the reward will be given is unpredictable. Variable-ratio schedules produce high, steady rates of behavior that are more resistant to extinction than the other three schedules.

Whereas ratio schedules of reinforcement are based on the *number* of behaviors that occur, interval reinforcement schedules are determined by the *time elapsed* since the last behavior was rewarded. A *fixed-interval schedule* reinforces the first behavior after a fixed amount of time has passed. If you take a class that has four scheduled exams, you might procrastinate most of the semester and cram just before each test. Fixed-interval schedules of reinforcement are also responsible for that fact that pets seem to be able to "tell time," eagerly sidling up to their food dish at 5 P.M. in anticipation of dinner. On a fixed-interval schedule, the rate of a behavior increases rapidly as the time approaches when the behavior likely will be reinforced. For example, a government official who is running for reelection may intensify her campaign activities as election day draws near.

A *variable-interval schedule* is a timetable in which a behavior is reinforced after a variable amount of time has elapsed. Pop quizzes occur on a variable-interval schedule. So does fishing—you do not know if the fish will bite in the next minute, in a half hour, in an hour, or ever. Because it is difficult to predict when a reward will come, behavior is slow and consistent on a variable-interval schedule (Staddon, Chelaru, & Higa, 2002).

This is why pop quizzes lead to more consistent levels of studying compared to the cramming that might be seen with scheduled tests.

To sharpen your sense of the differences between fixed and variable interval schedules, consider the following example. Penelope and Edith both design slot machines for their sorority's charity casino night. Penelope puts her slot machine on a variable-interval schedule of reinforcement; Edith puts hers on a fixed-interval schedule of reinforcement. On average, both machines will deliver a reward every 20 minutes. Whose slot machine is likely to make the most money for the sorority charity? Edith's machine is likely to lead to long lines just before the 20-minute mark, but people will be unlikely to

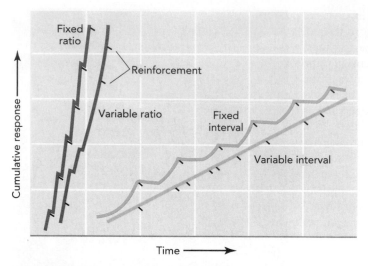

FIGURE 5.10
Schedules of Reinforcement and Different Patterns of Responding In this figure, each hash mark indicates the delivery of reinforcement. Notice on the fixed-ratio schedule the dropoff in responding after each response; on the variable-ratio schedule the high, steady rate of responding; on the fixed-interval schedule the immediate dropoff in responding after reinforcement, and the increase in responding just before reinforcement (resulting in a scalloped curve); and on the variable-interval schedule the slow, steady rate of responding.

Punishment is sometimes confused with negative reinforcement. Reinforcement increases behavior. Punishment is meant to decrease it.

What are some of your long-term goals? How do you balance your hoped-for long-term rewards with immediate pleasures?

play on it at other times. In contrast, Penelope's is more likely to entice continuous play, because the players never know when they might hit a jackpot. The magic of variable schedules of reinforcement is that the learner can never be sure exactly when the reward is coming. Figure 5.10 shows how the different schedules of reinforcement result in different rates of responding.

Punishment We began this section by noting that behaviors can be followed by something good or something bad. So far, we have explored only the good things—reinforcers that are meant to increase behaviors. Sometimes, however, the goal is to decrease a behavior, and in such cases the behavior might be followed by something unpleasant. **Punishment** is a consequence that decreases the likelihood that a behavior will occur. For instance, a child plays with a matchbox and gets burned when he or she lights one of the matches; the child consequently is less likely to play with matches in the future. As another example, a student interrupts the instructor, and the instructor scolds the student. This consequence—the teacher's verbal reprimand—makes the student less likely to interrupt in the future. In punishment, a response decreases because of its unpleasant consequences.

Just as the positive–negative distinction applies to reinforcement, it can also apply to punishment. As was the case for reinforcement, "positive" means adding something, and "negative" means taking something away. Thus, in **positive punishment,** a behavior decreases when it is followed by the presentation of an unpleasant stimulus, whereas in **negative punishment,** a behavior decreases when a positive stimulus is removed. Examples of positive punishment include spanking a misbehaving child and scolding a spouse who forgot to call when she was running late at the office; the coach who makes his team run wind sprints after a lackadaisical practice is also using positive punishment. *Time-out* is a form of negative punishment in which a child is removed from a positive reinforcer, such as his or her toys. Getting grounded is also a form of negative punishment as it involves taking a teenager away from the fun things in his or her life. Figure 5.11 compares positive reinforcement, negative reinforcement, positive punishment, and negative punishment.

The use of positive punishment, especially physical punishment such as spanking, with children has been a topic of some debate. To learn how psychologists view the use of physical punishment with children, see Challenge Your Thinking.

Timing, Reinforcement, and Punishment How does the timing of reinforcement and punishment influence behavior? And does it matter whether the reinforcement is small or large?

Immediate Versus Delayed Reinforcement As is the case in classical conditioning, in operant conditioning learning is more efficient when the interval between a behavior and its reinforcer is a few seconds rather than minutes or hours, especially in lower animals (Church & Kirkpatrick, 2001). If a food reward is delayed for more than 30 seconds after a rat presses a bar, it is virtually ineffective as reinforcement. Humans, however, have the ability to respond to delayed reinforcers (Holland, 1996).

punishment
A consequence that decreases the likelihood that a behavior will occur.

positive punishment
The presentation of an unpleasant stimulus following a given behavior in order to decrease the frequency of that behavior.

negative punishment
The removal of a positive stimulus following a given behavior in order to decrease the frequency of that behavior.

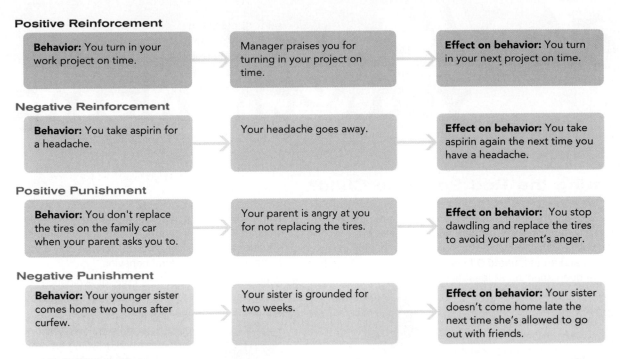

Positive Reinforcement

| Behavior: You turn in your work project on time. | → | Manager praises you for turning in your project on time. | → | Effect on behavior: You turn in your next project on time. |

Negative Reinforcement

| Behavior: You take aspirin for a headache. | → | Your headache goes away. | → | Effect on behavior: You take aspirin again the next time you have a headache. |

Positive Punishment

| Behavior: You don't replace the tires on the family car when your parent asks you to. | → | Your parent is angry at you for not replacing the tires. | → | Effect on behavior: You stop dawdling and replace the tires to avoid your parent's anger. |

Negative Punishment

| Behavior: Your younger sister comes home two hours after curfew. | → | Your sister is grounded for two weeks. | → | Effect on behavior: Your sister doesn't come home late the next time she's allowed to go out with friends. |

FIGURE 5.11

Positive Reinforcement, Negative Reinforcement, Positive Punishment, and Negative Punishment The fine distinctions here can sometimes be confusing. With respect to reinforcement, note that positive reinforcement means rewarding good behaviors and that negative reinforcement means taking away something unpleasant. With respect to the words *positive* and *negative* punishment, refer to whether the response to behavior is adding something unpleasant (positive punishment such as scolding) or taking away something pleasant (negative punishment such as being grounded or receiving a time-out).

Sometimes important life decisions involve whether to seek and enjoy a small, immediate reinforcer or to wait for a delayed but more highly valued reinforcer (Martin & Pear, 2007). For example, you might spend your money now on clothes, concert tickets, and the latest iPod, or you might save your money and buy a car later. You might choose to enjoy yourself now in return for immediate small reinforcers, or you might opt to study hard in return for delayed stronger reinforcers such as good grades, a scholarship to graduate school, and a better job.

© Mark Parisi. Atlantic Feature Syndicate.

Immediate Versus Delayed Punishment As with reinforcement, in most instances of research with lower animals, immediate punishment is more effective than delayed punishment in decreasing the occurrence of a behavior. However, also as with reinforcement, delayed punishment can have an effect on human behavior. Not studying at the beginning of a semester can lead to poor grades much later, and humans have the capacity to notice that this early behavior contributed to the negative outcome.

Immediate Versus Delayed Reinforcement and Punishment Many daily behaviors revolve around rewards and punishments, both immediate and delayed. We might put off going to the dentist to avoid a small punisher (such as the discomfort that comes with getting a cavity filled). However, this procrastination might contribute to greater pain later (such as the pain of having a tooth pulled). Sometimes life is about enduring a little pain *now* to avoid a lot of pain *later*.

challenge your thinking

Will Sparing the Rod Spoil the Child?

For centuries, experts considered corporal (physical) punishment such as spanking a necessary and even desirable method of disciplining children. Corporal punishment is legal in every U.S. state, and an estimated 94 percent of American 3- and 4-year-olds have been spanked at least once in any given year (Straus & Stewart, 1999). A cross-cultural comparison found that individuals in the United States and Canada were among the most favorable toward corporal punishment and remembered their parents' using it (Curran & others, 2001).

There have been surprisingly few research studies on physical punishment, and those that have been conducted are correlational (Kazdin & Benjet, 2003). Recall that cause and effect cannot be determined in a correlational study. In one such study, the researchers found a link between parents' spanking and children's antisocial behavior, including cheating, telling lies, being mean to others, bullying, getting into fights, and being disobedient (Straus, Sugarman, & Giles-Sims, 1997). Moreover, culture seems to play a big role in the outcomes associated with spanking. A longitudinal study tracked children from before the age of 2 until they were 6 years old. Spanking before the age of 2 is especially associated with increased behavior problems at age 6 but only for non-Latino White children (Slade & Wissow, 2004).

A research review concluded that although corporal punishment by parents is associated with children's higher levels of immediate compliance, it is also associated with aggression among children, as well as with lower levels of moral internalization and mental health (Gershoff, 2002). High and harsh levels of corporal punishment are especially harmful to children's well-being (Alyahri & Goodman, 2008; Aucoin, Frick, & Bodin, 2006; de Zoysa, Newcombe, & Rajapakse, 2008) and may affect adolescents as well (Bender & others, 2007). Some critics, though, argue that the research evidence is not sound enough to warrant making corporal punishment illegal, especially mild corporal punishment (Baumrind, Larzelere, & Cowan, 2002; Landrum & Kauffman, 2006). Further, animal studies reveal that punishment often reduces undesired behaviors (Domjan, 2006).

What are some reasons for avoiding spanking or similar punishments?

■ When adults yell, scream, or spank, they are presenting children with out-of-control models for handling stressful situations (Sim & Ong, 2005). Children may imitate this aggressive, out-of-control behavior.

■ Punishment can instill fear, rage, or avoidance. For example, spanking may cause the child to avoid being around the parent and to fear the parent.

■ Punishment tells children what not to do rather than what to do. It would be preferable to give children feedback such as "Why don't you try this?"

■ Punishment can be abusive. Even if parents do not so intend, they might get so carried away during the act of punishing that they become abusive (Dunlap & others, 2009).

For such reasons, Sweden passed a law in 1979 forbidding parents to punish children physically (to spank or slap them, for example). Since the law's enactment, youth rates of delinquency, alcohol abuse, rape, and suicide have dropped in Sweden (Durrant, 2008). Because this study is correlational in nature, however, we cannot assume that the anti-spanking law caused these social changes. These improvements may have occurred for other reasons, such as shifting attitudes and broadened opportunities for youth. Nonetheless, the Swedish experience suggests that the physical punishment of children may be unnecessary.

When asked why they use corporal punishment, parents often respond that their children need strong discipline to learn how to behave. Parents also sometimes reason that they were spanked by their own parents and they turned out okay, so there is nothing wrong with corporal punishment.

What Do You Think?

■ Should the United States outlaw the physical punishment of children? Why or why not?

■ Did your parents spank you when you were a child? If so, what effect do you think physical punishment had on your behavior?

■ Might negative punishment, such as time-outs, be more effective than positive punishment, such as spanking? Explain.

How does receiving immediate small reinforcement versus delayed strong punishment affect human behavior (Martin & Pear, 2007)? One reason that obesity is such a major health problem is that eating is a behavior with immediate positive consequences—food tastes great and quickly provides a pleasurable, satisfied feeling. Although the potential delayed consequences of overeating are negative (obesity and other possible health risks), the immediate consequences are difficult to override. When the delayed consequences of behavior are punishing and the immediate consequences are reinforcing, the immediate consequences usually win, even when the immediate consequences are minor reinforcers and the delayed consequences are major punishers.

Smoking and drinking follow a similar pattern. The immediate consequences of smoking are reinforcing for most smokers—the powerful combination of positive reinforcement (enhanced attention, energy boost) and negative reinforcement (tension relief, removal of craving). The primarily long-term effects of smoking are punishing and include shortness of breath, a chronic sore throat and/or coughing, chronic obstructive pulmonary disease (COPD), heart disease, and cancer. Likewise, the immediate pleasurable consequences of drinking override the delayed consequences of a hangover or even alcoholism and liver disease.

Now think about the following situations. Why are some of us so reluctant to take up a new sport, try a new dance step, run for office on campus or in local government, or do almost anything different? One reason is that learning new skills often involves minor punishing consequences, such as initially looking and feeling stupid, not knowing what to do, and having to put up with sarcastic comments from others. In these circumstances, reinforcing consequences are often delayed. For example, it may take a long time to become a good enough golfer or a good enough dancer to enjoy these activities, but persevering through the rough patches just might be worth it.

Applied Behavior Analysis

Some thinkers have criticized behavioral approaches for ignoring mental processes and focusing only on observable behavior. Nevertheless, these approaches do provide an optimistic perspective for individuals interested in changing their behaviors. That is, rather than concentrating on factors such as the type of person you are, behavioral approaches imply that you can modify even longstanding habits by changing the reward contingencies that maintain those habits (Watson & Tharp, 2007).

One real-world application of operant conditioning principles to promote better functioning is applied behavior analysis. **Applied behavior analysis** (also called *behavior modification*) is the use of operant conditioning principles to change human behavior. In applied behavior analysis, the rewards and punishers that exist in a particular setting are carefully analyzed and manipulated to change behaviors. Applied behavior analysis seeks to identify the rewards that might be maintaining unwanted behaviors and to enhance the rewards of more appropriate behaviors. From this perspective, we can understand all human behavior as being influenced by rewards and punishments. If we can figure out what rewards and punishers are controlling a person's behavior, we can change them—and eventually the behavior itself.

applied behavior analysis (behavior modification) The use of operant conditioning principles to change human behavior.

A manager who rewards his or her staff with a casual-dress day or a half day off if they meet a particular work goal is employing applied behavior analysis. So are a therapist and a client when they establish clear consequences of the client's behavior in order to reinforce more adaptive actions and discourage less adaptive ones (Chance, 2009; Umbreit & others, 2007). A teacher who notices that a troublesome student seems to enjoy the attention he receives—even when that attention is scolding—might use applied behavior analysis by changing her responses to the child's behavior, ignoring it instead.

Note that the teacher-student example involves negative punishment.

These examples show how attending to the consequences of behavior can be used to improve performance in settings such as the workplace and a classroom. Advocates of applied behavior analysis believe that many emotional and behavioral problems stem from inadequate or inappropriate consequences (Alberto & Troutman, 2009).

Applied behavior analysis has been effective in a wide range of situations. Practitioners have used it, for example, to train autistic individuals (Koegel & others, 2008), children and adolescents with psychological problems (Miltenberger, 2008), and residents of mental health facilities (Phillips & Mudford, 2008); to instruct individuals in effective parenting (Phaneuf & McIntyre, 2007); to enhance environmentally conscious behaviors such as recycling and not littering (Geller, 2002); to get people to wear seatbelts (Streff & Geller, 1986); and to promote workplace safety (Geller, 2006). Applied behavior analysis can help people improve their self-control in many aspects of mental and physical health (Spiegler & Guevremont, 2010). If you are interested in exploring the use of applied behavior analysis to make positive changes in your own life, you might consult the book *Self-Directed Behavior: Self-Modification for Personal Adjustment,* by David L. L. Watson and Roland Tharp (2007).

4 Observational Learning

Would it make sense to teach a 15-year-old boy how to drive with either classical conditioning or operant conditioning procedures? Driving a car is a voluntary behavior, so classical conditioning would not apply. In terms of operant conditioning, we could ask him to try to drive down the road and then reward his positive behaviors. Not many of us would want to be on the road, though, when he makes mistakes. Albert Bandura (2007b, 2008, 2009) believes that if we learned only in such a trial-and-error fashion, learning would be exceedingly tedious and at times hazardous. Instead, he says, many complex behaviors are the result of exposure to competent models. By observing other people, we can acquire knowledge, skills, rules, strategies, beliefs, and attitudes (Schunk, 2008).

Bandura's *observational learning,* also called *imitation* or *modeling,* is learning that occurs when a person observes and imitates behavior. The capacity to learn by observation eliminates trial-and-error learning. Often observational learning takes less time than operant conditioning. Bandura (1986) described four main processes that are involved in observational learning: attention, retention, motor reproduction, and reinforcement.

In observational learning, the first process that must occur is *attention* (which we initially considered in Chapter 3 due to its crucial role in perception). In order to reproduce a model's actions, you must attend to what the model is saying or doing. You might not hear what a friend says if the stereo is blaring, and you might miss your instructor's analysis of a problem if you are admiring someone sitting in the next row. As a further example, imagine that you decide to take a class to improve your drawing skills. To succeed, you need to attend to the instructor's words and hand movements. Characteristics of the model can influence attention to the model. Warm, powerful, atypical people, for example, command more attention than do cold, weak, typical people.

Retention is the second process required for observational learning to occur. To reproduce a model's actions, you must encode the information and keep it in

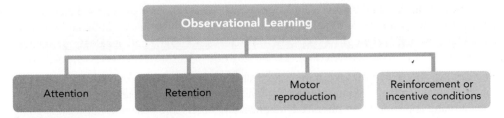

FIGURE 5.12

Bandura's Model of Observational Learning In terms of Bandura's model, if you are learning to ski, you need to attend to the instructor's words and demonstrations. You need to remember what the instructor did and his or her tips for avoiding disasters. You also need the motor abilities to reproduce what the instructor has shown you. Praise from the instructor after you have completed a few moves on the slopes should improve your motivation to continue skiing.

memory so that you can retrieve it. A simple verbal description, or a vivid image of what the model did, assists retention. (Memory is such an important cognitive process that Chapter 6 is devoted exclusively to it.) In the example of taking a class to sharpen your drawing skills, you will need to remember what the instructor said and did in modeling good drawing skills.

Motor reproduction, a third element of observational learning, is the process of imitating the model's actions. People might pay attention to a model and encode what they have seen, but limitations in motor development might make it difficult for them to reproduce the model's action. Thirteen-year-olds might see a professional basketball player do a reverse two-handed dunk but be unable to reproduce the pro's play. Similarly, in your drawing class, if you lack fine motor reproduction skills, you might be unable to follow the instructor's example.

Reinforcement is a final component of observational learning. In this case, the question is whether the model's behavior is followed by a consequence. Seeing a model attain a reward for an activity increases the chances that an observer will repeat the behavior—a process called *vicarious reinforcement*. On the other hand, seeing the model punished makes the observer less likely to repeat the behavior—a process called *vicarious punishment*. Unfortunately, vicarious reinforcement and vicarious punishment are often absent in, for example, media portrayals of violence and aggression.

Observational learning can be an important factor in the functioning of role models in inspiring people and changing their perceptions. Whether a model is similar to us can influence that model's effectiveness in modifying our behavior. The shortage of role models for women and minorities in science and engineering has often been suggested as a reason for the lack of women and minorities in these fields. After the election of Barack Obama as president of the United States, many commentators noted that for the first time, African American children could see concretely they might also attain the nation's highest office someday.

Figure 5.12 summarizes Bandura's model of observational learning.

1. Another name for observational learning is
   A. replication.
   B. modeling.
   C. trial-and-error learning.
   D. visualization.

2. According to Bandura, _____ occurs first in observational learning.
   A. motor reproduction
   B. retention
   C. attention
   D. reinforcement

3. A friend shows you how to do a card trick. However, you forget the second step in the trick and are thus unable to replicate the card trick. There has been a failure in
   A. motor reproduction.
   B. retention.
   C. attention.
   D. reinforcement.

Apply It! 4. Shawna is a 15-year-old high school girl whose mother is a highly paid accountant. Shawna's mom works long hours, often complains about her workplace and how much she hates her boss, and seems tired most of the time. When she is asked what she might do when she grows up, Shawna says she does not think she wants to pursue a career in accounting. Her mother is shocked and cannot understand why Shawna would not want to follow in her footsteps. Which of the following is the most likely explanation for this situation?
   A. Shawna has not observed her mother being reinforced for her behavior. She has only experienced vicarious punishment.
   B. Shawna is not aware that her mother is an accountant.
   C. Shawna is too different from her mother for her mother to be an effective role model.
   D. Shawna has not been paying attention to her mother.

5 Cognitive Factors in Learning

In learning about learning, we have looked at cognitive processes only as they apply in observational learning. Skinner's operant conditioning perspective and Pavlov's classical conditioning approach focus on the environment and observable behavior, not what is going on in the head of the learner. Many contemporary psychologists, including some behaviorists, recognize the importance of cognition and believe that learning involves more than environment–behavior connections (Bandura, 2007b, 2008, 2009; Schunk, 2008). A good starting place for considering cognitive influences in learning is the work of E. C. Tolman.

Purposive Behavior

E. C. Tolman (1932) emphasized the *purposiveness* of behavior—the idea that much of behavior is goal-directed. Tolman believed that it is necessary to study entire behavioral sequences in order to understand why people engage in particular actions. For example, high school students whose goal is to attend a leading college or university study hard in their classes. If we focused only on their studying, we would miss the purpose of their behavior. The students do not always study hard because they have been reinforced for studying in the past. Rather, studying is a means to intermediate goals (learning, high grades) that in turn improve their likelihood of getting into the college or university of their choice (Schunk, 2008).

We can see Tolman's legacy today in the extensive interest in the role of goal setting in human behavior (Gollwitzer & Oettingen, 2007). Researchers are especially curious about how people self-regulate and self-monitor their behavior to reach a goal (Schunk, Pintrich, & Meece, 2008).

Expectancy Learning and Information

In studying the purposiveness of behavior, Tolman went beyond the stimuli and responses of Pavlov and Skinner to focus on cognitive mechanisms. Tolman said that when classical conditioning and operant conditioning occur, the organism acquires certain expectations. In classical conditioning, the young boy fears the rabbit because he expects it will hurt him. In operant conditioning, a woman works hard all week because she expects a paycheck on Friday. Expectancies are acquired from people's experiences with their environment. Expectancies influence a variety of human experiences. We set the goals we do because we believe that we can reach them.

Expectancies also play a role in the placebo effect, described earlier. Many painkillers have been shown to be more effective in reducing pain if patients can see the intravenous injection sites than when they cannot (Price, Finniss, & Benedetti, 2008). If patients can see that they are getting a drug, they can harness their own expectations for pain reduction.

Tolman (1932) emphasized that the information value of the CS is important as a signal or an expectation that a UCS will follow. Anticipating contemporary thinking, Tolman believed that the information that the CS provides is the key to understanding classical conditioning.

One contemporary view of classical conditioning describes an organism as an information seeker, using logical and perceptual relations among events, along with preconceptions, to form a representation of the world (Rescorla, 2003, 2004, 2005, 2006a, 2006b, 2006c, 2009).

A classic experiment conducted by Leon Kamin (1968) illustrates the importance of an organism's history and the information provided by a conditioned stimulus in classical conditioning. Kamin conditioned a rat by repeatedly pairing a tone (CS) and a shock (UCS) until the tone alone produced fear (CR). Then he continued to pair the tone with the shock, but he turned on a light (a second CS) each time the tone sounded. Even though he repeatedly paired the light (CS) and the shock (UCS), the rat showed no conditioning to the light (the light by itself produced no CR). Conditioning to the light was blocked, almost as if the rat had not paid attention. The rat apparently used the tone as a signal to predict that a shock would be coming; information about the light's pairing with the shock was redundant with the information already learned about the tone's pairing with the shock. In this experiment, conditioning was governed not by the contiguity of the CS and UCS but instead by the rat's history and the information it received. Contemporary classical conditioning researchers are further exploring the role of information in an organism's learning (Beckers & others, 2006; Rescorla & Wagner, 2009; Schultz, Dayan, & Montague, 2009).

Latent Learning   Experiments on latent learning provide other evidence to support the role of cognition in learning. **Latent learning** (or *implicit learning*) is unreinforced learning that is not immediately reflected in behavior. In one study, researchers put two groups of hungry rats in a maze and required them to find their way from a starting point to an end point (Tolman & Honzik, 1930). The first group found food (a reinforcer) at the end point; the second group found nothing there. In the operant conditioning view, the first group should learn the maze better than the second group, which is exactly what happened. However, when the researchers subsequently took some of the rats from the non-reinforced group and gave them food at the end point of the maze, they quickly began to run the maze as effectively as the reinforced group. The non-reinforced rats apparently had learned a great deal about the maze as they roamed around and explored it. However, their learning was *latent,* stored cognitively in their memories but not yet expressed behaviorally. When these rats were given a good reason (reinforcement with food) to run the maze speedily, they called on their latent learning to help them reach the end of the maze more quickly.

Outside a laboratory, latent learning is evident when you walk around a new setting to get "the lay of the land." The first time you visited your college campus, you may have wandered about without a specific destination in mind. Exploring the environment made you better prepared when the time came to find that 8 A.M. class.

latent learning (implicit learning)
Unreinforced learning that is not immediately reflected in behavior.

www.CartoonStock.com

Insight Learning

Like E. C. Tolman, the German gestalt psychologist Wolfgang Köhler believed that cognitive factors play a significant role in learning. Köhler spent four months in the Canary Islands during World War I observing the behavior of apes. There he conducted two fascinating experiments—the stick problem and the box problem. Although these two experiments are basically the same, the solutions to the problems are different. In both situations, the ape discovers that it cannot reach an alluring piece of fruit, either because the fruit is too high or because it is outside of the ape's cage and beyond reach. To solve the stick problem, the ape has to insert a small stick inside a larger stick to reach the fruit. To master the box problem, the ape must stack several boxes to reach the fruit (Figure 5.13).

According to Köhler (1925), solving these problems does not involve trial and error or simple connections between stimuli and responses. Rather, when the ape realizes that its customary actions are not going to help it get the fruit, it often sits for a period of time and appears to ponder how to solve the problem. Then it quickly rises, as if it has had a sudden flash of insight, piles the boxes on top of one another, and gets the fruit. **Insight learning** is a form of problem solving in which the organism develops a sudden insight into or understanding of a problem's solution.

Insight learning requires that we think "outside the box," setting aside previous expectations and assumptions. One way that insight learning can be enhanced in human beings is through multicultural experiences (Leung & others, 2008). Correlational studies have shown that time spent living abroad is associated with higher insight learning performance

insight learning
A form of problem solving in which the organism develops a sudden insight into or understanding of a problem's solution.

FIGURE 5.13

Insight Learning Sultan, one of Köhler's brightest chimps, is faced with the problem of reaching a cluster of bananas overhead. He solves the problem by stacking boxes on top of one another to reach the bananas. Köhler called this type of problem solving "insight learning."

among MBA students (Maddux & Galinsky, 2007). Furthermore, experimental studies have shown that exposure to other cultures can influence insight learning. In one study, U.S. college students were randomly assigned to view one of two slide shows—one about Chinese and U.S. culture and the other about a control topic. Those who saw the multicultural slide show scored higher on measures of creativity and insight, and these changes persisted for a week (Leung & others, 2008). Being exposed to other cultures and other ways of thinking can be a key way to enhance insight and creativity.

1. E. C. Tolman emphasized the *purposiveness* of behavior—the idea that much of behavior is oriented toward the achievement of
   A. immortality.
   B. altruism.
   C. goals.
   D. self-esteem.

2. When the answer to a problem just "pops" into your head, you have experienced
   A. latent learning.
   B. insight learning.
   C. implicit learning.
   D. expectancy learning.

3. A type of learning that does *not* involve trial and error is
   A. insight learning
   B. latent learning.
   C. expectancy learning.
   D. implicit learning.

Apply It! 4. Derek is rehearsing his lines and songs for an upcoming production of *Grease*. He is playing the lead role of Danny Zucco. His friend Maria helps him practice his lines and learn the words to his songs. Maria is not in the play and wouldn't even think of appearing onstage. On opening night, Maria is in the audience, and halfway through "Summer Lovin'" people sitting around her are complaining because she is singing along. She also has been saying all of Danny's lines under her breath. What is the explanation?
   A. Maria is demonstrating the power of latent learning.
   B. Maria is demonstrating insight learning.
   C. Maria is showing purposive behavior.
   D. Maria secretly dreams of playing Danny Zucco in an all-female version of *Grease* someday.

6 Biological, Cultural, and Psychological Factors in Learning

Albert Einstein had many special talents. He combined enormous creativity with keen analytic ability to develop some of the twentieth century's most important insights into the nature of matter and the universe. Genes obviously endowed Einstein with extraordinary intellectual skills that enabled him to think and reason on a very high plane, but cultural factors also contributed to his genius. Einstein received an excellent, rigorous European education, and later in the United States he experienced the freedom and support believed to be important in creative exploration. Would Einstein have been able to develop his skills fully and to make such brilliant insights if he had grown up in a less advantageous environment? It is unlikely. Clearly, both biological *and* cultural factors contribute to learning.

Biological Constraints

Humans cannot breathe under water, fish cannot ski, and cows cannot solve math problems. The structure of an organism's body permits certain kinds of learning and inhibits others (Chance, 2009). For example, chimpanzees cannot learn to speak English because they lack the necessary vocal equipment.

Service dogs also illustrate the limits of learning principles. One type of service dog, the seizure-alert dog, warns individuals with epilepsy of an oncoming attack minutes or even hours before the seizure takes place. These dogs may whine, bark, or paw their owners prior to a seizure. No one knows how these canines sense an oncoming seizure, though learning principles of reward are used in their training. Dogs that show sensitivity to seizures receive treats when they successfully anticipate a seizure. Using rewards, trainers also teach the dogs to stay with their human companions after a seizure and to press a button to call 911. However, as one trainer noted, "I can train a dog to sit . . . and fetch, but I can't teach a dog to alert" (Mott, 2004). That is, if the dog does not have a natural sensitivity to seizures, no amount of training will produce it.

Instinctive Drift Keller and Marion Breland (1961), students of B. F. Skinner, used operant conditioning to train animals to perform at fairs and conventions and in television advertisements. They applied Skinner's techniques to teach pigs to cart large wooden nickels to a piggy bank and deposit them. They also trained raccoons to pick up a coin and place it in a metal tray. Although the pigs and raccoons, as well as chickens and other animals, performed most of the tasks well (raccoons became adept basketball players, for example—see Figure 5.14), some of the animals began acting strangely. Instead of picking up the large wooden nickels and carrying them to the piggy bank, the pigs dropped the nickels on the ground, shoved them with their snouts, tossed them in the air, and then repeated these actions. The raccoons began to hold on to their coins rather than dropping them into the metal tray. When two coins were introduced, the raccoons rubbed them together in a miserly fashion. Somehow these behaviors overwhelmed the strength of the

instinctive drift
The tendency of animals to revert to instinctive behavior that interferes with learning.

reinforcement. This example of biological influences on learning illustrates **instinctive drift,** the tendency of animals to revert to instinctive behavior that interferes with learning.

Why were the pigs and the raccoons misbehaving? The pigs were rooting, an instinct that is used to uncover edible roots. The raccoons were engaging in an instinctive food-washing response. Their instinctive drift interfered with learning.

preparedness
The species-specific biological predisposition to learn in certain ways but not others.

Preparedness Some animals learn readily in one situation but have difficulty learning in slightly different circumstances (Garcia & Koelling, 1966, 2009). The difficulty might result not from some aspect of the learning situation but from the organism's biological predisposition (Seligman, 1970). **Preparedness** is the species-specific biological predisposition to learn in certain ways but not others.

Much of the evidence for preparedness comes from research on taste aversion (Garcia, 1989; Garcia & Koelling, 2009). Recall that taste aversion involves a single trial of learning the association between a particular taste and nausea. Rats that experience low levels of radiation after eating show a strong aversion to the food they were eating when the radiation made

FIGURE 5.14

Instinctive Drift This raccoon's skill in using its hands made it an excellent basketball player, but because of instinctive drift, the raccoon had a much more difficult time dropping coins in a tray.

them ill. This aversion can last for as long as 32 days. Such long-term effects cannot be accounted for by classical conditioning, which would argue that a single pairing of the conditioned and unconditioned stimuli would not last that long (Garcia, Ervin, & Koelling, 1966). Taste aversion learning occurs in animals, including humans, that choose their food based on taste and smell. Other species are prepared to learn rapid associations between, for instance, colors of foods and illness.

Another example of preparedness comes from research on conditioning humans and monkeys to associate snakes with fear. Susan Mineka and Arne Ohman (2002; Ohman & Mineka, 2003) have investigated the fascinating natural power of snakes to evoke fear in many mammals. Many monkeys and humans fear snakes, and both monkeys and humans are very quick to learn the association between snakes and fear. In classical conditioning studies, when pictures of snakes (CS) are paired with electrical shocks (UCS), the snakes are likely to quickly and strongly evoke fear (the CR). Interestingly, pairing pictures of, say, flowers (CS) with electrical shocks produces much weaker associations (Mineka & Ohman, 2002; Ohman & Soares, 1998). Even more significantly, pictures of snakes can serve as conditioned stimuli for fearful responses, even when the pictures are presented so rapidly that they cannot be consciously perceived (Ohman & Mineka, 2001).

The link between snakes and fear has been demonstrated not only in classical conditioning paradigms. Monkeys that have been raised in the lab and that have never seen a snake rapidly learn to fear snakes, even entirely by observational learning. Lab monkeys that see a videotape of a monkey expressing fear toward a snake learn to be afraid of snakes faster than monkeys seeing the same fear video spliced so that the feared object is a rabbit, a flower, or a mushroom (Ohman & Mineka, 2003).

Mineka and Ohman (2002) suggest that these results demonstrate preparedness among mammals to associate snakes with fear and aversive stimuli. They suggest that this association is related to the amygdala (the part of the limbic system that is related to emotion) and is difficult to modify. These researchers suggest that this preparedness for fear of snakes has emerged out of the threat that reptiles likely posed to our evolutionary ancestors.

Cultural Influences

Traditionally, interest in the cultural context of human learning has been limited, partly because the organisms in those contexts typically were animals. The question arises, how might culture influence human learning? Most psychologists agree that the principles of classical conditioning, operant conditioning, and observational learning are universal and are powerful learning processes in every culture. However, culture can influence the *degree* to which these learning processes are used (Matsumoto & Juang, 2008). For example, Mexican American students may learn more through observational learning, while Euro-American students may be more accustomed to learn through direct instruction (Mejia-Arauz, Rogoff, & Paradise, 2005).

In addition, culture can determine the *content* of learning (Shiraev & Levy, 2007). We cannot learn about something we do not experience. The 4-year-old who grows up among the Bushmen of the Kalahari Desert is unlikely to learn about taking baths and eating with a knife and fork. Similarly, a child growing up in Chicago is unlikely to be skilled at tracking animals and finding water-bearing roots in the desert. Learning often requires practice, and certain behaviors are practiced more often in some cultures than in others. In Bali, many children are skilled dancers

On the Indonesian island of Bali, young children learn traditional dances, whereas in Norway children commonly learn to ski early in life. As cultures vary, so does the content of learning.

by the age of 6, whereas Norwegian children are much more likely to be good skiers and skaters by that age.

Psychological Constraints

Are there psychological constraints on learning? For animals, the answer is probably no. For humans, the answer may well be yes. This section opened with the claim that fish cannot ski. The truth of this statement is clear. Biological circumstances make it impossible. If we put biological considerations aside, we might ask ourselves about times in our lives when we feel like a fish trying to ski—when we feel that we just do not have what it takes to learn a skill or master a task.

Carol Dweck (2006) uses the term *mindset* to describe the way our beliefs about ability dictate what goals we set for ourselves, what we think we *can* learn, and ultimately what we *do* learn. Individuals have one of two mindsets: a *fixed mindset,* in which they believe that their qualities are carved in stone and cannot change; or a *growth mindset,* in which they believe their qualities can change and improve through their effort. These two mindsets have implications for the meaning of failure. From a fixed mindset, failure means lack of ability. From a growth mindset, however, failure tells the person what he or she still needs to learn. Your mindset influences whether you will be optimistic or pessimistic, what your goals will be, how hard you will strive to reach those goals, and how successful you are in college and after.

Dweck (2006) studied first-year pre-med majors taking their first chemistry class in college. Students with a growth mindset got higher grades than those with a fixed mindset. Even when they did not do well on a test, the growth-mindset students bounced back on the next test. Fixed-mindset students typically read and re-read the text and class notes or tried to memorize everything verbatim. The fixed-mindset students who did poorly on tests concluded that chemistry and maybe pre-med were not for them. By contrast, growth-mindset students took charge of their motivation and learning, searching for themes and principles in the course and going over mistakes until they understood why they made them. In Dweck's analysis (2006, p. 61), "They were studying to learn, not just ace the test. And, actually, this is why they got higher grades—not because they were smarter or had a better background in science."

Following are some effective strategies for developing a growth mindset (Dweck, 2006):

- *Understand that your intelligence and thinking skills are not fixed but can change.* Even if you are extremely bright, with effort you can increase your intelligence.

- *Become passionate about learning and stretch your mind in challenging situations.* It is easy to withdraw into a fixed mindset when the going gets tough; but as you bump up against obstacles, keep growing, work harder, stay the course, and improve your strategies; you will become a more successful person.

- *Think about the growth mindsets of people you admire.* Possibly you have a hero, someone who has achieved something extraordinary. You may have thought his or her accomplishments came easy because the person is so talented. However, find out more about this person and how he or she works and thinks. You likely will discover that much hard work and effort over a long period of time were responsible for his or her achievements.

- *Begin now.* If you have a fixed mindset, commit to changing now. Think about when, where, and how you will begin using your new growth mindset.

An early study on 5- to 7-year-old children demonstrated the power of these mindsets (Elliott & Dweck 1988). When faced with math problems that were beyond their age level, the children responded quite differently, depending on their mindset. Children whose views reflected a fixed mindset were threatened by the difficult task, withdrew from it, and were more likely to criticize the task and put themselves down. In contrast, the children who revealed a growth mindset seemed energized by the challenging task. They remained focused and persisted in trying to solve the "impossible" problems. Amazingly, some of them actually did—they achieved the impossible.

Dweck's work challenges us to consider the limits we place on our own learning. When we think of the relative absence of women and minorities in math and science professions, we might consider the messages these groups have received about whether they have what it takes to succeed in these domains. Our beliefs about ability profoundly influence what we try to learn. As any 7-year-old with a growth mindset would tell you, you never know what you can do until you try.

1. When a pig's rooting behavior interferes with its learning, the phenomenon is an example of
   A. preparedness.
   B. learned helplessness.
   C. a taste aversion.
   D. instinctive drift.

2. Mineka and Ohman suggest that humans' preparedness for fear of snakes emerged because of
   A. cultural myths.
   B. the religious symbolism of snakes.

C. the danger that snakes and other reptiles posed to earlier humans.
D. the limitations of human learning.

3. Believing that studying hard will result in a good grade in a course is an example of
   A. a growth insight.
   B. a growth mindset.
   C. preparedness.
   D. a fixed mindset.

Apply It! 4. Frances is a dog person who has just adopted her first-ever cat. Given her experience in housebreaking her pet dogs, Frances is shocked that her new kitty, Tolman, uses the litter box the very first day and never has an accident in the house. Frances thinks that Tolman must be a genius cat. Tolman's amazing ability demonstrates
A. psychological constraints on learning.
B. biological preparedness.
C. cultural constraints on learning.
D. that dog people are not very bright.

summary

① Types of Learning

Learning is a systematic, relatively permanent change in behavior that occurs through experience. Associative learning involves learning by making a connection between two events. Observational learning is learning by watching what other people do.

Conditioning is the process by which associative learning occurs. In classical conditioning, organisms learn the association between two stimuli. In operant conditioning, they learn the association between behavior and a consequence.

② Classical Conditioning

Classical conditioning occurs when a neutral stimulus becomes associated with a meaningful stimulus and comes to elicit a similar response. Pavlov discovered that an organism learns the association between an unconditioned stimulus (UCS) and a conditioned stimulus (CS). The UCS automatically produces the unconditioned response (UCR). After conditioning (CS–UCS pairing), the CS elicits the conditioned response (CR) by itself. Acquisition in classical conditioning is the initial linking of stimuli and responses, which involves a neutral stimulus being associated with the UCS so that the CS comes to elicit the CR. Two important aspects of acquisition are contiguity and contingency.

Generalization in classical conditioning is the tendency of a new stimulus that is similar to the original conditioned stimulus to elicit a response that is similar to the conditioned response. Discrimination is the process of learning to respond to certain stimuli and not to others. Extinction is the weakening of the CR in the absence of the UCS. Spontaneous recovery is the recurrence of a CR after a time delay without further conditioning. Renewal is the occurrence of the CR (even after extinction) when the CS is presented in a novel environment.

In humans, classical conditioning has been applied to eliminating fears, treating addiction, understanding taste aversion, and explaining such different experiences as pleasant emotions and drug overdose.

③ Operant Conditioning

Operant conditioning is a form of learning in which the consequences of behavior produce changes in the probability of the behavior's occurrence. Skinner described the behavior of the organism as operant: The behavior operates on the environment, and the environment in turn operates on the organism. Whereas classical conditioning involves respondent behavior, operant conditioning involves operant behavior. In most instances, operant conditioning is better at explaining voluntary behavior than is classical conditioning.

Thorndike's law of effect states that behaviors followed by positive outcomes are strengthened, whereas behaviors followed by negative outcomes are weakened. Skinner built on this idea to develop the notion of operant conditioning.

Shaping is the process of rewarding approximations of desired behavior in order to shorten the learning process. Principles of reinforcement include the distinction between positive reinforcement (the frequency of a behavior increases because it is followed by a rewarding stimulus) and negative reinforcement (the frequency of behavior increases because it is followed by the removal of an aversive, or unpleasant, stimulus). Positive reinforcement can be classified as primary reinforcement (using reinforcers that are innately satisfying) and secondary reinforcement (using reinforcers that acquire positive value through experience). Reinforcement can also be continuous (a behavior is reinforced every time) or partial (a behavior is reinforced only a portion of the time). Schedules of reinforcement—fixed ratio, variable ratio, fixed interval, and variable interval—determine when a behavior will be reinforced.

Operant conditioning involves generalization (giving the same response to similar stimuli), discrimination (responding to stimuli that signal that a behavior will or will not be reinforced), and extinction (a decreasing tendency to perform a previously reinforced behavior when reinforcement is stopped).

Punishment is a consequence that decreases the likelihood that a behavior will occur. In positive punishment, a behavior decreases when it is followed by an unpleasant stimulus. In negative punishment, a behavior decreases when a positive stimulus is removed from it.

Applied behavior analysis involves the application of operant conditioning principles to a variety of real-life behaviors.

④ Observational Learning

Observational learning occurs when a person observes and imitates someone else's behavior. Bandura identified four main processes in observational learning: attention, retention, motor reproduction, and reinforcement.

⑤ Cognitive Factors in Learning

Tolman emphasized the purposiveness of behavior. Purposiveness refers to Tolman's belief that much of behavior is goal-directed. In studying purposiveness, Tolman went beyond stimuli and responses to discuss cognitive mechanisms. Tolman believed that expectancies, acquired through experiences with the environment, are an important cognitive mechanism in learning.

Köhler developed the concept of insight learning, a form of problem solving in which the organism develops a sudden insight into or understanding of a problem's solution.

⑥ Biological, Cultural, and Psychological Factors in Learning

Biological constraints restrict what an organism can learn from experience. These constraints include instinctive drift (the tendency of animals to revert to instinctive behavior that interferes with learned behavior), preparedness (the species-specific biological predisposition to learn in certain ways but not in others), and taste aversion (the biological predisposition to avoid foods that have caused sickness in the past).

Although most psychologists agree that the principles of classical conditioning, operant conditioning, and observational learning are universal, cultural customs can influence the degree to which these learning processes are used. Culture also often determines the content of learning.

In addition, what we learn is determined in part by what we believe we can learn. Dweck emphasizes that individuals benefit enormously from having a growth mindset rather than a fixed mindset.

key terms

learning, p. 155
behaviorism, p. 155
associative learning, p. 156
observational learning, p. 156
classical conditioning, p. 157
unconditioned stimulus (UCS), p. 158
unconditioned response (UCR), p. 158
conditioned stimulus (CS), p. 158
conditioned response (CR), p. 158
acquisition, p. 159

generalization (classical conditioning), p. 160
discrimination (classical conditioning), p. 160
extinction (classical conditioning), p. 160
spontaneous recovery, p. 160
renewal, p. 161
counterconditioning, p. 162
systematic desensitization, p. 162
aversive conditioning, p. 163
operant conditioning (instrumental conditioning), p. 167

law of effect, p. 167
shaping, p. 169
reinforcement, p. 169
positive reinforcement, p. 170
negative reinforcement, p. 170
primary reinforcer, p. 171
secondary reinforcer, p. 171
generalization (operant conditioning), p. 172
discrimination (operant conditioning), p. 172
extinction (operant conditioning), p. 172

schedules of reinforcement, p. 172
punishment, p. 174
positive punishment, p. 174
negative punishment, p. 174
applied behavior analysis (behavior modification), p. 177
latent learning (implicit learning), p. 181
insight learning, p. 181
instinctive drift, p. 183
preparedness, p. 183

self-test

Multiple Choice

1. Salivation in response to food, shivering from exposure to a low temperature, and coughing in reaction to throat congestion are examples of automatic stimulus–response connections, or

   A. contractions.
   B. reflexes.
   C. associations.
   D. acquisitions.

2. Researchers found that raccoons that were trained to deposit coins in a tray began to rub the coins together instead of dropping them in the tray. Why?

   A. extinction
   B. spontaneous recovery
   C. instinctive drift
   D. counterconditioning

3. When a child hears a loud noise, he cries. The loud noise is
   A. the unconditioned stimulus.
   B. the conditioned stimulus.
   C. the unconditioned response.
   D. the conditioned response.

4. Which of the following is consistent with the law of effect?
   A. A child who is rewarded for getting good grades begins to do poorly in school.
   B. A dog that is punished for barking barks more.
   C. A cat that is yelled at when it scratches the sofa stops scratching the sofa.
   D. An adult who is fired from his job for being late is late at his next job.

5. Meghan is scared of flying. When she goes on vacation with her husband, he helps her to relax by holding her hand, having her breathe deeply, and imagining herself on a sandy beach. After several flights with her husband, Meghan is no longer afraid of flying. Which of the following processes occurred?
   A. counterconditioning
   B. extinction
   C. discrimination
   D. spontaneous recovery

6. Every sixth time Miguel cleans his room, his mother takes him to dinner as a reward. On what type of reinforcement schedule is Miguel?
   A. variable-ratio schedule
   B. variable-interval schedule
   C. fixed-ratio schedule
   D. fixed-interval schedule

7. The schedule of reinforcement that is most resistant to extinction is the
   A. variable-ratio schedule.
   B. variable-interval schedule.
   C. fixed-ratio schedule.
   D. fixed-interval schedule.

8. Putting a child who misbehaves in time-out is an example of
   A. a negative reinforcer.
   B. negative punishment.
   C. a positive reinforcer.
   D. positive punishment.

9. Sally witnesses her friend get arrested for drug possession. As a result, Sally avoids drugs. Sally has experienced what type of learning?
   A. negative reinforcement
   B. classical conditioning
   C. operant learning
   D. observational learning

10. _____ accounts for the finding that taste aversions develop more quickly than other types of learning.
    A. Instinctive drift
    B. Preparedness
    C. Insight learning
    D. Contingency

Apply It!

11. Imagine that you are about to begin an internship in an organization that you would like join someday as a professional. Use the processes of observational learning to describe your strategy for making the most of your intern experience.

6 Memory

Remarkable Memories: Making Pi a Piece of Cake

On March 14, 2008, Boston College senior James Niles-Joyal won the Pi Day competition at Harvard University by reciting the first 3,141 digits of pi from memory (Wiedeman, 2008). Though it set the Harvard record, Niles-Joyal's achievement was only a fraction of the world record. That honor was held by Akira Haraguchi, who in 2005 recited the digits of pi to the first 83,431 decimal places (BBC News, 2005). Think about memorizing a list of over 80,000 numbers.

Mnemonists are people with astonishing memory abilities such as Niles-Joyal's and Haraguchi's. Psychologists have learned a good deal about memory from such exceptional individuals (Takahashi & others, 2006). Yet even "ordinary" people routinely demonstrate the amazing capacity of memory.

Imagine that you are at an upscale restaurant with six friends. After reciting your rather complicated order to the server, you notice that *he is not writing anything down*. Waiting patiently through your friends' orders, you wonder, "How can he possibly remember all this?" When the meal arrives, however, everything is exactly right. Waiters seem to commit remarkable acts of memory routinely. How do they do it?

Asked to share their secrets, a few college students who moonlight in food service explained their methods: "I always try to remember the person's face and imagine him eating the food he's ordered"; "if it's something really off the wall, you'll never forget it"; "repetition is the key." As we will see, research on memory supports these techniques surprisingly well. ■

- What strategies do you use when memorizing?
- Does your strategy depend on whether you need to remember the information for school, for a job, or for a social relationship?
- What is one experience you know you will never forget?

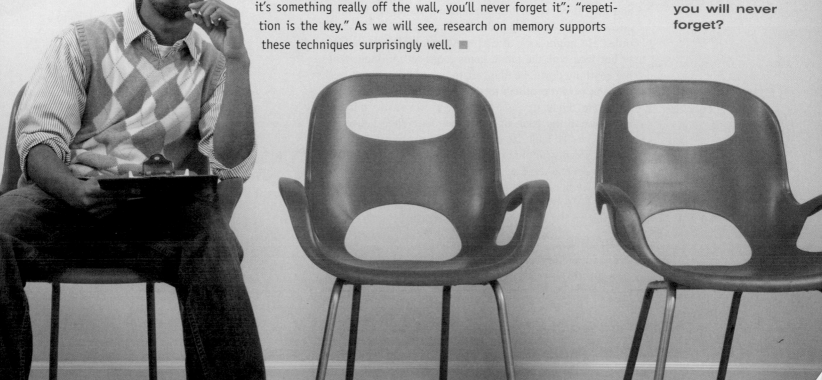

Through memory, we weave the past into the present. In this chapter, we explore key processes of memory, including how information gets into our memory and how it is stored, retrieved, and sometimes forgotten. We also probe what the science of memory can teach us about the best way to study and retain course material, and we look at various ways memory processes enrich our lives.

1 The Nature of Memory

The stars are shining and the moon is full. A beautiful evening is coming to a close. You look at your significant other and think, "I'll never forget this night." How is it possible that in fact you never will forget it? Years from now, you might tell your children about that one special night so many years ago, even if you had not thought about it in the years since. How does one perfect night become a part of your enduring life memories?

memory
The retention of information or experience over time as the result of three key processes: encoding, storage, and retrieval.

Psychologists define **memory** as the retention of information or experience over time. Memory occurs through three important processes: encoding, storage, and retrieval. For memory to work, we have to take in information (encode the sights and sounds of that night), store it or represent it in some manner (retain it in some mental storehouse), and then retrieve it for a later purpose (recall it when someone asks, "So, how did you two end up together?"). In the next three sections, we focus on these phases of memory: encoding, storage, and retrieval (Figure 6.1).

Except for the annoying moments when our memory fails, or the upsetting situation where someone we know experiences memory loss, we do not think about how much everything we do or say depends on the smooth operation of our memory systems (Schacter, 2001, 2007). Let's return to our server in the restaurant. He has to attend to the orders he receives—who is asking for what and how they would like it prepared. To do so, he must encode the information about each customer and each order. He might look at each customer and associate his or her face with the menu items requested. Without writing anything down, he must retain the information, at least until he gets the orders to the kitchen or onto the computer. He might rehearse the orders over in his mind as he walks to the back of the restaurant. When delivering the food to the table, he must accurately retrieve the information about who ordered what. Human memory systems truly are remarkable when we consider how much information we put into our memories and how much we must retrieve to perform life's activities (Kellogg, 2007).

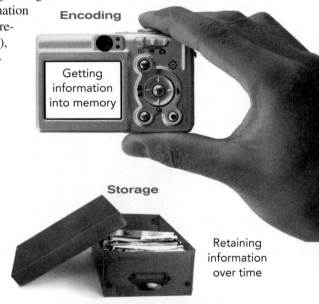

Encoding
Getting information into memory

Storage
Retaining information over time

Retrieval
Taking information out of storage

FIGURE 6.1

Processing Information in Memory As you read about the many aspects of memory in this chapter, think about the organization of memory in terms of these three main activities.

1. Memory is the _____ of information or experience over a period of time.
   A. rehearsal
   B. intake
   C. association
   D. retention

2. When we take in information in the course of daily life, such as the words and diagrams presented during a lecture, we are using the memory process of
   A. retention.
   B. encoding.
   C. retrieval.
   D. fixation.

3. The three processes of memory are encoding, _____, and retrieval.
   A. storage
   B. rehearsal
   C. recollection
   D. fixation

Apply It! 4. James and Adam are very good friends and often sit next to each other in Intro Psych. James spends a lot of time in class working on homework for his biology lab, while Adam listens to the lecture and takes lots of notes. Before the first exam, James asks to borrow Adam's notebook from Intro and studies those notes very carefully. In fact, both James and Adam study for 10 hours for the test. After the exam, James finds out he got a *C*, while Adam got an *A*. James cannot understand how they could have studied the same notes yet gotten such different grades. The most likely, most accurate explanation is that

A. James and Adam encoded the information differently.
B. Adam simply has a better memory than James.
C. James is taking too many hard courses and couldn't retrieve the information as well as Adam because of stress.
D. Adam probably gave James fake notes to torpedo his work.

2 Memory Encoding

The first step in memory is **encoding,** the process by which information gets into memory storage. When you are listening to a lecture, watching a play, reading a book, or talking with a friend, you are encoding information into memory. Some information gets into memory virtually automatically, whereas encoding other information takes effort. Let's examine some of the encoding processes that require effort. These include attention, deep processing, elaboration, and the use of mental imagery.

encoding
The first step in memory; the process by which information gets into memory storage.

Attention

To begin the process of memory encoding, we have to pay attention to information (Posner & Rothbart, 2007). Recall from Chapter 3 that selective attention involves focusing on a specific aspect of experience while ignoring others. Attention is selective because the brain's resources are limited—they cannot attend to everything. These limitations mean that we have to attend selectively to some things in our environment and ignore others (Dixon & others, 2009). So, on that special night, you never noticed the bus that roared by or the people whom you passed while you strolled along the street with your significant other. Those aspects of that night did not make it into your enduring memory.

Divided attention also affects memory encoding. Divided attention occurs when we attend to several things simultaneously—that is, when we multitask (Skinner & Fernandes, 2009). Dividing attention among three or more activities—for example, simultaneously doing homework, instant messaging, surfing the web, and scanning an iTunes playlist—is not unusual for youth (Bauerlein, 2008). Divided attention leads to worse memory. In a number of studies, individuals who are allowed to give their full attention to information they are asked to remember do much better on subsequent memory tests of the information than do their counterparts whose attention is divided (Naveh-Benjamin, Kilb, & Fisher, 2006; Pomplum, Reingold, & Shen, 2001).

 *Remember that the next time you sit down to study in front of the TV.*

Levels of Processing

Another factor that influences memory is whether we engage with information superficially or really get into it. Fergus Craik and Robert Lockhart (1972) first suggested that encoding can be influenced by levels of processing. The term **levels of processing** refers

levels of processing
A continuum of memory processing from shallow to intermediate to deep, with deeper processing producing better memory.

FIGURE 6.2

Depth of Processing

According to the levels of
processing principle, deeper
processing of stimuli produces
better memory of them.

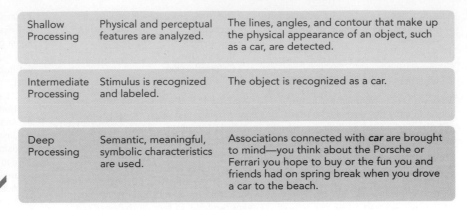

to a continuum from shallow to intermediate to deep, with deeper processing producing better memory.

Imagine that you are asked to memorize a list of words, including the word *mom*. Shallow processing includes noting the physical features of a stimulus, such as the shapes of the letters in the word *mom*. Intermediate processing involves giving the stimulus a label, as in reading the word *mom*. The deepest level of processing entails thinking about the meaning of a stimulus—for instance, thinking about the meaning of the word *mom* and about your own mother, her face, and her special qualities.

The more deeply we process, the better the memory (Howes, 2006; Ragland & others, 2006). For example, researchers have found that if we encode something meaningful about a face and make associations with it, we are more likely to remember the face (Harris & Kay, 1995). The restaurant server who strives to remember the face of the customer and to imagine her eating the food she has ordered is using deep processing (Figure 6.2).

Elaboration

elaboration
The number of different
connections that are made
around a stimulus at a given
level of memory encoding.

Effective encoding of a memory depends on more than just depth of processing. Within deep processing, the more extensive the processing, the better the memory (Terry, 2009). **Elaboration** refers to the number of different connections that are made around a stimulus at any given level of memory encoding. Elaboration is like creating a huge spider web of links between some new information and everything one already knows, and it can occur at any level of processing. In the case of the word *mom,* a person can elaborate on *mom* even at a shallow level—for example, by thinking of the shapes of the letters and how they relate to the shapes of other letters, say, how an *m* looks like two *n*'s. At a deep level of processing, a person might focus on what a mother is or might think about various mothers he or she knows, images of mothers in art, and portrayals of mothers on television and in film. Generally speaking, the more elaborate the processing, the better memory will be. Deep, elaborate processing is a powerful way to remember.

For example, rather than trying to memorize the definition of *memory,* you would do better to weave a complex spider web around the concept of memory by coming up with a real-world example of how information enters your mind, how it is stored, and how you can retrieve it. Thinking of concrete examples of a concept is a good way to understand it. Self-reference—relating material to your own experience—is another effective way to elaborate on information, drawing mental links between aspects of your own life and new information (Hunt & Ellis, 2004) (Figure 6.3).

The process of elaboration is evident in the physical activity of the brain. Neuroscience research has shown a link between elaboration during encoding and brain activity (Kirchhoff & Buckner, 2006). In one study, researchers placed individuals in magnetic resonance imaging (MRI) machines (see Chapter 2) and flashed one word every 2 seconds on a screen inside (Wagner & others, 1998). Initially, the individuals simply noted whether the words were in uppercase or lowercase letters. As the study progressed, they were asked to determine whether each word was concrete, such as *chair* or *book,* or abstract, such as *love* or *democracy*. In this study, the participants showed more neural activity in the left frontal lobe of the brain during the concrete/abstract task than they did when they were asked merely to state whether the words were in uppercase or lowercase letters. Further, they demonstrated better memory in the concrete/abstract task. The researchers concluded that greater elaboration of information is linked with neural activity, especially in the brain's left frontal lobe, and with improved memory.

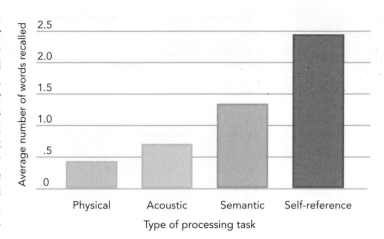

FIGURE 6.3

Memory Improves When Self-Reference Is Used In one study, researchers asked participants to remember lists of words according to the words' physical, acoustic (sound), semantic (meaning), or self-referent characteristics. As the figure illustrates, when individuals generated self-references for the words, they remembered them better.

Imagery

One of the most powerful ways to make memories distinctive is to use mental imagery (Murray, 2007; Quinn & McConnell, 2006). Psychologist Alexander Luria (1968/1987) chronicled the life of S., whose unique visual imagination allowed him to remember an extraordinary amount of detail. Luria had become acquainted with S. in the 1920s in Russia. Luria began with some simple research to test S.'s memory. For example, he asked S. to recall a series of words or numbers, a standard method of testing memory skills. Luria concluded that S. had no apparent limits to his ability to recall. In such tests, people typically remember at most five to nine numbers. Not only could S. remember as many as 70 numbers, but he could also recall them accurately in reverse order. Moreover, S. could report the sequence flawlessly with no warning or practice even as long as 15 years after his initial exposure to the sequence. In addition, after the 15-year interval, S. could describe what Luria had been wearing and where he had been sitting when S. learned the list.

How could S. manage such tasks? As long as each number or word was spoken slowly, S. could represent it as a visual image that was meaningful to him. These images were durable—S. easily remembered the image he created for each sequence long after he learned the sequence. Imagery helped S. remember complicated lists of items and information. For example, S. once was asked to remember the following formula:

$$N \cdot \sqrt{d^2 \cdot \frac{85}{VX}} \cdot 3\sqrt{\frac{276^2 \cdot 86x}{n^2V \cdot \pi264}} \, n^2 b$$
$$= sv \, \frac{1624}{32^2} \cdot r^2 s$$

S. studied the formula for 7 minutes and then reported how he memorized it. Notice in his account of this process, which follows, how he used imagery:

> Neiman (N) came out and jabbed at the ground with his cane ($\cdot$). He looked up at a tall tree, which resembled the square-root sign ($\sqrt{}$), and thought to himself: "No wonder this tree has withered and begun to expose its roots. After all, it was here when I built these two houses" (d^2). Once again he poked his cane ($\cdot$). Then he said: "The houses are old, I'll have to get rid of them; the sale will bring in far more money." He had originally invested 85,000 in them (85). . . . (Luria, 1968/1987)

S.'s complete story was four times this length, but the imagery in the story must have been powerful, because S. remembered the formula perfectly 15 years later without any advance notice.

Memorization of...	Record Holder	Country	Year	Record
Written numbers in 1 minute, without errors	Gunther Karsten	Germany	2007	102 numbers
Random words in 15 minutes*	Boris-Nikolai Konrad	Germany	2008	255 words
Speed to recall a single deck of 52 shuffled playing cards, without errors	Ben Pridmore	Great Britain	2007	26.28 seconds
Historic dates in 5 minutes	Johannes Mallow	Germany	2008	110.5 dates
Abstract images in 15 minutes	Gunther Karsten	Germany	2008	276 images

Participants view random words in columns of 25 words. Scoring is tabulated by column: one point for each word. One mistake reduces the score for that column by half, and the second mistake reduces the score for that column to zero.

FIGURE 6.4

World Champions of Memory For memorization wizards such as these world record holders, imagery is a powerful encoding tool.

Source: http:www.recordholders.org/en/list/memory.html#numbers-1min

Imagery functions as a powerful encoding tool for all of us, certainly including the memory record holders listed in Figure 6.4. James Niles-Joyal, the student in the opening story of this chapter, who recited more than 3,000 digits of pi, imagined various sets of numbers of characters, emotions, and actions to aid his memory. One of the student waiters mentioned imagining the person eating the food to remember the customer's order. Classic studies by Allan Paivio (1971, 1986, 2007) have documented how imagery can improve memory. Paivio argues that memory is stored in one of two ways: as a verbal code (a word or a label) or an image code. Paivio thinks that the image code, which is highly detailed and distinctive, produces better memory than the verbal code. His *dual-code hypothesis* claims that memory for pictures is better than memory for words because pictures—at least those that can be named—are stored as both image codes and verbal codes. Thus, when we use imagery to remember, we have two potential avenues by which we can retrieve information.

self-quiz

1. Shane is studying for a vocabulary test. When he studies the word *braggart,* he thinks of how his friend Bill acts whenever Bill wins a tennis match. Shane is processing this word at a(n)
   A. shallow level.
   B. intermediate level.
   C. deep level.
   D. personal level.

2. The extensiveness of processing information at a given level is called
   A. scope of processing.
   B. depth of processing.
   C. span of memory.
   D. elaboration.

3. One of the most effective ways to make our memories distinctive is to use mental
   A. cues.
   B. rehearsal.
   C. imagery.
   D. concentration.

Apply It! 4. Linus and Polly are arguing over the best way to study for an upcoming psychology exam. Polly tries to tell Linus that the best way to remember things is to use flashcards, but Linus, an astrophysics major, spends a lot of time jotting down the connections between his psychology class and various concepts from astrophysics. Polly warns him, "You are wasting your time. You're just going to get confused." What do you think of Polly's warning?
   A. Linus should listen to Polly. There truly is one best way to remember things.
   B. Polly should back off. Linus is elaborating on the material at a deep level, and this approach will probably pay off on the exam.
   C. Linus is likely to get confused when the exam has no astrophysics questions.
   D. Polly will do better because flashcards require shallow processing.

3 Memory Storage

The quality of encoding does not alone determine the quality of memory. A memory also needs to be stored properly after it is encoded. **Storage** encompasses how information is retained over time and how it is represented in memory.

We remember some information for less than a second, some for half a minute, and some for minutes, hours, years, or even a lifetime. Richard Atkinson and Richard Shiffrin (1968) formulated an early popular theory of memory that acknowledged the varying life span of memories (Figure 6.5). The **Atkinson-Shiffrin theory** states that memory storage involves three separate systems:

- *Sensory memory:* time frames of a fraction of a second to several seconds
- *Short-term memory:* time frames up to 30 seconds
- *Long-term memory:* time frames up to a lifetime

As you read about these three memory storage systems, you will find that time frame is not the only thing that makes them different from one another. Each type of memory also operates in a distinctive way and has a special purpose.

storage
The retention of information over time and how this information is represented in memory.

Atkinson-Shiffrin theory
Theory stating that memory storage involves three separate systems: sensory memory, short-term memory, and long-term memory.

Sensory Memory

sensory memory
Memory system that involves holding information from the world in its original sensory form for only an instant, not much longer than the brief time it is exposed to the visual, auditory, and other senses.

Sensory memory holds information from the world in its original sensory form for only an instant, not much longer than the brief time it is exposed to the visual, auditory, and other senses. Sensory memory is very rich and detailed, but we lose the information in it quickly unless we use certain strategies that transfer it into short-term or long-term memory.

Think about the sights and sounds you encounter as you walk to class on a typical morning. Literally thousands of stimuli come into your field of vision and hearing—cracks in the sidewalk, chirping birds, a noisy motorcycle, the blue sky, faces and voices of hundreds of people. You do not process all of these stimuli, but you do process a number of them. In general, you process many more stimuli at the sensory level than you consciously notice. Sensory memory

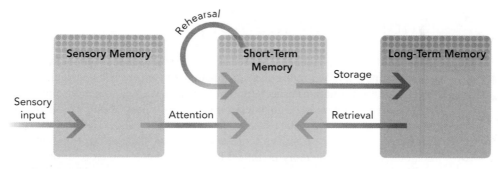

FIGURE 6.5
Atkinson and Shiffrin's Theory of Memory In this model, sensory input goes into sensory memory. Through the process of attention, information moves into short-term memory, where it remains for 30 seconds or less unless it is rehearsed. When the information goes into long-term memory storage, it can be retrieved over a lifetime.

retains this information from your senses, including a large portion of what you think you ignore. However, sensory memory does not retain the information very long.

Echoic memory (from the word *echo*) refers to auditory sensory memory, which is retained for up to several seconds. Imagine standing in an elevator with a friend who suddenly asks, "What was that song?" about the piped-in tune that just ended. If your friend asks his question quickly enough, you just might have a trace of the song left on your sensory registers.

Iconic memory (from the word *icon,* which means "image") refers to visual sensory memory, which is retained only for about ¼ of a second (Figure 6.6). Visual sensory memory is responsible for our ability to "write" in the air using a sparkler on the Fourth of July—the residual iconic memory is what makes a moving point of light appear to be a line. The sensory memory for other senses, such as smell and touch, has received little attention in research studies.

The first scientific research on sensory memory focused on iconic memory. In George Sperling's (1960) classic study, participants viewed patterns of stimuli such as those in Figure 6.7. As you look at the letters, you have no trouble recognizing them. However, Sperling flashed the letters on a screen for very brief intervals, about 1/20 of a second. Afterward, the participants could report only four or five letters. With such a short exposure, reporting all nine letters was impossible.

Some participants in Sperling's study reported feeling that for an instant, they could see all nine letters within a briefly flashed pattern. They ran into trouble when they tried to name all the letters they had initially seen. One hypothesis to explain this experience is that all nine letters were initially processed as far as the iconic sensory memory level. This is why all nine letters were seen. However, forgetting from iconic memory occurred so rapidly that the participants did not have time to transfer all the letters to short-term memory, where they could be named.

Sperling reasoned that if all nine letters are actually processed in sensory memory, they should all be available for a brief time. To test this possibility, Sperling sounded a low, medium, or high tone just after a pattern of letters was shown. The participants were told that the tone was a signal to report only the letters from the bottom, middle, or top row. Under these conditions, the participants performed much better, and this outcome suggests a brief memory for most or all of the letters in the display.

FIGURE 6.7
Sperling's Sensory Memory Experiment
This array of stimuli is similar to those flashed for about 1/20 of a second to the participants in Sperling's study.

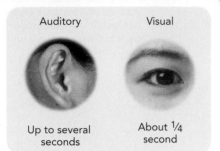

Type of sensory register

Auditory	Visual
Up to several seconds	About ¼ second

FIGURE 6.6
Auditory and Visual Sensory Memory If you hear this bird's call while walking through the woods, your auditory sensory memory holds the information for several seconds. If you see the bird, your visual sensory memory holds the information for only about ¼ of a second.

Sperling showed that an entire array of information is briefly present in iconic memory. To experience this phenomenon, glance at this page for just a second. All of the letters are present in your sensory memory for an instant, creating a mental image that momentarily exists in its entirety. By giving the participants the signal, Sperling helped them to scan their mental image quickly so that they could find specific pieces of the information that it contained in various places. Their ability to do so demonstrates that all the material was actually there. Fantastic!

Short-Term Memory

Much information goes no further than the stage of auditory and visual sensory memory. We retain this information for only a brief instant. However, some information, especially that to which we pay attention, proceeds into short-term memory. **Short-term memory** is a limited-capacity memory system in which information is usually retained for only as long as 30 seconds unless we use strategies to retain it longer. Compared with sensory memory, short-term memory is limited in capacity, but it can store information for a longer time.

George Miller (1956) examined the limited capacity of short-term memory in the classic paper "The Magical Number Seven, Plus or Minus Two." Miller pointed out that on many tasks individuals are limited in how much information they can keep track of without external aids. Usually the limit is in the range of 7 ± 2 items.

short-term memory
Limited-capacity memory system in which information is usually retained for only as long as 30 seconds unless we use strategies to retain it longer.

The most widely cited example of this phenomenon involves *memory span,* the number of digits an individual can report back in order after a single presentation of them. Most college students can remember eight or nine digits without making errors (think about how easy it is to remember a phone number). Longer lists pose problems because they exceed short-term memory capacity. If you rely on simple short-term memory to retain longer lists, you probably will make errors.

Chunking and Rehearsal   Two ways to improve short-term memory are chunking and rehearsal. *Chunking* involves grouping or "packing" information that exceeds the 7 ± 2 memory span into higher-order units that can be remembered as single units. Chunking works by making large amounts of information more manageable (Gobet & Clarkson, 2004).

To get a sense of chunking, consider this list: *hot, city, book, forget, tomorrow,* and *smile.* Hold these words in memory for a moment; then write them down. If you recalled the words, you succeeded in holding 30 letters, grouped into six chunks, in memory. Now hold the following list in memory and then write it down:

O   LDH   ARO   LDAN   DYO   UNGB   EN

How did you do? Do not feel bad if you did poorly. This string of letters is very difficult to remember, even though it is arranged in chunks. The problem is that the chunks lack meaning. If you re-chunk the letters to form the meaningful words "Old Harold and Young Ben," they become much easier to remember.

What are some numbers that are important in your life? Do they follow the 7 ± 2 rule?

Another way to improve short-term memory involves *rehearsal,* the conscious repetition of information (Theeuwes, Belopolsky, & Olivers, 2009). Information stored in short-term memory lasts half a minute or less without rehearsal. However, if rehearsal is not interrupted, information can be retained indefinitely. Rehearsal is often verbal, giving the impression of an inner voice, but it can also be visual or spatial, giving the impression of a private inner eye (Guérard, Tremblay, & Saint-Aubin, 2009).

Rehearsal works best when we must briefly remember a list of numbers or items such as entrées from a dinner menu. When we need to remember information for longer periods of time, as when we are studying for a test coming up next week or even an hour from now, other strategies usually work better. A main reason rehearsal does not work well for retaining information over the long term is that rehearsal often involves just mechanically repeating information, without imparting meaning to it. The fact that, over the long term, we remember information best when we add meaning to it demonstrates the importance of deep, elaborate processing.

Working Memory   Though useful, Atkinson and Shiffrin's theory of the three time-linked memory systems fails to capture the dynamic way short-term memory functions (Baddeley, 2008). Some key questions remain, such as how do things get in and out of memory, and where does problem solving take place?

An alternative approach to explaining short-term memory comes from British psychologist Alan Baddeley (1993, 1998, 2001, 2003, 2006, 2007, 2008). Baddeley proposed the concept of **working memory,** a three-part system that allows us to hold information temporarily as we perform cognitive tasks. Working memory is a kind of mental workbench on which the brain manipulates and assembles information to help us understand, make decisions, and solve problems. If, say, all of the information on the hard drive of your computer is like long-term memory, then working memory is comparable to what you actually have open and active at any given moment. Working memory has a limited capacity, and, to take the computer metaphor further, the capacity of the working memory is like RAM. Working memory is not a passive storehouse with shelves to store information until it moves to long-term memory, but rather it is an active memory system (De Smedt & others, 2009; Laine & others, 2009).

working memory
A three-part system that allows us to hold information temporarily as we perform cognitive tasks; a kind of mental workbench on which the brain manipulates and assembles information to help us understand, make decisions, and solve problems.

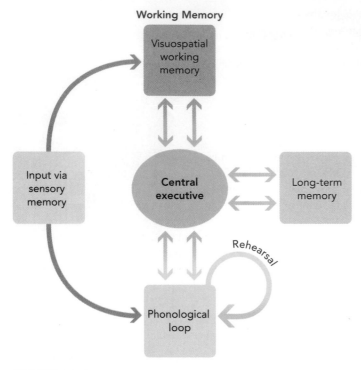

Working Memory

FIGURE 6.8

Working Memory In Baddeley's working memory model, working memory consists of three main components: the phonological loop, visuospatial working memory, and the central executive. The phonological loop and visuospatial working memory serve as assistants, helping the central executive do its work. Input from sensory memory goes to the phonological loop, where information about speech is stored and rehearsal takes place, and to visuospatial working memory, where visual and spatial information, including imagery, is stored. Working memory is a limited capacity system, and information is stored there for only a brief time. Working memory interacts with long-term memory, drawing information from long-term memory and transmitting information to long-term memory for longer storage.

Figure 6.8 shows Baddeley's view of the three components of working memory. Think of them as a boss (the central executive) who has two assistants (the phonological loop and visuospatial working memory) to help do the work.

1. The *phonological loop* is specialized to briefly store speech-based information about the sounds of language. The phonological loop contains two separate components: an acoustic code (the sounds we heard), which decays in a few seconds, and rehearsal, which allows us to repeat the words in the phonological store.

2. *Visuospatial working memory* stores visual and spatial information, including visual imagery. As in the case of the phonological loop, the capacity of visuospatial working memory is limited. If we try to put too many items in visuospatial working memory, we cannot represent them accurately enough to retrieve them successfully. The phonological loop and visuospatial memory function independently. We can rehearse numbers in the phonological loop while making spatial arrangements of letters in visuospatial working memory.

3. The *central executive* integrates information not only from the phonological loop and visuospatial working memory but also from long-term memory. In Baddeley's (2006, 2007) view, the central executive plays important roles in attention, planning, and organizing. The central executive acts like a supervisor who monitors which information deserves our attention and which we should ignore. It also selects which strategies to use to process information and solve problems. Like the phonological loop and visuospatial working memory, the central executive has a limited capacity. If working memory is like the files you have open on your computer, the central executive is *you*. You pull up information you need, close out other things, and so forth.

Though it is compelling, Baddeley's notion of working memory is merely a conceptual model describing processes in memory. Neuroscientists have only just begun to search for brain areas and activity that might be responsible for these processes (Buchsbaum & D'Esposito, 2008; Budson, 2009; Glascher & others, 2009).

Long-Term Memory

long-term memory
A relatively permanent type of memory that stores huge amounts of information for a long time.

Long-term memory is a relatively permanent type of memory that stores huge amounts of information for a long time. The capacity of long-term memory is staggering. John von Neumann, a distinguished mathematician, put the size at $2.8 \cdot 10^{20}$ (280 quintillion) bits, which in practical terms means that our storage capacity is virtually unlimited. Von Neumann assumed that we never forget anything; but even considering that we do forget things, we can hold several billion times more information than a large computer.

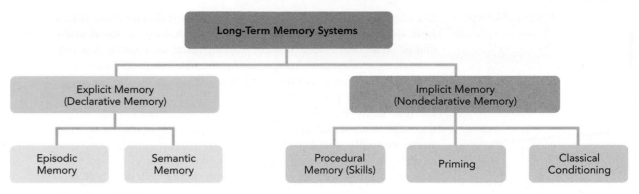

FIGURE 6.9

Systems of Long-Term Memory Long-term memory stores huge amounts of information for long periods of time, much like a computer's hard drive. The hierarchy in the figure shows the division of long-term memory at the top level into explicit memory and implicit memory. Explicit memory can be further divided into episodic and semantic memory; implicit memory includes procedural memory, priming, and classical conditioning.

Components of Long-Term Memory

Long-term memory is complex, as Figure 6.9 shows. At the top level, it is divided into substructures of explicit memory and implicit memory. Explicit memory can be further subdivided into episodic and semantic memory. Implicit memory includes the systems involved in procedural memory, classical conditioning, and priming.

In simple terms, explicit memory has to do with remembering who, what, where, when, and why; implicit memory has to do with remembering how. To explore the distinction, let's look at the case of a person known as H. M. Afflicted with severe epilepsy, H. M. underwent surgery in 1953 that involved removing the hippocampus and a portion of the temporal lobes of both hemispheres in his brain. (We examined the location and functions of these brain areas in Chapter 2.) H. M.'s epilepsy improved, but something devastating happened to his memory. Most dramatically, he developed an inability to form new memories that outlive working memory. H. M.'s memory time frame was only a few minutes at most, so he lived, until his death in 2007, in a perpetual present and could not remember past events (explicit memory). In contrast, his memory of *how* to do things (implicit memory) was less affected. For example, he could learn new physical tasks, even though he had no memory of how or when he learned them.

H. M.'s situation demonstrates a distinction between explicit memory, which was dramatically impaired in his case, and implicit memory, which in his case was less influenced by his surgery. Let's explore the subsystems of explicit and implicit memory more thoroughly.

Explicit Memory

Explicit memory (declarative memory) is the conscious recollection of information, such as specific facts and events and, at least in humans, information that can be verbally communicated (Tulving, 1989, 2000). Examples of using explicit, or declarative, memory include recounting the events in a movie you have seen and recalling which politicians are in the president's cabinet.

How long does explicit memory last? Explicit memory includes things you are learning in your classes even now. Will it stay with you? Research by Harry Bahrick has examined this very question. Ohio Wesleyan University, where Bahrick is a professor of psychology, is a small (about 1,800 students) liberal arts school that boasts very loyal alumni who faithfully return to campus for reunions and other events. Bahrick (1984) took advantage of this situation to conduct an ingenious study on the retention of course material over time. He gave vocabulary tests to individuals who had taken Spanish in college as well as to a control group of college students who had not taken Spanish

explicit memory (declarative memory)
The conscious recollection of information, such as specific facts or events and, at least in humans, information that can be verbally communicated.

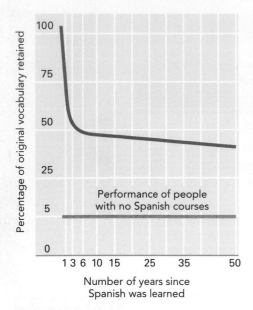

FIGURE 6.10

Memory for Spanish as a Function of Age Since Spanish Was Learned
An initial steep drop over about a three-year period in remembering the vocabulary learned in Spanish classes occurred. However, there was little dropoff in memory for Spanish vocabulary from three years after taking Spanish classes to 50 years after taking them. Even 50 years after taking Spanish classes, individuals still remembered almost 50 percent of the vocabulary.

Think about what is getting into your own memory right now that you will never forget.

Your memory of your first day on campus involves episodic memory. If you take a history class, your memory of the information you need to know to do well on the next test involves semantic memory.

in college. The individuals chosen for the study had used Spanish very little since their college courses. Some individuals were tested at the end of an academic year (just after having taken the courses), but others were tested years after graduation—as many as 50 years later. When Bahrick assessed how much the participants had forgotten, he found a striking pattern (Figure 6.10): Forgetting tended to occur in the first three years after taking the classes and then leveled off, so that adults maintained considerable knowledge of Spanish vocabulary words up to 50 years later.

Bahrick (1984) assessed not only how long ago adults studied Spanish but also how well they did in Spanish during college. Those who got an *A* in their courses 50 years earlier remembered more Spanish than adults who got a *C* grade when taking Spanish only one year earlier. Thus, how well students initially learned the material was even more important than how long ago they studied it. Bahrick (2000) calls information that is retained for such a long time "permastore" content. Permastore memory represents that portion of original learning that appears destined to be with the person virtually forever, even without rehearsal. In addition to focusing on course material, Bahrick and colleagues (1974) have probed adults' memories for the faces and names of their high school classmates. Thirty-five years after graduation, the participants visually recognized 90 percent of the portraits of their high school classmates, with name recognition being almost as high. These results held even in relatively large classes (the average class size in the study was 294).

Canadian cognitive psychologist Endel Tulving (1972, 1989, 2000) has been the foremost advocate of distinguishing between two subtypes of explicit memory: episodic and semantic. **Episodic memory** is the retention of information about the where, when, and what of life's happenings—basically, how we remember life's episodes. Episodic memory is autobiographical. For example, episodic memory includes the details of where you were when your younger brother or sister was born, what happened on your first date, and what you ate for breakfast this morning.

Semantic memory is a person's knowledge about the world. It includes your areas of expertise, general knowledge of the sort you are learning in school, and everyday knowledge about the meanings of words, famous individuals, important places, and common things. For example, semantic memory is involved in a person's knowledge of chess, of geometry, and of who the Dalai Lama, Barack Obama, and Kate Winslet are. An important aspect of semantic memory is that it appears to be independent of an individual's personal identity with the past. You can access a fact—such as the detail that Lima is the capital of Peru—and not have the foggiest notion of when and where you learned it.

The difference between episodic and semantic memory is also demonstrated in certain cases of amnesia (memory loss). A person with amnesia might forget entirely who she is—her name, family, career, and all other vital information about herself—yet still be able to talk, know what words mean, and have general knowledge about the world, such as what day it is or who currently holds the office of U.S. president (Rosenbaum & others, 2005). In such cases, episodic memory is impaired, but semantic memory is functioning.

Figure 6.11 summarizes some aspects of the episodic/semantic distinction. The differences that are listed are controversial. One criticism is that many cases of explicit, or declarative, memory are neither purely episodic nor purely semantic but fall in a gray area in between. Consider your memory for what you studied last night. You probably added knowledge to your semantic memory—that was, after all, the reason you were studying. You probably remember where you were studying, as well as about when you started and when you stopped. You

episodic memory
The retention of information about the where, when, and what of life's happenings— that is, how individuals remember life's episodes.

semantic memory
A person's knowledge about the world.

probably also can remember some minor occurrences, such as a burst of loud laughter from the room next door or the coffee you spilled on the desk. Is episodic or semantic memory involved here? Tulving (1983, 2000) argues that semantic and episodic systems often work together in forming new memories. In such cases, the memory that ultimately forms might consist of an autobiographical episode *and* semantic information.

Implicit (Nondeclarative) Memory In addition to explicit memory, there is a type of long-term memory that is related to nonconsciously remembering skills and sensory perceptions rather than consciously remembering facts. **Implicit memory (nondeclarative memory)** is memory in which behavior is affected by prior experience without a conscious recollection of that experience. Implicit memory comes into play, for example, in the skills of playing tennis and snowboarding, as well as in the physical act of text messaging. Another example of implicit memory is the repetition in your mind of a song you heard playing in the supermarket, even though you did not notice that song playing.

Three subsystems of implicit memory are procedural memory, classical conditioning, and priming. All of these subsystems refer to memories that you are not aware of but that influence behavior (Slotnick & Schacter, 2006).

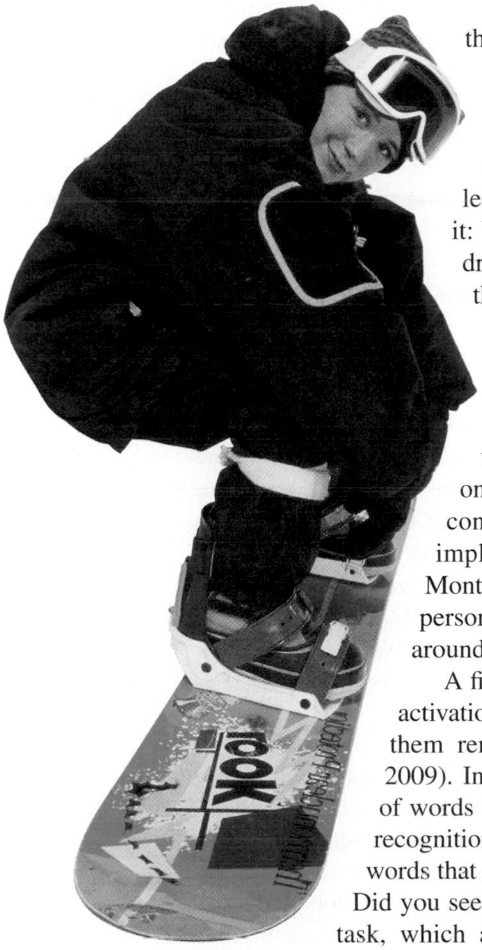

Procedural memory is a type of implicit memory process that involves memory for skills. For example (assuming that you are an expert typist), as you type a paper, you are not conscious of where the keys are for the various letters, but your well-learned, nonconscious skill of typing allows you to hit the right keys. Similarly, once you have learned to drive a car, you remember how to go about it: You do not have to remember consciously how to drive the car as you put the key in the ignition, turn the steering wheel, depress the gas pedal, and step on the brake pedal.

Another type of implicit memory involves *classical conditioning*, a form of learning discussed in Chapter 5. Recall that classical conditioning involves the automatic learning of associations between stimuli, so that one comes to evoke the same response as the other. Classically conditioned associations such as this involve nonconscious, implicit memory (Pearce & Hall, 2009; Schultz, Dayan, & Montague, 2009). So without realizing it, you might start to like the person who sits next to you in your favorite class, because she is around while you are feeling good.

A final type of implicit memory process is priming. **Priming** is the activation of information that people already have in storage to help them remember new information better and faster (Hare & others, 2009). In a common demonstration of priming, individuals study a list of words (such as *hope, walk,* and *cake*). Then they are given a standard recognition task to assess explicit memory. They must select all of the words that appeared in the list—for example, "Did you see the word *hope*? Did you see the word *form*?" Then participants perform a stem-completion task, which assesses implicit memory. In this task, they view a list of

Margin glossary

implicit memory (nondeclarative memory)
Memory in which behavior is affected by prior experience without a conscious recollection of that experience.

procedural memory
Memory for skills.

priming
The activation of information that people already have in storage to help them remember new information better and faster.

Margin handwritten notes

This is why you might find yourself knowing all the words to a song you hate. You have heard it so many times that you have memorized it without knowing it.

To grasp the distinction between explicit memory and procedural memory, imagine trying to describe in words exactly how to tie a shoe—something you can do successfully in just a few seconds—without having a shoe around.

Figure table

Characteristic	Episodic Memory	Semantic Memory
Units	Events, episodes	Facts, ideas, concepts
Organization	Time	Concepts
Emotion	More important	Less important
Retrieval process	Deliberate (effortful)	Automatic
Retrieval report	"I remember"	"I know"
Education	Irrelevant	Relevant
Intelligence	Irrelevant	Relevant
Legal testimony	Admissible in court	Inadmissible in court

FIGURE 6.11
Some Differences Between Episodic and Semantic Memory
These characteristics have been proposed as the main ways to differentiate episodic from semantic memory.

incomplete words (for example, *ho___*, *wa___*, *ca___*), called word stems, and must fill in the blanks with whatever word comes to mind. The results show that individuals more often fill in the blanks with the previously studied words than would be expected if they were filling in the blanks randomly. For example, they are more likely to complete the stem *ho___* with *hope* than with *hole*. This result occurs even when individuals do not recognize the words on the earlier recognition task. Because priming takes place even when explicit memory for previous information is not required, it is assumed to be an involuntary and nonconscious process (Soldan & others, 2009).

Priming occurs when something in the environment evokes a response in memory—such as the activation of a particular concept. Priming a term or concept makes it more available in memory (Kelly & McNamara, 2009). John Bargh and other social psychologists have demonstrated that priming can have a surprising influence on social behavior (Bargh, 2005, 2006; Bargh & Morsella, 2009; McCulloch & others, 2008; P. K. Smith & Bargh, 2008). For example, in one study, college students were asked to unscramble a series of words to make a sentence (Bargh, Chen, & Burrows, 1996). For some of the participants, the items in the series included such words as *rude, aggressively, intrude,* and *bluntly.* For other students, the words included *polite, cautious,* and *sensitively.*

Upon completing the scrambled sentences, participants were to report to the experimenter, but each participant encountered the experimenter deep in conversation with another person. Who was more likely to interrupt the ongoing conversation? Among those who were primed with words connoting rudeness, 67 percent interrupted the experimenter. Among those in the "polite" condition, 84 percent of the participants waited the entire 10 minutes, never interrupting the ongoing conversation.

Priming can also spur goal-directed behavior. For example, Bargh and colleagues (2001) asked students to perform a word-find puzzle. Embedded in the puzzle were either neutral words (*shampoo, robin*) or achievement-related words (*compete, win, achieve*). Participants who were exposed to the achievement-related words did better on a later puzzle task, finding 26 words in other puzzles, while those with the neutral primes found only 21.5. Other research has shown that individuals primed with words like *professor* and *intelligent* performed better at a game of Trivial Pursuit than those primed with words like *stupid* and *hooligan* (Dijksterhuis & Van Knippenberg, 1998). These effects occur without awareness, with no participants reporting suspicion about the effects of the primes on their behavior.

Note that this study was an experiment. Participants were randomly assigned to be primed with rude words or polite words. We know that the primes caused the differences between the groups because they were randomly assigned.

How Memory Is Organized

Explaining the forms of long-term memory does not address the question of how the different types of memory are organized for storage. The word *organized* is important: Memories are not haphazardly stored but instead are carefully sorted.

Here is a demonstration. Recall the 12 months of the year as quickly as you can. How long did it take you? What was the order of your recall? Chances are, you listed them within a few seconds in chronological order (January, February, March, and so on). Now try to remember the months in alphabetical order. How long did it take you? Did you make any errors? It should be obvious that your memory for the months of the year is organized in a particular way. Indeed, one of memory's most distinctive features is its organization.

Researchers have found that if people are encouraged to organize material simply, their memories of the material improve even if they receive no warning that their memories will be tested (Mandler, 1980). Psychologists have developed a variety of theories of how long-term memory is organized. Let's consider two of these more closely: schemas and connectionist networks.

Because you have a schema for what happens in a restaurant, you know that someone is going to take your order and eventually bring you food.

Schemas

You and a friend have taken a long drive to a new town where neither of you has ever been before. You stop at the local diner, have a seat, and look over the menu. You have never been in this diner before, but you know exactly what is going to happen. Why? Because you have a schema for what happens in a restaurant. When we store information in memory, we often fit it into the collection of information that already exists, as you do even in a new experience with a diner. A **schema** is a preexisting mental concept or framework that helps people to organize and interpret information. Schemas from prior encounters with the environment influence the way we handle information—how we encode it, the inferences we make about it, and how we retrieve it (R. G. Morris, 2006).

Schemas can also be at work when we recall information. Schema theory holds that long-term memory is not very exact. We seldom find precisely the memory that we want, or at least not all of what we want; hence, we have to *reconstruct* the rest. Our schemas support the reconstruction process, helping us fill in gaps between our fragmented memories.

We have schemas for lots of situations and experiences—for scenes and spatial layouts (a beach, a bathroom), as well as for common events (playing football, writing a term paper). A **script** is a schema for an event (Schank & Abelson, 1977). Scripts often have information about physical features, people, and typical occurrences. This kind of information is helpful when people need to figure out what is happening around them. For example, if you are enjoying your after-dinner coffee in an upscale restaurant and a man in a tuxedo comes over and puts a piece of paper on the table, your script tells you that the man probably is a waiter who has just given you the check. Scripts help to organize our storage of memories about events.

If someone asked you about the trip to the diner, you might not remember ever getting the bill, but you know, because of your restaurant script, that someone probably did, so you can fill in that gap in memory with information from this script.

Connectionist Networks

Schema theory has little or nothing to say about the role of the physical brain in memory. Thus, a new theory based on brain research has generated a wave of excitement among psychologists. **Connectionism,** or **parallel distributed processing (PDP),** is the theory that memory is stored throughout the brain in connections among neurons, several of which may work together to process a single memory (Goldman, 2009; Janata, 2009). We initially considered the concept of neural networks in Chapter 2 and the idea of parallel sensory processing pathways in Chapter 3. These concepts also apply to memory.

In the connectionist view, memories are not large knowledge structures (as in schema theories). Instead, memories are more like electrical impulses, organized only to the extent that neurons, the connections among them, and their activity are organized. Any piece of knowledge—such as your dog's name—is embedded in the strengths of hundreds or thousands of connections among neurons and is not limited to a single location.

Shown here are representative scripts from a Japanese tea ceremony, a Western dinner, and an Ethiopian meal. With which script do you feel most comfortable?

How does the connectionist process work? A neural activity involving memory, such as remembering your dog's name, is spread across a number of areas of the cerebral cortex. The locations of neural activity, called *nodes,* are interconnected. When a node reaches a critical level of activation, it can affect another node across synapses. We know that the human cerebral cortex contains millions of neurons that are richly interconnected through hundreds of millions of synapses. Because of these synaptic connections, the activity of one neuron can be influenced by many other neurons. Because of these simple reactions, the connectionist view argues that changes in the strength of synaptic connections are the fundamental bases of memory (Canals & others, 2009). From the connectionist network perspective, memories are organized sets of neurons that are routinely activated together.

Part of the appeal of the connectionist view is that it is consistent with what we know about brain function and allows psychologists to simulate human memory studies using computers (Marcus, 2001). Connectionist approaches also help to explain how priming a concept (rudeness) can influence behavior (interrupting someone). Furthermore, insights from this connectionist view support brain research undertaken to determine where memories are stored in the brain (McClelland & Rumelhart, 2009), another fascinating and complex topic.

Indeed, so far we have examined the many ways cognitive psychologists think about how information is stored. The question remains, *where?* The puzzle of the physical location of memories has long fascinated psychologists. In the 1960s, researchers examined this question using planaria (worms) (Walker & Milton, 1966). In this study, the researchers first trained worms to travel through a maze. Then they killed the trained worms and fed them to naive (untrained) worms. Remarkably, the worms that had eaten the trained worms learned the maze more quickly than the worms that had not cannibalized their maze-skilled comrades. Clearly, human memory is not the same as worm memory—and cannibalism is not an effective means of gaining information. However, this old research does highlight the notion that although memory may seem to be a mysterious phenomenon, it, like all psychological processes, must occur in a physical place: the brain.

Almost as gross as salivating cockroaches (see Chapter 5)—but not quite.

Where Memories Are Stored

Karl Lashley (1950) spent a lifetime looking for a location in the brain in which memories are stored. He trained rats to discover the correct pathway in a maze and then cut out various portions of the animals' brains and retested their memory of the maze pathway. Experiments with thousands of rats showed that the loss of various cortical areas did not affect rats' ability to remember the pathway, leading Lashley to conclude that memories are not stored in a specific location in the brain. Other researchers, continuing Lashley's quest, agreed that memory storage is diffuse, but they developed additional insights. Canadian psychologist Donald Hebb (1949, 1980) suggested that assemblies of cells, distributed over large areas of the cerebral cortex, work together to represent information, just as the connectionist network perspective would predict.

Neurons and Memory

Today many neuroscientists believe that memory is located in specific sets or circuits of neurons. Brain researcher Larry Squire, for example, says that most memories are probably clustered in groups of about 1,000 neurons (1990, 2004, 2007). At the same time, single neurons are also at work in memory (Squire, 2007). Researchers who measure the electrical activity of single cells have found that some respond to faces and others to eye or hair color, for example. Still, in order for you to recognize your Uncle Albert, individual neurons that provide information about hair color, size, and other characteristics must act together.

Researchers also believe that brain chemicals may be the ink with which memories are written. Remember that neurotransmitters are the chemicals that allow neurons to communicate across the synapse. These chemicals play a crucial role in forging the connections that represent memory.

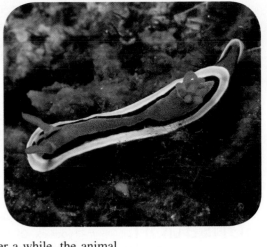

Ironically, some of the answers to complex questions about the neural mechanics of memory come from studies on a very simple experimental animal—the inelegant sea slug. Eric Kandel and James Schwartz (1982) chose this large snail-without-a-shell because of the simple architecture of its nervous system, which consists of only about 10,000 neurons. (You might recall from Chapter 2 that the human brain has about 100 billion neurons.)

The sea slug is hardly a quick learner or an animal with a good memory, but it is equipped with a reliable reflex. When anything touches the gill on its back, it quickly withdraws it. First the researchers accustomed the sea slug to having its gill prodded. After a while, the animal ignored the prod and stopped withdrawing its gill. Next the researchers applied an electric shock to its tail when they touched the gill. After many rounds of the shock-accompanied prod, the sea slug violently withdrew its gill at the slightest touch. The researchers found that the sea slug remembered this message for hours or even weeks. They also determined that shocking the sea slug's gill releases the neurotransmitter serotonin at the synapses of its nervous system, and this chemical release basically provides a reminder that the gill was shocked. This "memory" informs the nerve cell to send out chemical commands to retract the gill the next time it is touched. If nature builds complexity out of simplicity, then the mechanism used by the sea slug may work in the human brain as well.

Researchers have proposed the concept of *long-term potentiation* to explain how memory functions at the neuron level. In line with connectionist theory, this concept states that if two neurons are activated at the same time, the connection between them—and thus the memory—may be strengthened (Hutchison, Chidiac, & Leung, 2009; S. J. Lee & others, 2009). Long-term potentiation has been demonstrated experimentally by administering a drug that increases the flow of information from one neuron to another across the synapse (Shakesby, Anwyl, & Rowan, 2002), raising the possibility of someday improving memory through drugs that increase neural connections (Schacter, 2001).

Imagine that what we experience as a memory is really a collection of well-worn pathways in our brain.

Brain Structures and Memory Functions

Whereas some neuroscientists are unveiling the cellular basis of memory, others are examining its broad-scale architecture in the brain. Many different parts of the brain and nervous system are involved in the rich, complex process that is memory (Addis & others, 2009; Schacter & Wagner, 2009). Although there is no one memory center in the brain, researchers have demonstrated that specific brain structures are involved in particular aspects of memory.

Figure 6.12 shows the location of brain structures active in different types of long-term memory. Note that implicit and explicit memory appear to involve different locations in the brain.

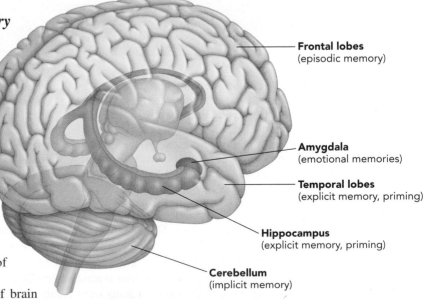

Frontal lobes
(episodic memory)

Amygdala
(emotional memories)

Temporal lobes
(explicit memory, priming)

Hippocampus
(explicit memory, priming)

Cerebellum
(implicit memory)

FIGURE 6.12
Structures of the Brain Involved in Different Aspects of Long-Term Memory Note that explicit memory and implicit memory appear to involve different locations in the brain.

intersection

You smell a turkey roasting in the oven, and suddenly you are once again 6 years old and eagerly anticipating your family's Thanksgiving dinner. The aroma of the tamales your *abuela* (grandmother) used to make reminds you of so many Christmases past. With less pleasure, you smell the cologne of a former romantic partner and vividly recall your last argument with your ex. Of all of the senses, smell seems to bear the strongest relationship to memory, and a smell can

Memory and Sensation: Why Does Smell Share a Special Relationship with Memory?

trigger rich emotional memories. Marcel Proust described this link so powerfully in his novel *Swann's Way* that the term the *Proust effect* has come to mean the ability of smell to transport us into vivid memory.

Rachel Herz (2004) found that autobiographical memories that were cued by odors (a campfire, fresh-cut grass, popcorn) were more emotional and more evocative than such memories cued by pictures or sounds. Indeed, smells can be powerful tools for memory. Herz and Gerald Cupchik (1995; Herz, 1998) found that individuals performed better on a surprise memory test if the same odor cue was present in the room during learning and recall. One implication of that study is that it might be a good idea to wear the same cologne to an exam that you typically wear to class.

However, showing that smells influence memory and that the brain evidently has evolved to give smell a privileged place does not help us understand why the special status of smell is adaptive. Why would it be adaptive to give smell a special link with emotion and memory? Many other animals detect important information about their environments from smell; that is why, for instance, dogs' noses are so close to the ground (and so sensitive). Animals use smells to navigate through the world—to detect what is good (the smell of a food) and what is bad (the scent of a predator). In humans, emotions play a similar role in that they tell us how we are doing in the world in terms of what matters to us. Perhaps for humans, the special link between smells and emotions allows us quickly to learn associations between particular smells and stimuli that are good (morning coffee) or bad (spoiled milk) for us.

Why does smell share such a special relationship with memory? At least part of the answer is anatomical. Recall from Chapter 3 that nerves in the nose send information about smells to the primary olfactory cortex in the brain. That cortex links directly to the amygdala and hippocampus. Thus, smells have a superhighway to the brain structures involved in emotion (the amygdala) and memory consolidation (the hippocampus) (Galan & others, 2006; Herz, Schankler, & Beland, 2004).

As the holiday dinner examples above suggest, smells may have a special power in the positive emotional experience of nostalgia. The right smells alone can transport us powerfully to the good old days.

Do you have any favorite smells? How are they related to your memories?

■ *Explicit memory:* Neuroscientists have found that the hippocampus, the temporal lobes in the cerebral cortex, and other areas of the limbic system play a role in explicit memory (Budson, 2009; van Strien, Cappaert, & Witter, 2009). In many aspects of explicit memory, information is transmitted from the hippocampus to the frontal lobes, which are involved in both retrospective (remembering things from the past) and prospective (remembering things that you need to do in the future) memory (McDaniel & Einstein, 2007). The left frontal lobe is especially active when we encode new information into memory; the right frontal lobe is more active when we subsequently retrieve it (Babiloni & others, 2006). In addition, the amygdala, which is part of the limbic system, is involved in emotional memories (Kishioka & others, 2009).

- *Implicit memory:* The cerebellum (the structure at the back and toward the bottom of the brain) is active in the implicit memory required to perform skills (Quintero-Gallego & others, 2006). Various areas of the cerebral cortex, such as the temporal lobes and hippocampus, function in priming (Kristjansson & others, 2006).

Neuroscientists studying memory have benefited greatly from the use of MRI scans, which allow the tracking of neural activity during cognitive tasks (Phillips & others, 2009; Raichle & Mintun, 2006). In one research study, participants viewed color photographs of indoor and outdoor scenes while in an MRI machine (Brewer & others, 1998). The experimenters told them that they would receive a memory test about the scenes. After the MRI scans, the participants were asked which pictures they remembered well, vaguely, or not at all. The researchers compared their memories with the brain scans and found that the greater the activation in both prefrontal lobes and a particular region of the hippocampus during viewing, the better the participants remembered the scenes.

Thus, current research is intensively studying the links between memory and neuroscience (Gamer & others, 2009; Ross, Brown, & Stern, 2009; Suzuki & others, 2009). The Intersection showcases another example of overlapping fields of psychology, this time involving memory and sensation.

1. You tell your friends about the great time you had at the local Six Flags park. Most of the information that you have forgotten about this experience was most likely processed in your
   A. personal memory.
   B. short-term memory.
   C. long-term memory.
   D. sensory memory.

2. Short-term memory has a _____ capacity than sensory memory and a _____ duration.
   A. more limited; longer
   B. less limited; longer
   C. larger; shorter
   D. more limited; shorter

3. According to the connectionist network view of memory, memories are _____, and according to the schema theory of memory, memories are _____.
   A. abstract concepts; large knowledge structures
   B. neural connections; large knowledge structures
   C. parallel concepts; electrical impulses
   D. concurrent concepts; nodes of information

Apply It! 4. Before an exam, Professor Sweetheart tells the class how brilliant they are. She tells the students that she has seen them learning the concepts in class and feels confident that everyone can remember the material. In contrast, Professor Meany tells her class that she realizes they have been bored most of the time, probably cannot remember most of the material, and that she does not expect much from this group of uninspired pupils. Although the material is the same and the tests are the same, Professor Sweetheart's students perform better on the test. What basic memory process might explain this difference?
   A. The professors are classically conditioning the students in their classes.
   B. The professors are priming different behavior, so that concepts related to learning and brilliance are more available to Professor Sweetheart's students.
   C. The professors are influencing the semantic memory of the students.
   D. The professors are influencing the episodic memory of the students.

4 Memory Retrieval

Remember that unforgettable night of shining stars with your romantic partner? Let's say the evening has indeed been encoded deeply and elaborately in your memory. Through the years you have thought about the night a great deal and told your best friends about it. The story of that night has become part of the longer story of your life with your significant other. Fifty years later, your grandson asks, "How did you two end up together?" You share that story you have been saving for just such a question. What are the retrieval processes that allow you to do so?

Memory **retrieval** takes place when information that was retained in memory comes out of storage. You might think of long-term memory as a library. You retrieve information in a fashion similar to the process you use to locate and check out a book in an actual library. To retrieve something from your mental data bank, you search your store of memory to find the relevant information.

The efficiency with which you retrieve information from memory is impressive. It usually takes only a moment to search through a vast storehouse to find the information you want. When were you born? What was the name of your first date? Who

retrieval
The memory process that occurs when information that was retained in memory comes out of storage.

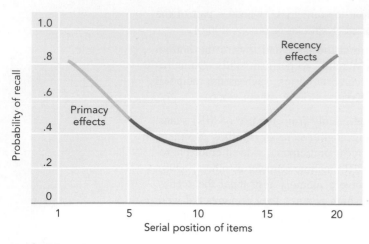

FIGURE 6.13
The Serial Position Effect When a person is asked to memorize a list of words, the words memorized last usually are recalled best, those at the beginning next best, and those in the middle least efficiently.

If you or some friends have ever tried speed dating, consider the role of the serial position effect. Which participant did you or they like best?

off the mark.com   by Mark Parisi

LOOK, I KNOW YOU TOLD ME YOUR NAME BUT I FORGOT TO SAVE IT...

MARK PARISI

offthemark.com   ©2006 MARK PARISI DIST. BY UFS INC.

© Mark Parisi. Atlantic Feature Syndicate.

developed the first psychology laboratory? You can, of course, answer all of these questions instantly. Retrieval of memory is a complex and sometimes imperfect process (Benoit & others, 2009).

Before examining ways that retrieval may fall short, let's look at some basic concepts and variables that are known to affect the likelihood that information will be accurately encoded, stored, and ultimately retrieved. As we will see, retrieval depends heavily on the circumstances under which a memory was encoded and the way it was retained (Mate & Baques, 2009).

Serial Position Effect

The **serial position effect** is the tendency to recall the items at the beginning and end of a list more readily than those in the middle. If you are a reality TV fan, you might notice that you always seem to remember the first person to get voted off and the last few survivors. All those people in the middle, however, are a blur. The *primacy effect* refers to better recall for items at the beginning of a list. The *recency effect* refers to better recall for items at the end of the list. Together with the relatively low recall of items from the middle of the list, this pattern makes up the *serial position effect* (Surprenant, 2001). See Figure 6.13 for a typical serial position effect that shows a weaker primacy effect and a stronger recency effect.

Psychologists explain these effects using principles of encoding. With respect to the primacy effect, the first few items in the list are easily remembered because they are rehearsed more or because they receive more elaborative processing than do words later in the list (Atkinson & Shiffrin, 1968; Craik & Tulving, 1975). Working memory is relatively empty when the items enter, so there is little competition for rehearsal time. Moreover, because the items get more rehearsal, they stay in working memory longer and are more likely to be encoded successfully into long-term memory. In contrast, many items from the middle of the list drop out of working memory before being encoded into long-term memory.

As for the recency effect, the last several items are remembered for different reasons. First, when these items are recalled, they might still be in working memory. Second, even if these items are not in working memory, the fact that they were just encountered makes them easier to recall.

Retrieval Cues and the Retrieval Task

Two other factors are involved in retrieval: the nature of the cues that can prompt your memory and the retrieval task that you set for yourself. We consider each in turn.

If effective cues for what you are trying to remember do not seem to be available, you need to create them—a process that takes place in working memory (Carpenter & DeLosh, 2006). For example, if you have a block about remembering a new friend's name, you might go through the alphabet, generating names that begin with each letter. If you manage to stumble across the right name, you will probably recognize it.

serial position effect
The tendency to recall the items at the beginning and end of a list more readily than those in the middle.

We can learn to generate retrieval cues (Allan & others, 2001). One good strategy is to use different subcategories as retrieval cues. For example, write down the names of as many of your classmates from middle or junior high school as you can remember. When you run out of names, think about the activities you were involved in during those school years, such as math class, student council, lunch, drill team, and so on. Does this set of cues help you to remember more of your classmates?

Although cues help, your success in retrieving information also depends on the retrieval task you set for yourself. For instance, if you are simply trying to decide whether something seems familiar, retrieval is probably a snap. Let's say that you see a short, dark-haired woman walking toward you. You quickly decide that she is someone who shops at the same supermarket as you do. However, remembering her name or a precise detail, such as when you met her, can be harder. Such distinctions have implications for police investigations: A witness might be certain she has previously seen a face, yet she might have a hard time deciding whether it was at the scene of the crime or in a mug shot.

Recall and Recognition   The presence or absence of good cues and the retrieval task required are factors in an important memory distinction: recall versus recognition. *Recall* is a memory task in which the individual has to retrieve previously learned information, as on essay tests. *Recognition* is a memory task in which the individual only has to identify (recognize) learned items, as on multiple-choice tests. Recall tests such as essay tests have poor retrieval cues. You are told to try to recall a certain class of information ("Discuss the factors that caused World War I"). In recognition tests such as multiple-choice tests, you merely judge whether a stimulus is familiar (such as that Archduke Franz Ferdinand was assassinated in 1914).

Some people say that they are better at essay tests, while others prefer multiple choice. What's your preference? From a memory perspective, multiple choice should always be easier. What might account for differences in actual experience?

You probably have heard some people say that they never forget a face. However, recognizing a face is far simpler than recalling a face "from scratch," as law enforcement officers know. In some cases, police bring in an artist to draw a suspect's face from witnesses' descriptions (Figure 6.14). Recalling faces is difficult, and artists' sketches of suspects are frequently not detailed or accurate enough to result in apprehension.

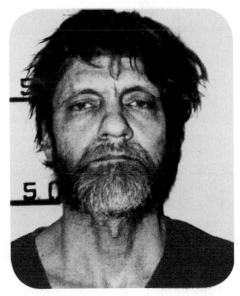

FIGURE 6.14

Remembering Faces (*Left*) The FBI artist's sketch of Ted Kaczynski. Kaczynski, also known as the Unabomber, is a serial killer who conducted a sequence of mail bombings targeting universities and airlines beginning in the late 1970s. (*Right*) A photograph of Kaczynski. The FBI widely circulated the artist's sketch, which was based on bits and pieces of observations people had made of the infamous Unabomber, in the hope that someone would recognize him. Would you have been able to recognize Kaczynski from the artist's sketch? Probably not. Although most people say they are good at remembering faces, they usually are not as good as they think they are.

Encoding Specificity

Another consideration in understanding retrieval is the *encoding specificity principle*, which states that information present at the time of encoding or learning tends to be effective as a retrieval cue (Raposo, Han, & Dobbins, 2009). For example, you know your instructors when they are in the classroom setting—you see them there all the time. If, however, you run into one of them in an unexpected setting and in more casual attire, such as at the gym in workout clothes, the person's name might escape you. Your memory might fail because the cues you encoded are not available for use.

Context at Encoding and Retrieval

An important consequence of encoding specificity is that a change in context between encoding and retrieval can cause memory to fail (Schwabe, Bohringer, & Wolf, 2009). In many instances, people remember better when they attempt to recall information in the same context in which they learned it—a process referred to as *context-dependent memory*. This better recollection is believed to occur because they have encoded features of the context in which they learned the information along with the actual information. Such features can later act as retrieval cues (Eich, 2007).

In one study, scuba divers learned information on land and under water (Godden & Baddeley, 1975). Later they were asked to recall the information when they were either on land or under water. The divers' recall was much better when the encoding and retrieval contexts were the same (both on land or both under water).

This result illustrates why you should sit in your usual seat for an exam.

psychology in our world

From the Courtroom to KFC: Making It Memorable

Understanding the processes that contribute to memory is a valuable skill in many realms of life, from the judicial system to the commercial marketplace. For example, legal consultants with expertise in memory are often hired to train law enforcers how to preserve witness memory and how to understand the recollections of crime victims. Such consultants may even provide legal testimony at trial, lending their expertise in controversial cases.

Memory processes also play a role in successful product marketing. Companies hire ad agencies to craft persuasive messages that will capture consumers' attention, be encoded, and later be retrieved. If you have ever found yourself humming a television jingle, you know that some advertiser has done a great job of influencing your memory.

To enhance the chances that a product will be remembered, an advertiser might target a promotion to be personally relevant to a particular consumer group, thereby increasing the associative network around the product. Think of the commercial where Dennis Hopper (a star in the classic 1969 film *Easy Rider,* about two countercultural bikers) persuades aging baby boomers to consider their financial retirement plans as the Steppenwolf song "Born to Be Wild" wails. In addition, to improve the chances that a product name will be retrieved, a message might include context cues that are likely to occur in a consumer's daily life. Thus, a fast food chain might use images of hungry teenagers pulling up to a drive-thru or hungry kids complaining to their mom about what they are going to have for dinner that night.

Special Cases of Retrieval

We began this discussion by likening memory retrieval to looking for and finding a book in the library. However, the process of retrieving information from long-term memory is not as precise as the library analogy suggests. When we search through our long-term memory storehouse, we do not always find the exact "book" we want—or we might find the book but discover that several pages are missing. We have to fill in these gaps somehow.

Our memories are affected by a number of things, including the pattern of facts we remember, schemas and scripts, the situations we associate with memories, and the personal or emotional context. Certainly, everyone has had the experience of remembering a shared situation with a particular individual, only to have him or her remind us, "Oh, that wasn't *me!*" Such moments provide convincing evidence that memory may well be best understood as "reconstructive." This subjective quality of memory certainly has implications for important day-to-day procedures such as eyewitness testimony (Greene, 1999).

While the factors that we have discussed so far relate to the retrieval of generic information, various kinds of special memory retrieval also have generated a great deal of research. These memories have special significance because of their relevance to the self, to their emotional or traumatic character, or because they show unusually high levels of apparent accuracy (Piolino & others, 2006). Researchers in cognitive psychology have debated whether these memories rely on processes that are different from those already described or are simply extreme cases of typical memory processes (Lane & Schooler, 2004; Schooler & Eich, 2000). We now turn to these special cases of memory.

autobiographical memory
A special form of episodic memory, consisting of a person's recollections of his or her life experiences.

Retrieval of Autobiographical Memories

Autobiographical memory, a special form of episodic memory, is a person's recollections of his or her life experiences (N. R. Brown & others, 2009; D. K. Thomsen, 2009). An intriguing discovery about autobiographical memory is the *reminiscence bump,* the effect that adults remember more events from the second and third decades of life than from other decades (Copeland, Radvansky, & Goodwin, 2009).

Autobiographical memories are complex and seem to contain unending strings of stories and snapshots, but researchers have found that they can be categorized (Roediger & Marsh, 2003). For example, based on their research, Martin Conway and David Rubin (1993) sketched a structure of autobiographical memory that has three levels (Figure 6.15). The most abstract level consists of *life time periods;* for example, you might remember something about your life in high school. The middle level in the hierarchy is made up of *general events,* such as a trip you took with your friends after you graduated from high school. The most concrete level in the hierarchy is composed of *event-specific knowledge;* for example, from your postgraduation trip, you might remember the exhilarating experience you had the first time you jet-skied. When people tell their life stories, all three levels of information are usually present and intertwined.

Write down a memory that you feel has been especially important in making you who you are. What are some characteristics of this self-defining memory? What do you think the memory says about you? How does it relate to your current goals and aspirations? Do you think of the memory often? You might find that this part of your life story can be inspiring when things are going poorly or when you are feeling down.

Level	Label	Description
Level 1	Life time periods	Long segments of time measured in years and even decades
Level 2	General events	Extended composite episodes measured in days, weeks, or months
Level 3	Event-specific knowledge	Individual episodes measured in seconds, minutes, or hours.

FIGURE 6.15
The Three-Level Hierarchical Structure of Autobiographical Memory When people relate their life stories, all three levels of information are typically present and intertwined.

Most autobiographical memories include some reality and some myth. Personality psychologist Dan McAdams argues that autobiographical memories are less about facts and more about meanings (2001, 2006; McAdams & others, 2006). They provide a reconstructed, embellished telling of the past that connects the past to the present.

Retrieval of Emotional Memories

When we remember our life experiences, the memories are often wrapped in emotion. Emotion affects the encoding and storage of memories and thus shapes the details that are retrieved. The role that emotion plays in memory is of considerable interest to contemporary researchers and has echoes in public life.

Flashbulb memory is the memory of emotionally significant events that people often recall with more accuracy and vivid imagery than everyday events (Talarico, 2009). Perhaps you can remember, for example, where you were when you first heard of the terrorist attacks on the United States on September 11, 2001. An intriguing dimension of flashbulb memories is that several decades later, people often remember where they were and what was going on in their lives at the time of such an emotionally charged event. These memories seem to be part of an adaptive system that fixes in memory the details that accompany important events so that they can be interpreted at a later time.

Most people express confidence about the accuracy of their flashbulb memories. However, flashbulb memories probably are not as accurately etched in our brain as we think. One way to gauge the accuracy of flashbulb memories is to probe how consistent the details of these memories remain over time. One study found that 25 percent of participants included

flashbulb memory
The memory of emotionally significant events that people often recall with more accuracy and vivid imagery than everyday events.

Do It!

It's time to become a memory detective and explore the accuracy of your own memory for major events. Think about an event for which you might have a flashbulb memory. You might choose from a major event in recent history, such as the 9/11 attacks, Hurricane Katrina, or the Indian Ocean tsunami. Then ask yourself some easily verifiable questions about it, such as what day of the week did it happen? What time of day? What were the date and year? How many people were involved? When you have done your best to answer these questions, go to the library or go online and check out the facts. Were your memories accurate?

Many people have flashbulb memories of where they were and what they were doing when terrorists attacked the World Trade Center towers in New York City on September 11, 2001.

contradictory information in their memories of the 1986 *Challenger* space shuttle disaster (Neisser & Harsch, 1992).

Still, on the whole, flashbulb memories do seem more durable and accurate than memories of day-to-day happenings (Davidson, Cook, & Glisky, 2006). One possible explanation is that flashbulb memories are quite likely to be rehearsed in the days following the event. However, it is not just the discussion and rehearsal of information that make flashbulb memories so long-lasting. The emotions triggered by flashbulb events also figure in their durability. Although we have focused on negative news events as typical of flashbulb memories, such memories can also occur for positive events. An individual's wedding day and the birth of a child are events that may become milestones in personal history and are always remembered.

For rescuers as well as victims in natural and other disasters, memories are typically longer-lasting and more accurate than are recollections of ordinary events. Here Coast Guard Petty Officer 2nd Class Shawn Beaty of Long Island, New York, looks for survivors in the wake of Hurricane Katrina in New Orleans in August 2005.

Memory for Traumatic Events

In 1890, the American psychologist and philosopher William James said that an experience can be so emotionally arousing that it almost leaves a scar on the brain. Personal traumas are candidates for such emotionally stirring experiences.

Some psychologists argue that memories of emotionally traumatic events are accurately retained, possibly forever, in considerable detail (Langer, 1991). There is good evidence that memory for traumatic events is usually more accurate than memory for ordinary events (Berntsen & Rubin, 2006; Schooler & Eich, 2000). Consider the traumatic experience of some children who were kidnapped at gunpoint on a school bus in Chowchilla, California, in 1983 and then buried underground for 16 hours before escaping. The children had the classic signs of traumatic memory: detailed and vivid recollections.

However, when a child psychiatrist interviewed the children four to five years after the chilling episode, she noted striking errors and distortions in the memories of half of them (Terr, 1988). How can a traumatic memory be so vivid and detailed yet at the same time have inaccuracies? A number of factors can be involved. Some children might have made perceptual errors while encoding information because the episode was so shocking. Others might have distorted the information and recalled the episode as being less traumatic than it was in order to reduce their anxiety about it. Other children, in discussing the terrifying event with others, might have incorporated bits and pieces of these people's recollections of what happened.

Usually, memories of real-life traumas are more accurate and longer-lasting than memories of everyday events. Where distortion often arises is in the details of the traumatic episode. Stress-related hormones likely play a role in memories that involve personal trauma. The release of stress-related hormones, signaled by the amygdala (see Figure 6.12), likely accounts for some of the extraordinary durability and vividness of traumatic memories (Bucherelli & others, 2006).

Repressed Memories

A great deal of debate surrounds the question, can an individual forget, and later recover, memories of traumatic events (Colangelo, 2009; Geraerts & others, 2009)? *Repression* is a defense mechanism by which a person is so traumatized by an event that he or she forgets it and then forgets the act of forgetting. According to psychodynamic theory, repression's main function is to protect the individual from threatening information.

How extensively repression occurs is a controversial issue. Most studies of traumatic memory indicate that a traumatic life event such as childhood sexual abuse is very likely to be remembered. However, there is at least some evidence that childhood sexual abuse may not be remembered. Linda Williams and her colleagues have conducted a number of investigations of memories of childhood abuse (Banyard & Williams, 2007; Liang,

Williams, & Siegel, 2006; L. M. Williams, 2003, 2004). One study involved 129 women for whom hospital emergency room records indicated a childhood abuse experience (L. M. Williams, 1995). Seventeen years after the abuse incident, the researchers contacted the women and asked (among other things) whether they had ever been the victim of childhood sexual abuse. Of the 129 women, most reported remembering and never having forgotten the experience. Ten percent of the participants reported having forgotten about the abuse at least for some portion of their lives.

motivated forgetting
Forgetting that occurs when something is so painful or anxiety laden that remembering it is intolerable.

If it does exist, repression can be considered a special case of **motivated forgetting,** which occurs when individuals forget something because it is so painful or anxiety-laden that remembering is intolerable (Fujiwara, Levine, & Anderson, 2008). This type of forgetting may be a consequence of the emotional trauma experienced by victims of rape or physical abuse, war veterans, and survivors of earthquakes, plane crashes, and other terrifying events. These emotional traumas may haunt people for many years unless they can put the details out of mind. Even when people have not experienced trauma, they may use motivated forgetting to protect themselves from memories of painful, stressful, or otherwise unpleasant circumstances.

Are so-called recovered memories authentic? See Challenge Your Thinking to explore this intriguing question.

Eyewitness Testimony By now, you should realize that memory is not a perfect reflection of reality. Understanding the distortions of memory is particularly important when people are called on to report what they saw or heard in relation to a crime. Eyewitness testimonies, like other sorts of memories, may contain errors (Laney & Loftus, 2009; Nelson & others, 2009), and faulty memory in criminal matters has especially serious consequences. When eyewitness testimony is inaccurate, the wrong person might go to jail or even be put to death, or the perpetrator of the crime might not be prosecuted. Estimates are that between 2,000 and 10,000 people are wrongfully convicted each year in the United States because of faulty eyewitness testimony (Cutler & Penrod, 1995). It is important to note that witnessing a crime is often traumatic for the individual, and so this type of memory typically fits in the larger category of memory for highly emotional events.

Much of the interest in eyewitness testimony focuses on distortion, bias, and inaccuracy in memory (Laney & Loftus, 2009; Steblay & Loftus, 2009). One reason for distortion is that memory fades. In one study, people were able to identify pictures with 100 percent accuracy after a 2-hour time lapse. However, four months later they achieved an accuracy of only 57 percent; chance alone accounts for 50 percent accuracy (Shepard, 1967).

Unlike a video, memory can be altered by new information (Dysart & Lindsay, 2007). In one study, researchers showed students a film

Faulty memories complicated the search for the perpetrators in the sniper attacks that killed 10 people in the Washington, D.C., area in 2002. Police released photos of the type of white truck or van that witnesses said they saw fleeing some of the crime scenes (right). In the end, however, the suspects were driving a blue car when law enforcement officials apprehended them (above).

of an automobile accident and then asked them how fast the white sports car was going when it passed a barn (Loftus, 1975). Although there was no barn in the film, 17 percent of the students mentioned the barn in their answer.

Bias is also a factor in faulty memory (Brigham & others, 2007). Studies have shown that people of one ethnic group are less likely to recognize individual differences among people of another ethnic group (Behrman & Davey, 2001). Latino eyewitnesses, for example, may have trouble distinguishing among several Asian suspects. In one experiment, a mugging was shown on a television news program (Loftus, 1993). Immediately after, a lineup of six suspects was broadcast, and viewers were asked to phone in and identify which one of the six individuals they thought had committed the robbery. Of the 2,000 callers, more than 1,800 identified the wrong person. In addition, even though the robber was a White Euro-American, one-third of the viewers identified an African American or a Latino suspect as the criminal.

Hundreds of individuals have been harmed by witnesses who have made a mistake (Loftus, 2009; Steblay & Loftus, 2009). One estimate indicates that each year approximately 7,500 people in the United States are arrested for and wrongly convicted of serious crimes (Huff, 2002).

Faulty memory is not just about accusing the wrong person. For example, faulty memories were evident in descriptions of the suspects' vehicle in the sniper attacks that killed 10 people in the Washington, D.C., area in 2002. Witnesses reported seeing a white truck or van fleeing several of the crime scenes. It appears that a white van may have been near one of the first shootings and that media repetition of this information contaminated the memories of witnesses to later attacks, making them more likely to remember a white truck or van. When caught, the sniper suspects were driving a blue car.

Before police even arrive at a crime scene, witnesses talk among themselves, and this dialogue can contaminate memories. This is why, during the Washington, D.C., sniper attacks in 2002, law enforcement officials advised any persons who might witness the next attack immediately to write down what they had seen—even on their hands if they did not have a piece of paper.

When DNA evidence has led to freeing falsely convicted individuals, eyewitness testimony was a key piece of evidence in 75 percent of these cases.

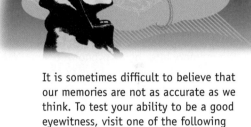

It is sometimes difficult to believe that our memories are not as accurate as we think. To test your ability to be a good eyewitness, visit one of the following websites:

http://www.pbs.org/wgbh/pages/frontline/shows/dna/

http://www.psychology.iastate.edu/faculty/gwells/theeyewitnesstest.html

Did this exercise change your opinion of the accuracy of eyewitness testimony? Explain.

self-quiz

1. The tendency to remember the items at the beginning and end of a list more easily than the items in the middle is the
   A. bookends effect.
   B. serial cues effect.
   C. serial position effect.
   D. endpoints effect.

2. Carrie prides herself on "never forgetting a face," although she frequently cannot put the correct name with a specific face. Carrie is really saying that she
   A. is better at recognition than at recall.
   B. is better at recall than at recognition.
   C. is better at memory retrieval than at memory reconstruction.
   D. is better at memory reconstruction than at memory recall.

3. Faulty memory can occur due to
   A. bias.
   B. receipt of new information.
   C. distortion.
   D. all of the above

Apply It! 4. Andrew is getting ready for a group interview for a job he really wants. The group session will take place at the beginning of the day, followed by individual interviews. When the manager who is conducting the interviews calls Andrew, he tells him that because he has not talked to any of the other candidates yet, Andrew can decide when he would like his individual interview to be. There are five candidates. Which position should Andrew take?

A. Andrew should go third because that way he will be right in the middle, and the interviewer will not be too nervous or too tired.
B. Andrew should go either first or last, to be the candidate most likely to be remembered.
C. Andrew should probably go second so that he will not be sitting around feeling nervous for too long—and besides, asking to go first might seem pushy.
D. It will not matter, so Andrew should just pick a spot randomly.

challenge your thinking

Memories: Recovered, Discovered, or False?

In 1990 a jury found George Franklin guilty of the murder of an 8-year-old girl. The murder had taken place in 1969, and the primary evidence against Franklin had been his daughter's memory of the murder, which she allegedly had repressed for over 20 years and recovered during therapy (Loftus & Ketcham, 1991). George Franklin spent nearly 7 years in prison until his conviction was overturned on appeal when it was revealed that his daughter had recovered the memory after being hypnotized, and DNA evidence proved that he could not have been the perpetrator of a second murder that his daughter also "remembered" witnessing. There is no question that George Franklin's daughter truly believed in the reality of her memories. How could she be so wrong? Can memories that seem real to the rememberer in fact be false?

Led by the research of memory expert Elizabeth Loftus, study after study has found that it is indeed possible to create false memories (Garry & Loftus, 2009; Kaasa & Loftus, 2009; Loftus, 2009). In one study, Loftus and Jacquie Pickrell (2001) persuaded people that they had met Bugs Bunny at Disneyland, even though Bugs is not a Disney character. In this study, 30 to 40 percent of participants who were simply shown a fake ad for Disneyland that included Bugs Bunny later reported remembering meeting Bugs when they had visited Disneyland. Such research has led some to question whether so-called recovered memories are ever authentic. Is there evidence that a traumatic life event might be forgotten and then recovered?

Cognitive psychologist Jonathan Schooler (2002) suggested that recovered memories are better termed *discovered memories* because, regardless of their accuracy, individuals do experience them as real. Schooler and his colleagues (1997) investigated a number of cases of discovered memories of abuse, in which they sought independent corroboration by others. They were able to identify actual cases in which the perpetrator or some third party could verify a discovered memory. For example, Frank Fitzpatrick's memory of previously "forgotten" abuse at the hands of a Catholic priest was corroborated by witnesses who had also been abused (*Commonwealth of Massachusetts v. Porter,* 1993).

The very existence of such cases suggests that it is inappropriate to reject all claims by adults that they were victims of long-forgotten childhood sexual abuse. Current consensus is still well represented by the American Psychological Association's (1995) interim report of a working group investigating memories of childhood abuse, which tentatively concludes:

1. Controversies regarding adult recollections should not be allowed to obscure the fact that child sexual abuse is a complex and pervasive problem in the United States that has historically gone unacknowledged.

2. Most people who were sexually abused as children remember all or part of what happened to them.

3. It is possible for memories of abuse that have been forgotten for a long time to be remembered, although the mechanism by which such delayed recall occurs is not currently well understood.

4. It is also possible to construct convincing false memories for events that never occurred, although the mechanism by which these false memories occur is not currently well understood.

5. There are gaps in our knowledge about the processes that lead to accurate and inaccurate recollections of childhood abuse.

What Do You Think?

- How should courts of law deal with "discovered" memories?

- How does our perspective on discovered memories affect our view of childhood abuse in general? If we cannot trust the testimony of adult survivors of abuse, how can we determine the frequency of childhood abuse today?

5 Forgetting

Human memory has its imperfections, as we have all experienced. It is not unusual for two people to argue about whether something did or did not happen, each supremely confident that his or her memory is accurate and the other person's is faulty. We all have had the frustrating experience of trying to remember the name of some person or some place but not quite being able to retrieve it. Missed appointments, misplaced keys, the failure to recall the name of a familiar face, and inability to recall your password for Internet access are everyday examples of forgetting. Why do we forget?

One of psychology's pioneers, Hermann Ebbinghaus (1850–1909), was the first person to conduct scientific research on forgetting. In 1885, he made up and memorized a list of 13 nonsense syllables and then assessed how many of them he could remember as time passed. (*Nonsense syllables* are meaningless combinations of letters that are unlikely to have been learned already, such as *zeq, xid, lek,* and *riy*.) Even just an hour later, Ebbinghaus could recall only a few of the nonsense syllables he had memorized. Figure 6.16 shows Ebbinghaus's learning curve for nonsense syllables. Based on his research, Ebbinghaus concluded that most forgetting takes place soon after we learn something.

If we forget so quickly, why put effort into learning something? Fortunately, researchers have demonstrated that forgetting is not as extensive as Ebbinghaus envisioned (Hsieh & others, 2009). Ebbinghaus studied meaningless nonsense syllables. When we memorize more meaningful material—such as poetry, history, or the content of this text—forgetting is neither so rapid nor so extensive. Following are some of the factors that influence how well we can retrieve information from long-term memory.

Hermann Ebbinghaus (1850–1909)
Ebbinghaus was the first psychologist to conduct scientific research on forgetting.

Encoding Failure

Sometimes when people say they have forgotten something, they have not really forgotten it; rather, they never encoded the information in the first place. *Encoding failure* occurs when the information was never entered into long-term memory.

As an example of encoding failure, think about what the U.S. penny looks like. In one study, researchers showed 15 versions of the penny to participants and asked them which one was correct (Nickerson & Adams, 1979). Look at the pennies in Figure 6.17 (but do not read the caption yet) and see whether you can tell which is the real penny. Most people do not do well on this task. Unless you are a coin collector, you probably have not encoded a lot of specific details about pennies. You may have encoded just enough information to distinguish them from other coins (pennies are copper-colored, dimes and nickels are silver-colored; pennies fall between the sizes of dimes and quarters).

The penny exercise illustrates that we encode and enter into long-term

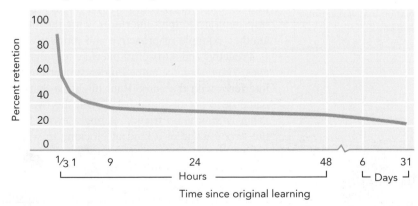

FIGURE 6.16
Ebbinghaus's Forgetting Curve The figure illustrates Ebbinghaus's conclusion that most forgetting occurs soon after we learn something.

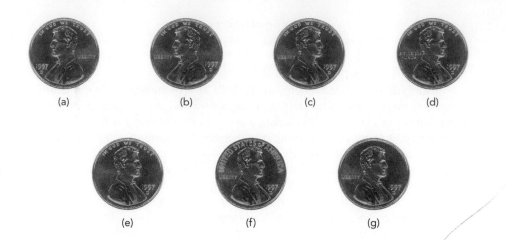

FIGURE 6.17
Which Is a Real U.S. Penny? In the original experiment, participants viewed 15 versions of pennies; only one version was an actual U.S. penny. This figure shows only 7 of the 15 versions, and as you likely can tell, the task is still very difficult. Why? By the way, the actual U.S. penny is (c).

(a)   (b)   (c)   (d)

(e)   (f)   (g)

memory only a small portion of our life experiences. In a sense, then, encoding failures really are not cases of forgetting; they are cases of not remembering.

Retrieval Failure

Problems in retrieving information from memory are clearly examples of forgetting (Del Missier & Terpini, 2009; Jaeger & others, 2009). Psychologists have theorized that the causes of retrieval failure include problems with the information in storage, the effects of time, personal reasons for remembering or forgetting, and the brain's condition (Schneider & Logan, 2009; Standing & others, 2008).

Interference   Interference is one reason that people forget (Barrouillet & Camos, 2009; Schmiedek, Li, & Lindenberger, 2009). According to **interference theory,** people forget not because memories are lost from storage but because other information gets in the way of what they want to remember.

There are two kinds of interference: proactive and retroactive. **Proactive interference** occurs when material that was learned earlier disrupts the recall of material learned later (Hedden & Yoon, 2006). Remember that *pro-* means "forward in time." For example, suppose you had a good friend 10 years ago named Prudence and that last night you met someone named Patience. You might find yourself calling your new friend Prudence because the old information (Prudence) interferes with retrieval of new information (Patience). **Retroactive interference** occurs when material learned later disrupts the retrieval of information learned earlier (Delprato, 2005). Remember that *retro-* means "backward in time." Suppose you have lately become friends with Ralph. In sending a note to your old friend Raul, you might mistakenly address it to Ralph because the new information (Ralph) interferes with the old information (Raul). Figure 6.18 depicts another example of proactive and retroactive interference.

Proactive and retroactive interference might both be explained as problems with retrieval cues. The reason the name Prudence interferes with the name Patience and the name Ralph interferes with the name Raul might be that the cue you are using to remember the one name does not distinguish between the two memories. For example, if the cue you are using is "my good friend," it might evoke both names. The result might be retrieval of the wrong name or a kind of blocking in which each name interferes with the other and neither comes to mind. Retrieval cues (such as "friend" in our example) can become overloaded, and when that happens we are likely to forget or to retrieve incorrectly.

Decay   Another possible reason for forgetting is the passage of time. According to **decay theory**, when we learn something new, a neurochemical memory trace forms, but over time this trace disintegrates. Decay theory suggests that the passage of time always increases forgetting.

interference theory
The theory that people forget not because memories are lost from storage but because other information gets in the way of what they want to remember.

retroactive interference
Situation in which material that was learned later disrupts the retrieval of information that was learned earlier.

proactive interference
Situation in which material that was learned earlier disrupts the recall of material that was learned later.

decay theory
Theory stating that when we learn something new, a neurochemical memory trace forms, but over time this trace disintegrates; suggests that the passage of time always increases forgetting.

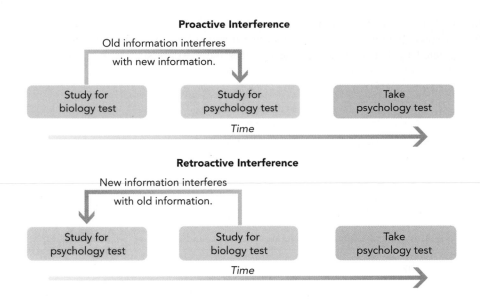

Proactive Interference

Old information interferes with new information.

| Study for biology test | Study for psychology test | Take psychology test |

Time

Retroactive Interference

New information interferes with old information.

| Study for psychology test | Study for biology test | Take psychology test |

Time

FIGURE 6.18
Proactive and Retroactive Interference
Pro- means "forward"; in proactive interference, old information has a forward influence by getting in the way of new material learned. *Retro-* means "backward"; in retroactive interference, new information has a backward influence by getting in the way of material learned earlier.

Memories often do fade with the passage of time, but decay alone cannot explain forgetting. For example, under the right retrieval conditions, we can recover memories that we seem to have forgotten. You might have forgotten the face or name of someone in your high school class, for instance, but when you return to the setting where you knew the person, you might remember. Similarly, you may not have thought about someone from your past for a very long time, but when the person "friends" you on Facebook or MySpace, you may remember a lot of prior experiences with him or her.

Many things we might think we've forgotten are just waiting for the right cues in order to pop back into our mental lives.

Tip-of-the-Tongue Phenomenon We are all familiar with the retrieval glitch called **tip-of-the-tongue (TOT) phenomenon**—a type of "effortful retrieval" that occurs when we are confident that we know something but cannot quite pull it out of memory (Hanley & Chapman, 2008). In a TOT state we usually can successfully retrieve characteristics of the word, such as the first letter and the number of syllables, but not the word itself. The TOT phenomenon arises when we can retrieve some of the desired information but not all of it (Maril, Wagner, & Schacter, 2001; Schacter, 2001).

The TOT phenomenon reveals some interesting aspects of memory. For one thing, it demonstrates that we do not store all of the information about a particular topic or experience in one way. If you have ever struggled to think of a specific word, you probably came up with various words that mean the same thing as the word you were looking for, but you still had a nagging feeling that none was quite right. Sometimes you might find the solution in an unexpected way. For example, imagine that you are doing a crossword puzzle with the clue "Colorful scarf" for a seven-letter word. You have a feeling you know this word. If you have not thought of the answer yet, say the following word aloud: *bandage.* If you were experiencing

tip-of-the-tongue (TOT) phenomenon A type of effortful retrieval that occurs when we are confident that we know something but cannot quite pull it out of memory.

"I can't remember it right now, but it's on the tips of my tongue . . ."
www.CartoonStock.com

the TOT phenomenon when doing the crossword, thinking of *bandage* might have helped you come up with the correct answer *bandana*. Although the meaning of *bandage* is unrelated to that of *bandana,* the fact that these words start with the same sounds (and therefore are linked in verbal memory) can lead you to the word *bandana* (Abrams & Rodriguez, 2005).

Prospective Memory: Remembering (or Forgetting) When to Do Something

The main focus of this chapter has been on **retrospective memory,** which is remembering the past. **Prospective memory** involves remembering information about doing something in the future; it includes memory for intentions (MacKinlay, Kliegel, & Mäntylä, 2009; Meeks & Marsh, 2009). Prospective memory includes both *timing*—when we have to do something—and *content*—what we have to do.

We can make a distinction between time-based and event-based prospective memory. *Time-based* prospective memory is our intention to engage in a given behavior after a specified amount of time has gone by, such as an intention to make a phone call to someone in one hour. In *event-based* prospective memory, we engage in the intended behavior when some external event or cue elicits it, as when we give a message to a roommate when we see her. The cues available in event-based prospective memory make it more effective than time-based prospective memory (McDaniel & Einstein, 2007).

Some failures in prospective memory are referred to as "absentmindedness." We are more absentminded when we become preoccupied with something else, are distracted by something, or are under a lot of time pressure (Matlin, 2001). Absentmindedness often involves a breakdown between attention and memory storage (Schacter, 2001). Fortunately, research has shown that our goals are encoded into memory along with the features of situations that would allow us to pursue them. Our memories, then, prepare us to recognize when a situation presents an opportunity to achieve those goals.

Researchers also have found that older adults perform worse on prospective memory tasks than younger adults do, but typically these findings are true only for artificial lab tasks (Bisiacchi, Tarantino, & Ciccola, 2008). In real life, older adults generally perform as well as younger adults in terms of prospective memory (Rendell & Craik, 2000). Generally, prospective memory failure (forgetting to do something) occurs when retrieval is a conscious, effortful (rather than automatic) process (Henry & others, 2004).

Amnesia

Recall the case of H. M. in the discussion of explicit and implicit memory. In H. M.'s surgery, the part of his brain that was responsible for laying down new memories was damaged beyond repair. The result was **amnesia,** the loss of memory. H. M. suffered from **anterograde amnesia,** a memory disorder that affects the retention of new information and events (*antero-* indicates amnesia that moves forward in time) (Levine & others, 2009). What he learned before the surgery (and thus before the onset of amnesia) was not affected. For example, H. M. could identify his friends, recall their names, and even tell stories about them—*if* he had known them before the surgery. People who met H. M. after the surgery remained strangers, even if they spent thousands of hours with him. H. M.'s postsurgical experiences were rarely encoded in his long-term memory.

Amnesia also occurs in a form known as **retrograde amnesia,** which involves memory loss for a segment of the past but not for new events (*retro-* indicates amnesia that moves back in time) (Collinson, Meyyappan, & Rosenfeld, 2009). Retrograde amnesia is much more common than anterograde amnesia and frequently occurs when the brain is assaulted by an electrical shock or a physical blow such as a head injury to a football player. In contrast to anterograde amnesia, in retrograde amnesia the forgotten information is *old*—it occurred prior to the event that caused the amnesia—and the ability to acquire new memories is not affected. Sometimes individuals have both anterograde and retrograde amnesia.

prospective memory
Remembering information about doing something in the future; includes memory for intentions.

retrospective memory
Remembering information from the past.

amnesia
The loss of memory.

anterograde amnesia
A memory disorder that affects the retention of new information and events.

retrograde amnesia
Memory loss for a segment of the past but not for new events.

1. The term for the failure of information to enter into long-term memory is
   A. rehearsal failure.
   B. encoding failure.
   C. proactive interference.
   D. retroactive interference.

2. Marco, a college freshman, is sure that he knows the name of his old Little League coach, but he cannot quite pull the name out of his memory. Marco is experiencing
   A. anterograde amnesia.
   B. retrograde amnesia.
   C. associative interference.
   D. tip-of-the-tongue phenomenon.

3. Retrospective memory involves remembering information about doing something in the _____, and prospective memory involves remembering information about doing something in the _____.
   A. past; present
   B. past; future
   C. present; future
   D. present; past

Apply It! 4. Carlos, who is fluent in Spanish, is planning a trip to Paris and decides to take a course in French. On Carlos's first French vocabulary quiz, his instructor notes that he has mixed up a lot of Spanish words with French words. Carlos cannot understand why, because he has always excelled at learning languages. What is happening to Carlos?
   A. Carlos is experiencing retroactive interference. His knowledge of Spanish is interfering with learning the new French words.
   B. Carlos is experiencing proactive interference. His knowledge of Spanish is interfering with learning the new French words.
   C. Carlos is experiencing anterograde amnesia. He seems unable to learn new words.
   D. Carlos has hit his limit on languages. He should stick to Spanish and visit Barcelona instead.

6 Tips from the Science of Memory— for Studying and for Life

How can you apply your new knowledge of memory processes to improving your academic performance—and your life? No matter what model of memory you use, you can sharpen your memory by thinking deeply about the "material" of life and connecting the information to other things you know. Perhaps the one most well-connected node or most elaborate schema to which you can relate something is the self—what you know and think about yourself. To make something meaningful and to secure its place in memory, you must make it matter to yourself.

If you think about memory as a physical event in the brain, you can see that memorizing material is like training a muscle. Repeated recruitment of sets of neurons creates the connection you want to have available not only at exam time but throughout life.

Organizing, Encoding, Rehearsing, and Retrieving Course Content

Organize Before you engage the powerful process of memory, the first step in improving your academic performance is to make sure that the information you are studying is accurate and well organized.

Tips for Organizing

■ Review your course notes routinely and catch potential errors and ambiguities early. There is no sense in memorizing inaccurate or incomplete information.

■ Organize the material in a way that will allow you to commit it to memory effectively. Arrange information, rework material, and give it a structure that will help you to remember it.

■ Experiment with different organizational techniques. One approach is to use a hierarchy such as an outline. You might create analogies (such as

Students sometimes complain about memorization, as if memorizing is not learning. Remember that how we memorize is key. Actively creating connections to new material and elaborating on it will help keep it in memory. In order to understand and critically evaluate information, you need to start with a strong foundation of knowledge. That's where memorization is key.

the earlier comparison of retrieval from long-term memory to finding a book in the library) that take advantage of your preexisting schemas.

Encode   Once you ensure that the material to be remembered is accurate and well organized, it is time to memorize. Although some types of information are encoded automatically, academic learning usually requires considerable effort (Bruning & others, 2004).

Tips for Encoding

- Pay attention. Remember that staying focused on one thing is crucial. In other words, no divided attention.

- Process information at an appropriate level. Think about the material meaningfully and process it deeply.

- Elaborate on the points to be remembered. Make associations to your life and to other aspects of the material you want to remember.

- Use imagery. Devising images to help you remember (such as the mental picture of a computer screen to help you recall the concept of working memory) allows you to "double-encode" the information.

- Understand that encoding is not simply something that you should do before a test. Rather, encode early and often. During class, while reading, or in discussing issues, take advantage of opportunities to create associations to your course material.

Rehearse   While learning material initially, relate it to your life and attend to examples that help you do so. After class, rehearse the course material over time to solidify it in memory.

Tips for Rehearsing

- Rewrite, type, or retype your notes. Some students find this exercise a good form of rehearsal.

- Talk to people about what you have learned and how it is important to real life in order to reinforce memory. You are more likely to remember information over the long term if you understand it and relate it to your world than if you just mechanically rehearse and memorize it. Rehearsal works well for information in short-term memory, but when you need to encode, store, and then retrieve information from long-term memory, it is much less efficient. Thus, for most information, understand it, give it meaning, elaborate on it, and personalize it.

- Test yourself. It is not enough to look at your notes and think, "Oh, yes, I know this." Sometimes recognition instills a false sense of knowing. If you look at a definition, and it seems so familiar that you are certain you know it, challenge yourself. What happens when you close the book and try to reconstruct the definition? Check your personal definition with the technical one in the book. How did you do?

- While reading and studying, ask yourself questions such as "What is the meaning of what I just read?" "Why is this important?" and "What is an example of the concept I just read about?" When you make a concerted effort to ask yourself questions about what you have read or about an activity in class, you expand the number of associations you make with the information you will need to retrieve later.

"Okay, here's the plan... "

www.CartoonStock.com

- Treat your brain kindly. If you are genuinely seeking to improve your memory performance, keep in mind that the brain is a physical organ. Perhaps the best way to promote effective memory storage is to make sure that your brain is able to function at maximum capacity. That means resting it, nourishing it by eating well, and keeping it free of mind-altering substances.

Retrieve   So, you have studied not just hard but deeply, elaborating on important concepts and committing lists to memory. You have slept well and eaten a nutritious breakfast, and now it is exam time. How can you best retrieve the essential information?

Tips for Retrieving

- Use retrieval cues. Sit in the same seat where you learned the material. Remember that the exam is full of questions about topics that you have thoughtfully encoded. Some of the questions on the test might help jog your memory for the answers to others.

- Sit comfortably, take a deep breath, and stay calm. Bolster your confidence by recalling that research on long-term memory has shown that material that has been committed to memory is there for a very long time—even among those who may experience a moment of panic when the test is handed out.

Naturally, one potential retrieval cue is out of the question—you have put aside your class notes.

Memory is clearly crucial for learning and academic success, but memory serves far more functions. It is the fundamental ingredient of our life stories, as we next consider.

Autobiographical Memory and the Life Story

Autobiographical memory may be one of the most important aspects of human life (N. R. Brown & others, 2009; Markowitsch, 2008). For instance, one of the many functions that autobiographical memory serves is to allow us to learn from our experiences (Pillemer, 1998). In autobiographical memory, we store the lessons we have learned from life. These memories become a resource to which we can turn when faced with life's difficulties.

Autobiographical memory also allows us to understand ourselves and provides us with a source of identity. In his studies of self-defining autobiographical memories, Jefferson Singer and his colleagues maintain that these internalized stories of personal experience serve as signs of the meaning we have created out of our life events and give our lives coherence (Baddeley & Singer, 2008; Singer & Blagov, 2004; Singer & Conway, 2008). According to Dan McAdams (2006, 2009) autobiographical memories form the core of our personal identity. A number of studies have now shown that the stories we tell about our lives have important implications. For instance, McAdams and his colleagues have demonstrated that individuals who describe important life experiences that go from bad to better (*redemptive stories*) are more *generative*—that is, they are the kind of people who make a contribution to future generations, people who leave a legacy that will outlive them (Bauer, McAdams,

Our memories are an intimate way to share a part of ourselves with others, as a grandfather does with his grandchild.

Do It!

Earlier in this chapter, you were invited to write about a self-defining memory. Pull out your description and see how it reflects the concepts of contamination and redemption. If the self-defining memory ends unhappily, think about stretching the story out further. Can you rewrite the memory so that it ends on a different note—not in a time of struggle and stress but now, as the person you are today?

& Sakaeda, 2005). These individuals are also better adjusted than those whose self-defining memories go from good to bad (labeled *contamination stories*). Clearly, the construction and reconstruction of autobiographical memory may reveal important aspects of how individuals function, grow, and discover meaning in their lives (King & Hicks, 2006).

A final function of autobiographical memory, and perhaps its most vital aspect, is its role in social bonding (Alea & Bluck, 2003; Bruce, 1989; K. Nelson, 1993). Our memories are a valuable way to share a part of ourselves with others. Sharing personal experience is a way to foster intimacy, create bonds, and deepen existing ties. When we know a person's most cherished autobiographical memory, we know that he or she is no longer just an acquaintance but clearly a friend. To the extent that social bonds are necessary for survival, it makes sense that human beings can remember and share those memories with one another and that sharing our memories is a key pathway for sharing ourselves.

Keeping Memory Sharp

As a process rooted in the brain, memory is also an indicator of brain functioning. Preserving memory is of vital importance as we age. A strong message from research on aging and memory is that, as for many things in life, the phrase "Use it or lose it" applies to memory.

Consider the case of Richard Wetherill, a retired lecturer and an uncommonly good chess player (Melton, 2005). Wetherill was so skilled that he was able to think eight moves ahead in a chess match. At one point, he noticed that he was having trouble playing chess—he could think only five moves ahead. He was sure that something was seriously wrong with him, despite his wife's assurances that she noticed no changes. A battery of cognitive tests revealed no abnormalities, and a brain scan was similarly reassuring. Two years later, Wetherill was dead, and the autopsy showed a brain ravaged by Alzheimer disease, a progressive, irreversible brain disorder that is characterized by gradual deterioration of memory, reasoning, language, and eventually physical functioning. Brain damage of this sort should indicate a person who was incapable of coherent thought. Wetherill's symptoms, however, had been limited to a small decline in his skill at playing chess.

Wetherill's case is surprising but also typical. Individuals who lead active intellectual lives seem to be protected against the mental decline generally associated with age. Indeed, research has shown that individuals who are educated, have high IQs, and remain mentally engaged in complex tasks tend to cope better with a variety of assaults to the brain, including Alzheimer disease, stroke, head injury, and even poisoning with neurotoxins (Melton, 2005). Some research has suggested that an active mental life leads to the accumulation of a "cognitive store"—an emergency stash of mental capacity that allows individuals to avoid the negative effects of harm to the brain.

Yaakov Stern found that among a group of individuals with Alzheimer disease who appeared to be equal in terms of their outward symptoms, those who were more educated were actually suffering from much worse brain damage—yet they were functioning at a level similar to others with relatively less damage (Stern & others, 1992). Stern and his colleagues (2004) have also shown that intellectual pursuits such as playing chess and reading reduce the severity of Alzheimer symptoms. Apparently, a lifetime of mental activity and engagement produces this cognitive reserve that allows the brain to maintain its ability to recruit new neural networks that compensate for damage. These brains are better able to move to a backup plan to maintain the individual's level of functioning (Andel & others, 2005). The clear message from these studies is the importance of building up a cognitive reserve by staying mentally active throughout life. In addition to educational achievement, staying physically active also seems to play a role in maintaining a sharp mind (Erickson & Kramer, 2009; Park & Reuter-Lorenz, 2009).

Before we leave the science of memory, let's consider the role of memory in shaping meaningful experiences in daily life. Think of the most meaningful event of your life. Clearly, that event is one that you remember, among *all* the things you have experienced in your life. We all have certain particularly vivid autobiographical memories that stand out as indicators of meaning, such as those studied by Jefferson Singer that we reviewed above. In fact, however, everyday life is filled with potentially remarkable moments—a beautiful sunrise, a delicious meal prepared just for you, an unexpected telephone call from an old friend. Experiencing everyday life in its richness requires us to be attentive and engaged. Sometimes the daily chores and hassles of life lead us to feel that we are just going through the motions. This sort of mindless living may be a way to survive, but it is unlikely to be a way to thrive.

The processes of attention and encoding that we have explored in this chapter suggest that actively engaging in life—investing ourselves in the events of the day (Cantor & Sanderson, 1999)—is the way we can be assured that our life stories are rich and nuanced. That way, when someone asks, "So, tell me about yourself," we have a story to tell.

self-quiz

1. To improve your performance in your courses, you must make sure the information you are studying is
   A. well organized.
   B. accurate.
   C. complete.
   D. all of the above

2. One way to improve the accuracy and efficiency of retrieval is through the use of
   A. retrieval cues.
   B. encoding cues.
   C. storage cues.
   D. none of the above

3. Factors associated with keeping a sharp mind as we age include all of the following *except*

   A. educational attainment.
   B. being physically active.
   C. engaging in comfortable, easy tasks.
   D. having a high IQ.

Apply It! 4. Albert is a retiree in his mid-60s. His wife, who is the same age, likes to read the latest novels and attend poetry readings. She also works the daily crossword puzzle in the *New York Times* and has started taking a language class. Albert thinks that she is wasting her time and that retirement should be a time of kicking back. They both worked hard in school and had great careers, so what more does she want, Albert protests. Which of the following might be a good piece of advice for Albert's wife?

   A. She should tell Albert that all of this mental activity will keep her mind sharp and that he should join her in some of her pursuits.
   B. She should probably relax more. After all, at her age, how much more can she really learn?
   C. She should leave Albert alone; he is taking retirement seriously.
   D. She should continue in her activities, but they will not have any impact on her later memory ability.

summary

① The Nature of Memory

Memory is the retention of information over time. The three processes involved in memory are encoding (getting information into storage), storage (retaining information over time), and retrieval (taking information out of storage).

② Memory Encoding

Encoding requires attention, but the attention must be selective. Memory is negatively influenced by divided attention.

According to the theory of levels of processing, information is processed on a continuum from shallow (sensory or physical features are encoded) to intermediate (labels are attached to stimuli) to deep (the meanings of stimuli and their associations with other stimuli are processed). Deeper processing produces better memory. Elaboration, the extensiveness of processing at any given level of memory encoding, improves memory. Using imagery, or mental pictures, as a context for information can improve memory.

③ Memory Storage

The Atkinson-Shiffrin theory describes memory as a three-stage process: sensory memory, short-term memory, and long-term memory.

Sensory memory holds perceptions of the world for only an instant. Visual sensory memory (iconic memory) retains information about ¼ of a second; auditory sensory memory (echoic memory) preserves information for several seconds.

Short-term memory is a limited-capacity memory system in which information is usually retained for as long as 30 seconds. Short-term memory's limitation is 7 ± 2 bits of information. Chunking and rehearsal can benefit short-term memory. Baddeley's concept of working memory characterizes short-term memory as active and complex. Working memory has three components: a central executive and two assistants (phonological loop and visuospatial working memory).

Long-term memory is a relatively permanent type of memory that holds huge amounts of information for a long time. Long-term memory has two main subtypes: explicit and implicit memory. Explicit memory is the conscious recollection of information, such as specific facts or events. Implicit memory affects behavior through prior experiences that are not consciously recollected. Explicit memory has two dimensions. One dimension includes episodic memory and semantic memory. The other dimension includes retrospective memory and prospective memory. Implicit memory is multidimensional too and includes systems for procedural memory, priming, and classical conditioning.

④ Memory Retrieval

The serial position effect is the tendency to recall items at the beginning and the end of a list better than the middle items. The primacy effect is the tendency to recall items at the beginning of the list better than the middle items. The recency effect is the tendency to remember the items at the end of a list better than the middle items.

Retrieval is easier when effective cues are present. Another factor in effective retrieval is the nature of the retrieval task. Simple recognition of previously remembered information in the presence of cues is generally easier than recall of the information.

According to the encoding specificity principle, information present at the time of encoding or learning tends to be effective as a retrieval cue, a process referred to as context-dependent memory.

Retrieval also benefits from priming, which activates particular connections or associations in memory. The tip-of-the-tongue phenomenon occurs when we cannot quite pull something out of memory.

Five special cases of retrieval are autobiographical memory, emotional memory, memory for trauma, repressed memory, and eyewitness testimony.

Autobiographical memory is a person's recollections of his or her life experiences. Autobiographical memory has three levels: life time periods, general events, and event-specific knowledge. Biographies of the self connect the past and the present to form our identity.

Emotional memories may be especially vivid and enduring. Particularly significant emotional memories, or flashbulb memories, capture emotionally profound events that people often recall accurately and vividly.

Memory for personal trauma also is usually more accurate than memory for ordinary events, but it too is subject to distortion and inaccuracy. People tend to remember the core information about a personal trauma but might distort some of the details. Personal trauma can cause individuals to repress emotionally laden information so that it is not accessible to consciousness.

Repression means forgetting a particularly troubling experience because it would be too upsetting to remember it. Eyewitness testimony may contain errors due to memory decay or bias.

⑤ Forgetting

Encoding failure is forgetting information that was never entered into long-term memory. Retrieval failure can occur for at least four reasons:

1. Interference theory stresses that we forget not because memories are lost from storage but because other information gets in the way of what we want to remember. Interference can be proactive (as occurs when material learned earlier disrupts the recall of material learned later) or retroactive (as occurs when material learned later disrupts the retrieval of information learned earlier).
2. Decay theory states that when we learn something new, a neurochemical memory trace forms, but over time this chemical trail disintegrates.
3. Motivated forgetting occurs when we want to forget something. It is common when a memory becomes painful or anxiety-laden, as in the case of emotional traumas such as rape and physical abuse.
4. Amnesia, the physiologically based loss of memory, can be anterograde, affecting the retention of new information or events; retrograde, affecting memories of the past but not memories of new events; or a combination of both.

⑥ Tips from the Science of Memory—for Studying and for Life

Effective encoding strategies when studying include paying attention and minimizing distraction, understanding the material rather than relying on rote memorization, asking yourself questions, and taking good notes. Research on memory suggests that the best way to remember course material is to relate it to many different aspects of your life.

Autobiographical memories, particularly self-defining memories, play a significant role in identity and social relationships. Our self-defining memories provide a unique source of identity, and sharing those memories with others plays a role in social bonding.

Taking on challenging cognitive tasks throughout life can stave off the effects of age on memory and lessen the effects of Alzheimer disease.

Engaging in everyday life means living memorably. Mindfulness to life events provides a rich reservoir of experiences upon which to build a storehouse of autobiographical memory.

key terms

memory, p. 190
encoding, p. 191
levels of processing, p. 191
elaboration, p. 192
storage, p. 195
Atkinson-Shiffrin theory, p. 195
sensory memory, p. 195
short-term memory, p. 196
working memory, p. 197
long-term memory, p. 198

explicit memory (declarative memory), p. 199
episodic memory, p. 200
semantic memory, p. 200
implicit memory (nondeclarative memory), p. 201
procedural memory, p. 201
priming, p. 201
schema, p. 203
script, p. 203

connectionism (parallel distributed processing: PDP), p. 203
retrieval, p. 207
serial position effect, p. 208
autobiographical memory, p. 211
flashbulb memory, p. 212
motivated forgetting, p. 214
interference theory, p. 218
proactive interference, p. 218

retroactive interference, p. 218
decay theory, p. 218
tip-of-the-tongue (TOT) phenomenon, p. 219
retrospective memory, p. 220
prospective memory, p. 220
amnesia, p. 220
anterograde amnesia, p. 220
retrograde amnesia, p. 220

self-test

Multiple Choice

1. The sensory memory for which of the following has been studied *least?*
   A. smell
   B. hearing
   C. sight
   D. walking

2. George Miller's classic paper on the phenomenon of "magical seven, plus or minus two" refers to a person's
   A. memory span.
   B. memory capacity.
   C. memory recall.
   D. memory lobe.

3. Chunking involves
   A. immediately scanning information for relevant details.
   B. elaboratively encoding information.
   C. immediately forgetting relevant information.
   D. using Miller's framework for memory retrieval.

4. After hearing a friend's telephone number for the first time, you are able to recite all seven digits in perfect order. This feat is made possible by your
   A. digit rehearsal system.
   B. performance increment capacity.
   C. number recall capacity.
   D. memory span.

5. Unrehearsed information stored in short-term memory lasts about
   A. 30 seconds.
   B. three minutes.
   C. two hours.
   D. one day.

6. Priming has been found to result in
   A. impaired explicit memories.
   B. enhanced procedural memories.
   C. enhanced retrieval of memories.
   D. impaired semantic memories.

7. An example of a hierarchical representation of information is
   A. the listings of addresses in a telephone directory.
   B. the listings of names in a telephone directory.
   C. the table of contents of your textbook.
   D. the index of your textbook.

8. People adapt quickly to the procedures and behaviors appropriate in a parade. The general knowledge of how to behave in a parade is called a
   A. script.
   B. social schema.
   C. hierarchical node.
   D. semantic reconstruction.

9. You have an important meeting with your advisor on Tuesday at 1:30, after your English class. This event is stored in your _____ memory.
   A. retrospective
   B. prospective
   C. proactive
   D. retroactive

10. In the systematic application of information from the science of memory to improving your study skills, the first step is to make sure
    A. the material you are studying is accurate.
    B. the material you are studying is relevant.
    C. the material you are studying is course-related.
    D. the material you are studying is appropriate.

Apply It!

11. Sasha loves watching a favorite drama on HBO, and she has a crush on an actor on the show. Her problem is that every time she watches the credits to find out his name, the cast information flies by too fast for her to read it. Sasha has no access to a VCR or DVR, and the show is not on DVD. Using the information about sensory memory and Sperling's classic study as a guide, devise a plan to solve Sasha's problem.

7 Thinking, Intelligence, and Language

From Alarm Clocks to Toilet Paper

So much of our everyday existence depends on the ingenious ideas of others. How did you wake up this morning? If you used an alarm clock, you owe gratitude to Levi Hutchins, who invented the device in 1787 so that he could wake up at 4 A.M. every morning. Did you make coffee? Then you might pay a moment of thanks to Melitta Bentz, the German housewife who patented the coffee filter in 1908. Did you turn on a light switch? Work on a computer? Make a phone call? Sit in an air-conditioned room? Use toilet paper? If so, a host of great minds played crucial roles in your life this morning (including Humphry Davy, Thomas Alva Edison, Stanley Mazor, Alexander Graham Bell, Willis Haviland Carrier, and Joseph Coyetty—who in 1857 invented toilet paper).

What we think of as necessities of living started out as someone else's idea. Bill Bowerman, the inventor of Nike shoes, asked, "What happens if I pour rubber over a waffle iron?" Masaru Ibuka, Sony's founder and the inspiration for the Walkman and the iPod, asked, "Why don't we remove the recording function and speaker from the portable music player and put the headphones directly on the player?" At first people ridiculed these questions and the ideas they spawned. Some Sony insiders told Ibuka that the Walkman would never sell. The doubters' skepticism aside, these dramatic inventions started with mental processes. They were physical expressions of critical thinking—of looking at the status quo, realizing that it could be improved, and devising creative solutions. ■

- ■ **What present-day inconveniences could new inventions help solve?**
- ■ **What thought processes led to inventions like Nike shoes and the Walkman?**
- ■ **What is the great idea behind your favorite everyday convenience?**

Cognitive psychology is the study of mental processes. This chapter investigates the basic cognitive processes of thinking, problem solving, reasoning, and decision making. We first define cognition and look at the cognitive revolution that led to new thinking about the workings of the human mind. We then review capacities associated with superior problem solving: critical thinking, creativity, expertise, and, perhaps most important, intelligence. We conclude by exploring the unique contribution of language to mental processes.

1 The Cognitive Revolution in Psychology

Cognitive psychologists study **cognition**—the way in which information is processed and manipulated in remembering, thinking, and knowing. Cognitive psychology is a relatively young field, scarcely more than a half-century old. We begin by tracing its history.

After the first decade of the twentieth century, behaviorism had a stranglehold on the thinking of experimental psychologists. Behaviorists such as B. F. Skinner believed that the human mind is a black box best left to philosophers, and they considered observable behavior to be psychologists' proper focus. The behaviorist perspective had little use for the mental processes occurring in that dark place between your ears.

In the 1950s psychologists' views began to change. The advent of computers provided a new way to think about the workings of the human mind. If we could "see" what computers were doing internally, maybe we could use our observations to study human mental processes, scientists reasoned. Indeed, computer science was a key motivator in the birth of the study of human cognition. The first modern computer, developed by mathematician John von Neumann in the late 1940s, showed that machines could perform logical operations. In the 1950s, researchers speculated that some mental operations might be modeled by computers, and they believed that such modeling might shed light on how the human mind works (Marcus, 2001).

Cognitive psychologists often use the computer as an analogy to help explain the relationship between cognition and the brain (Forsythe, Bernard, & Goldsmith, 2006). They describe the physical brain as the computer's hardware, and cognition as its software. Herbert Simon (1969) was among the pioneers in comparing the human mind to computer processing systems. In this analogy, the sensory and perceptual systems provide an "input channel," similar to the way data are entered into the computer

cognition
The way in which information is processed and manipulated in remembering, thinking, and knowing.

Mathematician John von Neumann (1903–1957) pioneered in the early development of computers. The fact that his computer could perform logical operations led researchers to imagine that some mental processes might be modeled by computers and that such modeling might shed light on how the human mind functions.

(Figure 7.1). As input (information) comes into the mind, mental processes, or operations, act on it, just as the computer's software acts on the data. The transformed input generates information that remains in memory much in the way a computer stores what it has worked on. Finally, the information is retrieved from memory and "printed out" or "displayed" (so to speak) as an observable response.

Computers provide a logical and concrete, but oversimplified, model of the mind's processing of information. Inanimate computers and human brains function quite differently in some respects. For example, most computers receive information from a human who has already coded the information and removed much of its ambiguity. In contrast, each brain cell, or neuron, can respond to ambiguous information transmitted through sensory receptors such as the eyes and ears.

Computers can do some things better than humans. Computers can perform complex numerical calculations much faster and more accurately than humans could ever hope to (Forouzan, 2007). Computers can also apply and follow rules more consistently and with fewer errors than humans and can represent complex mathematical patterns better than humans.

Still, the brain's extraordinary capabilities will probably not be mimicked completely by computers at any time in the near future. Attempts to use computers to process visual information or spoken language have achieved only limited success in specific situations. The human brain also has an incredible ability to learn new rules, relationships, concepts, and patterns that it can generalize to novel situations. In comparison, computers are quite limited in their ability to learn and generalize. Although a computer can improve its ability to recognize patterns or use rules of thumb to make decisions, it does not have the means to develop new learning goals.

Furthermore, the human mind is aware of itself; the computer is not. Indeed, no computer is likely to approach the richness of human consciousness (Hudson, 2009; Reder, Park, & Kieffaber, 2009).

Nonetheless, the computer's role in cognitive psychology continues to increase. An entire scientific field called **artificial intelligence (AI)** focuses on creating machines capable of performing activities that require

FIGURE 7.1

Computers and Human Cognition An analogy is commonly drawn between human cognition and the way computers work. The physical brain is analogous to a computer's hardware, and cognition is analogous to a computer's software.

Human

Input

↓

Brain, mind, cognition (memory, problem solving, reasoning, consciousness)

↓

Output

Computers

Input

↓

Hardware and software (memory, operations)

↓

Output

artificial intelligence (AI) A scientific field that focuses on creating machines capable of performing activities that require intelligence when they are done by people.

Artificial intelligence (AI) researchers are exploring frontiers that were once the context for sci-fi movie plots. Cog is a human-form robot built by the Humanoid Robotics Group at the Massachusetts Institute of Technology. The sensors and structures in Cog's AI system model human sensory and motor activity as well as perception. Cog's creators have sought to achieve humanlike functioning and interactions with people—both of which, they hope, will lead to new, humanlike learning experiences for the robot. Think about it: How might research findings from experiments such as Cog be applied to real-world situations?

intelligence when they are done by people. AI is especially helpful in tasks requiring speed, persistence, and a vast memory (Cassimatis, Murugesan, & Bignoli, 2009). AI systems also assist in diagnosing medical illnesses and prescribing treatment, examining equipment failures, evaluating loan applicants, and advising students about which courses to take (Lopes & Santos-Victor, 2007; Soltesz & Cohn, 2007). Computer scientists continue to develop computers that more closely approximate human thinking.

By the late 1950s the cognitive revolution was in full swing, and it peaked in the 1980s. The term *cognitive psychology* became a label for approaches that sought to explain observable behavior by investigating mental processes and structures that we cannot directly observe (Ashcraft & Radvansky, 2009; Sternberg, 2009). In Chapter 6, we examined the operations involved in memory. We now build on that knowledge by exploring the processes of thinking, problem solving, and decision making.

Have you ever noticed that whether it's The Sarah Connor Chronicles or 2001: A Space Odyssey, intelligent computers on TV and in the movies almost always turn out to be evil? Why do you think that fictional treatments of A.I. often portray smart computers as scary?

self-quiz

1. Behaviorists thought that psychology should properly focus on
   A. mental processes.
   B. the subconscious mind.
   C. private behavior.
   D. observable behavior.

2. The name for the scientific field that is concerned with making machines that mimic human information processing is
   A. cognitive science.
   B. cognitive neuroscience.
   C. artificial intelligence.
   D. computer science.

3. Cognition involves
   A. manipulating information.
   B. processing information.
   C. thinking.
   D. all of the above

Apply It! 4. When Demarre plays chess against his friend, he almost always wins, but when he plays against his computer, he typically loses. What is the *most likely* explanation for Demarre's experience?
   A. Computers are smarter than human beings.
   B. When playing against his friend, Demarre always cheats.
   C. When playing against his friend, Demarre is able to use his human cognitive skills to "read" his opponent's facial expressions and predict what the latter will do. These cues are missing when he plays against his computer.
   D. Demarre's computer is better than his friend at picking up on Demarre's cues and predicting what he will do next.

2 Thinking

When you save a file you have completed on a computer, you hear a sound from inside, and you know the computer is processing the work you have just done. Unlike a computer, the brain does not make noise to let us know it is working. Rather, the brain's processing is the silent operation of thinking. **Thinking** involves manipulating information mentally by forming concepts, solving problems, making decisions, and reflecting in a critical or creative manner.

In this section we probe the nature of concepts—the basic components of thinking. We then explore the cognitive processes of problem solving, reasoning, and decision making. We also examine three capacities related to enhanced problem solving: critical thinking, creativity, and expertise.

thinking
The mental process of manipulating information mentally by forming concepts, solving problems, making decisions, and reflecting critically or creatively.

Concepts

One fundamental aspect of thinking is the notion of concepts. **Concepts** are mental categories that are used to group objects, events, and characteristics. Humans have a special ability for creating categories to help us make sense of information in our world (Hemmer & Steyvers, 2009; Shea, Krug, & Tobler, 2008). We know that apples and oranges are both fruits. We know that poodles and collies are both dogs and that cockroaches and ladybugs are both insects. These items differ from one another in various ways, and yet we recognize that they belong together because we have concepts for fruits, dogs, and insects.

concept
A mental category that is used to group objects, events, and characteristics.

Concepts are important for four reasons. First, concepts allow us to generalize. If we did not have concepts, each object and event in our world would be unique and brand new to us each time we encountered it. Second, concepts allow us to associate experiences and objects. Basketball, ice hockey, and track are sports. The concept *sport* gives us a way to compare these activities. Third, concepts aid memory by making it more efficient so that we do not have to reinvent the wheel each time we come across a piece of information. Imagine having to think about how to sit in a chair every time we find ourselves in front of one. Fourth, concepts provide clues about how to react to a particular object or experience. Perhaps you have had the experience of trying an exotic new cuisine and feeling puzzled as you consider the contents of your plate. If a friend tells you reassuringly, "That's food!" you know that given the concept *food*, it is okay to dig in.

As we will see later, prototypes can also lead to mistakes, especially when they are applied to people.

One way that psychologists explain the structure of concepts is the prototype model. The **prototype model** emphasizes that when people evaluate whether a given item reflects a certain concept, they compare the item with the most typical item(s) in that category and look for a "family resemblance" with that item's properties. Birds generally fly and sing, so we know that robins and sparrows are both birds. We recognize exceptions to these properties, however—we know that a penguin is still a bird even though it does not fly or sing. The prototype model maintains that people use characteristic properties to create a representation of the average or ideal member—the prototype—for each concept. Comparing individual cases to our mental prototypes may be a good way to decide quickly whether something (or someone) fits a particular category.

prototype model
A model emphasizing that when people evaluate whether a given item reflects a certain concept, they compare the item with the most typical item(s) in that category and look for a "family resemblance" with that item's properties.

Although it has a ducklike bill and lays eggs, the platypus is nevertheless a mammal like the tiger, as platypus females produce milk with which they feed their young. The prototypical birdlike characteristics of the platypus can lead us to think mistakenly that the platypus is a bird. Its atypical properties place the platypus on the extreme of the concept of mammal.

Problem Solving

Concepts tell us *what* we think about but not *why* we think (Patalano, Wengrovitz, & Sharpes, 2009). *Why* do we bother to engage in the mental effort of thinking? Consider Levi Hutchins, the ambitious young clockmaker. *Why* did he go to the trouble of inventing the alarm clock? The reason is that he had a specific goal—he wanted to get up before sunrise every morning—yet he faced a dilemma in accomplishing that goal. **Problem solving** means finding an appropriate way to attain a goal when the goal is not readily available. Problem solving entails following several steps, overcoming mental obstacles, and developing expertise.

problem solving
The mental process of finding an appropriate way to attain a goal when the goal is not readily available.

Following the Steps in Problem Solving Psychological research points to four steps in the problem-solving process.

1. Find and Frame Problems Recognizing a problem is the first step toward a solution (Mayer, 2000). Finding and framing problems involves asking questions in creative ways and "seeing" what others do not. The positive psychology movement began, for example, because some psychologists noticed a lack of research on human strengths (Seligman, 2000).

The ability to recognize and frame a problem is difficult to learn. Furthermore, many real-world problems are ill-defined or vague and have no clear-cut solutions (Schunk, 2008). The inventors whose stories we considered at the beginning of this chapter—the visionaries who developed the microcomputer, telephone, light bulb, and toilet paper—saw problems that everyone else was content to live with. Recognizing problems involves being aware of and open to experiences (two mental habits we will examine later). It also means listening carefully to that voice in your head that occasionally sighs, "There must be a better way."

2. Develop Good Problem-Solving Strategies

Once we find a problem and clearly define it, we need to develop strategies for solving it. Among the effective strategies are subgoals, algorithms, and heuristics.

Subgoaling involves setting intermediate goals or defining intermediate problems that put us in a better position for reaching the final goal or solution. Imagine that you are writing a paper for a psychology class. What are some subgoaling strategies for approaching this task? One might be locating the right books and research journals on your chosen topic. At the same time that you are searching for the right publications, you will likely benefit from establishing some subgoals within your time frame for completing the project. If the paper is due in two months, you might set a subgoal of a first draft of the paper two weeks before it is due, another subgoal of completing your reading for the paper one month before it is due, and still another subgoal of starting your library research tomorrow. Notice that in establishing the subgoals for meeting the deadline, we worked backward. Working backward in establishing subgoals is a good strategy. You first create the subgoal that is closest to the final goal and then work backward to the subgoal that is closest to the beginning of the problem-solving effort.

Algorithms are strategies that guarantee a solution to a problem. Algorithms come in different forms, such as formulas, instructions, and the testing of all possible solutions (Bocker, Briesemeister, & Klau, 2009; Voyvodic, Petrella, & Friedman, 2009). We use algorithms in cooking (by following a recipe) and driving (by following directions to an address).

An algorithmic strategy might take a long time. Staring at a rack of letters during a game of Scrabble, for example, you might find yourself moving the tiles around and trying all possible combinations to make a high-scoring word. Instead of using an algorithm to solve your Scrabble problem, however, you might rely on some rules of thumb about words and language. **Heuristics** are such shortcut strategies or guidelines that suggest a solution to a problem but do not guarantee an answer (Cranley & others, 2009; Redondo & others, 2009). In your Scrabble game, you know that if you have a Q, you are going to need a U. If you have an X and a T, the T is probably not going to come right before the X. In this situation, heuristics allow you to be more efficient than algorithms would. In the real world, we are more likely to solve the types of problems we face by heuristics than by algorithms. Heuristics help us to narrow down the possible solutions and to find one that works.

3. Evaluate Solutions

Once we think we have solved a problem, we will not know how effective our solution is until we find out if it works. It helps to have in mind a clear criterion for the effectiveness of the solution. For example, what will your criterion be for judging the effectiveness of your solution to the psychology assignment, your psychology paper? Will you judge your solution to be effective if you simply complete the paper? If you get an A? If the instructor says that it is one of the best papers a student ever turned in on the topic?

4. Rethink and Redefine Problems and Solutions over Time

An important final step in problem solving is to rethink and redefine problems continually (Bereiter & Scardamalia, 1993). Good problem solvers tend to be more motivated than the average

subgoaling
The process of setting intermediate goals or defining intermediate problems that put us in a better position for reaching the final goal or solution.

algorithms
Strategies—including formulas, instructions, and the testing of all possible solutions—that guarantee a solution to a problem.

heuristics
Shortcut strategies or guidelines that suggest a solution to a problem but do not guarantee an answer.

We'll be coming back to heuristics later. Keep in mind that these are shortcuts in problem solving.

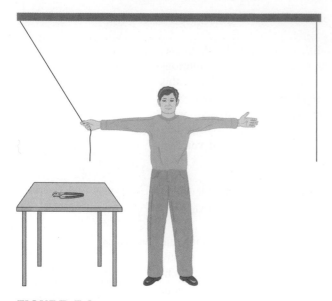

FIGURE 7.2
Maier String Problem How can you tie the two strings together if you cannot reach them both at the same time?

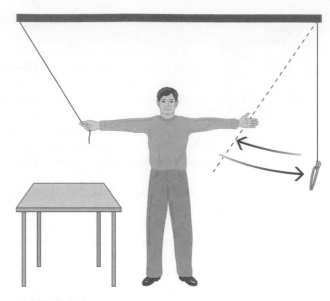

FIGURE 7.3
Solution to the Maier String Problem Use the pliers as a weight to create a pendulum motion that brings the second string closer.

person to improve on their past performances and to make original contributions. Can we make the computer faster and more powerful? Can we make the iPod Shuffle even smaller?

An Obstacle to Problem Solving: Becoming Fixated

A key ingredient of being a good problem solver is to acknowledge that one does not know everything—that one's strategies and conclusions are always open to revision. Optimal problem solving may require a certain amount of humility, or the ability to admit that one is not perfect and that there may be better ways than one's tried and true methods to solve life's problems. It is easy to fall into the trap of becoming fixated on a particular strategy for solving a problem.

fixation
Using a prior strategy and failing to look at a problem from a fresh, new perspective.

Fixation involves using a prior strategy and failing to look at a problem from a fresh, new perspective. **Functional fixedness** occurs when individuals fail to solve a problem because they are fixated on a thing's usual functions. If you have ever used a shoe to hammer a nail, you have overcome functional fixedness to solve a problem.

functional fixedness
Failing to solve a problem as a result of fixation on a thing's usual functions.

An example of a problem that requires overcoming functional fixedness is the Maier string problem, depicted in Figure 7.2 (Maier, 1931). The problem is to figure out how to tie two strings together when you must stand in one spot and cannot reach both at the same time. It seems as though you are stuck. However, there is a pair of pliers on a table. Can you solve the problem?

The solution is to use the pliers as a weight, tying them to the end of one string (Figure 7.3). Swing this string back and forth like a pendulum and grasp the stationary string. Your past experience with pliers and your fixation on their usual function makes this a difficult problem to solve. To do so, you need to find an unusual use for the pliers—in this case, as a weight to create a pendulum.

Effective problem solving often necessitates trying something new, or thinking outside the box—that is, exploring novel ways of approaching tasks and challenges and finding solutions. This might require admitting that one's past strategies were not ideal or do not readily translate to a particular situation. Students who are used to succeeding in high school by cramming for tests and relying on parental pressure to get homework done may find that in college these strategies are no longer viable ways to succeed. To explore how fixation might play a role in your own problem solving, see Figure 7.4.

Recall from Chapter 5 that multicultural experiences are one way to increase insight and creativity.

The Candle Problem

How would you mount a candle on a wall so that it won't drip wax on a table or a floor while it is burning?

The Nine-Dot Problem

Take out a piece of paper and copy the arrangement of dots shown below. Without lifting your pencil, connect the dots using only four straight lines.

The Six-Matchstick Problem

Arrange six matchsticks of equal length to make four equilateral triangles, the sides of which are one matchstick long.

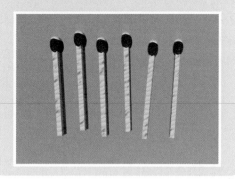

Solutions to the problems are presented at the end of the chapter on page 259.

FIGURE 7.4

Examples of How Fixation Impedes Problem Solving These tasks help psychologists measure creative problem solving.

Reasoning and Decision Making

In addition to forming concepts and solving problems, thinking includes the higher-order mental processes of reasoning and decision making. These activities require rich connections among neurons and the ability to apply judgment. The end result of this type of thinking is an evaluation, a conclusion, or a decision.

Reasoning **Reasoning** is the mental activity of transforming information to reach conclusions. Reasoning is involved in problem solving and decision making. It is also a skill closely tied to critical thinking (Kemp & Tenenbaum, 2009). Reasoning can be either inductive or deductive (Figure 7.5).

Inductive reasoning involves reasoning from specific observations to make generalizations (Tenenbaum, Griffiths, & Kemp, 2006). Inductive reasoning is in play, for example, when we form a concept about all members of a category on the basis of observing only some members. Inductive reasoning is an important way that we form beliefs about the world. For instance, having turned on your cell phone many times without having it explode, you have every reason to believe that it will not explode the next time you turn it on. From your prior experiences with the phone, you form the general belief that it is not likely to become a dangerous object.

A great deal of scientific knowledge is the product of inductive reasoning. We know, for instance, that men and women are genetically different, with women having two X chromosomes and men having an X and a Y chromosome, though no one has actually tested every single human being's chromosomes to verify this generalization. Psychological research is often inductive as well, studying a sample of participants in order to yield conclusions about the population from which the sample is drawn.

inductive reasoning
Reasoning from specific observations to make generalizations.

reasoning
The mental activity of transforming information to reach conclusions.

Imagine taking a sip of milk from a container and finding that it tastes sour. Inductive reasoning is at work when you throw out the whole container, even though you haven't tasted every drop.

Inductive Reasoning

General

Specific

Deductive Reasoning

Specific

General

FIGURE 7.5

Inductive and Deductive Reasoning

(*Left*) The upside-down pyramid represents inductive reasoning—going from specific to general. (*Right*) The right-side-up pyramid represents deductive reasoning—going from general to specific.

In contrast, **deductive reasoning** is reasoning from a general case that we know to be true to a specific instance (Demeure, Bonnefon, & Raufaste, 2009; Reverberi & others, 2009). Using deductive reasoning, we draw conclusions based on facts. For example, we might start with the general premise that all Texans love the Dallas Cowboys. Thus, if John is a Texan, we logically might surmise that John loves the Dallas Cowboys. Notice, however, that the logic of this deductive reasoning requires that the first statement be true; if all Texans do not love the Cowboys, John just might be a Philadelphia Eagles fan.

When psychologists and other scientists use theories to make predictions and then evaluate their predictions by making further observations, deductive reasoning is at work. When psychologists develop a hypothesis from a theory, they are using a form of deductive reasoning, because the hypothesis is a specific, logical extension of the general theory. If the theory is true, then the hypothesis will be true as well.

deductive reasoning Reasoning from a general case that is known to be true to a specific instance.

© Mark Parisi. Atlantic Feature Syndicate.

Decision Making

Think of all the decisions, large and small, that you have to make in life. Should you major in biology, psychology, or business? Should you go to graduate school right after college or get a job first? Should you establish yourself in a career before settling down to have a family? Do you want fries with that? **Decision making** involves evaluating alternatives and choosing among them.

Reasoning uses established rules to draw conclusions. In contrast, in decision making, such rules are not established, and we may not know the consequences of the decisions (Bongers & Djiksterhuis, 2009; Palomo & others, 2008). Some of the information might be missing, and we might not trust all of the information we have. Making decisions means weighing information and coming to some conclusion that we feel will maximize our outcome: Yes, we will be able to see the movie from this row in the theater; no, we will not run that red light to get to class on time.

decision making The mental activity of evaluating alternatives and choosing among them.

Reasoning and Decision Making Without Awareness

Cognitive psychology is about mental processes, and many of the ones we have considered so far are part of conscious awareness. There is evidence, however, that reasoning and decision making can occur outside of our awareness. That is, sometimes we can be thinking without knowing it (Dijksterhuis & Nordgren, 2006). Some very important information processing can be going on in our brain without our realizing it is happening.

No doubt you have had the experience of consciously grappling with a problem and spending a good deal of time trying to solve it, with no success. Then you take a break to listen to music or go running, and suddenly the solution pops into your head. Recent research by Ap Dijksterhuis and colleagues (2006) might ring a bell for you. In a series of laboratory studies, the experimenters gave the participants complex problems to solve after a few minutes of thought. Half of the participants, however, were distracted during the thinking period and were not permitted to concentrate consciously on the problems. The results showed that the distracted participants performed better than the individuals who were allowed to think the problems through consciously. Clearly, we sometimes solve problems without a great deal of conscious effort.

Biases and Heuristics

Another fruitful subject of decision-making research is the biases and heuristics (rules of thumb) that affect the quality of decisions. In many cases, our decision-making strategies are well adapted to deal with a variety of problems (Nisbett & Ross, 1980). Heuristics, for example, are

Confirmation bias

Description

Tendency to search for and use information that supports rather than refutes one's ideas

Example: A politician accepts news that supports his views, and dismisses evidence that runs counter to these views.

Base rate fallacy

Description

Tendency to ignore information about general principles in favor of very specific but vivid information

Example: You read a favorable expert report on a TV you are intending to buy, but you decide not to buy it when a friend tells you about a bad experience with that model.

Hindsight bias

Description

Tendency to report falsely, after the fact, that one accurately predicted an outcome

Example: You read about the results of a particular psychological study and say, "I always knew that," though in fact you have little knowledge about the issues examined in the study.

Representativeness heuristic

Description

Tendency to make judgments about group membership based on physical appearances or one's stereotype of a group rather than available base rate information

Example: The victim of a holdup, you view police photos of possible perpetrators. The suspects look very similar to you, but you choose the individual whose hair and clothing look dirtiest and most disheveled.

Availability heuristic

Description

Prediction about the probability of an event based on the ease of recalling or imagining similar events

Example: A girl from an extended family in which no family member ever attended college tells her mother that she wants to be a doctor. Her mother cannot imagine her daughter in such a career and suggests that she become a home health-care aide.

FIGURE 7.6

Decision-Making Problems: Biases and Heuristics Biases and heuristics (rules of thumb) affect the quality of many of the decisions we make.

intuitive and efficient ways of solving problems and making decisions; they are often at work when we make a decision by following a gut feeling. However, heuristics and gut feelings can lead to mistakes. Here we look at a few biases and heuristic errors, summarized in Figure 7.6.

Confirmation bias is the tendency to search for and use information that supports our ideas rather than refutes them (Cook & Smallman, 2008). Our decisions can also become further biased because we tend to seek out and listen to people whose views confirm our own while we avoid those with dissenting views. It is easy to detect the confirmation bias in the way that many people think. Consider politicians. They often accept news that supports their views and dismiss evidence that runs counter to their views. Avoiding confirmation bias means applying the same rigorous analysis to both sides of an argument.

confirmation bias
The tendency to search for and use information that supports our ideas rather than refutes them.

Hindsight bias is our tendency to report falsely, after the fact, that we accurately predicted an outcome. It is sometimes referred to as the "I knew it all along effect." With this type of bias, people tend to view events that have happened as more predictable than they were, and to represent themselves as being more accurate in their predictions than they actually were (Nestler, Blank, & von Collani, 2008). For instance, at the end of a long baseball season, fans might say they knew all along that a particular team would win the World Series. One reason for hindsight bias is that actual events are more vivid in our minds than all those things that failed to happen, an effect called the availability heuristic.

hindsight bias
The tendency to report falsely, after the fact, that we accurately predicted an outcome.

The **availability heuristic** refers to a prediction about the probability of an event based on the ease of recalling or imagining similar events (McDermott, 2009). Have you ever experienced a sudden fear of flying right after hearing about an airplane crash?

To give your hindsight bias a workout, consider: What is the worst idea you've had lately? Why did it seem like a good idea at first?

availability heuristic
A prediction about the probability of an event based on the ease of recalling or imagining similar events.

Shocking events such as plane crashes stick in our minds, making it seem as if such disasters are common. The chance of a dying in plane crash in a given year, however, is tiny (1 in 400,000) compared to the chance of dying in a car accident (1 in 6,500). Because car accidents are less newsworthy, they are less likely to catch our attention and remain in our awareness. The availability heuristic can reinforce generalizations about others in daily life. Imagine that Elvedina, a Mexican American girl, tells her mother that she wants to be a doctor. Her mother, who has never seen a Latina doctor, finds it hard to conceive of her daughter's pursuing such a career and might suggest that she try nursing instead.

Also reflective of the impact of vivid cases on decision making is the **base rate fallacy,** the tendency to ignore information about general principles in favor of very specific but vivid information. Let's say that as a prospective car buyer, you read *Consumer Reports* and find that a particular vehicle is rated exceptionally well by a panel of experts. You might still be swayed in your purchasing decision, however, if a friend tells you about her bad experiences with that car.

To experience another heuristic in action, consider the following example. Your psychology professor tells you she has assembled 100 men in the hallway outside your classroom. The group consists of 5 librarians and 95 members of the Hells Angels motorcycle club. She is going to randomly select one man into the room, and you can win $100 if you accurately guess whether he is a librarian or a Hells Angel. The man stands before you. He is in his 50s, with short graying hair, and he wears thick glasses, a button-down white shirt, a bow tie, neatly pressed slacks, and loafers. Is he a librarian or a Hells Angel? If you guessed librarian, you have just fallen victim to the representativeness heuristic.

The **representativeness heuristic** is the tendency to make judgments about group membership based on physical appearances or the match between a person and one's stereotype of a group rather than on available base rate information (Nilsson, Justin, & Olsson, 2008). In the example just described, the base rate information tells you that the man in your class is likely to be a Hells Angel 95 times out of 100. The best approach to winning the $100 might be simply to shut your eyes and guess Hells Angel, no matter what the man looks like.

The representativeness heuristic can be particularly damaging in the context of social judgments. Consider a scenario where a particular engineering corporation seeks to hire a new chief executive officer (CEO). Lori, a top-notch candidate with an undergraduate engineering degree and an MBA from an outstanding business school, applies. Because there are few women in upper management at the firm, the company's board of directors might inaccurately view Lori as unqualified—and miss the chance to hire an exceptional CEO.

Thus, heuristics help us make decisions rapidly. To solve problems accurately and make the best decisions, however, we must sometimes override these shortcuts and think more deeply, critically, and creatively.

base rate fallacy
The tendency to ignore information about general principles in favor of very specific but vivid information.

representativeness heuristic
The tendency to make judgments about group membership based on physical appearances or the match between a person and one's stereotype of a group rather than on available base rate information.

Thinking Critically and Creatively

Problem solving and decision making are basic cognitive processes that we use multiple times each day. Certain strategies lead to better solutions and choices than others, and some people are particularly good at these cognitive exercises. In this section we examine two skills associated with superior problem solving: critical thinking and creativity.

Critical Thinking   *Critical thinking* means thinking reflectively and productively and evaluating the evidence. Recall from Chapter 1 that scientists are critical thinkers. Critical thinkers grasp the deeper meaning of ideas, question assumptions, and decide for themselves what to believe or do (Campbell, Whitehead, & Finkelstein, 2009; Vacek, 2009). Critical thinking requires maintaining a sense of humility about what we know (and what we do not know). It means being motivated to see past the obvious.

Critical thinking is vital to effective problem solving. However, few schools teach students to think critically and to develop a deep understanding of concepts (Brooks & Brooks, 2001). Instead, especially in light of pressures to maximize students' scores on standardized tests, teachers concentrate on getting students to give a single correct answer in an imitative way rather than on encouraging new ideas (Bransford & others, 2006). Further, many people are inclined to stay on the surface of problems rather than to stretch their minds. The cultivation of two mental habits is essential to critical thinking: mindfulness and open-mindedness.

Mindfulness means being alert and mentally present for one's everyday activities. The mindful person maintains an active awareness of the circumstances of his or her life. According to Ellen Langer (1997, 2000, 2005), mindfulness is a key to critical thinking. Langer distinguishes mindful behavior from *mindless* behaviors—automatic activities we perform without thought.

mindfulness
The state of being alert and mentally present for one's everyday activities.

In a classic study, Langer found that people (as many as 90 percent) would mindlessly give up their place in line for a copy machine when someone asked, "Can I go first? I need to make copies" as compared to when the same person simply said, "Can I go first?" (just 60 percent) (Langer, Blank, & Chanowitz, 1978). For the mindless persons in the study, even a completely meaningless justification—after all, everyone in line was there to make copies—was reason enough to step aside. A mindless person engages in automatic behavior without careful thinking. In contrast, a mindful person is engaged with the environment, responding in a thoughtful way to various experiences.

Open-mindedness means being receptive to other ways of looking at things. People often do not even know that there is another side to an issue or evidence contrary to what they believe. Simple openness to other viewpoints can help to keep individuals from jumping to conclusions. As Socrates once said, knowing what it is you do not know is the first step to true wisdom.

open-mindedness
The state of being receptive to other ways of looking at things.

Being mindful and maintaining an open mind may be more difficult than the alternative of going through life on automatic pilot. Critical thinking is valuable, however, because it allows us to make better predictions about the future, to evaluate situations objectively, and to effect appropriate changes. In some sense, critical thinking requires courage. When we expose ourselves to a broad range of perspectives, we risk finding out that our assumptions might be wrong. When we engage our critical minds, we may discover problems, but we are also more likely to have opportunities to make positive changes.

creativity
The ability to think about something in novel and unusual ways and to devise unconventional solutions to problems.

Creative Thinking In addition to thinking critically, coming up with the best solution to a problem may involve thinking creatively. The word *creative* can apply to an activity or a person, and creativity as a process may be open even to people who do not think of themselves as creative. When we talk about **creativity** as a characteristic of a person, we are referring to the ability to think about something in novel and unusual ways and to devise unconventional solutions to problems (Abraham & Windmann, 2007; Sternberg, 2009b; T. B. Ward, 2007).

We can look at the thinking of creative people in terms of divergent and convergent thinking. **Divergent thinking** produces many solutions to the same problem. **Convergent thinking** produces the single best solution to a problem. Creative thinkers do *both* types of thinking. Divergent thinking occurs during *brainstorming,* when a group of people openly throw out a range of possible solutions to a problem,

divergent thinking
Thinking that produces many solutions to the same problem.

convergent thinking
Thinking that produces the single best solution to a problem.

To get a sense of the roles of divergent and convergent thinking in creativity, try the following exercise. First take 10 minutes and jot down all of the uses that you can think of for a cardboard box. Don't hold back—include every possibility that comes to mind. That list represents divergent thinking. Now look the list over. Which of the possible uses are most unusual or most likely to be worthwhile? That's convergent thinking.

Do you have to get into a bad mood to do well at math? Studies that link mood and thinking might lead you to think so. Researchers have examined the ways that our moods influence how we think (Blanchette & others, 2007; Moberly & Watkins, 2009). They have shown that negative moods and positive moods are related to two different styles of problem solving and decision making.

Negative moods are associated with narrow, analytical thinking (Clore, Gasper, & Garvin, 2001). People who are feeling crabby are less likely to use heuristic shortcuts (Isbell, 2004) and are more likely to think problems through carefully, reaching conclusions based on logic. What about being in a good mood? Compared to people who are in a bad

Emotion and Cognition: How Are You Feeling and Thinking Today?

mood, happy individuals tend to use more heuristics, which means sometimes making errors. Do positive moods have value for thinking?

Social psychologist Alice Isen pioneered the study of the adaptive effects of positive mood on cognition. In the early 1970s, when no one else was interested in the potential benefits of positive moods, Isen began a program of research that changed the way psychologists think about the role of positive emotional experience in thinking.

In her lab, Isen found ways to make people happy—by offering cookies, money, or showing funny movies—and she

examined the effects of positive mood on the way people think. Isen has uncovered strong evidence for the role of positive mood in creativity, originality, and efficient thinking. In a good mood, people are likely to be more cognitively flexible and to be more creative in their concept formations and structures (Compton & others, 2004; Isen, 2007a). Positive moods are related to enhanced creative problem solving (Isen, 1984, 2007b, 2008). Positive moods allow us to be better brainstormers—to come up with more ideas in response to a task and to be more open to all of the fantastic or crazy possibilities we think of (Gasper, 2004).

In contrast to previous research showing that positive moods are related to mindlessness, Isen's work (2004) revealed that a positive mood makes people more likely to engage thoughtfully with problems and to learn from new experiences. In one study, happy doctors were more likely to make the appropriate diagnosis faster than unhappy doctors (Estrada, Isen, & Young, 1997). Happy people, compared to unhappy ones, are better able to ignore unimportant information (Isen & Means, 1983).

We face such an array of choices in today's world, from the kind of orange juice we buy to the kind of college we attend. Happy moods allow us to be more efficient at settling on a satisfying choice, while unhappy moods leave us lost in thought in the juice aisle (Schwartz & others, 2002).

Try using this research on mood and cognition to study for an upcoming exam or to write a creative paper for a class. What would the best mood be for each of these activities?

even some that might seem crazy. Having a lot of possible solutions, however, still requires that they come up with the solution that is best. That is where convergent thinking comes in. Convergent thinking means taking all of those possibilities and finding the right one for the job. Convergent thinking is best when a problem has only one right answer.

Humans can think in many different ways, analyzing problems or following our gut, thinking divergently or convergently. To explore the role of our moods in these types of thinking, check out the Intersection.

Individuals who think creatively also show the following characteristics (Perkins, 1994).

- *Flexibility and playful thinking:* Creative thinkers are flexible and play with problems. This trait gives rise to the paradox that, although creativity takes hard work, the work goes more smoothly if it is taken lightly. In a way, humor greases the wheels of creativity (Goleman, Kaufman, & Ray, 1993). When you are joking around, you are more likely to consider any possibility and to ignore the inner censor who can condemn your ideas as off base.

- *Inner motivation:* Creative people often are motivated by the joy of creating. They tend to be less inspired than less creative people by grades, money, or favorable feedback from others. Thus, creative people are motivated more internally than externally.

- *Willingness to face risk:* Creative people make more mistakes than their less imaginative counterparts because they come up with more ideas and more possibilities. They win some; they lose some. Creative thinkers know that being wrong is not a failure—it simply means that they have discovered that one possible solution does not work.

- *Objective evaluation of work.* Most creative thinkers strive to evaluate their work objectively. They may use established criteria to make judgments or rely on the judgments of respected, trusted others. In this manner, they can determine whether further creative thinking will improve their work.

"Ug, this is okay, but what we really need is for you to start thinking outside the rocks."

www.CartoonStock.com

psychology in our world

Help Wanted: Critical and Creative Thinkers

It is hard to imagine any occupation where critical thinking and creativity would not be useful traits. Each year, the Great Place to Work Institute conducts a survey to identify the best workplaces in the United States, which are then announced in *Fortune* magazine. Today, the best places to work are characterized as flexible, diverse, learning-oriented, and open in communication.

In 2007, Google, the Internet search engine company, was voted the number 1 best place to work in the United States (Moskowitz & Levering, 2007). Google gets 472,771 job applicants a year. What do Google managers look for in potential employees? They seek to hire creative, brainy, and hardworking people who work well in a context that is relatively free of structure.

In both hiring decisions and the day-to-day work flow, many organizations seek creativity and thinking outside the box. Some organizations even hire consultants to help promote creative and critical thinking in managers and employees. Being a great problem solver involves not only know-how and motivation but also the capacity to meet every challenge with an open mind.

1. An example of a concept is
   A. a basketball.
   B. a daisy.
   C. a vegetable.
   D. an eagle.

2. Deductive reasoning starts at
   _____ and goes to _____.
   A. the general; the specific
   B. the specific; the general
   C. fixation; function
   D. function; fixation

3. All of the following are characteristic
   of creative thinkers *except*
   A. inner motivation.
   B. functional fixedness.
   C. objectivity.
   D. risk taking.

Apply It! 4. The students in an architecture class are given the assignment to design a new student center for their campus. They have one week to submit their first drafts. Jenny and David, two students in the class, spend the first day very differently. Jenny quickly decides on what her building will look like and starts designing it. David spends the first day doodling and devises 20 different styles he might use, including a Gothic version, a spaceship design, a blueprint with a garden growing on top, and another plan that looks like a giant elephant (the school's mascot).

When Jenny sees David's sketches, she scoffs, "You're wasting your time. We have only a week for the first draft!" On the second day, David selects his best effort and works on that one until he finishes it. Which of the following is true of these strategies?
A. Jenny is effectively using divergent thinking in her strategy.
B. David should be using heuristics given the limited time for the project.
C. Jenny is criticizing David for engaging in deductive reasoning.
D. David is using divergent thinking first and will get to convergent thinking later, while Jenny has only engaged in convergent thinking.

3 Intelligence

Like *creative,* the word *intelligent* can apply to a behavior or a person. We might say that someone who decides to quit smoking has made an intelligent choice. When we apply the word to a person, however, defining *intelligent* can be trickier.

Cultures vary in the ways they define intelligence (Sternberg & Grigorenko, 2008; Zhang & Sternberg, 2009). Most Euro-Americans think of intelligence in terms of reasoning and thinking skills, but people in Kenya consider responsible participation in family and social life an integral part of intelligence. An intelligent person in Uganda is someone who knows what to do and follows through with appropriate action. Intelligence to the Iatmul people of Papua New Guinea involves the ability to remember the names of 10,000 to 20,000 clans. The residents of the widely dispersed Caroline Islands incorporate the talent of navigating by the stars into their definition of intelligence (Figure 7.7). In the United States, we generally define **intelligence** as an all-purpose ability to do well on cognitive tasks, to solve problems, and to learn from experience.

intelligence
All-purpose ability to do well on cognitive tasks, to solve problems, and to learn from experience.

FIGURE 7.7
Iatmul and Caroline Island Intelligence The intelligence of the Iatmul people of Papua New Guinea involves the ability to remember the names of many clans. On the 680 Caroline Islands in the Pacific Ocean east of the Philippines, the intelligence of the inhabitants includes the ability to navigate by the stars.

Measuring Intelligence

Psychologists measure intelligence using tests that produce a score known as the person's *intelligence quotient (IQ)*. To understand how IQ is derived and what it means, let's first examine the criteria for a good intelligence test: validity, reliability, and standardization.

validity
The extent to which a test measures what it is intended to measure.

In the realm of testing, **validity** refers to the extent to which a test measures what it is intended to measure. If a test is supposed to measure intelligence, then it should measure intelligence, not some other characteristic, such as anxiety. One of the most important indicators of validity is the degree to which it predicts an individual's performance when that performance is assessed by other measures, or criteria, of the attribute (Neukrug & Fawcett, 2010). For example, a psychologist might validate an intelligence test by asking employers of the individuals who took the test how intelligent they are at work. The employers' perceptions would be a criterion for measuring intelligence. When the scores on a measure relate to important outcomes (such as employers' evaluations), we say the test has high *criterion validity*.

> *Test validity means that a scale measures what it says it measures. You might recall from Chapter 1 that in experiments, validity refers to the soundness of the conclusions that a researcher draws from an experiment.*

reliability
The extent to which a test yields a consistent, reproducible measure of performance.

Reliability is the extent to which a test yields a consistent, reproducible measure of performance. That is, a reliable test is one that produces the same score over time and repeated testing. Reliability and validity are related. If a test is valid, then it must be reliable, but a reliable test need not be valid. People can respond consistently on a test, but the test might not be measuring what it purports to measure.

Good intelligence tests are not only reliable and valid but also standardized (Salvia, Ysseldyke, & Bolt, 2010). **Standardization** involves developing uniform procedures for administering and scoring a test, as well as creating *norms,* or performance standards, for the test. Uniform testing procedures require that the testing environment be as similar as possible for all individuals. Norms are created by giving the test to a large group of individuals representative of the population for whom the test is intended. Norms tell us which scores are considered high, low, or average. Many tests of intelligence are designed for individuals from diverse groups. So that the tests are applicable to such different groups, many of them have norms for individuals of different ages, socioeconomic statuses, and ethnic groups (Kaplan & Saccuzzo, 2009). Figure 7.8 summarizes the criteria for test construction and evaluation.

standardization
The development of uniform procedures for administering and scoring a test and the creation of norms (performance standards) for the test.

mental age (MA)
An individual's level of mental development relative to that of others.

IQ Tests   In 1904, the French Ministry of Education asked psychologist Alfred Binet to devise a method that would determine which students did not learn effectively from regular classroom instruction. School officials wanted to reduce overcrowding by placing such students in special schools. Binet and his student Theophile Simon developed an intelligence test to meet this request. The test consisted of 30 items ranging from the ability to touch one's nose or ear on command to the ability to draw designs from memory and to define abstract concepts. To measure intelligence, Binet came up with the idea of comparing a person's mental abilities to the mental abilities that are typical for a particular age group.

Binet developed the concept of **mental age (MA),** which is an individual's level of mental development relative to that of others. Binet reasoned that a mentally retarded child would perform like a normal child of a younger age. To think about a person's level of intelligence, then, we might compare the person's mental age (MA) to his or her chronological age (CA), or age from birth. A very bright child has an MA considerably above CA; a less bright child has an MA considerably below CA.

Alfred Binet (1857–1911)
Binet constructed the first intelligence test after being asked to create a measure to determine which children would benefit from instruction in France's schools.

Validity

| Does the test measure what it purports to measure? |

Reliability

| Is test performance consistent? |

Standardization

| Are uniform procedures for administering and scoring the test used? |

FIGURE 7.8
Test Construction and Evaluation Tests are a tool for measuring important abilities such as intelligence. Good tests show high reliability and validity and are standardized so that people's scores can be compared.

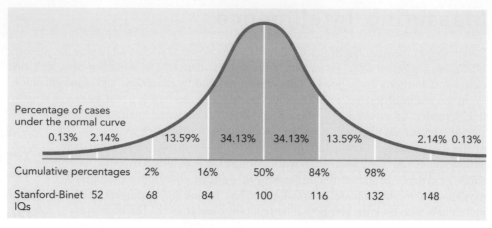

FIGURE 7.9

The Normal Curve and Stanford-Binet IQ Scores The distribution of IQ scores approximates a normal curve. Most of the population falls in the middle range of scores, between 84 and 116. Extremely high and extremely low scores are rare. Only about 1 in 50 individuals has an IQ of more than 132 or less than 68.

Percentage of cases under the normal curve

0.13%   2.14%   13.59%   34.13%   34.13%   13.59%   2.14% 0.13%

Cumulative percentages   2%   16%   50%   84%   98%

Stanford-Binet   52   68   84   100   116   132   148
IQs

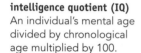

intelligence quotient (IQ) An individual's mental age divided by chronological age multiplied by 100.

The German psychologist William Stern devised the term **intelligence quotient (IQ)** in 1912. IQ consists of an individual's mental age divided by chronological age multiplied by 100:

$$IQ = (MA/CA) \times 100$$

If mental age is the same as chronological age, then the individual's IQ is 100 (average); if mental age is above chronological age, the IQ is more than 100 (above average); if mental age is below chronological age, the IQ is less than 100 (below average). For example, a 6-year-old child with a mental age of 8 has an IQ of 133, whereas a 6-year-old child with a mental age of 5 has an IQ of 83.

In childhood, mental age increases as the child ages, but once he or she reaches about age 16, the concept of mental age loses its meaning. That is why many experts today prefer to examine IQ scores in terms of how unusual a person's score is when compared to that of other adults. For this purpose, researchers and testers use standardized norms that they have identified in the many people who have been tested.

In fact, over the years, the Binet test has been given to thousands of children and adults of different ages selected at random from different parts of the United States. Administering the test to large numbers of individuals and recording the results have revealed that intelligence measured by the Binet test approximates a normal distribution (Figure 7.9). A **normal distribution** is a symmetrical, bell-shaped curve, with a majority of the scores falling in the middle of the possible range and few scores appearing toward the extremes of the range. The Stanford-Binet continues to be one of the most widely used individual tests of intelligence (Kamphaus & Kroncke, 2004).

normal distribution A symmetrical, bell-shaped curve, with a majority of the scores falling in the middle of the possible range and few scores appearing toward the extremes of the range.

Individuals from the age of 2 through adulthood take the current Stanford-Binet test (the name reflects the fact that the revisions were completed at Stanford University). It includes a wide variety of items, some requiring verbal responses, others nonverbal responses. For example, items that characterize a 6-year-old's performance on the test include the verbal ability to define at least six words, such as *orange* and *envelope,* and the nonverbal ability to trace a path through a maze. Items that reflect the average adult's intelligence include defining such words as *disproportionate* and *regard,* explaining a proverb, and comparing idleness and laziness.

Cultural Bias in Testing

Many early intelligence tests were culturally biased, favoring people who were from urban rather than rural environments, of middle rather than low socioeconomic status, and White rather than African American (Provenzo, 2002). For example, a question on an early test asked what one should do if one finds a 3-year-old child in the street. The correct answer was "call the police." However, children from inner-city families who perceive the police as scary are unlikely to choose this answer. Similarly, children from rural areas might not choose this answer if there is no police force nearby. Such questions clearly do not measure the knowledge necessary to adapt to one's environment or to be "intelligent" in an inner-city or a rural neighborhood

(Scarr, 1984). In addition, members of minority groups may not speak English or may speak nonstandard English. Consequently, they may be at a disadvantage in trying to understand verbal questions that are framed in standard English, even if the content of the test is appropriate (Cathers-Shiffman & Thompson, 2007).

The experience of Gregory Ochoa illustrates how cultural bias in intelligence tests can affect people. As a high school student, Gregory and his classmates took an IQ test. Looking at the test questions, Gregory understood only a few words because he did not speak English well and spoke Spanish at home. Several weeks later, Gregory was placed in a special class for mentally retarded students. Many of the students in the class, it turns out, had last names such as Ramirez and Gonzales. Gregory lost interest in school, dropped out, and eventually joined the navy, where he took high school courses and earned enough credits to attend college later. He graduated from San Jose City College as an honor student, continued his education, and became a professor of social work at the University of Washington in Seattle.

As a result of cases such as Gregory's, researchers have sought to develop tests that accurately reflect a person's intelligence, regardless of cultural background (Reynolds, Livingston, & Willson, 2006). **Culture-fair tests** are intelligence tests that are intended to be culturally unbiased. One type of culture-fair test includes questions that are familiar to people from all socioeconomic and ethnic backgrounds. A second type contains no verbal questions. Figure 7.10 shows a sample question from the Raven Progressive Matrices Test. Even though tests such as the Raven Progressive Matrices are designed to be culture-fair, people with more education still score higher than do those with less education.

Why is it so hard to create culture-fair tests? Just as the definition of intelligence may vary by culture, most tests of intelligence reflect what is important to the dominant culture. If tests have time limits, the test will be biased against groups not concerned with time. If languages differ, the same words might have different meanings for different language groups. Even pictures can produce bias, because some cultures have less experience with drawings and photographs (Anastasi & Urbina, 1996). Because of such difficulties, Robert Sternberg and his colleagues (Sternberg & Grigorenko, 2008; Zhang & Sternberg, 2009) conclude that there are no culture-fair tests, only *culture-reduced tests.*

Moreover, within the same culture, different groups can have different attitudes, values, and motivation, and these variations can affect their performance on intelligence tests (Ang & van Dyne, 2009; Sternberg, 2009c). Questions about railroads, furnaces, seasons of the year, distances between cities, and so on can be biased against groups who have less experience than others with these contexts. One explanation for the effects of education on IQ test scores is that education (and other environmental factors) may influence intelligence, a possibility to which we now turn.

culture-fair tests Intelligence tests that are intended to be culturally unbiased.

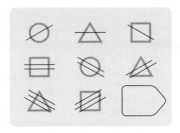
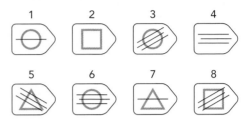

FIGURE 7.10

Sample Item from the Raven Progressive Matrices Test For this item, the respondent must choose which of the numbered figures would come next in the order. Can you explain why the right answer is number 6?

Simulated item similar to those found in the Raven's Progressive Matrices (Advanced Progressive Matrices). Copyright © 1998 NCS Pearson, Inc. Reproduced with permission. All rights reserved. "Raven's Progressive Matrices" is a trademark, in the US and/or other countries, of Pearson Education, Inc. or its affiliates.

Genetic and Environmental Influences on Intelligence

There is no doubt that genes influence intelligence (Chiang & others, 2009; Friedman & others, 2008). Researchers have found *genetic markers* (unique genetic locations) for intelligence on chromosomes 4, 6, and 22 (Plomin & Craig, 2001). Research has shown that the genetic marker on chromosome 6 is carried by approximately one-third of children with high IQs but by only one-sixth of children with average IQs (Chorney & others, 1998). So, the question with respect to genetics and intelligence is not whether genes matter but *how much* they matter to intelligence.

Scientists often use a statistic called heritability to describe the extent to which the observable differences among people in a group can be explained by the genetic differences of the group's members. **Heritability** is the proportion of observable differences in a group that can be explained by differences in the genes of the group's members. For intelligence, that means that heritability tells us how much of the differences we observe in intelligence is attributable to differences in genes. Because heritability is a proportion, the highest degree of heritability is 100 percent. A committee of respected researchers convened by the American Psychological Association concluded that by late adolescence, the heritability of intelligence is about 75 percent, a finding that reflects a strong genetic influence (Neisser & others, 1996). Researchers have found that the heritability of intelligence increases with age (from as low as 35 percent in childhood to as high as 75 percent in adulthood) (McGue & others, 1993).

Why might hereditary influences on intelligence increase with age? Possibly, as we grow older, our interactions with the environment are shaped less by the influence of others and more by our ability to choose environments that allow the expression of genetic tendencies we have inherited (Neisser & others, 1996). For example, parents might push their child into an environment that is incompatible with the child's genetic inheritance (pressuring the child to become a doctor or an engineer, for example), but as an adult, the son or daughter might choose to follow his or her own personal interests (say, becoming a sculptor or a hardware store owner).

As you consider this discussion of genetic influences on intelligence, you might find yourself reflecting on some of the less than brilliant things your parents have done over the years and feeling a bit discouraged. If IQ is heritable, is there any hope? The heritability statistic has certainly been an important way for researchers to gauge the influence of genetics on psychological characteristics including intelligence, but we must understand this statistic for what it can and cannot tell us about intelligence or any characteristic. First and most important, heritability is a statistic that provides information about a group, not a single individual (Sesardic, 2006). That means that finding out that heritability for intelligence is 75 percent tells us nothing at all about the source of an individual person's intelligence. We cannot dissect your intelligence and determine that you got 75 percent of it from your parents and 25 percent from your schooling. Heritability has no meaning when applied to a single case.

Also, heritability estimates can change over time and across different groups (Turkheimer & others, 2003). If a group of individuals lives in the same advantageous setting (with good nutrition, supportive parents, great schools, stable neighborhoods, and plenty of opportunities), heritability estimates for intelligence might be quite high, as this optimal environment allows genetic characteristics to flourish to their highest potential. However, if a group of individuals lives in a highly variable environment (with some individuals experiencing rich, nurturing environments full of opportunity and others experiencing less supportive contexts), genetic characteristics may be less predictive of differences in intelligence in that group, relative to environmental factors.

Even if the heritability of a characteristic is very high, the environment still matters. Take height, for example. More than 90 percent of the variation in height is explained by genetic variation. Humans continue to get taller and taller, however, and this trend demonstrates that environmental factors such as nutrition have an impact. Similarly, in the case of intelligence, most researchers agree that for most people, modifications in environment can change their IQ scores considerably (F. A. Campbell, 2006; Ramey, Ramey, & Lanzi, 2006; Rutter, 2007a). Enriching an environment can improve school achievement and develop crucial workplace skills. Children who come from impoverished socioeconomic backgrounds who are adopted into more economically advantaged families often have IQs that are higher then their biological parents (Sternberg, Grigorenko, & Kidd, 2005). Although genetics may influence intellectual ability, environmental factors and opportunities make a difference (Sternberg & Grigorenko, 2008).

Researchers are increasingly interested in manipulating the early environment of children who are at risk for impoverished intelligence (Ramey, Ramey, & Lanzi, 2006). Programs that educate parents to be more sensitive caregivers and that train them to be

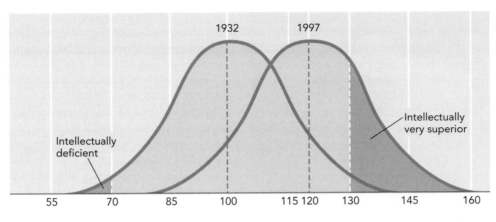

better teachers can make a difference in a child's intellectual development, as can support services such as high-quality child-care programs (Sameroff, 2006).

One effect of education on intelligence is evident in rapidly increasing IQ test scores around the world, a phenomenon called the *Flynn effect* (Flynn, 1999, 2006). Scores on these tests have been rising so fast that a high percentage of people regarded as having average intelligence at the turn of century would be regarded as having below average intelligence today (Figure 7.11). Because the increase has taken place in a relatively short period of time, it cannot be due to heredity but rather may be due to rising levels of education attained by a much greater percentage of the world's population or to other environmental factors, such as the explosion of information to which people are now exposed.

Environmental influences are complex (Bronfenbrenner & Morris, 2006). Growing up with all the advantages does not guarantee success. Children from wealthy families may have easy access to excellent schools, books, tutors, and travel, but they may take such opportunities for granted and not be motivated to learn and to achieve. Alternatively, poor or disadvantaged children may be highly motivated and successful. Caregivers who themselves lacked educational opportunities may instill a strong sense of the value of learning and achievement in their children. Oprah Winfrey, the offspring of an unwed teenage couple, was reared in the inner city by her grandmother, who instilled in her a love of reading and a strong belief that she had the ability to do great things.

Let's return for a moment to the idea that the word *intelligent* describes not only people but also behaviors. Mastering skills, thinking about life actively, and making life decisions thoughtfully are intelligent behaviors that people can engage in regardless of the numerical intelligence quotient on their permanent record. Intelligent behavior is always an option, no matter one's IQ score. As we saw in Chapter 5, our beliefs about cognitive ability, specifically whether it is fixed or changeable, have important implications for the goals we set for learning new skills (Dweck, 2006). We never know what we might accomplish if we try, and no one is doomed because of a number, no matter how powerful that number may seem.

Extremes of Intelligence

Intelligence, then, appears to emerge from a combination of genetic heritage and environmental factors. As we have seen, scores on IQ tests generally conform to the bell-shaped normal curve. We now examine the implications of falling on either tail of that curve.

Many different intelligence tests are available online, such as at http://www.iqtest.com/ Give this one a try and then do a web search for intelligence tests and see if you get the same results when you take a different test. Do the websites tell you how reliable the tests are? Do they provide information on standardization or validity? If your scores on the two tests are very different, what might account for this difference?

Olympic speed skating gold medalist Joey Cheek well illustrates giftedness. Beyond his accomplishments on the ice, he is studying economics and Chinese at Princeton University and is co-founder of Team Darfur, an organization dedicated to raising awareness of human rights abuses in Sudan.

Giftedness There are people whose abilities and accomplishments outshine those of others—the *A*+ student, the star athlete, the natural musician. People who are **gifted** have high intelligence (an IQ of 130 or higher) and/or superior talent in a particular area. Lewis Terman (1925) conducted a study of 1,500 children whose Stanford-Binet IQs averaged 150, a score that placed them in the top 1 percent. A popular myth is that gifted children are maladjusted, but Terman found that his participants (the "Termites") were not only academically gifted but also socially well adjusted. Many of them later became successful doctors, lawyers, professors, and scientists. Do gifted children grow into gifted and highly creative adults? In Terman's research, gifted children typically did become experts in a well-established domain, such as medicine, law, or business; but the Termites did not become major creators or innovators (Winner, 2000, 2006).

gifted
Possessing high intelligence (an IQ of 130 or higher) and/or superior talent in a particular area.

In light of the sweeping social and economic changes of the information age, are today's gifted children perhaps better able than the Termites to use their gifts in innovative and important ways in adulthood? The results from a longitudinal study of profoundly gifted children begun by Julian Stanley at Johns Hopkins University in 1971 seem to indicate just that. The Study of Mathematically Precocious Youth includes 320 participants whom researchers recruited before age 13 based on IQ scores, with the group's average IQ estimated at 180. This group is said to represent the top 1 in 10,000 IQ scores (Lubinski & others, 2001). Following up on these individuals in their 20s, David Lubinski and colleagues (2006) found that these strikingly gifted young people were doing remarkable things. At age 23, they were pursuing doctoral degrees at a rate 50 times higher than the average. Some reported achievements such as receiving creative writing awards, creating original art and music, publishing in scholarly journals, and developing commercially viable software and video games. Thus, unlike the Termites, this group has been quite creative and innovative (Wai, Lubinski, & Benbow, 2005).

Like intelligence itself, giftedness is likely a product of both heredity and environment. Experts who study giftedness point out that gifted individuals recall showing signs of high ability in a particular area at a very young age, prior to or at the beginning of formal training (Howe & others, 1995). This result suggests the importance of innate ability in giftedness. However, researchers also have found that the individuals who enjoy world-class status in the arts, mathematics, science, and sports all report strong family support and years of training and practice (Bloom, 1985). Deliberate practice is an important characteristic of individuals who become experts in a particular domain (Grigorenko & others, 2009).

An increasing number of experts argue that typical U.S. classrooms often do not meet the educational needs of gifted children (Karnes & Stephens, 2008; Sternberg, 2009e). Some educators conclude that the problem of inadequate education of gifted adolescents has been compounded by the federal government's No Child Left Behind policy, which seeks to raise the achievement level of students who are not doing well in school at the expense of enriching the education of gifted children (Clark, 2008; Cloud, 2008). Ellen Winner (1996, 2006) recommends that when children and adolescents are underchallenged,

This is a serious policy question in the United States. What's your opinion? Should resources be spent mostly to bring everyone up to a level of proficiency, or should public schools focus on enhancing the education of those who are gifted? How much money would you be willing to pay in taxes every year to accomplish both?

they be allowed to attend advanced classes in their domain of exceptional ability, as did Bill Gates, Microsoft's founder, who took college math classes at 13, and famed cellist Yo-Yo Ma, who graduated from high school at 15 and then attended the Juilliard School of Music.

Mental Retardation

Just as some individuals are at the high extreme of intelligence, others are at the lower end. **Mental retardation,** more recently termed *intellectual disability,* is a condition of limited mental ability in which an individual has a low IQ, usually below 70 on a traditional intelligence test, and has difficulty adapting to everyday life; he or she would have exhibited these characteristics by age 18. In the United States, about 5 million people fit this definition of mental retardation. Note that for a person to be described as mentally retarded, low IQ and low adaptiveness are evident in childhood. We do not usually think of a college student who suffers massive brain damage in a car accident, resulting in an IQ of 60, as mentally retarded.

Individuals with Down syndrome may excel in sensitivity toward others. The possibility that other strengths or intelligences coexist with cognitive ability (or disability) has led some psychologists to propose the need for expanding the concept of intelligence.

Mental retardation may have an organic cause, or it may be social and cultural in origin (Hallahan, Kauffman, & Pullen, 2009). *Organic retardation* is mental retardation caused by a genetic disorder or by brain damage; *organic* refers to the tissues or organs of the body, so there is some physical damage in organic retardation. Down syndrome, one form of organic mental retardation, occurs when an extra chromosome is present in the individual's genetic makeup. Most people who suffer from organic retardation have IQs between 0 and 50.

Cultural-familial retardation is a mental deficit with no evidence of organic brain damage. Individuals with this type of retardation have IQs between 55 and 70. Psychologists suspect that such mental deficits result at least in part from growing up in a below-average intellectual environment. As children, individuals with familial retardation can be identified in school, where they often fail, need tangible rewards (candy rather than grades, for example), and are highly sensitive to what peers and adults expect of them (Vaughn, Bos, & Schumm, 2003). However, as adults, these individuals usually go unnoticed, perhaps because adult settings do not tax their cognitive skills as much. It may also be that the intelligence of such individuals increases as they move toward adulthood.

There are several classifications of mental retardation. In one classification system, retardation ranges from mild, to moderate, to severe or profound (Hallahan, Kauffman, & Pullen, 2009). The large majority of individuals diagnosed with mental retardation fall in the mild category. Most school systems still use this system. However, because these categories are based on IQ ranges, they are not perfect predictors of functioning. Indeed, it is not unusual to find clear *functional* differences between two people who have the same low IQ. For example, looking at two individuals with a similarly low IQ, we might find that one of them is married, employed, and involved in the community and the other requires constant supervision in an institution. Such differences in social competence have led psychologists to include deficits in adaptive behavior in their definition of mental retardation (Hallahan, Kauffman, & Pullen, 2009). The American Association on Mental Retardation (1992) has developed a different classification based on the degree of support required for a person with mental retardation to function at the highest level; these categories of support are *intermittent, limited, extensive,* and *pervasive.* These categories reflect not IQ but rather what the individual is capable of accomplishing and how much help he or she needs to negotiate life.

A person with Down syndrome may never accomplish the amazing academic feats of gifted individuals. However, he or she may be capable of building close, warm relations with others, serving as an inspiration to loved ones, and bringing smiles into an otherwise gloomy day (Van Riper, 2007). Individuals with Down syndrome moreover might possess different kinds of intelligence, even if they are low on general cognitive ability. The possibility that other intelligences exist alongside cognitive ability (or disability) has inspired some psychologists to suggest that we need more than one concept of intelligence.

Theories of Multiple Intelligences

Is it more appropriate to think of an individual's intelligence as a general ability or as a number of specific abilities? Traditionally, most psychologists have viewed intelligence as a general, all-purpose problem-solving ability, sometimes referred to as "g," first discovered and named by Charles Spearman (1904). Others have proposed that we think about different kinds of intelligence, such as *emotional intelligence,* the ability to perceive emotions in ourselves and others accurately (Mayer, Salovey, & Caruso, 2008). Robert Sternberg and Howard Gardner have developed influential theories presenting the viewpoint that there are *multiple intelligences.*

Sternberg's Triarchic Theory and Gardner's Multiple Intelligences

triarchic theory of intelligence
Sternberg's theory that intelligence comes in three forms: analytical, creative, and practical.

Robert J. Sternberg (1986, 2004, 2008, 2009, 2009b, 2009c, 2009d) developed the **triarchic theory of intelligence,** which says that intelligence comes in multiple (specifically, three) forms. These forms are

Analytical intelligence: The ability to analyze, judge, evaluate, compare, and contrast.

Creative intelligence: The ability to create, design, invent, originate, and imagine.

Practical intelligence: The ability to use, apply, implement, and put ideas into practice.

Howard Gardner (1983, 1993, 2002) suggests there are nine types of intelligence, or "frames of mind." These are described here, with examples of the types of vocations in which they are reflected as strengths (Campbell, Campbell, & Dickinson, 2004):

Verbal: The ability to think in words and use language to express meaning. Occupations: author, journalist, speaker.

Mathematical: The ability to carry out mathematical operations. Occupations: scientist, engineer, accountant.

Spatial: The ability to think three-dimensionally. Occupations: architect, artist, sailor.

Bodily-kinesthetic: The ability to manipulate objects and to be physically adept. Occupations: surgeon, craftsperson, dancer, athlete.

Musical: The ability to be sensitive to pitch, melody, rhythm, and tone. Occupations: composer, musician

Interpersonal: The ability to understand and interact effectively with others. Occupations: teacher, mental health professional.

Intrapersonal: The ability to understand oneself. Occupations: theologian, psychologist.

Naturalist: The ability to observe patterns in nature and understand natural and human-made systems. Occupations: farmer, botanist, ecologist, landscaper.

Existentialist: The ability to grapple with the big questions of human existence, such as the meaning of life and death, with special sensitivity to issues of spirituality. Gardner has not identified an occupation for existential intelligence, but one career path would likely be philosopher.

Do you know some people you might call "book smart" and others you think of as "people smart"? Which kinds of intelligence do they show?

According to Gardner, everyone has all of these intelligences to varying degrees. As a result, we prefer to learn and process information in different ways. People learn best when they can do so in a way that uses their stronger intelligences.

Evaluating the Approaches of Multiple Intelligences

Sternberg's and Gardner's approaches have stimulated teachers to think broadly about what makes up children's competencies. They have motivated educators to develop programs that instruct students in multiple domains. These theories have also contributed to interest in assessing intelligence and classroom learning in innovative ways, such as by evaluating student portfolios (May, 2006; Robinson, Shore, & Enerson, 2007).

Doubts about multiple-intelligences approaches persist, however. A number of psychologists think that the proponents of multiple intelligences have taken the concept of specific intelligences too far (Reeve & Charles, 2008). Some critics argue that a research base to support the three intelligences of Sternberg or the nine intelligences of Gardner has not yet emerged. One expert on intelligence, Nathan Brody (2007), observes that people who excel at one type of intellectual task are likely to excel in others. Thus, individuals who do well at memorizing lists of digits are also likely to be good at solving verbal problems and spatial layout problems. Other critics ask, if musical skill, for example, reflects a distinct type of intelligence, why not also label the skills of outstanding chess players, prize fighters, painters, and poets as types of intelligence? In sum, controversy still characterizes whether it is more accurate to conceptualize intelligence as a general ability, specific abilities, or both (Brody, 2007; Sternberg, 2009, 2009b, 2009c).

Our examination of cognitive abilities has highlighted how individuals differ in the quality of their thinking and how thoughts may differ from one another. Some thoughts reflect critical thinking, creativity, or intelligence. Other thoughts are perhaps less inspired. One thing thoughts have in common is that they often involve language. Even when we talk to ourselves, we do so with words. The central role of language in cognitive activity is the topic to which we now turn.

4 Language

Language is a form of communication, whether spoken, written, or signed, that is based on a system of symbols. We need language to speak with others, listen to others, read, and write (Berko Gleason, 2009). Language is not just how we speak to others but how we talk to ourselves. Consider an occasion, for example, when you have experienced the feeling of a guilty conscience, of having done something you should not have. That little voice in your head that clamors, "You shouldn't have done that! *Why* did you do it?" speaks to you in your mother tongue. In this section we first examine the fundamental characteristics of language and then trace the links between language and cognition.

language
A form of communication, whether spoken, written, or signed, that is based on a system of symbols.

The Basic Properties of Language

All human languages have **infinite generativity,** the ability to produce an endless number of meaningful sentences. This superb flexibility comes from five basic rule systems:

infinite generativity
The ability of language to produce an endless number of meaningful sentences.

phonology
A language's sound system.

- ■ **Phonology:** a language's sound system. Language is made up of basic sounds, or *phonemes.* Phonological rules ensure that certain sound sequences occur (for example, *sp, ba,* or *ar*) and others do not (for example, *zx* or *qp*) (Menn & Stoel-Gammon, 2009). A good example of a phoneme in the English language is /k/, the sound represented by the letter *k* in the word *ski* and the letter *c* in the word *cat*. Although the /k/ sound is slightly different in these two words, the /k/ sound is described as a single phoneme in English.

morphology
A language's rules for word formation.

- **Morphology:** a language's rules for word formation. Every word in the English language is made up of one or more morphemes. A morpheme is the smallest unit of language that carries meaning. Some words consist of a single morpheme—for example, *help*. Others are made up of more than one; for example, *helper* has two morphemes, *help + er*. The morpheme *-er* means "one who"—in this case, "one who helps." As you can see, not all morphemes are words; for example, *pre-, -tion,* and *-ing* are morphemes. Just as the rules that govern phonemes ensure that certain sound sequences occur, the rules that govern morphemes ensure that certain strings of sounds occur in particular sequences.

syntax
A language's rules for combining words to form acceptable phrases and sentences.

- **Syntax:** a language's rules for combining words to form acceptable phrases and sentences (Tager-Flusberg & Zukowski, 2009). If someone says, "John kissed Emily" or "Emily was kissed by John," you know who did the kissing and who was kissed in each case because you share that person's understanding of sentence structure. You also understand that the sentence "You didn't stay, did you?" is a grammatical sentence but that "You didn't stay, didn't you?" is unacceptable.

semantics
The meaning of words and sentences in a particular language.

- **Semantics:** the meaning of words and sentences in a particular language. Every word has a unique set of semantic features (Pan & Uccelli, 2009). *Girl* and *woman,* for example, share many semantic features (for instance, both signify female human beings), but they differ semantically in regard to age. Words have semantic restrictions on how they can be used in sentences. The sentence "The bicycle talked the boy into buying a candy bar" is syntactically correct but semantically incorrect. The sentence violates our semantic knowledge that bicycles do not talk.

pragmatics
The useful character of language and the ability of language to communicate even more meaning than is said.

- **Pragmatics:** the useful character of language and the ability of language to communicate even more meaning than is said (Bryant, 2009). The pragmatic aspect of language allows us to use words to get the things we want. If you ever find yourself in a country in which you know only a little of the language, you will certainly take advantage of pragmatics. Wandering the streets of, say, Madrid, you might approach a stranger and ask, simply, "Autobus?" (the Spanish word for *bus*). You know that given your inflection and perhaps your desperate facial expression, the person will understand that you are looking for the bus stop.

With this basic understanding of language in place, we can examine the connections between language and cognition.

Language and Cognition

Language is a vast system of symbols capable of expressing most thoughts. Language is the vehicle for communicating most of our thoughts to one another. Although we do not always think in words, our thinking would be greatly impoverished without words.

The connection between language and thought has been of considerable interest to psychologists. Some have even argued that we cannot think without language. This proposition has produced heated controversy. Is thought dependent on language, or is language dependent on thought?

The Role of Language in Cognition

Recall from Chapter 6 that memory is stored not only in the form of sounds and images but also in words. Language helps us think, make inferences, tackle difficult decisions, and solve problems (Horst & others, 2009). Language is a tool for representing ideas (Kovacs, 2009).

Today, most psychologists would accept these points. However, linguist Benjamin Whorf (1956) went a step further: He argued that language determines the way we think, a view that has been called the *linguistic relativity hypothesis*. Whorf and his student Edward Sapir were specialists in Native American languages, and they were fascinated by the possibility that people might perceive the world differently as the result of the different languages they speak. The Inuit people in Alaska, for instance, have a dozen or more words to describe the various textures, colors, and physical states of snow. In contrast, English has relatively few words

Think of all the words we have in our society for coffee drinks. What might this say about our society?

Whorf's view is that our cultural experiences with a particular concept shape a catalog of names that can be either rich or poor. Consider how rich your mental library of names for camel might be if you had extensive experience with camels in a desert world, and how poor your mental library of names for snow might be if you lived in a tropical world of palm trees and parrots. Despite its intriguing appeal, Whorf's view is controversial, and many psychologists do not believe it plays a pivotal role in shaping thought.

to describe snow, and thus, according to Whorf's view, English speakers *cannot see* the different kinds of snow because they have no words for them.

Whorf's bold claim appealed to many scholars. Some even tried to apply Whorf's view to gender differences in color perception. Asked to describe the colors of two sweaters, a woman might say, "One is mauve and the other is magenta," while a man might say, "They're both pink." Whorf's view of the influence of language on perceptual ability might suggest that women are able to see more colors than men simply because they have a richer color vocabulary (Hepting & Solle, 1973). It turns out, however, that men can learn to discriminate among the various hues that women use, and this outcome suggests that Whorf's view is not quite accurate.

Indeed, critics of Whorf's ideas say that words merely reflect, rather than cause, the way we think. The Inuits' adaptability and livelihood in Alaska depend on their capacity to recognize various conditions of snow and ice. A skier or snowboarder who is not Inuit might also know numerous words for snow, far more than the average person, and a person who does not know the words for the different types of snow might still be able to perceive these differences.

Interestingly, research has shown that Whorf might have been accurate for information that is presented to the left hemisphere of the brain. That is, when colors were presented in the right visual field (and therefore went to the left brain), having names for the colors enhanced perception of and discrimination between those colors (Gilbert & others, 2006).

Although research has not supported Whorf's view with regard to gender differences in vocabulary, is it true that men and women do not differ linguistically in other ways? To explore this question, read Challenge Your Thinking.

Although the strongest form of Whorf's hypothesis—that language determines perception—seems doubtful, research has continued to demonstrate the influence of language on how we think, even about something as fundamental as our own personalities. For example, in a series of studies, researchers interviewed bilingual individuals (that is, people who fluently speak two languages, in this case Spanish and English) (Ramirez-Esparza & others, 2006). Each person rated his or her own personality characteristics,

challenge your thinking

Does Gender Influence Language?

Common stereotypes suggest that women are the talkative sex. The best-seller *The Female Brain* by Louann Brizendine (2006) claims that women talk three times as much as men. Brizendine suggests that women's brains are wired from birth to be extraordinarily sensitive to social information. Women, she says, have an "eight-lane superhighway" for processing emotion, whereas men have only "a single country road."

The notion that men are somehow missing out on an emotional expressway is also reflected in the *extreme male brain theory* of autism. Recall from Chapter 4 that autism is a disorder in which individuals have particular difficulty processing social information. Simon Baron-Cohen (2002, 2003, 2008; Baron-Cohen, Knickmeyer, & Belmonte, 2006) has suggested that characteristics associated with autism might be considered simply extreme forms of the "male brain" (that is, one that is well suited to math and spatial reasoning but less well geared to verbal and social skills). This controversial notion certainly shows that people seem to be prone to extreme positions and stereotypes when discussing gender differences.

Recent research challenges the idea that women are the talkers of the world. Matthias Mehl and his colleagues (Mehl & others, 2007) examined this notion in an innovative way. Nearly 400 male and female college students wore a device that recorded them for a few minutes every 12½ minutes as they went about their daily routines. The device allowed the researchers to count how much each participant spoke in the

course of the day. The results of the study showed that women uttered slightly more than 16,000 words a day. And men? They spoke slightly less than 16,000 words a day. No significant difference emerged. Interestingly, the biggest talkers in the study (averaging 47,000 words per day) were all men. So was the quietest person in the study, speaking just 700 words per day.

The sheer number of best-selling books about gender differences highlights our fascination with male–female contrasts. Boys, men, girls, and women live in a social world that poses different expectations and different challenges. It is easy to think of male–female differences as rooted exclusively in the biological differences of sex. A more realistic and balanced viewpoint might acknowledge that men and women are, after all, human beings and that working out our conflicts with the other sex is about negotiating common human needs rather than simply living with biologically programmed characteristics.

What Do You Think?

- Is research on gender differences in language ability potentially damaging to men or women? Why?

- Why are gender differences so fascinating to people in general?

- Who are the biggest talkers you know? Do they have any characteristics (aside from gender) in common?

once in Spanish and once in English. Across all studies, and regardless of whether the individuals lived in a Spanish-speaking or an English-speaking country, respondents reported themselves as more outgoing, nicer, and more responsible when responding to the survey in English.

The Role of Cognition in Language

Clearly, then, language can influence cognition. Researchers also study the possibility that cognition is an important foundation for language (Bohannon & Bonvillian, 2009). If language is a reflection of cognition in general, we would expect to find a close link between language ability and general intellectual ability. In particular, we would expect to find that problems in cognition are paralleled by problems in language. We would anticipate, for example, that general mental retardation is accompanied by lowered language abilities.

It is often but not always the case that individuals with mental retardation have a reduced language proficiency. For instance, individuals with Williams syndrome, a genetic disorder that affects about 1 in 20,000 births, tend to show extraordinary verbal, social, and musical abilities while having an extremely low IQ and difficulty with motor tasks and numbers. Williams syndrome demonstrates that mental retardation is not always accompanied by poor language skills.

In summary, although thought influences language and language influences thought, there is increasing evidence that language and thought are not part of a single system. Instead, they seem to have evolved as separate but related components of the mind.

Note the deductive reasoning in this paragraph.

Biological and Environmental Influences on Language

Everyone who uses language in some way "knows" its rules and has the ability to create an infinite number of words and sentences. Is this knowledge the product of biology, or is language learned and influenced by experiences in the environment?

STAY TUNED FOR, ARE YOU SMARTER THAN A MONKEY?

www.CartoonStock.com

Biological Influences   Scientists believe that humans acquired language about 100,000 years ago. In evolutionary time, then, language is a very recent human ability. However, a number of experts believe that biological evolution that occurred long before language emerged undeniably shaped humans into linguistic creatures (Chomsky, 1975). The brain, nervous system, and vocal apparatus of our predecessors changed over hundreds of thousands of years. Physically equipped to do so, *Homo sapiens* went beyond grunting and shrieking to develop abstract speech. This sophisticated language ability gave humans an enormous edge over other animals and increased their chances of survival (Pinker, 1994).

Noam Chomsky (b. 1928)
MIT linguist Noam Chomsky was one of the early architects of the view that children's language development cannot be explained by environmental input. In Chomsky's view, language has strong biological underpinnings, with children biologically prewired to learn language at a certain time and in a certain way.

Language Universals   American linguist Noam Chomsky (1975) has argued that humans come into the world biologically prewired to learn language at a certain time and in a certain way. According to Chomsky and many other language experts, the strongest evidence for language's biological basis is the fact that children all over the world reach language milestones at about the same time and in about the same order, despite vast variations in the language input they receive from their environments. For example, in some cultures adults never talk to infants under 1 year of age, yet these infants still acquire language.

In Chomsky's view, children cannot possibly learn the full rules and structure of languages by only imitating what they hear. Rather, nature must provide children with a biological, prewired, universal grammar, allowing them to understand the basic rules of all languages and to apply these rules to the speech they hear. They learn language without an awareness of its underlying logic. Think about it: The terms we used above to define the characteristics of language—*phonology, morphology, semantics,* and so forth—may be new to you, but on some level you have mastered these principles. This mastery is demonstrated by your reading of this book, writing a paper for class, and talking with a friend. Like all other humans, you are engaged in the use of a rule-based language system even without knowing that you know those rules.

Language and the Brain   There is strong evidence to back up experts who believe language has a biological foundation. Neuroscience research has shown that the brain contains particular regions that are predisposed to language use (Tremblay, Monetta, & Joanette, 2009). As we saw in Chapter 2, accumulating evidence suggests that language processing, such as speech and grammar, mainly occurs in the brain's left hemisphere (Harpaz, Levkovitz, & Lavidor, 2009; Hornickel, Skoe, & Kraus, 2009). Recall the importance of Broca's area, which contributes to speech production, and Wernicke's area, which is involved in language comprehension. Using brain-imaging techniques such as PET scans, researchers have found that when an infant is about 9 months old, the part of the brain that stores and indexes many kinds of memory becomes fully functional (Bauer, 2009). This is also the time at which infants appear to be able to attach meaning to words, for instance to look at the ball if someone says "ball"—a development suggesting links among language, cognition, and the development of the brain.

Environmental Influences   Decades ago, behaviorists opposed Chomsky's hypothesis and argued that language represents nothing more than chains of responses acquired through reinforcement (Skinner, 1957). A baby happens to babble "ma-ma"; mama rewards the baby with hugs and smiles; the baby says "mama" more and more. Bit by bit, said the behaviorists, the baby's language is built up. According to behaviorists, language is a complex learned skill, much like playing the piano or dancing.

Such a view of language development is simply not tenable, however, given the rapid way children learn language, as well as the lack of evidence that social environments carefully reinforce language skills (R. Brown, 1973). This is not to say the environment has no role in language development. Many language experts argue that a child's experiences, the particular language to be learned, and the context in which learning takes place can strongly influence language acquisition (Berko Gleason, 2009; Goldfield & Snow, 2009).

Cases of children who have lacked exposure to language provide evidence for the important role of the environment in language development. In 1970, a California social worker made a routine visit to the home of a partially blind woman who had applied for public assistance. The social worker discovered that the woman and her husband had kept their 13-year-old daughter, Genie, locked away in almost total isolation during her childhood. Genie could not speak or stand erect. She had spent every day bound naked to a child's potty seat. She could move only her hands and feet. At night, she had been placed in a kind of straightjacket and caged in a crib with wire mesh sides and a cover. Whenever Genie had made a noise, her father had beaten her. He had never communicated with her in words; he had growled and barked at her instead (Rymer, 1993).

After she was rescued from her parents, Genie spent a number of years in extensive rehabilitation programs, including speech and physical therapy (Curtiss, 1977). She eventually learned to walk, although with a jerky motion, and to use the toilet. Genie also learned to recognize many words and to speak in rudimentary sentences. Gradually, she was able to string together two-word combinations such as "Big teeth," "Little marble," and "Two hand" and then

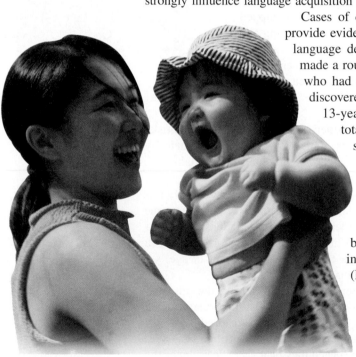

FIGURE 7.12

The Power of Smile and Touch Research has shown that when mothers immediately smiled and touched their 8-month-old infants after they had babbled, the infants subsequently made more complex speechlike sounds than when mothers responded randomly to their infants.

three-word combinations such as "Small two cup." As far as we know, unlike normal children, Genie did not learn to ask questions and did not develop a language system that allowed her to understand English grammar. As an adult, she speaks in short, mangled sentences such as "Father hit leg," "Big wood," and "Genie hurt."

Children who, like Genie, are abused and lack exposure to language for many years rarely speak normally. Some language experts have argued that these cases support the idea that there is a "critical period" for language development, a special time in a child's life (usually the preschool years) during which language must develop or it never will. Because these children also suffer severe emotional trauma and possible neurological deficits, however, the issue is still far from clear. Whether or not these cases suggest such a critical period, they certainly support the idea that the environment is crucial for the development of language.

Clearly, most humans do not learn language in a social vacuum. Most children are bathed in language from a very early age (Berko Gleason, 2009). The support and involvement of caregivers and teachers greatly facilitate a child's language learning (Goldfield & Snow, 2009; Pan & Uccelli, 2009). For example, one study showed that when mothers immediately smiled and touched their 8-month-old infants after they had babbled, the infants subsequently made more complex speechlike sounds than when mothers responded to their infants in a random manner (Goldstein, King, & West, 2003) (Figure 7.12).

Research findings about environmental influences on language learning complicate the understanding of its foundations. In the real world of language learning, children appear to be neither exclusively biologically programmed linguists nor exclusively socially driven language experts (Ratner, 1993). We have to look at how biology and environment interact when children learn language. That is, children are biologically prepared to learn language but benefit enormously from being immersed in a competent language environment from an early age (Goldfield & Snow, 2009; Pan & Uccelli, 2009).

Language Development over the Life Span

Most individuals develop a clear understanding of their language's structure, as well as a large vocabulary, during childhood. Most adults in the United States have acquired a vocabulary of nearly 50,000 words. Researchers have taken a great interest in the process by which these aspects of language develop (Hollich & Huston, 2007). Their many studies have provided an understanding of the milestones of language development (Figure 7.13).

Language researchers are fascinated by babies' speech even before the little ones say

0–6 Months	Cooing Discrimination of vowels Babbling present by 6 months
6–12 Months	Babbling expands to include sounds of spoken language Gestures used to communicate about objects First words spoken 10–13 months
12–18 Months	Understands 50+ words on average
18–24 Months	Vocabulary increases to an average of 200 words Two-word combinations
2 Years	Vocabulary rapidly increases Correct use of plurals Use of past tense Use of some prepositions
3–4 Years	Mean length of utterances increases to 3–4 morphemes in a sentence Use of "yes" and "no" questions, wh- questions Use of negatives and imperatives Increased awareness of pragmatics
5–6 Years	Vocabulary reaches an average of about 10,000 words Coordination of simple sentences
6–8 Years	Vocabulary continues to increase rapidly More skilled use of syntactical rules Conversational skills improve
9–11 Years	Word definitions include synonyms Conversational strategies continue to improve
11–14 Years	Vocabulary increases with addition of more abstract words Understanding of complex grammar forms Increased understanding of function a word plays in a sentence Understands metaphor and satire
15–20 Years	Understands adult literary works

Note: This list is meant not to be exhaustive but rather to highlight some of the main language milestones. Also keep in mind that there is a great deal of variation in the ages at which children can reach these milestones and still be considered within the normal range of language development.

FIGURE 7.13

Language Milestones All children are different and acquire language at varying rates, but these milestones provide a general sense of how language emerges in human life.

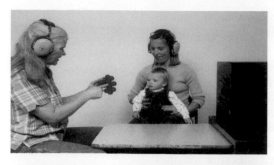

FIGURE 7.14

From Universal Linguist to Language-Specific Listener A baby is shown in Patricia Kuhl's research laboratory. In this research, babies listen to recorded voices that repeat syllables. When the sounds of the syllables change, the babies quickly learn to look at the bear. Using this technique, Kuhl has demonstrated that babies are universal linguists until about 6 months of age but in the next 6 months become language-specific listeners.

Around the world, young children learn to speak in two-word utterances at 18 to 24 months of age.

their first words (Pan & Uccelli, 2009). *Babbling*—endlessly repeating sounds and syllables, such as *bababa* or *dadada*—begins at the age of about 4 to 6 months and is determined by biological readiness, not by the amount of reinforcement or the ability to hear (Menn & Stoel-Gammon, 2009). Even deaf babies babble for a time (Lenneberg, Rebelsky, & Nichols, 1965). Babbling probably allows babies to exercise their vocal cords and helps develop the ability to articulate different sounds.

Patricia Kuhl's research reveals that long before they begin to learn words, infants can sort through a number of spoken sounds in search of the ones that have meaning (Kuhl, 1993, 2000, 2007; Kuhl & Damasio, 2009). Kuhl argues that from birth to about 6 months of age, children are "universal linguists" who are capable of distinguishing each of the sounds that make up human speech. By about 6 months of age, they have started to specialize in the speech sounds (or phonology) of their native language (Figure 7.14).

A child's first words, uttered at the age of 10 to 13 months, name important people (*dada*), familiar animals (*kitty*), vehicles (*car*), toys (*ball*), food (*milk*), body parts (*eye*), clothes (*hat*), household items (*clock*), and greetings (*bye*). These were babies' first words a century ago, and they are babies' first words still (Bloom, 2004).

By the time children reach the age of 18 to 24 months, they usually utter two-word statements. They quickly grasp the importance of expressing concepts and the role that language plays in communicating with others (Sachs, 2009). To convey meaning in two-word statements, the child relies heavily on gesture, tone, and context. Although these two-word sentences omit many parts of speech, they are remarkably effective in conveying many messages. When a toddler demands, "Pet doggie!" parents know he means, "May I please pet the doggie?" Very young children learn that language is a good way to get what they want, suggesting that they grasp another aspect of language—its pragmatics.

Although childhood is an important time for language learning, we continue to learn language (new words, new skills) throughout life (Obler, 2009). For many years, it was claimed that if individuals did not learn a second language prior to puberty, they would never reach native-language learners' levels in the second language (Johnson & Newport, 1991). However, recent research indicates a more complex conclusion: Sensitive periods likely vary across different language systems (Thomas & Johnson, 2008). Thus, for late second-language learners, such as adolescents and adults, new vocabulary is easier to learn than new sounds or new grammar (Neville, 2006). For example, children's ability to pronounce words with a native-like accent in a second language typically decreases with age, with an especially sharp drop occurring after about 10 to 12 years of age.

For adults, learning a new language requires a special kind of cognitive exercise. As we have seen, a great deal of language learning in infancy and childhood involves recognizing the sounds that are part of one's native tongue. This process also entails learning to ignore sounds that are *not* important to one's first language. For instance, in Japanese, the phonemes /l/ and /r/ are not distinguished from each other, so that, for a Japanese adult, the word *lion* is not distinguishable from the name *Ryan*. Recent research suggests that mastering a new language in adulthood may involve overriding such learned habits and learning to listen to sounds that one previously ignored. Indeed, adults can learn to hear and discriminate sounds that are part of a new language, and this learning can contribute to speech fluency and language skill (Evans & Iverson, 2007).

Thus, learning a new language in adulthood involves cognitively stretching ourselves away from our assumptions. Such a process might play a role in enhancing not only our language skills but also our cognitive ability generally. Susanne Jaeggi and colleagues found that undertaking complex memory tasks led to enhanced reasoning ability (Jaeggi & others, 2008). In this work, the participants engaged in a complicated memory game similar to the card game Concentration, in which all the cards are placed face down and players have to remember where each one is in order to find matches. After training for a half hour a day for several days, participants increased their scores on reasoning ability, compared to a control group who did not complete the training. The more the participants trained, the smarter they got. One aspect of the study is particularly interesting. The researchers designed the memory game so that as participants mastered it, it became harder and harder. In short, getting smarter is not just a matter of mastering a skill and then resting on our laurels. Reasoning ability can increase, but for that to happen, we have to keep challenging ourselves to think about things in increasingly new, and sometimes difficult, ways.

This study is an experiment, so we know that playing the memory game actually caused changes in reasoning ability.

1. The rules of language are known as _____, whereas the meaning of language is known as _____.
   A. phonology; morphology
   B. morphology; phonology
   C. semantics; syntax
   D. syntax; semantics

2. Noam Chomsky's view of language acquisition centers on
   A. environmental factors.
   B. biological factors.
   C. social factors.
   D. person-specific factors.

3. Williams syndrome demonstrates that
   A. mental retardation always leads to language deficits.
   B. extraordinary language ability can exist even in a person with mental retardation.
   C. without high intelligence, verbal ability is always low.
   D. mental retardation never leads to language deficits.

Apply It! 4. Susan and her husband Terence adopted a baby boy from another country. Their son is 4 months old, and they are worried because they are not sure he was exposed to a lot of talking before they adopted him. What advice would you give these nervous new parents?

A. They should be worried. They should bombard their new son with words and reward any indication of talking throughout his childhood.
B. They do not have to worry. In some cultures children are rarely talked to, but all kids (except in extreme cases) learn to talk. They should enjoy talking with and reading to their new little guy but also feel confident that he will certainly acquire language.
C. They should be worried, especially because their child is a boy.
D. We simply cannot know what the future holds for their son, because language is mostly genetic anyway.

The Candle Problem

The solution requires a unique perception of the function of the box in which the matches came. It can become a candleholder when tacked to the wall.

The Nine-Dot Problem

Most people have difficulty with this problem because they try to draw the lines within the boundaries of the dots. Notice that by extending the lines beyond the dots, the problem can be solved.

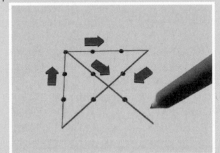

The Six-Matchstick Problem

Nothing in the instructions said that the solution had to be two-dimensional.

Solutions to problems from Figure 7.4.

summary

① The Cognitive Revolution in Psychology

Cognition is the way in which information is processed and manipulated in remembering, thinking, and knowing. The advent of the computer in the mid-twentieth century spurred a cognitive revolution in which psychologists took on the challenge of understanding human information processing. Artificial intelligence (AI), the science of creating machines capable of performing activities that require intelligence when they are done by people, is a by-product of the cognitive revolution.

② Thinking

Concepts are mental categories used to group objects, events, and characteristics. Concepts help us to generalize; they improve our memories; and they keep us from having to learn new things with every new instance or example of a concept. The prototype model suggests that members of a concept vary in terms of their similarity to the most typical item.

Problem solving is an attempt to find a way to attain a goal when the goal is not readily available. The four steps in problem solving are to (1) find and frame the problem, (2) develop good problem-solving strategies, (3) evaluate solutions, and (4) rethink and redefine problems and solutions over time. Among effective strategies for solving problems are subgoaling (the setting of intermediate goals that put you in a better position to reach your goal), algorithms (strategies that guarantee a solution), and heuristics (shortcuts that suggest, but do not guarantee, a solution to a problem).

Reasoning is the mental activity of transforming information to reach conclusions. Inductive reasoning is reasoning from the specific to the general. Deductive reasoning is reasoning from the general to the specific. Decision making involves evaluating alternatives and making choices among them. Biases and heuristics that may lead to problematic decision making include confirmation bias, hindsight bias, the availability heuristic, and the representativeness heuristic.

Critical thinking and creativity improve problem solving. Critical thinking involves thinking productively, evaluating the evidence, being mindful, and keeping an open mind. Creativity is the ability to think in novel and unusual ways and to come up with unconventional solutions. Creative thinkers are flexible and playful, self-motivated, willing to face risk, and objective in evaluating their work. Creativity has often been described as occurring in a five-step process: preparation, incubation, insight, evaluation, and elaboration.

③ Intelligence

Intelligence consists of the ability to solve problems and to adapt to and learn from everyday experiences. Traditionally, intelligence has been measured by tests designed to compare people's performance on cognitive tasks.

A good test of intelligence meets three criteria: validity, reliability, and standardization. Validity is the extent to which a test measures what it is intended to measure. Reliability is how consistently an individual performs on a test. Standardization focuses on uniform procedures for administering and scoring a test and establishing norms.

Binet developed the first intelligence test. Individuals from age 2 through adulthood take the current Stanford-Binet test (so called because the revisions were completed at Stanford University). Some intelligence tests are unfair to individuals from different cultures. Culture-fair tests are intelligence tests that are intended to be culturally unbiased.

Genes are clearly involved in intelligence. The proportion of differences in intelligence that is explained by genetic variation (or heritability) is substantial. Environmental influences on intelligence have also been demonstrated. The fact that intelligence test scores have risen considerably around the world in recent decades—called the Flynn effect—supports the role of environment in intelligence.

At the extreme ends of intelligence are giftedness and mental retardation. People who are gifted have high intelligence (IQ of 130 or higher) and/or superior talent for a particular domain. Research has shown that individuals who are gifted are likely to make important and creative contributions. Mental retardation is a condition of limited mental ability in which the individual has a low IQ, usually below 70; has difficulty adapting to everyday life; and has an onset of these characteristics during childhood. Mental retardation can have an organic cause (called organic retardation) or can be social and cultural in origin (called cultural-familial retardation).

Instead of focusing on intelligence as a single, broad cognitive ability, some psychologists have broken intelligence up into a variety of areas of life skills. Sternberg's triarchic theory states there are three main types of intelligence: analytical, creative, and practical. Gardner identifies nine types of intelligence, involving skills that are verbal, mathematical, spatial, bodily-kinesthetic, musical, interpersonal, intrapersonal, naturalist, and existential. The multiple-intelligences approaches have broadened the definition of intelligence and motivated educators to develop programs that instruct students in different domains. Critics maintain that multiple-intelligences theories include factors that really are not part of intelligence, such as musical skills. Critics also say that there is not enough research to support the concept of multiple intelligences.

④ Language

Language is a form of communication that is based on a system of symbols. All human languages have common aspects, including infinite generativity and organizational rules about structure. Any language has five characteristics: phonology, the sound system of a language; morphology, the rules for combining morphemes, which are meaningful strings of sounds that contain no smaller meaningful parts; syntax, the ways words are combined to form acceptable phrases and sentences; semantics, the meaning of words and sentences; and pragmatics, the uses of language.

Although language and thought influence each other, there is increasing evidence that they evolved as separate, modular, biologically prepared components of the mind. Evolution shaped humans into linguistic creatures. Chomsky said that humans are biologically prewired to learn language at a certain time and in a certain way. In addition, there is strong evidence that particular regions in the left hemisphere of the brain are predisposed to be used for language. Experience is also crucial to language development. It is important for children to interact with language-skilled people. Children are biologically prepared to learn language but benefit enormously from being in a competent language environment from early in development.

Although we often think of language, thinking, and intelligence as fixed when we are adults, research shows that we can continue to master skills and even increase intelligence by engaging in challenging mental tasks.

key terms

cognition, p. 229
artificial intelligence
  (AI), p. 230
thinking, p. 231
concept, p. 231
prototype model, p. 232
problem solving, p. 232
subgoaling, p. 233
algorithms, p. 233
heuristics, p. 233
fixation, p. 234
functional fixedness, p. 234

reasoning, p. 235
inductive reasoning, p. 235
deductive reasoning, p. 236
decision making, p. 236
confirmation bias, p. 237
hindsight bias, p. 237
availability heuristic, p. 237
base rate fallacy, p. 238
representativeness heuristic, p. 238
mindfulness, p. 239
open-mindedness, p. 239
creativity, p. 239

divergent thinking, p. 239
convergent thinking, p. 239
intelligence, p. 242
validity, p. 243
reliability, p. 243
standardization, p. 243
mental age (MA), p. 243
intelligence quotient
  (IQ), p. 244
normal distribution, p. 244
culture-fair tests, p. 245
heritability, p. 246

gifted, p. 248
mental retardation (intellectual
  disability), p. 249
triarchic theory of
  intelligence, p. 250
language, p. 251
infinite generativity, p. 251
phonology, p. 251
morphology, p. 252
syntax, p. 252
semantics, p. 252
pragmatics, p. 252

self-test

Multiple Choice

1. Cognitive psychology was considered a revolutionary development in psychology because
   A. it was a radical departure from behaviorism.
   B. it was a radical departure from psychoanalysis.
   C. it was a radical departure from the study of mental processes.
   D. John von Neumann used basic cognitive principles to develop the first modern computer.

2. Shantae, a sales representative, uses MapQuest to get driving directions to her clients' offices. Shantae is using a(n) _____ to reach her destinations.
   A. algorithm
   B. heuristic
   C. prototype
   D. category

3. Categories by which the mind groups things, events, and characteristics are called
   A. algorithms.
   B. cognitions.
   C. concepts.
   D. heuristics.

4. Someone who has difficulty exploring more than one possible solution to a problem is demonstrating
   A. functional fixedness.
   B. deductive reasoning.
   C. inductive reasoning.
   D. subgoaling.

5. Looking for available information that is consistent with our viewpoint is an example of
   A. the availability heuristic.
   B. hindsight bias.
   C. functional fixedness.
   D. confirmation bias.

6. The relationship between reliability and validity is that
   A. a reliable test is valid.
   B. a valid test is reliable.
   C. a reliable test is not valid.
   D. a valid test is not reliable.

7. The common criterion for determining mental retardation is
   A. an IQ below 100.
   B. an IQ below 85.
   C. an IQ below 70.
   D. an IQ below 55.

8. The sentence "the book ate the yellow house" is problematic because
   A. it has incorrect syntax.
   B. it has incorrect semantics.
   C. it has incorrect phonology.
   D. it has incorrect morphology.

9. Children begin saying words at the age of
   A. 4 to 6 months.
   B. 10 to 13 months.
   C. 18 to 24 months.
   D. 24 to 30 months.

10. Infinite generativity refers to the ability of languages
    A. to produce an unlimited number of meaningful sentences.
    B. to produce an unlimited number of sounds.
    C. to keep adding new words.
    D. to keep changing over time.

Apply It!

11. Jeremy's Uncle Ted, who is 70 years old, is taking a course in French for the first time. Jeremy tells you, "I don't know why he's bothering—you can't learn a language at that age." Respond to Jeremy's assertion using material from the text. Can Uncle Ted learn French? What challenges is he likely to face?

8 Human Development

Welcome to the World

On any given day, about 384,000 babies are born worldwide. In the time it takes you to read these few words, about 16 people enter the world and begin the journey of life. For their parents it is a life-changing moment: a Monday or a Thursday that becomes not just a square on the calendar but a date they will never forget. Children are being born everywhere, in homes and hospitals, at birthing centers, and even in parking lots—as was the case for Cole Hickson, who was born in his parents' car in a Charlotte, North Carolina, hospital parking lot on November 11, 2008. Newborn babies are cute and fascinating, a few pounds of complete mystery. Is it a boy or a girl? Whom does she look like? What will she be when she grows up?

Think about your birthday—not the date but the actual day you were born. You cannot remember it, but you were much smaller, completely helpless, and full of possibilities. Those possibilities have been unfolding throughout your life. Today, you are quite a bit taller and heavier (not to mention toilet trained). Some of these developments—physical growth, for instance—have just happened. Some, such as reading and writing, you have learned through instruction and practice. Other things—such as getting a tattoo, exercising to get in shape, and studying psychology—have happened because you have wanted them to. Just as learning to walk was a developmental milestone, accomplishing the goals you set for yourself as a mature adult may also qualify as developmental changes. ∎

- What characteristics of yourself have remained the same as you have grown from a small child into the person you are today?

- What does the word *mature* mean to you?

- Who is the most mature person you know? What makes that individual mature?

Developmental psychologists are interested in tracking and understanding the changes that occur throughout a person's life—all the steps toward being the person you are now and the person you are becoming. We begin this chapter by examining the meaning of development and some key issues in the field. We then review the processes of development throughout the life span: prenatally (before birth), during childhood, and in adolescence and adulthood. We round off our tour of the human life span with a look at successful aging. Throughout, we consider how the active developer—whether an infant, a toddler, a teenager, or an adult—can influence the meaning of development itself.

1 Exploring Human Development

Development refers to the pattern of continuity and change in human capabilities that occurs throughout the course of life. Most development involves growth, although it also consists of decline (for example, physical abilities may decline with age). Researchers who study development are intrigued by its universal characteristics and by its individual variations. The pattern of development is complex because it is the product of several processes:

development
The pattern of continuity and change in human capabilities that occurs throughout life, involving both growth and decline.

- *Physical processes* involve changes in an individual's biological nature. Genes inherited from parents, the hormonal changes of puberty and menopause, and changes throughout life in the brain, height and weight, and motor skills all reflect the developmental role of biological processes. Such biological growth processes are called *maturation*.

- *Cognitive processes* involve changes in an individual's thought, intelligence, and language. Observing a colorful mobile as it swings above a crib, constructing a sentence about the future, imagining oneself as a movie star, memorizing a new telephone number—these activities reflect the role of cognitive processes in development.

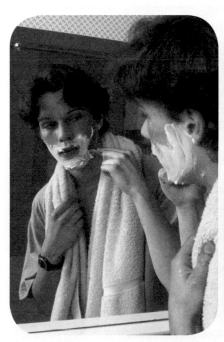
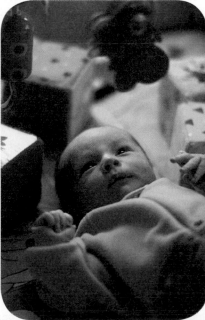

Human development is complex because it is the product of several processes. The hormonal changes of puberty, a baby's observation of a mobile, and an older couple's embrace reflect physical, cognitive, and socioemotional processes, respectively.

- *Socioemotional processes* involve changes in an individual's relationships with other people, changes in emotions, and changes in personality. An infant's smile in response to her mother's touch, a girl's development of assertiveness, an adolescent's joy at the senior prom, a young man's aggressiveness in sport, and an older couple's affection for each other all reflect the role of socioemotional processes.

These physical, cognitive, and socioemotional processes are intricately interwoven. Think of Hannah, an infant whose parents place a teddy bear in her crib. As an infant she might simply look at the teddy bear when her parents jiggle it in front of her. Over time, she not only can see the teddy bear but also can reach for it. She might even remember that the teddy bear exists and might cry for it when it is not with her. As a toddler, when she carries it around, she is demonstrating her physical abilities to do so, as well as her capacity to use the teddy bear as a source of comfort. As an adolescent, Hannah might no longer sleep with her teddy, but she might give him a place of honor on a shelf. As you read this chapter's separate sections on childhood, adolescence, and adulthood, remember that you are studying the development of an integrated human being in whom body, mind, and emotion are interdependent.

How Do Nature and Nurture Influence Development?

nature
An individual's biological inheritance, especially his or her genes.

nurture
An individual's environmental and social experiences.

Developmental psychologists are interested in understanding how nature and nurture contribute to development. The term **nature** refers to a person's biological inheritance, especially his or her genes. The term **nurture** refers to the individual's environmental and social experiences.

When we look at how nature and nurture contribute to development, we must take into account the influence of both genes (nature) and the environment (nurture) on behavior and characteristics. In Chapter 2 we considered the concept of *genotype* (the individual's genetic heritage—the actual genetic material). We also examined the idea of *phenotype* (the person's observable characteristics). The phenotype shows the contributions of both nature (genetic heritage) and nurture (environment). The genotype may be expressed in various ways, depending on the environment as well as characteristics of the genotype itself. Recall that a recessive gene, though part of the genotype, will not show up in the phenotype at all if it is paired with a dominant gene.

One example of the role of environmental influences on genetic expression is a genetic condition called *phenylketonuria* (PKU). Caused by two recessive genes, PKU results in an inability to metabolize the amino acid phenylalanine. Decades ago, it was thought that the genotype for PKU led to a specific phenotype, namely, irreversible brain damage, mental retardation, and seizures. However, experts now know that as long as individuals with the genotype for PKU stick to a diet that is very low in phenylalanine, these characteristics in the phenotype can be avoided. This special diet means avoiding or restricting consumption of a variety of foods that contain phenylalanine, including breast milk, meat, chicken, and other high-protein foods. In short, these environmental precautions can change the phenotype associated with this genotype. In most developed nations, infants are tested for PKU shortly after birth. Incidentally, you might know phenylalanine as a major component of the artificial sweetener aspartame.

Thus, a person's observable and measurable characteristics (phenotype) might not reflect his or her genetic heritage (genotype) very precisely because of the particular experiences the person has had. Instead, for each genotype, a *range* of phenotypes may be expressed, depending on environmental experiences. In concrete terms, an individual can inherit the genetic potential to grow very tall, but good nutrition, an environmental factor, is important for achieving that potential. The person whom we see before us emerges out of an interplay of genetic and environmental experiences. In short, development is the product of nature,

Wolfgang Amadeus Mozart composed some of the most beautiful classical music the world has known. His family history suggests that some of that talent was genetic, but his environment clearly mattered too: His father pressured him to practice and perform constantly. What are some of the things that were present in your childhood environment that influenced your expression of your gifts and abilities?

nurture, and the complex interaction of the two. Heredity and environment operate together to produce such characteristics as height, weight, and athletic ability (Diamond, 2009a; Mader, 2010).

Thus, although it might be easy to think of genes as the blueprint for a person, development is not a process that follows a genetic master plan. In fact, it is difficult to tell a simple story about how development occurs. One way that scientists and philosophers think about complex processes such as development is through the concept of *emergent properties*. An emergent property is a big entity (like a person) that is a consequence of the interaction of multiple lower-level factors (Gottlieb, 2007). Again, development is about the complex interactions of genes and experience that build the whole person. In many ways, your development is as mysterious as the newborn baby you once were. One of the factors that must be considered in the emergence of development is the developer himself or herself.

When you see a flock of birds flying in formation in the sky, you are observing an emergent property. It may look as if the birds are simply following the leader, but they aren't actually doing so. Instead, each individual bird is following its own local rules. What you see as a flock of birds is in fact a collection of individual birds, each one "doing its own thing" but creating the formation (the emergent property) that you recognize as a flock.

Nature, Nurture, and You

Nature and nurture have at least one thing in common. Because we cannot pick our genes or our parents, each of us would seem to be stuck with the genes and environment we got at birth. However, it is important to recognize that the developing human being has a role to play in development (Brandstadter, 2006). Although you might think of nature and nurture as the raw ingredients of yourself as a person, the fact is that you take those ingredients and make them into the person you are.

Indeed, some psychologists believe that we can develop beyond what our genetic inheritance and our environment give us. They argue that a key aspect of development involves seeking optimal experiences in life (Armor, Massey, & Sackett, 2008). They cite examples of individuals who go beyond what life has given them to achieve extraordinary things. These individuals build and construct their own lives, authoring a unique developmental path and sometimes transforming negative characteristics into real strengths.

In our effort to experience our lives in optimal ways, we develop *life themes* that involve activities, social relationships, and life goals (Csikszentmihalyi & Rathunde, 1998; Rathunde & Csikszentmihalyi, 2006). Some individuals are more successful at constructing optimal life experiences than others. Among the public figures who have succeeded are Martin Luther King, Jr., Mother Teresa, Nelson Mandela, Bill and Melinda Gates, and Oprah Winfrey. These people looked for and found meaningful life themes as they developed. Their lives were not restricted to simple biological survival or to simply settling for their particular life situations. A person does not have to be famous to take an active role in shaping development.

Do Early Experiences Rule Us for Life?

A key question in developmental psychology is the extent to which childhood experiences (nurture) determine aspects of later life. Developmental psychologists debate whether early experiences or later experiences are more important (McElwain, 2009; Park & Reuter-Lorenz, 2009; Thompson, 2009a). Some believe that unless infants experience warm, nurturing caregiving in the first year or so of life, they will not develop to their full potential (Berlin, Cassidy, & Appleyard, 2008). Other psychologists emphasize the power of later experience, arguing that important development occurs in later life as well. Lifespan developmentalists, who focus on both children and adults, stress

Microsoft founder Bill Gates and his wife Melinda have quested after—and carved out—meaningful life experiences as they have progressed through their development.

that researchers have given too little attention to adult development (Park & Reuter-Lorenz, 2009). They argue that although early experiences are important contributors to development, they are not necessarily more influential than later experiences. Both early and later experience make significant contributions to development, these experts say, and so no one is doomed to be a prisoner of his or her childhood.

1. The late Diana, Princess of Wales, devoted a considerable amount of her time on efforts to eliminate land mines. Her work illustrates
   A. a life theme.
   B. a genotype.
   C. a socioemotional process.
   D. a phenotype.

2. Development can be best described as
   A. due entirely to nature.
   B. due entirely to nurture.
   C. the product of the interaction of nature and nurture.
   D. none of the above

3. An example of an optimal experience is
   A. cooking food to eat.

   B. getting a great buy on those boots you wanted.
   C. volunteering time to teach adults to read.
   D. competing with others.

Apply It! 4. Sonja and Pete are both engineers who met during college. They share a love of mathematics and science and are both quite successful. When their daughter Gabriella is born, they decorate her room with numbers and spend a great deal of time counting objects and talking about mathematics with her. When she starts school, they are not surprised to find out that Gabriella is particularly gifted in mathematics. Gabriella does not become an

engineer, but she does have a career as a terrific math teacher. Which statement is most accurate in describing Gabriella?
A. Her math ability is a direct result of her genetic heritage.
B. Her math ability is a direct result of her environmental experiences.
C. The fact that she became a teacher instead of an engineer shows that neither genetics nor environment matters that much to development.
D. Gabriella's development shows the influence of genetics, environment, their interaction, and Gabriella's capacity to forge a life theme that is meaningful to her.

2 Child Development

To understand childhood in all its dimensions, we must begin before it even starts, with *prenatal* ("before birth") development. Childhood continues through the elementary school years. In this section we focus on the three fundamental developmental processes of childhood—physical, cognitive, and socioemotional. We revisit the nature–nurture theme and explore the importance of resilience—the ability to cope effectively with difficult life experiences—as a factor in helping children grow up to become capable adults.

Prenatal Development

Prenatal development is a time of astonishing change, beginning with conception. *Conception* occurs when a single sperm cell from the male merges with the female's ovum (egg) to produce a *zygote,* a single cell with 23 chromosomes from the mother and 23 from the father.

The Course of Prenatal Development
Development from zygote to fetus is divided into three periods:

- *Germinal period—weeks 1 and 2:* The germinal period begins with conception. After 1 week and many cell divisions, the zygote is made up of 100 to 150 cells. By the end of 2 weeks, the mass of cells has attached to the uterine wall.

  Note that 28 days is before most women even know they are pregnant. That's why doctors recommend that all women who might become pregnant take folic acid supplements (about 400 micrograms a day) to prevent neural tube defects.

- *Embryonic period—weeks 3 through 8:* The rate of cell differentiation intensifies, support systems for the cells develop, and the beginnings of organs appear (Figure 8.1a). In the third week, the neural tube, which eventually becomes the spinal cord, starts to take shape. Within the first 28 days after conception, the neural tube is formed and closes, encased inside the embryo. Problems in neural tube development can lead to birth defects such as spina bifida, in which the spinal cord is not completely enclosed by the spinal column, or severe underdevelopment of the brain. Folic acid, a B vitamin

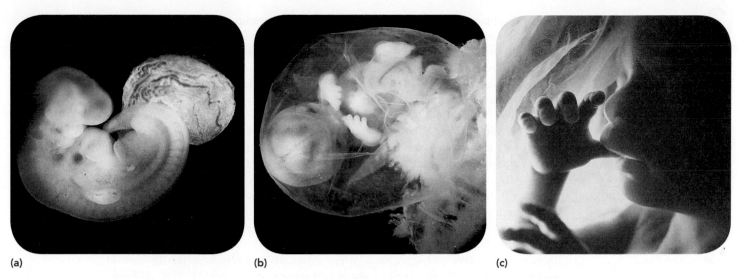

(a) (b) (c)

FIGURE 8.1

From Embryo to Fetus (*a*) At about 4 weeks, an embryo is about 0.2 inch (less than 1 centimeter) long. The head, eyes, and ears begin to show; the head and neck are half the length of the body; the shoulders will be located where the whitish arm buds are attached. (*b*) At 8 weeks, the developing individual is about 1.6 inches (4 centimeters) long and has reached the end of its embryonic phase. It has become a fetus. Everything that will be found in the fully developed human being has now begun to form. The fetal stage is a period of growth and perfection of detail. The heart has been beating for a month, and the muscles have just begun their first exercises. (*c*) At 4½ months, the fetus is just over 7 inches (about 18 centimeters) long. When the thumb comes close to the mouth, the head may turn, and the lips and tongue begin their sucking motions—a reflex for survival.

found in orange juice and leafy green vegetables like spinach, greatly reduces the chances of neural tube defects. By the end of the embryonic period, the heart begins to beat, the arms and legs become more differentiated, the face starts to form, and the intestinal tract appears (Figure 8.1b).

■ *Fetal period—months 2 through 9:* At 2 months, the fetus is the size of a kidney bean and has already started to move around. At 4 months, the fetus is 5 inches long and weighs about 5 ounces (Figure 8.1c). At 6 months, the fetus has grown to a pound and a half. The last three months of pregnancy are the time when organ functioning increases, and the fetus puts on considerable weight and size, adding baby fat. The average newborn is about 19 inches long and weighs about 7 pounds.

Until about 50 years ago, mothers and their doctors were unaware of the role that maternal diet and behavior might play for the developing fetus. Although it floats in a comfortable, well-protected womb, the fetus is not immune to the larger environment surrounding the mother (Derbyshire, 2007). Indeed, sometimes normal development is disrupted by environmental insults.

Threats to the Fetus A *teratogen* is any agent that causes a birth defect. Teratogens include chemical substances ingested by the mother (such as nicotine, if the mother smokes) and certain illnesses (such as rubella, or German measles). Substances that are ingested by the mother can lead to serious birth defects. Heroin is an example of a teratogen. Babies born to heroin users are at risk for many problems, including premature birth, low birth weight, physical defects, breathing problems, and death.

Fetal alcohol spectrum disorders (FASD) are a cluster of abnormalities and problems that appear in the offspring of mothers who drink alcohol heavily during pregnancy (Olson, King, & Jirkowic, 2008). These abnormalities include a small head; facial characteristics such as wide-spaced eyes, a flattened nose, and an underdeveloped upper lip; defects in the limbs and heart; and below-average intelligence (Caley & others, 2008). Heavy drinking is linked to FASD, but even moderate drinking can lead to serious problems

Some pregnant women who smoke feel that it would be too stressful to quit smoking during what is an already stressful period. As a useful reality check, though, they might imagine something even more stressful: a baby with a lit cigarette in his or her mouth. That image is certainly more troubling than giving up an unhealthy habit for 9 months. A pregnant woman who smokes is smoking for two.

(Sayal & others, 2007). The best advice for a woman who is pregnant or thinking of becoming pregnant is to avoid alcohol.

The effects of chemical teratogens depend on the timing of exposure. The body part or organ system that is developing when the fetus encounters the teratogen is most vulnerable. Genetic characteristics may buffer or worsen the effects of a teratogen. Perhaps most importantly, the environment the child encounters *after birth* can influence the ultimate effects of prenatal insults.

Sexually transmitted infections (STIs) also threaten the fetus. Some STIs, such as gonorrhea, can be transferred to the baby during delivery. Others, including syphilis and the human immunodeficiency virus (HIV), the virus that causes AIDS, can also infect the fetus while it is in the womb. Because HIV leads to an incurable infection, antiviral medications are given to HIV-positive mothers to reduce the chances that they will pass the virus to their fetus. HIV can also be transferred to newborns through breastfeeding. Besides transmission of infections to the fetus and newborns, STI exposure enhances the risk of stillbirth, as well as a number of other problems, such as eye infections and blindness (in the case of gonorrhea). Many STIs also increase the risk of preterm birth.

A *preterm infant,* one who is born prior to 37 weeks after conception, may also be at risk for developmental difficulties. Whether a preterm infant will have developmental problems is a complex issue, however. Very small preterm infants are more likely than their larger counterparts to have developmental problems (Minde & Zelkowitz, 2008). Preterm infants who grow up in poverty are more likely to have problems than are those who live in better socioeconomic conditions (Madan & others, 2006). Indeed, many larger preterm infants from middle- and high-income families do not have developmental problems. Postnatal experience plays a crucial role in determining the ultimate effects of preterm birth. Research has shown that massage can improve developmental outcomes for premature infants (Diego, Field, & Hernandez-Reif, 2008; T. Field, 2001, 2003, 2007). In one study, massaging infants for 15 minutes three times a day for five consecutive days had a stress-reducing effect on preterm infants, which is especially important because they encounter numerous stressors while they are hospitalized (Hernandez-Reif, Diego, & Field, 2008). Massaged infants were more active and alert and performed better on developmental tests.

Prenatal and newborn development sets the stage for development in childhood. The changes in every realm of childhood—physical, cognitive, and socioemotional—establish the foundation for our development as adults.

Physical Development in Childhood

Human infants are among the world's most helpless newborns. One reason for their helplessness is that they are born not quite finished. From an evolutionary perspective, what sets humans apart from other animals is our enormous brain. Getting that big brain out of the relatively small birth canal is a challenge, and nature has met that challenge by sending human babies out of the womb before the brain has fully developed. The first months and years of life allow the developing human (and his or her environment) to put the finishing touches on that important organ. During infancy (the period from birth to about 18 to 24 months), children change from virtually immobile beings to creatures who toddle as fast as their legs can carry them.

Reflexes   Newborns come into the world equipped with several genetically wired reflexes that are crucial for survival. Babies are born with the ability to suck and swallow. If they are dropped in water, they will naturally hold their breath, contract their throats to keep water out, and move their arms and legs to stay afloat at least briefly. Some reflexes persist throughout life—coughing, blinking, and yawning, for example. Others, such as automatically grasping something that touches the fingers, disappear in the months following birth as higher brain functions mature and infants develop voluntary control over many behaviors. Figure 8.2 shows some examples of infant reflexes.

Rooting

What provokes the response? Stroking of the infant's cheek

What the infant does Head turns in the direction of the touch, and the infant opens his or her mouth for feeding.

Gripping

What provokes the response? Something that is placed in the infant's hand

What the infant does The infant grasps the item and can hold on very well—almost enough to support his or her own weight.

Toe curling

What provokes the response? Stroking of the inner or outer sole of the infant's foot

What the infant does If the inner sole is stroked, the infant curls his or her toes. If the outer sole is stroked, the toes spread out.

Moro or startle

What provokes the response? Sudden noise or movement

What the infant does The infant throws his or her head back and arms and legs out (and then cries).

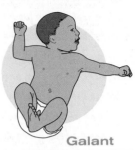
Galant

What provokes the response? Stroking of the infant's lower back, next to the spinal cord

What the infant does The infant curves toward the side that was stroked—and looks like a fencer when doing so.

FIGURE 8.2
Some Infant Reflexes Infants are born with a number of reflexes to get them through life, and they are incredibly cute when they perform them. These reflexes disappear as infants mature.

Motor and Perceptual Skills

Relative to the rest of the body, a newborn's head is gigantic, and it flops around uncontrollably. Within 12 months, the infant becomes capable of sitting upright, standing, stooping, climbing, and often walking. During the second year, growth decelerates, but rapid gains occur in such activities as running and climbing. Researchers used to think that motor milestones (such as sitting up, crawling, and walking) unfolded as part of a genetic plan. Psychologists now recognize that motor development is not the consequence of nature or nurture alone. The focus of research has shifted to discovering *how* motor skills develop and away from simply describing the age at which they develop (Adolph & Joh, 2009; Needham, 2009).

Infants are active developers. When infants are motivated to do something, they may create a new motor behavior, such as reaching out to grab a new toy or mommy's earrings (Thelen & Smith, 2006). That new behavior is the result of many converging factors: the developing nervous system, the body's physical properties and its movement possibilities, the goal the infant is motivated to reach, and environmental support for the skill.

Environmental experiences play a role in reaching and grasping (Needham, 2009). In one study, 3-month-old infants participated in play sessions wearing "sticky mittens"—mittens with palms that stick to the edges of toys and allow the infants to pick up the toys (Needham, Barrett, & Peterman, 2002, p. 279) (Figure 8.3). Infants who participated in sessions with the mittens grasped and manipulated objects earlier in their development than a control group of infants who did not receive the "mitten" experience. The experienced infants looked at the objects longer, swatted at them, and were more likely to put the objects in their mouths.

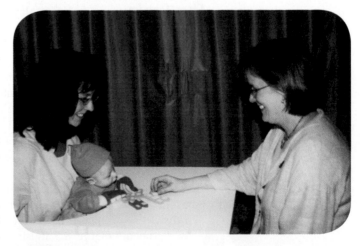

FIGURE 8.3
Infants' Use of "Sticky Mittens" to Explore Objects Amy Needham and her colleagues (2002) found that "sticky mittens" enhance young infants' object exploration skills.

preferential looking
A research technique that involves giving an infant a choice of what object to look at.

habituation
Decreased responsiveness to a stimulus after repeated presentations.

Motor skills and perceptual skills are coupled and depend on each other. Babies are continually coordinating their movements with information they perceive through their senses to learn how to maintain their balance, reach for objects in space, and move across various surfaces and terrains (Adolph & others, 2009). Consider what happens when a baby sees a fun toy across the room. Because she can see it, she is motivated to get it. She must perceive the current state of her body and learn how to use her limbs to get to the goal. Action also educates perception. For example, watching an object while holding and touching it helps infants to learn about its texture, size, and hardness. Moving from place to place in the environment teaches babies how objects and people look from different perspectives and whether surfaces will support their weight (Gibson, 2001).

Psychologists face a daunting challenge in studying infant perception. Infants cannot talk, so how can scientists learn whether they can see or hear certain things? Psychologists who study infants have no choice but to become extraordinarily clever methodologists, relying on what infants can do to understand what they know (Aslin & Lathrop, 2008). One thing infants can do is look. The **preferential looking** technique involves giving an infant a choice of what object to look at. If an infant shows a reliable preference for one stimulus (say, a picture of a face) over another (a scrambled picture of a face) when these are repeatedly presented in differing locations, we can infer that the infant can tell the two images apart.

Another way to examine infant perception is to habituate the infant on a particular stimulus. **Habituation** refers to decreased responsiveness to a stimulus after repeated presentations (Snyder & Torrence, 2008). Simply put, habituation means boring the baby with the object. For example, a square filled with vertical black and white stripes is presented to the infant until it is no longer interesting. Then a new stimulus (such as a square with slightly broader stripes) is presented. If the infant does not notice the change (or does not start looking at the new stimulus), we can infer that he or she does not perceive the new stimulus as different from the first.

Using these techniques, researchers have found that as early as *7 days old,* infants are already engaged in organized perception of faces and are able to put together sights and sounds. If presented with two faces with mouths moving, infants will watch the face whose mouth matches the sounds they are hearing (Pascalls & Kelly, 2008). At 3 months, infants prefer real faces to scrambled faces, and their mother's face to a stranger's (Slater, Field, & Reif-Hernandez, 2007). These techniques have provided a great deal of information about infant's remarkable abilities, but they are also limited. Research using brain imaging suggests that infants may know more than even these clever strategies can tell us.

The Brain   As an infant plays, crawls, shakes a rattle, smiles, and frowns, his or her brain is changing dramatically. At birth and in early infancy, the brain's 100 billion neurons have only minimal connections. The infant brain literally is ready and waiting for the experiences that will create these connections (Moulson & Nelson, 2008; C. A. Nelson, 2009). During the first 2 years of life, the dendrites of the neurons branch out, and the neurons become far more interconnected (Figure 8.4). Myelination, the process of encasing axons with fat cells (the myelin sheath described in Chapter 2), begins prenatally and continues after birth.

During childhood, *synaptic connections* increase dramatically (Fischer & Immordino-Yang, 2008). Recall from Chapter 2 that a *synapse* is a gap between neurons that is bridged by chemical neurotransmitters. Nearly twice as many synapses are available as will ever be used (Huttenlocher & Dabholkar, 1997). The connections that are made become stronger and will survive; the unused ones will be replaced by other neural pathways or disappear. In the language of neuroscience, these unused connections will be "pruned." Figure 8.5 illustrates the steep growth and later pruning of synapses during infancy in specific areas of the brain.

Using brain scanning tools such as MRI and CT, scientists have discovered that children's brains also undergo amazing anatomical changes (Paus, 2009; Toga, Thompson, & Sowell, 2006). Repeated brain scans of the same children for up to

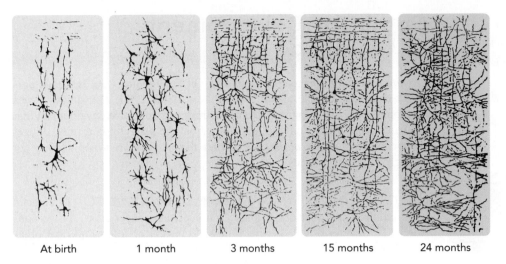

| At birth | 1 month | 3 months | 15 months | 24 months |

FIGURE 8.4

Dendritic Spreading Note the increase in connections among neurons over the course of the first 2 years of life.

Reprinted by permission of the publisher from *The Postnatal Development of the Human Cerebral Cortex, Vols. I-VIII* by Jesse Leroy Conel, Cambridge, Mass.: Harvard University Press, Copyright © 1939, 1975 by the President and Fellows of Harvard College.

four years show that the amount of brain material in some areas can nearly double within as little as a year, followed by a drastic loss of tissue as unneeded cells are purged and the brain continues to reorganize itself. The overall size of the brain does not change very much, but local patterns within the brain change tremendously. From 3 to 6 years of age, the most rapid growth takes place in the frontal lobe areas, which are involved in planning and organizing new actions and in maintaining attention to tasks (Thompson & others, 2000). These brain changes are not simply the result of nature; new experiences in the world also promote brain development (de Haan & Martinos, 2008). Thus, as in other areas of development, nature and nurture operate together (Diamond, 2010).

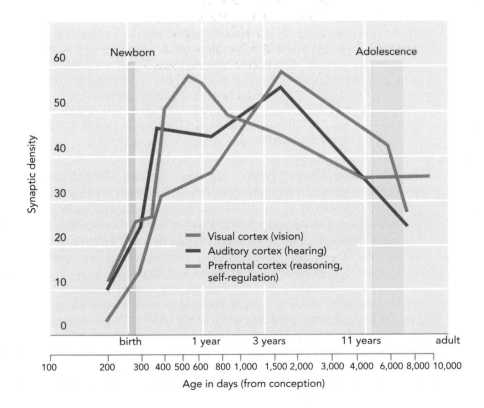

FIGURE 8.5

Synaptic Density in the Human Brain from Infancy to Adulthood The graph shows the dramatic increase and then pruning in synaptic density in three regions of the brain: visual cortex, auditory cortex, and prefrontal cortex. Synaptic density is believed to be an important indication of the extent of connectivity between neurons.

Cognitive Development in Childhood

Jean Piaget (1896–1980)
Piaget, the famous Swiss developmental psychologist, changed the way we think about the development of children's minds.

Cognitive development refers to how thought, intelligence, and language processes change as people mature. Jean Piaget (1896–1980), the famous Swiss developmental psychologist, presented a theory of cognitive development that has had lasting impact on how we think about the way children think. Piaget believed that children *actively construct* their cognitive world as they go through a series of stages.

Piaget's Theory of Cognitive Development

In Piaget's view, children use schemas to make sense of their experience. As we considered in Chapter 6, a *schema* is a mental concept or framework that organizes information and provides a structure for interpreting it. Schemas are expressed as various behaviors and skills that the child can exercise in relation to objects or situations. For example, sucking is an early, simple schema. Later and more complex schemas include licking, blowing, crawling, and hiding.

Piaget (1952) described two processes responsible for how people use and adapt their schemas:

assimilation
An individual's incorporation of new information into existing knowledge.

■ **Assimilation** occurs when individuals incorporate new information into existing knowledge. That is, people *assimilate* the environment into a schema. Consider the schema of sucking. Newborns reflexively suck everything that touches their lips. Their experience in sucking various objects allows them to assimilate those objects into other schemas of taste, texture, shape, and so on. The first time a child realizes that she might suck her thumb, she is assimilating the category "thumb" into the schema of sucking.

■ **Accommodation** occurs when individuals adjust their schemas to new information. That is, people *accommodate* their schemas to the environment. After several months of experience, the infant who has been sticking everything in her mouth might begin to accommodate the sucking schema by being more selective with it. For example, she might discover that some objects, such as fingers and the mother's breasts, can be sucked, whereas others, such as fuzzy stuffed toys, are better not. With experience, the schema sucking changes into different schemas (such as snuggling) that accommodate the realities of different types of objects.

accommodation
An individual's adjustment of his or her schemas to new information.

According to Piaget, we go through four stages in understanding the world (Figure 8.6). Each stage involves a qualitatively different way of making sense of the world than the one before it.

Sensorimotor Stage

Piaget's first stage, the **sensorimotor stage**, lasts from birth to about 2 years of age. In this stage, infants construct an understanding of the world by coordinating sensory experiences (such as seeing and hearing) with motor (physical) actions—hence the term *sensorimotor*. As newborns they have little more than reflexive patterns with which to work. By the end of this stage, 2-year-olds show complex sensorimotor patterns and are beginning to use symbols or words in their thinking.

Object permanence is Piaget's term for the crucial accomplishment of understanding that objects and events continue to exist even when they cannot directly be seen, heard, or touched. Piaget believed that "out of sight" literally was "out of mind" for very young infants. The most common way to study object permanence was to show an infant an interesting toy and then cover the toy with a blanket. Piaget reasoned that if infants understood that the toy still existed, they would try to uncover it (Figure 8.7). Piaget thought the development of object permanence continues throughout the sensorimotor period.

sensorimotor stage
Piaget's first stage of cognitive development, lasting from birth to about 2 years of age, during which infants construct an understanding of the world by coordinating sensory experiences with motor (physical) actions.

⊙ *Without object permanence, the world and its objects change from one moment to the next. Once the infant knows that objects still exist even if he or she can't see them, the infant can become attached to things and can wonder, "Where did I leave my teddy bear?" The infant starts thinking about future events, as in "When will I see Mommy again?" The child can take comfort in the knowledge that Mommy will be back. Object permanence also means getting a first taste of the human capacity for longing—for missing someone who is not there.*

Sensorimotor Stage	**Preoperational Stage**	**Concrete Operational Stage**	**Formal Operational Stage**
The infant constructs an understanding of the world by coordinating sensory experiences with physical actions. An infant progresses from reflexive, instinctual action at birth to the beginning of symbolic thought toward the end of the stage.	The child begins to represent the world with words and images. These words and images reflect increased symbolic thinking and go beyond the connection of sensory information and physical action.	The child can now reason logically about concrete events and classify objects into different sets.	The adolescent reasons in more abstract, idealistic, and logical ways.
Birth to 2 Years of Age	**2 to 7 Years of Age**	**7 to 11 Years of Age**	**11 Years of Age Through Adulthood**

FIGURE 8.6
Piaget's Four Stages of Cognitive Development Jean Piaget described how human beings, through development, become ever more sophisticated thinkers about the world.

Preoperational Stage Piaget's second stage of cognitive development, the **preoperational stage,** lasts from approximately 2 to 7 years of age. Preoperational thought is more symbolic than sensorimotor thought. In preschool years, children begin to represent their world with words, images, and drawings. Thus, their thoughts begin to exceed simple connections of sensorimotor information and physical action.

The type of symbolic thinking that children are able to accomplish during this stage is limited. They still cannot perform what Piaget called *operations,* by which he meant mental

preoperational stage
Piaget's second stage of cognitive development, lasting from about 2 to 7 years of age, during which thought is more symbolic than sensorimotor thought.

FIGURE 8.7
Object Permanence Piaget regarded object permanence as one of infancy's landmark cognitive accomplishments. For this 5-month-old boy, out of sight is literally out of mind. The infant looks at the toy dog (*left*), but when his view of the toy is blocked (*right*), he does not search for it. In a few more months, he will search for hidden toys, a development reflecting the presence of object permanence.

FIGURE 8.8

Piaget's Conservation Task The beaker test determines whether a child can think operationally—that is, can mentally reverse action and understand conservation of the substance. (*a*) Two identical beakers are presented to the child, each containing the same amount of liquid. As the child watches, the experimenter pours the liquid from B into C, which is taller and thinner than A and B. (*b*) The experimenter then asks the child whether beakers A and C have the same amount of liquid. The preoperational child says no. When asked to point to the beaker that has more liquid, the child points to the tall, thin one.

representations that are "reversible." Preoperational children have difficulty understanding that reversing an action may restore the original conditions from which the action began.

A well-known test of whether a child can think "operationally" is to present a child with two identical beakers, A and B, filled with liquid to the same height (Figure 8.8). Next to them is a third beaker, C. Beaker C is tall and thin, whereas beakers A and B are short and wide. The liquid is poured from B into C, and the child is asked whether the amounts in A and C are the same. The 4-year-old child invariably says that the amount of liquid in the tall, thin beaker (C) is greater than that in the short, wide beaker (A). The 8-year-old child consistently says the amounts are the same. The 4-year-old child, a preoperational thinker, cannot mentally reverse the pouring action; that is, she cannot imagine the liquid going back from container C to container B. Piaget said that such a child has not grasped the concept of *conservation*, a belief in the permanence of certain attributes of objects despite superficial changes.

Parents of preschoolers take heart. They are not intentionally trying to make you crazy. Children at this age may say things that seem remarkably cruel, but they are not able to gauge what their words might feel like to someone else.

The child's thought in the preoperational stage is egocentric. This does not mean that the child is self-centered or arrogant but that preoperational children cannot put themselves in someone else's shoes. They cannot take another person's mental states into account.

Preoperational thinking is also intuitive. This means that preoperational children make judgments based on gut feelings rather than logic. In reaching a basic level of operational understanding, the child progresses to the third of Piaget's cognitive stages.

concrete operational stage Piaget's third stage of cognitive development, lasting from about 7 to 11 years of age, during which the individual uses operations and replaces intuitive reasoning with logical reasoning in concrete situations.

Concrete Operational Stage Piaget's **concrete operational stage** (7 to 11 years of age) involves using operations and replacing intuitive reasoning with logical reasoning in concrete situations. Children in the concrete operational stage can successfully complete the beaker task described above. They are able to mentally imagine the operation of reversing the pouring of the liquid back into the wide beaker. Many of the concrete operations identified by Piaget are related to the properties of objects. For instance, when playing with Play-doh, the child in the concrete operational stage realizes that *the amount* of Play-doh is not changed by changing its shape. One important skill at this stage of reasoning is the ability to classify or divide things into different sets or subsets and to consider their inter-relations. (You might remember learning the childhood song that goes, "One of these things is not like the other," which effectively aimed to coax you into concrete operations.)

Concrete operational thought involves operational thinking, classification skills, and logical reasoning in concrete but not hypothetical contexts. According to Piaget, this kind of abstract, logical reasoning occurs in the fourth, and final, cognitive stage.

Formal Operational Stage

Individuals enter the **formal operational stage** of cognitive development at 11 to 15 years of age. This stage continues through the adult years. Formal operational thought is more abstract and logical than concrete operational thought. Most importantly, formal operational thinking includes thinking about things that are not concrete, making predictions, and using logic to come up with hypotheses about the future.

Unlike elementary schoolchildren, adolescents can conceive of hypothetical, purely abstract possibilities. This type of thinking is called idealistic because it involves comparing how things are to how they might be. Adolescents also think more logically. They begin to think more as a scientist thinks, devising plans to solve problems and systematically testing solutions. Piaget called this type of problem solving *hypothetical-deductive reasoning*. The phrase denotes adolescents' ability to develop hypotheses, or best hunches, about ways to solve a problem such as an algebraic equation. It also denotes their ability to systematically deduce, or come to a conclusion about, the best path for solving the problem. In contrast, before adolescence, children are more likely to solve problems by trial and error.

In summary, over the course of Piaget's four developmental stages, a person progresses from sensorimotor cognition to abstract, idealistic, and logical thought. Piaget based his stages on careful observation of children's behavior, but there is always room to evaluate theory and research. Let's consider the current thinking about Piaget's theories of cognitive development.

formal operational stage
Piaget's fourth stage of cognitive development, which begins at age 11 to 15 and continues through the adulthood; it features thinking about things that are not concrete, making predictions, and using logic to come up with hypotheses about the future.

Evaluating Piaget's Theory

Piaget opened up a new way of looking at how children's minds develop. We owe him for a long list of masterful concepts that have enduring power and fascination. These include the concepts of schemas, assimilation, accommodation, cognitive stages, object permanence, egocentrism, and conservation. We owe Piaget for the currently accepted vision of children as active, constructive thinkers who play a role in their own development.

Nevertheless, just as other psychological theories have been criticized and amended, so have Piaget's. As methods have improved for testing infants and children, researchers have found that many cognitive abilities emerge earlier in children than Piaget thought (S. P. Johnson, 2009; Spelke & Kinzler, 2009). Piaget's object permanence task, for example, has been criticized for not giving infants a chance to show their stuff. Rather than indicating that small children do not have a sense of object permanence, such a task might be demonstrating that these children simply are not able to enact the plan of getting the toy back.

Indeed, Renee Baillargeon (1997; Baillargeon & others, 2009) has documented that infants as young as 3 months of age know that objects continue to exist even when hidden, and that even these very young infants have expectations about objects in the world that seem quite a bit more sophisticated than Piaget imagined. In one study (Luo & Baillargeon, 2005), researchers showed 3-month-old infants a puppet show of Minnie Mouse. In the center of the stage was a flat cardboard cut-out of a castle, with an open door in the middle. Minnie entered stage right and proceeded toward the castle, disappearing behind. When Minnie went behind the castle walls from one side, the infants looked for her to come out on the other side. Furthermore, if, as she made her way behind the castle walls, Minnie did not appear in the open doorway, infants as young as 3 months were surprised. Not only did they realize that Minnie still existed, but they also had expectations about where she was heading, and they believed that she certainly should appear in the door as she passed behind the castle. Also, memory and other forms of symbolic activity occur by at least 6 months of age—much earlier than Piaget thought possible (Bauer, 2009).

This study used looking not only to gauge where the babies expected Minnie to be but also to monitor infant facial expressions. Can you picture all those cute 3-month-old jaws dropping in shock?

Just as Piaget may have *under* estimated infants, he may have *over* estimated adolescents and adults. Formal operational thought does not emerge as consistently and universally in early adolescence as Piaget envisioned (Kuhn, 2008, 2009), and many adolescents and even adults do not reason as logically as Piaget proposed.

Piaget did not think that culture and education play important roles in children's cognitive development. However, researchers have found that the age at which children acquire conservation skills is related to whether their culture provides relevant practice (Cole & Gajdamaschko, 2007). For Piaget, the child's active interaction with the physical world was all that was needed to go through these stages.

The Russian psychologist Lev Vygotsky (1962) took a different approach, recognizing that cognitive development is very much an interpersonal process that happens in a cultural context. Vygotsky thought of children as apprentice thinkers who develop as they interact in dialogue with more knowledgeable others, such as parents and teachers (Holzman, 2009; Wertsch, 2008). Vygotsky believed that these expert thinkers spur cognitive development by interacting with a child in a way that is just above the level of sophistication the child has mastered. In effect, these interactions provide *scaffolding* that allows the child's cognitive abilities to be built higher and higher. Teachers and parents, then, provide a framework for thinking that is always just at a level the child can strive to attain. Furthermore, in Vygotsky's view, the goal of cognitive development is to learn the skills that will allow the individual to be competent in his or her particular culture. These expert thinkers are not simply guiding a child into a level of cognitive sophistication but also, along the way, sharing with the child important aspects of culture, such as language and customs. For Vygotsky, a child is not simply learning to think about the world—he or she is learning to think about *his or her own world*.

Scaffolding is a way of learning that we use throughout life. Do you have friends who have taught you something important about life? Whenever we interact with someone who has more expertise, we have a new scaffold to climb.

Socioemotional Development in Childhood

As children grow and develop, they are socialized by and socialize others, including parents, siblings, peers, and teachers. This section probes several key aspects of children's socioemotional development.

Temperament   When we observe the newborns behind the window of a hospital nursery, one thing is clear: Humans differ from one another in terms of their emotional demeanor from the very beginnings of life. Some are easygoing, and some are prone to distress. **Temperament** refers to an individual's behavioral style and characteristic way of responding.

There are a number of ways to think about infant temperament. For example, psychiatrists Alexander Chess and Stella Thomas (1977) identified three basic types of temperament in children:

temperament
An individual's behavioral style and characteristic way of responding.

- *The easy child* generally is in a positive mood, quickly establishes regular routines in infancy, and easily adapts to new experiences.

- *The difficult child* tends to react negatively and to cry frequently, engages in irregular daily routines, and is slow to accept new experiences.

- *The slow-to-warm-up child* has a low activity level, is somewhat negative, is inflexible, and displays a low intensity of mood.

Other researchers have suggested that we should think about infants as being high or low on different dimensions, such as *effortful control* or *self-regulation* (controlling arousal and not being easily agitated), *inhibition* (being shy and showing distress in an unfamiliar situation), and *negative affectivity* (tending to be frustrated or sad)

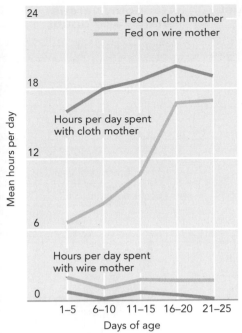

FIGURE 8.9
Contact Time with Wire and Cloth Surrogate Mothers
Regardless of whether the infant monkeys were fed by a wire or a cloth mother, they overwhelmingly preferred to spend contact time with the cloth mother.

(Kagan, 2008; Rothbart & Gartstein, 2008). Thus, psychologists have not reached agreement about the basic core dimensions of temperament (Bates & Pettit, 2007). The emotional characteristics that a child brings into the world serve as a foundation for later personality, and the child's earliest social bonds might set the stage for later social relationships.

Attachment in Infancy   Just as infants require nutrition and shelter, they need warm social interaction to survive and develop. A classic study by Harry Harlow (1958) demonstrates the essential importance of warm contact. Harlow separated infant monkeys from their mothers at birth and placed them in cages in which they had access to two artificial "mothers." One of the mothers was a physically cold wire mother; the other was a warm, fuzzy cloth mother (the "contact comfort" mother). Each mother could be outfitted with a feeding mechanism. Half of the infant monkeys were fed by the wire mother, half by the cloth mother. The infant monkeys nestled close to the cloth mother and spent little time on the wire one, even if it was the wire mother that gave them milk (Figure 8.9). When afraid, the infant monkeys ran to the comfy mom. This study clearly demonstrates that what the researchers described as "contact comfort," not feeding, is crucial to the attachment of an infant to its caregiver.

You might find it hard to believe that psychologists required proof that snuggling with Mommy matters to babies. Remember, though, scientists are skeptical, and so it was important that Harlow demonstrated that even if the warm, snuggly mother didn't provide food, she was still a source of comfort.

infant attachment
The close emotional bond between an infant and its caregiver.

Infant attachment is the close emotional bond between an infant and its caregiver. British psychiatrist John Bowlby (1969, 1989) theorized that the infant and the mother instinctively form an attachment. He viewed the newborn as innately equipped to stimulate the caregiver to respond; it cries, clings, smiles, and coos. Bowlby thought that our early relationships with our caregiver are internalized so that they serve as our schemas for our sense of self and the social world. A number of developmental psychologists conclude that attachment to the caregiver during the first year provides an important foundation for later development (Berlin, Zeanah, & Lieberman, 2008; Cassidy, 2008).

Mary Ainsworth devised a way to study differences in children's attachment, called the *strange situation* test (Ainsworth, 1979; Ainsworth & others, 1978). In this procedure, caregivers leave infants alone with a stranger and then return. Reponses of children

Trust versus mistrust	**Autonomy versus shame and doubt**	**Initiative versus guilt**	**Industry versus inferiority**
Developmental period: Infancy (Birth to 1½ years)	**Developmental period:** Toddlerhood (1½ to 3 years)	**Developmental period:** Early childhood (preschool years, ages 3–5)	**Developmental period:** Middle and late childhood (elementary school years, 6 years–puberty)
Characteristics: A sense of trust requires a feeling of physical comfort and minimal amount of fear about the future. Infants' basic needs are met by responsive, sensitive caregivers.	**Characteristics:** After gaining trust in their caregivers, infants start to discover that they have a will of their own. They assert their sense of autonomy, or independence. They realize their will. If infants are restrained too much or punished too harshly, they are likely to develop a sense of shame and doubt.	**Characteristics:** As preschool children encounter a widening social world, they are challenged more and need to develop more purposeful behavior to cope with these challenges. Children are now asked to assume more responsibility. Uncomfortable guilt feelings may arise, though, if the children are irresponsible and are made to feel too anxious.	**Characteristics:** At no other time are children more enthusiastic than at the end of early childhood's period of expansive imagination. As children move into the elementary school years, they direct their energy toward mastering knowledge and intellectual skills. The danger at this stage involves feeling incompetent and unproductive.

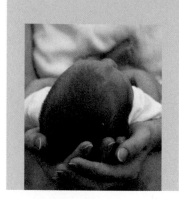

FIGURE 8.10
Erikson's Eight Stages of Human Development Erikson changed the way psychologists think about development by tracing the process of growth over the entire life span.

to this situation are used to classify their attachment style. Ainsworth devised the term **secure attachment** to describe how infants use the caregiver, usually the mother, as a secure base from which to explore the environment. In the strange situation, the secure infant is upset when the mother leaves, but calms down and appears happy to see her when she returns. Infants who are securely attached are more likely to have mothers who are responsive and accepting and who express affection toward them than are infants who are insecurely attached (Sroufe & others, 2005). The securely attached infant moves freely away from the mother but also keeps tabs on her by periodically glancing at her. An insecurely attached infant, in contrast, avoids the mother or is ambivalent toward her. In the strange situation, such an infant might not even notice the mother has gone, or conversely might respond with intense distress, only to rage at the mother when she returns.

One criticism of attachment theory is that it does not adequately account for cultural variations (van IJzendoorn & Sagi-Schwartz, 2008). For example, in some cultures infants show strong attachments to many people, not just their primary caregiver. In the African Hausa culture, both grandmothers and siblings provide a significant amount of care to infants (Harkness & Super, 1995). Infants in agricultural societies tend to form attachments to older siblings who are assigned a major responsibility for younger siblings' care.

Another critique of attachment theory is that it may not account for temperamental differences among infants that might color the attachment relationship. In addition, caregivers and infants likely share genetic characteristics, and it might be that the attachment relationship is really a product of these shared genes. Despite such criticisms there is ample evidence that secure attachment is important to development (Cassidy, 2008; Thompson & Newton, 2009).

Erikson's Theory of Socioemotional Development
The life-span development theory of the influential psychologist Erik Erikson (1902–1994), who trained as a psychoanalyst under Sigmund Freud, proposed eight psychosocial stages of development from infancy through old age. In Erikson's (1968) view, the first four stages take

secure attachment The ways that infants use their caregiver, usually their mother, as a secure base from which to explore the environment.

Identity versus identity confusion	**Intimacy versus isolation**	**Generativity versus stagnation**	**Integrity versus despair**
Developmental period: Adolescence (10–20 years) **Characteristics:** Individuals are faced with finding out who they are, what they are all about, and where they are going in life. An important dimension is the exploration of alternative solutions to roles. Career exploration is important.	**Developmental period:** Eary adulthood (20s, 30s) **Characteristics:** Individuals face the developmental task of forming intimate relationships with others. Erikson described intimacy as finding oneself yet losing oneself in another person.	**Developmental period:** Middle adulthood (40s, 50s) **Characteristics:** A chief concern is to assist the younger generation in developing and leading useful lives.	**Developmental period:** Late adulthood (60s–) **Characteristics:** Individuals look back and evaluate what they have done with their lives. The retrospective glances can either be positive (integrity) or negative (despair).

place in childhood; the last four, in adolescence and adulthood (Figure 8.10). Each stage represents the kind of developmental task that the individual must master at a particular place in physical and emotional development. According to Erikson, these developmental tasks are represented by two possible outcomes, such as trust versus mistrust (Erikson's first stage). If an infant's physical and emotional needs are well taken care of, he or she will experience an enduring sense of trust in others. If these needs are frustrated, the person might carry concerns about trust throughout his or her life, with bits of this unfinished business being reflected in the rest of the stages. For Erikson, each stage is a turning point with two opposing possible outcomes: one, greater personal competence; and the other, greater weakness and vulnerability.

Erik Erikson (1902–1994)
Erikson generated one of the most important developmental theories of the twentieth century.

Erikson's Childhood Stages
We examine Erikson's adolescence and adult stages later in this chapter. His four childhood stages are:

1. *Trust versus mistrust* (the first 18 months of life): Trust is built when a baby's basic needs—such as comfort, food, and warmth—are met. If infants' needs are not met by responsive, sensitive caregivers, the result is mistrust. Trust in infancy sets the stage for a lifelong expectation that the world will be a good and pleasant place to live.

2. *Autonomy versus shame and doubt* (18 months through 3 years): Children can develop either a positive sense of independence and autonomy or negative feelings of shame and doubt. In seeking autonomy, they are likely to develop a strong sense of independence.

3. *Initiative versus guilt* (3 to 5 years): During these years, children's social worlds are widening. When asked to assume more responsibility for themselves, children can develop initiative. When allowed to be irresponsible or made to feel anxious, they can develop too much guilt.

4. *Industry versus inferiority* (age 6 to puberty): Children can achieve industry by mastering knowledge and intellectual skills. When they do not, they can feel inferior. At

psychology in our world

The Joy of the Toy

When kids are playing, they are often playing with toys. Toys have been around for a very long time. Archaeologists have dated the first toy, an ancient Egyptian doll made of paper, cloth, and string, to 2000 B.C.E. Today, toys are a huge U.S. industry: In 2004 and 2005, Americans spent *$22 billion* on them ("Americans spent billions on toys," 2006).

Toy manufacturers are well aware of the importance of understanding developmental psychology when designing toys. As noted by toy designer Barry Kudrowitz (quoted in Benson, 2006), "Before brainstorming, the designer should know what types of behaviors are typical for that age group; . . . the social, mental, and physical abilities of the age group, and what types of play are most common." Developmental psychology courses are required in the toy design degree program at the Fashion Institute of Technology in New York City, where the first U.S. toy design program was founded in the 1980s.

Toy manufacturers conduct a great deal of research examining toys and children's cognitive and perceptual abilities. Outside the toy industry, psychologists have investigated such topics as the effects of advertising on toy preferences and the influence of toys on children's body images. They have found, for example, that boys are more susceptible than girls to gender in ads (Pike & Jennings, 2005) and that exposure to Barbie can predict lowered body image among girls (Dittmar, Halliwell, & Ive, 2006).

The value of a toy lies in its capacity to capture a child's imagination. How many parents have stood by in shock as their child tossed aside an expensive new toy and played for hours with the box it came in? In that box, the child may have discovered a house, a cave, a car, or a spaceship. Is it any surprise that in 2008, the humble *stick* was inducted into the Toy Hall of Fame? As long as there is a stick around, an imaginative child has a horse, a sword, a baton, and a superpowered laser cannon.

the end of early childhood, children are ready to turn their energy to learning academic skills. If they do not, they can develop a sense of being incompetent and unproductive.

Evaluating Erikson's Theory

Like Piaget's theory, Erikson's conclusions have had their critics (Kroger, 2007). Erikson mainly practiced case study research, which some reject as the sole research foundation for his approach. Critics also argue that Erikson's attempt to capture each stage with a single concept leaves out other important developmental tasks. For example, Erikson said that the main task for young adults is to resolve the conflict between intimacy and isolation. However, another important developmental task in early adulthood involves careers and work. Such criticisms do not tarnish Erikson's monumental contributions, however. Like Piaget, he is a giant in developmental psychology.

Parenting and Developmental Outcomes

Even though many American children spend a great deal of time in child care in their early years, and nearly all children in the United States spend many hours in school as they grow older, parents

are still the main caregivers for most children. Various researchers have tried to identify styles of parenting associated with positive developmental outcomes. Diana Baumrind (1991, 1993) described four basic styles of interaction between parents and their children:

■ **Authoritarian parenting** is a restrictive, punitive style in which the parent exhorts the child to follow the parent's directions and to value hard work and effort. The authoritarian parent firmly limits and controls the child with little verbal exchange. In a difference of opinion about how to do something, for example, the authoritarian parent might say, "You do it my way or else." Children of authoritarian parents sometimes lack social skills, show poor initiative, and compare themselves with others.

    However, culture influences the effects of authoritarian parenting. In one study (Rudy & Grusec, 2006), collectivist mothers (in this case Iranian, Indian, Egyptian, and Pakistani) described themselves as more authoritarian but did not express negative attitudes about their children, and the children did not show these more negative outcomes. Further, with respect to Latino families, some psychologists have suggested that authoritarian parenting may express culturally valued child-rearing goals such as family, respect, and education and that this parenting style must be understood in the context of these cultural ideals (Halgunseth, Ispa, & Rudy, 2006).

authoritarian parenting
A restrictive, punitive style in which the parent exhorts the child to follow the parent's directions and to value hard work and effort.

■ **Authoritative parenting** encourages the child to be independent but still places limits and controls on behavior. Extensive verbal give-and-take is allowed, and parents are warm and nurturing toward the child. An authoritative father might put his arm around the child in a comforting way and say, "You know you should not have done that; let's talk about how you can handle the situation better next time." Children whose parents are authoritative tend to be socially competent, self-reliant, and socially responsible.

authoritative parenting
A parenting style that encourages the child to be independent but that still places limits and controls on behavior.

■ **Neglectful parenting** is distinguished by a lack of parental involvement in the child's life. Children of neglectful parents might develop a sense that other aspects of the parents' lives are more important than they are. Children whose parents are neglectful tend to be less competent socially, to handle independence poorly, and (especially) to show poor self-control.

neglectful parenting
A parenting style characterized by a lack of parental involvement in the child's life.

■ **Permissive parenting** is characterized by parental involvement with the child in a context where there are few limits on the child's behavior. A permissive parent lets the child do what he or she wants. Some parents deliberately rear their children this way because they believe that the combination of warm involvement and few limits will produce a creative, confident child. However, children with very permissive parents typically rate poorly in social competence. They often fail to learn respect for others, expect to get their own way, and have difficulty controlling their behavior.

permissive parenting
A parenting style characterized by the placement of few limits on the child's behavior.

    A recent debate about parenting focuses on whether "super parenting" is necessary. To examine this issue, see Challenge Your Thinking.

Divorce and Developmental Outcomes

Although the U.S. divorce rate has been declining in the last two decades, the rate is still very high (Amato, 2006). As a result, the United States has the highest percentage of children growing up in single-parent families (many of which are the result of divorce) of all industrialized countries.

    Many children are highly vulnerable to stress during the experience of divorce. According to leading researcher E. Mavis Hetherington, adjustment difficulties characterize approximately 25 percent of children and adolescents in divorced families, compared with only 10 percent of children and adolescents in non-divorced families (Hetherington, 2006; Hetherington & Stanley-Hagen, 2002). This finding means that approximately 75 percent of children in divorced families do *not* have adjustment problems. Among

challenge your thinking

Should Parents Be Superheroes?

Long ago, most parents held firmly to the adage "Children should be seen and not heard." These traditional parents expected children to be independent, to play among themselves, and to stay out of the way. Today parents are more likely to be preoccupied with their children's lives, even to the point of obsessing over enrolling their little ones in the "right" preschool and kindergarten. Is this obsession necessary for healthy development?

Some experts would give that question a definite no. Judith Harris (1998), in her book *The Nurture Assumption,* argues that what parents do makes no difference in children's behavior. Instead, Harris says, genes and peers are far more important than parents in children's development. For her part, developmental researcher Sandra Scarr (1992, 2000) contends that "super-parenting" is unnecessary. Scarr argues that the genotype is so strong that it makes most environmental experiences unimportant. She suggests that the only parenting that significantly affects a child's development is parenting that is far outside the normal range, such as chronic physical abuse. Apart from such extremes, Scarr asserts, genes are the primary determinant of developmental outcomes. So, maybe parents can take a breather.

Not so fast. Such claims have met with a firestorm of criticism. Diane Baumrind (1993) countered that "good enough" parenting *is not* good enough, and cited evidence that highly demanding and highly responsive parents are more likely to have high-achieving

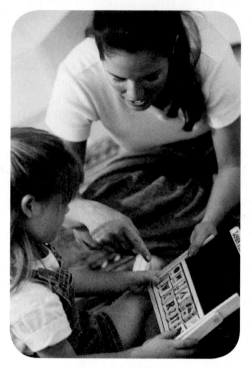

and socially well-adjusted children. A longitudinal study by W. Andrew Collins and his colleagues (2000) supported Baumrind's claims; it showed that even with genetic influences taken into account, parenting practices made a difference in children's lives.

Sometimes, however, very attentive parents forget the importance of simply letting a kid be a kid. Parents can overemphasize academic achievement over the fun that childhood should always include. A recent study of over 300 preschoolers found that the children who were best prepared for school were those whose parents taught them not only their ABCs but also how to play—and in particular, how to play well with others (Bierman & others, 2008). In short, there must be a happy medium—parents who allow children enough freedom to make their own mistakes yet who attend to their children in responsive ways. Parenting may be serious business, but it can also be a great excuse to play again, like a child.

What Do You Think?

- If you have children or decide to have them in the future, how might this debate affect your approach to parenting?

- Why might today's parents be more likely than parents in the past to try to be super-parents?

---

the factors that predict better adjustment for children in divorced families are harmony between the divorced parents, authoritative parenting, good schools, and the child's possession of an easy rather than a difficult temperament (Amato, 2006; Fine & Harvey, 2006; Hetherington, 2006).

Moral Development   Moral development involves changes with age in thoughts, feelings, and behaviors regarding the principles and values that guide what people should do. Psychologists have studied how people reason and think about moral matters, how they feel about them, and how they actually behave. Research on moral reasoning and thinking has revolved around Lawrence Kohlberg's theory of moral development and reactions to it.

Kohlberg's Theory Kohlberg (1958) began his study of moral thinking by creating a series of stories and asking children, adolescents, and adults questions about the stories. One of the stories goes something like this: A man, Heinz, whose wife is dying of cancer, knows about a drug that might save her life. He approaches the pharmacist who has the drug, but the pharmacist refuses to give it to him without being paid a very high price. Heinz is unable to scrape together the money and eventually decides to steal the drug.

After reading the story, the interviewee was asked a series of questions about the moral dilemma. Was stealing it right or wrong? Why? Based on the answers that people gave to the questions about this story and other moral dilemmas, Kohlberg (1986) evaluated their level of moral development. Kohlberg's stages of moral development consisted of three levels, with two stages at each level (Figure 8.11):

Lawrence Kohlberg (1927–1987)
Kohlberg created a provocative theory of moral development. In his view, "Moral development consists of a sequence of qualitative changes in the way an individual thinks."

1. The *preconventional level* is based primarily on punishments (stage 1) or rewards (stage 2) that come from the external world. In regard to the Heinz story, at stage 1 an individual might say that Heinz should not steal the drug because he might get caught and sent to jail. At stage 2, the person might say he should not steal the drug because the druggist needs to make a profit on the drug.

2. At the *conventional level,* the individual abides by standards such as those learned from parents (stage 3) or society's laws (stage 4). At stage 3, an individual might say that Heinz should steal the drug for his wife because that is what people expect a good husband to do. At stage 4, the person might say that it is natural for Heinz to want to save his wife but that the law says it still is always wrong to steal.

3. At the *postconventional level,* the individual recognizes alternative moral courses, explores the options, and then develops a personal moral code. The code reflects the principles generally accepted by the community (stage 5) or it reflects more abstract principles for all of humanity (stage 6). At stage 5, a person might say that the law was not set up for these circumstances, so Heinz can steal the drug. It is not really right, but he is justified in doing it. At stage 6, the individual evaluates alternatives but recognizes that Heinz's wife's life is more important than a law.

LEVEL 1	LEVEL 2	LEVEL 3
Preconventional Level **No Internalization**	**Conventional Level** **Intermediate Internalization**	**Postconventional Level** **Full Internalization**
Stage 1 Heteronomous Morality	**Stage 3** Mutual Interpersonal Expectations, Relationships, and Interpersonal Conformity	**Stage 5** Social Contract or Utility and Individual Rights
Individuals pursue their own interests but let others do the same. What is right involves equal exchange.	*Individuals value trust, caring, and loyalty to others as a basis for moral judgments.*	*Individuals reason that values, rights, and principles undergird or transcend the law.*
Stage 2 Individualism, Purpose, and Exchange	**Stage 4** Social System Morality	**Stage 6** Universal Ethical Principles
Children obey because adults tell them to obey. People base their moral decisions on fear of punishment.	*Moral judgments are based on understanding and the social order, law, justice, and duty.*	*The person has developed moral judgments that are based on universal human rights. When faced with a dilemma between law and conscience, a personal, individualized conscience is followed.*

FIGURE 8.11
Kohlberg's Three Levels and Six Stages of Moral Development Kohlberg proposed that human moral development could be characterized by a sequence of age-related changes.

Carol Gilligan (b. 1936)
Gilligan argues that Kohlberg's approach does not give adequate attention to relationships. In Gilligan's view, "Many girls seem to fear, most of all, being alone—without friends, family and relationships."

Go online and google "Parenting Discussion Boards." Click on one or two of the many sites that come up, and see what parents are talking about. What issues seem to concern them most? Do these parents appear to have a sense of the issues addressed by developmental psychologists? Does the advice that parents share with one another seem to be based on the science of psychology?

Kohlberg thought that advances in moral development occur because of the maturation of thought, opportunities for role taking, and the chance to discuss moral issues with a person who reasons at a stage just above one's own.

Evaluating Kohlberg's Theory   Kohlberg's ideas have stimulated considerable research about how people think about moral issues (Lapsley, 2006; Power & others, 2008). At the same time, his theory has numerous critics. One criticism is that moral *reasoning* does not necessarily mean moral *behavior.* When people are asked about their moral reasoning, what they say might fit into Kohlberg's advanced stages, but their actual behavior might involve cheating, lying, and stealing. The cheaters, liars, and thieves might know what is right but still do what is wrong.

Another criticism is that Kohlberg's view does not adequately reflect concern for other people and social bonds (Carlo, 2006). Kohlberg's theory is called a *justice perspective* because it focuses on the rights of the individual, who stands alone and independently makes moral decisions. In contrast, the *care perspective,* which lies at the heart of Carol Gilligan's (1982) approach to moral development, views people in terms of their connectedness with others and emphasizes interpersonal communication, relationships, and concern for others. From Gilligan's perspective this weakness in Kohlberg's approach explains why, using his measures, women generally score lower than men on moral development. Similarly, culture can influence whether a person approaches a moral dilemma from the perspective of justice or care (Gibbs, 2009). Individuals in Western cultures, who more generally tend toward an individualistic sense of self and who therefore are inclined to take a justice perspective, might score higher in Kohlberg's scheme than individuals in Asian cultures that stress collectivism and a sense of the self as part of a larger group.

Recent Studies of Moral Development   Researchers interested in moral development have increasingly studied **prosocial behavior,** behavior that is intended to benefit other people (Eisenberg & others, 2009). For example, researchers are probing how, when, and why children engage in everyday acts of kindness toward others (Carlo, 2006). Studies have found that supportive parenting and parental monitoring relate to increased helping and comforting of others (Dodge, Coie, & Lynam, 2006).

Other recent work has focused on when a child first shows signs of possessing a conscience (Kochanska & others, 2008; R. A. Thompson, 2009b). Having a conscience means hearing that voice in our head that tells us that something is morally good or bad. Deborah Laible and Ross Thompson (2000, 2002, 2007) have examined the conversations between mothers and toddlers at times when the child did something well or got into trouble. They have found that by 3 years of age, children begin to show signs of early conscience development. This development is fostered by parent–child interactions that are clear, elaborate, and rich with emotional content and that include shared positive emotion. Childhood characteristics are important because longitudinal research shows that kind, moral children are more likely to be kind, moral adults (Eisenberg, Fabes, & Sprinrad, 2006).

How can parents successfully rear a child to be considerate of others and to understand the difference between right and wrong? The following parenting strategies have most often been found to be helpful in rearing a moral child (Eisenberg & Murphy, 1995; Eisenberg & Valiente, 2002; Eisenberg & others, 2009):

- Being warm and supportive rather than overly punishing and rigid
- When disciplining, using reasoning the child can understand
- Providing opportunities for the child to learn about others' perspectives and feelings

prosocial behavior
Behavior that is intended to benefit other people.

- Involving children in family decision making and in thinking about moral decisions
- Modeling moral behaviors and thinking, and providing children with opportunities to engage in such behaviors and thought

Gender Development

Gender Development Following prenatal tests, or when a baby is born, the first question often is, "Is it a boy or a girl?" *Gender* refers to the social and psychological aspects of being male or female. Gender includes not only biological sex but also one's understanding of the meaning of gender in one's life. Although checking off "male" or "female" on a questionnaire may seem like a pretty simple decision, gender is a complex variable influenced by both nature and nurture.

Biology and Gender Development Humans normally have 46 chromosomes arranged in pairs. The 23rd pair may have two X-shaped chromosomes, which produces a female, or it may have both an X-shaped and an (upside-down) Y-shaped chromosome, which produces a male.

In the first few weeks after conception, male and female embryos look alike. When the Y chromosome in the male embryo triggers the secretion of **androgens,** the main class of male sex hormones, male sex organs start to differentiate from female sex organs. Low levels of androgen in a female embryo allow the normal development of female sex organs. Long after conception, hormones still play a powerful role in shaping sex characteristics and possibly in influencing gender-related behaviors (Blakemore, Berenbaum, & Liben, 2009).

androgens
The main class of male sex hormones.

Social Experience and Gender Development Social experiences also influence gender behavior. As children grow up, they adopt **gender roles,** which involve expectations for how females and males should think, act, and feel (Leaper & Friedman, 2007). Recall from our earlier discussion of Piaget's theory that a schema is a mental framework that organizes and guides an individual's thoughts. One theory proposes that children develop a gender schema based on what is considered appropriate behavior for females and males in their culture (Zosuls, Lurye, & Ruble, 2008). This gender schema then serves as a cognitive framework for interpreting further experiences related to gender. As their gender schema develops, children knit together all sorts of ideas in the context of gender, such as "Girls are expected to be nurturing" and "Boys are expected to be independent."

gender roles
Roles that reflect the individual's expectations for how females and males should think, act, and feel.

Some cultures emphasize that children should be reared to adopt traditional gender roles (Shiraev & Levy, 2010). Parents in these cultures bring up boys to be "masculine" (say, powerful, aggressive, and independent) and girls to be "feminine" (sensitive to others, good at relationships, and less assertive). Other cultures, especially in recent times, have emphasized rearing boys and girls to be more similar— raising boys to be just as caring toward others as girls and raising girls to be just as assertive as boys. Egypt and China are two countries in which traditional gender roles continue to dominate, but the United States has moved toward more diversity in gender roles. Still, even in the United States, parents often dress infant boys in blue and infant girls in pink. Boys receive trucks to play with; girls get dolls.

Peers also play an important role in gender development (Rose & Smith, 2009). Starting in middle and late childhood (6 to 10 or 11 years of age or until puberty begins) especially, peer groups are often segregated into boy groups and girl groups (Maccoby, 2002) (Figure 8.12). Peers are stricter than most parents in rewarding gender-appropriate behavior and punishing gender-inappropriate behavior. As we see in the Intersection, gender plays a role in the effects of friends on children's well-being.

Psychologists have increasingly viewed gender, like many other aspects of human life, as a complex product of nature and nurture

Very young children may believe that a person's sex can change depending on superficial features. They may reason, for instance, that girls have long hair, and so if that hair is cut short, a girl becomes a boy.

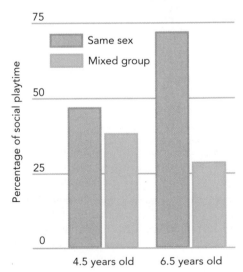

FIGURE 8.12
Developmental Changes in Percentage of Time Spent in Same-Sex and Mixed-Group Settings
Observations of children show that they are more likely to play in same-sex than mixed-sex groups. This tendency increases between 4 and 6 years of age.

intersection

Making and keeping friends and being a friend are all tasks that face the developing human being. Friends are important to children's self-esteem, well-being, and school adjustment (Rubin, Bukowski, & Parker, 2006). Having friends means that there is someone to talk to when we have problems and to celebrate with when things go well. Are all friendships equally supportive, however? Research indicates that some friends have a knack for making problems seem worse, not better.

Developmental psychologist Amanda Rose and her colleagues (Rose, 2002; Rose, Carlson, & Waller, 2007; Rose & Smith, 2009) have studied how young friends' responses to their friends' problems influence children's and adolescents' mental health. Rose (2002) introduced the concept of *co-rumination* to describe the ways that some friends might make matters worse by giving their pals more to worry about than they had originally realized. For example, if Janisa

Developmental Psychology and Clinical Psychology: Is "Girl Talk" Always a Good Thing?

tells her friend Robin about doing poorly on a spelling test, does Robin encourage Janisa to study harder, or does she remind Janisa that not doing well now is a bad sign because the words are only going to get harder in the future? Rumination is a way of thinking that involves worrying without finding a resolution. When we ruminate, we might dwell on all the possible horrible consequences of some negative life event or imagine everything that might go wrong in the future. Co-rumination is like that too, but it involves engaging in a conversation with someone and making a negative event that the person is going through seem even worse.

In a study of hundreds of grade-school and middle-school children, Rose (2002) found that girls were more likely than boys to co-ruminate, and this difference was particularly large among adolescents. Furthermore, longitudinal research has shown that co-rumination, even in the context of good friends, was associated with increased feelings of depression and anxiety, especially for girls (Rose, Carlson, & Waller, 2007). Rose and colleagues suggest that some friends represent a trade-off, notably in the case of girls. Having close friends might be a sign of social functioning, but when those friends hurt more than help, they can negatively influence well-being.

Why do you think co-ruminators often accentuate the negatives? Why might co-rumination be a greater problem for girls than boys?

(Hyde, 2007; Lippa, 2005; Ruble, Martin, & Berenbaum, 2006). John Money, a sex researcher who coined the term *gender role,* believed strongly that nurture was the main determinant of gender behavior. In the late 1960s, a case presented itself that gave Money the opportunity to test this theory. In 1965 twin boys were born, and a few months after birth, one twin's penis was destroyed during circumcision. Money persuaded the boy's parents to allow him to surgically transform the injured male genitals into female genitals and to agree to raise the child as a girl. The "John/Joan" case became famous—the former boy was reared as a girl, dressed like a girl, and treated like a girl in every way possible (Money & Tucker, 1975).

For many years, this case was used as evidence for the amazing flexibility of gender. In fact, until recently, many psychology textbooks still described the case of "John/Joan" as a story of the triumph of nurture over nature. However, Milton Diamond, a biologist and strong critic of Money's theory, decided to follow up on Money's most famous case study (Diamond & Sigmundson, 1997). Diamond found that over time, "Joan" became less and less interested in being a girl and eventually refused to continue the process of feminization that Money had devised. Indeed, we now know that "Joan" was really David, whose biography, *As Nature Made Him,* written by John Colapinto (2000), revealed the difficulties of his life as a boy, then girl, then boy, and finally man. David struggled with traumatic gender-related life experiences and also depression, eventually committing suicide in 2004. Although this case seems to indicate that nature is quite powerful, similar cases have had more positive outcomes, supporting the flexibility aspect of gender (Bradley & others, 1998; Lippa, 2005).

Resilience in Childhood

resilience
A person's ability to recover from or adapt to difficult times.

Even in the worst circumstances, individuals sometimes overcome hardships, thrive, and achieve great things. **Resilience** refers to a person's ability to recover from or adapt to difficult times. Despite hardship, time and time again, resilient children grow up to be capable adults. Why does one person who is subjected to violence, poverty, racism, or the divorce of parents remain mired in lifelong misfortune, while another rises above those obstacles to succeed in business, the community, or family life?

Researchers have found that resilient children have one or more advantages that help them to overcome their disadvantages (Masten, 2007; Masten, Obradovic, & Burt, 2006). These advantages include individual factors (such as strong intellectual functioning), family factors (such as a close, caring relationship with at least one parent), and extrafamilial factors (for example, bonds to supportive, competent adults outside the family). Not all of them need to be present to help a child develop successfully. If a child does not have responsible, caring parents, then high self-esteem and a bond to a caring adult outside the home could make the child resilient enough to overcome negative family factors.

Extrafamilial factors, such as contact with supportive, competent adults outside the home, can contribute powerfully to childhood resiliency.

self-quiz

1. The first two weeks after conception are referred to as the
   A. fetal period.
   B. germinal period.
   C. embryonic period.
   D. zygotic period.

2. In Piaget's theory, object permanence occurs in the stage of cognitive development called the
   A. concrete operational stage.
   B. formal operational stage.
   C. preoperational stage.
   D. sensorimotor stage.

3. Vygotsky stressed that cognitive development is an interpersonal process that happens in a _____ context.
   A. historical
   B. physical

C. cultural
D. positive

Apply It! 4. Tyrone is babysitting for his younger cousins, who are ages 3, 4, and 9. For lunch, each child will be drinking apple juice, which they all love. Tyrone only has three serving cups—one that is short and wide, and two that are long and thin. Although Tyrone pours the same amount of juice into all the cups, the younger kids fuss and fight over who gets stuck with the short, wide cup. The 9-year-old shrugs and takes the wide cup. Tyrone later proclaims, "Those other two kids are really spoiled brats! Thank

goodness the oldest is not so selfish." Which of the following best applies to Tyrone's conclusion?
A. Tyrone is right—young kids are more likely to be spoiled and whiny.
B. Tyrone does not understand that the younger kids do not recognize that the amount of juice in the cups is the same. The 9-year-old is not being unselfish; he or she knows the amounts are the same.
C. The 9-year-old probably does not understand that the wider cup contains the same amount of juice as the other two.
D. Tyrone probably got an *A* in Developmental Psychology.

3 Adolescence

Adolescence is the developmental period of transition from childhood to adulthood, beginning around 10 to 12 years of age and ending at 18 to 21 years of age. Adolescents are not all the same (Diamond & Savin-Williams, 2009). Ethnic, cultural, historical, gender, socioeconomic, and lifestyle variations characterize their life trajectories (Galambos, Berenbaum, & McHale, 2009). Any image of adolescents should take into account the particular adolescent or group of adolescents we are considering.

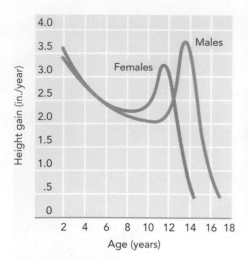

FIGURE 8.13

Pubertal Growth Spurt On average, the pubertal growth spurt begins and peaks about two years earlier for girls (starts at 9, peaks at 11½) than for boys (starts at 11½, peaks at 13½).

From J. M. Tanner et al., in *Archives of Diseases in Childhood* 41, 1966. Reproduced with permission from the BMJ Publishing Group.

Physical Development in Adolescence

Dramatic physical changes characterize adolescence, especially early adolescence. Among the major physical changes of adolescence are those involving puberty and the brain.

Pubertal Change   The signature physical change in adolescence is **puberty,** a period of rapid skeletal and sexual maturation that occurs mainly in early adolescence. In general, we know when an individual is going through puberty, but we have a hard time pinpointing its beginning and its end. Except for *menarche* (girls' first menstrual cycle), no single marker defines it. For boys the first whisker or first nocturnal ejaculation (or wet dream) could mark its appearance, but both may go unnoticed.

The jump in height and weight that characterizes pubertal change occurs about two years earlier for girls than for boys (Figure 8.13). In the United States today, the average beginning of the growth spurt is 9 years of age for girls and 11 years for boys. The peak of pubertal change occurs at an average age of 11½ for girls and 13½ for boys.

Hormonal changes lie at the core of pubertal development. The concentrations of certain hormones increase dramatically during puberty (Susman & Dorn, 2009). *Testosterone,* an androgen, is associated in boys with the development of genitals, an increase in height, and voice change. *Estradiol,* an estrogen, is associated in girls with breast, uterine, and skeletal development. Developmental psychologists believe that hormonal changes account for at least some of the emotional ups and downs of adolescence, but hormones are not alone responsible for adolescent behavior (Graber, 2007).

Remember that physical and socioemotional development are intertwined. Nowhere is this link more apparent than in the timing of puberty. Boys who mature earlier than their peers tend to show more positive socioemotional outcomes, such as being popular with their peers and having higher self-esteem (Graber, Brooks-Gunn, & Warren, 2006). In one study, boys who matured early in adolescence were more successful and less likely to drink alcohol or smoke cigarettes than late-maturing boys some *39 years later* (Taga, Markey, & Friedman, 2006). In contrast, girls who are early bloomers tend to be less outgoing and less popular, and they are more likely to smoke, use drugs, become sexually active, and engage less in academic pursuits (Susman & Dorn, 2009).

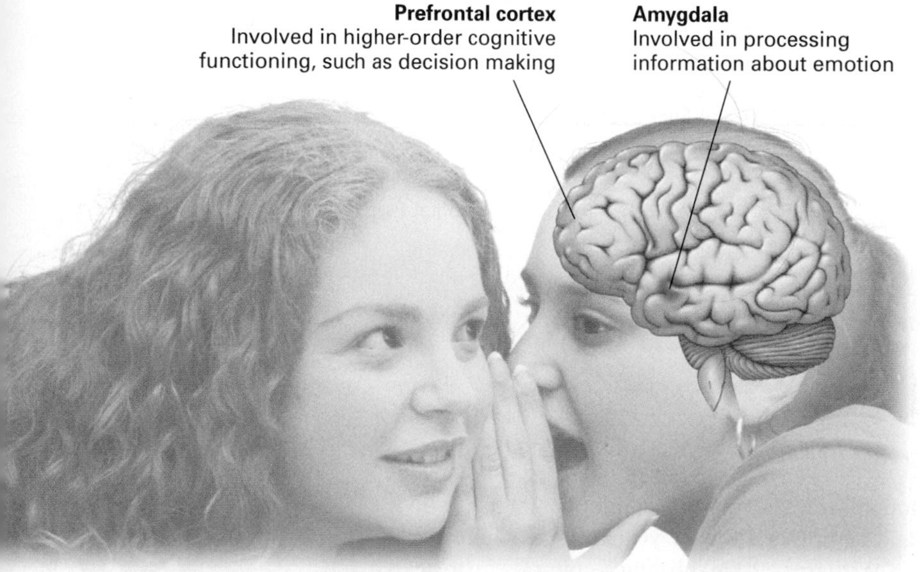

The Brain   Advances in imaging the human brain have allowed researchers to discover some important changes in the brain during adolescence (Paus, 2009; Steinberg, 2009). These changes focus on the earlier development of the amygdala, which involves emotion, and the later development of the prefrontal cortex, which is concerned with reasoning and decision making (Figure 8.14). These changes in the brain may help to explain why adolescents often display very strong emotions but cannot yet control these

puberty
A period of rapid skeletal and sexual maturation that occurs mainly in early adolescence.

Prefrontal cortex
Involved in higher-order cognitive functioning, such as decision making

Amygdala
Involved in processing information about emotion

FIGURE 8.14

Developmental Changes in the Adolescent's Brain The amygdala, which is responsible for processing information about emotion, matures earlier than the prefrontal cortex, which is responsible for making decisions and other higher-order cognitive functions.

passions. It is as if their brains do not have the brakes to slow down their emotions. Because of the relatively slow development of the prefrontal cortex, which continues to mature into early adulthood, adolescents may lack the cognitive skills to control their pleasure seeking effectively. This developmental disjunction may account for increased risk taking and other problems in adolescence (Steinberg, 2009).

A major question is which comes first—biological changes in the brain or experiences that stimulate these changes (Lerner, Boyd, & Du, 2008)? Consider a recent study in which the prefrontal cortex thickened and more brain connections formed when adolescents resisted peer pressure (Paus & others, 2008). Were the results due to biology or to experience? This correlational study cannot answer that question, and once again we encounter the nature–nurture issue that is so prominent in examining development.

Cognitive Development in Adolescence

Adolescents undergo significant cognitive changes (Byrnes, 2008; Kuhn, 2009), including advancing into Piaget's stage of formal operational thinking, which we examined earlier. Another characteristic of adolescent thinking, especially in early adolescence, is egocentrism. Although egocentrism has been noted as an aspect of children's cognitions, *adolescent egocentrism* involves the belief that others are as preoccupied with the adolescent as he or she is, that one is unique, and that one is invincible (meaning that one cannot be harmed) (Elkind, 1978). With egocentrism at this developmental stage, individuals perceive others to be noticing and watching them more than actually is the case. Think of the eighth-grade boy who senses that everyone has noticed the small pimple on his face, and the teenage girl who says, "My mother has no idea about how much pain I'm going through. She has never been hurt like me! Why did he break up with me?"

The sense of invincibility is the most dangerous aspect of adolescent egocentrism. This belief may lead to behaviors such as drag racing, drug use, and unsafe sex. In one study of sixth- through twelfth-graders, feeling invincible was linked to risky behaviors such as smoking cigarettes, drinking alcohol, and delinquency (Aalsma, Lapsley, & Flannery, 2006). On a positive note, the adolescent's feelings of invincibility may also lead to courageous efforts to save people's lives in hazardous circumstances.

At every age we put our own special stamp on egocentrism. Have you ever noticed that each of your instructors seems to think that his or her class is the only one you're taking?

Socioemotional Development in Adolescence

Adolescence is a time when many of us ask ourselves, "Who am I?" Adolescents spend time thinking about who they are, who they want to be, and trying on different identities. Erikson's theory addresses the manner in which adolescents seek their identities.

Erikson's Theory and Identity Development

As we saw in the section on children's socioemotional development, Erik Erikson's life-span theory states that people go through eight psychosocial stages of development. Within the eight stages that Erikson (1968) proposed, his ideas about the formation of identity during adolescence are among his most important contributions to psychology. They changed the way we think about adolescence (Kroger, 2007). Erikson encouraged us to look at adolescents not just as hormone-driven beings but also as individuals finding out who they are and searching for their niche in the world.

Erikson's theory characterizes the main concern of the fifth stage of socioemotional development as **identity versus identity confusion.** In seeking an *identity,* adolescents face the challenges of finding

identity versus identity confusion Erikson's fifth psychological stage, in which adolescents face the challenge of finding out who they are, what they are all about, and where they are going in life.

"Relax, Ted, it's only a phase!"

www.CartoonStock.com

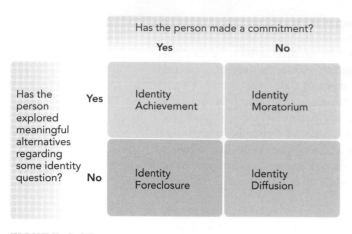

		Has the person made a commitment?	
		Yes	**No**
Has the person explored meaningful alternatives regarding some identity question?	**Yes**	Identity Achievement	Identity Moratorium
	No	Identity Foreclosure	Identity Diffusion

FIGURE 8.15

Marcia's Four Statuses of Identity Who are you? When you think of how you have come to identify yourself, which of these four statuses does your answer best represent?

out who they are, what they are all about, and where they are going in life. Adolescents are confronted with many new roles and adult statuses—from the vocational to the romantic. If they do not adequately explore their identities during this stage, they emerge confused about who they are. Therefore, Erikson argues, parents should allow adolescents to explore many different roles and many paths within a particular role. Adolescents who spend this time in their lives exploring alternatives can reach some resolution of the identity crisis and emerge with a new sense of self that is both refreshing and acceptable. Those who do not successfully resolve the crisis become confused, suffering what Erikson calls *identity confusion*. This confusion is expressed in one of two ways: Either individuals withdraw, isolating themselves from peers and family, or they lose themselves in the crowd.

Marcia's Theory of Identity Status Building on Erikson's ideas, James Marcia (1980, 2002) proposed the concept of *identity status* to describe a person's position in the development of an identity. In his view, two dimensions of identity are important. *Exploration* refers to a person's exploring various options for a career and for personal values. *Commitment* involves making a decision about which identity path to follow and making a personal investment in attaining that identity. Various combinations of exploration and commitment give rise to one of four identity statuses (Figure 8.15).

Ethnic Identity Developing an identity in adolescence can be especially challenging for individuals from ethnic minority groups (Phinney & Ong, 2007). As they mature cognitively, many adolescents become acutely aware of the evaluation of their ethnic group by the majority culture. In addition, an increasing number of minority adolescents face the challenge of *biculturalism*—identifying in some ways with their ethnic minority group and in other ways with the majority culture (Phinney & others, 2006).

Research has shown that for ethnic minority youth, feeling both a positive attachment to their minority group and an attachment to the larger culture is related to more positive academic and emotional outcomes (Oyserman, 2008; Yip, Kiang, & Fuligni, 2008). Although it might seem that being a member of an ethnic minority would make life more stressful, studies have indicated that having a strong ethnic identity can buffer adolescents from the effects of discrimination (Sellers & Shelton, 2003; Sellers & others, 2006). For both minority and majority adolescents, developing a positive identity is an important life theme (Cote, 2006; Kroger, 2007). In addition to ethnic identity, adolescence can be a time when other aspects of one's identity come to the fore, such a sexual orientation or gender role.

Parents and Peers Parents and peers both powerfully influence adolescents' development (Brown & Dietz, 2009; McElhaney & others, 2009). An important developmental task in adolescence is to acquire the ability to make competent decisions with increasing independence (Kuhn, 2009). To help adolescents reach their full potential, a key parental role is to be an effective manager—one who locates information, makes contacts, helps to structure their offsprings' choices, and provides guidance. By assuming this managerial role, parents help adolescents to avoid pitfalls and to work their way through the many decisions they face (Parke & others, 2008).

A crucial aspect of the managerial role of parenting is effective monitoring of the adolescent (Collins & Steinberg, 2006). Monitoring includes supervising the adolescent's choice of social settings, activities, and friends, as well as his or her academic efforts. A recent research review concluded that when African American parents monitored their sons' academic achievement—by ensuring that they completed homework and restricted the time spent on things like video games and TV, and by participating in a consistent, positive dialogue with teachers—their sons' academic achievement benefited (Mandara, 2006).

During adolescence, individuals spend more time with peers than they did in childhood. These peer influences can be positive or negative (Asher & McDonald, 2009). A key aspect of positive peer relations is having one or more close friends. Adolescents can learn to be skilled and sensitive partners in intimate relationships by forging close friendships with selected peers. However, some peers and friends can negatively impact adolescents' development. Researchers have found that hanging out with delinquent peers in adolescence can be a strong predictor of substance abuse, delinquent behavior, and depression (Dishion & Piehler, 2009; Farrington, 2009).

Rethinking Adolescence

Adolescence is a time of evaluation, decision making, and commitment—a stage when the individual carves out a place in the world (Kroger, 2007). It is wrong to confuse the adolescent's enthusiasm for trying on new identities and enjoying moderate amounts of outrageous behavior with hostility toward parents and society. Searching for an identity is a way in which the adolescent moves toward accepting, rather than rejecting, parental and societal values.

Who were your best friends during adolescence? Are you still close? How did those individuals shape your development?

How competent the adolescent will eventually become often depends on access to legitimate opportunities for growth—such as a quality education, community and societal support for achievement and involvement, and good jobs. Especially important in adolescent development is long-term, deeply caring support from adults (Lerner & others, 2009).

self-quiz

1. Puberty is generally characterized by all of the following *except*
   A. a decrease in concentrations of certain hormones.
   B. a dramatic increase in height and weight.
   C. an increase in idealistic and abstract thinking.
   D. the development of thought.

2. The hormone associated with girls' breast, uterine, and skeletal development during puberty is
   A. testosterone.
   B. estradiol.
   C. androgen.
   D. norepinephrine.

3. With regard to ethnic identity, psychological research indicates that
   A. adolescents who downplay the importance of their ethnic identity do better in school.
   B. adolescents use their ethnic identity to avoid developmental tasks.
   C. adolescents who have a strong ethnic identity are better able to cope with stress.
   D. adolescents from different racial groups face the same challenges to their ethnic identity.

Apply It! 4. Alicia's parents are both medical doctors, and Alicia never doubted for a minute what she would be when she grew up. She did very well in high school

and college and started medical school early. Even though she experiences great success, she feels strangely unfulfilled and does not enjoy her training or her work as a doctor. What explains her feelings?
   A. Alicia is low on identity commitment; she needs to dedicate herself more to her goals.
   B. Alicia never explored her identity. She needs to think more about what she wants to do and who she wants to be.
   C. Alicia is not using formal operational thinking.
   D. Alicia is too goal focused and probably needs to branch out and make some friends.

4 Emerging Adulthood, Adult Development, and Aging

Development continues throughout adulthood. Developmental psychologists identify three approximate periods in adult development: early adulthood (20s and 30s), middle adulthood (40s and 50s), and late adulthood (60s until death). Each phase features some distinctive physical, cognitive, and socioemotional changes.

Leading up to the first period of adulthood is the transitional life stage called *emerging adulthood*. If you are a traditional-age college student, you are at this point in the life span.

Emerging Adulthood

Emerging adulthood is the transitional period from adolescence to adulthood (Arnett, 2004, 2006, 2007). The age range for emerging adulthood is approximately 18 to 25 years of age. Experimentation and exploration characterize the emerging adult. At this point in their development, many individuals are still exploring which career path they want to follow, what they want their identity to be, and what kinds of close relationships they will have.

emerging adulthood
The transitional period from adolescence to adulthood, spanning approximately 18 to 25 years of age.

Key Features of Emerging Adulthood

Jeffrey Arnett (2006) identified five main features of emerging adulthood:

■ *Identity exploration, especially in love and work:* Emerging adulthood is the time of significant changes in identity for many individuals.

■ *Instability:* Residential changes peak during emerging adulthood, a time during which there also is often instability in love, work, and education.

■ *Self-focus:* Emerging adults "are self-focused in the sense that they have little in the way of social obligations, little in the way of duties and commitments to others, which leaves them with a great deal of autonomy in running their own lives" (Arnett, 2006, p. 10).

■ *Feeling "in between":* Many emerging adults consider themselves neither adolescents nor full-fledged adults.

■ *The age of possibilities, a time when individuals have an opportunity to transform their lives:* Arnett (2006) describes two ways in which emerging adulthood is the age of possibilities: (1) Many emerging adults are optimistic about their future, and (2) for emerging adults who have experienced difficult times while growing up, emerging adulthood presents an opportunity to guide their lives in a more positive direction.

Some people enter adulthood earlier than others. Some marry, start a family, and take up full-time employment right out of high school. Do you think these individuals experience "emerging adulthood"?

For the most part, life gets better for most emerging adults. From age 18 to 26, steady increases in well-being have been reported (Schulenberg & Zarrett, 2006). One possible reason for this improvement is that emerging adults have more choices and more control over those choices in their daily lives. Emerging adulthood provides an opportunity for individuals who engaged in problem behavior during adolescence to get their lives together.

Physical Development in Adulthood

Like other developmental periods, our bodies change during adulthood. Here we review some of these transitions.

Physical Changes in Early Adulthood
Most adults reach their peak physical development during their 20s and are the healthiest then. Early adulthood, however, is also the time when many physical skills begin to decline. The decline in strength and speed often is noticeable in the 30s.

Young adults may not think about the consequences of their current behaviors for later physical well-being. Perhaps because of their robust physical skills and overall health, they rarely recognize that bad nutrition, heavy drinking, and smoking in early adulthood can impair their health as they age. A special concern is heavy drinking by college students (Karam, Kypri, & Salamoun, 2007).

Another realm in which physical changes occur with age is in our ability to perceive the world around us. Hearing loss is very common with age. In fact, starting at about age 18, hearing begins a gradual decline. This decline is so slow that most people do not notice it until the age of 50 or so. Vision also changes with age, as we will see.

Physical Changes in Middle Adulthood

One of the most visible physical changes in middle adulthood is appearance. By the 40s or 50s, the skin has begun to wrinkle and sag because of the loss of fat and collagen in underlying tissues. Small, localized areas of pigmentation in the skin produce age spots, especially in areas exposed to sunlight such as the hands and face (McCullough & Kelly, 2006). Hair becomes thinner and grayer due to a lower replacement rate and a decline in melanin production. Because U.S. culture values a youthful appearance, these physical changes of middle adulthood can be difficult for the individual to handle.

Individuals lose height in middle age, and many gain weight (Page & others, 2009). The decrease in height is due to bone loss in the vertebrae. On average, body fat accounts for about 10 percent of body weight in adolescence; it makes up 20 percent or more in middle age.

Once a person hits his or her 40s, age-related vision changes usually become apparent, especially difficulty in seeing things up close (*presbyopia*). The individual might notice the need to hold a magazine or book with outstretched arms in order to read the words. Even someone with previously excellent vision may need reading glasses to read a newspaper or menu.

For women, entering middle age means that menopause will soon occur. Usually in the late 40s or early 50s, a woman's menstrual periods cease completely. The average age at which women have their last period is 52, but 10 percent of women undergo menopause before age 40. With menopause comes a dramatic decline in the ovaries' production of estrogen. Estrogen decline produces uncomfortable symptoms in some menopausal women, such as *hot flashes* (sudden, brief flushing of the skin and a feeling of elevated body temperature), nausea, fatigue, and rapid heartbeat. Some menopausal women report depression and irritability (K. A. Matthews & others, 2007), but these feelings can be related to other circumstances, such as becoming divorced, losing a job, or caring for a sick parent (Soares, 2008). Menopause does not produce psychological or physical problems for most women (Bauld & Brown, 2009; Weismiller, 2009).

When individuals reach their 60s, they may find that seeing in dim light is more difficult. Driving at night may be difficult, and restaurants may be too dark to see the menu. Vision can continue to decline into late adulthood, with the field of vision narrowing and risk of cataracts increasing.

Physical Changes in Late Adulthood

The concept of a period called late adulthood is a recent one: Until the twentieth century, most individuals died before age 65. Many societies around the world have become less youthful, however, and so we need to develop a better understanding of the later years of life (Markides, 2007; Schaie, 2007).

The term *life expectancy* describes the number of years that the average person born in a particular year will probably live. Improvements in medicine, nutrition, exercise, and lifestyle have increased human life expectancy an average of 31 additional years since 1900. The life expectancy of individuals born today in the United States is 77.8 years—80.4 for women, 75.2 for men (National Center for Health Statistics, 2008). One in three women born today is expected to live to be 100 or more. According to the United Nations (2002), the world's population of individuals 65 years and older tripled from 1950 to 2000, and the fastest-growing segment of the population is 85 years and older.

Individuals live longer on the Japanese island of Okinawa than anywhere else in the world, and Okinawa has the world's highest prevalence of *centenarians*—individuals who live to 100 years or older. Examination of Okinawans' lives provides insights into why they live so long. Specific factors are diet (they eat nutritious foods such as grains, fish, and vegetables); lifestyle (they are easygoing and experience low stress); community (Okinawans look out for one another and do not isolate or ignore older adults); activity

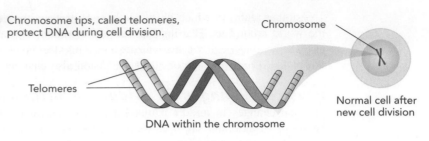

1 Chromosome tips, called telomeres, protect DNA during cell division.

Telomeres

DNA within the chromosome

Chromosome

Normal cell after new cell division

2 Telomeres shorten as cell undergoes many cell divisions.

Dividing cell

3 Ultimately, telomeres become too short, exposing DNA, which becomes damaged, and the cell dies. This is the normal life and death cycle of a cell.

Cell death

FIGURE 8.16

Telomeres and Aging The photograph shows telomeres lighting up the tips of chromosomes. The figure illustrates how the telomeres shorten every time a cell divides. Eventually, after about 100 divisions, the telomeres are greatly reduced in length. As a result, the cell can no longer reproduce and it dies.

(they lead active lifestyles, and many older adults continue to work); and spirituality (they find a sense of purpose in spiritual matters) (Willcox & others, 2008).

Biological Theories of Aging   Of the many proposed biological theories of aging, three especially merit attention: cellular-clock theory, free-radical theory, and hormonal stress theory.

 People often say life is short, and it surely is. But imagine living to be 120. At the age of 30 a person would still have 90 years to fill with life.

The *cellular-clock theory* is Leonard Hayflick's (1977) view that cells can divide a maximum of about 100 times and that, as we age, our cells become less capable of dividing. Hayflick found that cells extracted from adults in their 50s to 70s had divided fewer than 100 times. The total number of cell divisions was roughly related to the age of the individual. Based on the way cells divide, Hayflick places the upper limit of the human life span at about 120 years.

Recently, scientists have been intensively examining why cells lose their ability to divide (Kaszubowska, 2008; Y. Zhao & others, 2008; Zou & others, 2009). The answer may lie at the tips of chromosomes. Each time a cell divides, the *telomeres* that protect the ends of chromosomes become shorter and shorter (Figure 8.16). After about 100 replications, the telomeres are dramatically reduced, and the cell no longer can reproduce (Shay & Wright, 2007). Currently, there is considerable interest in discovering ways to maintain high levels of the telomere-extending enzyme—telomerase—through genetic manipulation of chemical telomerase activators (Effros, 2009).

The *free-radical theory* of aging states that people age because unstable oxygen molecules known as *free radicals* are produced inside their cells. These molecules ricochet around in the cells, damaging DNA and other cellular structures (Hepple, 2009; van Remmen & Jones, 2009). The damage done by free radicals may lead to a range of disorders, including cancer and arthritis.

Hormonal stress theory argues that aging in the body's hormonal system can lower resistance to stress and increase the likelihood of disease. As individuals age, the hormones stimulated by stress stay in the bloodstream longer than when they were younger (Brown-Borg, 2008). These prolonged, elevated levels of stress hormones are linked to increased risks for many diseases, including cardiovascular disease, cancer, and diabetes. Recently, the hormonal stress theory of aging has focused on the role of chronic stress in reducing immune system functioning (Bauer, Jeckel, & Luz, 2009).

Aging and the Brain Just as the aging body has a greater capacity for renewal than previously thought, so does the aging brain (Hillman, Erickson, & Kramer, 2008; Imayoshi & others, 2009). For decades, scientists believed that no new brain cells are generated past early childhood. However, researchers have recently discovered that adults can grow new brain cells throughout life (Eisch & others, 2008; Gould & others, 1999), although evidence is limited to two areas of the brain: the hippocampus and the olfactory bulb (Libert, Cohen, & Guarente, 2008).

Even in late adulthood, the brain has remarkable repair capability (Grady, 2008). Stanley Rapaport (1994) compared the brains of younger and older adults when they were engaged in the same tasks. The older adults' brains literally rewired themselves to compensate for losses. If one neuron was not up to the job, neighboring neurons helped to pick up the slack. Rapaport concluded that as brains age, they can shift responsibilities for a given task from one region to another.

Changes in lateralization may provide one type of adaptation in aging adults (Kramer, Fabiani, & Colcombe, 2006). *Lateralization* is the specialization of function in one hemisphere of the brain or the other. Using neuroimaging techniques, researchers have found that brain activity in the prefrontal cortex is lateralized less in older adults than in younger adults when they are engaging in cognitive tasks (Cabeza, 2002; Cabeza, Nyberg, & Park, 2005). For example, when younger adults are given the task of recognizing words they have previously seen, they process the information primarily in the right hemisphere, whereas older adults are more likely to use both hemispheres (Madden & others, 1999). The decrease in lateralization in older adults might play a compensatory role in the aging brain. That is, using both hemispheres may improve the cognitive functioning of older adults.

Research on the aging brain, including the Nun Study (described in Chapter 1), gives cause for hope. Recall that this study involves nearly 700 nuns in a convent in Mankato, Minnesota (Snowdon, 2003, 2007) (Figure 8.17). Although in Chapter 1 we surveyed the aspects of the study related to happiness, this research has also investigated brain functioning. By examining the nuns' donated brains as well as others, neuroscientists have documented the aging brain's remarkable ability to grow and change. Even the oldest Mankato nuns lead intellectually challenging lives, and neuroscientists believe that stimulating mental activities increase dendritic branching. Keeping the brain actively engaged in challenging activities can help to slow the effects of age, as we noted in Chapter 6.

FIGURE 8.17
The Brains of the Mankato Nuns
At 90 years old, Nun Study participant Sister Rosella Kreuzer, SSND, remains an active contributing member of her community of sisters. Sister Rosella articulated the Nun Study's mission as "That You May Have Life to the Full." (*Inset*) A neuroscientist holds a brain donated by one of the Mankato Nun Study participants.

Cognitive Development in Adulthood

We have seen that considerable changes take place in children's and adolescents' cognitive development. What kind of cognitive changes occur in adults?

Cognition in Early Adulthood Piaget theorized that formal operational thought is the highest level of thinking, and he argued that no new qualitative changes in cognition take place in adulthood. He did not believe that a person with a PhD in physics thinks any differently than a young adolescent who has reached the stage of formal operational thought. The only difference is that the physicist has more knowledge in a specific scientific domain. The physicist and the young adolescent both use logical thought to develop alternatives for solving a problem and to deduce a solution from the options. Piaget was right about some adolescents and some adults—but not about all of them. As you learned earlier, some adolescents are not formal operational thinkers; as well, many adults never reach that stage.

Some experts on cognitive development argue that the typical idealism of Piaget's formal operational stage is replaced in young adulthood by more realistic, pragmatic thinking. Gisela Labouvie-Vief (2006) proposed that the increasing complexity of cultures in the past century has generated a greater need for reflective, more complex thinking that takes into account the changing nature of knowledge and the kinds of challenges contemporary thinkers face. She emphasizes that key aspects of cognitive development for young adults include deciding on a particular worldview, recognizing that the worldview is subjective, and understanding that diverse worldviews should be acknowledged. In her perspective, considerable individual variation characterizes the thinking of emerging adults, with the highest level of thinking attained only by some. She argues that the level of education individuals achieve influences how likely they are to maximize their thinking potential.

So, taking this course is good for your cognitive development.

In sum, for the most part, intellectual skills are strong in early adulthood (Kitchener, King, & DeLuca, 2006). Do they begin to decline in middle age?

Cognition in Middle Adulthood
The answer to the question of whether cognitive abilities decline with age depends on the methods researchers use to address this issue. In *cross-sectional studies,* a number of people of different ages are assessed at one point in time. By examining how the ages of these individuals relate to the cognitive abilities measured, researchers can find out whether younger individuals differ from older ones. Research using cross-sectional designs has compared individuals in early and middle adulthood on two forms of cognitive abilities: *crystallized intelligence,* an individual's accumulated information and verbal skills, and *fluid intelligence,* the ability to reason abstractly. The results show that crystallized intelligence is higher in middle adulthood compared to early adulthood, but fluid intelligence is higher in early adulthood compared to middle adulthood (Horn & Donaldson, 1980).

One problem in cross-sectional studies is cohort effects. *Cohort effects* are differences between individuals that stem not necessarily from their ages but from the historical and social time period in which they were born and developed. For instance, individuals who were born in the 1940s might be less likely to have attended college than those born in the 1990s. Differences observed between these groups might be due not to their age but rather to these differing educational opportunities.

What are some unique experiences that characterize people in your cohort? How might these experiences lead you and your peers to be different from other generations?

In contrast to cross-sectional research, a *longitudinal study* assesses the same participants over a lengthy period. A longitudinal study of intelligence in middle adulthood might consist of giving the same intelligence test to the same individuals over a 20-year time span, when they are 40, 50, and 60 years of age. As we consider next, whether data on intelligence are collected cross-sectionally or longitudinally can make a difference in the conclusions we draw about cognitive ability in middle adulthood (Schaie, 2009).

K. Warner Schaie is conducting an extensive longitudinal study of intellectual abilities in adulthood. Five hundred individuals initially were tested in 1956 and have been tested repeatedly over the years (Schaie, 1994, 2007; Schaie & Zanjani, 2006). New waves of participants are added periodically. In his work, Schaie has measured a host of different cognitive abilities. As shown in Figure 8.18, the highest level of functioning for four of the six intellectual abilities occurred in middle adulthood (Schaie, 2006). Only two of the six abilities—numerical ability and perceptual speed—declined in middle age. Perceptual speed showed the earliest decline, beginning in early adulthood. Schaie found middle adulthood to be a time of peak performance for some aspects of both crystallized intelligence (vocabulary) and fluid intelligence (spatial orientation and inductive reasoning). Based on the longitudinal data he has collected so far, Schaie (2006, 2007) concluded that middle adulthood, not early adulthood, is the period when many people reach their peak for many intellectual skills.

Cognition in Late Adulthood
Many contemporary psychologists believe that, as in middle adulthood, some dimensions of intelligence decline in late adulthood, whereas others are maintained or may even increase.

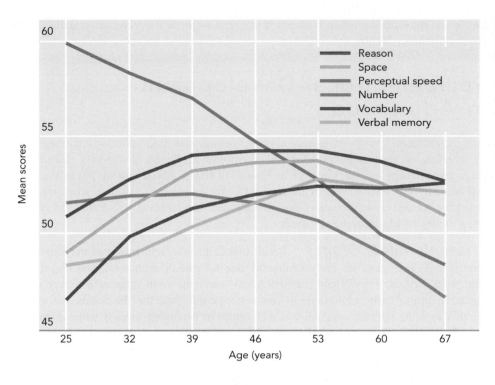

One of the most consistent findings is that when the speed of processing information is involved, older adults do more poorly than their younger counterparts (Figure 8.19). This decline in speed of processing is apparent in middle-aged adults and becomes more pronounced in older adults (Salthouse, 2009). Older adults also tend to do more poorly than younger adults in most aspects of memory (Towse, 2008). Older adults do not remember the "where" and "when" of life's happenings as well as younger adults (Tulving, 2000). For example, your grandmother may remember that you are going to Hawaii for spring break but not recall that you told her that on the phone last Tuesday. In the area of memory involving knowledge of the world (for instance, the capital of Peru or the chemical formula for water), older adults usually take longer than younger adults to remember the information, but they often are able to remember it (Houer & Roodin, 2009). Further, in the important area of memory in which individuals manipulate and assemble information to solve problems and make decisions, decline occurs in older adults.

wisdom
Expert knowledge about the practical aspects of life.

However, some aspects of cognition might improve with age. One such area is **wisdom,** expert knowledge about the practical aspects of life (Staudinger & Dorner, 2007). Wisdom may increase with age because of the buildup of life experiences, but individual variations characterize people throughout their lives (Sternberg, 2009f). Thus, not every older person has wisdom, and some young people are wise beyond their years.

For younger people, wisdom sometimes comes at a cost—they might gain wisdom from living through very difficult life experiences.

Do we all face the prospect of gradually becoming less competent intellectually? Not necessarily. Even for those aspects of cognitive aging that decline, training older adults can improve their cognitive skills (Schaie, 2006; Willis & Schaie, 2005). Researchers have demonstrated that training older adults to use specific strategies can improve their memories, and there is increasing evidence that physical fitness training sharpens the thinking skills of older adults (Hillman, Erickson, & Kramer, 2008; Park & Reuter-Lorenz, 2009). However, many experts conclude that older adults are less able to adapt than younger

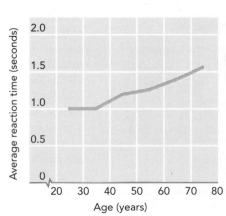

FIGURE 8.19

The Relationship Between Age and Reaction Time In one study, the average reaction time slowed in the 40s, and this decline accelerated in the 60s and 70s (Salthouse, 1994). The task used to assess reaction time required individuals to match numbers with symbols on a computer screen.

adults and thus are limited in how much they can improve their cognitive skills (Finch, 2009; Salthouse, 2009).

Socioemotional Development in Adulthood

Infancy, childhood, and adolescence all have demarcated time periods—they begin and end and lead to another period of development. For adulthood, in contrast, these beginnings and endings are much less clear. Our adult life is driven less by physical change and more by our own pursuit of meaningful goals. In order to examine what psychologists have learned about socioemotional development in adulthood, let's return to Erikson's stage theory of life-span development.

Erikson's Adult Stages   Recall that Erikson's eight stages of the human life span include one stage for early adulthood, one for middle adulthood, and one for late adulthood. Erikson (1968) said that individuals enter the sixth stage of *intimacy versus isolation* during early adulthood. At this time, people face the developmental task of either forming intimate relationships with others or becoming socially isolated. Erikson describes intimacy as both finding oneself and losing oneself in another. If the young adult develops healthy friendships and an intimate relationship with a partner, intimacy will likely be achieved.

Generativity versus stagnation, Erikson's seventh stage, occurs in middle adulthood. A main concern in middle adulthood is to help the younger generation in developing useful lives—this is what Erikson means by generativity. The feeling of having done nothing to help the next generation is stagnation.

Integrity versus despair, Erikson's eighth stage, occurs in late adulthood. In the later years of life, we look back and evaluate what we have done with our lives. If the older adult has resolved many of the earlier stages negatively, looking back likely will produce doubt or gloom—the despair Erikson speaks of. If, however, the older adult has successfully negotiated most or all of the previous stages of development, looking back will reveal a picture of a life well spent, and the person will feel a sense of satisfaction—integrity will be attained.

> *Generativity can also be experienced through mentoring others. A mentor is someone who takes a new person under his or her wing at work or in any organization. A mentor helps the newbie learn the ropes, gives advice, and acts as a sounding board. Mentors are special people who commit themselves to someone else's success.*

Marriage   Although it sometimes seems that the institution of marriage is on the decline, most people will eventually marry. Even among those who have divorced, remarriage is the norm (Popenoe, 2007). Nonetheless, some aspects of marriage have changed with time. In the last two decades or so, it is clear that men and women are waiting longer to marry. For example, in 2005, the average age for a first marriage in the United States climbed to just over 27 years for men and 26 years for women (U.S. Bureau of the Census, 2005). This may be very good news, because the age of a woman at her first marriage is related to the ultimate survival of the marriage. As many as 59 percent of marriages in which the wife is less than 18 years old end in divorce within 15 years, compared to just 36 percent of marriages in which the woman is age 20 or older (Center for Family and Demographic Research, 2002). The U.S. divorce rate, while slowing down in recent years, increased astronomically in the 1970s and remains high—the highest rate of any industrialized society. The average duration of a marriage in the United States currently is about 9 years.

What makes a marriage work? John Gottman has been studying married couples' lives since the early 1970s (Gottman, 1994, 2006; Gottman, Gottman, & Declaire, 2006; Gottman & Silver, 1999). He interviews couples about the history of their marriage, their philosophy about marriage, and their views of their parents'

"We only live once. Hop in."

marriages. He films them talking with each other about how their day went and evaluates what they say about the good and bad times of their marriage. He uses physiological measures to assess a variety of physical reactions, including heart rate and blood pressure, while they discuss these topics. He also checks back with the couples every year to see how their marriages are faring. He and his colleagues continue to follow married couples, as well as same-sex partners, to try to understand what makes relationships successful. A key issue, according to Gottman, is getting past the notion that love is a magical thing. From his perspective, love is a decision and a responsibility, and we have control over extramarital temptations (Gottman, Gottman, & Declaire, 2006).

Gottman (2006) has found these four principles at work in successful marriages:

- *Nurturing fondness and admiration:* Partners sing each other's praises. When couples put a positive spin on their talk with and about each other, the marriage tends to work.

- *Turning toward each other as friends:* Partners see each other as friends and turn toward each other for support in times of stress and difficulty.

- *Giving up some power:* Bad marriages often involve one partner who is a power-monger. This is more common in husbands, but some wives have the problem as well.

- *Solving conflicts together:* Couples work to solve problems, regulate their emotion during times of conflict, and compromise to accommodate each other.

Parenting   Having children is a key way by which individuals meet Erikson's challenge of generativity. By procreating, they contribute to the next generation. Research shows that engaged parenting may have benefits not only for children but for parents as well. John Snarey (1993) followed fathers and their children for four decades. He found that children, especially girls, were better off if their fathers were actively engaged in their lives—especially with regard to athletic pursuits. In addition, and perhaps more importantly for fathers, those who were constructively engaged in child rearing were themselves better off in terms of marital satisfaction, life satisfaction, and even career success.

Midlife Crises   If a man turns 50 and suddenly buys a hot new red Corvette, family and friends might roll their eyes and conclude, "Midlife crisis." The notion of midlife crisis was introduced by Daniel Levinson (1978) in his book *The Seasons of a Man's Life*. However, research on middle-aged adults reveals that few experience what people think of as a midlife crisis (Kirasic, 2004; Lachman, 2004). Rather than a time of crisis, midlife is perhaps more accurately a time of heightened awareness of the finite nature of one's life and the importance of contributing a legacy to future generations. During middle age, people do become aware of the gap between being young and being old and the shrinking time left in their lives, and many individuals increasingly contemplate the meaning of life.

Socioemotional Aspects of Aging   Although people are in the evening of their life in late adulthood, they need not live out their remaining years lonely and unhappy. The more active and involved older people are, the more satisfied they are and the more likely they are to stay healthy (Hendricks & Hatch, 2006). Researchers have found that older people who go to church, attend meetings, take trips, and exercise are happier than those who simply sit at home (George, 2006).

However, older adults may become more selective about their social networks (Carstensen, 2006, 2008). Because they place a high value on emotional satisfaction, older adults often are motivated to spend more time with familiar individuals—close friends and family members—with whom they have had rewarding relationships. They may deliberately withdraw from social contact with individuals on the fringes of their lives. This narrowing of social interaction maximizes positive emotional experiences and minimizes emotional risks as individuals become older (Charles & Carstensen, 2007).

Researchers also have found that across diverse samples—Norwegians, Catholic nuns, African Americans, Chinese Americans, and Euro-Americans—older adults report better control of their emotions than younger adults (Carstensen &

These effects are not just about age. Even young people will do the same kinds of things when their time is limited. Imagine that you are leaving on an extended trip and won't see your family and friends for a long time. What would you do with the last few days you have left? You would probably do the same things older adults do when they realize that time on earth is limited.

Charles, 2003). Research moreover suggests that this superior emotional regulation pays off. One study of a very large U.S. sample examined emotions at different ages (Charles, Reynolds, & Gatz, 2001; Mroczek & Kolarz, 1998). Older adults reported experiencing more positive emotion and less negative emotion than younger adults, and positive emotion increased with age in adults at an accelerating rate (Figure 8.20).

Consider a recent large-scale U.S. study of approximately 28,000 individuals aged 18 to 88 indicating that happiness increased with age (Yang, 2008). About 33 percent of the participants were very happy at 88 years of age, compared to only about 24 percent of those in their late teens and early 20s. Why might the older people have reported being happier and more satisfied with their lives than the younger participants? Some reasons may be that despite the losses and the increased physical problems that older adults experience, they may be more content with what they have in their lives, enjoy better relationships with the people who matter to them, have more time for leisure pursuits, and have many more years of experience to help them adapt to their circumstances with wisdom, as compared to younger adults (Cornwell, Schumm, & Laumann, 2008; Ram & others, 2008).

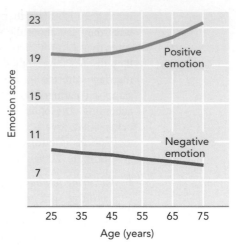

FIGURE 8.20
Changes in Positive and Negative Emotion Across the Adult Years
Positive and negative scores had a possible range of 6 to 30, with higher scores reflecting positive emotion and lower scores negative emotion. Positive emotion increased in the middle adulthood and late adulthood years while negative emotion declined.

Active Development and Aging

Until fairly recently, middle-aged and older adults were perceived as enduring a steady decline in physical, cognitive, and socioemotional functioning, and research ignored the positive dimensions of aging (Rowe & Kahn, 1997). Once developmental psychologists focused on the positive aspects of aging, they discovered that far more robust, healthy middle-aged and older adults are among us than they previously envisioned. Further, as we just saw, older adults are happier and more satisfied with their lives than younger adults are.

When you think about developmental psychology, child development may still be the first thing that pops into your mind. However, development characterizes adulthood as well. Graying hair? Loss of mobility? Cognitive decline? How can those be considered development? In fact, it may be that adult development is especially important *because* it occurs in the context of some declines. Unlike childhood growth, adult growth is more likely to be a conscious process and therefore a truer mark of an individual's accomplishment (King & Hicks, 2007; Levenson & Crumpler, 1996).

How do adults "grow themselves"? One way that adults develop is through coping with life's difficulties. Psychologist Carolyn Aldwin and her colleagues have suggested that stress and coping play a role in development (Aldwin, 2007; Aldwin, Levenson, & Kelly, 2009; Aldwin, Spiro, & Park, 2006; Aldwin, Yancura, & Boeninger, 2007; Boeninger & others, 2009). When we encounter a negative life circumstance such as an illness or a loss, we have the opportunity to develop and to mature (Davis & others, 2007). Research suggests that individuals who are faced with difficulties in life are more likely than others to come to a rich, complex view of themselves and the world (Helson, 1992; Helson & Roberts, 1994).

One of the negative events that people begin to experience in middle adulthood is death, especially the death of parents and older relatives. Also faced with less time in their own lives, many individuals think more deeply than before about what life is all about and what they want the rest of their lives to be like. Austrian psychiatrist Victor Frankl confronted this issue personally and then shared his insights with the world. His mother, father, brother, and wife died in the concentration camps and gas chambers in Auschwitz, Germany. Frankl survived the camps and went on to write *Man's Search for Meaning* (1963/1984), in which he emphasized each person's uniqueness and the finiteness of life. If life were not finite, said Frankl, we could spend our lives doing just about anything we please, because time would go on forever. Frankl proposed that people need to ask themselves such questions as why they exist, what they want from life, and what their lives really mean.

Frankl's ideas fit with the concept of a life theme. As we have seen earlier in this chapter, a life theme involves a person's efforts to cultivate meaningful optimal experiences (Csikszentmihalyi & Rathunde, 1998; Massimini & Delle Fave, 2000; Rathunde & Csikzentmihalyi, 2006). For example, consider someone who has spent much of his or her adult life pursuing wealth and career success but then turns to more selfless pursuits in middle age. To contribute to the well-being of the next generation, the individual devotes more energy and resources to helping others—for example, by volunteering or working with young people. This reorientation can ease the individual into a positive and meaningful old age. Remaining actively engaged in life is an essential part of successful adulthood (Hillman, Erickson, & Kramer, 2008).

These motivations are demonstrated by numerous individuals who are using their successes for the betterment of the world. Consider Bono, the lead singer of the rock group U2. Enriched by tremendous music sales and concert proceeds, the Grammy Award winner has spent the last few years lobbying political leaders on behalf of African nations beset with debt. More recently, he has been an advocate for DATA, a nonprofit organization dedicated to eradicating AIDS and poverty in Africa.

Bono has turned his energies and celebrity to addressing urgent global problems such as poverty and AIDS.

As children, our psychological development occurs in tandem with physical development. As we become strong and skilled enough to walk, the horizons of our world open up to new discoveries. In adulthood, we receive our developmental cues from ourselves—where do we go, once we have managed the many tasks that human beings face in childhood and adolescence? This chapter began by reminding you of the day of your birth, a day when you were the center of attention and a mystery waiting to unfold. From a developmental psychology perspective, today could be as important a day as that one. On the day you were born, you were full of possibilities—and you still are.

self-quiz

1. Of the following activities, the one that uses crystallized intelligence is
   A. reciting facts about the Civil War.
   B. solving a jigsaw puzzle.
   C. using a mathematical formula to solve a problem.
   D. visualizing the way an object would look if rotated.

2. The life expectancy of humans born in the United States is currently
   A. approximately 50 years.
   B. approximately 65 years.
   C. approximately 80 years.
   D. approximately 95 years.

3. The theory that aging is caused by damage to DNA is known as the
   A. cellular-clock theory.
   B. life expectancy theory.
   C. hormonal stress theory.
   D. free-radical theory.

Apply It! 4. Rosemary's Grandpa Jack is 80 years old and wears a hearing aid and glasses, and he has always been very active. He and Rosemary's grandmother spend a great deal of time with their children and grandchildren, and both laugh a lot and seem genuinely to enjoy life. Grandpa Jack recently resigned his position as a member of the local senior citizen's council. He tells Rosemary that the council had become a hassle. Rosemary wonders whether this decision is normal and reasonable or whether her granddad is feeling depressed. Based on your reading of this example and this chapter, should Rosemary be worried?

A. Rosemary should be worried because it appears that Grandpa Jack is withdrawing from opportunities for generativity.
B. Rosemary should be worried because Grandpa Jack should stay involved in community activities given that such involvement is related to being happier and healthier.
C. Rosemary should probably not be worried. Grandpa Jack just sounds as if he is going through what most people do when they are faced with limited time: maximizing meaningful social contacts.
D. Rosemary should not be worried because Grandpa Jack has completed Erikson's stages, and it makes sense that he is probably preparing for death by withdrawing from the world.

summary

① Exploring Human Development

Development is the pattern of change in human capabilities that begins at conception and continues throughout the life span. Both nature (biological inheritance) and nurture (environmental experience) influence development extensively. However, people are not at the mercy of either their genes or their environment when they actively construct optimal experiences.

② Child Development

Prenatal development progresses through the germinal, embryonic, and fetal periods. Certain drugs, such as alcohol, can have an adverse effect on the fetus. Preterm birth is another potential problem, especially if the infant is very small or grows up in an adverse environment.

The infant's physical development is dramatic in the first year, and a number of motor milestones are reached in infancy. Extensive changes in the brain, including denser connections between synapses, take place in infancy and childhood.

With regard to cognitive development, in Piaget's view, children use schemas to actively construct their world, either assimilating new information into existing schemas or adjusting schemas to accommodate it. Piaget identified four stages of cognitive development: the sensorimotor stage, the preoperational stage, the concrete operational stage, and the formal operational stage.

Socioemotional development in childhood includes consideration of Erikson's psychosocial stages as well as moral development and gender issues. Erikson presented a major, eight-stage psychosocial view of life-span development; its first four stages occur in childhood. In each stage, the individual seeks to resolve a particular socioemotional conflict. Kohlberg proposed a cognitive-developmental theory of moral development with three levels (preconventional, conventional, and postconventional). Gender development includes biology, social experience, and cognitive factors.

Resilience is the capacity of some children to thrive despite adverse circumstances.

③ Adolescence

Puberty is a period of rapid skeletal and sexual maturation that occurs mainly in early adolescence. Its onset occurs about two years earlier in girls than in boys. Hormonal changes lie at the core of pubertal development.

According to Piaget, cognitive development in adolescence is characterized by the appearance of formal operational thought, the final stage in his theory. This stage involves abstract, idealistic, and logical thought.

One of the most important aspects of socioemotional development in adolescence is identity. Erikson's fifth stage of psychosocial development is identity versus identity confusion. Marcia proposed four statuses of identity based on crisis and commitment. A special concern is the development of ethnic identity. Despite great differences among adolescents, the majority of them develop competently.

④ Emerging Adulthood, Adult Development, and Aging

Psychologists refer to the period between adolescence and adulthood as emerging adulthood. This period is characterized by the exploration of identity through work and relationships, instability, and self-focus.

Most adults reach their peak physical performance during their 20s and are healthiest then. However, physical skills begin to decline during the 30s. The cellular-clock, free-radical, and hormonal stress theories are three important biological theories of aging. Even in late adulthood, the brain has remarkable repair capacity and plasticity.

Piaget argued that no new cognitive changes occur in adulthood. However, some psychologists have proposed that the idealistic thinking of adolescents is replaced by the more realistic, pragmatic thinking of young adults. Longitudinal research on intelligence shows that many cognitive skills peak in middle age. Overall, older adults do not do as well on memory and other cognitive tasks and are slower to process information than younger adults. However, older adults may have greater wisdom than younger adults.

Erikson's three stages of socioemotional development in adulthood are intimacy versus isolation (early adulthood), generativity versus stagnation (middle adulthood), and integrity versus despair (late adulthood). A special concern, beginning in the 50s, is the challenge of understanding the meaning of life. Researchers have found that remaining active increases the likelihood that older adults will be happier and healthier. They also have found that older adults often reduce their general social affiliations. Instead, they are motivated to spend more time with close friends and family members. Older adults also experience more positive emotion, are happier, and are more satisfied with their lives than younger adults.

The positive dimensions of aging were largely ignored until recently. Developmentalists now recognize that many adults can sustain or even improve their functioning as they age. Development in adulthood can be viewed as a self-motivated process whose limits are set by the individual's capacity to imagine.

key terms

self-test

Multiple Choice

1. The phrase "out of sight, out of mind" is true of children's cognitive processing in the _____ of development.
   A. sensorimotor stage
   B. preoperational stage
   C. concrete operational stage
   D. formal operational stage

2. The period of prenatal development that occurs just before birth is the
   A. embryonic period.
   B. zygotic period.
   C. fetal period.
   D. germinal period.

3. Of the following, the activity that is consistent with the concept of a life theme is
   A. competing against others.
   B. making a great deal of money.
   C. procreating.
   D. being altruistic.

4. A baby who is shown an image of a lion and an image of a tractor gazes at the tractor more. This finding is an example of
   A. preferential looking.
   B. visual development.
   C. habituation.
   D. object permanence.

5. During the course of successful prenatal development, a human organism begins as a(n)
   A. zygote and finally develops into an embryo.
   B. embryo and finally develops into a fetus.
   C. zygote and finally develops into a fetus.
   D. fetus and finally develops into an embryo.

6. A developmental stage characteristic of early childhood (3–5 years) is
   A. identity versus identity confusion.
   B. trust versus mistrust.
   C. intimacy versus isolation.
   D. initiative versus guilt.

7. The theory of aging that focuses on the division of cells is the
   A. telomere theory.
   B. life expectancy theory.
   C. cellular-clock theory.
   D. free-radical theory.

8. The ability to think abstractly is known as
   A. fluid intelligence.
   B. cohort effects.
   C. crystallized intelligence.
   D. accommodation.

9. A newly pregnant woman is warned by a doctor about teratogens. She does not know what these are and asks whether you know. You explain, and you tell her that the teratogens named in your psychology text include
   A. testosterone.
   B. serotonin.
   C. dopamine.
   D. alcohol.

10. A person who does not do something because he or she is fearful of getting in trouble is at the level of moral reasoning called
    A. preconventional.
    B. conventional.
    C. postconventional.
    D. formal operational.

Apply It!

11. Based on this chapter's definition of wisdom, what are three wise decisions you have made? Why do you think they qualify as wise?

9

Motivation and Emotion

Climbing Unseen Mountains

In 1995, Erik Weihenmayer and his team were ascending Mount McKinley, the highest peak in North America. His wife and family arranged to fly over them in a plane. All the climbers in the team were dressed in red gear, and as they waved their ski poles madly at the plane overhead, Weihenmayer asked a friend, "Do you think they know which one is me?" His friend assured him that they probably did, because he was the only one waving in the wrong direction.

Erik Weihenmayer, an exceptional athlete, skier, and marathon runner, has been completely blind since age 13. He is also one of an elite group that has made it to the top of all the Seven Summits, including Mount Everest, which he climbed in 2001. Considering Weihenmayer's achievements, we might ask, why did he do it? More pointedly, why did he *even imagine* doing it? For Weihenmayer, part of the motivation has been to inspire others to look beyond physical disabilities and to imagine the possible in every human circumstance. Although he has shattered stereotypes about what a blind person can accomplish, his tremendous efforts have also allowed him to stand on the peak of Everest as "just another climber."

When we ask why, we are asking about motivation. The terms *motivation* and *emotion* come from the Latin word *movere,* which means "to move." Motivation and emotion are the "go" of human life, providing the steam that propels us to overcome obstacles and to accomplish the great and little things we do every day. Our emotions often define for us what we really want: We feel joy or sorrow depending on how events influence our most cherished life dreams. ■

- ■ **What is one really big goal you want to accomplish?**
- ■ **What do you think are the most important human needs?**
- ■ **What is your motivation for taking introductory psychology?**

This chapter examines the ways psychologists study motivation and emotion. We first review some general approaches to motivation and consider two important physiological sources of motivation: hunger and sex. We then examine motivation as it applies to everyday life. Finally, we turn to the rich topic of emotion and take a close-up look at psychologists' approaches to such emotions as anger, gratitude, and happiness.

1 Theories of Motivation

Motivation is the force that moves people to behave, think, and feel the way they do. Motivated behavior is energized, directed, and sustained. Psychologists have proposed a variety of theories about why organisms are motivated to do what they do. In this section we explore some of the main theoretical approaches to motivation.

motivation
The force that moves people to behave, think, and feel the way they do.

The Evolutionary Approach

In the early history of psychology, the evolutionary approach emphasized the role of instincts in motivation. *Ethology*—the study of animal behavior—also has described motivation from an evolutionary perspective.

An **instinct** is an innate (unlearned) biological pattern of behavior that is assumed to be universal throughout a species. Generally, an instinct is set in motion by a "sign stimulus"—something in the environment that turns on a fixed pattern of behavior. Instincts may explain a great deal of nonhuman animal behavior. In addition, some human behavior is instinctive. For example, you might recall the discussion of infant reflexes in Chapter 8. Babies do not have to learn to suck; they instinctively do it when something is placed in their mouth. So, for infants, an object touching the lips is a sign stimulus. After infancy, though, it is hard to think of specific behaviors that all human beings engage in when presented with a particular stimulus.

instinct
An innate (unlearned) biological pattern of behavior that is assumed to be universal throughout a species.

You might think that some stimuli provide a strong case for instinctive responses. Doesn't everyone respond to chocolate with the behavior of eating? Not so fast—some people don't even like chocolate!

According to evolutionary psychologists, the motivations for sex, aggression, achievement, and other behaviors are rooted in our evolutionary past (Bjorklund, 2007; Buss, 2008; Geary, 2006), and we can understand similarities among members of the human species through these shared evolutionary roots. Because evolutionary approaches emphasize the passing on of one's genes, these theories focus on domains of life that are especially relevant to reproduction. For example, evolutionary theorists note that in terms of romantic partners, across many cultures, men prefer younger women to older women, and women prefer men who have resources (Buss, 2008). In general, however, most human behavior is far too complex to be explained on the basis of instinct. Indeed, it would hardly seem adaptive for humans to have a fixed action pattern that is invariably set in motion by a particular signal in the environment. To understand human behavior, psychologists have developed a variety of other approaches, as we now consider.

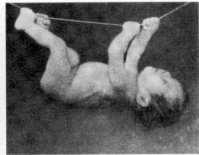

Human newborns display behavioral reflexes such as holding on to a rope so that they can be lifted. In our evolutionary past, this gripping reflex appeared in primates, allowing an infant to cling to its mother's hair while she moved about.

Drive Reduction Theory

need
A deprivation that energizes the drive to eliminate or reduce the deprivation.

Another way to think about motivation is through the constructs of drive and need. A **drive** is an aroused state that occurs because of a physiological need. You can think of a drive as a psychological itch that requires scratching. A **need** is a deprivation that energizes the drive to eliminate or reduce the deprivation. Generally, psychologists think of needs as underlying our drives. You may have a need for water; the drive that accompanies that need is your feeling of being thirsty. Usually but not always, needs and drives are closely associated. For example, when your body needs food, your hunger drive will probably be aroused. An hour after you have eaten a hamburger, your body might still need essential nutrients (thus you need food), but your hunger drive might have subsided.

This example should reinforce the concept that drive pertains to a psychological state, whereas need involves a physiological state. Drives do not always follow from needs. For example, if you are deprived of oxygen because of a gas leak, you may feel light-headed but may not realize that your condition is the result of a gas leak that is creating a need for air. However, this need for air fails to create a drive for oxygen that might lead you to open a window. Moreover, drives sometimes seem to come out of nowhere. Imagine having eaten a fine meal and feeling full to the point of not wanting another single bite—until the waiter wheels over the dessert cart. Suddenly you feel ready to tackle the double chocolate oblivion, despite your lack of hunger.

Drive reduction theory explains that as a drive becomes stronger, we are motivated to reduce it. The goal of drive reduction is **homeostasis,** the body's tendency to maintain an equilibrium, or steady state. Literally hundreds of biological states in our bodies must be maintained within a certain range: temperature, blood sugar level, potassium and sodium levels, oxygenation, and so on. When you dive into an icy swimming pool, your body uses energy to maintain its normal temperature. When you walk out of an air-conditioned room into the heat of a summer day, your body releases excess heat by sweating. These physiological changes occur automatically to keep your body in an optimal state of functioning.

drive
An aroused state that occurs because of a physiological need.

homeostasis
The body's tendency to maintain an equilibrium, or steady state.

Most psychologists believe that drive reduction theory does not provide a comprehensive framework for understanding motivation because people often behave in ways that increase rather than reduce a drive. For example, when dieting, you might choose to skip meals, but this tactic can increase your hunger drive rather than reduce it. Similarly, many other things that you might opt to do involve increasing (not decreasing) tensions—for example, taking a challenging course in school, raising a family, and working at a difficult job.

Performance under high-arousal conditions, such as those that faced pilot Chesley Sullenberger when he had to land his damaged plane in the Hudson River, requires being trained to the point of overlearning.

Optimum Arousal Theory

When psychologists talk about arousal, they are generally referring to a person's feelings of being alert and engaged. When we are very excited, our arousal levels are high. When we are bored, they are low. You have probably noticed that motivation influences arousal levels. Sometimes you can want something (for example to do well on a test) so much that you feel "over-motivated" and anxious. On the other hand, you might be so unmotivated for a task (such as doing dishes) that you can hardly force yourself to complete it.

Early in the twentieth century, two psychologists described how arousal can influence performance. According to their formulation, now known as the **Yerkes-Dodson law,** performance is best under conditions of moderate arousal rather than either low

Yerkes-Dodson law
The psychological principle stating that performance is best under conditions of moderate arousal rather than either low or high arousal.

or high arousal. At the low end of arousal, you may be too lethargic to perform tasks well; at the high end, you may not be able to concentrate. Think about how aroused you were the last time you took a test. If your arousal was too high, you might have felt too nervous to concentrate, and your performance likely suffered. If it was too low, you may not have worked fast enough to finish the test. Also think about performance in sports. Being too aroused usually harms athletes' performance; a thumping heart and rapid breathing have accompanied many golfers' missed putts. However, if athletes' arousal is too low, they may not concentrate well on the task at hand.

The relationship between arousal and performance is one reason that individuals who have to perform well under stressful conditions (such as EMTs and lifeguards) are trained to overlearn important procedures so that they do not require much thought. With this extra learning, when these individuals are under conditions of high arousal, they can rely on automatic pilot to do what needs to be done.

self-quiz

1. The force that moves people to behave, think, and feel the way they do is
   A. emotion.
   B. instinct.
   C. need.
   D. motivation.

2. Natalie will be taking an exam today. According to the Yerkes-Dodson law, the condition that will allow Natalie to score highest on the exam is
   A. no anxiety.
   B. moderate anxiety.
   C. high anxiety.
   D. high relaxation.

3. Which of the following statements is correct?

   A. Instincts have little to do with animal behavior.
   B. Instincts are learned patterns of behavior.
   C. Instincts direct most aspects of human behavior.
   D. Instincts are innate and biological.

Apply It! 4. Jared is a star basketball player on his school's team. In a crucial game, the score is tied with just a few seconds left on the clock, and Jared finds himself at the free-throw line preparing to shoot the winning baskets. The opponents' coach calls a time-out to "ice" Jared's nerves. Finally, as Jared steps up to the line, the rival team's student section goes crazy, screaming and jumping around in an attempt to psyche Jared out. His heart racing, Jared sinks both baskets, and his team wins. Which of the following is most likely true of this situation?

   A. The opposing team's coach and student fans know that low arousal leads to poor performance.
   B. Jared has practiced free throws so many times that he can land them even when he is highly aroused.
   C. Jared is showing the effects of very high arousal on performance.
   D. Jared is generally a sluggish person, and his performance is helped by his low levels of arousal.

2 Hunger and Sex

Some of the influence of motivation in our lives is tied to physiological needs. Two behaviors that are central to the survival of our species are eating and sex. In this section we examine the basic motivational processes underlying eating and sex.

The Biology of Hunger

You know you are hungry when your stomach growls and you feel those familiar hunger pangs. What role do such signals play in hunger?

Gastric Signals In 1912, Walter Cannon and A. L. Washburn conducted an experiment that revealed a close association between stomach contractions and hunger (Figure 9.1). As part of the procedure, a partially inflated balloon was passed through a tube inserted in Washburn's mouth and pushed down into his stomach. A machine that measures air pressure was connected to the balloon to monitor Washburn's stomach contractions. Every time Washburn reported hunger pangs, his stomach was also contracting. Sure enough, a growling stomach needs food. The stomach tells the brain not only how full it is but also how much nutrient is present, which is why rich food stops hunger faster than the same amount of water. The hormone *cholecystokinin* (CCK) helps start the digestion of food, travels to the brain through the bloodstream, and signals us to stop eating (Nefti & others, 2009). Hunger involves a lot more than an empty stomach, however.

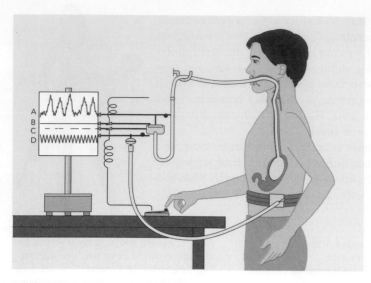

FIGURE 9.1

Cannon and Washburn's Classic Experiment on Hunger In this experiment, the researchers demonstrated that stomach contractions, which were detected by the stomach balloon, accompany a person's hunger feelings, which were indicated by pressing the key. Line A in the chart records increases and decreases in the volume of the balloon in the participant's stomach. Line B records the passage of time. Line C records the participant's manual signals of feelings of hunger. Line D records a reading from the belt around the participant's waist to detect movements of the abdominal wall and ensure that such movements are not the cause of changes in stomach volume.

Blood Chemistry Three key chemical substances play a role in hunger, eating, and *satiety* (the state of feeling full): glucose, insulin, and leptin.

Glucose (blood sugar) is an important factor in hunger, probably because the brain critically depends on sugar for energy. One set of sugar receptors, located in the brain itself, triggers hunger when sugar levels fall too low. Another set of sugar receptors is in the liver, which stores excess sugar and releases it into the blood when needed. The sugar receptors in the liver signal the brain when its sugar supply falls, and this signal also can make you hungry.

The hormone *insulin* also plays a role in glucose control (Oliver & others, 2009). When we eat complex carbohydrates such as bread and pasta, insulin levels go up and fall off gradually. When we consume simple sugars such as candy, insulin levels rise and then fall sharply—the all-too-familiar "sugar low" (Rodin, 1984). Blood glucose levels are affected by complex carbohydrates and simple sugars in similar ways, so we are more likely to eat within the next several hours after eating simple sugars than after eating complex carbohydrates.

The chemical substance *leptin* (from the Greek word *leptos,* which means "thin"), released by fat cells, decreases food intake and increases energy expenditure or metabolism (Bluher & Mantzoros, 2009; Farooqui & O'Rahilly, 2009). Leptin's functions were discovered in a strain of genetically obese mice, called *ob mice* (Pelleymounter & others, 1995). Because of a genetic mutation, the fat cells of ob mice cannot produce leptin. The ob mouse has a low metabolism, overeats, and gets extremely fat. Leptin appears to act as an anti-obesity hormone (Friedman, 2009; Wang & Eckel, 2009). If ob mice are given daily injections of leptin, their metabolic rate increases, and they become more active, eat less, and lose weight. Figure 9.2 shows an untreated ob mouse and an ob mouse that has received injections of leptin.

In humans, leptin concentrations have been linked with weight, body fat, and weight loss in response to dieting (Lee & Fried, 2009). Scientists continue to explore the possibility that disorders in the production and uptake of leptin may explain human obesity (Leibel, 2008).

Brain Processes Chapter 2 described the central role of the hypothalamus in regulating important body functions, including hunger. More specifically, activity in two areas of the hypothalamus contributes to our understanding of hunger. The *lateral hypothalamus* is involved in stimulating eating. When this area is electrically stimulated in a well-fed animal, the animal begins to eat. If this part of the hypothalamus is destroyed, even a

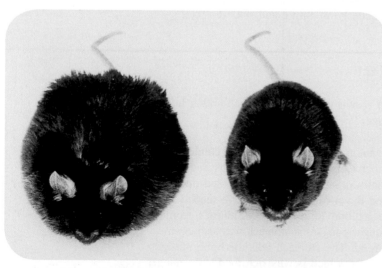

FIGURE 9.2

Leptin and Obesity The ob mouse on the left is untreated; the one on the right has been given injections of leptin.

starving animal will show no interest in food. The *ventromedial hypothalamus* is involved in reducing hunger and restricting eating. When this area of an animal's brain is stimulated, the animal stops eating. When the area is destroyed, the animal eats profusely and quickly becomes obese.

Although the lateral and ventromedial hypothalamuses both influence hunger, there is much more to the brain's role in determining hunger than these on/off centers in the hypothalamus. Neurotransmitters (the chemical messengers that convey information from neuron to neuron) and neural circuits (clusters of neurons that often involve different parts of the brain) also function in hunger (Minor, Chang, & de Cabo, 2009). Leptin influences eating by inhibiting the production of a neurotransmitter in the hypothalamus that induces eating. The neurotransmitter serotonin is partly responsible for the satiating effect of CCK, and serotonin antagonists have been used to treat obesity in humans (Garfield & Heisler, 2009; Hayes & others, 2006).

Obesity

Given that the brain and body are so elegantly wired to regulate eating behavior, why do so many people in the United States overeat and suffer the effects of overeating? Sixty percent of Americans are overweight, and one-third are considered obese (dangerously overweight) (Center for Disease Control & Prevention, 2009). Being obese or overweight raises one's risk for a variety of health problems (Cameron, Zimmet, & Alberti, 2009; Weiss & others, 2009). Currently, the number of people considered overweight around the world is 20 percent higher than the number suffering from hunger. Overweight and obesity are worldwide health problems.

The worldwide problem of obesity has been termed "globesity" by the World Health Organization.

Why so many people overeat to the point of becoming obese is a motivational puzzle, because it involves eating when one is not in need of nutrition. As is the case with much behavior, in eating, biological, cognitive, and sociocultural factors interact in diverse ways in different individuals, making it difficult to point to a specific cause (Adler & Stewart, 2009).

The Biology of Obesity Obesity clearly has a genetic component. After the discovery of an ob gene in mice, researchers found a similar gene in humans. Some individuals do inherit a tendency to be overweight (Walley, Blakemore, & Froguel, 2006). Only 10 percent of children who do not have obese parents become obese themselves, whereas 40 percent of children who have one obese parent become obese, and 70 percent of children who have two obese parents become obese. Identical human twins have similar weights, even when they are reared apart (Maes, Neal, & Eaves, 1997).

set point
The weight maintained when the individual makes no effort to gain or lose weight.

Another factor in weight is **set point,** the weight maintained when the individual makes no effort to gain or lose weight. Set point is determined in part by the amount of stored fat in the body (Fehm, Kern, & Peters, 2006). Fat is stored in *adipose cells,* or fat cells. When these cells are filled, you do not get hungry. When people gain weight—because of genetic predisposition, childhood eating patterns, or adult overeating—the number of their fat cells increases, and they might not be able to get rid of extra ones. A normal-weight individual has 10 to 20 billion fat cells. An obese individual can have up to 100 billion fat cells (Fried, 2008). Consequently, an obese individual has to eat more to feel satisfied.

Psychological Factors in Hunger and Obesity
Psychologists used to think that obesity stemmed from factors such as unhappiness and external food cues. These ideas make some sense; drowning one's sorrows in chocolate or eating some cookies just because they are there seems common enough to explain overeating.

www.CartoonStock.com

However, a number of factors are more important than emotional state and external stimuli (Rodin, 1984).

Time and place affect our eating. Learned associations of food with a particular place and time are characteristic of many organisms (Fiese, Foley, & Spagnola, 2006). If it is noon, we are likely to feel hungry even if we ate a big breakfast. We also associate eating with certain places. Many people link watching television with eating and feel uncomfortable if they are not eating something while watching TV.

From an evolutionary framework, we might note that human taste preferences developed at a time when reliable food sources were scarce. Our earliest ancestors probably developed a preference for sweets and fatty foods because ripe fruit, a concentrated source of sugar (and calories), was accessible and because high-fat foods carried much-needed calories. Today many people still have a taste for such foods, but unlike our ancestors' ripe fruit (containing sugar *plus* vitamins and minerals), the soft drinks and candy bars we snack on fill us with nutrient-free calories. Furthermore, in modern life we rarely require the calorie counts that our ancestors needed to survive.

Dieting is a continuing obsession in the United States. Furthermore, some people who focus on losing weight should not. In Chapter 12, we will examine eating disorders that involve extremely unhealthy patterns of eating. In Chapter 14, we will take up the question of how individuals successfully and healthfully lose weight.

Even if we are trying to lose weight, we know we have to eat to survive. For our species to survive, we have to have sex. Like hunger, sex has a strong physiological basis, as well as cognitive and sociocultural components. Let's review some of the key issues involved in the human need for sex.

The Biology of Sex

What brain areas are involved in sex? What role do hormones play in sexual motivation? What is the nature of the human sexual response pattern? This section uncovers the answers to these central questions about the biology of sex.

The Hypothalamus, Cerebral Cortex, and Limbic System
Motivation for sexual behavior is centered in the hypothalamus (Paredes, 2009). However, like many other areas of motivation, brain functioning related to sex radiates outward to connect with a wide range of other brain areas in both the limbic system and the cerebral cortex.

Researchers have shown the importance of the hypothalamus in sexual activity by electrically stimulating or surgically removing it. Electrical stimulation of certain hypothalamic areas increases sexual behavior; surgical removal of some hypothalamic areas produces sexual inhibition. Electrical stimulation of the hypothalamus in a male can lead to as many as 20 ejaculations in an hour. The limbic system, which runs through the hypothalamus, also seems to be involved in sexual behavior. Its electrical stimulation can produce penile erection in males and orgasm in females.

In humans, the temporal lobes of the neocortex (located on the sides of the brain) play an important role in moderating sexual arousal and directing it to an appropriate goal object (Carroll, 2007). Temporal lobe damage in male cats has been shown to impair the animals' ability to select an appropriate partner. Male cats with temporal lobe damage try to copulate with everything in sight, including teddy bears, chairs—and even researchers! Temporal lobe damage in humans also has been associated with changes in sexual activity (Mendez & others, 2000).

The brain tissues that produce sexual feelings and behaviors are activated by various neurotransmitters in conjunction with sex hormones. Like scratching an itch, sexual motivation also is characterized by a basic urge-reward-relief cycle. That means that we become sexually aroused, feel a strong urge to engage in sexual behavior, engage in that behavior, and then experience a rewarding sensation, followed by feelings of calm relief.

The motivation for sex is generated by excitatory neurotransmitters (Hull & Dominguez, 2006). The intense reward of orgasm is caused by a massive rush of dopamine, and the deep feeling of relaxation that follows is linked with the hormone oxytocin, which we examined in Chapter 2 (Clement & others, 2009).

Sex Hormones

estrogens
The class of sex hormones that predominate in females, produced mainly by the ovaries.

androgens
The class of sex hormones that predominate in males, produced by the testes in males and by the adrenal glands in both males and females.

The two main classes of sex hormones are estrogens and androgens. **Estrogens,** the class of sex hormones that predominate in females, are produced mainly by the ovaries. **Androgens,** such as testosterone, the class of sex hormones that predominates in males, are produced by the testes in males and by the adrenal glands in both males and females. For men, higher androgen levels are associated with sexual motivation and orgasm frequency (Thiessen, 2002). Recent research suggests that increasing testosterone in women increases sex drive and the frequency of satisfying sexual experiences (Braunstein, 2007), although it may carry a heightened risk for breast cancer.

One substance that is known to decrease testosterone is black licorice. Some researchers have participants eat black licorice as a way to manipulate testosterone levels.

The Human Sexual Response Pattern

What physiological changes do humans experience during sexual activity? To answer this question, William Masters and Virginia Johnson (1966) carefully observed and measured the physiological responses of 382 female and 312 male volunteers as they masturbated or had sexual intercourse. Masters and Johnson identified a **human sexual response pattern** consisting of four phases: excitement, plateau, orgasm, and resolution.

human sexual response pattern
According to Masters and Johnson, the characteristic sequence of physiological changes that humans experience during sexual activity, consisting of four phases: excitement, plateau, orgasm, and resolution.

The *excitement phase* begins the process of erotic responsiveness. It lasts from several minutes to several hours, depending on the nature of the sex play involved. Engorgement of blood vessels and increased blood flow in genital areas and muscle tension characterize the excitement phase. The most obvious signs of response in this phase are lubrication of the vagina and partial erection of the penis.

The second phase of the human sexual response, the *plateau phase,* is a continuation and heightening of the arousal begun in the excitement phase. The increases in breathing, pulse rate, and blood pressure that occurred during the excitement phase become more intense, penile erection and vaginal lubrication are more complete, and orgasm is closer.

The third phase of the human sexual response cycle is *orgasm.* How long does orgasm last? Some individuals sense that time is standing still when it takes place, but in fact orgasm lasts for only about 3 to 15 seconds. Orgasm involves an explosive discharge of neuromuscular tension and an intensely pleasurable feeling.

Following orgasm, the individual enters the *resolution phase,* in which blood vessels return to their normal state. A sex difference in this phase is that females may be stimulated to orgasm again without delay. Males enter a *refractory period* during which they cannot have another orgasm.

Cognitive and Sensory/ Perceptual Factors

From experience, we know that our cognitive world plays an important role in our sexuality (Kelly, 2006). We might be sexually attracted to someone but understand that we must inhibit our sexual urges until the relationship has time to develop. We have the cognitive capacity to think about the importance of respecting our partners and not taking sexual advantage of someone. We also have the cognitive capacity to generate sexual images—to become sexually aroused just by thinking about erotic images (Whipple, Ogden, & Komisaruk, 1992).

Recall from the discussion of memory in Chapter 6 that *scripts* are schemas for events. Sexual motivation is influenced by *sexual scripts,* stereotyped patterns of expectancies for how people should behave sexually. We carry these scripts with us in our memories. Typically, women and men have different sexual scripts (R. Jones, 2006). Women tend to link sexual intercourse with love more than men do, and men are more likely to

This difference in sexual scripts might explain why erotic magazines and movies are directed more toward men than toward women.

emphasize sexual conquest. Some sexual scripts involve a double standard: For example, it is okay for male but not female adolescents to have sex, and women bear the blame if they become pregnant.

Cognitive interpretation of sexual activity also involves our perceptions of the individual with whom we are having sex and his or her perceptions of us (Miller, Perlman, & Brehm, 2009). We imbue our sexual acts with perceptual questions such as, is he loyal to me and what will our future relationship be like? Amid the wash of hormones in sexual activity is the cognitive ability to control, reason about, and try to make sense of the activity.

Sensation and perception are also involved in sexual behavior. The sensory system of touch usually predominates during sexual intimacy, but vision also plays a powerful role for some individuals. In general, women are more aroused by touch; men, by what they see.

Cultural Factors

Sexual motivation also is influenced by cultural factors (Shiraev & Levy, 2010; Strong & others, 2008). Some cultures consider sexual pleasures to be normal or desirable; other cultures view sexual pleasures as abnormal or unappealing.

The influence of culture on sexuality was demonstrated dramatically in a classic analysis by John Messenger (1971) of the people living on the small island of Inis Beag off the coast of Ireland. They knew nothing about tongue kissing or hand stimulation of the penis, and they detested nudity. For both females and males, premarital sex was out of the question. Men avoided most sexual experiences because they believed that sexual intercourse reduced their energy level and was bad for their health. Under these repressive conditions, sexual intercourse occurred only at night, taking place as quickly as possible. As you might suspect, female orgasm was rare in this culture (Messenger, 1971).

What are some aspects of your own culture that influence your sexual behavior?

In contrast, around the same time that Messenger was studying the people of Inis Beag, Donald Marshall (1971) was studying the Mangaian culture in the South Pacific. In Mangaia, young boys were taught about masturbation and encouraged to engage in it as much as they liked. At age 13, the boys underwent a ritual, initiating them into sexual manhood. First, their elders instructed them about sexual strategies, including how to aid their female partner in having orgasms. Two weeks later, the boy had intercourse with an experienced woman who helped him hold back from ejaculation until she experienced orgasm with him. By the end of adolescence, Mangaians had sex nearly every day. Mangaian women reported a high frequency of orgasm.

Sexual Behavior and Orientation

Few cultures are as isolated and homogeneous as are Inis Beag and Mangaia. In the United States, sexual behaviors and attitudes reflect the country's diverse multicultural population, and Americans fall somewhere in the middle of a continuum going from repressive to liberal. We are more conservative in our sexual habits than once thought but somewhat more open-minded regarding sexual orientation than a century ago.

Recall from Chapter 1 the importance of having a representative sample. Kinsey's research included only those who were willing to talk about their sex lives—a biased sample.

Sexual Attitudes and Practices Describing sexual practices in the United States has always been challenging (Dunne, 2002). The earliest research on this topic, including the groundbreaking research of Alfred Kinsey and his colleagues in 1948, indicated that Americans were engaging in a lot of very wild sex. However such research was limited by the lack of representative samples. Kinsey was certainly a pioneer in studying sexuality, but

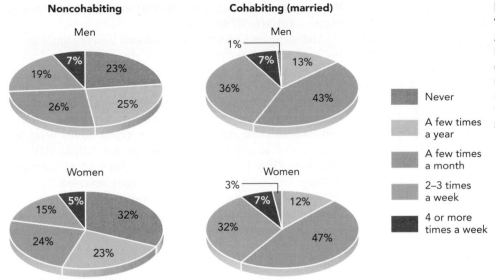

Noncohabiting

Men

23% | 25% | 26% | 19% | 7%

Women

32% | 23% | 24% | 15% | 5%

Cohabiting (married)

Men

1% | 7% | 13% | 43% | 36%

Women

3% | 7% | 12% | 47% | 32%

- Never
- A few times a year
- A few times a month
- 2–3 times a week
- 4 or more times a week

FIGURE 9.3

The 1994 Sex in America Survey

Percentages show noncohabiting and cohabiting (married) males' and females' responses to the question "How often have you had sex in the past year?"

he collected data wherever he could find it, from anyone willing to discuss the intimate details of his or her sex life.

Not until 1994 were more accurate data obtained from a well-designed, comprehensive study of U.S. sexual patterns. Robert Michael and his colleagues (1994) interviewed nearly 3,500 randomly selected people from 18 to 50 years of age. One of the most powerful messages to emerge from the 1994 survey was that Americans' sexual lives are more ordinary than was previously believed. Although 17 percent of the men and 3 percent of the women said they had had sex with at least 21 partners, the overall impression from the survey was that for most Americans, marriage and monogamy rule sexual behavior. Married couples have sex most often and are the most likely to have orgasms when they do. Figure 9.3 portrays the frequency of sex for married and non-cohabiting individuals in the year before the survey was taken. Nearly 75 percent of the married men and 85 percent of the married women indicated that they had never been unfaithful. More recent surveys have shown similar results. For instance, in 2004 ABC polled a nationally representative sample and found that individuals in committed relationships had more sex than singles, and the vast majority reported themselves as sexually faithful.

Men and women differ sexually in some ways. Men think about sex far more often than women do. The 1994 survey found that 54 percent of the men said they think about it every day or several times a day, whereas 67 percent of the women said they think about it only a few times a week or a few times a month. Men report more frequent feelings of sexual arousal, have more frequent sexual fantasies, and rate the strength of their own sex drive higher than women do (Baumeister, Catanese, & Vohs, 2001). Men also are more likely to masturbate, have more permissive attitudes about casual premarital sex, and have a more difficult time adhering to their vows of sexual fidelity when they become married (Oliver & Hyde, 1993; Peplau, 2003). Compared to men, women tend to show more changes in their sexual patterns and desires over their lifetime (Baumeister, 2000; Baumeister & Stillman, 2006; Diamond, 2008). Women are more likely than men, for instance, to have had sexual experiences with same- and opposite-sex partners, even if they identify themselves strongly as heterosexual or lesbian.

Sex is a topic about which, as a society, we have had difficulty talking plainly. Moreover, there is reason to believe that many of us are not sure about what qualifies as sex and what does not. For example, as Figure 9.4 shows, rates of oral sex during adolescence have sharply increased (Brady & Halpern-Felsher, 2007; Brewster & Harker Tillman, 2008). Especially worrisome about the increase in oral sex during adolescence is how casually individuals engage in it. For many adolescents, oral sex appears to be a recreational activity, and because many adolescents do not view oral sex as "sex,"

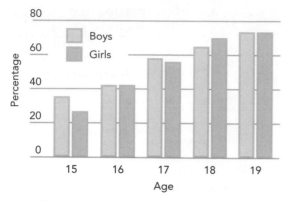

FIGURE 9.4

Percentage of U.S. 15- to 19-Year-Old Boys and Girls Who Report Engaging in Oral Sex

Is it "really sex"? This figure shows the percentage of young people under the age of 20 who report having engaged in oral sex.

SOURCE: National Center for Health Statistics (2002).

they believe it is a safe alternative to intercourse (Cornell & Halpern-Felsher, 2006).

Although some people have expressed concern that educating children and young adolescents about sex might lead to early sexual experimentation, research suggests the opposite. Currently, a major controversy in sex education is whether schools should have an abstinence-only program or a program that emphasizes contraceptive knowledge. Two recent research reviews found that abstinence-only programs do not delay the initiation of sexual intercourse and do not reduce HIV-risk behaviors (Kirby, Laris, & Rolleri, 2007; Underhill, Montgomery, & Operario, 2007). Further, a recent study revealed that adolescents who experienced comprehensive sex education were less likely to report adolescent pregnancies than those who were given abstinence-only sex education or no education (Kohler, Manhart, & Lafferty, 2008). A number of leading experts on adolescent sexuality now conclude that sex education programs that emphasize contraceptive knowledge do not increase the incidence of sexual intercourse and are more likely to reduce the risk of adolescent pregnancy and sexually transmitted infections (STIs) than abstinence-only programs (Constantine, 2008; Eisenberg & others, 2008; Hampton, 2008).

Sexual Orientation Sex is clearly an important and powerful motivation, but we might also wonder about the related issue of the direction of a person's sexual feelings. An individual's **sexual orientation** refers to the direction of his or her erotic interests. An individual who identifies himself or herself as heterosexual is generally sexually attracted to members of the opposite sex. An individual who identifies himself or herself as homosexual is generally sexually attracted to members of the same sex.

Today, sexual orientation is commonly viewed as a continuum from exclusive male–female relations to exclusive same-sex relations (B. M. King, 2005). Some individuals self-identify as *bisexual,* meaning that they are sexually attracted to people of both sexes.

sexual orientation The direction of an individual's erotic interests, today viewed as a continuum from exclusive male–female relations to exclusive same-sex relations.

Despite the widespread use of labels such as "homosexual," "gay," "lesbian," and "bisexual," some researchers argue that they are misleading. Because a person's erotic attractions may be fluid, these commentators say, references to a construct such as a fixed sexual orientation ignores the potential flexibility of human sexual attraction and behavior (Diamond, 2008).

It is difficult to know precisely how many gays, lesbians, and bisexuals there are in the world because fears of discrimination may prevent individuals from answering honestly on surveys. Estimates of the frequency of homosexuality range from between 1 percent and 10 percent of the population and are typically higher for men than women (Zietsch & others, 2008). In 2000 the U.S. Bureau of the Census added the category "unmarried partners" to the options for respondents, and from the census data (combined with the information on the sex of respondents) experts estimate that at least 1.2 million Americans are living in same-sex households. Such households exist in 99 percent of counties throughout the United States, and approximately one in four of these households includes children (O'Barr, 2006).

Research shows that gay and lesbian individuals are similar to their heterosexual counterparts in many ways. Regardless of their sexual orientation, all people have similar physiological responses during sexual arousal and seem to be aroused by the same types of tactile stimulation. Investigators typically find no differences among lesbians, gays, bisexuals, and heterosexuals in a wide range of attitudes, behaviors, and psychological

An individual's sexual orientation is most likely determined by a combination of genetic, hormonal, cognitive, and environmental factors.

adjustment (Savin-Williams & Diamond, 2004). Many gender differences that appear in heterosexual relationships occur in same-sex relationships (Peplau & Fingerhut, 2007; Savin-Williams & Diamond, 2004).

Essentially, gay men are quite similar to heterosexual men, and lesbians are quite similar to heterosexual women.

What explains a person's sexual orientation? Speculation about this question has been extensive (Kelly, 2006; Rahman, 2005). Twin studies show that genes do play a role in sexual orientation, with some studies suggesting heritability as high as 60 percent (Kendler & others, 2000). More recently, a study of nearly 4,000 twins in Sweden indicated much lower heritability, about 35 percent in men, and just 19 percent in women (Langstrom & others, 2009). These heritability estimates suggest that while genes play a role in sexual orientation, they are not as strong in explaining sexuality as they are for other characteristics, such as intelligence.

Another recent study examined the role of genes in the *potential* for same-sex activity. In this study (Santtila & others, 2008), over 9,000 twins and their siblings were asked not only about their same-sex behavior but about their potential for such behavior. The researchers asked the participants whether they would be able to engage in sexual activity with an attractive same-sex person whom they liked, if no one would find out about it. The researchers found that 33 percent of men and 65 percent of women said they would, even though over 90 percent of these individuals had had no same-sex sexual contacts in the previous year. Furthermore, twins were more similar in their responses to the question about potential same-sex behavior than non-twin siblings. The researchers concluded that the potential for same-sex activity is more common than previously considered and that the potential for same-sex sexual behavior is at least partially genetic.

Genetic explanations for homosexuality present a puzzle for evolutionary psychologists. How can a characteristic that seems to decrease a person's likelihood of reproducing be passed down genetically? One possibility is that some of the same genes that contribute to homosexuality may also lead to reproductive success for *heterosexual* individuals who possess them (Iemmola & Ciani, 2009). Research has examined twin pairs in which one twin is heterosexual and the other homosexual (Zietsch & others, 2008). Heterosexual twins of homosexual individuals are likely to possess attractive qualities (such as, for men, being caring and gentle; and for women, being assertive and sexually open) and to have more sex partners than heterosexual individuals with heterosexual twins (Zietsch & others, 2008).

Homosexual behavior has been observed in nearly 1,500 species of animals, including rats, nonhuman primates, ostriches, goats, guppies, cats, bison, dolphins, and fruit flies (Bagemhi, 1999; Sommer and Vasey, 2006).

Although genes clearly play a role in sexual orientation, much remains to be explained by other factors. Similar to many other psychological characteristics, an individual's sexual orientation most likely depends on a combination of genetic, hormonal, cognitive, and environmental factors (Langstrom & others, 2009). Most experts on sexual orientation believe that no one factor alone causes sexual orientation and that the relative weight of each factor can vary from one individual to the next. Importantly, no particular parenting style has been shown to relate to the development of children's sexual orientation. Whether heterosexual, homosexual, or bisexual, a person cannot be talked out of his or her sexual orientation. Homosexuality is present in all cultures, regardless of whether a culture is accepting or intolerant.

In the United States, gay marriage and gay parenting have inspired strong controversy, especially in political election years. In addressing these issues, psychologists rely on scientific evidence. After reviewing that evidence, the American Psychological Association issued a press release supporting gay marriage and opposing

Same-sex marriage is a contentious social issue in the United States.

discrimination against gay men and lesbians in matters such as parenting, adoption, and child custody (APA, 2004). The APA's stand on gay marriage was based on the considerable research supporting the central role of committed intimate relationships in human functioning. With regard to gay parenting, the APA drew on studies showing that children reared by gay men and lesbians tend to be as well adjusted as those from heterosexual households, are no more likely to be homosexual themselves, and are no less likely to be accepted by their peers (Chan, Raboy, & Patterson, 1998).

This endorsement represents a turn-around, as the APA classified homosexuality as a mental disorder until the 1970s. Attitudes about gays and lesbians have become more positive in society in general (Kaiser Family Foundation, 2001). This increased acceptance likely stems in part from gay men's and lesbians' greater openness with others about their lives. In 2001, 73 percent of the general public reported knowing someone who is gay, compared to just 24 percent in 1984. Indeed, 70 percent or more of those surveyed in 2001 said that they believed there should be laws protecting gays and lesbians from discrimination at work and in housing.

Younger Americans are especially likely to support gay rights. A recent survey of members of Generation Next (those born between 1981 and 1988) found that 58 percent believed that homosexuality ought to be accepted, and nearly half felt that same-sex marriage should be legal (Pew Research Center, 2007). Further, a recent USA Today/ Gallup poll found that 6 in 10 Americans believe that same-sex marriage should be a private decision between two adults, not an issue for government regulation (Grossman, 2008). For gay, lesbian, and bisexual individuals, being open about their sexual orientation is not only related to progress in changing attitudes but is also a strong predictor of psychological and physical health (Savin-Williams, 2006).

self quiz

1. Obesity
   A. does not have a genetic component.
   B. is linked to good health.
   C. is associated with the body's set point.
   D. has most recently decreased in the United States.

2. The brain structure(s) *primarily* involved in motivation for sexual behavior is (are) the
   A. hypothalamus.
   B. temporal lobes.
   C. hippocampus.
   D. medulla.

3. Among lesbians and gay men, the relationship between openness about one's sexual orientation and well-being is that
   A. openness is related to increased depression.
   B. openness puts one at risk for victimization.
   C. there is no clear link between openness and well-being.
   D. openness is related to increased psychological and physical health.

Apply It! 4. A small town's school board is considering what sort of sex education to adopt for the high school. A number of individuals have expressed concern that giving students information about contraception will only send the message that it is okay to engage in sexual activity. Which of the following reflects the research relevant to this issue?
   A. Students who are given information about contraception generally have sex earlier and more frequently than individuals who are not given this information.
   B. Students who are given abstinence-only education are least likely to engage in sex at all.
   C. Sex education in schools has shown no relationship to adolescent sexual activity.
   D. Students who are given comprehensive information about contraception are less likely to become pregnant during adolescence and are not more likely to engage in sexual activity.

3 Beyond Hunger and Sex: Approaches to Motivation in Everyday Life

Food and sex are unquestionably crucial to human survival. Surviving is not all we do, however. Think about the wide range of human actions and achievements reported in the news, such as a man's donation of his kidney to a best friend and the appointment of a woman who grew up in poverty as the CEO of a major corporation. Such individuals' behaviors are not easily explained by motivational approaches that focus on physiological needs. Psychologists have begun to appreciate the role of the goals that people set for themselves in motivation. In this section, we explore the ways that psychologists have come to understand the processes that underlie everyday human behavior.

Maslow's Hierarchy of Human Needs

hierarchy of needs
Maslow's theory that human needs must be satisfied in the following sequence: physiological needs, safety, love and belongingness, esteem, and self-actualization.

Humanistic theorist Abraham Maslow (1954, 1971) proposed a **hierarchy of needs** that must be satisfied in the following sequence: physiological needs, safety, love and belongingness, esteem, and self-actualization (Figure 9.5). The strongest needs are at the base of the hierarchy (physiological) and the weakest are at the top (self-actualization). According to this hierarchy, people are motivated to satisfy their need for food first and to satisfy their need for safety before their need for love. If we think of our needs as calls for action, hunger and safety needs shout loudly, while the need for self-actualization beckons with a whisper. Maslow asserted that each lower need in the hierarchy comes from a deficiency, such as being hungry, afraid, or lonely, and that we see the higher-level needs in a person who is relatively sated in these basic needs. Such an individual can turn his or her attention to the fulfillment of a higher calling.

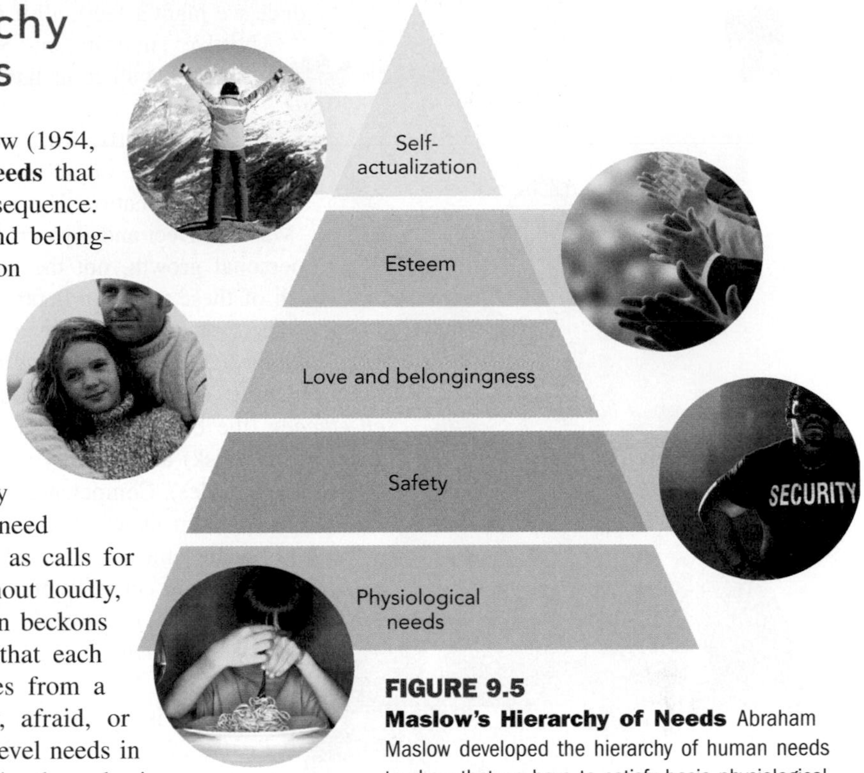

FIGURE 9.5
Maslow's Hierarchy of Needs Abraham Maslow developed the hierarchy of human needs to show that we have to satisfy basic physiological needs before we can satisfy other, higher needs.

self-actualization
The motivation to develop one's full potential as a human being—the highest and most elusive of Maslow's proposed needs.

Self-actualization, the highest and most elusive of Maslow's needs, is the motivation to develop one's full potential as a human being. According to Maslow, self-actualization is possible only after the other needs in the hierarchy are met. Maslow cautions that most people stop moving up the hierarchy after they have developed a high level of esteem and thus do not become self-actualized. We will return to Maslow's notion of self-actualization in Chapter 10.

The idea that human motives are hierarchically arranged is appealing; however, Maslow's ordering of the needs is debatable. Some people might seek greatness in a career to achieve self-esteem, while putting on hold their needs for love and belongingness. Certainly history is full of examples of individuals who, in the most difficult circumstances, were still able to engage in acts of kindness that seem to come from higher-level needs. Often, the poorest individuals are most likely to give generously to others.

Perhaps Maslow's greatest contribution to our understanding of motivation is that he asked the key question about motivation for modern people: How can we explain what humans do, once their bellies are full? That is, how do we explain the "why" of human behavior when survival is not the most pressing need? This is the kind of questioning that inspired *self-determination theory* (Deci & Ryan, 2002).

Near the end of his life, Maslow added self-transcendence as a need even higher than self-actualization. Self-transcendence involves a level of experience that is beyond the self, including spirituality, compassion, and morality. What other needs do you think Maslow left out of his original hierarchy?

Self-Determination Theory

self-determination theory
Deci and Ryan's theory asserting that all humans have three basic, innate organismic needs: competence, relatedness, and autonomy.

Building from Maslow's humanistic perspective, Edward Deci and Richard Ryan (2000) have explored the role of motivation in optimal human functioning from a perspective that emphasizes particular kinds of needs as factors in psychological and physical well-being. Their **self-determination theory** asserts that there are three basic organismic needs: competence, relatedness, and autonomy. These psychological needs are innate and exist in every person. They are basic to human growth and functioning, just as water, soil, and sunshine are necessary for plant growth. This metaphor is especially apt, because once we plant a seed, all it requires to thrive and grow is a supportive environment. Similarly, self-determination theory holds that all of us have the capacity for growth and fulfillment in us, ready to emerge if given the right context.

Importantly, from the perspective of self-determination theory, these organismic needs do not arise from deficits. Self-determination theory is not a drive reduction theory. Like Maslow, Deci and Ryan (2000) argue that these needs concern personal growth, not the filling of deficiencies. Let's examine each of these needs in depth.

The first organismic need described by self-determination theory, *competence,* is met when we feel that we are able to bring about desired outcomes (Reis & others, 2000). Competence motivation involves *self-efficacy* (the belief that you have the competence to accomplish a given goal or task) and *mastery* (the sense that you can gain skills and overcome obstacles). Competence is also related to expectancies for success. One domain in which competence needs may be met is in the realm of achievement. Some individuals are highly motivated to succeed and spend considerable effort striving to excel.

The second organismic need described by self-determination theory is *relatedness,* the need to engage in warm relations with other people. Some psychologists have proposed that the need to belong is the strongest human motivator (Baumeister & Leary, 2000). The need for relatedness is reflected in the importance of parents' nurturing children's development, the intimate moments of sharing private thoughts in friendship, the uncomfortable feelings we have when we are lonely, and the powerful attraction we have for someone else when we are in love.

The third need proposed by self-determination theory is *autonomy*—the sense that we are in control of our own life. Autonomy means being independent and self-reliant, and it is a key aspect of feeling that one's behavior is self-motivated and emerging from genuine interest. Of course, many of the behaviors we engage in may feel like things we are forced to do, but a sense of autonomy is strongly related to well-being (Sheldon & others, 2005). Kennon Sheldon and colleagues (2005) have found that age relates to the experience of autonomy. For example, older Americans feel more autonomous than younger Americans when paying taxes, voting, and tipping.

Research on the role of motivation in well-being supports the idea that progress on goals that serve the three organismic needs is strongly related to well-being (Sheldon & Elliot, 1998). Further, valuing more extrinsic qualities—such as money, prestige, and physical appearance—over these organismic concerns is associated with lowered well-being, lowered self-actualization, and physical illness (Kasser & Ryan, 1996; Kasser & others, 2004).

Like any theory, self-determination theory has its controversies. One important issue is the extent to which the three needs are indeed universal. Cultures vary in how strongly they promote the needs for competence, relatedness, and autonomy. Many Western cultures—among them, the United States, Canada, and western European countries—are termed *individualistic* because they emphasize individual achievement, independence, and self-reliance. In contrast, many Eastern cultures—such as China, Japan, and Korea—are called *collectivist* because they stress affiliation, cooperation, and interdependence (Triandis, 2000). However, cross-cultural evidence suggests that the needs emphasized by self-determination theory are likely to be valued in both Western and Eastern cultures (Sheldon & others, 2001).

Self-determination theory maintains that one of the most important aspects of healthy motivation is the sense that we do the things we do because we have freely chosen to do them. When we can choose our behaviors and feel ownership over those choices, we are likely to experience heightened fulfillment (Blumenfeld, Kempler, & Krajcik, 2006).

When our behaviors follow from the needs for competence, autonomy, and relatedness, we experience intrinsic motivation. When our behavior serves needs for other values, such as prestige, money, or approval, our behavior is extrinsically motivated (Deci & Ryan, 1994; Ryan & Deci, 2000, 2001). We examine this important distinction between intrinsic and extrinsic motivation next.

Intrinsic Versus Extrinsic Motivation

One way psychologists understand the "why" of our goals is by distinguishing between intrinsic and extrinsic motivation. **Intrinsic motivation** is based on internal factors such as organismic needs (competence, relatedness, and autonomy), as well as curiosity, challenge, and fun. When we are intrinsically motivated, we engage in a behavior because we enjoy it. **Extrinsic motivation** involves external incentives such as rewards and punishments. When we are extrinsically motivated, we engage in a behavior for some external pay-off or to avoid an external punishment. Some students study hard because they are internally motivated to put forth considerable effort and achieve high quality in their work (intrinsic motivation). Other students study hard because they want to make good grades or avoid parental disapproval (extrinsic motivation).

intrinsic motivation
Motivation based on internal factors such as organismic needs (competence, relatedness, and autonomy), as well as curiosity, challenge, and fun.

extrinsic motivation
Motivation that involves external incentives such as rewards and punishments.

"Mr. Frimley, sir, can I have a word about the motivational artwork . . ."

www.CartoonStock.com

If someone is producing shoddy work, seems bored, or has a negative attitude, offering an external incentive may improve motivation. There are times, though, when external rewards can diminish intrinsic motivation. The problem with using a reward as an incentive is that individuals may perceive that the reward rather than their own motivation caused their achievement behavior. Many psychologists believe that intrinsic motivation has more positive outcomes than extrinsic motivation (Blumenfeld, Kempler, & Krajcik, 2006; Patell, Cooper, & Robinson, 2008; Ryan & Deci, 2001). They argue that intrinsic motivation is more likely to produce competent behavior and mastery. Indeed, research comparisons often reveal that people whose motivation is intrinsic show more interest, excitement, and confidence in what they are doing than those whose motivation is extrinsic. Intrinsic motivation often results in improved performance, persistence, creativity, and self-esteem (Ryan & Deci, 2001).

Some psychologists stress that many very successful individuals are both intrinsically motivated (they have high personal standards of achievement and emphasize personal effort) and extrinsically motivated (they are strongly competitive). For the most part, however, psychologists believe that intrinsic motivation is the key to achievement (Blumenfeld, Kempler, & Krajcik, 2006), although elite athletes, such as members of Olympic teams, may be motivated by both intrinsic and extrinsic rewards. Indeed, many of us might think of the ideal occupation as one in which we get paid (an extrinsic reward) for doing the very thing we love to do (intrinsic motivation).

Self-Regulation: The Successful Pursuit of Goals

Today many psychologists approach motivation in the way that you yourself might—by asking about goals and values and seeking to understand how these motivational forces shape behavior. Psychologists have referred to goals by various names, including *personal projects, best possible selves, life tasks,* and *personal strivings* (King, 2008). All of these terms reflect the goals a person is trying to accomplish in everyday life.

Self-generated goals can range from trivial matters (such as letting a bad haircut grow out) to life tasks (such as becoming a good parent).

Goal approaches to motivation include the concept of self-regulation. **Self-regulation** is the process by which an organism effortfully controls behavior in order to pursue important objectives (Carver & Scheier, 2000). A key aspect of self-regulation is getting feedback about how we are doing in our goal pursuits. Our daily mood has been proposed as a way that we may receive this feedback—that is, we feel good or bad depending on how we are doing in the areas of life we value. Note that the role of mood in self-regulation means that we cannot be happy all the time. In order to effectively pursue our goals, we have to be open to the bad news that might occasionally come our way (King, 2008).

Putting our personal goals into action is a potentially complex process that involves setting goals, planning for their implementation, and monitoring our progress. Individuals' success improves when they set goals that are specific and moderately challenging (Bandura, 1997; Schunk, 2008). A fuzzy, nonspecific goal is "I want to be successful." A concrete, specific goal is "I want to have a 3.5 average at the end of the semester." You can set both long-term and short-term goals. When you set long-term goals, such as "I want to be a clinical psychologist," make sure that you also create short-term goals as steps along the way, such as "I want to get an *A* on my next psychology test." Make commitments in manageable chunks. Planning how to reach a goal and monitoring progress toward the goal are critical aspects of achievement (Wigfield & others, 2006). Researchers have found that high-achieving individuals monitor their own learning and systematically evaluate their progress toward their goals more than low-achieving individuals do (Schunk, 2008; Schunk, Pintrich, & Meece, 2008).

Even as we keep our nose to the grindstone in pursuing short-term goals, it is also important to have a sense of the big picture. Dedication to a long-term dream or personal mission can enhance the experience of purpose in life. In his book *The Path to Purpose: Helping Our Children Find Their Calling in Life,* William Damon (2008) describes how purpose is a missing ingredient in many adolescents' and emerging adults' achievement orientation and career success. For Damon, *purpose* is an intention to accomplish a goal that is meaningful to oneself and to contribute something to the world. Finding purpose involves answering such questions as "Why am I doing this? Why does it matter? Why is it important for me and the world beyond me? Why do I strive to accomplish this end?" (Damon, 2008, pp. 33–34). While short-term goals can provide a sense of accomplishment, attaching these goals to a future dream can allow a person to experience a sense of meaning and to maintain his or her efforts in the face of short-term failure (Houser-Marko & Sheldon, 2008).

It can be difficult to recruit all of your willpower to pursue a goal you have consciously chosen. To learn more about the ways motivation and cognition relate to sticking with a goal, see the Intersection.

self-quiz

1. Rank-order the following needs according to Maslow's hierarchy: hunger, self-esteem, social relationships, safety.
   A. Social relationships must be fulfilled first, followed by hunger, safety, and finally self-esteem.
   B. Self-esteem must be fulfilled first, followed by social relationships, safety, and hunger.
   C. Hunger must be fulfilled first, followed by safety, social relationships, and finally self-esteem.
   D. Safety must be fulfilled first, followed by hunger, social relationships, and finally self-esteem.

2. According to self-determination theory, self-efficacy is most related to the need for
   A. autonomy.
   B. relatedness.
   C. competence.
   D. self-actualization.

3. Of the following, the individual who will likely perform best is someone with
   A. high extrinsic motivation.
   B. low extrinsic motivation.
   C. high intrinsic motivation.
   D. low intrinsic motivation.

Apply It! 4. Kim just bought a new game for her Xbox and cannot wait to play with it. Unfortunately, she has an exam tomorrow and needs to study instead of trying out her new game. Which of the following strategies should help Kim do well on the exam?
   A. Kim should put the new game cartridge up on her bookshelf as a reminder that she can have fun soon if she studies.
   B. Kim should allow herself to look the game over and maybe even play a little before settling down to study.
   C. Kim should put the game away where she cannot even see it or think about it. She will then be able to study without distraction.
   D. Kim should play with the game for as long as she likes, to get it out of her system.

intersection

It's bound to happen. On Friday you commit to studying all weekend, and then a friend invites you to a party that night. You commit to losing 10 pounds, and without fail the Girl Scouts show up peddling their delicious cookies. Motivation is about committing to the pursuit of valued goals, but often it seems that the world conspires against you, dangling temptation at every turn (Mischel & Ayduk, 2004). How do you stick with the program when life tries to derail you from pursuing your goals?

Motivation and Cognition: How Do We Resist Temptation?

Psychologists from a variety of fields have been interested in the human capacity to resist temptation. Research on animal learning, social cognition, and self-control has significant implications for our ability to stay the course. One of the most important underlying problems in resisting temptation is *delay of gratification*—putting off a pleasurable experience in the interest of some larger but later reward. Successful delay of gratification is evident in the student who does not go out with friends but instead stays in and studies for an upcoming test, perhaps thinking, "There will be plenty of time to party after the test." Delaying gratification is challenging. Think about it—future payoffs are simply much less certain than current rewards. If an organism is in a situation where rewards are few and far between, it might make sense to eat or drink or be merry based on whatever is around right now (Logue, 1995).

Walter Mischel and his colleagues (Mischel, Cantor, & Feldman, 1996; Mischel & Moore, 1980) examined how children managed to delay gratification. They placed children in a difficult situation—alone in a room with a tempting cookie in their reach. The children were told that if they wanted to at any time, they could ring a bell and eat the cookie. Otherwise, they could wait until the experimenter returned, and then they would get two cookies. The children were then left alone to face this self-control dilemma. In truth, the experimenter was not coming back. The researchers were interested in measuring how long the children could wait before giving in to temptation and eating the cookie.

The children responded in various ways. Some kids sat dead still, focused on the tempting cookie. Some smelled the cookie. Others turned away, sang songs, picked their noses, or did anything but pay attention to the cookie. How did the children who were able to resist temptation do it? Mischel and colleagues found that the kids who distracted themselves from the cookie by focusing on "cool thoughts" (non-cookie-related things) were better able to delay gratification. In contrast, children who remained focused on the cookie and all its delightful qualities—what Mischel called "hot thoughts"—ate the cookie sooner (Metcalfe & Mischel, 1999).

These findings have implications for self-control. Say that you are in a long-term romantic relationship that you wish to continue, and you meet someone new to whom you are physically attracted. Should you cultivate a friendship with that individual? Maybe not, if you want to avoid temptation and preserve your current relationship. Think about all the current and potential "cookies" in your life—those things that have the power to distract you from achieving your long-term plans. Mischel's research with children demonstrates that avoiding these hot issues might be a good way to see a long-term plan through to completion.

What are your biggest temptations in life? How do you resist them?

4 Emotion

Motivation and emotion are closely linked. We can feel happy or sad depending on how events influence the likelihood of our getting the things we want in life. Sometimes our emotions take us by surprise and give us a reality check about what we really want. We might think, for example, that we have lost interest in our romantic partner until that person initiates a breakup. Suddenly, we realize how much he or she really means to us. Anyone who has watched an awards show on television surely knows the link between motivation and emotion. Strolling in on the red carpet, the celebrities stress how honored they are to be nominated; but behind the Hollywood smiles is the longing to win. When the announcement is made, "And the Oscar goes to . . . ," the cameras zoom in to catch a glimpse of real emotion: the winner's face lighting up with joy and, of course, the moment of disappointment for the others.

Emotions are certainly complex. The body, the mind, and the face play key roles in emotion, although psychologists debate which of these components is most significant in emotion and how they mix to produce emotional experiences (Davidson, Scherer, & Goldsmith, 2002). For our purposes, **emotion** is feeling, or affect, that can involve physiological arousal (such as a fast heartbeat), conscious experience (thinking about being in love with someone), and behavioral expression (a smile or grimace).

emotion
Feeling, or affect, that can involve physiological arousal (such as a fast heartbeat), conscious experience (thinking about being in love with someone), and behavioral expression (a smile or grimace).

Biological Factors in Emotion

A friend whom you have been counseling about a life problem calls you to say, "We need to talk." As the time of your friend's visit approaches, you get nervous. What could be going on? You feel burdened—you have a lot of work to do, and you do not have time for a talk session. You also worry that she is angry or disappointed about something you have done. When she arrives with a gift-wrapped package and a big smile, your nerves give way to relief. She announces, "I wanted to give you this present to say thanks for all your help over the last few weeks." Your heart warms, and you feel a strong sense of your enduring bond with her. As you moved through the emotions of worry, relief, and joy, your body changed. Indeed, the body is a crucial part of our emotional experience.

Arousal   Recall from Chapter 2 that the *autonomic nervous system* (ANS) takes messages to and from the body's internal organs, monitoring such processes as breathing, heart rate, and digestion. The ANS is divided into the sympathetic and the parasympathetic nervous systems (Figure 9.6). The *sympathetic nervous system* (SNS) is involved in the body's arousal; it is responsible for a rapid reaction to a stressor, sometimes referred to as the fight-or-flight response. The SNS immediately causes an increase in blood pressure, a faster heart rate, more rapid breathing for greater oxygen intake, and more efficient blood flow to the brain and major muscle groups. All of these changes prepare us for action. At the same time, the body stops digesting food, because it is not necessary for immediate action (which could explain why just before an exam, students usually are not hungry).

The *parasympathetic nervous system* (PNS) calms the body. Whereas the sympathetic nervous system prepares the individual for fighting or running away, the parasympathetic nervous system promotes relaxation and healing. When the PNS is activated, heart rate and blood pressure drop, stomach activity and food digestion increase, and breathing slows down.

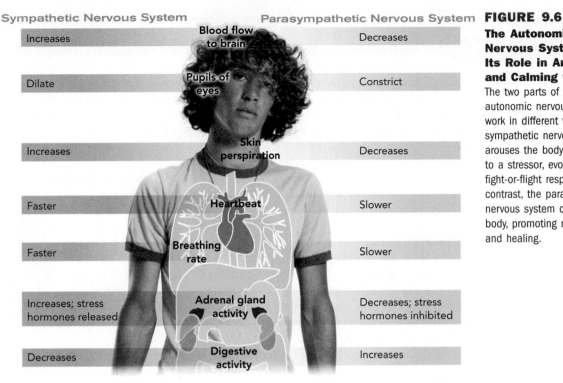

Sympathetic Nervous System		Parasympathetic Nervous System	
Increases	Blood flow to brain	Decreases	
Dilate	Pupils of eyes	Constrict	
Increases	Skin perspiration	Decreases	
Faster	Heartbeat	Slower	
Faster	Breathing rate	Slower	
Increases; stress hormones released	Adrenal gland activity	Decreases; stress hormones inhibited	
Decreases	Digestive activity	Increases	

FIGURE 9.6

The Autonomic Nervous System and Its Role in Arousing and Calming the Body The two parts of the autonomic nervous system work in different ways. The sympathetic nervous system arouses the body in reaction to a stressor, evoking the fight-or-flight response. In contrast, the parasympathetic nervous system calms the body, promoting relaxation and healing.

The sympathetic and parasympathetic nervous systems evolved to improve the human species' likelihood for survival, but it does not take a life-threatening situation to activate them. Emotions such as anger and fear are associated with elevated SNS activity as exemplified in heightened blood pressure and heart rate. States of happiness and contentment also activate the SNS to a lesser extent.

Measuring Arousal Because arousal includes a physiological response, researchers have been intrigued by how to measure it accurately. One aspect of emotional arousal is *skin conductance level* (SCL) response, a rise in the skin's electrical conductivity when sweat gland activity increases. A sweaty palm conducts electricity better than a dry palm, and this difference provides the basis for SCL, which produces an index of arousal that has been used in many studies of emotion.

Another measure of arousal is the **polygraph** or lie detector, a machine examiners use to try to determine whether someone is lying. The polygraph monitors changes in the body—heart rate, breathing, and SCL—thought to be influenced by emotional states.

In a typical polygraph test, the examiner asks the individual a number of neutral questions and several key, less neutral questions. If the individual's heart rate, breathing, and SCL responses increase substantially when the key questions are asked, the individual is assumed to be lying. Lying also has been linked with certain emotional facial expressions (Porter & ten Brinke, 2008; Warren, Schertler, & Bull, 2009).

How accurate is the lie detector? Although it measures the degree of arousal to a series of questions, no one has found a unique physiological response to telling lies (Lykken, 1987, 2001; Seymour & others, 2000). Heart rate and breathing can increase for reasons other than lying, and this effect can make it difficult to interpret the physiological indicators of arousal. Accurately identifying truth or deception is linked with the skill of the examiner and the skill of the individual being examined. Body movements and the presence of certain drugs in the person's system can interfere with the polygraph's accuracy. Sometimes the mere presence of the polygraph and the individual's belief that it is accurate in detecting deception trigger a confession of guilt. Police may use the polygraph in this way to get a suspect to confess. However, in too many instances it has been misused and misrepresented. Experts argue that the polygraph errs just under 50 percent

polygraph
A machine, commonly called a lie detector, that monitors changes in the body, used to try to determine whether someone is lying.

of the time, especially as it cannot distinguish between such feelings as anxiety and guilt (Iacono & Lykken, 1997).

The Employee Polygraph Protection Act of 1988 restricts polygraph testing outside government agencies, and most courts do not accept the results of polygraph testing. However, some psychologists defend the polygraph's use, saying that polygraph results are as sound as other admissible forms of evidence, such as hair fiber analysis (Grubin & Madsen, 2006; Honts, 1998). The majority of psychologists, though, argue against the polygraph's use because of its inability to tell who is lying and who is not (Iacono & Lykken, 1997; Lykken, 1998; Saxe, 1998; Steinbrook, 1992).

Physiological Theories of Emotion

Imagine that you are on a picnic in the country. Suddenly, a bull runs across the field toward you. Why are you afraid?

Common sense tells you that you are trembling and fleeing from the bull because you are afraid, but William James (1950) and Carl Lange (1922) said emotion works in the opposite way. According to the **James-Lange theory,** emotion results from physiological states triggered by stimuli in the environment. Essentially, the theory proposes that after the initial perception of a stimulus, the experience of the emotion results from the perception of one's own physiological changes (changes in heart rate, breathing, and sweating patterns, for example). In the case of the charging bull, you see the bull approaching and you run away. Your aroused body then sends sensory messages to your brain, at which point emotion is perceived. You do not run away because you are afraid; rather, you are afraid because you are running away.

Walter Cannon (1927) presented an alternative physiologically based theory of emotion. To understand it, imagine the bull and the picnic once again. Seeing the bull approaching causes your brain's thalamus simultaneously to (1) stimulate your autonomic nervous system to produce the physiological changes involved in emotion (increased heart rate, rapid breathing) and (2) send messages to your cerebral cortex, where the experience of emotion is perceived. Philip Bard (1934) supported this analysis, and the theory became known as the **Cannon-Bard theory**—the proposition that emotion and physiological reactions occur simultaneously. In the Cannon-Bard theory, the body plays a less important role than in the James-Lange theory.

James-Lange theory
The theory that emotion results from physiological states triggered by stimuli in the environment.

Cannon-Bard theory
The proposition that emotion and physiological reactions occur simultaneously.

Neural Circuits and Neurotransmitters

Contemporary researchers are keenly interested in charting the neural circuitry of emotions and in discovering the role of neurotransmitters (Kindt, Soeter, & Vervliet, 2009; Pessoa, 2009). The focus of much of their work has been on the amygdala, the almond-shaped structure in the limbic system that we considered in Chapter 2. The amygdala houses circuits that are activated when we experience negative emotions.

Research by Joseph LeDoux and his colleagues has investigated the neural circuitry of one particular emotion: fear (LeDoux, 1996, 2002, 2008; Schiller & others, 2008; Sotres-Bayon & others, 2009). The amygdala plays a central role in fear. When the amygdala determines that danger is present, it shifts into high gear, marshaling the brain's resources in an effort to protect the organism from harm. This fear system evolved to detect and respond to predators and other types of natural dangers that threaten survival or territory.

The brain circuitry that involves the emotion of fear can follow two pathways: a direct pathway from the thalamus to the amygdala or an indirect pathway from the thalamus through the sensory cortex to the amygdala (Figure 9.7). The direct pathway does not convey detailed information about the stimulus, but it has the advantage of speed—and speed clearly is an important characteristic of information for an organism facing a threat to its survival. The indirect pathway carries nerve impulses from the sensory organs (eyes and ears, for example) to the thalamus (recall that the thalamus is a relay station for incoming sensory stimuli); from the thalamus, the nerve impulses travel to the sensory cortex, which then sends appropriate signals to the amygdala.

FIGURE 9.7

Direct and Indirect Brain Pathways in the Emotion of Fear Information about fear can follow two pathways in the brain when an individual sees a snake. The direct pathway (*broken arrow*) conveys information rapidly from the thalamus to the amygdala. The indirect pathway (*solid arrows*) transmits information more slowly from the thalamus to the sensory cortex (here, the visual cortex) and then to the amygdala.

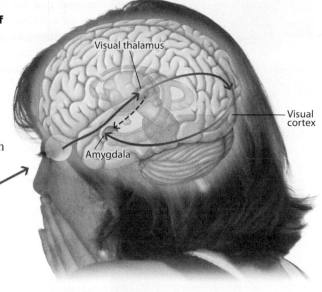

Recall from Chapter 6 that the amygdala is linked with emotional memories. LeDoux and his colleagues say that the amygdala hardly ever forgets (Debiec & LeDoux, 2006; Duvarci, Nader, & LeDoux, 2008; LeDoux, 2000, 2001, 2008). This quality is useful, because once we learn that something is dangerous, we do not have to relearn it. However, we pay a penalty for this ability. Many people carry fears and anxieties around with them that they would like to get rid of but cannot seem to shake. We will look at such fears when we explore phobias in Chapter 12. Part of the reason fears are so difficult to change is that the amygdala is well connected to the cerebral cortex, in which thinking and decision making primarily occur (Rauch, Shin, & Phelps, 2006). The amygdala is in a much better position to influence the cerebral cortex than the other way around, because it sends more connections to the cerebral cortex than it gets back. This may explain why it is so hard to control our emotions, and why, once fear is learned, it is so hard to erase.

The amygdala is not only involved in negative emotions but appears to participate in positive emotions as well. A research review concluded that various regions of the limbic system, including the amygdala, are involved in the experience of positive emotions (Burgdorf & Panksepp, 2006; Koepp & others, 2009). The neurotransmitter dopamine was especially active in the limbic system during positive emotions.

Researchers are also finding that the cerebral hemispheres may be involved in understanding emotion. Richard Davidson and his colleagues have shown that the cerebral hemispheres work differently in positive and negative emotions (Davidson, 2000; Davidson, Shackman, & Pizzagalli, 2002; Light & others, 2009; Reuter-Lorenz & Davidson, 1981; Urry & others, 2004). Recall that research we reviewed in Chapter 2 suggests that people who show relatively more left than right prefrontal activation tend to be happier. Researchers are also intrigued by the roles that neurotransmitters play in the neural pathways of emotions. Endorphins and dopamine are involved in positive emotions such as happiness (Koepp & others, 2009), and norepinephrine functions in regulating arousal (Berridge & Kringelbach, 2008; Greeson & others, 2009).

Cognitive Factors in Emotion

Does emotion depend on the tides of the mind? Are we happy only when we think we are happy? Cognitive theories of emotion center on the premise that emotion always has a cognitive component (Derryberry & Reed, 2002; Frijda, 2007; Johnson-Laird, Mancini, & Gangemi, 2006). Thinking is said to be responsible for feelings of love and hate, joy and sadness. While cognitive theorists do recognize the role of the brain and body in emotion, they give cognitive processes the main credit for these responses.

The Two-Factor Theory of Emotion In the **two-factor theory of emotion** developed by Stanley Schachter and Jerome Singer (1962), emotion is determined by two factors: physiological arousal and cognitive labeling. Schachter and Singer

two-factor theory of emotion Schachter and Singer's theory that emotion is determined by two factors: physiological arousal and cognitive labeling.

FIGURE 9.8

Capilano River Bridge Experiment: Misinterpreted Arousal Intensifies Emotional Experiences (*Top*) The precarious Capilano River Bridge in British Columbia. (*Bottom*) The experiment in progress. An attractive woman approached the men while they were crossing the bridge; she asked them to make up a story to help her with a creativity project. She also made the same request on a lower, much safer bridge. The men on the Capilano River Bridge told more sexually oriented stories, probably because they were aroused by the fear or excitement of being up so high on a swaying bridge and interpreted their arousal as sexual attraction for the female interviewer.

argued that we look to the external world for an explanation of why we are aroused. We interpret external cues and label the emotion. For example, if you feel good after someone has made a pleasant comment to you, you might label the emotion "happy." If you feel bad after you have done something wrong, you may label the feeling "guilty."

To test their theory of emotion, Schachter and Singer (1962) injected volunteer participants with epinephrine, a drug that produces high arousal. After participants received the drug, they observed someone else behave in either a euphoric way (shooting papers at a wastebasket) or an angry way (stomping out of the room). As predicted, the euphoric and angry behavior influenced the participants' cognitive interpretation of their own arousal. When they were with a happy person, they rated themselves as happy; when they were with an angry person, they said they were angry. This effect occurred, however, only when the participants were not told about the true effects of the injection. When they were told that the drug would increase their heart rate and make them jittery, they said the reason for their own arousal was the drug, not the other person's behavior.

In general, research supports the belief that misinterpreted arousal intensifies emotional experiences (Leventhal & Tomarken, 1986). An intriguing study by Donald Dutton and Arthur Aron (1974) substantiates this conclusion. In the study, an attractive woman approached men while they were walking across the Capilano River Bridge in British Columbia. Only men without a female companion were approached. The woman asked the men to make up a brief story for a project she was doing on creativity. The Capilano River Bridge sways dangerously more than 200 feet above rapids and rocks (Figure 9.8). The female interviewer made the same request of other men crossing a much safer, lower bridge. The men on the Capilano River Bridge told more sexually oriented stories and rated the female interviewer more attractive than did men on the lower, less frightening bridge.

Imagine that you are late for class on an important exam day. You sprint across campus as fast as you can, arriving just in time for the test. As you look over the questions, your heart is racing, your breathing is fast, and you feel sweaty. Are you nervous about the test or just recovering from your run to the classroom? The two-factor theory suggests that you just might mistake your bodily sensations as indications that you are scared of the test.

The Primacy Debate: Cognition or Emotion?

Which comes first, thinking or feeling? Fans of vintage episodes of TV's *Star Trek* may recognize this theme from the frequent arguments between Mr. Spock, the logical Vulcan, and Bones, the emotional doctor on the *Enterprise*. In the 1980s and 1990s, two eminent psychologists, Richard Lazarus (1922–2002) and Robert Zajonc (whose name sounds like the word *science*) debated the question of which is central, cognition or emotion.

Lazarus (1991) argued for the primacy of thinking—he believed cognitive activity to be a precondition for emotion. Lazarus said that we cognitively appraise ourselves and our social circumstances. These appraisals—which include values, goals, commitments, beliefs, and expectations—determine our emotions. People may feel happy because they have a deep religious commitment, angry because they did not get the raise they anticipated, or fearful because they expect to fail an exam. Zajonc (1984) disagreed with Lazarus. Emotions are primary, he said, and our thoughts are a result of them. Zajonc famously argued that "preferences need no inferences," meaning that the way we feel about something on a "gut level" requires no thought.

Which of the two psychologists is right? *Both* are likely correct. Lazarus talked mainly about a cluster of related events that occur over a period of time, whereas Zajonc described single events or a simple preference for one stimulus over another. Lazarus was concerned with love over the course of months and years, a sense of value to the community, and plans for retirement; Zajonc spoke about a car accident, an encounter with a snake, and a preference for ice cream rather than spinach.

Some of our emotional reactions are virtually instantaneous and probably do not involve cognitive appraisal, such as shrieking upon detecting a snake. Other emotional circumstances, especially long-term feelings such as a depressed mood or anger toward a friend, are more likely to involve cognitive appraisal. Indeed, the direct and indirect brain pathways described earlier support the idea that some of our emotional reactions do not involve deliberate thinking, whereas others do (LeDoux, 2001).

Vintage Star Trek *episodes explored the question, what comes first—thinking or feeling?*

Behavioral Factors in Emotion

Remember that our definition of emotion includes not only physiological and cognitive components but also a behavioral component. The behavioral component can be verbal or nonverbal. Verbally, a person might show love for someone by professing it in words or might display anger by saying nasty things. Nonverbally, a person might smile, frown, show a fearful expression, look down, or slouch.

The most interest in the behavioral dimension of emotion has focused on the nonverbal behavior of facial expressions (Sacco & Hugenberg, 2009). Emotion researchers have been intrigued by people's ability to detect emotion from a person's facial expression (Eichmann, Kugel, & Suslow, 2009; Yoon, Joorman, & Gotlib, 2009). In a typical research study, participants, when shown photographs like those in Figure 9.9, are usually able to identify six emotions: happiness, anger, sadness, surprise, disgust, and fear (Ekman & O'Sullivan, 1991).

facial feedback hypothesis
The idea that facial expressions can influence emotions as well as reflect them.

Might our facial expressions not only reflect our emotions but also influence them? According to the **facial feedback hypothesis,** facial expressions can influence emotions as well as reflect them (Davis, Senghas, & Ochsner, 2010). In this view, facial muscles send signals to the brain that help us to recognize the emotion we are experiencing (Keillor & others, 2002). For example, we feel happier when we smile and sadder when we frown.

Support for the facial feedback hypothesis comes from an experiment by Paul Ekman and his colleagues (1983). In this study, professional actors moved their facial muscles in very precise ways, such as raising their eyebrows and pulling them together, raising their upper eyelids, and stretching their lips horizontally back to their ears (you might want to try this yourself). They were asked to hold their expression for 10 seconds, during which time the researchers measured their heart rate and body temperature. When the actors moved facial muscles in the ways described, they showed a rise in heart rate and a steady body temperature—physiological reactions that characterize fear. When they made an angry facial expression (with a penetrating stare, brows drawn together and downward, and lips pressed together or opened and pushed forward), their heart rate and body temperature both increased. The facial feedback hypothesis provides support for the James-Lange theory of emotion discussed earlier—namely, that emotional experiences can be generated by changes in and awareness of our own bodily states.

Consider what this might mean for someone who is forced to wear a smile at work all the time, such as a flight attendant or waiter.

If you've ever taken an acting class, you might recognize that this description fits with Stanislavski's "method acting," which suggests that to feel a particular emotion, an actor should imitate the behavior of someone feeling that emotion.

FIGURE 9.9

Recognizing Emotions in Facial Expressions

Look at the six photographs and determine the emotion reflected in each of the six faces. (*Top*) Happiness, anger, sadness (*bottom*) Surprise, disgust, fear.

Sociocultural Factors in Emotion

Are the facial expressions that are associated with different emotions largely innate, or do they vary across cultures? Are there gender variations in emotion? Answering these questions requires a look at research findings on sociocultural influences in emotions.

Culture and the Expression of Emotion   In *The Expression of the Emotions in Man and Animals,* Charles Darwin stated that the facial expressions of human beings are innate, not learned; are the same in all cultures around the world; and have evolved from the emotions of animals (1965). Today psychologists still believe that emotions, especially facial expressions of emotion, have strong biological ties (Gelder & others, 2006; Peleg & others, 2006). For example, children who are blind from birth and have never observed the smile or frown on another person's face smile or frown in the same way that children with normal vision do. If emotions and facial expressions that go with them are unlearned, then they should be the same the world over. Is that in fact the case?

Extensive research has examined the universality of facial expressions and the ability of people from different cultures accurately to label the emotion that lies behind facial expressions. Paul Ekman's careful observations reveal that the many faces of emotion do not differ significantly from one culture to another (Ekman, 1980, 1996, 2003). For example, Ekman and his colleague photographed people expressing emotions such as happiness, fear, surprise, disgust, and grief. When they showed the photographs to people from the United States, Chile, Japan, Brazil, and Borneo (an Indonesian island in the western Pacific), the participants recognized the emotions the faces were meant to show, across the various cultures (Ekman & Friesen, 1969). Another study focused on the way the Fore tribe, an isolated Stone Age culture in New Guinea, matched descriptions of emotions with facial expressions (Ekman & Friesen, 1971). Before Ekman's visit, most of the Fore had never seen a Caucasian face. Ekman's team showed them photographs of people's faces expressing emotions such as fear, happiness, anger, and surprise. Then they read stories about people in emotional situations and asked the tribespeople to pick out the face that matched the story. The Fore were able to match the descriptions of emotions with the facial expressions in the photographs. Figure 9.10 shows the similarity of facial expressions of emotions by persons in New Guinea and the United States.

Whereas facial expressions of basic emotions appear to be universal, display rules for emotion vary (Fischer, 2006; Fok & others, 2008). **Display rules** are sociocultural standards that determine when, where, and how emotions should be expressed. For example, although happiness is a universally expressed emotion, when, where, and how people display it may vary from one culture to another. The same is true for other emotions, such as fear, sadness, and anger. Members of the Utku culture in Alaska, for example, discourage anger by cultivating acceptance and by dissociating themselves from any display of anger. If an unexpected snowstorm hampers a trip, the Utku do not express frustration but accept the storm and build an igloo. The importance of display rules is especially evident when we evaluate the emotional expression of another. Does that grieving husband on a morning talk show seem appropriately distraught over his wife's murder? Or might he be a suspect?

display rules
Sociocultural standards that determine when, where, and how emotions should be expressed.

Like facial expressions, some other nonverbal signals appear to be universal indicators of certain emotions. For example, regardless of where they live, when people are depressed, their emotional state shows not only in their sad facial expressions but also in their slow body movements, downturned heads, and slumped posture. Many nonverbal signals of emotion, though, vary from one culture to another (Mesquita, 2002). For example, male-to-male kissing is commonplace in Yemen but uncommon in the United States. The "thumbs up" sign, which in most cultures means either that everything is okay or that one wants to hitch a ride, is an insult in Greece, similar to a raised third finger in the United States—a cultural difference to keep in mind if you find yourself backpacking through Greece.

FIGURE 9.10
Emotional Expressions in the United States and New Guinea (*Top*) Two women from the United States. (*Bottom*) Two men from the Fore tribe in New Guinea. Notice the similarity in their expressions of disgust and happiness. Psychologists believe that the facial expression of emotion is virtually the same in all cultures.

Gender Influences
Unless you have been isolated on a mountaintop, you probably know the stereotype about gender and emotion: She is emotional; he is not. This stereotype is a powerful and pervasive image in U.S. culture (Shields, 1991).

Does research on emotional experiences support this stereotype? Researchers have found that men and women are often more alike in the way they experience emotion than the stereotype would lead us to believe. Women and men often use the same facial expressions, adopt the same language, and describe their emotional experiences similarly when they keep diaries about their experiences. For many emotional experiences, researchers do not find gender differences—both sexes are equally likely to experience love, jealousy, anxiety in new social situations, anger when they are insulted, grief when close relationships end, and embarrassment when they make mistakes in public (Tavris & Wade, 1984).

When we go beyond stereotypes and consider some specific emotional experiences, contexts in which emotion is displayed, and certain beliefs about emotion, gender does

psychology in our world

Expressing Ourselves Online: The Psychology of Emoticons

Computer science professor Scott Fahlman of Carnegie Mellon University noticed that people using an online message board were getting into conflicts because it was difficult to communicate when they were "just kidding." He posted the suggestion that they use the symbol **:-)** to express humor—and the *emoticon* was born (Fahlman, 2003). In today's world of e-mail and instant messaging, it is hard to imagine a time *without* emoticons. We use emoticons to express a variety of feelings, from joy **:D** to sadness **:-(** to silliness **;P** to great shock and dismay **: - 0.**

Psychologists are examining the place of emoticons in human communication. Emoticons are a form of *computer-mediated communication*. They allow us to compensate for the loss of information from other expressive channels, such as vocal tone and facial expression. Emoticons seem to work by capturing attention and conveying emotions and attitudes (Derks, Bos, & von Grumbkow, 2008; Lo, 2008). People use emoticons as they do other displays of emotions, such as laughter, often at the end of the statement they are trying to clarify (Provine, Spencer, & Mandell, 2007).

Women use emoticons more than men (Wolf, 2000). Men, especially when they are in all-male groups, use emoticons infrequently. In mixed-gender groups, however, men's emoticon use increases drastically (Wolf, 2000). Moreover, just as culture influences emotional expressions, it has influenced emoticons as well. For instance, East Asian emoticons are less likely to be presented sideways, so that a Japanese student might convey her level of exhaustion with **(-.-)Zzzzzz** rather than **1-)Zzzzzz.** Even with emoticons, display rules can be important. A Japanese student expressing a thumbs up **d(^_^)b** might encounter an American who thinks he is saying he has big ears.

Emoticons reveal a unique aspect of computer-mediated communication. Consider that when people communicated by writing letters (an art that would seem to share the limitations of e-mail and texting), they did not use smileys and frownies to explain their feelings. In effect, computer-mediated communication such as instant messaging might be considered a blend of spoken conversation and the written word (Tagliamonte & Denis, 2008).

As texting and IMing have become more common, it is no wonder that humans have come up with a way to inject emotional meanings into their online discourse. Emoticons powerfully demonstrate how crucial emotions are to our communications with one another.

matter in understanding emotion (Brannon, 1999; Brody, 1999; Shields, 1991). Research has shown that women are more accurate at recognizing the emotional content of faces, especially when the task is made challenging by showing the faces for a very short time (Hall & Matsumoto, 2004), and this finding suggests a gender difference in emotional intelligence (mentioned in Chapter 7). Women also report themselves as experiencing emotions for a longer period than men (Birditt & Fingerman, 2003).

It is important to keep in mind that both women and men are certainly aware of the gender-specific expectations for emotional behavior (Blakemore, Berenbaum, &

Liben, 2009). Indeed, men who embrace a stereotypically masculine gender identity are more likely to report themselves as less emotional (Jakupcak & others, 2003). Gender differences in emotion are much more tied to social context than to biological sex (Brody, 1999).

Classifying Emotions

There are more than 200 words for emotions in the English language, indicating the complexity and variety of emotions. Not surprisingly, psychologists have created ways to classify emotions—to summarize these many emotions along various dimensions (Izard, 2009), including their valence and arousal.

Valence   The *valence* of an emotion refers to whether it feels pleasant or unpleasant. You probably are not surprised to know that happiness, joy, pleasure, and contentment are positively valenced emotions. In contrast, sadness, anger, worry, and feeling upset are negatively valenced emotions. Research has shown that emotions tend to go together based on their valence, so that if someone is sad, he or she is also likely to be angry or worried, and if a person is happy, he is or she is also likely to be feeling confident, joyful, and content (D. Watson, 2001).

We can classify many emotional states on the basis of valence. Indeed, according to some experts in emotion (D. Watson, 2001), there are two broad dimensions of emotional experience: negative affect and positive affect. **Negative affect** refers to emotions such as anger, guilt, and sadness. **Positive affect** refers to emotions such as joy, happiness, and interest. Although it seems essential to consider the valence of emotions as a way to classify them, valence does not fully capture all that we need to know about emotional states. The joy a person experiences at the birth of a child and the mild high at finding a $5 bill are both positive states, but they clearly differ in important ways.

positive affect
Positive emotions such as joy, happiness, and interest.

negative affect
Negative emotions such as anger, guilt, and sadness.

Arousal Level   The *arousal level* of an emotion is the degree to which the emotion is reflected in an individual's being active, engaged, or excited versus more passive, relatively disengaged, or calm. Positive and negative emotions can be high or low in arousal. Ecstasy and excitement are examples of high-arousal positive emotions, whereas contentment and tranquility are low-arousal positive emotions. Examples of high-arousal negative emotion are rage, fury, and panic, while irritation and boredom represent low-arousal negative emotions.

Valence and arousal level are independent dimensions that together describe a vast number of emotional states. Using these dimensions, we can effectively create a wheel of mood states (Figure 9.11). The illustration shows what psychologists call a *circumplex model* of mood (Posner, Russell, & Peterson, 2005). A circumplex is simply a type of graph that creates a circle from two independent dimensions. Using the two dimensions of valence and arousal level, we can arrange emotional states in an organized fashion.

We carry our moods with us into various situations, and these situations, in turn, can influence our moods. One context in which our moods might be particularly important is at work. Are people who are happy on the job more successful or less so? To explore this question, see Challenge Your Thinking.

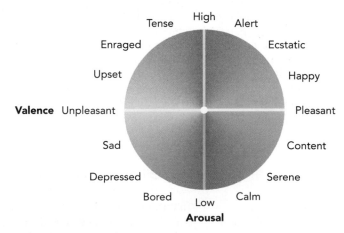

FIGURE 9.11
A Circumplex Model of Mood Using the dimensions of valence and arousal, this wheel-like figure shows a variety of emotional states.

challenge your thinking

Is a Happy Worker a More Productive Worker?

Many of us have seen TV ads that show dot-com workers playing ping-pong on the job or a warehouse manager cruising around on a Segway. At the Internet technology company Google, lunch is free, the dress code is jeans and sweatshirts, and pets are allowed. After one particularly successful run of FDA approvals for its drugs, Genentech, a cancer research firm, held a celebratory rock concert featuring Elton John, Mary J. Blige, and Matchbox 20.

It sounds like a lot of fun, but Google and Genentech are businesses that keep a close eye on the bottom line. To what extent are policies and practices that enhance employees' positive feelings good for business? Are happy workers more productive? Research in I/O (industrial and organizational) psychology, the subfield that examines psychology in the workplace, has examined this question.

To begin, you might think of happiness as a consequence of work success. That is, people who do well at work probably feel happier as a result. What is most fascinating about research on the relationship between happiness and productivity is that longitudinal studies have demonstrated that often it is the other way around: The happiness comes first (Lyubomirsky, King, & Diener, 2005). Indeed, happy individuals are more likely to graduate from college and to receive an interview for a job or a callback for a second interview than their unhappy counterparts (Burger & Caldwell, 2000; Frisch & others, 2004). One study found that happiness at age 18 was related to financial independence, occupational attainment, and work autonomy at age 26 (Roberts, Caspi, & Moffitt, 2003).

Once happy individuals get a job, they are more likely to succeed than unhappy individuals. Happy employees receive relatively more favorable performance evaluations (Wright & Staw, 1999). In one study, managers in three organizations gave higher evaluations to happy employees than to unhappy employees, based on work quality, productivity, dependability, and creativity (Staw, Sutton, & Pelled, 1994). In two studies, job performance (as judged by supervisors) was significantly related to well-being regardless of how much people liked their jobs (Wright & Cropanzano, 2000).

One reason that happy workers are more likely to be high performers is that they are less likely to miss work, leave a job, or experience burnout (Donovan, 2000; Thoresen & others, 2003). Those who experience calmer types of positive emotions on the job, such as serenity and contentment, are less likely to want to quit and to be in conflict with other workers (Van Katwyk & others, 2000).

So, are happy workers productive workers? The research reviewed above suggests that investing in workers' overall well-being just might make great business sense.

What Do You Think?

- Are free lunches and relaxed dress codes good business practices or gimmicks? Why?

- If you were a manager, how would you use the research discussed above?

The Adaptive Functions of Emotions

broaden-and-build model
Fredrickson's model of positive emotion, stating that the function of positive emotions lies in their effects on an individual's attention and ability to build resources.

In considering the functions of emotions, it is fairly easy to come up with a good reason for us to have emotions such as fear and anger. Negative emotions carry direct and immediate adaptive benefits in situations that threaten survival. Negative emotions indicate clearly that something is wrong and that we must take action. Positive emotions do not signal a problem. So, what is the adaptive function of positive emotions?

Confronting this question, Barbara Fredrickson proposed the **broaden-and-build model** of positive emotion (Fredrickson, 1998, 2001, 2006, 2009). She argues that the function of positive emotions lies in their effects on our attention and our ability to build resources. The broaden-and-build model begins with the influence of positive emotions on cognitive processing.

Positive moods, such as contentment and humor, have been shown to broaden our attentional focus; they allow us to see the forest for the trees. As a result, when in a good mood, we may be more disposed to think outside the box—to see unusual possibilities that escaped us before. In addition, a good mood, Fredrickson says, gives us a chance to build resources—to make friends, to exercise to promote our health, to branch out in new ways. These activities allow us to build up strengths that we can use when we encounter life's difficulties (Kok, Catalino, & Fredrickson, 2008). For example, joy broadens people by creating the urge to play, push the limits, and be creative. Interest broadens people by creating the motivation to explore, absorb new information and experiences, and expand the self (Csikszentmihalyi, 1990; Ryan & Deci, 2000). Positive emotions facilitate "approach" behavior (Otake & others, 2006; D, Watson, 2001), meaning that when we are feeling good, we are more likely to go after the rewards we want and to face our problems head on.

Resilience   Resilience is a characteristic that has been associated with the capacity to thrive during difficult times (Masten, 2006). Resilience refers to the ability to bounce back from negative experiences, to be flexible and adaptable when things are not going well. Resilient individuals might be thought of as tall trees that have the ability to bend but do not break in response to strong winds. In contrast, people who lack resilience might be characterized as more brittle—more likely to snap or break in the face of adversity (Block & Kremen, 1996).

Positive emotions might play an important role in the ability of resilient individuals to cope successfully with life's challenges. Resilient individuals are zestful, optimistic, and energetic in their approach to life (Block & Kremen, 1996; Klohnen, 1996). They cultivate positive emotion in their lives through the use of humor (Segerstrom, 2006). Michelle Tugade, Barbara Fredrickson, and Lisa Feldman Barrett (2004) found that the superior coping of resilient individuals came from their ability to use positive emotions to bounce back from negative emotional experiences. Using measures of cardiovascular activity, they found that resilient individuals were better able to regulate their responses to stressful situations (for instance, being told they were about to give an important speech) by strategically experiencing positive emotion. Resilient individuals seem to show a kind of emotional wisdom; they capitalize on the capacity of positive emotions to reverse the stress of negative feelings. This skill has been demonstrated in response to a specific stressful event: the terrorist attacks of September 11, 2001.

Resilience and 9/11   Fredrickson, Tugade, and their colleagues (2003) had begun a study of resilience and positive emotion in early 2001. As part of that study, they had measured resilience and a variety of other psychological characteristics. Following the 9/11 attacks, these researchers realized that they had an opportunity to examine how resilience might relate to coping with this horrific crisis. They followed up on the individuals whom they had studied earlier that year (none of whom had been directly affected by the attacks) and examined their experiences in the weeks following 9/11.

The results were striking. All participants felt a broad range of negative emotions—including fear, anxiety, horror, anger, and sadness. However,

Recall from Chapter 7 that some psychologists believe that the ability to identify and regulate one's emotions is a kind of intelligence. Emotionally intelligent people are also thought to be better at reading the emotional expressions of others. Do a web search for *emotional intelligence tests* and take some online quizzes, or just try the one at http://www.testcafe.com/ei/ Do you think you are emotionally intelligent? Does your performance on the test seem to reflect your actual experience? What is your opinion of the test you tried? Is there information on the site for its validity and reliability?

they also experienced positive emotions such as gratitude, love, and an increased closeness to others.

Individuals who had previously scored high on resilience were particularly likely to demonstrate growth in psychological resources, such as optimism and feelings of well-being, through the difficult experience of 9/11. Resilient individuals were also less likely to experience depressive symptoms. The capacity of resilient individuals to grow and to avoid depression was explained by their capacity for the experience of positive emotions. The experience of positive emotions even during a crisis was the key to the benefits of resilience. Resilient people felt profoundly distressed by 9/11, yet they nevertheless flourished because of their openness to the positive things in life—perhaps a smile from a friend, a warm hug, the reassurance of family.

self-quiz

1. The James-Lange theory of emotion states that
   A. emotion happens first, followed by physiological reactions.
   B. physiological reactions happen first, followed by emotion.
   C. physiological reactions and emotion happen simultaneously.
   D. the body plays a minimal role in emotion.

2. In the case of fearful stimuli, *indirect* neural pathways go first to the thalamus and
   A. then to the hypothalamus, followed by the amygdala.
   B. then to the sensory cortex, followed by the amygdala.
   C. then to the hippocampus.
   D. then to the hypothalamus, followed by the sensory cortex, and finally the hippocampus.

3. The facial feedback hypothesis is consistent with the theory of emotion known as
   A. the James-Lange theory.
   B. the Cannon-Bard theory.
   C. direct theory.
   D. indirect theory.

Apply It! 4. Seymour is talking to his friend about his recent breakup with his girlfriend. Seymour is describing how sad he feels about this lost relationship. His girlfriend cheated on him, but Seymour was willing to forgive her. She was not interested, though, and broke things off. As Seymour talks, his friend notices that Seymour is clenching his teeth, making fists with his hands, and generally getting pretty angry. The friend says, "You know, you sound more angry than sad." Why might Seymour have confused anger and sadness?
   A. Sadness and anger are similar in terms of their arousal level.
   B. Seymour's friend is probably wrong given that sadness produces the same facial expression as anger.
   C. Because he is a man, Seymour probably does not understand emotion very well.
   D. Sadness and anger have the same valence, so someone who is feeling sad is likely to also feel angry. Seymour is probably feeling both of these negative emotions.

5 Motivation and Emotion: The Pursuit of Happiness

Motivation is about what people want, and a quick scan of the best-seller list or the self-help section of any bookstore would seem to indicate that one thing people want very much is to be happy or happier. Can people get happier? Let's consider the evidence.

Biological Factors in Happiness

As we have seen, the brain is certainly at work in the experience of positive emotions. Genes also play a role. For instance, research on the heritability of well-being has tended to show that a substantial proportion of well-being differences among people can be explained by genetic differences. The heritability estimates for happiness range from 50 to 80 percent (Lykken, 1999). Remember from Chapter 7 that heritability is a statistic that describes characteristics of a group, that heritability estimates can vary across groups and over time, and that even highly heritable characteristics can be influenced by experience. Thus, a person is not necessarily doomed to an unhappy life, even if the person knows that he or she has particularly miserable parents.

Recall the concept of *set point* in our discussion of weight. There may also be a happiness set point, basically a person's general level of happiness that exists when the individual is not trying to increase happiness (Sheldon & Lyubomirsky, 2007). Like our weight, our happiness levels may fluctuate around this set point. In trying to increase happiness, we must consider the role of this powerful starting spot that is likely the result of genetic factors and personal dispositions.

Given these potential biological limitations, other factors also complicate the pursuit of happiness, including the hedonic treadmill and the dangers of striving for happiness itself.

Obstacles in the Pursuit of Happiness

The first key dilemma in increasing happiness is the hedonic (meaning "related to pleasure") treadmill (Brickman & Campbell, 1971; Fredrick & Loewenstein, 1999). The term *hedonic treadmill* captures the idea that any aspect of life that enhances our positive feelings is likely to do so for only a short period of time. That is, we are likely to adapt quite rapidly to any change that might occur in our life that would presumably influence our happiness. So winning the lottery, moving to a dream home in California, or falling in love may lead to temporary gains in our experience of joy, but eventually we go back to our baseline (Schkade & Kahneman, 1998). Whether it is the switch from CDs to iTunes or from dial-up to wireless, what we first experience as a life-changing improvement eventually fades to a routine (but still necessary) aspect of life, all too soon to be taken for granted. How can we increase happiness if such happiness enhancers quickly lose their power? Clearly, happiness is not about shopping at the right stores, because things we can buy will likely only lead to a momentary burst of pleasure, eventually giving way to our set point.

A second challenge to the goal of enhancing happiness is that pursuing happiness for its own sake is rarely a good way to do it. When happiness is the goal, the pursuit is likely to backfire (Schooler, Ariely, & Loewenstein, 2003). That is, explicitly focusing on trying to be happier is not a good way to be happier. Indeed, those who explicitly link the pursuit of their everyday goals to happiness fare quite poorly (McIntosh, Harlow, & Martin, 1995).

How can the many among us who are interested in being happier navigate this difficult path? In other words, how can we enhance our happiness without having this new capacity for joy become ho-hum, and how might we achieve happiness without really pursuing it?

Happiness Activities and Goal Striving

Sonja Lyubomirsky (2008) and her colleagues (Sheldon & Lyubomirsky, 2007) have proposed a promising approach to enhancing happiness. Lyubomirsky suggests that the place to begin is in intentional activities. A variety of activities, she notes, are associated with enhanced positive emotion. Physical activity, kindness, positive self-reflection, and experiencing meaning have all been shown to enhance positive affect (Sheldon & Lyubomirsky, 2007). Indeed, the strong link between altruistic behavior and positive affect is all but inescapable. Habitually helping others is one way to enhance happiness. Engaging in acts of kindness, especially trying out a wide range of different acts of service (keeping the hedonic treadmill at bay), can be especially powerful (Lyubomirsky, 2008).

One way to engage in positive self-reflection and experience meaning is to keep a gratitude journal. Robert Emmons and Michael McCullough (2004) have conducted a number of studies demonstrating the ways that being grateful can lead to enhanced happiness and psychological well-being. In one study, they asked participants to keep a diary in which they counted their blessings every day. Those who counted their blessings were better off on a variety of measures of well-being. Although some individuals do seem to be more grateful than others, what is most encouraging about this research is that experimental evidence indicates that even those who are not naturally grateful can benefit by taking a moment to count their blessings (Emmons & McCullough, 2003; McCullough, Emmons, & Tsang, 2002).

Another potentially useful approach to enhancing happiness is to commit ourselves to the pursuit of personally meaningful goals. Stop for a minute and write down the things you are typically trying to accomplish in your everyday behavior. You might identify a goal such as "to get better grades," "to be a good friend (or partner or parent)," or "to fight injustice when I see it happening." Such everyday goals and our pursuit of them have been shown to relate strongly to our subjective well-being (Brunstein, 1993; Sheldon, 2002). Simply having important, valued goals is associated with heightened feelings of well-being, as is making progress on those goals. Goal pursuit provides the glue that meaningfully relates a chain of life events, endowing life with beginnings, middles, and ends (King, 2008).

The considerable scientific literature on goal investment offers a variety of ideas about the types of goals that are likely to enhance happiness. To optimize the happiness payoffs of goal pursuit, one ought to pursue goals that are important and personally valuable and that reflect the intrinsic needs of relatedness, competence, and autonomy (Sheldon, 2002). These goals should be moderately challenging and should share an instrumental relationship with each other—so that the pursuit of one goal facilitates the accomplishment of another (Emmons & King, 1988).

With regard to the hedonic treadmill, goal pursuit has a tremendous advantage over many other ways of trying to enhance happiness. Goals change and are changed by life experience. As a result, goal pursuit may be less susceptible to adaptation over time. One reason why goals may allow us to maintain traction on the hedonic treadmill is that goals accentuate the positive but do not necessarily eliminate the negative. Goals may increase not only subjective well-being, but also momentary unhappiness—the latter effect perhaps being a very good thing. Sometimes a particular goal just does not work out, no matter doggedly we pursue it. Indeed, setting a goal includes not only the promise of fulfillment but also the potential for failure. Emotionally investing in one's daily life may mean experiencing worry over whether one will succeed (Pomerantz, Saxon, & Oishi, 2000) and experiencing disappointment when things do not go well (Kernis & others, 2000; Marsh, 1995).

So, overall, goal pursuit may lead to a happier life. Goals also keep life emotionally interesting. By fostering a rich emotional life that is also coherent and comprehensible, goals keep the positive possible and interesting. The conclusion, assuming that you want to enhance your happiness, is to strive mightily for the goals that you value. You may fail now and then but missing the mark will only make your successes all the sweeter.

Another advantage of goals as an entryway to enhanced happiness is that goals allow you to enjoy happiness without necessarily pursuing it. Goals pave the way for you to pursue happiness while you are pursuing other things. As pleasant as happiness is, even the very happiest people in the world are unhappy sometimes (Diener & Seligman, 2002). Even in the pursuit of happiness, it is important to keep in mind that positive and negative emotions are both adaptive and that the best life is one that is emotionally rich.

self-quiz

1. Studies have demonstrated that variance in well-being is
   A. quite heritable.
   B. surprisingly unpredictable.
   C. extreme.
   D. dependent on the cultural context.

2. Similarly to our body weight, our personal happiness levels may fluctuate around
   A. our popularity.
   B. our stress levels.
   C. a set point.
   D. the seasons of the year.

3. Researchers have discovered that one way for individuals to engage in positive self-reflection and experience meaning in life is to

   A. write down what they are thankful for in a diary.
   B. pursue the hedonic treadmill.
   C. practice transience.
   D. refresh their coping skills.

Apply It! 4. Bonita works at a small advertising agency. She is very much committed to her work goals and always gives her all when she has a task to perform. She is deeply disappointed when a potential client decides to go with another firm after Bonita put a whole week into her presentation. A co-worker notices Bonita's distress and says, "You know, you only feel so bad because you care too much. You should be like me. I don't care about anything, and

I'm never disappointed." What does the psychology of happiness tell us about this situation?
   A. Although Bonita feels disappointed now, her overall approach will likely lead to greater happiness in the long term.
   B. Bonita's colleague is right on. Bonita should disengage from her goals, and then she will never be disappointed.
   C. Bonita's colleague will probably be happier than Bonita in the long term and will likely have a greater sense of purpose in life.
   D. Bonita's happiness depends more on her genetic makeup than on any particular life experience.

summary

① Theories of Motivation

Motivated behavior is energized, directed, and sustained. Early evolutionary theorists considered motivation to be based on instinct—the innate biological pattern of behavior.

A drive is an aroused state that occurs because of a physiological need or deprivation. Drive reduction theory was proposed as an explanation of motivation, with the goal of drive reduction being homeostasis: the body's tendency to maintain equilibrium.

Optimum arousal theory focuses on the Yerkes-Dodson law, which states that performance is best under conditions of moderate rather than low or high arousal. Moderate arousal often serves us best, but there are times when low or high arousal is linked with better performance.

② Hunger and Sex

Stomach signals are one factor in hunger. Glucose (blood sugar) and insulin both play an important role in hunger. Glucose is needed for the brain to function, and low levels of glucose increase hunger. Insulin can cause a rise in hunger.

Leptin, a protein secreted by fat cells, decreases food intake and increases energy expenditure. The hypothalamus plays an important role in regulating hunger. The lateral hypothalamus is involved in stimulating eating; the ventromedial hypothalamus, in restricting eating.

Obesity is a serious problem in the United States. Heredity, basal metabolism, set point, and fat cells are biological factors involved in obesity. Time and place affect eating. Our early ancestors ate fruits to satisfy nutritional needs, but today we fill up on the empty calories in sweets.

Motivation for sexual behavior involves the hypothalamus. The role of sex hormones in human sexual behavior, especially in women, is not clear. Masters and Johnson mapped out the human sexual response pattern, which consists of four physiological phases: excitement, plateau, orgasm, and resolution.

Thoughts and images are central in the sexual lives of humans. Sexual scripts influence sexual behavior, as do sensory/perceptual factors. Females tend to be more sexually aroused by touch; males, by visual stimulation.

Sexual values vary across cultures. These values influence sexual behavior.

Describing sexual practices in the United States has been challenging due to the difficulty of surveying a representative sample of the population. In general, research shows that people are less sexually active and less likely to cheat than popular beliefs may suggest. Sex education has sometimes been a controversial issue, but research shows that nations with comprehensive sex education have far lower rates of teen pregnancy and sexually transmitted infections than does the United States.

Sexual orientation refers to the direction of a person's erotic attraction. Sexual orientation—heterosexual, homosexual, or bisexual—is most likely determined by a combination of genetic, hormonal, cognitive, and environmental factors. Based on scientific evidence, the APA recently supported gay marriage and argued against discriminating against gay men and lesbians in parenting, custody, and adoption.

③ Beyond Hunger and Sex: Approaches to Motivation in Everyday Life

According to Maslow's hierarchy of needs, our main needs are satisfied in this sequence: physiological needs, safety, love and belongingness, esteem, and self-actualization. Maslow gave the most attention to self-actualization: the motivation to develop to one's full potential.

Self-determination theory states that intrinsic motivation occurs when individuals are engaged in the pursuit of organismic needs that are innate and universal. These needs include competence, relatedness, and autonomy. Intrinsic motivation is based on internal factors. Extrinsic motivation is based on external factors, such as rewards and punishments.

Self-regulation involves setting goals, monitoring progress, and making adjustments in behavior to attain desired outcomes. Research suggests that setting subgoals to reach a long-term goal is a good strategy.

④ Emotion

Emotion is feeling, or affect, that has three components: physiological arousal, conscious experience, and behavioral expression. The biology of emotion focuses on physiological arousal involving the autonomic nervous system and its two subsystems. Skin conductance level and the polygraph have been used to measure emotional arousal.

The James-Lange theory states that emotion results from physiological states triggered by environmental stimuli: Emotion follows physiological reactions. The Cannon-Bard theory states that emotion and physiological reactions occur simultaneously. Contemporary biological views of emotion increasingly highlight neural circuitry and neurotransmitters. LeDoux has charted the neural circuitry of fear, which focuses on the amygdala and consists of two pathways, one direct and the other indirect. It is likely that positive and negative emotions use different neural circuitry and neurotransmitters.

Schachter and Singer's two-factor theory states that emotion is the result of both physiological arousal and cognitive labeling. Lazarus believed that cognition always directs emotion, but Zajonc has argued that emotion directs cognition. Both probably are right.

Research on the behavioral component of emotion focuses on facial expressions. The facial feedback hypothesis states that facial expressions can influence emotions, as well as reflect them.

Most psychologists believe that facial expressions of basic emotions are the same across cultures. However, display rules, which involve nonverbal signals of body movement, posture, and gesture, vary across cultures.

Emotions can be classified based on valence (pleasant or unpleasant) and arousal (high or low). Using the dimensions of valence and arousal, emotions can be arranged in a circle, or circumplex model.

Positive emotions likely play an important role in well-being by broadening our focus and allowing us to build resources. Resilience is an individual's capacity to thrive even during difficult times. Research has shown that one way resilient individuals thrive is by experiencing positive emotions.

⑤ Motivation and Emotion: The Pursuit of Happiness

Happiness is highly heritable, and there is reason to consider each person as having a happiness set point. Still, many people would like to increase their level of happiness. One obstacle to changing happiness is the hedonic treadmill: the idea that we quickly adapt to changes that might enhance happiness. Another obstacle is that pursuing happiness for its own sake often backfires.

Ways to enhance happiness include engaging in physical activity, helping others, and engaging in positive self-reflection and experiencing meaning (such as by keeping a gratitude journal). Another way to enhance happiness is to pursue personally valued goals passionately.

key terms

motivation, p. 305
instinct, p. 305
drive, p. 306
need, p. 306
homeostasis, p. 306
Yerkes-Dodson law, p. 306
set point, p. 309
estrogens, p. 311

androgens, p. 311
human sexual response
   pattern, p. 311
sexual orientation, p. 314
hierarchy of needs, p. 317
self-actualization, p. 317
self-determination theory, p. 317
intrinsic motivation, p. 319

extrinsic motivation, p. 319
self-regulation, p. 321
emotion, p. 322
polygraph, p. 323
James-Lange theory, p. 324
Cannon-Bard theory, p. 324
two-factor theory of
   emotion, p. 325

facial feedback
   hypothesis, p. 327
display rules, p. 329
negative affect, p. 331
positive affect, p. 331
broaden-and-build
   model, p. 332

self-test

Multiple Choice

1. A physiological requirement is a(n) _____; the resulting arousal is a(n) _____.
   A. instinct; motivation
   B. motivation; instinct
   C. drive; need
   D. need; drive

2. Tamesha has an upcoming test. She is so nervous about it that she develops a rash. What would the Yerkes-Dodson law predict about her performance on the test?
   A. Tamesha will do well because she has high arousal.
   B. Tamesha will do well because she has low arousal.
   C. Tamesha will do poorly because she has high arousal.
   D. Tamesha will do poorly because she has low arousal.

3. Factors that are likely related to sexual orientation include all of the following *except*
   A. hormonal factors.
   B. genetic factors.
   C. cognitive factors.
   D. socioeconomic factors.

4. Psychological research shows that lesbian women are most like
   A. heterosexual men.
   B. gay men.
   C. heterosexual women.
   D. transgender individuals.

5. The beginning of the human sexual response pattern is the
   A. orgasm.
   B. resolution phase.
   C. plateau phase.
   D. excitement phase.

6. An example of an extrinsic motivation is
   A. fulfillment.
   B. competence.
   C. money.
   D. curiosity.

7. All of the following are a component of self-determination theory *except*
   A. autonomy.
   B. competition.
   C. relatedness.
   D. competence.

8. The view that emotional responses and physiological reactions occur simultaneously is consistent with the
   A. Cannon-Bard theory.
   B. broaden-and-build theory.
   C. facial feedback theory.
   D. James-Lange theory.

9. The biology of emotion is connected with physiological arousal involving
   A. the circulatory system.
   B. the sympathetic nervous system.
   C. the endocrine system.
   D. none of the above

10. According to the facial feedback hypothesis, facial expressions can influence, as well as reflect, a person's
    A. needs.
    B. motivations.
    C. drives.
    D. emotions.

Apply It!

11. A commercial about a new diet pill promises, "Lose weight without ever feeling hungry!" Based on research on hunger and obesity, evaluate the likelihood that this claim is true.

10 Personality

What Makes You *You*?

A parent or grade-school teacher probably told you that people are like snowflakes, with no two exactly alike. What makes you like a snowflake? How are you unique?

Fans of *CSI, Law & Order,* and other crime dramas know that one thing that can uniquely identify a person is fingerprints. In the hundred years that fingerprints have been collected (with nearly 100 million fingers printed), no two people have had the same fingerprints. The irises of our eyes also distinguish us from all other people. Unlike fingerprints, irises cannot be worn down (or filed away, if you are thinking like a hit man). Further, irises have six times the number of distinguishing characteristics that fingerprints have. Irises are so unique to each individual that a recent technology known as iris recognition (similar to taking a photograph) is used for security screening at some airports and immigration-inspection locations.

But the person who told you that people are unique was not talking about fingerprints or irises. Your uniqueness comes from the *person* you are, with all of your traits, abilities, and experiences. That is what personality psychology is all about. To paraphrase personality psychologist Henry Murray, "All of us are in some ways like all other people, in some ways like some other people, and in some ways like no other person." Murray meant that although we share attributes with all other human beings (such as our anatomy), and we share attributes with some others (for example, people who are the same age as we are), in other ways we are truly unique. Personality psychology explores the psychological attributes that make us who we are—the unified and enduring core characteristics that account for our existence as the same person throughout our lives. Personality psychology is the science of what makes you *you*. ■

- ■ **How would you describe your personality?**
- ■ **In what ways are you like your friends and family?**
- ■ **What makes you unique?**

In this chapter, we survey classic theories of personality from the major psychological perspectives. We also review contemporary research on personality. We conclude the chapter with a look at personality assessment.

1 Psychodynamic Perspectives

Personality is a pattern of enduring, distinctive thoughts, emotions, and behaviors that characterize the way an individual adapts to the world. Psychologists have approached these enduring characteristics in a variety of ways, focusing on different aspects of the person.

Psychodynamic perspectives on personality emphasize that personality is primarily unconscious (that is, beyond awareness). According to this viewpoint, those enduring patterns that make up personality are largely unavailable to our conscious awareness, and they powerfully shape our behaviors in ways that we cannot consciously comprehend. Psychodynamic theorists use the word *unconscious* differently from how other psychologists might use the term. From the psychodynamic perspective, aspects of our personality are unconscious because they *must* be; this lack of awareness is motivated. These mysterious, unconscious forces are simply too frightening to be part of our conscious awareness.

Psychodynamic theorists believe that behavior is only a surface characteristic and that to truly understand someone's personality, we have to explore the symbolic meanings of that behavior and the deep inner workings of the mind (Westen, Gabbard, & Soto, 2008). Psychodynamic theorists also stress the role of early childhood experience in adult personality. From this perspective, the adult is a reflection of those childhood experiences that shape our earliest conceptions of ourselves and others. These characteristics were sketched by the architect of psychoanalytic theory, Sigmund Freud.

psychodynamic perspectives
Theoretical views emphasizing that personality is primarily unconscious (beyond awareness).

personality
A pattern of enduring, distinctive thoughts, emotions, and behaviors that characterize the way an individual adapts to the world.

If we knew the dark truth of our existence, we might do something as desperate as the tragic Greek hero Oedipus, who unwittingly murdered his father and married his mother—and then gouged out his eyes.

Freud's Psychoanalytic Theory

Sigmund Freud, one of the most influential thinkers of the twentieth century, was born in Freiberg, Moravia (today part of the Czech Republic), in 1856 and died in London at the age of 83. Freud spent most of his life in Vienna, but he left the city near the end of his career to escape the Holocaust.

Freud has had such a phenomenal impact that just about everyone has an opinion about him, even those who have never studied his work. If you ask others what they think of Freud, you will likely get a variety of interesting answers. Some might comment that Freud was a cocaine addict. Freud did use cocaine early in his career, but he stopped using the drug when he discovered its harmful effects. Others might claim that Freud hated women. As we will see, Freud's theory of development did include the notion that women are morally inferior to men. In truth, however, Freud was never satisfied with his approach to the psychology of women. He welcomed women interested in pursuing careers in psychoanalysis, and many of his earliest and most influential followers were women. Finally, people might declare that Freud thought everything was about sex. That claim, it turns out, is quite true, except by *sex* Freud did not mean sexual activity in the usual sense.

So, if you hear someone describe the joys of eating a decadent dessert like double-chocolate fudge cake as "better than sex," remember that in Freud's view, eating that cake is sex.

Instead, Freud defined sex as organ pleasure. *Anything* that is pleasurable is sex, according to Freud.

For Freud, the sexual drive was the most important motivator of all human activity. As we will see, Freud thought that the human sexual drive was the main determinant of personality development, and he felt that psychological disorders, dreams, and all human behavior represent the conflict between this unconscious sexual drive and the demands of civilized human society.

Freud developed *psychoanalysis,* his approach to personality, through his work with patients suffering from hysteria. *Hysteria* refers to physical symptoms that have no physical cause. For instance, a person might be unable to see, even with perfectly healthy eyes, or unable to walk, despite having no physical injury.

In Freud's day (the Victorian era, a time marked by strict rules regarding sex), many young women suffered from physical problems that could not be explained by actual physical illness. In his practice, Freud spent many long hours simply listening to these women talk about their symptoms. Freud came to understand that the hysterical symptoms stemmed from unconscious psychological conflicts. These conflicts centered on experiences in which the person's drive for pleasure was thwarted by the social pressures of Victorian society. Furthermore, the particular symptoms were symbolically related to these underlying conflicts. One of Freud's patients, Fraulein Elisabeth Von R., suffered from horrible leg pains that prevented her from standing or walking. The fact that Fraulein Elisabeth could not walk was no accident. Through analysis, Freud discovered that Fraulein Elisabeth had had a number of experiences in which she wanted nothing more than to take a walk but had been prevented from doing so by her duty to her ill father.

TV and movie portrayals of hysterical symptoms typically culminate in a psychologist's unlocking of the unconscious secret of the person's problem. For example, a young soap opera heroine's problems may be solved in one climactic episode revealing that she is hysterically blind because she has witnessed her father cheating on her mother. Importantly, however, Freud believed that hysterical symptoms were *overdetermined*—that is, they had *many* causes in the unconscious. Thus, although unlocking one unconscious traumatic memory might work for Hollywood, it does not accurately represent Freud's view. Eventually, Freud came to use hysterical symptoms as his metaphor for understanding dreams, slips of the tongue, and all human behavior. Everything we do, he said, has a multitude of unconscious causes.

Drawing from his work in analyzing patients (as well as himself), Freud developed his model of the human personality. He described personality as like an iceberg, existing mostly below the level of awareness, just as the massive part of an iceberg lies beneath the surface of the water. Figure 10.1 illustrates this analogy and depicts how extensive the unconscious part of our mind is, in Freud's view.

Sigmund Freud (1856–1939)
Freud's theories have strongly influenced how people in Western cultures view themselves and the world.

Today, we call hysterical symptoms **somatoform** disorders—physical symptoms with no physical cause.

We call it a **Freudian** slip when someone makes a mistake in speech or action that seems to express unconscious wishes—such as a typo spelling "Freud" as "Fraud."

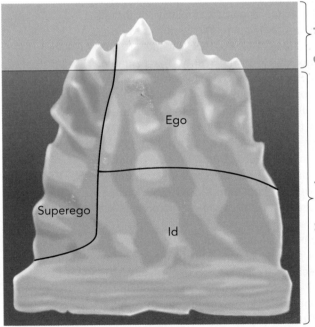

FIGURE 10.1
The Conscious and Unconscious Mind: The Iceberg Analogy The iceberg analogy illustrates how much of the mind is unconscious in Freud's theory. The conscious mind is the part of the iceberg above water; the unconscious mind, the part below water. Notice that the id is totally unconscious, whereas the ego and the superego can operate at either the conscious or the unconscious level.

Structures of Personality

The three parts of the iceberg in Figure 10.1 reflect the three structures of personality described by Freud. Freud (1917) called these structures the id, the ego, and the superego. You can get a better feel for these Latin labels by considering their English translations: The id is literally the "it," the ego is the "I," and the superego is the "above-I."

⊙ One of Freud's most famous essays, "The Ego and the Id," was titled "Das Ich und Das Ess" in German, meaning "The I and the It."

The **id** consists of unconscious drives and is the individual's reservoir of sexual energy. This "it" is a pool of amoral and often vile urges pressing for expression. In Freud's view, the id has no contact with reality. The id works according to the *pleasure principle,* the Freudian concept that the id always seeks pleasure.

The world would be dangerous and scary, however, if personalities were all id. As young children mature, they learn that they cannot slug other children in the face, that they have to use the toilet instead of diapers, and that they must negotiate with others to get the things they want. As children experience the constraints of reality, a new element of personality is formed—the **ego,** the Freudian structure of personality that deals with the demands of reality. Indeed, according to Freud, the ego abides by the *reality principle.* That is, it tries to bring the individual pleasure within the norms of society. The ego helps us to test reality, to see how far we can go without getting into trouble and hurting ourselves. Whereas the id is completely unconscious, the ego is partly conscious. It houses our higher mental functions—reasoning, problem solving, and decision making, for example.

The id and ego do not consider whether something is right or wrong. Rather, the **superego** is the harsh internal judge of our behavior. The superego is reflected in what we often call conscience and evaluates the morality of our behavior. Like the id, the superego does not consider reality; it considers only whether the id's impulses can be satisfied in acceptable moral terms.

The ego acts as a mediator between the conflicting demands of the id and the superego, as well as the real world. Your ego might say, for example, "I will have sex only in a committed relationship and always practice safe sex." Your id, however, screams, "Sex! Now!" and your superego commands, "Sex? Don't even think about it."

Defense Mechanisms

The conflicts that erupt among the demands of the id, the superego, and reality create a great deal of anxiety for the ego. The ego has strategies for dealing with this anxiety, called defense mechanisms. **Defense mechanisms** are tactics the ego uses to reduce anxiety by unconsciously distorting reality. For example, imagine that Jason's id is pressing to express an unconscious desire to have sex with his mother. Clearly, acting on this impulse would not please the superego or society at large. If he became aware of this impulse, Jason might recoil in horror. Instead, Jason's ego might use the defense mechanism of *displacement,* and he might develop a relationship with a girlfriend who looks and acts like his mother. Displacement means directing unacceptable impulses at a less threatening target. Through displacement, the ego allows Jason to express his id impulse in a way that will not land him in trouble. Of course, Jason's friends might chuckle at the resemblance between his mother and his girlfriend, but you can bet that Jason will never notice.

Figure 10.2 describes several defense mechanisms, many of which were introduced and developed by Freud's daughter Anna, who followed in her father's career footsteps. All these mechanisms work to reduce anxiety.

Repression is the most powerful and pervasive defense mechanism. Repression pushes unacceptable id impulses back into the unconscious mind. Repression is the foundation for *all* of the psychological defense mechanisms, whose goal is to *repress* threatening impulses, that is, to push them out of awareness. Freud said, for example, that our early childhood experiences, many of which he believed were sexually laden, are too threatening for us to deal with consciously, so we reduce the anxiety of childhood conflict through repression.

Two final points about defense mechanisms are important. First, defense mechanisms are unconscious; we are not aware that we are calling on them.

ego
The Freudian structure of personality that deals with the demands of reality.

superego
The Freudian structure of personality that serves as the harsh internal judge of our behavior; what we often call conscience.

id
The part of the person that Freud called the "it," consisting of unconscious drives; the individual's reservoir of sexual energy.

defense mechanisms
Tactics the ego uses to reduce anxiety by unconsciously distorting reality.

Anna Freud (1895–1982)
The youngest of Sigmund Freud's six children, Anna Freud not only did influential work on defense mechanisms but also pioneered in the theory and practice of child psychoanalysis.

Defense Mechanism	How It Works	Example
Repression	The master defense mechanism; the ego pushes unacceptable impulses out of awareness, back into the unconscious mind.	A young girl was sexually abused by her uncle. As an adult, she can't remember anything about the traumatic experience.
Rationalization	The ego replaces a less acceptable motive with a more acceptable one.	A college student does not get into the fraternity of his choice. He tells himself that the fraternity is very exclusive and that a lot of students could not get in.
Displacement	The ego shifts feelings toward an unacceptable object to another, more acceptable object.	A woman can't take her anger out on her boss so she goes home and takes it out on her husband.
Sublimation	The ego replaces an unacceptable impulse with a socially acceptable one.	A man with strong sexual urges becomes an artist who paints nudes.
Projection	The ego attributes personal shortcomings, problems, and faults to others.	A man who has a strong desire to have an extramarital affair accuses his wife of flirting with other men.
Reaction Formation	The ego transforms an unacceptable motive into its opposite.	A woman who fears her sexual urges becomes a religious zealot.
Denial	The ego refuses to acknowledge anxiety-producing realities.	A man won't acknowledge that he has cancer even though a team of doctors has diagnosed his cancer.
Regression	The ego seeks the security of an earlier developmental period in the face of stress.	A woman returns home to mother every time she and her husband have a big argument.

FIGURE 10.2
Defense Mechanisms Defense mechanisms reduce anxiety by distorting reality.

Second, when used in moderation or on a temporary basis, defense mechanisms are not necessarily unhealthy (Cramer, 2008a). For example, the defense mechanism of *denial* can help a person cope upon first getting the news that his or her death is impending, and the defense mechanism of *sublimation* involves transforming unconscious impulses into activities that benefit society. Note that the defense mechanism of sublimation means that even the very best things that human beings accomplish—a beautiful work of art, an amazing act of kindness—are still explained by unconscious sexual drives and defenses.

Psychosexual Stages of Personality Development

Freud believed that human beings go through universal stages of personality development and that at each developmental stage we experience sexual pleasure in one part of the body more than in others. Each stage is named for the location of sexual pleasure at that stage. *Erogenous zones* are parts of the body that have especially strong pleasure-giving qualities at particular stages of development. Freud thought that our adult personality is determined by the way we resolve conflicts between these early sources of pleasure—the mouth, the anus, and then the genitals—and the demands of reality.

- *Oral stage (first 18 months):* The infant's pleasure centers on the mouth. Chewing, sucking, and biting are the chief sources of pleasure that reduce tension in the infant.

- *Anal stage (18 to 36 months):* During a time when most children are experiencing toilet training, the child's greatest pleasure involves the anus and urethra and their functions. Freud recognized that there is pleasure in "going" and "holding it" as well as in the experience of control over one's parents in deciding when to do either.

- *Phallic stage (3 to 6 years):* The name of Freud's third stage comes from the Latin word *phallus,* which means "penis." Pleasure focuses on the genitals as the child discovers that self-stimulation is enjoyable.

In Freud's view, the phallic stage has a special importance in personality development because it triggers the Oedipus complex. This name comes from the Greek tragedy, mentioned earlier, in which Oedipus kills his father and marries his mother. The **Oedipus complex** is the boy's intense desire to replace his father and enjoy the affections of his mother. Eventually, the boy recognizes that his father might punish him for these incestuous wishes, specifically by cutting off the boy's penis. *Castration anxiety* refers to the boy's intense fear of being mutilated by his father. To reduce this conflict, the boy identifies with his father, adopting the male gender role. The intense castration anxiety is repressed into the unconscious and serves as the foundation for the development of the superego.

Freud recognized that there were differences between boys and girls in the phallic stage. Because a girl does not have a penis, she cannot experience castration anxiety, Freud reasoned. Instead, she compares herself to boys and realizes that she is missing something—a penis. Without experiencing the powerful force of castration anxiety, a girl cannot develop a superego in the same sense that boys do. Given this inability, Freud concluded, women were morally inferior to men, and this inferiority explained their place as second-class citizens in Victorian society. Freud believed that girls experience "castration completed," resulting in penis envy—the intense desire to obtain a penis by eventually marrying and bearing a son.

While noting that his views ran counter to the early feminist thinkers of his time, Freud stood firm that the sexes are not equal in every way. He considered women to be somewhat childlike in their development and thought it was good that fathers, and eventually husbands, should guide them through life. He asserted that the only hope for women's moral development was education.

- *Latency period (6 years to puberty):* This phase is not a developmental stage but rather a kind of psychic time-out. After the drama of the phallic stage, the child sets aside all interest in sexuality. Although we now consider these years extremely important to development, Freud felt that this was a time in which no psychosexual development occurred.

- *Genital stage (adolescence and adulthood):* The genital stage is the time of sexual reawakening, a point when the source of sexual pleasure shifts to someone outside the family. Freud believed that in adulthood the individual becomes capable of the two hallmarks of maturity: love and work. However, Freud felt that human beings are inevitably subject to intense conflict, reasoning that everyone, no matter how healthy or well adjusted, still has an id pressing for expression. Adulthood, even in the best of circumstances, still involves reliving the unconscious conflicts of childhood.

Freud argued that the individual may become stuck in any of these developmental stages if he or she is underindulged or overindulged at a given stage. For example, a parent might wean a child too early, be too strict in toilet training, punish the child for masturbating, or smother the child with too much attention. *Fixation* occurs when a particular psychosexual stage colors an individual's adult personality. For instance, an *anal retentive* person (someone who is obsessively neat and organized) is fixated at the anal stage. The construct of fixation thus explains how, according to Freud's view, childhood experiences can have an enormous impact on adult personality. Figure 10.3 illustrates possible links between adult personality characteristics and fixation at the oral, anal, and phallic stages.

The superego wields a lot of power—it is essentially the internalized castrating father.

In Freud's view, anatomy is destiny. By this he meant that anatomy (whether a person has a penis or not) determines whether he or she will develop a superego.

Oedipus complex According to Freud, a boy's intense desire to replace his father and enjoy the affections of his mother.

Stage	Adult Extensions (Fixations)	Sublimations	Reaction Formations
Oral	Smoking, eating, kissing, oral hygiene, drinking, chewing gum	Seeking knowledge, humor, wit, sarcasm, being a food or wine expert	Speech purist, food faddist, prohibitionist, dislike of milk
Anal	Notable interest in one's bowel movements, love of bathroom humor, extreme messiness	Interest in painting or sculpture, being overly giving, great interest in statistics	Extreme disgust with feces, fear of dirt, prudishness, irritability
Phallic	Heavy reliance on masturbation, flirtatiousness, expressions of virility	Interest in poetry, love of love, interest in acting, striving for success	Puritanical attitude toward sex, excessive modesty

FIGURE 10.3

Defense Mechanisms and Freudian Stages If a person is fixated at a psychosexual stage, the fixation can color his or her personality in many ways, including the defense mechanisms the person might use to cope with anxiety.

Psychodynamic Critics and Revisionists

Because Freud was among the first theorists to explore personality, some of his ideas have needed updating and revision over time, while others have been tossed out altogether. In particular, Freud's critics have said that his ideas about sexuality, early experience, social factors, and the unconscious mind were misguided (Adler, 1927; Erikson, 1968; Fromm, 1947; Horney, 1945; Jung, 1917; Kohut, 1977; Rapaport, 1967; Sullivan, 1953). They stress the following points:

- Sexuality is not the pervasive force behind personality that Freud believed it to be. Furthermore, the Oedipus complex is not as universal as Freud maintained. Freud's concepts were heavily influenced by the setting in which he lived and worked—turn-of-the-century Vienna, a society that, compared with contemporary society, was sexually repressed and male-dominated.

- The first five years of life are not as powerful in shaping adult personality as Freud thought. Later experiences deserve more attention.

- The ego and conscious thought processes play a more dominant role in our personality than Freud believed; he claimed that we are forever captive to the instinctual, unconscious clutches of the id. In addition, the ego has a separate line of development from the id, so achievement, thinking, and reasoning are not always tied to sexual impulses.

- Sociocultural factors are much more important than Freud believed. In stressing the id's dominance, Freud placed more emphasis on the biological basis of personality. More contemporary psychodynamic scholars have especially emphasized the interpersonal setting of the family and the role of early social relationships in personality development.

A number of dissenters and revisionists to Freud's theory have been influential in the development of psychodynamic theories. Erik Erikson, whose psychosocial stages we examined in Chapter 8, is among these. Here we consider three other thinkers—Karen Horney, Carl Jung, and Alfred Adler—who made notable revisions to Freud's approach.

Horney's Sociocultural Approach Karen Horney (1885–1952) rejected the classical psychoanalytic concept that anatomy is destiny and cautioned that some of Freud's most popular ideas were only hypotheses. She insisted that these hypotheses be supported with observable data before

Karen Horney (1885–1952) *Horney developed the first feminist criticism of Freud's theory. Horney's view emphasizes women's positive qualities and self-evaluation.*

being accepted as fact. She also argued that sociocultural influences on personality development should be considered.

Consider Freud's concept of penis envy, which attributed some of the behavior of his female patients to their repressed desire to have a penis. Horney pointed out that women might envy the penis not because of some neurotic tendencies but because of the status that society bestows on those who have one. Further, she suggested that both sexes envy the attributes of the other, with men coveting women's reproductive capacities (Horney, 1967).

Horney also believed that the need for security, not for sex, is the prime motive in human existence. Horney reasoned that an individual whose needs for security are met should be able to develop his or her capacities to the fullest extent. She viewed psychological health as allowing the person to express his or her talents and abilities freely and spontaneously.

Jung's Analytical Theory

Freud's contemporary Carl Jung (1875–1961) had a different complaint about psychoanalytic theory. Jung shared Freud's interest in the unconscious, but he believed that Freud underplayed the unconscious mind's role in personality. In fact, Jung believed that the roots of personality go back to the dawn of human existence. The **collective unconscious** is Jung's name for the impersonal, deepest layer of the unconscious mind, shared by all human beings because of their common ancestral past. In Jung's theory, the experiences of a common past have made a deep, permanent impression on the human mind.

Jung posited that the collective unconscious contains **archetypes,** emotionally laden ideas and images that have rich and symbolic meaning for all people. Jung concluded that these archetypes emerge in art, literature, religion, and dreams (Faber & Mayer, 2009; Kradin, 2009; Merchant, 2006). He used archetypes to help people understand themselves (Urban, 2008). Archetypes are essentially predispositions to respond to the environment in particular ways.

Jung used the terms *anima* and *animus* to identify two common archetypes. He believed each of us has a passive feminine side—the anima—and an assertive masculine side—the animus. Another archetype, the *persona*, represents the public mask that we all wear during social interactions. Jung believed that the persona is an essential archetype because it allows us always to keep some secret part of ourselves hidden from others.

Adler's Individual Psychology

Alfred Adler (1870–1937) was one of Freud's earliest followers, although his relationship with Freud was quite brief and his approach to personality was drastically different. In Adler's **individual psychology,** people are motivated by purposes and goals—thus, perfection, not pleasure, is the key motivator in human life. Adler argued that people have the ability to take their genetic inheritance and their environmental experiences and act upon them creatively to become the person they want to be.

Adler thought that everyone strives for superiority by seeking to adapt, improve, and master the environment. Striving for superiority is our response to the uncomfortable feelings of inferiority that we experience as infants and young children when we interact with bigger, more powerful people. *Compensation* is Adler's term for the individual's attempt to overcome imagined or real inferiorities or weaknesses by developing one's own abilities. Adler believed that compensation is normal, and he said that we often make up for a weakness in one ability by excelling in a different ability. For example, a person of small stature and limited physical abilities (like Adler himself) might compensate by excelling in academics.

Adler believed that birth order could influence how successfully a person could strive for superiority. He viewed firstborn children to be in a particularly vulnerable state given that they begin life as the center of attention but then are knocked off their pedestal by their siblings. Adler in fact believed that the firstborn are more likely to suffer from

Carl Jung (1875–1961)
Swiss psychoanalytic theorist Carl Jung developed the concepts of the collective unconscious and archetypes.

archetypes
Emotionally laden ideas and images that have rich and symbolic meaning for all people.

collective unconscious
Jung's name for the impersonal, deepest layer of the unconscious mind, shared by all human beings because of their common ancestral past.

individual psychology
Adler's view that people are motivated by purposes and goals and that perfection, not pleasure, is thus the key motivator in human life.

psychological disorders and to engage in criminal behavior. Youngest children, however, also are potentially in trouble because they are most likely to be spoiled. The healthiest birth order? According to Adler, all of us (including Adler himself) who are middle-born are in a particularly advantageous situation because we have our older siblings as built-in inspiration for superiority striving. Importantly, though, Adler did not believe that anyone was doomed by birth order. Rather, sensitive parents could help children at any place in the family to negotiate their needs for superiority.

Evaluating the Psychodynamic Perspectives

Although psychodynamic theories have diverged from Freud's original psychoanalytic version, they share some core principles:

- Personality is determined both by current experiences and, as the original psychoanalytic theory proposed, by early life experiences.

- Personality can be better understood by examining it developmentally—as a series of stages that unfold with the individual's physical, cognitive, and socioemotional development.

- We mentally transform our experiences, giving them meaning that shapes our personality.

- The mind is not all consciousness; unconscious motives lie behind some of our puzzling behavior.

- The individual's inner world often conflicts with the outer demands of reality, creating anxiety that is not easy to resolve.

- Personality and adjustment—not just the experimental laboratory topics of sensation, perception, and learning—are rightful and important topics of psychological inquiry.

Psychodynamic perspectives have come under fire for a variety of reasons. Some critics say that psychodynamic theorists overemphasize the influence of early family experiences on personality and do not acknowledge that people retain the capacity for change and adaptation throughout life. Some psychologists believe moreover that Freud and Jung put too much faith in the unconscious mind's ability to control behavior. Others object that Freud placed too much importance on sexuality in explaining personality; we humans are not born into the world with only a bundle of sexual and aggressive instincts, this camp insists.

Some have argued, too, that psychoanalysis is not a theory that researchers can test through empirical studies. However, numerous empirical studies on concepts such as defense mechanisms and the unconscious have proved this criticism to be unfounded (Cramer, 2008a; Jorgensen & Zachariae, 2006). At the same time, another version of this argument may be accurate. Although it is certainly possible to test hypotheses derived from psychoanalytic theory through research, the question remains whether psychoanalytically oriented individuals who believe strongly in Freud's ideas would be open to research results that call for serious changes in the theory.

In light of these criticisms, it may be hard to appreciate why Freud continues to have an impact on psychology. It is useful to keep in mind that Freud made a number of important contributions, including being the first to propose that childhood is crucial to later functioning, that development might be understood in terms of stages, and that unconscious processes might play a significant role in human life.

1. According to Freud, our conscience is a reflection of the
   A. ego.
   B. collective unconscious.
   C. id.
   D. superego.

2. All of the following are examples of defense mechanisms *except*
   A. sublimation.
   B. repression.
   C. latency.
   D. displacement.

3. A theorist who focused on archetypes is
   A. Karen Horney.
   B. Sigmund Freud.
   C. Alfred Adler.
   D. Carl Jung.

Apply It! 4. Simone and her older sister have long had an intense sibling rivalry. Simone has tried to best her sister in schoolwork, fashion sense, and sporting achievements. Simone's sister complains that Simone needs to get a life of her own. What would Alfred Adler say about Simone's behavior?

A. Simone is engaging in the defense mechanism of displacement, striving to conquer her sister when it is really her mother she wishes to defeat.

B. Simone is expressing her animus archetype by engaging in masculine-style competition.

C. Simone is expressing superiority striving by trying to overcome her sister—a healthy way for middle children to pursue superiority.

D. Simone lacks a sense of basic trust in the world, and her parents must have been neglectful of her.

2 Humanistic Perspectives

Humanistic perspectives stress a person's capacity for personal growth and positive human qualities. Humanistic psychologists believe that we all have the ability to control our lives and to achieve what we desire (Cain, 2001; M. B. Smith, 2001).

Humanistic perspectives contrast with both psychodynamic perspectives and behaviorism, discussed in Chapter 5. Humanistic theorists sought to move beyond Freudian psychoanalysis and behaviorism to a theory that might capture the rich and potentially positive aspects of human nature.

humanistic perspectives
Theoretical views stressing a person's capacity for personal growth and positive human qualities.

Maslow's Approach

A leading architect of the humanistic movement was Abraham Maslow (1908–1970), whose hierarchy of needs we considered in Chapter 9. Maslow referred to humanistic psychology as "third force" psychology because it stressed neither Freudian drives nor the stimulus–response principles of behaviorism. Maslow believed that we can learn the most about human personality by focusing on the very best examples of human beings— self-actualizers.

Recall that at the top of Maslow's (1954, 1971) hierarchy was the need for self-actualization. Self-actualization is the motivation to develop one's full potential as a human being. Maslow described self-actualizers as spontaneous, creative, and possessing a childlike capacity for awe. According to Maslow, a person at this optimal level of existence would be tolerant of others, have a gentle sense of humor, and be likely to pursue the greater good. Self-actualizers also maintain a capacity for "peak experiences," or breathtaking moments of spiritual insight. As examples of self-actualized individuals, Maslow included Pablo Casals (cellist), Albert Einstein (physicist), Ralph Waldo Emerson (writer), William James (psychologist), Thomas Jefferson (politician), Eleanor Roosevelt (humanitarian, diplomat), and Albert Schweitzer (humanitarian).

Created nearly 40 years ago, Maslow's list of self-actualized individuals is clearly biased. Maslow focused on highly successful individuals who he thought represented the best of the human species. Because Maslow concentrated on people who were successful in a particular historical context, his self-actualizers were limited to those who had opportunities for success in that context. Maslow thus named considerably more men than women, and most of the individuals were from Western cultures and of European ancestry. Today, we might add to Maslow's list individuals such as the Dalai Lama (Tenzin Gyatso), Tibetan spiritual and political leader; Wangari Maathai, a Kenyan woman acclaimed for her work on behalf of democracy and the environment; and

Muhammad Yunus, a Bangladeshi banker and crusader against poverty. All are recipients of the Nobel Peace Prize in recent years.

Rogers's Approach

The other key figure in the development of humanistic psychology, Carl Rogers (1902–1987), began his career as a psychotherapist struggling to understand the unhappiness of the individuals he encountered in therapy. Rogers's groundbreaking work established the foundations for more contemporary studies of personal growth and self-determination.

Carl Rogers (1902–1987)
Rogers was a pioneer in the development of the humanistic perspective.

Like Freud, Rogers began his inquiry into human nature with troubled people. In the knotted, anxious verbal stream of his clients, Rogers (1961) noted the things that seemed to be keeping them from reaching their full potential. Based on his clinical observations, Rogers devised his own approach to personality. Rogers believed that we are all born with the raw ingredients of a fulfilling life. We simply need the right conditions to thrive. Just as a sunflower seed, once planted in rich soil and given water and sunshine, will grow into a strong and healthy flower, all humans will flourish in the appropriate environment.

This analogy is particularly apt and reveals the differences between Rogers's view of human nature and Freud's. A sunflower seed does not have to be shaped away from its dark natural tendencies by social constraints, nor does it have to reach a difficult compromise between its vile true impulses and reality. Instead, given the appropriate environment, it will grow into a beautiful flower. Rogers believed that, similarly, each person is born with natural capacities for growth and fulfillment. We are also endowed with an innate sense—a gut feeling—that allows us to evaluate whether an experience is good or bad for us. Finally, we are all born with a need for positive regard from others. We need to be loved, liked, or accepted by people around us. As children interacting with our parents, we learn early on to value the feeling that they value us, and we gain a sense of valuing ourselves.

unconditional positive regard
Rogers's construct referring to the individual's need to be accepted, valued, and treated positively regardless of his or her behavior.

conditions of worth
The standards that the individual must live up to in order to receive positive regard from others.

Explaining Unhappiness If we have innate tendencies toward growth and fulfillment, why are so many people so unhappy? The problem arises when our need for positive regard from others is not met *unconditionally*. **Unconditional positive regard** is Rogers's term for being accepted, valued, and treated positively regardless of one's behavior. Unfortunately, others often value us only when we behave in particular ways that meet what Rogers called *conditions of worth*. **Conditions of worth** are the standards we must live up to in order to receive positive regard from others. For instance, parents might give their son positive regard only when he achieves in school, succeeds on the soccer field, or chooses a profession that they themselves value. According to Rogers, as we grow up, people who are central to our lives condition us to move away from our genuine feelings, to earn their love by pursuing those goals that they value, even if those goals do not reflect our deepest wishes.

Rogers's theory includes the idea that we develop a *self-concept,* our conscious representation of who we are and who we wish to become, during childhood. Optimally, this self-concept reflects our genuine, innate desires, but it also can be influenced by conditions of worth. Conditions of worth can become part of who we think we ought to be. As a result, we can become alienated from our genuine feelings and strive to actualize a self that is not who we were meant to be. A person who dedicates himself or herself to such goals might be very successful by outward appearances but might feel utterly unfulfilled. Such an individual might be able to check off all the important boxes in life's to-do lists, and to do all that he or she is "supposed to do," but never feel truly happy.

Promoting Optimal Functioning   To remedy this situation, Rogers believed that the person must reconnect with his or her true feelings and desires. He proposed that to achieve this reconnection, the individual must experience a relationship that includes three essential qualities: unconditional positive regard, as defined above; empathy; and genuineness. We consider each in turn.

First, Rogers said that regardless of what they do, people need unconditional positive regard. Although an individual might lack unconditional positive regard in childhood, he or she can experience this unconditional acceptance from others later, in friendships and/ or romantic relationships or during sessions with a therapist. Even when a person's behavior is inappropriate, obnoxious, or unacceptable, he or she still needs the respect, comfort, and love of others (Assor, Roth, & Deci, 2004).

Second, Rogers said that individuals can become more fulfilled by interacting with people who are empathic toward them. Empathy involves being a sensitive listener and understanding another's true feelings.

Genuineness is a third requirement in the individual's path to become fully functioning. Being genuine means being open with one's feelings and dropping all pretenses and facades. The importance that Rogers placed on the therapist's acting genuinely in the therapeutic relationship demonstrates his strong belief in the positive character of human nature. For Rogers, we can help others simply by being present for them as the authentic individuals we are.

Thus, according to Rogers, unconditional positive regard, empathy, and genuineness are three essential ingredients of healthy human relations. Anyone—a manager, teacher, counselor, member of the clergy—who is interested in promoting optimal human functioning can apply these principles.

Evaluating the Humanistic Perspectives

The humanistic perspectives emphasize that the way we perceive ourselves and the world around us is an essential element of personality. Humanistic psychologists also stress that we need to consider the whole person and the positive bent of human nature (Schneider, 2009). Their emphasis on conscious experience has given us the view that personality contains a well of potential that can be developed to its fullest (C. E. Hill, 2000).

Some critics believe that humanistic psychologists are too optimistic about human nature and that they overestimate people's freedom and rationality. Others say that the humanists may promote excessive self-love and narcissism by encouraging people to think so positively about themselves. Still others argue that humanistic approaches do not hold individuals accountable for their behaviors, if all negative human behavior is seen as emerging out of negative situations.

Self-determination theory, which we considered in Chapter 9, demonstrates the way that psychologists have tested humanistic ideas that might appear too abstract and difficult to test. Their work bears witness to the enduring impact of humanistic perspectives on contemporary personality psychology.

1. In Maslow's theory, the motivation to develop one's full potential as a human being is called
   A. self-satisfaction.
   B. self-actualization.
   C. self-sufficiency.
   D. self-determination.

2. Rogers proposed that in order to become fulfilled, the individual requires all of the following *except*
   A. unconditional positive regard.
   B. genuineness.
   C. self-actualization.
   D. empathy.

3. A child who consistently strives for an *A* in math and science in order to secure the affection of her parents is trying to establish
   A. unconditional positive regard.
   B. conditions of worth.
   C. self-actualization.
   D. empathy.

Apply It! 4. Phoebe and Joey are parents to little Jennifer. These parents believe that because so many things in life involve hard work, it is important for Jennifer to earn the good things that happen to her. They make it very clear to Jennifer that one of the things she must earn is their approval, and they tell her that they love her only when she does well in school and behaves according to their standards. They are certain that this training will instill in Jennifer the importance of working hard and valuing the good things that she gets in life. What would Carl Rogers say about Phoebe and Joey's parenting style?
   A. They are on the right track, as all children need strict limits and must learn discipline.
   B. What they are doing is fine but will have little influence on Jennifer, because genes matter most to personality.
   C. They are likely to be creating a fixation in Jennifer, and she will spend a lifetime working out her unconscious conflicts.
   D. They are setting Jennifer up to value herself only when she meets certain standards and would be better advised to love her unconditionally.

3 Trait Perspectives

If you are setting up a friend on a blind date, you are likely to describe the person in terms of his or her *traits*, or lasting personality characteristics. Trait perspectives on personality have been the dominant approach for the past two decades.

Trait Theories

According to **trait theories,** personality consists of broad, enduring dispositions (traits) that tend to lead to characteristic responses. In other words, we can describe people in terms of the ways they behave, such as whether they are outgoing, friendly, private, or hostile. People who have a strong tendency to behave in certain ways are referred to as "high" on the traits; those with a weak tendency to behave in these ways are "low" on the traits. Although trait theorists differ about which traits make up personality, they agree that traits are the fundamental building blocks of personality (Ashton & Kibeom, 2008; McCrae & Sutin, 2009).

Gordon Allport (1897–1967), sometimes referred to as the father of American personality psychology, was particularly bothered by the negative view of humanity that psychoanalysis portrayed. He rejected the notion that the unconscious was central to an understanding of personality. He further believed that to understand healthy people, we must focus on their lives in the present, not on their childhood experiences. Allport, who took a pragmatic approach to understanding the person, asserted that if you want to know something about someone, you should "just ask him" (or her).

Allport believed that personality psychology should focus on understanding healthy, well-adjusted individuals. He described such persons as showing a positive but objective sense of self and others, interest in issues beyond their own experience, a sense of humor, common sense, and a unifying philosophy of life—typically but not always provided by religious faith (Allport, 1961). Allport dedicated himself to the idea that psychology should have relevance to social issues facing modern society, and his scholarship has influenced not only personality psychology but also the psychology of religion and prejudice.

In defining personality, Allport (1961) stressed each person's uniqueness and capacity to adapt to the environment. For Allport, the unit we should use to understand personality is the trait. He defined traits as mental structures that make different situations the same for the person. For Allport, traits are structures that are inside a person that cause behavior to be similar even in different situations. For instance, if Carly is sociable, she is likely to behave in an outgoing, happy fashion whether she is at a party or in a group study session. Allport's definition implies that behavior should be consistent across different situations.

trait theories
Theoretical views stressing that personality consists of broad, enduring dispositions (traits) that tend to lead to characteristic responses.

It's called "lexical" because
a lexicon is a dictionary or vocabulary.
These researchers are generally
starting with the words we use
to describe other people.

We get a sense of the down-to-earth quality of Allport's approach to personality by looking at his study of traits. In the late 1930s, Allport and his colleague H. S. Odbert (1936) sat down with two big unabridged dictionaries and pulled out all the words that could be used to describe a person—a method called the *lexical approach*. This approach reflects the idea that if a trait is important to people in real life, it ought to be represented in the natural language people use to talk about one another. Furthermore, the more important a trait is, the more likely it is that it should be represented by a single word. Allport and Odbert started with 18,000 words and gradually pared down that list to 4,500.

As you can appreciate, 4,500 traits make for a very long questionnaire. Imagine that you are asked to rate a person, Ignacio, on some traits. You use a scale from 1 to 5, with 1 meaning "not at all" and 5 meaning "very much." If you give Ignacio a 5 on "outgoing," what do you think you might give him on "shy"? Clearly, we may not need 4,500 traits to summarize the way we describe personality. Still, how might we whittle down these descriptors further without losing something important?

With advances in statistical methods and the advent of computers, the lexical approach became considerably less unwieldy, as researchers began to analyze the words to look for underlying structures that might account for their overlap. Specifically, a statistical procedure called *factor analysis* allowed researchers to identify which traits go together in terms of how they are rated. Factor analysis essentially tells us what items on a scale people are responding to as if they mean the same thing. For example, if Ignacio got a 5 on "outgoing," he probably would get a 5 on "talkative" and a 1 or 2 on "shy." One important characteristic of factor analysis is that it relies on the scientist to interpret the meaning of the factors, and the researcher must make some decisions about how many factors are enough to explain the data (Goldberg & Digman, 1994). In 1963, W. T. Norman reanalyzed the Allport and Odbert traits and concluded that only five factors were needed to summarize these traits. Norman's research set the stage for the dominant approach in personality psychology today: the five-factor model (Digman, 1990).

The Five-Factor Model of Personality

Pick a friend and jot down 10 of that person's most notable personality traits. Did you perhaps list "reserved" or "a good leader"? "Responsible" or "unreliable"? "Sweet," "kind," or "friendly"? Maybe even "creative"? Researchers in personality psychology have found that there are essentially five broad personality dimensions that are represented in the natural language and that also summarize the various ways psychologists have studied traits (Costa & McCrae, 1998, 2006; Digman, 2002; Hogan, 2006).

Take a good look at Figure
10.4 so that you understand
each of these traits. Openness
to experience is often the
trickiest one.

The **big five factors of personality**—the supertraits that are thought to describe the main dimensions of personality—are neuroticism (emotional instability), extraversion, openness to experience, agreeableness, and conscientiousness. Although personality psychologists typically refer to the traits as N, E, O, A, and C on the basis of the order in which they emerged in a factor analysis, if you create an anagram from these first letters of the trait names, you get the word *OCEAN*. Figure 10.4 more fully defines the traits.

Each of the five traits has been the topic of extensive research (McCrae & Sutin, 2007; Ozer & Benet-Martinez, 2006). We consider a sampling of research findings on each trait here to give you a sense of the interesting work that the five-factor model has inspired:

- Neuroticism is related to feeling negative emotion more often than positive emotion in one's daily life and to experiencing more lingering negative states (Widiger, 2009). Neuroticism has been shown to relate to more health complaints (Goodwin, Cox, & Clara, 2006). In a recent longitudinal study, individuals were studied for nearly seven years. Neuroticism was associated with dying during the study (Fry & Debats, 2009). Neurotic individuals are more likely to report negative events happening to them (Magnus & others 1993).

big five factors of personality The five supertraits that are thought to describe the main dimensions of personality: neuroticism (emotional instability), extraversion, openness to experience, agreeableness, and conscientiousness.

Openness	**C**onscientiousness	**E**xtraversion	**A**greeableness	**N**euroticism (emotional stability)
• Imaginative or practical • Interested in variety or routine • Independent or conforming	• Organized or disorganized • Careful or careless • Disciplined or impulsive	• Sociable or retiring • Fun-loving or somber • Affectionate or reserved	• Softhearted or ruthless • Trusting or suspicious • Helpful or uncooperative	• Calm or anxious • Secure or insecure • Self-satisfied or self-pitying

FIGURE 10.4

The Big Five Factors of Personality Each of the broad supertraits encompasses more narrow traits and characteristics. Use the acronym OCEAN to remember the big five personality factors (openness, conscientiousness, extraversion, agreeableness, and neuroticism).

- Extraverts are more likely than others to engage in social activities (Emmons & Diener, 1986) and to report more positive life events happening to them (Magnus & others, 1993). Extraversion is related to experiencing gratitude (McCullough, Emmons, & Tsang, 2002), being more forgiving (Thompson & others, 2005), and feeling a strong sense of meaning in life (King & others, 2006).

- Openness is related to higher IQ, liberal values, open-mindedness, and tolerance (McCrae & Sutin, 2009). Openness to experience is linked to creativity and creative accomplishments (King, McKee-Walker, & Broyles, 1996).

- Agreeableness (Graziano & Tobin, 2009) is related to generosity. When asked to make a wish for anything at all, agreeable people are more likely to make altruistic wishes such as "for world peace" (King & Broyles, 1997). Agreeableness is also related to reports of religious faith (MacDonald, 2000) and to more satisfying romantic relationships (Donnellan, Larsen-Rife, & Conger, 2005).

- Conscientiousness is increasingly showing up as a key factor in achievement, relationships, health, and even longevity (Roberts & others, 2009; Soto & others, 2008). Researchers have found that conscientiousness is positively related to high school and college students' grade point averages (Noftie & Robins, 2007), is linked to better-quality friendships (Jensen-Campbell & Malcolm, 2007), and, in a longitudinal study of more than 1,200 individuals across seven decades, predicted lower mortality risk from childhood through late adulthood (Martin, Friedman, & Schwartz, 2007). Low levels of conscientiousness are associated with criminal behavior (Wiebe, 2004) and substance abuse (Walton & Roberts, 2004).

Keep in mind that because the five factors are theoretically independent of one another, a person can be any combination of them. Do you know a neurotic extravert or an agreeable introvert, for example?

Cross-Cultural and Animal Studies on the Big Five

Some research on the big five factors addresses the extent to which the factors appear in personality profiles in different cultures (Lingjaerde, Foreland, & Engvik, 2001; Miacic & Goldberg, 2007; Pukrop, Sass, & Steinmeyer, 2000). Do the five factors show up in the assessment of personality in cultures around the world? There is increasing evidence that they do (McCrae & Costa, 2006; Ozer & Riese, 1994).

Researchers have found that some version of the five factors appears in people in countries as diverse as Canada, Finland, Poland, China, and Japan (Paunonen & others, 1992; X. Zhou &

others, 2009). Research has generally supported the concept of the big five traits. Researchers have even begun to find evidence for at least some of the big five personality traits in animals, including domestic dogs (Gosling, 2008; Gosling, Kwan, & John, 2003) and hyenas (Gosling & John, 1999). In addition, evidence for general personality traits (such as overall outgoingness) has been found in orangutans, geese, lizards, and squid (Sinn, Gosling, & Moltschaniwskyj, 2008; Weinstein, Capitanio, & Gosling, 2008).

Despite this strong evidence, some personality researchers say that the big five might not end up being the final list of broad supertraits; they argue that more specific traits are better predictors of behavior (Fung & Ng, 2006; Saucier, 2001; Simms, 2007). One alternative, the HEXACO model, incorporates a sixth dimension, honesty/humility, to capture the moral dimensions of personality (Ashton & Kibeom, 2008).

Neuroticism, Extraversion, and Well-Being

A great deal of research in personality psychology has examined the relationship between personality traits and a person's level of happiness, or what psychologists call subjective well-being (Diener, Kesebir, & Tov, 2009; Lucas, 2009; Steel, Schmidt, & Schultz, 2008). You have probably noticed that some people seem to go through life having fun, while others appear to feel distress at even the slightest problem. You might think that most happiness can be explained by the events that happen to us—of course, you reason, a person is going to be happy if she is doing well in school and has a loving romantic partner, but unhappy if she is doing poorly and has just experienced a painful breakup. In fact, research has shown that life events explain relatively little about a person's overall well-being.

On average, some people appear to be happier than others. Among the most consistent findings in personality research is the strong relationship between personality traits and well-being. Specifically, extraversion is related to higher levels of well-being, and neuroticism is strongly related to lower levels of well-being (Steel, Schmidt, & Schultz, 2008; Wilt & Revelle, 2009). These links between extraversion and higher levels of well-being, and between neuroticism and lower levels of well-being, are consistent and have even been found in orangutans (Weiss, King, & Perkins, 2006). What explains these connections?

Traits, Mood, and Subjective Well-Being

To begin, it might be helpful to define *well-being* as psychologists do. **Subjective well-being** is a person's assessment of his or her own level of positive affect relative to negative affect, and an evaluation of his or her life in general (Diener, 2000). When psychologists measure subjective well-being, they often focus first on a person's positive and negative mood and then on his or her life satisfaction.

subjective well-being
A person's assessment of his or her own level of positive affect relative to negative affect, and an evaluation of his or her life in general.

When psychologists measure subjective well-being, they often focus first on a person's positive and negative mood and then on his or her life satisfaction.

This definition of subjective well-being provides a clue as to why the traits of neuroticism and extraversion might be so strongly related to one's level of well-being. Neuroticism is the tendency to worry, to feel distressed, and to experience negative emotion. Neurotic individuals experience more negative mood than others, and their moods are more changeable. David Watson, a personality and clinical psychologist who specializes in the study of mood, has suggested that negative emotion is at the core of the trait of neuroticism, while positive emotion is at the core of the trait of extraversion (Watson & Clark, 1997). To the extent that neurotic individuals are more prone to negative emotion, it would seem that this trait might take a toll on overall well-being. Interestingly, however, research has shown that neurotics can be happy—especially if they are also extraverted (Hotard & others, 1989). That is, for neurotic individuals, extraversion is especially strongly related to well-being. Why is extraversion so strongly linked to happiness?

An early theory about the relationship between extraversion and high levels of well-being was that extraverts engage in behaviors that are themselves related to higher well-being and positive mood, such as socializing with others. Thus, the thinking went, maybe extraverts are happier because they choose to spend more time with other people.

Remember that you took the Satisfaction with Life Scale in Chapter 1.

Despite the logic of this explanation, research has shown that extraverts are happier than introverts even when they are alone (Lucas, 2009).

In fact, research has supported the conclusion that extraverts are simply happier regardless of what they are doing or with whom they are doing it (Lucas, 2007). Richard Lucas and Brendan Baird (2004) conducted a series of studies to examine the relationship between extraversion and positive mood. They exposed students who differed on the trait of extraversion to a variety of positive or neutral stimuli. The positive mood conditions included writing about a dream vacation or winning the lottery, viewing pleasant film clips about gardening or a Bill Cosby comedy routine, or reading jokes and cartoons. The neutral mood conditions included writing about taking a drive or going grocery shopping or watching a financial news report from PBS. In all of the studies, the strong relationship between extraversion and positive affect was found even in the neutral conditions. In other words, the extraverts were happier than the introverts regardless of whether the researchers had tried to put them in a pleasant mood; even when they had just read a financial news report, the extraverts were happier.

www.CartoonStock.com

Traits and States If you are neurotic or an introvert—or even a neurotic introvert—you may be feeling your mood deflating like a helium-filled balloon in a heat wave. If personality is stable, what good is it to find out that your personality might make you miserable?

One way to think about these issues is to focus on the difference between traits and states (Marine & others, 2006). As we have seen, traits are enduring characteristics—the way you generally are. In contrast, states (such as positive or negative moods) are briefer experiences. Having a trait, such as neuroticism, that predisposes you to feelings of worry (a state) does not mean that your overall well-being must suffer. Instead, recognizing that you tend to be neurotic may be an important step in noting when your negative moods are potentially being fed by traits and are not necessarily the result of objective events. Finding out that you have a personality style associated with lowered levels of happiness should not lead you to conclude that you are doomed. Rather, this information can allow you to take steps to improve your life, to foster good habits, and to make the most of your unique qualities.

In addition to happiness, researchers have examined how the big five traits might influence another important set of behaviors—leadership. To read about how personality relates to whether a person is likely to be a good leader, see the Intersection.

Evaluating the Trait Perspectives

Studying people in terms of their personality traits has practical value. Identifying a person's traits allows us to know that individual better. Psychologists have learned a great deal about the connections between personality and our health, ways of thinking, career success, and relations with others using traits (Fry & Debats, 2009; Leary & Hoyle, 2009a; Levenson & Aldwin, 2006; Roberts & others, 2007).

The trait approach has been faulted, however, for missing the importance of situational factors in personality and behavior (Leary & Hoyle, 2009b). For example, a person might say that she is introverted when meeting new people but very outgoing when with family and friends. Further, some have criticized the trait perspective for painting an individual's personality with very broad strokes. Traits can tell us much about someone whom we have never met but reveal little about the nuances of each individual's personality.

intersection

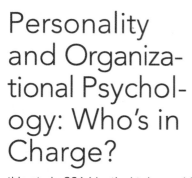

At the beginning of a group project, as you meet with your co-workers for the first time, there is that moment of tension over the question, who will be in charge? What characteristics do *you* think are important for effective leadership? Intelligence, trustworthiness, responsibility, and assertiveness may come to mind. Are these in fact the traits of good leaders? What factors best predict who shall lead? *Industrial and organizational psychologists*—specialists who study the workplace and workers—and personality psychologists have examined the ways that individuals' characteristics are related to whether they emerge as leaders.

Personality and Organizational Psychology: Who's in Charge?

Some aspects of leadership may be genetic, and these genetic influences may underlie the personality traits we think of as part of a "good leader" (Ilies, Arvey, & Bouchard, 2006). Consider a longitudinal study of twins that focused on the contribution of genetics to the attainment of leadership positions (Arvey & others, 2006). In this study, 331 identical twins and 315 fraternal twins provided biographical information about all of the leadership positions they had ever occupied, including leadership in groups such as high school and college clubs, professional organizations, and work groups. In comparing the overlap in leadership experience between identical and fraternal twins, the researchers found that the identical twins were more similar than the fraternal twins. The heritability for leadership positions was 30 percent. These data add to research indicating that leadership styles are influenced by genetics (Arvey & others, 2007; A. M. Johnson & others, 2004). So, perhaps leaders really are, at least to some degree, "born, not made."

Of course, leadership is not the same thing as eye color—genes do not simply "turn leadership on." More likely, genes influence other psychological characteristics that in turn enhance the chances for a person to become a leader. In the study described above, the genetic influence was partially explained by differences in the personality traits measured (Arvey & others, 2006). Genes may provide a person with traits, such as extraversion and achievement motivation, that can pave the way to leadership (Anderson & Kilduff, 2009; Avolio, Walumbwa, & Weber, 2009).

In terms of the big five personality traits, studies have shown that high extraversion, high conscientiousness, and low neuroticism are associated with being a leader (Judge & others, 1999, 2001). Members of sororities and fraternities at the University of Illinois participated in a study of personality traits and leadership (Harms, Roberts, & Woods, 2007). Each participant completed a measure of personality traits and was then rated by others in their organization for status and leadership. Extraversion and conscientiousness were both related to others' perceiving the person as having status and making a difference—in short, being a leader.

It might strike you as odd that so much research has considered the personality qualities of leaders without examining the type of group the persons are going to lead. However, the results of these studies seem to indicate that leadership is not the same as being the best at whatever the group does. (If you think about the captain of your favorite sports team, rarely is that person the team's best player.) Rather, leadership is a social process, and it likely emerges out of an individual's disposition to get noticed, to assert himself or herself, and to demonstrate responsibility. A good leader may not be the person who knows the most but rather the one whose temperament predisposes him or her to flourish as the "top dog."

> Who is the best leader you know? What makes him or her so effective?

self quiz

1. All of the following are among the big five factors of personality *except*
   A. openness to experience.
   B. altruism.
   C. conscientiousness.
   D. extraversion.

2. Researchers have found that some version of the big five factors appears in
   A. people in diverse countries around the world.
   B. domestic dogs.
   C. lizards.
   D. all of the above

3. The personality factor that is most linked with a higher IQ is
   A. neuroticism.
   B. conscientiousness.
   C. agreeableness.
   D. openness to experience.

Apply It! 4. Sigmund is a very high-achieving psychoanalyst. He always sees his patients in a timely manner and completes his written work well ahead of deadline. A brilliant public speaker, he is often surrounded by enthusiastic admirers, and he enjoys being the center of attention. He has some pretty wild, abstract ideas and has developed a complex theory to explain all of human behavior. He is an unconventional thinker, to say the least. He does not respond to criticism particularly well and is rather extreme in his response to even slight disapproval. Which of the following best describes Sigmund's personality?
   A. low conscientiousness, high extraversion, low neuroticism, high openness to experience
   B. high conscientiousness, high extraversion, high openness to experience, high neuroticism
   C. high conscientiousness, low extraversion, low openness to experience, low neuroticism
   D. low conscientiousness, high extraversion, low openness to experience, high neuroticism

4 Personological and Life Story Perspectives

Imagine giving 1,000 people a questionnaire measuring them on each of the big five traits. In looking at their scores, you might conclude that people are *not* like snowflakes after all but rather like Chips Ahoy cookies: They differ in small ways, but there are plenty who share very similar traits.

If two people have the same levels of the big five traits, do they essentially have the same personality? Researchers who approach personality from the personological and life story perspectives do not think so (McAdams & Olson, 2010). We began this chapter with the notion that each of us is unique and in some ways like no other human being on earth. **Personological and life story perspectives** stress that the way to understand the person is to focus on his or her life history and life story—aspects that distinguish the individual from all the other "snowflakes."

Murray's Personological Approach

Henry Murray (1893–1988) was a young biochemistry graduate student when he became interested in the psychology of personality after meeting Carl Jung and reading his work. Murray went on to become the director of the Psychological Clinic at Harvard at the same time that Gordon Allport was on the faculty there. Murray and Allport saw personality very differently. Whereas Allport was most comfortable focusing on conscious experience and traits, Murray embraced the psychodynamic notion of unconscious motivation.

Murray coined the word *personology* to refer to the study of the whole person. He famously stated that "the history of the organism is the organism," meaning that in order to understand a person, we have to understand that person's history, including all aspects of the person's life.

Murray applied his insights into personality during World War II, when he was called upon by the Office of Strategic Services (or OSS, a precursor to the CIA) to develop a psychological profile of Adolf Hitler. That document, produced in 1943, accurately predicted that Hitler would commit suicide rather than be taken alive by the Allies. Murray's analysis of Hitler was the first "offender profile," and it has served as a model for modern criminal profiling.

Henry Murray's psychological profile of Adolf Hitler, developed in 1943 during World War II, serves as a model for criminal profiling today.

The aspect of Murray's research that has had the most impact on contemporary personality psychology is his approach to motivation. Murray believed that our motives are largely unknown to us, so that measures of motivation must be developed that do not just ask people to say what it is they want. Thus, along with Christiana Morgan, Murray developed the Thematic Apperception Test (or TAT), to which we return later in this chapter (Morgan & Murray, 1935).

Moreover, a variety of scoring procedures have been devised for analyzing the unconscious motives that are revealed in imaginative stories (C. P. Smith, 1992). These scoring procedures involve *content analysis,* a procedure in which a psychologist takes the person's story and codes it for different images, words, and so forth. Murray posited 22 different unconscious needs to explain behavior. The three needs that have been the focus of most current research are the need for achievement (an enduring concern for attaining excellence and overcoming obstacles), for affiliation (an enduring concern for establishing and maintaining interpersonal connections), and for power (an enduring concern for having impact on the social world).

Motivation is a central part of personality psychology. Personality psychologists consider motivation an enduring part of the person and examine how individuals vary on their levels of different motives.

David Winter (2005) analyzed the motives revealed in inaugural addresses of U.S. presidents. He found that certain needs revealed in these speeches corresponded to later events during the person's presidency. For instance, presidents who scored high on need for achievement (such as Jimmy Carter) were less successful during their terms. Note that the need for achievement is about striving for personal excellence and may have little to do with playing politics, negotiating interpersonal relationships, or delegating responsibility. Presidents who scored high on need for power tended to be judged as more successful (John F. Kennedy, Ronald Reagan), and presidents whose addresses included a great deal of warm, interpersonal imagery (suggesting a high need for affiliation) tended to experience scandal during their presidencies (Richard M. Nixon).

The Life Story Approach to Identity

Following in the Murray tradition, Dan McAdams (2001, 2006) developed the *life story approach* to identity. His work centers on the idea that each of us has a unique life story, full of ups and downs. These stories represent our memories of what makes us who we are. McAdams found that the life story is a constantly changing narrative that serves to provide our lives with a sense of coherence. Just as Murray said that the history of the organism is the organism, McAdams suggests that our life stories are our identities.

Pick a potentially negative experience from your life and write the story of that experience. Is the ending happy or sad? In reading your story, what might a personality psychologist learn about you?

McAdams has conducted research using large samples of individuals who have undergone "life story interviews." Interview responses are coded for themes that are relevant to differing life stages and transitions. For example, McAdams and his colleagues found that kindergarten teachers (who are assumed to be high in generativity, which we considered in Chapter 8) are more likely to tell life stories characterized by a redemption pattern, with things going from bad to good.

McAdams (1989) also introduced the concept of intimacy motivation. The *intimacy motive* is an enduring concern for warm interpersonal encounters for their own sake. Intimacy motivation is revealed in the warm, positive interpersonal imagery in the stories people tell. Intimacy motive has been shown to relate to positive outcomes. For instance, college men who were high on intimacy motivation showed heightened levels of happiness and lowered work strain some 30 years later (McAdams & Bryant, 1987). A study of the coming out stories of gay men and lesbians demonstrated that intimacy-related imagery (for example, experiencing falling in love or warm acceptance from others) was associated with both measures of well-being and personality development (King & Smith, 2005).

Other personality psychologists have relied on narrative accounts of life experiences as a means of understanding how individuals create meaning in life events (King & others, 2000). In one study, parents of children with Down syndrome wrote down the story of how they found out about their child's diagnosis. Parents whose stories ended happily scored higher on measures of happiness, life meaning, and personal growth (King & others, 2000) than others. By using narratives, personal documents (such as diaries), and even letters and speeches, personality psychologists look for the deeper meaning that cannot be revealed through tests that ask people directly about whether specific items capture their personality traits.

Psychobiographies have been written about a wide variety of individuals, including Jesus Christ (Capps, 2004), Elvis Presley (Elms and Heller, 2005), and Osama bin Laden (Dennis, 2005), as well as Sigmund Freud, Carl Rogers (J. W. Anderson, 2005), and Gordon Allport (Berenbaum, 2005).

Finally, some personality psychologists take very seriously Murray's commitment to understanding the whole person, by focusing on just one case. *Psychobiography* is a means of inquiry in which the personality psychologist attempts to apply a personality theory to a single person's life (Runyon, 2007; Schultz, 2005). Freud himself wrote the first psychobiography in his analysis of Michelangelo. However, some problems with his interpretations of Michelangelo's life have caused his work to become a road map for what a psychobiographer ought *not* to do (Elms, 2005).

Evaluating the Life Story Approach and Similar Perspectives

Studying individuals through narratives and personal interviews provides an extraordinarily rich opportunity for the researcher. Imagine having the choice of reading someone's diary versus seeing that person's scores on a questionnaire measuring traits. Not many would pass up the chance to read the diary.

However, life story studies are difficult and time-consuming. Personologist Robert W. White (1992) referred to the study of narratives as exploring personality "the long way." Collecting interviews and narratives is often just the first step. In order for these personal stories to become scientific data, they must be transformed into numbers, a process involving extensive coding and content analysis. Further, for narrative studies to be worthwhile, they must tell us something we could not have found out in a much easier way (King, 2003). Psychobiographical inquiries moreover are prone to the biases of the scholars who conduct them and may not serve the scientific goal of generalizability.

Recall that generalizability refers to whether a particular finding is true of all people or just a narrow sample or even just one person.

self-quiz

1. Murray's personological approach is consistent with the
   A. humanistic perspective.
   B. psychodynamic perspective.
   C. trait perspective.
   D. lexical perspective.

2. Personology focuses primarily on
   A. objective tests.
   B. genetic factors.
   C. traits.
   D. unconscious motivations.

3. McAdams suggests that our identities are dependent on our

   A. heredity.
   B. cultural context.
   C. life stories.
   D. social networks.

Apply It! 4. Larry takes a test that involves looking at a series of pictures and telling stories about them. Based on his stories, he receives feedback that he is very high on need for power, and that means that he might be a good leader. Larry is shocked at this information, as he has never been put in charge before, and he cannot believe the score. According to the

personological approach to motivation, what likely explains Larry's experience?
   A. Need for power is unconscious, and so Larry is not aware that he is high on this motive.
   B. The measure used to assess need for power is probably not appropriate.
   C. Larry is likely low on need for power. It is very unlikely that a personality measure would tell you something you do not already know about yourself.
   D. Larry is probably a neurotic introvert.

5 Social Cognitive Perspectives

social cognitive perspectives
Theoretical views emphasizing conscious awareness, beliefs, expectations, and goals.

Social cognitive perspectives on personality emphasize conscious awareness, beliefs, expectations, and goals. While incorporating principles from behaviorism (see Chapter 5), social cognitive psychologists explore the person's ability to reason; to think about the past, present, and future; and to reflect on the self. They emphasize the person's individual interpretation of situations and thus focus on the uniqueness of each person by examining how behavior is tailored to the diversity of situations in which people find themselves.

Social cognitive theorists are not interested in broad traits. Rather, they investigate how more specific factors, such as beliefs, relate to behavior and performance. In this section we consider the two major social cognitive approaches, developed respectively by Albert Bandura and Walter Mischel.

Bandura's Social Cognitive Theory

B. F. Skinner, whose work we examined in Chapter 5, believed that there is no such thing as "personality"; rather, he emphasized behavior and felt that internal mental states were irrelevant to psychology. Albert Bandura (1986, 2001, 2006a, 2007a, 2008, 2009) found Skinner's approach to be far too simplistic for understanding human functioning. Bandura took the basic tenets of behaviorism and added a recognition of the role of mental processes

Albert Bandura (b. 1925)
Bandura's practical, problem-solving social cognitive approach has made a lasting mark on personality theory and therapy.

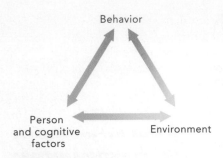

FIGURE 10.5
Bandura's Social Cognitive Theory
Bandura's social cognitive theory emphasizes reciprocal influences of behavior, environment, and person/cognitive factors.

in determining behavior. While Skinner saw behavior as caused by the situation, Bandura pointed out that the person can cause situations, and sometimes the very definition of the situation itself depends on the person's beliefs about it. For example, is that upcoming exam an opportunity to show your stuff or a threat to your ability to achieve your goals? The test is the same either way, but a person's unique take on the test can influence a host of behaviors (studying hard, worrying, and so on).

Bandura's social cognitive theory states that behavior, environment, and person/cognitive factors are *all* important in understanding personality. Bandura coined the term *reciprocal determinism* to describe the way behavior, environment, and person/cognitive factors interact to create personality (Figure 10.5). The environment can determine a person's behavior, and the person can act to change the environment. Similarly, person/cognitive factors can both influence behavior and be influenced by behavior. From Bandura's perspective, then, behavior is a product of a variety of forces, some of which come from the situation and some of which the person brings to the situation. We now review the important processes and variables Bandura used to understand personality.

Observational Learning

Recall from Chapter 5 Bandura's belief that observational learning is a key aspect of how we learn. Through observational learning, we form ideas about the behavior of others and then possibly adopt this behavior ourselves. For example, a young boy might observe his father's aggressive outbursts and hostile exchanges with people; when the boy is with his peers, he might interact in a highly aggressive way, showing the same characteristics as his father's behavior. Social cognitive theorists believe that we acquire a wide range of behaviors, thoughts, and feelings through observing others' behavior and that these observations strongly shape our personalities.

Personal Control

Social cognitive theorists emphasize that we can regulate and control our own behavior despite our changing environment (Bandura, 2008, 2009; Mischel, 2004). For example, a young executive who observes her boss behave in an overbearing and sarcastic manner toward his subordinates may find the behavior distasteful and go out of her way to encourage and support her own staff. Psychologists commonly describe a sense of behavioral control as coming from inside the person (an *internal locus of control*) or outside the person (an *external locus of control*). When we feel that we ourselves are controlling our choices and behaviors, the locus of control is internal, but when other influences are controlling them, the locus of control is external.

Consider the question of whether you will perform well on your next test. With an internal locus of control, you believe that you are in command of your choices and behaviors, and your answer will depend on what you can realistically do (for example, study hard or attend a special review session). From the perspective of an external locus of control, however, you might say that you cannot predict how things will go because so many factors influence performance, such as whether the test is difficult and if the exam room is too hot or too cold.

Feeling a strong sense of personal control is vital to many aspects of performance, well-being, and physical health (Bandura, 2009). Self-efficacy is an important aspect of the experience of control, as we next consider.

Self-Efficacy

Self-efficacy is the belief that one has the competence to accomplish a given goal or task.

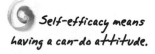
Self-efficacy means having a can-do attitude.

Bandura and others have shown that self-efficacy is related to a number of positive developments in people's lives, including solving problems, becoming more sociable, initiating and maintaining a diet or an exercise program, and quitting smoking (Bandura, 2001, 2009; Schunk, 2008; Schunk, Pintrich, & Meece, 2008). Self-efficacy influences whether people even try to develop healthy habits, as well as how much effort they expend in coping with stress, how long they persist in the face of obstacles, and how much stress and pain they experience (Brister & others, 2006; Clark & Dodge, 1999; Sarkar, Fisher, & Schillinger, 2006). Self-efficacy is also related to whether people initiate psychotherapy to deal with

self-efficacy
The belief that one can master a situation and produce positive change.

their problems and whether it succeeds (Longo, Lent, & Brown, 1992). In addition, researchers have found that self-efficacy is linked with successful job interviewing and job performance (Tay, Ang, & Van Dyne, 2006). We will return to the topics of personal control and self-efficacy in Chapter 14, in the context of making healthy changes in behavior.

Mischel's Contributions

Like Bandura, Walter Mischel is a social cognitive psychologist who has explored how personality influences behavior. Mischel has left his mark on the field of personality in two notable ways. First, his critique of the idea of consistency in behavior ignited a flurry of controversy. Second, he has proposed the CAPS model, a new way of thinking about personality.

Mischel's Critique of Consistency
Whether we are talking about unconscious sexual conflicts, traits, or motives, all of the approaches we have considered so far maintain that these various personality characteristics are an enduring influence on behavior. This shared assumption was attacked in 1968 with the publication of Walter Mischel's *Personality and Assessment,* a book that nearly ended the psychological study of personality.

To understand Mischel's argument, recall Gordon Allport's definition of a trait as a characteristic that ought to make different situations equivalent for a given person. This quality of traits suggests that a person should behave consistently in different situations—in other words, the individual should exhibit *cross-situational consistency.* For example, an outgoing person should act highly sociably whether she is at a party or in the library. However, Mischel looked at the research compiled on trait prediction of behavior and found it to be lacking. He concluded that there was no evidence for cross-situational consistency in behavior—and thus no evidence for the existence of personality as it had been previously assumed to exist.

Rather than understanding personality as consisting of broad, internal traits that make for consistent behavior across situations, Mischel said that personality often changes according to a given situation. Mischel asserted that behavior is discriminative—that is, a person looks at each situation and responds accordingly. Mischel's view is called *situationism,* the idea that personality and behavior often vary considerably from one context to another.

Personality psychologists responded to Mischel's situationist attack in a variety of ways (Funder, 2009; Hogan, 2009). Researchers were able to show that it is not a matter of *whether* personality predicts behavior, but *when and how* it does so, often in combination with situational factors. The research findings were that

1. The narrower and more limited a trait is, the more likely it will predict behavior.

2. Some people are consistent on some traits, and other people are consistent on other traits.

3. Personality traits exert a stronger influence on an individual's behavior when situational influences are less powerful. A very powerful situation is one that contains many clear cues about how a person is supposed to behave. For example, even a highly talkative person typically sits quietly during a class lecture. In weaker situations, however, such as during his or her leisure time, the person may spend most of the time talking.

Moreover, individuals select the situations they are in. This means that even if situations determine behavior, traits play a role in determining which situations people choose—such as going to a party or staying home to study (Emmons & Diener, 1986).

Let's pause and consider what it means to be consistent. You might believe that being consistent is part of being a genuine, honest person and that tailoring behavior to different situations means being fake. On the other hand, consider that someone who never changes his or her behavior to fit a situation might be unpleasant—"a drag"—to have around. Think for example about someone who cannot put aside his competitive drive even when playing checkers with a 4-year-old. Clearly, adaptive behavior might involve sometimes being consistent and sometimes tailoring behavior to the situation.

Over time, Mischel (2004, 2009) has developed an approach to personality that he feels is better suited to capturing the nuances of the relationship between the individual and situations in producing behavior. Imagine trying to study personality without using traits or broad motives. What would you focus on? Mischel's answer to this dilemma is his CAPS theory.

CAPS Theory Recall Mischel's (2004) work on delay of gratification from Chapter 9. In that work, children were left in a room with a tempting cookie. Mischel measured the amount of time the kids were able to delay eating the cookie, and he and his colleagues continued to study those children for many years. They found that the amount of time the children were able to delay gratification predicted their academic performance in high school and even college (Mischel, 2004). These results indicate remarkable stability in personality over time.

Mischel's revised approach to personality is concerned with just such stability (or coherence) in the pattern of behavior *over time,* not with consistency across differing situations. That is, Mischel and his colleagues have studied how behaviors in very different situations have a coherent pattern, such as a child's waiting to eat the cookie versus that same individual's (as a grown college student) deciding to stay home and study instead of going out to party.

In keeping with the social cognitive emphasis on the person's cognitive abilities and mental states, Mischel conceptualizes personality as a set of interconnected **cognitive affective processing systems (CAPS)** (Mischel, 2004, 2009; Mischel & Shoda, 1999; Orom & Cervone, 2009). According to this approach, our thoughts and emotions about ourselves and the world affect our behavior and become linked in ways that matter to behavior. Personal control and self-efficacy are connections of sorts that a person has made among situations, beliefs, and behaviors. Imagine someone—let's call him Raoul—who is excited by the challenge of a new assignment given by his boss. Raoul may think about all the possible strategies to complete the project and get down to work immediately. Yet this go-getter may respond differently to other challenges, depending on who gives the assignment, what it is, or whether he feels he can do a good job.

CAPS is concerned with how personality works, not with what it is (Shoda & Mischel, 2006). From the CAPS perspective, it makes no sense to ask a person "How extraverted are you?" because the answer is always, "It depends." A person may be outgoing in one situation (on the first day of class) and not another (right before an exam), and that unique pattern of flexibility is what personality is all about.

Not surprisingly, CAPS theory focuses on how people behave in different situations and how they uniquely interpret situational features. From this perspective, knowing that Crystal is an extravert tells us little about how she will behave in a group discussion in her psychology class. We need to know about Crystal's beliefs and goals in the discussion. For example, does she want to impress the instructor? Is she a psychology major? Are several members of the class good friends of hers? We also need to know about her personal understanding of the situation itself: Is this an opportunity to shine, or is she thinking about her test for the next class? Research using the CAPS approach generally involves observing individuals behaving in a variety of contexts in order to identify the patterns of associations that exist among beliefs, emotions, and behavior for each individual person across different situations.

Mischel focused on coherence, or whether behaviors make sense across different situations, not whether they are the very same behavior.

cognitive affective processing systems (CAPS) Mischel's theoretical model for describing that our thoughts and emotions about ourselves and the world affect our behavior and become linked in ways that matter to behavior.

Is your own behavior mostly consistent across different situations?

Evaluating the Social Cognitive Perspectives

Social cognitive theory focuses on the interactions of individuals with their environments. The social cognitive approach has fostered a scientific climate for understanding personality that highlights the observation of behavior. Social cognitive theory emphasizes the influence of cognitive processes in explaining personality and suggests that people have the ability to control their environment.

Critics of the social cognitive perspective on personality take issue with one or more aspects of the theory. For example, they charge that

■ The social cognitive approach is too concerned with change and situational influences on personality. It does not pay adequate tribute to the enduring qualities of personality.

■ Social cognitive theory ignores the role biology plays in personality.

■ In its attempt to incorporate both the situation and the person into its view of personality, social cognitive psychology tends to lead to very specific predictions for each person in any given situation, making generalizations impossible.

self-quiz

1. The following are components of Bandura's social cognitive theory *except*
   A. self-efficacy.
   B. unconscious motivations.
   C. personal control.
   D. observational learning.

2. According to Mischel's 1968 book, behavior is determined by
   A. traits.
   B. biology.
   C. situations and the person's perceptions of them.
   D. unconscious motives.

3. The cognitive affective processing systems (CAPS) approach is centrally concerned with
   A. how personality works in different situations.
   B. how genetic inheritance affects personality.
   C. what biological factors influence personality.
   D. what personality is.

Apply It! 4. Omri thinks of himself as an extravert, but he rarely speaks up in his classes. He is especially quiet when he meets new people, especially authority figures such as a new boss. What would Walter Mischel say about Omri's behavior?
   A. Omri is not really an extravert at all; he just does not understand that.
   B. Omri is being discriminative in his behavior. He is probably extraverted in some situations and introverted in others, and that should not be surprising.
   C. Omri is probably fixated at the phallic stage of development.
   D. Omri was not given enough unconditional positive regard in his childhood.

6 Biological Perspectives

The notion that physiological processes influence personality has been around since ancient times. Around 400 B.C.E., Hippocrates, the father of medicine, described human beings as having one of four basic personalities based on levels of particular bodily fluids (called *humours*). For Hippocrates, a "sanguine" personality was a happy, optimistic individual who happened to have an abundance of blood. A "choleric" person was quick-tempered with too much yellow bile. A "phlegmatic" personality referred to a placid, sluggish individual with too much phlegm (mucus), and a "melancholic" pessimist had too much black bile.

Of course, Hippocrates' ideas about bodily fluids have fallen by the wayside. Still, personality psychologists have long acknowledged that personality involves the brain and biological processes, although they often have assumed the processes to exist rather than actually studying them. Freud's psychosexual stages bear witness to his strong belief in the connection between the mind (personality) and the body. Allport defined traits as "*neuro*psychic" structures and personality as a "psycho*physical*" system. Murray once declared, "No brain, no personality." More recently, advances in method and theory have led to fascinating research on the role of biological processes in personality.

Personality and the Brain

The brain is clearly important in personality as in other psychological phenomena. Recall the case of Phineas Gage, described in Chapter 2. One of the key effects of Gage's horrific accident was that it changed his personality. He went from being gentle, kind, and reliable to being angry, hostile, and untrustworthy.

A great deal of research is addressing the ways in which brain activity is associated with various personality traits. For example, research has shown an extraverted person's

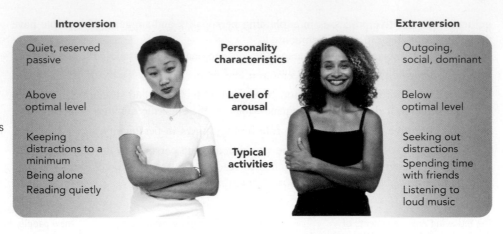

FIGURE 10.6
Eysenck's Reticular Activation System Theory Eysenck viewed introversion and extraversion as characteristic behavioral patterns that aim to regulate arousal around the individual's baseline level.

Introversion

| Personality characteristics | Extraversion |

Quiet, reserved passive — **Personality characteristics** — Outgoing, social, dominant

Above optimal level — **Level of arousal** — Below optimal level

Keeping distractions to a minimum
Being alone
Reading quietly — **Typical activities** — Seeking out distractions
Spending time with friends
Listening to loud music

left frontal cortex is more responsive to positive stimuli and that the same area in neurotic individuals is more responsive to negative stimuli (Canli, 2008a, 2008b; Haas & others, 2007; Schmidtke & Heller, 2004). Extraverts' amygdalas are more responsive to seeing happy faces than are introverts' amygdalas (Canli & others, 2002). Two theoretical approaches to the biology of personality, by Hans Eysenck and Jeffrey Gray, have garnered the most interest.

Eysenck's Reticular Activation System Theory

British psychologist Hans Eysenck (1967) was among the first to describe the role of a particular brain system in personality. He developed an approach to extraversion/introversion based on the *reticular activation system* (RAS).

Recall from Chapter 2 that the reticular formation is located in the brain stem and plays a role in wakefulness or arousal. The RAS is the name given to the reticular formation and its connections. Eysenck posited that all of us share an optimal arousal level, a level at which we all feel comfortably engaged with the world. However, Eysenck proposed, the RAS of extraverts and introverts differs with respect to the baseline level of arousal. You know that an extravert tends to be outgoing, sociable, and dominant and that an introvert is quieter and more reserved and passive. According to Eysenck, these outward differences in behavior reflect different arousal regulation strategies (Figure 10.6). Extraverts wake up in the morning under-aroused, *below* the optimal level, whereas introverts start out *above* the optimal level.

If *you* were feeling under-engaged with life, what might you do? You might listen to loud music or hang out with friends—in other words, behave like an extravert. If, on the other hand, you were feeling over-aroused or too stimulated, what would you do? You might spend time alone, keep distractions to a minimum, maybe sit quietly and read a book—in other words, you might act like an introvert.

Thus, from Eysenck's perspective, we can understand the traits of extraversion/introversion as characteristic patterns of behavior that aim to regulate arousal around our baseline. Research has not shown that extraverts and introverts differ in terms of baseline arousal, but rather that introverts may be more sensitive to arousing stimuli.

Gray's Reinforcement Sensitivity Theory

Building from Eysenck's work, Jeffrey Gray (1987; Gray & McNaughton, 2000) proposed a neuropsychology of personality, called *reinforcement sensitivity theory,* that has been the subject of much research. On the basis of animal learning principles, Gray posited that two neurological systems—the *behavioral activation system* (BAS) and the *behavioral inhibition system* (BIS)—could be viewed as underlying personality, as Figure 10.7 shows. According to Gray, these systems explain differences in an organism's attention to rewards and punishers in the environment. An organism sensitive to rewards is more likely to learn associations between behaviors and rewards and therefore to show a characteristic pattern of seeking out rewarding opportunities. In contrast, an organism with a heightened sensitivity to punishers in the environment is more likely to learn associations between behaviors and negative consequences. Such an organism shows a characteristic pattern of avoiding such consequences.

In Gray's theory, the BAS is sensitive to rewards in the environment, predisposes one to feelings of positive emotion, and underlies the trait of extraversion. In contrast, the BIS is sensitive to punishments and is involved in avoidance learning; it predisposes the individual to feelings of fear and underlies the trait of neuroticism (Corr, 2008; Gray & McNaughton, 2000). Psychologists often measure BAS and BIS in humans by using questionnaires that assess a person's attention to rewarding or punishing outcomes. As the description of these systems suggests, those high on BAS measures (extraverts) are more susceptible to positive mood, and those high on BIS measures (neurotics) are more susceptible to negative mood (Larsen & Ketelaar, 1991).

Gray's conceptual model of reinforcement sensitivity proposed interacting brain systems as primarily responsible for the behavioral manifestations of BAS and BIS. Research has provided some evidence for the biological underpinnings of these systems. The amygdala, the prefrontal cortex, and the anterior cingulated cortex appear to serve together as a system for affective style (Davidson, 2005; McNaughton & Corr, 2008) and are particularly implicated in the BAS or extraversion (Pickering & Smillie, 2008).

The Role of Neurotransmitters

Neurotransmitters have also been implicated in personality in ways that fit Gray's model. Recall from Chapter 5 the function of the neurotransmitter dopamine in the experience of reward. Dopamine is a "feel good" neurotransmitter vital to learning that certain behaviors are rewarding and to sending the message to "do it again!" Research has shown that dopamine is also a factor in BAS or extraversion (Depue & Collins, 1999; Pickering & Gray, 1999). Studies have suggested that early encounters with warm caregivers and positive life experiences can promote the growth of dopamine-producing cells and receptors. These early experiences can make the brain especially sensitive to rewards, setting the neurochemical stage for extraversion (Depue & Collins, 1999).

Perhaps even stronger than the link between dopamine and extraversion is the relationship between the neurotransmitter serotonin and neuroticism (Brummett & others, 2008; Middeldorp & others, 2007; Schinka, Busch, & Robichaux-Keene, 2004). Neuroticism is especially related to a certain serotonin transporter gene and to the binding of serotonin in the thalamus (Canli & Lesch, 2007; Gonda & others, 2009; Harro & others, 2009). Individuals who have less circulating serotonin are prone to negative mood; giving them drugs that inhibit the reuptake of serotonin tends to decrease negative mood and enhance feelings of sociability (Ksir, Hart, & Ray, 2008). Serotonin is also implicated in aggressive behavior, as we will see in Chapter 11, as well as in the experience of depression, as we will consider in Chapter 12.

Keep in mind that finding associations between brain activity or neurotransmitters and personality does not tell us about the potential causal pathways between these variables. Behavior can influence brain processes, and patterns of behavior can therefore determine brain activity. One thing that behavior cannot influence, at least not yet, is genes, another important biological factor in personality.

Behavioral Approach System

Sensitive to
Environmental reward

Behavior
Seek positive consequences/rewards

Character of emotion
Positive

Personality trait
Extraversion

Behavioral Inhibition System

Sensitive to
Environmental punishment

Behavior
Avoid negative consequences/punishments

Character of emotion
Negative

Personality trait
Neuroticism

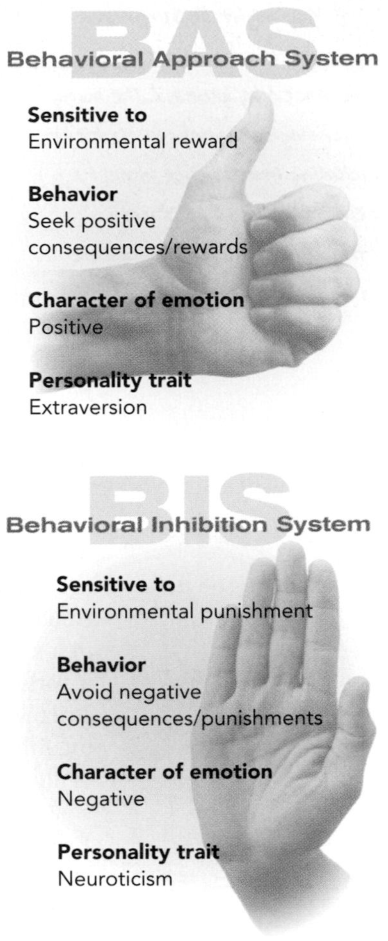

FIGURE 10.7

Gray's Reinforcement Sensitivity Theory Gray theorized that two neurological systems, the BAS and the BIS, explain differences in an organism's attention to environmental rewards and punishments and in this way shape personality.

Personality and Behavioral Genetics

Behavioral genetics is the study of the inherited underpinnings of behavioral characteristics. A great deal of research in behavioral genetics has involved twin studies, and the hub of this work is, appropriately, the University of Minnesota, Twin Cities.

Twin study findings demonstrate that genetic factors explain a substantial amount of the observed differences in each of the big five traits. Heritability estimates for the five factors are about 50 percent (Bouchard & Loehlin, 2001; Jang, Livesley, & Vernon, 1996;

behavioral genetics
The study of the inherited underpinnings of behavioral characteristics.

You might be surprised to learn that well-being is influenced by genes. Like many psychological characteristics— including intelligence, traits, religiosity, and political attitudes—genes play a role in how happy we are.

South & Krueger, 2008). Remember that to do these studies, researchers compare identical twins, who share 100 percent of their genes, with fraternal twins, who share just 50 percent. All of the participants complete questionnaires measuring their traits. Then the researchers see if the identical twins are more similar to each other than the fraternal twins. One potential explanation for the strong relationship between personality characteristics and well-being is that the same genetic factors may play a role in traits such as extraversion, neuroticism, and well-being (Carprara & others, 2009; Weiss, Bates, & Luciano, 2008).

Even aspects of personality that are not traits reveal some genetic influence. For example, research has shown that autobiographical memories about one's childhood and early family experiences (the kind of data that the personologist might find interesting) are influenced by genetics. Robert Krueger and his colleagues (Krueger, Markon, & Bouchard, 2003) examined retrospective reports on the quality of family environments in a sample of twins who were reared apart. Participants rated their adoptive families on a variety of characteristics such as parental warmth, feelings of being wanted, and the strictness of their parents. These twins, though obviously sharing genetics, were reared by different families, so they were describing different experiences. Yet their recollections of their early family experiences were similar, and the heritability estimate for family cohesion ranged from 40 to 60 percent.

As we saw in Chapter 7's discussion of intelligence and Chapter 9's examination of happiness, the heritability statistic describes a group, not an individual, and heritability does not mean that traits are set in stone. Understanding the role of genetic factors in personality is enormously complex. Research on non-twin samples often suggests much lower heritability, for reasons that are not well understood (South & Krueger, 2008). Furthermore, because genes and environment are often intertwined, it is very difficult to tease apart whether, and how, genes or experience explains enduring patterns of behavior. For instance, a child who is genetically predisposed to disruptive behavior may often find himself or herself in a time-out or be involved in arguments with parents or teachers. When that child emerges as an adult with a "fighting spirit" or lots of "spunk," are those adult traits the product of genes, experiences, or both? Finally, most traits are probably influenced by multiple genes (Savitz & Ramesar, 2004), making the task of identifying specific molecular links very challenging.

Consider how genes might influence the processes of autobiographical memory—encoding, retention, and recall. In which memory process would genes matter most?

Evaluating the Biological Perspectives

Research that explores the biological aspects of personality is clearly important, and it is likely to remain a key avenue of research. This work ties the field of personality to animal learning models, advances in brain imaging, and evolutionary theory (Revelle, 2008). However, a few cautions are necessary in thinking about biological variables and their place in personality.

As we considered above, biology can be the effect, not the cause, of personality. To be sure that you grasp this idea, first recall that personality is the individual's characteristic pattern of behavior, thoughts, and feelings. Then recall from previous chapters that behavior, thoughts, and feelings are physical events in the body and brain. If traits predispose individuals to particular, consistent behaviors, thoughts, and emotional responses, traits may play a role in forging particular habitually used pathways in the brain. Recall, too, from Chapter 6 that memory may be thought of as patterns of activation among neurons. The autobiographical memories that interest personologists, then, might be

challenge your thinking

Can Personality Change?

As you talk with a friend, she tells you for what seems like the hundredth time about her boyfriend troubles. He never calls when he says he will. He always "forgets" his wallet when they go out. Now she thinks he might be cheating on her *again*. As you count silently to 10, you are tempted to blurt it out: "Dump him already! He's never going to change!"

Of course, your friend might be banking on the notion that he *will* change. Can people genuinely change? The answer to this question has implications for a variety of important life domains. For example, can criminals be rehabilitated? Can addicts truly recover from addictions? Will those self-help books ever help you to stop worrying and enjoy life? Will that lousy boyfriend turn out to be suitable husband material after all?

Whether personality can change has been a topic of controversy throughout the history of the field of personality. Freud thought that personality was essentially fixed by the age of 6, with little development occurring over the rest of life. Jung split with Freud on this issue, believing that the most important personality development occurred in middle age. William James wrote that "it is well for the world that in most of us, by the age of thirty, the character has set like plaster, and will never soften again." Trait psychologists Paul Costa and Robert McCrae concluded from their own work that James was on target: They suggested that most traits are indeed "essentially fixed" by age 30, with little meaningful change occurring throughout the rest of adulthood (Costa & McCrae, 1992, 2006; McCrae & Costa, 2006). However, other research has found that meaningful personality change continues over time (Roberts & Mroczek, 2008; Roberts, Wood, & Caspi, 2008).

Evidence that personality traits may change is provided by longitudinal studies that follow the same individuals over a long

period. Brent Roberts and his colleagues (Edmonds & others, 2007; Roberts, Walton, & Viechtbauer, 2006; Roberts, Wood, & Caspi, 2008; Roberts & others, 2009) analyzed 92 different longitudinal studies that included thousands of participants ranging from 12 to over 80 years old and that measured aspects of the big five across the life course. They found strong, consistent evidence for trait changes throughout life, even into adulthood. Social dominance (a facet of extraversion), conscientiousness, and emotional stability (the opposite of neuroticism) were found to increase especially between the ages of 20 and 40. Agreeableness showed a steady rise over the life course. Over time, people were not just getting older—they were getting more responsible, kinder, and less worried.

Other research has shown that individuals become more confident, warm, responsible, and calm as they age. Such positive changes equate with becoming more socially mature (Blonigen & others, 2008; Klimstra & others, 2009; Roberts & Mroczek, 2008).

What do these findings mean for your friend and her loser boyfriend? He just might shape up, but she might have to wait a long time. Maybe there are other, more agreeable and conscientious fish in the sea.

What Do You Think?

- In your opinion, can personality change throughout life? Explain.

- Reflect on what you were like five years ago. Which aspects of your personality have changed? Which have stayed the same?

- What advice would you give to a friend who wants to be more outgoing?

---

viewed as well-worn patterns of activation. To the extent that personality represents a person's characteristic pattern of thought or the accumulation of memories over the life span, personality may not only be influenced by the brain—it may also play a role in the brain's very structure and functions.

One issue that biological approaches bring to the fore is the question of whether personality is plastic—that is, whether it can change throughout a person's life. If personality is "caused" by biological processes, does that mean it is fixed? To explore this issue, see Challenge Your Thinking.

1. Eysenck suggested that introversion and extraversion are influenced by the brain's
   A. amygdala.
   B. reticular activation system.
   C. thalamus.
   D. prefrontal cortex.

2. Gray's reward sensitivity theory of personality suggests that extraversion and neuroticism can be understood as two neurological systems linked to _____ in the individual's environment.
   A. stability and consistency
   B. stability and change

C. rewards and punishments
D. opportunities for growth

3. A technique commonly used by researchers in the specialized field known as behavioral genetics is
   A. life story interviews.
   B. naturalistic observation.
   C. case studies.
   D. twin studies.

Apply It! 4. Dorian's parents are both very outgoing, while Dorian is quiet and reserved. Her parents often embarrass her in public with their loud voices and crazy antics. When Dorian learns that extraversion

is 50 percent heritable, she starts to wonder if she will eventually become as irritating as her parents. What is your advice for Dorian?
A. She should start getting used to the idea of being an extravert—she's doomed.
B. She has nothing to worry about, because heritability is only about twins.
C. She should remember that heritability is a statistic that applies only to a group, not to a single case.
D. She should be glad, because as an extravert she is likely to be happier.

7 Personality Assessment

One of the great contributions of personality psychology to the science of psychology is its development of rigorous methods for measuring mental processes. Psychologists use a number of scientifically developed methods to evaluate personality. They assess personality for different reasons, from clinical evaluation to career counseling and job selection (Heine & Buchtel, 2009).

Self-Report Tests

self-report test
Also called an objective test or an inventory, a method of measuring personality characteristics that directly asks people whether specific items describe their personality traits.

The most commonly used method of measuring personality characteristics is the self-report. A **self-report test** directly asks people whether specific items describe their personality traits. Self-report personality tests include items such as

I am easily embarrassed.

I love to go to parties.

I like to watch cartoons on TV.

Respondents choose from a limited number of answers (yes or no, true or false, agree or disagree).

One problem with self-report tests is a factor called *social desirability*. To grasp the idea of social desirability, imagine answering the item "I am lazy at times." This statement is probably true for everyone, but would you feel comfortable admitting it? When motivated by social desirability, individuals say what they think the researcher wants to hear or what they think will make them look better. One way to measure the influence of social desirability is to give individuals a questionnaire that is designed to tap into this tendency. Such a scale typically contains many universally true but threatening items ("I like to gossip at times," "I have never said anything intentionally to hurt someone's feelings"). If scores on a trait measure correlate with this measure of social desirability, we know that the test takers were probably not being straightforward with respect to the trait measure. That is, if a person answers one questionnaire in a socially desirable fashion, he or she is probably answering all the questionnaires that way.

Another way to get around social desirability issues is to design scales so that it is virtually impossible for the respondent

"I like the way I look, but I hate my personality."

empirically
keyed test
A type of self-
report test that
presents many
questionnaire
items to two
groups that are
known to be dif-
ferent in some
central way.

to know what the researcher is trying to measure. One means of accomplishing this goal is to use an **empirically keyed test,** a type of self-report test that is created by first identifying two groups that are known to be different. The researcher would give these two groups a large number of questionnaire items and then see which items show the biggest differences between the groups. Those items would then become part of the scale to measure the group difference. For instance, a researcher might want to develop a test that distinguishes between individuals with a history of substance abuse and those with no such history. The researcher might generate a long list of true/false items that ask about a variety of different topics but that do not even mention substance abuse. These many questions are presented to the members of the two groups, and on the basis of the responses, the researcher can then select the items that best discriminate between the members of the differing groups (Segal & Coolidge, 2004).

An empirically keyed test can have items that seem to have nothing to do with the variable of interest.

Note that an empirically keyed test avoids the issue of social desirability because the items that distinguish between the two groups are not related in any obvious way to the actual purpose of the test. For instance, those without a substance abuse history might typically respond "true" to the item "I enjoy taking long walks," while those with a history of substance abuse might respond "false"; but this item does not mention substance use, and there is no clear reason why it should distinguish between these groups.

Indeed, an important consideration with respect to empirically keyed tests is that researchers often do not know why a given test item distinguishes between two groups. Imagine, for example, that an empirically keyed test of achievement motivation includes an item such as "I prefer to watch sports on TV instead of romantic movies." A researcher might find that this item does a good job of distinguishing between higher-paid versus lower-paid managers in a work setting. However, does an item such as this example measure achievement motivation or, instead, simply the respondents' gender?

Minnesota
Multiphasic
Personality
Inventory (MMPI)
The most widely
used and re-
searched empiri-
cally keyed
self-report per-
sonality test.

MMPI   The **Minnesota Multiphasic Personality Inventory (MMPI)** is the most widely used and researched empirically keyed self-report personality test. The MMPI was initially constructed in the 1940s to assess "abnormal" personality tendencies. The most recent version of the inventory, the MMPI-2, is still widely used around the world to assess personality and predict outcomes (Butcher & others, 2006; Tellegen, Ben-Porath, & Sellbom, 2009; Thomas & Youngjohn, 2009; Veltri & others, 2009). The scale features 567 items and provides information on a variety of personality characteristics. The MMPI also includes a variety of items meant to assess whether the respondent is lying or trying to make a good impression.

Some of the MMPI-2 scales measure characteristics associated with psychological disorders, such as depression and schizophrenia, which we will examine in Chapter 12. Other scales include masculinity/femininity and introversion.

The MMPI is not only used by clinical psychologists to assess mental health; it is also a tool for predicting which individuals will make the best job candidates and which career an individual should pursue. With computers now widely employed to score the MMPI-2 (Forbey & Ben-Porath, 2007), critics warn that the availability of computer scoring has tempted some untrained individuals to use the test in ways for which it has not been validated.

Assessment of the Big Five Factors

Paul Costa and Robert McCrae (1992) constructed the Neuroticism Extraversion Openness Personality Inventory—Revised (or NEO-PI-R, for short), a self-report test geared to assessing the five-factor model: openness, conscientiousness, extraversion, agreeableness, and neuroticism (emotional instability). The test also evaluates six subdimensions that make up the five main factors. Other measures of the big five traits have relied on the lexical approach and offer the advantage of being available without a fee.

face validity
The quality of
seeming, on the
surface, to fit a
particular trait in
question.

Unlike empirically keyed tests, measures of the big five generally contain items that are quite straightforward; for instance, the trait "talkative" might show up on an extraversion scale. These items have what psychologists call face validity. A test item has **face validity** if it seems on the surface to fit the trait in question. Measures of the big five typically involve items that are obvious in terms of what they measure, but not all self-report assessments have this quality.

For example, an item measuring neuroticism that is very face valid would be, "I am a worrier."

psychology
in our world

Hey, What's Your Type?

Personality assessment has become increasingly useful in business settings. One of the most popular assessment tools for personnel decisions is the Myers Briggs Type Indicator (MBTI; Briggs & Myers, 1998), developed in the 1940s by the mother–daughter team of Katherine Briggs and Isabel Briggs Myers, neither of whom was trained in psychology or assessment (Saunders, 1991). Based on a book by Carl Jung, the Myers Briggs questionnaire provides people with feedback on their personality "type" based on four dimensions:

- *Extraversion* (basing one's actions on outward conditions) versus *introversion* (being more introspective)

- *Sensing* (relying on what can be sensed about reality) versus *intuiting* (relying on gut feelings and unconscious processes)

- *Thinking* (relying on logic) versus *feeling* (relying on emotion)

- *Judgment* (using thinking and feeling) versus *perception* (using sensing and intuiting)

These MBTI dimensions are used to create categories that are labeled with letters; for example, an extraverted person who relies on sensation, thinking, and judgment would be called an ESTJ. The MBTI has become so popular that people in some organizations introduce themselves as an INTJ or an INSP in the same way that people might exchange their astrological signs. Unfortunately, as in the case of astrology, strong evidence for the actual value of the MBTI types for personnel selection and job performance is very weak at best (Hunsley, Lee, & Wood, 2004; Pittenger, 2005). In fact, the MBTI is neither reliable (people get different scores with repeated testing) nor valid (it does not predict what it should). For example, there is no evidence that particular MBTI types are better suited to particular occupations (Bjork & Druckman, 1991; Boyle, 1995; Gardner & Martinko, 1996).

Given this lack of empirical support, why does MBTI remain popular? Some practitioners have found it to be quite useful in their own work (McCaulley, 2000) and may be unaware of the lack of scientific evidence for the types. The MBTI has been well marketed, and those who pay for the scale and its training may be motivated to find evidence in their own lives to support the notion that it works (recall from Chapter 7 the problem of the confirmation bias).

It can be fun to learn about our personalities and to be given these letter labels. When we read that an INTJ is someone who is "introspective and likely to sometimes argue a point just for the sake of argument," we might think, "They really figured me out." In truth, however, this description could be true of virtually anyone, as is the case for most astrological-sign profiles. The tendency to see ourselves in such vague descriptions is called the *Barnum effect*, after P. T. Barnum, the famous showman. The wily Barnum—simply by dispensing vague, general descriptions that would likely be true of anyone—convinced people that he could read minds.

The popularity of the Myers Briggs letter typology attests to the power of marketing, the persistence of confirmation bias, and the Barnum effect. Most troubling to personality psychologists is that although other psychological measures may not be as exciting and mysterious as those four letters, they are more likely to provide reliable and valid information about job performance (Hunsley, Lee, & Wood, 2004).

ESTP

INTJ

It is likely that you would be able to give a reasonably good assessment of your own levels of traits such as neuroticism and extraversion. What about the more mysterious aspects of yourself and others? If you are like most people, you think of psychological assessments as tools to find out things you do not already know about yourself. For that objective, psychologists might turn to projective tests.

Projective Tests

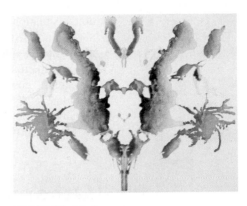

projective test
A personality assessment test that presents individuals with an ambiguous stimulus and asks them to describe it or tell a story about it—to project their own meaning onto the stimulus.

A **projective test** presents individuals with an ambiguous stimulus and asks them to describe it or tell a story about it—in other words, to *project* their own meaning onto the stimulus. Projective tests are based on the assumption that the ambiguity of the stimulus allows individuals to interpret it based on their feelings, desires, needs, and attitudes. The test is especially designed to elicit the individual's unconscious feelings and conflicts, providing an assessment that goes deeper than the surface of personality (Aiken & Groth-Marnat, 2006; Husain, 2009; Leichtman, 2004). Projective tests attempt to get inside the mind to discover how the test taker really feels and thinks; that is, they aim to go beyond the way the individual overtly presents himself or herself. Projective tests are theoretically aligned with the psychodynamic perspectives on personality, which give more weight to the unconscious than do other perspectives. Projective techniques also require content analysis. The examiner must code the responses for the underlying motivations revealed in the story.

FIGURE 10.8

Type of Stimulus Used in the Rorschach Inkblot Test What do you see in this figure? Do you see two green seahorses? Or a pair of blue spiders? A psychologist who relies on the Rorschach test would examine your responses to find out who you are.

Rorschach inkblot test
A famous projective test that uses an individual's perception of inkblots to determine his or her personality.

Perhaps the most famous projective test is the **Rorschach inkblot test,** developed in 1921 by the Swiss psychiatrist Hermann Rorschach. The test consists of 10 cards, half in black and white and half in color, which the individual views one at a time (Figure 10.8). The person taking the Rorschach test is asked to describe what he or she sees in each of the inkblots. For example, the individual may say, "I see two fairies having a tea party" or "This is the rabbit's face from the movie *Donnie Darko*." These responses are scored based on indications of various underlying psychological characteristics (Exner, 2003; Leichtman, 2009).

The Rorschach's usefulness in research is controversial. From a scientific perspective, researchers are skeptical about the Rorschach (Feshbach & Weiner, 1996; Garb & others, 2001; Hunsley & Bailey, 2001; Weiner, 2004). The test's reliability and validity have both been criticized. If the Rorschach were reliable, two different scorers would agree on the personality characteristics of the individual being tested. If the Rorschach were valid, it would predict behavior outside of the testing situation; that is, it would predict, for example, whether an individual will attempt suicide, become severely depressed, cope successfully with stress, or get along well with others. Conclusions based on research evidence suggest that the Rorschach does not meet these criteria of reliability and validity (Lilienfeld, Wood, & Garb, 2000). Thus, many psychologists have serious reservations about the Rorschach's use in diagnosis and clinical practice.

FIGURE 10.9

Picture from the Thematic Apperception Test (TAT) What are these two women thinking and feeling? How did they come to this situation, and what will happen next? A psychologist who uses the TAT would analyze your story to find out your unconscious motives.

Reprinted by permission of the publishers from *Thematic Apperception Test* by Henry A. Murray, Card 12F, Cambridge, Mass.: Harvard University Press. Copyright © 1943 by the President and the Fellows of Harvard College. Copyright © 1971 by Henry A. Murray.

Thematic Apperception Test (TAT)
A projective test that is designed to elicit stories that reveal something about an individual's personality.

Although still administered in clinical circles, the Rorschach is not commonly used in personality research. However, the projective method itself remains a tool for studying personality, especially in the form of the Thematic Apperception Test (TAT).

The **Thematic Apperception Test (TAT),** developed by Henry Murray and Christiana Morgan in the 1930s, is designed to elicit stories that reveal something about an individual's personality. The TAT consists of a series of pictures like the one in Figure 10.9, each on an individual card or slide. The TAT test taker is asked to tell a story about each of the pictures, including events leading up to the situation described, the characters' thoughts and feelings, and the way the situation turns out. The tester assumes that the person projects his or her own unconscious feelings and thoughts into the story (Woike, 2008). In addition to being administered as a projective test in clinical practice, the TAT is used in research on people's need for achievement, affiliation, power, intimacy, and a variety of other needs (Brunstein & Maier, 2005; Schultheiss & Brunstein, 2005; C. P. Smith, 1992); unconscious defense mechanisms (Cramer, 2008, 2008a; Cramer & Jones, 2007); and cognitive styles (Woike, 2008; Woike & Matic, 2004; Woike, Mcleod, & Goggin, 2003). In contrast to the Rorschach, TAT measures have shown high inter-rater reliability and validity (Woike, 2001).

Other Assessment Methods

Self-report questionnaires and projective techniques are just two of the multitude of assessment methods developed and used by personality psychologists. Personality psychologists might also measure behavior directly, by observing a person either live or in

Approach	Summary	Assumptions	Typical Methods	Sample Research Question
Psychodynamic	Personality is characterized by unconscious processes. Childhood experiences are of great importance to adult personality.	The most important aspects of personality are unconscious.	Case studies, projective techniques.	How do unconscious conflicts lead to dysfunctional behavior?
Humanistic	Personality evolves out of the person's innate, organismic motives to grow and actualize the self. These healthy tendencies can be undermined by social pressure.	Human nature is basically good. By getting in touch with who we are and what we really want, we can lead happier, healthier lives.	Questionnaires, interviews, observation.	Can situations be changed to support individuals' organismic values and enhance their well-being?
Social Cognitive	Personality is the pattern of coherence that characterizes a person's interactions with the situations he or she encounters in life. The individual's beliefs and expectations, rather than global traits, are the central variables of interest.	Behavior is best understood as changing across situations. To understand personality, we must understand what each situation means for a given person.	Multiple observations over different situations; videotaped behaviors rated by coders; questionnaires.	When and why do individuals respond to challenging tasks with fear vs. excitement?
Trait	Personality is characterized by five general traits that are represented in the natural language that people use to describe themselves and others.	Traits are relatively stable over time. Traits predict behavior.	Questionnaires, observer reports.	Are the five factors universal across cultures?
Personology and Life Story	To understand personality we must understand the whole person. We all have unique life experiences, and the stories we tell about those experiences make up our identities.	The life story provides a unique opportunity to examine the personality processes associated with behavior, development, and well-being.	Written narratives, TAT stories, autobiographical memories, interviews, and psychobiography.	How do narrative accounts of life experiences relate to happiness?
Biological	Personality characteristics reflect underlying biological processes such as those carried out by the brain, neurotransmitters, and genes. Differences in behaviors, thoughts, and feelings depend on these processes.	Biological differences among individuals can explain differences in their personalities.	Brain imagining, twin studies, molecular genetic studies.	Do genes explain individual differences in extraversion?

FIGURE 10.10

Approaches to Personality Psychology This figure summarizes the broad approaches to personality described in this chapter. Many researchers in personality do not stick with just one approach but apply the various theories and methods that are most relevant to their research questions.

a video. In addition, cognitive assessments have become more common in personality psychology, as researchers probe such topics as the relationship between personality and processes of attention and memory. Many personality psychologists incorporate friend or peer ratings of individuals' traits or other characteristics. Personality psychologists also employ a host of psychophysiological measures, such as heart rate and skin conductance. Increasingly, personality psychologists are incorporating brain imaging as well.

Whether personality assessments are being used by clinical psychologists, psychological researchers, or other practitioners, the choice of assessment instrument depends on the researcher's theoretical perspective. Figure 10.10 lists which methods are associated with each perspective, summarizes each approach and its major assumptions, and gives a sample research question for each. Personality psychology is a diverse field, unified by a shared interest in understanding the person—that is, *you*.

1. An empirically keyed test is one that
   A. has right and wrong answers.
   B. discriminates between different groups.
   C. has face validity.
   D. has both easy and difficult questions.

2. A problem with self-report tests, and one that researchers try to overcome, is the issue of
   A. social desirability.
   B. memory lapse.
   C. participant bias.
   D. scorer bias.

3. The assessment technique that asks participants to tell a story about the stimuli they see is the

A. Rorschach inkblot test.
B. Minnesota Multiphasic Personality Inventory (MMPI).
C. NEO-P-I.
D. Thematic Apperception Test (TAT).

Apply It! 4. Hank applies for a job as a ticket taker at a movie theater. After his initial interview, he is asked to complete a set of questionnaires. That night, talking with friends, he brags, "They had me answer all these questions about whether I would ever steal from work, gossip about people, or sneak into a movie theater without paying. Of course, I just lied about everything! They'll never know. The job is mine." One of Hank's friends has taken

introductory psychology and has news for Hank. Which of the following best captures what he will say?
A. Good job, Hank. They have no way of knowing you lied. Good luck with job!
B. Hank, if you lied on all the questions to make yourself look good, they will be able to detect it. It's called social desirability, and you fell for it.
C. Hank, unless the measures involved telling stories, your lies will never be revealed.
D. Hank, you will probably get the job, but your future employer sounds naïve. Didn't they know you could just lie on those tests?

summary

① Psychodynamic Perspectives

Freud developed psychoanalysis through his work with patients suffering from hysterical symptoms (physical symptoms with no physical cause). Freud viewed these symptoms as representing conflicts between sexual drive and duty. Freud believed that most personality—which, in his theory, includes components he called the id, ego, and superego—is unconscious. The ego uses various defense mechanisms, Freud said, to reduce anxiety.

A number of theorists criticized and revised Freud's approach. Horney said that the need for security, not sex or aggression, is our most important need. Jung developed the concept of the collective unconscious, a storehouse of archetypes. Adler's individual psychology stresses that people are striving toward perfection.

Weaknesses of the psychodynamic perspectives include overreliance on reports from the past and overemphasis of the unconscious mind. Strengths of psychodynamic approaches include recognizing the importance of childhood, conceptualizing development through stages, and calling attention to the role of unconscious processes in behavior.

② Humanistic Perspectives

Humanistic perspectives stress a person's capacity for personal growth and positive human qualities. Maslow developed the concept of a

hierarchy of needs, with self-actualization being the highest human need. In Rogers's approach, each of us is born with a tendency toward growth, a sense of what is good and bad for us, and a need for unconditional positive regard. Because we are often denied unconditional positive regard, we may become alienated from our innate growth tendencies. In order to reconnect with these innate tendencies, Rogers felt, a person required a relationship that included unconditional positive regard, empathy, and genuineness.

The humanistic perspectives promote the positive capacities of human beings. The weaknesses of the approach are a tendency to be too optimistic and an inclination to downplay personal responsibility.

③ Trait Perspectives

Trait theories emphasize that personality consists of traits—broad, enduring dispositions that lead to characteristic responses. Allport stated that traits should produce consistent behavior in different situations, and he used the lexical approach to personality traits, which involves using all the words in the natural language that could describe a person as a basis for understanding the traits of personality.

The current dominant perspective in personality psychology is the five-factor model. The big five traits include neuroticism, extraversion, openness to experience, agreeableness, and conscientiousness.

Extraversion is related to enhanced well-being, and neuroticism is linked to lowered well-being.

Studying people in terms of their traits has value. However, trait approaches are criticized for focusing on broad dimensions and not attending to each person's uniqueness.

④ Personological and Life Story Perspectives

Murray described personology as the study of the whole person. Contemporary followers of Murray study personality through narrative accounts and interviews. McAdams introduced the life story approach to identity, which views identity as a constantly changing story with a beginning, a middle, and an end. Psychobiography is a form of personological investigation that applies personality theory to one person's life.

Life story approaches to personality reveal the richness of each person's unique life story. However, this work can be very difficult to carry out.

⑤ Social Cognitive Perspectives

Social cognitive theory states that behavior, environment, and person/cognitive factors are important in understanding personality. In Bandura's view, these factors reciprocally interact.

Two key concepts in social cognitive theory are self-efficacy and personal control. Self-efficacy is the belief that one can master a situation and produce positive outcomes. Personal control refers to individuals' beliefs about whether the outcomes of their actions depend on their own internal acts or on external events.

In 1968, Mischel published a controversial book, *Personality and Assessment,* that stressed that people do not behave consistently across different situations but rather tailor their behavior to suit particular situations. Personality psychologists countered that personality does predict behavior for some people some of the time. Very specific personality characteristics predict behavior better than very general ones, and personality characteristics are more likely to predict behavior in weak versus strong situations.

Mischel developed a revised approach to personality centered on a cognitive affective processing system (CAPS). According to CAPS, personality is best understood as a person's habitual emotional and cognitive reactions to specific situations.

A particular strength of social cognitive theory is its focus on cognitive processes. However, social cognitive approaches have not given adequate attention to enduring individual differences, to biological factors, and to personality as a whole.

⑥ Biological Perspectives

Eysenck suggested that the brain's reticular activation system (RAS) plays a role in introversion/extraversion. He thought of these traits as the outward manifestations of arousal regulation. Gray developed a reward sensitivity theory of personality, suggesting that extraversion and neuroticism can be understood as two neurological systems that respond to rewards (the behavioral approach system, or BAS) and punishments (the behavioral inhibition system, or BIS) in the environment.

Dopamine is associated with behavioral approach (extraversion), and serotonin with behavioral avoidance (neuroticism). Behavioral genetics studies have shown that the heritability of personality traits is about 50 percent. Studies of biological processes in personality are valuable but can overestimate the causal role of biological factors.

⑦ Personality Assessment

Self-report tests assess personality by asking participants about their preferences and behaviors. One problem in self-report research is the tendency for individuals to respond in socially desirable ways. Empirically keyed tests avoid social desirability problems by using items that distinguish between groups even if we do not know why the items do so.

The most popular test for assessing the big five traits is the NEO-PI-R, which uses self-report items to measure each of the traits. The Minnesota Multiphasic Personality Inventory (MMPI) is the most widely used empirically keyed personality test.

Projective tests, designed to assess unconscious aspects of personality, present individuals with an ambiguous stimulus, such as an inkblot or a picture, and ask them to tell a story about it. Projective tests are based on the assumption that individuals will project their personalities onto these stimuli. The Thematic Apperception Test (TAT) is a projective test that has been used in personality research. Other assessment methods include behavioral observation, obtaining peer reports, and psychophysiological and neuropsychological measures.

key terms

self-test

Multiple Choice

1. Psychologists who study personality investigate
   A. the distinctive thoughts, emotions, and behavior that individuals demonstrate over time.
   B. relatively permanent changes in behavior due to experience.
   C. the organization of sensation into a meaningful interpretation.
   D. the pleasantness or sociability of an individual.

2. The strongest proponents of the role of the unconscious mind in personality are
   A. humanists.
   B. psychodynamic theorists.
   C. behaviorists.
   D. trait theorists.

3. According to Freud, the personality structure that negotiates the pull between a person's baser needs and higher conscience is the
   A. superego.
   B. alter ego.
   C. ego.
   D. id.

4. The theorist who emphasized unconditional positive regard was
   A. Carl Jung.
   B. Karen Horney.
   C. Henry Murray.
   D. Carl Rogers.

5. Broad, enduring dispositions that produce characteristic responses are called
   A. attitudes.
   B. traits.
   C. schemas.
   D. archetypes.

6. Jaime is punctual, hardworking, shy, and conservative. Jaime is likely to be
   A. high in agreeableness, low in extraversion, and high in openness to experience.
   B. low in extraversion, high in conscientiousness, and low in openness to experience.
   C. high in conscientiousness, low in neuroticism, and high in extraversion.
   D. low in conscientiousness, low in openness to experience, and high in extraversion.

7. The perspective on understanding personality that focuses on situational factors is the
   A. psychodynamic approach.
   B. trait approach.
   C. personological approach.
   D. social cognitive approach.

8. Gray's reinforcement sensitivity theory is based on an organism's attention and sensitivity to
   A. cues and feedback from others.
   B. rewards and punishments in the organism's environment.
   C. stressors in the organism's environment.
   D. the impact of experiences early in the life span.

9. The Thematic Apperception Test (TAT) is consistent with
   A. personology.
   B. the humanistic approach to personality.
   C. the social cognitive approach to personality.
   D. trait perspectives.

10. The Minnesota Multiphasic Personality Inventory (MMPI) is a
    A. projective test.
    B. reliable but not valid test.
    C. face valid test.
    D. self-report test.

Apply It!

11. Personality psychologists often consider the role of childhood experience in adult personality. Choose something about your childhood (a particularly vivid memory or pattern of experiences) and describe how it is reflected in your current personality, drawing on the work of Freud, Adler, and Rogers.

11 Social Psychology

Rosa Parks: Spurring Social Action

Humans are social animals. The influence of other people is evident in just about every aspect of our lives. For example, it is highly unlikely that you have made all of your own clothes, built your own home, and hunted and gathered your own food.

Groups of people can do more than any individual acting alone, and social progress often occurs through group action. Rosa Parks (1913–2005) became a heroine of the civil rights movement when, on December 1, 1955, in Montgomery, Alabama, she refused to give up her seat on a bus to a White man. Ms. Parks is rightfully recognized as an individual who stood up (or, actually, sat down) for social equality, but she was also part of a larger social movement. Her defiant actions triggered a massive bus boycott that would spur many other such group protests and bring civil rights reforms to U.S. society.

Groups can also have powerful negative effects. Acting as part of a group, individuals may engage in abominable behavior that they would never do if acting alone. The lynchings that occurred in the South in reaction to Blacks' efforts to achieve racial equality exemplify the negative influence that groups can have on behavior. ■

- **When was the last time you stood up against group pressure?**

- **Does your behavior change when you are in a group?**

- **How have social movements influenced your life?**

We begin the chapter by examining humans' social cognitive nature and by subsequently exploring social behavior, zeroing in on its extreme forms: altruism and aggression. We next look at the two-way street of social influence: how we influence others and how they influence us. After that we consider how the groups to which we belong shape our interactions with other groups. Finally, we probe the world of close relationships, including attraction and love.

1 Social Cognition

Social psychology is the study of how people think about, influence, and relate to other people. There are probably few issues reported in the news today that social psychologists have not studied. As you will see, social psychologists take many of the topics we have covered so far—including perception, cognition, emotion, and personality—and examine them in a social context.

Social cognition is the area of social psychology that explores how people select, interpret, remember, and use social information (Augoustinos, Walker, & Donaghue, 2006). Essentially, it is the way in which individuals think in social situations (Strack & Forster, 2009; Wyer, 2007).

social psychology
The study of how people think about, influence, and relate to other people.

We've discussed cognition in previous chapters. Some have argued that social cognition—thinking about other people—is more fundamental than thinking about anything else.

Person Perception

Person perception refers to the processes by which we use social stimuli to form impressions of others (Smith & Collins, 2009). One important social cue is the face (Hall & others, 2009). Alexander Todorov and his colleagues (2005) asked people to rate the competence of individuals from photographs of their faces. The faces belonged to candidates in the 2000, 2002, and 2004 U.S. House and Senate elections. Respondents' ratings accurately predicted the outcome for about *70 percent* of the elections. Apparently, those faces gave away information about the candidates that was meaningful to the perceivers. Other aspects of faces can also have important implications for social perception, as we now consider.

Physical Attractiveness and Other Perceptual Cues
Physical attractiveness is a powerful social cue. Judith Langlois and her colleagues (Hoss & Langlois, 2003; Ramsey & others, 2004) found that even infants as young as 3 to 6 months of age prefer looking at attractive faces versus unattractive faces (as rated by adults). Attractive individuals are generally assumed to have a variety of other positive characteristics, including being better adjusted, socially skilled, friendly, likable, extraverted, and likely to achieve superior job performance (Langlois & others, 2000). These positive expectations for physically attractive individuals are called the "beautiful is good" stereotype.

stereotype
A generalization about a group's characteristics that does not consider any variations from one individual to another.

A **stereotype** is a generalization about a group's characteristics that does not consider any variations from one individual to another. Stereotypes are a natural extension of the limits on human cognitive processing and our reliance on concepts in cognitive processing (Wegener, Clark, & Petty, 2006). We simplify the task of understanding people by classifying them as members of groups or categories with which we are familiar. It takes more mental effort to consider a person's individual characteristics than it does to label him or her as a member of a particular group. Thus, when we categorize an individual, that categorization often reflects stereotyping.

Recall the discussion of concepts in Chapter 7—we use concepts to simplify the world. However, when we use concepts to understand groups of people, we are stereotyping.

Is there any truth to the "beautiful is good" stereotype? Research has shown that attractive people may indeed possess a number of positive characteristics (Langlois & others, 2000). Does that mean that attractiveness is naturally related to, for example, better social skills? Not necessarily.

How do you think the teachers influenced the late bloomers? What kinds of behaviors led to the kids' enhanced performance?

One way that stereotypes can influence individuals is through a phenomenon called *self-fulfilling prophecy*. In a self-fulfilling prophecy, expectations cause individuals to act in ways that serve to make the expectations come true. Robert Rosenthal and Lenore Jacobsen conducted the classic self-fulfilling prophecy study in 1968. The researchers told grade-school teachers that five students were likely to be "late bloomers"—that these students had high levels of ability that would likely shine forth over time. In reality, the students had been randomly selected by the researchers. Nonetheless, a year later, the researchers found that teachers' expectations for the "late bloomers" were reflected in student performance—the academic performance of the "late bloomers" was beyond that of other students. Self-fulfilling prophecy effects show the potential power of stereotypes and other sources of expectations on human behavior.

How might self-fulfilling prophecy effects apply when people interact with physically attractive versus unattractive individuals? Consider that attractive people may receive differential treatment from others throughout their lives. This special treatment increases the likelihood that the attractive individuals might well develop enhanced social skills and be more self-confident than others.

Another relevant question is, what makes a face attractive? *People* magazine's "50 Most Beautiful People" issue might lead you to conclude that attractiveness is about being exceptional in some way: Consider Angelina Jolie's sensuous lips or George Clooney's dreamy eyes. Research has examined what specifically makes a face attractive, with some surprising results. Using computer technology that allowed them to average together digitized photographs of a large group of individuals of varying attractiveness, Langlois and her colleagues (1994) created composite faces. A large sample of college students then rated the individual faces and the composites. The results showed that individual faces were less attractive than faces that were created by averaging 8, 16, or 32 other faces. The researchers concluded that attractive faces are actually "just average." Although "averageness" is not the only predictor of attractiveness, Langlois and her colleagues suggest that being average is an essential component (along with variables such as symmetry and youthfulness) of facial attractiveness.

Check out this website to see how the averaging of faces works: http://www.faceresearch.org/demos/average. Pick some faces you consider unattractive. What happens when you average them together? If you have a digital photograph of yourself and some friends, see what happens when you average those faces. Do you agree that average faces are more attractive than any single face?

Cornered
by Mike Baldwin

"Thank God we're cute. You only get one chance to make a good first impression."

First Impressions
When we first meet someone, typically the new acquaintance makes a quick impression on us. That first impression can have lasting effects (Bar, Neta, & Linz, 2006). Recall the primacy effect from Chapter 6—people's tendency to attend to and remember what they learned first (Anderson, 1965). The power of first impressions is likely due to just such an effect. In one recent study, judgments made after just a 100-millisecond exposure time to unfamiliar faces was sufficient for individuals to form an impression (Willis & Todorov, 2006).

Of course, once you become acquainted with someone, you have a lot more information to use to form an opinion about him or her. The process by which we come to understand the causes of others' behavior and form an impression of them as individuals is called *attribution*.

Attribution

Trying to understand why people do the things they do—this puzzle fascinates not only psychologists but all of us. Finding causal explanations for the many things that people do is a complex task (Hilton, 2007). We can observe people's behavior and listen to what they say, but to determine the underlying cause of their behavior, we often have to make inferences from these observations. We take the information we have and come up with a good guess about who they are and what they are likely to do in the future (Gaunt & Trope, 2007; Krueger, 2007).

Attribution theory (Heider, 1958; Kelley, 1973; Weiner, 2006) views people as motivated to discover the underlying causes of behavior as part of their effort to make sense of the behavior. Attributions vary along three dimensions (Jones, 1998):

attribution theory
The view that people are motivated to discover the underlying causes of behavior as part of their effort to make sense of the behavior.

- *Internal/external causes:* Internal attributions include causes inside and specific to the person, such as his or her traits and abilities. External attributions include causes outside the person, such as social pressure, aspects of the social situation, and the weather. Did Beth get an *A* on the test because she is smart or because the test was easy?

- *Stable/unstable causes:* Is the cause relatively enduring and permanent, or is it temporary? Did Aaron blow up at his girlfriend because he is a hostile guy or because he was in a bad mood that day?

- *Controllable/uncontrollable causes:* We perceive that we have power over some causes (for instance, by preparing delicious food for a picnic) but not others (rain on picnic day).

Attributional Errors and Biases

fundamental attribution error
Observers' over-estimation of the importance of internal traits and underestimation of the importance of external situations when they seek explanations of an actor's behavior.

In attribution theory, the person who produces the behavior to be explained is called the *actor*. The person who offers a causal explanation of the actor's behavior is called the *observer*. Actors often explain their own behavior in terms of external causes. In contrast, observers frequently explain the actor's behavior in terms of internal causes. Susannah might explain that she honked her car horn at someone who was slow to move when the light turned green because she was in a hurry to get to the hospital to see her ill father, but the driver she honked at might think she was rude.

In committing the **fundamental attribution error,** observers overestimate the importance of internal traits and underestimate the importance of external situations when they seek explanations of an actor's behavior (Gilbert & Malone, 1995; Jones & Harris, 1967) (Figure 11.1). For example, news coverage of Hurricane Katrina conveyed grim images of individuals who had not evacuated and were left homeless and helpless in the storm's aftermath. An observer might have concluded, "They were foolish not to get out in time." In fact, situational factors, including lacking financial resources or a means of transportation, may have prevented them from leaving.

Heuristics in Social Information Processing

Heuristics, as described in Chapter 7, are cognitive shortcuts that allow us to make decisions rapidly. Just as heuristics are useful in information processing generally, they can play a role in social information processing (Chaiken & Ledgerwood, 2007; Reimer & Rieskamp, 2007). Indeed, heuristics are sometimes helpful tools for navigating the complex social

Observer Tends to give internal, trait explanations of actor's behavior

"She's late with her report because she can't concentrate on her own responsibilities."

Actor Tends to give external, situational explanations of own behavior

"I'm late with my report because other people keep asking me to help them with their projects."

FIGURE 11.1
The Fundamental Attribution Error In this situation, the supervisor is the observer, and the employee is the actor.

landscape, although they can lead to mistakes (Weaver & others, 2007). Stereotypes can be considered a type of heuristic in that they allow us to make quick judgments using very little information.

Recall that the availability heuristic is the tendency to confuse the probability of an event's occurrence with the ease with which you can imagine it. For example, having never met an African American physician, an African American student might not consider pre-med as a major.

Another common heuristic is the false consensus effect. Ask yourself: "How many students at your school support the death penalty?" Your answer is likely to depend on whether *you* support the death penalty. The **false consensus effect** is the overestimation of the degree to which everybody else thinks or acts the way we do. False consensus effects can be important in social interactions. Imagine for example that someone in a group to which you belong makes a racially insensitive remark. According to the false consensus effect, that person is likely to interpret silence on the part of others in the group as agreement.

The fundamental attribution error and the false consensus effect are related to the special significance of our personal thoughts and circumstances as we process social information. Both effects reflect the vast amount of information we have about ourselves relative to the more limited information we have about others, and they suggest the special place of the self in social information processing.

false consensus effect Observers' overestimation of the degree to which everybody else thinks or acts the way they do.

The Self as a Social Object

Each of us carries around mental representations of ourselves. We can think of the self as our schema for who we are, what we are like, and how we feel about these perceptions. The self is different from other social objects because we know so much more about ourselves than we do about others. While we are more likely to think that behavior is very important to understanding who other people really are, we are more likely to think that our private thoughts and feelings are most indicative of our true self (Johnson, Robinson, & Mitchell, 2004).

 *Recall from Chapter 4 how important consciousness is to our sense of self.*

The self is special not only because we have direct access to these private experiences but also because we value ourselves. One of the most important self-related variables is *self-esteem,* the degree to which we have positive or negative feelings about ourselves (Harter, 2006). In general, research has shown that it is good to feel good about oneself (Bosson & Swann, 2009).

Individuals with high self-esteem often possess a variety of **positive illusions**—favorable views of themselves that are not necessarily rooted in reality. Constantine Sedikides and his colleagues have shown that many of us think of ourselves as above average on a number of valued characteristics, including how trustworthy and attractive we are (Sedikides, 2007, 2009; Sedikides, Gaertner, & Vevea, 2005; Sedikides & Gregg, 2008; Sedikides & Skowronski, 2009). Of course, the very definition of *average* indicates that not all of us can be "above average."

positive illusions Favorable views of the self that are not necessarily rooted in reality.

Shelley Taylor and her colleagues (2003a, 2003b, 2007; Taylor & Sherman, 2008) have demonstrated that having positive illusions about the self is often related to heightened well-being. Individuals who tend to have positive illusions about themselves are psychologically healthier and more likely to be judged positively by others. Self-esteem also affects our attributions about our own behavior. Individuals with high self-esteem, for instance, tend to give themselves breaks when it comes to judging their own behavior.

Self-serving bias refers to the tendency to take credit for our successes and to deny responsibility for our failures. Think about taking a psychology exam. If you do well, you are likely to take credit for that success ("I'm smart" or "I knew that

self-serving bias The tendency to take credit for our successes and to deny responsibility for our failures.

stuff")—that is, to make internal attributions. If you do poorly, however, you are more likely to blame situational factors ("The test was too hard")—that is, to make external attributions.

Stereotype Threat

Stereotypes can influence the members of stereotyped groups (Seacat & Mickelson, 2009; Wout & others, 2009). **Stereotype threat** is an individual's fast-acting, self-fulfilling fear of being judged based on a negative stereotype about his or her group. A person who experiences stereotype threat is well aware of stereotypical expectations for him or her as a member of the group. In stereotype-relevant situations, the individual experiences anxiety about living "down" to expectations and consequently underperforms (Schmader & others, 2009). Claude Steele and Eliot Aronson (1995, 2004) have shown that when a test is presented to African American and Euro-American students who have first simply checked a box indicating their ethnicity, the African Americans perform more poorly. In situations where ethnicity was not made salient, no differences in performance emerged.

Imagine what might happen to scores if standardized tests did not ask questions about gender or ethnicity until the end of the test.

Research has also demonstrated that stereotype threat affects performance on math tests by women compared to men, even when both groups have equally strong math training (Spencer, Steele, & Quinn, 1999). White men, too, can fall prey to stereotype threat; in a study of golf ability, Euro-American men performed more poorly than African American men when they were told the test measured "natural athletic ability" (Stone, 2002). Asian women perform better on a math test if asked first for their ethnicity, but more poorly if asked first about their gender (Shih & others, 2007).

Social Comparison

Have you ever felt a sense of accomplishment about getting a *B* on a test, only to feel deflated when you found out that your friend in the class got an *A?* We gain self-knowledge from our own behavior, of course, but we also acquire it from others through **social comparison,** the process by which we evaluate our thoughts, feelings, behaviors, and abilities in relation to others. Social comparison helps us to evaluate ourselves, tells us what our distinctive characteristics are, and aids us in building an identity.

Over 50 years ago, Leon Festinger (1954) proposed a theory of social comparison. According to this theory, when we lack objective means to evaluate our opinions and abilities, we compare ourselves with others. Furthermore, to get an accurate appraisal of ourselves, we are most likely to compare ourselves with others who are similar to us. Social comparison theory has been extended and modified over the years and continues to provide an important rationale for how we come to know ourselves (Mussweiler, 2009).

Festinger concentrated on comparisons with those who are similar to us; other researchers have focused on downward social comparisons, that is, comparisons with people whom we consider inferior to us. Individuals under threat (from negative feedback or low self-esteem, for example) try to feel better by comparing themselves with others who are less fortunate (Wayment & O'Mara, 2008).

What are your attitudes about social issues such as the death penalty, the right to bear arms, and the growing scarcity of natural resources? How do these views influence your behavior?

Attitudes

Attitudes are our feelings or opinions about people, objects, and ideas. We have attitudes about all sorts of things. Social psychologists are interested in how attitudes relate to behavior and in whether and how attitudes can change (Jost, Federico, & Napier, 2009).

Can Attitudes Predict Behavior?

People sometimes say one thing but do another. You might report positive attitudes about recycling on a survey but still pitch an aluminum soda can in the trash. Studies over the past half-century indicate some of the conditions under which attitudes guide actions (McGuire, 2004; Schomerus, Matschinger, & Angermeyer, 2009):

■ *When the person's attitudes are strong* (Ajzen, 2001): For example, senators whose attitudes toward the president are "highly favorable" are more likely to vote for the president's policies than are senators who have only "moderately favorable" attitudes toward the chief executive.

■ *When the person shows a strong awareness of his or her attitudes and when the person rehearses and practices them* (Fazio & Olsen, 2007; Fazio & others, 1982): For example, a person who has been asked to give a speech about the benefits of recycling is more likely to recycle than is an individual with the same attitude about recycling who has not put the idea into words or defined it in public.

■ *When the person has a vested interest:* People are more likely to act on attitudes when the issue at stake will affect them personally. For example, a classic study examined whether students would show up for a rally protesting a change that would raise the legal drinking age from 18 to 21 (Sivacek & Crano, 1982). Although students in general were against the change, only those in the critical age group (from 18 to 20) turned out to protest.

Can Behavior Predict Attitudes?

Just as attitudes guide behavior, ample evidence also exists that changes in behavior sometimes precede changes in attitudes. Social psychologists offer two main explanations of why behavior influences attitudes: cognitive dissonance theory and self-perception theory.

Cognitive Dissonance Theory

Cognitive dissonance, a concept developed by Festinger (1957), is an individual's psychological discomfort (*dissonance*) caused by two inconsistent thoughts. According to the theory, we feel uneasy when we notice an inconsistency between what we believe and what we do.

> **cognitive dissonance**
> An individual's psychological discomfort (dissonance) caused by two inconsistent thoughts.

Remember, random assignment is used to make sure the groups are equal in every way except for the independent variable—which in this study was how much they were paid for the lie.

In a classic study of cognitive dissonance, Festinger and J. Merrill Carlsmith (1959) asked college students to engage in very boring tasks such as sorting spools into trays and turning wooden pegs. The participants were later asked to persuade another student (who was in fact a confederate) to participate in the study by telling him that the task was interesting and enjoyable. Half of the participants were randomly assigned to be paid $1 for telling this white lie, and the other half received $20. Afterward, all of the participants rated how interesting and enjoyable the task really was.

This rating of enjoyment was the dependent variable.

Interestingly, those who were paid only $1 to tell the lie rated the task as significantly more enjoyable than those who were paid $20. Festinger and Carlsmith reasoned that those paid $20 to tell the lie could attribute their behavior to the high value of the money they received. On the other hand, those who were paid $1 experienced cognitive dissonance. The inconsistency between what they *did* (tell a lie) and what they *were paid for it* (just $1) moved these individuals to change their attitudes about the task ("I wouldn't lie for just $1. If I said I liked the task, I must have really liked it").

We can reduce cognitive dissonance in one of two ways: change our behavior to fit our attitudes or change our attitudes to fit our behavior. In the classic study above, participants changed their attitudes about the task to match their behavior. Thus, when our attitudes and behavior are at odds, our behavior can influence our attitudes. After you have pitched that soda can, for example, you might feel guilty and relieve that guilt by deciding, "Recycling is not really that important."

Effort justification, one type of dissonance reduction, means rationalizing the amount of effort we put into something. Effort justification explains strong feelings of loyalty toward a group based on the effort it takes to get into that group. Working hard to get into an organization (such as a Greek society or the Marines) or a profession (such as medicine or law) can change our attitudes about it. According to cognitive dissonance theory, individuals in these situations are likely to think, "If it's this tough to get into, it must be worth it."

self-perception theory
Bem's theory on how behaviors influence attitudes, stating that individuals make inferences about their attitudes by perceiving their behavior.

Self-Perception Theory   **Self-perception theory** is Daryl Bem's (1967) explanation of how behaviors influence attitudes. According to this theory, individuals make inferences about their attitudes by perceiving their behavior. That is, behaviors can cause attitudes because when we are questioned about our attitudes, we think back on our behaviors for information. When asked about your attitude toward exercise, for instance, you might think, "Well, I run every morning, so I must like it." From Bem's perspective, your behavior has led you to recognize something about yourself that you had not noticed before. Bem believes that we are especially likely to look to our own behavior to determine our attitudes when our attitudes are not completely clear, and research has supported this assertion (Olson & Stone, 2005).

Figure 11.2 compares cognitive dissonance theory and self-perception theory. Both theories have merit in explaining the connection between attitudes and behavior, and these opposing views bring to light the complexity that may exist in this connection.

Festinger Cognitive Dissonance Theory	**Bem Self-Perception Theory**
We are motivated toward consistency between attitudes and behavior and away from inconsistency.	We make inferences about our attitudes by perceiving and examining our behavior and the context in which it occurs, which might involve inducements to behave in certain ways.
Example: "I hate my job. I need to develop a better attitude toward it or else quit."	*Example: "I am spending all of my time thinking about how much I hate my job. I really must not like it."*

FIGURE 11.2

Two Theories of the Connections Between Attitudes and Behavior Although we often think of attitudes as causing behavior, behavior can change attitudes, through either dissonance reduction or self-perception.

If you have ever played devil's advocate in an argument (arguing a point just for the sake of argument), you might have found yourself realizing that maybe you do hold the views you have pretended to advocate. That's self-perception theory at work.

Persuasion

Persuasion involves trying to change someone's attitude—and often his or her behavior as well. Two central questions with respect to persuasion are, what makes an individual decide to give up an original attitude and adopt a new one, and what makes a person decide to act on an attitude that he or she has not acted on before? Teachers, lawyers, and sales representatives study techniques that will help them sway their audiences (children, juries, and buyers). Presidential candidates have arsenals of speechwriters

Hillary Clinton called on her powers of persuasion when she ran for president in 2008, and she relies on persuasion today in her role as secretary of state.

Social Cognition   **383**

and image consultants to help ensure that their words are persuasive. Perhaps the most skilled persuaders of all are advertisers, who combine a full array of techniques to sell everything from cornflakes to carpets to cars. Carl Hovland and his colleagues originally identified the elements of persuasion as follows (Hovland, Janis, & Kelley, 1953; Janis & Hovland, 1959):

- *The communicator (source):* Suppose you are running for student body president. You tell your fellow students that you are going to make life at your college better. Will they believe you? Most likely, that will depend on your characteristics as a communicator. Whether they believe you will depend in large part on your credibility—that is, how much other students trust what you say. Trustworthiness, expertise, power, attractiveness, likeability, and similarity are all credibility characteristics that help a communicator change people's attitudes or convince them to act.

- *The message:* What kind of message is persuasive? One line of research has focused on whether a rational strategy (presenting logic and fact) or an emotional strategy (using fear or anger) is more effective.

    Emotional appeals are very powerful (Visser & Cooper, 2007). In the 2004 presidential race, a group called the Swift Boat Veterans launched a scathing attack on Democratic candidate and Vietnam veteran John Kerry that people on both sides of the party fence condemned. The term *swift boating* has become synonymous with unjustified negative political attacks. Such negative appeals play to the audience's emotions.

- *The medium:* Another persuasion factor is the medium or technology used to get the message across. Consider the difference between watching a presidential debate on television and reading about it in the newspaper. Because it presents live images, television is generally a more powerful medium than print sources for changing attitudes.

- *The target (audience):* Age and attitude strength are two characteristics of the audience that determine whether a message will be effective. Younger people are more likely to change their attitudes than older ones. Weaker attitudes on the part of the audience make attitude change more likely than do strong attitudes.

A strong argument should work, no matter who it comes from or how it is presented, right? One model that seeks to explain how different aspects of appeals influence persuasion is the **elaboration likelihood model.** This theory identifies two ways to persuade: a central route and a peripheral route (DeMarree & Petty, 2007; Petty & Brinol, 2008; Petty & Cacioppo, 1986). The central route works by engaging someone thoughtfully, with a sound, logical argument. The peripheral route involves non-message factors such as the source's credibility and attractiveness or emotional appeals. The peripheral route is effective when people are not paying close attention to or do not have the time or energy to think about the message. Television advertisers often use the peripheral route to persuasion on the assumption that during commercials, you are probably not paying full attention to the screen. However, the central route is more persuasive when people have the ability and the motivation to pay attention to the facts (Sparks & Areni, 2008).

Attitudes that are changed using the central route are more likely to persist than attitudes that are changed using the peripheral route.

elaboration likelihood model Theory identifying two ways to persuade: a central route and a peripheral route.

How can we resist persuasion? William McGuire (2003; McGuire & Papageorgis, 1961) has suggested that *inoculation* is one way not to fall victim to persuasion. McGuire proposed that just as administering a vaccine inoculates individuals from a virus by introducing a weakened or dead version of that virus to the immune system, giving people a weak version of a persuasive message and allowing them time to argue against it can help them avoid persuasion. Research has shown that such inoculation helps college students resist plagiarism (Compton & Pfau, 2008) as well as credit card marketing appeals (Compton & Pfau, 2004)

Consider yourself warned: Credit card companies often prey on college students.

psychology
in our world

Clinching the Sale

At some point, nearly everyone is in the position of having to sell something. Social psychologists have studied a variety of ways in which social psychological principles influence whether a seller makes that sale.

One strategy for closing a sale is the *foot-in-the-door* technique (Freedman & Fraser, 1966). The foot-in-the-door strategy involves making a smaller request (Would you be interested in a three-month trial subscription to a magazine?) at the beginning and saving the biggest demand (How about a full year?) for last. The foot-in-the-door strategy relies on the notion that in agreeing to the smaller offer, the customer has developed a relationship of trust with the seller.

Robert Cialdini and his colleagues (Cialdini & others, 1975) introduced a different strategy, the *door-in-the-face* technique. The door-in-the-face strategy involves making the biggest pitch at the beginning (Would you be interested in a full-year subscription?), which the customer probably will reject, and then making a smaller, "concessionary" demand (Okay, then, how about a three-month trial?). The door-in-the-face technique relies on the fact that the customer experiences a sense of reciprocity and obligation: Because you let him off the hook with that big request, maybe he should be nice and take that smaller offer.

Cognitive dissonance can also be used as a powerful tool in sales. Sometimes the harder we work to buy something, the more we want it. After all, did you *buy* that strange lamp on e-Bay—or did you *win* it?

self quiz

1. Stereotype threat refers to
   A. the damage potentially caused by stereotyping others.
   B. the strategy of changing someone's behavior by threatening to use a stereotype.
   C. humans' tendency to categorize people using broad generalizations.
   D. an individual's self-fulfilling fear of being judged based on a negative stereotype about his or her group.

2. In committing the fundamental attribution error, we overemphasize _____ and underemphasize _____ when making attributions about others' behavior.

   A. internal factors; external factors
   B. external factors; internal factors
   C. controllability; stability
   D. stability; controllability

3. Which of the following statements about positive illusions is *true*?
   A. Positive illusions are more common in people with low self-esteem.
   B. Positive illusions are accurate.
   C. Positive illusions have been linked to better well-being.
   D. Positive illusions are focused on actors rather than observers.

Apply It! 4. Thomas has spent long hours working to get his candidate elected president of the student body. When he talks to his mother on election night, Thomas is overjoyed to report that his candidate won by a landslide. His mom points out that Thomas never cared about campus politics before, and she asks him about his sudden interest. Thomas admits that she is right, but notes that he now cares deeply about campus issues and is likely to continue to be involved in politics. What theory best explains Thomas's change?
A. social comparison theory
B. self-perception theory
C. stereotype threat
D. the elaboration likelihood model

2 Social Behavior

We do not just think socially; we also behave in social ways. Two particular behaviors that have interested psychologists represent the extremes of human social activity: altruism and aggression.

Altruism

In 1998, Joyce Rush, a nurse and mother of five, presented herself to the surgeons at the Johns Hopkins Hospital transplant unit and offered to donate one of her kidneys to whoever might need it. Once news of her selfless act hit the media, the hospital received calls from numerous other potential live organ donors.

Other selfless acts of kindness include the huge relief efforts that have followed disasters like the massive China earthquake and the cyclone in Myanmar in 2008. In everyday life, we witness and perform "random acts of kindness"—maybe adding a quarter to someone's expired parking meter or giving up our seat on a bus to someone in need. We may volunteer for the Special Olympics or act as a literacy tutor. What all of these acts have in common is **altruism,** an unselfish interest in helping another person (Eisenberg & others, 2009).

Critical thinking means questioning what "everyone knows."

In examining potentially altruistic behavior (or *prosocial behavior*), psychologists commonly have questioned just how genuinely selfless it is, because "everyone knows" that people are naturally selfish. Dale Miller (1999, 2001) challenged this pessimistic view of humanity, which he called *homo-economicus*—the assumption that each person is out for his or her own gain. Miller suggested that although we are socialized to believe that humans are naturally selfish, a great deal of research indicates that humans are not necessarily self-centered and do not engage in selfish acts as a natural response (Holmes, Miller, & Lerner, 2002).

Do you think altruism is a puzzle to be solved—or a natural expression of human nature?

Altruism has presented a puzzle for evolutionary psychologists (Stewart-Williams, 2008; Van Vugt & Van Lange, 2006). How can a behavior that rewards others, and not oneself, be adaptive? Interestingly, kindness is not exclusive to humans. Ethologists studying nonhuman primates have shown that altruistic acts of kindness also occur in other species (de Waal, 1996, 2006; de Waal, Leimgruber, & Greenberg, 2008).

altruism
Unselfish interest in helping another person.

An example of animal altruism—a baboon plucking bugs from another baboon. Most acts of animal altruism involve kin.

Psychological Components of Altruism   A key aspect of altruism is *reciprocity,* which means acting kindly toward others because we assume that they will do the same for us in return. Reciprocity involves an expression of trust for another person, as well as feelings of obligation and guilt. Reciprocity was in evidence in a study in which college students were more likely to pledge to the charity of an individual who had previously bought them candy (Webster & others, 1999).

Not all seemingly altruistic behavior is unselfish. Some psychologists even argue that true altruism has never been demonstrated (Cialdini, 1991; Maner & others, 2002). **Egoism** involves giving to another person to ensure reciprocity; to gain self-esteem; to present oneself as powerful, competent, or caring; or to avoid social and self-censure for failing to live up to society's expectations. In contrast, true altruism means giving to another person with the ultimate goal of benefiting that person.

Another psychological component of altruistic behavior is mood. A strong conclusion from the research literature is that happy people are more likely to help (Snyder & Lopez, 2007). Does it then follow that when they are in a bad mood, people are less likely to help? Not necessarily, because adults (especially) generally understand that doing good for another person can be a mood booster. Thus, when in a bad mood, they might be likely to help if they think that doing so will improve their mood. Furthermore, sometimes those who have experienced

egoism
Giving to another person to ensure reciprocity; to gain self-esteem; to present oneself as powerful, competent, or caring; or to avoid social and self-censure for failing to live up to society's expectations.

distressing traumatic events find helping others to be an effective and meaningful way of coping (Staub & Vollhardt, 2008).

A key social emotion involved in altruism is empathy (Saarni & others, 2006). **Empathy** is a person's feeling of oneness with the emotional state of another. Daniel Batson (2002, 2006; Batson & others, 2007) has spent the better part of his career searching for proof that truly altruistic behavior does exist. The key to such altruism is the extent to which we can put ourselves in another's shoes. Empathy for someone else's plight moves us to action—not to make ourselves feel better but out of genuine concern for the other person. Empathy can produce altruistic behavior even toward members of rival groups and even when we believe no one will ever hear about our kind act (Fultz & others, 1986).

empathy
A feeling of oneness with the emotional state of another person.

What was the last altruistic act you committed? What led to your behavior?

Altruism and Gender

Given the role of empathy in helping, we might think that women should be more likely to help than men. After all, stereotypes tell us that women are more prone to empathy than men. However, as in most domains, it is a good idea to think about gender in context (Eisenberg & others, 2009). Researchers have found that women are more likely than men to help when the context involves nurturing, such as volunteering time to help a child with a personal problem. Men, on the other hand, are more likely to help in situations in which a perceived danger is present (for instance, picking up a hitchhiker) and in which they feel competent to help (as in assisting someone with a flat tire) (Eagly & Crowley, 1986).

The Bystander Effect

More than 45 years ago, a young woman named Kitty Genovese was brutally murdered in New York City. She was attacked at about 3 A.M. in a courtyard surrounded by apartment buildings. It took the slayer approximately 30 minutes to kill Genovese. Thirty-eight neighbors watched the gory scene from their windows and heard Genovese's screams. No one helped or called the police.

Inspired by the Genovese case, social psychologists John Darley and Bibb Latané (1968) conducted a number of studies on the **bystander effect,** the tendency for an individual who observes an emergency to help less when other people are present than when the observer is alone. Most bystander studies show that when alone, a person will help 75 percent of the time, but when another bystander is present, the figure drops to 50 percent. Apparently the difference is due to diffusion of responsibility among witnesses and the tendency to look to the behavior of others for cues about what to do. We may think that someone else will call the police or that, because no one else is helping, possibly the person does not need help.

bystander effect
The tendency for an individual who observes an emergency to help less when other people are present than when the observer is alone.

The bystander effect is still in evidence today. In August 2007, security cameras recorded the rape of a woman in the hallway of a St. Paul apartment building as 10 or so witnesses walked past. No one called the police (Volpe, 2007).

Whether people help can also depend on characteristics of the person in need of help or on the situation (Hardy & Van Vugt, 2006). Among these characteristics are the degree of need shown, the needy person's responsibility for his or her plight, the cost of assisting the needy person, and the extent to which reciprocity is expected (Batson, 2003, 2006; Penner & others, 2005). From an evolutionary perspective, helping is especially likely to occur between family members, because helping a relative also means promoting the survival of our own genes.

Some evolutionary scientists have suggested that altruism, especially when directed at members of our own group, is likely to exist alongside hostile feelings toward other groups (Arrow, 2007; Choi & Bowles, 2007). A soldier who fights for his country may be a hero of selfless altruism for members of his group, but for a person on the other side of combat, his behavior is harmful. Thus, altruism within a group may be linked to aggression, our next topic.

Aggression

Aggression refers to social behavior whose objective is to harm someone, either physically or verbally. Aggression is common in contemporary society. Murders in the United States take place at the rate of about 20,000 per year (U.S. Department of Justice, 2007).

aggression
Social behavior whose objective is to harm someone, either physically or verbally.

Perhaps the greatest puzzle of aggression is that a species capable of incredible acts of kindness can also perpetrate horrifying acts of violence.

Biological Influences   There is nothing new about human aggression. The primate ancestors of human beings and the earliest humans are thought to have committed aggressive acts against others of their own kind. Researchers who approach aggression from a biological viewpoint examine the influence of evolutionary tendencies, genetics, and neurobiological factors.

In the animal world, aggression often is ritualistic and typically involves threat displays such as a cat's arching its back, baring its teeth, and hissing.

Evolutionary Views   Ethologists say that certain stimuli release innate aggressive responses (Lorenz, 1965; Tinbergen, 1969). For example, a male robin will attack another male bird when it sees the red patch on the other bird's breast. When the patch is removed, no attack takes place. However, in the animal kingdom, most hostile encounters do not escalate to killing or even severe harm. Much of the fighting is ritualistic and involves threat displays, for example, a cat arching its back, baring its teeth, and hissing or a chimpanzee staring, stomping the ground, and screaming.

Evolutionary theorists believe that human beings are not much different from other animals. A basic theme of their theory is the survival of the fittest (Barber, 2009; Kardong, 2008). Thus, they conclude that early in human evolution the survivors were probably aggressive individuals.

Genetic Basis   Genes are important in explaining the biological basis of aggression (Brooker, 2009). The selective breeding of animals provides evidence for genetic influences in aggression. After a number of breedings among only aggressive animals and among only docile animals, vicious and timid strains of animals emerge.

The genetic basis for aggression is more difficult to demonstrate in humans than animals and may depend on the type of aggression studied (Baker & others, 2008; Brendgen & others, 2008). Twin studies have shown that physical aggression that is proactive in nature may be more influenced by genes, but more reactive aggression and social aggression (for instance, starting rumors about someone) may be more susceptible to environmental effects. Genetic influences may be stronger for males than females (Baker & others, 2008).

Neurobiological Factors   In 1966, Charles Whitman climbed to the top of the campus tower at the University of Texas at Austin and killed 15 people below with a high-powered rifle before he was felled by police bullets. Shortly before the rampage, he had murdered his wife and mother in their homes. An autopsy revealed a tumor in the limbic system of Whitman's brain, an area associated with emotion. Although humans do not appear to have a specific aggression center in the brain, aggressive behavior often results when areas such as the limbic system are stimulated by electric currents (Herbert, 1988; Wood & Liossi, 2006).

The brain's frontal lobes—the areas most involved in executive functions such as planning and self-control—have also been implicated in aggression. Research by Adriane Raine and his colleagues (Raine, 2008; Yang, Glen, & Raine, 2008) have examined the brains of individuals who have committed the ultimate act of violence: murder. The results indicate that murderers may differ from others in deficits in the functioning of these areas of the brain.

Neurotransmitters, and in particular lower levels of serotonin, have been linked to aggressive behavior (Carrillo & others, 2009). In one study, young men whose serotonin levels were low relative to those of other men their age were far more likely to have committed a violent crime (Moffitt & others, 1998). Similarly, aggressive children have lower levels of serotonin than do children who display low rates of aggression (Blader, 2006).

Hormones may also play a role in aggression (Susman & Dorn, 2009). Research on rats and other animals has shown that the hormone testosterone in particular relates to aggression (Cunningham & McGinnis, 2007). Results with humans have been less consistent (van Bokhoven & others, 2006), although higher testosterone levels have been found in incarcerated individuals convicted of especially ruthless murders (Dabbs, Riad, & Chance, 2001).

Importantly, behaving aggressively may itself increase a person's level of testosterone.

A fascinating study examined how testosterone is influenced by experience and how experience and testosterone together might help explain aggression (Klinesmith, Kasser, & McAndrew, 2006). In this study, college men interacted with either a gun or a child's toy. Testosterone was measured before and after this phase of the study. Men who interacted with the gun showed higher increases in testosterone, compared to the control group. Furthermore, later in the study, those men who had interacted with the gun were more aggressive (in this case, they put more hot sauce in a cup of water they thought someone else was going to drink). The fact that testosterone at least partially explains this increase in aggression suggests that testosterone changes may shed light on why some people respond to violent cues with more violent behavior than others (Klinesmith, Kasser, & McAndrew, 2006).

Note that many studies of aggression that have been conducted in social psychology laboratories rely on behaviors that may be considered aggressive even if they do not involve a violent physical act such as punching someone in the face. In studies on aggression, participants might have an opportunity to "aggress" against another, for instance, by subjecting the individual to a blast of loud noise, dispensing a mild electrical shock, or even, as described above, administering a large dose of Tabasco to swallow. Whether these operational definitions of aggression are applicable to real-life violence is a matter of much debate (Savage & Yancey, 2008).

This controversy over the operational definitions of aggression reflects concern over the external validity of this work.

Psychological Factors
Numerous psychological factors appear to be involved in aggression. They include individuals' responses to circumstances, as well as cognitive and learning factors.

Frustrating and Aversive Circumstances
Many years ago, John Dollard and his colleagues (1939) proposed the *frustration-aggression hypothesis,* which states that frustration—the blocking of an individual's attempts to reach a goal—always leads to aggression. However, psychologists subsequently found that aggression is not the only

Aversive circumstances that might stimulate aggression include factors in the physical environment such as noise, crowding, and heat waves.

possible response to frustration: Some individuals who experience frustration become passive, for example (Miller, 1941).

Psychologists later recognized that besides frustration, a broad range of aversive experiences can cause aggression. They include physical pain, personal insults, crowding, and unpleasant events. Aversive circumstances also include factors in the physical environment, such as the weather. Murder, rape, and assault increase when temperatures are the highest, as well as in the hottest years and the hottest cities (Anderson & Bushman, 2002).

Cognitive Determinants

Aspects of the environment may prime us to behave aggressively (Englander, 2006). Recall from Chapter 6 that priming can involve making something salient to a person, even subliminally or without the person's awareness. Leonard Berkowitz (1993; Berkowitz & LePage, 1996) has shown how the mere presence of a weapon (such as a gun) may prime hostile thoughts and produce aggression (Anderson, Benjamin, & Bartholow, 1998). Indeed, in accordance with Berkowitz's ideas, a famous study found that individuals who lived in a household with a gun were 2.7 times more likely to be murdered than those dwelling in a household without a gun (Kellerman & others, 1993).

> *This is a correlational study. What are some third variables that might explain the association between gun ownership and murder?*

A variety of other cognitive factors determine whether an individual responds aggressively to aversive situations (Baumeister, 1999; Berkowitz, 1990; DeWall & others, 2009). For instance, if a person perceives that another's actions are unfair or intentionally hurtful, aggression is more likely to occur. Indeed, in the workplace, individuals who perceive that they have been treated unfairly are more likely to aggress, verbally and physically, against supervisors (Dupre & Barling, 2006).

Observational Learning

Social cognitive theorists believe that aggression is learned through reinforcement and observational learning (Englander, 2006). Aggression can be learned by watching others engage in aggressive actions (Bandura, 1986). One of the most frequent opportunities people have to observe aggression in our culture is to watch violence on television, which we consider further in the discussion below on media violence.

Sociocultural Factors

Aggression involves not only biological and cognitive factors but also factors in the wider social world. Among the sociocultural factors in aggression are variations in economic inequity, the "culture of honor," and the extent to which people watch violence in the media.

Cultural Variations and the Culture of Honor

Aggression and violence are more common in some cultures than others (Kitayama & Cohen, 2007; Sorrentino & others, 2005). The U.S. homicide rate does not compare well with rates for other countries. For example, the U.S. homicide rate in 2004 was 5.5 per 100,000 (U.S. Bureau of Justice Statistics, 2006), five times the rate in Germany (BKA, 2006) and more than twice that of Canada (Canadian Statistics, 2005). Also, crime rates *in general* tend to be higher in countries and communities with a considerable gap between the rich and poor (Messner, Raffalovich, & Shrock, 2002; Popp, 2006).

Dov Cohen has examined the ways in which some cultural norms about masculine pride and family honor may foster aggressive behavior (Cohen, 2001; Vandello & Cohen, 2004). In a *culture of honor,* a man's reputation is thought to be an essential aspect of his economic survival. Such a culture sees insults to a man's honor as diminishing his reputation and views violence as a way to compensate for that loss. Cultures of honor are in evidence in countries where family pride might lead to so-called honor killings—in which, for example, a female rape victim is slain by her male family members so that they are not "contaminated" by the rape. In April 2009, a Jordanian man confessed to stabbing his pregnant sister with a meat cleaver because she had left her husband and he believed she was seeing other men. He felt that he had to kill her to protect his family honor (Gavlak, 2009).

> *Cognitive dissonance could lead to even greater valuing of one's personal honor. That honor would have to be really important for a person to harm someone else physically or to kill his own sister.*

Cohen has examined how, in the United States, southerners are more likely than northerners to be aggressive when honor is at stake. In one study, Cohen and his colleagues (1996) had White men who were from either the North or the South take part in an experiment that required them to walk down a hallway. A confederate passed all the men, bumping against them and quietly calling them a derogatory name. The southerners were more likely than the northerners to think their masculine reputation was threatened, to become physiologically aroused by the insult, and to engage in actual aggressive or dominant acts. In contrast, the northerners were less likely to perceive a random insult as "fightin' words."

Media Violence   Images of violence pervade the U.S. popular media. Moreover, television shows, movies, video games, and song lyrics usually portray violence unrealistically and without showing its lasting effects. It is easy to get the message that aggression and violence are the norm.

Although some critics have disputed the conclusion that TV violence causes aggression (Savage & Yancey, 2008), many scholars insist that television violence can prompt aggressive or antisocial behavior in children (Anderson & Huesmann, 2007; Comstock & Scharrer, 2003, 2006; Dubow, Huesmann, & Greenwood, 2007). Of course, television violence is not the only cause of aggression in children or adults. Aggression, like all other social behaviors, has multiple determinants. The link between TV violence and aggression in children is influenced by children's aggressive tendencies, by their attitudes toward violence, and by the monitoring of children's exposure to it. Perhaps the strongest predictor of aggression is witnessing aggression in one's own family (Ferguson & others, 2008).

Another type of media violence that has interested social psychologists is violent pornography—films, videos, and magazines portraying the degradation of women in a sexual context. The question most often posed about such media is whether they can foster violence toward women.

Based on several meta-analyses and on research of their own, Neil Malamuth and his colleagues concluded that pornography consumption does have a small effect on male sexual aggression, but they caution that it is only one of a number of factors that may lead to sexual violence against women (Malamuth, Addison, & Koss, 2000; Vega & Malamuth, 2007). The most problematic materials are those that depict women enjoying being the victims of male sexual violence (Malamuth, Addison, & Koss, 2000). Such violent pornography reinforces the rape myth—the false belief that women desire coercive sex.

Violent video games are another form of media that might influence aggressive behavior. To read about this topic, see Challenge Your Thinking.

NON SEQUITUR © Wiley Miller. Dist. by Universal Press Syndicate. Reprinted with permission. All rights reserved.

Aggression and Gender   Generally, research has supported stereotypes that tag males as more aggressive than females. As children, boys are more likely to engage in rough-and-tumble play and get in more fights in which they are physically aggressive (Blakemore, Berenbaum, & Liben, 2009). As adolescents, males are more likely to be members of gangs and to commit violent acts (Farrington, 2009). Children and adolescents who are diagnosed with conduct disorder (a pattern of offensive behavior that violates the basic rights of others) are three times more likely to be boys than girls (Kjelsberg, 2005). As adults, men are more likely to be chronically hostile and to commit violent crimes than are women (White & Frabutt, 2006).

Despite strong evidence for gender differences in aggression, we need to remind ourselves that when we say that males are more aggressive than females, we cannot jump to the conclusion that *all* males are more aggressive than *all* females (Hyde, 2005, 2007). In any given culture, some females will be more aggressive than some males.

challenge your thinking

Do Violent Video Games Lead to Violence?

On April 20, 1999, Eric Harris and Dylan Klebold carried out a shooting rampage at Columbine High School near Littleton, Colorado. Before killing themselves, the two teens shot and killed 12 fellow students and a teacher and wounded 24 others. The media reported that Harris and Klebold had been fans of violent video games. Some people began to wonder if the boys had been so obsessively occupied with these games that they could no longer distinguish fantasy from reality. Is it possible that video games promote violence?

Psychologists have examined the role of violent video games in empathy, attitudes about violence, and aggression. A recent research review concluded that children and adolescents who play violent video games extensively are more aggressive, less sensitive to real-life violence, more likely to engage in delinquent acts, and more likely to get lower grades in school than their counterparts who spend less time playing the games or do not play them at all (Escobar-Chaves & Anderson, 2008).

In light of such research conclusions, social psychologist Craig Anderson has been a vocal spokesperson against media violence, especially violent video games (Anderson, 2003; Anderson, Gentile, & Buckley, 2007; Anderson & Huesmann, 2007; Buckley & Anderson, 2006; Bushman & Anderson, 2007; Gentile & Anderson, 2006). However, some experts have challenged research results relating violent video games to violence and aggression on the grounds that acts of aggression studied in the laboratory are not generalizable to real-world criminal violence (Ritter & Elsea, 2005; Savage, 2008; Savage & Yancey, 2008). Furthermore, critics stress that many studies have not measured important third variables, such as family violence, in predicting both video game use and aggression (Ferguson & others, 2008). Critics have also pointed out that the media rarely note when acts of extreme violence such as the Virginia Tech shootings in 2007 have been perpetrated by individuals who do not play violent video games (Ferguson, 2007). Some have suggested that the movement against violent video games has created a hysteria fueled by individuals who have little personal experience with these games (Ferguson, 2007; Ferguson & others, 2008).

The controversy over violent video games and aggression highlights the links among social psychology, public policy, and current events. Every innovation in technology opens a new set of questions for social psychologists to address.

What Do You Think?

■ Do you or people whom you know play violent video games? What impact, if any, do you think this activity has on your or their thoughts and feelings?

■ Would you allow your child to play violent video games? Why or why not?

Reducing Aggression   Social cognitive theorists believe that people who act aggressively often are rewarded for their aggression and that individuals learn to be aggressive by watching others behave aggressively. Research has supported this view (Bandura, 1997). Thus, promising strategies for reducing aggression are to decrease rewards for aggression and to lessen exposure to it. Parents have been especially targeted to help children to reduce aggression (Leaper & Friedman, 2007). Recommended parenting strategies include encouraging young children to develop empathy toward others and more closely monitoring adolescents' activities (Denham, Bassett, & Wyatt, 2007; Eisenberg, & others, 2009).

1. With respect to *homo-economicus,* psychological research indicates that
   A. human behavior can be predicted using economic theory.
   B. humans are innately selfish.
   C. human actions are based on the supply of natural resources.
   D. humans are not necessarily self-centered and do not naturally act selfishly.

2. The following are ways to reduce aggression *except*
   A. minimizing the amount of violence witnessed.
   B. increasing empathy.
   C. rewarding aggressive actions.
   D. not modeling aggressive behaviors at home.

3. With respect to aggressiveness in women and men,
   A. men are more aggressive than women.
   B. women are more aggressive than men.
   C. men and women are equally aggressive.
   D. it depends on the context.

Apply It! 4. Driving down a country road one night, Nate sees an elderly man struggling to change a flat tire. He stops and helps the man and then continues to his girlfriend's house. When Nate tells his girlfriend about his random act of kindness, she says, "I would never have done that." Nate suggests that he just must be a lot nicer than she is. Considering the social psychology of helping, is Nate right?
   A. Nate is right because men are generally more helpful then women.
   B. Nate is right because he engaged in a selfless act of altruism.
   C. Nate is not right because his girlfriend may not have felt safe stopping to help someone on a country road at night.
   D. Nate is not right because he probably got a lot of praise from his girlfriend, rendering his act selfish.

3 Social Influence

Another topic of interest to social psychologists is how our behavior is influenced by other individuals and groups (Judd & Park, 2007; Monin, 2007). This section explores key aspects of social influence: conformity, obedience, and group influence.

Conformity and Obedience

Research on conformity and obedience started in earnest after World War II. Psychologists sought answers to the disturbing question of how ordinary people could be influenced to commit the sort of atrocities inflicted on Jews, Gypsies, and other minorities during the Holocaust. A central question is, how extensively will people change their behavior to coincide with what others are doing or dictating?

Conformity **Conformity** is a change in a person's behavior to coincide more closely with a group standard. Conformity takes many forms and affects many aspects of people's lives, in negative and positive ways. Conformity is at work, for example, when a person comes to college and starts to drink alcohol heavily at parties, even though he or she might have never been a drinker before. Conformity is also involved when we obey the rules and regulations that allow society to run smoothly. Consider how chaotic it would be if people did not conform to social norms such as stopping at a red light and not punching others in the face. Conformity can also be a powerful way to increase group cohesion. Even something as simple as marching in step together or singing a song with a group can lead to enhanced cooperation among group members (Wiltermuth & Heath, 2009).

conformity
A change in a person's behavior to coincide more closely with a group standard.

Asch's Experiment Put yourself in this situation: You are taken into a room where you see five other people seated along a table. A person in a white lab coat enters the room and announces that you are about to participate in an experiment on perceptual accuracy. The group is shown two cards—the first having only a single vertical line on it and the second having three vertical lines of varying length. You are told that the task is to determine which of the three lines on the second card is the same length as the line on the first card. You look at the cards and think, "What a snap. It's so obvious which is the same" (Figure 11.3).

What you do not know is that the other people in the room are confederates working with the experimenter. On the first several trials, everyone agrees about which line

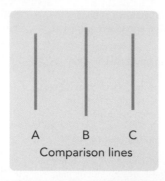

Standard line   Comparison lines
                       A   B   C

FIGURE 11.3

Asch's Conformity Experiment The figures at the top show the stimulus materials for the Asch conformity experiment on group influence. The photograph captures the puzzlement of one student after five confederates of the experimenter chose the incorrect line.

matches the standard. Then on the fourth trial, each of the others picks the same incorrect line. As the last person to make a choice, you have the dilemma of responding as your eyes tell you or conforming to what the others before you said. How would you answer?

Solomon Asch conducted this classic experiment on conformity in 1951. Asch instructed the confederates to give incorrect responses on 12 of 18 trials. To his surprise, Asch (1951) found that the volunteer participants conformed to the incorrect answers 35 percent of the time. Subsequent research has supported the notion that the pressure to conform is strong (Fein & others, 1993; Pines & Maslach, 2002)—but *why* do people go along with the group even when faced with clear-cut information such as the lines in the Asch experiment?

Going Along to Be Right and Going Along to Be Liked
Two main factors have been identified as contributing to conformity: informational social influence and normative social influence.

Informational social influence refers to the influence other people have on us because we want to be right. The social group can provide us with information that we did not know, or may help us see things in ways that had not occurred to us. As a result, we may conform because we have come to agree with the group. The tendency to conform based on informational social influence depends especially on two factors: how confident we are in our own independent judgment and how well informed we perceive the group to be. For example, if you know little about computers and three of your acquaintances who are IT geeks tell you not to buy a particular brand of computer, you are likely to conform to their recommendation.

In contrast, **normative social influence** is the influence others have on us because we want them to like us. Whether the group is an inner-city gang or members of a profession such as medicine or law, if a particular group is important to us, we might adopt a clothing style that people in the group wear or use the same slang words, and we might assume a certain set of attitudes that characterizes the group's members (Hewlin, 2009).

Conformity is a powerful social force, but why is it so important to us to fit in with a group? Recent research in social psychology and neuroscience has provided an interesting answer, as we shall see in the Intersection.

To feel the pressure of conformity, the next time you get on an elevator with other people, do not turn around to face the door.

Obedience
Obedience is behavior that complies with the explicit demands of the individual in authority. We are obedient when an authority figure demands that we do something, and we do it. Note that in conformity, people change their thinking or behavior so that it will be more like that of others, while in obedience, there is an explicit demand to comply (Blass, 2007).

Obedient behavior, such as that involved in the Nazi crimes against Jews and others during World War II, can sometimes be distressingly cruel. More recent examples include the obedience of radical Muslims instructed to participate in suicide attacks

informational social influence
The influence other people have on us because we want to be right.

normative social influence
The influence others have on us because we want them to like us.

obedience
Behavior that complies with the explicit demands of the individual in authority.

intersection

Just as the brain is involved in all human behavior, it is involved in conformity. Recent research has provided intriguing insights into the ways the brain responds to moments when we do not fit in with a group. The research results suggest that our brain may actually "feel better" when we fit in.

Social Psychology and Cognitive Neuroscience: Is the Brain Wired for Conformity?

In a recent study using fMRI, Vasily Klucharev and his colleagues (Klucharev & others, 2009) examined what happens in the brain when people find out that their opinions conflict with those of others. Women were asked to rate a variety of female faces for attractiveness, and their brains were scanned while they received feedback about whether their ratings agreed with those of the other group members. When participants were told that their ratings differed from the group's ratings, they showed enhanced activation in the brain area typically associated with monitoring for errors. In other words, the brain responded to judgments that differed from the group judgments as if they were *mistakes*. Furthermore, when the women's ratings were different from the group's ratings, women experienced less activation in the nucleus accumbens (NAc) and the ventral tegmental area (VTA), the brain's reward centers. The more the women's brains responded to being different as an error and as not rewarding, the more they tended to conform when given a chance to re-rate the faces at the end of the study. Klucharev and colleagues suggest that their findings demonstrate that humans *learn* that conformity is rewarding.

In a second study, the researchers found that these effects were specific to social conformity. When the women were given feedback about a *computer's* ratings of the faces, the brain did not mind being different from a computer nearly as much as it minded being different from a group of other humans.

Why would humans be wired for conformity? Could the brain learn to enjoy being different?

against Israelis and Westerners (McCauley & Segal, 2009), as well as the behavior of U.S. military personnel at Abu Ghraib prison in Iraq, who justified their horrendous abuse of detainees by asserting that they were "just following orders" (Miller, 2004).

A classic series of experiments by Stanley Milgram (1965, 1974) provides insight into such obedience. Imagine that as part of an experiment, you are asked to deliver a series of painful electric shocks to another person. You are told that the purpose of the study is to determine the effects of punishment on memory. Your role is to be the "teacher" and to punish the mistakes made by the "learner." Each time the learner makes a mistake, you are to increase the intensity of the shock.

You are introduced to the learner, a nice 50-year-old man who mumbles something about having a heart condition. He is strapped to a chair in the next room; he communicates with you through an intercom. The apparatus in front of you has 30 switches, ranging from 15 volts (light shock) to 450 volts (marked as "severe shock XXX").

As the trials proceed, the learner runs into trouble and is unable to give the correct answers. Should you shock him? As you increase the intensity of the shock, the learner says that he is in pain. At 150 volts, he demands to have the experiment stopped. At 180 volts, he cries out that he cannot stand it anymore. At 300 volts, he yells about his heart condition and pleads to be released. If you hesitate in shocking the learner, however, the experimenter tells you that you have no choice; the experiment must continue. Eventually the learner stops responding altogether, and the experimenter tells you that not responding is the same as a wrong answer. At this point, the learner appears to be injured or even dead. Would you keep going?

© Betsy Streeter. Used with permission.

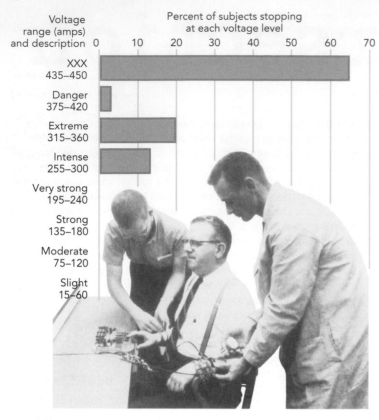

Voltage range (amps) and description | Percent of subjects stopping at each voltage level
0 10 20 30 40 50 60 70

XXX 435–450
Danger 375–420
Extreme 315–360
Intense 255–300
Very strong 195–240
Strong 135–180
Moderate 75–120
Slight 15–60

FIGURE 11.4

Milgram Obedience Study A 50-year-old man, the "learner," is strapped into a chair. The experimenter makes it look as if a shock generator is being connected to his body through several electrodes. The chart shows the percentage of "teachers" who stopped shocking the learner at each voltage level.

Prior to doing the study, Milgram asked 40 psychiatrists how they thought individuals would respond to this situation. The psychiatrists predicted that most teachers would go no farther than 150 volts, that fewer than 1 in 25 would go as far as 300 volts, and that only 1 in 1,000 would deliver the full 450 volts. The psychiatrists were way off. As shown in Figure 11.4, the majority of the teachers obeyed the experimenter: Almost two-thirds delivered the full 450 volts.

By the way, the 50-year-old man was a confederate in the experiment. In Milgram's study, the learner was not being shocked at all. Of course, the teachers were unaware that the learner was only pretending to be shocked.

At very strong voltage levels, the learner quit responding. When the teacher asked the experimenter what to do, the experimenter simply replied, "You must go on. The experiment requires that you continue." Imagine that with those simple statements the experimenter was able to command people calmly to (as far as they knew) shock a man to unconsciousness and possibly death. Such is the power of obedience to authority.

In variations of the experiment, Milgram discovered that more people would disobey in certain circumstances. Specifically, disobedience was more common when participants could see others disobey, when the authority figure was not perceived to be legitimate and was not close by, and when the victim was made to seem more human.

Milgram's studies became the subject of a 1976 TV movie called The Tenth Level. *The film starred William Shatner as Stephen Hunter—a character based on Stanley Milgram.*

The ethics of Milgram's studies has been a subject of controversy since he began them. The teachers in the experiment clearly felt anguish; some were very disturbed about "harming" another individual. All of the participants had been deceived by Milgram as part of the study. Even though they found out that they had not actually shocked or harmed anyone, was the anguish imposed on them ethical? Milgram's studies certainly revealed a great deal about human nature, and none of the volunteers expressed regret that they had taken part.

Under today's ethical guidelines, it is unlikely that these experiments would have been approved. Nonetheless, we are still learning from Milgram's data. A recent meta-analysis of his experiments suggested that the critical decision was at the 150-volt level, when the learner first requested that the experiment be halted. At that point, 80 percent of those who were going to stop did so (Packer, 2008). Apparently, individuals who were going to disobey were those who responded not to the later anguished cries of pain but to the learner's first request to be set free.

Burger had to exclude participants who had heard of Milgram's studies. In effect, people who had learned the lessons of Milgram's work were not given a chance to show their stuff.

You might wonder whether Milgram's results would still apply today. To examine this question, in 2006 social psychologist Jerry Burger (2009) attempted to re-create Milgram's study at Santa Clara University in California. Burger's study was similar to Milgram's except that in Burger's experiment the participants were never allowed to go higher than 150 volts. At 150 volts, the confederate asked to end the study, and immediately after participants decided whether to continue, the experiment was ended. Surprisingly, Burger's participants were only slightly less likely to obey than Milgram's had been. In a diverse sample of individuals in the California study, 70 percent of participants chose to continue even when the confederate asked to be released from the study. Notably, Burger's study employed safeguards to protect his participants.

Exerting Personal Control

It is safe to say that as we go through life, we are both conformists and nonconformists. Sometimes we go with the flow, and other times we stand up and stand out.

Our relationship to the social world is reciprocal. Individuals may try to control us, but we can exert personal control over our actions and influence others in turn (Bandura, 2007a, 2007b; Knowles, Nolan, & Riner, 2007; Knowles & Riner, 2006). Although it may not be easy to resist authority, living with the knowledge that you compromised your own moral integrity may be more difficult in the long run.

Can you think of a time when you resisted conformity or obedience? Do you think you would have obeyed in Milgram's study?

Group Influence

On February 2, 2005, Chico State University student Matthew Carrington died following a fraternity hazing. He and another pledge were verbally taunted and forced to do push-ups in raw sewage. They were also compelled to drink gallons of water. Eventually, Matthew Carrington suffered a seizure and died of water intoxication. Among those convicted in his death were four fraternity brothers who had never been in trouble before. The group's ringleader was Gabriel Maestretti, a religious former altar boy, high school homecoming king, and volunteer coach. Why do individuals who would never perform destructive acts when alone perpetrate them when in a group? This central question has driven research in the social psychology of group influence.

Deindividuation

deindividuation
The reduction in personal identity and erosion of the sense of personal responsibility when one is part of a group.

One process that sheds light on the behavior of individuals in groups is **deindividuation,** which occurs when being part of a group reduces personal identity and erodes the sense of personal responsibility (Dietz-Uhler, Bishop-Clark, & Howard, 2005; Zimbardo, 2007). The effects of deindividuation are visible in the wild street revelry that erupts after a team's victory in the World Series or Super Bowl, as well as in mass civic observances such as big-city Fourth of July celebrations.

One explanation for the effects of deindividuation is that groups give us anonymity. When we are part of a group, we may act in an uninhibited way because we believe that no one will be able to identify us.

Social Contagion

social contagion
Imitative behavior involving the spread of behavior, emotions, and ideas.

Have you ever noticed that a movie you watched in a crowded theater seemed funnier than it did when you watched the DVD alone at home? People laugh more when others are laughing. Babies cry when other babies are crying. The effects of others on our behavior can take the form of **social contagion,** imitative behavior involving the spread of behavior, emotions, and ideas (Cohen & Prinstein, 2006; Gino, Ayal, & Ariely, 2009). Social contagion effects can be observed in such varied phenomena as social fads, the popularity of dog breeds (Herzog, 2006), the spread of unhealthy behaviors such as smoking and drinking among adolescents (Rodgers, 2007), and symptoms of eating disorders among young women (Crandall, 2004; Forman-Hoffman & Cunningham, 2008).

One way to observe social contagion is to sit in a quiet but crowded library and start coughing. You will soon notice others doing the same thing. Similarly, imagine that you are walking down the sidewalk and come upon a group of people who are all looking up. How likely is it that you can avoid the temptation of looking up to see what is so interesting to them?

The Ku Klux Klan demonstrates a variety of ways that human beings can deindividuate: turning out in groups, acting under cover of darkness, and wearing white hoods to conceal identity.

Group Performance
Are two or three heads better than one? Some studies reveal that we do better in groups; others show that we are more productive when we work alone (Paulus, 1989). We can make sense out of these contradictory findings by looking closely at the circumstances in which performance is being analyzed (Nijstad, 2009).

Social Facilitation
If you have ever given a presentation in a class, you might have noticed that you did a much better job standing in front of your classmates than during any of your practice runs. **Social facilitation** occurs when an individual's performance improves because of the presence of others (Mendes, 2007). Robert Zajonc (1965) argued that the presence of other individuals arouses us. The arousal produces energy and facilitates our performance in groups. If our arousal is too high, however, we are unable to learn new or difficult tasks efficiently. Social facilitation, then, improves our performance on well-learned tasks. For new or difficult tasks, we might be best advised to work things out on our own before trying them in a group.

social facilitation
Improvement in an individual's performance because of the presence of others.

Social Loafing
Another factor in group performance is the degree to which one's behavior is monitored. **Social loafing** refers to each person's tendency to exert less effort in a group because of reduced accountability for individual effort. The effect of social loafing is lowered group performance (Latané, 1981). The larger the group, the more likely it is that an individual can loaf without detection.

social loafing
Each person's tendency to exert less effort in a group because of reduced accountability for individual effort.

Social loafing commonly occurs when a group of students is assigned a class project, and it is one reason that some students intensely dislike group assignments. These same individuals will not be surprised to learn that under certain conditions, working with others can increase individual effort (Levine, 2000). For example, a person who views the group's task as important (say, a student who strongly wants an *A* on the project) and who does not expect other group members to contribute adequately is likely to work harder than usual—and perhaps to do most of the work himself or herself.

Researchers have identified ways to decrease social loafing. They include making individuals' contributions more identifiable and unique, simplifying the evaluation of these contributions, and making the group's task more attractive (Karau & Williams, 1993).

The research of Norman Triplett (1898) of Indiana University, viewed by some to be the first North American sport psychologist, found that cyclists performed better when they raced in groups than when they rode by themselves, against the clock.

Group Decision Making
Many social decisions take place in groups—juries, teams, families, clubs, school boards, and the U.S. Senate, for example (Crampton, 2007; Gastil, 2009). What happens when people put their minds to the task of making a group decision? How do they decide whether a criminal is guilty, whether one country should attack another country, whether a family should stay home or go on vacation, or whether sex education should be part of a school curriculum? Three aspects of group decision making bear special mention: risky shift and group polarization; groupthink; and majority and minority influence.

Risky Shift and Group Polarization
Imagine that you have a friend, Lisa, who works as an accountant. All her life Lisa has longed to be a writer. In fact, she believes that she has the next great American novel in her head and that she just needs time and energy to devote to writing it. Would you advise Lisa to quit her job and go for it? What

if you knew beforehand that her chances of success were 50-50? How about 60-40? How much risk would you advise her to take?

In one investigation, fictitious dilemmas like this one were presented, and participants were asked how much risk the characters in the dilemmas should take (Stoner, 1961). When the individuals discussed the dilemmas as a group, they were more willing to endorse riskier decisions than when they were queried alone. The so-called **risky shift** is the tendency for a group decision to be riskier than the average decision made by the individual group members. Many studies have been conducted on this topic with similar results (Goethals & Demorest, 1995).

We do not always make riskier decisions in a group than when alone, however; hundreds of research studies show that being in a group moves us more strongly in the direction of the position we initially held (Moscovici, 1985). The **group polarization effect** is the solidification and further strengthening of an individual's position as a consequence of a group discussion. Initially held views often become more polarized because of group discussion. Group polarization may occur because, during the discussion, people hear new, more persuasive arguments that strengthen their original position. Group polarization also might arise because of social comparison. We may find that our opinion is not as extreme as others' opinions, and we might be influenced to take a stand at least as strong as the most extreme advocate's position.

risky shift
The tendency for a group decision to be riskier than the average decision made by the individual group members.

group polarization effect
The solidification and further strengthening of an individual's position as a consequence of a group discussion.

Groupthink: Getting Along but Being Very Wrong

Groupthink refers to the impaired group decision making that occurs when making the right decision is less important than maintaining group harmony. Instead of engaging in an open discussion of all the available information, in groupthink, members of a group place the highest value on conformity and unanimity. Members are encouraged to "get with the program," and dissent meets with very strong disapproval.

Groupthink can result in disastrous decisions. Irving Janis (1972) introduced the concept of groupthink to explain a number of enormous decision-making errors throughout history. Such errors include the lack of U.S. preparation for the Japanese bombing of Pearl Harbor during World War II, the escalation of the Vietnam War in the 1960s, the Watergate cover-up in 1974, and the *Challenger* space shuttle disaster in 1986. After the September 11, 2001, terrorist attacks, the possibility that groupthink interfered with the proper implementation of intelligence reared its head. Whistleblower Colleen Rowley, an FBI special agent, revealed that the FBI power hierarchy had been unresponsive to information that might have helped prevent the attacks. Similarly, many people criticized President George W. Bush and his cabinet for not listening to dissenting voices in the days leading up to the Iraq War.

Symptoms of groupthink include overestimating the power and morality of one's group, lack of willingness to hear all sides of an argument, and pressure for uniformity. Groupthink can occur whenever groups value conformity over accuracy (Degnin, 2009). However, groupthink can be prevented if groups avoid isolation, allow the airing of all sides of an argument, have an impartial leader, include outside experts in the debate, and when members who are strongly identified with the group speak out in dissent (Packer, 2009).

groupthink
The impaired group decision making that occurs when making the right decision is less important than maintaining group harmony.

Majority and Minority Influence

Most groups make decisions by voting, and, even in the absence of groupthink, the majority usually wins. The majority exerts influence on group decision making through both informational influence (they have greater opportunity to share their views) and normative influence (they set group norms). Those who do not go along may be ignored or even given the boot.

Even so, minority opinion holders *can* make a difference. Because it is outnumbered, the minority cannot win through normative pressure. Instead, it must do its work through informational pressure. If the minority presents its views consistently and confidently, then the majority is more likely to listen to the minority's perspectives. A powerful way that minority opinion holders can have influence is by winning over former majority members to their points of view.

A great example of minority influence is depicted in Twelve Angry Men, *a 1957 film (based on the play of the same name) starring Henry Fonda.*

1. All of the following are related to deindividuation *except*
   A. doing something as part of a large group.
   B. hearing someone explicitly call your name and express recognition of you.
   C. losing your sense of personal responsibility while taking part in a group activity.
   D. wearing a disguise while taking part in a group activity.

2. A difference between conformity and obedience is that
   A. conformity has a stronger influence on behavior than obedience.
   B. conformity does not involve an explicit command from others.
   C. conformity happens in small groups, whereas obedience happens in large groups.
   D. conformity is based on wanting to be right; obedience is based on wanting to be liked.

3. Social contagion is
   A. the tendency of people to perform worse when in the presence of others.
   B. the rapid spread of bad ideas among the members of a group.
   C. behavior that imitates others' actions, thoughts, or emotions.
   D. the influence of minority groups on the majority group.

Apply It! 4. Serena is serving on a jury in a driving-under-the-influence case. When she first enters the jury room with the other jurors, she is pretty sure the suspect is not guilty. During deliberations, one juror points out that in his testimony, the suspect made inconsistent remarks, first saying that he'd had only one beer and later mentioning that he'd drunk whiskey that night. Serena had completely missed those details. When the jury votes, Serena finds the suspect guilty. What explains Serena's change of heart?
   A. risky shift
   B. normative social influence
   C. informational social influence
   D. groupthink

4 Intergroup Relations

Conflicts between groups, especially ethnic and cultural groups, are rampant around the world (Stevens & Gielen, 2007; Tyler & De Cremer, 2006). The Islamic terrorist organization al Qaeda attacks countries that its members perceive to be too secular and materialistic. The wronged nations retaliate. Israelis and Palestinians fight over territory in the Middle East, each claiming religious and historical rights to the disputed land. Across Africa, tribal chiefs try to craft new social orders favorable to their own rule. A variety of social psychological concepts can help us understand the intensity of such cultural and ethnic conflicts and can provide insights into how to reduce them (Sanchez-Burks, 2007).

Group conflict such as that between Israelis and Palestinians in the Middle East is rampant in the world today.

Group Identity: Us Versus Them

Think about the groups of which you are a member—religious and social organizations, your ethnic group, your nationality. When someone asks you to identify yourself, how often do you respond by mentioning these group memberships? How much does it matter to you whether the people you associate with are members of the same groups as you?

Social Identity
Social identity refers to the way we define ourselves in terms of our group membership. In contrast to personal identity, which can be highly individualized, social

social identity
The way we define ourselves in terms of our group membership.

Ethnicity & Religion	Relationships	Vocations & Avocations	Political Affiliation	Stigmatized Identities
Jewish Asian American Southern Baptist West Indian	Parent Mother Son Widow	Artist Athlete Psychologist Military veteran	Environmentalist Feminist Republican	Overweight person Person with AIDS Homeless person Alcoholic

   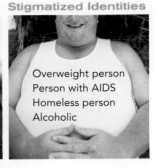

FIGURE 11.5

Types of Identity When we identify ourselves, we draw on a host of different characteristics associated with the various social groups to which we belong.

identity assumes some commonalities with others (Dovidio, Gaertner, & Saguy, 2009; Wenzel, 2009). A person's social identity might include identifying with a religious group, a country, a social organization, a political party, and many other groups (Carney & others, 2007; Haslam & Reicher, 2006). These diverse forms of social identity reflect the numerous ways people connect to groups and social categories (Abrams & Hogg, 2004; Hogg & Abrams, 2007; Postmes & Jetten, 2006). Social psychologist Kay Deaux (2001) identified five distinct types of social identity: ethnicity and religion, political affiliation, vocations and avocations, personal relationships, and stigmatized groups (Figure 11.5).

For many people, ethnic identity and religious identity are central to their social identity (Fuligni, Hughes, & Way, 2009; King & Roeser, 2009). Ethnic identity can be a source of pride for individuals. In the United States, special events celebrate the rich cultural contributions of many different groups to the society. Such experiences may provide individuals with an important resource in coping with biases they may encounter in life (Crocker, Major, & Steele, 1998). Feeling connected to one's ethnic group may buffer individuals from the stressful effects of injustice (Sellers & Shelton, 2003; Sellers & others, 2006).

Social psychologist Henry Tajfel (1978), a Holocaust survivor, wanted to explain the extreme violence and prejudice that his religious group (Jews) experienced. Tajfel's **social identity theory** states that our social identities are a crucial part of our self-image and a valuable source of positive feelings about ourselves. To feel good about ourselves, we need to feel good about the groups to which we belong. For this reason, individuals invariably think of the group to which they belong as an *in-group,* a group that has special value in comparison with other groups, called *out-groups.* To improve our self-image, we continually compare our in-groups with out-groups (Parks, 2007). In the process, we often focus more on the differences between the two groups than on their similarities.

Research by Tajfel (1978), along with many others who have used his theory, showed how easy it is to lead people to think in terms of "us" and "them." In one experiment, Tajfel had participants look at a screen featuring a huge number of dots and estimate how many dots were displayed. He then assigned the participants to groups based one whether they overestimated or underestimated the number of dots. Once assigned to one of the two groups, the participants were asked to award money to other participants. Invariably, individuals awarded money only to members of their own group. If we favor the members of a group that was formed on such trivial bases, it is no wonder that we show intense in-group favoritism when differences are not so trivial.

Such groups are referred to as minimal groups because group assignment is arbitrary and meaningless.

Ethnocentrism The tendency to favor one's own ethnic group over other groups is called **ethnocentrism.** Ethnocentrism does not simply mean taking pride in one's group; it also involves asserting the group's superiority over other groups. As such,

social identity theory
The view that our social identities are a crucial part of our self-image and a valuable source of positive feelings about ourselves.

ethnocentrism
The tendency to favor one's own ethnic group over other groups.

Ethnic identity evokes pride in many people. Here, Italian American soccer fans in Boston's North End rejoice at the Italian soccer team's World Cup win, and a Native American boy honors his heritage.

⟳ *As noted in the description of altruism, there may be a thin line between positive feelings and behaviors toward one's own group and hostile feelings and behaviors toward out-groups.*

ethnocentrism encourages in-group/out-group, we/they thinking (Brewer, 2007; Smith, Bond, & Kagitcibasi, 2006). Consequently, ethnocentrism implies that ethnic out-groups are not simply different; they are worse than one's group. Hence ethnocentrism may underlie prejudice.

Prejudice

Prejudice is an unjustified negative attitude toward an individual based on the individual's membership in a group. The group can be made up of people of a particular ethnicity, sex, age, religion—essentially, people who are different in some way from a prejudiced person (Amodio & Devine, 2006; T. D. Nelson, 2009; Sanchez-Burks, 2007). Prejudice can be seen in many eruptions of hatred in human history. In the Balkan Peninsula of eastern Europe, Serbs were so prejudiced against Bosnians that they pursued a policy of "ethnic cleansing." Hutus in Rwanda were so prejudiced against Tutsis that they went on a murderous rampage, hacking off their arms and legs with machetes.

A powerful example of destructive prejudice within U.S. society is racial prejudice against African Americans. When Africans were brought to colonial America as slaves, they were considered property and treated inhumanely. In the first half of the twentieth century, most African Americans still lived in the South and remained largely segregated from White society by law.

Despite progress in racial equality over the years, a much higher percentage of African Americans than Whites still live in impoverished neighborhoods and lack access to good schools, jobs, and healthcare, even decades after the abolition of legal segregation. Recent national events also make clear that there is still work to be done. Following Hurricane Katrina, news reports referred to White victims as "finding" food but described African Americans who were doing the same things as "looting" (Kinney, 2005).

Because racial prejudice is socially unacceptable, few people today would readily admit to racist or prejudicial views. In a CNN poll (2006), 88 percent of individuals answered no to the question "Are you racist?" It is not clear whether such results reflect a genuine change of heart or simply the recognition of this shifting social

prejudice
An unjustified negative attitude toward an individual based on the individual's membership in a group.

standard. Today, prejudiced individuals are more likely than before to appear unprejudiced on the surface while nevertheless holding racist views at a deeper level (Sears, 2008; Sears & Henry, 2007). Indeed, individuals may not be consciously aware of their own racial (or gender or age) biases.

To confront this problem, social psychologists examine prejudicial attitudes on two levels—explicit or overt racism and implicit or covert racism. *Explicit racism* is a person's conscious and openly shared attitude, which might be measured using a questionnaire. *Implicit racism* refers to attitudes that exist on a deeper, hidden level. Implicit attitudes must be measured with a method that does not require awareness. For example, implicit racism is sometimes measured using the Implicit Associations Test (IAT), a computerized survey that assesses the ease with which a person can associate a Black or White person with good things (for example, flowers) or bad things (for example, misery) (Greenwald & others, 2009; Nosek & Banaji, 2007; Sriram & Greenwald, 2009). This test is based on the idea that preexisting biases may make it easier to associate some social stimuli with positive rather than negative items.

Many people are surprised by the results of the IAT when they take this implicit measure. Try it out at https://implicit. harvard.edu/implicit. Do you think your results are valid?

In one study, a sample of White college students completed measures of explicit and implicit attitudes toward Black people (Dovidio, Kawakami, & Gaertner, 2002) using an implicit measure similar to the IAT. The students then interacted with a Black student partner. Explicit prejudice predicted what people said to a person of a different race—that is, White students who said they were not prejudiced were unlikely to say overtly racist things. Explicit prejudice also predicted how friendly White individuals felt they had behaved toward their Black partner. However, implicit prejudice related to nonverbal aspects of the interaction, such as how close the White students sat to their partners, as well as their facial expressions.

Social psychologists have explored some possible reasons why people develop prejudice. Competition between groups, especially when resources are scarce, can contribute to prejudice. For example, immigrants often compete with established low-income members of a society for jobs—a situation that can lead to prejudice. Cultural learning is also clearly involved. Children can adopt the prejudicial attitudes of their families and friends before they even meet a person from an out-group. In addition, when people feel bad about themselves, they might bolster their self-esteem by demeaning out-group members.

What are your attitudes toward individuals of an ethnic background different from your own? How do these attitudes compare with those of your parents?

A final factor that might underlie prejudice comes from the limits on our information-processing abilities. Human beings are limited in their capacity for effortful thought, but they face a complex social environment. To simplify the challenge of understanding others' behavior, people use categories or stereotypes. Stereotypes can be a powerful force in developing and maintaining prejudicial attitudes.

Stereotyping and Prejudice

Recall that stereotypes are generalizations about a group that deny variations within the group. Researchers have found that we are less likely to detect variations among individuals who belong to "other" groups than among individuals who belong to "our" group. So, we might see the people in our in-group as varied, unique individuals while viewing the members of out-groups as "all the same." Thinking that "they all look alike" can be a particular concern in the context of eyewitness identification (Brigham, 1986). At the root of prejudice is a particular kind of stereotype: a generalization about a group that contains negative information that is applied to all members of that group (Stangor, 2009).

Discrimination

Discrimination refers to an unjustified negative or harmful action toward a member of a group simply because the person belongs to that group. Discrimination results when negative emotional reactions combine with prejudicial beliefs

discrimination
An unjustified negative or harmful action toward a member of a group simply because the person belongs to that group.

and are translated into behavior (Bretherton, 2007; Major & Sawyer, 2009). Many forms of discrimination are illegal in the American workplace. Since the Civil Rights Act of 1964 (revised in 1991), it has been unlawful to deny someone employment on the basis of gender or ethnicity (Parker, 2006).

sexual harassment
Unwelcome behavior or conduct of a sexual nature that offends, humiliates, or intimidates another person.

A particular form of discrimination is **sexual harassment,** unwelcome behavior or conduct of a sexual nature that offends, humiliates, or intimidates another person. In the workplace and schools, sexual harassment includes unwanted sexual advances, requests for sexual favors, and other verbal or physical conduct of a sexual nature against an employee's, a teacher's, or a peer's wishes (Berdahl & Acquino, 2009; Petersen & Hyde, 2009; Swim & Hyers, 2009). In the United States, sexual harassment is an illegal form of sexual discrimination. Victims include not only the person harassed but also anyone affected by the offensive conduct. For example, a man who works in a setting in which women are routinely demeaned may experience the environment as a toxic place to work.

Ways to Improve Intergroup Relations

Martin Luther King, Jr., said, "I have a dream that my four little children will one day live in a nation where they will not be judged by the color of their skin but by the content of their character." How might we attain the world that King envisioned?

One way might be for people to come to know one another better so that they can get along. However, in daily life many people interact with individuals from other ethnic groups, and this contact does not necessarily lead to tolerance or warm relations. Indeed, researchers have consistently found that contact by itself—attending the same school or working in the same company—does not necessarily improve relations among people of different ethnic backgrounds. So, rather than focusing on contact per se, researchers have examined how *various features* of a contact situation may be optimal for reducing prejudice and promoting intergroup harmony.

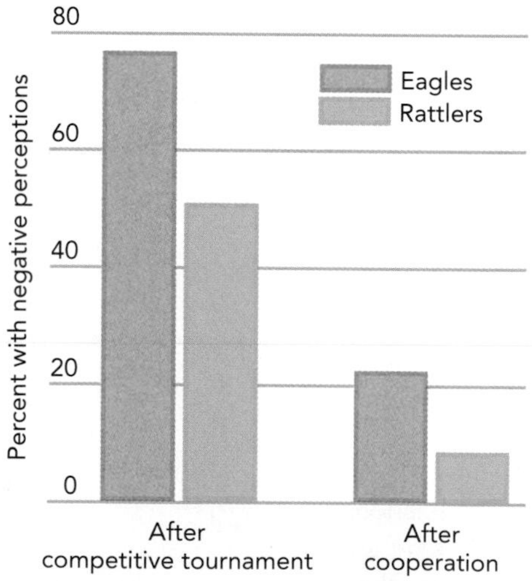

Studies have shown that contact is more effective if the people involved think that they are of equal status, feel that an authority figure sanctions their positive relationships, and believe that friendship might emerge from the interaction (Pettigrew & Tropp, 2006). Another important feature of optimal intergroup contact is *task-oriented cooperation*— working together on a shared goal. An example of the power of task-oriented cooperation is Muzafer Sherif's Robbers Cave study.

It may be hard to imagine in our post-*Survivor* era, but even before Jeff Probst started handing out color-coded "buffs" on the TV show *Survivor*, Sherif and his colleagues (1961) had the idea of exploring group processes by assigning 11-year-old boys to two competitive groups (the "Rattlers" and the "Eagles") in a summer camp called Robbers Cave. Sherif, disguised as a janitor so that he could unobtrusively observe the Rattlers and the Eagles, arranged for the two groups to compete in baseball, touch football, and tug-of-war. If you have watched reality television, you have some idea how this experiment went. In short order, relations between the groups got downright ugly. Members of each group expressed negative opinions of members of the other group, and the Rattlers and Eagles became battling factions. What would bring these clashing groups together? Sherif created tasks that required the joint efforts of both groups, such as working together to repair the camp's only water supply and pooling their money to rent a movie. When the groups were required to work cooperatively to solve problems, the Rattlers and Eagles developed more positive relationships. Figure 11.6 shows how competitive and cooperative activities changed perceptions of the out-group.

FIGURE 11.6

Attitudes Toward the Out-Group Following Competitive and Cooperative Activities In Sherif's research, hostility peaked after an athletic tournament, as reflected in the high percentage of Eagles and Rattlers who perceived the other group unfavorably following this event. However, after the groups worked together to reach a goal, their unfavorable attitudes toward each other dropped considerably.

1. With respect to groups, social identity theory says that
   A. groups naturally cooperate with one another.
   B. members of the in-group feel positively about members of the out-group.
   C. groups tend to highlight the differences rather than the similarities between themselves.
   D. group membership has little to do with our sense of self.

2. All of the following statements are true about ethnocentrism *except*
   A. ethnocentrism involves asserting one group's superiority over other groups.
   B. ethnocentrism leads to we-versus-they thinking.
   C. ethnocentrism is unrelated to prejudice.
   D. ethnocentrism is related to group pride.

3. A White woman says she is not racist but avoids sitting near Black individuals. She has
   A. high explicit racism, low implicit racism.
   B. high explicit racism, high implicit racism.
   C. low explicit racism, low implicit racism.
   D. low explicit racism, high implicit racism.

Apply It! 4. Whenever he eats in the campus commons, Will is bothered by the way students segregate themselves, with all the African American students generally eating in one area, the Latinos in another, the Asians in another, and the Euro-Americans in another. Bill starts the Students Together program to get students to interact more and to promote interethnic harmony. Which of the following strategies is most likely to work, based on the social psychological evidence?
   A. Assign seats in the lunchroom so that students have to sit with members of other ethnic groups.
   B. Identify problems of common interest to students of all groups and initiate ethnically diverse discussion groups aimed at solving those problems.
   C. Post signs in the commons that encourage interethnic contact.
   D. None of the above, because nothing will work.

5 Close Relationships

If you are asked to make three wishes for anything at all, chances are that one will be for love, marriage, or a partner to share your life (King & Broyles, 1997). Along with good health and happiness, close relationships figure prominently in most notions of a good life. Every day we see commercials lauding the ability of this or that Internet dating service to link us up with the love of our life. U.S. consumers spent more than $490 million on Internet personals and dating services in 2005 (Online Publishers Association, 2005).

Because close romantic relationships are so crucial for most of us, it is no wonder that social psychologists should be interested in studying this fascinating aspect of human existence. Indeed, a vast literature has accumulated in social psychology, examining attraction, love, and intimacy.

Attraction

At the beginning of this chapter, we discussed one key factor in interpersonal attraction, namely, physical attractiveness. Research on interpersonal attraction has illuminated a variety of other factors that play a role in the process of becoming attracted to someone.

Proximity, Acquaintance, and Similarity

Even in the age of Internet dating, it is very unlikely that you are going to become attracted to someone without meeting the person. *Proximity*, or physical closeness, is a strong predictor of attraction. You are more likely to become attracted to an individual you pass in the hall every day than someone you rarely see. One potential mechanism for the role of proximity in attraction is the mere exposure effect (Zajonc, 1968, 2001). The **mere exposure effect** means that the more we encounter someone or something (a person, a word, an image), the more likely we are to start liking the person or thing even if we do not realize we have seen it before.

We are not only more likely to be attracted to people whom we have seen before, but also more likely to like someone if we are led to believe we will be meeting that person. Let's say you are sitting in a room and an experimenter tells you there are two strangers next door, one of whom you will be meeting and the other not. Research shows that you are likely to begin to like the first

mere exposure effect
The phenomenon that the more we encounter someone or something, the more likely we are to start liking the person or thing even if we do not realize we have seen it before.

Potential matchmakers, take note: If you want to pair up two friends in a romantic relationship, tell each of them how much the other liked his or her Facebook page.

Friends often share similar attitudes, behavior, taste in clothing, personalities, and lifestyles.

person, in anticipation of your interaction (Insko & Wilson, 1977). In addition, if you find out that someone whom you do not yet know already likes you, that is a sure sign that you will find yourself attracted to that person.

Similarity also plays an important role in attraction (Qian, 2009). We have all heard that opposites attract, but what is true of magnets is not typically true of human beings. We like to associate with people who are similar to us (Berscheid, 2000). Our friends and lovers are much more like us than unlike us: We share with them similar attitudes, behavior patterns, taste in clothes, intelligence, personality, other friends, values, lifestyle, physical attractiveness, and so on.

The concept of *consensual validation* explains why people are attracted to others who are similar to them. Our own attitudes and behavior are supported when someone else's attitudes and behavior are similar to ours—their attitudes and behavior validate ours. Another reason that similarity matters is that we tend to shy away from the unknown. Similarity implies that we will enjoy doing things with another person who has similar tastes and attitudes.

Evolutionary Approaches to Attraction

Evolutionary psychologists focus on gender differences in the variables that account for attraction (Buss, 2008). Evolutionary psychologists argue that women and men have faced different pressures in the course of human evolution (Geary, 2006). They stress that the sexes' different statuses in reproduction are the key to understanding how this evolution took place (Buss, 2008).

From the perspective of evolutionary psychology, the goal for both men and women is to procreate. For men, this evolutionary task is complicated by the fact that in the human species, paternity is somewhat more mysterious than motherhood. To be sure that a woman is not already pregnant with another man's child, evolutionary psychologists say, men should be more strongly attracted to younger women. Youth is also likely to indicate a woman's fertility. For women, the task of producing offspring is an innately difficult one. Although a man might focus on quantity of sexual partners, a woman must focus on quality and search for a mate who will invest his resources in her and her offspring (Caporeal, 2007).

Personal ads show evidence of these evolutionary differences. When men place ads seeking women, they typically look for youth and beauty (a potential proxy for health and fertility), and they offer tangible resources—for example, by describing themselves as a "professional homeowner" (Buss, 2008). When women place ads seeking men, they are more likely to offer youth and beauty and to seek resources. The personal ads of gay men and lesbians offer an intriguing context for consideration. In general, research has shown that gay men seek youth and beauty, whereas lesbians seek personal qualities such as stability and a sense of humor. Evolutionary thinkers suggest that such results provide evidence for strong sex-linked adaptive patterns.

Critics of evolutionary psychology theory argue that humans have the decision-making ability to change their gender behavior and thus are not locked into their evolutionary past. They cite extensive cross-cultural variation in gender behavior and mate preference as proof that social experience affects gender behavior (Matlin, 2008; B. Smith, 2007). For example, the *social role view* of gender asserts that *social,* not evolutionary, experiences have led to differences in gender behavior (Eagly & Koenig, 2006; Wood & Eagly, 2007). The social role approach acknowledges the biological differences between men and women but stresses the ways these differences are played out in a range of cultures and societal contexts. Indeed, in cultures that view the sexes more equally, women appear to be less likely to prefer mates with economic resources (Kasser & Sharma, 1999).

Love

Some relationships never progress much beyond the attraction stage. Others deepen to friendship and perhaps even to love (Berscheid, 2006). Here we consider two types of love: romantic and affectionate.

Poets, playwrights, and musicians through the ages have celebrated the fiery passion of romantic love—and lamented the searing pain when it fails. Think about songs and books that hit the top of the charts. Chances are, they are about romantic love.

romantic love
Love with strong components of sexuality and infatuation, often predominant in the early part of a love relationship; also called passionate love.

Romantic love, also called passionate love, is love with strong components of sexuality and infatuation, and it often predominates in the early part of a love relationship (Hendrick & Hendrick, 2006). Ellen Berscheid (1988) says that it is romantic love we mean when we say that we are "in love" with someone. It is romantic love that she believes we need to understand if we are to learn what love is all about. Berscheid judges sexual desire to be the most important ingredient of romantic love. Although we often think of romantic love as a "chick thing," men, not women, are the ones who fall in love more quickly and easily (Dion & Dion, 2001).

As love matures, romantic love tends to evolve into affectionate love.

Love is more than just passion, however. **Affectionate love,** also called *companionate love,* is the type of love that occurs when an individual has a deep, caring affection for another person and desires to have that person near. There is a growing belief that the early stages of love have more romantic ingredients and that as love matures, passion tends to give way to affection (Berscheid & Regan, 2005).

affectionate love
Love that occurs when an individual has a deep, caring affection for another person and desires to have that person near; also called companionate love.

Models of Close Relationships

A bewildering question is, how do we make love last? The United States is the most divorce-prone nation in the world, with 50 percent of marriages ending in divorce (Popenoe & Whitehead, 2006). Several factors predict whether a relationship will end in divorce. Couples who marry after age 20, who come from stable two-parent homes, and who are well- and similarly educated are less likely to divorce (Myers, 2000). Successful marriage partners talk positively about their relationship, are friends, do not try to control their partner, and solve conflicts together (Gottman, 2006). These factors are generally applicable whether the couple is heterosexual or homosexual (Peplau & Fingerhut, 2007).

Social Exchange Theory
The social exchange approach to close relationships focuses on the costs and benefits of one's romantic partner. **Social exchange theory** is based on the notion of social relationships as involving an exchange of goods, the objective of which is to minimize costs and maximize benefits. From this perspective, the most important predictor of relationship success is *equity*—that is, having both partners feel that each is doing his or her "fair share." Essentially, social exchange theory asserts that we keep a mental balance sheet, tallying the plusses and minuses associated

social exchange theory
The view of social relationships as involving an exchange of goods, the objective of which is to minimize costs and maximize benefits.

Surely we can all think of long-term couples in which one partner remains committed even when the benefits are hard for the outsider to see, as when a person's romantic partner is gravely ill for a long time.

with our romantic partner—what we put in ("I paid for our last date") and what we get out ("He brought me flowers").

As relationships progress, however, equity may no longer apply. Happily married couples are less likely to keep track of "what I get versus what I give," and they avoid thinking about the costs and benefits of their relationships (Buunk & Van Yperen, 1991; Clark & Chrisman, 1994).

The Investment Model

Another way to think about long-term romantic relationships is to focus on the underlying factors that characterize stable, happy relationships compared to others. The **investment model** examines the ways that commitment, investment, and the availability of attractive alternative partners predict satisfaction and stability in relationships (Rusbult & others, 2004). From this perspective, long-term relationships are likely to continue when both partners are committed to, and have invested a great deal in, the relationship and when there are few tempting alternatives—other attractive partners—around.

Commitment to the relationship is especially important and predicts a willingness to sacrifice for a romantic partner. In one study, individuals were given a chance to climb up and down a short staircase, over and over, to spare their partner from having to do so. Those who were more committed to their partner worked harder to climb up and down repeatedly, to spare their loved one the burden (Van Lange & others, 1997).

A loving intimate relationship is surely a part of most notions of a fulfilling life. In every couple, two individuals come together. In turn, each couple is embedded in a social network, including their families, friends, and the social groups and societies to which they belong. Social psychologists are dedicated to understanding these many, varied social forces and their influence on our lives and behavior.

> **investment model**
> A model of long-term relationships that examines the ways that commitment, investment, and the availability of attractive alternative partners predict satisfaction and stability in relationships.

self-quiz

1. With regard to happy relationships, social exchange theory tells us that
   A. we are happiest when we are giving in a relationship.
   B. we are happiest when we are receiving in a relationship.
   C. we are happiest when there is a balance between giving and receiving in a relationship.
   D. equity is important to happiness only in long-lasting relationships.

2. Consensual validation would predict
   A. that opposites attract.
   B. that relationships with more give and take are best.
   C. that we are attracted to people who are similar to us.
   D. that romantic love is more important than affectionate love.

3. Affectionate love is more common _____, whereas romantic love is more common _____.
   A. in men; in women
   B. in women; in men
   C. early in a relationship; later in a relationship
   D. later in a relationship; early in a relationship

Apply It! 4. Daniel and Alexa, two college students, have been dating for two years. Alexa meets a new guy during spring break and cheats on Daniel. When she tells Daniel about it, he is crushed but forgives her. He reasons that because the two of them have worked together on their relationship for two years, it makes no sense to throw it all away based on one mistake. Which of the following theories would predict that Daniel is likely to cheat on Alexa in the future?
   A. the investment model
   B. social exchange theory
   C. evolutionary theory
   D. theory of affectionate love

summary

① Social Cognition

The face conveys information to social perceivers, including attractiveness. Self-fulfilling prophecy means that our expectations of others can have a powerful impact on their behavior.

Attributions are our thoughts about why people behave as they do and about who or what is responsible for the outcome of events. Attribution theory views people as motivated to discover the causes of behavior as part of their effort to make sense of it. The dimensions used to make sense of the causes of human behavior include internal/external, stable/unstable, and controllable/uncontrollable.

The fundamental attribution error is observers' tendency to overestimate traits and to underestimate situations when they explain an actor's behavior. Self-serving bias means attributing our successes to internal causes and blaming our failures on external causes. Heuristics are used as shortcuts in social information processing. One such heuristic is a stereotype—a generalization about a group's characteristics that does not consider any variations among individuals in the group.

The self is our mental representation of our own characteristics. Self-esteem is important and is related to holding unrealistically positive views of ourselves. Stereotype threat is an individual's fast-acting, self-fulfilling fear of being judged based on a negative stereotype about his or her group. In order to understand ourselves better, we might engage in social comparison, evaluating ourselves by comparison with others.

Attitudes are our feelings—about people, objects, and ideas. We are better able to predict behavior on the basis of attitudes when an individual's attitudes are strong, when the person is aware of his or her attitudes and expresses them often, and when the attitudes are specifically relevant to the behavior. Sometimes changes in behavior precede changes in attitude.

According to cognitive dissonance theory, our strong need for cognitive consistency causes us to change our behavior to fit our attitudes or to change our attitudes to fit our behavior. Self-perception theory stresses the importance of making inferences about attitudes by observing our own behavior, especially when our attitudes are not clear.

② Social Behavior

Altruism is an unselfish interest in helping someone else. Reciprocity often is involved in altruism. Individuals who are in a good mood are more helpful. Empathy is also linked to helping. The bystander effect means that individuals who observe an emergency help less when someone else is present than when they are alone.

Women are more likely to help in situations that are not dangerous and involve caregiving. Men are more likely to help in situations that involve danger or in which they feel competent.

One view of the biological basis of aggression is that early in human evolution, the most aggressive individuals were likely to be the survivors. Neurobiological factors involved in aggressive behavior include the neurotransmitter serotonin and the hormone testosterone. Psychological factors in aggression include frustrating and aversive circumstances. Sociocultural factors include cross-cultural variations, the culture of honor, and violence in the media. Males are consistently more physically aggressive than females.

③ Social Influence

Conformity involves a change in behavior to coincide with a group standard. Factors that influence conformity include informational social influence (going along to be right) and normative social influence (going along to be liked).

Obedience is behavior that complies with the explicit demands of an authority. Milgram's classic experiment demonstrated the power of obedience.

People often change their behaviors when they are in a group. Deindividuation refers to the lack of inhibition and diffusion of responsibility that can occur in groups. Social contagion refers to imitative behaviors involving the spread of behavior, emotions, and ideas. Our performance in groups can be improved through social facilitation and lowered because of social loafing.

Risky shift refers to the tendency for a group decision to be riskier than the average decision made by the individual group members. The group polarization effect is the solidification and further strengthening of a position as a consequence of group discussion. Groupthink involves impaired decision making and avoidance of realistic appraisal to maintain harmony in the group.

④ Intergroup Relations

Social identity is our definition of ourselves in terms of our group memberships. Social identity theory states that when individuals are assigned to a group, they invariably think of it as the in-group. Identifying with the group allows the person to have a positive self-image. Ethnocentrism is the tendency to favor one's own ethnic group over others.

Prejudice is an unjustified negative attitude toward an individual based on membership in a group. The underlying reasons for prejudice include the presence of competition between groups over scarce resources, a person's motivation to enhance his or her self-esteem, cognitive processes that tend to categorize and stereotype others, and cultural learning. Prejudice is also based on stereotypes. The cognitive process of stereotyping can lead to discrimination, an unjustified negative or harmful action toward a member of a group simply because he or she belongs to that group. Discrimination results when negative emotional reactions combine with prejudicial beliefs and are translated into behavior.

An effective strategy for enhancing the effects of intergroup contact is to set up task-oriented cooperation among individuals from different groups.

⑤ Close Relationships

We tend to be attracted to people whom we see often, whom we are likely to meet, and who are similar to us. Romantic love (passionate love) includes feelings of infatuation and sexual attraction. Affectionate love (companionate love) is more akin to friendship and includes deep, caring feelings for another.

Social exchange theory states that a relationship is likely to be successful if individuals feel that they get out of the relationship what they put in. The investment model focuses on commitment, investment, and the availability of attractive alternatives in predicting relationship success.

key terms

self-test

multiple choice

1. Which of the following is *true* about stereotypes?
   A. Stereotypes take mental effort.
   B. Stereotypes are accurate.
   C. Stereotypes do not account for individual variation.
   D. Stereotypes are always negative.

2. Believing that everyone shares the same view as you is known as
   A. the availability heuristic.
   B. the false consensus effect.
   C. a stereotype.
   D. stereotype threat.

3. If 10 people are competing as one team in a tug-of-war contest, their combined effort level is likely to be
   A. more than the sum of their individual abilities.
   B. less than the sum of their individual abilities.
   C. the same as the sum of their individual abilities.
   D. the same as the sum of their individual abilities for men, but less than the sum of their individual abilities for women.

4. Despite evidence to the contrary, Denise thinks she is smarter than most others in her class. Denise's unfounded attitude about herself is an example of
   A. a positive illusion.
   B. a self-serving bias.
   C. a negative illusion.
   D. a self-fulfilling prophecy.

5. "Am I as popular as Cathy?" This question is an example of gaining self-knowledge through the process of
   A. peer review.
   B. peripheral attribute.
   C. wishful thinking.
   D. social comparison.

6. The fifth-grade teacher was surprised when her Japanese American student, Hiroko, performed poorly in math. The teacher's reaction was due to
   A. polarization.
   B. stereotyping.
   C. groupthink.
   D. deindividuation.

7. Marilyn smokes; however, she is well aware of the negative health consequences of smoking. As a result, Marilyn feels guilty about smoking. Marilyn is most likely experiencing
   A. effort justification.
   B. a negative illusion.
   C. a fundamental attribution error.
   D. cognitive dissonance.

8. Having negative views of an out-group is
   A. explicit bias.
   B. implicit bias.
   C. prejudice.
   D. discrimination.

9. A defining characteristic of groupthink is
   A. accurate decision making.
   B. decisions that are more extreme than normal.
   C. the discouragement of minority viewpoints.
   D. group discord.

10. The results of the Milgram study are disturbing because
    A. the majority of participants who went all the way to 450 volts did so quite happily.
    B. Milgram violated the ethical principles of his time.
    C. the experimenter had no real power to force the subjects to comply.
    D. the subjects volunteered to be the "teacher" rather than the "learner."

Apply It!

11. Organizations are using the Internet as a way to put many heads together to solve problems. This technique, called *crowd sourcing,* involves posting problems to the Internet and having huge numbers of individuals post their solutions to the problems. Evaluate the possible effectiveness of crowd sourcing. Is it more or less likely to demonstrate processes such as social loafing, social facilitation, group polarization, and groupthink than face-to-face group interactions? Why?

12 Psychological Disorders

Moe Armstrong's Pretty Good Life

What makes for a good life? Good health, a happy marriage, close friends, and a satisfying career may come to mind.

Consider the life of Moe Armstrong. Moe is the 66-year-old director of consumer and family affairs for the Vinfen Corporation. A sought-after public speaker who holds two master's degrees, Moe has appeared on *Larry King Live* and the *CBS Evening News*. Married for 10 years, he enjoys writing poetry, cartooning, and photography. When he takes stock of his rich experiences, Moe is grateful, noting, "I've had a pretty good life" (Bonfatti, 2005).

Moe's "pretty good life" is in fact remarkable—not only because of his accomplishments but also because he has schizophrenia, a psychological disorder characterized by profoundly disturbed thought. At age 21, while serving in Vietnam as a Marine medical corpsman, Moe experienced a psychotic break. Dead Vietcong soldiers appeared to talk to him and beg him for help; in Moe's visions, they did not seem to realize that they were dead. After the war, Moe struggled for many years, turning to alcohol and drugs as a way of coping with the bizarre, terrifying visions that continued to haunt him. Today he takes antipsychotic medication for his disorder. In his own words, "I have many more limitations than other people, and that's very hard." He tries to avoid relapse by cultivating "supportive, gentle, loving environments" (Boodman, 2002).

Moe lives every day with worries—about the return of those visions, his continuing need for medication, and the effects of schizophrenia on his body, mind, and social interactions. These burdens affect him in ways that few of us can grasp. Life with schizophrenia can be so difficult that the suicide risk for individuals with the disorder is eight times that of the general population (Pompili & others, 2007).

Although few of us experience psychological struggles as severe as Moe's, everyone faces obstacles in creating a good life. These obstacles can include one or more of a range of psychological disorders, our focus in this chapter. ▪

- Persistent abnormal behavior can indicate a psychological disorder. How would you define *abnormal?*

- When you think of the term *psychological disorder*, what first comes to mind?

- If you (or someone you know) has experienced a psychological disorder, how has it affected your (or that other person's) life?

In this chapter we explore the meaning of the word *abnormal* as it relates to psychology. We examine various theoretical approaches to understanding abnormal behavior and survey the main psychological disorders. In the concluding section, we delve into how stigma plays a role in the lives of individuals struggling with psychological disorders, and we consider how even difficult, troubled lives remain valuable and meaningful.

1 Defining and Explaining Abnormal Behavior

What makes behavior "abnormal"? The American Psychiatric Association (2001, 2006) defines abnormal behavior in medical terms: a mental illness that affects or is manifested in a person's brain and can affect the way the individual thinks, behaves, and interacts with others. Three criteria help distinguish normal from abnormal behavior: **Abnormal behavior** is *deviant, maladaptive,* or *personally distressful* over a relatively long period of time. Let's take a closer look at what each of the three characteristics of abnormal behavior entails.

abnormal behavior
Behavior that is deviant, maladaptive, or personally distressful over a relatively long period of time.

■ Abnormal behavior is *deviant.* Abnormal behavior is certainly atypical or statistically unusual. For example, Oprah Winfrey, LeBron James, and Steve Jobs are atypical in many of their behaviors—and yet we do not categorize them as abnormal. We do often consider atypical behavior abnormal, though, when it deviates from what is acceptable in a culture. A woman who washes her hands three or four times an hour and takes seven showers a day is abnormal because her behavior deviates from what we see as acceptable.

■ Abnormal behavior is *maladaptive.* Maladaptive behavior interferes with one's ability to function effectively in the world. A man who believes that he can endanger others through his breathing may go to great lengths to isolate himself from people for what he believes is their own good. His belief negatively affects his everyday functioning; thus, his behavior is maladaptive. Behavior that presents a danger to the person or those around him or her is also considered maladaptive (and abnormal).

Which of these three qualities—deviation from what is acceptable, maladaptiveness, and personal distress—do you think is most important to calling a behavior abnormal? Why?

■ Abnormal behavior involves *personal distress* over a long period of time. The person engaging in the behavior finds it troubling. A woman who

Accomplished people such as Cleveland Cavaliers superstar LeBron James and Apple Computer co-founder Steve Jobs are atypical but not abnormal. However, when atypical behavior deviates from cultural norms, it often is considered abnormal.

secretly makes herself vomit after every meal may never be seen by others as deviant (because they do not know about it), but this pattern of behavior may cause her to feel intense shame, guilt, and despair.

Only one of these criteria need be present for behavior to be labeled "abnormal," but typically two or all three may be present. Note that the context may contribute to whether a behavior is abnormal. For instance, if the woman who washes her hands three or four times an hour and takes repeated showers works in a sterile lab with toxic chemicals or live viruses, her behavior might be quite adaptive. When abnormal behavior persists, it may lead to the diagnosis of a psychological disorder.

Spend 15 to 20 minutes observing an area with a large number of people, such as a mall, a cafeteria, or a stadium during a game. Identify and make a list of behaviors you would classify as abnormal. How does your list of behaviors compare with the definition of *abnormal* provided above? What would change in the list if you were in a different setting, such as a church, a bar, or a library? What does this exercise tell you about the meaning of *abnormal?*

Theoretical Approaches to Psychological Disorders

What causes people to develop a psychological disorder, that is, to behave in deviant, maladaptive, and personally distressful ways? Theorists have suggested various approaches to this question.

The Biological Approach

The biological approach attributes psychological disorders to organic, internal causes. This perspective primarily focuses on the brain, genetic factors, and neurotransmitter functioning as the sources of abnormality.

medical model
The view that psychological disorders are medical diseases with a biological origin.

The biological approach is evident in the **medical model,** which describes psychological disorders as medical diseases with a biological origin. From the perspective of the medical model, abnormalities are called *mental illnesses,* the afflicted individuals are *patients,* and they are treated by *doctors.*

The Psychological Approach

The psychological approach emphasizes the contributions of experiences, thoughts, emotions, and personality characteristics in explaining psychological disorders. Psychologists might focus, for example, on the influence of childhood experiences, personality traits, learning experiences, or cognitions in the development and course of psychological disorders.

The Sociocultural Approach

The sociocultural approach emphasizes the social contexts in which a person lives, including gender, ethnicity, socioeconomic status, family relationships, and culture. For instance, poverty is related to rates of psychological disorders (Kohrt & others, 2009).

The sociocultural perspective stresses the ways that cultures influence the understanding and treatment of psychological disorders. The frequency and intensity of psychological disorders vary and depend on social, economic, technological, and religious aspects of cultures (Shiraev & Levy, 2010). Some disorders are culture-related, such as windigo, a disorder recognized by Algonquin Indian hunters that involves fear of being bewitched and turned into a cannibal. Anorexia nervosa, which we will consider later in this chapter, tends to occur only in Western cultures, especially the United States.

The Biopsychosocial Model

Abnormal behavior can be influenced by biological factors (such as genes), psychological factors (such as childhood experiences), and sociocultural factors (such as gender). These factors can operate alone, but they often act in combination with one another.

To appreciate how these factors work together, let's back up for a moment. Consider that not everyone with a genetic predisposition to schizophrenia develops the disorder. Similarly, not everyone who experiences childhood neglect develops depression. Moreover, even women who live in cultures that strongly discriminate against them do not always develop psychological disorders. Thus, to understand the development of psychological disorders, we must consider a variety of *interacting* factors from each of the domains of experience.

Sometimes this approach is called *biopsychosocial*. From the biopsychosocial perspective, none of the factors considered is necessarily viewed as more important than another; rather, biological, psychological, and social factors are *all* significant ingredients in producing both normal and abnormal behavior. Furthermore, these ingredients may combine in unique ways, so that one depressed person might differ from another in terms of the key factors associated with the development of the disorder.

Classifying Abnormal Behavior

To understand, prevent, and treat abnormal behavior, psychiatrists and psychologists have devised systems classifying those behaviors into specific psychological disorders. Classifying psychological disorders provides a common basis for communicating. If one psychologist says that her client is experiencing depression, another psychologist understands that a particular pattern of abnormal behavior has led to this diagnosis. A classification system can also help clinicians make predictions about how likely it is that a particular disorder will occur, which individuals are most susceptible to it, how the disorder progresses, and what the prognosis (or outcome) for treatment is (Canino & others, 2004).

Further, a classification system may benefit the person suffering from psychological symptoms. Having a name for a problem can be a comfort and a signal that treatments are available. On the other hand, officially naming a problem can also have serious negative implications for the person because of the potential for creating *stigma,* a mark of shame that may cause others to avoid or to act negatively toward an individual. Being diagnosed with a psychological disorder can profoundly influence a person's life because of what the diagnosis means with respect to the person and his or her family and larger social world. We discuss stigma further at the end of this chapter.

The DSM-IV *Classification System* In 1952, the American Psychiatric Association (APA) published the first major classification of psychological disorders in the United States, the *Diagnostic and Statistical Manual of Mental Disorders*. Its current version, the **DSM-IV** (APA, 1994), was introduced in 1994 and revised in 2000, producing the *DSM-IV-TR* (text revision) (APA, 2000). *DSM-V* is due in 2011. Throughout the development of the *DSM,* the number of diagnosable disorders has increased dramatically. The first *DSM* listed 112 disorders; the *DSM-IV-TR* includes 374.

The *DSM-IV* classifies individuals on the basis of five dimensions, or *axes,* that take into account the individual's history and highest level of functioning in the previous year. The system's creators meant to ensure that the individual is not merely assigned to a psychological disorder category but instead is characterized in terms of a number of factors. The five axes of *DSM-IV* are:

Axis I: All diagnostic categories except personality disorders and mental retardation

Axis II: Personality disorders and mental retardation

Axis III: General medical conditions

Axis IV: Psychosocial and environmental problems

Axis V: Current level of functioning

Axes I and II are concerned with the classification of psychological disorders. Figure 12.1 describes the major categories of these disorders. Axes III through V may not be needed to diagnose a psychological disorder, but

Not all changes involved adding diagnoses. You might recall from Chapter 9 that homosexuality was considered a psychological disorder until 1973.

The DSM-IV was the work of more than 200 mental health professionals, including more women, ethnic minorities, and non-psychiatrists than any previous version.

DSM-IV
The *Diagnostic and Statistical Manual of Mental Disorders,* Fourth Edition; the major classification of psychological disorders in the United States.

Major Categories of Psychological Disorders	Description
Axis I Disorders	
Disorders usually first diagnosed in infancy, childhood, or adolescence and communication disorders	Include disorders that appear before adolescence, such as attention deficit hyperactivity disorder, autism, and learning disorders (stuttering, for example).
Anxiety disorders	Characterized by motor tension, hyperactivity, and apprehensive expectations/thoughts. Include generalized anxiety disorder, panic disorder, phobic disorder, obsessive-compulsive disorder, and post-traumatic stress disorder.
Somatoform disorders	Occur when psychological symptoms take a physical form even though no physical causes can be found. Include hypochondriasis and conversion disorder.
Factitious disorders	Characterized by the individual's deliberate fabrication of a medical or mental disorder, but not for external gain (such as a disability claim).
Dissociative disorders	Involve a sudden loss of memory or change of identity. Include the disorders of dissociative amnesia, dissociative fugue, and dissociative identity disorder.
Delirium, dementia, amnesia, and other cognitive disorders	Consist of mental disorders involving problems in consciousness and cognition, such as substance-induced delirium or dementia related to Alzheimer disease.
Mood disorders	Disorders in which there is a primary disturbance in mood; include depressive disorders and bipolar disorder (which involves wide mood swings from deep depression to extreme euphoria and agitation).
Schizophrenia and other psychotic disorders	Disorders characterized by distorted thoughts and perceptions, odd communication, inappropriate emotion, and other unusual behaviors.
Substance-related disorders	Include alcohol-related disorders, cocaine-related disorders, hallucinogen-related disorders, and other drug-related disorders.
Sexual and gender identity disorders	Consist of three main types of disorders: gender-identity disorders (person is not comfortable with identity as a female or male), paraphilias (person has a preference for unusual sexual acts to stimulate sexual arousal), and sexual dysfunctions (impairments in sexual functioning).
Eating disorders	Include anorexia nervosa, bulimia nervosa, and binge eating disorder.
Sleep disorders	Consist of primary sleep disorders, such as insomnia and narcolepsy (see Chapter 4), and sleep disorders due to a general medical condition.
Impulse control disorders not elsewhere classified	Include kleptomania, pyromania, and compulsive gambling.
Adjustment disorders	Characterized by distressing emotional or behavioral symptoms in response to an identifiable stressor.
Axis II Disorders	
Mental retardation	Low intellectual functioning and an inability to adapt to everyday life (see Chapter 7).
Personality disorders	Develop when personality traits become inflexible and maladaptive. Include antisocial personality disorder and borderline personality disorder.
Other conditions that may be a focus of clinical attention	Include relational problems (with a partner, sibling, and so on), problems related to abuse or neglect (physical abuse of a child, for example), or additional conditions (such as bereavement, academic problems, religious or spiritual problems).

FIGURE 12.1

Main Categories of Psychological Disorders in the *DSM-IV* The *DSM-IV* provides a way for mental health professionals and researchers to communicate with one another about these well-defined psychological disorders.

challenge your thinking

Are Psychological Disorders a Myth?

In a 2005 broadcast of NBC's *Today Show,* Matt Lauer interviewed Tom Cruise, who was embroiled in a heated media debate with fellow actor Brooke Shields. Shields had published a book about her experience with *postpartum* (that is, following childbirth) depression and her positive experience with prescription antidepressants to treat her disorder. Cruise vehemently criticized the very idea of depression and scorned the use of prescription drugs to treat psychological disorders. Cruise's words provoked strong responses. The National Alliance for the Mentally Ill (NAMI), the American Psychiatric Association, and the National Mental Health Association (NMHA) issued a joint statement declaring, "While we respect the right of individuals to express their own points of view, they are not entitled to their own facts. Mental illnesses are real medical conditions that affect millions of Americans" (NAMI/APA/NMHA, 2005).

Cruise's argument was very similar to one made nearly 50 years ago by psychiatrist Thomas Szasz (1961) in his book *The Myth of Mental Illness.* Szasz argued that psychological disorders are not illnesses and are better labeled "problems of living." If a man's bizarre beliefs do nothing more than offend or frighten other people, what right do we have to label him "mentally ill" and to administer drugs to him?

The controversy over attention deficit hyperactivity disorder provides a thought-provoking example. In **attention deficit hyperactivity disorder (ADHD),** individuals show one or more of the following symptoms: inattention, hyperactivity, and impulsivity. ADHD is one of the most common psychological disorders of childhood, and the growth in diagnosis of this disorder in recent years is staggering (Jensen, 2006). Whereas in 1988 just 500,000 cases were diagnosed, currently *4 million* children are diagnosed with ADHD each year (Bloom & Cohen, 2007). The sheer number of ADHD diagnoses has prompted some observers to wonder whether psychiatrists, parents, and teachers are in fact labeling what is normal childhood behavior as psychopathology (Carey, 2002). This issue is significant because animal research has shown that in the absence of ADHD, exposure to stimulants such as Ritalin (a common drug treatment for ADHD) can predispose individuals to later addiction problems (Leo, 2005).

In response to the controversy, the National Institute of Mental Health reviewed the scientific evidence. The resulting "consensus statement," signed by 75 psychiatrists and psychologists, declared that ADHD is a real psychological disorder with a biological basis in the brain, associated with a number of problems, including dropping out of school, teen pregnancy, and antisocial behavior (Barkley & 74 others, 2002). In turn, however, critics of the consensus statement argued that the biological basis of ADHD is not unique to ADHD but is a pattern shared with other childhood disorders (Timimi, 2004). Furthermore, the critics argued, the use of prescription drugs removes responsibility from parents and teachers and leads society to ignore possible environmental factors in ADHD. Finally, critics pointed out that some of those signing the statement were researchers funded by the pharmaceutical companies that produce the drugs used to treat ADHD.

Does this debate have a resolution? Clearly, psychological disorders are "real" in the sense that they lead to objectively negative outcomes in people's lives. The controversy over ADHD is a reminder of the important role of research in clarifying and defining diagnostic categories. Nobody wants to label inappropriately, to misdiagnose, or to mistreat people who are already suffering.

In 2005, actor Tom Cruise denounced fellow actor Brooke Shields (left) after she publicized her experience with postpartum depression. On the Today Show, *Cruise (right, with host Matt Lauer) attacked the very idea of depression and called psychiatry a "pseudo science."*

What Do You Think?

■ When do you think it is appropriate to label someone as having a psychological disorder?

■ When do you think medical treatments for psychological disorders are appropriate?

■ If a teacher suggested that your child be tested for ADHD, what would you do?

they are included so that the person's overall life situation is considered. Axis III information helps to clarify if symptoms may be rooted in physical illness. On Axis V, the clinician evaluates the highest level of adaptive functioning the person has attained in the preceding year in social, occupational, or school activities.

Critiques of the *DSM-IV*

The most controversial aspect of the *DSM-IV* is that the manual classifies individuals based on their symptoms, using medical terminology in the psychiatric tradition of thinking about mental disorders in terms of disease (Oltmanns & Emery, 2007). This emphasis implies that the abnormalities have an internal cause that is relatively independent of environmental factors (Kring & others, 2007). So, even though researchers have begun to shed light on the complex interaction of biological, psychological, and environmental factors in psychological disorders, the *DSM-IV* continues to reflect the medical model (American Psychiatric Association, 2006).

Another criticism is that the *DSM-IV* focuses strictly on pathology and problems. Critics argue that emphasizing *strengths* as well as weaknesses might help to destigmatize labels such as "schizophrenic." Indeed, professionals avoid such labels, using what is called *people-first language*. Moe Armstrong is a "person with schizophrenia," not a "schizophrenic." Identifying a person's strengths can be an important step toward maximizing his or her ability to contribute to society (Roten, 2007).

Labels such as those described by the *DSM* are based on the idea that psychological disorders are real. However, some individuals have questioned this very assumption. To read about this controversy, see Challenge Your Thinking.

attention deficit hyperactivity disorder (ADHD)
One of the most common psychological disorders of childhood, in which individuals show one or more of the following: inattention, hyperactivity, and impulsivity.

Labeling Moe Armstrong as having schizophrenia does not reveal that he is also capable of love, creativity, and productive work.

self-quiz

1. All of the following are characteristics of abnormal behavior *except*
   A. it is typical.
   B. it causes distress.
   C. it is maladaptive.
   D. it is deviant.

2. The medical model interprets psychological disorders as medical diseases with a/an
   A. environmental origin.
   B. sociocultural origin.
   C. biological origin.
   D. biopsychosocial origin.

3. Mental retardation is classified on _____ of the *DSM-IV*.
   A. Axis I
   B. Axis II
   C. Axis III
   D. Axis IV

Apply It! 4. Since she was a little girl, 19-year-old Francesca has believed that whenever she walks through a doorway, she must touch the door frame 12 times and silently count to 12 or else her mother will die. She has never told anyone about this ritual, which she feels is harmless, similar to carrying a lucky charm. Which of the following is true of Francesca's behavior?
   A. Francesca's behavior is abnormal only because it is different from the norm. It is not maladaptive, nor does it cause her distress.
   B. Francesca's behavior fits all three characteristics of abnormal behavior.
   C. Francesca's behavior is maladaptive, but it is not abnormal because she does not feel personal distress over her ritual.
   D. Francesca's behavior does not fit any of the characteristics of abnormal behavior.

2 Anxiety Disorders

Think about how you felt before a make-or-break exam or a big presentation—or perhaps as you noticed police lights flashing behind your speeding car. Did you feel jittery and nervous and experience tightness in your stomach? These are the feelings of normal anxiety, an unpleasant feeling of fear and dread.

In contrast, **anxiety disorders** involve fears that are uncontrollable, disproportionate to the actual danger the person might be in, and disruptive of ordinary life. They feature motor tension (jumpiness, trembling), hyperactivity (dizziness, a racing heart), and apprehensive expectations and thoughts. In this section we survey five types of anxiety disorders:

anxiety disorders
Disabling (uncontrollable and disruptive) psychological disorders that feature motor tension, hyperactivity, and apprehensive expectations and thoughts.

- Generalized anxiety disorder
- Panic disorder
- Phobic disorder
- Obsessive-compulsive disorder
- Post-traumatic stress disorder

Generalized Anxiety Disorder

When you are worrying about getting a speeding ticket, you know why you are anxious; there is a specific cause. **Generalized anxiety disorder** is different from such everyday feelings of anxiety in that sufferers experience persistent anxiety for at least 6 months and are unable to specify the reasons for the anxiety (Kendler & others, 2007). People with generalized anxiety disorder are nervous most of the time. They may worry about their work, relationships, or health. That worry can also take a physical toll and cause fatigue, muscle tension, stomach problems, and difficulty sleeping.

What is the etiology of generalized anxiety disorder? (*Etiology* means the causes or significant preceding conditions.) Among the biological factors are genetic predisposition, deficiency in the neurotransmitter GABA, and respiratory system abnormalities (Garner & others, 2009; Katzman, 2009). The psychological and sociocultural factors include having harsh (or even impossible) self-standards, overly strict and critical parents, automatic negative thoughts when feeling stressed, and a history of uncontrollable traumas or stressors (such as an abusive parent).

Recall from Chapter 2 that GABA is the neurotransmitter that inhibits neurons from firing—it's like the brain's brake pedal. Problems with GABA are often implicated in anxiety disorders.

A panic attack can be a one-time occurrence. People with panic disorder have recurrent attacks that sometimes lead them to be afraid to even leave their homes, a condition called agoraphobia.

generalized anxiety disorder Psychological disorder marked by persistent anxiety for at least 6 months, and in which the individual is unable to specify the reasons for the anxiety.

Panic Disorder

Much like everyone else, you might sometimes have a specific experience that sends you into a panic. For example, you work all night on a paper, only to have your computer crash before you saved your last changes, or you are about to dash across a street when you see a large truck coming right at you. Your heart races, your hands shake, and you might break into a sweat.

In a **panic disorder,** however, a person experiences recurrent, sudden onsets of intense terror, often without warning and with no specific cause. Panic attacks can produce severe palpitations, extreme shortness of breath, chest pains, trembling, sweating, dizziness, and a feeling of helplessness (Dammen & others, 2006). People with panic disorder may feel that they are having a heart attack or going to die. Charles Darwin, the scientist who proposed the theory of evolution, suffered from intense panic disorder (Barloon & Noyes, 1997). Actor Kim Basinger and former NFL running back Earl Campbell also have dealt with this disorder.

What is the etiology of panic disorder? In terms of biological factors, individuals may have a genetic predisposition to the disorder (Battaglia & others, 2009). One biological view is that individuals who experience panic disorder may have an autonomic nervous system that is predisposed to be overly active (Barlow, 1988). Another biologically based possibility is that panic disorder may stem from problems involving either or both of two neurotransmitters: norepinephrine and GABA (Zwanzger & Rupprecht, 2005).

panic disorder Anxiety disorder in which the individual experiences recurrent, sudden onsets of intense terror, often without warning and with no specific cause.

Many experts interpret Edvard Munch's painting The Scream *as an expression of the terror brought on by a panic attack.*

With respect to psychological factors, one theory about panic disorder is that individuals misinterpret harmless indicators of physiological arousal (for example, a slightly raised heartbeat) as an emergency (such as a heart attack). However, this model of panic disorder remains controversial (Austin & Richards, 2006).

In terms of sociocultural factors, American women are twice as likely as American men to have panic attacks (Altemus, 2006). Possible reasons for this difference include biological differences in hormones and neurotransmitters (Altemus, 2006; Fodor & Epstein, 2002). Research also suggests that women may cope with anxiety-provoking situations differently than men, and these differences may explain the gender difference in panic disorder (Schmidt & Koselka, 2000).

Phobic Disorder

Many people are afraid of spiders and snakes; indeed, thinking about letting a tarantula crawl over one's face is likely to give anyone the willies. It is not uncommon to be afraid of particular objects or specific environments such as extreme heights. For most of us, these fears do not interfere with daily life. Some of us, however, have an irrational, overwhelming, persistent fear of a particular object or situation—an anxiety disorder called a **phobic disorder (phobia).** Whereas individuals with generalized anxiety disorder cannot pinpoint the cause of their nervous feelings, individuals with phobias can (Schienle & others, 2009).

A fear becomes a phobia when a situation is so dreaded that an individual goes to almost any length to avoid it. As with any anxiety disorder, phobias are fears that are uncontrollable, disproportionate, and disruptive. A snake phobia that keeps a city-dweller from leaving his apartment is clearly disproportionate to the actual chances of encountering a snake. John Madden—former NFL coach, recently retired football commentator, and successful video game consultant—has a famous fear of flying that led him to take a bus to the games that he broadcast.

Another phobic disorder, *social phobia,* is an intense fear of being humiliated or embarrassed in social situations (Rapee, Gaston, & Abbott, 2009). Successful singers Carly Simon and Barbra Streisand have dealt with social phobia.

Phobias usually begin in childhood (National Institute of Mental Health, 2008) and come in many forms. Figure 12.2 labels and describes a number of phobias.

What is the etiology of phobic disorder? Genes appear to play a role in social phobia (Reich, 2009). Researchers have proposed that there is a neural circuit for social phobia that includes the thalamus, amygdala, and cerebral cortex (Damsa, Kosel, & Moussally, 2009). Also, a number of neurotransmitters may be involved in social phobia, especially serotonin (Nash & Nutt, 2005).

With regard to psychological factors, learning theorists consider phobias learned fears (Clark & others, 2006). Perhaps, for example, the individual with the fear of falling off a building experienced a fall from a high place earlier in life and therefore associates heights with pain (a classical conditioning explanation). Alternatively, he or she may have heard about or watched others who demonstrated terror of high places (an observational-learning explanation), as when a little girl develops a fear of heights after sitting next to her terrified mother and observing her clutch the handrails, white-knuckled, as the roller coaster creeps steeply uphill.

phobic disorder (phobia)
Anxiety disorder characterized by an irrational, overwhelming, persistent fear of a particular object or situation.

Whenever you encounter gender differences in this discussion, ask yourself whether men or women might be more likely to report themselves as having problems or to seek treatment. Research on psychological disorders is often based on individuals who have reported symptoms or sought help. If men are less likely to report symptoms or seek treatment, the data may underestimate their levels of psychological disorders.

"Stephen's fear of heights is particularly bad today."
www.CartoonStock.com

Systematic desensitization, described in Chapter 5, involves the application of learning principles to the unlearning of phobias.

Acrophobia	Fear of high places	Arachnophobia	Fear of spiders	Mysophobia	Fear of dirt
Aerophobia	Fear of flying	Astrapophobia	Fear of lightning	Nyctophobia	Fear of darkness
Ailurophobia	Fear of cats	Cynophobia	Fear of dogs	Ophidiophobia	Fear of non-
Algophobia	Fear of pain	Gamophobia	Fear of marriage		poisonous snakes
Amaxophobia	Fear of vehicles, driving	Hydrophobia	Fear of water	Thanatophobia	Fear of death
		Melissophobia	Fear of bees	Xenophobia	Fear of strangers

FIGURE 12.2

Phobias This figure features some examples of phobic disorder—an anxiety disorder characterized by irrational and overwhelming fear of a particular object or situation.

© Mike Baldwin / Cornered

"Since you have a complete record of my life, could you tell me if I remembered to turn the stove off?"

www.CartoonStock.com

As long as the person performs the ritual, the terrible outcome doesn't happen. Of course, it wouldn't happen anyway, but as long as she goes through the ritual, she never finds that out. The easing of the anxiety is an example of negative reinforcement (having something bad taken away after performing a behavior).

Obsessive-Compulsive Disorder

Just before leaving on a long road trip, you find yourself checking to be sure you locked the front door. As you pull away in your car, you are stricken with the thought that you forgot to turn off the coffeemaker. Going to bed the night before an early flight, you check your alarm clock a few times to be sure you will wake up on time. This kind of checking behavior is normal.

In contrast, the anxiety disorder known as **obsessive-compulsive disorder (OCD)** features anxiety-provoking thoughts that will not go away and/or urges to perform repetitive, ritualistic behaviors to prevent or produce some future situation. *Obsessions* are recurrent thoughts, and *compulsions* are recurrent behaviors. Individuals with OCD dwell on their doubts and repeat their routines sometimes hundreds of times a day (Abramowitz, 2009). Game show host Howie Mandel has coped with OCD; soccer star David Beckham and actor Leonardo DiCaprio have each described mild cases.

The most common compulsions are excessive checking, cleansing, and counting. An individual with OCD might believe that she has to touch the doorway with her left hand whenever she enters a room and count her steps as she walks across the room. If she does not complete this ritual, she may be overcome with a sense of fear that something terrible will happen (Victor & Bernstein, 2009).

What is the etiology of obsessive-compulsive disorder? In terms of biological factors, there seems to be a genetic component (Gelernter & Stein, 2009; Wang, Simpson, & Dulawa, 2009). Also, brain-imaging studies have suggested neurological links for OCD (Nakao & others, 2009). One interpretation of these data is that the frontal cortex or basal ganglia are so active in OCD that numerous impulses reach the thalamus, generating obsessive thoughts or compulsive actions (Figure 12.3) (Rotge & others, 2009).

A study using fMRI examined the brain activity of individuals with OCD before and after treatment. The results demonstrated that following effective treatment,

obsessive-compulsive disorder (OCD) Anxiety disorder in which the individual has anxiety-provoking thoughts that will not go away and/or urges to perform repetitive, ritualistic behaviors to prevent or produce some future situation.

a number of areas in the frontal cortex showed decreased activation (Nakao & others, 2005). Interestingly, the amygdala, which is associated with the experience of anxiety, may be smaller (Atmaca & others, 2008) in individuals with OCD compared to those who do not have the disorder. Low levels of the neurotransmitters serotonin and dopamine likely are involved in the brain pathways linked with OCD (Olver & others, 2009; Pampaloni & others, 2009).

In terms of psychological factors, OCD sometimes occurs during a period of life stress such as that surrounding the birth of a child or a change in occupational or marital status (Uguz & others, 2007). According to the cognitive perspective, what differentiates individuals with OCD from those who do not have it is the ability to turn off negative, intrusive thoughts by ignoring or effectively dismissing them (Najmi, Riemann, & Wegner, 2009; Wu, Aardema, & O'Connor, 2009).

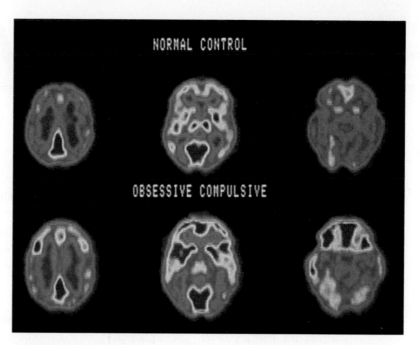

FIGURE 12.3

PET Scans of Individuals with Obsessive-Compulsive Disorder
(*Top*) Brain images of normal individuals. (*Bottom*) Brain images of individuals with obsessive-compulsive disorder (OCD). The brain images of the individuals with OCD show more activity in the frontal cortex, basal ganglia, and thalamus than the scans of normal individuals.

Post-Traumatic Stress Disorder

If you have ever been in even a minor car accident, you may have had a nightmare or two about it. You might have even found yourself reliving the experience for some time. This normal recovery process takes on a particularly devastating character in post-traumatic stress disorder. **Post-traumatic stress disorder (PTSD)** is an anxiety disorder that develops through exposure to a traumatic event that has overwhelmed the person's abilities to cope (Friedman, Keane, & Resick, 2007). The symptoms of PTSD vary but include:

post-traumatic stress disorder (PTSD)
Anxiety disorder that develops through exposure to a traumatic event, a severely oppressive situation, cruel abuse, or a natural or an unnatural disaster.

- Flashbacks in which the individual relives the event. A flashback can make the person lose touch with reality and reenact the event for seconds, hours, or, very rarely, days. A person having a flashback—which can come in the form of images, sounds, smells, and/or feelings—usually believes that the traumatic event is happening all over again (Speckens & others, 2007).

- Avoiding emotional experiences and avoiding talking about emotions with others.

- Reduced ability to feel emotions, often reported as feeling numb, resulting in an inability to experience happiness, sexual desire, or enjoyable interpersonal relationships.

- Excessive arousal, resulting in an exaggerated startle response or an inability to sleep.

- Difficulties with memory and concentration.

- Feelings of apprehension, including nervous tremors.

- Impulsive outbursts of behavior, such as aggressiveness, or sudden changes in lifestyle.

PTSD symptoms can follow a trauma immediately or after months or even years (Breslau & Alvarado, 2007). Most individuals who are exposed to a traumatic event experience

The Psychological Wounds of War

PTSD has been a concern for soldiers in Iraq and Afghanistan (Ling & others, 2009). In an effort to prevent PTSD, the U.S. military gives troops stress-management training before deployment (Ritchie & others, 2006). Branches of the armed forces station mental health professionals in combat zones around the world to help prevent PTSD and to lessen the effects of the disorder (Rabasca, 2000). These measures appear to be paying off: Researchers have found that PTSD sufferers from the Iraq and Afghanistan wars are generally less likely to be unemployed or incarcerated, and more likely to maintain strong social bonds following their term of service, than veterans of earlier wars (Fontana & Rosenheck, 2008).

Historically, the stigma associated with psychological disorders has been particularly strong within the military ranks, where struggling with a psychological problem is commonly viewed as a sign of weakness or incompetence. Yet individuals engaged in combat are at considerable risk of developing PTSD, and the disorder can profoundly affect their lives. A survey of almost 3,000 soldiers who had just returned from the Iraq War revealed that 17 percent met the criteria for PTSD (Hoge & others, 2007). This figure is likely an underestimate given the stigma linked to psychological disorders in the military.

In 2008, military psychologist John Fortunato suggested that veterans with PTSD ought to be eligible for the Purple Heart, the prestigious military decoration awarded to those who have been physically wounded or killed in combat (Schogol, 2009). Awarding PTSD sufferers the Purple Heart, Fortunato argued, would not only acknowledge their sacrifice but also reduce the stigma attached to psychological disorders. That year, the military did consider whether PTSD sufferers in its ranks ought to be awarded the Purple Heart. However, the Pentagon decided against awarding the Purple Heart to military personnel with PTSD, on the grounds that the disorder is not limited to victims of physical trauma from enemy fire but also can affect eyewitnesses (Schogol, 2009). Still, the fact that the top brass considered the possibility suggests that the military is becoming more aware of the serious problems facing those who are traumatized while serving their country in combat.

Prior to deployment, U.S. troops receive stress-management training aimed at helping to prevent PTSD and other disorders that might be triggered by the high-stress conditions of war.

some of the symptoms in the days and weeks following exposure (National Center for Post-Traumatic Stress Disorder, 2006). However, not every individual exposed to the same event develops PTSD (Gil & Caspi, 2006; Nemeroff & others, 2006).

Researchers have examined PTSD associated with various different experiences. These include combat and war-related traumas (Johnson & Thompson, 2007; Thabet & others, 2009); sexual abuse and assault (Weich & others, 2009); natural disasters such as hurricanes and earthquakes (Parvaresh & Bahramnezhad, 2009); and unnatural disasters such as plane crashes and terrorist attacks (Dedert & others, 2009).

Clearly, one cause of PTSD is the traumatic event itself. However, because not everyone who experiences the same traumatic life event develops PTSD, other factors (aside from the event) must influence a person's vulnerability to the disorder (Markowitz & others 2009). These include a history of previous traumatic events and conditions, such as abuse and psychological disorders (Courtois & Ford, 2009), as well as genetic predisposition (H. Cohen & others, 2008; Voisey & others, 2009).

1. Sudden episodes of extreme anxiety or terror that involve symptoms such as heart palpitations, trembling, sweating, and fear of losing control are characteristic of
   A. generalized anxiety disorder.
   B. post-traumatic stress disorder.
   C. obsessive-compulsive disorder.
   D. panic disorder.

2. Which of the following is *true* of post-traumatic stress disorder?
   A. It is caused by panic attacks.
   B. It is the natural outgrowth of experiencing trauma.
   C. It involves flashbacks.
   D. The symptoms always occur immediately following a trauma.

3. Intense fear of something that provokes an individual's efforts to avoid the feared stimulus is a defining characteristic of
   A. post-traumatic stress disorder.
   B. phobic disorder.
   C. panic disorder.
   D. generalized anxiety disorder.

Apply It! 4. Although Tina's mother has always been a worrier, lately Tina has noticed that her mother appears to be overwhelmed with worry about everything. Her mother has told Tina that she is having trouble sleeping and is experiencing racing thoughts of all the terrible things that might happen at any given moment. Tina's mother is showing signs of
A. panic disorder.
B. obsessive-compulsive disorder.
C. generalized anxiety disorder.
D. post-traumatic stress disorder.

3 Mood Disorders

Mood disorders are psychological disorders in which there is a primary disturbance of *mood:* prolonged emotion that colors the individual's entire emotional state. This mood disturbance can include cognitive, behavioral, and somatic (physical) symptoms, as well as interpersonal difficulties. In this section we examine the two main types of mood disorders, depressive disorders and bipolar disorder. In addition, we consider a tragic correlate of these disorders—suicide.

mood disorders
Psychological disorders—the main types of which are depressive disorders and bipolar disorder—in which there is a primary disturbance of mood: prolonged emotion that colors the individual's entire emotional state.

Depressive Disorders

depressive disorders
Mood disorders in which the individual suffers from depression—an unrelenting lack of pleasure in life.

major depressive disorder (MDD)
Psychological disorder involving a major depressive episode and depressed characteristics, such as lethargy and hopelessness, for at least two weeks.

Everyone feels blue sometimes. A romantic breakup, the death of a loved one, or a personal failure can cast a dark cloud over life. Sometimes, however, a person might feel unhappy and not know why. **Depressive disorders** are mood disorders in which the individual suffers from *depression:* an unrelenting lack of pleasure in life. The severity of depressive disorders varies. Some individuals experience what is classified as *major depressive disorder,* whereas others are given the diagnosis of *dysthymic disorder,* a more chronic depression with fewer symptoms than major depression (Ingram, 2009).

Depressive disorders are common, and a number of successful individuals have been diagnosed with depression. They include musicians Sheryl Crow and Eric Clapton, actors Drew Barrymore and Jim Carrey, artist Pablo Picasso, astronaut Buzz Aldrin (the second moon walker), and famed American architect Frank Lloyd Wright.

Major depressive disorder (MDD) involves a significant depressive episode and depressed characteristics, such as lethargy and hopelessness, for at least two weeks. MDD impairs daily functioning, and it has been called the leading cause of disability in the United States (National Institute of Mental Health, 2006). Nine symptoms (at least

This painting by Vincent Van Gogh, Portrait of Dr. Gachet, *reflects the extreme melancholy that characterizes the depressive disorders.*

five of which must be present during a two-week period) define a major depressive episode:

- Depressed mood most of the day
- Reduced interest or pleasure in all or most activities
- Significant weight loss or gain or significant decrease or interest in appetite
- Trouble sleeping or sleeping too much
- Psychomotor agitation or retardation
- Fatigue or loss of energy
- Feeling worthless or guilty in an excessive or inappropriate manner
- Problems in thinking, concentrating, or making decisions
- Recurrent thoughts of death and suicide
- No history of manic episodes (periods of euphoric mood)

dysthymic disorder (DD)
Mood disorder that is generally more chronic and has fewer symptoms than major depressive disorder.

Dysthymic disorder (DD) is a mood disorder that is generally more chronic and has fewer symptoms than MDD. The individual is in a depressed mood for most days for at least two years as an adult or at least one year as a child or adolescent. To be classified as having dysthymic disorder, the individual must not have experienced a major depressive episode, and the two-year period of depression must not have been broken by a normal mood lasting more than two months. Two or more of these six symptoms must be present:

- Poor appetite or overeating
- Sleep problems
- Low energy or fatigue
- Low self-esteem
- Poor concentration or difficulty making decisions
- Feelings of hopelessness

What are the causes of depressive disorder? A variety of biological, psychological, and sociocultural factors have been implicated in the development of these disorders.

Biological Factors

Genetic influences play a role in depression (Craddock & Forty, 2006). In addition, specific brain structures are involved in depressive disorders. For example, depressed individuals show lower levels of brain activity in a section of the prefrontal cortex that is involved in generating actions (Clark, Chamberlain, & Sahakian, 2009; Friedel & others, 2009) as well as in regions of the brain associated with the perception of rewards in the environment (Keedwell & others, 2005; Tye & Janak, 2007). A depressed person's brain may not recognize opportunities for pleasurable experiences.

Depression also likely involves problems in the regulation of a number of neurotransmitters. Recall from Chapter 2 that neurotransmitters are chemicals that carry impulses from neuron to neuron. In order for the brain to function smoothly, these neurotransmitters must ebb and flow, often in harmony with one another. Individuals with major depressive disorder appear to have too few receptors for the neurotransmitters serotonin and norepinephrine (Asghar-Ali & Braun, 2009; Cipriani & others, 2009). Still other research suggests that problems in regulating a neurotransmitter called substance P might be involved in depression (Norman & Burrows, 2007). Substance P is thought to play an important role in the psychological experience of pain.

Psychological Factors

learned helplessness
An individual's acquisition of feelings of powerlessness when he or she is exposed to aversive circumstances, such as prolonged stress, over which that individual has no control.

Psychological explanations of depression have drawn on behavioral learning theories and cognitive theories. One behavioral view of depression focuses on **learned helplessness,** an individual's acquisition of feelings of powerlessness when exposed to aversive circumstances, such as prolonged stress, over which the individual has no control. Martin Seligman (1975) proposed that learned helplessness is one reason that some individuals become depressed. When individuals cannot control their stress, they eventually feel helpless and stop trying to change their situations. This helplessness spirals into hopelessness (Becker-Weidman & others, 2009).

Cognitive explanations of depression focus on the thoughts and beliefs that contribute to this sense of hopelessness (Fiske, Wetherell, & Gatz, 2009; Smith, Calam, & Bolton, 2009). Psychiatrist Aaron Beck (1967) proposed that negative thoughts reflect self-defeating beliefs that shape depressed individuals' experiences. These habitual negative thoughts magnify and expand depressed persons' negative experiences (Joorman, Teachman, & Gotlib, 2009; Kuyken & Beck, 2007). For example, a depressed individual might overgeneralize about a minor occurrence—say, turning in a work assignment late—and think that he or she is worthless. A depressed person might view a minor setback such as getting a D on a paper as the end of the world. The accumulation of such cognitive distortions can lead to depression (Joorman & others, 2009).

The *way* people think can also influence the course of depression (Brinker & Dozois, 2009). Depressed individuals may ruminate on negative experiences and negative feelings, playing them over and over again in their minds (Nolen-Hoeksema & others, 2007). This tendency to ruminate is associated with the development of depression as well as other psychological problems such as binge eating and substance abuse (Nolen-Hoeksema & others, 2007).

Another cognitive view of depression focuses on people's *attributions*—their attempts to explain what caused something to happen (Hartley & Maclean, 2009; Northoff, 2007). Depression is thought to be related to a pessimistic attributional style. In this style, individuals regularly explain negative events as having internal causes ("It is my fault I failed the exam"), stable causes ("I'm going to fail again and again"), and global causes ("Failing this exam shows that I won't do well in any of my courses"). Pessimistic attributional style means blaming oneself for negative events and expecting the negative events to recur (Abramson, Seligman, & Teasdale, 1978). This pessimistic style can be contrasted with an optimistic attributional style, which is essentially its opposite. Optimists make external attributions for bad things that happen ("I did badly on the test because it's hard to know what a professor wants on the first exam"). They also recognize that these causes can change ("I'll do better on the next one") and that they are specific ("It was only one test"). Optimistic attributional style has been related to lowered depression and decreased suicide risk in a variety of samples (Giltay, Zitman, & Kromhout, 2006; Hirsch & others, 2009).

Sociocultural Factors

Individuals with a low socioeconomic status (SES), especially people living in poverty, are more likely to develop depression than their higher-SES counterparts (Boothroyd & others, 2006). A longitudinal study of adults revealed that depression increased as standard of living and employment circumstances worsened (Lorant & others, 2007). Studies have found very high rates of depression in Native American groups, among whom poverty, hopelessness, and alcoholism are widespread (Teesson & Vogl, 2006).

Women are nearly twice as likely as men to develop depression (Yuan & others, 2009). This gender difference occurs in many countries (Figure 12.4; Inaba & others, 2005). Incidence of depression is high, too, among single women who are the heads of households and among young married women who work at unsatisfying, dead-end jobs (Whiffen & Demidenko, 2006). Minority women also are a high-risk group for depression (Diefenbach & others, 2009).

We have concentrated so far on adult depression. However, there also is concern about depression during childhood, as the Intersection explores.

Lifetime rate per 100 people

Korea 4 / 2.5
Puerto Rico 6.5 / 4.5
United States 8.5 / 3.5
Edmonton, Canada 13 / 7.5
New Zealand 16 / 8
West Germany 17 / 5
Florence, Italy 19 / 6.5
Paris, France 22 / 11
Beirut, Lebanon 24 / 14

☐ Males   ☐ Females

FIGURE 12.4

Gender Differences in Depression Across Cultures One study showed that women were more likely than men to have major depression in nine cultures (Weissman & Olfson, 1995).

Another gender difference to consider: Why might men show lower levels of depression than women?

I magine once again being 3 years old. Your routine would likely revolve around eating, playing, and napping. For most 3-year-olds and even older children, life would seem to be a time of simple happiness. For some children, however, childhood is clouded by depression. Between 1.5 and 2.5 percent of school-age children and 15 to 20 percent of adolescents experience major depression (Graber & Sontag, 2009).

Clinical and Developmental Psychology: A Happier Future for Depressed Children?

Childhood depression is a significant problem (Domenech-Llaberia & others, 2009; Korczak & Goldstein, 2009). Because childhood is a time of building skills and abilities that are essential in later life, childhood depression may interfere with normal development. Children who develop depression face a higher risk of substance abuse, academic problems, physical illness, future depression, and suicide (Cullen, Klimes-Dougan, & Kumra, 2009; Horowitz & Garber, 2006). How can we as a society come to better understand, treat, and prevent this debilitating childhood disorder?

Developmental psychopathology represents the merging of developmental and clinical psychology to understand, treat, and prevent childhood psychological disorders (Fontaine & others, 2009; Masten, 2006; Obradovic & others, 2009). Rather than applying knowledge about adult psychological disorders to children, developmental psychopathologists focus on the special developmental circumstances of children.

Using longitudinal studies to track the relationships that exist in the unfolding of abnormal and normal behavior patterns (Ge & others, 2009; Zimmer-Gembeck & others, 2009), developmental psychopathology seeks to identify *risk factors* that might predispose a child to depression (Bureau, Easterbooks, & Lyons-Ruth, 2009; Cicchetti & Toth, 2006), as well as *protective factors*, that is, aspects of a child's psychological or social experience that may provide a shield against the development of depression. The identification of risk factors might suggest avenues for both prevention and treatment. For example, researchers have identified parental psychopathology as a risk factor for childhood depression: Parents who suffer from depression, an anxiety disorder, or substance abuse are more likely to have children who experience depression (Shaw & others, 2009). A recent research review revealed that interventions aimed at youth who were at risk for depression promoted wellness in the targeted groups (Horowitz & Garber, 2006). Interventions might include training at-risk children to engage in more effective attributions for negative events, or to manage their emotions in a healthy way. Protective factors might include a supportive adult who provides the child with love, encouragement, and a role model or a strong extended family that supports the child's attempts to cope with difficulties.

Childhood is a time of extraordinary development and learning. Developmental psychopathologists are taking the problems of persistently sad and disengaged children seriously and striving to understand the sources of their suffering in order to give them a more promising future (Graber & Sontag, 2009).

Do you know a child who might be at risk for depression? How might *you* be a protective factor?

Bipolar Disorder

bipolar disorder
Mood disorder characterized by extreme mood swings that include one or more episodes of mania, an overexcited, unrealistically optimistic state.

Just as we all have down times, there are times when things seem to be going phenomenally well. For individuals with bipolar disorder, the ups and downs of life take on an extreme and often harmful tone. **Bipolar disorder** is a mood disorder that is characterized by extreme mood swings that include one or more episodes of *mania,* an overexcited, unrealistically optimistic state. A manic episode is like the flip-side of a depressive episode (Last, 2009). The person who experiences mania feels on top of the world. He or she has tremendous energy and might sleep very little. A manic state also features an impulsivity that can get the individual in trouble. For example, the sufferer might spend his or her life savings on a foolish business venture.

Most bipolar individuals experience multiple cycles of depression interspersed with mania, usually separated by six months to a year. Unlike depressive disorders, which are more likely to occur in women, bipolar disorder is equally common in women and men. Bipolar disorder does not prevent a person from being successful. Tony Award–winning actor Patty Duke, famed American dancer and choreographer Alvin Ailey, and actor Carrie Fisher (Princess Leia) have been diagnosed with bipolar disorder.

What factors play a role in the development of bipolar disorder? Genetic influences are stronger predictors of bipolar disorder than depressive disorder (Craddock & Forty, 2006). An individual with an identical twin who has bipolar disorder has a more than 60 percent probability of also having the disorder, and a fraternal twin more than 10 percent (Figure 12.5). Researchers are zeroing in on the specific genetic location of bipolar disorder (Barnett & Smoller, 2009; Zhou & others, 2009a).

Other biological processes are also a factor. Like depression, bipolar disorder is associated with differences in brain activity. Figure 12.6 shows the metabolic activity in the cerebral cortex of an individual cycling through depressive and manic phases. Notice the decrease in metabolic activity in the brain during depression and the increase in metabolic activity during mania (Baxter & others, 1995). In addition to high levels of norepinephrine and low levels of serotonin, studies show that high levels of the neurotransmitter glutamate occur in bipolar disorder (Kugaya & Sanacora, 2005; Sourial-Bassilious & others, 2009). These differences between depression and bipolar disorder have led to differences in treatment, as we will see in Chapter 13.

Suicide

It is not uncommon for individuals to contemplate suicide at some point in life. Thinking about suicide is not necessarily abnormal. However, attempting or completing the act of suicide *is* abnormal. Approximately

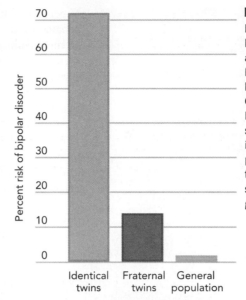

FIGURE 12.5

Risk of Bipolar Disorder in Identical and Fraternal Twins If One Twin Has the Disorder, and in the General Population Notice how much stronger the similarity of bipolar disorder is in identical twins, compared with fraternal twins and the general population. These statistics suggest a strong genetic role in the disorder.

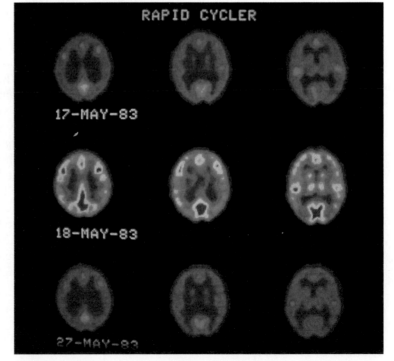

FIGURE 12.6

Brain Metabolism in Mania and Depression PET scans of an individual with bipolar disorder, who is described as a rapid-cycler because of how quickly severe mood changes occurred. (*Top and bottom*) The person's brain in a depressed state. (*Middle*) A manic state. The PET scans reveal how the brain's energy consumption falls in depression and rises in mania. The red areas in the middle row reflect rapid consumption of glucose.

What to Do

1. Ask direct, straightforward questions in a calm manner. For example, "Are you thinking about hurting yourself?"
2. Be a good listener and be supportive. Emphasize that unbearable pain can be survived.
3. Take the suicide threat very seriously. Ask questions about the person's feelings, relationships, and thoughts about the type of method to be used. If a gun, pills, rope, or other means is mentioned and a specific plan has been developed, the situation is dangerous. Stay with the person until help arrives.
4. Encourage the person to get professional help and assist him or her in getting help. If the person is willing, take the person to a mental health facility or hospital.

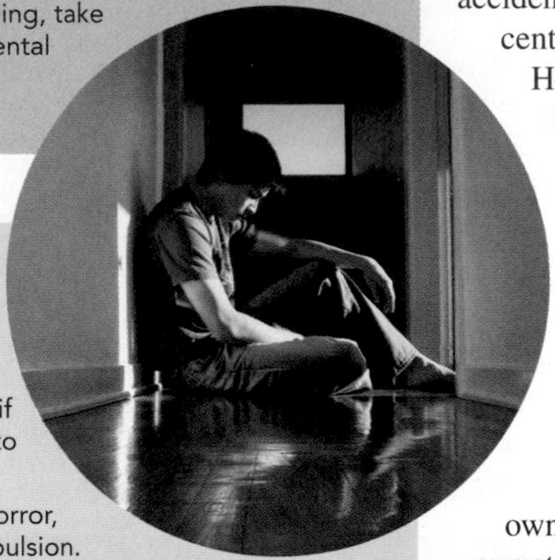

What Not to Do

1. Don't ignore the warning signs.
2. Don't refuse to talk about suicide if the person wants to talk about it.
3. Don't react with horror, disapproval, or repulsion.
4. Don't offer false reassurances ("Everything will be all right") or make judgments ("You should be thankful for . . .").
5. Don't abandon the person after the crisis seems to have passed or after professional counseling has begun.

FIGURE 12.7
When Someone Is Threatening Suicide Do not ignore the warning signs if you think someone you know is considering suicide. Talk to a counselor if you are reluctant to say anything to the person yourself.

90 percent of individuals who commit suicide are estimated to have a diagnosable mental disorder (NIMH, 2008), and the most common disorders among individuals who commit suicide are depression and anxiety (Boden, Fergusson, & Horwood, 2006, 2007; Zonda, 2006). Depressed individuals are also likely to attempt suicide more than once (da Silva Cais & others, 2009).

According to the National Institute of Mental Health (NIMH), in 2004, 32,439 people in the United States committed suicide, and suicide was the 11th-highest cause of death (NIMH, 2008). Research indicates that for every completed suicide, 8 to 25 attempted suicides occur (NIMH, 2008). Suicide is the third-leading cause (after automobile accidents and homicides) of death today among U.S. adolescents 13 through 19 years of age (National Center for Health Statistics, 2005a). Even more shocking, suicide is the third-leading cause of death among children in the United States age 10 to 14 (Centers for Disease Control and Prevention, 2007). Given these grim statistics, psychologists work with individuals to reduce the frequency and intensity of suicidal impulses. You can do your part. Figure 12.7 provides good advice on what to do and what not to do if you encounter someone who is threatening suicide.

What might prompt an individual to end his or her own life? Biological, psychological, and sociocultural circumstances can be contributing factors.

Biological Factors Genetic factors appear to play a role in suicide, which tends to run in families (Brezo & others, 2009; Must & others, 2009). The Hemingways are one famous family who have been plagued by suicide. Five Hemingways, spread across generations, committed suicide, including the writer Ernest Hemingway and his granddaughter Margaux, a model and actor. Similarly, in 2009, Nicholas Hughes—a successful marine biologist and the son of Sylvia Plath, a poet who had killed herself—tragically hanged himself.

A number of studies have linked suicide with low levels of the neurotransmitter serotonin (Ryding & others, 2006). Individuals who attempt suicide and who have low serotonin levels are 10 times more likely to attempt suicide again than are attempters who have high serotonin levels (Courtet & others, 2004). Poor physical health, especially when it is long-standing and chronic, is another risk factor for suicide.

These individuals grew up in families where a parent had ended his or her life. That experience might have made them more likely to consider suicide as an option. So, environment still matters.

Psychological Factors Psychological factors that can contribute to suicide include mental disorders and traumas such as sexual abuse. Struggling with the stress of a psychological disorder can leave a person feeling hopeless, and the disorder itself may tax the person's ability to cope with life difficulties. Indeed, approximately 90 percent of individuals who commit suicide are estimated to have a diagnosable mental disorder (NIMH, 2008).

An immediate and highly stressful circumstance—such as the loss of a loved one or a job, flunking out of school, or an unwanted pregnancy—can lead people to threaten and/or to commit suicide (Videtic & others, 2009). Substance abuse is linked with suicide more today than in the past (Galaif & others, 2007; Seguin & others, 2006).

In research focusing on suicide notes, Thomas Joiner and his colleagues found that having a sense of belongingness or of being needed separates individuals who attempt suicide from those who complete it (Conner & others, 2007; Joiner, 2005; Joiner, Hollar, & Van Orden, 2006; Van Orden & others, 2008). Essentially, people who feel that someone will miss them or still need them are less likely than others to complete a suicide.

Sociocultural Factors

Chronic economic hardship can be a factor in suicide (Ferretti & Coluccia, 2009). Cultural and ethnic contexts also are related to suicide attempts. In the United States, adolescents' suicide attempts vary across ethnic groups. As Figure 12.8 illustrates, more than 20 percent of American Indian/Alaska Native (AI/AN) female adolescents reported that they had attempted suicide in the previous year, and suicide accounts for almost 20 percent of AI/AN deaths in 15- to 19-year-olds (Goldston & others, 2008). As the figure also shows, African American and non-Latino White males reported the lowest incidence of suicide attempts. A major risk factor in the high rate of suicide attempts by AI/AN adolescents is their elevated rate of alcohol abuse.

Worldwide, Hungary, Austria, Russia, Sri Lanka, and Japan are among the nations with the highest suicide rates, and Egypt, Guatemala, Iran, Peru, and the Dominican Republic are among those with the lowest rates (World Health Organization, 2003). Suicide rates for the United States and Canada fall between the rates in these countries. The reasons for the variations include the degree to which there are cultural and religious norms against suicide.

There are gender differences in suicide as well (Fortuna & others, 2007). Women are three times more likely to attempt suicide than men. Men, however, are four times more likely to complete suicide than women (Kochanek & others, 2004). Men are also more likely than women to use a firearm in a suicide attempt (Maris, 1998). The highest suicide rate is among non-Latino White men aged 85 and older (NIMH, 2008).

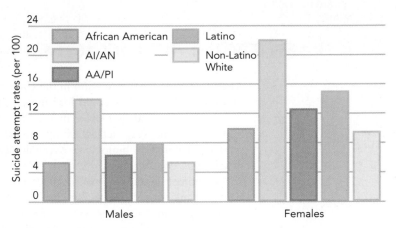

FIGURE 12.8

Suicide Attempts by U.S. Adolescents from Different Ethnic Groups Note that the data shown are for one-year rates of self-reported suicide attempts. AI/AN = American Indian/Alaska Native; AA/PI = Asian American/Pacific Islander.

Men are less likely than women to report being depressed but are more likely to commit suicide. Clearly, depression in men might be underestimated.

1. To be diagnosed with bipolar disorder, an individual must experience
   A. a manic episode.
   B. a depressive episode.
   C. a manic episode and a depressive episode.
   D. a dysthymic episode.

2. All of the following are a symptom of major depressive disorder *except*
   A. fatigue.
   B. weight change.
   C. thoughts of death.
   D. substance use.

3. A *true* statement about suicide and gender is that
   A. women are more likely to attempt suicide than men.
   B. men are more likely to attempt suicide than women.
   C. men and women are equally likely to attempt suicide.
   D. men and women are equally likely to complete suicide.

Apply It! 4. During his first two college years, Barry has felt "down" most of the time. He has had trouble concentrating and difficulty making decisions. Sometimes he is so overwhelmed with deciding on his major and struggling to focus that he feels hopeless. Otherwise, Barry is doing fairly well; he has no problems with loss of appetite or sleeping, and in general his energy level is fine. Which of the following is most likely to be true of Barry?
   A. Barry is suffering from major depressive disorder.
   B. Barry is entering the depressive phase of bipolar disorder.
   C. Barry has dysthymic disorder.
   D. Barry is experiencing the everyday blues that everyone gets from time to time.

4 Eating Disorders

Dieting is a national obsession in the United States. Many Americans feel that life would improve greatly if they could lose those last 5 pounds. However, for some people, concerns about weight and body image become a serious, debilitating disorder. For such individuals, the very act of eating, essential for survival, becomes an arena where a variety of complex biological, psychological, and cultural issues are played out, often with tragic consequences.

A number of famous people have coped with eating disorders, including Princess Diana, Paula Abdul, and Kelly Clarkson. Eating disorders are characterized by extreme disturbances in eating behavior—from eating very, very little to eating a great deal. In this section we examine three eating disorders—anorexia nervosa, bulimia nervosa, and binge eating disorder.

Anorexia Nervosa

anorexia nervosa
Eating disorder that involves the relentless pursuit of thinness through starvation.

Anorexia nervosa is an eating disorder that involves the relentless pursuit of thinness through starvation. Anorexia nervosa is much more common in girls and women than boys and men and affects between 0.5 and 3.7 percent of young women (NIMH, 2009). The American Psychiatric Association (2005) lists these main characteristics of anorexia nervosa:

- Weight less than 85 percent of what is considered normal for age and height and refusing to maintain weight at a healthy level.
- An intense fear of gaining weight that does not decrease with weight loss.
- A distorted body image. Even when individuals with anorexia nervosa are extremely thin, they never think they are thin enough. They weigh themselves frequently, take their body measurements often, and gaze critically at themselves in mirrors.
- Amenorrhea (lack of menstruation) in girls who have reached puberty.

Over time, anorexia nervosa can lead to physical changes, such as the growth of fine hairs all over the body, thinning of bones and hair, severe constipation, and low blood pressure (NIMH, 2009). Serious and even life-threatening complications of anorexia nervosa include damage to the heart and thyroid. Anorexia nervosa is said to have the highest mortality rate (about 5.6 percent of individuals with anorexia nervosa die per decade) of any psychological disorder (Hoek, 2006; NIMH, 2009).

Individuals with anorexia nervosa lack personal distress over their symptoms. Recall that personal distress over one's behavior is an aspect of the definition of abnormal.

Anorexia nervosa is difficult to treat and may require hospitalization. The first target of intervention is promoting weight gain, in extreme cases through the use of a feeding tube. A key obstacle in the treatment of anorexia nervosa is that individuals with the disorder deny that anything is wrong. They maintain the belief that thinness and restrictive dieting are correct and not a sign of psychopathology (Wilson, Grilo, & Vitousek, 2007).

Anorexia nervosa typically begins in the teenage years, often following an episode of dieting and some type of life stress (Lo Sauro & others, 2008; Sigel, 2008). Most individuals with anorexia

Uruguayan model Eliana Ramos posed for the camera in her native country. Tragically, the super-thin Eliana died at age 18 in February 2007, two years after this picture was taken, reportedly from health problems associated with anorexia nervosa.

nervosa are non-Latino White female adolescents or young adults from well-educated, middle- and upper-income families. They are often high-achieving perfectionists (Forbush, Heatherton, & Keel, 2007). In addition to perfectionism, obsessive-compulsive tendencies are related to anorexia nervosa (Finzi-Dottan & Zubery, 2009).

Bulimia Nervosa

Bulimia nervosa is an eating disorder in which an individual (typically a girl or woman) consistently follows a binge-and-purge eating pattern. The individual goes on an eating binge and then purges by self-induced vomiting or the use of laxatives. Most people with bulimia nervosa are preoccupied with food, have a strong fear of becoming overweight, and are depressed or anxious (Speranza & others, 2003). Because bulimia nervosa occurs within a normal weight range, the disorder is often difficult to detect (Mizes & Miller, 2000). A person with bulimia nervosa usually keeps the disorder a secret and experiences a great deal of disgust and shame.

Bulimia nervosa can lead to complications such as a chronic sore throat, kidney problems, dehydration, and gastrointestinal disorders (NIMH, 2009). The disorder is also related to dental problems, as persistent exposure to the stomach acids in vomit can wear away tooth enamel. Drug therapies and psychotherapy are standard treatments for bulimia nervosa.

Bulimia nervosa typically begins in late adolescence or early adulthood (Levine, 2002). The disorder affects between 1 and 4 percent of young women (NIMH, 2008). Like those with anorexia nervosa, many young women who develop bulimia nervosa are highly perfectionistic (Forbush, Heatherton, & Keel, 2007). At the same time, they tend to have low levels of self-efficacy (Bardone-Cone & others, 2006). In short, these are young women with very high standards but very low confidence that they can achieve their goals. Impulsivity, negative affect, and childhood OCD are also related to bulimia (Tchanturia & others, 2004; Vervaet, van Heeringen & Audenaert, 2004). Bulimia nervosa is associated, too, with a high incidence of sexual and physical abuse in childhood (Lo Sauro & others, 2008).

bulimia nervosa
Eating disorder in which an individual (typically a girl or woman) consistently follows a binge-and-purge eating pattern.

Dentists and dental hygenists are sometimes the first to recognize the signs of bulimia nervosa.

Causes of Anorexia Nervosa and Bulimia Nervosa

What is the etiology of anorexia nervosa and bulimia nervosa? For many years researchers thought that sociocultural factors, such as media images of very thin women, were the central determinant of these disorders. Certainly the U.S. popular media bombard their audiences with images of extremely thin women. Media images that glorify extreme thinness can influence women's body image, and emphasis on the thin ideal is related to anorexia nervosa and bulimia nervosa (Harrison & Hefner, 2006; Stice & others, 2007). However, as powerful as these media messages might be, countless girls and women are exposed to media images of unrealistically thin women, but relatively few develop eating disorders. Thus, since the 1980s, researchers have moved beyond a sole focus on sociocultural factors and have increasingly probed the potential biological underpinnings of these disorders.

Genes play a substantial role in both anorexia nervosa and bulimia nervosa (Collier & Treasure, 2004; Sokol & others, 2009). In fact, many personality characteristics (for example, perfectionism, impulsivity, obsessive-compulsive tendencies, and thinness drive) and behaviors (restrained eating, binge eating, self-induced vomiting) that are associated with anorexia nervosa and bulimia nervosa are influenced by genes (Bulik & others, 2000; Devlin & others, 2002; Ribases & others, 2004). These genes are also factors in the regulation of serotonin, and problems in regulating serotonin are related to both anorexia nervosa and bulimia nervosa (Capasso, Putrella, & Milano, 2009).

Binge Eating Disorder

Unlike individuals with anorexia nervosa or bulimia nervosa, most people with binge eating disorder (BED) are overweight or obese.

Binge eating disorder (BED) is characterized by recurrent episodes of eating large amounts of food during which the person feels a lack of control over eating (NIMH, 2009; Striegel-Moore & Franko, 2008). Unlike a person with bulimia nervosa, someone with BED does not try to purge. Most individuals with BED are overweight or obese. BED was added as a provisional diagnosis in the *DSM-IV* in 1994, and some have argued for its inclusion as a full-fledged diagnostic category in the *DSM-V* (Striegel-Moore & Franko, 2008; Wilfley & others, 2007).

Individuals with BED often eat quickly, eat a great deal when they are not hungry, and eat until they are uncomfortably full. They frequently eat alone because of embarrassment or guilt, and they experience disgust and shame after overeating. BED is the most common of all eating disorders—affecting men, women, and ethnic groups within the United States more similarly than anorexia nervosa or bulimia nervosa (Striegel-Moore & Franko, 2008). An estimated 2 to 5 percent of Americans will suffer from BED in their lifetime (NIMH, 2009). BED is thought to characterize approximately 8 percent of individuals who are obese. Unlike obese individuals who do not suffer from BED, binge eaters are more likely to place great value on their physical appearance, weight, and body shape (Wilson, Grilo, & Vitousek, 2007). The complications of BED are those of obesity more generally, including diabetes, hypertension, and cardiovascular disease.

Just as treatment for anorexia nervosa focuses on weight gain first, some believe that treatment for BED should focus on weight loss first (De Angelis, 2002). Others argue that individuals with BED must be treated for disordered eating per se, and insist that if the underlying psychological issues are not addressed, weight loss will not be successful or permanent (Wilfley & others, 2000; de Zwaan & others, 2005).

Researchers have begun to examine the role of biological and psychological factors in BED. Genes do play a role (Collier & Treasure, 2004), as does dopamine, the neurotransmitter related to reward pathways in the brain (Davis & others, 2008). Binge eating often occurs after stressful life events, suggesting that binge eaters use food as a way to regulate their emotions (Wilson, Grilo, & Vitousek, 2007). There is evidence that the areas of the brain and endocrine system that respond to stress are overactive in individuals with BED (Lo Sauro & others, 2008), leading to high levels of circulating cortisol, the hormone most associated with stress. Individuals with BED may be more likely to perceive events as stressful and then seek to manage that stress by binge eating.

binge eating disorder (BED) Eating disorder characterized by recurrent episodes of eating large amounts of food during which the person feels a lack of control over eating.

selfquiz

1. The main characteristics of anorexia nervosa include all of the following *except*
   A. absence of menstrual periods after puberty.
   B. distorted image of one's body.
   C. strong fears of weight gain even as weight loss occurs.
   D. intense and persistent tremors.

2. A person with bulimia nervosa typically
   A. thinks a lot about food.
   B. is considerably underweight.
   C. is a male.
   D. is not overly concerned about gaining weight.

3. The most common of all eating disorders is
   A. bulimia nervosa.
   B. anorexia nervosa.
   C. binge eating disorder.
   D. gastrointestinal disease.

Apply It! 4. Nancy is a first-year pre-med major. She is getting *A*s in all of her challenging classes. Nancy's roommate Luci notices that Nancy has lost a great deal of weight and is extremely thin. Luci observes that Nancy works out a lot, rarely finishes meals, and wears bulky sweaters even when it is not very cold. Luci also notices that Nancy's arms have fine hairs growing on them. When Luci asks Nancy about her weight loss, Nancy replies that she is very concerned that she not gain the "freshman 15" and is feeling pretty good about her ability to keep up with her work and keep off those extra pounds. Which of the following is the *most likely* explanation for what is going on with Nancy?
   A. Nancy has bulimia nervosa.
   B. Despite her lack of personal distress about her symptoms, Nancy has anorexia nervosa.
   C. Nancy has binge eating disorder.
   D. Given Nancy's overall success, it seems unlikely that she is suffering from a psychological disorder.

5 Dissociative Disorders

Have you ever been on a long car ride and completely lost track of time, so that you could not even remember a stretch of miles along the road? Have you been so caught up in a daydream that you were unaware of the passage of time? These are examples of normal dissociation. *Dissociation* refers to psychological states in which the person feels disconnected from immediate experience.

At the extreme of dissociation are individuals who feel a sense of disconnection *persistently*. **Dissociative disorders** are psychological disorders that involve a sudden loss of memory or change in identity. Under extreme stress or shock, the individual's conscious awareness becomes *dissociated* (separated or split) from previous memories and thoughts (Espirito-Santo & Pio-Abreu, 2009). Individuals who develop dissociative disorders may have problems putting together different aspects of consciousness, so that experiences at different levels of awareness might be felt as if they are happening to someone else (Dell & O'Neil, 2007).

Psychologists believe that dissociation is an individual's way of dealing with extreme stress (Spiegel, 2006). Through dissociation the individual mentally protects his or her conscious self from the traumatic event. Dissociative disorders often occur in individuals who also show signs of PTSD (Zucker & others, 2006). Both psychological disorders are thought to be rooted, in part, in extremely traumatic life events (Foote & others, 2006). The notion that dissociative disorders are related to problems in pulling together emotional memories is supported by findings showing lower volume in the hippocampus and amygdala in individuals with dissociative disorders (Vermetten & others, 2006). The hippocampus is especially involved in consolidating memory and organizing life experience into a coherent whole (Spiegel, 2006). Dissociative disorders are perhaps the most controversial of all diagnostic categories, with some psychologists believing that they are often mistakenly diagnosed (Freeland & others, 1993) while others believe that they are underdiagnosed (Sar, Akyuz, & Dogan, 2007; Spiegel, 2006).

Three kinds of dissociative disorders are dissociative amnesia, dissociative fugue, and dissociative identity disorder.

dissociative disorders Psychological disorders that involve a sudden loss of memory or change in identity due to the dissociation (separation) of the individual's conscious awareness from previous memories and thoughts.

> Chapter 4 was all about consciousness. In dissociative disorders, consciousness itself is split off from experience—the "stream of consciousness" is disrupted. Hypnosis is often used in treating dissociative disorders.

Dissociative Amnesia and Fugue

Amnesia is the inability to recall important events (Cipolotti & Bird, 2006). Amnesia can result from a blow to the head that produces trauma in the brain. In contrast, **dissociative amnesia** is characterized by extreme memory loss that is caused by extensive psychological stress. A person experiencing dissociative amnesia remembers things like how to hail a cab and use a phone but forgets aspects of his or her identity and autobiographical experiences. For example, an individual showed up at a hospital and said that he did not know who he was. After several days in the hospital, he awoke one morning and demanded to be released. Eventually he remembered that he had been involved in an automobile accident in which a pedestrian had died. The extreme stress of the accident and the fear that he might be held responsible triggered the amnesia.

Dissociative fugue (*fugue* means "flight") is a dissociative disorder in which the individual not only develops amnesia but also unexpectedly travels away from home and sometimes assumes a new identity. What makes dissociative fugue different from dissociative amnesia is this tendency to run away.

A recent case of dissociative fugue involved the disappearance of a middle school teacher in New York City. Twenty-three-year-old Hannah Upp disappeared while out for a run on August 28, 2008 (Marx & Didziulis, 2009). She had no wallet, no identification, no cell phone, and no money. Her family, friends, and roommates posted flyers around the city and messages on the

dissociative amnesia Dissociative disorder characterized by extreme memory loss that is caused by extensive psychological stress.

dissociative fugue Dissociative disorder in which the individual not only develops amnesia but also unexpectedly travels away from home and assumes a new identity.

> Matt Damon's character, Jason Bourne, in the **Bourne Identity** films is named after Ansel Bourne, who in 1887 became the first known real-life case of dissociative fugue.

At one point during her fugue, Hannah was approached by someone who asked if she was the Hannah everyone was looking for, and she answered no.

Internet. As days went by, they became increasingly concerned that something terrible had happened. Finally, Hannah was found floating face down in the New York harbor on September 16, sunburned and dehydrated but alive. She remembered nothing of her experiences. To her, it felt like she had gone out for a run and 10 minutes later was being pulled from the harbor. To this day, she does not know what event might have led to her dissociative fugue, nor does she remember how she survived during her two-week disappearance.

Dissociative Identity Disorder

dissociative identity disorder (DID)
Formerly called multiple personality disorder, a dissociative disorder in which the individual has two or more distinct personalities or selves, each with its own memories, behaviors, and relationships.

Dissociative identity disorder (DID), formerly called *multiple personality disorder,* is the most dramatic, least common, and most controversial dissociative disorder. Individuals with this disorder have two or more distinct personalities or identities. Each identity has its own memories, behaviors, and relationships. One identity dominates at one time, another takes over at another time.

Individuals sometimes report that a wall of amnesia separates their different identities (Dale & others, 2009). However research suggests that memory does transfer across these identities (Kong, Allen, & Glisky, 2008). The shift between identities usually occurs under distress (Sar & others, 2007) but sometimes can also be controlled by the person (Kong, Allen, & Glisky, 2008).

One of the most famous real-life cases of dissociative identity disorder involves the "three faces of Eve" (Thigpen & Cleckley, 1957) (Figure 12.9). Eve White was the original dominant personality. She had no knowledge of her second personality, Eve Black, although Eve Black had been alternating with Eve White for a number of years. Eve White was bland, quiet, and serious. By contrast, Eve Black was carefree, mischievous, and uninhibited. Eve Black would emerge at the most inappropriate times, leaving Eve White with hangovers, bills, and a reputation in local bars that she could not explain. During treatment, a third personality, Jane, emerged. More mature than the other two, Jane seems to have developed as a result of therapy. More recently, former Heisman Trophy winner and legendary NFL running back Herschel Walker (2008) revealed his experience with dissociative disorder in his book *Breaking Free: My Life with Dissociative Identity Disorder.*

Research on dissociative identity disorder suggests that a high rate of extraordinarily severe sexual or physical abuse during early childhood is related to the condition (Sar, Akyuz, & Dogan, 2007). Some psychologists believe that a child can cope with intense trauma by dissociating from the experience and developing other alternate selves as protectors. Sexual abuse has occurred in as many as 70 percent or more of dissociative identity disorder cases (Foote & others, 2006); however, the majority of individuals who have been sexually abused do not develop dissociative identity disorder. The vast majority of individuals with dissociative identity disorder are women. A genetic predisposition might also exist, as the disorder tends to run in families (Dell & Eisenhower, 1990).

Until the 1980s, only about 300 cases of dissociative identity disorder had ever

FIGURE 12.9
The Three Faces of Eve Chris Sizemore, the subject of *The Three Faces of Eve,* is shown here with a work she painted, titled *Three Faces in One.*

been reported (Suinn, 1984). In the past 25 years, hundreds more cases have been labeled as "dissociative identity disorder." Social cognitive psychologists point out that reports of the disorder have tended to increase whenever the popular media present a case of it, such as in the film *The Three Faces of Eve,* the miniseries *Sybil,* and the Showtime drama *The United States of Tara.* From this perspective, individuals develop multiple identities through social contagion (see Chapter 11) or by adopting the disorder because it makes sense out of their conflicting experiences (Spanos, 1996). Rather than being a single person with many conflicting feelings, wishes, and potentially awful experiences, the individual compartmentalizes different aspects of the self into independent identities.

In some cases, therapists have been accused of creating alternate personalities. Encountering an individual who appears to have a fragmented sense of self, the therapist may begin to treat each fragment as its own "personality" (Spiegel, 2006). Thus, some observers believe that dissociative identity is a *social construction*—that it represents a category of disorder that therapists and patients have created to explain their experiences.

Therapists and patients are making **attributions to** *understand abnormal behavior.*

self-quiz

1. Dissociative identity disorder is associated with unusually high rates of
   A. anxiety.
   B. abuse during early childhood.
   C. depression.
   D. divorce.

2. Someone who suffers memory loss after a psychological trauma is said to have
   A. dissociative identity disorder.
   B. dissociative fugue.
   C. dissociative amnesia.
   D. schizophrenia.

3. In cases of dissociative fugue, the individual not only experiences amnesia but also
   A. has frequent thoughts of suicide.
   B. takes on multiple different identities.
   C. refuses to leave his or her home.
   D. travels away from home.

Apply It! 4. Eddie often loses track of time. He is sometimes late for appointments because he is so engrossed in whatever he is doing. While working on a term paper in the library, he gets so caught up in what he is reading that he is shocked when he looks up and sees that that sun has set and it is night. Which of the following best describes Eddie?
   A. Eddie is showing signs of dissociative identity disorder.
   B. Eddie is showing signs of dissociative fugue.
   C. Eddie is showing normal dissociative states.
   D. Eddie is at risk for dissociative amnesia.

6 Schizophrenia

Have you had the experience of watching a movie and suddenly noticing that the film bears an uncanny resemblance to your life? Have you ever listened to a radio talk show and realized that the host was saying exactly what you were just thinking? Do these moments mean something special about you, or are they coincidences? For people with schizophrenia, such experiences may take on special and personal meaning.

schizophrenia
Severe psychological disorder characterized by highly disordered thought processes, referred to as psychotic because they are so far removed from reality.

Schizophrenia is a severe psychological disorder that is characterized by highly disordered thought processes. These disordered thoughts are referred to as *psychotic* because they are far removed from reality. Indeed, the world of the person with schizophrenia is deeply frightening and chaotic.

Schizophrenia is usually diagnosed in early adulthood, around age 18 for men and 25 for women. Individuals with schizophrenia may see things that are not there, hear voices inside their heads, and live in a strange world of twisted logic. They may say odd things, show inappropriate emotion, and move their bodies in peculiar ways. Often, they are socially withdrawn and isolated.

As much as schizophrenia may sound disturbing to an outsider, we can only imagine the ordeal of those living with it. Indeed, schizophrenia can be debilitating. About one-half of the patients in psychiatric hospitals are afflicted with schizophrenia. The suicide risk for individuals with schizophrenia is eight times that for the general population (Pompili & others, 2007). For many with the disorder, controlling it means using powerful medications to combat symptoms. The most common cause of relapse is that individuals stop taking their

Seeking treatment for schizophrenia takes courage. It requires individuals to accept that their perception of the world—their very sense of reality—is mistaken.

medication. They might do so because they feel better, because they do not realize that their thoughts are disordered, or because the side effects of the medications are so unpleasant.

Symptoms of Schizophrenia

Psychologists generally classify the symptoms of schizophrenia as positive symptoms, negative symptoms, and cognitive deficits (NIMH, 2006).

Positive Symptoms

The *positive symptoms* of schizophrenia are marked by a distortion or an excess of normal function. They are "positive" because they reflect something added above and beyond normal behavior. Positive symptoms of schizophrenia include hallucinations, delusions, thought disorders, and disorders of movement.

Hallucinations are sensory experiences in the absence of real stimuli. Hallucinations are usually auditory—the person might complain of hearing voices—or visual and much less commonly can take the form of smells or tastes (Bhatia & others, 2009). Hallucinations can also involve seeing things that are not there. Viewers of the movie *A Beautiful Mind* might have been surprised to find out at the end of the film that John Nash's friend from college was in fact a hallucination.

Delusions are false, unusual, and sometimes magical beliefs that are not part of an individual's culture. A delusional person might think that he is Jesus Christ or Muhammad. Another might imagine that her thoughts are being broadcast over the radio. It is crucial to distinguish delusions from cultural ideas such as the religious belief that a person can have divine visions or communicate personally with a deity. Generally, psychology and psychiatry do not treat these ideas as delusional.

Thought disorder refers to the unusual, sometimes bizarre thought processes that are characteristic positive symptoms of schizophrenia. The thoughts of persons with schizophrenia can be disorganized and confused. Often individuals with schizophrenia do not make sense when they talk or write. For example, someone with schizophrenia might say, "Well, Rocky, babe, happening, but where, when, up, top, side, over, you know, out of the way, that's it. Sign off." These incoherent, loose word associations, called *word salad,* have no meaning for the listener. The individual might also make up new words (Kerns & others, 1999). In addition, a person with schizophrenia can show **referential thinking,** which means giving personal meaning to completely random events. For instance, the individual might believe that a traffic light has turned red *because* he or she is in a hurry.

A final type of positive symptom is *disorders of movement.* A person with schizophrenia may show unusual mannerisms, body movements, and facial expressions. The individual may repeat certain motions over and over or, in extreme cases, may become catatonic. **Catatonia** is a state of immobility and unresponsiveness that lasts for long periods of time (Figure 12.10).

Negative Symptoms

Whereas schizophrenia's positive symptoms are characterized by a distortion or an excess of normal functions, schizophrenia's *negative symptoms* reflect social withdrawal, behavioral deficits, and the loss or decrease of normal functions. One negative symptom is **flat affect,** which means the display of little or no emotion (Alvino & others, 2007). Individuals with schizophrenia also may be lacking in the ability to read the emotions of others (Chambon, Baudouin, & Franck, 2006). They may experience a lack of positive emotional experience in daily life and show a deficient ability to plan, initiate, and engage in goal-directed behavior.

FIGURE 12.10
Disorders of Movement in Schizophrenia Unusual motor behaviors are positive symptoms of schizophrenia. Individuals may cease to move altogether (a state called catatonia), sometimes holding bizarre postures.

referential thinking
Ascribing personal meaning to completely random events.

Because negative symptoms are not as obviously part of a psychiatric illness, people with schizophrenia may be perceived as lazy and unwilling to better their lives.

hallucinations
Sensory experiences that occur in the absence of real stimuli.

delusions
False, unusual, and sometimes magical beliefs that are not part of an individual's culture.

catatonia
State of immobility and unresponsiveness, lasting for long periods of time.

flat affect
The display of little or no emotion—a common negative symptom of schizophrenia.

Cognitive Symptoms

Cognitive Symptoms Cognitive symptoms of schizophrenia include difficulty sustaining attention, problems holding information in memory, and inability to interpret information and make decisions (Kerns, 2007; Sitnikova, Goff, & Kuperberg, 2009). These cognitive symptoms may be quite subtle and are often detected only through neuropsychological tests.

Causes of Schizophrenia

A great deal of research has investigated schizophrenia's causes. Here we consider the biological, psychological, and sociocultural factors involved in the disorder.

Biological Factors Research provides strong support for biological explanations of schizophrenia. Particularly compelling is the evidence for a genetic predisposition, but structural abnormalities and neurotransmitters also are linked to this severe psychological disorder (Picchioni & others, 2006; Ross & others, 2006).

Heredity Research supports the notion schizophrenia is at least partially due to genetic factors (Hall & others, 2007). As genetic similarity to a person with schizophrenia increases, so does a person's risk of developing schizophrenia, as Figure 12.11 shows (Cardno & Gottesman, 2000). Such data strongly suggest that genetic factors play a role in schizophrenia. Researchers are seeking to pinpoint the chromosomal location of genes involved in susceptibility to schizophrenia (Holliday & others, 2009; Potkin & others, 2009).

Structural Brain Abnormalities Studies have found structural brain abnormalities in people with schizophrenia. Imaging techniques such as MRI scans clearly show enlarged ventricles in their brains (Killgore & others, 2009). Ventricles are fluid-filled spaces, and enlargement of the ventricles indicates the deterioration in other brain tissue. Individuals with schizophrenia also have a small frontal cortex (the area in which thinking,

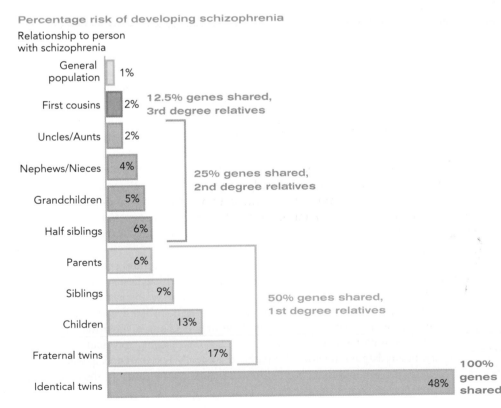

FIGURE 12.11
Lifetime Risk of Developing Schizophrenia, According to Genetic Relatedness As genetic relatedness to an individual with schizophrenia increases, so does the risk of developing schizophrenia.

planning, and decision making take place) and show less activity in this area than individuals who do not have schizophrenia (Cotter & others, 2002).

Still, the differences between the brains of healthy individuals and those with schizophrenia are small (NIMH, 2006). Microscopic studies of brain tissue after death reveal small changes in the distribution or characteristics of brain cells in persons with schizophrenia. It appears that many of these changes occurred prenatally because they are not accompanied by glial cells, which are always present when a brain injury occurs after birth. It may be that problems in prenatal development such as prenatal infections (A. S. Brown, 2006) predispose a brain to developing schizophrenic symptoms during puberty and young adulthood (Fatemi & Folsom, 2009).

Problems in Neurotransmitter Regulation

An early biological explanation for schizophrenia linked excess dopamine production to schizophrenia. The link between dopamine and psychotic symptoms was first noticed when the drug L-dopa (which increases dopamine levels) was given to individuals as a treatment for Parkinson disease. In addition to relieving their Parkinson symptoms, L-dopa caused some individuals to experience disturbed thoughts (Janowsky, Addario, & Risch, 1987). Furthermore, drugs that reduce psychotic symptoms often block dopamine (Kapur, 2003). Whether it is differences in the amount, the production, or the uptake of dopamine, there is good evidence that dopamine plays a role in schizophrenia (Howes & others, 2009; Tamminga, 2006).

As noted in the chapters about states of consciousness (Chapter 4) and learning (Chapter 5), dopamine is a "feel good" neurotransmitter that helps us recognize rewarding stimuli in the environment. As described in the chapter on personality (Chapter 10), dopamine is related to being outgoing and sociable. How can a neurotransmitter that is associated with good things play a crucial role in the most devastating psychological disorder?

One way to think about this puzzle is view dopamine as a neurochemical messenger that in effect shouts out, "Hey! This is important!" whenever we encounter opportunities for reward. Imagine what it might be like to be bombarded with such messages about even the smallest details of life (Kapur, 2003). The person's own thoughts might take on such dramatic proportions that they sound like someone else's voice talking inside the person's head. Fleeting ideas, such as "It's raining today *because* I didn't bring my umbrella to work," suddenly seem not silly but true. Shitij Kapur (2003) has suggested that hallucinations, delusions, and referential thinking may be expressions of the individual's attempts to make sense of such extraordinary feelings.

> *Excess dopamine basically tells the person that* **everything** *is important.*

A problem with the dopamine explanation of schizophrenia is that antipsychotic drugs reduce dopamine levels very quickly, but delusional beliefs take much longer to disappear. Even after dopamine levels are balanced, a person might still cling to the bizarre belief that members of a powerful conspiracy are watching his or her every move. If dopamine causes these symptoms, why do the symptoms persist even after the dopamine is under control? According to Kapur, delusions serve as explanatory schemes that have helped the person make sense of the random and chaotic experiences caused by out-of-control dopamine. Bizarre beliefs might disappear only after experience demonstrates that such schemes no longer carry their explanatory power (Kapur, 2003). That is, with time, experience, and therapy, the person might come to realize that there is, in fact, no conspiracy.

Psychological Factors

Psychologists used to explain schizophrenia as rooted in an individual's difficult childhood experiences with parents. Such explanations have mostly fallen by the wayside, but contemporary theorists do recognize that stress may contribute to the development of this disorder. The **diathesis-stress model** argues that a combination of biogenetic disposition and stress causes schizophrenia (Meehl, 1962). (*Diathesis* means "physical vulnerability or predisposition to a particular disorder.") For instance, genetic characteristics might produce schizophrenia only when (and if) the individual experiences extreme stress.

> *Recall that Moe Armstrong experienced his first symptoms during the extremely stressful experience of the Vietnam War.*

diathesis-stress model
View of schizophrenia emphasizing that a combination of biogenetic disposition and stress causes the disorder.

Sociocultural Factors   Individuals living in poverty are more likely to have schizophrenia than people at higher socioeconomic levels, but poverty is not considered a cause of schizophrenia (Schiffman & Walker, 1998). However, sociocultural factors do appear to affect the *course* of schizophrenia—how it progresses. Individuals with schizophrenia in developing, nonindustrialized nations tend to have better outcomes than those in developed, industrialized nations (Jablensky, 2000). This difference may be due to the fact that in developing nations, family and friends are more accepting and supportive of individuals with schizophrenia. In addition, in Western samples, marriage, warm supportive friends (Jablensky & others, 1992; Wiersma & others, 1998), and employment are related to better outcomes for people diagnosed with schizophrenia (Rosen & Garety, 2005). At the very least, this research suggests that some individuals with schizophrenia enjoy marriage, productive work, and friendships (Drake, Levine, & Laska, 2007; Fleischhaker & others, 2005; Marshall & Rathbone, 2006). Whether their lives include psychiatric medication, therapy, or other treatment, some individuals with schizophrenia, like Moe Armstrong, live pretty good lives.

If you have never met anyone with schizophrenia, why not get to know Moe Armstrong online? He has a blog at http://www.moearmstrong.com/Site/Welcome.html and a speech on YouTube at http://www.youtube.com/watch?v=p-_j1ZNKzsg

self-quiz

1. A *negative* symptom of schizophrenia is
   A. hallucinations.
   B. flat affect.
   C. delusions.
   D. catatonia.

2. Joel believes that he has superhuman powers. He is likely suffering from
   A. hallucinations.
   B. delusions.
   C. negative symptoms.
   D. referential thinking.

3. The biological causes of schizophrenia include
   A. problems with the body's regulation of dopamine.
   B. abnormalities in brain structure such as enlarged ventricles and a small frontal cortex.
   C. both A and B.
   D. neither A nor B.

Apply It! 4. During an internship at a psychiatric hospital, Tara sees a young man sitting alone in the corner. She approaches him and they have a short conversation. He asks her if she is with the government, and she tells him that she is not. She asks him a few more questions and then walks away. She tells her advisor later that what disturbed her about the conversation was not so much what the young man said, but that she had this feeling that he just was not really there. Tara was noticing the _____ symptoms of schizophrenia.
   A. positive
   B. negative
   C. cognitive
   D. genetic

7 Personality Disorders

Are there aspects of your personality that you would like to change? Maybe you worry too much or fall in love too easily. Imagine that your very personality—the thing about you that makes you you—is the core of your life difficulties. That is what happens with **personality disorders,** which are chronic, maladaptive cognitive-behavioral patterns that are thoroughly integrated into an individual's personality. Personality disorders are relatively common. In a study of a representative sample of Americans, researchers found that 15 percent had a personality disorder (Grant & others, 2004).

The *DSM-IV* lists 10 different personality disorders. Below we survey the two that have been the object of greatest study: antisocial personality disorder and borderline personality disorder. These disorders are associated with dire consequences, including criminal activity and violence (in the case of antisocial personality disorder) and self-harm and suicide (borderline personality disorder).

personality disorders
Chronic, maladaptive cognitive-behavioral patterns that are thoroughly integrated into an individual's personality.

Antisocial Personality Disorder

Antisocial personality disorder (ASPD) is a psychological disorder characterized by guiltlessness, law-breaking, exploitation of others, irresponsibility, and deceit. Although they may be superficially charming, individuals with ASPD do not play by the rules, and

antisocial personality disorder (ASPD)
Psychological disorder characterized by guiltlessness, law-breaking, exploitation of others, irresponsibility, and deceit.

they often lead a life of crime and violence. ASPD is far more common in men than in women and is related to criminal behavior, vandalism, substance abuse, and alcoholism (Cale & Lilienfeld, 2002).

The *DSM-IV* criteria for antisocial personality disorder include

- Failure to conform to social norms or obey the law
- Deceitfulness, lying, using aliases, or conning others for personal profit or pleasure
- Impulsivity or failure to plan ahead
- Irritability and aggressiveness; getting into physical fights or perpetrating assaults
- Reckless disregard for the safety of self or others
- Consistent irresponsibility, inconsistent work behavior; not paying bills
- Lack of remorse, indifference to the pain of others, or rationalizing; hurting or mistreating another person

Generally, ASPD is not diagnosed unless a person has shown persistent antisocial behavior before the age of 15.

Although ASPD is associated with criminal behavior, not all individuals with ASPD engage in crime, and not all criminals suffer from ASPD. Some individuals with ASPD can have successful careers. There are antisocial physicians, clergy members, lawyers, and just about any other occupation. Still, such individuals tend to be exploitative of others, and they break the rules, even if they are never caught.

What is the etiology of ASPD? Biological factors include genetic, brain, and autonomic nervous system differences. We consider these in turn.

ASPD is genetically heritable (Rhee & Waldman, 2007). Certain genetic characteristics associated with ASPD may interact with testosterone (the hormone most associated with aggressive behavior) to promote antisocial behavior (Sjoberg & others, 2008). Although the experience of childhood abuse may be implicated in ASPD, there is evidence that genetic differences may distinguish abused children who go on to commit violent acts themselves from those who do not (Caspi & others, 2002).

Lack of autonomic nervous system activity suggests why individuals with ASPD might be able to fool a polygraph (lie detector).

In terms of the brain, research has linked ASPD to low levels of activation in the prefrontal cortex and has related these brain differences to poor decision making and problems in learning (Raine & others, 2000). With regard to the autonomic nervous system, researchers have found that individuals with ASPD are less stressed than others by aversive circumstances, including punishment (Fung & others, 2005), and that they have the ability to keep their cool while engaging in deception (Verschuere & others, 2005). The underaroused autonomic nervous system may be

John Wayne Gacy (left) and Ted Bundy (right) exemplify the subgroup of people with ASPD who are also psychopathic.

a key difference between adolescents who become antisocial adults and those whose behavior improves during adulthood (Raine, Venables, & Williams, 1990).

Psychopaths are one subgroup of individuals with ASPD (Weber & others, 2008). Psychopaths are remorseless predators who engage in violence to get what they want. Examples of psychopaths include serial killers John Wayne Gacy, who murdered 33 boys and young men, and Ted Bundy, who confessed to murdering at least 30 young women.

Psychopaths tend to show less prefrontal activation than normal individuals and to have structural abnormalities in the amygdala, as well as the hippocampus, the brain structure most closely associated with memory (Weber & others, 2008). Importantly, these brain differences are most pronounced in "unsuccessful psychopaths"—individuals who have been arrested for their behaviors (Yang & others, 2005). In contrast, "successful psychopaths"—individuals who have engaged in antisocial behavior but have not gotten caught—are more similar to healthy controls in terms of brain structure and function. However, in their behavior, successful psychopaths show a lack of empathy and a willingness to act immorally; they victimize other people to enrich their own lives. Psychopaths show deficiencies in learning about fear and have difficulty processing information related to the distress of others, such as sad or fearful faces (Dolan & Fullam, 2006).

Their functioning frontal lobes might help successful psychopaths succeed.

A key challenge in treating individuals with ASPD, including psychopaths, is their ability to con even sophisticated mental health professionals. Many never seek therapy, and others end up in prison, where treatment is rarely an option.

Borderline Personality Disorder

According to the *DSM-IV,* **borderline personality disorder (BPD)** is a pervasive pattern of instability in interpersonal relationships, self-image, and emotions, and of marked impulsivity beginning by early adulthood and present in various contexts. Individuals with BPD are insecure, impulsive, and emotional (Aggen & others, 2009; Crowell, Beauchaine, & Linehan, 2009). BPD is related to self-harming behaviors such as cutting (injuring oneself with a sharp object but without suicidal intent) and also to suicide (Soloff & others, 1994).

The *DSM-IV* specifies that BPD is indicated by the presence of five or more of the following symptoms:

borderline personality disorder (BPD) Psychological disorder characterized by a pervasive pattern of instability in interpersonal relationships, self-image, and emotions, and of marked impulsivity beginning by early adulthood and present in a variety of contexts.

- Frantic efforts to avoid being abandoned
- Unstable and intense interpersonal relationships characterized by extreme shifts between idealization and devaluation
- Markedly and persistently unstable self-image or sense of self
- Impulsivity in at least two areas that are potentially self-damaging (for example, spending, sex, substance abuse, reckless driving, and binge eating)
- Recurrent suicidal behavior, gestures, or threats or self-mutilating behavior
- Unstable and extreme emotional responses
- Chronic feelings of emptiness
- Inappropriate, intense anger or difficulty controlling anger
- Temporary stress-related *paranoia* (a pattern of disturbed thought featuring delusions of grandeur or persecution) or severe dissociative symptoms

Individuals with BPD are prone to wild mood swings and are very sensitive to how others treat them. They often feel as if they are riding a nonstop emotional rollercoaster (Selby & others, 2009), and their loved ones may have to work hard to avoid upsetting them. Individuals with BPD tend to see the world in black and white terms, a thinking style called *splitting*. For example, they typically view other people as either hated enemies with no positive qualities or as beloved, idealized friends who can do no wrong.

Borderline personality disorder is far more common in women than men. Women make up 75 percent of those with the disorder (Korzekwa & others, 2008).

Film depictions of BPD include Fatal Attraction, Single White Female, and Obsessed. Where these films get it wrong is that they show BPD as leading to more harm to others than to the self.

The potential causes of BPD are likely complex and include biological factors as well as childhood experiences. The role of genes in BPD has been demonstrated in a variety of studies and across cultures. The heritability of BPD is about 40 percent (Distel & others, 2008; Livesley, 2008; Tadic & others, 2008).

Many individuals with borderline personality disorder report experiences of childhood sexual abuse, as well as physical abuse and neglect (Al-Alem & Omar, 2008; Soloff, Feske, & Fabio, 2008; Zanarini & others, 2000). It is not clear, however, whether abuse is a primary cause of the disorder (Trull & Widiger, 2003). Childhood abuse experiences may combine with genetic factors in promoting BPD.

This would be a diathesis-stress model explanation for BPD.

Cognitive factors associated with BPD include a tendency to hold a set of irrational beliefs. These include thinking that one is powerless and innately unacceptable and that other people are dangerous and hostile (Arntz, 2005). Individuals with BPD also display *hypervigilance:* the tendency to be constantly on the alert, looking for threatening information in the environment (Sieswerda & others, 2007).

Because of the severe toll on individuals with BPD and their families and friends, in 2008 the U.S. House of Representatives declared the month of May National Borderline Personality Disorder Awareness Month.

As recently as within the past 20 years, experts thought that BPD was unlikely to be treatable. Newer evidence, however, suggests that many individuals with BPD show improvement over time. As many as 50 percent of individuals with BPD improve within two years (Gunderson, 2008). One key aspect of successful treatment appears to be a reduction in social stress, such as that due to leaving an abusive romantic partner or establishing a sense of trust in a therapist (Gunderson & others, 2003).

self-quiz

1. Individuals with ASPD
   A. are incapable of having successful careers.
   B. are typically women.
   C. are typically men.
   D. rarely engage in criminal behavior.

2. People with BPD
   A. pay little attention to how others treat them.
   B. rarely have problems with anger or strong emotion.
   C. tend to have suicidal thoughts or engage in self-harming actions.
   D. tend to have a balanced viewpoint of people and things rather than to see them as all black or all white.

3. All of the following are true of BPD *except*
   A. BPD can be caused by a combination of nature and nurture—genetic inheritance and childhood experience.
   B. Recent research has shown that people with BPD respond positively to treatment.
   C. A common symptom of BPD is impulsive behavior such as binge eating and reckless driving.
   D. BPD is far more common in men than women.

Apply It! 4. Your new friend Maureen tells you that she was diagnosed with borderline personality disorder at the age of 23. She feels hopeless when she considers that her mood swings and unstable self-esteem are part of her very personality. Despairing, she asks, "How will I ever change?" Which of the following statements about Maureen's condition is accurate?
   A. Maureen should seek therapy and strive to improve her relationships with others, as BPD is treatable.
   B. Maureen's concerns are realistic, because a personality disorder like BPD is unlikely to change.
   C. Maureen should seek treatment for BPD because there is high likelihood that she will end up committing a criminal act.
   D. Maureen is right to be concerned, because BPD is most often caused by genetic factors.

8 Combating Stigma

Putting a label on a person with a psychological disorder can make the disorder seem like something that happens only to other people (Baumann, 2007). The truth is that psychological disorders are not just about *other* people; they are about people, period. Over 26 percent of Americans age 18 and older suffer from a diagnosable psychological disorder in a given year—an estimated 57.7 million U.S. adults (Kessler & others, 2005; NIMH, 2008). Chances are that you or someone you know will experience a psychological disorder. Figure 12.12 shows how common many psychological disorders are in the United States.

A classic and controversial study illustrated that labels of psychological disorder can be very "sticky"—that is, once applied to a person, a label is hard to remove. David Rosenhan (1973) recruited eight adults (including a stay-at-home mom, a psychology graduate student, a pediatrician, and some psychiatrists), none with a psychological disorder, to see a psychiatrist at various hospitals. These "pseudo-patients" were instructed to act in a normal way except to complain about hearing voices that said things like "empty" and "thud." All eight expressed an interest in leaving the hospital and behaved cooperatively. Nevertheless, all eight were labeled with schizophrenia and kept in the hospital from 3 to 52 days. None of the mental health professionals they encountered ever questioned the diagnosis that was given to these individuals, and all were discharged with the label "schizophrenia in remission." The label "schizophrenia" had stuck to the pseudo-patients and caused the professionals around them to interpret their quite normal behavior as abnormal. Clearly, once a person has been labeled with a psychological disorder, that label colors how we perceive everything else he or she does.

Labels of psychological disorder carry with them a wide array of implications for the individual. Is he or she still able to be a good friend? A good parent? A competent worker? A significant concern for individuals with psychological disorders is the negative attitudes that others might have about people struggling with mental illness (Phelan & Basow, 2007). Stigma can be a significant barrier for individuals coping with a psychological disorder, as well as for their families and loved ones (Corrigan, 2007, Hinshaw, 2007). Fear of stigma can prevent individuals from seeking treatment and from talking about their problems with family and friends. To test your own attitudes about people with psychological disorders, complete the exercise in Figure 12.13.

	Number of Americans in a given year (millions)	Percentage of Americans
Anxiety Disorders		
General anxiety disorder	6.8	3.1%
Panic disorder	6.0	2.7%
Phobic disorder	19.2	8.7%
PTSD	7.7	3.5%
Mood Disorders		
Major depressive disorder	14.8	6.7%
Dysthymic disorder	3.3	1.5%
Bipolar disorder	5.7	2.6%
Schizophrenia	2.4	1.1%

FIGURE 12.12

The 12-Month Prevalence of the Most Common Psychological Disorders If you add up the numbers in this figure, you will see that the totals are higher than the numbers given in the text. The explanation is that people are frequently diagnosed with more than one psychological disorder. An individual who has both a depressive and an anxiety disorder would be counted in both of those categories.

Consequences of Stigma

The stigma attached to psychological disorders can provoke prejudice and discrimination toward individuals who are struggling with these problems, thus adding a complication to an already difficult situation. Having a disorder and experiencing the stigma associated with it can also negatively affect the physical health of such individuals.

Prejudice and Discrimination Labels of psychological disorders can be damaging because they may lead to negative stereotypes, which, as reviewed in Chapter 11, play a role in prejudice. For example, the label "schizophrenic" often has negative connotations such as "frightening" and "dangerous."

This is why psychologists have moved to people-first language as described at the beginning of this chapter.

Vivid cases of extremely harmful behavior by individuals with psychological disorders can perpetuate the stereotype that people with such disorders are violent. For example, Cho Seung-Hui, a 23-year-old college student, murdered 32 students and faculty at Virginia Tech University in April 2007 before killing himself. The widely reported fact that Cho had struggled with psychological disorders throughout his life may have reinforced the notion that individuals with disorders are dangerous. In fact, however, people with psychological disorders (especially those in treatment) are no more likely to commit violent acts than the general population. Cho was no more

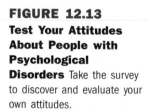

Rate the following items using a scale of 1–5, with 1 indicating that you completely *disagree* with the statement and 5 indicating that you completely *agree* with the statement.

1=completely disagree 2=slightly agree
3=moderately agree 4=strongly agree
5=completely agree

_____ 1. I would rather not live next door to a person with a psychological disorder.

_____ 2. A person with a psychological disorder is unfit to raise children.

_____ 3. I would be afraid to be around a person with a psychological disorder.

_____ 4. I would not want to live in the same neighborhood as a group home for persons with psychological disorders.

_____ 5. A person with a psychological disorder cannot hold a job.

_____ 6. A person with a psychological disorder is dangerous or potentially violent.

Total _____

Add up your score and divide by 6. If your score is 3 or higher, you may want to rethink your attitudes about individuals with psychological disorders.

It may be revealing to ask yourself how you would respond to these statements if the words "person with a psychological disorder" were replaced with "woman," "African American," or "gay man or lesbian." Sometimes even individuals who would not think of themselves a being prejudiced against other groups find themselves biased against the mentally ill.

FIGURE 12.13
Test Your Attitudes About People with Psychological Disorders Take the survey to discover and evaluate your own attitudes.

representative of people with psychological disorders than he was representative of students at Virginia Tech.

Individuals with psychological disorders are often aware of the negative stigma attached to these conditions. They themselves may have previously held such negative attitudes. They need help, but seeking that assistance may involve accepting a stigmatized identity (Thornicroft & others, 2009; Yen & others, 2009). Even mental health professionals can fall prey to prejudicial attitudes toward those who are coping with psychological disorders (Nordt, Rossler, & Lauber, 2006).

Among the most feared aspects of stigma is discrimination. As described in Chapter 11, discrimination means acting prejudicially toward a person who is a member of a stigmatized group. In the workplace, discrimination against a person with a psychological disorder is against the law. The Americans with Disabilities Act (ADA) of 1990 made it illegal to refuse employment or a promotion to someone with a psychological disorder when the person's condition does not prevent performance of the job's essential functions (Cleveland, Barnes-Farrell, & Ratz, 1997). A person's appearance or behavior may be unusual or irritating, but as long as that individual is able to complete the duties required of a position, he or she cannot be denied employment or promotion.

Physical Health   Individuals with psychological disorders are more likely to be physically ill and two times more likely to die than their psychologically healthy counterparts (Gittelman, 2008; Kumar, 2004). They are also more likely to be obese, to smoke, to drink excessively, and to lead sedentary lives (Kim & others, 2007; Lindwall & others, 2007; Mykletun & others, 2007; Osborn, Nazareth, & King, 2006).

You might be thinking that these physical health issues are the least of their worries. If someone struggling with schizophrenia wants to smoke, why not just let him or her? This type of thinking sells short the capacity of psychological and psychiatric treatments to help those with psychological disorders. Research has shown that health-promotion programs can work well even for individuals with a severe psychological disorder (Addington & others, 1998; Chafetz & others, 2008). When we disregard the potential of physical health interventions for people with psychological disorders to make positive life changes, we reveal our biases.

Overcoming Stigma

How can we effectively combat the stigma of psychological disorders? One obstacle to changing people's attitudes toward individuals with psychological disorders is that mental illness is often "invisible." That is, sometimes a person can have a disorder without those of us around him or her ever knowing. Indeed, we may be unaware of

Although Sheila Hollingsworth struggles with schizophrenia, her story is one of success, not failure. She has refused to allow her disorder to rob her of a good life.

many good lives around us that are being lived under a cloud of psychological disorder, because worries about being stigmatized keep the affected individuals from "coming out." Thus, stigma leads to a catch-22: Positive examples of individuals coping with psychological disorders are often missing from our experience because those who are doing well shun public disclosure of their disorders (Jensen & Wadkins, 2007).

A critical step toward eliminating stigma is to resist thinking of people with disorders as limited individuals whose disorder colors everything they do. Instead, it is vital to recognize their strengths—both in confronting their disorder and in carrying on despite their problems—and their achievements. By creating a positive environment for people with disorders, we encourage more of them to become confidently "visible," and we empower them to be positive role models for others.

Sheila Hollingsworth—a 51-year-old divorced mother of two—is such a role model. She has a master's degree and works at the Baltic Street Mental Health Board. She is so beloved at work that everyone calls her "Sheila Love." She sings in her church choir, takes calligraphy classes, and is determined to lose 30 pounds (Bonfatti, 2005). Notably, Sheila has schizophrenia. However, she has not allowed the stigma of this disorder to rob her of a good life. She works as a peer counselor and helps others by leading groups and modeling effective treatment. It can be enormously positive for individuals coping with severe psychological disorders to have a role model like Sheila, who is struggling but making it, one day at a time.

After reading this chapter, you know that many admired individuals have dealt with psychological disorders. Their diagnoses do not detract from their accomplishments. To the contrary, their accomplishments are all the more remarkable in the context of the challenging lives in which they have occurred.

Do It!

Although we might think of people who contend with psychological disorders as troubled and downtrodden, they (like all people) have the capacity to be astonishingly creative. Check out the website maintained by the National Art Exhibitions of the Mentally Ill (NAEMI) to experience some amazing creations of artists who suffer from mental illness. Go to http://www.naemi.org and click on "Artists." How does your exploration of this artwork influence your feelings about mental illness?

self-quiz

1. The percentage of Americans 18 years of age and older who suffer from a diagnosable psychological disorder in a given year is closest to
   A. 15 percent.
   B. 26 percent.
   C. 40 percent.
   D. 46 percent.

2. The stigma attached to psychological disorders can have implications for
   A. the physical health of an individual with such a disorder.
   B. the psychological well-being of an individual with such a disorder.
   C. other people's attitudes and behaviors toward the individual with such a disorder.
   D. all of the above

3. Labeling psychological disorders can lead to damaging
   A. stereotyping.
   B. discrimination.
   C. prejudice.
   D. all of the above

Apply It! 4. Liliana has applied for a full-time job after graduation doing data entry for a polling firm. She held a similar job last summer and is excited when she sees that the procedures are very much like the ones she learned in the previous year. During her second interview, Liliana asks the human resources manager whether the health benefits for the job include prescription drug coverage, as she is on anti-anxiety medication for generalized anxiety disorder. Which of the following statements is most applicable, legally and otherwise, in light of Liliana's request?
   A. The human resources manager should tell the hiring committee to avoid hiring Liliana because she has a psychological disorder.
   B. It is illegal for the firm to deny Liliana employment simply because she has a psychological disorder.
   C. Liliana should not have asked that question because she will not be hired.
   D. Liliana must be given the job, or the firm could face a lawsuit.

summary

① Defining and Explaining Abnormal Behavior

Abnormal behavior is deviant, maladaptive, or personally distressful. Theoretical perspectives on the causes of psychological disorders include biological, psychological, sociocultural, and biopsychosocial approaches.

Biological approaches to disorders describe psychological disorders as diseases with origins in structural, biochemical, and genetic factors. Psychological approaches include the behavioral, social cognitive, and trait perspectives. Sociocultural approaches place emphasis on the larger social context in which a person lives, including marriage, socioeconomic status, ethnicity, gender, and culture. Biopsychosocial approaches view the interactions among biological, psychological, and social factors as significant forces in producing both normal and abnormal behavior.

The classification of disorders provides a shorthand for communication, allows clinicians to make predictions about disorders, and helps them to decide on appropriate treatment. The *Diagnostic and Statistical Manual of Mental Disorders* (*DSM*) is the classification system clinicians use to diagnose psychological disorders. Some psychologists contend that the *DSM-IV* perpetuates the medical model of psychological disorders, labels everyday problems as psychological disorders, and fails to address strengths.

② Anxiety Disorders

Generalized anxiety disorder is anxiety that persists for at least 6 months with no specific reason for the anxiety. Panic disorder involves attacks marked by the sudden onset of intense terror. Biological, psychological, and sociocultural factors may contribute to the development of panic disorder.

Phobic disorders involve an irrational, overwhelming fear of a particular object, such as snakes, or a situation, such as flying. Obsessive-compulsive disorder is an anxiety disorder in which the individual has anxiety-provoking thoughts that will not go away (obsession) and/or urges to perform repetitive, ritualistic behaviors to prevent or produce some future situation (compulsion). Post-traumatic stress disorder (PTSD) is an anxiety disorder that develops through exposure to traumatic events, sexual abuse and assault, and natural and unnatural disasters. Symptoms include flashbacks, emotional avoidance, emotional numbing, and excessive arousal. A variety of experiential, psychological, and genetic factors have been shown to relate to these disorders.

③ Mood Disorders

Two types of mood disorders are depressive disorders and bipolar disorder.

The depressive disorders include major depressive disorder and dysthymic disorder. In major depressive disorder, the individual experiences a serious depressive episode and depressed characteristics such as lethargy and hopelessness. Dysthymic disorder is generally more chronic and has fewer symptoms than major depressive disorder.

Biological explanations of depressive disorders focus on heredity, neurophysiological abnormalities, and neurotransmitter deregulation. Psychological explanations include behavioral and cognitive perspectives. Sociocultural explanations emphasize socioeconomic and ethnic factors, as well as gender.

Bipolar disorder is characterized by extreme mood swings that include one or more episodes of mania (an overexcited, unrealistic, optimistic state). Most individuals with bipolar disorder go through multiple cycles of depression interspersed with mania. Genetic influences are stronger predictors of bipolar disorder than depressive disorder, and biological processes are also a factor in bipolar disorder.

Severe depression and other psychological disorders can cause individuals to want to end their lives. Theorists have proposed biological, psychological, and sociocultural explanations of suicide.

④ Eating Disorders

Three eating disorders are anorexia nervosa, bulimia nervosa, and binge eating disorder. Anorexia nervosa is characterized by extreme underweight and starvation. The disorder is related to perfectionism and obsessive-compulsive tendencies. Bulimia nervosa involves a pattern of binge eating followed by purging through self-induced vomiting. In contrast, binge eating disorder involves binge eating without purging.

Anorexia nervosa and bulimia nervosa are much more common in women than men, but there is no gender difference in binge eating disorder. Although sociocultural factors were once thought to be primary in explaining eating disorders, more recent evidence points to the role of biological factors.

⑤ Dissociative Disorders

Dissociative amnesia involves memory loss caused by extensive psychological stress. Dissociative fugue also involves memory loss, but individuals with this disorder unexpectedly travel away from home or work, sometimes assume a new identity, and do not remember the old one. In dissociative identity disorder, formerly called multiple personality disorder, two or more distinct personalities are present in the same individual; this disorder is rare.

⑥ Schizophrenia

Schizophrenia is a severe psychological disorder characterized by highly disordered thought processes. Positive symptoms of schizophrenia are behaviors and experiences that are present in individuals with schizophrenia but absent in healthy people; they include hallucinations and delusions. Negative symptoms of schizophrenia are behaviors and experiences that are part of healthy human life that are absent for those with this disorder; they include flat affect and an inability to plan or engage in goal-directed behavior.

Biological factors (heredity, structural brain abnormalities, and problems in neurotransmitter regulation, especially dopamine), psychological factors (diathesis-stress model), and sociocultural factors may be involved in schizophrenia. Psychological and sociocultural factors are not viewed as stand-alone causes of schizophrenia, but they are related to the course of the disorder.

⑦ Personality Disorders

Personality disorders are chronic, maladaptive cognitive-behavioral patterns that are thoroughly integrated into an individual's personality. Two common types are antisocial personality disorder (ASPD) and borderline personality disorder (BPD).

Antisocial personality disorder is characterized by guiltlessness, law-breaking, exploitation of others, irresponsibility, and deceit. Individuals with this disorder often lead a life of crime and violence. Psychopaths—remorseless predators who engage in violence to get what they want—are a subgroup of individuals with ASPD.

Borderline personality disorder is a pervasive pattern of instability in interpersonal relationships, self-image, and emotions, and of marked impulsivity beginning by early adulthood and present in a variety of contexts. This disorder is related to self-harming behaviors such as cutting and suicide.

Biological factors for ASPD include genetic, brain, and autonomic nervous system differences. The potential causes of BPD are complex and include biological and cognitive factors as well as childhood experiences.

⑧ Combating Stigma

Stigma can create a significant barrier for people coping with a psychological disorder, as well as for their loved ones. Fear of being labeled can prevent individuals with a disorder from getting treatment and from talking about their problems with family and friends. In addition, the stigma attached to psychological disorders can lead to prejudice and discrimination toward individuals who are struggling with these problems. Having a disorder and experiencing the stigma associated with it can also negatively affect the physical health of such individuals.

We can help to combat stigma by acknowledging the strengths and the achievements of individuals coping with psychological disorders. By creating a positive environment for people with disorders, we encourage more of them to be open about their struggles and to thrive, with the result that they can become positive role models for others.

key terms

abnormal behavior, p. 412
medical model, p. 413
DSM-IV, p. 414
attention deficit hyperactivity
    disorder (ADHD), p. 417
anxiety disorders, p. 417
generalized anxiety
    disorder, p. 418
panic disorder, p. 418
phobic disorder (phobia), p. 419

obsessive-compulsive disorder
    (OCD), p. 420
post-traumatic stress disorder
    (PTSD), p. 421
mood disorders, p. 423
depressive disorders, p. 423
major depressive disorder
    (MDD), p.423
dysthymic disorder (DD), p. 424
learned helplessness, p. 424

bipolar disorder, p. 426
anorexia nervosa, p. 430
bulimia nervosa, p. 431
binge eating disorder (BED), p. 432
dissociative disorders, p. 433
dissociative amnesia, p. 433
dissociative fugue, p. 433
dissociative identity disorder
    (DID), p. 434
schizophrenia, p. 435

hallucinations, p. 436
delusions, p. 436
referential thinking, p. 436
catatonia, p. 436
flat affect, p. 436
diathesis-stress model, p. 438
personality disorders, p. 439
antisocial personality disorder
    (ASPD), p. 439
borderline personality disorder
    (BPD), p. 441

self-test

Multiple Choice

1. The name for a mark of shame that may cause people to avoid, or act negatively toward, an individual is
   A. disfigurement.
   B. mortification.
   C. stigma.
   D. prejudice.

2. Feeling an overwhelming sense of dread and worry without a specific cause is known as
   A. obsessive-compulsive disorder.
   B. generalized anxiety disorder.
   C. phobic disorder.
   D. panic disorder.

3. A characteristic of post-traumatic stress disorder is
   A. panic attacks.
   B. an exaggerated startle response.

   C. persistent nervousness about a variety of things.
   D. extreme fear of an object or place.

4. All of the following are a mood disorder *except*
   A. generalized anxiety disorder.
   B. dysthymic disorder.
   C. major depressive disorder.
   D. bipolar disorder.

5. The diagnostic criteria for major depressive disorder include the standard that a depressive episode must last at least
   A. one week.
   B. two weeks.
   C. two months.
   D. two years.

6. Insistently focusing on being depressed is characteristic of
   A. catastrophic thinking.
   B. a ruminative coping style.
   C. dysthymic disorder.
   D. learned helplessness.

7. The eating disorder that involves binge eating followed by purging through self-induced vomiting is
   A. binge eating disorder.
   B. bulimia nervosa.
   C. anorexia nervosa.
   D. compulsive eating disorder.

8. A dissociative disorder accompanied by unexpected sudden travel is
   A. dissociate disorder.
   B. dissociative amnesia.
   C. dissociative identity disorder.
   D. dissociative fugue.

9. _____ symptoms of schizophrenia reflect a loss of normal functioning, while _____ symptoms reflect the addition of abnormal functioning.
   A. Cognitive; behavioral
   B. Behavioral; cognitive
   C. Positive; negative
   D. Negative; positive

10. Antisocial personality disorder is characterized by _____, whereas borderline personality disorder is characterized by _____.
    A. avoidance of impulsive behavior; avoidance of physical aggression
    B. avoidance of physical aggression; avoidance of impulsive behavior
    C. a tendency to harm oneself; violence toward others
    D. violence toward others; a tendency to harm oneself

Apply It!

11. What is the diathesis-stress model? In the text this model was applied to schizophrenia. Apply it to one eating disorder and one anxiety disorder.

13 Therapies

Rebuilding Houses and Lives

On Monday, August 29, 2005, a category 5 hurricane named Katrina made violent landfall in the city of New Orleans and elsewhere along the Gulf Coast. Katrina would be the costliest—and one of the deadliest—hurricanes in U.S. history. Years later, the rebuilding of the city is ongoing.

The physical reconstruction of their city has been only one part of the recovery for the people of New Orleans. In addition, these uprooted survivors have been rebuilding their sense of hope and their very lives, with the help of teams of psychologists. Clinical psychologists from all over the United States have flocked to New Orleans many times since that day in the summer of 2005, lending an ear, teaching new skills, and dispensing therapies to help the stricken residents manage their sense of loss and develop new goals. Just as Habitat for Humanity, a nonprofit organization dedicated to constructing decent and affordable housing, has helped the victims repair the storm's physical damage and rebuild their homes, psychologists have helped them repair the psychological damage of trauma and rebuild their lives (Borchardt, 2008).

For countless Katrina survivors, asking for help to rebuild their city was natural, but asking for psychological help was a different—and often difficult—matter. Indeed, for many of us, seeking aid when we are troubled seems a mark of weakness. To the contrary, however, seeking help is a sign that we are strong and courageous enough to admit that we cannot go it alone. ■

- Have you, or has anyone you know, ever sought therapy for a psychological problem?

- How is seeking treatment for a psychological disorder a sign of strength?

- When you think of treatments for psychological disorders, what comes to mind?

The science of psychology has led to the development of various treatment approaches to help relieve psychological suffering. These different forms of therapy are the subject of this chapter. We review biological, psychological, and sociocultural approaches to the use of therapy to improve the lives of individuals with psychological disorders. We close by examining the effectiveness of therapy and its broad array of benefits and by exploring the factors that contribute to its success.

1 Biological Therapies

Biological therapies (biomedical therapies) are treatments that reduce or eliminate the symptoms of psychological disorders by altering aspects of body functioning. Drug therapy is the most common form of biomedical therapy. Electroconvulsive therapy and psychosurgery are much less widely used biomedical therapies.

As medical doctors, psychiatrists can administer drugs as part of therapy. Family doctors can also prescribe drugs for psychological disorders. In contrast, psychologists, who are not trained as medical doctors, cannot administer drugs therapeutically in most states.

biological therapies (biomedical therapies) Treatments that reduce or eliminate the symptoms of psychological disorders by altering aspects of body functioning.

Have you taken a prescription drug for a psychological problem? As you read, see if that medication is described. Does the description fit with your experiences?

Drug Therapy

Although people have long used medicine and herbs to alleviate symptoms of emotional distress, it was not until the twentieth century that drug treatments revolutionized mental healthcare. Psychotherapeutic drugs are used mainly in three diagnostic categories: anxiety disorders, mood disorders, and schizophrenia. In this section we explore the effectiveness of drugs for these various disorders—antianxiety drugs, antidepressant drugs, and antipsychotic drugs.

antianxiety drugs Commonly known as tranquilizers, drugs that reduce anxiety by making individuals calmer and less excitable.

Antianxiety Drugs **Antianxiety drugs** are commonly known as *tranquilizers*. These drugs reduce anxiety by making individuals calmer and less excitable. Benzodiazepines are the antianxiety drugs that generally offer the greatest relief for anxiety symptoms, though these drugs are potentially addictive. They work by binding to the receptor sites of neurotransmitters that become overactive during anxiety (Poisnel & others, 2009). The most frequently prescribed benzodiazepines include Xanax, Valium, and Librium. A nonbenzodiazepine—buspirone, or BuSpar—is commonly used to treat generalized anxiety disorder (Pollack, 2009).

Benzodiazepines are relatively fast-acting, taking effect within hours. In contrast, buspirone must be taken daily for two to three weeks before the patient feels benefits. Side effects of benzodiazepines include drowsiness, loss of coordination, fatigue, and mental slowing (Fields, 2010). These effects can be hazardous when a person is driving or operating machinery, especially when the individual first starts taking the medication. Benzodiazepines also have been linked to abnormalities in babies born to mothers who took them during pregnancy (Istaphanous & Loepke, 2009). Further, the combination of benzodiazepines with alcohol and with other medications—including anesthetics, antihistamines, sedatives, muscle relaxants, and some prescription pain medicines—can lead to problems such as depression (Vakily & others, 2009).

Why are antianxiety drugs so widely used? Many individuals experience stress, anxiety, or both. Family physicians and psychiatrists prescribe these drugs to improve people's ability to cope with their problems. Antianxiety medications are best used only

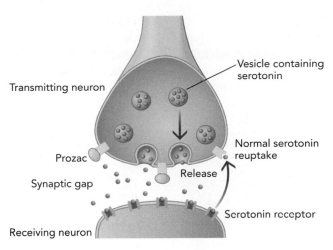

temporarily for symptomatic relief. Too often, they are overused and can become addictive (Lader, Tylee, & Donoghue, 2009).

Antidepressant Drugs

antidepressant drugs Drugs that regulate mood.

Antidepressant drugs regulate mood. The three main classes of antidepressant drugs are tricyclics, such as Elavil; monoamine oxidase (MAO) inhibitors, such as Nardil; and selective serotonin reuptake inhibitors, such as Prozac. These antidepressants are all thought to help depressed mood through their effects on neurotransmitters in the brain. In different ways, they all allow the depressed person's brain to increase or maintain its level of important neurotransmitters, especially serotonin and norepinephrine.

Tricyclics, so-called because of their three-ringed molecular structure, are believed to work by increasing the level of certain neurotransmitters, especially norepinephrine and serotonin (Lopez-Munoz & Alamo, 2009). You might recall the role of low serotonin levels in negative mood (Chapter 10) and aggression (Chapter 11). Tricyclics reduce the symptoms of depression in approximately 60 to 70 percent of cases. Tricyclics usually take two to four weeks to improve mood. Adverse side effects may include restlessness, faintness, trembling, sleepiness, and memory difficulties.

FIGURE 13.1

How the Antidepressant Prozac Works Secreted by a transmitting neuron, serotonin moves across the synaptic gap and binds to receptors in a receiving neuron. Excess serotonin in the synaptic gap is normally reabsorbed by the transmitting neuron. The antidepressant Prozac blocks this reuptake of serotonin by the transmitting neuron, however, leaving excess serotonin in the synaptic gap. The excess serotonin is transmitted to the receiving neuron and circulated through the brain. The result is a reduction of the serotonin deficit found in depressed individuals.

MAO inhibitors are thought to work by blocking the enzyme monoamine oxidase, which breaks down the neurotransmitters serotonin and norepinephrine in the brain (Hazell, 2009). Scientists believe that the blocking action of MAO inhibitors allows these neurotransmitters to stick around and help regulate mood. MAO inhibitors are not as widely used as tricyclics because they are more potentially harmful. However, some individuals who do not respond to tricyclics do respond to MAO inhibitors. MAO inhibitors may be especially risky because of their potential interactions with certain foods and drugs (Nishida & others, 2009). Cheese and other fermented foods—including alcoholic beverages, such as red wine—can interact with the inhibitors to raise blood pressure and, over time, cause a stroke.

Psychiatrists increasingly are prescribing a type of antidepressant drug called *selective serotonin reuptake inhibitors* (SSRIs). SSRIs target serotonin and work mainly by interfering with the reabsorption of serotonin in the brain (Cipriani & others, 2009; Z. Zhou & others, 2009). Figure 13.1 shows how this process works.

Just as their name suggests, these drugs selectively inhibit the reuptake of serotonin.

Three widely prescribed SSRIs are Prozac (fluoxetine), Paxil (paroxetine), and Zoloft (sertraline). The increased prescription of these drugs reflects their effectiveness in reducing depression symptoms with fewer side effects than other antidepressants (Ksir, Hart, & Ray, 2008). Nonetheless, they can have negative effects, including insomnia, anxiety, headache, and diarrhea (Keeton, Kolos, & Walkup, 2009). They also can impair sexual functioning and produce severe withdrawal symptoms if their use is ended too abruptly (Frohlich & Meston, 2005).

Beyond their usefulness in treating mood disorders, antidepressant drugs are often effective for a number of anxiety disorders, including generalized anxiety disorder, panic disorder, obsessive-compulsive disorder, social phobia, and post-traumatic stress disorder (Davidson, 2009; Pampaloni & others, 2009). In addition, eating disorders, especially bulimia nervosa, may be amenable to treatment with antidepressant drugs (Grilo, Masheb, & Wilson, 2006).

lithium The lightest of the solid elements in the periodic table of elements, widely used to treat bipolar disorder.

Lithium is widely used to treat bipolar disorder. Lithium is the lightest of the solid elements in the periodic table of elements. If you have ever used a lithium battery (or are a fan of Nirvana or Evanescence), you know that

The diagnosis of bipolar disorder may be made because the person is responsive to lithium.

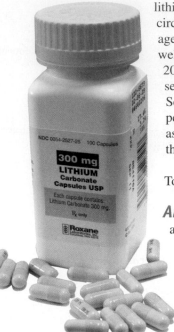

lithium has uses beyond treating psychological disorders. The amount of lithium that circulates in the bloodstream must be carefully monitored because the effective dosage is precariously close to toxic levels. Kidney and thyroid gland complications as well as weight gain can arise as a consequence of lithium therapy (Bauer & others, 2007). Lithium is thought to stabilize moods by influencing norepinephrine and serotonin, but the exact mechanism of its effect is unknown (Perlis & others, 2009; Serretti, Drago, & DeRonchi, 2009). The effectiveness of lithium depends on the person's staying on the medication. Some consumers may be troubled by the association between lithium and weight gain, and others may go off the drug when they are feeling well.

The use of antidepressant drugs to treat depression in children is controversial. To read more about this issue, see Challenge Your Thinking.

Antipsychotic Drugs

Antipsychotic drugs are powerful drugs that diminish agitated behavior, reduce tension, decrease hallucinations, improve social behavior, and produce better sleep patterns in individuals who have a severe psychological disorder, especially schizophrenia (Smith, Weston, & Lieberman, 2009; Uchida & Mamo, 2009). Before antipsychotic drugs were developed in the 1950s, few, if any, interventions brought relief from the torment of psychotic symptoms.

Neuroleptics are the most extensively used class of antipsychotic drugs (Garver, 2006). Numerous well-controlled investigations reveal that when taken in sufficient doses, neuroleptics reduce schizophrenic symptoms (Nasrallah & others, 2009; Thomas & others, 2009). The most widely accepted explanation for the effectiveness of neuroleptics is their ability to block dopamine's action in the brain (Agatonovic-Kustrin, Davies, & Turner, 2009).

Neuroleptics do not cure schizophrenia; they treat its symptoms, not its causes. If an individual with schizophrenia stops taking the drug, the symptoms return. Neuroleptic drugs have substantially reduced the length of hospital stays for individuals with schizophrenia. However, when these individuals are able to return to the community (because the drug therapy reduces their symptoms), many have difficulty coping with the demands of society. In the absence of symptoms, many struggle to justify to themselves that they should continue to take the very medications that have reduced their symptoms—particularly because neuroleptic drugs can have severe side effects. Specifically, drugs that treat disturbed thought by reducing dopamine can also induce a lack of pleasure (Kapur, 2003).

Another potential side effect of neuroleptic drugs is *tardive dyskinesia,* a neurological disorder characterized by involuntary random movements of the facial muscles, tongue, and mouth, as well as extensive twitching of the neck, arms, and legs (Go & others, 2009). Up to 20 percent of individuals with schizophrenia who take neuroleptics develop this disorder. As you may recall from Chapter 12, movement disorders are a positive symptom of schizophrenia, and tardive dyskinesia can also occur in individuals suffering from psychiatric disorders who have not taken neuroleptic drugs (Chouinard, 2006).

Newer antipsychotic drugs called *atypical antipsychotic medications*, introduced in the 1990s, appear to influence dopamine as well as serotonin (Leucht, Kissling, & Davis, 2009; Lin & others, 2009). The two most widely used medications in this group, Clozaril (clozapine) and Risperdal (risperidone), show promise for reducing schizophrenia's symptoms without the side effects of neuroleptics (Keith, 2009; Smith, Weston, & Lieberman, 2009).

Strategies to increase the effectiveness of antipsychotic drugs involve administering small dosages over time, rather than a large initial dose, and combining drug therapy with psychotherapy. Along with drug treatment, individuals with schizophrenia may need training in vocational, family, and social skills.

Recall from Chapter 12 that people with schizophrenia have difficulty regulating the neurotransmitter dopamine. Dopamine is also associated with the experience of reward.

antipsychotic drugs
Powerful drugs that diminish agitated behavior, reduce tension, decrease hallucinations, improve social behavior, and produce better sleep patterns in individuals with a severe psychological disorder, especially schizophrenia.

LAB RAT REHAB

challenge your thinking

Do Antidepressants Increase Suicide Risk in Children?

In 2000, Caitlin McIntosh, a 12-year-old straight-A student, artist, and musician, hanged herself with her shoelaces. Caitlin had been struggling with depression and had begun taking antidepressants shortly before her suicide. Tragic cases such as Caitlin's have stirred deep concerns among parents and mental health professionals. Could the very drugs prescribed to alleviate depression be causing children to become suicidal?

In 2004, the FDA held hearings to address these concerns about the risk of suicide as an unexpected, tragic side effect of antidepressant treatment. The testimonies of many parents indicated no apparent previous risk of suicide and starkly illustrated the impulsiveness of their children's suicides. Some of the children had made plans for activities for the day after their suicides. Some had left sad evidence of the apparent randomness of their acts—a half-drunk glass of soda, an unfinished letter on the computer. Are such real-life case studies generalizable to the population as a whole? What does the scientific evidence say?

During the hearings, the FDA reviewed clinical trials of antidepressant use with children, including 23 trials involving 4,300 children who were randomly assigned to receive either an antidepressant or a placebo (Hammad, 2004). None of the children in the studies committed or attempted suicide. Some studies included participants' self-report ratings of their suicidal thoughts and behaviors. The research showed no differences between the antidepressant and placebo groups on this variable. Another variable examined was "adverse event reports"—spontaneous statements of thoughts about suicide reported by the participants or their parents. The research did show an increase in adverse event reports by the participants in the treatment group, namely a 4 percent rate of such reports, versus 2 percent for the placebo group. This last finding, along with the dramatic personal cases presented by families, appears to have been the basis of the FDA's subsequent action.

In October 2004, the FDA required prescription antidepressants to carry the severest "black box" warning, describing the potential of antidepressants to be associated with suicidal thoughts and behaviors in children and adolescents (FDA, 2004). The warning had a chilling effect: Between March 2004 and June 2005, the number of prescriptions fell 20 percent compared to the same time frame the year before (Rosack, 2007). This drop in prescriptions might indicate that health professionals were being more careful about prescribing antidepressants to youth. It might also indicate, however, that professionals were hesitant to prescribe these drugs even when they might be of real help.

Since the FDA called for the black box warning, a number of studies have found no link between antidepressants and suicide in either adults or children (Hammond, Laughren, & Racoosin, 2006; Markowitz & Cuellar, 2007). One study revealed that Prozac and cognitive-behavior therapy were both effective in reducing depression in children and adolescents, with a drop in suicidal thoughts from 29 percent to 10 percent in the treatment groups (March & others, 2004).

Importantly, drug therapy may not be the first-choice treatment for depressed children. Many children and adolescents have uncomplicated depression that responds well to psychotherapy alone (Kennard & others, 2008). In Great Britain, guidelines allow the prescription of Prozac only in conjunction with ongoing psychotherapy (Boseley, 2006). In the United Kingdom and France, Paxil and Zoloft are not approved for pediatric use.

This controversy highlights issues we have addressed throughout this book. How do we weigh dramatic case study evidence against less vivid scientific data that do not bear out those cases? Are special considerations required when professionals suggest drug therapy in children? How can we best balance the potential benefits and risks of drug treatment? Throughout the debate, the tragedy of suicide has loomed, and professionals have been moved to change their thinking and practices with regard to treating depression in youth.

What Do You Think?

- Have antidepressants helped anyone you know? If so, were you aware of negative side effects? Positive side effects? What was the nature of these effects?

- Do you think occasional bouts of depression might play a normal role in psychological development? Why or why not?

Psychological Disorder	Drug	Effectiveness	Side Effects
Everyday Anxiety and Anxiety Disorders			
Everyday anxiety	Antianxiety drugs; antidepressant drugs	Substantial improvement short term	Antianxiety drugs: less powerful the longer people take them; may be addictive Antidepressant drugs: see below under depressive disorders
Generalized anxiety disorder	Antianxiety drugs	Not very effective	Less powerful the longer people take them; may be addictive
Panic disorder	Antianxiety drugs	About half show improvement	Less powerful the longer people take them; may be addictive
Agoraphobia	Tricyclic drugs and MAO inhibitors	Majority show improvement	Tricyclics: restlessness, fainting, and trembling MAO inhibitors: toxicity
Specific phobias	Antianxiety drugs	Not very effective	Less powerful the longer people take them; may be addictive
Mood Disorders			
Depressive disorders	Tricyclic drugs, MAO inhibitors, and SSRI drugs	Majority show moderate improvement	Tricyclics: cardiac problems, mania, confusion, memory loss, fatigue MAO inhibitors: toxicity SSRI drugs: nausea, nervousness, insomnia, and, in a few cases, suicidal thoughts
Bipolar disorder	Lithium	Large majority show substantial improvement	Toxicity
Schizophrenic Disorders			
Schizophrenia	Neuroleptics; atypical antipsychotic medications	Majority show partial improvement	Neuroleptics: irregular heartbeat, low blood pressure, uncontrolled fidgeting, tardive dyskinesia, and immobility of face Atypical antipsychotic medications: less extensive side effects than with neuroleptics, but can have a toxic effect on white blood cells

FIGURE 13.2

Drug Therapy for Psychological Disorders This figure summarizes the types of drugs used to treat various psychological disorders.

Figure 13.2 lists the drugs used to treat various psychological disorders, their effectiveness, and their side effects. Note that for some anxiety disorders, such as agoraphobia, MAO inhibitors (antidepressant drugs) might be used instead of antianxiety drugs.

Electroconvulsive Therapy

electroconvulsive therapy (ECT)
Also called shock therapy, a treatment, commonly used for depression, that sets off a seizure in the brain.

The goal of **electroconvulsive therapy (ECT)**, commonly called *shock therapy,* is to set off a seizure in the brain, much like what happens spontaneously in some forms of epilepsy (Brown, 2007; Moss & Vaidya, 2006). The notion of causing a seizure to help cure a psychological disorder has been around for quite some time. Hippocrates, the ancient Greek "father of medicine," first noticed that malaria-induced convulsions would sometimes cure individuals who were thought to be insane (Endler, 1988). Following Hippocrates, many other medical doctors noted that head traumas, seizures, and convulsions brought on by fever would sometimes lead to the apparent cure of psychological problems.

In the early twentieth century, doctors induced seizures by insulin overdose and other means and used this procedure primarily to treat schizophrenia. In 1937, Ugo Cerletti, an Italian neurologist specializing in epilepsy, developed the procedure by which seizures could be induced using electrical shock. With colleagues, he developed a fast, efficient

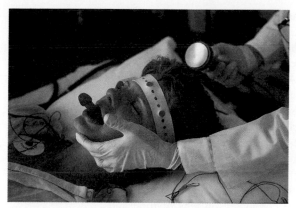

Electroconvulsive therapy (ECT), commonly called shock therapy, causes a seizure in the brain. ECT is given to as many as 100,000 people a year, mainly to treat major depressive disorder.

means of causing seizures in humans, and ECT gained wide use in mental institutions (Endler, 1988). Unfortunately, in earlier years, ECT was used indiscriminately, sometimes even to punish patients, as illustrated in the classic film *One Flew Over the Cuckoo's Nest*. Among the individuals who underwent ECT were Ernest Hemingway and Sylvia Plath, both of whom struggled with depression and ultimately committed suicide.

Other famous people who have received ECT include actress Vivien Leigh (Scarlett O'Hara in Gone With the Wind), singer and actress Judy Garland (Dorothy in The Wizard of Oz), and novelist William Styron (the author of Sophie's Choice).

Today, doctors use ECT primarily to treat severe depression. As many as 100,000 individuals a year undergo ECT, primarily as treatment for major depressive disorder (Mayo Foundation, 2006). Fortunately, the contemporary use of ECT bears little resemblance to its earlier uses. A small electric current lasting for one second or less passes through two electrodes placed on the individual's head. The current excites neural tissue, stimulating a seizure that lasts for approximately a minute. Today, ECT is given mainly to individuals who have not responded to drug therapy or psychotherapy, and its administration involves little discomfort. The patient receives anesthesia and muscle relaxants before the current is applied; this medication allows the individual to sleep through the procedure, minimizes convulsions, and reduces the risk of physical injury. Increasingly ECT is applied only to the brain's right side. The individual awakens shortly afterward with no conscious memory of the treatment.

One analysis of studies of the use of ECT compared its effectiveness in treating depression with that of cognitive therapy and antidepressant drugs (Seligman, 1994). ECT was as effective as cognitive therapy or drug therapy, with about four of five individuals showing marked improvement in all three therapies. However, as with the other therapies, the relapse rate for ECT is moderate to high. What sets ECT apart from other treatments is the rapid relief it can produce in a person's mood (Merkl, Heuser, & Bajbouj, 2009; Popeo, 2009). ECT may be especially effective as a treatment for acute depression in individuals who are at great risk of suicide (Kellner & others, 2006).

ECT is controversial. Its potential side effects remain a source of debate and contradictory findings (Crowley & others, 2008). These possible effects include memory loss and other cognitive impairments and are generally more severe than drug side effects (Caverzasi & others, 2008). Some individuals treated with ECT report prolonged and profound memory loss (Koitabashi, Oyaizu, & Ouchi, 2009; Robertson & Pryor, 2006). Side effects are typically lessened if only one side of the brain is stimulated. Despite the potential problems of ECT, some psychiatrists argue that for certain individuals, this invasive treatment can have life-enhancing—and even life-saving—benefits (O'Connor & others, 2009; Sherman, 2009).

Psychosurgery

Psychosurgery is a biological intervention that involves the removal or destruction of brain tissue. Its effects are irreversible.

In the 1930s, Portuguese physician Antonio Egas Moniz developed a procedure that became known as a *prefrontal lobotomy*. In this operation, a surgical instrument is inserted into the brain and rotated, severing fibers that connect the frontal lobe, which is important in higher thought processes, and the thalamus, which plays a key role in emotion. Moniz theorized that by breaking the connections between these structures, the surgeon could alleviate the symptoms of severe mental disorders. In 1949, Moniz received

psychosurgery
A biological therapy, with irreversible effects, that involves removal or destruction of brain tissue.

the Nobel Prize for developing this procedure. However, although some patients may have benefited from these lobotomies, many were left in a vegetable-like state because of the massive assaults on their brains. Moniz himself felt that the procedure should be used with extreme caution and only as a last resort.

After hearing about Moniz's procedure, American physician and neurologist Walter Freeman became the champion of prefrontal lobotomies (a term he coined). With his colleague James Watts, he performed the first lobotomy in the United States in 1936 (El-Hai, 2005). Freeman developed his own technique, which he performed using a device similar to an ice pick, in surgeries that lasted mere minutes. A charismatic showman who argued strongly for the usefulness of the technique, Freeman in the 1950s and 1960s traveled the country in a van he called the "lobotomobile," demonstrating the surgery in state-run mental institutions. In his career, Freeman performed over 3,000 lobotomies (El-Hai, 2005). Prefrontal lobotomies were conducted on tens of thousands of patients from the 1930s through the 1960s. These numbers speak not only to Freeman's persuasive charm but also to the desperation many physicians felt in treating institutionalized patients with severe psychological disorders (Lerner, 2005).

Subsequent research challenged the effectiveness of lobotomies in enhancing the lives of individuals who had undergone the procedure, pointing instead to the considerable damage that resulted (Landis & Erlick, 1950; Mettler, 1952). Many individuals who received lobotomies suffered permanent and profound brain damage (Whitaker, 2002). Ethical concerns were raised because in many instances, giving consent for the lobotomy was a requirement for release from a mental hospital. Like ECT, lobotomies were used as a form of punishment and control.

By the 1950s drug therapies had emerged as alternatives to lobotomy (Juckel & others, 2009). By the late 1970s new regulations classified the procedure as experimental and established safeguards for patients. Fortunately, Freeman's crude techniques are not typical of contemporary psychosurgery. In current practice, psychosurgery is more precise (Heller & others, 2006; Kopell, Machado, & Rezai, 2006) and involves making just a small lesion in the amygdala or another part of the limbic system (Fountas & Smith, 2007).

Today, only several hundred patients who have severely debilitating conditions undergo psychosurgery each year. The procedure is now used only as a last resort—and with the utmost caution (Ruck, 2003). Psychiatrists and psychologists recognize that science should tamper with the brain only in extreme cases (Pressman, 1998).

In the twenty-first century, practitioners have shifted from traditional psychosurgery to deep brain stimulation in treating psychological disorders (Sachdev & Chen, 2009). In deep brain stimulation, electrodes that are surgically implanted in the brain emit signals that alter the brain's circuitry (Mayo Clinic, 2009). Deep brain stimulation involving the transmission of high-frequency electrical impulses to targeted areas of the brain is now being used for some cases of treatment-resistant depression and obsessive-compulsive disorder (Juckel & others, 2009).

self-quiz

1. _____ are used to treat schizophrenia, whereas _____ are used to treat anxiety.
   A. Benzodiazepines; neuroleptics
   B. Neuroleptics; benzodiazepines
   C. MAO inhibitors; tricyclics
   D. Tricyclics; MAO inhibitors

2. Atypical antipsychotic medications work by
   A. increasing the release of presynaptic neurotransmitters.
   B. acting as an antagonist to dopamine.
   C. stopping the reuptake of serotonin.
   D. inhibiting enzymes that break down norepinephrine.

3. A *true* statement about electroconvulsive therapy is that
   A. it is less effective than medication.
   B. it takes several weeks to see results.
   C. its side effects are more severe than those for medication.
   D. it is painful.

Apply It! 4. Serena experienced times when her mood was very negative for prolonged periods. She was deeply troubled by her feelings and lacked a sense of pleasure in life. At other times, she felt on top of the world. Antidepressant medications brought her no relief. Finally, her psychiatrist prescribed a different drug, which is helping Serena. Not only have her dark moods leveled out, but she is experiencing more stable positive moods. Which of the following is likely true of Serena's experience?
   A. Serena has a depressive disorder, and the drug is an MAO inhibitor.
   B. Serena has an anxiety disorder, and the drug is a benzodiazipene.
   C. Serena has bipolar disorder, and the drug is lithium.
   D. Serena has an eating disorder, and the drug is an SSRI.

2 Psychotherapy

Although their ability to prescribe drugs is limited, psychologists and other mental health professionals may provide **psychotherapy,** a nonmedical process that helps individuals with psychological disorders recognize and overcome their problems. Psychotherapy may be given alone or in conjunction with biological therapy administered by psychiatrists and other medical doctors (Davidson, 2009). In many instances, a combination of psychotherapy and medication is a desirable course of treatment (Nolen-Hoeksema, 2010). Psychotherapists employ a number of strategies to alleviate symptoms of psychological disorders: talking, interpreting, listening, rewarding, and modeling, for example (Prochaska & Norcross, 2010).

Psychotherapy is practiced by a variety of mental health professionals, including clinical psychologists, psychiatrists, counselors, and social workers (Figure 13.3). Society retains control over psychotherapy practitioners through state laws that address licensing and certification. These laws vary in toughness from state to state, but invariably they specify the training the mental health professional must have, and they provide for assessment of an applicant's skill through formal examination. Regardless of their particular

psychotherapy
A nonmedical process that helps individuals with psychological disorders recognize and overcome their problems.

Professional Type	Degree	Education Beyond Bachelor's Degree	Nature of Training
Clinical psychologist	PhD or PsyD	5–7 years	Requires both clinical and research training. Includes a 1-year internship in a psychiatric hospital or mental health facility. Some universities have developed PsyD programs, which have a stronger clinical than research emphasis. The PsyD training program takes as long as the clinical psychology PhD program and also requires the equivalent of a 1-year internship.
Psychiatrist	MD	7–9 years	Four years of medical school, plus an internship and residency in psychiatry, is required. A psychiatry residency involves supervision in therapies, including psychotherapy and biomedical therapy.
Counseling psychologist	MA, PhD, PsyD, or EdD	3–7 years	Similar to clinical psychologist but with emphasis on counseling and therapy. Some counseling psychologists specialize in vocational counseling. Some counselors complete master's degree training, others PhD or EdD training, in graduate schools of psychology or education.
School psychologist	MA, PhD, PsyD, or EdD	3–7 years	Training in graduate programs of education or psychology. Emphasis on psychological assessment and counseling practices involving students' school-related problems. Training is at the master's or doctoral level.
Social worker	MS W/DSW or PhD	2–5 years	Graduate work in a school of social work that includes specialized clinical training in mental health facilities.
Psychiatric nurse	RN, MA, or PhD	0–5 years	Graduate work in a school of nursing with special emphasis on care of mentally disturbed individuals in hospital settings and mental health facilities.
Occupational therapist	BS, MA, or PhD	0–5 years	Emphasis on occupational training with focus on physically or psychologically handicapped individuals. Stresses getting individuals back into the mainstream of work.
Pastoral counselor	None to PhD or DD (Doctor of Divinity)	0–5 years	Requires ministerial background and training in psychology. An internship in a mental health facility as a chaplain is recommended.
Counselor	MA or MEd	2 years	Graduate work in a department of psychology or department of education with specialized training in counseling techniques.

FIGURE 13.3

Main Types of Mental Health Professionals A wide range of professionals with varying levels of training have taken on the challenge of helping people with psychological disorders.

occupation, psychotherapists use a variety of techniques to help alleviate suffering. This section focuses on four main approaches to psychotherapy: psychodynamic, humanistic, behavioral, and cognitive.

Psychodynamic Therapies

psychodynamic therapies
Treatments that stress the importance of the unconscious mind, extensive interpretation by the therapist, and the role of early childhood experiences in the development of an individual's problems.

The **psychodynamic therapies** stress the importance of the unconscious mind, extensive interpretation by the therapist, and the role of early childhood experiences in the development of an individual's problems. The goal of psychodynamic therapies is to help individuals gain insight into the unconscious conflicts that are the source of their problems. Many psychodynamic approaches grew out of Freud's psychoanalytic theory of personality. Today some therapists with a psychodynamic perspective practice Freudian techniques, but others do not (Busch, Milrod, & Sandberg, 2009; Cardoso Zoppe & others, 2009).

psychoanalysis
Freud's therapeutic technique for analyzing an individual's unconscious thoughts.

Psychoanalysis Psychoanalysis is Freud's therapeutic technique for analyzing an individual's unconscious thoughts. Freud believed that a person's current problems could be traced to childhood experiences, many of which involved unconscious sexual conflicts. Only through extensive questioning, probing, and analyzing was Freud able to put together the pieces of the client's personality and help the individual become aware of how these early experiences were affecting present behavior. The psychoanalyst's goal is to bring unconscious conflicts into conscious awareness, thus giving the client insight into his or her core problems and freeing the individual from unconscious influences.

To reach the shadowy world of the unconscious, psychoanalytic therapists use the therapeutic techniques of free association, interpretation, dream analysis, analysis of transference, and analysis of resistance. We survey each in turn.

free association
A psychoanalytic technique that involves encouraging individuals to say aloud whatever comes to mind, no matter how trivial or embarrassing.

Free association involves encouraging individuals to say aloud whatever comes to mind, no matter how trivial or embarrassing. When Freud detected a person resisting the spontaneous flow of thoughts, he probed further. He believed that the crux of the person's problem probably lurked below this point of resistance. Encouraging people to talk freely, Freud reasoned, would allow their deepest thoughts and feelings to emerge. *Catharsis* is the release of emotional tension a person experiences when reliving an emotionally charged and conflicting experience.

To encourage his patients to relax, Freud had them recline on this couch while he sat in the chair on the left, out of their view.

Interpretation plays an important role in psychoanalysis. The analyst does not take the patient's statements and behavior at face value. To understand what is causing the person's conflicts, the therapist constantly searches for symbolic, hidden meanings in what the individual says and does. From time to time, the therapist suggests possible meanings of the person's statements and behavior.

interpretation
A psychoanalyst's search for symbolic, hidden meanings in what the client says and does during therapy.

Dream analysis is a psychoanalytic technique for interpreting a person's dreams. Psychoanalysts believe that dreams contain information about unconscious thoughts, wishes, and conflicts (Freud, 1899/1911). From this perspective, dreams provide our unconscious with an outlet to express our unconscious wishes, a mental theater in which our deepest and most secret desires can be played out (Ferro, 2009; Ferruta, 2009). According to Freud, every dream, even our worst nightmare, contains a hidden, disguised wish. Nightmares might express a wish for punishment, or the sheer horror we feel during the nightmare might itself be the disguise.

dream analysis
A psychoanalytic technique for interpreting a person's dreams.

Freud distinguished between the dream's manifest content and latent content. *Manifest content* refers to the conscious, remembered aspects of a dream. If you wake up remembering a dream about being back in sixth grade with your teacher scolding you for not turning in your homework, that is the dream's manifest content. *Latent content* refers to the unconscious, hidden aspects that are symbolized by the manifest content. To understand your dream, a psychoanalyst might ask you to free-associate to each of the elements of the manifest content. What comes to your mind when you think of being in sixth grade or of your teacher? According to Freud, the latent meaning of a dream is locked inside the dreamer's unconscious mind. The psychoanalyst's goal is to unlock that secret meaning by probing into the deeper layers of the person's mind through having the individual free-associate about the manifest dream elements. The analyst interprets the dream by examining the manifest content for disguised unconscious wishes and needs, especially those that are sexual and aggressive. Dream symbols can mean different things to different dreamers. Freud (1899/1911) recognized that the true meaning of any dream symbol depends on the individual.

The dreamer "knows" what the dream means, but this meaning is locked in his or her unconscious mind.

Freud believed that transference was an inevitable—and essential—aspect of the analyst–patient relationship. **Transference** is the psychoanalytic term for the person's relating to the analyst in ways that reproduce or relive important relationships in the individual's life. A person might interact with an analyst as if the analyst were a parent or lover, for example. According to Freud, transference is a necessary part of the psychoanalytic relationship. Transference can be used therapeutically as a model of how individuals relate to important people in their lives (Meissner, 2009).

transference
A client's relating to the psychoanalyst in ways that reproduce or relive important relationships in the individual's life.

resistance
Unconscious defense strategies on the part of a client that prevent the psychoanalyst from understanding the individual's problems.

Resistance is the psychoanalytic term for the client's unconscious defense strategies that prevent the analyst from understanding the person's problems. Resistance occurs because it is painful for the client to bring conflicts into conscious awareness. By resisting analysis, the individual does not have to face the threatening truths that underlie his or her problems (Hoffman, 2006). Showing up late or missing sessions, arguing with the psychoanalyst, and faking free associations are examples of resistance. A major goal of the analyst is to break through this resistance.

Freud would say that the appearance of resistance means that the analyst is getting very close to the truth.

Contemporary Psychodynamic Therapies Psychodynamic therapy has changed extensively since its beginnings almost a century ago. Nonetheless, many contemporary psychodynamic therapists still probe unconscious thoughts about early childhood experiences to get clues to their clients' current problems, and they try to help individuals gain insight into their emotionally laden, repressed conflicts (Gotthold, 2009; Rustin, 2009). However, contemporary psychoanalysts accord more power to the conscious mind and to a person's current relationships, and they generally place less emphasis on sex (Knoblauch, 2009). In addition, clients today rarely lie on a couch as they did in Freud's time (see the photo on the previous page) or see their therapist several times a week, as was the norm in early psychodynamic therapy. Instead, they sit in a comfortable chair facing the therapist, and weekly appointments are typical.

Some contemporary psychodynamic therapists (Busch, 2007) focus on the self in social contexts, as Heinz Kohut suggested (1977). In Kohut's view, early social relationships with attachment figures such as parents are critical. As we develop, we internalize those relationships, and they serve as the basis for our sense of self. Kohut (1977) believed that the therapist's job is to replace unhealthy childhood relationships with the healthy relationship the therapist provides. In Kohut's view, the therapist needs to interact with the client in empathic and understanding ways. Empathy and understanding are also cornerstones for humanistic therapies, our next topic.

Humanistic Therapies

The underlying philosophy of humanistic therapies is captured by the metaphor of how an acorn, if provided with appropriate conditions, will grow in positive ways, pushing naturally toward its actualization as an oak (Schneider, 2002). In **humanistic therapies,** people are encouraged to understand themselves and to grow personally. The humanistic therapies are unique in their emphasis on the person's self-healing capacities. In contrast to psychodynamic therapies, humanistic therapies emphasize conscious rather than unconscious thoughts, the present rather than the past, and growth and self-fulfillment rather than illness.

Client-centered therapy (also called *Rogerian therapy* or *nondirective therapy*) is a form of humanistic therapy, developed by Carl Rogers (1961, 1980), in which the therapist provides a warm, supportive atmosphere to improve the client's self-concept and to encourage the client to gain insight into problems. Compared with psychodynamic therapies, which emphasize analysis and interpretation by the therapist, client-centered therapy places far more emphasis on the client's self-reflection (Hill, 2000). In client-centered therapy, the goal is not to unlock the deep secrets of the unconscious but rather to help the client identify and understand his or her own genuine feelings (Hazler, 2007). One way to achieve this goal is through active listening and **reflective speech,** a technique in which the therapist mirrors the client's own feelings back to the client. For example, as a woman is describing her grief over the traumatic loss of her husband in a drunk-driving accident, the therapist, noting her voice and facial expression, might suggest, "You sound angry" to help her identify her feelings.

Importantly, in Rogers's therapy, the therapist must enter into an authentic relationship with the client, not as a physician diagnosing a disease but as one human being connecting to another. Indeed, in talking about those he was trying to help, Rogers referred to the "client" and, eventually, to the "person" rather than to the "patient."

Rogers believed that each of us is born with the potential to be fully functioning but that we live in a world in which we are valued only if we live up to conditions of worth. That is, others value us only if we meet certain standards, and we come to apply those standards to ourselves. Each of us needs to feel the positive regard of others, but this positive regard is often conditional—it comes with strings attached.

Rogers believed that humans require three essential elements to grow: unconditional positive regard, empathy, and genuineness. These three elements are reflected in his approach to therapy. To free a person from conditions of worth, the therapist engages in unconditional positive regard, which involves creating a warm, caring environment and never disapproving of the client as a person. Rogers believed unconditional positive regard provides a context for personal growth and self-acceptance, just as soil, water, and sunshine provide a context for the acorn to become an oak. The Rogerian therapist's role is *nondirective*—that is, he or she does not lead the client to any particular revelation. The therapist is there to listen

client-centered therapy
Also called Rogerian therapy or nondirective therapy, a form of humanistic therapy, developed by Rogers, in which the therapist provides a warm, supportive atmosphere to improve the client's self-concept and to encourage the client to gain insight into problems.

humanistic therapies
Treatments, unique in their emphasis on people's self-healing capacities, that encourage clients to understand themselves and to grow personally.

reflective speech
A technique in which the therapist mirrors the client's own feelings back to the client.

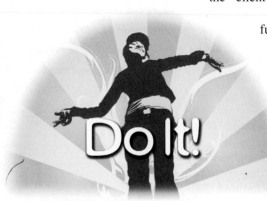

To experience Rogerian therapy firsthand, watch a video of Carl Rogers describing his approach and participating in a session with a client at http://www.viddler.com/explore/digizen/videos/14/.

empathetically to the client's problems and to encourage positive self-regard, independent self-appraisal, and decision making.

In addition to unconditional positive regard, Rogers emphasized the importance of empathy and genuineness. Through empathy the therapist strives to put himself or herself in the client's shoes—to feel the client's emotions. Genuineness requires the therapist to let the client openly know the therapist's own feelings. Genuineness is meant to coexist with unconditional positive regard. The therapist must provide the client with positive regard no matter what, but at the same time that regard must be a genuine expression of the therapist's true feelings.

The therapist may distinguish between the person's behavior and the person himself or herself. Although the client is always acknowledged as a valuable human being, his or her behavior can be evaluated negatively: "You are a good person but your actions are not." Rogers's positive view of humanity extended to his view of therapists. He believed that by being genuine with the client, the therapist could help the client improve.

Put yourself in the shoes of the therapist who must maintain positive regard for a client while also being genuine with that person. Imagine that your client talks about physically harming a child. Could you successfully offer your client unconditional positive regard?

Behavior Therapies

Psychodynamic and humanistic methods are called *insight therapies* because they encourage self-awareness as the path to psychological health. We now turn to therapies that take a different approach: behavior therapies. Insight and self-awareness are not the keys to helping individuals develop more adaptive behavior patterns, behavior therapists say. Rather, changing behavior is the key. Behavior therapies offer action-oriented strategies to help people change behavior, not underlying thoughts or emotions (Spiegler & Guevremont, 2010).

behavior therapies
Treatments, based on the behavioral and social cognitive theories, that use principles of learning to reduce or eliminate maladaptive behavior.

Behavior therapies, based on the behavioral and social cognitive theories, use principles of learning to reduce or eliminate maladaptive behavior. Behavior therapists assume that overt symptoms are the client's central problem. They say that individuals can become aware of why they are depressed and yet still be depressed. Behavior therapists strive to eliminate the depressed symptoms or behaviors rather than trying to get individuals to gain insight into, or awareness of, why they are depressed (Yamanishi & others, 2009).

Although initially based almost exclusively on the learning principles of classical and operant conditioning, behavior therapies have become more diverse in recent years. As social cognitive theory grew in popularity, behavior therapists increasingly included observational learning, cognitive factors, and self-instruction in their treatments (Vassilopoulos & Watkins, 2009). In self-instruction, therapists try to get people to change what they say to themselves.

Classical Conditioning Techniques As described in Chapter 5, classical conditioning has been used in treating phobias. Recall that systematic desensitization means pairing a feared stimulus with a state of deep relaxation.

Figure 13.4 shows a desensitization hierarchy. Desensitization involves exposing someone to a feared situation in a real or an imagined way (Figueroa-Moseley & others, 2007). A more intense form of exposure is *flooding,* that is, exposing an individual to feared stimuli to an excessive degree while not allowing him or her to avoid the stimuli (Berry, Rosenfield, & Smits, 2009; Wolitzky & Telch, 2009). In flooding, the patient is essentially forced to confront the

1 A month before an examination
2 Two weeks before an examination
3 A week before an examination
4 Five days before an examination
5 Four days before an examination
6 Three days before an examination
7 Two days before an examination
8 One day before an examination
9 The night before an examination
10 On the way to the university on the day of an examination
11 Before the unopened doors of the examination room
12 Awaiting distribution of examination papers
13 The examination paper lies facedown before her
14 In the process of answering an examination paper

FIGURE 13.4

A Desensitization Hierarchy Involving Test Anxiety In this hierarchy, the individual begins with her least feared circumstance (a month before the exam) and moves through each of the circumstances until reaching her most feared circumstance (answering the exam questions on test day). At each step, the person replaces fear with deep relaxation and successful visualization.

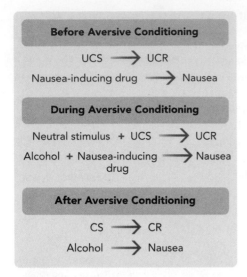

| Before Aversive Conditioning |
| UCS $\longrightarrow$ UCR |
| Nausea-inducing drug $\longrightarrow$ Nausea |

| During Aversive Conditioning |
| Neutral stimulus + UCS $\longrightarrow$ UCR |
| Alcohol + Nausea-inducing drug $\longrightarrow$ Nausea |

| After Aversive Conditioning |
| CS $\longrightarrow$ CR |
| Alcohol $\longrightarrow$ Nausea |

FIGURE 13.5

Classical Conditioning: The Backbone of Aversive Conditioning Classical conditioning can provide a conditional aversion to alcohol. After the association of the drug with alcohol, the alcohol becomes a conditioned stimulus for nausea. Recall the abbreviations UCS (unconditioned stimulus), UCR (unconditioned response), CS (conditioned stimulus), and CR (conditioned response).

frightening situation and survive. Desensitization and flooding are based on the process of extinction in classical conditioning. During extinction, the conditioned stimulus is presented without the unconditioned stimulus, leading to a decreased conditioned response.

Recall from Chapter 5 that aversive conditioning consists of repeated pairings of an undesirable behavior with aversive stimuli to decrease the behavior's positive associations. Through aversive conditioning people can learn to avoid such behaviors as smoking, overeating, and drinking alcohol. Electric shocks, nausea-inducing substances, and verbal insults are some of the noxious stimuli used in aversive conditioning (Sommer & others, 2006). Figure 13.5 illustrates how classical conditioning is the backbone of aversive conditioning.

Operant Conditioning Techniques The idea behind using operant conditioning as a therapy is that just as maladaptive behavior patterns are learned, they can be unlearned. Therapy involves conducting a careful analysis of the person's environment to determine which factors need modification. Especially important is changing the consequences of the person's behavior to ensure that healthy, adaptive replacement behaviors are followed by positive reinforcement.

Applied behavior analysis, described in Chapter 5, involves establishing positive reinforcement connections between behaviors and rewards so that individuals engage in appropriate behavior and extinguish inappropriate behavior. Consider a woman with obsessive-compulsive disorder (OCD) who engages in a compulsive ritual such as touching the door frame three times every time she enters a room. If she does not complete her ritual, she is overcome with anxiety that something dreadful will happen. Note that whenever she completes the ritual, nothing dreadful does happen and her anxiety is relieved. Her compulsion is a behavior that is rewarded by the relief of anxiety and the fact that nothing dreadful happens. Such a ritual, then, might be viewed as avoidance learning. An operant conditioning-based therapy might involve stopping the behavior to extinguish this avoidance. Specifically, allowing the woman to experience the lack of catastrophic consequences in the absence of the touching the door frame, as well as training her to relax, might help to eliminate the compulsive rituals. Indeed, behavior therapy has been shown to be effective in treating OCD (Bonchek, 2009; Rosa-Alcazar & others, 2008).

It may strike you as unusual that behavioral approaches do not emphasize gaining insight and self-awareness. However, for the very reason that they do not stress these goals, such treatments may be particularly useful in individuals with limited cognitive abilities, such as people with developmental disabilities. Applied behavior analysis can be used, for instance, with individuals with autism who engage in self-injurious behaviors such as head banging. Such interventions may also be useful with children, who lack the cognitive abilities of adults.

Because it does not rely on the cognitive ability of the client, therapy directed at changing behaviors can be remarkably useful.

Cognitive Therapies

cognitive therapies
Treatments that emphasize that cognitions (thoughts) are the main source of psychological problems and that attempt to change the individual's feelings and behaviors by changing cognitions.

Cognitive therapies emphasize that cognitions, or thoughts, are the main source of psychological problems, and they attempt to change the individual's feelings and behaviors by changing cognitions. *Cognitive restructuring,* a general concept for changing a pattern of thought that is presumed to be causing maladaptive behavior or emotion, is central to cognitive therapies.

Cognitive therapies differ from psychoanalytic therapies by focusing more on overt symptoms than on deep-seated unconscious thoughts, by providing more structure to the individual's thoughts, and by being less concerned about the origin of the problem.

Compared with humanistic therapies, cognitive therapies provide more of a framework and more analysis, and they are based on specific cognitive techniques.

Cognitive therapists guide individuals in identifying their irrational and self-defeating thoughts. Then they get clients to challenge these thoughts and to consider more positive ways of thinking. Cognitive therapies all involve the basic assumption that human beings have control over their feelings and that how individuals feel about something depends on how they think about it. In this section we examine three main types of cognitive therapy: Albert Ellis's rational-emotive behavior therapy, Aaron Beck's cognitive therapy, and cognitive-behavior therapy.

Rational-Emotive Behavior Therapy

Rational-emotive behavior therapy, or **REBT,** was developed by Albert Ellis (1913–2007), who believed that individuals develop a psychological disorder because of their irrational and self-defeating beliefs. Ellis said our emotional reactions to life events are a product of our irrational beliefs and expectations along with the central false belief that we cannot control our feelings (1962, 1996, 2000, 2002, 2005). Ellis was a very confrontational therapist who aggressively attacked these irrational beliefs.

Ellis (2000, 2002) believed that many individuals construct three basic demands for themselves, which he called *musterbating*: (1) I absolutely *must* perform well and win the approval of other people; (2) other people *must* treat me kindly and fairly; and (3) my life conditions *must* not be frustrating but rather should be enjoyable. Once people convert their important desires into demands, they often create dysfunctional, exaggerated beliefs such as "Because I'm not performing well, as I absolutely must, I'm an inadequate person."

The goal of REBT is to get the individual to eliminate self-defeating beliefs by rationally examining them (Sava & others, 2009). A client is shown how to dispute his or her dysfunctional beliefs—especially those "musts"—and how to convert them to realistic and logical thoughts. Homework assignments provide opportunities to engage in the new self-talk and to experience the positive results of not viewing life in such a catastrophic way. For Ellis, a successful outcome meant getting the client to live in reality, where life is sometimes tough and bad things happen.

Beck's Cognitive Therapy

Aaron Beck developed a somewhat different form of cognitive therapy to treat psychological problems, especially depression (1976, 1993). A basic assumption Beck makes is that a psychological problem such as depression results when people think illogically about themselves, their world, and the future (2005, 2006). Beck's approach shares with Ellis's method the idea that therapy's goal should be to help people to recognize and discard self-defeating cognitions.

In the initial phases of Beck's therapy, individuals learn to make connections between their patterns of thinking and their emotional responses. From Beck's perspective, emotions are a product of cognitions. By changing cognitions, people can change how they feel. Unfortunately, thoughts that lead to emotions can happen so rapidly that a person is not even aware of them. Thus, the first goal of therapy is to bring these automatic thoughts into awareness so that they can be changed. The therapist helps clients to identify their own automatic thoughts and to keep records of their thought content and emotional reactions.

With the therapist's assistance, clients learn to recognize logical errors in their thinking and to challenge the accuracy of these automatic thoughts. Logical errors in thinking can lead individuals to the following erroneous beliefs (Carson, Butcher, & Mineka, 1996):

■ Perceiving the world as harmful while ignoring evidence to the contrary—for example, when a young woman still feels worthless after a friend has just told her how much other people genuinely like her.

rational-emotive behavior therapy (REBT)
A therapy based on Ellis's assertion that individuals develop a psychological disorder because of irrational and self-defeating beliefs and whose goal is to get clients to eliminate these beliefs by rationally examining them.

Ellis believed that our thoughts determine all of our emotional responses and that we have the capacity to never be miserable. What do you think?

Aaron Beck's method stresses that the goal of therapy should be to help people to recognize and eliminate illogical and self-defeating thinking.

When was the last time something upset you? What kinds of thoughts did you have about that event or development?

- Overgeneralizing on the basis of limited examples, such as a man's seeing himself as worthless because one individual stopped dating him.
- Magnifying the importance of undesirable events, such as seeing the loss of a dating partner as the end of the world.
- Engaging in absolutist thinking, such as exaggerating the importance of someone's mildly critical comment and perceiving it as proof of total inadequacy.

Figure 13.6 describes some of the most widely used cognitive therapy techniques.

Cognitive Therapy Technique	Description	Example
Challenge idiosyncratic meanings	Explore personal meaning attached to the client's words and ask the client to consider alternatives.	When a client says he will be "devastated" by his spouse leaving, ask just how he would be devastated and ways he could avoid being devastated.
Question the evidence	Systematically examine the evidence for the client's beliefs or assertions.	When a client says she can't live without her spouse, explore how she lived without the spouse before she was married.
Reattribution	Help the client distribute responsibility for events appropriately.	When a client says that his son's failure in school must be his fault, explore other possibilities, such as the quality of the school.
Examine options and alternatives	Help the client generate alternative actions to maladaptive ones.	If a client considers leaving school, explore whether tutoring or going part-time to school are good alternatives.
Decatastrophize	Help the client evaluate whether he is overestimating the nature of a situation.	If a client states that failure in a course means he or she must give up the dream of medical school, question whether this is a necessary conclusion.
Fantasize consequences	Explore fantasies of a feared situation: if unrealistic, the client may recognize this; if realistic, work on effective coping strategies.	Help a client who fantasizes "falling apart" when asking the boss for a raise to role-play the situation and develop effective skills for making the request.
Examine advantages and disadvantages	Examine advantages and disadvantages of an issue, to instill a broader perspective.	If a client says he "was just born depressed and will always be that way," explore the advantages and disadvantages of holding that perspective versus other perspectives.
Turn adversity to advantage	Explore ways that difficult situations can be transformed to opportunities.	If a client has just been laid off, explore whether this is an opportunity for her to return to school.
Guided association	Help the client see connections between different thoughts or ideas.	Draw the connections between a client's anger at his wife for going on a business trip and his fear of being alone.
Scaling	Ask the client to rate her emotions or thoughts on scales to help gain perspective.	If a client says she was overwhelmed by an emotion, ask her to rate it on a scale from 0 (not at all present) to 100 (I fell down in a faint).
Thought stopping	Provide the client with ways of stopping a cascade of negative thoughts.	Teach an anxious client to picture a stop sign or hear a bell when anxious thoughts begin to snowball.
Distraction	Help the client find benign or positive distractions to take attention away from negative thoughts or emotions temporarily.	Have a client count to 200 by 13s when he feels himself becoming anxious.
Labeling of distortions	Provide labels for specific types of distorted thinking to help the client gain more distance and perspective.	Have a client keep a record of the number of times a day she engages in all-or-nothing thinking—seeing things as all bad or all good.

FIGURE 13.6

Cognitive Therapy Techniques Cognitive therapists develop strategies to help change the way people think.

Ellis's and Beck's cognitive therapies share some differences as well as similarities. Ellis's rational-emotive behavior therapy is directive, persuasive, and confrontational; in contrast, Beck's cognitive therapy involves more of an open-ended dialogue between therapist and client. The aim of this dialogue in Beck's approach is to get individuals to reflect on personal issues and discover their own misconceptions. Beck also encourages clients to gather information about themselves and to try out unbiased experiments that reveal the inaccuracies of their beliefs. So whereas Ellis's approach was to bring a sledge hammer down on irrational beliefs, Beck's therapy involves a more subtle process of coaxing a client to recognize that these beliefs promote thoughts that influence feelings. A recent study revealed that Ellis's rational-emotive behavior therapy and Beck's cognitive therapy were more effective in treating depression than drug therapy (Sava & others, 2009).

The Beck Institute maintains a website chronicling the latest developments in cognitive therapy and including a variety of videos of Beck himself. Check out the site at http://www .beckinstituteblog.org/.

cognitive-behavior therapy
A therapy that combines cognitive therapy and behavior therapy with the goal of developing self-efficacy.

Cognitive-Behavior Therapy
Cognitive-behavior therapy is a combination of cognitive therapy, with its emphasis on reducing self-defeating thoughts, and behavior therapy, with its emphasis on changing behavior (Watson & Tharp, 2007). An important aspect of cognitive-behavior therapy is *self-efficacy,* Albert Bandura's concept that one can master a situation and produce positive outcomes (1997, 2001, 2006b, 2007a, 2007b, 2008). Bandura believes that self-efficacy is the key to successful therapy. At each step of the therapy, clients need to bolster their confidence by telling themselves messages such as "I'm going to master my problem," "I can do it," and "I'm improving." As they gain confidence and engage in adaptive behavior, the successes become intrinsically motivating. Before long, individuals persist (with considerable effort) in their attempts to solve personal problems because of the positive outcomes that were set in motion by self-efficacy.

Self-instructional methods are cognitive-behavior techniques aimed at teaching individuals to modify their own behavior (Spiegler & Guevremont, 2010). Using self-instructional techniques, cognitive-behavior therapists prompt clients to change what they say to themselves. The therapist gives the client examples of constructive statements, known as *reinforcing self-statements,* that the client can repeat in order to take positive steps to cope with stress or meet a goal. The therapist also encourages the client to practice the statements through role playing and strengthens his or her newly acquired skills through reinforcement.

Use of Cognitive Therapy to Treat Psychological Disorders
Cognitive therapy has successfully treated some anxiety disorders, mood disorders, schizophrenia, and personality disorders (Parker & Fletcher, 2007; Sava & others, 2009). In many instances, cognitive therapy used together with drug therapy is an effective treatment for psychological disorders (Starcevic, 2006).

Panic disorder is among the anxiety disorders to which cognitive therapy has been applied (Bohni & others, 2009; Smit & others, 2009). The central concept in the cognitive model of panic is that individuals catastrophically misinterpret relatively harmless physical or psychological events. In cognitive therapy, the therapist encourages individuals to test the catastrophic misinterpretations by inducing an actual panic attack. The individuals then can test the notion that they will die or go crazy, which they find out is not the case. Cognitive therapy also shows considerable promise in the treatment of post-traumatic stress disorder, especially when therapists encourage clients to relive traumatic experiences so that they can come to grips with the threatening cognitions precipitated by those experiences (Vickerman & Margolin, 2009). In addition, cognitive therapy has been successful in treating generalized anxiety disorder, certain phobias, and obsessive-compulsive disorder (Jaurrieta & others, 2008).

One of the earliest applications of cognitive therapy was in the treatment of depression. A number of studies have shown that cognitive therapy can be just as successful as, or in some cases superior to, drug therapy in the treatment of depressive disorders

	Cause of Problem	Therapy Emphasis	Nature of Therapy and Techniques
Psychodynamic Therapies	Client's problems are symptoms of deep-seated, unresolved unconscious conflicts.	Discover underlying unconscious conflicts and work with client to develop insight.	Psychoanalysis, including free association, dream analysis, resistance, and transference: therapist interprets heavily, operant conditioning.
Humanistic Therapies	Client is not functioning at an optimal level of development.	Develop awareness of inherent potential for growth.	Person-centered therapy, including unconditional positive regard, genuineness, accurate empathy, and active listening; self-appreciation emphasized.
Behavior Therapies	Client has learned maladaptive behavior patterns.	Learn adaptive behavior patterns through changes in the environment or cognitive processes.	Observation of behavior and its controlling conditions; specific advice given about what should be done; therapies based on classical conditioning, operant conditioning.
Cognitive Therapies	Client has developed inappropriate thoughts.	Change feelings and behaviors by changing cognitions.	Conversation with client designed to get him or her to change irrational and self-deflating beliefs.

FIGURE 13.7

Therapy Comparisons Different therapies address the same problems in very different ways. Many therapists use the tools that seem right for any given client and his or her problems.

(Sado & others, 2009; Sava & others, 2009). Some studies also have demonstrated that individuals treated with cognitive therapy are less likely to relapse into depression than those treated with drug therapy (Jarrett & others, 2001).

Consider that cognitive therapy lacks the side effects of drug therapies.

Practitioners have made considerable strides in recent years in applying cognitive therapy to the treatment of schizophrenia. Although not a substitute for drug therapy in the treatment of this disorder, cognitive therapy has been effective in reducing some schizophrenia symptoms, such as belief in delusions and acting out impulsively (Christopher Frueh & others, 2009). Cognitive therapy also has proved effective in treating personality disorders (McMain & Pos, 2007). The focus is on using cognitive therapy to change individuals' core beliefs and to reduce their automatic negative thoughts.

So far, we have studied the biological therapies and psychotherapies. The four psychotherapies—psychodynamic, humanistic, behavior, and cognitive—are compared in Figure 13.7.

The increasing interest in cognitive and cognitive-behavior therapy and the dramatic advances in neuroscience have stimulated researchers to explore what happens to the brain during therapy. To read about this fascinating research, see the Intersection.

Therapy Integrations

integrative therapy
A combination of techniques from different therapies based on the therapist's judgment of which particular methods will provide the greatest benefit for the client.

As many as 50 percent of therapists identify themselves as not adhering to one particular method. Rather, they refer to themselves as "integrative" or "eclectic." **Integrative therapy** is a combination of techniques from different therapies based on the therapist's judgment of which particular methods will provide the greatest benefit for the client (Prochaska & Norcross, 2010). Integrative therapy is characterized by openness to various ways of applying diverse therapies. For example, a therapist might use a behavioral approach to treat an individual with panic disorder and a cognitive approach to treat a client with major depressive disorder.

Because clients present a wide range of problems, it makes sense for therapists to use the best tools in each case rather than a "one size fits all" program. Sometimes a given psychological disorder is so difficult to treat that it requires the therapist to bring all of his or her tools to bear (de Groot, Verheul, & Trijsburg, 2008; Kozaric-Kovacic, 2008). For example, borderline personality disorder (see Chapter 12) involves emotional instability,

The cognitive approach to therapy assumes that how we think is an important part of how we feel. Its practitioners believe that if we change how we think about things, we can feel better. Thus, a goal for cognitive-behavior therapy is to help us to alter our routine, automatic thinking habits (Jaurrieta & others, 2008).

When we change these thinking patterns, we are also making physical changes in the brain. Remarkably, brain-imaging technology such as fMRI has allowed researchers to examine what actually happens in the brain when, through therapy, we change the way we think (Costafreda & others, 2009). We might be activating brain areas we have not used, and we might be establishing new physical connections.

Clinical Psychology and Neuroscience: Brain Change Through Therapy?

Emotion regulation means bringing our automatic emotional reactions under our cognitive control. Regulating emotion involves using cognitive strategies to change our emotional reactions, either heightening or lessening our feelings. Automatic emotional responses involve activation in the amygdala, while the cognitive control of emotion is associated with activation in the prefrontal cortex (the very front of the brain, just behind the forehead) (Banks & others, 2007; Koenigsberg & others, 2009). One goal of cognitive therapy may be to help Individuals gain control over automatic emotional reactions (in the amygdala) with control processes (in the prefrontal cortex). Research using fMRI has in fact shown that controlling emotions involves activation in the left prefrontal cortex and that activation in this area is associated with changes in the amygdala (Ray & others, 2005).

Research has also revealed that therapeutic interventions "wake up" dormant parts of the brain. Schizophrenia is associated with low levels of activity in the prefrontal cortex, the brain area thought to be associated with high-order functions such as problem solving, judgment, and planning. In one study, a treatment called *cognitive-remediation therapy* (CRT) was administered to a group of individuals who were profoundly disabled by schizophrenia for 10 years or more (Wykes & others, 2002).

CRT is a psychological intervention that involves giving individuals practice in problem solving and information processing. The client completes paper-and-pencil tasks that require skills such as cognitive flexibility, planning, and the use of working memory. Individuals with schizophrenia, who were on medication, and a control group of healthy individuals were scanned while engaging in a problem-solving task before and after those with schizophrenia completed CRT. Before CRT, the individuals with schizophrenia showed lower activation in the prefrontal cortex when solving such problems compared with the healthy individuals. After CRT, prefrontal activation of participants with schizophrenia was no longer different from the healthy participants. This result shows that a psychological intervention that engages particular brain areas can produce changes in the brain, even for patterns that were previously thought to be stable characteristics of a disorder.

The growing literature applying sophisticated scanning techniques to therapeutic interventions sheds light on how researchers can use knowledge about the brain to track psychological processes such as emotion regulation and to pinpoint brain changes associated with improved functioning (Kross & others, 2009; Pine, 2009). Because the brain is a physical organ, we might assume that it is most sensitive to biological interventions. However, research is showing that psychological interventions also can powerfully affect the brain. In a sense, the dramatic findings are revealing how, with the help of therapy, the brain is capable of changing itself.

Like everything else we do or experience, therapy influences (and is influenced by) the brain.

impulsivity, and self-harming behaviors. This disorder responds to a therapy called *dialectical behavior therapy,* or DBT (Dimeff, Koerner, & Linehan, 2007; Harley & others, 2008). Like psychodynamic approaches, DBT assumes that early childhood experiences are important to the development of borderline personality disorder. DBT employs a variety of techniques, including homework assignments, cognitive interventions, intensive individual therapy, and group sessions involving others with the disorder. Group sessions focus on mindfulness training as well as emotional and interpersonal skills training.

Another integrative method is to combine psychotherapy with drug therapy. Combined cognitive therapy and drug therapy has been effective in treating anxiety and depressive

In most states psychologists cannot prescribe drugs.

disorders (Dunner, 2001), eating disorders (Wilson, Grilo, & Vitousek, 2007), and schizophrenia (Rector & Beck, 2001). This integrative therapy might be conducted by a mental health team that includes a psychiatrist and a clinical psychologist.

At their best, integrative therapies are effective, systematic uses of a variety of therapeutic approaches (Prochaska & Norcross, 2010). However, one worry about integrative therapies is that their increased use will result in an unsystematic, haphazard use of therapeutic techniques that some therapists say would be no better than a narrow, dogmatic approach (Lazarus, Beutler, & Norcross, 1992).

Therapy integrations are conceptually compatible with the biopsychosocial model of abnormal behavior described in Chapter 12. That is, many therapists believe that abnormal behavior involves biological, psychological, and social factors. Many single-therapy approaches concentrate on one aspect of the person more than others; for example, drug therapies focus on biological factors, and cognitive therapies probe psychological factors. Therapy integrations take a broader look at individuals' problems, and such breadth is also implied in sociocultural approaches to therapy, our next topic.

self-quiz

1. A behavioral therapy technique that is often used for treating phobic disorder is
   A. aversive conditioning.
   B. self-instruction.
   C. systematic desensitization.
   D. counterconditioning.

2. The psychotherapy approach that focuses on the ways in which early childhood relationships have taught people how to behave in current relationships is
   A. client-centered therapy.
   B. psychodynamic therapy.
   C. cognitive therapy.
   D. rational-emotive behavior therapy.

3. The therapy that has unconditional positive regard at its core is
   A. psychodynamic therapy.
   B. cognitive therapy.
   C. dialectical behavior therapy.
   D. client-centered therapy.

Apply It! 4. Cara has taken a few psychology classes. When she decides to see a therapist for help with her relationship with her mother, she is certain that the therapist will make her lie on a couch and talk about her childhood. When her appointments begin, Cara is surprised that the therapist asks her to just talk about her feelings and offers little feedback. At other times, the therapist talks to Cara about her thoughts and beliefs and gives her homework. On other appointments, the therapist asks Cara about her dreams and childhood. The kind of therapy Cara is getting is
   A. cognitive-behavioral.
   B. humanistic.
   C. psychodynamic.
   D. integrative.

3 Sociocultural Approaches and Issues in Treatment

In the treatment of psychological disorders, biological therapies change the person's body, behavior therapies modify the person's behavior, and cognitive therapies alter the person's thinking. This section focuses on sociocultural approaches to the treatment of psychological disorders. These methods view the individual as part of a system of relationships that are influenced by various social and cultural factors (Nolen-Hoeksema, 2010). We first review common sociocultural approaches and then survey various cultural perspectives on therapy.

Group Therapy

Individuals who share a psychological problem may benefit from observing others cope with a similar problem. In turn, helping others cope can improve individuals' feelings of competence and efficacy. The sociocultural approach known as **group therapy** brings together individuals who share a psychological disorder in sessions that are typically led by a mental health professional.

Advocates of group therapy point out that individual therapy puts the client outside the normal context of the relationships—family, marital, or

What might the popularity of integrative therapy mean for the training of future psychotherapists?

group therapy
A sociocultural approach to the treatment of psychological disorders that brings together individuals who share a particular psychological disorder in sessions that are typically led by a mental health professional.

peer-group relationships, for example—where many psychological problems develop. Yet such relationships may hold the key to successful therapy, these advocates say. By taking the context of important groups into account, group therapy may be more successful than individual therapy.

Group therapy takes many diverse forms, including psychodynamic, humanistic, behavior, and cognitive therapy, plus approaches that do not reflect the major psychotherapeutic perspectives (Hornsey & others, 2009; van Ingen & Novicki, 2009). Six features make group therapy an attractive treatment format (Yalom & Leszcz, 2006):

- *Information:* Individuals receive information about their problems from either the group leader or other group members.

- *Universality:* Many individuals develop the sense that no one else has frightening and unacceptable impulses. In the group, individuals observe that others feel anguish and suffering as well.

- *Altruism:* Group members support one another with advice and sympathy and learn that they have something to offer others.

- *Experiencing a positive family group:* A therapy group often resembles a family (in family therapy, the group is a family), with the leaders representing parents and the other members siblings. In this new family, old wounds may be healed, and new, more positive family ties made.

- *Development of social skills:* Feedback from peers may correct flaws in the individual's interpersonal skills. Self-centered individuals may see that they are self-centered if five other group members inform them about this quality; in one-on-one therapy, the individual might not believe the therapist.

- *Interpersonal learning:* The group can serve as a training ground for practicing new behaviors and relationships. A hostile person may learn that he or she can get along better with others by behaving less aggressively, for example.

A group of people in therapy together is still a group, so processes described in Chapter 11, such as informational and normative social influence, apply.

In family therapy, the assumption is that particular patterns of interaction among the family members cause the observed abnormal symptoms.

Family and Couples Therapy

Relationships with family members and significant others are certainly an important part of human life. Sometimes these vital relationships can benefit from a helpful outsider. **Family therapy** is group therapy among family members. **Couples therapy** is group therapy with married or unmarried couples whose major problem lies within their relationship. These approaches stress that although one person may have psychological symptoms, these symptoms are a function of the family or couple relationships (Gehar, 2010; Hazell, 2009; Keitner, Ryan, & Solomon, 2009).

family therapy
Group therapy with family members.

couples therapy
Group therapy with married or unmarried couples whose major problem lies within their relationship.

Four of the most widely used family therapy techniques are

1. *Validation:* The therapist expresses an understanding and acceptance of each family member's feelings and beliefs and thus validates the person. When the therapist talks with each family member, he or she finds something positive to say.

2. *Reframing:* The therapist helps families reframe problems as family problems, not an individual's problems. A delinquent adolescent boy's problems are reframed in terms of how each family member contributed to the situation. The parents' lack of attention to the boy or marital conflict may be involved, for example.

© David Sipress

3. *Structural change:* The family therapist tries to restructure the coalitions in a family. In a mother–son coalition, the therapist might suggest that the father take a stronger disciplinarian role to relieve the mother of some burden. Restructuring might be as simple as suggesting that the parents explore satisfying ways of being together, such as going out once a week for a quiet dinner.

4. *Detriangulation:* In some families, one member is the scapegoat for two other members who are in conflict but pretend not to be. For example, parents of a girl with anorexia nervosa might insist that their marriage is fine but find themselves in subtle conflict over how to handle the child. The therapist tries to disentangle, or detriangulate, this situation by shifting attention away from the child to the conflict between the parents.

Couples therapy proceeds similarly to family therapy. Conflict in marriages and in relationships between unmarried individuals frequently involves poor communication. In some instances, communication has broken down entirely. The therapist tries to improve the communication between the partners (Kauffman & Silberman, 2009; Ro & Wampler, 2009). In some cases, the therapist will focus on the roles partners play: One may be strong, the other weak; one may be responsible, the other spoiled, for example. Couples therapy addresses diverse problems such as alcohol abuse, jealousy, sexual issues, infidelity, gender roles, two-career families, divorce, remarriage, and the special concerns of stepfamilies (Hernandez, Siegel, & Almeida, 2009).

Self-Help Support Groups

Self-help support groups are voluntary organizations of individuals who get together on a regular basis to discuss topics of common interest. The groups are not conducted by a professional therapist but by a paraprofessional or a member of the common interest group. A *paraprofessional* is an individual who has been taught by a professional to provide some mental health services but who does not have *formal* mental health training. The paraprofessional may have personally had a disorder; for example, a chemical dependency counselor may also be a recovering addict. The group leader and members provide support to help individuals with their problems.

Self-help support groups play a key and valuable role in our nation's mental health. A survey in 2002 revealed that for mental health support alone, nearly 7,500 such groups existed in the United States, with more than 1 million members (Goldstrom & others, 2006).

In addition to reaching so many people in need of help, these groups are important because they use community resources and are relatively inexpensive. They also serve people who are less likely to receive help otherwise, such as less educated adults and individuals with low incomes.

Self-help support groups provide members with a sympathetic audience for social sharing and emotional release. The social support, role modeling, and sharing of concrete strategies for solving problems that unfold in self-help groups add to their effectiveness. A woman who has been raped might not believe a male therapist who tells her that, with time, she will put the pieces of her shattered life back together. The same message from another rape survivor—someone who has had to work through the same feelings of rage, fear, and violation—might be more believable.

Alcoholics Anonymous (AA), founded in 1935 by a reformed alcoholic and a physician, is one of the best-known self-help groups. Mental health professionals often recommend AA for their clients struggling with alcoholism (Kaskutas & others, 2009; Slaymaker & Sheehan, 2008). Some studies show a positive effect for AA but others do not (Kaskutas, 2009). Another self-help organization is Compeer, which matches community volunteers

BLOGGERS ANONYMOUS

www.CartoonStock.com

psychology in our world

Finding Therapy and Support in Cyberspace

Many contemporary therapists communicate with clients through e-mail or text messaging (Berger, Hohl, & Caspar, 2009; Wangberg, Gammon, & Spitznogle, 2007). Another recent development is *e-therapy*, or *cybertherapy*, in which an online source helps people who are seeking therapy for psychological disorders (Marks & Cavanaugh, 2009; Reger & Gahm, 2009). However, e-therapy websites are controversial among mental health professionals (Smith & Reynolds, 2002). For one thing, many of these sites do not include the most basic information about the therapists' qualifications (Recupero & Rainey, 2006). In addition, because cybertherapy occurs at a distance, such sites typically exclude individuals who are having thoughts of suicide. Further, confidentiality, a crucial aspect of the therapeutic relationship, cannot always be guaranteed on a website. On the plus side, though, individuals who might be unwilling or unable to seek out face-to-face therapy may be more disposed to pursue getting help online (Postel, de Jong, & de Haan, 2005; Van Voorhees & others, 2009).

A multitude of online support groups has also emerged (Andersson & others, 2006; Davison, Pennebaker, & Dickerson, 2000). Online support groups have promise, but they can have downsides. In the absence of guidance from a trained professional, members may lack the expertise and knowledge to provide optimal advice. The emergence of pro-anorexia (or "pro-ana") websites, which *promote* anorexia, exemplifies the potentially negative side of the online "support" phenomenon (Bardone-Cone & Cass, 2006; Mulveen & Hepworth, 2006).

Technological advances have influenced therapy in positive ways. However, they also present their own challenges—and even dangers.

in supportive friendship relationships with children and adults receiving mental health treatment (McCorkle & others, 2008). There are myriad other self-help groups, including groups for gays, lesbians, cocaine abusers, dieters, victims of child abuse, and people with various medical conditions (heart disease, cancer, diabetes, and so on).

For individuals who tend to cope by seeking information and affiliation with similar peers, self-help support groups can reduce stress and promote adjustment. However, as with any group therapy, there is a possibility that negative emotions will spread through the group, especially if the members face circumstances that deteriorate over time, as terminal cancer patients do. Group leaders who are sensitive to the spread of negative emotions can minimize such effects.

Problems such as social contagion and groupthink can arise in support groups.

Community Mental Health

The community mental health movement was born in the 1960s, when society recognized that locking away individuals with psychological disorders and disabilities was inhumane and inappropriate. The deplorable conditions inside some psychiatric facilities spurred the movement as well. The central idea behind the community mental health movement was that individuals with disorders ought to remain within society and with their families and should receive treatment in community mental health centers. This movement also reflected economic concerns, as it was thought that institutionalizing people was more expensive than treating them in the community at large. Thus, with the passage of the Community Mental Health Act of 1963, large numbers of individuals with psychological disorders were transferred from mental institutions to community-based facilities, a process called *deinstitutionalization.* Although at least partially motivated by a desire to help individuals with psychological disorders more effectively, deinstitutionalization has been implicated in rising rates of homelessness. The success of community mental health services depends on the resources and commitment of the communities in which they occur.

Community mental health involves training teachers, ministers, family physicians, nurses, and others who directly interact with community members to offer lay counseling and workshops on such topics as coping with stress, reducing drug use, and assertiveness training (Moritsugu, Wong, & Duffy, 2010). Advocates and providers of community mental health believe that the best way to treat a psychological disorder is through prevention (Shinn & Thaden, 2010).

An explicit goal of community mental health is to help people who are disenfranchised from society, such as those living in poverty, to lead happier, more productive lives (Jackson & others, 2009). A key objective in this effort is empowerment—assisting individuals to develop skills for controlling their own lives. All community mental health programs may rely on financial support from local, state, and federal governments.

That means taxes. How much would you be willing to pay in taxes to support community mental health programs?

Cultural Perspectives

The psychotherapies discussed earlier in this chapter—psychodynamic, humanistic, behavior, and cognitive—center on the individual. This focus is generally compatible with the needs of people in Western cultures such as the United States, where the emphasis is on the individual rather than the group (family, community, or ethnic group). However, these psychotherapies may not be as effective with people who live in cultures that place more importance on the group—called *collectivist cultures.* Some psychologists argue that family therapy is likely to be more effective with people in cultures that place a high value on the family, such as Latino and Asian cultures (Guo, 2005).

Ethnicity   Many ethnic minority individuals prefer discussing problems with parents, friends, and relatives rather than mental health professionals (Sue, Sue, & Sue, 2010). Might therapy progress best, then, when the therapist and the client are from the same ethnic background? Researchers have found that when there is an ethnic match between the therapist and the client and when ethnic-specific services are provided, clients are less likely to drop out of therapy early and in many cases have better treatment outcomes (Jackson & Greene, 2000). Ethnic-specific services include culturally appropriate greetings and arrangements (for example, serving tea rather than coffee to Chinese American clients), providing flexible hours for treatment, and employing a bicultural/bilingual staff (Nystul, 1999).

Nonetheless, therapy can be effective when the therapist and client are from different ethnic backgrounds if the therapist has excellent clinical skills and is culturally sensitive (Akhtar, 2006). Culturally skilled psychotherapists have good knowledge of their clients' cultural groups, understand sociopolitical influences on clients, and have competence in working with culturally diverse groups (Austad, 2009).

Would you be comfortable receiving treatment from a therapist who is different from you in terms of ethnic background? Gender? Religion?

Gender   One byproduct of changing gender roles for women and men is reevaluation of the goal of psychotherapy (Gilbert & Kearney, 2006; Nolen-Hoeksema, 2010). Traditionally, the goal has been autonomy or self-determination for the client. However, autonomy and self-determination are often more central characteristics for men than for women, whose lives generally are more characterized by relatedness and connection with others. Thus, some psychologists argue that therapy goals should involve increased attention to relatedness and connection with others, especially for women, or an emphasis on both autonomy/self-determination and relatedness/connection to others (Notman & Nadelson, 2002).

Feminist therapists believe that traditional psychotherapy continues to carry considerable gender bias and has not adequately addressed the specific concerns of women. Thus, several alternative, nontraditional therapies have arisen that aim to help clients break free from traditional gender roles and stereotypes. In terms of improving clients' lives, the goals of feminist therapists are no different from those of other therapists. However, feminist therapists maintain that clients' improvement depends in part on understanding how the nature of women's roles in U.S. society can contribute to the development of a psychological disorder. In other words, feminist therapists believe that women must become alert to the possibility of bias and discrimination in their own lives in order to achieve their mental health goals (Herlihy & McCollum, 2007).

self-quiz

1. A family therapist who attempts to change the alliances among members of a family is using the technique of
   A. reframing.
   B. structural change.
   C. detriangulation.
   D. validation.

2. A paraprofessional is
   A. someone who helps a therapist to conduct therapy.
   B. an unlicensed therapist.
   C. the leader of a therapy group.
   D. someone who has training in helping but lacks formal training as a therapist.

3. Deinstitutionalization is
   A. the release of a convict from the prison system.
   B. the transfer of mental health clients from institutions to community agencies.
   C. the process of having someone admitted to a treatment center against his or her will.
   D. discharging someone with a psychological disorder from treatment.

Apply It! 4. Frank, an Asian American, is struggling with depression. When he tells a friend that he plans to get therapy, Frank mentions that he hopes the therapist is Asian American. His friend responds that Frank is biased and that he should be open to a therapist from any background. Based on research findings, what is Frank's wisest course of action if he genuinely wants his therapy to succeed?
   A. Frank should insist on an Asian American therapist because he can benefit from counseling only if his therapist shares his ethnicity.
   B. Frank is being close-minded and should take whatever therapist he gets.
   C. Frank should be open to a therapist who understands the cultural issues that might affect Frank's life.
   D. Frank should seek out a therapist who does not share his ethnicity because that way he will be forced to think outside the box.

4 The Effectiveness of Psychotherapy

Do individuals who go through therapy get better? Are some approaches more effective than others? How would we know if a therapy worked? During the past several decades, a large volume of research has addressed these questions (Kazdin, 2007).

Research on the Effectiveness of Psychotherapy

A large body of research points to the conclusion that psychotherapy works (Beck, 2005; Butler & others, 2006; Lambert, 2001; Luborsky & others, 2002). Researchers have carried out hundreds of studies examining the effects of psychotherapy. The strategy used to analyze these diverse studies is meta-analysis, in which the researcher statistically combines the results of many different studies (Rosenthal & DiMatteo, 2001). A number of persuasive meta-analyses have concluded that psychotherapy does work, and works well, for many psychological disorders (Lipsey & Wilson, 1993; Wampold, 2001).

Figure 13.8 provides a summary of numerous studies and reviews of research in which clients were randomly assigned to a no-treatment control group, a placebo control group, or a psychotherapy treatment (Lambert, 2001). As can be seen, some individuals who did not get treatment improved. These cases tell us that some psychological symptoms are likely to improve on their own, although it is also possible that these individuals sought help from friends, family, or clergy. Individuals in a placebo control group fared better than untreated individuals, probably because of having contact with a therapist, expectations of being helped, or the reassurance and support that they got during the study. However, by far the best outcomes occurred for individuals who received psychotherapy.

Individuals contemplating seeing a psychotherapist want to know not only *whether* psychotherapy in general is effective but also *which form* is most effective. The situation is similar to that of the Dodo bird in *Alice's Adventures in Wonderland*. Dodo was asked to judge the winner of a race. He decided, "Everybody has won and all must have prizes." Many studies of psychotherapy have supported the *Dodo bird hypothesis*—all "win" and all must have "prizes." That is, although research confirms that therapy works, no one therapy has been shown to be significantly better than the others (Hubble & Miller, 2004; Lambert, 2001; Luborsky & others, 2002; Wampold, 2001). These results suggest that consumers should find out all they can about the available therapies and think about which might best suit their personality and problem.

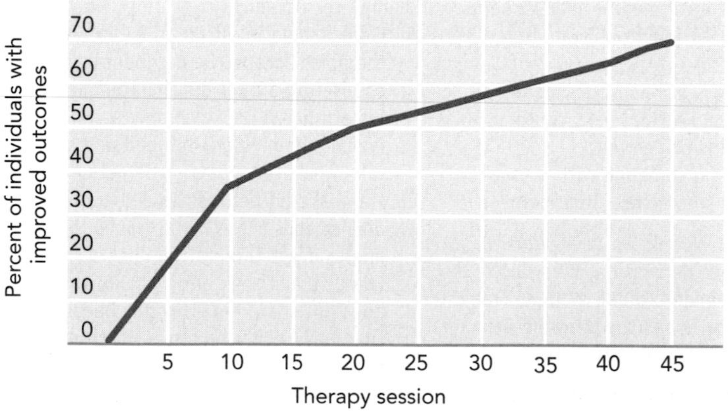

Individuals who see a therapist also want to know how long it will take them to get better. In one study, individuals in therapy showed substantial improvement over the first six months, with diminishing returns after that (Howard & others, 1996). In another study, individuals rated their symptoms, interpersonal relations, and quality of life weekly before each treatment session (Anderson & Lambert, 2001). Figure 13.9 shows that one-third of the individuals had improved outcomes by the 10th

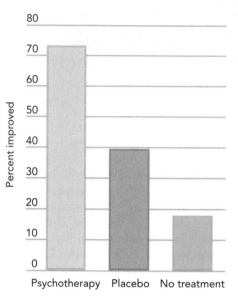

FIGURE 13.8
The Effects of Psychotherapy In a review of studies, more than 70 percent of individuals who saw a therapist improved, whereas less than 40 percent who received a placebo and less than 20 percent who received no treatment improved (Lambert, 2001).

FIGURE 13.9
Number of Therapy Sessions and Improvement In one study, a large number of people undergoing therapy rated their well-being (based on symptoms, interpersonal relations, and quality of life) before each treatment session (Anderson & Lambert, 2001). The percentage of people who showed improved outcomes after each additional session of treatment indicated that about one-third of the individuals recovered by the 10th session, 50 percent by the 20th session, and 70 percent by the 45th session.

session, 50 percent by the 20th session, and 70 percent by the 45th session. In sum, therapy benefits individuals with psychological problems at least through the first six months of treatment and possibly longer.

Health and Wellness Benefits of Psychotherapy

Therapy generally targets the relief of psychological symptoms. A therapy is considered effective if it frees a person from the negative effects of psychological disorders. Does therapy have larger implications related to a person's psychological wellness and even physical health?

For example, receiving a cancer diagnosis is stressful for diagnosed individuals. Might psychotherapeutic help aimed at reducing this stress improve patients' ability to cope with the disease? New research is indicating that therapy has such a positive effect. One recent study revealed that group-based cognitive therapy that focused on sharpening prostate cancer patients' stress management skills was effective in improving their quality of life (Penedo & others, 2006). Another recent study found that individual cognitive-behavior therapy reduced symptom severity in cancer patients undergoing chemotherapy (Sikorskii & others, 2006).

Psychotherapy might also have benefits for physical health. Depression is associated with coronary heart disease, for example (Linke & others, 2009). Psychotherapy that reduces depression is likely, then, to reduce the risk of heart disease (K. W. Davidson & others, 2006). A research review also revealed evidence of positive effects of psychotherapy on health behavior and physical illness, including habits and ailments such as smoking, chronic pain, chronic fatigue syndrome, and asthma (Eells, 2000).

Psychotherapy might even be a way to *prevent* psychological and physical problems. In one study (Smit & others, 2006), individuals waiting to see their primary healthcare provider were assigned to receive either physical health treatment as usual or that same treatment plus brief psychotherapy (a simple version of minimal contact cognitive-behavior therapy). The brief psychotherapy included a self-help manual, instructions in mood management, and six short telephone conversations with a prevention worker. The overall rate of depression was significantly lower in the psychotherapy group, and this difference was cost effective. That is, the use of brief psychotherapy as a part of regular physical checkups was psychologically and economically advantageous.

Finally, although typically targeted at relieving distressing symptoms, might psychotherapy enhance psychological well-being? This question is important because the absence of psychological symptoms (the goal of most psychotherapy) is not the same thing as the presence of psychological wellness. Just as an individual who is without serious physical illness is not necessarily at the height of physical health, a person who is relatively free of psychological symptoms still might not show the qualities we associate with psychological thriving. Studies have found that a lack of psychological wellness may predispose individuals to relapse or make them vulnerable to problems (Ryff & Singer, 1998; Ryff, Singer, & Love, 2004; Thunedborg, Black, & Bech, 1995). Research has revealed that individuals who show not only a decrease in symptoms but also an increase in well-being are less prone to relapse (Fava, 2006; Ruini & Fava, 2004).

Recently, therapists have developed a new type of treatment specifically aimed at enhancing well-being. **Well-being therapy (WBT)** is a short-term, problem-focused, directive therapy that encourages clients to accentuate the

well-being therapy (WBT) A short-term, problem-focused, directive therapy that encourages clients to accentuate the positive.

The question is whether an individual whose symptoms have been treated can go on to enjoy a productive work life, a rewarding relationship with a romantic partner, and close friendships.

positive (Fava, 2006; Ruini & Fava, 2009). The first step in WBT is recognizing the positive in one's life when it happens. The initial WBT homework assignment asks clients to monitor their own happiness levels and to keep track of moments of well-being. Clients are encouraged to note even small pleasures—a beautiful spring day, a relaxing chat with a friend, the great taste of morning coffee. Clients then identify thoughts and feelings that are related to the premature ending of these moments. WBT is about learning to notice and savor positive experiences and coming up with ways to promote and celebrate life's good moments. WBT is effective in enhancing well-being, and it may also allow individuals to enjoy sustained recovery from mental disorders (Fava, Ruini, & Belaise, 2007; Ruini & Fava, 2009; Ruini & others, 2006).

Common Themes in Effective Psychotherapy

In this final section, we look at common threads in successful psychotherapy. Two factors that play a key role in successful therapy are the therapeutic alliance and client factors.

- Participates actively
- Draws on personal strengths, abilities, skills, and motivation
- Develops confidence and trust in therapist
- Becomes more hopeful and less alienated

- Participates actively
- Provides genuine support
- Monitors quality of relationship with client

FIGURE 13.10

Factors in a Successful Therapeutic Alliance This figure emphasizes the qualities and behaviors of the therapist and the client that are necessary to make the therapeutic alliance succeed.

The Therapeutic Alliance   The **therapeutic alliance** is the relationship between the therapist and client. This alliance is an important element of successful psychotherapy (Prochaska & Norcross, 2010; Strupp, 1995). A relationship in which the client has confidence and trust in the therapist is essential to effective psychotherapy (Knapp, 2007; McLeod, 2007).

In one study, the most common ingredient in the success of different psychotherapies was the therapist's supportiveness of the client (Wallerstein, 1989). The client and therapist engage in a healing ritual that requires the active participation of both parties (Figure 13.10). As part of this ritual, the client becomes more hopeful and less alienated. It also is important for the therapist to monitor the quality of the relationship with the client. Clients of therapists who did not assess the quality of the alliance were two times more likely to drop out of therapy (Hubble & Miller, 2004). Among those who completed therapy, clients of therapists who failed to assess their alliance were three to four times more likely to have a negative outcome (Hubble & Miller, 2004).

Client Factors   In all of the meta-analyses of therapeutic outcome studies, one major factor in predicting therapeutic outcome is the client himself or herself. Indeed, the quality of the client's participation is the chief determinant of therapy outcome (McKay, Imel, & Wampold, 2006; Wampold, 2001). Even though the individual may seek therapy from a place of vulnerability, it is that person's strengths, abilities, skills, and motivation that account for therapeutic success (Hubble & Miller, 2004; Wampold & Brown, 2005). In a review of the extensive evidence on therapeutic efficacy, it was noted that "the data make abundantly clear that therapy does not make clients work, but rather clients make therapy work" (Hubble & Miller, 2004, p. 347). Therapy becomes a catalyst for bringing the person's own strengths to the forefront of his or her life.

Life is complicated and filled with potential pitfalls. We all need help at times, and therapy is one way to improve oneself physically and psychologically—to grow and become the best person we can be. Therapy is as complex as any other human relationship and

therapeutic alliance
The relationship between the therapist and client—an important element of successful psychotherapy.

potentially as rewarding, producing positive changes in one person's life through a meaningful association with another person (Joseph & Linley, 2004).

summary

① Biological Therapies

Biological approaches to therapy include drugs, electroconvulsive therapy (ECT), and psychosurgery. Psychotherapeutic drugs that treat psychological disorders fall into three main categories: antianxiety drugs, antidepressant drugs, and antipsychotic drugs.

Benzodiazepines are the most commonly used antianxiety drugs. Antidepressant drugs regulate mood; the three main classes are tricyclics, MAO inhibitors, and SSRI drugs. Lithium is used to treat bipolar disorder. Antipsychotic drugs are administered to treat severe psychological disorders, especially schizophrenia.

Practitioners use electroconvulsive therapy to alleviate severe depression when other interventions have failed. Psychosurgery is an irreversible procedure in which brain tissue is destroyed. Though rarely used anymore, psychosurgery is more precise today than in the days of prefrontal lobotomies.

② Psychotherapy

Psychotherapy is the process that mental health professionals use to help individuals recognize, define, and overcome their disorders and improve their adjustment. In Freudian psychoanalysis, psychological disorders stem from unresolved unconscious conflicts, believed to originate in early family experiences. A therapist's interpretation of free association, dreams, transference, and resistance provides paths for understanding the client's unconscious conflicts. Although psychodynamic therapy has changed, many contemporary psychodynamic therapists still probe the unconscious mind for early family experiences that might provide clues to clients' current problems.

In humanistic therapies, the analyst encourages clients to understand themselves and to grow personally. Client-centered therapy, developed by Rogers, is a type of humanistic therapy that includes active listening, reflective speech, unconditional positive regard, empathy, and genuineness.

Behavior therapies use learning principles to reduce or eliminate maladaptive behavior. They are based on the behavioral and social cognitive theories of personality. Behavior therapies seek to eliminate symptoms or behaviors rather than to help individuals gain insight into their problems.

The two main behavior therapy techniques based on classical conditioning are systematic desensitization and aversive conditioning. In systematic desensitization, anxiety is treated by getting the individual to associate deep relaxation with increasingly intense anxiety-producing situations. In aversive conditioning, repeated pairings of the undesirable behavior with aversive stimuli decrease the behavior's pleasant associations.

In operant conditioning approaches to behavior therapy, an analysis of the person's environment determines which factors need modification. Applied behavior analysis is the application of operant conditioning to change behavior. Its main goal is to replace maladaptive behaviors with adaptive ones.

Cognitive therapies emphasize that the individual's cognitions (thoughts) are the root of abnormal behavior. Cognitive therapies attempt to change the person's feelings and behaviors by changing cognitions. Three main forms of cognitive therapy are Ellis's rational-emotive behavior therapy (REBT), Beck's cognitive therapy, and cognitive-behavior therapy.

Ellis's approach is based on the idea that individuals develop psychological disorders because of their beliefs, especially irrational beliefs. In Beck's cognitive therapy, the therapist assists the client in learning about logical errors in thinking and guides the client in challenging these thinking errors. Cognitive-behavior therapy combines cognitive and behavior therapy techniques and emphasizes self-efficacy and self-instructional methods.

③ Sociocultural Approaches and Issues in Treatment

Group therapies emphasize that relationships can hold the key to successful therapy. Family therapy is group therapy with family members. Four widely used family therapy techniques are validation, reframing, structural change, and detriangulation. Couples therapy is group therapy with married or unmarried couples whose major problem is within their relationship.

Self-help support groups are voluntary organizations of individuals who get together on a regular basis to discuss topics of common interest. They are conducted without a professional therapist.

The community mental health movement was born out of the belief that the mental healthcare system was not adequately reaching people in poverty and deinstitutionalized individuals. Empowerment is a common goal of community mental health.

Psychotherapies' traditional focus on the individual may be successful in individualist cultures, but individual-centered psychotherapies may not work as well in collectivist cultures. Therapy is often more effective when there is an ethnic match between the therapist and the client, although culturally sensitive therapy can be provided by a therapist from a different ethnic background.

The emphasis on autonomy in psychotherapies may produce a problem for many women, who place a strong emphasis on connectedness in relationships. Some feminist-based therapies have emerged.

As many as 50 percent of practicing therapists refer to themselves as "integrative" or "eclectic." Integrative therapy combines techniques from different therapies based on the therapist's judgment of which methods will provide the greatest benefit.

④ The Effectiveness of Psychotherapy

Meta-analysis has found that psychotherapies are successful in treating psychological disorders. Psychotherapy has been shown to help individuals cope with serious physical diseases as well. Psychotherapy can aid individuals by alleviating physical symptoms directly or by reducing psychological problems that are related to physical illness.

Brief psychotherapy may be a cost-effective way to prevent serious disorders before they occur. Psychotherapy can also enhance wellness. Individuals who gain in wellness are less likely to fall prey to recurrent problems.

The therapeutic alliance and specific client factors are important variables influencing therapeutic success. The key to successful therapy may lie in the quality of participation of the client. Although an individual may come into the therapeutic situation in distress, it may be that his or her internal resources and strengths are brought forth by therapy, as a result of which the individual might expect a healthier, more satisfying life.

key terms

biological therapies (biomedical therapies), p. 450
antianxiety drugs, p. 450
antidepressant drugs, p. 451
lithium, p. 451
antipsychotic drugs, p. 452
electroconvulsive therapy (ECT), p. 454

psychosurgery, p. 455
psychotherapy, p. 457
psychodynamic therapies, p. 458
psychoanalysis, p. 458
free association, p. 458
interpretation, p. 459
dream analysis, p. 459
transference, p. 459

resistance, p. 459
humanistic therapies, p. 460
client-centered therapy, p. 460
reflective speech, p. 460
behavior therapies, p. 461
cognitive therapies, p. 462
rational-emotive behavior therapy (REBT), p. 463

cognitive-behavior therapy, p. 465
integrative therapy, p. 466
group therapy, p. 468
family therapy, p. 469
couples therapy, p. 469
well-being therapy (WBT), p. 476
therapeutic alliance, p. 476

self-test

Multiple Choice

1. Prozac is an example of
   A. a benzodiazepine.
   B. a selective serotonin reuptake inhibitor.
   C. a neuroleptic.
   D. a tricyclic.

2. Sharon is seeing a new doctor after various medications have failed to help with her condition. This doctor tells her that many well-designed studies suggest that electroconvulsive therapy is effective in the treatment of
   A. epilepsy.
   B. panic attack disorder.
   C. schizophrenia.
   D. depression.

3. A client who pinches herself each time she has a craving for a cigarette is using the technique of
   A. extinction.
   B. systematic desensitization.

C. aversive conditioning.

D. cognitive restructuring.

4. *Catharsis* is a term used to describe the
   A. client's resistance to the therapist's suggestions.
   B. client's transfer of parental conflicts onto the therapist.
   C. release of emotions a person experiences when reliving an emotionally charged experience.
   D. process of redirecting unacceptable motives into a socially acceptable form.

5. Transference is an advantage in the therapeutic situation because
   A. it provides an opportunity to re-create difficult relationships.
   B. it reduces anxiety.
   C. it increases conflict.
   D. it stimulates resistance.

6. According to Freudian dream interpretation, the obvious content of a person's dream hides the true meaning or content of the dream, called the _____ content.
   A. obtuse
   B. subliminal
   C. latent
   D. manifest

7. Cognitive-behavior therapy attempts to produce change by
   A. bringing the unconscious to consciousness.
   B. helping clients unlearn and then relearn specific behaviors.
   C. helping clients develop self-awareness and self-acceptance.
   D. asking clients to give up irrational beliefs.

8. Therapy is most effective during the first
   A. week.
   B. three months.
   C. six months.
   D. year.

9. Helping a family to understand that the problems in their relationships are not exclusively the fault of an individual family member is an example of
   A. reframing.
   B. structural change.
   C. detriangulation.
   D. validation.

10. Self-help support groups
    A. do not play a significant role in promoting the nation's mental health.
    B. rely on community resources.
    C. are relatively expensive to run.
    D. typically serve people who are also receiving help from other sources.

Apply It!

11. Compare and contrast psychodynamic, humanistic, and cognitive-behavior therapies. For each, give an example of the type of person and problem for which the particular therapy might be best suited.

14 Health Psychology

Do New Year's Resolutions Work?

Worldwide, New Year's Eve is celebrated with rituals to ensure good luck in the coming year. In the United States, some people eat black-eyed peas. In Spain, revelers eat a grape with each stroke of midnight. In Italy, New Year's Eve is a time for "out with old," and folks throw unwanted possessions out the window.

The start of a new year is a time for new beginnings. Every December 31, millions of Americans resolve to change their lives in positive ways. New Year's resolutions date back to ancient Rome. January is named for Janus, the god of beginnings. Janus has two faces: one looking back on the past, and the other looking ahead to the future.

Nearly half of all Americans make New Year's resolutions, the most common being to stop smoking, to lose weight, and to exercise more (ABC/AOL, 2006). Do such health-related resolutions work? In one study (Norcross, Mrykalo, & Blagys, 2002), researchers contacted participants by telephone between December 26 and December 31. Groups of individuals who were pursuing the same goals (mostly losing weight, exercising, and quitting smoking) were identified. About half were planning to make a New Year's resolution and half were not. How did making a New Year's resolution relate to actual success? Six months later, 46 percent of the resolvers had succeeded in maintaining their resolutions. Only 4 percent of those who did not make a resolution achieved such success. Although adopting a healthier lifestyle can be difficult, success is possible if a person is ready to make a commitment. ■

■ **If you made a New Year's resolution this year, how did it turn out—and what might explain the outcome?**

■ **Why do so many of us engage in unhealthy behaviors?**

■ **What role might psychological processes play in physical health and illness?**

In this chapter, we focus on health psychology, the field devoted to promoting healthy practices and understanding the psychological processes that underlie health and illness. We begin by defining the field. Then we examine the various ways that psychologists explain the process of making healthy life changes and the resources on which individuals can draw to achieve positive change. Next we survey what psychologists know about stress and coping, and we consider psychological perspectives on making wise choices in four vital areas: physical activity, diet, the decision to smoke or not to smoke, and sex. We end with a look at psychology's role in shaping a good life.

1 Health Psychology and Behavioral Medicine

health psychology
A subfield of psychology that emphasizes psychology's role in establishing and maintaining health and preventing and treating illness.

Health psychology emphasizes psychology's role in establishing and maintaining health and preventing and treating illness. Health psychology reflects the belief that lifestyle choices, behaviors, and psychological characteristics can play important roles in health (Friedman & Silver, 2007; Taylor, 2007, 2009). A related discipline, **behavioral medicine,** is an interdisciplinary field that focuses on developing and integrating behavioral and biomedical knowledge to promote health and reduce illness. The concerns of health psychology and behavioral medicine overlap: Health psychology primarily focuses on behavioral, social, and cognitive factors (Lawton, Conner, & McEachan, 2009; Norris & others, 2009; Welch & Poulton, 2009), whereas behavioral medicine centers on behavioral, social, and biomedical factors (Mann & others, 2009; Pedersen & others, 2009).

behavioral medicine
An interdisciplinary field that focuses on developing and integrating behavioral and biomedical knowledge to promote health and reduce illness; overlaps with and is sometimes indistinguishable from health psychology.

The Biopsychosocial Model

The interests of health psychologists and behavioral medicine researchers are broad (Baker & others, 2009). The biopsychosocial model we examined in Chapter 12 in the context of psychological disorders applies to health psychology as well, because health psychology integrates biological, psychological, and social factors in health (Mihashi & others, 2009).

For example, stress is a focal point of study across the broad field of psychology. Study of the brain and behavior (Chapter 2 of this book), for instance, acknowledges the impact of stress on the autonomic nervous system. Furthermore, an individual's state of consciousness (Chapter 4), as well as his or her process of thinking about events in particular ways (Chapter 7), can influence the experience of stress. Stressful events also affect our emotions (Chapter 9), which are themselves psychological and physical events. Aspects of our personalities, too, may be associated with stress (Chapter 10) and can influence our health. Finally, social context (Chapter 11) can shape both an individual's experience of stress and his or her ability to cope with it.

The Relationship Between Mind and Body

From the biopsychosocial perspective, the many diverse aspects of each human being are strongly intertwined. Our bodies and minds are deeply connected, a link introduced in Chapter 1. After suffering a heart attack, one health psychologist ruefully noted that none of his colleagues in the field had thought to ask him whether heart disease was part of his family history, ignoring the obvious question that a medical doctor would ask first. Although the mind is responsible for much of what happens in the body, it is not the only factor. Even as we consider the many ways that psychological processes contribute to health and disease, we must understand that sometimes illness happens for other reasons—affecting even those who have led healthy lives.

While it might be fascinating to think about how the mind may influence bodily health, it is also important to appreciate that the body may influence the mind as well. Health psychology and behavioral medicine are concerned not only with how psychological states influence health, but also with how health and illness may influence the person's psychological experience, including cognitive abilities, stress, and coping (Mellon & others, 2009; Sherman & others, 2009). A person who is feeling psychologically rundown may not realize that the level of fatigue is the beginning stage of an illness. In turn, being physically healthy can be a source of psychological wellness.

2 Making Positive Life Changes

health behaviors
Practices that have an impact on physical well-being.

One of health psychology's missions is to help individuals identify and implement ways they can effectively change their behaviors for the better (Norris & others, 2009; Taylor, 2009). **Health behaviors**—practices that have an impact on physical well-being—include adopting a healthy approach to stress, exercising, eating right, brushing one's teeth, performing breast and testicular exams, not smoking, drinking in moderation (or not at all), and practicing safe sex. Before exploring what health psychologists have learned about the best ways to make healthy behavioral changes, we focus on the process of change itself.

Theoretical Models of Change

In many instances, changing behaviors begins by changing attitudes. Psychologists have sought to understand how changing attitudes can lead to behavioral changes.

theory of reasoned action
Theoretical model stating that effective change requires individuals to have specific intentions about their behaviors, as well as positive attitudes about a new behavior, and to perceive that their social group looks positively on the new behavior as well.

A number of theoretical models have addressed the factors that likely play roles in effective health behavior changes. For example, the **theory of reasoned action** suggests that effective change requires individuals to have specific intentions about their behaviors, as well as positive attitudes about a new behavior, and to perceive that their social group looks positively on the new behavior as well (Ajzen & Albarracin, 2007; Ajzen & Fishbein, 1980, 2005). If you smoke and want to quit smoking, you will be more successful if you devise an explicit intention of quitting, feel good about it, and believe that your friends support you. Icek Ajzen (pronounced "I-zen") modified the theory of reasoned action to include the fact that not all of our behaviors are under our control. The

theory of planned behavior Theoretical model that includes the basic ideas of the theory of reasoned action but adds the person's perceptions of control over the outcome.

theory of planned behavior includes the basic ideas of the theory of reasoned action but adds the person's perceptions of control over the outcome (Ajzen, 2002). The theory of reasoned action and its extension, the theory of planned behavior, have accurately predicted whether individuals successfully engage in healthy behaviors (Ajzen & Manstead, 2007), including cancer screening (Ross & others, 2007), HIV prevention (Kalichman, 2007), prevention of smoking and marijuana use in youth (Guo & others, 2007; Lac & others, 2009), and exercise (B. H. Park & others, 2009).

As we will see later, perceiving that one has control can have important implications for a number of life domains.

The Stages of Change Model

stages of change model Theoretical model describing a five-step process by which individuals give up bad habits and adopt healthier lifestyles.

The **stages of change model** describes the process by which individuals give up bad habits and adopt healthier lifestyles. The model breaks down behavioral changes into five steps, recognizing that real change does not occur overnight with one monumental decision, even if that night is New Year's Eve (Prochaska, DiClemente, & Norcross, 1992; Prochaska, Norcross, & DiClemente, 1994) (Figure 14.1). Rather, change occurs in progressive stages, each characterized by particular issues and challenges. Those stages are

- Precontemplation
- Contemplation
- Preparation/Determination
- Action/Willpower
- Maintenance

Have you made a healthy life change recently? As we go over these stages, ask yourself whether they apply to your experience.

Precontemplation The *precontemplation stage* occurs when individuals are not yet genuinely thinking about changing. They may even be unaware that they have a problem behavior. Individuals who drink to excess but are not aware that their drinking

Stage	Description	Example
1 Precontemplation	Individuals are not yet ready to think about changing and may not be aware that they have a problem that needs to be changed.	Overweight individuals are not aware that they have a weight problem.
2 Contemplation	Individuals acknowledge that they have a problem but may not yet be ready to change.	Overweight individuals know they have a weight problem but aren't yet sure they want to commit to losing weight.
3 Preparation/ Determination	Individuals are preparing to take action.	Overweight individuals explore options they can pursue in losing weight.
4 Action/Willpower	Individuals commit to making a behavioral change and enact a plan.	Overweight individuals begin a diet and start an exercise program.
5 Maintenance	Individuals are successful in continuing their behavior change over time.	Overweight individuals are able to stick with their diet and exercise regimens for 6 months.

FIGURE 14.1 Stages of Change Model Applied to Losing Weight The stages of change model has been applied to many different health behaviors, including losing weight.

is affecting their work may be in the precontemplation phase. At this stage, raising one's consciousness about the problem is crucial.

A woman who smokes may find her consciousness raised by the experience of becoming pregnant. A man who is stopped for drunk driving may be forced to take a good look at his drinking. Similarly, overweight individuals may not recognize their problem until they see photos of themselves taken at a family reunion—or until they learn that an order of a McDonald's Big Mac, large fries, and large chocolate shake amounts to over 2,000 calories, the recommended adult caloric intake for an entire day. If you have seen Morgan Spurlock's documentary film *Super Size Me,* you probably have had your consciousness raised about how harmful fast food consumption can be to health. Spurlock ate every meal at McDonald's for a month. By the end of filming he felt ill, had gained weight (he jumped from 185 to 210 pounds), and could not wait for the experience to end.

It is common for individuals in the precontemplation phase to deny that their behavior is a problem and to defend it, claiming that "I don't drink/smoke/eat that much." Overweight individuals may discover that they do eat "that much" when they start keeping track of calories.

Contemplation
In the *contemplation stage,* individuals acknowledge the problem but may not be ready to commit to change. As the name of the stage suggests, at this point individuals are actively thinking about change. They might reevaluate themselves and the place of this behavior in their life. They understandably may have mixed feelings about giving up a bad habit. For example, how will they deal with missing their friends on a smoke break? Or going out drinking? Or packing a healthy lunch instead of heading to the drive-thru? They may weigh the short-term gains of the harmful behavior against the long-term benefits of changing. As we considered in Chapter 5, future rewards can be difficult to pursue when immediate pleasures beckon. Sure, it would be nice to be thinner, but losing weight is going to take time, and that hot fudge sundae is right there, looking very delicious.

Preparation/Determination
In the *preparation/determination stage,* individuals are getting ready to take action. At this point, self-belief and especially beliefs about one's ability to "see it through" are very important. A key consideration is whether individuals truly feel they are ready to change. In the study described in the chapter introduction, readiness to change predicted success at achieving New Year's resolutions (Norcross, Mrykalo, & Blagys, 2002).

During this stage, individuals start thinking concretely about how they might take on their new challenge. For example, they explore options of the best ways to quit smoking or drinking or to start an exercise program. Some smokers might consider trying a nicotine patch or participating in a support group for people wanting to quit. Individuals who are seeking to lose weight might think about joining a gym or setting the alarm clock for a 6:00 A.M. run.

Action/Willpower
At the *action/willpower stage,* individuals commit to making a real behavioral change and enact an effective plan. An important challenge at this stage is to find ways to support the new, healthy behavior pattern. One approach is to find reinforcements or rewards for the new behavior. Individuals who have quit smoking might focus on how much better food tastes after they have given up cigarettes. Successful dieters might treat themselves to a shopping trip to buy new, smaller-size clothes. Acknowledging, enjoying, and celebrating accomplishments can motivate consistent behavior.

Another source of support for new behaviors is the individual's social network (Taylor, 2009). Friends, family, and members of a support group can help through their encouraging words and behaviors. Members of a family might all quit smoking at the same time or join the individual in physical activities or healthier eating.

Finally, individuals may focus on alternative behaviors that replace the unhealthy ones. Instead of bar hopping, they might join a group dedicated to activities

Can you quit smoking if you are spending time with smokers? Can you avoid binge drinking if you regularly go to keg parties?

not associated with drinking alcohol, such as a dance club or community theater group. In other words, effective change also involves avoiding temptations.

Maintenance

In the *maintenance stage,* individuals successfully avoid temptation and consistently pursue healthy behaviors. They may become skilled at anticipating tempting situations and avoid them or actively prepare for them. If smokers seeking to kick the habit know that they always enjoy a cigarette after a big meal out with friends, they might mentally prepare themselves for that temptation before going out. Successful dieters might post a consciousness-raising photograph on the refrigerator.

At some point, individuals in maintenance may find that actively fighting the urge to indulge in unhealthy behaviors is no longer necessary. *Transcendence* means that they are no longer consciously engaged in maintaining their healthy lifestyle; rather, the lifestyle has become a part of who they are. They are now nonsmokers, healthy eaters, or committed runners.

Relapse

relapse
A return to former unhealthy patterns.

One challenge during the maintenance stage is to avoid **relapse,** a return to former unhealthy patterns. Contrary to popular belief, relapse is a common aspect of change; and it can be discouraging. However, the *majority* of people who eventually do change do not succeed on the first try. Rather, they try and fail and try again, cycling through the five stages several times before achieving a stable healthy lifestyle. Consequently, individuals who are experts in changing health behavior consider relapse to be normal (Prochaska & Norcross, 2007; Prochaska, Norcross, & DiClemente, 1994).

If you have ever tried to adopt a healthier lifestyle by dieting, starting an exercise program, or quitting smoking, you might know how bad you feel when you experience relapse. One slip, however, does not mean that you are a failure and will never reach your goal. Rather, when a slipup occurs, you have an opportunity to learn, to think about what led to the relapse, and to devise a strategy for preventing it in the future. Successful dieters, for example, do not let one lapse ruin the week (Phelan & others, 2003).

off the mark.com   by Mark Parisi

Journal Entry for Jan. 1
Sadly, I have already broken one of my New Year's resolutions and fear I may soon break the other...

offthemark.com

© Mark Parisi. Atlantic Feature Syndicate.

Relapse is a normal part of change. What does this principle suggest about recovery from drug addiction?

Evaluation of the Stages of Change Model

The stages of change model has been applied successfully to a broad range of behaviors. These include cigarette smoking (C. L. Kohler & others, 2008; Schumann & others, 2006), exercise (Lippke & Plotnikoff, 2006), safe-sex practices (Arden & Armitage, 2008; Naar-King & others, 2006), substance use and abuse (DiClemente, 2006; Migneault, Adams, & Read, 2005; Walker & others, 2006), and weight loss (MacQueen, Brynes, & Frost, 2002).

Despite its relevance to a variety of behaviors, the stages of change model is controversial (Brug & others, 2004; Joseph, Breslin, & Skinner, 1999). Some critics have questioned whether the stages are mutually exclusive and whether individuals move from one stage to another in the order proposed (Littrell & Girvin, 2002). Critics of the model also point out that it refers more to attitudes that change than to behaviors (West, 2005).

Remember from Chapter 11 that the relationship between attitudes and behavior can be complex.

On the more positive side, recent evidence suggests that the stages of change model does a good job of capturing the ways that individuals make positive life changes (Lippke & others, 2009; Schuz & others, 2009). Experts have argued that the model can be a tool for therapists who are trying to help clients institute healthy behavior patterns. Sometimes, sharing the model with individuals who are trying to change provides them with a useful language for understanding the change process, for reducing uncertainty, and for developing realistic expectations for the difficult journey (Hodgins, 2005; Schuz & others, 2009).

1. The theoretical model that breaks down behavioral change into five distinct steps is the
   A. theory of planned behavior.
   B. theory of reasoned action.
   C. cognitive theory of change.
   D. stages of change model.

2. When someone who is trying to change a behavior returns to unhealthy patterns, we say that he or she is in a state of
   A. denial.
   B. relapse.
   C. plateau.
   D. maintenance.

3. The stages of change model
   A. is not at all controversial.
   B. applies to a wide variety of behaviors.
   C. does not apply to cigarette smoking.
   D. does not apply to safe-sex practices.

Apply It! 4. Malcolm has been trying to quit smoking for the past two years. During his last attempt, he went three full months without smoking but then had a cigarette after a big fight with his girlfriend. He is feeling hopeless about his chances of quitting. What does the stages of change model have to say about Malcolm's situation?
   A. Relapse is a normal part of change. Malcolm might think about why he relapsed and try to move on from there with a new strategy.
   B. Malcolm has blown it and will probably never quit smoking.
   C. Malcolm is stuck in the contemplation phase of change.
   D. Malcolm is unusual in that he had a relapse after three full months. He probably has a particularly strong addiction to cigarettes.

3 Resources for Effective Life Change

Making positive changes to promote health can be very challenging. Fortunately, we all have various psychological, social, and cultural resources at our disposal to help us in the journey to a healthier lifestyle. In this section we consider some of these tools that can help us achieve effective change and, ultimately, a healthier life.

Motivation

Recall from Chapter 9 that motivation refers to the "why" of behavior. Motivational tools for self-change involve changing for the right reasons. Change is most effective when you are doing it for you—because you want to. An analysis of intervention programs aimed at reducing childhood and adolescent obesity found that those who had joined voluntarily were more likely to lose weight than their counterparts who had been required to join (Stice, Shaw, & Marti, 2006).

Self-determination theory (SDT), presented in Chapter 9, distinguishes between intrinsic motivation (doing something because you want to) and extrinsic motivation (doing something for external rewards). Research has shown that creating a context in which people feel more in control, more autonomous, and more competent is associated with enhanced outcomes for a broad array of health behaviors, including controlling diabetes through diet (Julien, Senecal, & Guay, 2009), quitting smoking (Gwaltney & others, 2009), and getting regular physical exercise (Neupert, Lachman, & Whitbourne, 2009). Individuals are more likely to succeed in their New Year's resolutions if they approach them with a sense of both self-efficacy and autonomy (Koestner & others, 2006).

Planning and goal setting are also crucial to making effective change. Researchers have found that individuals who come up with specific strategies, or **implementation intentions,** for dealing with the challenges of making a life change are more successful than others at navigating change (Armitage, 2006; De Vet & others, 2009; Gallo & others, 2009). Setting short-term, achievable goals also allows individuals to experience the emotional payoff of small successes along the way to self-change (Kushner, 2007). The novice exerciser who catches a glimpse of his new biceps in the mirror gets a mood boost. These feelings of satisfaction can help to motivate continued effort toward achieving health goals (Finch & others, 2005).

implementation intentions Specific strategies for dealing with the challenges of making a life change.

M otivation can be a powerful force for positive life change. What about behaviors that are not so positive, such as drinking too much, smoking, and having unsafe sex? Are these behaviors motivated as well? Health psychologists recognize that probing the motives that guide even unhealthy behaviors is important for understanding, changing, and preventing these behaviors.

Health Psychology and Motivation: Why Do We Do the Things We Shouldn't Do?

Some health psychologists have been especially interested in analyzing why individuals consume alcohol. Lynne Cooper and her colleagues have identified three motivations for drinking (Cooper, 1994; Cooper & others, 1992):

- *Social motives* include drinking alcohol because it is what your friends do or because you want to be sociable.
- *Coping motives* center on drinking alcohol to relax, to deal with stress, or to forget your worries.
- *Enhancement motives* include drinking because it is fun, because you like how it feels, or because it is exciting.

Research has shown that young adults most commonly drink for social reasons, with enhancement motives coming in a distant second (Kuntsche & others, 2006). Like enhancement motives, coping motives are not as common in young adults. Although all three motives for drinking are related to higher levels of drinking frequency (with enhancement motives being especially linked to drinking for men—Cooper & others, 1992), the motives that drive drinking can have implications for whether the behavior is harmful or harmless. Drinking to cope with life's negative events is typically associated with negative outcomes such as social and work problems and potential substance abuse.

Research has related drinking motives to difficulties an individual might experience in reducing alcohol consumption. Individuals who drink because of coping or enhancement motives—that is, for internal reasons—are more likely to experience preoccupation with drinking when they try to limit their alcohol consumption (Stewart & Chambers, 2000).

Researchers conclude that motivation is a factor even in behaviors that might seem obviously self-defeating, such as smoking and unsafe sex (Cooper & others, 2006, 2008; Gynther & others, 1999). Viewing maladaptive behavior from a motivational perspective helps us to consider how we might meet our needs for social interaction, coping, and enhancement without alcohol (or cigarettes or unsafe sex). If you recognize that you drink—and occasionally drink too much—because of a desire for positive social interactions, you might think about ways to enjoy your social network without putting your health at risk.

What are some personal behaviors you'd like to change?

What motives do you think drive these behaviors?

Enjoying the payoffs of our efforts to change also means that we must monitor our goal progress. As anyone who has watched *The Biggest Loser* will attest, stepping on a scale can be a scary prospect for someone who is trying to lose weight. However, it is important to get feedback on one's progress in the pursuit of any goal. If an individual finds out that she is falling short, she can try to identify areas that need work. On the other hand, discovering that she is doing well can be a potent motivator for future progress.

Whether the news is good or bad, information is always important for making real progress.

As we have seen, motivation is instrumental to engaging in healthier behaviors. For further insight into its influence on health, see the Intersection.

Social Relationships

Research has shown, again and again, that social ties are an important, if not the most important, variable in predicting health. In a landmark study, social isolation had six times the effect on mortality rates that cigarette smoking had (House, Landis, & Umberson, 1988). In another study involving 1,234 heart attack patients, those living alone were nearly twice as likely to have a second heart attack (Case & others, 1992). Loneliness is linked with impaired physical health (Cacioppo & others, 2002, 2006; Hawkley, Thisted, & Cacioppo, 2009; Munoz-Laboy, Hirsch, & Quispe-Lazaro, 2009), and chronic loneliness can even lead to an early death (Cornwell & Waite, 2009; Cuijpers, 2001). Being connected to others is crucial to survival. One way that social connections make a difference in our lives is through social support.

social support
Information and feedback from others indicating that one is loved and cared for, esteemed and valued, and included in a network of communication and mutual obligation.

Social support is information and feedback from others indicating that one is loved and cared for, esteemed and valued, and included in a network of communication and mutual obligation. Social support has three types of benefits (Taylor, 2009):

- *Tangible assistance*: Family and friends can provide goods and services in stressful circumstances, as when gifts of food are given after the death of a loved one.

- *Information:* Individuals who extend support can also recommend specific strategies to help the person under stress cope. Friends may notice that a co-worker is overloaded with work and suggest ways of better managing time or delegating tasks.

- *Emotional support*: Individuals under stress often suffer emotionally and may develop depression, anxiety, or loss of self-esteem. Friends and family can reassure the stressed person that he or she is valuable and loved. Knowing that others care allows a person to manage stress with greater assurance.

One way that people gain support during difficult times is through *social sharing*—turning to others who act as a sounding board or a willing ear. Individuals who are striving to make healthy life changes might join a group of others who are also struggling with the same issue. Such social sharing can also occur in online support groups.

Sometimes social sharing does not have to be very social to be helpful. James Pennebaker and his colleagues have demonstrated that writing about traumatic life events for 20 minutes a day over two or three days is associated with improved health, fewer illnesses, greater immune system function, and superior reactions to vaccines (Pennebaker, 1997a, 1997b, 2004). Although writing about trauma is usually linked to increased distress in the short term, over the long run it brings physical and psychological health benefits (Frattaroli, 2006; Pennebaker & Chung, 2007; Smyth, 1998). In most of these studies, the participants were college students writing about their most traumatic life events, and the studies' results suggest that anyone can benefit from writing about negative life events. Subsequent studies have found health benefits for writing about life goals and intensely positive life experiences (Burton & King, 2004, 2008; King, 2002). If you would like to give this simple intervention a try, see Figure 14.2.

Getting support from others is important, but *giving* support can also have benefits. A study of 423 older adult couples who were followed for five years revealed how helping others benefits physical health (S. L. Brown & others, 2003). At the beginning of the study, the couples were asked about the extent to which they had given or received emotional or practical help in the past year. Five years later, those who said they had helped others were half as likely to have died.

Find a quiet place to write.

Pick just one topic to explore through writing.

Dedicate yourself to at least 20 minutes of writing about that topic.

While writing, do not be concerned with grammar or spelling; just let yourself go and write about all of the emotions, thoughts, and feelings associated with the experience you are writing about.

If you feel that writing about something negative is not for you, try writing about your most positive life experiences, about the people you care about, or all the things you feel grateful for in life.

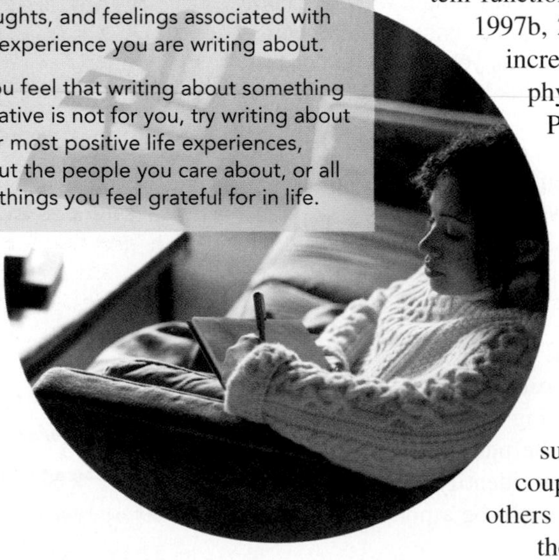

FIGURE 14.2
Harnessing the Healing Power of Writing Try this simple exercise to explore the health benefits of writing.

One possible reason for this finding is that helping others may reduce the output of stress hormones, an effect that improves cardiovascular health and strengthens the immune system (Cacioppo, Berntson, & Aue, 2009; Hawkley & Cacioppo, 2009).

Having many different social ties may be especially important during difficult times (Hawkley & Cacioppo, 2009; Taylor, 2009). People who participate in more diverse social networks—for example, having a close relationship with a partner; interacting with family members, friends, neighbors, and fellow workers; and belonging to social and religious groups—live longer than people with fewer types of social relationships (Vogt & others, 1992). One study investigated the effects of diverse social ties on the susceptibility to getting a common cold (S. Cohen & others, 1998). Individuals reported the extent of their participation in 12 types of social ties. Then they were given nasal drops containing a cold virus and monitored for the appearance of a cold. Individuals with more diverse social ties were less likely to get a cold than their counterparts with less diverse social networks.

For this study to be ethical, participants must have given informed consent, meaning they agreed to have a cold virus injected into their noses.

Religious Faith

As Figure 14.3 shows, religious faith is strongly related to maintaining a healthy lifestyle and to good health (Krause, 2006; C. L. Park, 2007). Many religions frown on excess and promote moderation. Indeed, weekly religious attendance relates to a host of healthy behaviors, including not smoking, taking vitamins, walking regularly, wearing seatbelts, exercising strenuously, sleeping soundly, and drinking moderately or not at all (T. D. Hill & others, 2006). A number of studies have definitively linked religious participation to a longer and healthier life (Campbell, Yoon, & Johnstone, 2009; Hummer & others, 2004; Krause, 2006; McCullough & Willoughby, 2009; McCullough & others, 2000).

Religious participation may also benefit health through its relationship to social support (George, 2009; Taylor, 2009). Belonging to a faith community may give people access to a warm group of others who are available during times of need. This community is there to provide transportation to the doctor, to check in with the individual during hard times, and simply to stand next to the individual during a worship service, as a fellow member of the community. The social connections promoted by religious activity can forestall anxiety and depression and help to prevent isolation and loneliness (Rosmarin, Krumrei, & Andersson, 2009; Ross & others, 2009a).

Religious faith and spirituality more generally may also be important factors in good health because they provide a sense of life meaning and a buffer against the effects of stressful life events (Emmons, 2005; C. Park, 2009). Religious thoughts can play a role in maintaining hope and stimulating motivation for positive life changes. Studies have

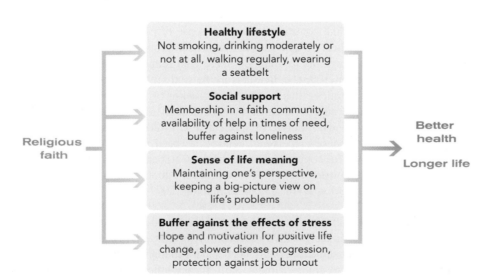

FIGURE 14.3

The Correlation Between Religious Faith and Good Health
Religious faith is closely linked with healthy living and good psychological and physical health.

shown that some individuals with AIDS who lived much longer than expected had used religion as a coping strategy—specific benefits came from participating in religious activities such as praying and attending church services (Ironson & others, 2001)—and that an increase in spirituality after testing positive for HIV is associated with slower disease progression over four years (Ironson, Stuetzle, & Fletcher, 2006). Faith may also help individuals to avoid burnout at work (Murray-Swank & others, 2006) and to negotiate life's difficulties without feeling overwhelmed (Mascaro & Rosen, 2006). Belief in the enduring meaningfulness of one's life can help one keep perspective and see life's hassles in the context of the big picture (C. Park, 2009).

How might these results apply to a person who is not religious at all?

Personality Characteristics

Personality traits are powerful instruments in the self-change toolbox. Here we survey some of the personality characteristics related to health.

Conscientiousness   Recall from Chapter 10 that conscientious individuals are responsible and reliable; they like structure and seeing a task to its completion. Conscientiousness is not the sexiest trait, but it might well be the most important of the big five traits when it comes to health, healthy living, and longevity (Roberts & Mroczek, 2008; Roberts & others, 2009). A variety of studies show that conscientious people tend to do all the things that they are told are good for their health, such as getting regular exercise, avoiding drinking and smoking, wearing seatbelts, and checking smoke detectors (D. B. O'Connor & others, 2009; Rush, Becker, & Curry, 2009). Research has also shown that conscientious individuals are less likely to die than their counterparts who are less conscientious (Fry & Debats, 2009; Iwassa & others, 2008, 2009; Kern & Friedman, 2008; R. S. Wilson & others, 2004).

Personal Control   Another personality characteristic associated with taking the right steps toward a long, healthy life is a sense of personal control, what we referred to in Chapter 10 as an internal locus of control (Baumeister & Alquist, 2009; Forgas, Baumeister & Tice, 2009). Feeling in control can reduce stress during difficult times (Taylor, 2006; S. C. Thompson, 2001) and can lead to the development of problem-solving strategies to deal with life difficulties. An individual with a good sense of personal control might reason, "If I stop smoking now, I will not develop lung cancer."

A person with a low level of personal control may feel that whatever happens happens—it was meant to be or just a matter of (good or bad) luck.

A sense of personal control has been linked to a lower risk for common chronic diseases such as cancer and cardiovascular disease (Sturmer, Hasselbach, & Amelang, 2006). Further, like conscientiousness, a sense of personal control might also help people avoid a risky lifestyle that involves health-compromising behaviors. Consider a study of East German migrants to West Germany who found themselves unemployed (Mittag & Schwarzer, 1993). Individuals in the study often turned to heavy drinking for solace—unless, that is, they had a sense of personal control (as measured by such survey items as "When I'm in trouble, I can rely on my ability to deal with the problem effectively"). Overall, across a wide range of studies, a sense of personal control has been related to emotional well-being, successful coping with a stressful event, healthy behavior change, and good health (Little, Snyder, & Wehmeyer, 2006; Stanton, Revenson, & Tennen, 2007; Taylor, 2006; Taylor & Stanton, 2007).

In Chapter 12 we examined the role of learned helplessness in depression. Learned helplessness means believing that one has no control over outcomes in one's life.

Self-Efficacy   Recall that *self-efficacy* is the individual's belief that he or she can master a situation and produce positive outcomes. Albert Bandura (1997, 2001, 2009) and others have shown that self-efficacy affects behavior in many situations, ranging from solving personal problems to going on diets. Self-efficacy influences whether individuals try to develop healthy habits, how much effort they expend in coping with stress, how long they persist in the face of obstacles, and how much stress they experience.

Research has shown that self-efficacy is related to success in a wide variety of positive life changes, including sticking to a New Year's resolution (Norcross, Mrykalo, & Blagys, 2002), achieving weight loss (Annesi, 2007; Finche & others, 2005; Linde & others, 2006), exercising regularly (Lippke & Plotnikoff, 2006), quitting smoking (Gwaltney & others, 2009), ending substance abuse (McPherson & others, 2006; Warren, Stein, & Grella, 2007), and practicing safe sex (Abbey & others, 2007). Recent evidence suggests that self-efficacy is strongly linked to cardiovascular functioning following heart failure and that individuals high in self-efficacy not only are less likely to suffer a second hospitalization due to heart failure but also are likely to live longer (Sarkar, Ali, & Whooley, 2009). If there is a problem to be fixed, self-efficacy—having a can-do attitude—is related to finding a solution.

BILL PROUD

"No, honestly, it's just diet and exercise."

www.CartoonStock.com

Throughout this book, we have examined the placebo effect as a positive response to a treatment that has no medicinal power. The placebo effect results from the individual's belief in the effectiveness of the treatment. Can you really lose those 10 pounds? Maybe or maybe not, but believing that you can allows you to harness the placebo effect. Self-efficacy is the power of belief in yourself.

Personal control and self-efficacy are related but different concepts. Personal control refers to whether the individual feels in charge of outcomes in his or her life, while self-efficacy refers to a can-do attitude about achieving those outcomes.

Optimism   One factor that is often linked to positive functioning and adjustment is optimism (C. Peterson, 2006; Peterson & Seligman, 2003; Seligman & Pawelski, 2003; Smith & MacKenzie, 2006). Martin Seligman (1990) views optimism as a matter of how a person explains the causes of bad events. Optimists identify the causes of bad events as external, unstable, and specific, whereas pessimists identify them as internal, stable, and global. Studies have associated explaining life events optimistically with a variety of positive outcomes (Reivich & Gillham, 2002).

Other researchers define optimism as the expectancy that good things are more likely and that bad things are less likely to occur in the future (Carver & Scheier, 2009; Solberg Nes, Evans, & Segerstrom, 2009; Solberg Nes & Segerstrom, 2006). This view focuses on how people pursue their goals and values. Even when faced with misfortune, optimists keep working to reach their goals, whereas pessimists give up.

Numerous studies reveal that optimists generally function more effectively and are physically and mentally healthier than pessimists (Segerstrom, 2006). Optimism has been linked to more effective immune system functioning and better health (Solberg Nes & Segerstrom, 2006; Segerstrom, 2003, 2005). Optimism can also be a powerful tool against hopelessness. One study found a connection between optimism and decreased thoughts of suicide in college students (Hirsch, Conner, & Duberstein, 2007).

Additional Perspectives on Personality, Health, and Illness

Reading about conscientiousness, personal control, self-efficacy, and optimism as they relate to health and healthy change can be unsettling if you recognize yourself as not particularly conscientious, low on personal control, not very efficacious, and pessimistic. It is vital to keep in mind that you can cultivate these qualities. After all, the title of Seligman's best-selling book was *Learned Optimism*. Studies have shown that even conscientiousness, the most stable of the characteristics we examined above, can increase, especially in young adulthood.

It is also important to confront another issue related to personality and health: victim blaming. If someone you love has a heart attack or gets a diagnosis of cancer, is it because the person was not optimistic enough or lacked sufficient personal control?

In thinking about that question, consider that the statistics underpinning the research findings are *group* statistics that do not apply to individual cases. Also note that even people who lead extraordinarily healthy lives may develop serious illness due to factors such as genetics and environmental exposure. Thus, instead of getting hung up on the possibility that the individual's personality characteristics led to the disease, it is more productive to focus, as optimists do, on the problem at hand and to rally your efforts around helping the ill individual confront the challenges ahead.

1. All of the following are powerful tools for self-change *except*
   A. ethnic heritage.
   B. religious faith.
   C. personality traits.
   D. motivation.

2. The benefits of social support include all of the following *except*
   A. information.
   B. tangible assistance.
   C. emotional support.
   D. victim blaming.

3. According to Seligman, optimists explain the causes of bad events as
   A. external.
   B. internal.
   C. global.
   D. stable.

Apply It! 4. Derek was recently diagnosed with diabetes. His doctor gave him a new diet to control his condition. Which of the following situations offers the *best* chances that Derek will stick with the diet?
   A. Derek loves junk food and does not want to follow the diet, but his mother and aunt, both diabetics, are pressuring him to follow the doctor's recommendations.
   B. Derek has always had trouble following through on doing what's good for him, though he says he wants more structure in his life.
   C. Clark, Derek's roommate, has a diabetic brother, and Clark tells Derek about how his brother has coped and what diet he follows; Clark offers to introduce them.
   D. Derek has a pessimistic personality and expects things to work out badly.

4 Toward a Healthier Mind (and Body): Controlling Stress

If you could change one thing about your behavior, what would you choose? Would the change perhaps have to do with feeling stressed out much of the time? Maybe you wish you could stop facing every daily challenge with tension. Let's look at the problems that can arise when you feel chronically stressed and the ways you can better manage your stress.

Stress and Its Stages

Getting married, having a baby, graduating from college—though they are positive life events, these achievements can be stressful because they are also major life changes.

As described in Chapter 2, *stress* is the response to environmental stressors, the circumstances and events that threaten individuals and tax their coping abilities. Hans Selye (1974, 1983), the founder of stress research, focused on the body's response to stressors, especially the wear and tear due to the demands placed on the body. After observing patients with different problems—the death of someone close, loss of income, arrest for embezzlement—Selye concluded that any number of environmental events or stimuli would produce the same stress symptoms: loss of appetite, muscular weakness, and decreased interest in the world.

General adaptation syndrome (GAS) is Selye's term for the common effects on the body when demands are placed on it (Figure 14.4). The GAS consists of three stages: alarm, resistance, and exhaustion. Selye's model is especially useful in helping us understand the link between stress and health.

The body's first reaction to a stressor, in the *alarm stage,* is a temporary state of shock during which resistance to illness and stress falls below normal limits. In trying to cope with the initial effects of stress, the body releases hormones that, in a short time, adversely affect the functioning of the immune system, the body's network of natural defenses. During this time the individual is prone to infections from illness and injury.

In the *resistance stage* of Selye's general adaptation syndrome, glands throughout the body manufacture different hormones that protect the individual. Endocrine and sympathetic

general adaptation syndrome (GAS) Selye's term for the common effects of demands on the body, consisting of three stages: alarm, resistance, and exhaustion.

nervous system activity are not as high as in the alarm stage, although they still are elevated. During the resistance stage, the body's immune system can fight off infection with remarkable efficiency. Similarly, hormones that reduce the inflammation normally associated with injury circulate at high levels.

If the body's all-out effort to combat stress fails and the stress persists, the individual moves into the *exhaustion stage*. At this point, wear and tear takes its toll—the person might collapse in exhaustion, and vulnerability to disease increases. Serious, possibly irreversible damage to the body, such as a heart attack, or even death may occur.

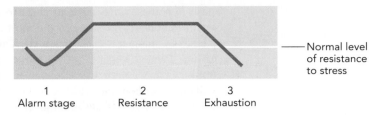

FIGURE 14.4

Selye's General Adaptation Syndrome The general adaptation syndrome (GAS) describes an individual's response to stress in terms of three stages: (1) alarm, in which the body mobilizes its resources; (2) resistance, in which the body strives mightily to endure the stressor; and (3) exhaustion, in which resistance becomes depleted.

Stress and the Immune System

In Chapter 2 we distinguished between acute stress and chronic stress. Chronic stress can have serious implications for the body, in particular for the immune system. Interest in links between the immune system and stress spawned a new field of scientific inquiry, **psychoneuroimmunology,** which explores connections among psychological factors (such as attitudes and emotions), the nervous system, and the immune system (Havelka, Lucanin, & Lucanin, 2009; Leonard & Myint, 2009).

The immune system and the central nervous system are similar in their modes of receiving, recognizing, and integrating signals from the external environment (Sternberg & Gold, 1996). The central nervous system and the immune system both possess "sensory" elements, which receive information from the environment and other parts of the body, and "motor" elements, which carry out an appropriate response. Both systems also rely on chemical mediators for communication. A key hormone shared by the central nervous system and the immune system is corticotropin-releasing hormone (CRH), which is produced in the hypothalamus and unites the stress and immune responses.

Stress can profoundly influence the immune system (Bellinger, Lubahn, & Lorton, 2008; Bob & others, 2009; Grippo & Johnson, 2009). Acute stressors (sudden, stressful, one-time life events) can produce immunological changes. For example, in relatively healthy HIV-infected individuals, as well as in individuals with cancer, acute stressors are associated with poorer immune system functioning (Pant & Ramaswamy, 2009). In addition to acute stressors, chronic stressors (long-lasting agents of stress) are associated with an increasing downturn in immune system responsiveness. This effect has been documented in a number of circumstances that include worries about living next to a damaged nuclear reactor, failures in close relationships (divorce, separation, and marital distress), and burdensome care giving for a family member with a progressive illness (Glaser & Kiecolt-Glaser, 2005; Gouin, Hantsoo, & Kiecolt-Glaser, 2009; Graham, Christian, & Kiecolt-Glaser, 2006).

Researchers hope to determine the precise links among psychological factors, the brain, and the immune system (Bauer, Jeckel, & Luz, 2009; Campbell & Edwards, 2009). Preliminary hypotheses about the interaction that causes vulnerability to disease include:

- Stressful experiences lower the efficiency of immune systems, making individuals more susceptible to disease.

- Stress directly promotes disease producing processes.

- Stressful experiences may cause the activation of dormant viruses that diminish the individual's ability to cope with disease.

psychoneuroimmunology
A new field of scientific inquiry that explores connections among psychological factors (such as attitudes and emotions), the nervous system, and the immune system.

Recall from Chapter 5 that the immune system can also learn through classical conditioning.

These hypotheses may lead to clues for more successful treatments for some of the most challenging diseases to conquer—cancer and AIDS among them (Armaiz-Pena & others, 2009; Bormann & others, 2008).

Sheldon Cohen and his colleagues have carried out a number of studies on the effects of stress, emotion, and social support on immunity and susceptibility to infectious disease (Cohen, Doyle, & Skoner, 1999; Cohen & Janicki-Deverts, 2009; Cohen & Lemay, 2007; Cohen & others, 2009; Horenstein & Cohen, 2009). In one such study, Cohen and his colleagues (1998) focused on 276 adults who were exposed to viruses and then quarantined for five days. Figure 14.5 shows the dramatic results. The longer the participants had experienced major stress in their lives before the study, the more likely they were to catch a cold. Cohen concluded that stress-triggered changes in the immune system and hormones might create greater vulnerability to infection. These findings suggest that when we are under stress, we need to take better care of ourselves than usual (Cohen & Janicki-Deverts, 2009; Cohen & others, 2009).

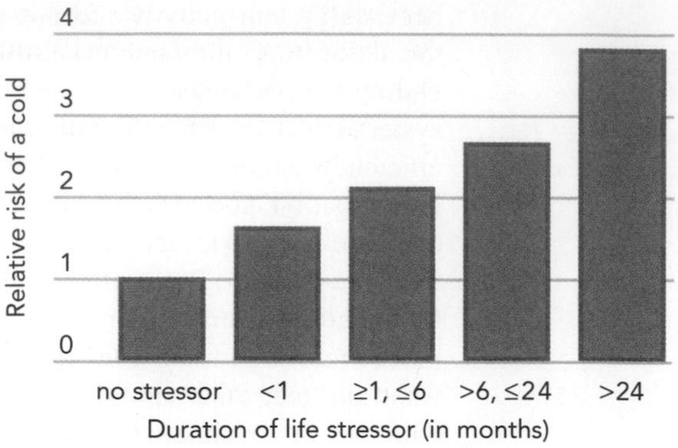

Meditation, described in Chapter 4, is a great way to cope with stress and has positive benefits for the immune system.

FIGURE 14.5
Stress and the Risk of Developing a Cold In a study by Cohen and others (1998), the longer individuals had a life stressor, the more likely they were to develop a cold. The four-point scale is based on the odds (0 = lower; 4 = higher) of getting a cold.

Stress and Cardiovascular Disease

There is also reason to believe that stress increases an individual's risk for cardiovascular disease (Kibler, 2009; Williams & Davidson, 2009). Chronic emotional stress is associated with high blood pressure, heart disease, and early death (Schulz, 2007). Apparently, the adrenaline surge caused by severe emotional stress causes the blood to clot more rapidly—and blood clotting is a major factor in heart attacks (Strike & others, 2006). Emotional stress can contribute to cardiovascular disease in other ways. Individuals who have had major life changes (such as the death of a spouse and the loss of a job) have a higher incidence of cardiovascular disease and early death (Taylor, 2009).

People in a chronically stressed condition are also more likely to take up smoking, start overeating, and avoid exercising. These stress-related behaviors are linked with cardiovascular disease (Kodama & others, 2009; Patel & others, 2009).

Just as personality characteristics such as a sense of control or self-efficacy can help buffer an individual against stress, other personality characteristics have been shown to worsen stress, with special significance for cardiovascular illness. In particular, people who are impatient or quick to anger or who display frequent hostility have an increased risk for cardiovascular disease (Chida & Steptoe, 2009).

In the late 1950s, a secretary for two California cardiologists, Meyer Friedman and Ray Rosenman, observed that the chairs in their waiting rooms were tattered and worn, but only on the front edges. The cardiologists had also noticed the impatience of their cardiac patients, who often arrived exactly on time and were in a great hurry to leave. Intrigued by this consistency, they conducted a study of 3,000 healthy men between the ages of 35 and 59 over eight years to find out whether people with certain behavioral characteristics might be prone to heart problems (Friedman & Rosenman, 1974). During the eight years, one group of men had twice as many heart attacks or other forms of heart disease as the other men. Further, autopsies of the men who died revealed that this same group had coronary arteries that were more obstructed than those of the other men.

Friedman and Rosenman described the common personality characteristics of the men who developed coronary disease as the **Type A behavior pattern.** They theorized that a cluster of characteristics—being excessively competitive, hard-driven, impatient,

Type A behavior pattern
A cluster of characteristics—including being excessively competitive, hard-driven, impatient, and hostile—that are related to a higher incidence of heart disease.

and hostile—is related to the incidence of heart disease. Rosenman and Friedman labeled the behavior of the healthier group, who were typically relaxed and easygoing, the **Type B behavior pattern.**

Further research on the link between Type A behavior and coronary disease indicates that the association is not as strong as Friedman and Rosenman believed (Suls & Swain, 1998; R. B. Williams, 2001, 2002). However, researchers have found that certain components of Type A behavior are more precisely linked with coronary risk (Spielberger, 2004). The Type A behavior component most consistently associated with coronary problems is hostility (Chida & Steptoe, 2009). People who are hostile outwardly or who turn anger inward are more likely to develop heart disease than their less angry counterparts (Eng & others, 2003; K. A. Matthews & others, 2004). Such people have been called "hot reactors" because of their intense physiological reactions to stress: Their hearts race, their breathing quickens, and their muscles tense up. One study found that hostility was a better predictor of coronary heart disease in older men than smoking, drinking, high caloric intake, or high levels of LDL cholesterol (Niaura & others, 2002).

Type B behavior pattern
A cluster of characteristics—including being relaxed and easygoing—that are related to a lower incidence of heart disease.

Stress and Cancer

Given the association of stress with poor health behaviors such as smoking, it is not surprising that stress has also been related to cancer risk (Hamer, Chida, & Molloy, 2009). Stress sets in motion biological changes involving the autonomic, endocrine, and immune systems. If the immune system is not compromised, it appears to help provide resistance to cancer and slow its progression. Researchers have found, however, that the physiological effects of stress inhibit a number of cellular immune responses (Anderson, Golden-Kreutz, & DiLillo, 2001). Cancer patients show diminished natural killer (NK)-cell activity in the blood (Bagnara & others, 2009) (Figure 14.6). Low NK-cell activity is linked with the development of further malignancies, and the length of survival for the cancer patient is related to NK-cell activity (Cho & Campana, 2009).

Thus, stress is clearly a factor not only in immune system functioning and cardiovascular health but also in the risk for cancer. In light of these links, understanding the

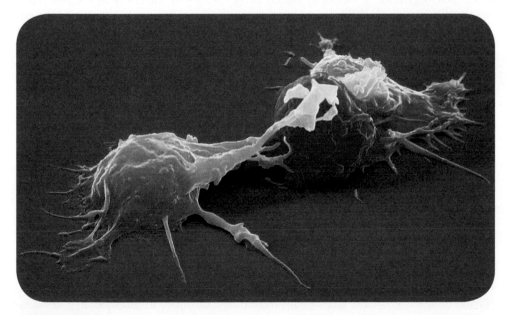

FIGURE 14.6
NK Cells and Cancer Two natural killer (NK) cells (*yellow*) are shown attacking a leukemia cell (*red*). Notice the blisters that the leukemia cell has developed to defend itself. Nonetheless, the NK cells are surrounding the leukemia cell and are about to destroy it.

psychological processes by which individuals can effectively handle stressful circumstances is a crucial topic in health psychology (Faul & others, 2009).

Cognitive Appraisal and Coping with Stress

What stresses you out? Stressors can be anything from losing irreplaceable notes from a class, to being yelled at by a friend, to failing a test, to being in a car wreck.

Although everyone's body may respond similarly to stressors, not everyone perceives the same events as stressful. Indeed, whether an experience "stresses us out" depends on how we think about that experience. For example, you may perceive an upcoming job interview as a threatening obligation, whereas your roommate may perceive it as a challenging opportunity—a chance to shine. You might view a *D* on a paper as a crushing blow; your roommate may view the same grade as an incentive to work harder. To some degree, then, what is stressful depends on how we think about events (Gidron & Nyklicek, 2009; Meade & others, 2009).

Let's face it. Just reading about the negative effects of stress can be stressful.

cognitive appraisal
An individual's interpretation of an event as either harmful, threatening, or challenging, and the person's determination of whether he or she has the resources to cope effectively with the event.

Steps in Cognitive Appraisal
Cognitive appraisal refers to an individual's interpretation of an event as either harmful, threatening, or challenging, and the person's determination of whether he or she has the resources to cope effectively with the event. **Coping** is essentially a kind of problem solving. It involves managing taxing circumstances, expending effort to solve life's problems, and seeking to master or reduce stress.

Richard Lazarus articulated the importance of cognitive appraisal to stress and coping (1993, 2000). In Lazarus's view, people appraise events in two steps: primary appraisal and secondary appraisal. In *primary appraisal,* individuals interpret whether an event involves *harm* or loss that has already occurred, a *threat* of some future danger, or a *challenge* to be overcome. Lazarus believed that perceiving a stressor as a challenge to be overcome rather than as a threat is a good strategy for reducing stress. To understand Lazarus's concept of primary appraisal, consider two students, each with a failing grade in a psychology class at midterm. Sam is almost frozen by the stress of the low grade and looks at the rest of the term as a threatening prospect. In contrast, Pam does not become overwhelmed by the harm already done and the threat of future failures. She sees the low grade as a challenge that she can address and overcome.

In *secondary appraisal,* individuals evaluate their resources and determine how effectively they can be marshaled to cope with the event. This appraisal is secondary because it both comes after primary appraisal and depends on the degree to which the event is appraised as harmful, threatening, or challenging. Sam might have some helpful resources for coping with his low midterm grade, but he views the stressful circumstance as so harmful and threatening that he does not take stock of and use his resources. Pam, in contrast, evaluates the resources she can call on to improve her grade. These include asking the instructor for suggestions about how to study better for the tests, managing time to include more study hours, and consulting with high-achieving classmates.

coping
A kind of problem solving that involves managing taxing circumstances, expending effort to solve life's problems, and seeking to master or reduce stress.

Types of Coping
Research has identified two types of coping. **Problem-focused coping** is the cognitive strategy of squarely facing one's troubles and trying to solve them. For example, if you are having trouble with a class, you might go to the campus study skills center and sign up for a program to learn how to study more effectively. Having done so, you have faced your problem and attempted to do something about it. Problem-focused coping might involve coming up with goals and implementation intentions, the problem-solving steps we examined earlier in this chapter.

Emotion-focused coping involves responding to the stress that you are feeling—trying to manage your emotional reaction—rather than confronting the root problem. If

emotion-focused coping
A coping strategy that involves responding to the stress that one is feeling—trying to manage one's emotional reaction—rather than focusing on the root problem.

problem-focused coping
The cognitive strategy of squarely facing one's troubles and trying to solve them.

you use emotion-focused coping, you might avoid going to a class that is a problem for you. Instead, you might say the class does not matter, deny that you are having difficulty with it, joke about it with your friends, or pray that you will do better.

In some circumstances, emotion-focused coping can be beneficial in dealing with life's problems. Denial is one of the main protective psychological mechanisms for navigating the flood of feelings that occurs when the reality of death or dying becomes too great. For example, one study found that following the death of a loved one, bereaved individuals who directed their attention away from their negative feelings had fewer health problems and were rated as better adjusted by their friends, compared to bereaved individuals who did not use this coping strategy (Coifman & others, 2007). Denial can be used to avoid the destructive impact of shock by postponing the time when we have to deal with stress. In other circumstances, however, emotion-focused coping can be a problem. Denying that the person we dated does not love us anymore when he or she has become engaged to someone else keeps us from getting on with our life.

Emotion-focused coping can be adaptive in situations in which there is no solution to a problem, such as grieving over a loved one's death, when in fact it makes sense to focus on feeling better and accepting the present circumstances.

Many individuals successfully use both problem-focused and emotion-focused coping when adjusting to a stressful circumstance. For example, in one study, individuals said they used both problem-focused and emotion-focused coping strategies in 98 percent of the stressful situations they encounter (Folkman & Lazarus, 1980). Over the long term, though, problem-focused coping rather than emotion-focused coping usually works best (Nagase & others, 2009).

Strategies for Successful Coping

A stressful circumstance becomes considerably less stressful when a person successfully copes with it. Successful coping is associated with a sense of personal control, a healthy immune system, personal resources, and positive emotions.

When one is experiencing stressful life events, multiple coping strategies often work better than a single strategy, as is true with any problem-solving challenge (Folkman & Moskowitz, 2004). People who have experienced a stressful life event or a cluster of difficulties might actively embrace problem solving and consistently take advantage of opportunities for positive experiences, even in the context of the bad times they are going through. Positive emotion can give them a sense of the big picture, help them devise a variety of possible solutions, and allow them to make creative connections.

Optimism can play a strong role in effective coping. Lisa Aspinwall has found, for example, that optimistic people are more likely to attend to and remember potentially threatening health-related information than are pessimists (Aspinwall, 1998; Aspinwall & Brunhart, 1996; Aspinwall, Leaf, & Leachman, 2009). Aspinwall views optimism as a resource that allows individuals to engage constructively with potentially frightening information. Optimists are more likely than others to seek out genetic testing in order to learn about their risk for disease (Aspinwall, Leaf, & Leachman, 2009). Optimists engage with life from a place of strength, so when an optimist finds out, for instance, that a favorite pastime, tanning, is related to an elevated risk of skin cancer, the information is important but not overwhelming. In contrast, pessimists are already living in a bleak world and prefer not to hear more bad news.

Optimists are not just denying that anything bad can happen. They are actively engaged with reality, even when it contains threatening news.

Another personality trait that appears to promote thriving during difficult times is hardiness. **Hardiness** is characterized by a sense of commitment (rather than alienation) and of control (rather than powerlessness) and a perception of problems as challenges (rather than threats) (Maddi & others, 2006). Consider the hardiness displayed by the basketball player whose team is down by two points with seconds remaining on the clock when he shouts, "Coach! Give me the ball!" In a time of high pressure and major stress, many of us might shrink from such a moment.

hardiness
A trait characterized by a sense of commitment rather than alienation and of control rather than powerlessness, and a perception of problems as challenges rather than threats.

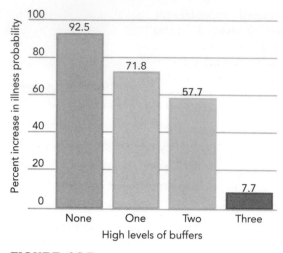

FIGURE 14.7

Illness in High-Stress Business Executives In one study of high-stress business executives, a low level of all three buffers (hardiness, exercise, and social support) involved a high probability of at least one serious illness in that year. High levels of one, two, and all three buffers decreased the likelihood of at least one serious illness occurring in the year of the study.

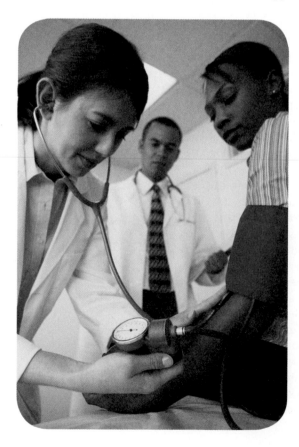

The links among hardiness, stress, and illness were the focus of the Chicago Stress Project, which studied male business managers 32 to 65 years of age over a five-year period (Kobasa, Maddi, & Kahn, 1982; Maddi, 1998). During the five years, most of the managers experienced stressful events such as divorce, job transfers, a close friend's death, inferior work-performance evaluations, and reporting to an unpleasant boss. Figure 14.7 shows how hardiness buffered these individuals from stress-related illness (Kobasa & others, 1986).

Other researchers also have found support for the role of hardiness in illness and health (Heckman & Clay, 2005). The results of hardiness research suggest the power of multiple factors, rather than any single factor, in cushioning individuals against stress and maintaining their health (Maddi, 1998, 2008; Maddi & others, 2006).

Stress Management Programs

Nearly every day we are reminded that stress is bad for our health. "Avoid stress" may be a good prescription, but life is full of potentially stressful experiences. Sometimes just checking e-mail or answering a phone can be an invitation for stress.

Because many people have difficulty regulating stress themselves, psychologists have developed techniques that individuals can learn (Greenberg, 2008; Marshall, Walizer, & Vernalis, 2009; Willert, Thulstrup, & Hertz, 2009). **Stress management programs** teach individuals how to appraise stressful events, develop coping skills, and put these skills into practical use. Some stress management programs teach a range of techniques to handle stress; others teach a specific technique, such as relaxation or assertiveness training.

Stress management programs are often taught through workshops, which are becoming more common in the workplace (Blonna & Paterson, 2007; Taylor, 2009). Aware of the high cost in lost productivity due to stress-related disorders, many organizations have become increasingly motivated to help their workers identify and cope with stressful circumstances. Colleges and universities similarly run stress management programs for students. If you are having difficulty coping with the pressures of college, you might consider enrolling in a stress management program at your school or in your community.

Do stress management programs work? In one study, researchers randomly assigned men and women with hypertension (blood pressure greater than 140/90) to one of three groups (Linden, Lenz, & Con, 2001). One group received 10 hours of individual stress management training; a second group was placed in a wait-list control group and eventually received stress management training; and a third group (a control group) received no such training (Linden, Lenz, & Con, 2001). The two groups that received the stress management training showed significantly reduced blood pressure. The control group experienced no reduction in blood pressure. Also, the reduced blood pressure in the first two groups was linked to a reported decrease in psychological stress and improved ability to cope with anger.

stress management program A regimen that teaches individuals how to appraise stressful events, how to develop skills for coping with stress, and how to put these skills into use in everyday life.

Coping effectively with stress is essential for physical and mental health (Fedler, Nestler, & Charney, 2009; Nagase & others, 2009). Still, there is a lot more we can do to promote our health. Healthful living—establishing healthy habits and evaluating and changing behaviors that interfere with good health—helps us avoid the damaging effects of stress (Frosch & others, 2009; Kodama & others, 2009). Just as the biopsychosocial perspective predicts, healthy changes in one area of life can have benefits that flow to other areas.

self-quiz

1. Selye's term for the pattern of common effects on the body when demands are placed on it is
   A. exhaustion syndrome.
   B. the Type A behavior pattern.
   C. the Type B behavior pattern.
   D. general adaptation syndrome.

2. A personality trait that is characterized by a sense of commitment and control, as well as by a perception of problems as challenges rather than threats, is
   A. self-efficacy.
   B. self-determination.
   C. hardiness.
   D. self-confidence.

3. Dealing with difficult circumstances, expending effort to solve life's problems, and seeking to control or reduce stress are key aspects of
   A. coping.
   B. cognitive appraisal.
   C. primary appraisal.
   D. secondary appraisal.

Apply It! 4. In addition to taking a full load of classes, Bonnie works at two part-time jobs and helps her sister care for two toddlers. Bonnie is achievement oriented and strives to get As in all of her courses. Because of her many commitments, she is often in a hurry and regularly does more than one thing at a time, but she tells people that she enjoys her busy routine. Which answer best assesses whether Bonnie is Type A and at risk for cardiovascular disease?
   A. Bonnie's hurriedness and achievement orientation indicate that she is Type A and probably at risk for cardiovascular disease.
   B. Although Bonnie may experience stress, the lack of hostility mentioned in this description suggests that she is not Type A or at risk for cardiovascular disease.
   C. Bonnie is a "hot reactor" and thus at risk for cardiovascular disease.
   D. Bonnie is Type A, but her enjoyment of life means that she is not at risk for cardiovascular disease.

5 Toward a Healthier Body (and Mind): Behaving as If Your Life Depends upon It

There is no escaping it: Getting stress under control is crucial for a healthy mind and body. It is also important to make wise behavioral choices in four additional life domains where healthy habits can have benefits for both body and mind. In this section we examine the advantages of becoming physically active, eating right, quitting smoking, and practicing safe sex.

Becoming Physically Active

Imagine that there was a time when, to change a TV channel, people had to get up and walk a few feet to turn a knob. Consider the time when people physically had to go to the library and hunt through card catalogs and shelves to find information rather than going online and Googling. As our daily tasks have become increasingly easy, we have become less active, and inactivity is a serious health problem (Whitt-Glover & others, 2009).

Any activity that expends physical energy can be part of a healthy lifestyle. It can be as simple as taking the stairs instead of an elevator, walking or biking to class instead of driving, or getting up and dancing instead of sitting at the bar. One study of older adults revealed that the more they expended energy in daily activities, the longer they were likely to live (Manini & others, 2006).

In addition to its relationship to longevity, physical activity corresponds with other positive outcomes, including a lower probability of developing cardiovascular disease (Sui & others, 2009), weight loss in overweight individuals (Ades & others, 2009),

FIGURE 14.8
The Jogging Hog Experiment Jogging hogs reveal the dramatic effects of exercise on health. In one investigation, a group of hogs was trained to run approximately 100 miles per week (Bloor & White, 1983). Then the researchers narrowed the arteries that supplied blood to the hogs' hearts. The hearts of the jogging hogs developed extensive alternate pathways for blood supply, and 42 percent of the threatened heart tissue was salvaged, compared with only 17 percent in a control group of non-jogging hogs.

improved cognitive functioning (Erickson & Kramer, 2009; Erickson & others, 2009), positive coping with stress (Collins & others, 2009), and increased self-esteem (Hallal & others, 2006). Physical exercise also reduces levels of anxiety (Rethorst, Wipfli, & Landers, 2009) and depression (Ryan, 2008). Even a real pig benefits from exercise; Figure 14.8 shows the positive effects of physical activity in hogs. Being physically active is like investing energy in a wellness bank account: Activity enhances physical well-being and gives us the ability to face life's potential stressors energetically.

Exercise is one special type of physical activity. **Exercise** formally refers to structured activities whose goal is to improve health. Although exercise designed to strengthen muscles and bones or to improve flexibility is important to fitness, many health experts stress the benefits of **aerobic exercise,** which is sustained activity—jogging, swimming, or cycling, for example—that stimulates heart and lung functioning.

In one study, exercise meant the difference between life and death for middle-aged and older adults (Blair & others, 1989). More than 10,000 men and women were divided into categories of low fitness, medium fitness, and high fitness (Blair & others, 1989). Then they were studied over eight years. As shown in Figure 14.9, sedentary participants (low fitness) were more than twice as likely to die during the study's eight-year time span than those who were moderately fit, and more than three times as likely to die as those who were highly fit. The positive effects of physical fitness occurred for both men and women. Further, a recent study revealed that adults aged 60 and over who were in the lowest fifth in terms of physical fitness as determined by a treadmill test were four times more likely to die over a 12-year period than their counterparts who were in the top fifth of physical fitness (Sui & others, 2007). This study also showed that older adults who were overweight but physically fit had a lower

exercise
Structured activities whose goal is to improve health.

aerobic exercise
Sustained activity—jogging, swimming, or cycling, for example—that stimulates heart and lung functioning.

mortality risk over the 12 years than their normal-weight counterparts who were low in fitness (Sui & others, 2007). In addition, a recent longitudinal study found that men who exercised regularly at 72 years of age had a 30 percent higher probability of being alive at 90 years of age than their sedentary counterparts (Yates & others, 2008).

⟳ "Fitness" here refers to the body's ability to supply fuel during sustained physical activity.

Health experts recommend that adults engage in at least 30 minutes of moderate physical activity on most, preferably all, days of the week and that children exercise for 60 minutes daily. Most specialists advise that exercisers raise their heart rate to at least 60 percent of their maximum rate. Only about one-fifth of adults are active at these recommended levels. Figure 14.10 lists physical activities that qualify as moderate and, for comparison, vigorous. Research suggests that both moderate and intense activities may produce important physical and psychological gains (Collins & others, 2009; Erickson & others, 2009; Sui & others, 2009).

⟳ Make time in your day to exercise. It might mean waking up earlier or forgoing watching TV. The benefits are well worth it.

One often welcome payoff for increasing physical activity is weight loss. Researchers have found that the most effective component of weight-loss programs is regular exercise (Hoeger & Hoeger, 2008; Kohl, 2009). Another way to combat weight problems is through changes in diet, our next topic.

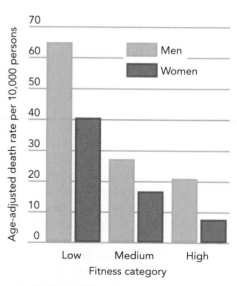

FIGURE 14.9
Physical Fitness and Mortality In this study of middle-aged and older adults, moderately fit or highly fit individuals were less likely to die over a period of eight years than their low-fitness (sedentary) counterparts (Blair & others, 1989).

Moderate	Vigorous
Walking briskly (3–4 mph)	Walking briskly uphill or with a load
Swimming, moderate effort	Swimming, fast treading crawl
Cycling for pleasure or transportation (≤10 mph)	Cycling, fast or racing (>10 mph)
Racket sports, table tennis	Racket sports, singles tennis, racketball
Conditioning exercise, general calisthenics	Conditioning exercise, stair ergometer, ski machine
Golf, pulling cart or carrying clubs	Golf, practice at driving range
Canoeing, leisurely (2.0–3.9 mph)	Canoeing, rapidly (≥4 mph)
Home care, general cleaning	Moving furniture
Mowing lawn, power mower	Mowing lawn, hand mower
Home repair, painting	Fix-up projects

FIGURE 14.10

Moderate and Vigorous Physical Activities At minimum, adults should strive for 30 minutes of moderate activity each day. That activity can become even more beneficial if we "pump it up" to vigorous.

Eating Right

The biggest health risk facing modern Americans is being overweight or obese. "Overweight" and "obese" are labels for ranges of weight that are greater than what experts consider healthy for an individual's height (National Center for Health Statistics, 2006a). In recent years, the percentage of individuals who are overweight or obese has been increasing at an alarming rate. As Figure 14.11 indicates, the prevalence of being overweight or obese in the United States changed little from 1960 to 1980 (National Center for Health Statistics, 2006a). However, the percentage of overweight and obese adults in the United States increased from less than 50 percent in 1960 to almost 70 percent in 2004. In that year, 30 percent of men and 34 percent of women were classified as obese. At this rate, by 2030, the percentage of overweight or obese Americans could reach *86 percent* (Beydoun & Wang, 2009).

Exercising regularly is one great way to lose weight. Making healthy dietary choices is another (Kersick & others, 2009; Ross & others, 2009b). Eating right means opting for sensible, nutritious foods that maximize health and wellness. Despite the growing variety of choices Americans can make in the grocery store, many of us are unhealthy eaters. We take in too much sugar and not enough foods high in vitamins, minerals, and fiber, such as fruits, vegetables, and grains. We eat too much fast food and too few well-balanced meals—choices that increase our fat and cholesterol intake, both of which are implicated in long-term health problems (Phelan & others, 2009).

Healthy eating does not mean trying out every new fad diet but rather incorporating tasty,

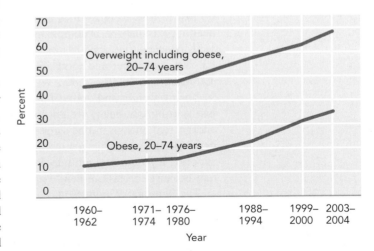

FIGURE 14.11

Changes in the Percentage of U.S. Adults 20 to 74 Years of Age Classified as Overweight or Obese, 1960–2004 Being overweight or obese poses the greatest overall health risk for Americans today.

challenge your thinking

Can You Be Fat *and* Fit?

What does a healthy body look like? During your spinning class, you notice that your instructor is overweight. Is she really healthy? Later, while watching your favorite baseball team, you check out the dugout. How many of the players are truly thin? Even Babe Ruth, perhaps the greatest baseball player of all time, was a rotund guy known for his hearty appetite. One day at Coney Island, Ruth ate four steaks and eight hot dogs and drank eight sodas. The workout favored by the Bambino was generally limited to running the bases after hitting one of his many home runs.

Body weight is certainly an important factor in physical health. Researchers have estimated that individuals who are obese at age 40 will live six to seven years less than their thin counterparts, and individuals who are overweight at 40 lose three years of life on average (Peeters & others, 2003).

How do we know if someone is overweight or obese? One of the most commonly used measures is the *body mass index* (BMI), which is calculated by multiplying weight in pounds by 704.5 and then dividing by height in inches, squared (National Heart, Lung, and Blood Institute, 2009):

$$\frac{\text{Weight (in pounds)} \times 704.5}{\text{Height (in inches)}^2}$$

Figure 14.12 shows a chart for determining BMI. According to the Centers for Disease Control and Prevention (2009b), a healthy BMI for an adult ranges between 18.5 and 24. Overweight refers to a BMI that is greater than or equal to 25, and obese is greater than or equal to 30. (Babe Ruth's BMI? A solidly overweight 28.)

Another important factor in physical health and the risk for serious illness is fitness. *Cardiorespiratory fitness* (CRF) refers to the ability of the body's circulatory and respiratory systems to supply fuel during sustained physical activity. CRF, usually measured with a treadmill test, is increased by engaging in aerobic exercise regularly (Kodama & others, 2009).

One study that compared BMI and CRF challenged the notion that BMI is an important risk factor for disease (Lee, Blair, & Jackson, 1999). The researchers measured leanness, obesity, and CRF in nearly 22,000 men 30 to 83 years of age. The men were followed over eight years. During that time, 428 died. Controlling for age, smoking, alcohol consumption, and parental history of heart disease and regardless of body size, unfit men were more likely to die than fit men. *Unfit lean* men had a higher risk of dying than *fit obese* men.

The idea that "fit and fat" might translate into good health set off a media frenzy. The news that it does not matter how fat people are, just whether they are active, spread like wildfire. Suddenly, it was safe to step on the scale again.

healthy foods into meals and snacks. Healthy eating is not something that people should do just to lose weight—it is about committing to lifelong healthy food habits. Several health goals can be accomplished through a sound nutritional plan. Not only does a well-balanced diet provide more energy, but it also can lower blood pressure and lessen the risk for cancer and tooth decay (Herder & Demmig-Adams, 2004; Levitan, Wolk, & Mittleman, 2009).

Losing weight and opting for healthier foods can be difficult, especially when one is just starting out. Many weight-loss fads promise weight loss with no effort, no hunger, and no real change in one's food consumption. These promises are unrealistic. Making genuine, enduring changes in eating behavior is hard work. This reality does not mean adopting a pessimistic attitude. Rather, positive expectations and self-efficacy are important because the task at hand is a challenging one.

The National Weight Control Registry is an ongoing study of people who have lost at least 40 pounds and kept it off for at least two years. Research on these successful dieters gives us important tips on how people who keep the weight off achieve this goal (Raynor & others, 2005). Successful dieters show consistency in what they eat, sticking to the same regimen even on weekends and during holidays (Gorin & others, 2004). A study of approximately 2,000 U.S. adults found that exercising 30 minutes a day, planning meals, and weighing themselves daily were the main strategies of successful dieters (Kruger, Blanck, & Gillespie, 2006).

One key practice is eating breakfast, especially whole-grain cereals.

Weight (pounds)

Height	120	130	140	150	160	170	180	190	200	210	220	230	240	250
4'6"	29	31	34	36	39	41	43	46	48	51	53	56	58	60
4'8"	27	29	31	34	36	38	40	43	45	47	49	52	54	56
4'10"	25	27	29	31	34	36	38	40	42	44	46	48	50	52
5'0"	23	25	27	29	31	33	35	37	39	41	43	45	47	49
5'2"	22	24	26	27	29	31	33	35	37	38	40	42	44	46
5'4"	21	22	24	26	28	29	31	33	34	36	38	40	41	43
5'6"	19	21	23	24	26	27	29	31	32	34	36	37	39	40
5'8"	18	20	21	23	24	26	27	29	30	32	34	35	37	38
5'10"	17	19	20	22	23	24	26	27	29	30	32	33	35	36
6'0"	16	18	19	20	22	23	24	26	27	28	30	31	33	34
6'2"	15	17	18	19	21	22	23	24	26	27	28	30	31	32
6'4"	15	16	17	18	20	21	22	23	24	26	27	28	29	30
6'6"	14	15	16	17	19	20	21	22	23	24	25	27	28	29
6'8"	13	14	15	17	18	19	20	21	22	23	24	25	26	28

☐ Underweight ☐ Healthy weight ☐ Overweight ☐ Obese

FIGURE 14.12
Determining Your Body Mass Index Body mass index is a measure of weight in relation to height. Anyone with a BMI of 25 or more is considered overweight, and people who have a body mass index of 30 or more (a BMI of 30 is roughly 30 pounds over a healthy weight) are considered obese, though BMI can overestimate body fat in very muscular people.

Within the scientific community, however, debate raged around the question, is it possible to avoid the negative effects of overweight and obesity by being physically fit? A wide range of studies have examined whether being fit can compensate for being fat. Although research has supported the importance of CRF (Gerson & Braun, 2006), studies have not found support for the idea that fitness can compensate for being overweight (Hu & others, 2004). Being fit does not protect a person from the health risks of being fat, and being thin does not protect the person from the risks associated with being unfit (Church & others, 2005; Sullivan & others, 2005).

Can a person be both fat and fit? Yes, but fat and fit people are not as healthy as lean and fit people. Similarly, fat and fit people may be healthier than lean sedentary individuals. Essentially, research has shown that there are two avenues to pursue for optimal health: being physically active *and* maintaining a reasonable weight.

This controversy has highlighted the common tendency to equate a healthy body with a thin one. However, lean individuals who are inactive, smoke, drink to excess, or otherwise fail to take care of their bodies are not healthier than individuals who carry a few extra pounds but engage in vigorous exercise and otherwise take good care of themselves. A healthy body is more than a number on a scale or a slim silhouette in the mirror. As with most things in life, it is what's on the inside that counts.

The truth is that keeping weight off is an ongoing process. Moreover, the longer a dieter keeps the weight off, the less likely he or she is to gain it back (McGuire & others, 1999). The goal is difficult, but an individual's ability to accomplish it is a testament to the power of self-belief. In Challenge Your Thinking, we explore a controversial question related to diet and health—whether a person can be fat *and* fit.

Quitting Smoking

Another health-related goal is giving up smoking. Evidence from a number of studies underscores the dangers of smoking and being around smokers (American Cancer Society, 2009). For example, smoking is linked to 30 percent of cancer deaths, 21 percent of heart disease deaths, and 82 percent of chronic pulmonary disease deaths. Secondhand smoke is implicated in as many as 9,000 lung cancer deaths a year. Children of smokers are at special risk for respiratory and middle-ear diseases (Goodwin & Cowles, 2008).

Fewer people smoke today than in the past, and almost half of the living adults who ever smoked have quit. In 2006, 20.8 percent of all adults in the United

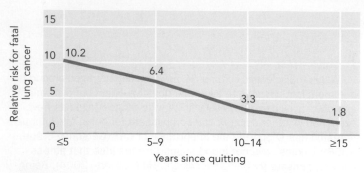

FIGURE 14.13

Fatal Lung Cancer and Years Since Quitting Smoking One study compared more than 43,000 former male smokers with almost 60,000 males who had never smoked (Enstrom, 1999). For comparison purposes, a zero level was assigned as the risk for fatal lung cancer for men who had never smoked. Over time, the relative risk for smokers who had quit declined, but even after 15 years it was still above that of nonsmokers.

States smoked, with men being more likely to smoke (23.6 percent) than women (18.1 percent) (National Center for Health Statistics, 2008a). Although these numbers represent a substantial decline from 40 years ago, when 50 percent of men smoked, many individuals still smoke.

Quitting smoking has enormous health benefits. Figure 14.13 shows that when individuals kick the habit, their risk of fatal lung cancer declines over time. There is little doubt that most smokers would like to quit, but their nicotine addiction makes quitting a challenge. Nicotine, the active drug in cigarettes, is a stimulant that increases the smoker's energy and alertness, a pleasurable and reinforcing experience. In addition, nicotine stimulates neurotransmitters that have a calming or pain-reducing effect (Johnstone & others, 2006).

Research confirms that giving up smoking can be difficult, especially in the early days of quitting (McCarthy & others, 2006). There are various ways to quit smoking (Fant & others, 2009; Glynn & others, 2009; Ramon & Bruguera, 2009), including:

- *"Going cold turkey":* Some individuals succeed by stopping smoking without making any major lifestyle changes. They decide they are going to quit, and they do. Lighter smokers usually have more success with this approach than heavier smokers.

- *Using a substitute source of nicotine:* Nicotine gum, the nicotine patch, the nicotine inhaler, and nicotine spray work on the principle of supplying small amounts of nicotine to diminish the intensity of withdrawal (Frishman & others, 2006e). *Nicotine gum,* available without a prescription, delivers nicotine orally when an individual gets the urge to smoke. The *nicotine patch* is a nonprescription adhesive pad that releases a steady dose of nicotine to the individual. The dose is gradually reduced over an 8- to 12-week period. *Nicotine spray* delivers a half-milligram squirt of nicotine to each nostril. The usual dosage is one to two administrations per hour and then as needed to reduce cravings. The spray is typically used for three to six months. Success rates for nicotine substitutes are encouraging. All of these nicotine replacement therapies enhance the chances of quitting and remaining smoke-free.

- *Seeking therapeutic help:* Some smokers get professional help to kick the habit. Therapies for helping smokers quit include prescribing medication such as antidepressants and teaching behaviorally based therapeutic techniques.

If you smoke, quit. Many smokers believe that they have to wait for the "perfect time" to quit—a moment when life is not stressful. The truth is that any moment is a good moment to quit smoking. Every cigarette you avoid smoking is a step in the right direction.

Bupropion SR, an antidepressant sold as Zyban, helps smokers control their cravings while they ease off nicotine. Zyban works at the neurotransmitter level in the brain by inhibiting the uptake of dopamine, serotonin, and norepinephrine. Smokers using Zyban to quit have had a 21 percent average success rate after 12 months of taking the antidepressant (Paluck & others, 2006), which is similar to results for individuals using nicotine replacement. More recently, varenicline (trade name Chantix) has been approved to help smokers quit. This drug partially blocks nicotine receptors, reducing cravings and also decreasing the pleasurable sensations of smoking. Varenicline, especially when combined with counseling/psychotherapy, is more effective for smoking cessation than buproprion SR (Garrison & Dugan, 2009; Nides, 2008; Ramon & Bruguera, 2009).

No one method is foolproof for quitting smoking (Fant & others, 2009). Often a combination of these approaches is the best strategy. Furthermore, quitting for good typically requires more than one try, as the stages of change model suggests.

psychology *in our world*

Making a Career of Good Health

Are you interested in pursuing a job that draws on your knowledge of health psychology? Two related occupations are health promotion and public health.

Health promotion involves helping people change their lifestyle to optimize health and assisting them in achieving balance in physical, emotional, social, spiritual, and intellectual health and wellness. Health promotion can be a goal of a company's human resources department, as well as state and city health departments, and it is sometimes a specialty for social workers and other members of the helping professions.

Public health is concerned with studying health and disease in large populations to guide policymakers. Public health experts identify public health concerns, set priorities, and design interventions for health promotion. An important goal of public health is to ensure that all populations have access to cost-effective healthcare and health promotion services.

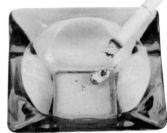

A job in health promotion or public health can involve creating attention-grabbing public service advertisements and brochures to alert the public to health-related issues. If you have noticed a "Click It or Ticket" sign on the highway or seen one of thetruth.com's antismoking ads on TV, you have a good feel for what health promotion and public health are all about.

Practicing Safe Sex

Sex is everywhere in U.S. society—online, on TV, and in films; in songs and music videos; in magazines and newspapers. We are fascinated by sex. Nonetheless, talking about sex is often uncomfortable. One thing that is certain is that satisfying sexual experience is part of a happy life (Strong & others, 2008). Sexual behavior also has important implications for physical health.

In this section we examine two aspects of physical health related to sexual behavior: preventing unwanted pregnancy and protecting oneself from sexually transmitted infections (STIs). Naturally, by simply not having sex, individuals can avoid these problems. However, even for those whose goal is abstinence, knowledge about protecting oneself from unwanted pregnancy and STIs is important, because as the stages of change model suggests, we sometimes fall short of our goals.

Preventing Unwanted Pregnancy   Inadequate knowledge about contraception, coupled with inconsistent use of effective contraceptive methods, has given the United States one of the highest rates of adolescent pregnancy and childbearing in the developed world (Holcombe, Peterson, & Manlove, 2009; Moore, 2009). Less than 20 percent of U.S. teen pregnancies are intended (Holcombe, Peterson, & Manlove, 2009). Births to adolescent girls in the United States had been falling in the last two decades, reaching a record low in 2004, but they increased in 2006 and 2007 (Hamilton, Martin, & Ventura, 2009). As can be seen in Figure 14.14, frequency of teen pregnancies in the United States is far higher than other developed countries. Although U.S. adolescents

Teen births per 1000 women

Niger	233
Mali	191
Ethiopia	100
Colombia	80
Mexico	64
United States	53
Romania	37
Sri Lanka	22
United Kingdom	20
Canada	16
Germany	11
France	9
Sweden	7
China, Netherlands, and Switzerland	5
Japan	4
South Korea	3
North Korea	2

FIGURE 14.14

Adolescent Pregnancy Rates Across Several Countries Comprehensive sex education is one reason for the difference in teen pregnancy rates among countries. What other factors might be at work?

are no more sexually active than their counterparts in countries such as France and Sweden, their adolescent pregnancy rate is much higher—perhaps because, compared to these other nations, the United States has less comprehensive sex education and less availability and use of condoms. Clearly, education and prevention are crucial to progress in reducing pregnancy among adolescents.

Condoms are a key tool in the efforts to prevent teen pregnancy. One advantage of condoms is that when properly used, they not only help to prevent unintended pregnancy but also protect the individual from some sexually transmitted infections.

sexually transmitted infection (STI)
An infection that is contracted primarily through sexual activity—vaginal intercourse as well as oral-genital and anal-genital sex.

Protecting Against Sexually Transmitted Infections   A **sexually transmitted infection (STI)** is an infection that is contracted primarily through sexual activity—vaginal intercourse as well as oral-genital and anal-genital sex. STIs affect about one of every six adults (National Center for Health Statistics, 2009). Some STIs are bacterial in origin, as in the case of gonorrhea and syphilis, and others are caused by viruses, as in the case of genital herpes and AIDS. STIs are an important health concern because they can have implications for a person's future fertility, risk of cancer, and life expectancy.

acquired immune deficiency syndrome (AIDS)
A disease caused by the human immunodeficiency virus (HIV), a sexually transmitted infection that destroys the immune system.

No single STI has had a greater impact on sexual behavior in the past decades than AIDS (Campbell, 2009). **Acquired immune deficiency syndrome (AIDS)** is caused by the sexually transmitted human immunodeficiency virus (HIV), which destroys the body's immune system. Without treatment, most people who contract AIDS are vulnerable to germs that a normal immune system can destroy. Through 2007, almost 600,000 AIDS deaths had occurred in the United States, including more than 14,000 in 2007 (Centers for Disease Control and Prevention, 2009a). In 2006, 56,300 new HIV infections were reported in the United States.

Recent improvements in drug therapies have given rise to the view that AIDS is a chronic rather than terminal condition. However, responses to treatment vary among individuals, and keeping up with the "cocktail" of drugs necessary to continuously fight HIV is challenging. The treatment known as *highly active antiretroviral therapy* (HAART) can involve taking between 6 and 22 pills each day, although the FDA has approved the first one-pill-per-day treatment for AIDS (Onen & others, 2009).

Because of increased education and the development of more effective drug therapies, deaths due to AIDS have begun to decline in the United States (National Center for Health Statistics, 2006). There are no solid estimates for the life expectancy of someone who is HIV-positive because the existing treatments have been around for only about a decade. Even in this era of improved treatments, however, AIDS remains incurable. Importantly, it has been estimated that as many as one-half of HIV-positive individuals are not in treatment and that one-fifth do not know that they have contracted the virus (Centers for Disease Control and Prevention, 2009a).

All sexually active people are at risk of contracting HIV and other STIs. The only 100 percent safe behavior is abstinence from sex, which many individuals do not view as an option. Sensual activities such as cuddling, massage, and mutual masturbation (without the exchange of bodily fluids) involve no risk of an STI. Sexual activities that involve penetration, including vaginal or anal intercourse as well as oral sex, are riskier behaviors that can be made less risky with the use of proper protection.

In your own sexual experience, it may be difficult to gauge the accuracy of a partner's estimates of risk and his or her HIV status. The wisest course is always to protect yourself from infection by using a latex condom. When correctly used, latex condoms help to block the transmission of many STIs. Condoms are most effective in preventing gonorrhea, syphilis, chlamydia, and AIDS. Recent research suggests that consistent condom use also significantly reduces the risk that males will transmit to their female partners the human papilloma virus (HPV), which can cause cervical cancer (Miksis, 2008). Although condoms are less effective against the spread of herpes than against other STIs, the consistent use of condoms significantly reduces the risk of herpes infection for both men and women (Steben & others, 2008; Tobian & others, 2009).

Anyone who thinks that condom use is inconvenient might well consider which is more inconvenient—using a condom or contracting gonorrhea or HIV.

Research has shown that safe-sex programs are especially effective if they include the eroticization of condom use—that is, making condoms part of the sensual experience of foreplay (Harper & others, 2003; Scott-Sheldon & Johnson, 2006). Recent analyses of HIV prevention programs (including over 350 intervention groups and 100 control groups) by Delores Albarracin and her colleagues have produced important recommendations for the best ways to influence behavior (Albarracin, Durantini, & Earl, 2006; Albarracin & others, 2005, 2008; Durantini & Albarracin, 2009). The studies have found that fear tactics are relatively less effective and that programs emphasizing active skill building (for example, role playing the use of condoms), self-efficacy, and positive attitudes about condom use are effective with most groups.

self-quiz

1. Regular physical activity, and in particular exercise, are associated with all of the following *except*
   A. weight loss.
   B. increased self-esteem.
   C. less incidence of depression.
   D. premature death in middle-age and older adults.

2. The biggest health risk facing most Americans today is
   A. heart disease.
   B. cancer.
   C. overweight and obesity.
   D. stress.

3. Typically, the *best* approach to quitting smoking is to
   A. go cold turkey.
   B. use a nicotine patch.
   C. use a combination of methods.
   D. get help from a therapist.

Apply It! 4. J. C. and Veronica promote student health causes on their college campus. This year, they are targeting wise sexual choices. Which of the following is the most promising strategy for their campaign?

A. They should focus on fear of disease as a motivator for condom use.
B. They should focus on promoting non-risky sexual activities, eroticizing condom use, and teaching students skills for effective condom use, reminding students that even if they do not intend to have sex, it is best to be safe.
C. They should focus only on students who are already engaging in sexual behavior.
D. They should encourage students, before having sex, simply to ask their partners how many sexual partners they have had.

6 Psychology and Your Good Life

In this discussion of health psychology, we have examined how the mental and physical aspects of your existence intertwine and influence each other in dynamic ways. The field of health psychology serves to illustrate how all of the various areas of psychology converge to reveal that interplay.

As a human being, you are both a physical entity and a system of mental processes that are themselves reflected in that most complex of physical organs, the brain. At every moment, both body and mind are present and affecting each other. Caring for your brain and mind—the resources that make it possible for you to read this book, study for tests, listen to lectures, fall in love, share with friends, help others, and make a difference in the world—is worthy of being a life mission.

Something as deceptively simple as taking in and perceiving a sunset (or a painting of a sunset) becomes stunningly complex in the context of a human life.

www.CartoonStock.com

Many pages ago, we defined psychology as the scientific study of behavior and mental processes, broadly meaning the things we do, think, and feel. Reflect for a moment on the psychological dimensions of vision. When we studied the human visual system, we examined the processes by which those amazing sense organs, our eyes, detect color, light, dark, shape, and depth. We probed the ways that the brain takes that information and turns it into perception—how a pattern of colors, shapes, and light come to be perceived as a flower, a fall day, a sunset. Visual systems, we discovered, are generally the same from one person to the next. Thus, you can memorize the different parts of the human eye and know that your understanding is true for just about all the human eyes you will encounter in life.

However, even something as deceptively simple as perceiving a sunset through the sense of vision becomes amazingly complex when we put it in the context of a human life. Is that sunset the first you see while on your honeymoon, or right after a painful romantic breakup, or as a new parent? Placing even the most ordinary moment in the context of a human life renders it extraordinary and fascinating.

This fascination is a primary motivation for the science of psychology itself. From time immemorial, individuals have pondered the mysteries of human behavior, thought, and emotion. Why do we do the things we do? How do we think and feel? In this book, we have explored the broad range of topics that have interested psychologists throughout the history of this young science.

Turn to the Table of Contents of this book. Consider which chapters or topics you found most interesting. Go to your school's library and locate the journals that are devoted to that subject (you can ask a librarian for help). Browse a recent issue of one of the journals. What topics are scientists studying? If a particular study described in this book sounded interesting, you can probably obtain it online. Do a Google "Scholar" search on the authors and take a look at the original article. What did the authors conclude? What did you learn?

Coming to the close of this introduction to psychology allows you, like the Roman god Janus, to look back but also ahead. It allows you to take stock of what psychology has come to mean to you now, as well as to consider what it might mean to you in the future. Whether or not you continue coursework in psychology, this book has highlighted opportunities for your future exploration about yourself and your world. In each of the real-life examples of human experience we have considered—moments of heroism, weakness, joy, pain, and more—psychology has had a lesson to share with respect to the person that is *you*. Making the most of what you have learned about psychology means making the most of yourself and your life.

summary

① Health Psychology and Behavioral Medicine

Health psychology emphasizes biological, psychological, and social factors in human health. Closely aligned with health psychology is behavioral medicine, which combines medical and behavioral knowledge to reduce illness and promote health. These approaches demonstrate the biopsychosocial model by examining the interaction of biological, psychological, and social variables as they relate to health and illness. Stress is an example of a biological, psychological, and social construct.

Health psychology and behavioral medicine bring the relationship of the mind and body to the forefront. These approaches examine the reciprocal mind-body relationship: how the body is influenced by psychological states and how mental life is influenced by physical health.

② Making Positive Life Changes

The theory of reasoned action suggests that we can make changes by devising specific intentions for behavioral change. We are more likely to follow through on our intentions if we feel good about the change and if we believe that others around us also support the change. The theory of planned behavior incorporates these factors as well as our perceptions of control over the behavior.

The stages of change model posits that personal change occurs in a series of five steps: precontemplation, contemplation, preparation/determination, action/willpower, and maintenance. Each stage has its own challenges. Relapse is a natural part of the journey toward change.

③ Resources for Effective Life Change

Motivation is an important part of sustaining behavioral change. Change is more effective when the person does it for intrinsic reasons (because he or she wants to) rather than extrinsic reasons (to gain rewards). Implementation intentions are the specific ways individuals plan to institute changes.

Social relationships are strongly associated with health and survival. Social support refers to the aid provided by others to a person in need. Support can take the form of tangible assistance, information, or emotional support. Social support is strongly related to functioning and coping with stress.

Religious faith is associated with enhanced health. One reason for this connection is that religions often frown on excess and promote healthy behavior. In addition, religious participation allows individuals to benefit from a social group, and religion provides a meaning system on which to rely in times of difficulty.

Personality characteristics related to positive health behaviors include conscientiousness, personal control, self-efficacy, and optimism. Conscientious individuals are likely to engage in healthy behaviors and live longer. Personal control is associated with better coping with stress. Self-efficacy is the person's belief in his or her own ability to master a situation and produce positive outcomes. Optimism refers to a particular explanatory style as well as to the inclination to have positive expectations for the future. Studies have shown that both of these types of optimism relate to positive health outcomes.

④ Toward a Healthier Mind (and Body): Controlling Stress

Stress is the response of individuals when life circumstances threaten them and tax their ability to cope. Selye characterized the stress response with his concept of a general adaptation syndrome (GAS), which has three stages: alarm, resistance, and exhaustion.

Chronic stress takes a toll on the body's natural disease-fighting abilities. Stress is also related to cardiovascular disease and cancer.

To kick the stress habit means remembering that stress is a product of how we think about events in our lives. Taking control of our appraisals allows us to see potentially threatening events as challenges. Hardiness is associated with thriving during stressful times.

The Type A behavior pattern, particularly the hostility component, is associated with stressing out angrily when things are going poorly. This hostility leads to poor health outcomes. When a person is unable to manage stress alone, stress management programs provide a viable option for help.

⑤ Toward a Healthier Body (and Mind): Behaving as If Your Life Depends upon It

Exercise has many positive psychological and physical benefits. Tips for increasing one's activity level include starting small by making changes in one's routine to incorporate physical activity and keeping track of progress.

Overweight and obesity pose the greatest health risks to Americans today. They can be largely avoided by eating right, which means selecting nutritious foods and maintaining healthy eating habits for a lifetime, not just while on a diet. A combination of healthy eating and exercise is the best way to achieve weight loss.

Despite widespread knowledge that smoking causes cancer, some people still smoke. Methods of quitting include going cold turkey, using a substitute source of nicotine, and seeking therapy. Quitting for good is difficult and usually takes more than one try. Usually a combination of methods is the best strategy for quitting.

Practicing safe sex is another aspect of health behavior of interest to health psychologists. Adolescent pregnancy is an especially significant social problem in the United States. Condoms help prevent both unwanted pregnancy and the transmission of sexually transmitted infections (STIs). Interventions to promote condom use are most successful when they include making condom use sexy, promoting contraceptive skills and self-efficacy, and encouraging positive attitudes about condoms.

⑥ Psychology and Your Good Life

Psychology is all about you. This book has aimed to show the relevance of psychology to your health and wellness and to help you appreciate the many, and deep, connections between this comparatively new science and your life.

key terms

health psychology, p. 481
behavioral medicine, p. 481
health behaviors, p. 482
theory of reasoned action, p. 482
theory of planned behavior, p. 483
stages of change model, p. 483
relapse, p. 485

implementation intentions, p. 486
social support, p. 488
general adaptation syndrome
    (GAS), p. 492
psychoneuroimmunology, p. 493
Type A behavior pattern, p. 494
Type B behavior pattern, p. 495

cognitive appraisal, p. 496
coping, p. 496
problem-focused coping, p. 496
emotion-focused coping, p. 496
hardiness, p. 497
stress management program, p. 498
exercise, p. 500

aerobic exercise, p. 500
sexually transmitted infection
    (STI), p. 506
acquired immune deficiency
    syndrome (AIDS), p. 506

self-test

multiple choice

1. If you are involved in the process of trying to change a maladaptive behavior, the stage in which you would most likely expend the most energy and effort is the
   A. preparation stage.
   B. contemplation stage.
   C. action stage.
   D. maintenance stage.

2. Individuals who have high self-efficacy are *least* likely to
   A. carry on when faced with challenges.
   B. expend effort in coping with stress.
   C. experience less stress in challenging situations.
   D. perceive that they have no control over the situation.

3. A distinct physiological pattern emerges when people are exposed to strong and prolonged stress. Selye labeled this response pattern the
   A. transactional stress response (TSR).
   B. two-factor theory of stress.
   C. general adaptation syndrome (GAS).
   D. chronic stress response (CSR).

4. When a rat is first introduced to an over-crowded cage, it will likely enter the _____ stage of the general adaptation syndrome.
   A. alarm
   B. resistance
   C. exhaustion
   D. none of the above

5. Numerous research studies support the idea that perhaps the most important variable in predicting health is
   A. life goals.
   B. social ties.
   C. consistent safe-sex practices.
   D. independence.

6. Religious faith is related to health because it promotes or is associated with all of the following *except*
   A. increased social support.
   B. sturdy moral fiber.
   C. a sense of meaning in life.
   D. moderation.

7. The aspect of Type A behavior that research most consistently associates with coronary problems is
   A. neuroticism.
   B. pessimism.
   C. conscientiousness.
   D. hostility.

8. According to the text, smoking contributes to all of the following *except*
   A. increased risk of middle-ear disease in children.
   B. death from cancer.
   C. death from heart disease.
   D. death from accidents.

9. A person who tries to quit smoking "cold turkey" is
   A. pairing unpleasant consequences (like smoking until he or she feels nauseated) with the undesirable behavior (smoking).
   B. taking antipsychotic drugs.
   C. trying to stop without making any major lifestyle changes.
   D. using nicotine substitutes.

10. The most probable reason that the United States has one of the highest rates of adolescent pregnancy in the developed world is that
   A. the contraceptive methods used by U.S. adolescents have higher failure rates than those used by adolescents in other developed countries.
   B. U.S. adolescents learn more about sex through school programs than adolescents in other developed countries do.
   C. U.S. adolescents are more sexually active than are adolescents in other developed countries.
   D. compared to other nations, the United States has less comprehensive sex education and less use and availability of condoms.

Apply It!

11. Cory is interested in becoming more physically active. Using the stages of change model, outline a plan for Cory to achieve his goal.

answers
to self-quizzes and self-tests

Chapter 1

Page 8:   1. A; 2. C; 3. B; 4. B
Page 13:   1. C; 2. D; 3. D; 4. C
Page 16:   1. D; 2. D; 3. B; 4. B
Page 27:   1. B; 2. B; 3. B; 4. A
Page 29:   1. C; 2. B; 3. A; 4. A
Page 33:   1. C; 2. D; 3. B; 4. B
Page 37:   1. A; 2. A; 3. B; 4. A; 5. B;
           6. D; 7. D; 8. D; 9. B; 10. A

Chapter 2

Page 42:   1. B; 2. D; 3. C; 4. A
Page 50:   1. D; 2. D; 3. A; 4. B
Page 66:   1. B; 2. C; 3. B; 4. C
Page 68:   1. A; 2. C; 3. D; 4. C
Page 70:   1. B; 2. C; 3. A; 4. B
Page 74:   1. C; 2. C; 3. C; 4. A
Page 76:   1. B; 2. B; 3. B; 4. B; 5. B;
           6. A; 7. D; 8. D; 9. C; 10. B

Chapter 3

Page 88:   1. C; 2. B; 3. A; 4. D
Page 100:   1. D; 2. A; 3. A; 4. B
Page 107:   1. A; 2. C; 3. B; 4. B
Page 114:   1. B; 2. B; 3. B; 4. B
Page 116:   1. B; 2. C; 3. C; 4. D; 5. C;
            6. A; 7. B; 8. B; 9. C; 10. B

Chapter 4

Page 123:   1. B; 2. A; 3. C; 4. B
Page 134:   1. D; 2. B; 3. B; 4. B
Page 146:   1. D; 2. D; 3. A; 4. C
Page 149:   1. A; 2. D; 3. D; 4. C
Page 151:   1. B; 2. D; 3. A; 4. C
Page 153:   1. A; 2. B; 3. C; 4. B; 5. B;
            6. D; 7. D; 8. D; 9. C; 10. D

Chapter 5

Page 157:   1. A; 2. C; 3. C; 4. C
Page 166:   1. B; 2. A; 3. D; 4. B
Page 178:   1. D; 2. B; 3. D; 4. A
Page 179:   1. B; 2. C; 3. B; 4. A
Page 182:   1. C; 2. B; 3. A; 4. A
Page 186:   1. D; 2. C; 3. B; 4. B
Pages 187–188:   1. B; 2. C; 3. A; 4. C; 5. A;
                 6. C; 7. A; 8. B; 9. D; 10. B

Chapter 6

Page 191:   1. D; 2. B; 3. A; 4. A
Page 194:   1. C; 2. D; 3. C; 4. B
Page 207:   1. D; 2. A; 3. B; 4. B
Page 215:   1. C; 2. A; 3. D; 4. B
Page 221:   1. B; 2. D; 3. B; 4. B
Page 225:   1. D; 2. A; 3. B; 4. A
Page 227:   1. A; 2. A; 3. B; 4. D; 5. A;
            6. C; 7. C; 8. A; 9. B; 10. A

Chapter 7

Page 231:   1. D; 2. C; 3. D; 4. C
Page 242:   1. C; 2. A; 3. B; 4. D
Page 251:   1. D; 2. B; 3. C; 4. A
Page 259:   1. D; 2. B; 3. B; 4. B
Page 261:   1. A; 2. A; 3. C; 4. A; 5. D;
            6. B; 7. C; 8. B; 9. B; 10. A

Chapter 8

Page 266:   1. A; 2. C; 3. C; 4. D
Page 287:   1. B; 2. D; 3. C; 4. B
Page 291:   1. A; 2. B; 3. C; 4. B
Page 301:   1. A; 2. C; 3. D; 4. C
Page 303:   1. A; 2. C; 3. D; 4. A; 5. C;
            6. D; 7. C; 8. A; 9. D; 10. A

Chapter 9

Page 307:   1. D; 2. B; 3. D; 4. B
Page 316:   1. C; 2. A; 3. D; 4. D
Page 320:   1. C; 2. C; 3. C; 4. C
Page 334:   1. B; 2. B; 3. A; 4. D
Page 336:   1. A; 2. C; 3. A; 4. A
Page 338:   1. D; 2. C; 3. D; 4. C; 5. D;
            6. C; 7. B; 8. A; 9. B; 10. D

Chapter 10

Page 348:   1. D; 2. C; 3. D; 4. C
Page 351:   1. B; 2. C; 3. B; 4. D
Page 356:   1. B; 2. D; 3. D; 4. B
Page 359:   1. B; 2. D; 3. C; 4. A
Page 363:   1. B; 2. C; 3. A; 4. B
Page 368:   1. B; 2. C; 3. D; 4. C
Page 373:   1. B; 2. A; 3. D; 4. B
Page 375:   1. A; 2. B; 3. C; 4. D; 5. B;
            6. B; 7. D; 8. B; 9. A; 10. D

Chapter 11

Page 385:   1. D; 2. A; 3. C; 4. B
Page 393:   1. D; 2. C; 3. A; 4. C
Page 400:   1. B; 2. B; 3. C; 4. C
Page 405:   1. C; 2. C; 3. D; 4. B
Page 408:   1. C; 2. C; 3. D; 4. B
Page 410:   1. C; 2. B; 3. B; 4. A; 5. D;
            6. B; 7. D; 8. C; 9. C; 10. C

Chapter 12

Page 417:   1. A; 2. C; 3. B; 4. A
Page 423:   1. D; 2. C; 3. B; 4. C
Page 429:   1. A; 2. D; 3. A; 4. C
Page 432:   1. D; 2. A; 3. C; 4. B
Page 435:   1. B; 2. C; 3. D; 4. C
Page 439:   1. B; 2. B; 3. C; 4. B
Page 442:   1. C; 2. C; 3. D; 4. A
Page 445:   1. B; 2. D; 3. D; 4. B
Pages 447–448:   1. C; 2. D; 3. B; 4. A; 5. B;
                 6. B; 7. B; 8. D; 9. D; 10. D

Chapter 13

Page 456:   1. B; 2. B; 3. C; 4. C
Page 468:   1. C; 2. B; 3. D; 4. D
Page 473:   1. B; 2. D; 3. B; 4. C
Page 477:   1. D; 2. B; 3. C; 4. B
Pages 478–479:   1. B; 2. D; 3. C; 4. C; 5. A;
                 6. C; 7. B; 8. C; 9. A; 10. B

Chapter 14

Page 482:   1. D; 2. B; 3. D; 4. B
Page 486:   1. D; 2. B; 3. B; 4. A
Page 492:   1. A; 2. D; 3. A; 4. C
Page 499:   1. D; 2. C; 3. A; 4. B
Page 507:   1. D; 2. C; 3. C; 4. B
Page 510:   1. C; 2. D; 3. C; 4. A; 5. B;
            6. B; 7. D; 8. D; 9. C; 10. D

glossary

A

abnormal behavior Behavior that is deviant, maladaptive, or personally distressful over a relatively long period of time.

absolute threshold The minimum amount of stimulus energy that a person can detect.

accommodation An individual's adjustment of his or her schemas to new information.

acquired immune deficiency syndrome (AIDS) A disease caused by the human immunodeficiency virus (HIV), a sexually transmitted infection that destroys the immune system.

acquisition The initial learning of the connection between the unconditioned stimulus and the conditioned stimulus when these two stimuli are paired.

action potential The brief wave of positive electrical charge that sweeps down the axon.

activation-synthesis theory The theory that dreaming occurs when the cerebral cortex synthesizes neural signals generated from activity in the lower brain and that dreams result from the brain's attempts to find logic in random brain activity that occurs during sleep.

addiction Either a physical or psychological dependence, or both, on a drug.

adrenal glands Glands at the top of each kidney that are responsible for regulating moods, energy level, and the ability to cope with stress.

aerobic exercise Sustained activity—jogging, swimming, or cycling, for example—that stimulates heart and lung functioning.

affectionate love Love that occurs when an individual has a deep, caring affection for another person and desires to have that person near; also called companionate love.

afferent nerves Also called sensory nerves; nerves that carry information about the external environment to the brain and spinal cord via sensory receptors.

aggression Social behavior whose objective is to harm someone, either physically or verbally.

agonist A drug that mimics or increases a neurotransmitter's effects.

alcoholism Disorder that involves long-term, repeated, uncontrolled, compulsive, and excessive use of alcoholic beverages and that impairs the drinker's health and social relationships.

algorithms Strategies—including formulas, instructions, and the testing of all possible solutions—that guarantee a solution to a problem.

all-or-nothing principle The principle that once the electrical impulse reaches a certain level of intensity (its threshold), it fires and moves all the way down the axon without losing intensity.

altruism Unselfish interest in helping another person.

amnesia The loss of memory.

amygdala An almond-shaped structure within the base of the temporal lobe that is involved in the discrimination of objects that are necessary for the organism's survival, such as appropriate food, mates, and social rivals.

androgens The class of sex hormones that predominate in males, produced by the testes in males and by the adrenal glands in both males and females.

anorexia nervosa Eating disorder that involves the relentless pursuit of thinness through starvation.

antagonist A drug that blocks a neurotransmitter's effects.

anterograde amnesia A memory disorder that affects the retention of new information and events.

antianxiety drugs Commonly known as tranquilizers, drugs that reduce anxiety by making individuals calmer and less excitable.

antidepressant drugs Drugs that regulate mood.

antipsychotic drugs Powerful drugs that diminish agitated behavior, reduce tension, decrease hallucinations, improve social behavior, and produce better sleep patterns in individuals with a severe psychological disorder, especially schizophrenia.

antisocial personality disorder (ASPD) Psychological disorder characterized by guiltlessness, lawbreaking, exploitation of others, irresponsibility, and deceit.

anxiety disorders Disabling (uncontrollable and disruptive) psychological disorders that feature motor tension, hyperactivity, and apprehensive expectations and thoughts.

apparent movement The perception that a stationary object is moving.

applied behavior analysis (behavior modification) The use of operant conditioning principles to change human behavior.

archetypes Emotionally laden ideas and images that have rich and symbolic meaning for all people.

artificial intelligence (AI) A scientific field that focuses on creating machines capable of performing activities that require intelligence when they are done by people.

assimilation An individual's incorporation of new information into existing knowledge.

association cortex Sometimes called *association areas,* the region of the cerebral cortex that is the site of the highest intellectual functions, such as thinking and problem solving.

associative learning Learning that occurs when we make a connection, or an association, between two events.

Atkinson-Shiffrin theory Theory stating that memory storage involves three separate systems: sensory memory, short-term memory, and long-term memory.

attention deficit hyperactivity disorder (ADHD) One of the most common psychological disorders of childhood, in which individuals show one or more of the following: inattention, hyperactivity, and impulsivity.

attitudes Our opinions and beliefs about people, objects, and ideas—how we feel about our world.

attribution theory The view that people are motivated to discover the underlying causes of behavior as part of their effort to make sense of the behavior.

auditory nerve The nerve structure that receives information about sound from the hair cells of the inner ear and carries these neural impulses to the brain's auditory areas.

authoritarian parenting A restrictive, punitive style in which the parent exhorts the child to follow the parent's directions and to value hard work and effort.

authoritative parenting A parenting style that encourages the child to be independent but that still places limits and controls on behavior.

autobiographical memory A special form of episodic memory, consisting of a person's recollections of his or her life experiences.

automatic processes States of consciousness that require little attention and do not interfere with other ongoing activities. Automatic processes require less conscious effort than controlled processes.

autonomic nervous system The body system that takes messages to and from the body's internal organs, monitoring such processes as breathing, heart rate, and digestion.

availability heuristic A prediction about the probability of an event based on the ease of recalling or imagining similar events.

aversive conditioning A form of treatment that consists of repeated pairings of a stimulus with a very unpleasant stimulus.

axon The part of the neuron that carries information away from the cell body toward other cells.

B

barbiturates Depressant drugs that decrease central nervous system activity.

basal ganglia Large neuron clusters located above the thalamus and under the cerebral cortex that work with the cerebellum and the cerebral cortex to control and coordinate voluntary movements.

base rate fallacy The tendency to ignore information about general principles in favor of very specific but vivid information.

behavior Everything we do that can be directly observed.

behavioral approach An approach to psychology emphasizing the scientific study of observable behavioral responses and their environmental determinants.

behavioral genetics The study of the inherited underpinnings of behavioral characteristics.

behavioral medicine An interdisciplinary field that focuses on developing and integrating behavioral and biomedical knowledge to promote health and reduce illness; overlaps with and is sometimes indistinguishable from health psychology.

behaviorism A theory of learning that focuses solely on observable behaviors, discounting the importance of such mental activity as thinking, wishing, and hoping.

behavior therapies Treatments, based on the behavioral and social cognitive theories of learning and personality, that use principles of learning to reduce or eliminate maladaptive behavior.

big five factors of personality The five supertraits that are thought to describe the main dimensions of personality: neuroticism (emotional instability), extraversion, openness to experience, agreeableness, and conscientiousness.

binding In the sense of vision, the bringing together and integration of what is processed by different neural pathways or cells.

binge eating disorder (BED) Eating disorder characterized by recurrent episodes of eating large amounts of food during which the person feels a lack of control over eating.

binocular cues Depth cues that depend on the combination of the images in the left and right eyes and on the way the two eyes work together.

biological approach An approach to psychology focusing on the body, especially the brain and nervous system.

biological rhythms Periodic physiological fluctuations in the body, such as the rise and fall of hormones and accelerated and decelerated cycles of brain activity, that can influence behavior.

biological therapies (biomedical therapies) Treatments that reduce or eliminate the symptoms of psychological disorders by altering aspects of body functioning.

bipolar disorder Mood disorder characterized by extreme mood swings that include one or more episodes of mania, an overexcited, unrealistically optimistic state.

borderline personality disorder (BPD) Psychological disorder characterized by a pervasive pattern of instability in interpersonal relationships, self-image, and emotions, and of marked impulsivity beginning by early adulthood and present in a variety of contexts.

bottom-up processing The operation in sensation and perception in which sensory receptors register information about the external environment and send it up to the brain for interpretation.

brain stem The stemlike brain area that includes much of the hindbrain (excluding the cerebellum) and the midbrain; connects with the spinal cord at its lower end and then extends upward to encase the reticular formation in the midbrain.

broaden-and-build model Fredrickson's model of positive emotion, stating that the function of positive emotions lies in their effects on an individual's attention and ability to build resources.

bulimia nervosa Eating disorder in which an individual (typically a girl or woman) consistently follows a binge-and-purge eating pattern.

bystander effect The tendency for an individual who observes an emergency to help less when other people are present than when the observer is alone.

C

Cannon-Bard theory The proposition that emotion and physiological reactions occur simultaneously.

case study Also called a case history, an in-depth look at a single individual.

catatonia State of immobility and unresponsiveness, lasting for long periods of time.

cell body The part of the neuron that contains the nucleus, which directs the manufacture of substances that the neuron needs for growth and maintenance.

central nervous system (CNS) The brain and spinal cord.

cerebral cortex Part of the forebrain, the outer layer of the brain, responsible for the most complex mental functions, such as thinking and planning.

chromosomes In the human cell, threadlike structures that come in 23 pairs, one member of each pair originating from each parent, and that contain DNA.

circadian rhythm Daily behavioral or physiological cycles that involve the sleep/wake cycle, body temperature, blood pressure, and blood sugar level.

classical conditioning Learning process in which a neutral stimulus becomes associated with a meaningful stimulus and acquires the capacity to elicit a similar response.

client-centered therapy Also called Rogerian or nondirective therapy, a form of humanistic therapy, developed by Rogers, in which the therapist provides a warm, supportive atmosphere to improve the client's self-concept and to encourage the client to gain insight into problems.

cognition The way in which information is processed and manipulated in remembering, thinking, and knowing.

cognitive affective processing systems (CAPS) Mischel's theoretical model for describing that our thoughts and emotions about ourselves and the world affect our behavior and become linked in ways that matter to behavior.

cognitive appraisal An individual's interpretation of events as either harmful and threatening or challenging, and the person's determination of whether he or she has the resources to cope effectively with the events.

cognitive approach An approach to psychology emphasizing the mental processes involved in knowing: how we direct our attention, perceive, remember, think, and solve problems.

cognitive-behavior therapy A therapy that combines cognitive therapy and behavior therapy with the goal of developing self-efficacy.

cognitive dissonance An individual's psychological discomfort (dissonance) caused by two inconsistent thoughts.

cognitive theory of dreaming Theory proposing that we can understand dreaming by applying the same cognitive concepts we use in studying the waking mind.

cognitive therapies Treatments that emphasize that cognitions (thoughts) are the main source of psychological problems and that attempt to change the individual's feelings and behaviors by changing cognitions.

collective unconscious Jung's name for the impersonal, deepest layer of the unconscious mind, shared by all human beings because of their common ancestral past.

concept A mental category that is used to group objects, events, and characteristics.

concrete operational stage Piaget's third stage of cognitive development, lasting from about 7 to 11 years of age, during which the individual uses operations and replaces intuitive reasoning with logical reasoning in concrete situations.

conditioned response (CR) The learned response to the conditioned stimulus that occurs after a conditioned stimulus–unconditioned stimulus pairing.

conditioned stimulus (CS) A previously neutral stimulus that eventually elicits a conditioned response after being paired with the unconditioned stimulus.

conditions of worth The standards that the individual must live up to in order to receive positive regard from others.

cones The receptor cells in the retina that allow for color perception.

confederate A person who is given a role to play in a study so that the social context can be manipulated.

confirmation bias The tendency to search for and use information that supports our ideas rather than refutes them.

conformity A change in a person's behavior to coincide more closely with a group standard.

connectionism (parallel distributed processing: PDP) The theory that memory is stored throughout the brain in connections among neurons, several of which may work together to process a single memory.

consciousness An individual's awareness of external events and internal sensations under a condition of arousal, including awareness of the self and thoughts about one's experiences.

control group The participants in an experiment who are as much like the experimental group as possible and who are treated in every way like the experimental group except for a manipulated factor, the independent variable.

controlled processes The most alert states of human consciousness, during which individuals actively focus their efforts toward a goal.

convergence A binocular cue to depth and distance in which the muscle movements in our two eyes provide information about how deep and/or far away something is.

convergent thinking Thinking that produces the single best solution to a problem.

coping Problem solving that involves managing taxing circumstances, expending effort to solve life's problems, and seeking to master or reduce stress.

corpus callosum The large bundle of axons that connects the brain's two hemispheres, responsible for relaying information between the two sides.

correlational research Research that examines the relationships between variables, whose purpose is to examine whether and how two variables change together.

counterconditioning A classical conditioning procedure for changing the relationship between a conditioned stimulus and its conditioned response.

couples therapy Group therapy with married or unmarried couples whose major problem lies within their relationship.

creativity The ability to think about something in novel and unusual ways and to devise unconventional solutions to problems.

critical thinking The process of thinking deeply and actively, asking questions, and evaluating the evidence.

culture-fair tests Intelligence tests that are intended to be culturally unbiased.

D

decay theory Theory stating that when we learn something new, a neurochemical memory trace forms, but over time this trace disintegrates; suggests that the passage of time always increases forgetting.

decision making The mental activity of evaluating alternatives and choosing among them.

deductive reasoning Reasoning from a general case that is known to be true to a specific instance.

defense mechanisms Tactics the ego uses to reduce anxiety by unconsciously distorting reality.

deindividuation The reduction in personal identity and erosion of the sense of personal responsibility when one is part of a group.

delusions False, unusual, and sometimes magical beliefs that are not part of an individual's culture.

demand characteristics Any aspects of a study that communicate to the participants how the experimenter wants them to behave.

dendrites Treelike fibers projecting from a neuron, which receive information and orient it toward the neuron's cell body.

deoxyribonucleic acid (DNA) A complex molecule in the cell's chromosomes that carries genetic information.

dependent variable The outcome—the factor that can change in an experiment in response to changes in the independent variable.

depressants Psychoactive drugs that slow down mental and physical activity.

depressive disorders Mood disorders in which the individual suffers from depression—an unrelenting lack of pleasure in life.

depth perception The ability to perceive objects three-dimensionally.

development The pattern of continuity and change in human capabilities that occurs throughout life, involving both growth and decline.

diathesis-stress model View of schizophrenia emphasizing that a combination of biogenetic disposition and stress causes the disorder.

difference threshold The degree of difference that must exist between two stimuli before the difference is detected.

discrimination An unjustified negative or harmful action toward a member of a group simply because the person belongs to that group.

discrimination (classical conditioning) The process of learning to respond to certain stimuli and not others.

discrimination (operant conditioning) Responding appropriately to stimuli that signal that a behavior will or will not be reinforced.

display rules Sociocultural standards that determine when, where, and how emotions should be expressed.

dissociative amnesia Dissociative disorder characterized by extreme memory loss that is caused by extensive psychological stress.

dissociative disorders Psychological disorders that involve a sudden loss of memory or change in identity due to the dissociation (separation) of the individual's conscious awareness from previous memories and thoughts.

dissociative fugue Dissociative disorder in which the individual not only develops amnesia but also unexpectedly travels away from home.

dissociative identity disorder (DID) Formerly called multiple personality disorder, a dissociative disorder in which the individual has two or more distinct personalities or selves, each with its own memories, behaviors, and relationships.

divergent thinking Thinking that produces many solutions to the same problem.

divided consciousness view of hypnosis Hilgard's view that hypnosis involves a splitting of consciousness into two separate components, one of which follows the hypnotist's commands and the other of which acts as a "hidden observer."

dominant-recessive genes principle The principle that if one gene of a pair is dominant and one is recessive, the dominant gene overrides the recessive gene. A recessive gene exerts its influence only if both genes of a pair are recessive.

double-blind experiment An experimental design in which neither the experimenter nor the participants are aware of which participants are in the experimental group and which are in the control group until the results are calculated.

dream analysis A psychoanalytic technique for interpreting a person's dreams.

drive An aroused state that occurs because of a physiological need.

DSM-IV The *Diagnostic and Statistical Manual of Mental Disorders,* Fourth Edition; the major classification of psychological disorders in the United States.

dysthymic disorder (DD) Mood disorder that is generally more chronic and has fewer symptoms than major depressive disorder.

E

efferent nerves Also called motor nerves; nerves that carry information out of the brain and spinal cord to other areas of the body.

ego The Freudian structure of personality that deals with the demands of reality.

egoism Giving to another person to ensure reciprocity; to gain self-esteem; to present oneself as powerful, competent, or caring; or to avoid social and self-censure for failing to live up to society's expectations.

elaboration The number of different connections that are made around a stimulus at a given level of memory encoding.

elaboration likelihood model Theory identifying two ways to persuade: a central route and a peripheral route.

electroconvulsive therapy (ECT) Also called shock therapy, a treatment, commonly used for depression, that sets off a seizure in the brain.

emerging adulthood The transitional period from adolescence to adulthood, spanning approximately ages 18 to 25 years.

emotion-focused coping A coping strategy that involves responding to the stress that one is feeling—trying to manage one's emotional reaction—rather than focusing on the problem itself.

empathy A feeling of oneness with the emotional state of another person.

empirically keyed test A type of self-report test that presents a host of questionnaire items to two groups that are known to be different in some central way.

emotion Feeling, or affect, that can involve physiological arousal (such as a fast heartbeat), conscious experience (thinking about being in love with someone), and behavioral expression (a smile or grimace).

encoding The first step in memory; the process by which information gets into memory storage.

endocrine system The body system consisting of a set of glands that regulate the activities of certain organs by releasing their chemical products into the bloodstream.

episodic memory The retention of information about the where, when, and what of life's happenings—that is, how individuals remember life's episodes.

estrogens The class of sex hormones that predominate in females, produced mainly by the ovaries.

ethnocentrism The tendency to favor one's own ethnic group over other groups.

evolutionary approach An approach to psychology centered on evolutionary ideas such as adaptation, reproduction, and natural selection as the basis for explaining specific human behaviors.

exercise Structured activities whose goal is to improve health.

experiment A carefully regulated procedure in which the researcher manipulates one or more variables that are believed to influence some other variable.

experimental group The participants in an experiment who receive the drug or other treatment under study—that is, those who are exposed to the change that the independent variable represents.

experimenter bias The influence of the experimenter's expectations on the outcome of research.

explicit memory (declarative memory) The conscious recollection of information, such as specific facts or events and, at least in humans, information that can be verbally communicated.

external validity The degree to which an experimental design actually reflects the real-world issues it is supposed to address.

extinction (classical conditioning) The weakening of the conditioned response when the unconditioned stimulus is absent.

extinction (operant conditioning) Decreases in the frequency of a behavior when the behavior is no longer reinforced.

extrinsic motivation Motivation that involves external incentives such as rewards and punishments.

F

face validity The quality of seeming, on the surface, to fit a particular trait in question.

facial feedback hypothesis The idea that facial expressions can influence emotions as well as reflect them.

false consensus effect Observers' overestimation of the degree to which everybody else thinks or acts the way they do.

family therapy Group therapy with family members.

feature detectors Neurons in the brain's visual system that respond to particular features of a stimulus.

figure-ground relationship The principle by which we organize the perceptual field into stimuli that stand out (*figure*) and those that are left over (*ground*).

fixation Using a prior strategy and failing to look at a problem from a fresh, new perspective.

flashbulb memory The memory of emotionally significant events that people often recall with more accuracy and vivid imagery than everyday events.

flat affect The display of little or no emotion—a common negative symptom of schizophrenia.

forebrain The brain's largest division and its most forward part.

formal operational stage Piaget's fourth stage of cognitive development, which begins at age 11 to 15 and continues through adulthood; it features thinking about things that are not concrete, making predictions, and using logic to come up with hypotheses about the future.

free association A psychoanalytic technique that involves encouraging individuals to say aloud whatever comes to mind, no matter how trivial or embarrassing.

frequency theory Theory on how the inner ear registers the frequency of sound, stating that the perception of a sound's frequency depends on how often the auditory nerve fires.

frontal lobes The portion of the cerebral cortex behind the forehead, involved in personality, intelligence, and the control of voluntary muscles.

functional fixedness Failing to solve a problem as a result of fixation on a thing's usual functions.

functionalism James's approach to mental processes, emphasizing the functions and purposes of the mind and behavior in the individual's adaptation to the environment.

fundamental attribution error Observers' overestimation of the importance of internal traits and underestimation of the importance of external situations when they seek explanations of an actor's behavior.

G

gender roles Roles that reflect the individual's expectations for how females and males should think, act, and feel.

general adaptation syndrome (GAS) Selye's term for the common effects of demands on the body, consisting of three stages: alarm, resistance, and exhaustion.

generalization (classical conditioning) The tendency of a new stimulus that is similar to the original conditioned stimulus to elicit a response that is similar to the conditioned response.

generalization (operant conditioning) Performing a reinforced behavior in a different situation.

generalized anxiety disorder Psychological disorder marked by persistent anxiety for at least 6 months, and in which the individual is unable to specify the reasons for the anxiety.

genes The units of hereditary information, consisting of short segments of chromosomes composed of DNA.

genotype A person's genetic heritage; his or her actual genetic material.

gestalt psychology A school of thought interested in how people naturally organize their perceptions according to certain patterns.

gifted Possessing high intelligence (an IQ of 130 or higher) and/or superior talent in a particular area.

glands Organs or tissues in the body that create chemicals that control many of our bodily functions.

glial cells Cells in the nervous system that provide support, nutritional benefits, and other functions and keep neurons running smoothly.

group polarization effect The solidification and further strengthening of an individual's position as a consequence of a group discussion.

group therapy A sociocultural approach to the treatment of psychological disorders that brings together individuals who share a particular psychological disorder in sessions that are typically led by a mental health professional.

groupthink The impaired group decision making that occurs when making the right decision is less important than maintaining group harmony.

H

habituation Decreased responsiveness to a stimulus after repeated presentations.

hallucinations Sensory experiences that occur in the absence of real stimuli.

hallucinogens Psychoactive drugs that modify a person's perceptual experiences and produce visual images that are not real.

hardiness A trait characterized by a sense of commitment rather than alienation and of control rather than powerlessness, and a perception of problems as challenges rather than threats.

health behaviors Practices that have an impact on physical well-being.

health psychology A subfield of psychology that emphasizes psychology's role in establishing and maintaining health and preventing and treating illness.

heritability The proportion of observable differences in a group that can be explained by differences in the genes of the group's members.

heuristics Shortcut strategies or guidelines that suggest a solution to a problem but do not guarantee an answer.

hierarchy of needs Maslow's theory that human needs must be satisfied in the following sequence: physiological needs, safety, love and belongingness, esteem, and self-actualization.

hindbrain Located at the skull's rear, the lowest portion of the brain, consisting of the medulla, cerebellum, and pons.

hindsight bias The tendency to report falsely, after the fact, that we accurately predicted an outcome.

hippocampus The structure in the limbic system that has a special role in the storage of memories.

homeostasis The body's tendency to maintain an equilibrium, or steady state.

hormones Chemical messengers that are produced by the endocrine glands and carried by the bloodstream to all parts of the body.

humanistic approach An approach to psychology emphasizing a person's positive qualities, the capacity for positive growth, and the freedom to choose any destiny.

humanistic perspectives Theoretical views stressing a person's capacity for personal growth and positive human qualities.

humanistic therapies Treatments, unique in their emphasis on people's self-healing capacities, that encourage clients to understand themselves and to grow personally.

human sexual response pattern According to Masters and Johnson, the characteristic sequence of physiological changes that humans experience during sexual activity, consisting of four phases: excitement, plateau, orgasm, and resolution.

hypnosis An altered state of consciousness or a psychological state of altered attention and expectation in which the individual is unusually receptive to suggestions.

hypothalamus A small forebrain structure, located just below the thalamus, that monitors three pleasurable activities—eating, drinking, and sex—as well as emotion, stress, and reward.

hypothesis An educated guess that derives logically from a theory; a prediction that can be tested.

I

id The part of the person that Freud called the "it," consisting of unconscious drives; the individual's reservoir of sexual energy.

identity versus identity confusion Erikson's fifth psychological stage, in which adolescents face the challenge of finding out who they are, what they are all about, and where they are going in life.

implementation intentions Specific strategies for dealing with the challenges of making a life change.

implicit memory (nondeclarative memory) Memory in which behavior is affected by prior experience without a conscious recollection of that experience.

independent variable A manipulated experimental factor, the variable that the experimenter changes to see what its effects are.

individual psychology Adler's view that people are motivated by purposes and goals and that perfection, not pleasure, is thus the key motivator in human life.

inductive reasoning Reasoning from specific observations to make generalizations.

infant attachment The close emotional bond between an infant and its caregiver.

infinite generativity The ability of language to produce an endless number of meaningful sentences.

informational social influence The influence other people have on us because we want to be right.

inner ear The part of the ear that includes the oval window, cochlea, and basilar membrane and whose function is to convert sound waves into neural impulses and send them to the brain.

insight learning A form of problem solving in which the organism develops a sudden insight into or understanding of a problem's solution.

instinct An innate (unlearned) biological pattern of behavior that is assumed to be universal throughout a species.

instinctive drift The tendency of animals to revert to instinctive behavior that interferes with learning.

integrative therapy A combination of techniques from different therapies based on the therapist's judgment of which particular methods will provide the greatest benefit for the client.

intelligence All-purpose ability to do well on cognitive tasks, to solve problems, and to learn from experience.

intelligence quotient (IQ) An individual's mental age divided by chronological age multiplied by 100.

interference theory The theory that people forget not because memories are lost from storage but because other information gets in the way of what they want to remember.

internal validity The degree to which changes in the dependent variable are due to the manipulation of the independent variable.

interpretation A psychoanalyst's search for symbolic, hidden meanings in what the client says and does during therapy.

intrinsic motivation Motivation based on internal factors such as organismic needs (competence, relatedness, and autonomy), as well as curiosity, challenge, and fun.

investment model A model of long-term relationships that examines the ways that commitment, investment, and the availability of attractive alternative partners predict satisfaction and stability in relationships.

J

James-Lange theory The theory that emotion results from physiological states triggered by stimuli in the environment.

K

kinesthetic senses Senses that provide information about movement, posture, and orientation.

L

language A form of communication, whether spoken, written, or signed, that is based on a system of symbols.

latent content According to Freud, a dream's hidden content; its unconscious and true meaning.

latent learning (implicit learning) Unreinforced learning that is not immediately reflected in behavior.

law of effect Thorndike's law stating that behaviors followed by positive outcomes are strengthened and that behaviors followed by negative outcomes are weakened.

learned helplessness An individual's acquisition of feelings of powerlessness when he or she is exposed to aversive circumstances, such as prolonged stress, over which that individual has no control.

learning A systematic, relatively permanent change in behavior that occurs through experience.

levels of processing A continuum of memory processing from shallow to intermediate to deep, with deeper processing producing better memory.

limbic system A loosely connected network of structures under the cerebral cortex, important in both memory and emotion. Its two principal structures are the amygdala and the hippocampus.

lithium The lightest of the solid elements in the periodic table of elements, widely used to treat bipolar disorder.

longitudinal design A special kind of systematic observation, used by correlational researchers, that involves obtaining measures of the variables of interest in multiple waves over time.

long-term memory A relatively permanent type of memory that stores huge amounts of information for a long time.

M

major depressive disorder (MDD) Psychological disorder involving a major depressive episode and depressed characteristics, such as lethargy and hopelessness, for at least two weeks.

manifest content According to Freud, the surface content of a dream, containing dream symbols that disguise the dream's true meaning.

medical model The view that psychological disorders are medical diseases with a biological origin.

memory The retention of information or experience over time as the result of three key processes: encoding, storage, and retrieval.

mental age (MA) An individual's level of mental development relative to that of others.

mental processes The thoughts, feelings, and motives that each of us experiences privately but that cannot be observed directly.

mental retardation (intellectual disability) A condition of limited mental ability in which an individual has a low IQ, usually below 70 on a traditional intelligence test, and has difficulty adapting to everyday life.

mere exposure effect The phenomenon that the more we encounter someone or something, the more likely we are to start liking the person or thing even if we do not realize we have seen it before.

midbrain Located between the hindbrain and forebrain, an area in which many nerve-fiber systems ascend and descend to connect the higher and lower portions of the brain; in particular, the midbrain relays information between the brain and the eyes and ears.

middle ear The part of the ear that channels sound through the eardrum, hammer, anvil, and stirrup to the inner ear.

mindfulness The state of being alert and mentally present for one's everyday activities.

Minnesota Multiphasic Personality Inventory (MMPI) The most widely used and researched empirically keyed self-report personality test.

monocular cues Powerful depth cues available from the image in one eye, either the right or the left.

mood disorders Psychological disorders—the main types of which are depressive disorders and bipolar disorder—in which there is a primary disturbance of mood: prolonged emotion that colors the individual's entire emotional state.

morphology A language's rules for word formation.

motivated forgetting Forgetting that occurs when something is so painful or anxiety laden that remembering it is intolerable.

motivation The force that moves people to behave, think, and feel the way they do.

motor cortex A region in the cerebral cortex that processes information about voluntary movement, located just behind the frontal lobes.

myelin sheath A layer of fat cells that encases and insulates most axons.

N

naturalistic observation The observation of behavior in a real-world setting.

natural selection Darwin's principle of an evolutionary process in which organisms that are best adapted to their environment will survive and produce offspring.

nature An individual's biological inheritance, especially his or her genes.

need A deprivation that energizes the drive to eliminate or reduce the deprivation.

negative affect Negative emotions such as anger, guilt, and sadness.

negative punishment The removal of a positive stimulus following a given behavior in order to decrease the frequency of that behavior.

negative reinforcement The removal of an unpleasant stimulus following a given behavior in order to increase the frequency of that behavior.

neglectful parenting A parenting style characterized by a lack of parental involvement in the child's life.

neocortex The outermost part of the cerebral cortex, making up 80 percent of the human brain's cortex.

nervous system The body's electrochemical communication circuitry.

neural networks Networks of nerve cells that integrate sensory input and motor output.

neurons One of two types of cells in the nervous system; neurons are the nerve cells that handle the information-processing function.

neuroscience The scientific study of the structure, function, development, genetics, and biochemistry of the nervous system, emphasizing that the brain and nervous system are central to understanding behavior, thought, and emotion.

neurotransmitters Chemical substances that are stored in very tiny sacs within the terminal buttons and involved in transmitting information across a synaptic gap to the next neuron.

noise Irrelevant and competing stimuli—not only sounds but also any distracting stimuli for our senses.

normal distribution A symmetrical, bell-shaped curve, with a majority of the scores falling in the middle of the possible range and few scores appearing toward the extremes of the range.

normative social influence The influence others have on us because we want them to like us.

nurture An individual's environmental and social experiences.

O

obedience Behavior that complies with the explicit demands of the individual in authority.

observational learning Learning that takes place when a person observes and imitates another's behavior.

obsessive-compulsive disorder (OCD) Anxiety disorder in which the individual has anxiety-provoking thoughts that will not go away and/or urges to perform repetitive, ritualistic behaviors to prevent or produce some future situation.

occipital lobes Structures located at the back of the head that respond to visual stimuli.

Oedipus complex According to Freud, a boy's intense desire to replace his father and enjoy the affections of his mother.

olfactory epithelium The lining the roof of the nasal cavity, containing a sheet of receptor cells for smell.

open-mindedness The state of being receptive to other ways of looking at things.

operant conditioning (instrumental conditioning) A form of associative learning in which the consequences of a behavior change the probability of the behavior's occurrence.

operational definition A definition that provides an objective description of how a variable is going to be measured and observed in a particular study.

opiates Opium and its derivatives; narcotic drugs that depress the central nervous system's activity and eliminate pain.

opponent-process theory Theory stating that cells in the visual system respond to complementary pairs of red-green and blue-yellow colors; a given cell might be excited by red and inhibited by green, whereas another cell might be excited by yellow and inhibited by blue.

optic nerve The structure at the back of the eye, made up of axons of the ganglion cells, that carries visual information to the brain for further processing.

outer ear The outermost part of the ear, consisting of the pinna and the external auditory canal.

ovaries Sex-related endocrine glands in the uterus that produce hormones related to women's sexual development and reproduction.

P

pain The sensation that warns us of damage to our bodies.

pancreas A dual-purpose gland under the stomach that performs both digestive and endocrine functions.

panic disorder Anxiety disorder in which the individual experiences recurrent, sudden onsets of intense apprehension or terror, often without warning and with no specific cause.

papillae Rounded bumps above the tongue's surface that contain the taste buds, the receptors for taste.

parallel processing The simultaneous distribution of information across different neural pathways.

parasympathetic nervous system The part of the autonomic nervous system that calms the body.

parietal lobes Structures at the top and toward the rear of the head that are involved in registering spatial location, attention, and motor control.

perception The process of organizing and interpreting sensory information so that it makes sense.

perceptual constancy The recognition that objects are constant and unchanging even though sensory input about them is changing.

perceptual set A predisposition or readiness to perceive something in a particular way.

peripheral nervous system (PNS) The network of nerves that connects the brain and spinal cord to other parts of the body.

permissive parenting A parenting style characterized by the placement of few limits on the child's behavior.

personality A pattern of enduring, distinctive thoughts, emotions, and behaviors that characterize the way an individual adapts to the world.

personality disorders Chronic, maladaptive cognitive-behavioral patterns that are thoroughly integrated into an individual's personality.

personological and life story perspectives Theoretical views stressing that the way to understand the person is to focus on his or her life history and life story.

phenotype An individual's observable characteristics.

phobic disorder (phobia) Anxiety disorder characterized by an irrational, overwhelming, persistent fear of a particular object or situation.

phonology A language's sound system.

physical dependence The physiological need for a drug that causes unpleasant withdrawal symptoms such as physical pain and a craving for the drug when it is discontinued.

pituitary gland A pea-sized gland just beneath the hypothalamus that controls growth and regulates other glands.

placebo In a drug study, a harmless substance that has no physiological effect, given to participants in a control group so that they are treated identically to the experimental group except for the active agent.

placebo effect The situation where participants' expectations, rather than the experimental treatment, produce an experimental outcome.

place theory Theory on how the inner ear registers the frequency of sound, stating that each frequency produces vibrations at a particular spot on the basilar membrane.

plasticity The brain's special capacity for change.

polygraph A machine, commonly called a lie detector, that monitors changes in the body, used to try to determine whether someone is lying.

population The entire group about which the investigator wants to draw conclusions.

positive affect Positive emotions such as joy, happiness, and interest.

positive illusions Favorable views of the self that are not necessarily rooted in reality.

positive punishment The presentation of an unpleasant stimulus following a given behavior in order to decrease the frequency of that behavior.

positive reinforcement The presentation of a rewarding stimulus following a given behavior in order to increase the frequency of that behavior.

post-traumatic stress disorder (PTSD) Anxiety disorder that develops through exposure to a traumatic event, a severely oppressive situation, cruel abuse, or a natural or an unnatural disaster.

pragmatics The useful character of language and the ability of language to communicate even more meaning than is said.

preferential looking A research technique that involves giving an infant a choice of what object to look at.

prejudice An unjustified negative attitude toward an individual based on the individual's membership in a group.

preoperational stage Piaget's second stage of cognitive development, lasting from about 2 to 7 years of age, during which thought is more symbolic than sensorimotor thought.

preparedness The species-specific biological predisposition to learn in certain ways but not others.

primary reinforcer A reinforcer that is innately satisfying; one that does not take any learning on the organism's part to make it pleasurable.

priming The activation of information that people already have in storage to help them remember new information better and faster.

proactive interference Situation in which material that was learned earlier disrupts the recall of material that was learned later.

problem-focused coping The cognitive strategy of squarely facing one's troubles and trying to solve them.

problem solving The mental process of finding an appropriate way to attain a goal when the goal is not readily available.

procedural memory Memory for skills.

projective test A personality assessment test that presents individuals with an ambiguous stimulus and asks them to describe it or tell a story about it—to project their own meaning onto the stimulus.

prosocial behavior Behavior that is intended to benefit other people.

prospective memory Remembering information about doing something in the future; includes memory for intentions.

prototype model A model emphasizing that when people evaluate whether a given item reflects a certain concept, they compare the item with the most typical item(s) in that category and look for a "family resemblance" with that item's properties.

psychoactive drugs Drugs that act on the nervous system to alter consciousness, modify perceptions, and change moods.

psychoanalysis Freud's therapeutic technique for analyzing an individual's unconscious thoughts.

psychodynamic approach An approach to psychology emphasizing unconscious thought, the conflict between biological drives (such as the drive for sex) and society's demands, and early childhood family experiences.

psychodynamic perspectives Theoretical views emphasizing that personality is primarily unconscious (beyond awareness).

psychodynamic therapies Treatments that stress the importance of the unconscious mind, extensive interpretation by the therapist, and the role of early childhood experiences in the development of an individual's problems.

psychological dependence The strong desire to repeat the use of a drug for emotional reasons, such as a feeling of well-being and reduction of stress.

psychology The scientific study of behavior and mental processes.

psychoneuroimmunology A new field of scientific inquiry that explores connections among psychological factors (such as attitudes and emotions), the nervous system, and the immune system.

psychosurgery A biological intervention, with irreversible effects, that involves removal or destruction of brain tissue to improve the individual's adjustment.

psychotherapy A nonmedical process that helps individuals with psychological disorders recognize and overcome their problems.

puberty A period of rapid skeletal and sexual maturation that occurs mainly in early adolescence.

punishment A consequence that decreases the likelihood that a behavior will occur.

R

random assignment Researchers' assignment of participants to groups by chance, to reduce the likelihood that an experiment's results will be due to preexisting differences between groups.

random sample A sample that gives every member of the population an equal chance of being selected.

rational-emotive behavior therapy (REBT) A therapy based on Ellis's assertion that individuals develop a psychological disorder because of irrational and self-defeating beliefs and whose goal is to get clients to eliminate these beliefs by rationally examining them.

reasoning The mental activity of transforming information to reach conclusions.

referential thinking Ascribing personal meaning to completely random events.

reflective speech A technique in which the therapist mirrors the client's own feelings back to the client.

reinforcement The process by which a rewarding stimulus or event (a reinforcer) following a particular behavior increases the probability that the behavior will happen again.

relapse A return to former unhealthy patterns.

reliability The extent to which a test yields a consistent, reproducible measure of performance.

REM (rapid eye movement) sleep An active stage of sleep during which dreaming occurs.

renewal The recovery of the conditioned response when the organism is placed in a novel context.

representativeness heuristic The tendency to make judgments about group membership based on physical appearances or the match between a person and one's stereotype of a group rather than on available base rate information.

research participant bias In an experiment, the influence of participants' expectations, and of their thoughts about how they should behave, on their behavior

resilience A person's ability to recover from or adapt to difficult times.

resistance Unconscious defense strategies on the part of a client that prevent the psychoanalyst from understanding the individual's problems.

resting potential The stable, negative charge of an inactive neuron.

reticular formation A system in the midbrain comprising a diffuse collection of neurons involved in stereotyped patterns of behavior such as walking, sleeping, and turning to attend to a sudden noise.

retina The multilayered light-sensitive surface in the eye that records electromagnetic energy and converts it to neural impulses for processing in the brain.

retrieval The memory process that occurs when information that was retained in memory comes out of storage.

retroactive interference Situation in which material that was learned later disrupts the retrieval of information that was learned earlier.

retrograde amnesia Memory loss for a segment of the past but not for new events.

retrospective memory Remembering information from the past.

risky shift The tendency for a group decision to be riskier than the average decision made by the individual group members.

rods The receptor cells in the retina that are sensitive to light but not very useful for color vision.

romantic love Love with strong components of sexuality and infatuation, often predominant in the early part of a love relationship; also called passionate love.

Rorschach inkblot test A famous projective test that uses an individual's perception of inkblots to determine his or her personality.

S

sample The subset of the population chosen by the investigator for study.

schedules of reinforcement Specific patterns that determine when a behavior will be reinforced.

schema A preexisting mental concept or framework that helps people to organize and interpret information. Schemas from prior encounters with the environment influence the way we encode, make inferences about, and retrieve information.

schizophrenia Severe psychological disorder characterized by highly disordered thought processes, referred to as psychotic because they are so far removed from reality.

science The use of systematic methods to observe the natural world, including human behavior, and to draw conclusions.

script A schema for an event, often containing information about physical features, people, and typical occurrences.

secondary reinforcer A reinforcer that acquires its positive value through an organism's experience; a secondary reinforcer is a learned or conditioned reinforcer.

secure attachment The ways that infants use their caregiver, usually their mother, as a secure base from which to explore the environment.

selective attention The act of focusing on a specific aspect of experience while ignoring others.

self-actualization The motivation to develop one's full potential as a human being—the highest and most elusive of Maslow's proposed needs.

self-determination theory Deci and Ryan's theory asserting that all humans have three basic, innate organismic needs: competence, relatedness, and autonomy.

self-efficacy The belief that one can master a situation and produce positive change.

self-perception theory Bem's theory on how behaviors influence attitudes, stating that individuals make inferences about their attitudes by perceiving their behavior.

self-regulation The process by which an organism effortfully controls behavior in order to pursue important objectives.

self-report test Also called an objective test or an inventory, a method of measuring personality characteristics that directly asks people whether specific items describe their personality traits.

self-serving bias The tendency to take credit for our successes and to deny responsibility for our failures.

semantic memory A person's knowledge about the world.

semantics The meaning of words and sentences in a particular language.

semicircular canals Three fluid-filled, circular tubes in the inner ear containing the sensory receptors that detect head motion caused when we tilt or move our heads and/or bodies.

sensation The process of receiving stimulus energies from the external environment and transforming those energies into neural energy.

sensorimotor stage Piaget's first stage of cognitive development, lasting from birth to about 2 years of age, during which infants construct an understanding of the world by coordinating sensory experiences with motor actions.

sensory adaptation A change in the responsiveness of the sensory system based on the average level of surrounding stimulation.

sensory memory Memory system that involves holding information from the world in its original sensory form for only an instant, not much longer than the brief time it is exposed to the visual, auditory, and other senses.

sensory receptors Specialized cells that detect stimulus information and transmit it to sensory (afferent) nerves and the brain.

serial position effect The tendency to recall the items at the beginning and end of a list more readily than those in the middle.

set point The weight maintained when the individual makes no effort to gain or lose weight.

sexual harassment Unwelcome behavior or conduct of a sexual nature that offends, humiliates, or intimidates another person.

sexually transmitted infection (STI) An infection that is contracted primarily through sexual activity—vaginal intercourse as well as oral-genital and anal-genital sex.

sexual orientation The direction of an individual's erotic interests, today viewed as a continuum from exclusive male–female relations to exclusive same-sex relations.

shaping Rewarding approximations of a desired behavior.

short-term memory Limited-capacity memory system in which information is usually retained for only as long as 30 seconds unless we use strategies to retain it longer.

social cognitive behavior view of hypnosis The perspective that hypnosis is a normal state in which the hypnotized person behaves the way he or she believes that a hypnotized person should behave.

social cognitive perspectives Theoretical views emphasizing conscious awareness, beliefs, expectations, and goals.

social comparison The process by which individuals evaluate their thoughts, feelings, behaviors, and abilities in relation to others.

social contagion Imitative behavior involving the spread of behavior, emotions, and ideas.

social exchange theory The view of social relationships as involving an exchange of goods, the objective of which is to minimize costs and maximize benefits.

social facilitation Improvement in an individual's performance because of the presence of others.

social identity The way we define ourselves in terms of our group membership.

social identity theory The view that our social identities are a crucial part of our self-image and a valuable source of positive feelings about ourselves.

social loafing Each person's tendency to exert less effort in a group because of reduced accountability for individual effort.

social psychology The study of how people think about, influence, and relate to other people.

social support Information and feedback from others indicating that one is loved and cared for, esteemed and valued, and included in a network of communication and mutual obligation.

sociocultural approach An approach to psychology that examines the ways in which social and cultural environments influence behavior.

somatic nervous system The body system consisting of the sensory nerves, whose function is to convey information from the skin and muscles to the central nervous system about conditions such as pain and temperature, and the motor nerves, whose function is to tell muscles what to do.

somatosensory cortex A region in the cerebral cortex that processes information about body sensations, located at the front of the parietal lobes.

spontaneous recovery The process in classical conditioning by which a conditioned response can recur after a time delay, without further conditioning.

stages of change model Theoretical model describing a five-step process by which individuals give up bad habits and adopt healthier lifestyles.

standardization The development of uniform procedures for administering and scoring a test and the creation of norms (performance standards) for the test.

stem cells Unique primitive cells that have the capacity to develop into most types of human cells.

stereotype A generalization about a group's characteristics that does not consider any variations from one individual to another.

stereotype threat An individual's fast-acting, self-fulfilling fear of being judged on the basis of a negative stereotype about his or her group.

stimulants Psychoactive drugs, including caffeine, nicotine, amphetamines, and cocaine, that increase the central nervous system's activity.

storage The retention of information over time and how this information is represented in memory.

stream of consciousness Term used by William James to describe the mind as a continuous flow of changing sensations, images, thoughts, and feelings.

stress The response of individuals to environmental stressors—circumstances and events that threaten them and tax their coping abilities.

stress management program A regimen that teaches individuals how to appraise stressful events, how to develop skills for coping with stress, and how to put these skills into use in everyday life.

stressors Circumstances and events that threaten individuals and tax their coping abilities and that cause physiological changes to ready the body to handle the assault of stress.

structuralism Wundt's approach to discovering the basic elements, or structures, of mental processes.

subgoaling The process of setting intermediate goals or defining intermediate problems that put us in a better position for reaching the final goal or solution.

subjective well-being A person's assessment of his or her own level of positive affect relative to negative affect, and an evaluation of his or her life in general.

subliminal perception The detection of information below the level of conscious awareness.

superego The Freudian structure of personality that serves as the harsh internal judge of our behavior; what we often call conscience.

suprachiasmatic nucleus (SCN) A small brain structure that uses input from the retina to synchronize its own rhythm with the daily cycle of light and dark; the body's way of monitoring the change from day to night.

sympathetic nervous system The part of the autonomic nervous system that arouses the body.

synapses Tiny spaces between neurons; the gaps between neurons are referred to as *synaptic gaps*.

syntax A language's rules for combining words to form acceptable phrases and sentences.

systematic desensitization A method of therapy that treats anxiety by teaching the client to associate deep relaxation with increasingly intense anxiety-producing situations.

T

temperament An individual's behavioral style and characteristic way of responding.

temporal lobes Structures in the cerebral cortex that are located just above the ears and are involved in hearing, language processing, and memory.

testes Sex-related endocrine glands in the scrotum that produce hormones related to men's sexual development and reproduction.

thalamus The forebrain structure that sits at the top of the brain stem in the brain's central core and serves as an important relay station.

Thematic Apperception Test (TAT) A projective test that is designed to elicit stories that reveal something about an individual's personality.

theory A broad idea or set of closely related ideas that attempts to explain observations and to make predictions about future observations.

theory of planned behavior Theoretical model that includes the basic ideas of the theory of reasoned action but adds the person's perceptions of control over the outcome.

theory of reasoned action Theoretical model stating that effective change requires individuals to have specific intentions about their behaviors, as well as positive attitudes about a new behavior, and to perceive that their social group looks positively on the new behavior as well.

therapeutic alliance The relationship between the therapist and client—an important element of successful psychotherapy.

thermoreceptors Sensory nerve endings under the skin that respond to changes in temperature at or near the skin and provide input to keep the body's temperature at 98.6 degrees Fahrenheit.

thinking The mental process of manipulating information mentally by forming concepts, solving problems, making decisions, and reflecting critically or creatively.

third variable problem The circumstance where a variable that has not been measured accounts for the relationship between two other variables.

tip-of-the-tongue (TOT) phenomenon Effortful retrieval that occurs when we are confident that we know something but cannot pull it out of memory.

tolerance The need to take increasing amounts of a drug to get the same effect.

top-down processing The operation in sensation and perception, launched by cognitive processing at the brain's higher levels, that allows the organism to sense what is happening and to apply that framework to information from the world.

trait theories Theoretical views stressing that personality consists of broad, enduring dispositions (traits) that tend to lead to characteristic responses.

tranquilizers Depressant drugs that reduce anxiety and induce relaxation.

transference A client's relating to the psychoanalyst in ways that reproduce or relive important relationships in the individual's life.

triarchic theory of intelligence Sternberg's theory that intelligence comes in three forms: analytical, creative, and practical.

trichromatic theory Theory stating that color perception is produced by three types of cone receptors in the retina that are particularly sensitive to different, but overlapping, ranges of wavelengths.

two-factor theory of emotion Schachter and Singer's theory that emotion is determined by two factors: physiological arousal and cognitive labeling.

Type A behavior pattern A cluster of characteristics— including being excessively competitive, hard-driven, impatient, and hostile—that are related to a higher incidence of heart disease.

Type B behavior pattern A cluster of characteristics— including being relaxed and easygoing—that are related to a lower incidence of heart disease.

U

unconditional positive regard Rogers's construct referring to the individual's need to be accepted, valued, and treated positively regardless of his or her behavior.

unconditioned response (UCR) An unlearned reaction that is automatically elicited by the unconditioned stimulus.

unconditioned stimulus (UCS) A stimulus that produces a response without prior learning.

unconscious thought According to Freud, a reservoir of unacceptable wishes, feelings, and thoughts that are beyond conscious awareness.

V

validity The soundness of the conclusions that a researcher draws from an experiment. In the realm of testing, the extent to which a test measures what it is intended to measure.

variable Anything that can change.

vestibular sense Sense that provides information about balance and movement.

volley principle Modification of frequency theory stating that a cluster of nerve cells can fire neural impulses in rapid succession, producing a volley of impulses.

W

Weber's law The principle that two stimuli must differ by a constant minimum percentage (rather than a constant amount) to be perceived as different.

well-being therapy (WBT) A short-term, problem-focused, directive therapy that encourages clients to accentuate the positive.

wisdom Expert knowledge about the practical aspects of life.

working memory A three-part system that allows us to hold information temporarily as we perform cognitive tasks; a kind of mental workbench on which the brain manipulates and assembles information to help us understand, make decisions, and solve problems.

Y

Yerkes-Dodson law The psychological principle stating that performance is best under conditions of moderate arousal rather than either low or high arousal.

references

A

Aalsma, M. C., Lapsley, D. K., & Flannery, D. J. (2006). Personal fables, narcissism, and adolescent adjustment. *Psychology in the Schools, 43,* 481–491.

Abbey, A., Parkhill, M. R., Buck, P. O., & Saenz, C. (2007). Condom use with a casual partner: What distinguishes college students' use when intoxicated? *Psychology of Addictive Behaviors, 21,* 76–83.

ABC/AOL. (2006, January 2). ABC News/AOL poll finds losing weight tops New Year's resolutions. American Online Press Release.

Abraham, A., & Windmann, S. (2007). Creative cognition: The diverse operations and the prospect of applying a cognitive neuroscience perspective. *Methods, 42,* 38–48.

Abramowitz, J. S. (2009). *Getting over OCD.* New York: Guilford.

Abrams, D., & Hogg, M. A. (2004). Metatheory: Lessons from social identity research. In A. W. Kruglanski & E. T. Higgins (Eds.), *Theory construction in social-personality psychology.* Mahwah, NJ: Erlbaum.

Abrams, L., & Rodriguez, E. L. (2005). Syntactic class influences phonological priming of tip-of-the-tongue resolution. *Psychonomic Bulletin & Review, 12* (6), 1018–1023.

Abramson, L. Y., Seligman, M. E. P., & Teasdale, J. (1978). Learned helplessness in humans: Critique and reformulation. *Journal of Abnormal Psychology, 87,* 49–74.

Accardi, M. C., & Milling, L. S. (2009). The effectiveness of hypnosis for reducing procedure-related pain in children and adolescents: A comprehensive methodological review. *Journal of Behavioral Medicine, 32,* 328–339.

Addington, J., el-Guebaly, N., Campbell, W., Hodgkins, D. C., & Addington, D. (1998). Smoking cessation treatment for patients with schizophrenia. *American Journal of Psychiatry, 155,* 974–976.

Addis, D. R., Pan, L., Vu, M. A., Laiser, N., & Schacter, D. L. (2009). Constructive episodic simulation of the future and the past: Distinct core brain network mediate imagining and remembering. *Neuropsychologia.* (in press)

Ader, R. (1974). Letter to the editor: Behaviorally conditioned immunosuppression. *Psychosomatic Medicine, 36,* 183–184.

Ader, R. (2000). On the development of psychoneuroimmunology. *European Journal of Pharmacology, 405,* 167–176.

Ader, R., & Cohen, N. (1975). Behaviorally conditioned immunosuppression. *Psychosomatic Medicine, 37,* 333–340.

Ader, R., & Cohen, N. (2000). Conditioning and immunity. In R. Ader, D. L. Felton, & N. Cohen (Eds.), *Psychoneuroimmunology* (3rd ed.). San Diego: Academic.

Ades, P. A., & others. (2009). High-calorie-expenditure exercise: A new approach to cardiac rehabilitation for overweight coronary patients. *Circulation, 119,* 2671–2678.

Adler, A. (1927). *The theory and practice of individual psychology.* Fort Worth: Harcourt Brace.

Adler, N. E., & Stewart, J. (2009). Reducing obesity: Motivating action while not blaming the victim. *Milbank Quarterly, 87,* 49–70.

Adolph, K. E. (2008). Motor and physical development. In M. M. Haith & J. B. Benson (Eds.), *Encyclopedia of infant and early childhood development.* Oxford, England: Elsevier.

Adolph, K. E., & Joh, A. S. (2009). Multiple learning mechanisms in the development of action. In A. Needham & A. Woodward (Eds.), *Learning and the infant mind.* New York: Oxford University Press.

Adolph, K. E., Joh, A. S., Franchak, J. M., Ishak, S., & Gill, S. V. (2009). Flexibility in the development of action. In J. Bargh, P. Gollwitzer, & E. Morsella (Eds.), *Oxford handbook of human action.* New York: Oxford University Press.

Agatonovic-Kustrin, S., Davies, P., & Turner, J. V. (2009). Structure-activity relationships for serotonin transporter and dopamine receptor selectivity. *Medicinal Chemistry, 5,* 271–278.

Aggen, S. H., Neale, M. C., Roysamb, E., Reichborn-Kjennerud, T., & Kendler, K. S. (2009). A psychometric evaluation of the DSM-IV borderline personality disorder criteria: Age and sex moderation of criterion functioning. *Psychological Medicine.* (in press)

Agresti, A., & Finlay, B. (2009). *Statistical methods for the social sciences* (4th ed.). Upper Saddle River, NJ: Prentice-Hall.

Ahmadi, J., Kampman, K. M., Oslin, D. M., Pettinati, H. M., Dackis, C., & Sparkman, T. (2009). Predictors of treatment outcome in outpatient cocaine and alcohol dependency treatment. *American Journal of Addiction, 18,* 81–86.

Ahn, S., & Phillips, A. G. (2007). Dopamine efflux in the nucleus accumbens during within-session extinction, outcome-dependent, and habit-based instrumental responding for food reward. *Psychopharmacology, 191,* 641–651.

Aiken, L. R., & Groth-Marnat, G. (2006). *Psychological testing and assessment* (12th ed.). Boston: Allyn & Bacon.

Aimone, J. B., Wiles, J., & Gage, F. H. (2009). Computational influence of adult neurogenesis on memory encoding. *Neuron, 61,* 187–202.

Ainsworth, M. D. S. (1979). Infant–mother attachment. *American Psychologist, 34,* 932–937.

Ainsworth, M. S., Blehar, M. C., Waters, E., & Wall, S. (1978). *Patterns of attachment: A psychological study of the strange situation.* Oxford, England: Erlbaum.

Ajzen, I. (2001). Nature and operation of attitudes. *Annual Review of Psychology* (vol. 52). Palo Alto, CA: Annual Reviews.

Ajzen, I. (2002). Perceived behavioral control, self-efficacy, locus of control, and the theory of planned behavior. *Journal of Applied Social Psychology, 32,* 665–683.

Ajzen, I., & Albarracin, D. (2007). Predicting and changing behavior: A reasoned action approach. In I. Ajzen, D. Albarracin, & R. Hornik (Eds.), *Prediction and change in health behavior.* Mahwah, NJ: Erlbaum.

Ajzen, I., & Fishbein, M. (1980). *Understanding attitudes and predicting social behavior.* Englewood Cliffs, NJ: Prentice-Hall.

Ajzen, I., & Fishbein, M. (2005). The influence of attitudes on behavior. In D. Albarracin, B. T. Johnson, & M. P. Zanna (Eds.), *The handbook of attitudes* (pp. 173–221). Mahwah, NJ: Erlbaum.

Ajzen, I., & Manstead, A. S. R. (2007). Changing health-related behaviours: An approach based on the theory of planned behaviour. In M. Hewstone, H. Schut, J. de Wit, K. van den Bos, & M. S. Stroebe (Eds.), *The scope of social psychology: Theory and applications* (pp. 43–63). New York: Psychology Press.

Akhtar, S. (2006). Technical challenges faced by the immigrant psychoanalyst. *Psychoanalytic Quarterly, 75,* 21–43.

Al-Alem, L., & Omar, H. A. (2008). Borderline personality: An overview of history, diagnosis, and treatment in adolescents. *International Journal of Adolescent Medicine, 20,* 395–404.

Albarracin, D., Durantini, M. R., & Earl, A. (2006). Empirical and theoretical conclusions of an analysis of outcomes of HIV-prevention interventions. *Current Directions in Psychological Science, 15,* 73–78.

Albarracin, D., Durantini, M. R., Earl, A., Gunnoe, J., & Leeper, J. (2008). Beyond the most willing audiences: A meta-intervention to increase participation in HIV prevention intervention. *Health Psychology, 27,* 638–644.

Albarracin, D., Gillette, J. C., Earl, A. N., Glasman, L. R., Durantini, M. R., & Ho, M. (2005). A test of major assumptions about behavior change: A comprehensive look at the effects of passive and active HIV-prevention interventions since the beginning of the epidemic. *Psychological Bulletin, 131,* 856–897.

Alberto, P. A., & Troutman, A. C. (2009). *Applied behavior analysis for teachers* (8th ed.). Upper Saddle River, NJ: Prentice-Hall.

Aldwin, C. M. (2007). *Stress, coping, and development* (2nd ed.). New York: Guilford.

Aldwin, C. M., Levenson, M. R., & Kelly, L. L. (2009). Lifespan developmental perspectives on stress-related growth. In C. L. Park, S. Lechner, A. Stanton, & M. Antoni (Eds.), *Positive life changes in the context of medical illness.* Washington, DC: APA Press.

Aldwin, C. M., Spiro, A., & Park, C. L. (2006). Health, behavior, and optimal aging. In J. E. Birren & K. W. Schaie (Eds.), *Handbook of the psychology of aging* (6th ed.). San Diego: Academic.

Aldwin, C. M., Yancura, L. A., & Boeninger, D. K. (2007). In C. M. Aldwin, C. L. Park, & A. Spiro (Eds.), *Handbook of health and aging.* New York: Guilford.

Alea, N., & Bluck, S. (2003). Why are you telling me that? A conceptual model of the social function of autobiographical memory. *Journal of Adult Development, 11,* 235–250.

Allan, K., Wolf, H. A., Rosenthal, C. R., & Rugg, M. D. (2001). The effects of retrieval cues on post-retrieval monitoring in episodic memory: An electrophysiological study. *Brain Research, 12,* 289–299.

Allen, J. J. B., Harmon-Jones, E., & Cavender, J. H. (2001). Manipulation of frontal EEG asymmetry through biofeedback alters self-reported emotional responses and facial EMG. *Psychophysiology, 38,* 685–693.

Allen, J. P., & Antonishak, J. (2008). Adolescent peer influences: Beyond the dark side. In M. J. Prinstein & K. A. Dodge (Eds.), *Understanding peer influence in childhood and adolescence.* New York: Guilford.

Allport, G. W. (1961). *Pattern and growth in personality.* New York: Holt, Rinehart & Winston.

Allport, G. W., & Odbert, H. (1936). Trait-names: A psycho-lexical study. No. 211. Princeton, NJ: Psychological Review Monographs.

Altemus, M. (2006). Sex differences in depression and anxiety disorders: Potential biological determinants. *Hormones and Behavior, 50,* 534–538.

Alvino, C., Kohlber, C., Barrett, F., Gur, R. E., Gur, R. C., & Verma, R. (2007). Computerized measurement of facial expression of emotions in schizophrenia. *Journal of Neuroscience Methods, 163,* 350–361.

Alyahri, A., & Goodman, R. (2008). Harsh corporal punishment of Yemeni children: Occurrence, type, and associations. *Child Abuse and Neglect, 32,* 766–773.

Amato, P. R. (2006). Marital discord, divorce, and children's well-being: Results from a 20-year longitudinal study of two generations. In A. Clarke-Stewart & J. Dunn (Eds.), *Families count.* New York: Cambridge University Press.

American Academy of Ophthalmology. (2003). *Use of marijuana to treat glaucoma.* San Francisco: Author.

American Association on Mental Retardation, Ad Hoc Committee on Terminology and Classification. (1992). *Mental retardation* (9th ed.). Washington, DC: Author.

American Cancer Society. (2009). *Information and resources for cancer.* www.cancer.org/ (accessed February 17, 2009)

American Psychiatric Association. (1994). *Diagnostic and statistical manual of mental disorders* (4th ed.). Washington, DC: Author.

American Psychiatric Association. (2000). *Diagnostic and statistical manual of mental disorders* (4th ed., text revision). Washington, DC: Author.

American Psychiatric Association. (2001). *Mental illness.* Washington, DC: Author.

American Psychiatric Association. (2005). *Let's talk about eating disorders.* Arlington, VA: Author.

American Psychiatric Association. (2006). *American Psychiatric Association practice guidelines for the treatment of psychiatric disorders.* Washington, DC: Author.

American Psychological Association. (1995). *Questions and answers about memories of child abuse.* Washington, DC: Author.

American Psychological Association. (2004, July 28). *APA supports legalization of same-sex civil marriages and opposes discrimination against lesbian and gay parents: Denying same-sex couples legal access to civil marriage is discriminatory and can adversely affect the psychological, physical, social, and economic well-being of gay and lesbian individuals.* Washington DC: Author.

American Sleep Apnea Association (ASAA). (2006). *Get the facts about sleep apnea.* Washington, DC: Author.

"Americans spent billions on toys." (2006). http://www.ksmu.org/content/view/3118/75/ (accessed March 6, 2009)

Amodio, D. M., & Devine, P. G. (2006). Stereotyping and evaluation in implicit race bias: Evidence for independent constructs and unique effects on behavior. *Journal of Personality and Social Psychology, 91,* 652–661.

Amunts, K., Schlaug, G., Jancke, L., Steinmetz, H., Schleicher, A., Dabringhaus, A., & Zilles, K. (1997). Motor cortex and hand motor skills: Structural compliance in the human brain. *Human Brain Mapping, 5* (3), 206–215.

Anastasi, A., & Urbina, S. (1996). *Psychological testing* (7th ed.). Upper Saddle River, NJ: Prentice-Hall.

Andel, R., Crowe, M., Pedersen, N. L., Mortimer, J., Crimmins, E., Johansson, B., & Gatz, M. (2005). Complexity of work and risk of Alzheimer's disease: A population-based study of Swedish twins. *Journals of Gerontology: Series B: Psychological Sciences and Social Sciences, 60B,* 251–258.

Anderson, B. A., Golden-Kreutz, D. M., & DiLillo, V. (2001). Cancer. In A. Baum, T. A. Revenson, & J. E. Singer (Eds.), *Handbook of health psychology.* Mahwah, NJ: Erlbaum.

Anderson, C., & Huesmann, L. R. (2007). Human aggression. In M. A. Hogg & J. Cooper (Eds.), *The Sage handbook of social psychology* (concise 2nd ed.). Thousand Oaks, CA: Sage.

Anderson, C., & Kilduff, G. J. (2009). Why do dominant personalities attain influence in face-to-face groups? The competence-signaling effects of trait dominance. *Journal of Personality and Social Psychology, 96,* 491–503.

Anderson, C. A. (2003). Video games and aggressive behavior. In D. Ravitch and J. P. Viteritti (Eds.), *Kid*

stuff: Marketing sex and violence to America's children* (pp. 143–167). Baltimore: Johns Hopkins University Press.

Anderson, C. A., Benjamin, A. J., Jr., & Bartholow, B. D. (1998). Does the gun pull the trigger? Automatic priming effects of weapon pictures and weapon names. *Psychological Science, 9,* 308–314.

Anderson, C. A., & Bushman, B. J. (2002). Human aggression. *Annual Review of Psychology* (vol. 53). Palo Alto, CA: Annual Reviews.

Anderson, C. A., Gentile, D. A., & Buckley, K. E. (2007). *Violent video game effects on children and adolescents: Theory, research, and public policy.* New York: Oxford University Press.

Anderson, E. M., & Lambert, M. J. (2001). A survival analysis of clinically significant change in outpatient psychotherapy. *Journal of Clinical Psychology, 57,* 875–888.

Anderson, J. W. (2005). The psychobiographical study of psychologists. In W. T. Schultz (Ed.), *Handbook of psychobiography* (pp. 203–210). Oxford, England: Oxford University Press.

Anderson, N. H. (1965). Primacy effects in personality impression formation using a generalized order effect paradigm. *Journal of Personality and Social Psychology, 2,* 1–9.

Andersson, G., Carlbring, P., Holmstrom, A., Sparthan, E., Furmark, T., Nilsson-Ihrfelt, E., Buhrman, M., & Ekselius, L. (2006). Internet-based self-help with therapist feedback and in vivo group exposure for social phobia: A randomized controlled trial. *Journal of Consulting and Clinical Psychology, 74,* 677–686.

Ang, S., & van Dyne, L. (Eds.). (2009). *Handbook on cultural intelligence.* New York: M. E. Sharpe.

Annesi, J. J. (2007). Relations of changes in exercise self-efficacy, physical self-concept, and body satisfaction with weight changes in obese white and African American women initiating a physical activity program. *Ethnicity and Disease, 17,* 19–22.

Arden, M., & Armitage, C. J. (2008). Predicting and explaining transtheoretical model stage transitions in relation to condom-carrying behaviour. *British Journal of Health Psychology, 13,* 719–735.

Arendt, J. (2009). Managing jet lag: Some of the problems and possible new solutions. *Sleep Medicine Reviews.* (in press).

Arias, A. J., Steinberg, K., Banga, A., & Trestman, R. L. (2006). Systematic review of the efficacy of meditation techniques as treatments for medical illness. *Journal of Alternative and Complementary Medicine, 12,* 817–832.

Armaiz-Pena, G. N., Lutgendorf, S. K., Cole, S. W., & Sood, A. K. (2009). Neuroendocrine modulation of cancer progression. *Brain, Behavior, and Immunity, 23,* 10–15.

Armitage, C. J. (2006). Evidence that implementation intentions promote transitions between the stages of change. *Journal of Consulting and Clinical Psychology, 74,* 141–151.

Armor, D. A., Massey, C., & Sackett, A. M. (2008). Prescribed optimism. *Psychological Science, 19,* 329–331.

Arnett, J. J. (2004). *Emerging adulthood.* New York: Oxford University Press.

Arnett, J. J. (2006). Emerging adulthood: Understanding the new way of coming of age. In J. J. Arnett & J. L. Tanner (Eds.), *Emerging adults in America.* Washington, DC: American Psychological Association.

Arnett, J. J. (2007). Socialization in emerging adulthood. In J. E. Grusec & P. D. Hastings (Eds.), *Handbook of socialization.* New York: Oxford University Press.

Arntz, A. (2005). Cognition and emotion in borderline personality disorder. *Journal of Behavior Therapy and Experimental Psychiatry, 36,* 167–172.

Arrow, H. (2007). The sharp end of altruism. *Science, 318,* 581–582.

Artazcoz, L., Cortes, I., Escriba-Aguir, V., Cascant, L., & Villegas, R. (2009). Understanding the relationship of long working hours with health status and health-related behaviors. *Journal of Epidemiology and Community Health, 63,* 521–527.

Arvey, R. D., Rotundo, M., Johnson, W., Zhang, Z., & McGue, M. (2006). The determinants of leadership role occupancy: Genetic and personality factors. *Leadership Quarterly, 17* (1), 1–20.

Arvey, R. D., Zhang, Z., Avolio, B. J., & Krueger, R. F. (2007). Developmental and genetic determinants of leadership role occupancy among women. *Journal of Applied Psychology, 92* (3), 693–706.

Asch, S. E. (1951). Effects of group pressure on the modification and distortion of judgments. In H. S. Guetzkow (Ed.), *Groups, leadership, and men.* Pittsburgh: Carnegie University Press.

Asghar-Ali, A., & Braun, U. K. (2009). Depression in geriatric patients. *Minerva Medica, 100,* 105–113.

Ash, M., & Sturm, T. (Eds.). (2007). *Psychology's territories.* Mahwah, NJ: Erlbaum.

Ashcraft, M. H., & Radvansky, G. (2009). *Cognition* (5th ed.). Upper Saddle River, NJ: Prentice-Hall.

Asher, S. R., & McDonald, K. L. (2009). Friendship in childhood and adolescence. In B. McGraw, P. L. Peterson, & E. Baker (Eds.), *International encyclopedia of education* (3rd ed.). Amsterdam: Elsevier. (in press)

Ashton, M. C., & Kibeom, L. (2008). The HEXACO model of personality structure and the importance of the H factor. *Social and Personality Psychology Compass, 2,* 1952–1962.

Aslin, R. N., & Lathrop, A. L. (2008). Visual perception. In M. M. Haith & J. B. Benson (Eds.), *Encyclopedia of infant and early childhood development.* Oxford, England: Elsevier.

Aspinwall, L. G. (1998). Rethinking the role of positive affect in self-regulation. *Motivation and Emotion, 22,* 1–32.

Aspinwall, L. G., & Brunhart, S. M. (1996). Distinguishing optimism from denial: Optimistic beliefs predict attention to health threats. *Personality and Social Psychology Bulletin, 22,* 993–1003.

Aspinwall, L. G., Leaf, S. L., & Leachman, S. A. (2009). Meaning and agency in the context of genetic testing for familial cancer. To appear in P. T. P. Wong (Ed.), *The human quest for meaning* (2nd ed.). Hillsdale, NJ: Erlbaum.

Assor, A., Roth, G., & Deci, E. L. (2004). The emotional costs of parents' conditional regard: A self-determination theory analysis. *Journal of Personality, 72,* 47–88.

Atkinson, R. C., & Shiffrin, R. M. (1968). Human memory: A proposed system and its control processes. In K. W. Spence & J. T. Spence (Eds.), *The psychology of learning and motivation* (vol. 2). San Diego: Academic.

Atmaca, M., Yildirim, H., Ozdemir, H. N., Ozler, S., Kara, B., Ozler, Z., Kanmaz, E., Mermi, O., & Tezcan, E. (2008). Hippocampus and amygdalar volumes in patients with refractory obsessive-compulsive disorder. *Progress in Neuro-Psychopharmacology & Biological Psychiatry, 32,* 1283–1286.

Aton, S. J., Seibt, J., Dumoulin, M., Steinmetz, N., Coleman, T., Naidoo, N., & Frank, M. G. (2009). Mechanisms of sleep-dependent consolidation of cortical plasticity. *Neuron, 61,* 454–466.

Aucoin, K. J., Frick, P. J., & Bodin, S. D. (2006). Corporal punishment and child adjustment. *Journal of Applied Developmental Psychology, 27,* 527–541.

Augoustinos, M., Walker, I., & Donaghue, N. (2006). *Social cognition.* Thousand Oaks, CA: Sage.

Austad, C. S. (2009). *Counseling and psychotherapy today.* New York: McGraw-Hill.

Austin, D. W., & Richards, J. C. (2006). A test of core assumptions of the catastrophic misinterpretation model of panic disorder. *Cognitive Therapy and Research, 30,* 53–68.

Avner, J. R. (2006). Altered states of consciousness. *Pediatric Review, 27,* 331–338.

Avolio, B. J., Walumbwa, F. O., & Weber, T. J. (2009). Leadership: Current theories, research, and future directions. *Annual Review of Psychology, 60,* 421–449.

Azboy, O., & Kaygisiz, Z. (2009). Effects of sleep deprivation on cardiorespiratory functions of the runners and volleyball players during rest and exercise. *Acta Physiologica Hungarica, 96,* 29–36.

B

Babiloni, C., Vecchio, F., Cappa, S., Pasqualetti, P., Rossi, S., Miniussi, C., & Rossini, P. M. (2006). Functional frontoparietal connectivity during encoding and retrieval processes follows HERA model: A high resolution study. *Brain Research Bulletin, 68,* 203–212.

Baddeley, A. (1993). Working memory and conscious awareness. In A. F. Collins, S. E. Gatherhole, M. A. Conway, & P. E. Morris (Eds.), *Theories of memory.* Mahwah, NJ: Erlbaum.

Baddeley, A. (1998). *Human memory* (rev. ed.). Boston: Allyn & Bacon.

Baddeley, A. (2001). *Is working memory still working?* Paper presented at the meeting of the American Psychological Association, San Francisco.

Baddeley, A. (2003). Working memory and language: An overview. *Journal of Communication Disorders, 36,* 189–208.

Baddeley, A. D. (2001). Is working memory still working? *American Psychologist, 56,* 851–864.

Baddeley, A. D. (2003). Working memory: Looking back and looking forward. *Nature Reviews: Neuroscience, 4,* 829–839.

Baddeley, A. D. (2006). Working memory: An overview. In S. Pickering (Ed.), *Working memory and education.* San Diego: Academic.

Baddeley, A. D. (2007). *Working memory, thought, and action.* New York: Oxford University Press.

Baddeley, A. D. (2008). What's new in working memory? *Psychological Review, 13,* 2–5.

Baddeley, J. L., & Singer, J. A. (2008). Telling losses: Personality correlates and functions of bereavement narratives. *Journal of Research in Personality, 42,* 421–438.

Badler, J. B., & Heinen, S. J. (2006). Anticipatory movement timing using prediction and external cues. *Journal of Neuroscience, 26,* 4519–4525.

Bagemihl, B. (1999). *Biological exuberance: Animal homosexuality and natural diversity.* New York: St. Martin's Press.

Bagnara, D., & others. (2009). Adoptive immunotherapy mediated by ex vivo expanded natural killer T cells against CD1d-expressing lymphoid neoplasms. *Haematologica.* (in press)

Bahrick, H. P. (1984). Semantic memory content in permastore: Fifty years of memory for Spanish learned in school. *Journal of Experimental Psychology: General, 113,* 1–29.

Bahrick, H. P. (2000). Long-term maintenance of knowledge. In E. Tulving & F. I. M. Craik (Eds.), *The Oxford handbook of memory* (pp. 347–362). New York: Oxford University Press.

Bahrick, H. P., Bahrick, P. O., & Wittlinger, R. P. (1974). Long-term memory: Those unforgettable high-school days. *Psychology Today, 8,* 50–56.

Baillargeon, R. (1997). The object concept revisited. In C. E. Granrud (Ed.), *Visual perception and cognition in infancy.* Mahwah, NJ: Erlbaum.

Baillargeon, R., Wu, D., Yan, S., Li, J., & Luo, Y. (2009). Young infants' expectations about self-propelled objects. In B. Hood & L. Santos (Eds.), *The origins of object knowledge.* New York: Oxford University Press.

Baker, C. K., Norris, F. H., Jones, E. C., & Murphy, A. D. (2009). Childhood trauma and adult physical health in Mexico. *Journal of Behavioral Medicine, 32,* 255–269.

Baker, L. A., Raine, A., Liu, J., & Jacobson, K. C. (2008). Differential genetic and environmental influences on reactive and proactive aggression in children. *Journal of Abnormal Child Psychology, 36,* 1265–1278.

Balaguer-Ballester, E., Clark, N. R., Krumbholz, K., & Denham, S. L. (2009). Understanding pitch perception as a hierarchical proces with top-down modulation. *PLoS Computational Biology, 5,* e1000301.

Bandura, A. (1986). *Social foundations of thought and action.* Englewood Cliffs, NJ: Prentice-Hall.

Bandura, A. (1997). *Self-efficacy.* New York: Freeman.

Bandura, A. (2001). Social cognitive theory. *Annual Review of Psychology* (vol. 52). Palo Alto, CA: Annual Reviews.

Bandura, A. (2006a). Going global with social cognitive theory: From prospect to paydirt. In D. E. Berger & K. Pezdek (Eds.), *The rise of applied psychology: New frontiers and rewarding careers.* Mahwah, NJ: Erlbaum.

Bandura, A. (2006b). Toward a psychology of human agency. *Perspectives on Psychological Science, 1,* 164–180.

Bandura, A. (2007a). Self-efficacy in health functioning. In S. Ayers & others (Eds.), *Cambridge handbook of psychology, health, and medicine.* New York: Cambridge University Press.

Bandura, A. (2007b). Social cognitive theory. In W. Donsbach (Ed.), *International handbook of communication.* Thousand Oaks, CA: Sage.

Bandura, A. (2008). Reconstrual of "free will" from the agentic perspective of social cognitive theory. In J. Baer, J. C. Kaufman, & R. F. Baumeister (Eds.), *Are we free? Psychology and free will.* Oxford, England: Oxford University Press.

Bandura, A. (2009). Social and policy impact of social cognitive theory. In M. Mark, S. Donaldson, & B. Campbell (Eds.), *Social psychology and program/policy evaluation.* New York: Guilford.

Banks, J. A. (2008). *Introduction to multicultural education* (4th ed.). Boston: Allyn & Bacon.

Banks, S. J., Eddy, K. T., Angstadt, M., Nathan, P. J., & Phan, K. L. (2007). Amygdala-frontal connectivity during emotion regulation. *Social Cognitive and Affective Neuroscience, 2,* 303–312.

Banyard, V. L., & Williams, L. M. (2007). Women's voices on recovery: A multi-method study of the complexity of recovery from child sexual abuse. *Child Abuse and Neglect, 31,* 275–290.

Bar, M., Neta, M., & Linz, H. (2006). Very first impressions. *Emotion, 6,* 269–278.

Barber, N. (2009). Evolutionary social science: A new approach to violent crime. *Aggression and Violent Behavior, 13,* 237–250.

Bard, P. (1934). Emotion. In C. Murchison (Ed.), *Handbook of general psychology.* Worcester, MA: Clark University Press.

Bardone-Cone, A. M., Abramson, L. Y., Vohs, K. D., Heatherton, T. F., & Joiner, T. E., Jr. (2006). Predicting bulimic symptoms: An interactive model of self-efficacy, perfectionism, and perceived weight status. *Behaviour Research and Therapy, 44,* 27–42.

Bardone-Cone, A. M., & Cass, K. M. (2006). Investigating the impact of pro-anorexia websites: A pilot study. *European Eating Disorders Review, 14,* 256–262.

Bargh, J. A. (2005). Bypassing the will: Towards demystifying the nonconscious control of social behavior. In R. Hassin, J. Uleman, & J. Bargh (Eds.), *The new unconscious.* New York: Oxford University Press.

Bargh, J. A., Chen, M., & Burrows, L. (1996). The automaticity of social behavior: Direct effects of trait concept and stereotype activation on action. *Journal of Personality and Social Psychology, 71,* 230–244.

Bargh, J. A., Gollwitzer, P. M., Lee-Chai, A., Barndollar, K., & Trotschel, R. (2001). The automated will: Nonconscious activation and pursuit of behavioral goals. *Journal of Personality and Social Psychology, 81,* 1014–1027.

Bargh, J. A., & McKenna, K. Y. A. (2004). The Internet and social life. *Annual Review of Psychology* (vol. 55). Palo Alto, CA: Annual Reviews.

Bargh, J. A., & Morsella, E. (2009). Unconscious behavioral guidance systems. In C. Agnew & others (Eds.), *Then a miracle occurs: Focusing on behavior and social psychological theory and research.* New York: Oxford University Press. (in press)

Barkley, R., & 74 others. (2002). International consensus statement on ADHD. *Clinical Child and Family Psychology, 5,* 89–111.

Barloon, T., & Noyes, R., Jr. (1997). Charles Darwin and panic disorder. *Journal of the American Medical Association, 277,* 138–141.

Barlow, D. H. (1988). *Anxiety and its disorders: The nature and treatment of anxiety and panic.* New York: Guilford.

Barnett, J. H., & Smoller, J. W. (2009). The genetics of bipolar disorder. *Neuroscience.* (in press)

Baron-Cohen, S. (1995). *Mindblindness: An essay on autism and theory of mind.* Cambridge, MA: MIT Press.

Baron-Cohen, S. (2002). The extreme male brain theory of autism. *Trends in Cognitive Science, 6,* 248–254.

Baron-Cohen, S. (2003). *The essential difference: Men, women, and the extreme male brain.* New York: Basic Books.

Baron-Cohen, S. (2006). The hyper-systemizing, assortative mating theory of autism. *Progress in Neuro-Psychopharmacology & Biological Psychiatry, 30,* 865–872.

Baron-Cohen, S. (2008). Autism, hypersystemizing, and the truth. *Quarterly Journal of Experimental Psychology, 61,* 64–75.

Baron-Cohen, S., Knickmeyer, R. C., & Belmonte, M. K. (2006). Sex differences in the brain: Implications for explaining autism. *Science, 311,* 952.

Barrouillet, P., & Camos, V. (2009). Interference: Unique source of forgetting in working memory. *Trends in Cognitive Science, 13,* 145–146.

Bartolo, A., Benuzzi, F., Nocetti, L., Baraldi, P., & Nichelli, P. (2006). Humor comprehension and appreciation: An fMRI study. *Journal of Cognitive Neuroscience, 18,* 1789–1798.

Bartoshuk, L. (2008). Chemical senses: Taste and smell. *Annual Review of Psychology* (vol. 59). Palo Alto, CA: Annual Reviews.

Bastien, C. H., St-Jean, G., Turcotte, I., Morin, C. M., Lavallee, M., & Carrier, J. (2009). Sleep spindles in chronic psychophysiological insomnia. *Journal of Psychosomatic Research, 66,* 59–65.

Bates, J. E., & Pettit, G. S. (2007). Temperament, parenting, and socialization. In J. E. Grusec & P. D. Hastings (Eds.), *Handbook of socialization.* New York: Oxford University Press.

Batson, C. D. (2002). Addressing the altruism question experimentally. In S. G. Post, L. G. Underwood, J. P. Schloss, & W. B. Hurlbut (Eds.), *Altruism and altruistic love.* New York: Oxford University Press.

Batson, C. D. (2003). Altruism and prosocial behavior. In I. B. Weiner (Ed.), *Handbook of Psychology* (vol. 5). New York: Wiley.

Batson, C. D. (2006). "Not all self-interest after all": Economics of empathy-induced altruism. In D. DeCremer, M. Zeelenberg, & J. K. Murnigham (Eds.), *Social psychology and economics* (pp. 281–299). Mahwah, NJ: Erlbaum.

Batson, C. D., Duncan, B. D., Ackerman, P., Buckley, T., Birch, K., Cialdini, R. B., Schaller, M., Houlihan, D., Arps, K., Fultz, J., & Beaman, A. L. (2007). Issue 17: Does true altruism exist? In J. A. Nier (Ed.), *Taking sides: Clashing views in social psychology* (2nd ed., pp. 348–371). New York: McGraw-Hill.

Battaglia, M., Pesenti-Gritti, P., Medland, S. E., Ogilari, A., Tambs, K., & Spatola, C. A. (2009). A genetically informed study of the association between childhood separation anxiety, sensitivity to CO(2), panic disorder, and the effect of childhood parental loss. *Archives of General Psychiatry, 66,* 64–71.

Bauer, J. J., McAdams, D. P., & Sakaeda, A. R. (2005). The crystallization of desire and the crystallization of discontent in narratives of life-changing decisions. *Journal of Personality, 73,* 1181–1213.

Bauer, M., & others. (2007). Using ultrasonography to determine thyroid size and prevalence of goiter in lithium-treated patients with affective disorders. *Journal of Affective Disorders, 104* (1–3), 45–51.

Bauer, M. E., Jeckel, C. M., & Luz, C. (2009). The role of stress factors during aging of the immune system. *Annals of the New York Academy of Sciences, 1153,* 139–152.

Bauer, P. (2009). Learning and memory: Like a horse and carriage. In A. Needham & A. Woodward (Eds.), *Learning and the infant mind.* New York: Oxford University Press.

Bauer, P. J. (2007). *Remembering the times of our lives.* Mahwah, NJ: Erlbaum.

Bauld, R., & Brown, R. F. (2009). Stress, psychological stress, psychosocial factors, menopause symptoms, and physical health in women. *Maturitas, 62,* 160–165.

Baumann, A. E. (2007). Stigmatization, social distance and exclusion because of mental illness: The individual with mental illness as a "stranger." *International Review of Psychiatry, 19,* 131–135.

Baumeister, R. F. (1999). *Evil: Inside human violence and cruelty.* New York: Freeman.

Baumeister, R. F. (2000). Gender differences in erotic plasticity: The female sex drive as socially flexible and responsive. *Psychological Bulletin, 126* (3), 347–374.

Baumeister, R. F., & Alquist, J. L. (2009). Self-regulation as limited resource: Strength model of control and depletion. In J. P. Forgas, R. F. Baumeister, & D. M. Tice (Eds.), *Psychology of self-regulation.* New York: Psychology Press.

Baumeister, R. F., Bushman, B. J., & Campbell, W. K. (2000). Self-esteem, narcissism, and aggression: Does violence result from low self-esteem or from threatened egotism? *Current Directions in Psychological Science, 9,* 26–29.

Baumeister, R. F., & Butz, D. A. (2005). Roots of hate, violence, and evil. In R. J. Sternberg (Ed.), *The psychology of hate* (pp. 87–102). Washington, DC: American Psychological Association.

Baumeister, R. F., Campbell, J. D., Krueger, J. I., Vohs, K. D., DuBois, D. L., & Tevendale, H. D. (2007). Issue 5: Applying social psychology: Are self-esteem programs misguided? In J. A. Nier (Ed.), *Taking sides: Clashing views in social psychology* (2nd ed., pp. 92–115). New York: McGraw-Hill.

Baumeister, R. F., Catanese, K. R., & Vohs, K. D. (2001). Is there a gender difference in strength of sex drive? *Personality and Social Psychology Review, 5,* 242–273.

Baumeister, R. F., & Leary, M. R. (2000). The need to belong: Desire for interpersonal attachments as a fundamental human motivation. In E. T. Higgins & A. W. Kruglanski (Eds.), *Motivational science: Social and personality perspectives* (pp. 24–49). New York: Psychology Press.

Baumeister, R. F., & Stillman, T. (2006). Erotic plasticity: Nature, culture, gender, and sexuality. In R. D. McAnulty & M. M. Burnette (Eds.), *Sex and sexuality: Sexuality today: Trends and controversies* (vol. 1, pp. 343–359, 377). Westport, CT: Praeger/Greenwood.

Baumrind, D. (1991). Parenting styles and adolescent development. In J. Brooks-Gunn, R. Lerner, & A. C. Petersen (Eds.), *The encyclopedia of adolescence* (vol. 2). New York: Garland.

Baumrind, D. (1993). The average expectable environment is not good enough: A response to Scarr. *Child Development, 64,* 1299–1307.

Baumrind, D., Larzelere, R. E., & Cowan, P. A. (2002). Ordinary physical punishment: Is it harmful? Comment on Gershoff (2002). *Psychological Bulletin, 128,* 590–595.

Bauerlein, M. (2008). *The dumbest generation.* New York: Tarcher.

Baxter, L. R., Jr., Phelps, M. E., Mazziotta, J. C., Schwartz, J. M., Gerner, R. H., Selin, C. E., & Sumida, R. M. (1995). Cerebral metabolic rates for glucose in mood disorders: Studies with positron emission tomography and fluorodeoxyglucose F 18. *Archives of General Psychiatry, 42,* 441–447.

Baylor, D. (2001). *Seeing, hearing, and smelling the world* [Commentary]. http://www.hhmi.org/senses (accessed October 2001)

BBC News. (2004, June 21). Creative side unlocked by stroke. http://news.bbc.co.uk/2/hi/health/3826857.stm (accessed July 25, 2006)

BBC News. (2005, July 5). Japanese breaks *pi* record. http://news.bbc.co.uk/2/hi/asia-pacific/4644103.stm (accessed October 10, 2006)

Beauchamp, M. S., Laconte, S., & Yasar, N. (2009). Distributed representation of single touches in somatosensory and visual cortex. *Human Brain Mapping.* (in press)

Beck, A. (1967). *Depression.* New York: Harper & Row.

Beck, A. T. (1976). *Cognitive therapies and the emotional disorders.* New York: International Universities Press.

Beck, A. T. (1993). Cognitive therapy: Past, present, and future. *Journal of Consulting and Clinical Psychology, 61,* 194–198.

Beck, A. T. (2005). The current state of cognitive therapy: A 40-year retrospective. *Archives of General Psychiatry, 62,* 953–959.

Beck, A. T. (2006). How an anomalous finding led to a new system of psychotherapy. *Nature Medicine, 12,* 1139–1141.

Beck, A. T., Rush, A. J., Shaw, B. F., & Emery, G. (1979). *Cognitive therapy of depression.* New York: Guilford.

Beckers, T., Miller, R. R., De Houwer, J., & Urushihara, K. (2006). Reasoning rats: Forward blocking in Pavlovian animal conditioning is sensitive to constraints of causal inference. *Journal of Experimental Psychology: General, 135,* 92–102.

Becker-Weidman, E. G., Reinecke, M. A., Jacobs, R. H., Martinovich, Z., Silva, S. G., & March, J. S. (2009). Predictors of hopelessness among clinically depressed youth. *Behavioral and Cognitive Psychotherapy.* (in press)

Beeli, G., Esslen, M., & Jancke, L. (2005). Synaesthesia: When coloured sounds taste sweet. *Nature, 434,* 38.

Beeson, M., Davison, I., Vostanis, P., & Windwo, S. (2006). Parenting programs for behavioral problems: Where do tertiary units fit in a comprehensive service? *Clinical Child Psychology and Psychiatry, 11,* 335–348.

Behrman, B. W., & Davey, S. L. (2001). Eyewitness identification in actual criminal cases: An archival analysis. *Law and Human Behavior, 25,* 475–491.

Beins, B. C. (2009). *Research methods* (2nd ed.). Upper Saddle River, NJ: Prentice-Hall.

Bekinschtein, T. A., Dehaene, S., Rohaut, B., Tadel, F., Cohen, L., & Naccache, L. (2009). Neural signature of the conscious processing of auditory regularites. *Proceedings of the National Academy of Sciences USA, 106,* 1672–1677.

Bellinger, D. L., Lubahn, C., & Lorton, D. (2008). Maternal and early life stress effects on immune function: Relevance to immunotoxicology. *Journal of Immunotoxicology, 5,* 419–444.

Bem, D. (1967). Self-perception: An alternative explanation of cognitive dissonance phenomena. *Psychological Review, 74,* 183–200.

Bender, H. L., Allen, J. P., McElhaney, K. B., Antonishak, J., Moore, C. M., Kello, H. O., & Davis, S. M. (2007). Use of harsh physical discipline and developmental outcomes in adolescence. *Development and Psychopathology, 19,* 227–242.

Benedetti, F., Pollo, A., Lopiano, L., Lanotte, M., Vighetti, S., and others. (2003). Conscious expectation and unconscious conditioning in analgesic; motor and hormonal placebo/nocebo responses. *Journal of Neuroscience, 23,* 4315–4323.

Benoit, R. G., Werkle-Bergner, M., Mecklinger, A., & Kray, J. (2009). Adapting to changing memory retrieval demands: Evidence from event-related potentials. *Brain and Cognition.* (in press)

Benoit-Bird, K. J., & Au, W. W. (2009). Phonation behavior of cooperatively foraging spinner dolphins. *Journal of the Acoustical Society of America, 125,* 539–546.

Benson, E. (2006). Toy stories. *Observer, 19* (12). http://ilabs.washington.edu/news/Toy_Stories_APS2006.pdf (accessed March 6, 2009)

Berdahl, J. L., & Acquino, K. (2009). Sexual behavior at work: Fun or folly? *Journal of Applied Psychology, 94,* 34–47.

Bereiter, C., & Scardamalia, M. (1993). *Surpassing ourselves: An inquiry into the nature and implications of expertise.* Chicago: Open Court.

Berenbaum, N. (2005). Four, two, or one? Gordon Allport and the unique personality. In W. T. Schultz (Ed.), *Handbook of psychobiography* (pp. 223–239). Oxford, England: Oxford University Press.

Berger, T., Hohl, E., & Caspar, F. (2009). Internet-based treatment for social phobia. *Journal of Clinical Psychology.* (in press)

Berko Gleason, J. (2009). The development of language: An overview. In J. Berko Gleason & N. Ratner (Eds.), *The development of language* (7th ed.). Boston: Allyn & Bacon.

Berkowitz, L. (1990). On the formation and regulation of anger and aggression: A cognitive neoassociationistic analysis. *American Psychologist, 45,* 494–503.

Berkowitz, L. (1993). *Aggression.* New York: McGraw-Hill.

Berkowitz, L., & LePage, A. (1996). Weapons as aggression-eliciting stimuli. In S. Fein & S. Spencer (Eds.), *Readings in social psychology: The art and science of research* (pp. 67–73). Boston: Houghton Mifflin.

Berlin, L. J., Cassidy, J., & Appleyard, K. (2008). The influence of early attachment on other relationships. In J. Cassidy & P. R. Shaver (Eds.), *Handbook of attachment* (2nd ed.). New York: Guilford.

Berlin, L. J., Zeanah, C. H., & Lieberman, A. F. (2008). Prevention and intervention programs for supporting early attachment. In J. Cassidy & P. R. Shaver (Eds.), *Handbook of attachment* (2nd ed.). New York: Guilford.

Bernstein, I. L., & Koh, M. T. (2007). Molecular signaling during taste aversion learning. *Chemical Senses, 32* (1), 99–103.

Berntsen, D., & Rubin, D. C. (2006). Flashbulb memories and posttraumatic stress reactions across the life span: Age-related effects of the German occupation of Denmark during World War II. *Psychology of Aging, 21,* 127–139.

Berridge, K. C., & Kringelbach, M. L. (2008). Affective neuroscience of pleasure: Reward in humans and animals. *Psychopharmacology, 199,* 457–480.

Berry, A. C., Rosenfeld, D., & Smits, J. A. (2009). Extinction retention predicts improvement in social anxiety symptoms following exposure therapy. *Depression and Anxiety, 26,* 22–27.

Berscheid, E. (1988). Some comments on love's anatomy. Or, whatever happened to an old-fashioned lust? In R. J. Sternberg & M. L. Barnes (Eds.), *Anatomy of love.* New Haven, CT: Yale University Press.

Berscheid, E. (2000). Attraction. In A. Kazdin (Ed.), *Encyclopedia of psychology.* Washington, DC, & New York: American Psychological Association and Oxford University Press.

Berscheid, E. (2006). Searching for the meaning of "love." In R. J. Sternberg & K. Weis (Eds.), *The new psychology of love* (pp. 171–183). New Haven, CT: Yale University Press.

Berscheid, E., & Regan, P. C. (2005). *The psychology of interpersonal relationships.* New York: Prentice-Hall.

Beste, C., Dziobek, I., Hielscher, H., Willemssen, R., & Falkenstein, M. (2009). Effects of stimulus-response compatibility on inhibitory processes in Parkinson's disease. *European Journal of Neuroscience, 29,* 855–860.

Beydoun, M. A., & Wang, Y. (2009). Gender-ethnic disparity in BMI and wait circumference distribution shifts in U.S. adults. *Obesity, 17,* 169–176.

Bhatia, T., Garg, K., Pogue-Geile, M., Nimaonkar, V. L., & Deshpande, S. N. (2009). Executive functions and cognitive deficits in schizophrenia: Comparisons between probands, parents, and controls in India. *Journal of Postgraduate Medicine, 55,* 3–7.

Bierman, K. L., Domitrovich, C. E., Nix, R. L., Gest, S. D., Welsh, J. A., Greenberg, M. T., Blair, C., Nelson, K. E., & Gill, S. (2008). Promoting academic and social-emotional school readiness: The Head Start REDI program. *Child Development, 79,* 1802–1817.

Birditt, K. S., & Fingerman, K. L. (2003). Age and gender differences in adults' descriptions of emotional reactions to interpersonal problems. *Journals of Gerontology: Series B: Psychological Sciences and Social Sciences, 58B,* 237–245.

Birren, J. E., & Schaie, K. W. (Eds.) (2007). *Encyclopedia of gerontology* (2nd ed.). Oxford, England: Elsevier.

Bisiacchi, P. S., Taratino, V., & Ciccola, A. (2008). Aging and prospective memory: The role of working memory and monitoring processes. *Aging: Clinical and Experimental Research, 20,* 569–577.

Biswas-Diener, R., Vitterso, J., & Diener, E. (2005). Most people are pretty happy, but there is cultural variation: The Inughuit, the Amish, and the Maasai. *Journal of Happiness Studies, 6,* 205–226.

Bjork, R. S., & Druckman, D. (1991). *In the mind's eye: Enhancing human performance.* Washington, DC: National Academy Books.

Bjorklund, D. F. (2007). *Why youth is not wasted on the young*. Malden, MA: Blackwell.

BKA. (2006). German federal crime statistics (German). http://www.bka.de/pks/pks2004/index2.html (accessed June 13, 2007)

Blader, J. C. (2006). Pharmacotherapy and postdischarge outcomes of child inpatients admitted for aggressive behavior. *Journal of Clinical Psychopharmacology, 26*, 419–425.

Blagrove, M., & Akehurst, L. (2000). Personality and dream recall frequency: Further negative findings. *Dreaming, 10*, 139–148.

Blair, S. N., Kohl, H. W., Paffenbarger, R. S., Clark, D. G., Cooper, K. H., & Gibbons, L. W. (1989). Physical fitness and all-cause mortality: A prospective study of healthy men and women. *Journal of the American Medical Association, 262*, 2395–2401.

Blake, R., & Sekuler, R. (2006). *Perception* (5th ed.). New York: McGraw-Hill.

Blakemore, J. E. O., Berenbaum, S. E., & Liben, L. S. (2009). *Gender development*. New York: Psychology Press.

Blanchette, I., Richards, A., Melnyk, L., & Lavda, A. (2007). Reasoning about emotional contents following shocking terrorist attacks: A tale of three cities. *Journal of Experimental Psychology: Applied, 13*, 47–56.

Blass, T. (2007). Unsupported allegations about a link between Milgram and the CIA: Tortured reasoning in *A Question of Torture. Journal of the History of the Behavioral Sciences, 43*, 199–203.

Block, J., & Kremen, A. M. (1996). IQ and ego-resiliency: Conceptual and empirical connections and separateness. *Journal of Personality and Social Psychology, 70*, 349–361.

Blonigen, D. M., Carlson, M. D., Hicks, B. M., Krueger, R. F., & Iacono, W. G. (2008). Stability and change in personality traits from late adolescence to early adulthood: A longitudinal twin study. *Journal of Personality, 76*, 229–266.

Blonna, R., & Paterson, W. (2007). *Coping with stress in a changing world* (4th ed.). New York: McGraw-Hill.

Bloom, B. (1985). *Developing talent in young people*. New York: Ballantine.

Bloom B., & Cohen, R. A. (2007). Summary health statistics for U.S. children: National Health Interview Survey, 2006. National Center for Health Statistics. *Vital Health Statistics, 10* (234).

Bloom, F., Nelson, C. A., & Lazerson, A. (2001). *Brain, mind, and behavior* (3rd ed.). New York: Worth.

Bloom, P. (2004). Myths of word learning. In D. G. Hall & S. R. Waxman (Eds), *Weaving a lexicon*. (pp. 205–224). Cambridge, MA: MIT Press.

Bloor, C., & White, F. (1983). Unpublished manuscript. LaJolla, CA: University of California, San Diego.

Bluher, S., & Mantzoros, C. S. (2009). Leptin in humans: Lessons from translational research. *American Journal of Clinical Nutrition, 89*, 991S–997S.

Blumenfeld, P. C., Kempler, T. M., & Krajcik, J. S. (2006). Motivation and cognitive engagement in learning environments. In R. K. Sawyer (Ed.), *The Cambridge handbook of learning sciences*. New York: Cambridge University Press.

Bob, P., & others. (2009). Depression, traumatic stress, and the individual. *Journal of Affective Disorders*. (in press)

Bocker, S., Briesemeister, S., & Klau, G. W. (2009). On optimal comparability editing with applications to molecular diagnostics. *BMC Bioinformatics, 10, Suppl. 1*, S61.

Boden, J. M., Fergusson, D. M., & Horwood, L. J. (2006, November). Anxiety disorders and suicidal behaviors in adolescence and young adulthood: Findings from a longitudinal study. *Psychological Medicine, 36*, 1–10.

Boden, J. M., Fergusson, D. M., & Horwood, L. J. (2007). Anxiety disorders and suicidal behaviours in adolescence and young adulthood: Findings from a longitudinal study. *Psychological Medicine, 37*, 431–440.

Boeninger, D. K., Shiraishi, R. W., Aldwin, C. M., & Spiro, A. (2009). Why do older men report lower stress ratings? Findings from the Normative Aging Study. *International Journal of Aging and Human Development, 2*, 149–170.

Bohannon, J. N., & Bonvillian, J. D. (2009). Theoretical approaches to language acquisition. In J. Berko Gleason & N. Ratner (Eds.), *The development of language* (7th ed.). Boston: Allyn & Bacon.

Bohni, M. K., Spindler, H., Arendt, M., Hougaard, E., & Rosenberg, N. K. (2009). A randomized study of massed three-week behavioral therapy schedule for panic disorder. *Acta Psychiatrica Scandinavica*. (in press)

Bonchek, A. (2009). What's broken with cognitive behavior therapy treatment of obsessive-compulsive disorder and how to fix it. *American Journal of Psychotherapy, 63*, 69–86.

Bonfatti, J. F. (2005). Hope holds the key: Finding inspiration. *Schizophrenia Digest*, (Summer), 31–34. www.schizophreniadigest.com

Bongers, K. C. A., & Dijksterhuis, A. (2009). Consciousness as a trouble shooting device? The role of consciousness in goal pursuit. In E. Morsella, J. A. Bargh, & P. Gollwitzer (Eds.), *The Oxford handbook of human action*. New York: Oxford University Press.

Bonnie, K. E., & de Waal, F. B. M. (2004). Primate social reciprocity and the origin of gratitude. In R. A. Emmons & M. E. McCullough (Eds.), *The psychology of gratitude* (pp. 213–229). Oxford, England: Oxford University Press.

Bono, G., McCullough, M. E., & Root, L. M. (2008). Forgiveness, feeling connected to others, and well-being: Two longitudinal studies. *Personality and Social Psychology Bulletin, 34*, 182–195.

Boodman, S. G. (2002, February 12). Beautiful but not rare recovery: John Nash's genius is extraordinary but recovery from schizophrenia is anything but. *Washington Post*.

Boothroyd, R. A., Best, K. A., Giard, J. A., Stiles, P. G., Suleski, J., Ort, R., & White, R. (2006). Poor and depressed, The tip of the iceberg: The unmet needs of enrollees in an indigent health care plan. *Administration and Policy in Mental Health and Mental Health Services Research, 33*, 172–181.

Borchardt, J. (2008, May 16). MU volunteers reach trauma victims worldwide. *Columbia Missourian*. http://www.Columbiamissourian.com/stories/2008/06/16/mu-volunteers-reach-trauma-victims-worldwide.htm (accessed April 15, 2009)

Borgs, L., Beukelaers, P., Vandenbosch, R., Belachew, S., Nguyen, L., & Malgrange, B. (2009). Cell "circadian" cycle: New role for mammalian core clock genes. *Cell Cycle, 8*, 832–837.

Bormann, J. E., Aschbacher, K., Wetherell, J. L., Roesch, S., & Redwine, L. (2008). Effects of faith/assurance on cortisol levels are enhanced by a spiritual mantram intervention in adults with HIV: A randomized trial. *Journal of Psychosomatic Research, 66*, 161–171.

Bornstein, M. (2006). Parenting science and practice. In W. Damon & R. Lerner (Eds.), *Handbook of child psychology* (6th ed.). New York: Wiley.

Boseley, S. (2006, June 12). Tough curbs on Prozac prescribed for children. *The Guardian*.

Bosson, J. K., & Swann, W. B. (2009). Self-esteem. In M. R. Leary & R. H. Hoyle (Eds.), *Handbook of individual differences in social behavior* (pp. 527–546). New York: Guilford.

Bouchard, T. J., & Loehlin, J. C. (2001). Genes, evolution, and personality. *Behavior Genetics, 31*, 243–273.

Bouchard, T. J., Lykken, D. T., Tellegen, A., & McGue, M. (1996). Genes, drives, environment, and experience. In D. Lubinski & C. Benbow (Eds.), *Psychometrics and social issues concerning intellectual talent*. Baltimore: Johns Hopkins University Press.

Bourne, V., & Todd, B. (2004, January). When left means right: An explanation of the left cradling bias in terms of right hemisphere specializations. *Developmental Science*.

Bowlby, J. (1969). *Attachment and loss* (vol. 1). London: Hogarth Press.

Bowlby, J. (1989). *Secure and insecure attachment*. New York: Basic Books.

Boyd, J. H. (2008). Have we found the holy grail? Theory of mind as a unifying concept. *Journal of Religion and Health, 47*, 366–385.

Boyle, G. J. (1995). Myers-Briggs Type Indicator (MBTI): Some psychometric limitations. *Australian psychologist, 30*, 71–74.

Bradley, S. J., Oliver, G. D., Chernick, A. B., & Zucker, K. J. (1998). Experiments of nurture: Ablatio penis at 2 months, sex reassignment at 7 months, and a psychosexual follow-up in young adulthood. *Pediatrics, 102*, e9.

Brady, S. S., & Halpern-Felsher, B. L. (2007). Adolescents' reported consequences of having oral sex versus vaginal sex. *Pediatrics, 119*, 229–236.

Brandstadter, J. (2006). Action perspectives in human development. In W. Damon & R. Lerner (Eds.), *Handbook of child psychology* (6th ed.). New York: Wiley.

Brannon, L. (1999). *Gender: Psychological perspectives* (2nd ed.). Boston: Allyn & Bacon.

Bransford, J., & others. (2006). Learning theories and education: Toward a decade of synergy. In P. A. Alexander & P. H. Winne (Eds.), *Handbook of educational psychology* (2nd ed.). Mahwah, NJ: Erlbaum.

Braunstein, G. D. (2007). Management of female sexual dysfunction in postmenopausal women by testosterone administration: Safety issues and controversies. *Journal of Sexual Medicine, 4*, 859–866.

Breer, H., Fleischer, J., & Strotmann, J. (2006). The sense of smell: Multiple olfactory subsystems. *Cellular and Molecular Life Sciences, 63*, 1465–1475.

Breland, K., & Breland, M. (1961). The misbehavior of organisms. *American Psychologist, 16*, 681–684.

Brendgen, M., Boivin, M., Vitaro, F., Bukowski, W. M., Dionne, G., Tremblay, R. E., & Perusse, D. (2008). Linkages between children's and their friends' social and physical aggression: Evidence for a gene-environment interaction? *Child Development, 79*, 13–29.

Breslau, N., & Alvarado, G. F. (2007). The clinical significance criterion in DSM-IV post-traumatic stress disorder. *Psychological Medicine, 37*, 1–8.

Bretherton, C. (2007). The social psychology of stereotyping, discrimination and prejudice. *Journal of Community & Applied Social Psychology, 17*, 159–165.

Brettell, C. B., & Sargent, C. F. (2009). *Gender in cross-cultural perspective*. Upper Saddle River, NJ: Prentice-Hall.

Brewer, J. B., Zuo, Z., Desmond, J. E., Glover, G. H., & Gabrieli, J. D. E. (1998). Making memories: Brain activity that predicts how well visual experience will be remembered. *Science, 281*, 1185–1187.

Brewer, M. B. (2007). The social psychology of intergroup relations: Social categorization, ingroup bias, and outgroup prejudice. In A. W. Kruglanski & E. Tory Higgins (Eds.), *Social psychology: Handbook of basic principles* (2nd ed.). New York: Guilford.

Brewster, K. L., & Harker Tillman, K. (2008). Who's doing it? Patterns and predictors of youths' oral sexual experiences. *Journal of Adolescent Health, 42*, 73–80.

Brezo, J., & others. (2009). Differences and similarities in the serotonergic diathesis for suicide attempts and mood disorders: A 22-year longitudinal gene-environment study. *Molecular Psychiatry*. (in press)

Brickman, P., & Campbell, D. T. (1971). Hedonic relativism and planning the good society. In M. H. Appley (Ed.), *Adaptation-level theory* (pp. 287–302). New York: Academic.

Briggs, K. C., & Myers, I. B. (1998). *Myers-Briggs Types Indicator*. Palo Alto, CA: Consulting Psychologists Press.

Briggs, S. R. (1988). Shyness: Introversion or neuroticism? *Journal of Research in Personality, 22*, 290–307.

Brigham, J. C. (1986). Race and eyewitness identifications. In S. Worschel & W. G. Austin (Eds.), *Psychology of intergroup relations*. Chicago: Nelson-Hall.

Brigham, J. C., Bennett, L. B., Meissner, C. A., & Mitchell, T. L. (2007). The influence of race on eyewitness memory. In R. C. L. Lindsay, D. F. Ross, J. D. Read, & M. P. Toglia (Eds.), *The handbook of eyewitness memory: Vol II*. Mahwah, NJ: Erlbaum.

Brink, S. (2001, May 7). Your brain on alcohol. *U.S. News & World Report, 130* (18), 50–57.

Brinker, J. K., & Dozois, D. J. (2009). Ruminative thought style and depressed mood. *Journal of Clinical Psychology, 65,* 1–19.

Brister, H., Turner, J. A., Aaron, L. A., & Manci, L. (2006). Self-efficacy is associated with pain, functioning, and coping in patients with chronic temporomandibular disorder pain. *Journal of Orofacial Pain, 20,* 115–124.

Brizendine, L. (2006). *The female brain.* New York: Morgan Road.

Broberg, D. J., & Bernstein, I. L. (1987). Candy as a scapegoat in the prevention of food aversions in children receiving chemotherapy. *Cancer, 60,* 2344–2347.

Brody, L. R. (1999). Gender emotion and the family. Cambridge, MA: Harvard University Press.

Brody, N. (2007). Does education influence intelligence? In P. C. Kyllonen, R. D. Roberts, & L. Stankov (Eds.), *Extending intelligence.* Mahwah, NJ: Erlbaum.

Bronfenbrenner, U., & Morris, P. A. (2006). The bio-ecological model of human development. In W. Damon & R. Lerner (Eds.), *Handbook of child psychology* (6th ed.). New York: Wiley.

Brooker, R. J. (2009). *Genetics* (3rd ed.). New York: McGraw-Hill.

Brooks, D. J. (2006). Dopaminergic action beyond its effects on motor function: Imaging studies. *Journal of Neurology, 253,* 8–15.

Brooks, J. G., & Brooks, M. G. (2001). *In search of understanding: The case for the constructivist classroom.* Upper Saddle River, NJ: Prentice-Hall.

Brown, A. L., & van Kamp, I. (2009). Response to a change in transport noise exposure: Competing explanations of change effects. *Journal of the Acoustical Society of America, 125,* 905–914.

Brown, A. S. (2006). Prenatal infection as a risk factor for schizophrenia. *Schizophrenia Bulletin, 32,* 200–202.

Brown, B. B., Bakken, J. P., Ameringer, S. W., & Mahon, S. D. (2008). A comprehensive conceptualization of the peer influence process in adolescence. In M. J. Prinstein & K. A. Dodge (Eds.), *Understanding peer influence in childhood and adolescence.* New York: Guilford.

Brown, B. B., & Dietz, E. L. (2009). Informal peer groups in middle childhood and adolescence. In K. H. Rubin, W. M. Bukowski, & B. Laursen (Eds.), *Handbook of peer interactions, relationships, and groups.* New York: Guilford.

Brown, G. M., Pandi-Perumal, S. R., Trakht, I., & Cardinali, D. P. (2009). Melatonin and its relevance to jet lag. *Travel Medicine and Infectious Disease, 7,* 69–81.

Brown, N. R., Lee, P. J., Krsiak, M., Conrad, F. G., Hansen, T., Havelka, J., & Reddon, J. R. (2009). Living in history: How war, terrorism, and natural disaster affect the organization of autobiographical memory. *Psychological Science, 20,* 399–405.

Brown, P. L., & Jenkins, H. M. (2009). On the law of effect. In D. Shanks (Ed.), *Psychology of learning.* Thousand Oaks, CA: Sage.

Brown, R. (1973). *A first language: The early stages.* Cambridge, MA: Harvard University Press.

Brown, S. L., Nesse, R. N., Vinokur, A. D., & Smith, D. M. (2003). Providing social support may be more beneficial than receiving it: Results from a prospective study of mortality. *Psychological Science, 14,* 320–327.

Brown, W. A. (2007). Treatment response in melancholia. *Acta Psychiatrica Scandinavica, 433,* 125–129.

Brown-Borg, H. M. (2008). Hormonal regulation of longevity in mammals. *Aging Research Reviews, 6,* 28–45.

Bruce, D. (1989). Functional explanations of memory. In L. W. Poon, D. C. Rubin, & B. A. Wilson (Eds.), *Everyday cognition in adulthood and late life* (pp. 44–58). Cambridge, England: Cambridge University Press.

Brug, J., Conner, M., Harré, N., Kremers, S., McKellar, S., & Whitelaw, S. (2004). The transtheoretical model and stages of change: A critique. Observations by five commentators on the paper by Adams, J. and White, M. (2004) Why don't stage-based activity promotion interventions work? *Health Education Research, 20,* 244–258.

Brummett, B. H., Boyle, S. H., Kuhn, C. M., Siegler, I. C., & Williams, R. B. (2008). Associations among central nervous system serotonergic function and neuroticism are moderated by gender. *Biological Psychology, 78,* 200–203.

Bruning, R. H., Schraw, G. J., Norby, M. M., & Ronning, R. R. (2004). *Cognitive psychology and instruction* (4th ed.). Upper Saddle River, NJ: Prentice-Hall.

Brunstein, J. (1993). Personal goals and subjective well-being: A longitudinal study. *Journal of Personality and Social Psychology, 65,* 1061–1070.

Brunstein, J., & Maier, G. W. (2005). Implicit and self-attributed motives to achieve: Two separate but interacting needs. *Journal of Personality and Social Psychology, 89,* 205–222.

Bryant, J. B. (2009). Language in social contexts: Communication competence in the preschool years. In J. Berko Gleason & N. Ratner (Eds.), *The development of language* (7th ed.). Boston: Allyn & Bacon.

Bucherelli, C., Baldi, E., Mariottini, C., Passani, M. B., & Blandina, P. (2006). Aversive memory reactivation engages in the amygdala only some neurotransmitters involved in consolidation. *Learning and Memory, 13,* 426–430.

Buchsbaum, B. R., & D'Esposito, M. (2008). The search for the phonological store: From loop to convolution. *Journal of Cognitive Neuroscience, 20* (5), 762–778.

Buckley, K. E., & Anderson, C. A. (2006). A theoretical model of the effects and consequences of playing video games. In P. Vorderer & J. Bryant (Eds.), *Playing video games—motives, responses, and consequences* (pp. 363–378). Mahwah, NJ: Erlbaum.

Bucur, B., & Madden, D. J. (2007). Information processing/cognition. In J. E. Birren (Ed.), *Encyclopedia of gerontology* (2nd ed.). Oxford, England: Elsevier.

Budson, A. E. (2009). Understanding memory dysfunction. *Neurologist, 15,* 71–79.

Bukach, C. M., Bub, D. N., Gauthier, I., & Tarr, M. J. (2006). *Journal of Cognitive Neuroscience, 18,* 48–63.

Bukowski, W., Velasquez, A. M., & Brendgen, M. (2008). Variations in patterns of peer influence: Considerations of self and other. In M. J. Prinstein & K. A. Dodge (Eds.), *Understanding peer influence in childhood and adolescence.* New York: Guilford.

Bulik, C. M., Sullivan, P. F., Wade, T. D., & others. (2000). Twin studies of eating disorders: A review. *International Journal of Eating Disorders, 27,* 1–20.

Bureau, J.-F., Easterbrooks, M. A., & Lyons-Ruth, K. (2009). Maternal depressive symptoms in infancy: Unique contribution to children's depressive symptoms in childhood and adolescence? *Development and Psychopathology, 21,* 519–537.

Burgdorf, J., & Panksepp, J. (2006). The neurobiology of positive emotions. *Neuroscience and Biobehavioral Reviews, 30,* 173–187.

Burger, J. (2009). Replicating Milgram: Would people still obey today? *American Psychologist, 64,* 1–11.

Burger, J. M., & Caldwell, D. F. (2000). Personality, social activities, job-search behavior and interview success: Distinguishing between PANAS trait positive affect and NEO extraversion. *Motivation and Emotion, 24,* 51–62.

Burkhalter, A. (2008). Many specialists for suppressing cortical excitation. *Frontiers in Neuoroscience, 2,* 155–167.

Burton, C. M., & King, L. A. (2004). The health benefits of writing about peak experiences. *Journal of Research in Personality, 38,* 150–163.

Burton, C. M., & King, L. A. (2008). The effects of (very) brief writing on health: The 2-minute miracle. *British Journal of Health Psychology, 13,* 9–14.

Busch, F. (2007). "I noticed": The emergence of self-observation in relationship to pathological attractor sites. *International Journal of Psychoanalysis, 88,* 423–441.

Busch, F. N., Milrod, B. L., & Sandberg, L. S. (2009). A study demonstrating efficacy of a psychoanalytic psychotherapy for panic disorder: Implications for psychoanalytic research, theory, and practice. *Journal of the American Psychoanalytic Association, 57,* 131–148.

Bushman, B. J., & Anderson, C. A. (2007). Measuring the strength of the effect of violent media on aggression. *American Psychologist, 62,* 253–254.

Bushman, B. J., & Baumeister, R. F. (2002). Does self-love or self-hate lead to violence? *Journal of Research in Personality, 36,* 543–545.

Buss, D. M. (2008). *Evolutionary psychology* (3rd ed.). Boston: Allyn & Bacon.

Butcher, J. N., Hamilton, C. K., Rouse, S. V., & Cumella, E. J. (2006). The deconstruction of the Hy Scale of MMPI-2: Failure of RC3 in measuring somatic symptom expression. *Journal of Personality Assessment, 87,* 186–192.

Butler, A. C., Chapman, J. E., Forman, E. M., & Beck, A. T. (2006). The empirical status of cognitive-behavioral therapy: A review of meta-analyses. *Clinical Psychology Review, 26,* 17–31.

Buunk, B. P., & Van Yperen, N. W. (1991). Referential comparisons, relational comparisons, and exchange orientation: Their relation to marital satisfaction. *Personality and Social Psychology Bulletin, 17,* 709–717.

Byrnes, J. P. (2008). Piaget's cognitive developmental theory. In M. M. Haith & J. B. Benson (Eds.), *Encyclopedia of infant and early childhood development.* Oxford, England: Elsevier.

C

Cabanac, M., Cabanac, A. J., & Parent, A. (2009). The emergence of consciousness in phylogeny. *Behavioral Brain Research, 198,* 267–272.

Cabeza, R. (2002). Hemispheric asymmetry reduction in older adults: The HAROLD model. *Psychology and Aging, 17,* 85–100.

Cabeza, R., Nyberg, L., & Park, D. (Eds.). (2005). *Cognitive neuroscience of aging.* New York: Oxford University Press.

Cacioppo, J. T., Berntson, G. G., & Aue, T. (2009). Social psychophysiology. In I. Weiner & E. Craighead (Eds.), *Corsini encyclopedia of psychology* (4th ed.). New York: Wiley. (in press)

Cacioppo, J. T., Hawkley, L. C., Berntson, G. C., Ernst, J. M., Gibbs, A. C., Stickgold, R., & Hobson, J. A. (2002). Do lonely days invade the nights? Potential social modulation of sleep efficiency. *Psychological Science, 13* (4), 384–387.

Cacioppo, J. T., Hawkley, L. C., Kalil, A., Hughes, M. E., Waite, L., & Thisted, R. A. (2008). Happiness and the invisible threads of social connection: The Chicago Health, Aging, and Social Relations Study. In M. Eid & R. Larsen (Eds.), *The science of well-being* (pp. 195–219). New York: Guilford.

Cacioppo, J. T., Hughes, M. E., Waite, L. J., Hawkley, L. C., & Thisted, R. A. (2006). Loneliness as a specific risk factor for depressive symptoms: Cross-sectional and longitudinal analyses. *Psychology and Aging, 21,* 140–151.

Caetano, R., & McGrath, C. (2005) Driving under the influence among U.S. ethnic groups. *Accident Analysis and Prevention, 37,* 217–224.

Cain, D. J. (2001). Defining characteristics, history, and evolution of humanistic psychotherapies. In D. J. Cain & J. Seeman (Eds.), *Humanistic psychotherapies.* Washington, DC: American Psychological Association.

Cale, E. M., & Lilienfeld, S. O. (2002). Sex differences in psychopathy and antisocial personality disorder: A review and integration. *Clinical Psychology Review, 22,* 1179–1207.

Caley, L., Syms, C., Robinson, L., Cederbaum, J., Henry, M., & Shipkey, N. (2008). What human service professionals know and want to know about fetal alcohol syndrome. *Canadian Journal of Clinical Pharmacology, 15,* e117–e123.

Cameron, A. J., Zimmet, P. Z., & Alberti, K. G. (2009). The metabolic syndrome: In need of a global mission statement. *Diabetic Medicine, 26,* 306–309.

Campbell, A., Whitehead, J., & Finkelstein, S. (2009). Why good leaders make bad decisions. *Harvard Business Review, 87,* 60–66.

Campbell, C. A. (2009). AIDS. In D. Carr (Ed.), *Encyclopedia of the life course and human development.* Boston: Gale Cengage.

Campbell, C. M., & Edwards, R. R. (2009). Mind-body interactions in pain: The neurophysiology of anxious and catastrophic pain-related thoughts. *Translational Research, 153,* 97–101.

Campbell, F. A. (2006). The malleability of the cognitive development of children of low income African-American families. In P. C. Kyllonen, R. D. Robers, & L. Stankov (Eds.), *Extending intelligence.* Mahwah, NJ: Erlbaum.

Campbell, J. D., Yoon, D. P., & Johnstone, B. (2009). Determining relationships between physical health and spiritual experience, religious practice, and congregational support in a heterogeneous sample. *Journal of Religion and Health.* (in press)

Campbell, L., Campbell, B., & Dickinson, D. (2004). *Teaching and learning through multiple intelligences.* Boston: Allyn & Bacon.

Campbell, W. K., Bonacci, A. M., Shelton, J., Exline, J. J., & Bushman, B. J. (2004). Psychological entitlement: Interpersonal consequences and validation of a self-report measure. *Journal of Personality Assessment, 83,* 29–45.

Canadian Statistics. (2005). Crime in Canada. http:// www.statcan.ca/Daily/English/050721/d050721a. htmltitle=Crime in Canada. (accessed June 13, 2007)

Canals, S., Beyerlein, M., Merkle, H., & Logothetis, N. K. (2009). Functional MRI evidence for LTP-induced neural network reorganization. *Current Biology, 19,* 398–403.

Canino, G., & others. (2004). The DSM-IV rates of child and adolescent disorders in Puerto Rico. *Archives of General Psychiatry, 61,* 85–93.

Canli, T. (2008a). Toward a neurogenetic theory of neuroticism. In D. W. Pfaff & B. L. Kieffer (Eds.), *Molecular and biophysical mechanisms of arousal, alertness, and attention.* (pp. 153–174). Malden, MA: Blackwell.

Canli, T. (2008b). Toward a "molecular psychology" of personality. In O. P. John, R. W. Robins, & L. A. Pervin (Eds.), *Handbook of personality theory and research* (3rd ed., pp. 311–327). New York: Guilford.

Canli, T., & Lesch, K. (2007). Long story short: The serotonin transporter in emotion regulation and social cognition. *Nature Neuroscience, 10,* 1103–1109.

Canli, T., Sivers, H., Whitfield, S. L., Gotlib, I. H., & Gabrieli, J. D. E. (2002). Amygdala response to happy faces as a function of extraversion. *Science, 296,* 2191.

Cannon, W. B. (1927). The James-Lange theory of emotions: A critical examination and an alternative theory. *American Journal of Psychology, 39,* 106–124.

Cantor, N., & Sanderson, C. A. (1999). Life task participation and well-being: The importance of taking part in daily life. In D. Kahneman, E. Diener, & N. Schwarz (Eds.), *Well-being: The foundations of hedonic psychology* (pp. 230–243). New York: Russell Sage Foundation.

Capasso, A., Putrella, C., & Milano, W. (2009). Recent clinical aspects of eating disorders. *Reviews on Recent Clinical Trials, 4,* 63–69.

Capetian, P., & others. (2009). Histological findings on fetal striatal grafts in Huntington's disease patient early after transplantation. *Neuroscience, 160,* 661–675.

Caporeal, L. R. (2007). Evolution. In A. W. Kruglanski & E. T. Higgins (Eds.), *Social psychology* (2nd ed.). New York: Guilford.

Capps, D. (2004). A psychobiography of Jesus. In J. H. Ellens & W. G. Rollins (Eds.), *Psychology and the Bible: A new way to read the scriptures, Vol. 4, From Jesus to Christ* (pp. 59–70). Westport, CT: Praeger.

Cardno, A. G., & Gottesman, I. I. (2000). Twin studies of schizophrenia: From bow-and-arrow concordances to Star Wars Mx and functional genomics. *American Journal of Medical Genetics, 97,* 12–17.

Cardoso Zoppe, E. H., Schoueri, P., Castro, M., & Neto, F. L. (2009). Teaching psychodynamics to psychiatric residents through psychiatric outpatient interviews. *Academic Psychiatry, 33,* 51–55.

Carey, W. B. (2002). Is ADHD a valid disorder? In P. Jensen & J. Cooper (Eds.), *Attention deficit hyperactivity disorder: State of the science, best practices.* Kingston, NJ: Civic Research Institute.

Carrillo, M., Ricci, L. A., Coppersmith, G. A., & Melloni, R. H. (2009). The effect of increased serontonergic neurotransmission on aggression: A critical meta-analytical review of preclinical studies. *Psychopharmacology.* (in press)

Carlo, G. (2006). Care-based and altruistically-based morality. In M. Killen & J. Smetana (Eds.), *Handbook of moral development.* Mahwah, NJ: Erlbaum.

Carmody, T. P., & others. (2008). Hypnosis for smoking cessation: A randomized trial. *Nicotine and Tobacco Research, 10,* 811–818.

Carmona, J. E., Holland, A. K., & Harrison, D. W. (2009). Extending the functional cerebral theory of emotion to the vestibular modality: A systematic and integrative approach. *Psychological Bulletin, 135,* 286–302.

Carney, D. R., Nosek, B. A., Greenwald, A. G., & Banaji, M. R. (2007). Implicit Association Test (IAT). In R. Baumeister & K. Vohs (Eds.), *Encyclopedia of social psychology.* Thousand Oaks, CA: Sage.

Carpenter, S. K., & DeLosh, E. L. (2006). Impoverished cue support enhances subsequent retention: Support for the elaborative retrieval explanation of the testing effect. *Memory and Cognition, 34,* 268–276.

Carprara, G. V., Gagnani, C., Alessandri, G., Steca, P., Gigantesco, A., Sforza, L. l., & Stazi, M. A. (2009). Human optimal functioning: The genetics of positive orientation towards self, life, and the future. *Behavior Genetics, 39,* 277–284.

Carroll, J. L. (2007). *Sexuality now* (2nd ed.). Belmont, CA: Thompson.

Carskadon, M. A. (2006, March). *Too little, too late: Sleep bioregulatory processes across adolescence.* Paper presented at the meeting of the Society for Research on Adolescence, San Francisco.

Carskadon, M. A., Mindell, J., & Drake, C. (2006, September). *Contemporary sleep patterns in the USA: Results of the 2006 National Sleep Foundation Poll.* Paper presented at the European Sleep Research Society, Innsbruck, Austria.

Carson, R. C., Butcher, J. N., & Mineka, S. (1996). *Abnormal psychology and life* (10th ed.). New York: HarperCollins.

Carstensen, L. L. (2006). The influence of a sense of time on human development. *Science, 312,* 1913–1915.

Carstensen, L. L. (2008, May). *Long life in the twenty-first century.* Paper presented at the meeting of the Association of Psychological Science, Chicago.

Carstensen, L. L., & Charles, S. T. (2003). Human aging: Why is even good news taken as bad? In L. A. Aspinall & U. M. Staudinger (Eds.), *A psychology of human strengths.* Washington, DC: American Psychological Association.

Carston, R. (2002). *Thoughts and utterances: The pragmatics of explicit communication.* Oxford, England: Blackwell.

Carter, C. S., Pournajafi-Nazarloo, H., Kramer, K. M., Ziegler, T. E., White-Traut, R., Bello, D., & Schwertz, D. (2007). Oxytocin: Behavioral associations and potential as a salivary biomarker. *Annals of the New York Academy of Sciences, 1098,* 312–322.

Carter, R. (1998). *Mapping the mind.* Berkeley: University of California Press.

Carver, C. S., & Scheier, M. F. (2000). Origins and functions of positive and negative affect: A control process view. In E. T. Higgins & A. W. Kruglanski, (Eds.), *Motivational science: Social and personality perspectives* (pp. 256–272). New York: Psychology Press.

Carver, C. S., & Scheier, M. F. (2004). *Perspectives on personality* (5th ed.). Boston: Allyn & Bacon.

Carver, C. S., & Scheier, M. F. (2009). Optimism. In M. R. Levy & R. H. Hoyle (Eds), *Handbook of individual differences in social behavior* (pp. 330–342). New York: Guilford.

Casale, R., Alaa, L., Mallick, M., & Ring, H. (2009). Phantom limb related phenomena and their rehabilitation after lower limb amputation. *European Journal of Physical and Rehabilitation Medicine.* (in press)

Case, R. B., Moss, A. J., Case, N., McDermott, M., & Eberly, S. (1992). Living alone after myocardial infarction. Impact on prognosis. *Journal of the American Medical Association, 267,* 515–519.

Caspi, A., McClay, J., Moffitt, T. E., Mill, J., Martin, J., Craig, I. W., Taylor, A., & Poulton, R. (2002). Role of genotype in the cycle of violence in maltreated children. *Science, 297,* 851–854.

Cassidy, J. (2008). The nature of the child's ties. In J. Cassidy & P. R. Shaver (Eds.), *Handbook of attachment* (2nd ed.). New York: Guilford.

Cassimatis, N. L., Murugesan, A., & Bignoli, P. G. (2009). Reasoning as simulation. *Cognitive Processing.* (in press)

Cathers-Schiffman, T. A., & Thompson, M. S. (2007). Assessment of English- and Spanish-speaking students with the WISC-III and Leiter-R. *Journal of Psychoeducational Assessment, 25,* 41–52.

Cattell, R. B. (1946). *The description and measurement of personality.* New York: Harcourt, Brace & World.

Cauller, L. (2001, May). *Review of Santrock, Psychology* (7th ed.). New York: McGraw-Hill.

Caverzasi, E., & others. (2008). Complications in major depressive disorder therapy: A review of magnetic resonance spectroscopy studies. *Functional Neurology, 23,* 129–132.

CBS News. (2006, March 15). Ambien may prompt sleep eating. http://www.cbsnews.com/stories/2006/03/15/earlyshow/health/health_news/main1404632.shtml (accessed December 15, 2006)

CBS News. (2009, February 8). Flight 1549: A routine take-off turns ugly. http://www.cbsnews.com/stories/2009/02/08/60minutes/main478380.shtml (accessed March 2, 2009)

Center for Family and Demographic Research. (2002). *Ohio population news: Marriage in U.S. and Ohio.* Bowling Green, Ohio: Author.

Centers for Disease Control and Prevention (CDC). (2005). National Youth Risk Behavior Survey: 1991–2005. U.S. Department of Health and Human Services, Centers for Disease Control and Prevention.

Centers for Disease Control and Prevention (CDC). (2006). *2006 Surgeon General's Report 2006.* Washington, DC: Author.

Centers for Disease Control and Prevention (CDC). (2007, September 7). Suicide trends among youths and young adults aged 10–24 Years—United States, 1990–2004. *Morbidity and Mortality Weekly Report, 56,* 905–908.

Centers for Disease Control and Prevention (CDC). (2009). *Obesity: Halting the epidemic by making health easier.* Atlanta: Author.

Centers for Disease Control and Prevention (CDC). (2009a). *HIV/AIDS.* Atlanta: Author.

Centers for Disease Control and Prevention (CDC). (2009b). *Defining obesity and overweight.* Atlanta: Author.

Chae, J. I., Kim, J., Wood, S. M., Han, H. W., Cho, Y. K., Oh, K. B., Nam, K. H., & Kang, Y. K. (2009). Cytoskeleton-associated proteins are enriched in human embryonic-cell-derived neuroelectrodermal spheres. *Proteomics, 9,* 1128–1141.

Chafetz, L., White, M., Collins-Bride, G., Cooper, B. A., & Nickens, J. (2008). Clinical trial of wellness training: Health promotion for severely mentally ill adults. *Journal of Nervous and Mental Disease, 196,* 475–483.

Chaiken, S., & Ledgerwood, A. (2007). Heuristic processing. In R. Baumeister & K. D. Vohs (Eds.), *Encyclopedia of social psychology.* Thousand Oaks, CA: Sage.

Chambon, V., Baudouin, J., & Franck, N. (2006). The role of configural information in facial emotion recognition in schizophrenia. *Neuropsychologia, 44,* 2437–2444.

Chan, R. W., Raboy, B., & Patterson, C. J. (1998). Psychosocial adjustment among children conceived via donor insemination by lesbian and heterosexual mothers. *Child Development, 69,* 326–332.

Chance, P. (2009). *Learning and behavior* (6th ed.). Belmont, CA: Cengage.

Charles, S. T., & Carstensen, L. L. (2007). Emotion and aging. In J. J. Gross (Ed.), *Handbook of emotion regulation.* New York: Guilford.

Charles, S. T., Reynolds, C. A., & Gatz, M. (2001). Age-related differences and changes in positive and negative affect over 23 years. *Journal of Personality and Social Psychology, 80,* 136–151.

Chassin, L., Hussong, A., & Beltran, I. (2009). Adolescent substance use. In R. M. Lerner & L. Steinberg (Eds.), *Handbook of adolescent psychology* (3rd ed.). New York: Wiley.

Chaves, J. F. (2000). Hypnosis. In A. Kazdin (Ed.), *Encyclopedia of psychology*. Washington DC, and New York: American Psychological Association and Oxford University Press.

Chen, C. C., Abrams, S., Pinhas, A., & Brumberg, J. C. (2009). Morphological heterogeneity of layer VI neurons in mouse barrel cortex. *Journal of Comparative Biology, 512,* 726–746.

Cheng, P. Y., & Chiou,W. B. (2009). Framing effects in group investment decision making: role of group polarization. *Psychological Reports, 102,* 283–292.

Chess, S., & Thomas, A. (1977). Temperamental individuality from childhood to adolescence. *Journal of Child Psychiatry, 16,* 218–226.

Chester, J. A., Rausch, E. J., June, H. L., & Froehlich, J. C. (2006). Decreased reward during acute alcohol withdrawal in rats selectively bred for low alcohol drinking. *Alcoholism, 38,* 165–172.

Chiang, M. C., & others. (2009). Genetics of brain fiber architecture and intellectual performance. *Journal of Neuroscience, 29,* 2214–2224.

Chichilnisky, E. J. (2007). Information processing in the retina. *Annual Review of Neuroscience* (vol. 30). Palo Alto, CA: Annual Reviews.

Chida, Y., & Steptoe, A. (2009). The association of anger and hostility with future coronary heart disease: A meta-analytic review of prospective evidence. *Journal of the American College of Cardiology, 53,* 936–946.

Cho, D., & Campana, D. (2009). Expansion and activation of natural killer cells for cancer immunotherapy. *Korean Journal of Laboratory Medicine, 29,* 89–96.

Choi, J. K., & Bowles, S. (2007). The co-evolution of parochial altruism and war. *Science, 318,* 636–640.

Chomsky, N. (1975). *Reflections on language.* New York: Pantheon.

Chorney, M. J., Chorney, K., Seese, N., Owen, M. J., Daniels, J., McGuffin, P., Thompson, L. A., Detterman, D. K., Benbow, C., Lubinski, D., Eley, T., & Plomin, R. (1998). A quantitative trait locus associated with cognitive ability in children. *Psychological Science, 9,* 159–166.

Chouinard, G. (2006). Interrelations between psychiatric symptoms and drug-induced movement disorder. *Journal of Psychiatry and Neuroscience, 31,* 177–180.

Christensen, L. B. (2007). *Experimental methodology* (10th ed.). Boston: Allyn & Bacon.

Christopher Frueh, B., Grubaugh, A. L., Cusack, K. J., Kimble, M. O., Elhai, J. D., & Knapp, R. G. (2009). Exposure-based cognitive-behavioral treatment of PTSD in adults with schizophrenia or schizoaffective disorder: A pilot study. *Journal of Anxiety Disorders, 23,* 665–675.

Church, R. M., & Kirkpatrick, K. (2001). Theories of conditioning and timing. In R. R. Mowrer & S. B. Klein (Eds.), *Handbook of contemporary learning theories.* Mahwah, NJ: Erlbaum.

Church, T. S., LaMonte, M. J., Barlow, C. E., & Blair, S. N. (2005). Cardiorespiratory fitness and body mass index as predictors of cardiovascular disease mortality among men with diabetes. *Archives of Internal Medicine, 165,* 2114–2120.

Cialdini, R. B. (1991). Altruism or egoism? That is (still) the question. *Psychological Inquiry, 2,* 124–126.

Cialdini, R. B., Vincent, J. E., Lewis, S. K., Catalan, J., Wheeler, D., & Darby, B. L. (1975). Reciprocal concessions procedure for inducing compliance: The door-in-the-face technique. *Journal of Personality and Social Psychology, 31,* 206–215.

Cicchetti, D., & Toth, S. L. (2006). Developmental psychopathology and preventive intervention. In W. Damon & R. Lerner (Eds.), *Handbook of child psychology* (6th ed.). New York: Wiley.

Cipolotti, L., & Bird, C. M. (2006). Amnesia and the hippocampus. *Current Opinion in Neuroscience, 19,* 593–598.

Cipriani, A., & others. (2009). Sertaline versus other antidepressive agents for depression. *Cochrane Database of Systematic Reviews, 2,* CD006117.

Clark, B. (2008). *Growing up gifted* (7th ed.). Upper Saddle River, NJ: Prentice-Hall.

Clark, D. M., Ehlers, A., Hackmann, A., McManus, F., Fennell, M., Grey, N., Waddington, L., & Wild, J. (2006). Cognitive therapy versus exposure and applied relaxation in social phobia: A randomized controlled trial. *Journal of Consulting and Clinical Psychology, 74,* 568–578.

Clark, L., Chamberlain, S. R., & Sahakian, B. J. (2009). Neurocognitive mechanisms in depression: Implications for treatment. *Annual Review of Neuroscience* (vol. 32). Palo Alto, CA: Annual Reviews.

Clark, M. S., & Chrisman, K. (1994). Resource allocation in intimate relationships: Trying to make sense of a confusing literature. In M. J. Lerner & G. Mikula (Eds.), *Entitlement and the affectional bond: Justice in close relationships* (pp. 65–88). New York: Plenum.

Clark, N. M., & Dodge, J. A. (1999). Exploring self-efficacy as a predictor of disease management. *Health Education & Behavior, 26,* 72–89.

Cleeremans, A., & Sarrazin, J. C. (2007). Time, action, and consciousness. *Human Movement Science, 26,* 180–202.

Clement, P., Pozzato, C., Heidbreder, C., Alexandre, L., Giuliano, F., & Melotto, S. (2009). Delay of ejaculation induced by SB-277011, a selective dopamine D3 receptor antagonist, in the rat. *Journal of Sexual Medicine.* (in press)

Cleveland, J. N., Barnes-Farrell, J. L., & Ratz, J. M. (1997). Accommodation in the workplace. *Human Resource Management Review, 7,* 77–107.

Clore, G. L., Gasper, K., & Garvin, E. (2001). Affect as information. In J. P. Forgas (Ed.), *Handbook of affect and social cognition* (pp. 121–144). Mahwah, NJ: Erlbaum.

Close, C. E., Roberts, P. L., & Berger, R. E. (1990). Cigarettes, alcohol, and marijuana are related to pyospermia in infertile men. *Journal of Urology, 144,* 900–903.

Cloud, J. (2008, August 27). Failing our geniuses. *Time,* 40–47.

CNN Poll. (2006, December 12). Most Americans see lingering racism—in others. http://www.cnn.com/2006/US/12/12/racism.poll/index.html (accessed June 13, 2007)

Coch, D., Fischer, K. W., & Dawson, G. (Eds.). (2007). *Human behavior, learning, and the developing brain.* New York: Guilford.

Cohen, D. (2001). Cultural variation: Considerations and implications. *Psychological Bulletin, 127,* 451–471.

Cohen, D., Nisbett, R. E., Bowdle, B. F., & Schwarz, N. (1996). Insult, aggression, and the southern culture of honor: An "experimental ethnography." *Journal of Personality and Social Psychology, 70,* 945–960.

Cohen, G. L., & Prinstein, M. J. (2006). Peer contagion of aggression and health risk behavior among adolescent males: An experimental investigation of effects on public conduct and private attitudes. *Child Development, 77,* 967–983.

Cohen, H., Geva, A. B., Matar, M. A., Zohar, J., & Kaplan, Z. (2008). Post-traumatic stress behavioural responses in inbred mouse strains: Can genetic predisposition explain phenotypic vulnerability? *International Journal of Neuropsychopharmacology, 11,* 331–349.

Cohen, K. R., & Henik, A. (2007). Can synaesthesia research inform cognitive science? *Trends in Cognitive Science, 11,* 177–184.

Cohen, S., Alper, C. M., Doyle, W. J., Treanor, J. J., & Turner, R. B. (2006). Positive emotional style predicts resistance to illness after experimental exposure to rhinovirus or influenza a virus. *Psychosomatic Medicine, 68,* 809–815.

Cohen, S., Doyle, W. J., & Skoner, D. P. (1999). Psychological stress, cytokine production, and severity of upper respiratory illness. *Psychosomatic Medicine, 61,* 175–180.

Cohen, S., Doyle, W. J., Alper, C. M., Janicki-Deverts, D., & Turner, R. B. (2009). Sleep habits and susceptibility to the common cold. *Archives of Internal Medicine, 169,* 62–67.

Cohen, S., Frank, E., Doyle, W., Skoner, D. P., Rabin, B. S., & Gwaltney, J. M. (1998). Types of stressors that increase susceptibility to the common cold in healthy adults. *Health Psychology, 17,* 214–223.

Cohen, S., Glass, D. C., & Singer, J. E. (1973). Apartment noise, auditory discrimination, and reading ability in children. *Journal of Experimental Psychology, 9,* 407–422.

Cohen, S., & Janicki-Deverts, D. (2009). Can we improve our physical health by altering our social networks? *Perspectives on Psychological Science.* (in press)

Cohen, S., & Lemay, E. (2007). Why would social networks be linked to affect and health practices? *Health Psychology, 27,* 410–417.

Coifman, K. G., Bonanno, G. A., Ray, R. D., & Gross, J. J. (2007). Does repressing coping promote resilience? Affective-autonomic response discrepancy during bereavement. *Journal of Personality and Social Psychology, 92,* 745–758.

Colangelo, J. J. (2009). The recovered memory controversy: A representative case study. *Journal of Child Sexual Abuse, 18,* 103–121.

Colapinto, J. (2000). *As nature made him.* New York: Harper Academic.

Cole, M., & Gajdamaschko, N. (2007). Vygotsky and culture. In H. Daniels, J. Wertsch, & M. Cole (Eds.), *The Cambridge companion to Vygotsky.* New York: Cambridge University Press.

Collier, D. A., & Treasure, J. L. (2004). The aetiology of eating disorders. *British Journal of Psychiatry, 185,* 363–365.

Collins, A., Hill, L. E., Chandramohan, Y., Witcomb, D., Droste, S. K., & Reul, J. M. (2009). Exercise improves cognitive responses to stress through enhancement of epigenetic mechanisms and gene expression in the dentate gyrus. *PLoS One, 4,* e4330.

Collins, W. A., Maccoby, E. E., Steinberg, L., Hetherington, E. M., & Bornstein, M. H. (2000). Contemporary research on parenting: The case for nature and nurture. *American Psychologist, 55,* 218–232.

Collins, W. A., & Steinberg, L. (2006). Adolescent development in interpersonal context. In W. Damon & R. Lerner (Eds.), *Handbook of child psychology* (6th ed.). New York: Wiley.

Collinson, S. L., Meyyappan, A., & Rosenfeld, J. V. (2009). Injury and recovery: Severe amnestic syndrome following traumatic brain injury. *Brain Injury, 23,* 71–76.

Commoner, B. (2002). Unraveling the DNA myth: The spurious foundation of genetic engineering. *Harper's Magazine, 304,* 39–47.

Commonwealth of Massachusetts vs. Porter 31285–330. (1993, Massachusetts).

Compton, J., & Pfau, M. (2008). Inoculating against pro-plagiarism justifications: Rational and affective strategies. *Journal of Applied Communication Research, 36,* 98–119.

Compton, J. A., & Pfau, M. (2004). Use of inoculation to foster resistance to credit card marketing targeting college students. *Journal of Applied Communication Research, 32,* 343–364.

Compton, R. J., Wirtz, D., Pajoumand, G., Claus, E., & Heller, W. (2004). Association between positive affect and attentional shifting. *Cognitive Therapy and Research, 28,* 733–744.

Comstock, G., & Scharrer, E. (2003). Meta-analyzing the controversy over television violence and aggression. In D. A. Gentile (Ed.), *Media violence and children: A complete guide for parents and professionals* (pp. 205–226). Westport, CT: Praeger/Greenwood.

Comstock, G., & Scharrer, E. (2006). Media and popular culture. In K. A. Renninger, I. E. Sigel, W. Damon, & R. M. Lerner (Eds.), *Handbook of child psychology* (6th ed., vol. 4, *Child psychology in practice,* pp. 817–863). Hoboken, NJ: Wiley.

Conner, K. R., Britton, P. C., Sworts, L. M., & Joiner, T. E., Jr. (2007). Suicide attempts among individuals with opiate dependence: The critical role of belonging. *Addictive Behaviors, 32,* 1395–1404.

Connor, C. M., & Zwolan, T. A. (2004). Examining multiples sources of influence on the reading comprehension skills of children who use cochlear implants. *Journal of Speech, Language and Hearing Research, 47,* 509–526.

Constantine, N. A. (2008). Converging evidence leaves policy behind: Sex education in the United States. *Journal of Adolescent Health, 42,* 324–326.

Conway, M., & Rubin, D. (1993). The structure of autobiographical memory. In A. F. Collins, S. E. Gathercole, M. A. Conway, & P. E. Morris (Eds.), *Theories of memory.* Hillsdale, NJ: Erlbaum.

Cook, M. B., & Smallman, H. S. (2008). Human factors of the confirmation bias in intelligence analysis: Decision support from graphical evidence landscapes. *Human Factors, 50,* 745–754.

Cooper, J. O., Heron, T. E., & Heward, W. L. (2007). *Applied behavior analysis* (2nd ed.). Upper Saddle River, NJ: Prentice-Hall.

Cooper, M., Talley, A., Sheldon, M. S., Levitt, A., & Barber, L. (2008). A dyadic perspective on approach and avoidance motives for sex. In A. J. Elliot (Ed.). *Handbook of approach and avoidance motivation.* New York: Psychology Press.

Cooper, M. L. (1994). Motivations for alcohol use among adolescents: Development and validation of a four-factor model. *Psychological Assessment, 6,* 117–128.

Cooper, M. L., Pioli, M., Levitt, A., Talley, A. E., Micheas, L., & Collins, N. L. (2006). Attachment styles, sex motives, and sexual behavior: Evidence for gender-specific expressions of attachment dynamics. In M. Mikulincer & G. S. Goodman (Eds.), *Dynamics of romantic love: Attachment, care-giving, and sex* (pp. 243–274). New York: Guilford.

Cooper, M. L., Russell, M., Skinner, J. B., & Windle, M. (1992). Development and validation of a three-dimensional measure of drinking motives. *Psychological Assessment, 4,* 123–132.

Cooper, R. M., & Zubek, J. P. (1958). Effects of enriched and restricted early environments on the learning ability of bright and dull rats. *Canadian Journal of Psychology, 12,* 159–164.

Copeland, D. E., Radvansky, G. A., & Goodwin, K. A. (2009). A novel study: Forgetting curves and the reminiscence bump. *Memory, 17,* 323–336.

Cornell, J. L., & Halpern-Felsher, B. L. (2006). Adolescents tell us why teens have oral sex. *Journal of Adolescent Health, 38,* 299–301.

Cornwell, B., Schumm, L. P., & Laumann, E. O. (2008). The social connectedness of older adults. *American Sociological Review, 73,* 185–203.

Cornwell, E. Y., & Waite, L. J. (2009). Social disconnectedness, perceived isolation, and health among older adults. *Journal of Health and Social Behavior, 50,* 31–48.

Corr, P. J. (2008). Reinforcement sensitivity theory (RST): Introduction. In P. J. Corr (Ed.), *The reinforcement sensitivity theory of personality* (pp. 1–43). New York: Cambridge University Press.

Correll, J., Park, B., Judd, C. M., & Wittenbrink, B. (2002). The police officer's dilemma: Using ethnicity to disambiguate potentially threatening individuals. *Journal of Personality and Social Psychology, 83,* 1314–1329.

Corrigan, P. W. (2007). How clinical diagnosis might exacerbate the stigma of mental illness. *Social Work, 52,* 31–39.

Costa, P. T., & McCrae, R. R. (1992). *Revised NEO personality inventory.* Odessa, FL: Psychological Assessment Resources.

Costa, P. T., & McCrae, R. R. (1998). Personality assessment. In H. S. Friedman (Ed.), *Encyclopedia of mental health* (vol. 3). San Diego: Academic.

Costa, P. T., & McCrae, R. R. (2006). Age changes in personality and their origins: Comment on Roberts, Walter, and Viechtbauer (2006). *Psychological Bulletin, 132,* 26–28.

Costafreda, S. G., Khanna, A., Mourao-Miranda, J., & Fu, C. H. (2009). Neural correlates of sad faces predict clinical remission to cognitive behavioral therapy in depression. *Neuroreport, 20,* 637–641.

Cote, J. E. (2006). Acculturation and identity: The role of individualization theory. *Human Development, 49,* 31–35.

Cotter, D., Mackay, D., Chana, G., Beasley, C., Landau, S., & Everall, I. P. (2002). Reduced neuronal size and glial density in area 9 of the dorsolateral prefrontal cortex in subjects with major depressive disorder. *Cerebral Cortex, 12,* 386–394.

Coulson, S., & Wu, Y. C. (2005). Right hemisphere activation of joke-related information: An event-related brain potential study. *Journal of Cognitive Neuroscience, 17,* 494–506.

Courtet, P., & others. (2004). Serotonin transporter gene may be involved in short-term risk of subsequent suicide attempts. *Biological Psychiatry, 55,* 46–51.

Courtois, C. A., & Ford, J. D. (Eds.). (2009). *Treating complex traumatic stress disorders.* New York: Guilford.

Cowan, R. L., Roberts, D. M., & Joers, J. M. (2008). Neuroimaging in human MDMA (Ecstasy) users. *Annals of the New York Academy of Sciences, 1139,* 291–298.

Cox, S. M. & others. (2009). Striatal dopamine responses to intranasal cocaine self-administration in humans. *Biological Psychiatry.* (in press)

Craddock, N., & Forty, L. (2006). Genetics of affective (mood) disorders. *European Journal of Human Genetics, 14,* 660–668.

Craik, F. I. M., & Lockhart, R. S. (1972). Levels of processing; A frame-work for memory research. *Journal of Verbal Learning and Verbal Behavior, 11,* 671–684.

Craik, F. I. M., & Tulving, E. (1975). Depth of processing and retention of words in episodic memory. *Journal of Experimental Psychology: General, 104,* 268–294.

Cramer, P. (2008). Longitudinal study of defense mechanisms: Late childhood to late adolescence. *Journal of Personality, 75,* 1–23.

Cramer, P. (2008a). Seven pillars of defense mechanism theory. *Social and Personality Psychology Compass, 2,* 1963–1981.

Cramer, P., & Jones, C. J. (2007). Defense mechanisms predict differential lifespan change in self-control and self-acceptance. *Journal of Research in Personality, 41,* 841–855.

Crampton, D. (2007). Research review: Family group decision-making: A promising practice in need of more programme theory and research. *Child & Family Social Work, 12,* 202–209.

Crandall, C. S. (2004). Social contagion of binge eating. In R. M. Kowalski & M. R. Leary (Eds.), *The interface of social and clinical psychology: Key readings* (pp. 99–115). New York: Psychology Press.

Cranley, L., Doran, D. M., Tourangeau, A. E., Kushniruk, A., & Nagle, L. (2009). Nurses' uncertainty in decision-making: A literature review. *Worldviews in Evidence-Based Nursing, 6,* 3–15.

Crocker, J., Major, B., & Steele, C. (1998). Social stigma. In D. T. Gilbert, S. T. Fiske, & G. Lindzey (Eds.), *Handbook of social psychology* (4th ed., vol. 2). New York: McGraw-Hill.

Crowell, S. E., Beauchaine, T. P., & Linehan, M. M. (2009). A biosocial developmental model of borderline personality: Elaborating and extending Linehan's theory. *Psychological Bulletin, 135,* 495–510.

Crowley, K., Pickle, J., Dale, R., & Fattal, O. (2008). A critical examination of bifrontal electroconvulsive therapy: Clinical efficacy, cognitive side effects, and directions for future research. *Journal of ECT, 24,* 268–271.

Csikszentmihalyi, M. (1990). *Flow: The psychology of optimal experience.* New York: Harper Perennial.

Csikszentmihalyi, M. (1996). *Creativity.* New York: HarperCollins.

Csikszentmihalyi, M., & Rathunde, K. (1998). The development of the person: An experiential perspective on the ontogenesis of psychological complexity. In W. Damon (Ed.), *Handbook of child psychology* (5th ed., vol. 1). New York: Wiley.

Cuijpers, P. (2001). Mortality and depressive symptoms in inhabitants of residential homes. *International Journal of Geriatric Psychiatry, 16,* 131–138.

Cullen, K., Klimes-Dougan, B., & Kumra, S. (2009). Pediatric depression: Issues and treatment recommendations. *Minnesota Medicine, 92,* 45–48.

Cunningham, R. L., & McGinnis, M. Y. (2007). Factors influencing aggression toward females by male rats exposed to anabolic androgenic steroids during puberty. *Hormones and Behavior, 51,* 135–141.

Curran, K., DuCette, J., Eisenstein, J., & Hyman, I. A. (2001, August). *Statistical analysis of the cross-cultural data: The third year.* Paper presented at the meeting of the American Psychological Association, San Francisco.

Curtiss, S. (1977). *Genie.* New York: Academic.

Cutler, B. L., & Penrod, S. D. (1995). *Mistaken identities: The eyewitness, psychology, and the law.* New York: Cambridge University Press.

D

Dabbs, J. M., Jr., Riad, J. K., & Chance, S. E. (2001). Testosterone and ruthless homicide. *Personality and Individual Differences, 31,* 599–603.

Dafters, R. I. (2006). Chronic ecstasy (MDMA) use is associated with deficits in task-switching but not inhibition or memory updating executive functions. *Drug and Alcohol Dependence, 83* (2), 181–184.

Dagher, A., & Robbins, T. W. (2009). Personality, addiction, dopamine: Insights from Parkinson's disease. *Neuron, 61,* 502–510.

Dahl, R., & Spear, L. P. (Eds.). (2004). Adolescent brain development: Vulnerabilities and opportunities. *Annals of the New York Academy of Sciences, 1021.*

Dale, K.Y., Berg, R., Elden, A., Odegard, A., & Holte, A. (2009). Testing the diagnosis of dissociative identity disorder through measures of dissociation, absorption, hypnotizability, and PTSD: A Norwegian pilot study. *Journal of Trauma and Dissociation, 10,* 102–112.

Dammen, T., Bringagar, C. B., Arnesen, H., Ekeberg, O., & Friis, S. (2006). A 1-year follow-up of chest-pain patients with and without panic disorder. *General Hospital Psychiatry, 28,* 516–524.

Damon, W. (2008). *The path to purpose: Helping our children find their calling in life.* New York: Free Press.

Damsa, C., Kosel, M., & Moussally, J. (2009). Current status of brain imaging in anxiety disorders. *Current Opinion in Psychiatry, 22,* 96–110.

Danner, D. D., Snowdon, D. A., & Friesen, W. V. (2001). Positive emotions in early life and longevity: Findings from the Nun Study. *Journal of Personality and Social Psychology, 80,* 804–813.

Darley, J. M., & Latané, B. (1968). Bystander intervention in emergencies: Diffusion of responsibility. *Journal of Personality and Social Psychology, 8,* 377–383.

Darwin, C. (1965). *The expression of the emotions in man and animals.* Chicago: University of Chicago Press. (original work published 1872)

Darwin, C. (1979). *The origin of species.* New York: Avenal Books. (original work published 1859)

da Silva Cais, C. F., Stefanello, S., Fabrício Mauro, M. L., Vaz Scavacini de Freitas, G., & Botega, N. J. (2009). Factors associated with repeated suicide attempts: Preliminary results of the WHO Multisite Intervention Study on Suicidal Behavior (SUPRE-MISS) from Campinas, Brazil. *Crisis: The Journal of Crisis Intervention and Suicide Prevention, 30,* 73–78.

Davidson, J. R. (2009). First-line pharmacotherapy approaches for generalized anxiety disorder. *Journal of Clinical Psychiatry, 70, Suppl. 2,* S25–S31.

Davidson, K. W., & others. (2006). Assessment and treatment of depression in patients with cardiovascular disease: National Heart, Lung, and Blood Institute Working Group Report. *Psychosomatic Medicine, 68,* 645–650.

Davidson, P. S., Cook, S. P., & Glisky, E. L. (2006). Flashbulb memories for September 11th can be preserved in older adults. *Neuropsychology, Development, and Cognition B, 13,* 196–206.

Davidson, R. J. (2000). Affective style, psychopathology, and resilience: Brain mechanisms and plasticity. *American Psychologist, 55,* 196–214.

Davidson, R. J. (2005). Neural substrates of affective style and value. In Y. Christen (Series Ed.) & J.-P. Changeux, A. R. Damasio, W. Singer, & Y. Christen

(Vol. Eds.), *Research and perspectives in neurosciences: Neurobiology of human values* (pp. 67–90). Germany: Springer-Verlag.

Davidson, R. J., Kabat-Zinn, J., Schumacher, J., Rosenkranz, M. M., Daniel, S., Saki, F., Urbanowski, F., Harrington, A., Bonus, K., & Sheridan, J. F. (2003). Alterations in brain and immune function produced by mindfulness meditation. *Psychosomatic Medicine, 65* (4), 564–570.

Davidson, R. J., & Lutz, A. (2008). Buddha's brain: Neuroplasticity and meditation. *IEEE Signal Processing, 25,* 171–174.

Davidson, R. J., Scherer, K. R., & Goldsmith, H. H. (Eds.). (2002). *Handbook of affective sciences.* New York: Oxford University Press.

Davidson, R. J., Shackman, A., & Pizzagalli, D. (2002). The functional neuroanatomy of emotion and affective style. In R. J. Davidson, K. R. Scherer, & H. H. Goldsmith (Eds.), *Handbook of affective sciences.* New York: Oxford University Press.

Davis, C., Levitan, R. D., Kaplan, A. S., Carter, J., Reid, C., Curtis, C., Patte, K., Hwang, R., & Kennedy, J. L. (2008). Reward sensitivity and the D2 dopamine receptor gene: A case-control study of binge eating disorder. *Progress in Neuro-Psychopharmacology & Biological Psychiatry, 32,* 620–628.

Davis, J. I., Senghas, A., & Ochsner, K. N. (2010). How does facial feedback modulate emotional experience? *Journal of Research in Personality.* (in press)

Davis, M. C., Zautra, A. J., Johnson, L. M., Murray, K. E., & Okvat, H. A. (2007). Psychosocial stress, emotion regulation, and resilience among older adults. In C. M. Aldwin, C. L. Park, & A. Spiro (Eds.), *Handbook of health and aging.* New York: Guilford.

Davison, K. P., Pennebaker, J. W., & Dickerson, S. S. (2000). Who talks? The social psychology of illness support groups. *American Psychologist, 55,* 205–217.

Dawson, A., & List, T. (2009). Comparison of pain thresholds and pain tolerance levels between Middle Easterners and Swedes and between genders. *Journal of Oral Rehabilitation.* (in press)

De Angelis, T. (2002). Binge-eating disorder: What's the best treatment? *Monitor on Psychology, 33.* http://www.apa.org/monitor/mar02/binge.html

Deaux, K. (2001). Social identity. In J. Worell (Ed.), *Encyclopedia of gender and women.* San Diego: Academic.

Debiec, J., & LeDoux, J. E. (2006). Noradrenergic signaling in the amygdale contributes to the reconsolidation of fear memory: Treatment implications for PTSD. *Annals of the New York Academy of Science, 1071,* 521–524.

Deci, E., & Ryan, R. (1994). Promoting self-determined education. *Scandinavian Journal of Educational Research, 38,* 3–14.

Deci, E. L., & Ryan, R. M. (2000). The "what" and "why" of goal pursuits: Human needs and the self-determination of behavior. *Psychological Inquiry, 4,* 227–268.

Deci, E. L., & Ryan, R. M. (Eds.). (2002). *Handbook of self-determination research.* Rochester, NY: University of Rochester Press.

Dedert, E. A., & others. (2009). Association of trauma exposure with psychiatric morbidity in military veterans who have served since September 11, 2001. *Journal of Psychiatric Research, 43,* 830–836.

Deeb, S. S. (2006). Genetics of variation in human color vision and the retinal cone mosaic. *Current Opinion in Genetics and Development, 16,* 301–307.

Degnin, F. D. (2009). Difficult patients, overmedication, and groupthink. *Journal of Clinical Ethics, 20,* 64–74.

de Groot, E. R., Verheul, R., & Trijsburg, R. W. (2008). An integrative perspective on psychotherapeutic treatments for borderline personality disorder. *Journal of Personality Disorders, 22,* 332–352.

de Haan, M., & Martinos, M. (2008). Brain function. In M. M. Haith & J. B. Benson (Eds.), *Encyclopedia of infant and early childhood development.* Oxford, England: Elsevier.

Dell, P. F., & Eisenhower, J. W. (1990). Adolescent multiple personality disorder: A preliminary study of eleven cases. *Journal of the American Academy of Child & Adolescent Psychiatry, 29,* 359–366.

Dell, P. F., & O'Neil, J. A. (Eds.). (2007). *Dissociation and the dissociative disorders: DSM-V and beyond.* New York: Routledge.

Del Missier, F., & Terpini, C. (2009). Part-set cueing in option generation. *Memory and Cognition, 37,* 265–276.

Delprato, D. J. (2005). Retroactive interference as a function of degree of interpolated study without overt retrieval practice. *Psychonomic Bulletin and Review, 12,* 345–349.

DeMarree, K. G., & Petty, R. E. (2007). The elaboration likelihood model of persuasion. In R. F. Baumeister & K. D. Vohs (Eds.), *Encyclopedia of social psychology.* Thousand Oaks, CA: Sage.

Demeure, V., Bonnefon, J. F., & Raufaste, E. (2009). Politeness and conditioned reasoning: Interpersonal cues to the indirect suppression of deductive inferences. *Journal of Experimental Psychology: Learning, Memory, and Cognition, 35,* 260–266.

Denham, S. A., Bassett, H. H., & Wyatt, T. (2007). The socialization of emotional competence. In J. E. Grusec & P. D. Hastings (Eds.), *Handbook of socialization.* New York: Guilford.

Dennis, A. (2005). Osama bin Laden: The sum of all fears. In W. T. Schultz (Ed.), *Handbook of psychobiography* (pp. 311–322). Oxford, England: Oxford University Press.

Depue, R. A., & Collins, P. F. (1999). Neurobiology of the structure of personality: Dopamine, facilitation of incentive motivation, and extraversion. *Behavoural and Brain Sciences, 22,* 491–569.

Derbyshire, E. (2007). The importance of adequate fluid and fiber intake during pregnancy. *Nursing Standard, 21,* 40–43.

Derks, D., Bos, A. E. R., & von Grumbkow, J. (2008). Emoticons in computer-mediated communication: Social motives and social context. *CyberPsychology & Behavior, 11,* 99–101.

Derryberry, D., & Reed, M. (2002). Information processing approaches to individual differences in emotional reactivity. In R. J. Davidson, K. R. Scherer, & H. H. Goldsmith (Eds.), *Handbook of affective sciences.* New York: Oxford University Press.

DeSantis-Moniaci, D., & Altshuler, L. (2007). Comprehensive behavioral treatment of overweight and the pediatric practice. *Pediatric Annals, 36,* 102–108.

Deschenes, C. L., & McCurry, S. M. (2009). Current treatments for sleep disturbances in individuals with dementia. *Current Psychiatry Reports, 11,* 20–26.

De Smedt, B., & others. (2009). Working memory and individual differences in mathematics achievement: A longitudinal study from first grade to second grade. *Journal of Experimental Child Psychology.* (in press)

De Vet, E., Oenema, A., Sheeran, P., & Brug, J. (2009). Should implantation intentions interventions be implemented in obesity prevention: the impact of if-then plans on daily physical activity in Dutch adults. *International Journal of Nutrition and Physical Activity, 6,* 11.

Devlin, B., Bacanu, S. A., Klump, K. L., & others. (2000). Linkage analysis of anorexia nervosa incorporating behavioral covariates. *Human Molecular Genetics, 11,* 689–696.

de Waal, F. (1996). *Good natured: The origins of right and wrong in humans and other animals.* Cambridge, MA: Harvard University Press.

de Waal, F. (2006). *Primates and philosophers: How morality evolved.* Princeton, NJ: Princeton University Press.

de Waal, F. B. M., Leimgruber, K., Greenberg, A. R. (2008). Giving is self-rewarding for monkeys. *PNAS Proceedings of the National Academy of Sciences USA, 105,* 13685–13689.

DeWall, C. N., Twenge, J. M., Gitter, S. A., & Baumeister, R. F. (2009). It's the thought that counts: The role of hostile cognition in shaping aggressive responses to social exclusion. *Journal of Personality and Social Psychology, 96,* 45–59.

de Wit, S., Niry, D., Wariyar, R., Aitken, M. R., & Dickinson, A. (2007). Stimulus–outcome interactions during instrumental discrimination learning by rats and humans. *Journal of Experimental Psychology: Animal Behavioral Processes, 33,* 1–11.

de Zoysa, P., Newcombe, P. A., & Rajapakse, L. (2008). Consequences of parental corporal punishment on 12-year-old children in the Colombo district. *Ceylon Medical Journal, 53,* 7–9.

de Zwaan, M., Mitchell, J. E., Crosby, R. D., Mussell, M. P., Raymond, N. C., Specker, S. M., & Seim, H. C. (2005). Short-term cognitive behavioral treatment does not improve outcome of a comprehensive very-low-calorie diet program in obese women with binge eating disorder. *Behavior Therapy, 36,* 89–99.

Diamond, A. (2009). The interplay of biology and the environment broadly defined. *Developmental Psychology, 45,* 1–8.

Diamond, A. (2009a). All or none hypothesis: A global-default mode that characterizes the brain and mind. *Developmental Psychology, 45,* 130–138.

Diamond, A. (2010). *Developmental cognitive neuroscience.* New York: Oxford University Press. (in press)

Diamond, L. (2008). *Sexual fluidity: Understanding women's love and desire.* Cambridge, MA: Harvard University Press.

Diamond, L. M., & Savin-Williams, R. C. (2009). Adolescent sexuality. In R. M. Lerner & L. Steinberg (Eds.), *Handbook of adolescent psychology* (3rd ed.). New York: Wiley.

Diamond, M., & Sigmundson, H. K. (1997). Sex reassignment at birth. *Archives of Pediatric and Adolescent Medicine, 151,* 298–304.

Diaz-Laplante, J. (2007). Humanistic psychology and social transformation: Path toward a likeable today and a just tomorrow. *Journal of Humanistic Psychology, 47,* 54–72.

DiClemente, C. C. (2006). Natural change and the troublesome use of substances: A life-course perspective. W. R. Miller & K. M. Carroll (Eds.), *Rethinking substance abuse: What the science shows, and what we should do about it* (pp. 81–96). New York: Guilford.

Diefenbach, G. J., Disch, W. B., Robinson, J. T., Baez, E., & Coman, E. (2009). Anxious depression among Puerto Rican and African American older adults. *Aging and Mental Health, 13,* 118–126.

Diego, M. A., Field, T., & Hernandez-Reif, M. (2008). Temperature increases in preterm infants during massage therapy. *Infant Behavior and Development, 31,* 149–152.

Diekelmann, S., Wilhelm, I., & Born, J. (2009). The whats and whens of sleep-dependent memory consolidation. *Sleep Medicine Reviews.* (in press)

Diener, E. (1999). Introduction to the special section on the structure of emotion. *Journal of Personality and Social Psychology, 76,* 803–804.

Diener, E. (2000). Subjective well-being: The science of happiness and a proposal for a national index. *American Psychologist, 55,* 34–43.

Diener, E., & Diener, C. (1996). Most people are happy. *Psychological Science, 7,* 181–185.

Diener, E., Emmons, R. A., Larsen, R. J., & Griffin, S. (1985). The Satisfaction with Life Scale. *Journal of Personality Assessment, 49,* 71–75.

Diener, E., Kesebir, P., & Tov, W. (2009). Happiness. In M. R. Leary & R. H. Hoyle (Eds.), *Handbook of individual differences in social behavior* (pp. 147–160). New York: Guilford.

Diener, E., & Seligman, M. E. P. (2002). Very happy people. *Psychological Science, 13,* 81–84.

Dietz-Uhler, B., Bishop-Clark, C., Howard, E. (2005). Formation of and adherence to a self-disclosure norm in an online chat. *CyberPsychology & Behavior, 8,* 114–120.

Digman, J. M. (1990). Personality structure: Emergence of the five-factor model. *Annual Review of Psychology, 41,* 417–440.

Digman, J. M. (2002). Historical antecedents of the five-factor model. In P. T. Costa & T. A. Widiger (Eds.), *Personality disorders and the five-factor model of personality* (2nd ed., pp. 17–22). Washington, DC: American Psychological Association.

Dijksterhuis, A., Bos, M. W., Nordgren, L. F., & van Baaren, R. B. (2006). On making the right choice: The deliberation-without-attention effect. *Science, 311,* 1005–1007.

Dijksterhuis, A., & Nordgren, L. F. (2006). A theory of unconscious thought. *Perspectives on Psychological Science, 1,* 95–109.

Dijksterhuis, A., & Van Knippenberg, A. (1998). The relation between perception and behavior or how to win a game of Trivial Pursuit. *Journal of Personality and Social Psychology, 74,* 865–877.

Dimeff, L. A., Koerner, K., & Linehan, M. M. (2007). *Dialectical behavior therapy in clinical practice: Applications across disorders and settings.* New York: Guilford.

Dion, K. K., & Dion, K. L. (2001). Gender and relationships. In R. K. Unger (Ed.), *Handbook of the psychology of women and gender* (pp. 256–271). Hoboken, NJ: Wiley.

Dishion, T. J., & Piehler, T. F. (2009). Deviant by design: Peer contagion in development, interventions, and schools. In K. H. Rubin, W. M. Bukowski, & B. Laursen (Eds.), *Handbook of peer interactions, relationships, and groups.* New York: Guilford.

Distel, M. A., Trull, T. J., Derom, C A., Thiery, E. W., Grimmer, M. A., Martin, N. G., Willemsen, G., & Boomsma, D. I. (2008). Heritability of borderline personality disorder features is similar across three countries. *Psychological Medicine, 38,* 1219–1229.

Dittmar, H., Halliwell, E., & Ive, S. (2006). Does Barbie make girls want to be thin? The effect of experimental exposure to images of dolls on the body image of 5–8-year-old girls. *Developmental Psychology, 42,* 283–292.

Dixon, M. L., Ruppel, J., Pratt, J., & De Rosa, E. (2009). Learning to ignore: Acquisition of sustained attentional suppression. *Psychonomic Bulletin and Review, 16,* 418–423.

Dodge, K. A., Coie, J. D., & Lynam, D. (2006). Aggression and antisocial behavior in youth. In W. Damon & R. Lerner (Eds.), *Handbook of child psychology* (6th ed.). New York: Wiley.

Doherty, M. (2008). *Theory of mind.* New York: Psychology Press.

Dolan, M., & Fullam, R. (2006). Face affect recognition deficits in personality disordered offenders: Associate with psychopathy. *Psychological Medicine, 36,* 1563–1569.

Dollard, J., Doob, L. W., Miller, N. E., Mowrer, O. H., & Sears, R. R. (1939). *Frustration and aggression.* New Haven, CT: Yale University Press.

Domenech-Llaberia, E., Vinas, F., Pla, E., Jane, M. C., Mitjavila, M., Corbella, T., & Canals, J. (2009). Prevalence of major depression in school children. *European Child and Adolescent Psychiatry.* (in press)

Domhoff, G. W. (2007). Realistic simulation and bizarreness in dream content: Past findings and suggestions for future research. In D. Barrett & P. McNamara (Eds.), *The new science of dreaming: Content, recall, and personality correlates* (vol. 2, pp. 1–27). Westport, CT: Praeger.

Domjan, M. (2006). *The principles of learning and behavior* (6th ed.). Belmont, CA: Wadsworth.

Donatelle, R. J. (2009). *Access to health* (11th ed.). Upper Saddle River, NJ: Pearson.

Donnellan, M. B., Larsen-Rife, D., & Conger, R. D. (2005). Personality, family history, and competence in early adult romantic relationships. *Journal of Personality and Social Psychology, 88,* 562–576.

Donnellan, M. B., Trzesniewski, K., & Robins, R. (2009). An emerging epidemic of narcissism or much ado about nothing? *Journal of Research in Personality.* (in press)

Donovan, M. A. (2000). Cognitive, affective, and satisfaction variables as predictors of organizational behaviors: A structural equation modeling examination of alternative models. *Dissertation Abstracts International, 60* (9-B), 4943 (UMI No. AAI9944835).

Doty, R. L. (2001). Olfaction. *Annual Review of Psychology, 52,* 423–452.

Dovidio, J. F., Gaertner, S. L., & Saguy, T. (2009). Commonality and the complexity of "we": Social attitudes and social change. *Personality and Social Psychology Review, 13,* 3–20.

Dovidio, J. F., Kawakami, K., & Gaertner, S. L. (2002). Implicit and explicit prejudice and interracial interaction. *Journal of Personality and Social Psychology, 82,* 62–68.

Downing, P. E. (2009). Visual neuroscience: A hat-trick for modularity. *Current Biology, 19,* R160–R162.

Drake, C., Levine, R., & Laska, E. A. (2007). Identifying prognostic factors that predict recovery in the presence of loss to follow-up. In K. Hopper, G. Harrison, A. Janca, & N. Sartorius (Eds.), *Recovery from schizophrenia: An international perspective: A report from the WHO Collaborative Project, the international study of schizophrenia* (pp. 69–72). New York: Oxford University Press.

Dricot, L., Sorger, B., Schiltz, C., Goebel, R., & Rossion, B. (2008). Evidence for individual face discrimination in non-face selective areas of the visual cortex in acquired prosopagnosia. *Behavioral Neuroscience, 19,* 75–79.

Dubow, E. F., Huesmann, L. R., & Greenwood, D. (2007). Media and youth socialization: Underlying processes and moderators of effects. In J. E. Grusec & P. D. Hastings (Eds.), *Handbook of socialization* (pp. 404–430). New York: Guilford.

Dunbar, R., & Barrett, L. (2007). *Oxford handbook of evolutionary psychology.* New York: Oxford University Press.

Dunbar, R. I. M., & Shultz, S. (2007). Evolution in the social brain. *Science, 317,* 1344–1347.

Duncan, A. E., Scherrer, J., Fu, Q., Bucholz, K. K., Heath, A. C., True, W. R., Haber, J. R., Howell, D., & Jacob, T. (2006). Exposure to paternal alcoholism does not predict development of alcohol-use disorders in offspring: Evidence from an offspring-of-twins study. *Journal of Studies on Alcohol, 67,* 649–656.

Dunlap, E., Golub, A., Johnson, B. D., & Benoit, E. (2009). Normalization of violence: Experiences of childhood abuse by inner-city crack users. *Journal of Ethnicity in Substance Abuse, 8,* 15–34.

Dunn, E. W., Aknin, L. B., & Norton, M. I. (2008). Spending money on others promotes happiness. *Science, 319,* 1687–1688.

Dunne, M. (2002). Sampling considerations. In M. W. Wiederman & B. E. Whitley (Eds.), *Handbook for conducting research on human sexuality.* Mahwah, NJ: Erlbaum.

Dunner, D. L. (2001). Acute and maintenance treatment of chronic depression. *Journal of Clinical Psychiatry, 62, Suppl. 6,* 10–16.

Dupoux, E., de Gardelle, V., & Kouider, S. (2008). Subliminal speech perception and auditory streaming. *Cognition, 109,* 267–273.

Dupre, K. E., & Barling, J. (2006). Predicting and preventing supervisory workplace aggression. *Journal of Occupational Health Psychology, 11,* 13–26.

Durantini, M. R., & Albarracin, D. (2009). Material and social incentives to participation in behavioral interventions: A meta-analysis of gender disparities in enrollment and retention in experimental HIV prevention interventions. *Health Psychology.* (in press)

Durrant, J. E. (2008). Physical punishment, culture, and rights: Current issues for professionals. *Developmental and Behavioral Pediatrics, 29,* 55–66.

Dutton, D., & Aron, A. (1974). Some evidence for heightened sexual attraction under conditions of high anxiety. *Journal of Personality and Social Psychology, 30,* 510–517.

Duvarci, S., Nader, K., & LeDoux, J. E. (2008). De novo mRNA synthesis is required for both consolidation and reconsolidation of fear memories in the amygdala. *Learning and Memory, 15,* 747–755.

Dweck, C. S. (2006). *Mindset.* New York: Random House.

Dysart, J. E., & Lindsay, R. C. L. (2007). The effects of delay on eyewitness identification witness accuracy: Should we be concerned? In R. C. L. Lindsay, D. F. Ross, J. D. Read, & M. P. Toglia (Eds.), *The handbook of eyewitness memory: Vol. II.* Mahwah, NJ: Erlbaum.

E

Eagly, A. H., & Crowley, M. (1986). Gender and helping behavior: A meta-analytic review of the social psychological literature. *Psychological Bulletin, 100,* 283–308.

Eagly, A. H., & Koenig, A. M. (2006). Social role theory of sex differences and similarities: Implications for prosocial behavior. In K. Dindia & D. J. Canary (Eds.), *Sex differences and similarities in communication.* Mahwah, NJ: Erlbaum.

Eaton, D. K., & others. (2008). Youth risk behavior surveillance—United States, 2007. *Morbidity and Mortality Weekly Reports, 57,* 1–131.

Edenberg, H. J., & Foroud, T. (2006). The genetics of alcoholism: Identifying specific genes through family studies. *Addiction Biology, 11,* 386–396.

Edinger, J. D., Wohlgemuth, W. K., Radtke, R. A., Marsh, G. R., & Quillian, R. E. (2001). Cognitive behavioral therapy for treatment of chronic primary insomnia. *Journal of the American Medical Association, 285,* 1856–1864.

Edmonds, G. W., Jackson, J. J., Fayard, J. V., & Roberts, B. R. (2007). Is character fate or is there hope to change my personality yet? *Social and Personality Psychology Compass, 2,* 399–413.

Edwards, W., Miles, R., & von Winterfeldt, D. (Eds.). (2007). *Advances in decision analysis.* New York: Cambridge University Press.

Eells, T. D. (2000). Can therapy affect physical health? *Journal of Psychotherapy Practice and Research, 9,* 100–104.

Effros, R. B. (2009). Kleemeir Award Lecture 2008—The canary in the cole mine: Telomeres and human healthspan. *Journals of Gerontology: Biological Sciences and Medical Sciences, 64,* 511–515.

Efklides, A. (2009). The role of metacognitive experiences in the learning process. *Psicothema, 21,* 76–82.

Eich, E. (2007). Mood, memory, and the concept of context. In H. L. Roediger, Y. Dubai, & S. Fitzpatrick (Eds.), *Science of memory: Concepts.* New York: Oxford University Press.

Eichmann, M., Kugel, H., & Suslow, T. (2008). Difficulty identifying feelings and automatic activation in the fusiform gyrus in response to facial emotion. *Perceptual and Motor Skills, 107,* 915–922.

Eisch, A. J., & others. (2008). Adult neurogenesis, mental health, and mental illness: Hope or hype? *Journal of Neuroscience, 28,* 11785–11791.

Eisenberg, M. E., & others. (2008). Support for comprehensive sexuality education: Perspectives from parents of school-age youth. *Journal of Adolescent Health, 42,* 352–359.

Eisenberg, N., Fabes, R. A., & Spinrad, T. L. (2006). Prosocial development. In W. Damon & R. Lerner (Eds.), *Handbook of child psychology* (2nd ed.). New York: Wiley.

Eisenberg, N., Morris, A. S., McDaniel, B., & Spinrad, T. L. (2009). Moral cognitions and prosocial responding. In R. M. Lerner & L. Steinberg (Eds.), *Handbook of adolescent psychology* (3rd ed.). New York: Wiley.

Eisenberg, N., & Murphy, B. (1995). Parenting and children's moral development. In M. H. Bornstein (Ed.), *Children and parenting* (vol. 4). Hillsdale, NJ: Erlbaum.

Eisenberg, N., & Valiente, C. (2002). Parenting and children's prosocial and moral development. In M. H. Bornstein (Ed.), *Handbook of parenting* (2nd ed.). Mahwah, NJ: Erlbaum.

Ekman, P. (1980). *The face of man.* New York: Garland.

Ekman, P. (1996). Lying and deception. In N. L. Stein, C. Brainerd, P. A. Ornstein, & B. Tversky (Eds.), *Memory for everyday emotional events.* Mahwah, NJ: Erlbaum.

Ekman, P. (2003). Emotions inside out: 130 years after Darwin's "The expression of emotions in man and animal." *Annals of the New York Academy of Science, 1000,* 1–6.

Ekman, P., Davidson, R. J., & Friesen, W. V. (1990). The Duchenne smile: Emotional expression and brain physiology: II. *Journal of Personality and Social Psychology, 58,* 342–353.

Ekman, P., Davidson, R. J., Ricard, M., & Wallace, B. A. (2005). Buddhist and psychological perspectives on emotions and well-being. *Current Directions in Psychological Science, 14,* 59–63.

Ekman, P., & Friesen, W. V. (1969). The repertoire of nonverbal behavior: Categories, origins, usage, and coding. *Semiotica, 1,* 49–98.

Ekman, P., & Friesen, W. V. (1971). Constants across cultures in the face and emotion. *Journal of Personality and Social Psychology, 17,* 124–129.

Ekman, P., Levenson, R. W., & Friesen, W. V. (1983). Autonomic nervous system activity distinguishes among emotions. *Science, 223,* 1208–1210.

Ekman, P., & O'Sullivan, M. (1991). Facial expressions: Methods, means, and moues. In R. S. Feldman & B. Rime (Eds.), *Fundamentals of nonverbal behavior.* Cambridge, England: Cambridge University Press.

El-Hai, J. (2005). *The lobotomist: A maverick medical genius and his tragic quest to rid the world of mental illness.* Hoboken, NJ: Wiley.

Eliot, L. (2001). *What's going on in there? How the brain and mind develop in the first five years of life.* New York: Bantam Doubleday.

Elkind, D. (1978). Understanding the young adolescent. *Adolescence, 13,* 127–134.

Elliott, E. S., & Dweck, C. S. (1988). Goals: An approach to motivation and achievement. *Journal of Personality and Social Psychology, 54,* 5–12.

Elliott, T., Kuang, X., Shadbolt, N. R., & Zauner, K. P. (2009). Adaptation in multisensory neurons: Impact of cross-modal enhancement. *Network, 20,* 1–31.

Ellis, A. (1962). *Reason and emotion in psychotherapy.* New York: Lyle Stuart.

Ellis, A. (1996). A rational-emotive behavior therapist's perspective on Ruth. In G. Corey (Ed.), *Case approach to counseling and psychotherapy.* Pacific Grove, CA: Brooks/Cole.

Ellis, A. (2000). Rational emotive behavior therapy. In A. Kazdin (Ed.), *Encyclopedia of Psychology.* Washington, DC, & New York: American Psychological Association and Oxford University Press.

Ellis, A. (2002). Rational emotive behavior therapy. In M. Hersen & W. H. Sledge (Eds.), *Encyclopedia of psychotherapy.* San Diego: Academic.

Ellis, A. (2005). Why I (really) became a therapist. *Journal of Clinical Psychology, 61,* 945–948.

Elms, A. C. (2005). Freud as Leonardo: Why the first psychobiography went wrong. In W. T. Schultz (Ed.), *The handbook of psychobiography* (pp. 210–222). New York: Oxford University Press.

Elms, A. C., & Heller, B. (2005). Twelve ways to say "lonesome": Assessing error and control in the music of Elvis Presley. In W. T. Schultz (Ed.), *Handbook of psychobiography* (pp. 142–157). Oxford, England: Oxford University Press.

Emmons, R. A. (2005). Striving for the sacred: Personal goals, life meaning, and religion. *Journal of Social Issues, 61,* 731–745.

Emmons, R. A., & Diener, E. (1986). Situation selection as a moderator of response consistency and stability. *Journal of Personality and Social Psychology, 51,* 1013–1019.

Emmons, R. A., & King, L. A. (1988). Conflict among personal strivings: Immediate and long-term implications for psychological and physical well-being. *Journal of Personality and Social Psychology, 48,* 1040–1048.

Emmons, R. A., & McCullough, M. E. (2003). Counting blessings versus burdens: An experimental investigation of gratitude and subjective well-being in daily life. *Journal of Personality and Social Psychology, 84,* 377–389.

Emmons, R. A., & McCullough, M. E. (Eds.). (2004). *The psychology of gratitude.* New York: Oxford University Press.

Endler, N. S. (1988). The origins of electroconvulsive therapy (ECT). *Convulsive Therapy, 4,* 5–23.

Eng, P. M., Fitzmaurice, G., Kubzansky, L. D., Rimm, E. B., & Kawachi, I. (2003). Anger expression and risk of stroke and coronary heart disease among male health professionals. *Psychosomatic Medicine, 65,* 100–110.

Engel, A. K., & Singer, W. (2001). Temporal binding and the neural correlates of sensory awareness. *Trends in Cognitive Science, 5,* 16–25.

Englander, E. K. (2006). *Understanding violence* (3rd ed.). Mahwah, NJ: Erlbaum.

Engler, B. (2009). *Personality theories* (8th ed.). Boston: Cengage.

Ensembl Human. (2008). *Explore the Homo sapiens genome.* www.ensembl.org/Homo_sapiens/index.html (accessed March 28, 2009)

Enstrom, J. E. (1999). Smoking cessation and mortality trends among two United States populations. *Journal of Clinical Epidemiology, 52,* 813–825.

Erdem, A., Acik, V., Leventoglu, A., Sarilar, C., & Cansu, A. (2009). A focalcortical dysplasia case whose seizure focuses were undetected using interhemispheric grid electrode: A technical case report. *Turkish Neurosurgery, 19,* 63–68.

Erickson, K. I., & others. (2009). Aerobic fitness is associated with hippocampal volume in elderly humans. *Hippocampus.* (in press)

Erickson, K. I., & Kramer, A. F. (2009). Aerobic exercise effects on cognitive and neural plasticity in older adults. *British Journal of Sports Medicine, 43,* 22–24.

Erikson, E. H. (1968). *Identity: Youth and crisis.* New York: Norton.

Erikson, E. H. (1969). *Gandhi's truth.* New York: Norton.

Escobar-Chaves, S. L., & Anderson, C. A. (2008). Media and risky behavior. *Future of Children, 18* (1), 147–180.

Espirito-Santo, H., & Pio-Abreu, J. L. (2009). Psychiatric symptoms and dissociation in conversion, somatization, and dissociative disorders. *Australian and New Zealand Journal of Psychiatry, 43,* 270–276.

Estrada, C., Isen, A. M., & Young, M. J. (1997). Positive affect influences creative problem solving and reported source of practice satisfaction in physicians. *Motivation and Emotion, 18,* 285–299.

Evans, B. G., & Iverson, P. (2007). Plasticity in vowel perception and production: A study of accent change in young adults. *Journal of the Acoustical Society of America, 121* (6), 3814–3826.

Exner, C., Kohl, A., Zaudig, M., Langs, G., Lincoln, T. M., & Rief, W. (2009). Metacognition and episodic memory in obsessive-compulsive disorder. *Journal of Anxiety Disorders.* (in press)

Exner, J. E. Jr. (2003). *The Rorschach: A comprehensive system* (4th ed.). Hoboken, NJ: Wiley.

Eysenck, H. J. (1967). *The biological basis of personality.* Springfield, IL: Thomas.

F

Faber, M. A., & Mayer, J. D. (2009). Resonance to archetypes in media: There's some accounting for taste. *Journal of Research in Personality, 43,* 307–322.

Fahlman, S. E. (2003). *Smiley lore.* http://www.cs.cmu.edu/~sef/sefSmiley.htm (accessed April 29, 2009)

Fant, R. V., Buchhalter, A. R., Buchman, A. C., & Heningfield, J. E. (2009). Pharmacotherapy for tobacco dependence. *Handbook of Experimental Pharmacology, 192,* 487–510.

Farooqui, I. S., & O'Rahilly, S. (2009). Leptin: A pivotal regulator of human energy homeostasis. *American Journal of Clinical Nutrition, 89,* 980S–984S.

Farrington, D. P. (2009). Conduct disorder, aggression, and delinquency. In R. M. Lerner & L. Steinberg (Eds.), *Handbook of adolescent psychology* (3rd ed.). New York: Wiley.

Fatemi, S. H., & Folsom, T. D. (2009). The neurodevelopmental hypothesis of schizophrenia, revisited. *Schizophrenia Bulletin, 35,* 528–548.

Faul, L. A., Jim, H. S., Williams, C., Loftus, L., & Jacobsen, P. B. (2009). Relationship of stress management skill to psychological distress and quality of life in adults with cancer. *Psychooncology.* (in press)

Fava, G. A. (2006). The intellectual crisis in psychiatric research. *Psychotherapy and Psychosomatics, 75,* 202–208.

Fava, G. A., Ruini, C., & Belaise, C. (2007). The concept of recovery in depression. *Psychological Medicine, 37,* 307–317.

Faymonville, M. E., Boly, M., & Laureys, S. (2006). Functional neuroanatomy of the hypnotic state. *Journal of Physiology, Paris, 99,* 463–469.

Fazio, R. H., Chen, J., McDonel, E. C., & Sherman, S. J. (1982). Attitude accessibility, attitude-behavior consistency, and the strength of the object-evaluation association. *Journal of Experimental Social Psychology, 18,* 339–357.

Fazio, R. H., & Olsen, A. (2007). Attitudes. In M. A. Hogg & J. Cooper (Eds.), *The Sage handbook of social psychology* (concise 2nd ed.). Thousand Oaks, CA: Sage.

Feder, A., Nestler, E. J., & Charney, D. S. (2009). Psychobiology and molecular genetics of resilience. *Nature Reviews: Neuroscience, 10,* 446–457.

Fehm, H. L., Kern, W., & Peters, A. (2006). The selfish brain: Competition for energy resources. *Progress in Brain Research, 153,* 129–140.

Fei-Fei, L., Iyer, A., Koch, C., & Perona, P. (2007). What do we perceive in a glance at a real-world scene? *Journal of Vision, 7,* 10.

Fein, S., Goethals, G. R., Kassin, S. M., & Cross, J. (1993, August). *Social influence and presidential debates.* Paper presented at the meeting of the American Psychological Association, Toronto.

Feldman, D. (2009). Synaptic mechanisms for plasticity in neocortex. *Annual Review of Neuroscience* (vol. 32). Palo Alto, CA: Annual Reviews.

Ferguson, C. J. (2007). Evidence for publication bias in video game violence effects literature: A meta-analytic review. *Aggression and Violent Behavior, 12,* 470–482.

Ferguson, C. J., Rueda, S. M., Cruz, A. M., Ferguson, D. E., Fritz, S., & Smith, S. M. (2008). Violent video games and aggression: Causal relationship or byproduct of family violence and intrinsic violence motivation? *Criminal Justice and Behavior, 35,* 311–332.

Fernandez, J. M., & Farell, B. (2008). A neural model for the integration of stereopsis and motion parallax in structure-from-motion. *Neurocomputing, 71,* 1629–1641.

Ferreira, G., Ferry, B., Meurise, M., & Levy, F. (2006). Forebrain structures specifically activated by conditioned taste aversion. *Behavioral Neuroscience, 120,* 952–962.

Ferretti, F., & Coluccia, A. (2009). Socio-economic factors and suicide rates in European Union countries. *Legal Medicine, 11.*

Ferro, A. (2009). Transformations in dreaming and characters in the psychoanalytic field. *International Journal of Psychoanalysis, 90,* 209–230.

Ferruta, A. (2009). The reality of the other: Dreaming of the analyst. *International Journal of Psychoanalysis, 90,* 93–108.

Feshbach, S., & Weiner, B. (1996). *Personality* (4th ed.). Lexington, MA: Heath.

Festinger, L. (1954). A theory of social comparison processes. *Human Relations, 7,* 117–140.

Festinger, L. (1957). *A theory of cognitive dissonance.* Evanston, IL: Row Peterson.

Festinger, L., & Carlsmith, J. M. (1959). Cognitive consequences of forced compliance. *Journal of Abnormal and Social Psychology, 58,* 203–211.

Field, C. D., & Chichilnisky, E. J. (2007). Information processing in the primate retina: Circuitry and coding. *Annual Review of Neuroscience* (vol. 30). Palo Alto, CA: Annual Reviews.

Field, T. (2007). *The amazing infant.* Malden, MA: Blackwell.

Field, T. M. (2001). Massage therapy facilitates weight gain in preterm infants. *Current Directions in Psychological Science, 10,* 51–53.

Field, T. M. (2003). Stimulation of preterm infants. *Pediatrics Review, 24,* 4–11.

Fields, R. (2010). *Drugs in perspective* (7th ed.). New York: McGraw-Hill.

Fiese, B. H., Foley, K. P., & Spagnola, M. (2006). Routine and ritual elements in family mealtimes: Contexts for child well-being and family identity. *New Directions in Child and Adolescent Development, 111,* 67–89.

Figueroa-Moseley, C., Jean-Pierre, P., Roscoe, J. A., Ryan, J. L., Kohli, S., Palesh, O. G., Ryan, E. P., Carroll, J., & Morrow, G. R. (2007). Behavioral interventions in treating anticipatory nausea and vomiting. *Journal of the National Comprehensive Cancer Network, 5,* 44–50.

Finch, C. E. (2009). The neurobiology of middle-age has arrived. *Neurobiology of Aging, 30,* 515–520.

Finch, E. A., Linde, J. A., Jeffery, R. W., Rothman, A. J., King, C. M., & Levy, R. L. (2005). The effects of outcome expectations and satisfaction on weight loss and maintenance: Correlational and experimental analyses—a randomized trial. *Health Psychology, 24* (6), 608–616.

Fine, M. A., & Harvey, J. H. (Eds.). (2006). *Divorce and relationship dissolution.* Mahwah, NJ: Erlbaum.

Finkbeiner, M., & Palermo, R. (2009). The role of spatial attention in nonconscious processing: A comparison of face and nonface stimuli. *Psychological Science, 20,* 42–51.

Finley, G. A., Kristjansdottir, O., & Forgeron, P. A. (2009). Cultural influences on the assessment of children's pain. *Pain Research and Management, 14,* 33–37.

Finzi-Dottan, R., & Zubery, E. (2009). The role of depression and anxiety in impulsive and obsessive-compulsive behaviors among anorexic and bulimic patients. *Eating Disorders, 17,* 162–182.

Fischer, K. W., & Immordino-Yang, M. H. (2008). The fundamental importance of the brain and learning for education. *The Jossey-Bass reader on the brain and learning.* San Francisco: Jossey-Bass.

Fischer, R. (2006). Congruence and functions of personal and cultural values: Do my values reflect my culture's values? *Personality and Social Psychology Bulletin, 32,* 1419–1431.

Fisher, M., & others. (2009). Update of stroke therapy academic industry roundtable preclinical recommendations. *Stroke, 40,* 2244–2250.

Fiske, A., Wetherell, J. L., & Gatz, M. (2009). Depression in older adults. *Annual Review of Clinical Psychology, 5,* 363–389.

Fitzpatrick, E., Olds, J., Durieux-Smith, A., McCrae, R., Schramm, D., & Gaboury, I. (2009). Pediatric cochlear implanation: How much hearing is too much? *International Journal of Audiology, 48,* 91–97.

Fleischhaker, S., Schulz, E., Tepper, K., Martin, M., Hennighausen, K., & Remschmidt, H. (2005). Long-term course of adolescent schizophrenia. *Schizophrenia Bulletin, 31,* 769–780.

Flint, M. S., Baum, A., Chambers, W. H., & Jenkins, F. J. (2007). Induction of DNA damage, alteration of DNA repair, and transcriptional activation by stress hormones. *Psychoneuroendocrinology. 32,* 470–479.

Flynn, J. R. (1999). Searching for justice: The discovery of IQ gains over time. *American Psychologist, 54,* 5–20.

Flynn, J. R. (2006). The history of the American mind in the 20th century: A scenario to explain gains over time and a case for the irrelevance of *g.* In P. C. Kyllonen, R. D. Roberts, & L. Stankov (Eds.), *Extending intelligence.* Mahwah, NJ: Erlbaum.

Fodor, I., & Epstein, J. (2002). Agoraphobia, panic disorder, and gender. In J. Worell (Ed.), *Encyclopedia of women and gender.* San Diego: Academic.

Fok, H., Hui, C., Bond, M. H., Matsumoto, D., & Yoo, S. H. (2008). Integrating personality, context, relationship, and emotion type into a model of display rules. *Journal of Research in Personality, 42,* 133–150.

Folkman, S., & Lazarus, R. S. (1980). An analysis of coping in a middle-aged community sample. *Journal of Health and Social Behavior, 21,* 219–239.

Folkman, S., & Moskowitz, J. T. (2004). Coping: Pitfalls and promises. *Annual Review of Psychology* (vol. 54). Palo Alto, CA: Annual Reviews.

Fontaine, R. G., Yang, C., Burks, V. S., Dodge, K. A., Price, J. M., Pettit, G. S., & Bates, J. E. (2009). Loneliness as a partial mediator of the relation between low social preference in childhood and anxious/depressed symptoms in adolescence. *Development and Psychopathology, 21,* 479–491.

Fontana, A., & Rosenheck, R. (2008). Treatment-seeking veterans of Iraq and Afghanistan: Comparison with veterans of previous wars. *Journal of Nervous and Mental Disease, 196,* 513–521.

Fontanini, A., Grossman, S. E., Figueroa, J. A., & Katz, D. B. (2009). Distinct subtypes of basolateral amygdala taste neurons reflect palatability and reward. *Journal of Neuroscience, 29,* 2486–2495.

Foote, B., Smolin, Y., Kaplan, M., Legatt, M. E., & Lipschitz, D. (2006). Prevalence of dissociative disorders in psychiatric outpatients. *American Journal of Psychiatry, 163,* 566–568.

Forbey, J. D., & Ben-Porath, Y. S. (2007). Computerized adaptive personality testing: A review and illustration with the MMPI-2 computerized adaptive version. *Psychological Assessment, 19,* 14–24.

Forbush, K., Heatherton, T. F., & Keel, P. K. (2007). Relationships between perfectionism and specific disordered eating behaviors. *International Journal of Eating Disorders, 40,* 37–41.

Forgas, J. P., Baumeister, R. F., & Tice, D. M. (2009). The psychology of self-regulation: An introduction. In J. P. Forgas, R. F. Baumeister, & D. M. Tice (Eds.), *Psychology of self-regulation.* New York: Psychology Press.

Forman-Hoffman, V. L., & Cunningham, C. L. (2008). Geographical clustering of eating disordered behaviors in U.S. high school students. *International Journal of Eating Disorders, 41,* 209–214.

Forouzan, B. A. (2007). *Data communication networking* (4th ed.). New York: McGraw-Hill.

Forsythe, C., Bernard, M. L., & Goldsmith, T. E. (Eds.). (2006). *Cognitive systems.* Mahwah, NJ: Erlbaum.

Fortuna, L. R., Perez, D. J., Canino, G., Sribney, W., & Alegria, M. (2007). Prevalence and correlates of lifetime suicidal ideation and suicide attempts among Latino subgroups in the United States. *Journal of Clinical Psychiatry, 68,* 572–581.

Foulkes, D. (1993). Cognitive dream theory. In M. A. Carskadon (Ed.), *Encyclopedia of sleep and dreams.* New York: Macmillan.

Foulkes, D. (1999). *Children's dreaming and the development of consciousness.* Cambridge, MA: Harvard University Press.

Fountas, K. N., & Smith, J. R. (2007). Historical evolution of stereotactic amygdalotomy for the management of severe aggression. *Journal of Neurosurgery, 106,* 710–713.

Fowler, K. A., Lilienfeld, S. O., & Patrick, C. J. (2009). Detecting psychopathy from thin slices of behavior. *Psychological Assessment, 21,* 68–78.

Fox, S. I. (2008). *Human physiology* (10th ed.). New York: McGraw-Hill.

Frankl, V. E. (1963/1984). *Man's search for meaning* (3rd ed.). New York: First Washington Square Press. (original work published 1946)

Frattaroli, J. (2006). Experimental disclosure and its moderators: A meta-analysis. *Psychological Bulletin, 132,* 823–865.

Fredrick, S., & Loewenstein, G. (1999). Hedonic adaptation. In D. Kahneman, E. Diener, & N. Schwarz (Eds.), *Well-being: The foundations of hedonic psychology* (pp. 302–329). New York: Russell Sage Foundation.

Fredrickson, B. L. (1998). What good are positive emotions? *Review of General Psychology, 2,* 300–319.

Fredrickson, B. L. (2001). The role of positive emotions in positive psychology. *American Psychologist, 56,* 218–226.

Fredrickson, B. L. (2006). Unpacking positive emotions: Investigating the seeds of human flourishing. *Journal of Positive Psychology, 1,* 57–60.

Fredrickson, B. L. (2009). *Positivity.* New York: Crown.

Fredrickson, B. L., Tugade, M. M., Waugh, C. E., & Larkin, G. R. (2003). What good are positive emotions in crisis? A prospective study of resilience and emotions following the terrorist attacks on the United States on September 11th, 2001. *Journal of Personality and Social Psychology, 84,* 365–376.

Freedman, J. L., & Fraser, S. C. (1966). Compliance without pressure: The foot-in-the-door technique. *Journal of Personality and Social Psychology, 4,* 195–202.

Freeland, A., Manchanda, R., Chiu, S., Sharma, V., & Merskey, H. (1993). Four cases of supposed multiple personality disorder: Evidence of unjustified diagnoses. *Canadian Journal of Psychiatry, 38,* 245–247.

Freeman, S., & Herron, J. C. (2007). *Evolutionary analysis* (4th ed.). Upper Saddle River, NJ: Prentice-Hall.

French, C. C., Santomauro, J., Hamilton, V., Fox, R., & Thalbourne, M. A. (2008). Psychological aspects of alien contact experience. *Cortex, 44,* 1387–1395.

Freud, S. (1899/1911). *The interpretation of dreams* (3rd ed.). A. A. Brill (Trans). New York: Macmillan.

Freud, S. (1917). *A general introduction to psychoanalysis.* New York: Washington Square Press.

Freud, S. (1953). The interpretation of dreams. In J. Strachey (Ed.), *The standard edition of the complete psychological works of Sigmund Freud.* New York: Washington Square Press. (original work published 1900)

Fried, S. (2008, October 9). Commentary in "Think fat just hangs around, does nothing." *USA Today,* 6D.

Friedel, E., & others. (2009). 5-HTT genotype effect on prefrontal-amygdala coupling differs between major depression and conrols. *Psychopharmacology.* (in press)

Friedman, H. S., & Schustack, M. W. (2009). *Personality* (4th ed.). Upper Saddle River, NJ: Prentice-Hall.

Friedman, H. S., & Silver, R. C. (Eds.). (2007). *Foundations of health psychology.* New York: Oxford University Press.

Friedman, J. M. (2009). Leptin at 14 y of age: An ongoing story. *American Journal of Clinical Nutrition, 89,* 973S–979S.

Friedman, M., & Rosenman, R. (1974). *Type A behavior and your heart.* New York: Knopf.

Friedman, M. J., Keane, T. M., & Resick, P. A. (Eds.). (2007). *Handbook of PTSD.* New York: Guilford.

Friedman, N. P., Miyake, A., Young, S. E., DeFries, J. C., Corley, R. P., & Hewitt, J. K. (2008). Individual differences in executive functions are almost entirely genetic in origin. *Journal of Experimental Psychology: General, 137 (2),* 201–225.

Friedman, R., Myers, P., & Benson, H. (1998). Meditation and the relaxation response. In H. S. Friedman (Ed.), *Encyclopedia of mental health* (vol. 2). San Diego: Academic.

Friese, R. S., Bruns, B., & Sinton, C. M. (2009). Sleep deprivation after septic insult increases mortality independent of age. *Journal of Trauma, 66,* 50–54.

Frijda, N. H. (2007). *The laws of emotion.* Mahwah, NJ: Erlbaum.

Frisch, M. B., Clark, M. P., Rouse, S. V., Rudd, M. D., Paweleck, J. K. Greenstone, A., & others. (2004). Predictive and treatment validity of life satisfaction and the Quality of Life Inventory. *Assessment, 10,* 1–13.

Frishman, W. H., Mitta, W., Kupersmith, A., & Ky, T. (2006). Nicotine and non-nicotine smoking cessation pharmacotherapies. *Cardiology in Review, 14,* 57–73.

Frohlich, P., & Meston, C. M. (2005). Fluoxetine-induced changes in tactile sensation and sexual functioning among clinically depressed women. *Journal of Sex & Marital Therapy, 31 (2),* 113–128.

Fromm, E. (1947). *Man for himself.* New York: Holt, Rinehart & Winston.

Frosch, Z. A., Dierker, L. C., Rose, J. S., & Waldinger, R. J. (2009). Smoking trajectories, health, and mortality across the adult lifespan. *Addictive Behaviors.* (in press)

Fry, P. S., & Debats, D. L. (2009). Perfectionism and the five-factor personality traits as predictors of mortality in older adults. *Journal of Health Psychology, 14,* 513–524.

Funder, D. C. (2009). Persons, behaviors, and situations: An agenda for personality psychology in the postwar era. *Journal of Research in Personality, 43,* 120–126.

Fujiwara, E., Levine, B., & Anderson, A. K. (2008). Intact implicit and reduced explicit memory for negative self-related information in repressive coping. *Cognitive, Affective, and Behavioral Neuroscience, 8,* 254–263.

Fuligni, A. J., Hughes, D. L., & Way, N. (2009). Ethnicity and immigration. In R. M. Lerner & L. Steinberg (Eds.), *Handbook of adolescent psychology* (3rd ed.). New York: Wiley.

Fultz, J., Batson, C. D., Fortenbach, V. A., McCarthy, P. M., & Varney, L. L. (1986). Social evaluation and the empathy-altruism hypothesis. *Journal of Personality and Social Psychology, 50,* 761–769.

Fung, H. H., & Ng, S. K. (2006). Age differences in the sixth personality factor: Age difference in interpersonal relatedness among Canadians and Hong Kong Chinese. *Psychology and Aging, 21,* 810–814.

Fung, M. T., Raine, A., Loeber, R., Lynam, D. R., Steinhauer, S. R., Venables, P. H., & Stouthamer-Loeber, M. (2005). Reduced electrodermal activity in psychopathy-prone adolescents. *Journal of Abnormal Psychology, 114,* 187–196.

Gage, F. H., & Bjorklund, A. (1986). Cholinergic septal grafts into the hippocampal formation improve spatial learning and memory in aged rats by an atropine-sensitive mechanism. *Journal of Neuroscience, 6,* 2837–2847.

Gail, T. L., Kritjansson, E., Charbonneau, C., & Florack, P. (2009). A longitudinal study on the role of spirituality in response to the diagnosis and treatment of breast cancer. *Journal of Behavioral Medicine, 32,* 174–186.

Galaif, E. R., Sussman, S., Newcomb, M. D., & Locke, T. F. (2007). Suicidality, depression, and alcohol use among adolescents: A review of empirical findings. *International Journal of Adolescent Medicine and Health, 19,* 27–35.

Galambos, N. L., Berenbaum, S. A., & McHale, S. M. (2009). Gender development in adolescence. In R. M. Lerner & L. Steinberg (Eds.), *Handbook of adolescent psychology* (3rd ed.). New York: Wiley.

Galan, R. F., Weidert, M., Menzel, R., Herz, A. V., & Galizia, C. G. (2006). Sensory memory for odors is encoded in spontaneous correlated activity between olfactory glomeruli. *Neural Computation, 18,* 10–25.

Gallo, I. S., Keil, A., McCulloch, K. C., Rockstroh, B., & Gollwitzer, P. M. (2009). Strategic automation of emotion regulation. *Journal of Personality and Social Psychology, 96,* 11–31.

Gamer, M., Klimecki, O., Bauermann, T., Stoeter, P., & Vossel, G. (2009). fMRI-activation patterns in the detection of concealed information rely on memory-related effects. *Social Cognitive and Affective Neuroscience.* (in press)

Gao, D., & Vasconcelos, N. (2009). Decision-theoretic saliency: Computational principles, biological plausibility, and implications for neurophysiology. *Neural Computation, 21,* 239–271.

Garb, H. N., Wood, J. M., Nezworski, M. T., Grove, W. M., & Stejskal, W. J. (2001). Toward a resolution of the Rorschach controversy. *Psychological Assessment, 13,* 433–448.

Garcia, J. (1989). Food for Tolman: Cognition and cathexis in concert. In T. Archer & L. Nilsson (Eds.), *Aversion, avoidance, and anxiety.* Mahwah, NJ: Erlbaum.

Garcia, J., Ervin, F. E., & Koelling, R. A. (1966). Learning with prolonged delay of reinforcement. *Psychonomic Science, 5,* 121–122.

Garcia, J., & Koelling, R. A. (1966). Relation of cue to consequence in avoidance learning. *Psychonomic Science, 4,* 123–124.

Garcia, J., & Koelling, R. A. (2009). Specific hungers and poison avoidance as adaptive specializations of learning. In D. Shanks (Ed.), *Psychology of learning.* Thousand Oaks, CA: Sage.

Gardner, H. (1983). *Frames of mind.* New York: Basic Books.

Gardner, H. (1993). *Multiple intelligences.* New York: Basic Books.

Gardner, H. (2002). The pursuit of excellence through education. In M. Ferrari (Ed.), *Learning from extraordinary minds.* Mahwah, NJ: Erlbaum.

Gardner, W. L., & Martinko, M. J. (1996). Using the Myers-Briggs Type Indicator to study managers: A literature review and research agenda. *Journal of Management, 22,* 45–83.

Garfield, A. S., & Heisler, L. K. (2009). Pharmacological targeting of the serotonergic system for the treatment of obesity. *Journal of Physiology, 587,* 49–60.

Garner, M., Mohler, H., Stein, D. J., Mueggler, T., & Baldwin, D. S. (2009). Research In anxiety disorders: From the bench to the beside. *European Neuropsychopharmacology, 19,* 381–390.

Garrison, G. D., & Dugan, S. E. (2009). Varenicline: A first-line treatment for smoking cessation. *Clinical Therapeutics, 31,* 463–491.

Garry, M., & Loftus, E. F. (2009). Repressed memory. In D. Clark (Ed.), *Encyclopedia of law and society* (pp. 555–556). Thousand Oaks, CA: Sage.

Garver, D. L. (2006). Evolution of antipsychotic intervention in the schizophrenic psychosis. *Current Drug Targets, 7,* 1205–1215.

Garzon, C., Guerrero, J. M., Aramburu, O., & Guzman, T. (2009). Effect of melatonin administration on sleep, behavioral disorders, and hypnotic drug discontinuation in the elderly: A randomized, double-blind, placebo-controlled study. *Aging: Clinical and Experimental Research, 21,* 38–42.

Gasper, K. (2004). Permission to seek freely? The effect of happy and sad moods on generating old and new ideas. *Creativity Research Journal, 16* (2–3), 215–229.

Gastil, J. W. (2009). *The group in society.* Thousand Oaks, CA: Sage.

Gaunt, R., & Trope, Y. (2007). Attribution and person perception. In M. A. Hogg & J. Cooper (Eds.), *The Sage handbook of social psychology* (concise 2nd ed.). Thousand Oaks, CA: Sage.

Gauthier, I., Behrmann, M., & Tarr, M. J. (2004). Are greebles like faces? Using the neuropsychological exception to test the rule. *Neuropsychologia, 42,* 1961–1970.

Gauthier, I., & Bukach, C. (2007). Should we reject the expertise hypothesis? *Cognition, 103,* 322–330.

Gauthier, I., Curran, T., Curby, K. M., & Collins, D. (2003). Perceptual inference supports a non-modular account of face processing. *Nature Neuroscience, 6,* 428–432.

Gauthier, I., Skudlarski, P., Gore, J. C., & Anderson, A. W. (2000). Expertise for cars and birds recruits brain areas involved in face recognition. *Nature Neuroscience, 3,* 191–197.

Gavlak, D. (2009, April, 12). Jordan honor killing: Man confesses to brutally stabbing to death pregnant sister. http://www.huffingtonpost.com/2009/04/12/jordan-honor-killing-man-_n_185977.html (accessed May 29, 2009)

Ge, X., Natsuaki, M. N., Neiderhiser, J. M., & Reiss, D. (2009). The longitudinal effects of stressful life events on adolescent depression are buffered by parent-child closeness. *Development and Psychopathology, 21,* 621–635.

Geary, D. (2006). Evolutionary developmental psychology: Current status and future directions. *Developmental Review, 26,* 113–119.

Gehar, D. R. (2010). *Mastering competencies in family therapy.* Boston: Cengage.

Gelder, B. D., Meeren, H. K., Righart, R., Stock, J. V., van de Riet, W. A., & Tamietto, M. (2006). Beyond the face: Exploring rapid influences of context on face processing. *Progress in Brain Research, 155PB,* 37–48.

Gelernter, J., & Stein, M. B. (2009). Heritability and genetics of anxiety disorders. In M. M. Antony & M. B. Stein (Eds.), *Oxford handbook of anxiety and related disorders* (pp. 87–96). New York: Oxford University Press.

Geller, E. S. (2002). The challenge of increasing pro-environmental behavior. In R. B. Bechtel & A. Churchman (Eds.), *Handbook of environmental psychology* (pp. 525–540). Hoboken, NJ: Wiley.

Geller, E. S. (2006). Occupational injury prevention and applied behavior analysis. In A. C. Gielen, D. A. Sleet, & R. J. DiClemente (Eds.), *Injury and violence prevention: Behavioral science theories, methods, and applications.* (pp. 297–322). San Francisco: Jossey-Bass.

Gelman, S. A. (2009). Learning from others: Children's constructions of concepts. *Annual Review of Psychology,* (vol. 60). Palo Alto, CA: Annual Reviews.

Gentile, D. A., & Anderson, C. A. (2006). Violent video games: Effects on youth and public policy implications. In N. Dowd, D. G. Singer, & R. F. Wilson (Eds.), *Handbook of children, culture, and violence* (pp. 225–246). Thousand Oaks, CA: Sage.

George, L. K. (2009). Perceived quality of life. In R. H. Binstock & L. K. George (Eds.), *Handbook of aging and the social sciences* (6th ed.). San Diego: Academic.

George, L. K. (2009). Religiousness and spirituality, later life. In D. Carr (Ed.), *Encyclopedia of the life course and human adjustment.* Boston: Gale Cengage.

Geraerts, E., Lindsay, D. S., Merckelbach, H., Jelicic, M., Raymaekers, L., Arnold, M. M., & Schooler, J. W. (2009). Cognitive mechanisms underlying recovered-memory experiences of childhood sexual abuse. *Psychological Science, 20,* 92–98.

Gershoff, E. T. (2002). Corporal punishment by parents and associated child behaviors and experiences: A meta-analysis and theoretical review. *Psychological Bulletin, 128,* 539–579.

Gerson, L. S., & Braun, B. (2006). Effect of high cardio-respiratory fitness and high body fat on insulin resistance. *Medicine and Science in Sports and Exercise, 38,* 1709–1715.

Giang, D. W., Goodman, A. D., Schiffer, R. B., Mattson, D. H., Petrie M., and others. (1996). Conditioning of cyclophosphamide-induced leukopenia in humans. *Journal of Neuropsychiatry and Clinical Neuroscience, 8,* 194–201.

Gibbs, J. C. (2009). Moral development and reality: Beyond the theories of Kohlberg and Hoffman (2nd ed.). Boston: Allyn & Bacon.

Gibson, E. J. (2001). *Perceiving the affordances.* Mahwah, NJ: Erlbaum.

Gidron, Y., & Nyklicek, I. (2009). Experimentally testing Taylor's stress, coping, and adaptation framework. *Anxiety, Stress, and Coping, 22,* 1477–2205.

Giedd, J. N. (2008). The teen brain: Insights from neuro-imaging. *Journal of Adolescent Medicine, 42,* 335–343.

Gil, S., & Caspi, Y. (2006). Personality traits, coping style, and perceived threat as predictors of posttraumatic stress disorder after exposure to a terrorist attack: A prospective study. *Psychosomatic Medicine, 68,* 904–909.

Gilbert, A. L., Regier, T., Kay, P., & Ivry, R. B. (2006). Whorf hypothesis is supported in the right visual field but not the left. *Proceedings of the National Academy of Sciences USA, 103* (2), 489–494.

Gilbert, D. T., & Malone, P. S. (1995). The correspondence bias. *Psychological Bulletin, 117,* 21–38.

Gilbert, L. A., & Kearney, L. K. (2006). The psychotherapeutic relationship as a positive and powerful resource for girls and women. In J. Worell & C. D. Goodheart (Eds.), *Handbook of girls' and women's psychological health: Gender and well-being across the lifespan.* New York: Oxford University Press.

Gillard, E., Van Dooren, W., Schaeken, W., & Verschaffel, L. (2009). Proportional reasoning as a heuristic-based processs. *Experimental Psychology, 56,* 92–99.

Gilligan, C. (1982). *In a different voice.* Cambridge, MA: Harvard University Press.

Giltay, E. J., Zitman, F. G., & Kromhout, D. (2006). Dispositional optimism and the risk of depressive symptoms during 15 years of follow-up: The Zutphen Elderly Study. *Journal of Affective Disorders, 91,* 45–52.

Gino, F., Ayal, S., & Ariely, D. (2009). Contagion and differentiation in unethical behavior: The effect of one bad apple on the barrel. *Psychological Science, 20,* 393–398.

Gittelman, M. (2008). Editor's introduction: Why are the mentally ill dying? *International Journal of Mental Health, 37,* 3–12.

Given, L. M. (2008). Qualitative research methods. In N. J. Salkind (Ed.), *Encyclopedia of educational psychology.* Thousand Oaks, CA: Sage.

Glascher, J., & others. (2009). Lesion mapping of cognitive abilities linked to intelligence. *Neuron, 61,* 681–691.

Glaser, R., & Kiecolt-Glaser, J. K. (2005). Stress-induced immune dysfunction: Implications for health. *Nature Reviews: Immunology, 5,* 243–251.

Glaw, X. M., Garrick, T. M., Terwee, P. J., Patching, J. R., Blake, H., & Harper, C. (2009). Brain donation: Who and why? *Cell and Tissue Banking.* (in press)

Glickstein, J. M., Strata, P., & Voogd, J. (2009). Cerebellum: History. *Neuroscience.* (in press)

Glynn, D. A., Cryan, J. F., Kent, P., Flynn, R. A., & Kennedy, M. P. (2009). Update on smoking cessation therapies. *Advances in Therapy, 26,* 369–382.

Go, C. L., Raosales, R. L., Caraos, R. J., & Fernandez, H. H. (2009). The current prevalence and factors associated with tardive dyskinesia among Filipino schizophrenic patients. *Parkinsonism and Related Disorders.* (in press)

Gobet, F., & Clarkson, G. (2004). Chunks in expert memory: Evidence for the magical number four . . . or is it two? *Memory, 12,* 732–747.

Godden, D. R., & Baddeley, A. D. (1975). Context-dependent memory in two natural environments: On land and under water. *British Journal of Psychology, 66,* 325–331.

Goodwin, R. D., & Cowles, R. A. (2008). Household smoking and childhood asthma in the United States: A state-level analysis. *Journal of Asthma, 45,* 607–610.

Goebel, M. U., Trebst, A. E., Steiner, J., Xie, Y. F., Exton, M. S., and others. (2002). Behavioral conditioning of immunosuppression is possible in humans. *Federation of American Societies for Experimental Biology Journal, 16,* 1869–1873.

Goel, N., & others. (2009). Circadian rhythm profiles in women with night eating syndrome. *Journal of Biological Rhythms, 24,* 85–94.

Goethals, G. R., & Demorest, A. P. (1995). The risky shift is a sure bet. In M. E. Ware & D. E. Johnson (Eds.), *Demonstrations and activities in teaching of psychology* (vol. 3). Mahwah, NJ: Erlbaum.

Goldberg, L. R., & Digman, J. M. (1994). Revealing structure in the data: Principles of exploratory factor analysis. In S. Strack & M. Lorr (Eds.), *Differentiating normal and abnormal personality* (pp. 216–242). New York: Springer.

Goldfield, B. A., & Snow, C. E. (2009). Individual differences: Implications for the study of language acquisition. In J. Berko Gleason & N. Ratner (Eds.), *The development of language* (7th ed.). Boston: Allyn & Bacon.

Goldman, M. S. (2009). Memory without feedback in a neural network. *Neuron, 61,* 621–634.

Goldman, S. E., & others. (2008). Sleep problems associated with daytime fatigue in community-dwelling older individuals. *Journals of Gerontology A: Biological Sciences and Medical Sciences, 63,* 1069–1075.

Goldstein, E. B. (2010). *Sensation and perception* (8th ed.). Boston: Cengage.

Goldstein, M. H., King, A. P., & West, M. J. (2003). Social interaction shapes babbling: Testing parallels between birdsong and speech. *Proceedings of the National Academy of Sciences USA, 100* (13), 8030–8035.

Goldston, D. B., Molock, S. D., Whibeck, L. B., Murakami, J. L., Zayas, L. H., & Hall, G. C. (2008). Cultural considerations in adolescent suicide prevention and psychosocial treatment. *American Psychologist, 63,* 14–31.

Goldstrom, I. D., Campbell, J., Rogers, J. A., Lambert, D. B., Blacklow, B., Henderson, M. J., & Manderscheid, R. W. (2006). National estimates for mental health mutual support groups, self-help organizations, and consumer-operated services. *Administration and Policy in Mental Health, 33,* 92–103.

Goleman, D., Kaufman, P., & Ray, M. (1993). *The creative mind.* New York: Plume.

Gollnick, D. M., & Chinn, P. C. (2009). *Multicultural education in a pluralistic society* (8th ed.). Boston: Allyn & Bacon.

Gollwitzer, P. M., & Oettingen, G. (2007). The role of goal setting and goal striving in medical adherence. In D. C. Park & L. L. Liu (Eds.), *Medical adherence and aging: Social and cognitive perspectives.* (pp. 23–47). Washington, DC: American Psychological Association.

Gonda, X., & others. (2009). Association of the s allele of the 5-HTTLPR with neuroticism-related traits and temperaments in a psychiatrically healthy population. *European Archives of Psychiatry and Clinical Neuroscience, 259,* 106–113.

Gonzalez-Maeso, J., & Sealfon, S. C. (2009). Psychodelics and schizophrenia. *Trends in Neuroscience, 32,* 225–232.

Goodwin, R. D., & Cowles, R. A. (2008). Household smoking and childhood asthma in the United States: A state-level analysis. *Journal of Asthma, 45,* 607–610.

Goodwin, R. D., Cox, B. J., & Clara, I. (2006). Neuroticism and physical disorders among adults in the community: Results from the National Comorbidity Survey. *Journal of Behavioral Medicine, 29,* 229–238.

Gordon, K. A., Valero, J., & Papsin, B. C. (2007). Binaural processing in children using bilateral cochlear implants. *Neuroreport, 18,* 613–617.

Gorin, A., Phelan, S., Wing, R. R., & Hill, J. O. (2004). Promoting long-term weight control: Does dieting consistency matter? *International Journal of Obesity Related Metabolic Disorder, 28,* 278–281.

Gosden, R. G. (2007). Menopause. In J. E. Birren (Ed.), *Encyclopedia of gerontology* (2nd ed.). Oxford, England: Elsevier.

Gosling, S. D. (2008). Personality in nonhuman animals. *Social and Personality Psychology Compass, 2,* 985–1001.

Gosling, S. D., & John, O. P. (1999). Personality dimensions in nonhuman animals: A cross-species review. *Current Directions in Psychological Science, 8,* 69–75.

Gosling, S. D., Kwan, V. S. Y., & John, O. (2003). A dog's got personality: A cross-species comparison of personality judgments in dogs and humans. *Journal of Personality and Social Psychology, 85,* 1161–1169.

Gotthold, J. J. (2009). Peeling the onion: Understanding layers of treatment. *Annals of the New York Academy of Sciences, 1159,* 301–312.

Gottlieb, G. (2007). Probabilistic epigenesis. *Developmental Science, 10,* 1–11.

Gottman, J. (2006, April, 29). Secrets of long term love. *New Scientist, 2549,* 40.

Gottman, J. M. (1994). *What predicts divorce?* Mahwah, NJ: Erlbaum.

Gottman, J. M., Gottman, J. S., & Declaire, J. (2006). *10 lessons to transform your marriage: America's love lab experts share their strategies for strengthening your relationship.* New York: Random House.

Gottman, J. M., & Silver, N. (1999). *The seven principles for making marriages work.* New York: Crown.

Gouin, J. P., Hantsoo, L., & Kiecolt-Glaser, J. K. (2008). Immune dysregulation and chronic stress among older adults: A review. *Neuroimmunomodulation, 15,* 251–259.

Gould, E., Reeves, A. J., Graziano, M. S., & Gross, C. G. (1999). Neurogenesis in the neocortex of adult primates, *Science, 286* (1), 548–552.

Graber, J. A. (2007). Pubertal and neuroendocrine development and risk for depressive disorders. In N. B. Allen & L. Sheeber (Eds.), *Adolescent emotional development and the emergence of depressive disorders.* New York: Cambridge University Press.

Graber, J. A., Brooks-Gunn, J., & Warren, M. P. (2006). Pubertal effects on adjustment in girls: Moving from demonstrating effects to identifying pathways. *Journal of Youth and Adolescence, 35,* 391–401.

Graber, J. A., & Sontag, L. M. (2009). Internalizing problems during adolescence. In R. M. Lerner & L. Steinberg (Eds.), *Handbook of adolescent psychology* (3rd ed.). New York: Wiley.

Grady, C. L. (2008). Cognitive neuroscience of aging. *Annals of the New York Academy of Sciences, 1124,* 127–144.

Graffin, N. F., Ray, W. J., & Lundy, R. (1995). EEG concomitants of hypnosis and hypnotic susceptibility. *Journal of Abnormal Psychology, 104,* 123–131.

Graham, J. E., Christian, L. M., & Kiecolt-Glaser, J. K. (2006). Stress, age, and immune function: Toward a lifespan approach. *Journal of Behavioral Medicine, 29,* 389–400.

Grant, B. F., Stinson, F. S., Dawson, D. A., Chou, P., Dufour, M. C., Compton, W., Pickering, R. P., & Kaplan, K. (2004). Prevalence and co-occurrence of substance use disorders and independent mood and anxiety disorders: Results from the national epidemiologic survey on alcohol and related conditions. *Archives of General Psychiatry, 61,* 807–816.

Gravetter, F. J. (2009). *Research methods for the behavioral sciences* (3rd ed.). Belmont, CA: Wadsworth.

Gray, J. A. (1987). *The psychology of fear and stress.* Cambridge, England: Cambridge University Press.

Gray, J. A., & McNaughton, N. (2000). *The neuropsychology of anxiety: An enquiry into the functions of the septo-hippocampal system.* Oxford, England: Oxford University Press.

Graziano, W. G., & Tobin, R. M. (2009). Agreeableness. In M. R. Leary & R. H. Hoyle (Eds.), *Handbook of individual differences in social behavior* (pp. 46–61). New York: Guilford.

Green, J. P., Page, R. A., Handley, G. W., & Rasekhy, R. (2005). The "hidden observer" and ideomotor responding: A real–simulator comparison. *Contemporary Hypnosis, 22,* 123–137.

Greenberg, J. S. (2008). *Comprehensive stress management* (10th ed.). New York: McGraw-Hill.

Greene, R. L. (1999). Applied memory research: How far from bankruptcy? *Contemporary Psychology, 44,* 29–31.

Greenfield, R. (2006). *Timothy Leary: A biography.* New York: Harcourt Books.

Greenwald, A. G., Poehlman, T. A., Uhlmann, E., & Banaji, M. R. (2009). Understanding and using the Implicit Association Test: III. Meta-analysis of predictive validity. *Journal of Personality and Social Psychology.* (in press)

Greeson, J. M., Lewis, J. G., Achanzar, K., Zimmerman, E., Young K. H., & Suarez, E. C. (2009). Stress-induced changes in the expression of monocytic beta-2-integrins: The impact of arousal of negative affect and adrenergic responses to the Anger Recall interview. *Brain, Behavior, and Immunity, 23,* 251–256.

Grigorenko, E. L., Jarvin, L., Tan, M., & Sternberg, R. J. (2009). Something new in the garden: Assessing creativity in academic domains. *Psychology Science Quarterly.* (in press)

Grilo, C. M., Masheb, R. M., & Wilson, G. T. (2006). Rapid response treatment to treatment for binge eating disorder. *Journal of Consulting and Clinical Psychology, 74,* 602–613.

Grippo, A. J., & Johnson, A. K. (2009). Stress, depression, and cardiovascular dysregulation: A review of neurobiological mechanisms and the integration of research from preclinical disease models. *Stress, 12,* 1–21.

Gronlund, N. E. (2006). *Assessment of student achievement* (8th ed.). Boston: Allyn & Bacon.

Grossi, A., Buscema, M. P., Snowdon, D., & Antuono, P. (2007). Neuropathological findings processed by artificial neural networks (ANNs) can perfectly distinguish Alzheimer's patients from controls in the Nun Study. *BMC Neurology, 7,* 15.

Grossman, C. L. (2008, June 4). Most say gay marriage private choice. *USA Today.* http://www.usatoday.com/news/nation/2008-06-03-gay-marriage-poll_N.htm?csp=34 (accessed March 10, 2009)

Gruber, A. J., & O'Donnell, P. (2009). Bursting activation of prefrontal cortex drives sustained up states in nucleus accumbens spin neurons in vivo. *Synapse, 63,* 173–180.

Grubin, D., & Madsen, L. (2006). Accuracy and utility of post-conviction polygraph testing of sex offenders. *British Journal of Psychiatry, 188,* 479–483.

Guérard, K., Tremblay, S., & Saint-Aubin, J. (2009). The processing of spatial information in short-term memory: Insights from eye-tracking the path length effect. *Acta Psychologica.* (in press)

Guerrini, I., Thomson, A. D., & Gurling, H. M. (2009). Molecular genetics of alcohol-related brain damage. *Alcohol and Alcoholism, 44,* 166–170.

Gueta, R., Barlam, D., Shneck, R. Z., & Rousso, I. (2006). Measurement of the mechanical properties of isolated tectorial membrane using atomic force microscopy. *Proceedings of the National Academy of Sciences USA, 103,* 14790–14795.

Gunderson, J. (2008). Borderline personality disorder: An overview. *Social Work in Mental Health, 6,* 5–12.

Gunderson, J. G., Bender, D., Sanislow, C., Yen, S., Rettew, J. B., Dolan-Sewell, R., Dyck, I., Morey, L. C., McGlashan, T. H., Shea, M. T., & Skodol, A. E. (2003). Plausibility and possible determinants of sudden "remissions" in borderline patients. *Psychiatry: Interpersonal and Biological Processes, 66,* 111–119.

Guo, Q., Johnson, C. A., Unger, J. B., Lee, L., Xie, B., Chou, C. P., Palmer, P. H., Sun, P., Gallaher, P., & Pentz, M. (2007). Utility of theory of reasoned action and theory of planned behavior for predicting Chinese adolescent smoking. *Addictive Behaviors, 32,* 1066–1081.

Guo, Y. (2005). Filial therapy for children's behavioral and emotional problems in mainland China. *Journal of Child and Adolescent Psychiatric Nursing, 18,* 171–180.

Guttman, N., & Kalish, H. I. (1956). Discriminability and stimulus generalization. *Journal of Experimental Psychology, 51,* 79–88.

Gwaltney, C. J., Metrik, J., Kahler, C. W., & Shiffman, S. (2009). Self-efficacy and smoking cessation: A meta-analysis. *Psychology of Addictive Behaviors, 23*, 56–66.

Gynther, L. M., Hewitt, J. K., Heath, A. C., & Eaves, L. J. (1999). Phenotypic and genetic factors in motives for smoking. *Behavior Genetics, 29*, 291–302.

H

Haas, B. W., Omura, K., Constable, R. T., & Canli, T. (2007). Emotional conflict and neuroticism: Personality-dependent activation in the amygdala and subgenual anterior cingulate. *Behavioral Neuroscience, 121*, 249–256.

Habbal, O. A., & Al-Jabri, A. A. (2009). Circadian rhythm and the immune system: A review. *International Reviews of Immunology, 28*, 93–108.

Habeck, C., Rakitin, B. C., Moeller, J., Scarmeas, N., Zarahn, E., Brown, T., & Stern, Y. (2004). An event-related fMRI study of the neurobehavioral impact of sleep deprivation on performance of a delayed-match-to-sample task. *Brain Research, 18*, 306–321.

Hackley, S. A. (2009). The speeding of voluntary reaction by a warning signal. *Psychophysiology, 46*, 225–233.

Hagg, T. (2009). From neurotransmitters to neurotrophic factors to neurogenesis. *Neuroscientist, 15*, 20–27.

Hahn, D. B., Payne, W. A., & Lucas, E. B. (2007). *Focus on health* (8th ed.). New York: McGraw-Hill.

Hales, D. (2008). *An invitation to health: 2009–2010 edition.* Boston: Cengage.

Halgunseth, L. C., Ispa, J. M., & Rudy, D. (2006). Parental control in Latino families: An integrated review of the literature. *Child Development, 77*, 1282–1297.

Hall, C. C., Goren, A., Chaiken, S., & Todorov, A. (2009). Shallow cues with deep effects: Trait judgments from faces and voting decisions. In E. Borgida, J. L. Sullivan, & C. M. Federico (Eds.), *The political psychology of democratic citizenship.* New York: Oxford University Press. (in press)

Hall, H., Lawyer, G., Sillen, A., Jonsson, E. G., Agartz, I., Terenius, L., & Arnborg, S. (2007). Potential genetic variants in schizophrenia: A Bayesian analysis. *World Journal of Biological Psychiatry, 8*, 12–22.

Hall, J. A., & Matsumoto, D. (2004). Gender differences in judgments of multiple emotions from facial expressions. *Emotion, 14*, 201–206.

Hallahan, D. P., Kauffmann, J. M., & Pullen, P. C. (2009). *Exceptional learners* (11th ed.). Boston: Allyn & Bacon.

Hallal, P. C., Victora, C. G., Azevedo, M. R., & Wells, J. C. (2006). Adolescent physical activity and health: A systematic review. *Sports Medicine, 36*, 1019–1030.

Halpern, J. H. (1996). The use of hallucinogens in the treatment of addiction. *Addiction Research, 4*, 177–189.

Halpern, J. H. (2003). Hallucinogens: An update. *Current Psychiatry Reports, 5*, 347–354.

Halpern, J. H., & Sewell, R. A. (2005). Hallucinogenic botanicals of America: A growing need for focused drug education and research. *Life Sciences, 78*, 519–526.

Halpern, J. H., Sherwood, A. R., Hudson, J. I., Yurgelun-Todd, D., & Pope, H. G. (2005). Psychological and cognitive effects of long-term peyote use among Native Americans. *Biological Psychiatry, 58*, 624–631.

Hamer, M., Chida, Y., & Molloy, G. J. (2009). Psychological distress and cancer mortality. *Journal of Psychosomatic Research, 66*, 255–258.

Hamilton, B. E., Martin, J. A., & Ventura, S. J. (2009). Births: Preliminary data for 2007. *National Vital Statistics Reports, 57* (12). Atlanta: National Center for Health Statistics.

Hamlin, A. S., Clemens, K. J., Choi, E. A., & McNally, G. P. (2009). Parventricular thalamus mediates context-induced reinstatement (renewal) of extinguished reward seeking. *European Journal of Neuroscience, 29*, 802–812.

Hammad, T. A. (2004, September 13). *Results of the analysis of suicidality in pediatric trials of newer antidepressants.* Presentation at the U.S. Food and Drug Administration, Psychopharmacologic Drugs Advisory Committee and the Pediatric Advisory Committee. www.fda.gov/ohrms/dockets/ac/04/slides/2004-4065S108 FDA-Hammad files/frame.htm (accessed July 26, 2006)

Hammond, D. C. (2007). Review of the efficacy of clinical hypnosis with headaches and migraines. *International Journal of Clinical and Experimental Hypnosis, 55*, 207–219.

Hammond, T. A., Laughren, T., & Racoosin, J. (2006). Suicidality in pediatric patients treated with antidepressant drugs. *Archives of General Psychiatry, 63*, 332–339.

Hampton, J. (2008). Abstinence-only programs under fire. *Journal of the American Medical Association, 17*, 2013–2015.

Hanley, J. R., & Chapman, E. (2008). Partial knowledge in a tip-of-the-tongue state about two- and three-word proper names. *Psychonomic Bulletin and Review, 15*, 156–160.

Hansimayr, S., Leipold, P., Pastotter, B., & Baumi, K. H. (2009). Anticipatory signatures of voluntary memory supression. *Journal of Neuroscience, 29*, 2742–2747.

Hardy, C. L., & Van Vugt, M. (2006). Nice guys finish first: The competitive altruism hypothesis. *Personality and Social Psychology Bulletin, 32*, 1402–1413.

Hare, M., Jones, M., Thomson, C., Kelly, S., & McRae, K. (2009). Activating event knowledge. *Cognition.* (in press)

Harker, L. A., & Keltner, D. (2001). Expressions of positive emotion in women's college yearbook pictures and their relationship to personality and life outcomes across adulthood. *Journal of Personality and Social Psychology, 80*, 112–124.

Harkness, S., & Super, C. M. (1995). Culture and parenting. In M. H. Bornstein (Ed.), *Children and parenting* (vol. 2). Hillsdale, NJ: Erlbaum.

Harley, R., Sprich, S., Safren, S., Jacobo, M., & Fava, M. (2008). Adaptation of dialetical behavior therapy skills training group for treatment-resistant depression. *Journal of Nervous and Mental Disease, 196*, 136–143.

Harlow, H. F. (1958). The nature of love. *American Psychologist, 13*, 673–685.

Harms, P., Roberts, B. W., & Woods, D. D. (2007). Who shall lead? An integrative personality approach to the study of the antecedents of status in informal social organizations. *Journal of Research in Personality, 41*, 689–699.

Harpaz, Y., Levkovitz, Y., & Lavidor, M. (2009). Lexical ambiguitiy resolution in Wernicke's area and its right homologue. *Cortex.* (in press)

Harper, G. W., Hosek, S. G., Contreras, R., & Doll, M. (2003). Psychosocial factors impacting condom use among adolescents: A review and theoretical integration. *Journal of HIV/AIDS Prevention & Education for Adolescents & Children, 5*, 33–69.

Harris, D. M., & Kay, J. (1995). I recognize your face but I can't remember your name: Is it because names are unique? *British Journal of Psychology, 86*, 345–358.

Harris, J. A. (2006). Elemental representations of stimuli in associative learning. *Psychological Review, 113*, 584–605.

Harris, J. R. (1998). *The nurture assumption: Why children turn out the way they do?* New York: Free Press.

Harris, M., & Grunstein, R. R. (2009). Treatments for sonambulism in adults: Assessing the evidence. *Sleep Medicine Reviews.* (in press)

Harrison, K., & Hefner, V. (2006). Media exposure, current and future body ideals, and disordered eating among preadolescent girls: A longitudinal panel study. *Journal of Youth and Adolescence, 35*, 153–163.

Harro, J., Merenakk, L., Nordquist, N., Konstabel, K., Comasco, E., & Oreland, L. (2009). Personality and the serotonin transporter gene: Associations in a longitudinal population-based study. *Biological Psychology, 81*, 9–13.

Hartenbaum, N., & others. (2006). Sleep apnea and commercial motor vehicle operators. *Chest, 130*, 902–905.

Harter, S. (2006). The development of self-esteem. In M. H. Kernis (Ed.), *Self-esteem issues and answers: A sourcebook of current perspectives* (pp. 144–150). New York: Psychology Press.

Hartley, S. L., & Maclean, W. E. (2009). Depression in adults with mild intellectual disability: Role of stress, attributions, and coping. *American Journal on Intellectual and Developmental Disabilities, 114*, 147–160.

Hartline, D. K., & Colman, D. R. (2007). Rapid conduction and the evolution of giant axons and myelinated fibers. *Current Biology, 17*, R29–R35.

Hartman, H., & Smith, T. F. (2009). The evolution of the cilium and the eukaryotic cell. *Cell Motility and the Cytoskeleton, 66*, 215–219.

Hartmann, E. (1993). Nightmares. In M. A. Carskadon (Ed.), *Encyclopedia of sleep and dreams.* New York: Macmillan.

Haselton, M. G. (2006, April 29). How to pick a perfect mate. *New Scientist, 2549*, 36.

Haslam, S. A., & Reicher, S. D. (2006). Debating the psychology of tyranny: Fundamental issues of theory, perspective and science. *British Journal of Social Psychology, 45*, 55–63.

Havelka, M., Lucanin, J. D., & Lucanin, D. (2009). Biopsychosocial model—the integrated approach to health and disease. *Collegium Antropologicum, 33*, 303–310.

Hawkley, L. C., & Cacioppo, J. T. (2009). Loneliness. In M. R. Leary & R. H. Hoyle (Eds.), *Handbook of individual differences in social behavior* (pp. 227–240). New York: Guilford.

Hawkley, L. C., Thisted, R. A., & Cacioppo, J. T. (2009). Loneliness predicts reduced physical activity: Cross-sectional and longitudinal analyses. *Health Psychology, 28*, 354–363.

Hayes, H., Geers, A. E., Treiman, R., & Moog, J. S. (2009). Receptive vocabulary development in deaf children with cochlear implants: Achievement in an intensive auditory-oral education setting. *Ear and Hearing, 30*, 128–135.

Hayes, M. R., Chory, F. M., Gallagher, C. A., & Covasa, M. (2006). Serotonin type-3 receptors mediate cholecystokinin-induced satiation through gastric distension. *American Journal of Physiology: Regulatory, Integrative, and Comparative Physiology, 291*, R112–R114.

Hayflick, L. (1977). The cellular basis for biological aging. In C. E. Finch & L. Hayflick (Eds.), *Handbook of the biology of aging.* New York: Van Nostrand.

Hazell, P. (2009). Depression in children and adolescents. *Clinical Evidence, 15*, 398–414.

Hazler, R. J. (2007). Person-centered therapy. In D. Capuzzi & D. Gross (Eds.), *Counseling and psychotherapy* (4th ed.). Upper Saddle River, NJ: Prentice-Hall.

Hebb, D. O. (1949). *The organization of behavior: A neuropsychological theory.* New York: Wiley.

Hebb, D. O. (1980). *Essay on mind.* Mahwah, NJ: Erlbaum.

Heckman, C. J., & Clay, D. L. (2005). Hardiness, history of abuse, and women's health. *Journal of Health Psychology, 10*, 767–777.

Hedden, T., & Yoon, C. (2006). Individual differences in executive processing predict susceptibility to interference in verbal working memory. *Neuropsychology, 20*, 511–528.

Heider, F. (1958). *The psychology of interpersonal relations.* Hoboken, NJ: Wiley.

Heine, S. J. (2005). Constructing good selves in Japan and North America. In R. M. Sorrentino, D. Cohen, J. M. Olson, & M. P. Zanna (Eds.), *Cultural and social behavior: The Ontario symposium* (vol. 10, pp. 95–116). Mahwah, NJ: Erlbaum.

Heine, S. J., & Buchtel, E. E. (2009). Personality: The universal and the culturally specific. *Annual Review of Psychology, 60*, 369–394.

Heller, A. C., Amar, A. P., Liu, C. Y., & Apuzzo, M. L. (2006). Surgery of the mind and mood: A mosaic of issues in time and evolution. *Neurosurgery, 59*, 720–733.

Helson, R. (1992). Women's difficult times and rewriting the life story. *Psychology of Women Quarterly, 16*, 331–347.

Helson, R., & Roberts, B. W. (1994). Ego development and personality change in adulthood. *Journal of Personality and Social Psychology, 66*, 911–920.

Hemmer, P., & Steyvers, M. (2009). Integrating episodic memories and prior knowledge at multiple levels of abstraction. *Psychonomic Bulletin and Review, 16,* 80–87.

Hendrick, C., & Hendrick, S. S. (2006). Styles of romantic love. In R. J. Sternberg & K. Weis (Eds.), *The new psychology of love* (pp. 149–170). New Haven, CT: Yale University Press.

Hendricks, R., & Hatch, L. R. (2006). Lifestyle and aging. In R. H. Binstock & L. K. George (Eds.), *Handbook of aging and the social sciences* (6th ed.). San Diego: Academic.

Henry, J. D., MacLeod, M. S., Phillips, L. H., & Crawford, J. R. (2004). A meta-analytic review of prospective memory and aging. *Psychology and Aging, 19,* 27–39.

Hepple, R. T. (2009). Why eating less keeps mitochondria working in aged skeletal muscle. *Exercise and Sport Sciences Reviews, 37,* 23–38.

Hepting, U., & Solle, R. (1973). Sex-specific differences in color coding. *Archiv fur Psychologie, 125 (2–3),* 184–202.

Herbert, J. (1988). The physiology of aggression. In J. Groebel & R. Hinde (Eds.), *Aggression and war: The biological and social bases.* New York: Cambridge University Press.

Herder, R., & Demmig-Adams, B. (2004). The power of a balanced diet and lifestyle in preventing cardiovascular disease. *Nutrition in Clinical Care, 7,* 46–55.

Hering, E. (1878). *Zur Lehre vom Lichtsinne* (illustration, 2nd ed.). Wien: C. Gerold's Sohn.

Herlihy, B., & McCollum, V. (2007). Feminist theory. In D. Capuzzi & D. Gross (Eds.), *Counseling and psychotherapy* (4th ed.). Upper Saddle River, NJ: Prentice-Hall.

Hernandez, P., Siegel, A., & Almeida, R. (2009). The cultural context model: How does it facilitate couples' therapeutic change? *Journal of Marital and Family Therapy, 35,* 97–110.

Hernandez-Reif, M., Diego, M., & Field, T. (2008). Preterm infants show reduced stress behaviors and activity after 5 days of massage therapy. *Infant Behavior and Development, 30,* 557–561.

Hernstein, R. J. (2009). Selection by consequences. In D. Shanks (Ed.), *Psychology of learning.* Thousand Oaks, CA: Sage.

Herz, R. S. (1998). Are odors the best cues to memory? A cross-modal comparison of associative memory stimuli. *Annals of the New York Academy of Sciences, 855,* 670–674.

Herz, R. S. (2004). A naturalistic analysis of autobiographical memories triggered by olfactory, visual, and auditory stimuli. *Chemical Senses, 29,* 217–224.

Herz, R. S., & Cupchik, G. C. (1995). The emotional distinctiveness of odor-evoked memories. *Chemical Senses, 20,* 517–528.

Herz, R. S., Schankler, C., & Beland, S. (2004). Olfaction, emotion and associative learning: Effects on motivated behavior. *Motivation and Emotion, 28,* 363–383.

Herzog, H. (2006). Forty-two thousand and one Dalmatians: Fads, social contagion, and dog breed popularity. *Society & Animals, 14,* 383–397.

Hetherington, E. M. (2006). The influence of conflict, marital problem solving, and parenting on children's adjustment in nondivorced, divorced, and remarried families. In A. Clarke-Stewart & J. Dunn (Eds.), *Families count.* New York: Cambridge University Press.

Hetherington, E. M., & Stanley-Hagan, M. (2002). Parenting in divorced and remarried families. In M. Bornstein (Ed.), *Handbook of parenting* (2nd ed.). Mahwah, NJ: Erlbaum.

Hewlin, P. F. (2009). Wearing the cloak: Antecedents and consequences of creating facades of conformity. *Journal of Applied Psychology, 94,* 727–741.

Hicks, J. A., & King, L. A. (2008). Mood and religion as information about meaning in life. *Journal of Research in Personality, 42,* 43–57.

Hilgard, E. R. (1965). *Hypnotic suggestibility.* Fort Worth: Harcourt Brace.

Hilgard, E. R. (1977). *Divided consciousness: Multiple controls in human thought and action.* New York: Wiley

Hilgard, E. R. (1992). Dissociation and theories of hypnosis. In E. Fromm & M. R. Nash (Eds.), *Contemporary hypnosis research.* New York: Guilford.

Hill, C. E. (2000). Client-centered therapy. In A. Kazdin (Ed.), *Encyclopedia of psychology.* Washington, DC, & New York: American Psychological Association and Oxford University Press.

Hill, P. D., & others. (2009). Association of serum prolactin and oxytocin with milk production in mothers of preterm and term infants. *Biological Research for Nursing, 10,* 340–349.

Hill, T. D., Burdette, A. M., Ellison, C. G., & Musick, M. A. (2006). Religious attendance and the health behaviors of Texas adults. *Preventive Medicine: An International Journal Devoted to Practice and Theory, 42,* 309–312.

Hillman, C. H., Erickson, K. I., & Kramer. A. F. (2008). Be smart, exercise your heart: Exercise effects on the brain and cognition. *Nature Reviews: Neuroscience, 9,* 58–65.

Hilton, D. J. (2007). Causal explanation. In A. W. Kruglanski & E. T. Higgins (Eds.), *Social psychology* (2nd ed.). New York: Guilford.

Hingson, R. W., Heeren, T., & Winter, M. R. (2006). Age at drinking onset and alcohol dependence: Age of onset, duration, and severity. *Archives of Pediatric and Adolescent Medicine, 160,* 739–746.

Hinshaw, S. P. (2007). *The mark of shame: Stigma of mental illness and an agenda for change.* New York: Oxford University Press.

Hirsch, J. K., Conner, K. R., & Duberstein, P. R. (2007). Optimism and suicide ideation among young college students. *Archives of Suicide Research, 11,* 177–185.

Hirsch, J. K., Wolford, K., Lalonde, S. M., Brunk, L., & Parker-Morris, A. (2009). Optimistic explanatory style as a moderator between negative life events and suicide ideation. *Crisis, 30,* 48–53.

Hobson, J. A. (1999). Dreams. In R. Conlan (Ed.), *States of mind.* New York: Wiley.

Hobson, J. A. (2000). Dreams: Physiology. In A. Kazdin (Ed.), *Encyclopedia of psychology.* Washington, DC, & New York: American Psychological Association and Oxford University Press.

Hobson, J. A. (2002). *Dreaming.* New York: Oxford University Press.

Hobson, J. A. (2004). Freud returns? Like a bad dream. *Scientific American, 290,* 89.

Hobson, J. A., Pace-Schott, E. F., & Stickgold, R. (2000). Dreaming and the brain. *Behavior and Brain Sciences, 23,* 793–842.

Hodgins, D. C. (2005). Weighing the pros and cons of changing change models: A comment on West (2005). *Addiction, 100,* 1042–1043.

Hoeger, W. W. K., & Hoeger, S. A. (2008). *Principles and labs for physical fitness* (6th ed.). New York: McGraw-Hill.

Hoek, H. W. (2006). Incidence, prevalence and mortality of anorexia nervosa and other eating disorders. *Current Opinion in Psychiatry, 19,* 389–394.

Hoelter, L. (2009). Divorce and separation. In D. Carr (Ed.), *Encyclopedia of the life course and human development.* Boston: Gale Cengage.

Hoffman, I. Z. (2006). The myths of free association and the potentials of the analytic relationship. *International Journal of Psychoanalysis, 87,* 43–61.

Hoffman, J. P. (2009). Drug use, adolescent. In D. Carr (Ed.), *Encyclopedia of the life course and human development.* Boston: Cengage.

Hogan, E. H., Hornick, B. A., & Bouchoux, A. (2002). Focus on communications: Communicating the message: Clarifying the controversies about caffeine. *Nutrition Today, 37,* 28–35.

Hogan, R. (2006). *Personality and the fate of organizations.* Mahwah, NJ: Erlbaum.

Hogan, R. (2009). Much ado about nothing. *Journal of Research in Personality, 43,* 249.

Hoge, C. W., Terhakoian, A., Castro, C. A., Messer, S. C., & Engel, C. C. (2007). Association of posttraumatic stress disorder with somatic symptoms, health care visits, and absenteeism among Iraq War veterans. *American Journal of Psychiatry, 164,* 150–153.

Hogg, M. A., & Abrams, D. (2007). Intergroup behavior and social identity. In M. A. Hogg & J. Cooper (Eds.), *The Sage handbook of social psychology* (concise 2nd ed.). Thousand Oaks, CA: Sage.

Holcombe, E., Peterson, K., & Manlove, J. (2009, March). Ten reasons to still keep the focus on teen childbearing. *Child Trends: Research Brief.* Pub. #2009–10, 1–7.

Holland, P. C. (1996). The effects of intertrial and feature-target intervals on operant serial feature-positive discrimination learning. *Animal Learning & Behavior, 24,* 411–428.

Hollich, G. J., & Huston, D. M. (2007). Language development: From speech to first words. In A. Slater & M. Lewis (Eds.), *Introduction to infant development* (2nd ed.). New York: Oxford University Press.

Holliday, E. G., Nyholt, D. R., Tirupati, S., John, S., Ramachandran, P., & others. (2009). Strong evidence for a novel schizophrenia risk locus on chromosome 1p31.1 in homogeneous pedigrees from Tamil Nadu, India. *American Journal of Psychiatry, 166,* 206–215.

Holmes, J. G., Miller, D. T., & Lerner, M. J. (2002). Committing altruism under the cloak of self-interest: The exchange fiction. *Journal of Experimental Social Psychology, 38* (2), 144–151.

Holmes, R. M., Little, K. C., & Welsh, D. (2009). Dating and romantic relationships, adulthood. In D. Carr (Ed.), *Encyclopedia of the life course and human development.* Boston: Gale Cengage.

Holmes, S. (1993). Food avoidance in patients undergoing cancer chemotherapy. *Support Care Cancer, 1* (6), 326–330.

Holsboer, F., & Ising, M. (2010). Stress hormones and stress regulation: Biological role and behavioral effects. *Annual Review of Psychology* (vol. 61). Palo Alto, CA: Annual Reviews.

Holt, J., Warren, L., Wallance, R., & Neher, J. O. (2006). Clinical inquiries: What behavioral interventions are safe for obesity? *Journal of Family Practice, 55,* 536–538.

Holzman, L. (2009). *Vygotsky at work and play.* Oxford, England: Routledge.

Honts, C. (1998, June). Commentary. *APA Monitor, 30.*

Hooper, J., & Teresi, D. (1993). *The 3-pound universe.* New York: Tarcher/Putnam.

Horenstein, J., & Cohen, S. (2009). Social support and depression. *International encyclopedia of depression.* New York: Springer. (in press)

Horgan, J. (2005, February 26). Psychedelic medicine: Mind bending, health giving. *New Scientist, 2488,* 36.

Horn, J. L., & Donaldson, G. (1980). Cognitive development II: Adulthood development of human abilities. In O. G. Brim & J. Kagan (Eds.), *Constancy and change in human development.* Cambridge, MA: Harvard University Press.

Horney, K. (1945). *Our inner conflicts.* New York: Norton.

Horney, K. (1967). *Feminine psychology (collected essays, 1922–1937).* New York: Norton.

Hornickel, J., Skoe, E., & Kraus, N. (2009). Subcortical laterality of speech encoding. *Audiology and Neuro-Otology, 14,* 198–207.

Hornsey, M. J., Dwyer, L., Oei, T. P., & Dingle, G. A. (2009). Group processes and outcomes in group psychotherapy: Is it time to let go of "cohesiveness"? *International Journal of Group Psychotherapy, 59,* 267–278.

Horowitz, J. L., & Garber, J. (2006). The prevention of depressive symptoms in children and adolescents: A meta-analytic review. *Journal of Consulting and Clinical Psychology, 74* (3), 401–415.

Horst, J. S., Ellis, A. E., Samuelson, L. K., Trejo, E., Worzalla, S. L., Peltan, J. R., & Oakes, L. M. (2009). Toddlers can adaptively change how they categorize: Same objects, same session, two different categorical distinctions. *Developmental Science, 12,* 96–105.

Hoss, R. A., & Langlois, J. H. (2003). Infants prefer attractive faces. In O. Pascalis & A. Slater (Eds.), *The development of face processing in infancy and early childhood: Current perspectives* (pp. 27–38). Hauppauge, NY: Nova Science Publishers.

Hotard, S. R., McFatter, R. M., McWhirter, R. M., & Stegall, M. E. (1989). Interactive effects of extraversion, neuroticism, and social relationships on subjective well-being. *Journal of Personality and Social Psychology, 57,* 321–331.

Houer, W. J., & Roodin, P. A. (2009). *Adult development and aging* (6th ed.). New York: McGraw-Hill.

House, J. S., Landis, K. R., & Umberson, D. (1988). Social relationships and health. *Science, 241,* 540–545.

Houser-Marko, L., & Sheldon, K. M. (2008). Eyes on the prize or nose to the grindstone? The effects of level of goal evaluation on mood and motivation. *Personality and Social Psychology Bulletin, 34,* 1556–1569.

Hovland, C. I., Janis, I. L., & Kelley, H. H. (1953). *Communication and persuasion.* New Haven, CT: Yale University Press.

Howard, K. I., Moras, K., Brill, P. L., Martinovich, Z., & Lutz, W. (1996). Evaluation of psychotherapy: Efficacy, effectiveness, and patient progress. *American Psychologist, 51,* 1059–1064.

Howe, M. J. A., Davidson, J. W., Moore, D. G., & Sloboda, J. A. (1995). Are there early childhood signs of musical ability? *Psychology of Music, 23,* 162–176.

Howell, D. C. (2008). *Fundamental statistics for the behavioral sciences* (6th ed.). Belmont, CA: Wadsworth.

Howes, M. B. (2006). *Human memory.* Thousand Oaks, CA: Sage.

Howes, O. D., & others. (2009). Elevated striatal dopamine function linked to prodomal signs of schizophrenia. *Archives of General Psychiatry, 66,* 13–20.

Hoyer, D., Hannon, J. P., & Martin, G. R. (2002). Molecular, pharmacological, and functional diversity of 5-HT receptors. *Pharmacology, Biochemistry, and Behavior, 71,* 533–554.

Hoyle, R. H. (2009). *Handbook of personality and social regulation.* Malden, MA: Blackwell.

Hsieh, L. T., Hung, D. L., Tzeng, O. J., Lee, J. R., & Cheng, S. K. (2009). An event-related potential investigation of the processing of remember/forget cues and item encoding in item-method directed forgetting. *Brain Research, 1250,* 190–201.

Hu, F. B., Willett, W. C., Li, T., Stampfer, M. J., Colditz, G. A., & Manson, J. E. (2004). Adiposity as compared with physical activity in predicting mortality among women. *New England Journal of Medicine, 351,* 2694–2703.

Huang, C. C., & Chang, Y. C. (2009). The long-term effects of febrile seizures on the hippocampal neuronal plasticity—clinical and experimental evidence. *Brain Development.* (in press)

Hubble, M. A., & Miller, S. D. (2004). The client: Psychotherapy's missing link for promoting a positive psychology. In A. Linley & S. Joseph (Eds.), *Positive psychology in practice* (pp. 335–353). Hoboken, NJ: Wiley.

Hubel, D. H., & Wiesel, T. N. (1963). Receptive fields of cells in striate cortex of very young, visually inexperienced kittens. *Journal of Neurophysiology, 26,* 994–1002.

Hudson, A. J. (2009). Consciousness: Physiological dependence on rapid memory access. *Frontiers in Biology, 14,* 2779–2800.

Huff, C. R. (2002). What can we learn from other nations about the problem of wrongful conviction? *Judicature, 86,* 91–97.

Hull, E. M., & Dominguez, J. M. (2006). Getting his act together: Roles of glutamate, nitric oxide, and dopamine in the medial preoptic area. *Brain Research, 1126,* 66–75.

"Human gene count tumbles again." (2008, January 15). *Science Daily,* 1.

Hummer, R. A., Ellison, C. G., Rogers, R. G., Moulton, B. C., & Romero, R. R. (2004). Religious involvement and adult mortality in the United States: Review and perspective. *Southern Medical Journal, 97,* 1223–1230.

Hunsley, J., & Bailey, J. M. (2001). Whither the Rorschach? An analysis of the evidence. *Psychological Assessment, 13,* 472–485.

Hunsley, J., Lee, C. M., & Wood, J. M. (2004). Controversial and questionable assessment techniques. In S. O. Lilienfeld, J. M. Lohr, & S. J. Lynn (Eds.), *Science and pseudoscience in clinical psychology* (pp. 39–76). New York: Guilford.

Hunt, R. R., & Ellis, H. C. (2004). *Fundamentals of cognitive psychology* (7th ed.). New York: McGraw-Hill.

Hurvich, L. M., & Jameson, D. (1969). Human color perception. *American Scientist, 57,* 143–166.

Husain, O. (2009). Paul Lerner and the heart of assessment: A tale of three relations. *Journal of Personality Assessment, 91,* 30–34.

Hutchison, R. M., Chidiac, P., & Leung, L. S. (2009). Hippocampal long-term potentiation is enhanced in urethane-anesthetized RGS2 knockout mice. *Hippocampus.* (in press)

Huttenlocher, P. R., & Dabholkar, A. S. (1997). Regional differences in synaptogenesis in human cerebral cortex. *Journal of Comparative Neurology, 37* (2), 167–178.

Hutton, J. L., Baracos, V. E., & Wismer, W. V. (2007). Chemosensory dysfunction is a primary factor in the evolution of declining nutrional status and quality of life in patients with advanced cancer. *Journal of Pain Symptom Management, 33* (2), 156–165.

Hyde, D. R. (2009). *Introduction to genetic principles.* New York: McGraw-Hill.

Hyde, J. S. (2005). The gender similarities hypothesis. *American Psychologist, 60,* 581–592.

Hyde, J. S. (2007). *Half the human experience* (7th ed.). Boston: Houghton Mifflin.

Hyde, M., & Power, D. (2006). Some ethical dimensions of cochlear implantation for deaf children and their families. *Journal of Deaf Studies and Deaf Education, 11,* 102–111.

Hyman, S. (2001, October 23). *Basic and clinical neuroscience in the post-genomic era.* Paper presented at the centennial symposium on the Celebration of Excellence in Neuroscience, the Rockefeller University, New York City.

Iacono, W. G., & Lykken, D. T. (1997). The validity of the lie detector: Two surveys of scientific opinion. *Journal of Applied Psychology, 82,* 426–433.

Ibrahim, R., & Eviatar, Z. (2009). Language status and hemispheric involvement in reading: Evidence from trilingual Arabic speakers tested in Arabic, Hebrew, and English. *Neuropsychology, 23,* 240–254.

Iemmola, F., & Ciani, A. C. (2009). New evidence of genetic factors influencing sexual orientation in men: Female fecundity increase in the maternal line. *Archives of Sexual Behavior, 38,* 393–399.

Ikeda, B. E., Collins, C. E., Alvaro, F., Marshall, G., & Garg, M. L. (2006). Well-being and nutrition-related side effects in children undergoing chemotherapy. *Nutrition and Dietetics, 63,* 227–239.

Ilies, R., Arvey, R. D., & Bouchard T. J., Jr. (2006). Darwinism, behavioral genetics, and organizational behavior: A review and agenda for future research. *Journal of Organizational Behavior, 27* (2), 121–141.

Imayoshi, I., Sakamoto, M., Ohtsuka, T., & Kageyama, R. (2009). Continuous neurogenesis in the adult brain. *Development, Growth, and Differentiation, 51,* 379–386.

Imeri, L., & Opp, M. R. (2009). How (and why) the immune system makes us sleep. *Nature Reviews: Neuroscience, 10,* 199–210.

Inaba, A., Thoits, P. A., Ueno, K., Gove, W. R., Evenson, R. J., & Sloan, M. (2005). Depression in the United States and Japan: Gender, marital status, and SES patterns. *Social Science & Medicine, 61,* 2280–2292.

Ingram, R. E. (Ed.). (2009). *The international encyclopedia of depression.* New York: Springer.

Insel, P. M., & Roth, W. T. (2008). *Core concepts in health* (10th ed.). New York: McGraw-Hill.

Insko, C. A., & Wilson, M. (1977). Interpersonal attraction as a function of social interaction. *Journal of Personality and Social Psychology, 35,* 903–911.

Institute of Medicine. (2006, April). *Sleep disorders and sleep deprivation: An unmet public health problem.* Washington, DC: National Academies.

Ironson, G., Solomon, G., Balbin, E., O'Cleirigh, C., George, A., Schneiderman, N., & Woods, T. (2001, March). *Religious behavior, religious coping, and compassionate view of others is associated with long-term survival with AIDS.* Paper presented at the meeting of the American Psychosomatic Society, Monterey, CA.

Ironson, G., Stuetzle, R., & Fletcher, M. A. (2006). An increase in religiousness/spirituality occurs after HIV diagnosis and predicts slower disease progression over 4 years in people with HIV. *Journal of General Internal Medicine, 21,* S62–S68.

Irwin, M. R., Wang, M., Campomayor, C. O., Coliado-Hidalgo, A., & Cole, S. (2006). Sleep deprivation and activation of morning levels of cellular and genomic markers of inflammation. *Archives of Internal Medicine, 166,* 1756–1762.

Isbell, L. M. (2004). Not all people are lazy or stupid: Evidence of systematic processing in happy moods. *Journal of Experimental Social Psychology, 40,* 341–349.

Isen, A. M. (1984). Toward understanding the role of affect in cognition. In R. S. Wyer, Jr., & T. K. Srull (Eds.), *Handbook of social cognition* (vol. 3, pp. 179–236). Hillsdale, NJ: Erlbaum.

Isen, A. M. (2004). Some perspectives on positive feelings and emotions: Positive affect facilitates thinking and problem solving. In A. S. R. Manstead, N. Frijda, & A. Fischer (Eds.). *Feelings and emotions: The Amsterdam symposium* (pp. 263–281). New York, NY: Cambridge University Press.

Isen, A. M. (2007a). Positive affect, cognitive flexibility, and self-control. In Y. Shoda, D. Cervone, & G. Downey (Eds.), *Persons in context.* New York: Guilford.

Isen, A. M. (2007b). Positive affect. In R. Baumeister & K. Vohs (Eds.), *Encyclopedia of social psychology.* Thousand Oaks, CA: Sage.

Isen, A. M. (2008). Some ways in which positive affect influences problem solving and decision making. In M. Lewis, J. Haviland-Jones, & L. F. Barrett (Eds.), *Handbook of emotions* (3rd ed.). New York: Guilford.

Isen, A. M., & Means, B. (1983). The influence of positive affect on decision-making strategy. *Social Cognition, 2,* 18–31.

Issa, E. B., & Wang, X. (2008). Sensory responses during sleep in primary and secondary auditory cortex. *Journal of Neuroscience, 28,* 14467–14480.

Istaphanous, G. K., & Loepke, A. W. (2009). General anesthetics and the developing brain. *Current Opinion in Anesthesiology, 22,* 368–373.

Iwassa, H., Masul, Y., Gondo, Y., Inagaki, H., Kawaal, C., & Suzuki, T. (2008). Personality and all-cause mortality among older adults dwelling in a Japanese community: A five-year population-based prospective study. *American Journal of Geriatric Psychiatry, 16,* 399–405.

Iwassa, H., & others. (2009). Personality and participation in mass health checkups among Japanese community-dwelling elderly. *Journal of Psycho-somatic Research, 66,* 155–159.

Izard, C. E. (2009). Emotion theory and research: Highlights, unanswered questions, and emerging issues. *Annual Review of Psychology* (vol. 60). Palo Alto, CA: Annual Reviews.

Jablensky, E. (2000). Epidemiology of schizophrenia: The global burden of disease and disability. *European Archives of Psychiatry and Clinical Neuroscience, 250,* 274–285.

Jablensky, E., Sartorius, N., Ernberg, G., & others. (1992). Schizophrenia: Manifestations, incidence and course in different cultures: A World Health Organization 10-country study. *Psychological Medicine, Monograph Suppl. 20,* 1–97.

Jackson, L., Langille, L., Lyons, R., Hughes, J., Martin, D., & Winstanley, V. (2009). Does moving from a high-poverty to lower-poverty neighborhood improve mental health? A realist view of "Moving to Opportunity." *Health and Place.* (in press)

Jackson, L. C., & Greene, B. (2000). *Psychotherapy with African-American women.* New York: Guilford.

Jackson, S. L. (2009). *Research methods and statistics* (4th ed.). Belmont, CA: Wadsworth.

Jacobsen, P. B., Bovbjerg, D. H., Schwartz, M. D., Andrykowski, M.A., Futterman, A. D., Gilewski, T., Norton, L., & Redd, W. H. (1993). Formation of food aversions in cancer patients receiving repeated infusions of chemotherapy. *Behavior Reseach Therapy, 31* (8), 739–748.

Jaeger, A., Johnson, J. D., Corona, M., & Rugg, M. D. (2009). ERP correlates of the incidental retrieval of emotional information: Effects of study-test delay. *Brain Research.* (in press)

Jaeggi, S. M., Buschkuehl, M., Jonides, J., & Perrig, W. J. (2008). Improving fluid intelligence with training on working memory. *Proceedings of the National Academy of Sciences USA, 105* (19), 6829–6833.

Jaffe, E. S. (2007). Pathobiology of peripheral T-cell lymphomas. *Hematology, 26,* 317–322.

Jakupcak, M., Salters, K., Gratz, K. L., & Roemer, L. (2003). Masculinity and emotionality: An investigation of men's primary and secondary emotional responding. *Sex Roles, 49,* 111–120.

James, W. (1950). *Principles of psychology.* New York: Dover. (original work published 1890)

Jameson, D., & Hurvich, L. M. (1989). Essay concerning color constancy. *Annual Review of Psychology* (vol. 40). Palo Alto, CA: Annual Reviews.

Janata, P. (2009). The neural architecture of music-evoked autobiographical memories. *Cerebral Cortex.* (in press)

Jang, K. L., Livesley, W. J., & Vernon, P. A. (1996). Heritability of the big five personality dimensions and their facets: A twin study. *Journal of Personality, 64,* 577–591.

Janis, I. (1972). *Victims of groupthink: A psychological study of foreign-policy decisions and fiascos.* Boston: Houghton Mifflin.

Janis, I. L., & Hovland, C. I. (1959). An overview of persuasability research. In C. I. Hovland & I. L. Janis (Eds.), *Personality and persuasability* (pp. 1–26). New Haven, CT: Yale University Press.

Janowsky, D. S., Addario, D., & Risch, S. C. (1987). *Psychopharmacology case studies* (2nd ed.). New York: Guilford.

Jarrett, R. B., Kraft, D., Doyle, J., Foster, B. M., Eaves, G. G., & Silver, P. C. (2001). Preventing recurrent depression using cognitive therapy with and without a continuation phase: A randomized clinical trial. *Archives of General Psychiatry, 58,* 381–388.

Jaurrieta, N., & others. (2008). Individual versus group cognitive behavioral treatment for obsessesive-compulsive disorder: Follow-up. *Psychiatry and Clinical Neuroscience, 62,* 697–704.

Jax, S. A., & Coslett, H. B. (2009). Disorders of the perceptual-motor system. *Advances in Experimental Medicine and Biology, 629,* 377–391.

Jellinger, K. A. (2009). Serotonin and sleep: Molecular, functional, and clinical aspects. *European Journal of Neurology.* (in press)

Jensen, L. W., & Wadkins, T. A. (2007). Mental health success stories: Finding paths to recovery. *Issues in Mental Health Nursing, 28,* 325–340.

Jensen, M. P. (2009). The neurophysiology of pain perception and hypnotic analgesia: Implications for clinical practice. *American Journal of Clinical Hypnosis, 51,* 123–148.

Jensen, P. S. (2006, October 24). *ADHD: A public health conference.* Atlanta: Centers for Disease Control and Prevention.

Jensen-Campbell, L. A., & Malcolm, K. T. (2007). The importance of conscientiousness in adolescent interpersonal relationships. *Personality and Social Psychology Bulletin, 33,* 368–383.

Jeong, J., Kim, D. J., Kim, S. Y., Chae, J. H., Go, H. J., & Kim, K. S. (2001). Effect of total sleep deprivation on the dimensional complexity of the waking EEG. *Sleep, 15,* 197–202.

Jermakowicz, W. J., Chen, X., Khaytin, I., Bonds, A. B., & Casagrande, V. A. (2009). Relationship between spontaneous and evoked spike-time correlations in primate visual cortex. *Journal of Neurophysiology, 101,* 2279–2289.

Jia, F., Goldstein, P. A., & Harrison, N. L. (2009). The modulation of synaptic GABA (A) receptors in the thalamus by eszopicione and zolpidem. *Journal of*

Pharmacology and Experimental Therapeutics, 328, 1000–1006.

Jimenez-Ruiz, C. A., Ulibarri, M. M., Besada, N. A., Guerrero, A. C., Garcia, A. G., & Cuadrado, A. R. (2009). Progressive reduction using nicotine gum as a prelude to quitting. *Nicotine and Tobacco Research.* (in press)

Jimenez-Sanchez, A. R., & others. (2009). Morphological background detection and enhancement of images with poor lighting. *IEEE Transactions on Image Processing, 18,* 613–623.

Johnson, A. M., Vernon, P. A., Harris, J. A., & Jang, K. L. (2004). Behavior genetic investigation of the relationship between leadership and personality. *Twin Research, 7* (1), 27–32.

Johnson, G. B. (2008). *The living world* (5th ed.). New York: McGraw-Hill.

Johnson, G. B., & Losos, J. (2008). *Essentials of the living world* (2nd ed.). New York: McGraw-Hill.

Johnson, H., & Thompson, A. (2007). The development and maintenance of post-traumatic stress disorder (PTSD) in civilian adult survivors of war trauma and torture: A review. *Clinical Psychology Review, 28,* 36–47.

Johnson, J. S., & Newport, E. L. (1991). Critical period effects on universal properties of language: The status of subjacency in the acquisition of a second language. *Cognition, 39,* 215–258.

Johnson, J. T., Robinson, M., & Mitchell, E. B. (2004). Inferences about the authentic self: When do actions say more than mental states? *Journal of Personality and Social Psychology, 87,* 615–630.

Johnson, M. R., & Johnson, M. K. (2009). Top-down enhancement and suppression of activity in category-selective extrastriate cortex from an act of reflective attention. *Journal of Cognitive Neuroscience.* (in press)

Johnson, S. P. (2009). Developmental origins of object perception. In A. Woodward & A. Needham (Eds.), *Learning and the infant mind.* New York: Oxford University Press.

Johnson-Laird, P. N., Mancini, F., & Gangemi, A. (2006). A hyper-emotion theory of psychological illnesses. *Psychological Review, 113,* 822–841.

Johnston, L. D., O'Malley, P. M., Bachman, J. G., & Schulenberg, J. E. (2008). *Monitoring the Future national survey results on drug use, 1975–2007.* Bethesda, MD: National Institute on Drug Abuse.

Johnston, L. D., O'Malley, P. M., Bachman, J. G., & Schulenberg, J. E. (2009). *Monitoring the Future: National results on adolescent drug use: Overview of key findings, 2008.* Bethesda, MD: National Institute on Drug Abuse.

Johnstone, E., Benowitz, N., Cargill, A., Jacob, R., Hinks, L., Day, I., Murphy, M., & Walton, R. (2006). Determinants of the rate of nicotine metabolism and the effects on smoking behavior. *Clinical Pharmacology and Therapeutics, 80,* 319–330.

Joiner, T. E., Jr. (2005). *Why people die by suicide.* Cambridge, MA: Harvard University Press.

Joiner, T. E., Jr., Hollar, D., & Van Orden, K. (2006). On Buckeyes, Gators, Super Bowl Sunday, and the miracle on ice: "Pulling together" is associated with lower suicide rates. *Journal of Social & Clinical Psychology, 25,* 179–195.

Jones, E. E. (1998). Major developments in five decades of social psychology. In D. T. Gilbert, S. T. Fiske, & G. Lindzey (Eds.), *Handbook of social psychology* (4th ed., vol. 1). New York: McGraw-Hill.

Jones, E. E., & Harris, V. A. (1967). The attribution of attitudes. *Journal of Experimental Social Psychology, 3,* 1–24.

Jones, R. (2006). Sex scripts and power: A framework to explain urban women's HIV sexual risk with male partners. *Nursing Clinics of North America, 41,* 425–436.

Joorman, J., Hertel, P. T., LeMoutl, J., & Gotlib, I. H. (2009). Training forgetting of negative material in depression. *Journal of Abnormal Psychology, 118,* 34–43.

Joorman, J., Teachman, B. A., & Gotlib, I. H. (2009). Sadder and less accurate? False memory for negative material in depression. *Journal of Abnormal Psychology, 118,* 412–417.

Jorgensen, M. M., & Zachariae, R. (2006). Repressive coping style and autonomic reactions to two experimental stressors in healthy men and women. *Scandinavian Journal of Psychology, 47,* 137–148.

Joscelyne, A., & Kehoe, E. J. (2007). Time and stimulus specificity in extinction of the conditioned nictitating membrane response in the rabbit (*Oryctolagus cuniculus*). *Behavioral Neuroscience, 121,* 50–62.

Joseph, J. (2006). *The missing gene.* New York: Algora.

Joseph, J., Breslin, C., & Skinner, H. (1999). Critical perspectives on the transtheoretical model and stages of change. In J. A. Tucker, D. M. Donovan, & G. A. Marlatt (Eds.), *Changing addictive behavior: Bridging clinical and public health strategies* (pp. 160–190). New York: Guilford.

Joseph, S., & Linley, P. A. (2004). Positive therapy: A positive psychological approach to therapeutic practice. In P. A. Linley & S. Joseph (Eds.), *Positive psychology in practice* (pp. 354–368). Hoboken, NJ: Wiley.

Jost, J. T., Federico, C. M., & Napier, J. L. (2009). Attitude structure. *Annual Review of Psychology, 60,* 307–337.

Joubert, O. R., Fize, D., Rousselet, G. A., & Fabre-Thorpe, M. (2008). Early interference of context congruence on object processing in rapid visual categorization of natural scences. *Journal of Vision, 8,* 1–18.

Joy, J. E., Watson, S. J., & Benson, J. A. (Eds.). (1999). *Institute of medicine. Marijuana and medicine: Assessing the science base.* Washington, DC: National Academy Press.

Juckel, G., Uhl, I., Padberg, F., Brune, M., & Winter, C. (2009). Psychosurgery and deep brain stimulation as ultima ratio treatment for refractory depression. *European Archives of Psychiatry and Clinical Neuroscience, 259,* 1–7.

Judd, C. M., & Park, B. (2007). Diverging ideological viewpoints on pathways to more harmonious intergroup relations. In E. Borgida & others (Eds.), *The political psychology of democratic citizenship.* New York: Cambridge University Press.

Judge, T., Higgins, C., Thoresen, C., & Barrick, M. (1999). The big five personality traits, general mental ability, and career success across the life span. *Personnel Psychology, 52,* 621–652.

Judge, T. A., Thorson, C. J., Bono, J. E., & Patton, G. K. (2001). The job satisfaction–job performance relationship: A qualitative and quantitative review. *Psychological Bulletin, 127,* 376–407.

Julien, E., Senecal, C., & Guay, F. (2009). Longi-tudinal relations among perceived autonomy support from health care practitioners, motivation, coping strategies and dietary compliance in a sample of adults with type 2 diabetes. *Journal of Health Psychology, 14,* 457–470.

Jung, C. (1917). *Analytic psychology.* New York: Moffat, Yard.

K

Kaasa, S. O., & Loftus, E. F. (2009). False memories. In F. T. L. Leong (Ed.), *Encyclopedia of counseling.* Thousand Oaks, CA: Sage. (in press)

Kabat-Zinn, J. (2006). Coming to our senses: Healing ourselves and the world through mindfulness. New York, NY: Hyperion.

Kabat-Zinn, J. (2009, March 18). This analog life; Reconnecting with what is important in an always uncertain world. Presentation at the 7th Annual Conference at the Center for Mindful Meditation, Worcester, MA.

Kabat-Zinn, J., Lipworth, L., & Burney, R. (1985). The clinical use of mindfulness meditation for the self-regulation of chronic pain. *Journal of Behavioral Medicine, 8,* 163–190.

Kabat-Zinn, J., Wheeler, E., Light, T., Skillings, A., Scharf, M. J., Cropley, T. G., Hosmer, D., & Bernhard, J. D. (1998). Influence of a mindfulness meditation-based stress reduction intervention on rates of skin clearing in patients with moderate to severe psoriasis undergoing phototherapy (UVB) and photochemotherapy (PUVA). *Psychosomatic Medicine, 60,* 625–632.

Kagan, J. (2008). Fear and wariness. In M. M. Haith & J. B. Benson (Eds.), *Encyclopedia of infant and early childhood development*. London: Elsevier.

Kaiser Family Foundation. (2001). *Inside-OUT: A report on the experiences of lesbians, gays, and bisexuals in America and the public's views on issues and policies related to sexual orientation*. Menlo Park, CA: Henry J. Kaiser Family Foundation.

Kalant, H. (2004). Adverse effects of cannabis on health: An update of the literature since 1996. *Progress in Neuropsychopharmacology, Biology, and Psychiatry, 28*, 849–863.

Kalichman, S. C. (2007). The theory of reasoned action and advances in HIV/AIDS prevention. In I. Ajzen, D. Albarracin, & R. Hornik (Eds.), *Prediction and change of health behavior*. Mahwah, NJ: Erlbaum.

Kalivas, P. W. (2007). Neurobiology of cocaine addiction: Implications for new pharmacotherapy. *American Journal of Addiction, 16*, 71–78.

Kalonia, H., Bishnoi, M., & Kumar, A. (2008). Possible mechanism involved in sleep-deprivation-induced memory dysfunction. *Methods and Findings in Experimental and Clinical Pharmacology, 30*, 529–535.

Kaltenbach, S. L., Yu, J. K., & Holland, N. D. (2009). The origin and migration of the earliest-developing sensory neurons in the peripheral nervous system of amphioxus. *Evolution and Development, 11*, 142–151.

Kamel, N. S., & Gammack, J. K. (2006). Insomnia in the elderly: Cause, approach, and treatment. *American Journal of Medicine, 119*, 463–469.

Kamin, L. J. (1968). Attention-like processes in classical conditioning. In M. R. Jones (Ed.), *Miami symposium on the prediction of behavior: Aversive stimuli*. Coral Gables, FL: University of Miami Press.

Kamphaus, R. W., & Kroncke, A. P. (2004). "Back to the future" of the Stanford-Binet Intelligence Scales. In M. Herson (Ed.), *Comprehensive handbook of psychological assessment* (vol. 1). New York: Wiley.

Kandel, E. R., & Schwartz, J. H. (1982). Molecular biology of learning: Modulation of transmitter release. *Science, 218*, 433–443.

Kantowitz, B. H., Roediger, H. L., & Elmes, D. G. (2009). *Experimental psychology* (9th ed.). Belmont, CA: Wadsworth.

Kanwisher, N. (2006). Neuroscience: What's in a face? *Science, 311*, 617–618.

Kanwisher, N., Livingstone, M. S., & Tsao, D. (2007). Face processing versus perceptual expertise: A debate. *Annual Review of Neuroscience* (vol. 30). Palo Alto, CA: Annual Reviews.

Kanwisher, N., & Yovel, G. (2009). Cortical specialization for face perception in humans. In J. T. Cacioppo & G. G. Berntson (Eds.), *Handbook of neuroscience for the behavioral sciences*. New York: Wiley. (in press)

Kaplan, R. M., & Saccuzzo, D. P. (2009). *Psychological testing* (7th ed.). Boston: Cengage.

Kapur, S. (2003). Psychosis as a state of aberrant salience: A framework linking biology, phenomenology, and pharmacology. *American Journal of Psychiatry, 160*, 13–23.

Karam, E., Kypri, K., & Salamoun, M. (2007). Alcohol use among college students: An international perspective. *Current Opinion in Psychiatry, 20*, 213–221.

Karau, S. J., & Williams, K. D. (1993). Social loafing: A meta-analytic review and theoretical integration. *Journal of Personality and Social Psychology, 65*, 681–706.

Kardong, K. (2008). *Introduction to biological evolution* (2nd ed.). New York: McGraw-Hill.

Karnes, F. A., & Stephens, K. R. (2008). *Achieving excellence: Educating the gifted and the talented*. Upper Saddle River, NJ: Prentice-Hall.

Kashdan, T. B., Biswas-Diener, R., & King, L. A. (2008). Reconsidering happiness: The costs of distinguishing between hedonics and eudaimonia. *Journal of Positive Psychology, 3*, 219–233.

Kaskutas, L. A. (2009). Alcoholics Anonymous effectiveness: Faith meets science. *Journal of Addictive Diseases, 28*, 145–157.

Kaskutas, L. A., Subbaraman, M. S., Witbordt, J., & Zemore, S. E. (2009). Effectiveness of making Alcoholics Anonymous easier: A group format 12-step facilitation approach. *Journal of Substance Abuse Treatment*. (in press)

Kasser, T., & Ryan, R. M. (1993). A dark side of the American dream: Correlates of financial success as a central life aspiration. *Journal of Personality and Social Psychology, 65*, 410–422.

Kasser, T., & Ryan, R. M. (1996). Further examining the American dream: Differential correlates of intrinsic and extrinsic goals. *Personality and Social Psychology Bulletin, 22*, 280–287.

Kasser, T., Ryan, R. M., Couchman, C. E., & Sheldon, K. M. (2004). Materialistic values: Their causes and consequences. In T. Kasser & A. D. Kanner (Eds.), *Psychology and consumer culture: The struggle for a good life in a materialistic world* (pp. 11–28). Washington, DC: American Psychological Association.

Kasser, T., & Sharma, Y. S. (1999). Reproductive freedom, educational equality, and females' preference for resource-acquisition characteristics in mates. *Psychological Science, 10*, 374–377.

Kaszubowska, L. (2008). Telomere shortening and aging of the immune system. *Journal of Physiology and Pharmacology, 59, Suppl. 9*, S169–S186.

Katzman, M. A. (2009). Current considerations in the treatment of generalized anxiety disorder. *CNS Drugs, 23*, 103–120.

Kauffman, C., & Silberman, J. (2009). Finding and fostering the positive in relationships: Positive interventions in couples therapy. *Journal of Clinical Psychology, 65*, 520–531.

Kazdin, A. E. (2007). Mediators and mechanisms of change in psychotherapy change. *Annual Review of Clinical Psychology* (vol. 3). Palo Alto, CA: Annual Reviews.

Kazdin, A. E., & Benjet, C. (2003). Spanking children: Evidence and issues. *Current Directions in Psychological Science, 12*, 99–103.

Keedwell, P. A., Andrew, C., Williams, S. C. R., Brammer, M. J., & Phillips, M. L. (2005). A double dissociation of ventromedial prefrontal cortical responses to sad and happy stimuli in depressed and healthy individuals. *Biological Psychiatry, 58*, 495–503.

Keeton, C. P., Kolos, A. C., & Walkup, J. T. (2009). Pediatric generalized anxiety disorder: Epidemiology, diagnosis, and management. *Pediatric Drugs, 11*, 171–183.

Keillor, J. M., Barrett, A. M., Crucian, G. P., Kortenkamp, S., & Heilman, K. M. (2002). Emotional experience and perception in the absence of facial feedback. *Journal of the International Neuropsychological Society, 8*, 130–135.

Keith, S. (2009). Use of long-acting risperidone in psychiatric disorders: Focus on efficacy, safety, and cost-effectiveness. *Expert Review of Neurotherapeutics, 9*, 9–31.

Keitner, G. I., Ryan, C. E., & Solomon, D. A. (2009). Family focused therapy shortens recovery time from depression but not mania in adolescents with bipolar disorder. *Evidence Based Mental Health, 12*, 48.

Kellerman, A. L., and others. (1993). Gun ownership as a risk factor for homicide in the home. *New England Journal of Medicine, 329*, 1084–1091.

Kelley, H. H. (1973). The processes of causal attribution. *American Psychologist, 28*, 107–128.

Kellner, C. H., Knapp, R. G., Petrides, G., Rummans, T. A., Husain, M. M., Rasmussen, K., Mueller, M., Bernstein, H. J., O'Connor, K., Smith, G., Biggs, M., Bailine, S. H., Malur, C., Yim, E., McClintock, S., Sampson, S., & Fink, M. (2006). Continuation electroconvulsive therapy vs pharmacotherapy for relapse prevention in major depression: A multisite study from the Consortium for Research in Electroconvulsive Therapy (CORE). *Archives of General Psychiatry, 63*, 1337–1344.

Kellogg, R. T. (2007). *Fundamentals of cognitive psychology*. Thousand Oaks, CA: Sage.

Kelly, G. F. (2006). *Sexuality today* (8th ed.). New York: McGraw-Hill.

Kelly, J. W., & McNamara, T. P. (2009). Facilitated pointing to remembered objects: Evidence for egocentric retrieval or for spatial priming. *Psychonomic Bulletin and Review, 16*, 295–300.

Kemp, C., & Tenenbaum, J. B. (2009). Structured statistical models of inductive reasoning. *Psychological Review, 116*, 20–58.

Kendler, K. S., Gardner, C. O., Gatz, M., & Pedersen, N. L. (2007). The sources of co-morbidity between major depression and generalized anxiety disorder in a Swedish national twin sample. *Psychological Medicine, 37*, 453–462.

Kendler, K. S., Thornton, L. M., Gilman, S. E., &. Kessler, R. C. (2000). Sexual orientation in a US national sample of twin and nontwin sibling pairs, *American Journal of Psychiatry, 157*, 1843–1846.

Kennard, B. D., & others. (2008). Cognitive-behavioral therapy to prevent relapse in pediatric responders to pharmacotherapy for major depressive disorder. *Journal of the American Academy of Child and Adolescent Psychiatry, 47*, 1395–1404.

Kensinger, E. A., & Choi, E. S. (2009). When side matters: Hemispheric processing and the visual specificity of emotional memories. *Journal of Experimental Psychology: Learning, Memory, and Cognition, 35*, 247–253.

Kern, M. L., & Friedman, H. S. (2008). Do conscientious individuals live longer? A quantitative review. *Health Psychology, 27*, 505–512.

Kernis, M. H., Paradise, A. W., Whitaker, D. J., Wheatman, S. R., & Goldman, B. N. (2000). Master of one's psychological domain? Not likely if one's self-esteem is unstable. *Personality and Social Psychology Bulletin, 26*, 1297–1305.

Kerns, J. G. (2007). Verbal communication impairments and cognitive control components in people with schizophrenia. *Journal of Abnormal Psychology, 116*, 279–289.

Kerns, J. G., Berenbaum, H., Barch, D. M., Banich, M. T., & Stolar, N. (1999). Word production in schizophrenia and its relationship to positive symptoms. *Psychiatry Research, 87*, 29–37.

Kersick, C., & others. (2009). Effects of a popular exercise and weight loss program on weight loss, body composition, energy expenditure, and health in obese women. *Nutrition and Metabolism, 6*, 23.

Kessler, R. C., Chiu, W. T., Demler, O., & Walters, E. E. (2005). Prevalence, severity, and comorbidity of twelve-month DSM-IV disorders in the National Comorbidity Survey Replication (NCS-R). *Archives of General Psychiatry, 62*, 617–627.

Khatapoush, S., & Hallfors, D. (2004). "Sending the wrong message": Did medical marijuana legalization in California change attitudes about and use of marijuana? *Journal of Drug Issues, 34*, 751–770.

Kibler, J. L. (2009). Posttraumatic stress and cardiovascular disease risk. *Journal of Trauma and Dissociation, 10*, 135–150.

Kihlstrom, J. (2005). Is hypnosis an altered state of consciousness or what?: Comment. *Contemporary Hypnosis. 22*, 34–38.

Killeen, P. R., Posadas-Sanchez, D., Johansen, E. B., & Thrailkill, E. A. (2009). Progressive ratio schedules of reinforcement. *Journal of Experimental Psychology: Animal Behavioral Processes, 35*, 35–50.

Killgore, W. D., Rosso, I. M., Gruber, S. A., & Yurgelun-Todd, D. A. (2009). Amygdala volume and verbal memory performance in schizophrenia and bipolar disorder. *Cognitive and Behavioral Neurology, 22*, 28–37.

Killgore, W. D. S., Killgore, D. B., Day, L. M., Li, C., Kamimori, G. H., & Balkin, T. J. (2007). The effects of 53 hours of sleep deprivation on moral judgment. *SLEEP, 30*, 345–352.

Kim, J. N., & Lee, B. M. (2007). Risk factors, health risks, and risk management for aircraft personnel and frequent flyers. *Journal of Toxicology and Environmental Health B: Critical Reviews, 10*, 223–234.

Kim, J. Y., Oh, D. J., Yoon, T. Y., Choi, J. M., & Choe, B. K. (2007). The impacts of obesity on psychological well-being: A cross-sectional study about depressive mood and quality of life. *Journal of Preventive Medicine and Public Health, 40*, 191–195.

Kindt, M., Soeter, M., & Vervliet, B. (2009). Beyond extinction: Erasing human fear responses and preventing the return of fear. *Nature Neuroscience, 12*, 256–258.

King, B. M. (2005). *Human sexuality today* (5th ed.). Upper Saddle River, NJ: Prentice-Hall.

King, L. A. (2002). Gain without pain: Expressive writing and self regulation. In S. J. Lepore & J. Smyth (Eds.), *The writing cure*. Washington, DC: American Psychological Association.

King, L. A. (2003). Measures and meanings: The use of qualitative data in social and personality psychology. In C. Sansone, C. Morf, & A. Panter (Eds.), *Handbook of methods in social psychology* (pp.173–194). New York: Sage.

King, L. A. (2008). Personal goals and life dreams: Positive psychology and motivation in daily life. In W. Gardner & J. Shah (Eds.), *Handbook of motivation science* (pp. 518–532). New York: Guilford.

King, L. A., & Broyles, S. (1997). Wishes, gender, personality, and well-being. *Journal of Personality, 65*, 50–75.

King, L. A., & Hicks, J. A. (2006). Narrating the self in the past and the future: Implications for maturity. *Research in Human Development, 3*, 121–138.

King, L. A., & Hicks, J. A. (2007). Whatever happened to "what might have been"? Regret, happiness, and maturity. *American Psychologist, 62*, 625–636.

King, L. A., Hicks, J. A., Krull, J., & Del Gaiso, A. K. (2006). Positive affect and the experience of meaning in life. *Journal of Personality and Social Psychology, 90*, 179–196.

King, L. A., McKee-Walker, L., & Broyles, S. (1996). Creativity and the five factor model. *Journal of Research in Personality, 30*, 189–203.

King, L. A., Scollon, C. K., Ramsey, C. M., & Williams, T. (2000). Stories of life transition: Happy endings, subjective well-being, and ego development in parents of children with Down syndrome. *Journal of Research in Personality, 34*, 509–536.

King, L. A., & Smith, S. N. (2005). Happy, mature, and gay: Intimacy, power, and difficult times in coming out stories. *Journal of Research in Personality, 39*, 278–298.

King, P. E., & Roeser, R. W. (2009). Religion and spirituality in adolescent development. In R. W. Lerner & L. Steinberg (Eds.), *Handbook of adolescent psychology* (3rd ed.). New York: Wiley.

Kinney, A. (2005, September 1). Looting or finding? *Salon.com*.http://dir.salon.com/story/news/feature/2005/09/01/photo_controversy/index.html (accessed March 21, 2009)

Kirasic, K. C. (2004). *Midlife in context*. New York: McGraw-Hill.

Kirby, D. B., Laris, B. A., & Rolleri, L. A. (2007). Sex and HIV education programs: Their impact on sexual behavior of young people throughout the world. *Journal of Adolescent Health, 40*, 206–217.

Kirchhoff, B. A., & Buckner, R. L. (2006). Functional-anatomic correlates of individual differences in memory. *Neuron, 51*, 263–274.

Kirsch, I., & Sapirstein, G. (1999). Listening to Prozac but hearing placebo: A meta-analysis of antidepressant medications. In I. Kirsch, (Ed), *How expectancies shape experience*. (pp. 303–320). Washington, DC: American Psychological Association.

Kishioka, A., & others. (2009). A novel form of memory for auditory fear conditioning at a low-intensity unconditioned stimulus. *PLoS One, 4*, e4157.

Kitayama, S., & Cohen, D. (Eds.). (2007). *Handbook of cultural psychology*. New York: Guilford.

Kitchener, K. S., King, P. M., & DeLuca, S. (2006). The development of reflective judgment in adulthood. In C. Hoare (Ed.), *Handbook of adult development and learning*. New York: Oxford University Press.

Kjelsberg, E. (2005). Conduct disordered adolescents hospitalised 1963–1990. Secular trends in criminal activity. *European Journal of Child and Adolescent Psychiatry, 14*, 191–199.

Klein, S. B. (2009). *Learning*. Thousand Oaks, CA: Sage.

Klimstra, T. A., Hale, W. W., Raaijmakers, Q. A., Branje, S. J., & Meeus, W. H. (2009). Maturation of personality in adolescence. *Journal of Personality and Social Psychology, 96*, 898–912.

Klinesmith, J., Kasser, T., & McAndrew, F. T. (2006). Guns, testosterone, and aggression: An experimental test of a mediational hypothesis. *Psychological Science, 17*, 568–571.

Klohnen, E. C. (1996). Conceptual analysis and measurement of the construct of ego-resiliency. *Journal of Personality and Social Psychology, 70*, 1067–1079.

Klosterhalfen, S., Rüttgers, A., Krumrey, E., Otto, B., Stockhorst, U., Riepl, R. L., Probst, T., & Enck, P. (2000). Pavlovian conditioning of taste aversion using a motion sickness paradigm. *Psychosomatic Medicine, 62*, 671–677.

Klucharev, V., Hytonen, K., Rijpkema, M., Smidts, A., & Fernandez, G. (2009). Reinforcement learning signal predicts social conformity. *Neuron, 61*, 140–151.

Klumpp, H., & Amir, N. (2009). Examination of vigilance and disengagement of threat in social anxiety with a probe detection task. *Anxiety, Stress, and Coping, 2*, 1–13.

Knapp, H. (2007). *Therapeutic communication*. Thousand Oaks, CA: Sage.

Knoblauch, S. H. (2009). From self psychology to selves in relationships: A radical process of micro and macro expansion in conceptual experience. *Annals of the New York Academy of Sciences, 1159*, 262–278.

Knott, V., McIntosh, J., Millar, A., Fisher, D., Villeneuve, C., Ilivitsky, V., & Horn, E. (2006). Nicotine and smoker status moderate brain and electric and mood activation induced by ketamine, an N-methyl-d-aspartate (NMDA) receptor antagonist. *Pharmacology, Biochemistry, and Behavior, 85*, 228–242.

Knowles, E. S., Nolan, J., & Riner, D. D. (2007). Resistance to persuasion. In R. Baumeister & K. Vohs (Eds), *Encyclopedia of social psychology*. Newbury Park, CA: Sage.

Knowles, E. S., & Riner, D. D. (2006). Omega approaches to persuasion: Overcoming resistance. In A. R. Pratkanis (Ed.), *Science of social influence*. New York: Psychology Press.

Kobasa, S., Maddi, S., & Kahn, S. (1982). Hardiness and health: A prospective study. *Journal of Personality and Social Psychology, 42*, 168–177.

Kobasa, S. C., Maddi, S. R., Puccetti, M. C., & Zola, M. (1986). Relative effectiveness of hardiness, exercise, and social support as resources against illness. *Journal of Psychosomatic Research, 29*, 525–533.

Kochanek, K. D., Murphy, S. L., Anderson, R. N, & Scott, C. (2004, October 12). Deaths: Final data for 2002. *National Vital Statistics Reports, 53* (5). Washington, DC: U.S. Department of Health and Human Services.

Kochanska, G., Aksan, N., Prisco, T. R., & Adams, E. E. (2008). Mother-child and father-child mutually responsive orientation in the first two years and children's outcomes at preschool age: Mechanisms of influence. *Child Development, 79*, 30–44.

Kodama, S., & others. (2009). Cardiorespiratory fitness as a quantitative predictor of all-cause mortality and cardiovascular events in healthy men and women: A meta-analysis. *Journal of the American Medical Association, 301*, 2024–2035.

Koegel, L. K., Koegel, R. L., Fredeen, R. M., & Gengoux, G. W. (2008). Naturalistic behavioral approaches to treatment. In K. Chawarska, A. Klin, & F. R. Volkmar (Eds.), *Autism spectrum disorders in infants and toddlers: Diagnosis, assessment, and treatment* (pp. 207–242). New York: Guilford.

Koenigsberg, H. W., & others. (2009). Neural correlates of emotional processing in borderline personality disorder. *Psychiatry Research, 172*, 192–199.

Koepp, M. J., Hammers, A., Lawrence, A. D., Asselin, M. C., Grasby, P. M., & Bench, C. J. (2009). Evidence for endogenous opioid release in the amygdale during positive emotion. *NeuroImage, 44*, 252–256.

Koestner, R., Horberg, E. J., Gaudreau, P., Powers, T., Di Dio, P., Bryan, C., Jochum, R., & Salter, N. (2006). Bolstering implementation plans for the long haul: The benefits of simultaneously boosting self-concordance or self-efficacy. *Personality and Social Psychology Bulletin, 32*, 1547–1558.

Kohl, H. W. (2009). Duration and intensity of exercise in weight loss among overweight women. *Clinical Journal of Sport Medicine, 19*, 151–152.

Kohlberg, L. (1958). *The development on modes of moral thinking and choice in the years 10 to 16*. Unpublished doctoral dissertation, University of Chicago.

Kohlberg, L. (1986). A current statement on some theoretical issues. In S. Modgil & C. Modgil (Eds.), *Lawrence Kohlberg*. Philadelphia: Falmer.

Kohler, C. L., Schoenberger, Y., Tseng, T., & Ross, L. (2008). Correlates of transitions in stage of change for quitting among adolescent smokers. *Addictive Behaviors, 33*, 1615–1618.

Kohler, P. K., Manhart, L. E., & Lafferty, W. E. (2008). Abstinence-only and comprehensive sex education and the initiation of sexual activity and teen pregnancy. *Journal of Adolescent Health, 42*, 344–351.

Köhler, W. (1925). *The mentality of apes*. New York: Harcourt Brace Jovanovich.

Kohrt, B. A., & others. (2009). Culture in psychiatric epidemiology: Using ethnography and multiple mediator models to assess the relationship of caste with depression and anxiety in Nepal. *Annals of Human Biology, 36*, 261–280.

Kohut, H. (1977). *Restoration of the self*. New York: International Universities Press.

Koitabashi, T., Oyaizu, T., & Ouchi, T. (2009). Low bispectral index values following electroconvulsive therapy associated with memory impairment. *Journal of Anesthesiology, 23*, 182–187.

Kok, B. E., Catalino, L. I., & Fredrickson, B. L. (2008). The broadening, building, buffering effects of positive emotion. In S. J. Lopez (Ed.), *Positive psychology: Exploring the best of people* (vol. 3). Westport, CT: Greenwood.

Kolb, B., & Whishaw, I. Q. (2007). *Fundamentals of human neuropsychology* (5th ed.). New York: Worth.

Kollewe, K., Jin, L., Krampfl, K., Dengler, R., & Mohammed, B. (2009). Treatment of phantom limb pain with botulinum toxin type A. *Pain Medicine*. (in press)

Kong, L. L., Allen, J. J. B., & Glisky, E. L. (2008). Interidentity memory transfer in dissociative identity disorder. *Journal of Abnormal Psychology, 117*, 686–692.

Konrath, S., Bushman, B. J., & Campbell, W. K. (2006). Attenuating the link between threatened egotism and aggression. *Psychological Science, 17*, 995–1001.

Koob, G. F. (2006). The neurobiology of addiction: A neuroadaptational view. *Addiction, 101*, Suppl. 1, S23–S30.

Kopell, B. H., Machado, A. G., & Rezai, A. R. (2006). Not your father's lobotomy: Psychiatric surgery revisited. *Clinical Neurosurgery, 52*, 315–330.

Koppes, L. L., & Pickren, W. (2007). Industrial and organizational psychology: An evolving science. In L. L. Koppes (Ed.), *Historical perspectives in industrial and organizational psychology*. Mahwah, NJ: Erlbaum.

Korczak, D. J., & Goldstein, B. I. (2009). Childhood onset major depressive disorder: Course of illness and psychiatric comorbidity in a community sample. *Journal of Pediatrics, 155*, 118–123.

Korzekwa, M. I., Dell, P. F., Links, P. S., Thabane, L., & Webb, S. P. (2008). Estimating the prevalence of borderline personality disorder in psychiatric outpatients using a two-phase procedure. *Comprehensive Psychiatry, 49* (4), 380–386.

Kosslyn, S. M., Thompson, W. L., Kim, I. J., Rauch, S. L., & Alpert, N. M. (1996). Individual differences in cerebral blood flow in Area 17 predict the time to evaluate visualized letters. *Journal of Cognitive Neuroscience, 8*, 78–82.

Kovacs, A. M. (2009). Early bilingualism enhances mechanisms of false-belief reasoning. *Developmental Science, 12*, 48–54.

Kozaric-Kovacic, D. (2008). Integrative psychotherapy. *Psychiatria Danubina, 20*, 352–363.

Kradin, R. (2009). The family myth: Its deconstruction and replacement with a balanced humanized narrative. *Journal of Analytical Psychology, 54*, 217–232.

Kramer, A. F., Fabiani, M., & Colcombe, S. J. (2006). Contributions of cognitive neuroscience to the understanding of behavior and aging. In J. E. Birren & K. W. Schaie (Eds.), *Handbook of the psychology of aging* (6th ed.). San Diego: Academic Press.

Krause, N. (2006). Religion and health in late life. In J. E. Birren & K. W. Schaie (Eds.), *Handbook of the psychology of aging* (6th ed.). San Diego: Academic.

Kriegstein, A., & Alvarez-Buylla, A. (2009). The glial nature of embryonic and adult neural stem cells. *Annual Review of Neuroscience* (vol. 32). Palo Alto, CA: Annual Reviews.

Kring, A. M., Davison, G. C., Neale, J. M., & Johnson, S. L. (2007). *Abnormal psychology* (10th ed.). New York: Wiley.

Kristjansson, A., Vuilleumier, P., Schwartz, S., Macaluso, E., & Driver, J. (2006). Neural basis for priming of pop-out during visual search revealed with fMRI. *Cerebral Cortex*, doi:10.1093/cercor/bhl072. (advance online publication)

Kroger, J. (2007). *Identity development* (2nd ed.). Thousand Oaks, CA: Sage.

Kross, E., Davidon, M., Weber, J., & Ochsner, K. (2009). Coping with emotions past: The neural bases of regulating affect associated with negative autobiographical memories. *Biological Psychiatry, 65,* 361–366.

Krueger, J. I. (2007). From social projection to social behaviour. *European Review of Social Psychology, 18,* 1–35.

Krueger, K. A., & Dayan, P. (2009). Flexible shaping: How learning in small steps helps. *Cognition, 110,* 380–394.

Krueger, R. F., Markon, K. E., & Bouchard, T. J. (2003). The extended genotype: The heritability of personality accounts for the heritability of recalled family environments in twins reared apart. *Journal of Personality, 71,* 809–833.

Kruger, J., Blanck, H. M., & Gillespie, C. (2006). Dietary and physical activity behaviors among adults successful at weight loss maintenance. *International Journal of Behavioral Nutrition and Physical Activity, 3,* 17.

Ksir, C. J., Hart, C. L., & Ray, O. S. (2008). *Drugs, society, and human behavior* (12th ed.). New York: McGraw-Hill.

Kugaya, A., & Sanacora, G. (2005). Beyond monoamines: Glutamatergic function in mood disorders. *CNS Spectrums, 10,* 808–819.

Kuhl, P. K. (1993). Infant speech perception: A window on psycholinguistic development. *International Journal of Psycholinguistics, 9,* 33–56.

Kuhl, P. K. (2000). A new view of language acquisition. *Proceedings of the National Academy of Sciences USA, 97,* 11850–11857.

Kuhl, P. K. (2007). Is speech learning "gated" by the social brain? *Developmental Science, 10,* 110–120.

Kuhl, P. K., & Damasio, A. (2009). In E. R. Kandel & others (Eds.), *Principles of neural science* (5th ed.). New York: McGraw-Hill. (in press)

Kuhn, D. (2008). Formal operations from a twenty-first century perspective. *Human Development, 51,* 48–55.

Kuhn, D. (2009). Adolescent thinking. In R. M. Lerner & L. Steinberg (Eds.), *Handbook of adolescent psychology* (3rd ed.). New York: Wiley.

Kumar, C. T. S. (2004). Physical illness and schizophrenia. *British Journal of Psychiatry, 184,* 541.

Kuntsche, E., Knibbe, R., Gmel, G., & Engels, R. (2006). Who drinks and why? A review of sociodemographic, personality, and contextual issues behind the drinking motives in young people. *Addictive Behaviors, 31,* 1844–1857.

Kurson, R. (2007). *Crashing through: A true story of risk, adventure, and the man who dared to see.* New York: Random House.

Kushner, M. G. (2007). The use of cognitive-behavioral therapy in the University of Minnesota's outpatient psychiatry clinic. *Minnesota Medicine, 90,* 31–33.

Kushner, R. F. (2007). Obesity management. *Gastroenterology Clinics of North America, 36,* 191–210.

Kuyken, W., & Beck, A. T. (2007). Cognitive therapy. In C. Freeman & M. J. Power (Eds.), *Handbook of evidence-based psychotherapy: A guide for research and practice.* New York: Wiley.

Kuyper, P. (1972). The cocktail party effect. *Audiology, 11,* 277–282.

Kwon, J. S., Jang, J. H., Choi, J. S., & Kang, D. H. (2009). Neuroimaging in obsessive-compulsive disorder. *Expert Review of Neurotherapeutics, 9,* 255–269.

Labouvie-Vief, G. (2006). Emerging structures of adult thought. In J. J. Arnett & J. L. Tanner (Eds.), *Emerging adults in America* (pp. 60–84). Washington, DC: American Psychological Association.

Lac, A., Alvaro, E. M., Crano, W. D., & Siegel, J. T. (2009). Pathways from parental knowledge and warmth to adolescent marijuana use: An extension to the theory of planned behavior. *Prevention Science, 10,* 22–32.

Lachman, M. E. (2004). Development in midlife. *Annual Review of Psychology* (vol. 54). Palo Alto, CA: Annual Reviews.

Lader, M., Tylee, A., & Donoghue, J. (2009). Withdrawing benzodiapines in primary care. *CNS Drugs, 23,* 19–34.

Laible, D. J., & Thompson, R. A. (2000). Mother–child discourse, attachment security, shared positive affect, and early conscience development. *Child Development, 71,* 1424–1440.

Laible, D. J., & Thompson, R. A. (2002). Mother–child conflict in the toddler years: Lessons in emotion, morality, and relationships. *Child Development, 73,* 1187–1203.

Laible, D. J., & Thompson, R. A. (2007). Early socialization: A relationship perspective. In J. E. Grusec & P. D. Hastings (Eds.), *Handbook of socialization.* New York: Guilford.

Laine, M., & others. (2009). Central executive function in mild cognitive impairment: A PET activation study. *Scandinavian Journal of Psychology, 50,* 33–40.

Lambert, M. J. (2001). The effectiveness of psychotherapy: What a century of research tells us about the effects of treatment. *Psychotherapeutically speaking—Updates from the Division of Psychotherapy* (29). Washington, DC: American Psychological Association.

Landau, M. E., & Barner, K. C. (2009). Vestibulocochlear nerve. *Seminars in Neurology, 29,* 66–73.

Landis, C., & Erlick, D. (1950). An analysis of the Porteus Maze Test as affected by psychosurgery. *American Journal of Psychology, 63,* 557–566.

Landrum, T. J., & Kauffman, J. M. (2006). Behavioral approaches to classroom management. In C. M. Evertson & C. S. Weinstein (Eds.), *Handbook of classroom management.* Mahwah, NJ: Erlbaum.

Lane, S. M., & Schooler, J. W. (2004). Skimming the surface: Verbal overshadowing of analogical retrieval. *Psychological Science, 15,* 715–719.

Lange, C. G. (1922). *The emotions.* Baltimore: Williams & Wilkins.

Laney, C., & Loftus, E. F. (2009). Eyewitness memory. In R. N. Kocsis (Ed.), *Applied criminal psychology.* Springfield, IL: Thomas.

Langer, E. (2005). *On becoming an artist.* New York: Ballantine.

Langer, E., Blank, A., & Chanowitz, B. (1978). The mindlessness of ostensibly thoughtful action: The role of "placebic" information in interpersonal interaction. *Journal of Personality and Social Psychology, 36* (6), 635–642.

Langer, E. J. (1997). *The power of mindful learning.* Reading, MA: Addison-Wesley.

Langer, E. J. (2000). Mindful learning. *Current Directions in Psychological Science, 9,* 220–223.

Langer, J. J. (1991). *Holocaust testimonies: The ruins of memory.* New Haven, CT: Yale University Press.

Langlois, J. H., Kalakanis, L., Rubenstein, A. J., Larson, A., Hallam, M., & Smoot, M. (2000). Maxims or myths of beauty? A meta-analytic and theoretical review. *Psychological Bulletin, 126,* 390–423.

Langlois, J. H., Roggman, L. A., & Musselman, L. (1994). What is average and what is not average about attractive faces? *Psychological Science, 5,* 214–220.

Langstrom, N., Rahman, Q., Carlstrom, E., & Lichtenstein, P. (2009). Genetic and environmental effects on same-sex sexual behaviour: A population study of twins in Sweden. *Archives of Sexual Behavior.* (in press)

Lapsley, D. K. (2006). Moral stage theory. In M. Killen & J. G. Smetana (Eds.), *Handbook of moral development* (pp. 37–66). Mahwah, NJ: Erlbaum.

Large, M. E., Cavina-Pratesi, C., Vilis, T., & Culham, J. C. (2008). The neural correlates of change detection in the face perception network. *Neuropsychologia, 46,* 2169–2176.

Larsen, R. J., & Ketelaar, T. (1991). Personality and susceptibility to positive and negative emotional states. *Journal of Personality and Social Psychology, 61,* 132–140.

Larson-Prior, L. J., Zempel, J. M., Nolan, T. S., Prior, F. W., Snyder, A. Z., & Rachlie, M. E. (2009). Cortical network functional connectivity in the descent to sleep. *Proceedings of the National Academy of Sciences USA, 106,* 4489–4494.

Lashley, K. (1950). In search of the engram. In *Symposium of the Society for Experimental Biology* (vol. 4). New York: Cambridge University Press.

Last, C. G. (2009). *When someone you love is bipolar.* New York: Guilford.

Latané, B. (1981). The psychology of social impact. *American Psychologist, 36,* 343–356.

Laurent, G., & others. (2008). Oxidative stress contributes to aging by enhancing angioigenesis and insulin signaling. *Cell Metabolism, 7,* 113–124.

Lawler-Row, K. A., Karremans, J. C., Scott, C., Edlis-Matityahou, M., & Edwards, L. (2008). Forgiveness, physiological reactivity, and health: The role of anger. *International Journal of Psychophysiology, 68,* 51–58.

Lawton, R., Conner, M., & McEachan, R. (2009). Desire or reason: Predicting health behaviors from affective and cognitive attitudes. *Health Psychology, 28,* 56–65.

Lazarus, A. A., Beutler, L. E., & Norcross, J. C. (1992). The future of technical eclecticism. *Psychotherapy, 29,* 11–20.

Lazarus, R. S. (1991). On the primacy of cognition. *American Psychologist, 39,* 124–129.

Lazarus, R. S. (1993). Coping theory and research: Past, present, and future. *Psychosomatic Medicine, 55,* 234–247.

Lazarus, R. S. (2000). Toward better research on stress and coping. *American Psychologist 55,* 665–673.

Lazarus, R. S. (2003). Does the positive psychology movement have legs? *Psychological Inquiry, 14,* 93–109.

Leaper, C., & Friedman, C. K. (2007). The socialization of gender. In J. E. Grusec & P. D. Hastings (Eds.), *Handbook of socialization.* New York: Guilford.

Leary, M. R. (2008). *Introduction to behavioral research methods* (5th ed.). Boston: Allyn & Bacon.

Leary, M. R., & Hoyle, R. H. (Eds.). (2009a). *Handbook of individual differences in social behavior.* New York: Guilford.

Leary, M. R., & Hoyle, R. H. (Eds.). (2009b). Situations, dispositions, and the study of social behavior. In M. R. Leary & R. H. Hoyle (Eds.), *Handbook of individual differences in social behavior.* (pp. 3–11). New York: Guilford.

Leasure, J. L., & Decker, L. (2009). Social isolation prevents exercise-induced proliferation of hippocampal progenitor cells in female rats. *Hippocampus.* (in press)

LeDoux, J. E. (1996). *The emotional brain: The mysterious underpinnings of emotional life.* New York: Simon & Schuster.

LeDoux, J. E. (2000). Emotion circuits in the brain. *Annual Review of Neuroscience, 23,* 155–184.

LeDoux, J. E. (2001). *Emotion, memory, and the brain.* http://www.cns.nyu.edu/home/ledoux.html (accessed October 15, 2001)

LeDoux, J. E. (2002). *The synaptic self.* New York: Viking.

LeDoux, J. E. (2008). Amygdala. *Scholarpedia, 3,* 2698.

Lee, C. D., Blair, S. N. & Jackson, A. S. (1999). Cardiorespiratory fitness, body composition, and all-cause and cardiovascular disease mortality in men. *American Journal of Clinical Nutrition, 69,* 373–380.

Lee, J., & Maunsell, J. H. (2009). A normalization model of attentional modulation of single unit responses. *PLoS One, 4,* e4651.

Lee, M. J., & Fried, S. K. (2009). Integration of hormonal and nutrient signals that regulate leptin synthesis and secretion. *American Journal of Physiology, Endocrinology, and Metabolism.* (in press)

Lee, S. J., Escobedo-Lozoya, Y., Szatmari, E. M., & Yasuda, R. (2009). Activation of CaMKII in single dendritic spines during long-term potentiation. *Nature, 458,* 299–304.

Legaree, T. A., Turner, J., & Lollis, S. (2007). Forgiveness and therapy: A critical review of conceptualizations, practices, and values in the literature. *Journal of Marital and Family Therapy, 33,* 192–213.

Legerstee, M., Barna, J., & DiAdamo, C. (2000). Precursors to the development of intention at 6 months: Understanding people and their actions. *Developmental Psychology, 36,* 627–634.

Leibel, R. L. (2008). Molecular physiology of weight regulation in mice and humans. *International Journal of Obesity, 32, Suppl. 7,* S98–S108.

Leichtman, M. (2004). Projective tests. In M. Hersen (Ed.), *Comprehensive handbook of psychological assessment* (vol. 2). New York: Wiley.

Leichtman, M. (2009). Concepts of development and the Rorschach: The contributions of Paul Lerner and John Exner in historical context. *Journal of Personality Assessment, 91,* 24–29.

Lenneberg, E. H., Rebelsky, F. G., & Nichols, I. A. (1965). The vocalization of infants born to deaf and hearing parents. *Human Development, 8,* 23–37.

Leo, J. L. (2005). Editorial: Methylphenidate-induced neuropathology in the developing rat brain: Implications for humans. *Ethical Human Psychology and Psychiatry, 7,* 107–110.

Leonard, B. E., & Myint, A. (2009). The psychoneuroimmunology of stress. *Human Psychopharmacology, 24,* 165–175.

Lerner, B. H. (2005). Last-ditch medical therapy—revisiting lobotomy. *New England Journal of Medicine, 353,* 119–121.

Lerner, J. V., Phelps, E., Forman, Y. E., & Bowers, E. (2009). Positive youth development. In R. M. Lerner & L. Steinberg (Eds.), *Handbook of adolescent psychology* (3rd ed.). New York: Wiley.

Lerner, R. D., Boyd, M., & Du, D. (2008). Adolescent development. In I. B. Weiner & C. B. Craighead (Eds.), *Encyclopedia of psychology* (4th ed.). New York: Wiley.

Leslie, A. M., German, T. P., & Polizzi, P. (2005). Belief-desire reasoning as a process of selection. *Cognitive Psychology, 50,* 45–85.

Leslie, J. C., Shaw, D., Gregg, G., McCormick, N., Reynolds, D. S., & Dawson, G. R. (2006). Effects of reinforcement schedule on facilitation of operant extinction by chlordiazepoxide. *Journal of the Experimental Analysis of Behavior, 84,* 327–338.

Letvin, N. L. (2007). Progress and obstacles in the development of an AIDS vaccine. *Nature Reviews: Immunology, 6,* 930–939.

Leucht, S., Kissling, W., & Davis, J. M. (2009). Second-generation antipsychotics for schizophrenia: Can we resolve the conflict? *Psychological Medicine.* (in press)

Leung, A. K., Maddux, W. W., Galinsky, A. D., & Chiu, C. (2008). Multicultural experience enhances creativity. *American Psychologist, 63,* 169–181.

Leung, J., Wang, N. Y., Yeagle, J. D., Chinnici, J., Bowditch, S., Francis, H. W., & Niparko, J. K. (2005). Predictive models for cochlear implantation in elderly candidates. *Archives of Otolaryngology Head and Neck Surgery, 131,* 1049–1054.

Levenson, M. R., & Aldwin, C. M. (2006). Change in personality processes and health outcomes. In D. K. Mroczek & T. D. Little (Eds.), *Handbook of personality development* (pp. 423–444). Mahwah, NJ: Erlbaum.

Levenson, M. R., & Crumpler, C. (1996). Three models of adult development. *Human Development, 39,* 135–149.

Leventhal, H., & Tomarken, A. J. (1986). Emotion: Today's problems. *Annual Review of Psychology* (vol. 37). Palo Alto, CA: Annual Reviews.

Levine, B., Svoboda, E., Turner, G. R., Mandic, M., & Mackey, A. (2009). Behavioral and functional neuroanatomical correlates of anterograde autobiographical memory in isolated retrograde amnesic patient M.L. *Neuoropsychologia.* (in press)

Levine, D. S. (2000). *Introduction to neural and cognitive modeling* (2nd ed.). Mahwah, NJ: Erlbaum.

Levine, R. L. (2002). Endocrine aspects of eating disorders in adolescents. *Adolescent Medicine, 13,* 129–144.

Levinson, D. J. (1978). *The seasons of a man's life.* New York: Knopf.

Levitan, E. B., Wolk, A., & Mittleman, M. A. (2009). Consistency with the DASH diet and the incidence of heart failure. *Archives of Internal Medicine, 169,* 851–857.

Levykh, M. G. (2008). The affective establishment and maintenance of Vygotsky's zone of proximal development. *Educational Theory, 58,* 83–111.

Liang, B., Williams, L. M., & Siegel, J. A. (2006). Relational outcomes of childhood sexual trauma in female survivors: A longitudinal study. *Journal of Interpersonal Violence, 21,* 42–57.

Libert, S., Cohen, D., & Guarente, L. (2008). Neurogenesis directed by Sirt1. *Nature: Cell Biology, 10,* 373–374.

Liefbroer, A. C., & Dourleijn, E. (2006). Unmarried cohabitation and union stability: Testing the role of diffusion using data from 16 European countries. *Demography, 43,* 203–221.

Light, S. N., Goldsmith, H. H., Coan, J. A., Frye, C., & Davidson, R. J. (2009). Dynamic variation in pleasure in children predicts non-linear change in lateral frontal activity. *Developmental Psychology, 45,* 525–533.

Lilienfeld, S. O., Wood, J. M., & Garb, H. N. (2000, November). The scientific status of projective techniques. *Psychological Science in the Public Interest, 1* (2).

Lin, C., & others. (2009). Haplotype analysis confirms association of serotonin transporter (5-HTT) gene with schizophrenia in the Han Chinese population. *Neuroscience Letters, 453,* 210–213.

Linde, J. A., Rothman, A. J., Baldwin, A. S., & Jeffery, R. W. (2006). The impact of self-efficacy on behavior change and weight change among overweight participants in a weight loss trial. *Health Psychology, 25,* 282–291.

Linden, W., Lenz, J. W., & Con, A. H. (2001). Individualized stress management for primary hypertension: A randomized trial. *Archives of Internal Medicine, 161,* 1071–1080.

Lindwall, M., Rennemark, M., Halling, A., Berglund, J., & Hassmen, P. (2007). Depression and exercise in elderly men and women: Findings from the Swedish national study on aging and care. *Journal of Aging and Physical Activity, 15,* 41–55.

Ling, G., Bandak, F., Armonda, R., Grant, G., & Ecklund, J. (2009). Explosive blast neurotrauma. *Journal of Neurotrauma.* (in press)

Lingjaerde, O., Foreland, A. R., & Engvik, H. (2001). Personality structure in patients with winter depression, assessed in a depression-free state according to the five-factor model of personality. *Journal of Affective Disorders, 62,* 165–174.

Linke, S. E., & others. (2009). Depressive symptom dimensions and cardiovascular prognosis among women with suspected myocardial ischemia: A report from the National Heart, Lung, and Blood Institute-sponsored women's Ischemia Syndrome Foundation. *Archives of General Psychiatry, 66,* 499–507.

Lippa, R. A. (2005). *Gender: Nature and nurture* (2nd ed.). Mahwah, NJ: Erlbaum.

Lippke, S., & Plotnikoff, R. C. (2006). Stages of change in physical exercise: A test of stage discrimination and nonlinearity. *American Journal of Health Behavior, 30,* 290–301.

Lippke, S., Ziegelmann, J. P., Schwarzer, R., & Velicer, W. F. (2009). Validity of stage assessment in the adoption and maintenance of physical activity and fruit and vegetable consumption. *Health Psychology, 28,* 183–193.

Lipsey, M. W., & Wilson, D. B. (1993). The efficacy of psychological, educational, and behavioral treatment: Confirmation from meta-analysis. *American Psychologist, 48,* 1181–1209.

Lisanby, S. H., Maddox, J. H., Prudic, J., Devanand, D. P., & Sackeim, H. A. (2000). The effects of electroconvulsive therapy on memory of autobiographical and public events. *Archives of General Psychiatry, 57,* 581–590.

Little, K. Y., Zhang, L., & Cook, E. (2006). Fluoxetine-induced alterations in human platelet serotonin transporter expression: Serotonin transporter polymorphism effects. *Psychiatry and Neuroscience, 31,* 333–339.

Little, T. D., Snyder, C. R., & Wehmeyer, M. (2006). The agentic self: On the nature and origins of personal agency across the life span. In D. K. Mroczek & T. D. Little (Eds.), *Handbook of personality development.* Mahwah, NJ: Erlbaum.

Littrell, J. H., & Girvin, H. (2002). Stages of change: A critique. *Behavior Modification, 26,* 223–273.

Liu, C. C., Doong, J. L., Hsu, W. S., Huang, W. S., & Jeng, M. C. (2009). Evidence from the selective attention mechanism and dual-task interference. *Applied Ergonomics, 40,* 341–347.

Livesley, J. (2008). Toward a genetically-informed model of borderline personality disorder. *Journal of Personality Disorders, 22,* 42–71.

Lo, S. (2008). The nonverbal communication functions of emotions in computer-mediated communication. *CyberPsychology & Behavior, 11,* 595–597.

Loftus, E. F. (1975). Spreading activation within semantic categories. *Journal of Experimental Psychology, 104,* 234–240.

Loftus, E. F. (1993). Psychologists in the eyewitness world. *American Psychologist, 48,* 550–552.

Loftus, E. F. (2006). Memory distortions: Problems solved and unsolved. In M. Garry & H. Hayne (Eds.), *Do justice and let the skies fall.* Mahwah, NJ: Erlbaum.

Loftus, E. F. (2009). Crimes of memory: False memories and social justice. In M. A. Gernsbacher, L. Hough, R. Pew, & J. Pomerantz (Eds.), *Psychology in the real world.* New York: Worth. (in press)

Loftus, E. F., & Ketcham, K. (1991). *Witness for the defense: The accused, the eyewitness, and the expert who puts memory on trial.* New York: St. Martin's Press.

Loftus, E. F., & Pickrell, J. E. (2001, June). *Creating false memories.* Paper presented at the meeting of the American Psychological Society, Toronto.

Logue, A. W. (1995). *Self control: Waiting until tomorrow for what you want today.* Upper Saddle River, NJ: Pearson Education.

Longo, D. A., Lent, R. W., & Brown, S. D. (1992). Social cognitive variables in the prediction of client motivation and attribution. *Journal of Counseling Psychology, 39,* 447–452.

Lopes, M., & Santos-Victor, J. (2007). A developmental roadmap for learning by imitation in robots. *IEEE Transactions on Systems, Man, and Cybernetics B, 37,* 308–321.

Lopez-Munoz, F., & Alamo, C. (2009). Monoaminergic neurotransmission: The history of the discovery of antidepressants from 1950s until today. *Current Pharmaceutical Design, 15,* 1563–1586.

Lorant, V., Croux, C., Weich, S., Deliege, D., Mackenbach, J., & Ansseau, M. (2007). Depression and socioeconomic risk factors: 7-year longitudinal population study. *British Journal of Psychiatry, 190,* 293–298.

Lorenz, K. Z. (1965). *Evolution and the modification of behavior.* Chicago: University of Chicago Press.

Lo Sauro, C., Ravaldi, C., Cabras, P. L., Faravelli, C., & Ricca, V. (2008). Stress, hypothalamic-pituitary-adrenal axis, and eating disorders. *Neuropsychobiology, 57,* 95–115.

Lu, J., Sherman, D., Devor, M., & Saper, C. B. (2006). A putative flip-flop switch for control of REM sleep. *Nature, 441,* 589–594.

Lubinski, D., Benbow, Camilla P., Webb, R. M., & Bleske-Rechek, A. (2006). Tracking exceptional human capital over two decades. *Psychological Science, 17,* 194–199.

Lubinski, D., Webb, R. M., Morelock, M. J., & Benbow, C. P. (2001). Top 1 in 10,000: A 10-year follow-up of the profoundly gifted. *Journal of Applied Psychology, 86,* 718–729.

Luborsky, L., Rosenthal, R., Diguer, L., Andrusyna, T. P., Berman, J. S., Levitt, J. T., Seligman, D. A., & Krause, E. D. (2002). The dodo bird verdict is alive and well—mostly. *Clinical Psychology: Science and Practice, 9,* 2–12.

Lucas, R. E. (2007). Extraversion. In R. Baumeister & K. Vohs (Eds.), *The encyclopedia of social psychology*. Thousand Oaks, CA: Sage.

Lucas, R. E. (2008). Personality and subjective well-being. In M. Eid & R. J. Larsen (Eds.), *The science of subjective well-being* (pp. 171–194). New York: Psychology Press.

Lucas, R. E. (2009). Personality and subjective well-being. In M. Eid & R. J. Larsen (Eds.), *The science of subjective well-being*. New York: Psychology Press.

Lucas, R. E., & Baird, B. (2004). Extraversion and emotional reactivity. *Journal of Personality and Social Psychology, 86,* 473–485.

Luo, Y., & Baillargeon, R. (2005). Can a self-propelled box have a goal? Psychological reasoning in 5-month-old infants. *Psychological Science, 16,* 601–608.

Luria, A. R. (1968/1987). *The mind of a mnemonist*. L. Solotaroff (Trans.). Cambridge, MA: Harvard University Press.

Luria, A. R. (1973). *The working brain*. New York: Penguin.

Lutz, A., Brefczynski-Lewis, J. A., Johnstone, T., & Davidson, R. J. (2008). Regulation of emotion by compassion meditation: Effects of expertise. *PLoS One, 3,* e1897.

Lykken, D. (1999). *Happiness: What studies on twins show us about nature, nurture, and the happiness setpoint*. New York: Golden Books.

Lykken, D. T. (1987). The probity of the polygraph. In S. M. Kassin & L. S. Wrightsman (Eds.), *The psychology of evidence and trial procedures*. Newbury Park, CA: Sage.

Lykken, D. T. (1998). A tremor in the blood: Uses and abuses of the lie detector (2nd ed.). New York: Plenum Press.

Lykken, D. T. (2001). Lie detection. In W. E. Craighead & C. B. Nemeroff (Eds.), *The Corsini encyclopedia of psychology and behavioral science* (3rd ed.). New York: Wiley.

Lynn, S. J. (2007). Hypnosis reconsidered. *American Journal of Clinical Hypnosis, 49,* 195–197.

Lynn, S. J., Boycheva, E., & Barnes, S. (2008). To assess or not assess hypnotic susceptibility? That is the question. *American Journal of Clinical Hypnosis, 51,* 161–165.

Lynn, S. J., & Cardena, E. (2007). Hypnosis and the treatment of posttraumatic conditions: An evidence-based approach. *International Journal of Clinical Hypnosis, 55,* 167–188.

Lynn, S. J., Das, L. S., Hallquist, M. N., & Williams, J. C. (2006). Mindfulness, acceptance, and hypnosis: Cognitive and clinical perspectives. *International Journal of Clinical and Experimental Hypnosis, 54,* 143–166.

Lythgoe, M. F., Pollak, T. A., Kalmas, M., de Haan, M., & Chong, W. (2005). Obsessive, prolific artistic output following subarachnoid hemorrhage. *Neurology, 64,* 397–398.

Lyubomirsky, S. (2008). *The how of happiness: A scientific approach to getting the life you want*. New York: Penguin.

Lyubomirsky, S., King, L. A., & Diener, E. (2005). The benefits of frequent positive affect: Does happiness lead to success? *Psychological Bulletin, 131,* 803–855.

M

Maccoby, E. E. (2002). Gender and group processes. *Current Directions in Psychological Science, 11,* 54–58.

MacDonald, D. A. (2000). Spirituality: description, measurement, and relation to the Five Factor model of personality. *Journal of Personality, 68,* 153–197.

Macdonald, J. S. P., & Lavie, N. (2008). Load induced blindness. *Journal of Experimental Psychology: Human Perception and Performance, 34,* 1078–1091.

Mack, A., & Rock, I. (1998). *Inattentional blindness*. Cambridge, MA: MIT Press.

Mackinlay, R. J., Kliegel, M., & Mäntylä, T. (2009). Predictors of time-based prospective memory in children. *Journal of Experimental Child Psychology, 102,* 251–264.

MacLeod, M. (2006, April 1). Mindless imitation teaches us how to be human. *New Scientist, 2545,* 42.

MacQueen, C. E., Brynes, A. E., & Frost, G. S. (2002). Treating obesity: A follow-up study. Can the stages of change model be used as a postal screening tool? *Journal of Human Nutrition and Dietetics, 15* (1), 3–7.

Madan, A., Palaniappan, L., Urizar, G., Wang, Y., Formann, S. P., & Gould, J. B. (2006). Sociocultural factors that affect pregnancy outcomes in two dissimilar immigrant groups in the United States. *Journal of Pediatrics, 148,* 341–346.

Madden, D. J., Gottlob, L. R., Denny, L. L., Turkington, T. G., Provenzale, J. M., Hawk, T. C., & others. (1999). Aging and recognition memory: Changes in regional cerebral blood flow associated with components of reaction time distributions. *Journal of Cognitive Neuroscience, 11,* 511–520.

Maddi, S. (1998). Hardiness. In H. S. Friedman (Ed.), *Encyclopedia of mental health* (vol. 3). San Diego: Academic.

Maddi, S. R. (2008). The courage and strategies of hardiness as helpful in growing despite major, disruptive stresses. *American Psychologist, 63,* 563–564.

Maddi, S. R., Harvey, R. H., Khoshaba, D. M., Lu, J. L., Persico, M., & Brow, M. (2006). The personality construct of hardiness, III: Relationships with repression, innovativeness, authoritarianism, and performance. *Journal of Personality, 74,* 575–597.

Mader, S. S. (2008). *Inquiry into life* (12th ed.). New York: McGraw-Hill.

Mader, S. S. (2009). *Concepts of biology*. New York: McGraw-Hill.

Mader, S. S. (2010). *Biology* (10th ed.). New York: McGraw-Hill.

Maddux, W. W., & Galinsky, A. D. (2007, September). *Cultural borders and mental barriers: Living in and adapting to foreign countries facilitates creativity*. Working Paper No. 2007/51/B. Fountainbleau, France: INSEAD.

Maes, H. H. M., Neal, M. C., & Eaves, L. J. (1997). Genetic and environmental factors in relative body weight and human adiposity. *Behavior Genetics, 27,* 325–351.

Mager, R. F. (1972). *Goals analysis*. Belmont, CA: Fearon.

Maggio, N., & Segal, M. (2009). Differential corticosteroid modulation of inhibitory synaptic currents in the dorsal and ventral hippocampus. *Journal of Neuroscience, 29,* 2857–2866.

Magnus, K., Diener, E., Fujita, F., & Payot, W. (1993). Extraversion and neuroticism as predictors of objective life events: A longitudinal analysis. *Journal of Personality and Social Psychology, 65,* 1046–1053.

Maguire, E. A., Gadian, G. D., Johnsrude, I. S., Good, C. D., Ashburner, J., Frackowiak, R. S. J., & Frith, C. D. (2000). Navigation-related structural change in the hippocampi of taxi drivers. *Proceedings of the National Academy of Sciences USA, 97,* 4398–4403.

Mahler, D. A., Murray, J. A., Waterman, L. A., Ward, J., Kraemer, W. J., Zhang, X., & Baird, J. C. (2009). Endogenous opioids modify dyspnosa during treadmill exercise in patients with COPD. *European Respiratory Journal, 33,* 771–777.

Maier, N. R. F. (1931). Reasoning in humans. *Journal of Comparative Psychology, 12,* 181–194.

Maier, S. F., & Seligman, M. E. P. (2009). Fears, phobias, and preparedness: Toward an evolved module of fear and fear learning. In D. Shanks (Ed.), *Psychology of learning*. Thousand Oaks, CA: Sage.

Major, B., & Sawyer, P. J. (2009). Attributions to discrimination: Antecedents and consequences. In T. D. Nelson (Ed.), *Handbook of prejudice, stereotyping, and discrimination*. New York: Psychology Press.

Malamuth, N. M., Addison, T., & Koss, M. (2000). Pornography and sexual aggression: Are there reliable effects and can we understand them? *Annual Review of Sex Research, 11,* 26–91.

Malcolm-Smith, S., Solms, M., Turnbull, O., & Tredoux, C. (2008). Threat in dreams: An adaptation? *Consciousness and cognition, 17,* 1281–1291.

Mandara, J. (2006). The impact of family functioning on African American males' academic achievement: A review and clarification of the empirical literature. *Teachers College Record, 108,* 206–233.

Mander, B. A., & others. (2008). Sleep deprivation alters functioning within the neural network underlying the covert orienting of attention. *Brain Research, 1217,* 148–156.

Mandler, G. (1980). Recognizing: The judgment of previous occurrence. *Psychological Review, 87,* 252–271.

Maner, J. K., Luce, C. L., Neuberg, S. L., Cialdini, R. B., Brown, S., & Sagarin, B. J. (2002). The effects of perspective taking on motivations for helping: Still no evidence for altruism. *Personality and Social Psychology Bulletin, 28,* 1601–1610.

Manini, T. M., & others. (2006). Daily activity energy expenditure and mortality among older adults. *Journal of the American Medical Association, 296,* 216–218.

Mann, D. M., Ponieman, D., Leventahl, H., & Halm, E. A. (2009). Predictors of adherence to diabetes medications: The role of disease and medication beliefs. *Journal of Behavioral Medicine, 32,* 278–284.

Mantere, T., Tupala, E., Hall, H., Sarkoja, T., Rasanen, P., Bergstrom, K., Callaway, J., & Tihonen, J. (2002). Serotinin transporter distribution and density in the cerebral cortex of alcoholic and nonalcoholic comparison subjects: A whole-hemisphere autoradiograph study. *American Journal of Psychiatry, 159,* 599–606.

March, J., Silva, S., Petrycki, S., Curry, J., Wells, K., Fairbank, J., Burns, B., Domino, M., McNulty, S., Vitiello, B., & Severe, J. (2004). Fluoxetine, cognitive-behavioral therapy, and their combination for adolescents with depression: Treatment for Adolescents with Depression Study (TADS) randomized controlled trial. *Journal of the American Medical Association, 292,* 807–820.

Marcia, J. E. (1980). Ego identity development. In J. Adelson (Ed.), *Handbook of adolescent psychology*. New York: Wiley.

Marcia, J. E. (2002). Identity and psychosocial development in adulthood. *Identity, 2,* 7–28.

Marcus, G. F. (2001). *The algebraic mind*. Cambridge, MA: MIT Books.

Maril, A., Wagner, A. D., & Schacter, D. L. (2001). On the tip of the tongue: An event-related fMRI study of semantic retrieval failure and cognitive conflict. *Neuron, 31,* 653–660.

Marine, A., Rutosalainen, J., Serra, C., & Verbeek, J. (2006). Preventing occupational stress in healthcare workers. *Cochrane Database System Review, 18* (4), CD002892.

Maris, R. W. (1998). Suicide. In H. S. Friedman (Ed.), *Encyclopedia of mental health* (vol. 3). San Diego: Academic.

Markessis, E., & others. (2009). Effect of presentation level on diagnosis of dead regions using the threshold equalizing noise test. *International Journal of Audiology, 48,* 55–62.

Markides, K. S. (Ed.). (2007). *Encyclopedia of health and aging*. Thousand Oaks, CA: Sage.

Marklund, P., Fransson, P., Cabeza, R., Petersson, K. M., Ingvar, M., & Nyberg, L. (2007). Sustained and transient neural modulations in prefrontal cortex related to declarative long-term memory, working memory, and attention. *Cortex, 43* (1), 22–37.

Markowitsch, H. J. (2008). Autobiographical memory: A biocultural relais between subject and environment. *European Archives of Psychiatry and Clinical Neuroscience, 258,* Suppl. 5, S98–S103.

Markowitz, J. C., Milrod, B., Bleiberg, K., & Marshall, R. D. (2009). Interpersonal factors in understanding and treating posttraumatic stress disorder. *Journal of Psychiatric Practice, 15,* 133–140.

Markowitz, S., & Cuellar, A. (2007). Antidepressants and youth: Healing or harmful? *Social Science Medicine, 64,* 2138–2151.

Marks, I., & Cavanaugh, K. (2009). Computer-aided psychological treatments. *Annual Review of Clinical Psychology, 5,* 121–141.

Marlow, A. (1999). *How to stop time: Heroin from A to Z*. New York: Basic Books.

Marsh, H. W. (1995). A Jamesian model of self-investment and self-esteem: Comment on Pelham

(1995). *Journal of Personality and Social Psychology, 69,* 1151–1160.

Marshall, D. A., Walizer, E. M., & Vernalis, M. N. (2009). Achievement of heart health characteristics through participation in an intensive lifestyle change program (Coronary Artery Disease Reversal Study). *Journal of Cardiopulmonary Rehabilitation and Prevention, 29,* 84–94.

Marshall, D. S. (1971). Sexual behavior in Mangaia. In D. S. Marshall & R. C. Suggs (Eds.), *Human sexual behavior: Variations in the ethnographic spectrum* (pp. 103–162). New York: Basic Books.

Marshall, M., & Rathbone, J. (2006). Early intervention for psychosis. *Cochrane Database of Systematic Reviews, 4,* CD004718.

Martin, D. W. (2008). *Doing psychology experiments* (7th ed.). Belmont, CA: Wadsworth.

Martin, G. L., & Pear, J. (2007). *Behavior modification* (8th ed.). Upper Saddle River, NJ: Prentice-Hall.

Martin, L. R., Friedman, H. S., & Schwartz, J. E. (2007). Personality and mortality risk across the lifespan: The importance of conscientiousness as biopsychosocial attribute. *Health Psychology, 26,* 428–436.

Martin, S. J., & Clark, R. E. (2007). The rodent hippocampus and spatial memory: From synapses to systems. *Cellular and Molecular Life Sciences, 64,* 401–431.

Martin-Soelch, C. (2009). Is depression associated with dysfunction of the central reward system? *Biochemical Society Transactions, 37,* 313–317.

Maruyama, Y., Pereira, M., Margolskee, R. F., Chaudhari, N., & Roper, S. D. (2006). Umami responses in mouse taste cells indicate more than one receptor. *Journal of Neuroscience, 26,* 2227–2234.

Marx, R. F., & Didziulis, V. (2009, March 1). A life, interrupted. *New York Times.*

Masaki, T., & Nakajima, S. (2006). Taste aversion in rats induced by forced swimming, voluntary running, forced running, and lithium chloride injection treatments. *Physiology and Behavior, 88,* 411–416.

Mascaro, N., & Rosen, D. H. (2006). The role of existential meaning as a buffer against stress. *Journal of Humanistic Psychology, 46,* 168–190.

Maslow, A. H. (1954). *Motivation and personality.* New York: Harper & Row.

Maslow, A. H. (1971). *The farther reaches of human nature.* New York: Viking.

Mason, T. B., & Pack, A. I. (2005). Sleep terrors in childhood. *Journal of Pediatrics, 147,* 388–392.

Massimini, F., & Delle Fave, A. (2000). Individual development in bio-cultural perspective. *American Psychologist, 55,* 24–33.

Masten, A. S. (2006). Developmental psychopathology: Pathways to the future. *International Journal of Behavioral Development, 31,* 46–53.

Masten, A. S. (2007). Resilience in developing systems: Progress and promise as the fourth wave rises. *Development and Psychopathology, 19,* 921–930.

Masten, A. S., Obradovic, J., & Burt, K. B. (2006). Resilience in emerging adulthood. In J. J. Arnett & J. L. Tanner (Eds.), *Emerging adults in America.* Washington, DC: American Psychological Association.

Masters, C. (2008, January 17). We just clicked. *Time,* 84–89.

Masters, W. H., & Johnson, V. E. (1966). *Human sexual response.* Boston: Little, Brown.

Mate, J., & Baques, J. (2009). Visual similarity at encoding and retrieval in an item recognition task. *Quarterly Journal of Experimental Psychology, 18,* 1–8.

Matis, G., & Birbilis, T. (2009). The Glasgow Coma Scale—A brief review. Past, present, future. *Acta Neurologica Belgica, 108,* 75–89.

Matlin, M. W. (2001). *Cognition* (5th ed.). Fort Worth, TX: Harcourt Brace.

Matlin, M. W. (2008). *Psychology of women* (6th ed.). Belmont, CA: Wadsworth.

Matsumoto, D., & Juang, L. (2008). *Culture and psychology* (4th ed.). Belmont, CA: Wadsworth.

Matsumoto, D., & others. (2008) Mapping expressive differences around the world: The relationship between emotional display rules and individualism versus collectivism. *Journal of Cross-Cultural Psychology, 39,* 55–74.

Matthews, K. A., Gump, B. B., Harris, K. F., Haney, T. L., & Barefoot, J. C. (2004). Hostile behaviors predict cardiovascular motality among men enrolled in the multiple risk factor intervention trial. *Circulation, 109,* 66–70.

Matthews, K. A., Schott, L. L., Bromberger, J., Cyranowski, J. Everson-Rose, S. A., & Sowers, M. F. (2007). Associations between depressive symptoms and inflammatory/hemostatic markers in women during the menopausal transition. *Psychosomatic Medicine, 69,* 124–130.

May, F. B. (2006). *Teaching reading creatively* (7th ed.). Upper Saddle River, NJ: Prentice-Hall.

May, M. (2003). *Vision diary.* http://www.guardian.co.uk/g2/story/0,3604,1029268,00.html (accessed October 11, 2006)

Mayer, J. D., Salovey, P., & Caruso, D. R. (2008). Emotional intelligence: New ability or eclectic traits? *American Psychologist, 63,* 503–517.

Mayer, R. (2000). Problem solving. In M. A. Runco & S. Pritzker (Eds.), *Encyclopedia of psychology.* San Diego: Academic.

Mayo Clinic. (2009). *Deep brain stimulation.* www.mayoclinic.com/health/deep-brain-stimulation/my00184 (accessed May 19, 2009)

Mayo Foundation. (2006). *Electroconvulsive therapy (ECT): Treating severe depression and mental illness.* Rochester, MN: Author. http://www.mayoclinic.com/health/electroconvulsive-therapy/MH00022

McAdams, D. P. (1989). *Intimacy: The need to be close.* New York: Doubleday.

McAdams, D. P. (2001). The psychology of life stories. *Review of General Psychology, 5,* 100–122.

McAdams, D. P. (2006). *The redemptive self: Stories Americans live by.* New York: Oxford University Press.

McAdams, D. P. (2009). *The person* (5th ed.). New York: Wiley.

McAdams, D. P., Bauer, J. J., Sakaeda, A. R., Anyidoho, N. A., Machado, M. A., Magrino-Failla, K., White, K. W., & Pals, J. L. (2006). Continuity and change in life story: A longitudinal study of autobiographical memories in emerging adulthood. *Journal of Personality, 74,* 1371–1400.

McAdams, D. P., & Bryant, F. B. (1987). Intimacy motivation and subjective mental health in a nation-wide sample. *Journal of Personality, 55,* 395–413.

McAdams, D. P., & Olson, B. D. (2010). Personality development: Continuity and change. *Annual Review of Psychology* (vol. 61). Palo Alto, CA: Annual Reviews. (in press)

McAllister, A. K. (2007). Dynamic aspects of synaptic maturation. *Annual Review of Neuroscience* (vol. 30). Palo Alto, CA: Annual Reviews.

McBurney, D. H., & White, T. L. (2007). *Research methods* (7th ed.). Belmont, CA: Wadsworth.

McCarthy, D. E., Piasecki, T. M., Fiore, M. C., & Baker, T. B. (2006). Life before and after quitting smoking: An electronic diary study. *Journal of Abnormal Psychology, 115,* 454–466.

McCauley, C., & Segal, M. E. (2009). Social psychology of terrorist groups. In J. Victoroff & A. W. Kruglanski (Eds), *Psychology of terrorism: Classic and contemporary insights* (pp. 331–346). New York: Psychology Press.

McCaulley, M. H. (2000). Myers Briggs Type Indicator: A bridge between counseling and consulting. *Consulting Psychology Journal: Practice and Research, 52,* 117–132.

McClelland, J. L., & Rumelhart, D. E. (2009). Why there are complementary learning systems in the hippocampus and neocortex: Insights from the successes and failures of connectionist models of learning and memory. In D. Shanks (Ed.), *Psychology of learning.* Thousand Oaks, CA: Sage.

McCloskey, M. S., Berman, M. E., Echevarria, D. J., & Coccaro, E. F. (2009). Effects of acute alcohol intoxication and paroxetine on aggression in men. *Alcoholism: Clinical and Experimental Research.* (in press)

McCorkle, B. H., Rogers, E. S., Dunn, E. C., Lyass, A., & Wan, Y. M. (2008). Increasing social support for individuals with serious mental illness: Evaluating the compeer model of intentional friendship. *Community Mental Health Journal, 44,* 359–366.

McCrae, R. R., & Costa, P. T. (1989). Reinterpreting the Myers-Briggs Type Indicator from the perspective of the five-factor model of personality. *Journal of Personality 57,* 17–40.

McCrae, R. R., & Costa, P. T. (2006). Cross-cultural perspectives on adult personality trait development. In D. K. Mroczek & T. D. Little (Eds.), *Handbook of personality development.* Mahwah, NJ: Erlbaum.

McCrae, R. R., & Sutin, A. R. (2007). New frontiers for the five factor model: A preview of the literature. *Social and Personality Psychology Compass, 1,* 423–440.

McCrae, R. R., & Sutin, A. R. (2009). Openness to experience. In M. R. Leary & R. H. Hoyle (Eds.), *Handbook of individual differences in social behavior* (pp. 257–273). New York: Guilford.

McCulloch, K. C., Ferguson, M. J., Kawada, C. C. K., & Bargh, J. A. (2008). Taking a closer look: On the operation of nonconscious impression formation. *Journal of Experimental Social Psychology, 44,* 614–623.

McCullough, J. L., & Kelly, K. M. (2006). Prevention and treatment of skin aging. *Annals of the New York Academy of Science, 1067,* 323–331.

McCullough, M. E., Bono, G., & Root, L. M. (2007). Rumination, emotion, and forgiveness: Three longitudinal studies. *Journal of Personality and Social Psychology, 92,* 490–505.

McCullough, M. E., Emmons, R. A., & Tsang, J. (2002). The grateful disposition: A conceptual and empirical topography. *Journal of Personality and Social Psychology, 82,* 112–127.

McCullough, M. E., Hoyt, W. T., Larson, D. B., Koenig, H. G., & Thoresen, C. (2000). Religious involvement and mortality: A meta-analytic review. *Health Psychology, 19,* 211–222.

McCullough, M. E., & Willoughby, B. L. (2009). Religion, self-regulation, and self-control: Associations, explanations, and implications. *Psychological Bulletin, 135,* 69–93.

McDaniel, M. A., & Einstein, G. O. (2007). *Prospective memory: An overview and synthesis of an emerging field.* Thousand Oaks, CA: Sage.

McDermott, R. (2009). Medical decision making: Lessons from psychology. *Urologic Oncology, 26,* 665–668.

McDonald, M. A., Hildebrand, J. A., Wiggins, S. M., Johnston, D. W., & Polovina, J. J. (2009). An acoustic survey of beaked whales at Cross Seamount near Hawaii. *Journal of the Acoustical Society of America, 125,* 624–627.

McElhaney, K. B., Allen, J. P., Stephenson, J. C., & Haer, A. L. (2009). Attachment and autonomy in adolescence. In R. M. Lerner & L. Steinberg (Eds.), *Handbook of adolescent psychology* (3rd ed.). New York: Wiley.

McElwain, N. L. (2009). Attachment theory. In D. Carr (Ed.), *Encyclopedia of the life course and human development.* Thousand Oaks, CA: Sage.

McEwen, B. S. (2006). Sleep deprivation as a neurobiologic and physiologic stressor: Allostasis and allostatic load. *Metabolism, 55,* Suppl. 2, S20–S23.

McGue, M., Bouchard, T. J., Iacono, W. G., & Lykken, D. T. (1993). Behavioral genetics of cognitive ability: A life-span perspective. In R. Plomin & G. E. McClearn (Eds.), *Nature, nurture, and psychology.* Washington, DC: American Psychological Association.

McGuire, M. T., Wing, R. R., Klem, M. L. Lang, W., & Hill, J. O. (1999). What predicts weight regain in a group of successful weight losers? *Journal of Consulting and Clinical Psychology, 67,* 177–185.

McGuire, W. J. (2003). Doing psychology my way. In R. J. Sternberg (Ed.), *Psychologists defying the crowd: Stories of those who battled the establishment and won.* (pp. 119–137). Washington, DC: American Psychological Association.

McGuire, W. J. (2004). The morphing of attitude-change into social-cognition. In G. V. Bodenhausen & A. J. Lambert (Eds.), *Foundations of social cognition.* Mahwah, NJ: Erlbaum.

McGuire, W. J., & Papageorgis, D. (1961). The relative efficacy of various types of prior belief-defense in producing immunity against persuasion. *Public Opinion Quarterly, 26,* 24–34.

McIntosh, W. D., Harlow, T. F., & Martin, L. L. (1995). Linkers and non-linkers: Goal beliefs as a moderator of the effects of everyday hassles on rumination, depression, and physical complaints. *Journal of Applied Social Psychology, 25,* 1231–1244.

McKay, K. M., Imel, Z. E., & Wampold, B. E. (2006). Psychiatrist effects in the psychopharmacological treatment of depression. *Journal of Affective Disorders, 92,* 287–290.

McKenny-Fick, N. M., Ferrie, C. D., Livingston, J. H., Taylor, J. C., & Allen, J. E. (2009). Prolonged recovery of consciousness in children following symptomatic epileptic seizures. *Seizure, 18,* 180–183.

McKim, W. (2007). *Drugs and behavior* (6th ed.). Upper Saddle River, NJ: Prentice-Hall.

McKone, E., Kanwisher, N., & Duchaine, B. C. (2007). Can generic expertise explain special processing for faces? *Trends in Cognitive Sciences, 11,* 8–15.

McLeod, J. (2007). *Counseling skill.* New York: McGraw-Hill.

McMahon, D. B., & Olson, C. R. (2009). Linearly additive shape and color signals in monkey inferotemporal cortex. *Journal of Neurophysiology, 101,* 1867–1875.

McMain, S., & Pos, A. E. (2007). Advances in psychotherapy of personality disorders: A research update. *Current Psychiatry Reports, 9,* 46–52.

McMillan, J. H. (2008). *Educational research* (5th ed.). Boston: Allyn & Bacon.

McNamara, P., McLaren, D., & Durso, K. (2007). Representation of the self in REM and NREM dreams. *Dreaming, 17,* 113–126.

McNaughton, N., & Corr, P. J. (2008). The neuropsychology of fear and anxiety: A foundation for reinforcement sensitivity theory. In P. J. Corr (Ed.), *The reinforcement sensitivity theory of personality* (pp. 44–94). New York: Cambridge University Press.

McPherson, T. L., Cook, R. F., Back, A. S., Hersch, R. K., & Hendrickson, A. (2006). A field test of a web-based substance abuse prevention training program for health promotion professionals. *American Journal of Health Promotion, 20,* 396–400.

Meade, C. S., Wang, J., Lin, X., Wu, H., & Poppen, P. J. (2009). Stress and coping in HIV-positive former plasma/blood donors in China: A test of cognitive appraisal theory. *AIDS Behavior.* (in press)

Meehl, P. (1962). Schizotonia, schizotypy, schizophrenia. *American Psychologist, 17,* 827–838.

Meeks, J. T., & Marsh, R. L. (2009). Implementation intentions about nonfocal event-based prospective memory tasks. *Psychological Research.* (in press)

Mehl, M. R., Vazire, S., Ramirez-Esparza, N., Slatcher, R. B., & Pennebaker, J. W. (2007). Are women really more talkative than men? *Science. 317,* 82.

Meissner, W. W. (2009). Religion in the psychoanalytic relationship—some aspects of transference and countertransference. *Journal of the American Academy of Psychoanalysis and Dynamic Psychiatry, 37,* 123–136.

Mejia-Arauz, R., Rogoff, B., & Paradise, R. (2005). Cultural variation in children's observation during a demonstration. *International Journal of Behavioral Development, 29,* 282–291.

Mellon, S., & others. (2009). Predictors of decision making in families at risk for inherited breast/ovarian cancer. *Health Psychology, 28,* 38–47.

Melton, L. (2005, December 17). How brain power can help you cheat old age. *New Scientist, 2530,* 32.

Melzack, R. (1973). *The puzzle of pain.* New York: Basic Books.

Mendes, W. B. (2007). Social facilitation. In R. Baumeister & K. Vohs (Eds.), *Encyclopedia of social psychology.* Thousand Oaks, CA: Sage.

Mendez, M. F., Chow, T., Ringman, J., Twitchell, G., & Hinkin, C. H. (2000). Pedophilia and temporal lobe disturbances. *Journal of Neuropsychiatry and Clinical Neurosciences, 12,* 71–76.

Menn, L., & Stoel-Gammon, C. (2009). Phonological development: Learning sounds and sound patterns. In J. Berko Gleason & N. Ratner (Eds.), *The development of language* (7th ed.). Boston: Allyn & Bacon.

Merchant, J. (2006). The developmental/emergent model of archetype, its implications and its applications to shamanism. *Journal of Analytical Psychology, 51,* 125–144.

Merkl, A., Heuser, I., & Bajbouj, M. (2009). Andipressant electroconvulsive therapy: Mechanism of action, recent advances, and limitations. *Experimental Neurology.* (in press)

Mesquita, B. (2002). Emotions as dynamic cultural phenomena. In R. J. Davidson, K. R. Scherer, & H. H. Goldsmith (Eds.), *Handbook of affective sciences.* New York: Oxford University Press.

Messenger, J. C. (1971). Sex and repression in an Irish folk community. In D. S. Marshall & R. C. Suggs (Eds.), *Human sexual behavior.* New York: Basic Books.

Messner, S. F., Raffalovich, L. E., & Shrock, P. (2002). Reassessing the cross-national relationship between income inequality and homicide rates: Implications of data quality control in the measurement of income distribution. *Journal of Quantitative Criminology, 18,* 377–395.

Metcalfe, J., & Mischel, W. (1999). A hot/cool system analysis of delay of gratification: Dynamics of will power. *Psychological Review, 106,* 3–19.

Mettler, F. A. (Ed.). (1952). *Psychosurgical problems.* Oxford: Blakiston.

Meyer, P. J., Meshul, C. K., & Phillips, T. J. (2009). Ethanol- and cocaine-induced locomotion are genetically related to increases in accumbal dopamine. *Genes, Brain, and Behavior, 8,* 346–355.

Miacic, B., & Goldberg, L. R. (2007). An analysis of a cross-cultural personality inventory: The IPIP big five factors markers in Croatia. *Journal of Personality Assessment, 88,* 168–177.

Michael, R. T., Gagnon, J. H., Laumann, E. O., & Kolata, G. (1994). *Sex in America.* Boston: Little, Brown.

Middeldorp, C. M., de Geus, E. J. C., Beem, A. L., Lakenberg, N., Hottenga, J., Slagboom, P. E., & Boomsma, D. I. (2007). Family based association analyses between the serotonin transporter gene polymorphism (5-HTTLPR) and neuroticism, anxiety and depression. *Behavior Genetics, 37,* 294–301.

Migneault, J. P., Adams, T. B., & Read, J. P. (2005). Application of the transtheoretical model to substance abuse: Historical development and future directions. *Drug and Alcohol Review, 24,* 437–448.

Mihashi, M., & others. (2009). Predictive factors of psychological disorder development during recovery following SARS outbreak. *Health Psychology, 28,* 91–100.

Miksis, S. (2008). A review of the evidence comparing the human papillomavirus versus condoms in the prevention of human papillomavirus infections. *Journal of Obstetric, Gynecologic, and Neonatal Nursing, 37,* 329–337.

Milgram, S. (1965). Some conditions of obedience and disobedience to authority. *Human Relations, 18,* 56–76.

Milgram, S. (1974). *Obedience to authority.* New York: Harper & Row.

Miller, A. G. (2004). What can the Milgram obedience experiments tell us about the Holocaust? Generalizing from the social psychology laboratory. In A. G. Miller (Ed.), *The social psychology of good and evil* (pp. 193–239). New York: Guilford.

Miller, D. B., & O'Callaghan, J. P. (2006). The pharmacology of wakefulness. *Metabolism, 55, Suppl. 2,* S13–S19.

Miller, D. T. (1999). The norm of self-interest. *American Psychologist, 54* (12), 1053–1060.

Miller, D. T. (2001).The norm of self-interest. In J. Dienhart, D. Moberg, & R. Duska (Eds.), *The next phase of business ethics: Integrating psychology and ethics* (pp. 193–210). New York: Elsevier Science/JAI Press.

Miller, G., Chen, E., & Cole, S. W. (2009). Health psychology: Developing biologically plausible models linking the social world and physical health. *Annual Review of Psychology* (vol. 60). Palo Alto, CA: Annual Reviews.

Miller, G. A. (1956). The magical number seven, plus or minus two: Some limits on our capacity for information processing. *Psychological Review, 48,* 337–442.

Miller, J. J., Fletcher, K., & Kabat-Zinn, J. (1995). Three-year follow-up and clinical implications of a mindfulness meditation-based stress reduction intervention in the treatment of anxiety disorders. *General Hospital Psychiatry, 17,* 192–200.

Miller, N. E. (1941). The frustration-aggression hypothesis. *Psychological Review, 48,* 337–442.

Miller, N. E. (1985). The value of behavioral research on animals. *American Psychologist, 40,* 432–440.

Miller, R., Perlman, D., & Brehm, S. S. (2009). *Intimate relationships* (5th ed.). New York: McGraw-Hill.

Milner, A. D., & Goodale, M. A. (1995). *The visual brain in action.* New York: Oxford University Press.

Miltenberger, R. G. (2008). Behavior modification. In M. Hersen & A. M. Gross (Eds.), *Handbook of clinical psychology, vol 2: Children and adolescents* (pp. 626–652). Hoboken, NJ: Wiley.

Minde, K., & Zelkowitz, P. (2008). Premature babies. In M. M. Haith & J. B. Benson (Eds.), *Encyclopedia of infant and early childhood development.* Oxford, England: Elsevier.

Mineka, S., & Ohman, A. (2002). Phobias and preparedness: The selective, automatic, and encapsulated nature of fear. *Biological Psychiatry, 52,* 927–937.

Minor, R. K., Chang, J. W., & de Cabo, R. (2009). Hungry for life: How the arcuate nucleus and neuropeptide Y may play a critical role in mediating the benefits of calorie restriction. *Molecular and Cellular Endocrinology, 299,* 79–88.

Mirochnic, S., Wolf, S., Staufenbiel, M., & Kempermann, G. (2009). Age effects on the regulation of adult hippocampal neurogenesis by physical activity and environmental enrichment in the APP23 mouse model of Alzheimer disease. *Hippocampus.* (in press)

Mischel, W. (1968). *Personality and assessment.* New York: Wiley.

Mischel, W. (2004). Toward an integrative science of the person. *Annual Review of Psychology* (vol. 55). Palo Alto, CA: Annual Reviews.

Mischel, W. (2009). From *Personality and Assessment* (1968) to Personality Science, 2009. *Journal of Research in Personality, 43,* 282–290.

Mischel, W., & Ayduk, O. (2004). Willpower in a cognitive-affective processing system: The dynamics of delay of gratification. In R. F. Baumeister & K. D. Vohs (Eds.), *Handbook of self-regulation: Research, theory, and applications* (pp. 99–129). New York: Guilford.

Mischel, W., Cantor, N., & Feldman, S. (1996). Principles of self-regulation: The nature of will power and self-control. In E. T. Higgins & A. W. Kruglanski (Eds.), *Social psychology: Handbook of basic principles.* New York: Guilford.

Mischel, W., & Moore, B. S. (1980). The role of ideation in voluntary delay for symbolically presented rewards. *Cognitive Therapy and Research, 4,* 211–221.

Mischel, W., & Shoda, Y. (1999). Integrating dispositions and processing dynamics within a unified theory of personality: The cognitive-affective personality system. In L. A. Pervin & O. P. John (Eds.), *Handbook of personality: Theory and research* (2nd ed., pp. 197–218). New York: Guilford.

Mitchell, D. L., Gallagher, T. V., & Thomas, R. E. (2008). The human factors of implementing shift work in logging operations. *Journal of Agricultural Safety and Health, 14,* 391–404.

Mittag, W., & Schwarzer, R. (1993). Interaction of employment status and self-efficacy on alcohol consumption: A two-wave study on stressful life transitions. *Psychology and Health, 8,* 77–87.

Miyamoto, M. (2009). Pharmacology of ramelteon, a selective MT1/MT2 receptor agonist: A novel therapeutic drug for sleep disorders. *CNS Neuroscience and Therapeutics, 15,* 32–51.

Mizes, J. S., & Miller, K. J. (2000). Eating disorders. In M. Herson & R. T. Ammerman (Eds.), *Advanced abnormal child psychology* (2nd ed.). Mahwah, NJ: Erlbaum.

Moberly, N. J., & Watkins, E. R. (2009). Negative affect and ruminative self-focus during everyday goal pursuit. *Cognition and Emotion.* (in press)

Moffitt, T. E., Brammer, G. L., Caspi, A., Fawcet, J. P., Raleigh, M., Yuwiler, A., & Silva, P. A. (1998).

Whole blood serotonin relates to violence in an epidemiological study. *Biological Psychiatry, 43,* 446–457.

Molles, M. C. (2010). *Ecology* (5th ed.). New York: McGraw-Hill.

Money, J. (1986). *Lovemaps: Clinical concepts of sexual/erotic health and pathology, paraphilia, and gender transposition in childhood, adolescence, and maturity.* New York: Irvington.

Money, J., & Tucker P. (1975). *Sexual signatures: On being a man or woman.* Boston: Little Brown.

Monin, B. (2007). Normative influence. In R. Baumeister & K. D. Vohs (Eds.), *Encyclopedia of social psychology.* Thousand Oaks, CA: Sage.

Moons, W. G., & Mackie, D. M. (2007). Thinking straight while seeing red: The influence of anger on information processing. *Personality and Social Psychology Bulletin, 33* (5), 706–720.

Moore, D. W. (2005, June 16). Three in four Americans believe in paranormal (press release). Washington, DC: Gallup News Service.

Moore, K. A. (2009, March). Teen births: Examining the recent increase. *Child Trends: Research Brief.* Pub. #2009–08, 1–5.

Morgan, C. D., & Murray, H. A. (1935). A method of investigating fantasies: The Thematic Apperception Test. *Archives of Neurology and Psychiatry, 34,* 289–306.

Moritsugu, J., Wong, F. Y., & Duffy, K. G. (2010). *Community psychology* (4th ed.). Boston: Allyn & Bacon.

Morris, R. G. (2006). Elements of neurobiological theory of hippocampal function: The role of synaptic plasticity, synaptic tagging, and schemas. *European Journal of Neuroscience, 23,* 2829–2846.

Morrish, E., King, M. A., Smith, I. E., & Shneerson, J. M. (2004). Factors associated with a delay in the diagnosis of narcolepsy. *Sleep Medicine, 5,* 37–41.

Moscovici, S. (1985). Social influence and conformity. In G. Lindzey & E. Aronson (Eds.), *Handbook of social psychology* (3rd ed., vol. 2). New York: Random House.

Moskowitz, M., & Levering, R. (2007). 2007 "100 Best Companies to Work For" in America. http://www.greatplacetowork.com/best/100best2007.php

Moss, L. E., & Vaidya, N. A. (2006). Electroconvulsive therapy as an alternative treatment for obese patients with mood disorders. *Journal of Electroconvulsive Therapy, 22,* 223–225.

Mott, M. (2004, February 11). Seizure-alert dogs save humans with early warnings. *National Geographic News.* http://news.nationalgeographic.com/news/2003/04/0416_030416_seizuredogs.html (accessed January 15, 2007)

Moulson, M. C., & Nelson, C. A. (2008). Brain development and behavior. In M. M. Haith & J. B. Benson (Eds.), *Encyclopedia of infant and early childhood development.* Oxford, England: Elsevier.

Moulton, S. T., & Kosslyn, S. M. (2008). Using neuroimaging to resolve the psi debate. *Journal of Cognitive Neuroscience, 20,* 182–192.

Mroczek, D. K., & Kolarz, C. M. (1998). The effect of age on positive and negative affect: A developmental perspective on happiness. *Journal of Personality and Social Psychology, 75,* 1333–1349.

Muggleton, N., Tsakanikos, E., Walsh, V., & Ward, J. (2007). Disruption of synaesthesia following TMS of the right posterior parietal cortex. *Neuropsychologia, 45,* 1582–1585.

Mullington, J. M., Haack, M., Toth, M., Serrador, J. M., & Meier-Ewert, H. K. (2009). Cardiovascular, inflammatory, and metabolic consequences of sleep deprivation. *Progress in Cardiovascular Diseases, 51,* 294–302.

Mulveen, R., & Hepworth, J. (2006). An interpretative phenomenological analysis of participation in a pro-anorexia internet site and its relationship with disordered eating. *Journal of Health Psychology, 11,* 283–296.

Mulvenna, C. M., & Walsh, V. (2006). Synaesthesia: Supernatural integration? *Trends in Cognitive Neuroscience, 10,* 350–352.

Munoz-Laboy, M., Hirsch, J. S., & Quispe-Lazaro, A. (2009). Loneliness as a sexual risk for male Mexican migrant workers. *American Journal of Public Health, 99,* 802–810.

Murray, E. A. (2007). Visual memory. *Annual Review of Neuroscience* (vol. 29). Palo Alto, CA: Annual Reviews.

Murray-Swank, A. B., Lucksted, A., Medoff, D. R., Yang, Y., Wohlheiter, K., & Dixon, L. B. (2006). Religiosity, psychosocial adjustment, and subjective burden of persons who care for those with mental illness. *Psychiatric Services, 57,* 361–365.

Must, A., Koks, S., Vasar, E., Tasa, G., Lang, A., Maron, E., & Vali, M. (2009). Common variations in 4p locus are related to male completed suicide. *Neuromolecular Medicine, 11,* 13–19.

Mussweiler, T. (2009). Social comparison. In F. Strack & J. Forster (Eds.), *Social cognition: The basis of human interaction.* New York: Psychology Press.

Myers, D. G. (2000). *A quiet world.* Hartford, CT: Yale University Press.

Mykletun, A., Bjerkeset, O., Dewey, M., Prince, M., Overland, S., & Stewart, R. (2007). Anxiety, depression, and cause-specific mortality: The Hunt Study. *Psychosomatic Medicine, 69,* 323–331.

N

Naar-King, S., Wright, K., Parsons, J. T., Frey, M., Templin, T., & Ondersma, S. (2006). Transtheoretical model and condom use in HIV-positive youths. *Health Psychology, 25,* 648–652.

Nagase, Y., & others. (2009). Coping strategies and their correlates with depression in the Japanese general population. *Psychiatry Research, 168,* 57–66.

Najmi, S., Riemann, B. C., & Wegner, D. M. (2009). Managing unwanted intrusive thoughts in obsessive-compulsive disorder: Relative effectiveness of suppresion, focused distraction, and acceptance. *Behavior Research and Therapy.* (in press)

Nakao, T., Nakagawa, A., Yoshiura, T., Nakatani, E., Nabeyama, M., Yoshizato, C., Kudoh, A., Tada, K., Yoshioka, K., & Kawamoto, M. (2005). A functional MRI comparison of patients with obsessive-compulsive disorder and normal controls during a Chinese character Stroop task. *Psychiatry Research: Neuroimaging, 139* (2), 101–114.

Nakao, T., & others. (2009). Working memory dysfunction in obsessive-compulsive disorder: A neuropsychological and functional MRI study. *Journal of Psychiatric Research, 43,* 784–791.

Nardi, P. M. (2006). *Doing survey research* (2nd ed.). Boston: Allyn & Bacon.

Nash, J. R., & Nutt, D. J. (2005). Pharmacotherapy of anxiety. *Handbook of Experimental Pharmacology, 169,* 469–501.

Nash, M. R. (2001). The truth and the hype about hypnosis. *Scientific American, 285,* 46–49, 52–55.

Nasrallah, H. A., & others. (2009). Proceedings and data from the Schizophrenia Summit: A critical appraisal to improve management of schizophrenia. *Journal of Clinical Psychiatry, 70,* Suppl. 1, 4–46.

National Alliance for the Mentally Ill, American Psychiatric Association, National Mental Health Association. (2005, June 24). *Joint statement in response to Tom Cruise's Today Show interview.* Author.

National Center for Health Statistics. (2002). *Sexual behavior and selected health measures: Men and women 15–44 years of age, United States, 2002.* Atlanta: Centers for Disease Control and Prevention.

National Center for Health Statistics. (2005). *Early release of selected estimates from Jan–Mar 2005 National Health Interview Survey.* Washington, DC: Author.

National Center for Health Statistics. (2005a). *Death statistics.* Atlanta: Centers for Disease Control and Prevention.

National Center for Health Statistics. (2006). *Vital and health statistics.* Atlanta: Centers for Disease Control and Prevention.

National Center for Health Statistics. (2006a). *Health United States, 2006.* Atlanta: Centers for Disease Control and Prevention.

National Center for Health Statistics. (2008). *Life expectancy.* www.cdc.gov/ (accessed May 25, 2008)

National Center for Health Statistics. (2008a). Table 63. Current cigarette smoking among adults 18 years of age and over, by sex, race, and age: United States, selected years 1965–2006. *Health, United States, 2008.* Atlanta: Centers for Disease Control and Prevention.

National Center for Health Statistics. (2009). *HIV/AIDS statistics and surveillance.* Atlanta: Centers for Disease Control and Prevention.

National Center for Post-Traumatic Stress Disorder (PTSD). (2006). *Facts about PTSD.* www.ncptsd.va.gov (accessed November 25, 2006)

National Heart, Lung, and Blood Institute. (2009). BMI calculator. http://www.nhlbisupport.com/bmi/

National Highway Traffic Safety Administration (NHTSA). (2001). *Traffic safety facts.* Washington, DC: Author.

National Highway Traffic Safety Administration (NHTSA). (2005. August). *Traffic safety facts: Alcohol-related fatalities in 2004.* Washington, DC: NHTSA's Center for Statistics and Analysis.

National Highway Traffic Safety Administration (NHTSA). (2007, December). *Traffic safety facts: Crash stats.* Washington, DC: NHTSA's Center for Statistics and Analysis.

National Institute on Drug Abuse (NIDA). (2009). *Research report series—MDMA (Ecstasy) abuse.* Bethesda, MD: Author.

National Institute of Mental Health (NIMH). (2006). *The numbers count: Mental disorders in America.* Fact Sheet. Washington, DC: National Institutes of Health.

National Institute of Mental Health (NIMH). (2008). *The numbers count: Mental disorders in America.* Bethesda, MD: US. Department of Health and Human Services. http://www.nimh.nih.gov/health/publications/the-numbers-count-mental-disorders-in-america/index.shtml

National Institute of Mental Health (NIMH). (2009). *Eating disorders.* Bethesda, MD: Author.

National Sleep Foundation. (2001). *2001 Sleep in America Poll.* Washington, DC: Author.

National Sleep Foundation. (2006). *2006 Sleep in America Poll.* Washington, DC: Author.

National Sleep Foundation. (2007, March 6). *Stressed-out American women have no time for sleep.* Washington DC: Author.

Naveh-Benjamin, M., Kilb, A., & Fisher, T. (2006). Concurrent task effects on memory encoding and retrieval: Further support for an asymmetry. *Memory and Cognition, 34,* 90–91.

Needham, A. (2009). Learning in infants' object perception, object-directed action, and tool use. In A. Woodward & A. Needham (Eds.), *Learning and the infant mind.* New York: Oxford University Press.

Needham, A., Barrett, T., & Peterman, K. (2002). A pick-me-up for infants' exploratory skills: Early simulated experiences reaching for objects using "sticky mittens" enhances young infants' object exploration skills. *Infant Behavior and Development, 25,* 279–295.

Needham, A., & Woodward, A. (Eds.) (2008). *Learning and the infant mind.* New York: Oxford University Press.

Nefti, W., Chaumontet, C., Fromentin, G., Tomé, D., & Darcel, N. (2009). A high fat diet attenuates the central response to within-meal satiation signals and modifies the receptor expression of vagal afferents in mice. *American Journal of Physiology: Regulatory, Integrative, and Comparative Physiology, 296,* R1681–R1686.

Neisser, U., Boodoo, G., Bouchard, T. J., Boykin, A. W., Brody, N., Ceci, S. J., Halpern, D. F., Loehlin, J. C., Perloff, R., Sternberg, R. J., & Urbina, S. (1996). Intelligence: Knowns & unknowns. *American Psychologist, 51,* 77–101.

Neisser, U., & Harsch, N. (1992). Phantom flashbulbs: False recollections of hearing the news about *Challenger.* In E. Winograd & U. Neisser (Eds.), *Affect and accuracy in recall: Studies of "flashbulb" memories* (pp. 9–31). New York: Cambridge University Press.

Nelson, C. A. (2009). Brain development and behavior. In A. M. Rudolph, C. Rudolph, L. First, G. Lister, &

A. A. Gersohon (Eds.), *Rudolph's pediatrics* (22nd ed.). New York: McGraw-Hill.

Nelson, D. L, & Gehlert, D. R. (2006). Central nervous system biogenic amine targets for control of appetite and energy expenditure. *Endocrine, 29* (1), 49–60.

Nelson, K. (1993). The psychological and social origins of autobiographical memory. *Psychological Science, 4,* 7–14.

Nelson, K. J., Bowman-Fowler, N., Berkowitz, S. R., & Loftus, E. F. (2009). Eyewitness testimony. In C. Edwards (Ed.), *Encyclopedia of forensic science.* New York: Wiley. (in press)

Nelson, T. D. (Ed.). (2009). *Handbook of prejudice, stereotyping, and discrimination.* New York: Psychology Press.

Nemeroff, C. B., Bremner, J. D., Foa, E. B., Mayberg, H. S., North, C. S., & Stein, M. B. (2006). Posttraumatic stress disorder: A state-of-the-science review. *Journal of Psychiatric Research, 40* (1), 1–21.

Nestler, S., Blank, H., & von Collani, G. (2008). Hindsight bias doesn't always come easy: Causal models, cognitive effort, and creeping determinism. *Journal of Experimental Psychology: Learning, Memory, and Cognition, 34,* 1043–1054.

Neukrug, E. S., & Fawcett, R. C. (2010). *Essentials of testing and assessment* (2nd ed.). Boston: Cengage.

Neuman, W.L. (2009). *Understanding research.* Upper Saddle River, NJ: Prentice-Hall.

Neumann, I. D. (2007). Oxytocin: The neuropeptide of love reveals some of its secrets. *Cell Metabolism, 5,* 231–233.

Neupert, S. D., Lachman, M. E., & Whitbourne, S. B. (2009). Exercise self-efficacy and control beliefs: Effects on exercise behavior after an exercise intervention with older adults. *Journal of Aging and Physical Activity, 17,* 1–16.

Neville, H. J. (2006). Different profiles of plasticity within human cognition. In Y. Munakata & M. H. Johnson (Eds.), *Attention and performance.* Oxford, England: Oxford University Press.

Niaura, R., Todaro, J. F., Strood, L., Spiro, A, Ward, K. D., & Weiss, S. (2002). Hostility, the metabolic syndrome, and incident coronary heart disease. *Health Psychology, 21,* 588–593.

Nickerson, R. S., & Adams, M. J. (1979). Long-term memory for a common object. *Cognitive Psychology, 11,* 287–307.

Nides, M. (2008). Update on pharmacological options for smoking cessation treatment. *American Journal of Medicine, 121, Suppl. 4,* S20–S31.

Nijstad, B. (2009). *Group performance.* New York: Psychology Press.

Nilsson, H., Juslin, P., & Olsson, H. (2008). Exemplars in the mist: The cognitive substrate of the representativeness heuristic. *Scandinavian Journal of Psychology, 49,* 201–212.

Niparko, J. K. (2004). Speech, language, and reading skills after early cochlear implantation. *Journal of the American Medical Association, 291,* 2378–2380.

Nisbett, R. E., & Ross, L. (1980). *Human inference.* Upper Saddle River, NJ: Prentice-Hall.

Nishida, A., Miyaoka, T., Inagaki, T., & Horiguchi, J. (2009). New approaches to antidepressant drug design: Cytokine-regulated pathways. *Current Pharmaceutical Design, 15,* 1683–1687.

Noel, N. E., Maisto, S. A., Johnson, J. D., & Jackson, L. A. (2009). The effects of alcohol and cue salience on young men's acceptance of sexual aggression. *Addictive Behaviors, 34,* 386–394.

Noftie, E. E., & Robins, R. W. (2007). Personality predictors of academic outcomes: Big five correlates of GPA and SAT scores. *Journal of Personality and Social Psychology, 93,* 116–130.

Nolen-Hoeksema, S. (2010). *Abnormal psychology* (5th ed.). New York: McGraw-Hill. (in press)

Nolen-Hoeksema, S., Stice, E., Wade, E., & Bohon, C. (2007). Reciprocal relations between rumination and bulimic, substance abuse, and depressive symptoms in female adolescents. *Journal of Abnormal Psychology, 116,* 198–207.

Nolte, J. (2009). *Essentials of the human brain.* London: Elsevier.

Norcross, J. C., Mrykalo, M. S., & Blagys, M. D. (2002). Auld lang syne: Success predictors, change processes, and self-reported outcomes of New Year's resolvers and nonresolvers. *Journal of Clinical Psychology, 58,* 397–405.

Nordt, C., Rossler, W., & Lauber, C. (2006). Attitudes of mental health professionals toward people with schizophrenia and major depression. *Schizophrenia Bulletin, 32,* 709–714.

Norenzayan, A., & Heine, S. J. (2005). Psychological universals: What are they and how can we know? *Psychological Bulletin, 131,* 763–784.

Norman, J. F., Lee, Y. L., Phillips, F., Norman, H. F., Jennings, L. R., & McBride, T. R. (2009). The perception of 3-D shape from shadows cast onto curved surfaces. *Acta Psychologica.*

Norman, T. R., & Burrows, G. D. (2007). Emerging treatments for major depression. *Expert Review of Neurotherapuetics, 7,* 203–213.

Norman, W. T. (1963). Toward an adequate taxonomy of personality attributes. *Journal of Abnormal and Social Psychology, 66,* 574–583.

Norris, J., & others. (2009). Cognitive mediation of alcohol's effects on women's in-the-moment sexual decision making. *Health Psychology, 28,* 20–28.

Northoff, G. (2007). Psychopathology and pathophysiology of the self in depression—neuropsychiatric hypothesis. *Journal of Affective Disorders, 104,* 1–14.

Nosek, B. A., & Banaji, M. R. (2007). Implicit attitude. In P. Wilken, T. Bayne, & A. Cleeremans (Eds.), *Oxford companion to consciousness.* Oxford: Oxford University Press.

Nosek, B. A., Greenwald, A. G., & Banaji, M. R. (2006). The Implicit Association Test at age 7: A methodological and conceptual review. In J. A. Bargh (Ed.), *Social psychology and the unconscious: The automaticity of higher mental processes* (pp. 265–292). New York: Psychology Press.

Notman, M. T., & Nadelson, C. C. (2002). Women's issues. In M. Hersen & W. H. Sledge (Eds.), *Encyclopedia of psychotherapy.* San Diego: Academic.

Nyberg, L. (2004, August). *Imaging Cognition.* Paper presented at the 28th International Congress of Psychology, Beijing, China.

Nystul, M. S. (1999). *Introduction to counseling.* Boston: Allyn & Bacon.

O'Barr, W. M. (2006). Multiculturalism in the marketplace: Targeting Latinas, African American women, and gay consumers. *Advertising and Society Review, 7* (4). http://muse.jhu.edu/journals/advertising_and_society_review/

Obler, L. K. (2009). Development in the adult years. In J. Berko Gleason & N. Ratner (Eds.), *The development of language* (7th ed.). Boston: Allyn & Bacon.

Obradovic, J., Long, J. D., Cutuli, J. J., Chan, C.-K., Hinz, E., Heistad, D., & Masten, A. S. (2009). Academic achievement of homeless and highly mobile children in an urban school district: Longitudinal evidence on risk, growth, and resilience. *Development and Psychopathology, 21,* 493–518.

O'Connor, D. B., Conner, M., Jones, F., McMillan, B., & Ferguson, E. (2009). Exploring the benefits of conscientiousness: An investigation of the role of daily stressors and health behaviors. *Annals of Behavioral Medicine.* (in press)

O'Connor, D. W., Gardner, B., Presnell, I., Singh, D., Tasanglis, M., & White, E. (2009). The effectiveness of continuation-maintenance ECT in reducing depressed older patients' re-admissions. *Journal of Affective Disorders.* (in press)

Ogilvie, R. D., & Wilkinson, R. T. (1988). Behavioral versus EEG-based monitoring of all-night sleep/wake patterns. *Sleep, 11* (2), 139–155.

Ohayon, M. M. (2009). Difficulty in resuming or inability to resume sleep and the links to daytime impairment: Definition, prevalence, and comorbidity. *Journal of Psychiatric Research.* (in press)

Ohman, A., & Mineka, S. (2001). Fears, phobias, and preparedness: Toward an evolved module of fear and fear learning. *Psychological Review, 108,* 483–522.

Ohman, A., & Mineka, S. (2003). The malicious serpent: Snakes as a prototypical stimulus for an evolved module of fear. *Current Directions in Psychological Science, 12,* 5–9.

Ohman, A., & Soares, J. J. P. (1998). Emotional conditioning to masked stimuli: Expectancies for aversive outcomes following nonrecognized fear-relevant stimuli. *Journal of Experimental Psychology, 127,* 69–82.

Olds, J. M. (1958). Self-stimulation experiments and differential reward systems. In H. H. Jasper, L. D. Proctor, R. S. Knighton, W. C. Noshay, & R. T. Costello (Eds.), *Reticular formation of the brain.* Boston: Little, Brown.

Olds, J. M., & Milner, P. M. (1954). Positive reinforcement produced by electrical stimulation of the septal area and other areas of the rat brain. *Journal of Comparative and Physiological Psychology, 47,* 419–427.

Oliver, M. B., & Hyde, J. S. (1993). Gender differences in sexuality: A meta-analysis. *Psychological Bulletin, 114,* 29–51.

Oliver, N. S., Toumazou, C., Cass, A. E., & Johnston, D. G. (2009). Glucose sensors: A review of current and emerging technology. *Diabetic Medicine, 26,* 197–2010.

Olness, K., & Ader, R. (1992). Conditioning as an adjunct in the pharmacotherapy of lupus erythematosus. *Journal of Developmental and Behavioral Pediatrics, 13,* 124–125.

Olson, H. C., King, S., & Jirkowic, T. (2008). Fetal alcohol spectrum disorders. In M. M. Haith & J. B. Benson (Eds.), *Encyclopedia of infant and early childhood development.* Oxford, England: Elsevier.

Olson, J. M., & Stone, J. (2005). The influence of behavior on attitudes. In D. Albarracin, B. T. Johnson, & M. P. Zanna (Eds), *The handbook of attitudes* (pp. 223–271). Mahwah, NJ: Erlbaum.

Olson, M., & Hergenhahn, B. R. (2009). *Introduction to theories of learning* (8th ed.). Upper Saddle River, NJ: Prentice-Hall.

Oltmanns, T. F., & Emery, R. E. (2007). *Abnormal psychology* (5th ed.). Upper Saddle River, NJ: Prentice-Hall.

Olver, J. S., & others. (2009). Dopamine D1 receptor binding in the striatum of patients with obsessive-compulsive disorder. *Journal of Affective Disorders, 114,* 321–326.

Onen, N. F., Overton, E. T., Presti, R., Blair, C., Powderly, W. G., & Mondy, K. (2009). Suboptimal CD4 recovery on long-term suppressive highly active antiretroviral therapy is associated with favorable outcome. *HIV Medicine.* (in press)

Online Publishers Association. (2005, October). *Online paid content U.S. market spending report.* New York: Online Publishers Association and Comscore Networks.

Orhan, G., Orhan, I., Subutay-Oztekin, N., Ak, F., & Sener, B. (2009). Contemporary anticholinesterase pharmaceuticals of natural origin and their synthetic analogues for the treatment of Alzheimer's disease. *Recent Patents on CNS Drug Discovery, 4,* 43–51.

Orom, H., & Cervone, D. (2009). Personality dynamics, meaning, and idiosyncrasy: Identifying cross-situational coherence by assessing personality architecture. *Journal of Research in Personality, 43,* 228–240.

Osborn, D. P. J., Nazareth, I., & King, M. B. (2006). Risk of coronary heart disease in people with severe mental illness: Cross-sectional comparative study in primary care. *British Journal of Psychiatry, 188,* 271–277.

Ostir, G. V., Markides, K. S., Black, S. A., & Goodwin, J. S. (2000). Emotional well-being predicts subsequent functional independence and survival. *Journal of the American Geriatrics Society, 48,* 473–478.

Otake, K., Shimai, S., Tanaka-Matsumi, J., Otsui, K., & Fredrickson, B. L. (2006). Happy people becoming happier through kindness: A counting kindnesses intervention. *Journal of Happiness Studies, 7,* 361–375.

Owen, A. M., Coleman, M. R., Boly, M., Davis, M. H., Laureys, S., & Pickard, J. D. (2006). Detecting awareness in the vegetative state. *Science, 313,* 1402.

Oyserman, D. (2008). Racial-ethnic self-schemas: Multidimensional identity-based motivation. *Journal of Research in Personality, 42,* 1186–1198.

Ozer, D. J., & Benet-Martinez, V. (2006). Personality and the prediction of consequential outcomes. *Annual Review of Psychology* (vol. 57). Palo Alto, CA: Annual Reviews.

Ozer, D. J., & Riese, S. P. (1994). Personality assessment. *Annual Review of Psychology* (vol. 45). Palo Alto, CA: Annual Reviews.

P

Packer, D. J. (2008). Identifying systematic disobedience in Milgram's obedience experiments: A meta-analytic review. *Perspectives on Psychological Science, 3,* 301–304.

Packer, D. J. (2009). Avoiding groupthink: Whereas weakly identified members stay silent, strongly identified members dissent about collective matters. *Psychological Science, 20,* 546–548.

Page, J. H., Rexrode, K. M., Hu, F., Albert, C. M., Chae, C. U., & Manson, J. E. (2009). Waist-height ratio as a predictor of coronary heart disease among women. *Epidemiology.* (in press)

Paivio, A. (1971). *Imagery and verbal processes.* New York: Holt, Rinehart & Winston.

Paivio, A. (1986). *Mental representations: A dual coding approach.* New York: Oxford University Press.

Paivio, A. (2007). *Mind and its evolution.* Mahwah, NJ: Erlbaum.

Paller, C. J., Campbell, C. M., Edwards, R. R., & Dobs, A. S. (2009). Sex-based differences in pain perception and treatment. *Pain Medicine.* (in press)

Palomo, T., Beninger, R. J., Kostrzewa, R. M., & Archer, T. (2008). Focusing on symptoms rather than diagnoses in brain dysfunction: Conscious and nonconscious expression in impulsiveness and decision-making. *Neurotoxicity Research, 14,* 1–20.

Paluck, E. C., McCormack, J. P., Ensom, M. H. H., Levine, M., Soon, J. A., & Fielding, D. W. (2006). Outcomes of bupropion therapy for smoking cessation during routine clinical use. *Annals of Pharmacotherapy, 40,* 185–190.

Pampaloni, I., & others. (2009). High-dose selective serotonin reuptake inhibitors In OCD: A systematic retrospective case notes survey, *Journal of Psychopharmacology.* (in press)

Pan, B. A., & Uccelli, P. (2009). Semantic development. In J. Berko Gleason & N. Ratner (Eds.), *The development of language* (7th ed.). Boston: Allyn & Bacon.

Pant, S., & Ramaswamy, B. (2009). Association of major stressors with elevated risk of breast cancer incidence or relapse. *Drugs Today, 45,* 115–126.

Paredes, R. G. (2009). Evaluating the neurobiology of sexual reward. *ILAR Journal, 50,* 15–27.

Parish, J. M. (2009) Sleep-related problems in common medical conditions. *Chest, 135,* 563–572.

Park, B. H., Lee, M. S., Hong, J. Y., Bas, S. H., Kim, E. Y., Kim, K. K., & Kim, D. K. (2009) The stages of physical activity and exercise behavior: An integrated approach to the theory of planned behavior. *Asia-Pacific Journal of Mental Health, 21,* 71–83.

Park, C. (2009). Meaning making in cancer survivorship. In P. T. P. Wong (Ed.), *Handbook of meaning* (2nd ed.). Thousand Oaks, CA: Sage. (in press)

Park, C. L. (2004). Positive and negative consequences of alcohol consumption in college students. *Addictive Behaviors, 29,* 311–321.

Park, C. L. (2007). Religious and spiritual issues in health and aging. In C. M. Aldwin, C. L. Park, & A. Spiro (Eds.), *Handbook of health psychology and aging.* New York: Guilford.

Park, D. C., Guchess, A. H., Meade, M. L., & Stine-Morrow, E. A. L. (2007). Improving cognitive function in older adults: Nontraditional approaches. *Journals of Gerontology: Psychological Sciences and Social Sciences, 62B, Special Issue 1,* P45–P52.

Park, D. C., & Reuter-Lorenz, P. (2009). The adaptive brain: Aging and neurocognitive scaffolding. *Annual Review of Psychology* (vol. 60). Palo Alto, CA: Annual Reviews.

Park, D. H., Eve, D. J., Borlongan, C. V., Klasko, S. K., Cruz, L. E., & Sanberg, P. R. (2009). From the basics to application of cell therapy, a steppingstone to the conquest of neurodegeneration: A meeting report. *Medical Science Monitor, 15,* RA23–31.

Park, I. S., Lee, K. J., Han, J. W., Lee, N. J., Park, K. A., & Rhyu, I. J. (2009). Experience-dependent plasticity of cerebellar vermis in basketball players. *Cerebellum.* (in press)

Parke, R. D., Leidy, M. S., Schofield, T. J., Miller, M. A., & Morris, K. L. (2008). Socialization. In M. M. Haith & J. B. Benson (Eds.), *Encyclopedia of infant and early childhood development.* Oxford, England: Elsevier.

Parker, G., & Fletcher, K. (2007). Treating depression with the evidence-based psychotherapies: A critique of the evidence. *Acta Psychiatrica Scandinavica, 115* (5), 352–359.

Parker, P. S. (2006). *Race, gender, and leadership.* Mahwah, NJ: Erlbaum.

Parks, M. R. (2007). *Personal relationships and personal networks.* Mahwah, NJ: Erlbaum.

Parry, A., & Matthews, P. M. (2002). Functional magnetic resonance imaging: A window into the brain. *Interdisciplinary Science Reviews, 27,* 50–60.

Partners for Life. (2007). *Partners for life: A service dog's tale.* http://cals.arizona.edu/agdiv/servicedog/ (accessed April 10, 2007)

Parvaresh, N., & Bahramnezhad, A. (2009). Post-traumatic stress disorder in bam-survived students who immigrated to Kerman, four months after the earthquake. *Archives of Iranian Medicine, 12,* 244–249.

Pascalls, O., & Kelly, D. J. (2008). Face processing. In M. M. Haith & J. B. Benson (Eds.), *Encyclopedia of infant and early childhood development.* Oxford, England: Elsevier.

Passie, T., Halpern, J. H., Stichtenoth, D. O., Emrich, H. M., & Hintzen, A. (2008). The pharmacology of lysergic acid diethlyamide: A review. *CNS Neuroscience and Therapeutics, 14,* 295–314.

Patalano, A. L., Wengrovitz, S. M., & Sharpes, K. M. (2009). The influence of category coherence on inference about cross-classified entities. *Memory and Cognition, 37,* 21–38.

Patel, A. R., Hui, H., J. T., Pandian, N. G., & Karas, R. H. (2009). Modestly overweight women have vascular endothelial dysfunction. *Clinical Cardiology, 32,* 269–273.

Patel, S. R., Zhu, X., Storfer-Isser, A., Mehra, A., Jenny, N. S., Tracy, R., & Redline, S. (2009). Sleep duration and biomarkers of inflammation. *Sleep, 32,* 200–204.

Patel, V. & others. (2009). Self-calibration of a cone-beam micro-CT scan. *Medical Physics, 36,* 48–58.

Patell, E. A., Cooper, H., & Robinson, J. C. (2008). The effects of choice on intrinsic motivation and related outcomes: A meta-analysis of research findings. *Psychological Bulletin, 134,* 270–300.

Patterson, C. J., & Hastings, P. D. (2007). Socialization in the context of family diversity. In J. E. Grusec & P. D. Hastings (Eds.), *Handbook of socialization.* New York: Guilford.

Patterson, T. G., & Joseph, S. (2007). Person-centered personality theory: Support from self determination theory and positive psychology. *Journal of Humanistic Psychology, 47,* 117–139.

Paulus, P. B. (1989). An overview and evaluation of group influence. In P. B. Paulus (Ed.), *Psychology of group influence.* Mahwah, NJ: Erlbaum.

Paunonen, S., Jackson, D., Trzebinski, J., & Forserling, F. (1992). Personality structures across cultures: A multimethod evaluation. *Journal of Personality and Social Psychology, 62,* 447–456.

Paus, T. (2009). Brain development. In R. M. Lerner & L. Steinberg (Ed.), *Handbook of adolescent psychology* (3rd ed.). New York: Wiley.

Paus, T., Toro, R., Leonard, G., Lerner, J. V., Lerner, R. M., Perron, M., Pike, G. B., Richer, L., Steinberg, L., Veillete, S., & Pausova, Z. (2008). Morphological properties of the action-observation cortical network in adolescents with low and high resistance to peer influence. *Social Neuroscience, 3,* 303–316.

Pavlov, I. P. (1927). *Conditioned reflexes.* G. V. Anrep (Trans.). New York: Dover.

Pavot, W., & Diener, E. (2008). The Satisfaction with Life Scale and the emerging construct of life satisfaction. *Journal of Positive Psychology, 3,* 137–152.

Payne, B. K. (2001). Prejudice and perception: The role of automatic and controlled processes in misperceiving a weapon. *Journal of Personality and Social Psychology, 81,* 181–192.

Payne, B. K. (2008). What mistakes disclose: A process dissociation approach to automatic and controlled processes in social psychology. *Social and Personality Psychology Compass, 2,* 10.1111/j.1751–9004.2008.00091.x (online journal).

Pearce, J. M., & Hall, G. (2009). A model for stimulus generalization in Pavlovian conditioning. In D. Shanks (Ed.), *Psychology of learning.* Thousand Oaks, CA: Sage.

Pearson, N. J., Johnson, L. L., & Nahin, R. L. (2006). Insomnia, trouble sleeping, and complementary and alternative medicine: Analysis of the 2002 National Health Interview Survey data. *Archives of Internal Medicine, 166,* 1775–1782.

Pedersen, S., Denollet, R., Erdman, R. A. M., Serruys, P. W., & van Domburg, R. T. (2009). Co-occurrence of diabetes and hopelessness predicts adverse prognosis following percutaneous coronary intervention. *Journal of Behavioral Medicine, 32,* 294–301.

Peel, J. B., Sui, X., Adams, S. A., Hebert, J. R., Hardin, J. W., & Blair, S. N. (2009). A prospective study of cardiorespiratory fitness and breast cancer mortality. *Medicine and Sciences in Sports and Exercise, 41,* 742–748.

Peeters, A., Barendregt, J. J., Willekens, F., Mackenbach, J. P., Al Mamun, A., Bonneux, L. (2003). Obesity in adulthood and its consequences for life expectancy: A Life-Table analysis. *Annals of Internal Medicine, 138,* 24–32.

Peleg, G., Katzier, G., Peleg, O., Kamara, M., Brodskey, L., Hel-Or, H., Keren, D., & Nevo, E. (2006). Hereditary family signature of facial expression. *Proceedings of the National Academy of Sciences USA, 103,* 15921–15926.

Pelleymounter, M. A., Bullen, M. J., Hecht, R., & others. (1995). Effects of the obese gene product on body weight regulation in ob/ob mice. *Science, 269,* 540–543.

Penedo, F. J., Molton, I., Dahn, J. R., Shen, B. J., Kinsigner, D., Traeger, L., Siegel, S., Schneiderman, N., & Antoni, M. (2006). A randomized clinical trial of group-based cognitive-behavioral stress management in localized prostate cancer: Development of stress management skills improves quality of life and benefit finding. *Annals of Behavioral Medicine, 31,* 261–270.

Penfield, W. (1947). Some observations in the cerebral cortex of man. *Proceedings of the Royal Society, 134,* 349.

Pennebaker, J. W. (1997a). *Opening up: The healing power of expressing emotions* (rev. ed.). New York: Guilford.

Pennebaker, J. W. (1997b). Writing about emotional experiences as a therapeutic experience. *Psychological Science, 8,* 162–166.

Pennebaker, J. W. (2004). *Writing to heal: A guided journal for recovering from trauma emotional upheaval.* Oakland, CA: New Harbinger Press.

Pennebaker, J. W., & Chung, C. K. (2007). Expressive writing, emotional upheavals, and health. In H. S. Friedman & R. C. Silver (Eds.), *Foundations of health psychology* (pp. 263–284). New York: Oxford University Press.

Penner, L. A., Dovidio, J. F., Piliavin, J. A., & Schroeder, D. A. (2005). Prosocial behavior: Multilevel perspectives. *Annual Review of Psychology* (vol. 56). Palo Alto, CA: Annual Reviews.

Peplau, L. A. (2003). Human sexuality: How do men and women differ? *Current Directions in Psychological Science, 12,* 37–40.

Peplau, L. A., & Fingerhut, A. W. (2007). The close relationships of lesbians and gay men. *Annual Review of Psychology* (vol. 58). Palo Alto, CA: Annual Reviews.

Perkins, D. (1994, September). Creativity by design. *Educational Leadership,* 18–25.

Perlis, R. H., & others. (2009). A genomewide association study of response to lithium for prevention of recurrence in bipolar disorder. *American Journal of Psychiatry, 166,* 718–725.

Pert, C. B. (1999). *Molecules of emotion.* New York: Simon & Schuster.

Pert, C. B., & Snyder, S. H. (1973). Opiate receptor: Demonstration in a nervous tissue. *Science, 179,* 1011.

Pessoa, L. (2009). How do emotion and motivation direct executive control? *Trends in Cognitive Science.* (in press)

Petersen, J. L., & Hyde, J. S. (2009). A longitudinal investigation of peer sexual harassment victimization in adolescence. *Journal of Adolescence.* (in press)

Peterson, C. (2006). *A primer in positive psychology.* New York: Oxford University Press.

Peterson, C., & Seligman, M. E. P. (2003). Character strengths before and after September 11. *Psychological Science, 14,* 381–384.

Peterson, C. C., Garnett, M., Kelly, A., & Attwood, T. (2009). Everyday social and conversation applications of theory-of-mind understanding by children with autism-spectrum disorders or typical development. *European Child and Adolescent Psychology, 18,* 105–115.

Pettigrew, T. F., & Tropp, L. R. (2006). A meta-analytic test of intergroup contact theory. *Journal of Personality and Social Psychology, 90,* 751–783.

Petty, R. E., & Brinol, P. (2008). Persuasion: From single to multiple to metacognitive processes. *Perspectives on Psychological Science, 3,* 137–147.

Petty, R. E., & Cacioppo, J. T. (1986). The elaboration likelihood of persuasion. In L. Berkowitz (Ed.), *Advances in experimental social psychology* (vol. 19). New York: Academic.

Pew Research Center. (2007, January 9). *A portrait of "Generation Next": How young people view their lives, futures and politics.* Washington, DC: Author.

Phaneuf, L., & McIntyre, L. L. (2007). Effects of individualized video feedback combined with group parent training on inappropriate maternal behavior. *Journal of Applied Behavior Analysis, 40* (4). 737–741.

Phelan, J. E., & Basow, S. A. (2007). College students' attitudes toward mental illness: An examination of the stigma process. *Journal of Applied Social Psychology, 37,* 2877–2902.

Phelan, S., Hill, J. O., Lang, W., Dibello, J. R., Wing, R. R. (2003). Recovery from relapse among successful weight maintainers. *American Journal of Clinical Nutrition, 78,* 1079–1084.

Phelan, S., Nallari, M., Daroch, F. E., & Wing, R. R. (2009). What do physicians recommend to their overweight obese patients? *Journal of the American Board of Family Medicine, 22,* 115–122.

Phillips, J. S., Velanova, K., Wolk, D. A., & Wheeler, M. E. (2009). Left posterior parietal cortex participates in both task preparation and episodic retrieval. *NeuroImage.* (in press)

Phillips, K. J., & Mudford, O. C. (2008). Functional analysis skills training for residential caregivers. *Behavioral Interventions, 23*(1), 1–12.

Phinney, J. S., Berry, J. W., Berry, D. L., & Vedder, S. P. (2006). Understanding immigrant youth: Conclusions and implications. In J. W. Berry, J. S. Phinney, D. L. Sam, & S. P. Vedder (Eds.), *Immigrant youth in cultural transmission.* Mahwah, NJ: Erlbaum.

Phinney, J. S., & Ong, A. D. (2007). Conceptualization and measurement of ethnic identity. *Journal of Counseling Psychology, 54,* 271–281.

Piaget, J. (1952). *The origins of intelligence in children.* New York: Oxford University Press.

Pierucci, M., Di Matteo, V., Benigno, A., Crescimanno, G., Esposito, E., & Di Giovanni, G. (2009). The unilateral nigral lesion induces dramatic belateral modification on a rat brain monoamine neurochemistry. *Annals of the New York Academy of Science, 1155,* 316–323.

Picchioni, M. M., Toulopoulou, T., Landau, S., Davies, N., Ribchester, T., & Murray, R. M. (2006). Neurological abnormalities in schizophrenic twins. *Biological Psychiatry, 59,* 341–348.

Pickering, A. D., & Gray, J. A. (1999). The neuroscience of personality. In L. A. Pervin & O. P. John (Eds.). *Handbook of personality: Theory and research* (2nd ed., pp. 277–299). New York: Guilford.

Pickering, A. D., & Smillie, L. D. (2008). The behavioral activation system: Challenges and opportunities. In P. J. Corr (Ed.), *The reinforcement sensitivity theory of personality* (pp. 120–154). New York: Cambridge University Press.

Pike, J. J., & Jennings, N. A. (2005). The effects of commercials on children's perceptions of gender appropriate toy use. *Sex Roles, 52,* 83–91.

Pillemer, D. B. (1998). *Momentous events: Vivid memories.* Cambridge, MA: Harvard University Press.

Pine, D. S. (2009). A social neuroscience approach to adolescent depression. In M. de Haan & M. R. Gunnar (Eds.), *Handbook of developmental social neuroscience.* New York: Guilford.

Pinel, J. P. J. (2009). *Biopsychology* (7th ed.). Upper Saddle River, NJ: Prentice-Hall.

Pinel, P., & Dehaene, S. (2009). Beyond hemispheric dominance: Brain regions underlying the joint lateralization of language and arithmetic to the left hemiphere. *Journal of Cognitive Neuroscience.* (in press)

Pines, A. M., & Maslach, C. (2002). *Experiencing social psychology* (4th ed.). New York: McGraw-Hill.

Pinker, S. (1994). *The language instinct.* New York: William Morrow.

Pinker, S. (2007). The mystery of consciousness. *Time, 169,* 58–62.

Piolino, P., Desgranges, B., Clarys, D., Guillery-Girard, B., Taconnat, L., Isingrini, M., & Eustache, F. (2006). Autobiographical memory, autonoetic consciousness, and self-perspective in aging. *Psychology and Aging, 21,* 510–525.

Pittenger, D. J. (2005). Cautionary comments regarding the Myers-Briggs Type Indicator. *Consulting Psychology Journal: Practice and Research, 57,* 210–221.

Plant, E. A., & Peruche, B. M. (2005). The consequences of race for police officers' responses to criminal suspects. *Psychological Science, 16,* 180–183.

Plante, G. E. (2006). Sleep and vascular disorders. *Metabolism, 55, Suppl. 2,* S45–S49.

Plomin, R., & Craig, I. (2001). Genetics, environment, and cognitive abilities: Review and work in progress toward a genome scan for quantitative trait locus associations using DNA pooling. *British Journal of Psychiatry, 40,* 41–48.

Plomin, R., DeFries, J. C., McClearn, G. E., & McGuffin, P. (2009). *Biological psychology and neuroscience* (5th ed.). New York: Worth.

Poisnel, G., Dhilly, M., Boisselier, R. L., Barre, L., & Debruyne, D. (2009). Comparison of five benzodiapine-receptor agnosts on buprenorphine-induced mu-opoid receptor regulation. *Journal of Pharmacological Sciences, 110,* 36–46.

Pollack, M. H. (2009). Refractory generalized anxiety disorder. *Journal of Clinical Psychiatry, 70, Suppl. 2,* S32–S38.

Pomerantz, E. M., Saxon, J. L., & Oishi, S. (2000). The psychological trade-offs of goal investment. *Journal of Personality and Social Psychology, 79,* 617–630.

Pompili, M., Amador, X. F., Girardi, P., Harkavy-Friedman, J., & others. (2007). Suicide risk in schizophrenia: Learning from the past to change the future. *Annals of General Psychiatry, 6,* 10.

Pomplum, M., Reingold, E. M., & Shen, J. (2001). Investigating the visual span in comparative search: The effects of task difficulty and divided attention. *Cognition, 81,* B57–67.

Poon, M. W. (2009). Hypnosis for complex trauma survivors: Four case studies. *American Journal of Hypnosis, 51,* 263–271.

Popenoe, D. (2007). *The future of marriage in America.* New Brunswick, NJ: Rutgers University, The Marriage Project.

Popenoe, D., & Whitehead, B. D. (2006). *The state of our unions: 2006.* New Brunswick, NJ: The National Marriage Project.

Popeo, D. M. (2009). Electroconvulsive therapy for depressive episodes: A brief review. *Geriatrics, 64,* 9–12.

Popp, A. (2006, November). *Inequality and segregation as correlates of urban crime rates.* Paper presented at the annual meeting of the American Society of Criminology (ASC), Los Angeles.

Porter, S., & ten Brinke, L. (2008). Reading between the lies: Identifying concealed and falsified emotions in universal facial expressions. *Psychological Science, 19,* 508–514.

Portnuff, C. D. F., & Fligor, B. J. (October, 2006). *Output levels of portable music players.* Presented at the American Auditory Society Conference, Cincinnati.

Posada, G. (2008). Attachment. In M. M. Haith & J. B. Benson (Eds.), *Encyclopedia of infant and early childhood development.* Oxford, England: Elsevier.

Posner J., Russell J., & Peterson, B. S. (2005). The circumplex model of affect: An integrative approach to affective neuroscience, cognitive development, and psychopathology. *Developmental Psychopathology, 17,* 715–734.

Posner, M. I., & Rothbart, M. K. (2007). Research on attention networks as a model for integration of psychological science. *Annual Review of Psychology* (vol. 58). Palo Alto, CA: Annual Reviews.

Postel, M. G., de Jong, C. A. J., de Haan, H. A. (2005). Does e-therapy for problem drinking reach hidden populations? *American Journal of Psychiatry, 162,* 2393.

Postmes, T., & Jetten, J. (2006). Reconciling individuality and the group. In T. Postmes & J. Jetten (Eds.), *Individuality and the group: Advances in social identity* (pp. 258–269). Thousand Oaks, CA: Sage.

Potkin, S. G., Turner, J. A., Guffanti, G., Lakatos, A., Fallon, J. H., Nguyen, D. D., Mathalon, D., Ford, J., Lauriello, J., & Macciardi, F. (2009). A genome-wide association study of schizophrenia using brain activation as a quantitative phenotype. *Schizophrenia Bulletin, 35,* 96–108.

Powell, R. A., Symbaluk, D. G., & Honey, P. L. (2009). *Introduction to learning and behavior* (3rd ed.). Belmont, CA: Cengage.

Power, F. C., Narvaez, D., Nuzzi, R., Lapsley, D., & Hunt, T. (Eds.). (2008). *Moral education: A handbook.* Westport, CT: Praeger/Greenwood.

Prescott, T. J., & Humphries, M. D. (2007). Who dominates the dark basements of the brain? *Behavioral and Brain Sciences, 30,* 104–105.

Pressman, J. (1998). *Last resort, Psychosurgery and the limits of medicine.* New York: Cambridge University Press.

Preston, T. J., Kourtzi, Z., & Welchman, A. E. (2009). Adaptive estimation of three-dimensional structure in the human brain. *Journal of Neuroscience, 29,* 1688–1699.

Price, D. D., Finniss, D. G., & Benedetti, F. (2008). A comprehensive review of the placebo effect. *Annual Review of Psychology, 59,* 565–590.

Prochaska, J. O., DiClemente, C. C., & Norcross, J. C. (1992). In search of how people change: Applications to addictive behaviors. *American Psychologist, 47,* 1102–1114.

Prochaska, J. O., & Norcross, J. C. (2010). *Systems of psychotherapy* (7th ed.). Pacific Grove, CA: Brooks/Cole. (in press)

Prochaska, J. O., Norcross, J. C., & DiClemente, C. C. (1994). *Changing for good: A revolutionary six-stage program for overcoming bad habits and moving your life positively forward.* New York: Avon Books.

Provenzo, E. F. (2002). *Teaching, learning, and schooling in American culture: A critical perspective.* Boston: Allyn & Bacon.

Provine, R. R., Spencer, R. J., & Mandell, D. L. (2007). Emotional expression online: Emoticons punctuate website text messages. *Journal of Language and Social Psychology, 26,* 299–307.

Puddicombe, A. (2008). Meditation in the workplace. *Management-Issues.* http://www.management-issues.com/2008/1/8/opinion/meditation-in-the-workplace.asp (accessed February 24, 2009)

Pukrop, R., Sass, H., & Steinmeyer, E. M. (2000). Circumplex models for the similarity relationships between higher-order factors of personality and personality disorders: An empirical analysis. *Contemporary Psychiatry, 41,* 438–445.

Pulver, C. A., & Kelly, K. R. (2008). Incremental validity of the Myers-Briggs Type Indicator in predicting academic major selection of undecided university students. *Journal of Career Assessment, 16,* 441–455.

Q

Qian, Z. (2009). Mate selection. In D. Carr (Ed.), *Encyclopedia of the life course and human development.* Boston: Gale Cengage.

Quera Salva, M. A., Vanier, B., Laredo, J., Hartley, S., Chapotot, F., Moulin, C., Lofaso, F., & Guilleminault, C. (2007). Major depressive disorder, sleep EEG, and agomelatine: An open-label study. *International Journal of Neuropsychopharmacology, 10,* 691–696.

Quinn, J. G., & McConnell, J. (2006). The interval for interference in conscious visual imagery. *Memory, 14,* 241–252.

Quintero-Gallego, E. A., Gomez, C. M., Casares, E. V., Marquez, J., & Perez-Santamaria, F. J. (2006). Declarative and procedural learning in children and adolescents with posterior fossa tumors. *Behavioral and Brain Functions, 15,* 9.

R

Rabasca, L. (2000, June). More psychologists in the trenches. *Monitor on Psychology, 31,* 50–51.

Rachlin, H., & Green, L. (2009). The neural basis of drug craving: An incentive-sensitization theory of addiction. In D. Shanks (Ed.), *Psychology of learning.* Thousand Oaks, CA: Sage.

Rachman, S. (2009). Psychological treatment of anxiety: The evolution of behavior therapy and cognitive-behavior therapy. *Annual Review of Clinical Psychology* (vol. 5). Palo Alto, CA: Annual Reviews.

Ragland, J. D., McCarthy, E., Bilker, W. B., Brensinger, C. M., Valdez, J., Kohler, C., Gur, R. E., & Gur, R. C. (2006). Levels-of-processing effect on internal source monitoring in schizophrenia. *Psychological Medicine, 36,* 641–648.

Rahman, Q. (2005). The neurodevelopment of human sexual orientation. *Neuroscience & Biobehavioral Reviews, 29,* 1057–1066.

Raichle, M. E., & Mintun, M. A. (2006). Brain work and brain imaging. *Annual Review of Neuroscience* (vol. 29). Palo Alto, CA: Annual Reviews.

Raine, A. (2008). From genes to brain to antisocial behavior. *Current Directions in Psychological Science, 17,* 323–328.

Raine, A., Lencz, T., Bihrle, S., LaCasse, L., & Colletti, P. (2000). Reduced prefrontal gray matter volume and reduced autonomic activity in antisocial personality disorder. *Archives of General Psychiatry, 57,* 119–127.

Raine, A., Venables, P. H., & Williams, M. (1990). Relationships between N1, P300 and CNV recorded at age 15 and criminal behavior at age 24. *Psychophysiology, 27,* 567–575.

Ram, N., Morelli, S., Lindberg, C., & Carstensen, L. L. (2008). From static to dynamic: The ongoing dialetic about human development. In K. W. Schaie & R. P. Abeles (Eds.), *Social structures and aging individuals.* Mahwah, NJ: Erlbaum.

Ramey, C. T., Ramey, S. L., & Lanzi, R. G. (2006). Children's health and education. In W. Damon & R. Lerner (Eds.), *Handbook of child psychology* (6th ed.). New York: Wiley.

Ramirez-Esparza, N., Gosling, S. D., Benet-Martinez, V., Potter, J. P., & Pennebaker, J. W. (2006). Do bilinguals have two personalities? A special case of cultural frame switching. *Journal of Research in Personality, 40,* 99–120.

Ramon, E., Mao, X., & Ridge, K. D. (2009). Studies on the stability of the human cone visual pigments. *Photochemistry and Photobiology, 85,* 509–516.

Ramon, J. M., & Bruguera, E. (2009). Real world study to evaluate the effectiveness of varenicline and cognitive-behavioral interventions for smoking cessation. *International Journal of Environmental Research and Public Health, 6,* 1530–1538.

Ramsey, J. L., Langlois, J. H., Hoss, R. A., Rubenstein, A. J., & Griffin, A. M. (2004) Origins of a stereotype: Categorization of facial attractiveness by 6-month-old infants. *Developmental Science 7* (2), 201–211.

Ranta, K., Kaltiaia-Heino, R., Rantanen, P., & Marttunen, M. (2009). Social phobia in Finnish general adolescent population: Prevalence, comorbidity, individual and family correlates, and service use. *Depression and Anxiety.* (in press)

Rao, U., Hammen, C. L., & Poland, R. E. (2009). Risk markers for depression in adolescents: Sleep and HPA measures. *Neuropsychopharmacology.* (in press)

Rapaport, D. (1967). On the psychoanalytic theory of thinking. In M. M. Gill (Ed.), *The collected papers of David Rapaport.* New York: Basic Books.

Rapaport, S. (1994, November 28). Interview. *U.S. News and World Report,* 94.

Rapee, R. M., Gaston, J. E., & Abbott, M. J. (2009). Testing the efficacy of theoretically derived improvements in the treatment of social phobia. *Journal of Consulting and Clinical Psychology, 77,* 317–327.

Raposo, A., Han, S., & Dobbins, I. G. (2009). Ventrolateral prefrontal cortex and self-initiated semantic elaboration during memory retrieval. *Neuropsychologia.* (in press)

Ratan, R. R., & Noble, M. (2009). Novel multimodal strategies to promote brain and spinal cord injury recovery. *Storke, 40, Suppl. 3,* S130–S132.

Rathunde, K., & Csikszentmihalyi, M. (2006). The developing person: An experiential perspective. In W. Damon & R. Lerner (Eds.), *Handbook of child psychology* (6th ed.). New York: Wiley.

Ratner, N. B. (1993). Learning to speak. *Science, 262,* 260.

Rauch, S. L., Shin, L. M., & Phelps, E. A. (2006). Neurocircuitry models of posttraumatic stress disorder and extinction: Human neuroimaging research—past, present, and future. *Biological Psychiatry, 60,* 376–382.

Ravassard, P., & others. (2009). Paradoxical (REM) sleep deprivation causes a large and rapidly reversible decrease in long-term potentiation, synaptic transmission, glutamate receptor protein levels, and ERK/MAPK activation in the dorsal hippocampus. *Sleep, 32,* 227–240.

Rawson, N. E., & Yee, K. K. (2006). Transduction and coding. *Advances in Otorhinolaryngology, 63,* 23–43.

Ray, R. D., Ochsner, K. N., Cooper, J. C., Robertson, E. R., Gabrieli, J. D. E., & Gross, J. J. (2005). Individual differences in trait rumination and the neural systems supporting cognitive reappraisal. *Cognitive, Affective & Behavioral Neuroscience, 5,* 156–168.

Ray, W. J. (2009). *Methods toward a science of behavior and experience* (9th ed.). Belmont, CA: Wadsworth.

Raynor, H. A., Jeffrey, R. W., Phelan, S., Hill, J. O., & Wing, R. R. (2005). Amount of food groups variety consumed in the diet and long term weight loss maintenance. *Obesity Research, 13,* 883–890.

Recanzone, G. H., & Sutter, M. L. (2008). The biological basis of audition. *Annual Review of Psychology* (vol. 59). Palo Alto, CA: Annual Reviews.

Rector, N. A., & Beck, A. T. (2001). Cognitive behavioral therapy for schizophrenia: An empirical review. *Journal of Nervous and Mental Disorders, 189,* 278–287.

Recupero, P. R., & Rainey, S. E. (2006). Characteristics of E-therapy, web sites. *Journal of Clinical Psychiatry, 67,* 1435–1440.

Reder, L. M., Park, H., & Kieffaber, P. D. (2009). Memory systems do not divide on consciousness: Reinterpreting memory in terms of activation and binding. *Psychological Bulletin, 135,* 23–49.

Redondo, J. L., Fernandez, J., Garcia, I., & Ortigosa, P. M. (2009). Solving the multiple competitive facilities location and design problem on the plane. *Evolutionary Computation, 17,* 21–53.

Reeve, C. (2000, May 1). Use the body's repair kit. *Time, 155,* 18.

Reeve, C. L., & Charles, J. E. (2008). Survey of opinions on the primacy of *g* and social consequences of ability testing: A comparison of expert and non-expert views. *Intelligence, 36,* 681–688.

Reger, M. A., & Gahm, G. A. (2009). A meta-analysis of the effects of internet- and computer-based cognitive-behavioral treatments for anxiety. *Journal of Clinical Psychology, 65,* 53–75.

Reich, J. (2009). Avoidant personality disorder and its relationship to social phobia. *Current Psychiatry Reports, 11,* 89–93.

Reimer, T., & Rieskamp, J. (2007). Fast and frugal heuristics. In R. F. Baumeister & K. D. Vohs (Eds.), *Encyclopedia of social psychology.* Thousand Oaks, CA: Sage.

Reis, H. T., Sheldon, K. M., Gable, S. L., Roscoe, J., & Ryan, R. M. (2000). Daily well-being: The role of autonomy, competence, and relatedness. *Personality and Social Psychology Bulletin, 26,* 419–435.

Reitz, C., Honig, L., Vonsattel, J. P., Tang, M. X,, & Mayeux, R. (2009). Memory performance is related to amyloid and tau pathology in the hippocampus. *Journal of Neurology, Neurosurgery, and Psychiatry.* (in press)

Reivich, K., & Gillham, J. (2003). Learned optimism: The measurement of explanatory style. In S. J. Lopez & C. R. Snyder (Eds.), *Positive psychological assessment: A handbook of models and measures.* (pp. 57–74). Washington, DC: American Psychological Association.

Rendell, P. G., & Craik, F. I. M. (2000). Virtual week and actual week: Age-related differences in prospective memory. *Applied Cognitive Psychology, 14,* S43–S62.

Rescorla, R. A. (1966). Predictability and number of pairings in Pavlovian fear conditioning. *Psychonomic Science, 4,* 383–384.

Rescorla, R. A. (1988). Pavlovian conditioning: It's not what you think it is. *American Psychologist, 43,* 151–160.

Rescorla, R. A. (2003). Contemporary study of Pavlovian conditioning. *Spanish Journal of Psychology, 6,* 185–195.

Rescorla, R. A. (2004). Spontaneous recovery varies inversely with the training-extinction interval. *Learning and Behavior, 32,* 401–408.

Rescorla, R. A. (2005). Spontaneous recovery of excitation but not inhibition. *Journal of Experimental Psychology: Animal Behavior Processes, 31,* 277–288.

Rescorla, R. A. (2006a). Stimulus generalization of excitation and inhibition. *Quarterly Journal of Experimental Psychology, 59,* 53–67.

Rescorla, R. A. (2006b). Spontaneous recovery from overexpectation. *Learning and Behavior, 34,* 13–20.

Rescorla, R. A. (2006c). Deepened extinction from compound stimulus presentation. *Journal of Experimental Psychology: Animal Behavior Processes, 32(2),* 135–144.

Rescorla, R. A. (2009). A theory of Pavlovian conditioning: Variations in the effectiveness of reinforcement and nonreinforcement. In D. Shanks (Ed.), *Psychology of learning.* Thousand Oaks, CA: Sage.

Rescorla, R. A., & Wagner, A. R. (2009). A theory of attention: Variations in the associability of stimuli with reinforcement. In D. Shanks (Ed.), *Psychology of learning.* Thousand Oaks, CA: Sage.

Rethorst, C. D., Wipfli, B. M., & Landers, D. M. (2009). The antidepressive effects of exercise: A meta-analysis of randomized trials. *Sports Medicine, 39,* 491–511.

Reuter-Lorenz, P., & Davidson, R. J. (1981). Differential contributions of the two cerebral hemispheres to the perception of happy and sad faces. *Neuropsychologia, 19,* 609–613.

Revelle, W. (2008). The contribution of reinforcement sensitivity theory to personality theory. In P. J. Corr (Ed.), *The reinforcement sensitivity theory of personality* (pp. 508–527). New York: Cambridge University Press.

Reverberi, C., Shallice, T., D'Agostini, S., Skrap, M., & Bonatti, L. L. (2009). Cortical bases of elementary deductive reasoning, inference, memory, and metadeduction. *Neuropsychologia, 47,* 1107–1116.

Reynolds, C. R., Livingston, R., & Willson, V. (2006). *Measurement and assessment in education.* Boston: Allyn & Bacon.

Rhee, S., & Waldman, I. D. (2007). Behavior-genetics of criminality and aggression. In D. J. Flannery, A. T. Vazsonyi, & I. D. Waldman (Eds.), *The Cambridge handbook of violent behavior and aggression* (pp. 77–90). New York: Cambridge University Press.

Ribases, M., Gratacos, M., Fernandez-Aranda, F., & others. (2004). Association of BDNF with anorexia, bulimia and age of onset of weight loss in six European populations. *Human Molecular Genetics, 13,* 1205–1212.

Ritchie, E. C., Benedek, D., Malone, R., & Carr-Malone, R. (2006). Psychiatry and the military: An update. *Psychiatric Clinics of North America, 29,* 695–707.

Ritskes, R., Ritskes-Hoitinga, M., Stodkilde-Jorgensen, H., Baerentsen, K., & Hartman, T. (2003). MRI scanning during Zen meditation: The picture of enlightenment? *Constructivism in the Human Sciences, 8* (1), 85–90.

Ritter, D., & Elsea, M. (2005). Hot sauce, toy guns, and graffiti: A critical account of current laboratory aggression paradigms. *Aggressive Behavior, 31,* 407–419.

Rizzolatti, G., & Craighero, L. (2004). The mirror-neuron system. *Annual Review of Neuroscience, 27,* 169–192.

Ro, H. S., & Wampler, R. S. (2009). What's wrong with these people? Clinicians' views of clinical couples. *Journal of Marital and Family Therapy, 35,* 3–17.

Roberts, B., Walton, K. E., & Viechtbauer, W. (2006). Patterns of mean level change in personality traits across the life course: A meta-analysis of longitudinal studies. *Psychological Bulletin, 132,* 1–25.

Roberts, B., Wood, D., & Caspi, A. (2008). Personality development. In O. P. John, R. W., Robins, & L. A. Pervin (Eds.), *Handbook of personality: Theory and research* (3rd ed.). New York: Guilford.

Roberts, B. W., Caspi, A., & Moffitt, T. E. (2003). Work experiences and personality development in young adulthood. *Journal of Personality and Social Psychology, 84,* 582–593.

Roberts, B. W., Jackson, J. J., Fayard, J. V., Edmonds, G., & Meints, J. O. (2009). Conscien-tiousness. In M. Leary & R. Hoyle (Eds.), *Handbook of individual differences in social behavior* (pp. 369–381). New York: Guilford.

Roberts, B. W., Kuncel, N., Shiner, R. N., Caspi, A., & Goldberg, L. (2007). The power of personality: A comparative analysis of the predictive validity of personality traits, SES, and IQ. *Perspectives on Psychological Science, 2,* 313–345.

Roberts, B. W., & Mroczek, D. (2008). Personality trait change in adulthood. *Current Directions in Psychological Science, 17,* 31–35.

Robertson, H., & Pryor, R. (2006). Memory and cognitive effects of ECT: Informing and assessing patients. *Advances in Psychiatric Treatment, 12,* 228–237.

Robinson, A., Shore, B. M., & Enersen, D. L. (2007). Best practices in gifted education: An evidence-based guide. Waco, TX: Prufrock Press.

Robinson-Riegler, G., & Robinson-Riegler, B. (2008). *Cognitive psychology* (2nd ed.). Upper Saddle River, NJ: Prentice-Hall.

Robinson-Wood, T. L. (2009). *The convergence of race, ethnicity, and gender* (3rd ed.). Upper Saddle River, NJ: Prentice-Hall.

Rodgers, J. L. (2007). The shape of things to come: Diagnosing social contagion from adolescent smoking and drinking curves. In T. D. Little, J. A. Bovaird, & N. A. Card (Eds), *Modeling contextual effects in longitudinal studies* (pp. 343–362). Mahwah, NJ: Erlbaum.

Rodin, J. (1984, December). Interview: A sense of control. *Psychology Today,* 38–45.

Rodrigues, S., Le Doux, J., & Sapolsky, R. M. (2009). The influence of stress hormones on fear circuitry. *Annual Review of Neuroscience* (vol. 32). Palo Alto, CA: Annual Reviews.

Roediger, H. L., & Marsh, E. J. (2003). Episodic and autobiographical memory. In I. B. Weiner (Ed.), *Handbook of psychology* (vol. 4). New York: Wiley.

Rogers, C. R. (1961). *On becoming a person.* Boston: Houghton Mifflin.

Rogers, G., & others. (2009). The harmful health effects of recreational ecstasy: A systematic review of observational evidence. *Health Technology Assessment, 13,* 1–315.

Rosa-Alcazar, A. I., Sanchez-Meca, J., Gomez-Conesa, A., & Marin-Martinez, F. (2008). Psychological treatment of obsessive-compulsive disorder: A meta-analysis. *Clinical Psychology Review, 28,* 1310–1325.

Rosack, J. (2007). Impact of FDA warning questioned in suicide rise. *Psychiatric News, 5,* 1.

Rose, A. J. (2002). Co-rumination in the friendships of girls and boys. *Child Development, 73,* 1830–1843.

Rose, A. J., Carlson, W., & Waller, E. M. (2007). Prospective associations of co-rumination with friendship and emotional adjustment: Considering the sociemotional trade-offs of co-rumination. *Developmental Psychology, 43,* 1019–1031.

Rose, A. J., & Smith, R. L. (2009). Sex differences in peer relationships. In K. H. Rubin, W. M. Bukowski, & B. Laursen (Eds.), *Handbook of peer interactions, relationships, and groups.* New York: Guilford.

Rose, R. J., Koskenvuo, M., Kaprio, J., Sarna, S., & Langinvainio, H. (1988). Shared genes, shared experiences, and similarity of personality: Data from 14,228 adult Finnish co-twins. *Journal of Personality and Social Psychology, 54,* 161–171.

Rosen, K., & Garety, P. (2005). Predicting recovery from schizophrenia: A retrospective comparison of characteristics at onset of people with single and multiple episodes. *Schizophrenia Bulletin, 31,* 735–750.

Rosenbaum, R. S., Kohler, S., Schacter, D. L., Moscovitch, M., Westmacott, R., Black, S. E., Gao, F., & Tulving, E. (2005). The case of K.C.: Contributions of a memory-impaired person to memory theory. *Neuropsychologia, 43,* 989–1021.

Rosenhan, D. L. (1973). On being sane in insane places. *Science, 179,* 250–258.

Rosenthal, R. (1966). *Experimenter effects in behavioral research.* New York: Appleton-Century-Crofts.

Rosenthal, R., & DiMatteo, M. R. (2001). Meta-analysis: Recent developments in quantitative methods for literature reviews. *Annual Review of Psychology, 52,* 59–62.

Rosenthal, R., & Jacobsen, L. (1968). *Pygmalion in the classroom.* Fort Worth: Harcourt Brace.

Rosmarin, D. H., Krumrei, E. J., & Andersson, G. (2009). Religion as a predictor of psychological distress in two religious communities. *Cognitive Behavior Therapy, 38,* 54–64.

Rosnow, R. L., & Rosenthal, R. (2008). *Beginning behavioral research* (6th ed.). Upper Saddle River, NJ: Prentice-Hall.

Ross, C. A., Margolis, R. L., Reading, S. A., Pletnikov, M., & Coyle, J. T. (2006). Neurobiology of schizophrenia. *Neuron, 52,* 139–153.

Ross, K., Handel, P. J., Clark, E. M., & Vander Wal, J. S. (2009a). The relationship between religion and religious coping: Religious coping as a moderator between coping and adjustment. *Journal of Religion and Health.*

Ross, K. M., Milsom, V. A., Debraganza, N., Gibbons, L. M., Murawski, M. E., & Perri, M. G. (2009b). The contributions of weight loss and increased physical fitness to improvements in health-related quality of life. *Eating Behaviors, 10,* 84–88.

Ross, L., Kohler, C. L., Grimley, D. M., & Anderson-Lewis, C. (2007). The theory of reasoned action and intention to seek cancer information. *American Journal of Health Behavior, 31,* 123–134.

Ross, R. S., Brown, T. I., & Stern, C. E. (2009). The retrieval of learned sequences engages the hippocampus: Evidence from fMRI. *Hippocampus.* (in press)

Rossi, E. L. (2009). The psychosocial genomics of therapeutic hypnosis, psychotherapy, and rehabilitation. *American Journal of Clinical Hypnosis, 51,* 281–298.

Roten, R. G. (2007). DSM-IV and the taxonomy of roles: How can the taxonomy of roles complement the DSM-IV to create a more holistic diagnostic tool? *The Arts in Psychotherapy, 34,* 53–68.

Rotge, J. Y., & others. (2009). Inverse relationship between thalamic and orbitofrontal volumes in obsessive-compulsive disorder. *Progress in Neuro-Psychopharmacology & Biological Psychiatry, 33,* 682–686.

Rothbart, M. K., & Gartstein, M. A. (2008). Temperament. In M. M. Haith & J. B. Benson (Eds.), *Encyclopedia of infant and early childhood development.* London: Elsevier.

Rowe, J. W., & Kahn, R. L. (1997). *Successful aging.* New York: Pantheon.

Roy, A. K., & others. (2009). Functional connectivity of the human amygdala using resting state fMRI. *NeuroImage, 45,* 614–626.

Rubin, K. H., Bukowski, W. M., & Parker, J. G. (2006). Peer interactions, relationships, and groups. In W. Damon & R. Lerner (Eds.), *Handbook of child psychology* (6th ed.). New York: Wiley.

Rubin, Z., & Mitchell, C. (1976). Couples research as couples counseling: Some unintended effects of studying close relationships. *American Psychologist, 31,* 17–25.

Ruble, D. N., Martin, C. L., & Berenbaum, S. A. (2006). Gender development. In W. Damon & R. Lerner (Eds.), *Handbook of child psychology* (6th ed.). New York: Wiley.

Ruck, C. (2003). Psychosurgery. *Journal of Neurosurgery, 99,* 1113–1114.

Rudy, D., & Grusec, J. E. (2006). Authoritarian parenting in individualist and collectivist groups: Associations with maternal emotion and cognition and children's self-esteem. *Journal of Family Psychology, 20,* 68–78.

Ruini, C., Belaise, C., Brombin, C., Caffo, E., & Fava, G. A. (2006). Well-being therapy in school settings: A pilot study. *Psychotherapy and Psychosomatics, 75,* 331–336.

Ruini, C., & Fava, G. A. (2004). Clinical applications of well-being therapy. In A. Linley & S. Joseph (Eds.), *Positive psychology in practice* (pp. 371–387). Hoboken, NJ: Wiley.

Ruini, C., & Fava, G. A. (2009). Well-being therapy for generalized anxiety disorder. *Journal of Clinical Psychology, 65,* 510–519.

Runyon, W. M. (2007). *Psychology and historical interpretation.* New York: Oxford University Press.

Rusbult, C. E., Kumashiro, M., Coolsen, M. K., & Kirchner, J. L. (2004). Interdependence, closeness, and relationships. In D. J. Mashek & A. P. Aaron (Eds.), *Handbook of closeness and intimacy.* (pp. 137–161). Mahwah, NJ: Erlbaum.

Rush, C. C., Becker, S. J., & Curry, J. F. (2009). Personality factors and styles among college students who binge eat and drink. *Psychology of Addictive Behaviors, 23,* 140–145.

Rustin, J. (2009). The interface of self psychology, infant research, and neuroscience in clinical practice. *Annals of the New York Academy of Sciences, 1159,* 204–217.

Rutter, M. (2007a). Gene-environment interplay and developmental psychopathology. In A. S. Masten (Ed.), *Multilevel dynamics in developmental psychology.* Mahwah, NJ: Erlbaum.

Ryan, M. P. (2008). The antidepressant effects of physical activity: Mediating self-esteem and self-efficacy mechanisms. *Psychology and Health, 23,* 279–307.

Ryan, R. M., & Deci, E. L. (2000). Self-determination theory and the facilitation of intrinsic motivation, social development, and well-being. *American Psychologist, 55,* 68–78.

Ryan, R. M., & Deci, E. L. (2001). On happiness and human potentials: A review of research on hedonic and eudaimonic well-being. *Annual Review of Psychology* (vol. 52). Palo Alto, CA: Annual Reviews.

Ryan, R. M., Huta, V., & Deci, E. L. (2008). Living well: A self-determination theory perspective on eudaimonia. *Journal of Happiness Studies, 9,* 139–170.

Ryding, E., Ahnlide, J. A., Lindstrom, M., Rosen, I., & Traskman-Bendz, L. (2006). Regional brain serotonin and dopamine transport binding capacity in suicide attempters relate to impulsiveness and mental energy. *Psychiatry Research, 148,* 195–203.

Ryff, C. D., & Singer, B. (1998). Contours of positive human health. *Psychological Inquiry, 9,* 1–28.

Ryff, C. D., Singer, B. H., & Love, G. D. (2004). Positive health: Connecting well-being with biology. *Philosophical Transactions of the Royal Society of London, 359,* 1383–1394.

Rymer, R. (1993). *Genie.* New York: HarperCollins.

S

Saad, L. (2008, December 26). Obama, Hillary Clinton share "Most Admired" billing. Gallup Press Release. http://www.gallup.com/poll/113572/Obama-Hillary-Clinton-Share-Most-Admired-Billing.aspx (accessed January 19, 2009)

Saarni, C., Campos, J. J., Camras, L. A., & Witherington, D. (2006). Emotional development: Action, communication, and understanding. In W. Damon & R. Lerner (Eds.), *Handbook of child psychology* (6th ed.). New York: Wiley.

Sacco, D. F., & Hugenberg, K. (2009). The look of anger and fear: Facial maturity modulates recognition of fearful and angry expressions. *Emotion, 9,* 39–49.

Sachdev, P. S., & Chen, X. (2009). Neurosurgical treatment of mood disorders: Traditional psychosurgery and the advent of deep brain stimulation. *Current Opinion in Psychiatry, 22,* 25–31.

Sachs, J. (2009). Communication development in infancy. In J. Berko Gleason & N. Ratner (Eds.), *The development of language* (7th ed.). Boston: Allyn & Bacon.

Sack, R. L. (2009). The pathology of jet lag. *Travel Medicine and Infectuous Disease, 7,* 102–110.

Sacks, O. (2006, June 19). Stereo Sue. *New Yorker,* 64–73.

Sadeghniiat-Haghighi, K., Aminian, O., Pouryaghoub, G., & Yazdi, Z. (2008). Efficacy and hypnotic effects of melatonin in shift-work nurses: double-blind, placebo-controlled crossover trial. *Journal of Circadian Rhythms, 6,* 10.

Sado, M., Knapp, M., Yamauchi, K., Fujisawa, D., So, M., Nakagawa, A., Kikuchi, T., & Ono, Y. (2009). Cost-effectiveness of combination therapy versus antidepressant therapy for management of depression in Japan. *Australian and New Zealand Journal of Psychiatry, 43,* 539–547.

Safren, S. A., & others. (2009). A randomized controlled trial of cognitive behavioral therapy for adherence and depression (CBT-AD) in HIV-infected individuals. *Health Psychology, 28,* 1–10.

Salkind, J. J. (Ed.). (2009). *Encyclopedia of educational psychology.* Thousand Oaks, CA: Sage.

Salthouse, T. A. (1994). The nature of the influence of speed on adult age differences in cognition. *Developmental Psychology, 30,* 240–259.

Salthouse, T. A. (2009). When does age-related cognitive decline begin? *Neurobiology of Aging, 30,* 507–514.

Salvia, J., Ysseldyke, J. E., & Bolt, S. (2010). *Assessment* (11th ed.). Boston: Cengage.

Sameroff, A. (2006). Identifying risk and protective factors for healthy child development. In A. Clarke-Stewart & J. Dunn (Eds.), *Families count.* New York: Oxford University Press.

Sampaio, C., & Brewer, W. F. (2009). The role of unconscious memory errors in judgments of confidence for sentence recognition. *Memory and Cognition, 37,* 158–163.

Sanchez-Burks, J. (2007). Cultural differences. In R. Baumeister & K. Vohs (Eds.), *Encyclopedia of social psychology.* Thousand Oaks: Sage.

Sandor, P. S., & Afra, J. (2005). Nonpharmacologic treatment of migraine. *Current Pain and Headache Reports, 9,* 202–205.

Sani, S., Shimamoto, S., Turner, R. S., Levesque, N., & Starr, P. A. (2009). Microelectrode recording in the posterior hypothalamic region in humans. *Neurosurgery, 64, Suppl. 3,* S161–S167.

Santtila, P., Sandnabba, N. K., Harlaar, N., Varjonen, M., Alanko, K., & von der Pahlen, B. (2008). Potential for homosexual response is prevalent and genetic. *Biological Psychology, 77,* 102–105.

Sapolsky, R. M. (2004). *Why zebras don't get ulcers* (3rd ed.). New York: Henry Holt.

Sar, V., Akyuz, G., & Dogan, O. (2007). Prevalence of dissociative disorders among women in the general population. *Psychiatry Research, 149,* 169–176.

Sar, V., Koyuncu, A., Ozturk, E., Yargic, L. I., Kundakci, T., Yazici, A., Kuskonmaz, E., & Aksut, D. (2007). Dissociative disorders in the psychiatric emergency ward. *General Hospital Psychiatry, 29,* 45–50.

Sarkar, U., Ali, S., & Whooley, M. A. (2009). Self-efficacy as a marker of cardiac function and predictor of heart failure hospitalization and mortality in patients with stable coronary heart disease: Findings from the Heart and Soul Study. *Health Psychology, 28,* 166–173.

Sarkar, U., Fisher, L., & Schillinger, D. (2006). Is self-efficacy associated with diabetes self-management across race/ethnicity and health literacy? *Diabetes Care, 29,* 323–329.

Sartor, C. E., Agrawal, A., Lynskey, M. T., Bucholz, K. K., Madden, P. A., & Heath, A. C. (2009). Common genetic influences on the timing of first use for alcohol, cigarettes, and cannibis in young African-American women. *Drug and Alcohol Dependence.* (in press)

Saucier, G. (2001, April). *Going beyond the big five.* Paper presented at the meeting of the Society for Research in Child Development, San Francisco.

Saul, S. (2006, March 8). Some sleeping pill users range far beyond bed. *New York Times.*

Saunders, F. W. (1991). *Katherine and Isabel: Mother's light, daughter's journey.* Palo Alto, CA: Consulting Psychologists Press.

Saurer, T. B., Ijames, S. G., Carrigan, K. A., & Lysle, D. T. (2008). Neuroimmune mechanisms of opioid-mediated conditioned immunomodulation. *Brain, Behavior, and Immunity, 22,* 89–97.

Sava, F. A., Yates, B. T., Lupu, V., Szentagotal, A., & David, D. (2009). Cost-effectiveness and cost-utility of cognitive therapy, rational emotive behavioral therapy, and fluoxetine (Prozac) in treating depression: A randomized clinical trial. *Journal of Clinical Psychology, 65,* 36–52.

Savage, J. (2008). The role of exposure to media violence in the etiology of violent behavior: A criminologist weighs in. *American Behavioral Scientist, 51,* 1123–1136.

Savage, J., & Yancey, C. (2008). The effects of media violence exposure on criminal aggression: A meta-analysis. *Criminal Justice and Behavior, 35,* 772–791.

Savin-Williams, R. (2006). *The new gay teenager.* Cambridge, MA: Harvard University Press.

Savin-Williams, R., & Diamond, L. (2004). Sex. In R. Lerner & L. Steinberg (Eds.), *Handbook of adolescent psychology* (2nd ed.). New York: Wiley.

Savitz J. B., & Ramesar R. S. (2004). Genetic variants implicated in personality: A review of the more promising candidates. *American Journal of Medical Genetics Part B, Neuropsychiatric Genetics, 131B,* 20–32.

Saxe, L. (1998, June). Commentary. *APA Monitor,* 30.

Sayal, K., Heron, J., Golding, J., & Emond, A. (2007). Prenatal alcohol exposure and gender differences in childhood mental health problems: A longitudinal population-based study. *Pediatrics, 119,* e426–e434.

Scarr, S. (1984, May). Interview. *Psychology Today,* 59–63.

Scarr, S. (1992). Keep our eyes on the prize: Family and child care policy in the United States, as it should be. In A. Booth (Ed.), *Child care in the 1990s: Trends and consequences* (pp. 215–222). Hillsdale, NJ: Erlbaum.

Scarr, S. (2000). Toward voluntary parenthood. *Journal of Personality, 68,* 615–623.

Schachter, S., & Singer, J. E. (1962). Cognitive, social, and physiological determinants of emotional state. *Psychological Review, 69,* 379–399.

Schacter, D. L. (2001). *The seven sins of memory.* Boston: Houghton Mifflin.

Schacter, D. L. (2007). Memory: Defining the core. In H. L. Roediger, Y. Dudai, & S. M. Fitzpatrick (Eds.), *Science of memory: Concepts.* New York: Oxford University Press.

Schacter, D. L., & Wagner, A. D. (2009). Learning and memory. In E. R. Kandel, J. R. Schwartz, & T. M. Jessell (Eds.), *Principles of neural science* (5th ed.). New York: McGraw-Hill. (in press)

Schaie, K. W. (1994). The life course of adult intellectual abilities. *American Psychologist, 49,* 304–313.

Schaie, K. W. (2006). Intelligence. In R. Schultz (Ed.), *Encyclopedia of aging* (4th ed.). New York: Springer.

Schaie, K. W. (2007). Generational differences: The age-cohort period model. In J. E. Birren & K. W. Schaie (Eds.), *Encyclopedia of gerontology.* Oxford, England: Elsevier.

Schaie, K. W. (2009). "When does age-related cognitive decline begin?" Salthouse again reifies the "cross-sectional fallacy." *Neurobiology of Aging, 30,* 528–529.

Schaie, K. W., & Zanjani, F. A. K. (2006). Intellectual development across adulthood. In C. Hoare (Ed.), *Handbook of adult development and learning.* New York: Oxford University Press.

Schank, R., & Abelson, R. (1977). *Scripts, plans, goals, and understanding.* Mahwah, NJ: Erlbaum.

Scheer, F. A., Hilton, M. F., Mantzoros, C. S., & Shea, S. A. (2009). Adverse metabolic and cardiovascular consequences for circadian misalignment. *Proceedings of the National Academy of Sciences USA, 106,* 4453–4458.

Scheier, M. F., & Carver, C. S. (1992). Effects of optimism on psychological and physical well-being: Theoretical overview and empirical update. *Cognitive Therapy and Research, 16,* 201–228.

Schienle, A., Schaefer, A., Stark, R., & Vaiti, D. (2009). Long-term effects of cognitive behavior therapy on brain activation in spider phobia. *Psychiatry Research, 172,* 99–102.

Schiffman, J., & Walker, E. (1998). Schizophrenia. In H. S. Friedman (Ed.), *Encyclopedia of mental health* (vol. 2). San Diego: Academic.

Schiller, D., Levy, I., Niv, Y., LeDoux, J. E., & Phelps, E. A. (2008). From fear to safety and back—reversal of fear in the human brain. *Journal of Neuroscience, 28,* 11517–11525.

Schinka, J. A., Busch, R. M., & Robichaux-Keene, N. (2004). A meta-analysis of the association between the serotonin transporter gene polymorphism (5-HTTLPR) and trait anxiety. *Molecular Psychiatry, 9,* 197–202.

Schkade, D. A., & Kahneman, D. (1998). Does living in California make people happy? A focusing illusion in judgments of life satisfaction. *Psychological Science, 9,* 340–346.

Schlosser, R. G., Nenadic, I., Wagner, G., Zysset, S., Koch, K., & Sauer, H. (2009). Dopaminergic modulation of brain systems subserving decision making under uncertainty: A study with fMRI and methylphenidate challenge. *Synapse, 63,* 429–442.

Schmader, T., Forbes, C. E., Zhang, S., & Berry Mendes, W. (2009). A metacognitive perspective on the cognitive deficits experiences in intellectually threatening environments. *Personality and Social Psychology Bulletin, 35,* 584–596.

Schmidt, N. B., & Koselka, M. (2000). Gender differences in patients with panic disorder: Evaluating cognitive mediation of phobic avoidance. *Cognitive Therapy and Research, 24,* 533–550.

Schmidtke, J. I., & Heller, W. (2004). Personality, affect, and EEG: Predicting patterns of regional brain activity related to extraversion and neuroticism. *Personality and Individual Differences, 36,* 717–732.

Schmiedek, F., Li, S. C., & Lindenberger, U. (2009). Interference and facilitation in spatial working memory: Age-associated differences in lure effects in the n-back paradigm. *Psychology and Aging, 24,* 203–210.

Schneider, D. W., & Logan, G. D. (2009). Selecting a response in task switching: Testing a model of compound cue retrieval. *Journal of Experimental Psychology: Learning, Memory, and Cognition, 35,* 122–136.

Schneider, K. J. (2002). Humanistic psychotherapy. In M. Hersen & W. H. Sledge (Eds.), *Encyclopedia of psychotherapy.* San Diego: Academic.

Schneider, K. J. (2009). Editor's commentary. *Journal of Humanistic Psychology, 49,* 6–8.

Schnitzer, M. (2009). New imaging methods. *Annual Review of Neuroscience* (vol. 32). Palo Alto, CA: Annual Reviews.

Schogol, J. (2009, January 6). Pentagon: No purple heart for PTSD. *Stars and Stripes.* http://www.stripes.com/article.asp?section=104&article=59810 (accessed March 27, 2009)

Scholnick, E. K. (2008). Formal operations from a twenty-first century perspective. *Human Development, 51,* 48–55.

Schomerus, G., Matschinger, H., & Angermeyer, M. C. (2009). Attitudes that determine willingness to seek psychiatric help for depression: A representative population survey applying the theory of planned behavior. *Psychological Medicine.* (in press)

Schooler, J. W. (2002). Re-representing consciousness: Dissociations between experience and meta-consciousness. *Trends in Cognitive Sciences, 6,* 339–344.

Schooler, J. W., Ambadar, Z., & Bendiksen, M. (1997). A cognitive corroborative case study approach for investigating discovered memories of sexual abuse. In J. D. Read & D. S. Lindsay (Eds.), *Recollections of trauma: Scientific evidence and clinical practice* (pp. 379–387). New York: Plenum Press.

Schooler, J. W., Ariely, D., & Loewenstein, G. (2003). The explicit pursuit and assessment of happiness can be self-defeating. In I. Brocas & J. Carrillo (Eds.), *The psychology of economic decisions.* Oxford, England: Oxford University Press.

Schooler, J. W., & Eich, E. (2000). Memory for emotional events. In E. Tulving & F. I. M. Craik (Eds.), *The Oxford handbook of memory* (pp. 379–392). New York: Oxford University Press.

Schredl, M. (2009). Dreams in patients with sleep disorders. *Sleep Medicine Reviews.* (in press)

Schredl, M., & Erlacher, D. (2008). Relation between waking sport activities, reading, and dream content in sport students and psychology students. *Journal of Psychology, 142,* 267–275.

Schuckit, M. A. (2009). Alcohol-use disorders. *Lancet, 373,* 492–501.

Schulenberg, J. E., & Zarrett, N. R. (2006). Mental health in emerging adulthood: Continuities and discontinuities in course, content, and meaning. In J. J. Arnett & J. Tanner (Eds.), *Advances in emerging adulthood.* Washington, DC: American Psychological Association.

Schultheiss, O. C., & Brunstein, J. C. (2005). An implicit motive perspective on competence. In A. J. Elliot & C. S. Dweck (Eds.), *Handbook of competence and motivation* (pp. 31–51). New York: Guilford.

Schultz, W. (2006). Behavioral theories and the neurophysiology of reward. *Annual Review of Psychology* (vol. 57). Palo Alto, CA: Annual Reviews.

Schultz, W., Dayan, P., & Montague, P. R. (1997). A neural substrate of prediction and reward. *Science, 275,* 1593–1599.

Schultz, W., Dayan, P., & Montague, P. R. (2009). Context, time, and memory retrieval in the interference paradigms of Pavlovian conditioning. In D. Shanks (Ed.), *Psychology of learning.* Thousand Oaks, CA: Sage.

Schultz, W. T. (Ed.) (2005). *The handbook of psychobiography.* New York: Oxford University Press.

Schultz-Bosbach, S., Tausche, P., & Weiss, C. (2009). Roughness perception during the rubber band illusion. *Brain and Cognition.* (in press)

Schulz, R. (2007). Cardiovascular health study. In K. S. Markides (Ed.), *Encyclopedia of health and aging.* Thousand Oaks, CA: Sage.

Schulz-Stubner, S., Krings, T., Meister, I. G., Rex, S., Thron, A., & Rossaint, R. (2004). Clinical hypnosis modulates functional magnetic resonance imaging signal intensities and pain perception in a thermal stimulation paradigm. *Regional Anesthesia and Pain Medicine, 29,* 549–556.

Schumann, A., John, U., Rumpf, H., Hapke, U., & Meyer, C. (2006). Changes in the "stages of change" as outcome measures of a smoking cessation intervention: A randomized controlled trial. *Preventive Medicine: An International Journal Devoted to Practice and Theory, 43,* 101–106.

Schunk, D. H. (2008). *Learning theories* (5th ed.). Upper Saddle River, NJ: Prentice-Hall.

Schunk, D. H., Pintrich, P. R., & Meece, J. L. (2008). *Motivation in education* (3rd ed.). Upper Saddle River, NJ: Prentice-Hall.

Schupak, C., & Rosenthal, J. (2009). Excessive daydreaming: A case history and discussion of mind wandering and high fantasy proneness. *Consciousness and Cognition, 18,* 290–292.

Schuz, B., Sniehotta, F. F., Mallach, N., Wiedemann, A. U., & Schwarzer, R. (2009). Predicting transitions from preintentional, intentional, and actional stages of change. *Health Education Research, 24,* 64–75.

Schwabe, L., Bohringer, A., & Wolf, O. T. (2009). Stress disrupts context-dependent memory. *Learning and Memory 16,* 110–113.

Schwartz, B., Ward, A. H., Monterosso, J., Lyubomirsky, S., White, K., & Lehman, D. (2002). Maximizing versus satisficing: Happiness is a matter of choice. *Journal of Personality and Social Psychology, 83,* 1178–1197.

Schwartz, R. H., Cooper, M. N., Oria, M., & Sheridan, M. J. (2003). Medical marijuana: A survey of teenagers and their parents. *Clinical Pediatrics, 42,* 547–551.

Scott, A. (2006). What I would say to a patient who asked me about this article. *Advances in Psychiatric Treatment, 12,* 237–238.

Scott, S. K., Rabito, F. A., Price, P. D., Butler, N. N., Schwartzbaum, J. A., Jackson, B. M., Love, R. L., & Harris, R. E. (2006). Comorbidity among the morbidly obese: A comparative study of 2002 U.S. hospital patient surcharges. *Surgery for Obesity and Related Disorders, 2,* 105–111.

Scott, T. R. (2000). Taste. In A. Kazdin (Ed.), *Encyclopedia of psychology.* Washington, DC, & New York: American Psychological Association and Oxford University Press.

Scott-Sheldon, L. A. J., & Johnson, B. T. (2006). Eroticizing creates safer sex: A research synthesis. *Journal of Primary Prevention, 27,* 619–640.

Seacat, J. D., & Mickelson, K. D. (2009). Stereotype threat and the exercise/dietary health intentions of overweight women. *Journal of Health Psychology, 14,* 556–567.

Sears, D. O. (2008). The American color line 50 years after *Brown v. Board:* Many "peoples of color" or Black exceptionalism? In G. Adams, M. Biernat, N. R. Branscombe, C. S. Crandall, & L. S. Wrightsman (Eds.), *Commemorating Brown: The social psychology of racism and discrimination.* Washington, DC: American Psychological Association.

Sears, D. O., & Henry, P. J. (2007). Symbolic racism. In R. Baumeister & K. Vohs (Eds.), *Encyclopedia of social psychology.* Newbury Park, CA: Sage.

Sedikides, C. (2007). Self-enhancement and self-protection: Powerful, pancultural, and functional. *Hellenic Journal of Psychology, 4,* 1–13.

Sedikides, C. (2009). On self-protection and self-enhancement regulation: The role of self-improvement and social norms. In J. P. Forgas, R. F. Baumeister, & D. Tice (Eds.), *The psychology of self-regulation.* New York: Psychology Press.

Sedikides, C., Gaertner, L., & Vevea, J. L. (2005). Pancultural self-enhancement reloaded: A meta-analytic reply to Heine (2005). *Journal of Personality and Social Psychology, 89,* 539–551.

Sedikides, C., & Gregg, A. P. (2008). Self-enchancement: Food for thought. *Perspectives on Psychological Science, 3,* 102–116.

Sedikides, C., & Skowronski, J. J. (2009). Social cognition and self-cognition: Two sides of the same evolutionary coin? *European Journal of Social Psychology.* (in press)

Segal, D. L., & Coolidge, F. L. (2004). Objective assessment of personality and psychopathology. In M. Hersen (Ed.), *Comprehensive handbook of psychological assessment* (vol. 2). New York: Wiley.

Segerstrom, S. C. (2003). Individual differences, immunity, and cancer: Lessons from personality psychology. *Brain, Behavior and Immunity, 17, Suppl. 1,* S92–S97.

Segerstrom, S. C. (2005). Optimism and immunity: Do positive thoughts always lead to positive effects? *Brain, Behavior and Immunity, 19,* 195–200.

Segerstrom, S. C. (2006). Breaking Murphy's law: How optimists get what they want from life and pessimists can too. New York: Guilford.

Seguin, M., Lesage, A., Chawky, N., Guy, A., Daigle, F., Girard, G., & Turecki, G. (2006) Suicide cases in New Brunswick from April 2002 to May 2003: The importance of better recognizing substance and mood disorder comorbidity. *Canadian Journal of Psychiatry, 51,* 581–586.

Selby, E. A., Anestis, M. D., Bender, T. W., & Joiner, T. E. (2009). An exploration of the emotional cascade model of borderline personality disorder. *Journal of Abnormal Psychology, 118,* 375–387.

Seligman, M. E. P. (1970). On the generality of the laws of learning. *Psychological Review, 77,* 406–418.

Seligman, M. E. P. (1975). *Helplessness: On depression, development and death.* San Francisco: Freeman.

Seligman, M. E. P. (1990). *Learned optimism.* New York: Knopf.

Seligman, M. E. P. (1994). *What you can change and what you can't.* New York: Knopf.

Seligman, M. E. P. (2000). Positive psychology. In J. E. Gillham (Ed.), *The science of optimism and hope: Research essays in honor of Martin E. P. Seligman* (pp. 415–429). West Conshohocken, PA: Templeton Foundation Press.

Seligman, M. E. P., & Csikszentmihalyi, M. (2000). Positive psychology: An introduction. *American Psychologist, 55,* 5–14.

Seligman, M. E. P., & Pawelski, J. O. (2003). Positive psychology: FAQs. *Psychological Inquiry, 14,* 159–163.

Sellers, R. M., Copeland-Linder, N., Martin, P. P., & Lewis, R. L. (2006). Racial identity matters: The relationship between racial discrimination and psychological functioning in African American adolescents. *Journal of Research on Adolescence, 16,* 187–216.

Sellers, R. M., & Shelton, J. N. (2003). The role of racial identity in perceived racial discrimination. *Journal of Personality and Social Psychology, 84,* 1079–1092.

Selye, H. (1974). *Stress without distress.* Philadelphia: Saunders.

Selye, H. (1983). The stress concept: Past, present, and future. In C. I. Cooper (Ed.), *Stress research.* New York: Wiley.

Serrano-Blanco, A., & others. (2009). Fluoxetine and imipramine: Are there differences in cost-utility for depression in primary care. *Journal of Evaluation in Clinical Practice, 15,* 195–203.

Serretti, A., Drago, A., & DeRonchi, D. (2009). Lithium pharmacogenetics. *Current Medicinal Chemistry, 16,* 1917–1948.

Sesardic, N. (2006). *Making sense of heritability.* New York: Cambridge University Press.

Sessa, B. (2007). Is there a case for MDMA-assisted psychotherapy in the UK? *Journal of Psychopharmacology, 21,* 220–224.

Sewell, R. A., Halpern, J. H., & Pope, H. G. (2006). Response of cluster headache to psilocybin and LSD. *Neurology, 66,* 1920–1922.

Seymour, K., Clifford, C. W., Logothetis, N. K., & Bartels, A. (2009). The coding of color, motion, and their conjunction in the human visual cortex. *Current Biology, 19,* 177–183.

Seymour, T. L., Seifert, C. M., Shafto, M. G., & Mosmann, A. L. (2000). Using response time measures to assess "guilty knowledge." *Journal of Applied Psychology, 85,* 30–37.

Shakesby, A. C., Anwyl, R., & Rowan, M. J. (2002). Overcoming the effects of stress on synaptic plasticity in the intact hippocampus: Rapid actions of serotonergic and antidepressant agents. *Journal of Neuroscience, 22,* 3638–3644.

Sharma, R., Gupta, N., & Bijiani, R. L. (2008). Effect of yoga based lifestyle intervention on subjective well-being. *Indian Journal of Physiolog and Pharmacology, 52,* 123–131.

Shaver, P., & Mikulincer, M. (2010). Recent advances in the study of close relationships. *Annual Review of Psychology* (vol. 61). Palo Alto, CA: Annual Reviews. (in press)

Shaw, D. S., Connell, A., Dishion, T. J., Wilson, M. N., & Gardner, F. (2009). Improvements in maternal depression as a mediator of intervention effects on early childhood problem behavior. *Development and Psychopathology, 21,* 417–439.

Shay, J. W., & Wright, W. E. (2007). Hallmarks of telomere aging research. *Journal of Pathology, 211,* 114–123.

Shea, N., Krug, K., & Tobler, P. N. (2008). Conceptual representations in goal-directed decision making.

Cognitive, Affective, and Behavioral Neuroscience, 8, 418–428.

Sheldon, K. M. (2002). The self-concordance model of healthy goal-striving: When personal goals correctly represent the person. In E. L. Deci & R. M. Ryan (Eds.), *Handbook of self-determination research* (pp. 65–86). Rochester, NY: University of Rochester Press.

Sheldon, K. M., & Elliot, A. J. (1998). Not all personal goals are personal: Comparing autonomous and controlled reasons for goals as predictors of effort and attainment. *Personality and Social Psychology Bulletin, 24,* 546–557.

Sheldon, K. M., Elliot, A. J., Kim, Y., & Kasser, T. (2001). What is satisfying about satisfying events? Testing 10 candidate psychological needs. *Journal of Personality and Social Psychology, 80,* 325–339.

Sheldon, K. M., Kasser, T., Houser-Marko, L., Jones, T., & Turban, D. (2005). Doing one's duty: Chronological age, felt autonomy, and subjective well-being. *European Journal of Personality, 19,* 97–115.

Sheldon, K. M., & Lyubomirsky, S. (2007). Is it possible to become happier? (And if so, how?). *Social and Personality Psychology Compass, 1,* 129–145.

Shepard, R. N. (1967). Recognition memory for words, sentences, and pictures. *Journal of Verbal Learning and Verbal Behavior, 6,* 156–163.

Sherif, M., Harvey, O. J., White, B. J., Hood, W. R., & Sherif, C. W. (1961). *Intergroup cooperation and competition: The Robbers Cave experiment.* Norman: University of Oklahoma Press.

Sherman, A. C., Plante, T. G., Simonton, U. L., & Anaissie, E. J. (2009). Prospective study of religious coping among patients undergoing autologous stem cell transplantation. *Journal of Behavioral Science, 32,* 118–128.

Sherman, F. T. (2009). Life-saving treatment for depression in the elderly: Always think of electroconvulsive therapy (ECT). *Geriatrics, 64,* 8, 12.

Sherman, R., & Hickner, J. (2008). Academic physicians use placebos in clinical practice and believe in the mind-body connection. *Journal of General Internal Medicine, 23,* 7–10.

Shetty, A. K., Rao, M. S., & Hattiangady, B. (2008). Behavior of hippocampal stem/progenitor cells following grafting into the injured hippocampus. *Journal of Neuroscience Research, 86,* 3062–3074.

Shields, S. A. (1991). Gender in the psychology of emotion. In K. T. Strongman (Ed.), *International Review of Studies of Emotion* (vol. 1). New York: Wiley.

Shier, D. N., Butler, J. L., & Lewis, R. (2007). *Hole's anatomy & physiology* (10th ed.). New York: McGraw-Hill.

Shier, D. N., Butler, J. L., & Lewis, R. (2010). *Hole's human anatomy and physiology* (12th ed.). New York: McGraw-Hill.

Shih, M., Bonam, C., Sanchez, D., & Peck, C. (2007). The social construction of race: Biracial identity and vulnerability to stereotypes. *Cultural Diversity & Ethnic Minority Psychology, 13,* 125–133.

Shinn, M., & Thaden, E. (2010). *Current directions in community psychology.* Boston: Allyn & Bacon.

Shipp, S., Adams, D. L., Moutoussis, K., & Zeki, S. (2009). Feature binding in the feedback layers of area V2. *Cerebral Cortex.* (in press)

Shiraev, E., & Levy, D. (2010). *Cross-cultural psychology* (4th ed.). Boston: Allyn & Bacon.

Shoda, Y., & Mischel, W. (2006). Applying meta-theory to achieve generalisability and precision in personality science: Comment. *Applied Psychology: An International Review, 55,* 439–452.

Shull, R. L., & Grimes, J. A. (2006). Resistance to extinction following variable-interval reinforcement: Reinforcer rate and amount. *Journal of the Experimental Analysis of Behavior, 85,* 23–39.

Sibbald, S. L., Singer, P. A., Upshur, R., & Martin, D. K. (2009). Priority setting: What constitutes success? A conceptual framework for successful priority setting. *BMC Health Services Research, 9,* 43.

Siegel, S. (1988). State dependent learning and morphine tolerance. *Behavioral Neuroscience, 102,* 228–232.

Sieswerda, S., Arntz, A., Mertens, I., & Vertommen, S. (2007). Hypervigilance in patients with borderline personality disorder: Specificity, automaticity, and predictors. *Behaviour Research and Therapy, 45,* 1011–1024.

Sigel, E. (2008). Eating disorders. *Adolescence Medicine: State of the Art Reviews, 19,* 547–572.

Sigurdsson, T., Doyere, V., Cain, C. K., & LeDoux, J. E. (2007). Long-term potentiation in the amygdale: A cellular mechanism of learning and memory. *Neuropharmacology, 52,* 215–227.

Sikorskii, A., Given, C., Given, B., Jeon, S., & McCorkle, R. (2006). Testing the effects of treatment complications on a cognitive-behavioral intervention for reducing symptom severity. *Journal of Pain and Symptom Management, 32,* 129–139.

Sim, T. N., & Ong, L. P. (2005). Parent punishment and child aggression in a Singapore Chinese preschool sample. *Journal of Marriage and the Family, 67,* 85–99.

Simm, A., Nass, N., Bartling, B., Hofmann, B., Silber, R. E., & Navarette Santos, A. (2008). Potential biomarkers of ageing. *Biological Chemistry, 389,* 257–265.

Simms, L. J. (2007). The big seven model of personality and its relevance to personality pathology. *Journal of Personality, 75,* 65–94.

Simon, H. A. (1969). *The sciences of the artificial.* Cambridge, MA: MIT Press.

Simons, D. J., & Chabris, C. F. (1999). Gorillas in our midst: Sustained inattentional blindness for dynamic events. *Perception, 28* (9), 1059–1074.

Singer, J. A., & Blagov, P. (2004). The integrative function of narrative processing: Autobiographical memory, self-defining memories, and the life story of identity. In D. R. Beike, J. M. Lampinen, & D. A. Behrend (Eds.), *The self and memory* (pp. 117–138). New York: Psychology Press.

Singer, J. A., & Conway, M. A. (2008). Should we forget about forgetting? *Memory Studies, 1,* 279–285.

Sinn, D. L., Gosling, S. D., & Moltschaniwskyj, N. A. (2008). Development of shy/bold behaviour in squid: Context-specific phenotypes associated with developmental plasticity. *Animal Behaviour, 75,* 433–442.

Sitnikova, T., Goff, D., & Kuperberg, G. R. (2009). Neurocognitive abnormalities during comprehension of real-world goal-directed behaviors in schizophrenia. *Journal of Abnormal Psychology, 118,* 256–277.

Sivacek, J., & Crano, W. D. (1982). Vested interest as a moderator of attitude-behavior consistency. *Journal of Personality and Social Psychology, 43* (2), 210–221.

Sjoberg, R. L., Ducci, F., Barr, C. S., Newman, T. K., Dell'Osso, L., Virkkunen, M., & Goldman, D. (2008). A non-additive interaction of a functional MAO-A VNTR and testosterone predicts antisocial behavior. *Neuropsychopharmacology, 33,* 425–430.

Skinner, B. F. (1938). *The behavior of organisms: An experimental analysis.* New York: Appleton-Century-Crofts.

Skinner, B. F. (1957). *Verbal behavior.* New York: Appleton-Century-Crofts.

Skinner, E. I., & Fernandes, M. A. (2009). Illusory recollection in older adults and younger adults under divided attention. *Psychology and Aging, 24,* 211–216.

Skolin, I., Wahlin, Y. B., Broman, D. A., Koivisto Hursti, U., Vikström, L. M., & Hernell, O. (2006). Altered food intake and taste perception in children with cancer after start of chemotherapy: Perspectives of children, parents and nurses. *Supportive Care in Cancer, 14,* 369–378.

Skowronski, M. D., & Fenton, M. B. (2009). Quantifying bat call detection performance of humans and machines. *Journal of the Acoustical Society of America, 125,* 513–521.

Slade, E. P., & Wissow, L. S. (2004). Spanking in early childhood and later behavior problems: A prospective study of infants and young toddlers. *Pediatrics, 113,* 1321–1330.

Slater, A., Field, T., & Hernandez-Reif, M. (2007). The development of the senses. In A. Slater & M. Lewis (Eds.), *Introduction to infant development* (2nd ed.). New York: Oxford University Press.

Slaymaker, V. J., & Sheehan, T. (2008). The impact of AA on professional treatment. *Recent Developments in Alcoholism, 18,* 59–70.

Slotnick, S. D., & Schacter, D. L. (2006). The nature of memory related activity in early visual areas. *Neuropsychologia, 44,* 2874–2886.

Slutske, W. S. (2005). Alcohol use disorders among US college students and their non-college-attending peers. *Archives of General Psychiatry, 62,* 321–327.

Smit, F., Willemse, G., Koopmanschap, M., Onrust, S., Cuijpers, P., & Beekman, A. (2006). Cost-effectiveness of preventing depression in primary care patients: Randomized trial. *British Journal of Psychiatry, 188,* 330–336.

Smit, F., & others. (2009). Preventing panic disorder: Cost-effectiveness analysis alongside a pragmatic randomized trial. *Cost Effectiveness and Resource Allocation.* (in press)

Smith, B. (2007). *The psychology of sex and gender.* Belmont, CA: Wadsworth.

Smith, C. P. (Ed.). (1992). *Thematic content analysis for motivation and personality research.* New York: Cambridge University Press.

Smith, E. R., & Collins, E. C. (2009). Contextualizing person perception. *Psychological Review, 116,* 343–364.

Smith, G. P. (1995) Dopamine and food reward. *Progress in Psychobiology and Physiological Psychology, 16,* 83–144.

Smith, M., Calam, R., & Bolton, C. (2009). Psychological factors linked to self-reported depression symptoms in late adolescence. *Behavioral and Cognitive Psychotherapy, 37,* 73–85.

Smith, P. B., Bond, M. H., & Kagitcibasi, C. (2006). *Understanding social psychology across cultures: Living and working in a changing world.* Thousand Oaks, CA: Sage.

Smith, P. K., & Bargh, J. A. (2008). Nonconscious effects of power on basic approach and avoidance tendencies. *Social Cognition, 26,* 1–24.

Smith, S. D., & Reynolds, C. (2002). Cyber-psychotherapy. *Annals of the American Psychotherapy Association, 5,* 20–22.

Smith, T. E., Weston, C. A., & Lieberman, J. A. (2009). Schizophrenia (maintenance treatment). *Clinical Evidence.* (in press)

Smith, T. W., & MacKenzie, J. (2006). Personality and risk of physical illness. *Annual Review of Clinical Psychology* (vol. 2). Palo Alto, CA: Annual Reviews.

Smyth, J. (1998). Written emotional expression: Effect sizes, outcome types, and moderating variables. *Journal of Consulting and Clinical Psychology, 66,* 174–184.

Snarey, J. R. (1993). *How fathers care for the next generation: A four-decade study.* Cambridge, MA: Harvard University Press.

Snowdon, D. A. (2003). Healthy aging and dementia: findings from the Nun study. *Annals of Internal Medicine, 139,* 450–454.

Snowdon, D. A. (2007, April). *Aging with grace: findings from the nun study.* Paper presented at the 22nd annual Alzheimer's regional conference, Seattle.

Snyder, A. R. (2008). Silent no more: Expression of RNA from telomeres may regulate telomere length. *Cancer Biology and Therapy, 7.*

Snyder, C. R., & Lopez, S. J. (Eds.). (2007). *Positive psychology: The scientific and practical explorations of human strengths.* Thousand Oaks, CA: Sage.

Snyder, K. A., & Torrence, C. M. (2008). Habituation and novelty. In M. M. Haith & J. B. Benson (Eds.), *Encyclopedia of infant and early childhood development.* Oxford, England: Elsevier.

Soares, C. N. (2008). Practical strategies for diagnosing and treating depression in women: Menopausal transition. *Journal of Clinical Psychiatry, 69,* e30.

Sokol, M. S., Carroll, A. K., Heebink, D. M., Hoffman-Riken, K. M., Goudge, C. S., & Ebers, D. D. (2009). Anorexia nervosa in identical triplets. *CNS Spectrums, 14,* 156–162.

Solberg Nes, L., Evans, D. R., & Segerstrom, S. C. (2009). Optimism and college retention: Mediation by motivation, performance, and adjustment. *Journal of Applied Social Psychology.* (in press)

Solberg Nes, L., & Segerstrom, S. C. (2006). Dispositional optimism and coping: A meta-analytic review. *Personality and Social Psychology Review, 10,* 235–251.

Soldan, A., Hilton, H. J., Cooper, L. A., & Stern, Y. (2009). Priming of familiar and unfamiliar visual objects over delays in young and older adults. *Psychology and Aging, 24,* 93–104.

Soloff, P. H., Feske, U., & Fabio, A. (2008). Mediators of the relationship between childhood sexual abuse and suicidal behavior in borderline personality disorder. *Journal of Personality Disorders, 22,* 221–232.

Soloff, P. H., Lis, J. A., Kelly, T., Cornelius, J., & others. (1994). Self-mutilation and suicidal behavior in borderline personality disorder. *Journal of Personality Disorders, 8,* 257–267.

Solomon, S. G., & Lennie, P. (2007). The machinery of color vision. *Nature Reviews: Neuroscience, 8,* 276–286.

Soltesz, E. G., & Cohn, L. H. (2007). Minimally invasive valve surgery. *Cardiology Review, 15,* 109–115.

Sommer, M., Hajak, G., Dohnel, K., Schwerdtner, J., Meinhardt, J., & Muller, J. L. (2006). Integration of emotion and cognition in patients with psychopathy. *Progress in Brain Research, 156C,* 457–466.

Sommer, V., & Vasey, P. L. (Eds.). (2006). *Homosexual behaviour in animals: An evolutionary perspective.* New York: Cambridge University Press.

Song, S. (2006, March 27). Mind over medicine. *Time, 167,* 13.

Soreth, M. E., & Hineline, P. N. (2009). The probability of small schedule values and preference for random-interval schedules. *Journal of Experimental Analysis of Behavior, 91,* 89–103.

Sorrentino, R., Cohen, D., Olson, J. M., & Zanna, M. P. (2005). *Cultural and social behavior: The Ontario symposium* (vol. 10). Mahwah, NJ: Erlbaum.

Soto, C. J., John, O., Gosling, S. D., & Potter, J. (2008). The development of psychometrics of big five reports: Acquiescence, factor structure, coherence, and differentiation from ages 10 to 20. *Journal of Personality and Social Psychology, 94,* 718–273.

Sotres-Bayon, F., Diaz-Mataix, L., Bush, D. E., & LeDoux, J. E. (2009). Dissociable roles for the ventromedial prefrontal cortex and amygdale in fear extinction: NR2B contribution. *Cerebral Cortex, 19,* 472–482.

Sourial-Bassillious, N., Rydelius, P. A., Aperia, A., & Aizman, O. (2009). Glutamate-mediated calcium signaling: A potential target for lithium action. *Neuroscience.* (in press)

South, S. C., & Krueger, R. F. (2008). An interactionist on genetic and environmental contributions to personality. *Social and Personality Psychology Compass, 2,* 929–948.

Soyka, M., Preuss, U. W., Hesselbrock, V., Zill, P., Koller, G., & Bondy, B. (2008). GABA-A2 receptor subunit gene (GABRAA2) polymorphisms and risk for alcohol dependence. *Journal of Psychiatric Research, 42,* 184–191.

Spanos, N. P. (1996). *Multiple identities and false memories: A sociocognitive perspective.* Washington, DC: American Psychological Association.

Spanos, N. P., & Chaves, J. F. (Eds.). (1989). *Hypnosis: The cognitive-behavior perspective.* Buffalo, NY: Prometheus.

Sparks, J. R., & Areni, C. S. (2008). Style versus substance: Multiple roles of language power in persuasion. *Journal of Applied Social Psychology, 38,* 37–60.

Spearman, C. (1904). "General intelligence" objectively determined and measured. *American Journal of Psychology, 15,* 201–293.

Speckens, A. E., Ehlers, A., Hackmann, A., Ruths, F. A., & Clark, D. M. (2007). Intrusive memories and rumination in patients with post-traumatic stress disorder: A phenomenological comparison. *Memory, 15,* 249–257.

Spelke, E. S., & Kinzler, K. D. (2009). Innateness, learning, and rationality. *Child Development Perspectives.* (in press)

Spellman, B. A. (2005). Could reality shows become reality experiments? *APS Observer, 18,* 34–35.

Spencer, S. J., Steele, C. M., & Quinn, D. M. (1999). Stereotype threat and women's math performance. *Journal of Experimental Social Psychology, 35,* 4–28.

Speranza, M., Corcos, M., Atger, F., Paterniti, S., & Jeammet, P. (2003). Binge eating behaviours, depression and weight control strategies. *Eating and Weight Disorders, 8,* 201–206.

Sperling, G. (1960). The information available in brief presentations. *Psychological Monographs, 74* (11).

Sperry, R. W. (1968). Hemisphere deconnection and unity in conscious awareness. *American Psychologist, 23,* 723–733.

Sperry, R. W. (1974). Lateral specialization in surgically separated hemispheres. In F. O. Schmitt & F. G. Worden (Eds.), *The neurosciences: Third study program.* Cambridge, MA: MIT Press.

Spiegel, D. (2006). Editorial: Recognizing traumatic dissociation. *American Journal of Psychiatry, 163,* 566–568.

Spiegler, M. D., & Guevremont, D. C. (2010). *Contemporary behavior therapy* (5th ed.). Boston: Cengage.

Spielberger, C. D. (2004, August). *Type A behavior, anger-hostility, and heart disease.* Paper presented at the 28th International Congress of Psychology, Beijing, China.

Squire, L. (1990, June). *Memory and brain systems.* Paper presented at the meeting of the American Psychological Society, Dallas.

Squire, L. (2007). Memory systems as a biological concept. In H. L. Roediger, Y. Dudai, & S. Fitzpatrick (Eds.), *Science of memory: Concepts.* New York: Oxford University Press.

Squire, L. (Ed.). (2009). *Encyclopedia of neuroscience.* London: Elsevier.

Squire, L. R. (2004). Memory systems of the brain: A brief history and current perspective. *Neurobiology of Learning and Memory, 82,* 171–177.

Sriram, N., & Greenwald, A. G. (2009). The Brief Implicit Association Test. *Experimental Psychology, 56,* 283–204.

Sroufe, L. A., Egeland, B., Carlson, E., & Collins, W. A. (2005). The place of early attachment in developmental context. In K. E. Grossmann, K. Grossmann, & E. Waters (Eds.), *The power of longitudinal research.* New York: Guilford.

Staddon, J. E., Chelaru, I. M., & Higa, J. J. (2002). A tune-trace theory of interval-timing dynamics. *Journal of the Experimental Analysis of Behavior, 77,* 105–124.

Standing, L. G., Bobbitt, K. E., Boisvert, K. L., Dayholos, K. N., & Gagnon, A. M. (2008). People, clothing, music, and arousal as contextual retrieval cues in verbal memory. *Perceptual and Motor Skills, 107,* 523–534.

Stangor, C. (2009). The study of stereotyping, prejudice, and discrimination within social psychology: A quick history of theory and research. In T. D. Nelson (Ed.), *Handbook of prejudice, stereotyping, and discrimination.* New York: Psychology Press.

Stanley, J., & Miall, R. C. (2009). Using predictive motor control processes in a cognitive task: Behavioral and neuroanatomical perspectives. *Advances in Experimental Medicine and Biology, 6239,* 337–354.

Stanovich, K. E. (2007). *How to think straight about psychology* (8th ed.). Boston: Allyn & Bacon.

Stanton, A. L., Revenson, T. A., & Tennen, H. (2007). Health psychology: Psychological adjustment to chronic disease. *Annual Review of Psychology* (vol. 58). Palo Alto, CA: Annual Reviews.

Starcevic, V. (2006). Anxiety states: A review of conceptual and treatment issues. *Current Opinions in Psychiatry, 19,* 79–83.

Stasiewicz, P. R., Brandon, T. H., & Bradizza, C. M. (2007). Effects of extinction context and retrieval cues on renewal of alcohol-cue reactivity among alcohol-dependent outpatients. *Psychology of Addictive Behaviors, 21* (2), 244–248.

Staub, E., & Vollhardt, J. (2008). Altruism born of suffering: The roots of caring and helping after victimization and other trauma. *American Journal of Orthopsychiatry, 78,* 267–280.

Staudinger, U., & Dorner, J. (2007). Wisdom. In J. E. Birren (Ed.), *Encyclopedia of gerontology* (2nd ed.). Oxford, England: Elsevier.

Staw, B. M., Sutton, R. I., & Pelled, L. H. (1994). Employee positive emotion and favorable outcomes at the workplace. *Organization Science, 5,* 51–71.

Steben, M., & others. (2008). Genital herpes: Gynecological aspects. *Journal of Obstetrics and Gynecology Canada, 30,* 347–361.

Steblay, N., & Loftus, E. (2009). Eyewitness memory and the legal system. In E. Shafir (Ed.), *The behavioral foundations of policy.* Princeton, NJ: Princeton University Press and the Russell Sage Foundation. (in press)

Steel, P., Schmidt, J., & Schultz, J. (2008). Refining the relationship between personality and subjective well-being. *Psychological Bulletin, 134,* 138–161.

Steele, C. M., & Aronson, J. (1995). Stereotype threat and the intellectual test performance of African-Americans. *Journal of Personality and Social Psychology, 69,* 797–811.

Steele, C. M., & Aronson, J. A. (2004). Stereotype threat does not live by Steele and Aronson (1995) alone. *American Psychologist, 59,* 47–48.

Steger, M. F., & Frazier, P. (2005). Meaning in life: One link in the chain from religion to well-being. *Journal of Counseling Psychology, 52,* 574–582.

Stein, R. (2003). *Blinded by the light.* http://www.theage.com.au/arti-cles/2003/09/01/1062403448264.html (accessed October 11, 2006)

Steinberg, L. (2009). Adolescent development and juvenile justice. *Annual Review of Clinical Psychology* (vol. 5). Palo Alto, CA: Annual Reviews.

Steinbrook, R. (1992). The polygraph test: A flawed diagnostic method. *New England Journal of Medicine, 327,* 122–123.

Stenfelt, S. (2006). Middle ear ossicles motion at hearing thresholds with air conduction and bone conduction stimulation. *Journal of the Acoustical Society of America, 119,* 2848–2858.

Stern, Y., Alexander, G. E., Prohovnik, I., & Mayeux, R. (1992). Inverse relationship between education and parietotemporal perfusion deficit in Alzheimer's disease. *Annals of Neurology, 32,* 371–375.

Stern, Y., Scarmeas, N., & Habeck, C. (2004). Imaging cognitive reserve. *International Journal of Psychology, 39,* 18–26.

Sternberg, E. M., & Gold, P. W. (1996). The mind–body interaction in disease. *Mysteries of the mind.* New York: Scientific American.

Sternberg, R. J. (1986). *Intelligence applied.* Fort Worth: Harcourt Brace.

Sternberg, R. J. (Ed.). (2004). Definitions and conceptions of giftedness. Thousand Oaks, CA: Corwin Press.

Sternberg, R. J. (2007a). *G, g's, or Jeez:* Which is the best model for developing abilities, competencies, and expertise? In P. C. Kyllonen, R. D. Roberts, & L. Stankov (Eds.), *Extending intelligence.* Mahwah, NJ: Erlbaum.

Sternberg, R. J. (2007b). Developing successful intelligence in all children: A potential solution to under-achievement in ethnic minority children. In M. C. Wang & R. D. Taylor (Eds.), *Closing the achievement gap.* Philadelphia: Laboratory for Student Success at Temple University.

Sternberg, R. J. (2008). The triarchic theory of human intelligence. In N. Salkind (Ed.), *Encyclopedia of educational psychology.* Thousand Oaks, CA: Sage.

Sternberg, R. J. (2009). *Cognitive psychology* (5th ed.). Belmont, CA: Wadsworth.

Sternberg, R. J. (2009b). Teaching for creativity. In R. A. Beghetto & J. C. Kaufman (Eds.), *Nurturing creativity in the classroom.* New York: Cambridge University Press. (in press)

Sternberg, R. J. (2009c). Successful intelligence as a framework for understanding cultural adaption. In S. Ang & L. van Dyne (Eds.), *Handbook on cultural intelligence.* New York: M. E. Sharpe. (in press)

Sternberg, R. J. (2009d). The triarchic theory of intelligence. In B. Kerr (Ed.), *Encyclopedia of giftedness, creativity, and talent.* Thousand Oaks, CA: Sage. (in press)

Sternberg, R. J. (2009e). Wisdom, intelligence, creativity, synthesized: A model of giftedness. In T. Balchin, B. Hymer, & D. Matthews (Eds.), *International companion to gifted education.* London: RoutledgeFalmer. (in press)

Sternberg, R. J. (2009f). Wisdom. In S. J. Lopez (Ed.), *Encyclopedia of positive psychology.* Amsterdam: Springer. (in press)

Sternberg, R. J., & Grigorenko, E. L. (2008). Ability testing across cultures. In L. Suzuki (Ed.), *Handbook of multicultural assessment* (3rd ed., pp. 335–359). New York: Jossey-Bass.

Sternberg, R. J., Grigorenko, E. L., & Kidd, K. K. (2005). Intelligence, race, and genetics. *American Psychologist, 60,* 46–59.

Sternberg, R. J., Jarvin, L., & Reznitskaya, A. (2008). Teaching for wisdom through history: Infusing wise thinking skills in the school curriculum. In M. Ferrari (Ed.), *Teaching for wisdom.* New York: Springer.

Sternberg, R. J., Roediger, H., & Halpern, D. (Eds.). (2007). *Critical thinking in psychology.* New York: Cambridge University Press.

Stevens, M. J., & Gielen, U. P. (Eds.). (2007). Toward a global psychology: Theory, research, intervention, and pedagogy. Mahwah, NJ: Erlbaum.

Stewart, S. H., & Chambers, L. (2000). Relationships between drinking motives and drinking restraint. *Addictive Behaviors, 25,* 269–274.

Stewart-Williams, S. (2008). Human beings as evolved nepotists: Exceptions to the rule and effects of cost of help. *Human Nature, 19,* 414–425.

Stice, E., Presnell, K., Gau, J., & Shaw, H. (2007). Testing mediators of intervention effects in randomized controlled trials: An evaluation of two eating disorder prevention programs. *Journal of Consulting and Clinical Psychology, 75,* 20–32.

Stice, E., Shaw, H., & Marti, C. N. (2006). A meta-analytic review of obesity prevention programs for children and adolescents: The skinny on interventions that work. *Psychological Bulletin, 132,* 667–691.

Stickgold, R. (2001). Watching the sleeping brain watch us: Sensory processing during sleep. *Trends in Neuroscience, 24,* 307–309.

Stickgold, R., & Hobson, J. A. (2000). Visual discrimination learning requires sleep after training. *Nature Neuroscience, 3,* 1237–1238.

Stickgold, R., & Walker, M. P. (2005). Sleep and memory: An ongoing debate. *Sleep, 28,* 1225–1227.

Stirling, J. D. (2002). *Introducing neuropsychology.* East Sussex, England: Psychology Press.

Stone, J. (2002). Battling doubt by avoiding practice: The effects of stereotype threat on self-handicapping in white athletes. *Personality and Social Psychology Bulletin, 28,* 1667–1678.

Stoner, J. (1961). *A comparison of individual and group decisions, including risk.* Unpublished master's thesis, School of Industrial Management, MIT.

Stores, G., Montgomery, P., & Wiggs, L. (2006). The psychosocial problems of children with narcolepsy and those with excessive daytime sleepiness of unknown origin. *Pediatrics, 118,* e1116–e1123.

Strack, F., & Forster, J. (2009). Social cognition: An introduction. In F. Strack & J. Forster (Eds.), *Social cognition: The basis of human interaction.* New York: Psychology Press.

Strahan, E., Spencer, S. J., & Zanna, M. P. (2002). Subliminal priming and persuasion: Striking while the iron is hot. *Journal of Experimental Social Psychology, 38,* 556–568.

Straus, M. A., & Stewart, J. H. (1999). Corporal punishment by American parents: National data on prevalence, chronicity, severity, and duration in relation to child and family characteristics. *Clinical Child and Family Psychology Review, 2,* 55–70.

Straus, M. A., Sugarman, D. B., & Giles-Sims, J. (1997). Spanking by parents and subsequent antisocial behavior of children. *Archives of Pediatric and Adolescent Medicine, 151,* 761–767.

Streff, F. M., & Geller, E. S. (1986). Strategies for motivating safety belt use: The application of applied behavior analysis. *Health Education Research, 1 (1),* 47–59.

Striegel-Moore, R. H., & Franko, D. L. (2008). Should binge eating disorder be included in the DSM-V? A critical review of the state of the evidence. *Annual Review of Clinical Psychology, 4,* 305–324.

Strike, P. C., Magid, K., Whitehead, D. L., Brydon, L., Bhattacharyya, M. R., & Steptoe, A. (2006). Pathophysiological processes underlying emotional triggering of acute cardiac events. *Proceedings of the National Academy of Sciences USA, 103,* 4322–4327.

Strong, B., Yarber, W., Sayad, B., & DeVault, C. (2008). *Human sexuality* (6th ed.). New York: McGraw-Hill.

Strupp, H. H. (1995). The psychotherapist's skills revised. *Clinical Psychology: Science and Practice, 2,* 70–74.

Sturmer, T., Hasselbach, P., & Amelang, M. (2006). Personality, lifestyle, and risk of cardiovascular disease and cancer: Follow-up of population-based cohort. *British Medical Journal, 332,* 1359.

Stuss, D. T. (2006). Frontal lobes and attention: Processes and networks, fractionation and integration. *Journal of the International Neuropsychological Society, 12,* 261–271.

Substance Abuse and Mental Health Services Administration (SAMHSA). (2006). *National survey on drug use and health report, 11.* Washington DC: Author.

Sue, D., Sue, D. W., & Sue, S. (2010). *Understanding abnormal behavior* (9th ed.). Boston: Cengage.

Sui, X., Laditka, J. N., Church, T. S., Hardin, J. W., Chase, N., Davis, K., & Blair, S. N. (2009). Prospective study of cardiovascular fitness and depressive symptoms in women and men. *Journal of Psychiatric Research, 43,* 546–552.

Sui, X., LaMonte, M. J., Laditka, J. N., Hardin, J. W., Chase, N., Hooker, S. P., & Blair, S. N. (2007). Cardiorespiratory fitness and adiposity as mortality predictors in older adults. *Journal of the American Medical Association, 298,* 2507–2516.

Suinn, R. M. (1984). *Fundamentals of abnormal psychology.* Chicago: Nelson-Hall.

Sullivan, H. S. (1953). *The interpersonal theory of psychiatry.* New York: Norton.

Sullivan, P. W., Morrato, E. H., Ghushchyan, V., Wyatt, H. R., & Hill, J. O. (2005). Obesity, inactivity, and the prevalence of diabetes and diabetes-related cardiovascular comorbidities in the U.S., 2000–2002. *Diabetes Care 28,* 1599–1603.

Suls, J., & Swain, A. (1998). Type A–Type B personalities. In H. S. Friedman (Ed.), *Encyclopedia of mental health* (vol. 3). San Diego: Academic.

Surprenant, A. M. (2001). Distinctiveness and serial position effects in tonal sequences. *Perception and Psychophysics, 63,* 737–745.

Susman, E. J., & Dorn, L. D. (2009). Puberty: Its role in development. In R. M. Lerner & L. Steinberg (Eds.), *Handbook of adolescent psychology* (3rd ed.). New York: Wiley.

Sutherland, N. S. (1989). *Macmillan dictionary of psychology.* Houndmills/Basingstoke/Hampshire, England: Palgrave-Macmillan.

Suzuki, C., Tsukiura, T., Mochiizuki-Kawai, H., Shigemune, Y., & Iijima, T. (2009). Prefrontal and medial temporal contributions to episodic memory-based reasoning. *Neuroscience Research, 63,* 177–183.

Swanson, J. (Ed.). (1999). *Sleep disorders sourcebook.* New York: Omnigraphics.

Swim, J. K., & Hyers, L. L. (2009). Sexism. In T. D. Nelson (Ed.), *Handbook of prejudice, stereotyping, and discrimination.* New York: Psychology Press.

Szasz, T. S. (1961). *The myth of mental illness: Foundations of a theory of personal conduct.* New York: Hoeber-Harper.

Tadic, A., Baskaya, O., Victor, A., Lieb, K., Hoppner, W., & Dahmen, N. (2008). Association analysis of SCN9A gene variants with borderline personality disorder. *Journal of Psychiatric Research, 43,* 155–163.

Taga, K. A., Markey, C. N., & Friedman, H. S. (2006). A longitudinal investigation of associations between boys' pubertal timing and adult behavioral health and well-being. *Journal of Youth and Adolescence, 35,* 380–390.

Tager-Flusberg, H., & Zukowski, A. (2009). Putting words together; Morphology and syntax in the preschool years. In J. Berko Gleason & N. Ratner (Eds.), *The development of language* (7th ed.). Boston: Allyn & Bacon.

Tagliamonte, S. A., & Denis, D. (2008). Linguistic ruin? LOL! Instant messaging and teen language. *American Speech, 83,* 3–34.

Tajfel, H. (1978). The achievement of group differentiation. In H. Tajfel (Ed.), *Differentiation between social groups.* London: Academic.

Takahashi, M., Shimizu, H., Saito, S., & Tomoyori, H. (2006). One percent ability and ninety-nine percent perspiration: A study of a Japanese memorist. *Journal of Experimental Psychology: Learning, Memory,and Cognition, 32,* 1195–1200.

Takeuchi, T., & De Valois, K. K. (2009). Visual motion mechanisms under low retinal illuminance revealed by motion-reversal. *Vision Research, 49,* 801–809.

Talarico, J. M. (2009). Freshman flashbulbs: Memories of unique and first-time events in starting college. *Memory, 17,* 256–265.

Tamminga, C. A. (2006). The neurobiology of cognition in schizophrenia. *Journal of Clinical Psychology, 67,* e11.

Tan, H. H., & Tan, M. L. (2008). Organizational citizenship and social loafing: The role of personality, motives, and contextual factors. *Journal of Psychology, 142,* 89–108.

Tang, Y., Fang, J. A., & Miao, Q. Y. (2009). Synchronization of stochastic delayed neural networks with markovian switching and its application. *International Journal of Neural Systems, 19,* 43–56.

Tanner, J. M. , & others. (1966). *Archives of Diseases in Childhood,* 41.

Tarokh, L., & Carskadon, M. A. (2008). In L. R. Squire (Ed.), *New Encyclopedia of Neuroscience.* London: Elsevier.

Tarr, M. J., & Gauthier, I. (2000). FFA: A flexible fusiform area for subordinate-level visual processing automatized by expertise. *Nature Neuroscience, 3,* 764–769.

Tarter, R. E., Vanyukov, M., Kirisci, L., Reynolds, M., & Clark, D. B. (2006). Predictors of marijuana use in adolescents before and after illicit drug use: Examination of the gateway hypothesis. *American Journal of Psychiatry, 163,* 2134–2140.

Tavris, C., & Wade, C. (1984). *The longest war: Sex differences in perspective* (2nd ed.). Fort Worth: Harcourt Brace.

Tay, C., Ang, S., & Van Dyne, L. (2006). Personality, biographical characteristics, and job interview success: A longitudinal study of the mediating effects of self-efficacy and the moderating effects of internal locus of causality. *Journal of Applied Psychology, 91,* 446–454.

Taylor, L. S., & Whittaker, C. R. (2009). *Bridging multiple worlds* (2nd ed.). Boston: Allyn & Bacon.

Taylor, S. E. (2001). Toward a biology of social support. In C. R. Snyder & S. J. Lopez (Eds.), *Handbook of positive psychology.* New York: Oxford University Press.

Taylor, S. E. (2006). *Health psychology* (6th ed.). New York: McGraw-Hill.

Taylor, S. E. (2007). Social support. In H. S. Friedman & R. C. Silver (Eds.), *Foundations of health psychology.* New York: Oxford University Press.

Taylor, S. E. (2009). *Health psychology* (7th ed.). New York: McGraw-Hill.

Taylor, S. E., Brown, J. D., Colvin, C. R., Block, J., & Funder, D. C. (2007). Issue 6: Do positive illusions lead to healthy behavior? In J. A. Nier (Ed.). *Taking sides: Clashing views in social psychology* (2nd ed., pp. 116–137). New York: McGraw-Hill.

Taylor, S. E., Lerner, J. S., Sherman, D. K., Sage, R. M., & McDowell, N. K. (2003a). Are self-enhancing cognitions associated with healthy or unhealthy biological profiles? *Journal of Personality and Social Psychology, 85,* 605–615.

Taylor, S. E., Lerner, J. S., Sherman, D. K., Sage, R. M., & McDowell, N. K. (2003b). Portrait of the self-enhancer: Well adjusted and well liked or maladjusted and friendless? *Journal of Personality and Social Psychology, 84,* 165–176.

Taylor, S. E., & Sherman, D. K. (2008). Self-enhancement and self-affirmation: The consequences of positive self-thoughts for motivation and health. In W. Gardner & J. Shah (Eds.), *Handbook of motivation science.* New York: Guilford.

Taylor, S. E., & Stanton, A. L. (2007). Coping resources, coping processes, and mental health. *Annual Review of Clinical Psychology* (vol. 3). Palo Alto, CA: Annual Reviews.

Tchantauria, K., Anderluh, B., Morris, R. G., & others. (2004). Cognitive flexibility in anorexia and bulimia nervosa. *Journal of the International Neuropsychological Society, 10,* 513–520.

Teesson, M., & Vogl, L. (2006). Major depressive disorder is common among Native Americans, women, the middle aged, the poor, the widowed, separated, or divorced people. *Evidence-Based Mental Health, 9,* 59.

Tellegen, A., Ben-Porath, Y. S., & Sellbom, M. (2009). Construct validity of the MMPI-2 restructured clinical (RC) scales: Reply to Rouse, Green, Butcher, Nichols, and Williams. *Journal of Personality Assessment, 91,* 211–221.

Tenenbaum, J. B., Griffiths, T. L., & Kemp, C. (2006). Theory-based Bayesian models of inductive learning and reasoning. *Trends in Cognitive Science, 10,* 309–318.

Teodorescu, M., & others. (2006). Correlates of daytime sleepiness in patients with asthma. *Sleep Medicine, 7,* 607–613.

Terman, L. (1925). *Genetic studies of genius. Vol. 1: Mental and physical traits of a thousand gifted children.* Stanford, CA: Stanford University Press.

Terr, L. C. (1988). What happens to early memories of trauma? *Journal of the American Academy of Child and Adolescent Psychiatry, 27,* 96–104.

Terry, S. (2009). *Learning and memory* (4th ed.). Upper Saddle River, NJ: Prentice-Hall.

Thabet, A. A., Ibraheem, A. N., Shhivram, R., Winter, E. A., & Vastanis, P. (2009). Parenting support and PTSD in children of a war zone. *International Journal of Social Psychiatry, 55,* 226–237.

Thankachan, S., Kaur, S., & Shiromani, P. J. (2009). Activity of pontine neurons during sleep and cataplexy in hypocretin knock-out mice. *Journal of Neuroscience, 29,* 1580–1585.

Theeuwes, J., Belopolsky, A., & Olivers, C. N. (2009). Interactions between working memory, attention, and eye movements. *Acta Psychologica.* (in press)

Thelen, E., & Smith, L. B. (2006). Dynamic development of action and thought. In W. Damon & R. Lerner (Eds.), *Handbook of child psychology* (6th ed.). New York: Wiley.

Thiessen, J. H. (2002). Relations of androgens and selected aspects of human behavior. *Maturitas, 41, Suppl.,* 47–54.

Thigpen, C. H., & Cleckley, H. M. (1957). *Three faces of Eve.* New York. McGraw-Hill.

Thomas, M., Sing, H., Belenky, G., Holcomb, H., Mayberg, H., Dannals, R., Wagner, H., Thorne, D., Popp, K., Rowland, L., Welsh, A., Balwinksi, S., & Redmond, D. (2001). Neural basis of alertness and cognitive performance impairments during sleepiness: I. Effects of 24 hours of sleep deprivation on waking human regional brain activity. *Journal of Sleep Research, 9,* 335–352.

Thomas, M., Tyers, P., Lazic, S. E., Barker, R. A., Beazley, L., & Ziman, M. (2009). Graft outcomes influences by co-expression of Pax7 in graft and host tissue. *Journal of Anatomy, 214,* 396–405.

Thomas, M. L., & Youngjohn, J. R. (2009). Let's not get hysterical: Comparing the MMPI-2 validity, clinical, and RC scales in TBI litigants tested for effort. *Clinical Neuropsychology, 31,* 1–18.

Thomas, M. S. C., & Johnson, M. H. (2008). New advances in understanding sensitive periods in brain development. *Current Directions in Psychological Science, 17,* 1–5.

Thompson, L., Snyder, C. R., Hoffman, L., Michael, S. T., Rasmussen, H. N., & others. (2005). Dispositional forgiveness of self, others, and situations. *Journal of Personality, 73,* 313–359.

Thompson, P. M., Giedd, J. N., MacDonald, D., Evans, A. C., & Toga, A. W. (2000). Growth patterns in the developing brain by using continuum sensor maps. *Nature, 404,* 190–193.

Thompson, R. A. (2009a). Emotional development. In R. A. Schweder (Ed.), *The Chicago companion to the child.* Chicago: University of Chicago Press. (in press)

Thompson, R. A. (2009b). Early foundations: Conscience and the development of moral character. In D. Narvaez & D. Lapsley (Eds.), *Moral self, identity,*

and character. New York: Cambridge University Press. (in press)

Thompson, R. A., & Newton, E. (2009). Infant-caregiver communication. In H. T. Rwid & S. Sprecher (Eds.), *Encyclopedia of human relationships.* Thousand Oaks, CA: Sage. (in press)

Thompson, S. C. (2001). The role of personal control in adaptive functioning. In C. R. Snyder & S. J. Lopez (Eds.), *Handbook of positive psychology.* New York: Oxford University Press.

Thomsen, D. K. (2009). There is more to life stories than memory. *Memory, 17,* 1–13.

Thomsen, M., Hall, F. S., Uhl, G. R., & Caine, S. B. (2009). Dramatically decreased cocaine self-administration in dopamine but not serotonin transporter knock-out mice. *Journal of Neuroscience, 29,* 1087–1092.

Thoresen, C. J., Kaplan, S. A., Barsky, A. P., Warren, C. R., & de Chermont, K. (2003). The affective underpinnings of job perceptions and attitudes: A meta-analytic review and integration. *Psychological Bulletin, 129,* 914–945.

Thorndike, E. L. (1898). *Animal intelligence: An experimental study of the associative processes in animals* (Psychological Review, monograph supplements, no. 8). New York: Macmillan.

Thornicroft, G., Brohan, E., Rose, D., Sartorius, N., Lees, M., & the INDIGO Study Group. (2009). Global pattern of experienced and anticipated discrimination against people with schizophrenia: A cross-sectional survey. *Lancet, 373,* 408–415.

Thunedborg, K., Black, C. H., & Bech, P. (1995). Beyond the Hamilton depression scores in long-term treatment of manic-melancholic patients: Prediction of recurrence of depression by quality of life measurements. *Psychotherapy and Psychosomatics, 64,* 131–140.

Timimi, S. (2004). A critique of the international consensus statement on ADHD. *Clinical Child and Family Psychology Review, 7* (1), 59–63.

Tinbergen, N. (1969). *The study of instinct.* New York: Oxford University Press.

Tobian, A. A., & others. (2009). Factors associated with the prevalence and incidence of herpes simplex virus type 2 infection among men in Rakai, Uganda. *Journal of Infectious Diseases.* (in press)

Todorov, A., Mandisodza, A. N., Goren, A., & Hall, C. C. (2005). Inferences of competence from faces predict election outcomes. *Science, 308* (5728), 1623–1626.

Toga, A. W., Thompson, P. M., & Sowell, E. R. (2006). Mapping brain maturation. *Trends in Neuroscience, 29,* 148–159.

Tolman, E. C. (1932). *Purposive behavior in animals and man.* New York: Appleton-Century-Crofts.

Tolman, E. C., & Honzik, C. H. (1930). Degrees of hunger, reward and non-reward, and maze performance in rats. *University of California Publications in Psychology, 4,* 21–256.

Tomasello, M. (2008). *Origins of human communication.* Cambridge, MA: MIT Press.

tom Dieck, S., & Brandstatter, J. H. (2006). Ribbon synapses in the retina. *Cell Tissue Research, 326,* 339–346.

Tong, F., Nakayama, K., Moscovitch, M., Weinrib, O., & Kanwisher, N. (2000). Response properties of the human fusiform face area. *Cognitive Neuropsychology, 17,* 257–279.

Towse, J. (2008). *Working memory and cognitive development.* Milton Park, England: Routledge.

Tremblay, T., Monetta, L., & Joanette, Y. (2009). Complexity and hemispheric abilities: Evidence for a differential impact on semantics and phonology. *Brain and Language, 108,* 67–72.

Triandis, H. C. (2000). Cross-cultural psychology: History of the field. In A. Kazdin (Ed.), *Encyclopedia of psychology.* Washington, DC, & New York: American Psychological Association and Oxford University Press.

Tribukait, A. (2006). Subjective visual horizontal in the upright posture and asymmetry in roll-tilt perception: Independent measures of vestibular function. *Journal of Vestibular Research, 16,* 35–43.

Triplett, N. (1898). The dynamogenic factors in pacemaking and competition. *American Journal of Psychology, 9,* 507–533.

Trull, T. J., & Widiger, T. A. (2003). Personality disorders. In I. B. Weiner (Ed.), *Handbook of Psychology* (vol. 8). New York: Wiley.

Tryon, R. C. (1940). Genetic differences in maze-learning ability in rats. In *39th Yearbook, National Society for the Study of Education.* Chicago: University of Chicago Press.

Trzesniewski, K. H., Donnellan, M. B., Moffitt, T. E., Robins, R. W., Poulton, R., & Caspi, A. (2006). Low self-esteem during adolescence predicts poor health, criminal behavior, and limited economic prospects during adulthood. *Developmental Psychology, 42,* 381–390.

Tsuchihashi-Makay, M., & others. (2009). Gene-environmental interaction regarding alcohol-metabolizing enzymes in the Japanese general population. *Hypertension Research, 32,* 207–213.

Tsushima, Y., Sasaki, Y., & Watanabe, T. (2006). Greater disruption due to failure of inhibitory control on an ambiguous distractor. *Science, 314,* 1786–1788.

Tugade, M. M., Fredrickson, B. L., & Feldman Barrett, L. (2004). Psychological resilience and positive emotional granularity: Examining the benefits of positive emotions on coping and health. *Journal of Personality, 72,* 1161–1190.

Tulving, E. (1972). Episodic and semantic memory. In E. Tulving & W. Donaldson (Eds.), *Origins of memory.* San Diego: Academic.

Tulving, E. (1983). *Elements of episodic memory.* New York: Oxford University Press.

Tulving, E. (1989). Remembering and knowing the past. *American Scientist, 77,* 361–367.

Tulving, E. (2000). Concepts of memory. In E. Tulving & F. I. M. Craik (Eds.), *The Oxford handbook of memory.* New York: Oxford University Press.

Turkheimer, E., Haley, A., Waldron, M., D'Onofrio, B., & Gottesman, I. I. (2003). Socioeconomic status modifies heritability of IQ in young children. *Psychological Science, 14,* 623–628.

Twenge, J. M. (2006). *Generation Me: Why today's young Americans are more confident, assertive, entitled—and more miserable than ever before.* New York: Free Press.

Twenge, J. M., & Foster, J. D. (2008). Mapping the scale of the narcissism epidemic: Increases in narcissism 2002–2007 within ethnic groups. *Journal of Research in Personality, 42,* 1619–1622.

Tyas, S. L., Salazar, J. C., Snowdon, D. A., Desrosier, M. F., Riley, K. P., Mendiondo, M. S., & Kryscio, R. J. (2007). Transitions to mild cognitive impairments, dementia, and death: Findings from the Nun Study. *American Journal of Epidemiology, 165,* 1231–1238.

Tye, K. M., & Janak, P. H. (2007). Amygdala neurons differentially encode motivation and reinforcement. *Journal of Neuroscience, 27,* 3937–3945.

Tyler, T. R., & De Cremer, D. (2006). Social psychology and economics. In P. A. M. Van Lange (Ed.), *Bridging social psychology.* Mahwah, NJ: Erlbaum.

U

Uchida, H., & Mamo, D. C. (2009). Dosing of antipsychotics across the life-spectrum. *Progress in Neuro-Psychopharmacology and Biological Psychiatry.* (in press)

Uguz, F., Akman, C., Kaya, N., & Cilli, A. S. (2007). Postpartum-onset obsessive-compulsive disorder: Incidence, clinical features, and related factors. *Journal of Clinical Psychiatry, 68,* 132–138.

Umbreit, J., Ferro, J., Liaupsin, C. J., & Lane, K. L. (2007). *Functional behavioral assessment and function-based intervention.* Upper Saddle River, NJ: Prentice-Hall.

Underhill, K., Montgomery, P., & Operario, D. (2007). Sexual abstinence programs to prevent HIV infection in high-income countries. *British Medical Journal, 335,* 248.

United Nations. (2002). *Demographic yearbook.* Geneva, Switzerland: Author.

United Nations Office on Drugs and Crime (UNODC). (2008). *World drug report.* Vienna: United Nations.

United Nations World Youth Report. (2005). *World youth report 2005: Young people today and in 2015.* Geneva, Switzerland: United Nations.

Urban, E. (2008). The "self" in analytical psychology: The function of the "central archetype" within Fordham's model. *Journal of Analytical Psychology, 53,* 329–350.

Urcelay, G. P., Wheeler, D. S., & Miller, R. R. (2009). Spacing extinction trials alleviates renewal and spontaneous recovery. *Learning and Behavior, 37,* 60–73.

Urry, H. L., Nitschke, J. B., Dolski, I., Jackson, D. C., Dalton, K. M., Mueller, C. J., Rosenkranz, M. A., Ryff, C. D., Singer, B. H., & Davidson, R. J. (2004). Making a life worth living: Neural correlates of well-being. *Psychological Science, 15,* 367–372.

U.S. Bureau of the Census. (2005). *Marriage.* Washington, DC: U.S. Department of Labor.

U.S. Bureau of Justice Statistics. (2006). All crimes in the US in 2004. Washington, DC: Author.

U.S. Department of Justice. (2007). *Homicide trends in the U.S.* http://www.ojp.usdoj.gov/bjs/homicide/tables/totalstab.htm (accessed May 29, 2009)

U.S. Food and Drug Administration. (2004, October 15). *FDA launches a multi-pronged strategy to strengthen safeguards for children treated with antidepressant medications.* News release. Washington, DC: Author.

U.S. Food and Drug Administration. (2005). *Office of Device Evaluation annual report fiscal year 2005.* Washington, DC: Center for Devices and Radiological Health.

V

Vacek, J. E. (2009). Using a conceptual approach with a concept map of psychosis as an exemplar to promote critical thinking. *Journal of Nursing Education, 48,* 49–53.

Vaillant, G. E. (1983). *The natural history of alcoholism.* Cambridge, MA: Harvard University Press.

Vaillant, G. E. (1992). Is there a natural history of addiction? In C. P. O'Brien & J. H. Jaffe (Eds.), *Addictive states.* Cambridge, MA: Harvard University Press.

Vakily, M., Lee, R. D., Wu, J., Gunawardhana, L., & Mulford, D. (2009). Drug interaction studies with dexlansoprazole modified release (TAK-390MR), a proton pump inhibitor with a dual delayed-release formulation. *Clinical Drug Investigation, 29,* 35–50.

Vallido, T., Jackson, D., & O'Brien, L. (2009). Mad, sad, and hormonal: The gendered nature of adolescent sleep disturbance. *Journal of Child Health Care, 13,* 7–18.

van Bokhoven, I., van Goozen, S. H. M., van Engeland, H., Schaal, B., Arseneault, L., Seguin, J. R., Assaad, J., Nagin, D. S., Vitaro, F., & Tremblay, R. E. (2006). Salivary testosterone and aggression, delinquency, and social dominance in a population-based longitudinal study of adolescent males. *Hormones and Behavior, 50,* 118–125.

Vandello, J. A., & Cohen, D. (2004). When believing is seeing: Sustaining norms of violence in cultures of honor. In M. Schaller & C. S. Crandall (Eds.). *The psychological foundations of culture* (pp. 281–304). Mahwah, NJ: Erlbaum.

Van der Borght, K., & others. (2009). Physical exercise leads to rapid adaptations in hippocampal vasculature: Temporal dynamics and relationship to cell proliferation and neurogenesis. *Hippocampus.* (in press)

van de Riet, W. A., Grezes, J., & de Gelder, B. (2009). Specific and common brain regions involved in the perception of faces and bodies and the representation of their emotional expressions. *Social Neuroscience, 4,* 101–120.

Van Deun, L., & others. (2009). Sound localization, sound lateralization, and binaural masking level differences in children with normal hearing. *Ear and Hearing, 30,* 178–190.

van Driel, M. A., & Brunner, H. G. (2006). Bioinformatics methods for identifying candidate disease genes. *Human Genomics. 2,* 429–432.

van Hateren, J. H. (2007). A model of spatiotemporal signal processing by primate cones and horizontal cells. *Journal of Vision, 7,* 3.

van IJzendoorn, M. H., & Sagi-Schwartz, A. (2008). Cross-cultural patterns of attachment: Universal and contextual dimensions. In J. Cassidy & P. R. Shaver (Eds.), *Handbook of attachment.* New York: Guilford.

van Ingen, D. J., & Novicki, D. J. (2009). An effectiveness study of group therapy for anxiety disorders. *International Journal of Group Psychotherapy, 59,* 243–251.

Van Katwyk, P. T., Fox, S., Spector, P. E., & Kelloway, E. K. (2000). Using the job-related affective well-being scale (JAWS) to investigate affective responses to work stressors. *Journal of Occupational Health Psychology, 52,* 219–230.

van Kempen, E. E., & others. (2009). Children's annoyance reactions to aircraft and road traffic noise. *Journal of the Acoustical Society of America, 125,* 895–904.

Van Lange, P. A. M., Rusbult, C. E., Drigotas, S. M., & Arriaga, X. B. (1997). Willingness to sacrifice in close relationships. *Journal of Personality and Social Psychology, 72,* 1373–1395.

van Leeuwen, W. M., & others. (2009). Sleep restriction increases the risk of developing cardiovascular diseases by augmenting proinflammatory responses through IL-17 and CRP. *PLoS One, 4,* e4589.

Van Orden, K. A., Whitte, T. K., Gordon, K. H., Bender, T. W., & Joiner, T. E. (2008). Suicidal desire and the capability of suicide: Tests of the interpersonal-psychological theory of suicidal behavior among adults. *Journal of Consulting and Clinical Psychology, 76,* 72–83.

van Reekum, C. M., Urry, H. L., Johnstone, T., Thurow, M. E., Frye, C. J., Jackson, J., Schaefer, H. S., Alexander, A. L., & Davidson, R. J. (2007). Individual differences in amygdala and ventromedial prefrontal cortex activity are associated with evaluation speed and psychological well-being. *Journal of Cognitive Neuroscience, 19,* 237–248.

Van Remmen, H., & Jones, D. P. (2009). Current thoughts on the role of mitochondria and free radicals in the biology of aging. *Journals of Gerontology A: Biological Sciences and Medical Sciences, 64,* 171–174.

Van Riper, M. (2007). Families of children with Down syndrome: Responding to "a change in plans" with resilience. *Journal of Pediatric Nursing, 22,* 116–128.

van Strien, N. M., Cappaert, N. L., & Witter, M. P. (2009). The anatomy of memory: An interactive overview of the parahippocampal-hippocampal network. *Nature Reviews: Neuoroscience, 10,* 272–282.

Van Voorhees, B. W., & others. (2009). Randomized clinical trial of an Internet-based depression prevention program for adolescents (Project CATCH-IT) in primary care: 12-week outcomes. *Journal of Developmental and Behavioral Pediatrics, 30,* 23–37.

Van Vugt, M., & Van Lange, P. A. M. (2006). The altruism puzzle: Psychological adaptations for prosocial behavior. In M. Schaller, J. S. Simpson, & D. T. Kenrick (Eds.), *Evolution and social psychology: Frontiers of social psychology* (pp. 237–261). Madison, CT: Psychosocial Press.

Vassilopoulos, S. P., & Watkins, E. R. (2009). Adaptive and maladaptive self-focus: A pilot extension study with individuals high and low in fear of negative evaluation. *Behavior Therapy, 40,* 181–189.

Vaughn, S., Bos, C. S., & Schumm, J. S. (2003). *Teaching exceptional, diverse, and at-risk students in the general education classroom* (3rd ed.). Boston: Allyn & Bacon.

Vazquez, J., Hall, S. C., Witkowska, H. E., & Greco, M. A. (2008). Rapid alterations in cortical protein profiles underlie spontaneous sleep and wake bouts. *Journal of Cellular Biochemistry, 105,* 1472–1484.

Vega, V., & Malamuth, N. M. (2007). Predicting sexual aggression: The role of pornography in the context of general and specific risk factors. *Aggressive Behavior, 33,* 104–117.

Veltri, C. O., & others. (2009). Correlates of MMPI-2—a scales in acute psychiatric and forensic samples. *Journal of Personality Assessment, 91,* 288–300.

Vermetten, E., Schmahl, C., Lindner, S., Loewenstein, R. J., & Bremner, J. D. (2006). Hippocampal and amygdalar volumes in dissociative identity disorder. *American Journal of Psychiatry, 163,* 630–636.

Verschuere, B., Crombez, G., De Clercq, A., & Koster, E. H. W. (2005). Psychopathic traits and autonomic responding to concealed information in a prison sample. *Psychophysiology, 42,* 239–245.

Vervaet, M., van Heeringen, C., & Audenaert, K. (2004). Personality-related characteristics in restricting versus binging and purging eating disordered patients. *Comprehensive Psychiatry, 45,* 37–43.

Vetter, I., Kapitzke, D., Hermanussen, S., Moneith, G. R., & Cabot, P. J. (2006). The effects of pH on beta-endorphin and morphine inhibition of calcium transients in dorsal root ganglion neurons. *Journal of Pain, 7,* 488–499.

Vickerman, K. A., & Margolin, G. (2009). Rape treatment outcome research: Empirical findings and state of the literature. *Clinical Psychology Review.* (in press)

Victor, A. M., & Bernstein, G. A. (2009). Anxiety disorders and posttraumatic stress disorder update. *Psychiatric Clinics of North America, 32,* 57–69.

Videtic, A., Zupanic, T., Pregelj, P., Balazic, J., Tomori, M., & Komel, R. (2009). Suicide, stress, and serotonin receptor 1A promotor polymorphism -1019>G in Slovenian suicide victims. *European Archives of Psychiatry and Clinical Neuroscience, 259,* 234–238.

Villemure, C., & Bushnell, M. C. (2009). Mood influences supraspinal pain processing separately from attention. *Journal of Neuroscience, 29,* 705–715.

Vimal, R. L., & others. (2009). Activation of the suprachiasmatic nuclei and primary visual cortex depends upon time of day. *European Journal of Neuroscience, 29,* 399–410.

Viney, W., & King, D. B. (2003). *History of psychology* (3rd ed.). Boston: Allyn & Bacon.

Visser, P. S., & Cooper, J. (2007). Attitude change. In M. A. Hogg & J. Cooper (Eds.), *The Sage handbook of social psychology* (concise 2nd ed.). Thousand Oaks, CA: Sage.

Vogt, T. M., Mullooly, J. P., Ernst, D., Pople, C. R., & Hollis, J. F. (1992). Social networks as predictors of ischemic heart disease, cancer, stroke, and hypertension. *Journal of Clinical Epidemiology, 45,* 659–666.

Voisey, J., Swagell, C. D., Hughes, I. P., Morris, C. P., van Daal, A., Noble, E. P., Kann, B., Heslop, K. A., Young, R. M., & Lawford, B. R. (2009). The DRD2 gene 957C > T polymorphism is associated with posttraumatic stress disorder in war veterans. *Depression and Anxiety, 26,* 28–33.

Volpe, T. (2007). Woman allegedly raped in St. Paul as bystanders look on. http://www.kare11.com/news/news_article.aspx?storyid=263021 (accessed September 15, 2008)

von Békésy, G. (1960). Vibratory patterns of the basilar membrane. In E. G. Wever (Ed.), *Experiments in hearing.* New York: McGraw-Hill.

von Helmholtz, H. (1852). On the theory of compound colors. *Philosophical Magazine, 4,* 519–534.

Voshaar, R. C., & others. (2006). Predictors of long-term benzodiazepine abstinence in participants of a randomized controlled benzodiazepine withdrawal program. *Canadian Journal of Psychiatry, 51,* 445–452.

Voss, J. L., & Paller, K. A. (2009). An electrophysiological signature of unconscious recognition memory. *Nature Neuroscience, 13,* 349–355.

Voss, H. U., Uluc, A. M., Dyke, J. P., Watts, R., Kobylarz, E. J., McCandliss, B. D., Heier, L. A., Beattie, B. J., Hamacher, K. A., Vallabhajosula, S., Goldsmith, S. J., Ballon, D., Giacino, J. T., & Schiff, N. D. (2006). Possible axonal regrowth in late recovery from the minimally conscious state. *Journal of Clinical Investigation, 116,* 2005–2011.

Voyvodic, J. T., Petrella, J. R., & Friedman, A. H. (2009). fMRI activation mapping as a percentage of local excitation: Consistent presurgical motor maps without threshold adjustment. *Journal of Magnetic Resonance Imaging, 29,* 751–759.

Vygotsky, L. S. (1962). *Thought and language.* Cambridge, MA: MIT Press.

W

Wagner, A. D., Schacter, D. L., Rotte, M., Koutstaal, B., Maril, A., Dale, A. M., Rosen, B. R., & Buckner, R. L. (1998). Building memories: Remembering and forgetting of verbal experiences as predicted by brain activity. *Science, 281,* 1185–1187.

Wai, J., Lubinski, D., & Benbow, C. P. (2005) Creativity and occupational accomplishments among intellectually precocious youths: An age 13 to age 33 longitudinal study. *Journal of Educational Psychology, 97,* 484–492.

Walker, D. D., Roffman, R. A., Stephens, R. S., Wakana, K., & Berghuis, J. (2006). Motivational enhancement therapy for adolescent marijuana users: A preliminary randomized controlled trial. *Journal of Consulting and Clinical Psychology, 74,* 628–632.

Walker, D. R., & Milton, G. A. (1966). Memory transfer vs. sensitization in cannibal planarians. *Psychonomic Science, 5,* 293–294.

Walker, H. (2008). *Breaking free: My life with dissociative disorder.* New York: Simon & Schuster.

Waller, E. A., Bendel, R. E., & Kaplan, J. (2008). Sleep disorders and the eye. *Mayo Clinic Proceedings, 83,* 1251–1261.

Wallerstein, R. S. (1989). The psychotherapy research project of the Menninger Foundation: An overview. *Journal of Consulting and Clinical Psychology, 57,* 195–205.

Walley, A. J., Blakemore, A. I., & Froguel, P. (2006). Genetics of obesity and the prediction of risk for health. *Human Molecular Genetics, 15, Suppl. 2,* R124–R130.

Walton, K. E., & Roberts, B. W. (2004). On the relationship between substance use and personality traits: Abstainers are not maladjusted. *Journal of Research in Personality, 38,* 515–535.

Wampold, B. E. (2001). *The great psychotherapy debate: Models, methods, and findings.* Mahwah, NJ: Erlbaum.

Wampold, B. E., & Brown, G. S. (2005). Estimating variability in outcomes attributable to therapists: A naturalistic study of outcomes of managed care. *Journal of Consulting and Clinical Psychology, 73,* 914–923.

Wanat, M. J., Sparta, D. R., Hopf, F. W., Bowers, M. S., Melis, M., & Bonci, A. (2009). Strain specific synaptic modifications on vental tegmental area dopamine neurons after ethanol exposure. *Biological Psychiatry, 65,* 646–653.

Wang, H., & Eckel, R. H. (2009). Liproprotein lipase: From gene to obesity. *American Journal of Physiology, Endocrinology, and Metabolism.* (in press)

Wang, J., Simpson, H. B., & Dulawa, S. C. (2009). Assessing the validity of current mouse genetic models of obsessive-compulsive disorder. *Behavioral Pharmacology, 20,* 119–133.

Wang, Y. F., & Hatton, G. I. (2009). Astrocytic plasticity and patterned oxytocin neuronalactivity: Dynamic interactions. *Journal of Neuroscience, 29,* 1743–1754.

Wangberg, S. C., Gammon, D., & Spitznogle, K. (2007). In the eyes of the beholder: Exploring psychologists' attitudes towards the use of e-therapy in Norway. *CyberPsychology and Behavior, 10,* 418–423.

Ward, J., Hall, K., & Haslam, C. (2006). Patterns of memory dysfunction in current and 2-year abstinent MDMA users. *Journal of Clinical and Experimental Neuropsychology, 28,* 306–324.

Ward, T. B. (2007). Creative cognition as a window on creativity. *Methods, 42,* 28–37.

Warnecke, R. B., Morera, O., Turner, L., Mermelstein, R., Johnson, T. P., Parsons, J., Crittenden, K., Freels, S., & Flay, B. (2001). Changes in self-efficacy and readiness for smoking cessation among women with high school or less education. *Journal of Health and Social Behavior, 42,* 97–109.

Warrant, E. J. (2009). Mammalian vision: Rods are a bargain. *Current Biology, 19,* R69–R71.

Warren, G., Schertler, E., & Bull, P. (2009). Detecting deception from emotional and unemotional cues. *Journal of Nonverbal Behavior, 33,* 59–69.

Warren, J. I., Stein, J. A., & Grella, C. E. (2007). Role of social support and self-efficacy in treatment outcomes among clients with co-occurring disorders. *Drug and Alcohol Dependence, 89,* 267–274.

Watanabe, H., & Mizunami, M. (2007). Pavlov's cockroach: Classical conditioning of salivation in an insect. *PloS One, 6,* e529.

Watkins, L. R., & Maier, S. F. (2000). The pain of being sick. *Annual Review of Psychology* (vol. 51). Palo Alto, CA: Annual Reviews.

Watson, A., El-Deredy, W., Bentley, D. E., Vogt, B. A., & Jones, A. K. (2006). Categories of placebo response in the absence of site-specific stimulation of analgesia. *Pain, 126,* 115–122.

Watson, D. (2001). Positive affectivity: The disposition to experience pleasurable emotional states. In C. R. Snyder & S. J. Lopez (Eds.), *Handbook of positive psychology.* New York: Oxford University Press.

Watson, D. (2009). Differentiation of mood and anxiety disorders. *Annual Review of Clinical Psychology* (vol. 5). Palo Alto, CA: Annual Reviews.

Watson, D., & Clark, L. A. (1997). Extraversion and its positive emotional core. In R. Hogan, J. A. Johnson, & S. R., Briggs (Eds.), *Handbook of personality psychology* (pp. 767–793). San Diego: Academic.

Watson, D. L., & Tharp, R. G. (2007). *Self-directed behavior* (9th ed.). Belmont, CA: Wadsworth.

Watson, J. B. (1928). *Psychological care of the infant and child.* Philadelphia: Lippincott.

Watson, J. B., & Rayner, R. (1920). Conditioned emotional reactions. *Journal of Experimental Psychology, 3,* 1–14.

Watt, J. A., Lo, D., Cranston, H. J., & Paden, C. M. (2009). CNTF receptor alpha is expressed by magnocellular neurons and expression in unregulated in the rate supraoptic nucleus during axonal sprouting. *Experimental Neurology, 215,* 135–141.

Wayment, H. A., & O'Mara, E. M. (2008). The collective and compassionate consequences of downward social comparisons. In H. A. Wayment & J. J. Bauer (Eds.), *Transcending self-interest: Psychological explorations of the quiet ego* (pp. 159–169). Washington, DC: American Psychological Association.

Weaver, K., Garcia, S. M., Schwarz, N., & Miller, D. T. (2007). Inferring the popularity of an opinion from its familiarity: A repetitive voice can sound like a chorus. *Journal of Personality and Social Psychology, 92,* 821–833.

Webb, W. B. (2000). Sleep. In A. Kazdin (Ed.), *Encyclopedia of psychology.* Washington, DC, & New York: American Psychological Association and Oxford University Press.

Weber, S., Habel, U., Amunts, K., & Schneider, F. (2008). Structural brain abnormalities in psychopaths—A review. *Behavorial Sciences and the Law, 26,* 7–28.

Webster, J. M., Smith, R. H., Rhodes, A., & Whatley, M. A. (1999). The effect of a favor on public and private compliance: How internalized is the norm of reciprocity? *Basic and Applied Social Psychology, 21,* 251–260.

Wechsler, H., Lee, J. E., Kuo, M., & Lee, H. (2000). College binge drinking in the 1990s—A continuing health problem: Results of the Harvard University School of Public Health 1999 College Alcohol Study. *Journal of American College Health, 48,* 199–210.

Wechsler, H., Lee, J. E., Kuo, M., Seibring, M., Nelson, T. F., & Lee, H. (2002). Trends in college binge drinking during a period of increased prevention efforts: Findings from 4 Harvard School of Public Health college alcohol study surveys: 1993–2001. *Journal of American College Health, 50,* 203–217.

Wecker, L., & others. (2010). *Brody's human pharmacology* (5th ed.). London: Elsevier.

Wegener, D. T., Clark, J. K., & Petty, R. E. (2006). Not all stereotyping is created equal: Differential consequences of thoughtful versus non-thoughtful stereotyping. *Journal of Personality and Social Psychology, 90,* 42–59.

Weich, S., Patterson, J., Shaw, R., & Stewart-Brown, S. (2009). Family relationships in childhood and common psychiatric disorders in later life: Systematic review of prospective studies. *British Journal of Psychiatry, 194,* 392–398.

Weidner, R., Krummenacher, J., Reimann, B., Muller, H. J., & Fink, G. R. (2009). Sources of top-down control in visual search. *Journal of Cognitive Neuroscience.* (in press)

Weiner, B. (2006). Social motivation, justice, and the moral emotions: An attributional approach. Mahwah, NJ: Erlbaum.

Weiner, I. B. (2004). Rorschach assessment: Current status. In M. Hersen (Ed.), *Comprehensive handbook of psychological assessment* (vol. 2). New York: Wiley.

Weinstein, T. A. R., Capitanio, J. P., & Gosling, S. D. (2008). Personality in animals. In O. P. John, R. W. Robins, & L. A. Pervin (Eds.), *Handbook of personality theory and research* (3rd ed., pp. 328–350). New York: Guilford.

Weir, W. (1984, October 15). Another look at subliminal "facts." *Advertising Age,* 46.

Weismiller, D. G. (2009). Menopause. *Primary Care, 36,* 199–226.

Weiss, A., Bates, T. C., & Luciano, M. (2008). Happiness is a personal(ity) thing: The genetics of personality and well-being in a representative sample. *Psychological Science, 19,* 205–210.

Weiss, A., Boaz, M., Belooseky, Y., Kornowski, R., & Grossman, E. (2009). Body mass index and risk of all-cause and cardiovascular mortality in hospitalized elderly patients with diabetes mellitus. *Diabetic Medicine, 26,* 253–259.

Weiss, A., King, J. E., & Perkins, L. (2006). Personality and subjective well-being in orangutans (Pongo pygmaeus and Pongo abelii). *Journal of Personality and Social Psychology, 90,* 501–511.

Weissman, M., & Olfson, M. (1995). Depression in women: Implications for health care research. *Science, 269,* 799–801.

Welch, D., & Poulton, R. (2009). Personality influences on change in smoking behavior. *Health Psychology, 28,* 292–299.

Wellman, H. M., & Woolley, J. D. (1990). From simple desires to ordinary beliefs: The early development of everyday psychology. *Cognition, 35,* 245–275.

Wenzel, M. (2009). Social identity and justice: Implications for intergroup relations. In S. Otten, K. Sassenberg, & T. Kessler (Eds.), *Intergroup relations.* New York: Psychology Press.

Wertsch, J. (2008). From social interaction to higher psychological processes. *Human Development, 51,* 66–79.

West, R. (2005). Time for a change: Putting the transtheoretical (stages of change) model to rest. *Addiction, 100,* 1036–1039.

Westen, D., Gabbard, G. O., & Soto, C. J. (2008). Psychoanalytic approaches to personality. In O. P. John, R. W. Robins, & L. A. Pervin (Eds.) *Handbook of personality theory and research* (3rd ed., pp. 61–113). New York: Guilford.

Weyers, P., Muhlberger, A., Kund, A., Hess, U., & Pauli, P. (2009). Modulation of facial reactions to avatar emotional faces by nonconscious competition priming. *Psychophysiology, 46,* 328–335.

Wheeler, D. S., & Miller, R. R. (2008). Determinants of cue interactions. *Behavioral Processes, 78,* 191–203.

Whiffen, V. E., & Demidenko, N. (2006). Mood disturbances across the lifespan. In J. Worell, & C. D. Goodheart (Eds.), *Handbook of girls' and women's health: Gender and well-being across the lifespan.* New York: Oxford University Press.

Whipple, B., Ogden, G., & Komisaruk, B. (1992). Analgesia produced in women by genital self-stimulation. *Archives of Sexual Behavior, 9,* 87–99.

Whitaker, R. (2002). Mad in America: Bad science, bad medicine, and the mistreatment of the mentally ill. Cambridge, MA: Perseus.

White, J. W., & Frabutt, J. M. (2006). Violence against girls and women: An integrative developmental perspective. In J. Worell & C. D. Goodheart (Eds.), *Handbook of girls' and women's psychological health: Gender and well-being across the lifespan* (pp. 85–93). New York: Oxford University Press.

White, R. C., & Aimola Davies, A. (2008). Attention set for numbers: Expectation and perceptual load in inattentional blindness. *Journal of Experimental Psychology: Human Perception and Performance, 34,* 1092–1107.

White, R. W. (1992). Exploring personality the long way: The study of lives. R. A. Zucker, A. I. Rabin, J.

Aronoff, & S. J. Frank (Eds.), *Personality structure in the life course: Essays on personology in the Murray tradition* (pp. 3–21). New York: Springer.

Whitt-Glover, M. C., Taylor, W. C., Floyd, M. F., Yore, M. M., Yancey, A. K., & Matthews, C. E. (2009). Disparities in physical activity and sedentary behaviors among U.S. children and adolescents: Prevalence, correlates, and intervention implications. *Journal of Public Health Policy, 30, Suppl. 1*, S309–S334.

Whorf, B. L. (1956). *Language, thought, and creativity.* New York: Wiley.

Widiger, T. A. (2009). Neuroticism. In M. R. Leary & R. H. Hoyle (Eds.), *Handbook of individual differences in social behavior* (pp. 129–146). New York: Guilford.

Wiebe, R. P. (2004). Delinquent behavior and the Five Factor model: Hiding in the adaptive landscape? *Individual Differences Research, 2*, 38–62.

Wiedeman, R. (2008, March 25). Digital man. *Boston Globe.* http://www.boston.com/news/education/higher/articles/2008/03/25/digital_man/

Wiersma, D., Nienhuis, F. J., Slooff, C. J., & Giel, R. (1998). Natural course of schizophrenic disorders: A 15-year follow up of a Dutch incidence cohort. *Schizophrenia Bulletin, 24*, 75–85.

Wierzynski, C. M., Lubenov, E. V., Gu, M., & Siapas, A. G. (2009). State-dependent spike-timing relationships between hippocampal and prefrontal circuits during sleep. *Neuron, 61*, 587–596.

Wigfield, A., Eccles, J. S., Schiefele, U., Roeser, R. W., & Davis-Kean, P. (2006). Development of achievement motivation. In W. Damon & R. Lerner (Eds.), *Handbook of child psychology* (6th ed.). New York: Wiley.

Wilfley, D. E., Bishop, M. E., Wilson, G. T., & Agras, W. S. (2007). Classification of eating disorders: Toward DSM-V. *International Journal of Eating Disorders, 40*, S123–S129.

Wilfley, D. E., Friedman, M. A., Dounchis, J. Z., Stein, R. I., Welch, R. R., & Ball, S. A. (2000). Comorbid psychopathology in binge eating disorder: Relation to eating disorder severity at baseline and following treatment. *Journal of Consulting and Clinical Psychology, 68*, 641–649.

Willcox, D. C., Willcox, B. J., He, Q., Wang, N. C., & Suzuki, M. (2008). They really are that old: A validation study of centenarian prevalence in Okinawa. *Journals of Gerontology A: Biological Sciences and Medical Sciences, 63*, 338–349.

Willert, M. V., Thulstrup, A. M., & Hertz, J. (2009). Changes in stress and coping from a randomized controlled trial of a three-month stress management intervention. *Scandinavian Journal of Work and Environmental Health, 35*, 145–152.

Williams, J. D., & Gruzelier, J. H. (2001). Differentiation of hypnosis and relaxation by analysis of narrow band theta and alpha frequencies. *International Journal of Clinical and Experimental Hypnosis, 49*, 185–206.

Williams, L. M. (1995). Recovered memories of abuse in women with documented child sexual victimization histories. *Journal of Traumatic Stress, 19*, 257–267.

Williams, L. M. (2003). Understanding child abuse and violence against women: A life-course perspective. *Journal of Interpersonal Violence, 18*, 441–451.

Williams, L. M. (2004). Researcher-advocate collaborations to end violence against women. *Journal of Interpersonal Violence, 19*, 1350–1357.

Williams, R. B. (2001). Hostility (and other psychosocial risk factors): Effects on health and the potential for successful behavioral approaches to prevention and treatment. In A. Baum, T. A. Revenson, & J. E. Singer (Eds.), *Handbook of health psychology.* Mahwah, NJ: Erlbaum.

Williams, R. B. (2002). Hostility, neuroendocrine changes, and health outcomes. In H. G. Koenig & H. J. Cohen (Eds.), *The link between religion and health.* New York: Oxford University Press.

Williams, S. K., & Davidson, K. W. (2009). Psychological distress and cardiovascular disease with emphasis on acute coronary syndromes. *Journal of the American College of Cardiology, 53*, 1339.

Willis, J., & Todorov, A. (2006). First impressions: Making up your mind after a 100-ms exposure to a face. *Psychological Science, 17*, 592–598.

Willis, S. L., & Schaie, K. W. (2005). Cognitive trajectories in midlife and cognitive functioning in old age. In S. L. Willis & M. Martin (Eds.), *Middle adulthood.* Thousand Oaks, CA: Sage.

Wilson, B., & Smallwood, S. (2008). The proportion of marriages ending in divorce. *Population Trends, 131*, 28–36.

Wilson, G. T., Grilo, C. M., & Vitousek, K. M. (2007). Psychological treatment of eating disorders. *American Psychologist, 62*, 199–216.

Wilson, R. S., Mendes de Leon, D. F., Bienias, J. L., Evans, D. A., & Bennett, D. A. (2004). Personality and mortality in old age. *Journals of Gerontology: Psychological Sciences and Social Sciences, 59B*, 110–116.

Wilt, J., & Revelle, W. (2009) Extraversion. In M. Leary & R. Hoyle (Eds.), *Handbook of individual differences in social behavior.* (pp. 27–45). New York: Guilford.

Wiltermuth, S. S., & Heath, C. (2009). Synchrony and cooperation. *Psychological Science, 20*, 1–5.

Winner, E. (1996). *Gifted children: Myths and realities.* New York: Basic Books.

Winner, E. (2000). The origins and ends of giftedness. *American Psychologist, 55*, 159–169.

Winner, E. (2006). Development in the arts. In W. Damon & R. Lerner (Eds.), *Handbook of child psychology* (6th ed.). New York: Wiley.

Winter, D. G. (2005). Measuring the motives of political actors at a distance. In J. M. Post (Ed.), *The psychological assessment of political leaders: With profiles of Saddam Hussein and Bill Clinton* (pp. 153–177). Ann Arbor: University of Michigan Press.

Wirtz, P. H., Redwine, L. S., Ehlert, U., & von Kanel, R. (2009).Independent association between lower level of social support and higher cagulation activity before and after acute psychosocial stress. *Psychosomatic Medicine, 71*, 30–37.

Wise, R. A. (2008). Dopamine and reward: The anhedonia hypothesis 30 years on. *Neurotoxicity Research, 14*, 169–183.

Wiseman, R., & Watt, C. (2006). Belief in psychic ability and the misattribution hypothesis: A qualitative review. *British Journal of Psychology, 97*, 323–338.

Witelson, S. F., Kigar, D. L., & Harvey, T. (1999). The exceptional brain of Albert Einstein. *Lancet, 353*, 2149–2153.

Wojtczak, M., & Oxenham, A. J. (2009). Pitfalls in behavioral estimates of basilar-membrane compression in humans. *Journal of the Acoustical Society of America, 125*, 270–281.

Woike, B. (2001). Working with free response data: Let's not give up hope. *Psychological Inquiry, 12*, 157–159.

Woike, B., & Matic, D. (2004). Cognitive complexity in response to traumatic experiences. *Journal of Personality, 72*, 633–657.

Woike, B., Mcleod, S., & Goggin, M. (2003). Implicit and explicit motives influence accessibility to different autobiographical knowledge. *Personality and Social Psychology Bulletin, 29*, 1046–1055.

Woike, B. A. (2008). The state of the story in personality psychology. *Social and Personality Psychology Compass, 2*, 434–443.

Wolf, A. (2000). Emotional expression online: Gender differences in emoticon use. *CyberPsychology & Behavior, 3*, 827–833.

Wolitzky, K. B., & Telch, M. J. (2009). Augmenting in vivo exposure with fear antagonistic actions: A preliminary test. *Behavior Therapy, 40*, 57–71.

Wolkove, N., Elkholy, O., Baltzan, M., & Palayew, M. (2007). Sleep and aging: 1. Sleep disorders commonly found in older people. *Canadian Medical Association Journal, 176*, 1299–1304.

Wolpe, J. (1963). Behavior therapy in complex neurotic states. *British Journal of Psychiatry, 110*, 28–34.

Wong, A. C-N., Jobard, G., James, K. H., James, T. W., & Gauthier, I. (2009). Expertise with characters in alphabetic and non-alphabetic writing systems engage overlapping occipito-temporal areas. *Cognitive Neuropsychology.* (in press)

Wong, A. C-N., Palmeri, T. J., & Gauthier, I. (2009) Conditions for face-like expertise with objects: Becoming a Ziggerin expert—but which type? *Psychological Science.* (in press)

Wood, R. L., & Liossi, C. (2006). Neuropsychological and neurobehavioral correlates of aggression following traumatic brain injury. *Journal of Neuropsychiatry & Clinical Neurosciences, 18*, 333–341.

Wood, S. C., Fay, J., Sage, J. R., & Anagnostaras, S. G. (2007). Cocaine and Pavlovian fear conditioning: Dose–effect analysis. *Behavioral Brain Research, 176*, 244–250.

Wood, W., & Eagly, A. H. (2007). Social structural origins of sex differences in human mating. In S. W. Gangestad & J. A. Simpson (Eds.), *The evolution of mind: Fundamental questions and controversies.* (pp. 383–390). New York: Guilford.

World Health Organization. (2003). *Suicide rates.* http://www.who.int/mental_health/prevention/suicide/suiciderates/en/ (accessed June 18, 2007)

Wout, D. A., Shih, M. J., Jackson, J. S., & Sellers, R. M. (2009). Targets as perceivers: How people determine if they will be negatively stereotyped. *Journal of Personality and Social Psychology, 96*, 349–362.

Wright, T. A., & Cropanzano, R. (2000). Psychological well-being and job satisfaction as predictors of job performance. *Journal of Occupational Health Psychology, 5*, 84–94.

Wright, T. A., & Staw, B. M. (1999). Affect and favorable work outcomes: Two longitudinal tests of the happy–productive worker thesis. *Journal of Organizational Behavior, 20*, 1–23.

Wu, K. D., Aardema, F., & O'Connor, K. P. (2009). Inferential confusion, obsessive beliefs, and obsessive-compulsive symptoms: A replication and extension. *Journal of Anxiety Disorders, 23*, 746–752.

Wyer, R. S. (2007). Principles of mental representation. In A.W. Kruglanski & E. T. Higgins (Eds.), *Social psychology: Handbook of basic principles* (2nd ed.). New York: Guilford.

Wyer, R. S., Chiu, C.-Y., & Hong, Y.-Y. (Eds.). (2009). *Understanding culture.* New York: Psychology Press.

Wykes, T., Brammer, M., Mellers, J., Bray, P., Reeder, C., Williams, C., & Corner, J. (2002). Effects on the brain of a psychological treatment: Cognitive remediation therapy: Functional magnetic resonance imaging in schizophrenia. *British Journal of Psychiatry, 181*, 144–152.

X

Xu, Y., & Cardena, E. (2008). Hypnosis as an adjunct therapy in the management of diabetes. *International Journal of Clinical and Experimental Hypnosis, 56*, 63–72.

Y

Yalom, I. D., & Leszcz, M. (2006). *Theory and practice of group psychotherapy* (5th ed.). New York: Basic Books.

Yamada, M., & Decety, J. (2009). Unconscious affective processing and empathy: An investigation of subliminal priming on the detection of painful facial expressions. *Pain, 143*, 71–75.

Yamanishi, T., & others. (2009). Changes after behavior therapy among responsive and nonresponsive patients with obsessive-compulsive disorder. *Psychiatry Research, 172*, 242–250.

Yang, Y. (2008). Social inequalities in happiness in the United States, 1972–2004: An age-period-cohort analysis. *American Sociological Review, 73*, 204–226.

Yang, Y., Glenn, A. L., & Raine, A. (2008). Brain abnormalities in antisocial individuals: Implications for the law. *Behavioral Sciences & the Law, 26*, 65–83.

Yang, Y., Raine, A., Lencz, T., Bihrle, S., LaCasse, L., & Colletti, P. (2005). Volume reduction in prefrontal gray matter in unsuccessful criminal psychopaths. *Biological Psychiatry, 57*, 1103–1108.

Yates, L. B., Djousse, L., Kurth, T., Buring, J. E., & Gaziano, J. M. (2008). Exceptional longevity in men: Modifiable factors associated with survival and function to age 90 years. *Archives of Internal Medicine, 168*, 284–290.

Yeates, K. O., & others. (2009). Longitudinal trajectories of postconcussive symptoms in children with mild traumatic brain injuries and their relationship to acute clinical status. *Pediatrics, 123,* 735–743.

Yen, C. F., Chen, C. C., Lee, Y., Tang, T. C., Ko, C. H., & Yen, J. Y. (2009). Association between quality of life and self-stigma, insight, and adverse effects of medication in patients with depressive disorders. *Depression and Anxiety.* (in press)

Yip, T., Kiang, L., & Fuligni, A. J. (2008). Multiple social identities and reactivity to daily stress among ethnically diverse young adults. *Journal of Research in Personality, 42,* 1160–1172.

Yoon, K. L., Joormann, J., & Gotlib, I. H. (2009). Judging the intensity of facial expressions of emotion: Depression-related biases in the processing of positive affect. *Journal of Abnormal Psychology, 118,* 223–228.

Young, L. J. (2009). Being human: Love: Neuroscience reveals all. *Nature, 457,* 148.

Young, S. (2008, March 19). For amputees, an unlikely painkiller: Mirrors. http://www.cnn.com/2008/HEALTH/03/19/mirror.therapy/index.html?iref=newssearch (accessed March 26, 2009)

Young, T. (1802). On the theory of light and colors. *Philosophical Transactions of the Royal Society of London, 92,* 12–48.

Yovel, G., & Kanwisher, M. (2008). The representation of spacing and part-based information are associated for upright faces but dissociated for objects: Evidence from individual differences. *Psychonomic Bulletin and Review, 15,* 933–939.

Yuan, J., Luo, Y., Yan, J. H., Meng, X., Yu, F., & Li, H. (2009). Neural correlates of the female's susceptibility to negative emotions: An insight into gender-related prevalence of affective disturbances. *Human Brain Mapping.* (in press)

Z

Zadra, A., Pilon, M., & Donderi, D. C. (2006). Variety and intensity of emotions in nightmares and bad dreams. *Journal of Nervous and Mental Disorders, 194,* 249–254.

Zajonc, R. B. (1965). Social facilitation. *Science, 149,* 269–274.

Zajonc, R. B. (1968). Attitudinal effects of mere exposure. *Journal of Personality and Social Psychology, 9,* 1–27.

Zajonc, R. B. (1984). On the primacy of affect. *American Psychologist, 39,* 117–123.

Zajonc, R. B. (2001). Mere exposure: A gateway to the subliminal. *Current Directions in Psychological Science, 10,* 224–228.

Zanarini, M. C., Frankenburg, F. R., Reich, D. B., & others. (2000). Biparental failure in the childhood experiences of borderline patients. *Journal of Personality Disorders, 14,* 264–273.

Zebrowitz, L. A., & Montepare, J. M. (2008). Social psychological face perception: Why appearance matters. *Social and Personality Psychology Compass, 2,* 1497–1517.

Zhang, L.-F., & Sternberg, R. J. (2009). Learning in a cross-cultural perspective. In T. Husén & T. N. Postlethwaite (Eds.), *International encyclopedia of education* (3rd ed.), *Learning and cognition.* Oxford, England: Elsevier. (in press)

Zhao, M., Ko, S. W., Wu, L., Toyoda, H., Xu, H., Quan, J., Li, J., Jia, Y., Ren, M., Xu, Z. C., & Zhuo, M. (2006). Enhanced presynaptic neurotransmitter release in the anterior cingulate cortex of mice with chronic pain. *Journal of Neuroscience, 26,* 8923–8930.

Zhao, Y., Hoshiyama, H., Shay, J. W., & Wright, W. E. (2008). Quantitative telomeric overhand determination using a double-strand specific nuclease. *Nucleic Acids Research, 36,* e14.

Zhou, Y.,& Saucier, G., Gao, D.,& Liu, J. (2009). The factor structure of Chinese personality terms. *Journal of Personality, 77,* 363–400.

Zhou, X., Tang, W., Greenwood, T. A., Guo, S., He, L., Geyer, M. A., & Kelsoe, J. R. (2009a). Transcription factor SP4 Is a susceptibility gene for bipolar disorder. *PLoS ONE, 4,* e5196.

Zhou, Z., Zhen, J., Karpowich, N. K., Law, C. J., Rith, M. E., & Wang, D. N. (2009). Antidepressant specificity of serotonin transporter suggested by three LeuT-SSRI structures. *Natural Structure and Molecular Biology.* (in press)

Zietsch, B. P., Morley, K. I., Shekar, S. N., Verweij, K. J. H., Keller, M. C., Macgregor, S., Wright, M. J., Bailey, J. M., & Martin, N. G. (2008). Genetic factors predisposing to homosexuality may increase mating success in heterosexuals. *Evolution and Human Behavior, 29,* 424–433.

Zimbardo, P. (2007). *The Lucifer effect: Understanding how good people turn evil.* New York: Random House.

Zimmer-Gembeck, M. J., Hunter, T. A., Waters, A. M., & Pronk, R. (2009). Depression as a longitudinal outcome and antecedent of preadolescents' peer relationships and peer-relevant cognitions. *Development and Psychopathology, 21,* 555–557.

Zonda, T. (2006). One-hundred cases of suicide in Budapest: A case-controlled autopsy study. *Crisis, 27,* 125–129.

Zosuls, K. M., Lurye, L. E., & Ruble, D. N. (2008). Gender: Awareness, identity, and stereotyping. In M. M. Haith & J. B. Benson (Eds.), *Encyclopedia of infant and early childhood development.* Oxford, England: Elsevier.

Zou, Y., Misri, S., Shay, J. W., Pandita, T. K., & Wright, W. E. (2009). Altered states of telomere deprotection and the two-stage mechanism of replicative aging. *Molecular and Cellular Biology.* (in press)

Zou, Y., Zheng, J., Ren, T., & Nuttall, A. (2006). Cochlear transducer operating point adaptation. *Journal of the Acoustical Society of America, 119,* 2232–2241.

Zucker, M., Spinazzola, J., Blaustein, M., & van der Kolk, B. A. (2006). Dissociative symptomatology in posttraumatic stress disorder and disorders of extreme stress. *Journal of Trauma & Dissociation, 7,* 19–31.

Zwanzger, P., & Rupprecht, R. (2005). Selective GABAergic treatment for panic? Investigations in experimental panic induction and panic disorder. *Journal of Psychiatry and Neuroscience, 30,* 167–175.

Text and Line Art Credits

Chapter 2
Figure 2.3: From R. Lewis, Life, 3rd Ed. Copyright © 1998 The McGraw-Hill Companies, Inc. Reproduced with permission by The McGraw-Hill Companies. **Figure 2.4:** From R. Lewis, Life, 3rd Ed. Copyright © 1998 The McGraw-Hill Companies, Inc. Reproduced with permission by The McGraw-Hill Companies. **Figure 2.6:** From Mapping the Mind by Rita Carter, 1998. Reprinted by permission of Weidenfeld & Nicholson Ltd, a division of The Orion Publishing Group (London). **Figure 2.11:** From Brain, Mind, and Behavior 3e by Floyd Bloom, Charles A. Nelson, and Arlyne Lazerson. © 1985, 1988, 2001 by Educational Broadcasting Corporation. Used with the permission of Worth Publishers. **Figure 2.17:** From Brain, Mind, and Behavior 3e by Floyd Bloom, Charles A. Nelson, and Arlyne Lazerson. © 1985, 1988, 2001 by Educational Broadcasting Corporation. Used with the permission of Worth Publishers.

Chapter 3
Figure 3.14: From Ishihara's Tests for Colour Deficiency. Published by Kanehara Trading, Inc. Tokyo, Japan. Used with permission. **Figure 3.15:** From Atkins/Hilgard/Smith/Hoeksema/Fredrickson. Atkinson and Hilgard's Introduction to Psychology, 14E. © 2003 Wadsworth, a part of Cengage Learning, Inc. Reproduced by permission. www.cengage.com/permissions. **Figure 3.22:** From James J. Gibson. The Perception of the Visual World. © 1950 Wadsworth, a part of Cengage Learning, Inc. Reproduced by permission. www.cengage.com/permissions. **Figure 3.24:** From Brain, Mind, and Behavior 3e by Floyd Bloom, Charles A. Nelson, and Arlyne Lazerson. © 1985, 1988, 2001 by Educational Broadcasting Corporation. Used with the permission of Worth Publishers.

Chapter 4
Figure 4.6: From Brain, Mind, and Behavior 3e by Floyd Bloom, Charles A. Nelson, and Arlyne Lazerson. © 1985, 1988, 2001 by Educational Broadcasting Corporation. Used with the permission of Worth Publishers. **Figure 4.8:** From John Santrock, Adolescence, 8th Ed. Copyright © 2001 The McGraw-Hill Companies, Inc. Reproduced with permission by The McGraw-Hill Companies. **Figure 4.12:** From Journal of the American Medical Association, 272, 1672–1677, 1994 data presented by H. Wechsler, Davenport, et al.

Used with permission by American Medical Association.

Chapter 6
Figure 6.10: From John Santrock, Life-Span Development, 11th Ed. Copyright © 2008 The McGraw-Hill Companies, Inc. Reproduced with permission by The McGraw-Hill Companies. **Figure 6.13:** From Human Memory: Theory and Data by B. Murdock, Jr. © 1974. Lawrence Erlbaum. **Figure 6.17:** David Barker, © Exploratorium, www.exploratorium.edu. Used with permission.

Chapter 7
Figure 7.9: From John Santrock, Children, 7th Ed. Copyright © 2003 The McGraw-Hill Companies, Inc. Reproduced with permission by The McGraw-Hill Companies. **Figure 7.11:** From "The Increase in IQ Scores from 1932–1997," by Ulric Neisser. Used with permission. **Figure 7.13:** From John Santrock, Educational Psychology. Copyright © 2001 The McGraw-Hill Companies, Inc. Reproduced with permission by The McGraw-Hill Companies.

Chapter 8
Figure 8.5: From John Santrock, Topical Life-Span Development, 2002. Copyright © The McGraw-Hill Companies, Inc. Reproduced with permission by The McGraw-Hill Companies. **Figure 8.8:** From John Santrock, Life-Span Development, 9th Ed. Copyright © The McGraw-Hill Companies, Inc. Reproduced with permission by The McGraw-Hill Companies. **Figure 8.12:** From John Santrock, Child Development, 10th Ed. Copyright © The McGraw-Hill Companies, Inc. Reproduced with permission by The McGraw-Hill Companies. **Figure 8.14:** From John Santrock, Life-Span Development, 11th Ed. Copyright © 2008 The McGraw-Hill Companies, Inc. Reproduced with permission by The McGraw-Hill Companies. **Figure 8.15:** From John Santrock, Life-Span Development, 8th Ed. Copyright © 2002 The McGraw-Hill Companies, Inc. Reproduced with permission by The McGraw-Hill Companies. **Figure 8.16 (graphic):** From Grant Jarding. USA Today. January 5, 1999. Reprinted with permission. **Figure 8.19:** From "The Nature of the Influence of Speed on Adult Age Differences in Cognition" from Developmental Psychology, 1994, 30, 240–259. Copyright © 1994 by the American Psychological Association. Adapted with permission. **Figure 8.20:** From L.L. Carstensen and S. Turk-Charles, Psychology and Aging, 9, 262. Copyright © 1994 by the American Psychological Association. Adapted with permission.

Chapter 9
Figure 9.3: From Sex in America by John Gagnon. Copyright © 1994 by CSG Enterprises, Inc., Edward O. Laumann, Robert T. Michael, and Gina Kolata. By permission of Little Brown & Company and Brockman, Inc.

Chapter 10
Figure 10.1: From Wrightsman/Sigelman/Sanford. Psychology: A Scientific Study of Human Behavior, 5E. © 1979 Wadsworth, a part of Cengage Learning, Inc. Reproduced with permission. www.cengage.com/permissions.

Chapter 11
Figure 11.5: This figure by K. Deaux was published in Encyclopedia of Women and Gender: Sex Similarities and Differences and the Impact of Society of Gender, 2 Volume Set, edited by Judith Worell, "Types of Identity." Copyright Elsevier 1969. **Figure 11.6:** Muzafer Sherif et al. Fig labeled "Attitudes Toward the Out-Group Following Competitive and Cooperative Activities." © 1988 by Muzafer Sherif and reprinted by permission of Wesleyan University Press.

Chapter 12
Figure 12.4: From Weissman and Olfson, Science 269:779, Figure 1 (1995). Copyright © 1995 American Association for the Advancement of Science. Used with permission. **Figure 12.5:** Reprinted with permission from the Annual Review of Neuroscience, Volume 20, © 1997 by Annual Reviews, www.annualreviews.org. **Figure 12.7:** From Living with 10–15-Year-Olds: A Parent Education Curriculum. Center for Early Adolescence, Carrboro, NC. **Figure 12.11:** © Irving Gottesman 2004. Used by permission.

Chapter 13
Figure 13.6: Adapted from A. Freeman and M.A. Reinecke, "Cognitive Therapy" in A.S. Gurman, ed., Essential Psychotherapies. Adapted with permission of The Guilford Press. **Figure 13.8:** Reprinted with permission of Michael J. Lambert, Brigham Young University. **Figure 13.9:** From "A Survival Analysis of Clinically Significant Change in Outpatient Psychotherapy" by Anderson & Lambert, from Journal of Clinical Psychology, 57, 875–888. Copyright © 2001. Reproduced with permission of John Wiley & Sons, Inc.

Chapter 14
Figure 14.4: From H. Selye et al, The Stress of Life. Copyright © 1976 The McGraw-Hill Companies, Inc. Reproduced with permission by The McGraw-Hill Companies. **Figure 14.5:** From S. Cohen, E. Frank, W.J. Doyle, D.P. Skoner, B.S. Rabin, and J.M. Gwaitney (1998). "Types of Stressors That Increase Susceptibility to the Common Cold in Adults." Health Psychology, 17, 214–233. Copyright © 1998 by the American Psychological Association. Used with permission. **Figure 14.7:** This article was published in Journal of Psychosomatic Research, Vol. 29, S.C. Kobasa, S.R. Maddi, M.C. Puccette, and M.A. Zola, pp. 525–533. Copyright Elsevier 1986. Used with permission. **Figure 14.9:** From John Santrock, Life-Span Development, 11th Ed. Copyright © 2008 The McGraw-Hill Companies, Inc. Reproduced with permission by The McGraw-Hill Companies. **Figure 14.12:** From John Santrock, Life-Span Development 11th Ed. Copyright © 2008 The McGraw-Hill Companies, Inc. Reproduced with permission by The McGraw-Hill Companies.

Photos

Chapter 1
Opener: © Bjorn Vinter/UpperCut Images/Getty; **p. 2 (both):** © age fotostock/SuperStock; **p. 5:** © William Thomas Cain/Stringer/Getty; **p. 7:** © James Warwick/The Image Bank/Getty; **p. 9:** Courtesy of Richard Davidson, University of Wisconsin, Madison. Photo by Jeff Miller.; **p. 10:** © Photofusion Picture Library/Alamy; **p. 13 (top):** © Creatas/Punchstock; **p. 13** (bottom): © George Doyle & Ciaran Griffin/Stockbyte/Getty; **p. 14 (left):** © Stockdisc/PunchStock; **p. 14 (right):** © Masterfile/Royalty Free; **p. 15:** © Peter Ciresa Cires/Index Stock; © Photodisc/Getty; **p. 17:** © Photodisc/Getty; **p. 18:** © Bettmann/Corbis; **Fig 1.4 (top left):** © Doug Menuez/Getty; **Fig 1.4 (top right):** © BananaStock/JupiterImages; **Fig 1.4 (bottom left):** © Veer; **Fig 1.4 (bottom right):** © Stockbyte/Punchstock; **p. 21:** © Photodisc/PunchStock; **p. 24:** © Stockbyte/Getty; **p. 25:** © Getty/Digital Vision; **Fig 1.5:** © Doug Mills-Pool/Getty; **p. 27 (left):** © Peter Arnold Inc.; **p. 27 (right):** © Elsa/Staff/Getty; **p. 29 (left):** © Michael Nichols/National Geographic/Getty; **p. 29 (right):** Courtesy of Barbara Fredrickson, University of North Carolina; **p. 30:** © The McGraw-Hill Companies, Inc./Lars A. Niki, photographer; **p. 31:** © American Images Inc./Photodisc Getty; **p. 32:** © M. Becker/American Idol 2009/Getty; **p. 33 (top):** © Royalty-Free/Corbis; **p. 33 (bottom):** © Stockbyte/Punchstock; **p. 35:** © Getty.

Chapter 2
Opener: © Julia Smith/Riser/Getty; **p. 40:** © David P. Hall/Corbis; **p. 41:** © RubberBall Productions; **p. 42:** © Ned Frisk Photography/Brand X/Corbis; **p. 44:** AP Photo/Richard

moodboard/Corbis; **Fig 11.5e:** © Stockbyte/ PunchStock; **p. 402 (left):** © Darren McCollester/Getty; **p. 402 (right):** © Bill Gillette/Stock Boston; **p. 404:** © SW Productions/Brand X Pictures/Getty; **p. 406:** © Mary Kate Denny/PhotoEdit; **p. 407:** © Ghislain & Marie David de Lossy.

Chapter 12
Opener: © Stuart Fox/Gallo Images/Getty; **p. 412 (left):** © Gregory Shamus/Getty; **p. 412 (right):** © John G. Mabanglo/epa/ Corbis; **p. 414:** © Editorial Image, LLC/Alamy; **p. 416 (left):** © Paul Hawthorne/Getty; **p. 416 (right):** © Virginia Sherwood/NBC. Photo courtesy of Everett Collection; **p. 418:** © Scala/Art Resource; **Fig 12.2 (lightning):** © Royalty-Free/Corbis; **Fig 12.2 (dog):** © Digital Archive Japan/Alamy; **Fig 12.2 (water):** © Comstock Images/Alamy; **Fig 12.2 (hand):** © Creatas/PunchStock;

Fig 12.2 (spider): © Photodisc/Getty; **Fig 12.3:** © Lewis Baxter/Peter Arnold, Inc.; **p. 422 (top):** © Photodisc/Getty; **p. 422 (bottom):** © John Moore/Getty; **p. 423:** © Erich Lessing/Art Resource; **p. 426:** © RubberBall/ Alamy; **Fig 12.6:** Courtesy Drs. Lewis Baxter and Michael Phelps, UCLA School of Medicine; **Fig 12.7:** © Nathan Lau/Design Pics/Corbis; **p. 430:** AP Photo/Ricardo Figueredo; **p. 431:** © Getty/Digital Vision; **p. 432:** © Digital Vision/Getty; **Fig 12.9:** The Washington Post. Photo by Gerald Martineau; **Fig 12.10:** © Grunnitus/Photo Researchers; **p. 440 (both):** © Bettmann/Corbis; **p. 445:** Courtesy of Sheila Hollingsworth.

Chapter 13
Opener: © Symphonie/Iconica/Getty; **p. 452:** © The McGraw-Hill Companies, Inc./Charles D. Winters, photographer; **p. 453:** © Nancy Richmond/The Image

Works; **p. 455:** © Will McIntyre/Photo Researchers; **p. 458:** © Historical Pictures/ Stock Montage; **p. 460:** © Perfect Picture Parts/Alamy; **p. 461:** © BananaStock/ PictureQuest; **p. 463:** © Leif Skoogfors/ Woodfin Camp & Associates; **p. 467:** © Geoffrey Stewart/The Medical File/Peter Arnold Inc.; **p. 469:** © Frank Pedrick/The Image Works; **p. 470:** © Digital Vision/ SuperStock; **p. 471:** © Veer; **p. 472:** © The McGraw-Hill Companies, Inc./Christopher Kerrigan, photographer; **p. 475:** © Zigy Kaluzny/Stone/Getty; **p. 476 (top):** © D Logan/ClassicStock/The Image Works; **Fig 13.10:** © Andrea Morini/Getty.

Chapter 14
Opener: © LWA/Taxi/Getty; **p. 484 (top):** © Photodisc/PunchStock; **p. 484 (bottom):** © Getty; **p. 486:** © Radius Images/Alamy; **p. 487:** © Bill Bachmann/The Image Works;

Fig 14.2: © Ryan McVay/Getty; **Fig 14.6:** © Eye of Science/Photo Researchers; **p. 496:** © image100 Ltd; **p. 498:** © John Lund/Tiffany Schoepp/Blend Images/Corbis; **Fig 14.8:** Courtesy of Colin M. Bloor; **Fig 14.10 (left):** © Reed Kaestner/Corbis; **Fig 14.10 (right):** © Stockbyte/PunchStock; **p. 503:** © Mike Schroeder/Peter Arnold Inc.; **p. 505:** © Ingram Publishing/Alamy; **Fig 14.14:** © Geoff Manasse/Getty.

Transparencies
p. 2: © iStockphoto.com/Arkadiusz Stachowski; **p. 3:** © Matt Gray/Getty; **p. 4:** © Getty; **p. 4:** © Robin Mouat; **p. 4:** © Burke/ Triolo Productions/Brand X Pictures/Getty; **p. 5:** © RubberBall Productions; **p. 5:** © Digital Vision; **p. 5:** © Kent Knudson/ PhotoLink/Getty; **p. 5:** © James Woodson/ Getty; **p. 5:** © James Woodson/Getty; **p. 5:** © Adri Berger/Getty.

name index

Logan, G. D., 218
Logothetis, N. K., 94, 204
Logue, A. W., 320
Lollis, S., 5
Long, J. D., 426
Longo, D. A., 361
Lopes, M., 231
Lopez, S. J., 386
Lopez-Munoz, F., 451
Lopiano, L., 164
Lorant, V., 425
Lorenz, K. Z., 388
Lorton, D., 493
Lo Sauro, C., 430, 431, 432
Losos, J., 55
Love, G. D., 475
Love, R. L., 132
Lu, J., 133
Lu, J. L., 497, 498
Lubahn, C., 493
Lubenov, E. V., 125
Lubinski, D., 245, 248
Luborsky, L., 474
Lucanin, D., 493
Lucanin, J. D., 493
Lucas, E. B., 110
Lucas, R. E., 354, 355
Luce, C. L., 386
Luciano, M., 366
Lucksted, A., 490
Lundy, R., 146
Luo, Y., 275, 425
Lupu, V., 463, 465, 466
Luria, A. R., 58, 193
Lurye, L. E., 285
Lutgendorf, S. K., 494
Lutz, A., 65
Lutz, W., 474
Luz, C., 294, 493
Lyass, A., 471
Lykken, D., 334
Lykken, D. T., 72, 246, 323, 324
Lynam, D. R., 284, 440
Lynn, S. J., 146, 148
Lynskey, M. T., 72
Lyons, R., 472
Lyons-Ruth, K., 426
Lysle, D. T., 164
Lythgoe, M. F., 38
Lyubomirsky, S., 240, 332, 334, 335

M

Macaluso, E., 207
Macciardi, F., 437
Maccoby, E. E., 282, 285
MacDonald, D., 271
MacDonald, D. A., 353
Macdonald, J. S. P., 84
Macgregor, S., 314, 315
Machado, A. G., 456
Machado, M. A., 212
Mack, A., 84
Mackay, D., 438
Mackenbach, J., 425
Mackenbach, J. P., 502
MacKenzie, J., 491
Mackey, A., 220
Mackinlay, R. J., 220
Maclean, W. E., 425
MacLeod, M., 156
MacLeod, M. S., 220
MacQueen, C. E., 485
Madan, A., 268
Madden, D. J., 295
Madden, P. A., 72
Maddi, S., 498
Maddi, S. R., 497, 498
Maddux, W. W., 181, 182
Mader, S. S., 7, 67, 79, 265
Madsen, L., 324
Maes, H. H. M., 309
Maggio, N., 42
Magid, K., 494
Magnus, K., 352, 353

Magrino-Failla, K., 212
Maguire, E. A., 38
Mahler, D. A., 49
Mahowald, M., 131
Maier, G. W., 372
Maier, N. R. F., 234
Maier, S. F., 110, 162
Maisto, S. A., 138
Major, B., 401, 404
Malamuth, N. M., 391
Malcolm, K. T., 353
Malcolm-Smith, S., 134
Malgrange, B., 123
Mallach, N., 485
Mallick, M., 81
Malone, P. S., 379
Malone, R., 422
Malur, C., 455
Mamo, D. C., 452
Manci, L., 360
Mancini, F., 325
Mandara, J., 291
Mandell, D. L., 330
Mander, B. A., 125
Manderscheid, R. W., 470
Mandic, M., 220
Mandisodza, A. N., 377
Mandler, G., 202
Maner, J. K., 386
Manhart, L. E., 314
Manini, T. M., 499
Manlove, J., 505
Mann, D. M., 481
Manson, J. E., 293, 503
Manstead, A. S. R., 483
Mantere, T., 137
Mäntylä, T., 220
Mantzoros, C. S., 123, 308
Mao, X., 91
March, J., 453
March, J. S., 425
Marcia, J. E., 290
Marcus, G. F., 204, 229
Margolin, G., 465
Margolis, R. L., 437
Margolskee, R. F., 111
Maril, A., 193, 219
Marine, A., 355
Marin-Martinez, F., 462
Mariottini, C., 213
Maris, R. W., 429
Markessis, E., 82
Markey, C. N., 288
Markides, K. S., 21, 293
Markon, K. E., 366
Markowitsch, H. J., 223
Markowitz, J. C., 423
Markowitz, S., 453
Marks, I., 471
Marlow, A., 166
Maron, E., 428
Marquez, J., 207
Marsh, E. J., 211
Marsh, G. R., 130
Marsh, H. W., 336
Marsh, R. L., 220
Marshall, D. A., 498
Marshall, D. S., 312
Marshall, G., 164
Marshall, M., 439
Marshall, R. D., 423
Marti, C. N., 486
Martin, C. L., 286
Martin, D., 472
Martin, D. K., 119
Martin, D. W., 3
Martin, G. L., 175, 177
Martin, G. R., 49
Martin, J., 440
Martin, J. A., 505
Martin, L. L., 335
Martin, L. R., 353
Martin, M., 439
Martin, N. G., 314, 315, 442

Martin, P. P., 290, 401
Martin, S. J., 51
Martinko, M. J., 370
Martinos, M., 271
Martinovich, Z., 425, 474
Martin-Soelch, C., 49
Maruyama, Y., 111
Marx, R. F., 433
Masaki, T., 164
Mascaro, N., 490
Masheb, R. M., 451
Maslach, C., 394
Maslow, A. H., 10, 26, 317, 348
Mason, T. B., 131
Massey, C., 265
Massimini, F., 301
Masten, A. S., 287, 333, 426
Masters, W. H., 311
Masul, Y., 490
Matar, M. A., 423
Mate, J., 208
Mathalon, D., 437
Matic, D., 372
Matis, G., 121
Matlin, M. W., 28, 220, 406
Matschinger, H., 382
Matsumoto, D., 11, 184, 329, 330
Matthews, C. E., 499
Matthews, K. A., 293, 495
Matthews, P. M., 52
Mattson, D. H., 164
Maunsell, J. H., 93
May, F. B., 250
May, M., 88, 93, 114
Mayberg, H., 125
Mayberg, H. S., 422
Mayer, J. D., 250, 346
Mayer, R., 232
Mayeux, R., 55, 224
Mayo Clinic, 456
Mayo Foundation, 455
Mazziotta, J. C., 427
McAdams, D. P., 26, 212, 223–224, 357, 358
McAllister, A. K., 46
McAndrew, F. T., 389
McBride, T. R., 96
McCandliss, B. D., 117
McCarthy, D. E., 504
McCarthy, E., 192
McCarthy, P. M., 387
McCauley, C., 395
McCauley, M. H., 370
McClay, J., 440
McClearn, G. E., 72
McClelland, J. L., 204
McClintock, S., 455
McCloskey, M. S., 138
McCollum, V., 473
McConnell, J., 193
McCorkle, B. H., 471
McCorkle, R., 475
McCormick, N., 172
McCrae, R., 105
McCrae, R. R., 351, 352, 353, 367, 369
McCulloch, K. C., 202, 486
McCullough, J. L., 293
McCullough, M. E., 5, 335, 353, 489
McCurry, S. M., 130
McDaniel, B., 284, 386, 387, 392
McDaniel, M. A., 206, 220
McDermott, M., 488
McDermott, R., 237
McDonald, K. L., 291
McDonald, M. A., 107
McDonel, E. C., 382
McDowell, N. K., 380
McEachan, R., 481
McElhaney, K. B., 176, 290
McElwain, N. L., 265
McFatter, R. M., 354
McGinnis, M. Y., 389
McGlashan, T. H., 442
McGrath, C., 137

McGue, M., 72, 246, 356
McGuffin, P., 72, 245
McGuire, M. T., 503
McGuire, W. J., 382, 384
McHale, S. M., 287
McHugh, T., 38
McIntosh, J., 140
McIntosh, W. D., 335
McIntyre, L. L., 178
McKay, K. M., 476
McKee-Walker, L., 353
McKellar, S., 485
McKenny-Fick, N. M., 118
McKone, E., 59
McLaren, D., 129
McLeod, J., 476
Mcleod, S., 372
McMahon, D. B., 94
McMain, S., 466
McManus, F., 419
McMillan, B., 455, 490
McMillan, J. H., 3, 29
McNally, G. P., 66
McNamara, P., 129
McNamara, T. P., 202
McNaughton, N., 364, 365
McNulty, S., 453
McPherson, T. L., 491
McRae, K., 201
McWhirter, R. M., 354
Meade, C. S., 496
Means, B., 240
Mecklinger, A., 208
Medland, S. E., 418
Medoff, D. R., 490
Meece, J. L., 180, 321, 360
Meehl, P., 438
Meeks, J. T., 220
Meeren, H. K., 328
Meeus, W. H., 367
Mehl, M. R., 254
Meier-Ewert, H. K., 125
Meinhardt, J., 163, 462
Meints, J. O., 353, 367, 490
Meissner, C. A., 215
Meissner, W. W., 459
Meister, I. G., 148
Mejia-Arauz, R., 184
Melis, M., 136
Mellers, J., 467
Mellon, S., 482
Melloni, R. H., 388
Melnyk, L., 240
Melotto, S., 311
Melton, L., 224
Melzack, R., 110
Mendel, G., 70, 71, 72
Mendes, W. B., 398
Mendes de Leon, D. F., 490
Mendez, M. F., 310
Mendiondo, M. S., 21
Meng, X., 425
Menn, L., 251, 258
Menzel, R., 206
Merchant, J., 346
Merckelbach, H., 213
Merenakk, L., 365
Merkl, A., 455
Merkle, H., 204
Mermi, O., 421
Mertens, I., 442
Meshul, C. K., 136, 139
Mesquita, B., 329
Messenger, J. C., 312
Messer, S. C., 422
Messner, S. F., 390
Meston, C. M., 451
Metcalfe, J., 320
Metrik, J., 486, 491
Mettler, F. A., 456
Meurise, M., 164
Meyer, C., 485
Meyer, P. J., 136, 139
Miacic, B., 353

subject index